Scott Foresman - Addison Wesley

MATH

AUTHORS

Randall I. Charles **John A. Dossey** **Steven J. Leinwand**
Cathy L. Seeley **Charles B. Vonder Embse**

L. Carey Bolster • Janet H. Caldwell • Dwight A. Cooley • Warren D. Crown
Linda Proudfit • Alma B. Ramírez • Jeanne F. Ramos • Freddie Lee Renfro
David Robitaille • Jane Swafford

Scott Foresman
Addison Wesley

Editorial Offices: Menlo Park, California • Glenview, Illinois
Sales Offices: Reading, Massachusetts • Atlanta, Georgia • Glenview, Illinois
Carrollton, Texas • Menlo Park, California

http://www.sf.aw.com

The friendly characters who help you in this book with math tips, remembering, and problem solving are Zoombinis™. They are used with the permission of Brøderbund Software and can be found in the interactive problem-solving software, *Logical Journey of the Zoombinis®*, © 1996 Brøderbund Software and TERC, available from Brøderbund Software, Novato, California. For more information, write Brøderbund at P.O. Box 6125, Novato, CA 94948-6125, or call (415) 382-4740.

Cover artist Robert Silvers, 29, started taking photographs and playing with computers at the same time, about 20 years ago. He always thought of computer programming as a way to express himself much as he does with photography. Silvers has melded his interests to produce the image on this cover.

Credits: Photographs xvBL Ellen Beach/Bruce Coleman Inc. xvMR (upper) Frank Rossotto/The Stock Market xvMR (lower) Jane Burton/Bruce Coleman Inc. xvBC Mac Tavish/Comstock xvC (upper) Paul Humann/Jeff Rotman Photography xvC (lower) Robie Price* **Illustrations** xvi Ginidir Marshall
*Photographs provided expressly for Scott Foresman-Addison Wesley

Printed in the United States of America

ISBN 0-201-36493-X

3 4 5 6 7 8 9 10-VH-01 00 99

CHAPTER 1 Statistics—Real-World Use of Whole Numbers 2

Data File 2

Team Project State of the Nations 4

Technology Resources

Reading and Interpreting Graphs 5

1-1 Reading Graphs 6
Mixed Review and Test Prep

1-2 Misleading Graphs 10
Mixed Review and Test Prep

1-3 Scatterplots and Trends 14
Mixed Review and Test Prep

Problem Solving Decision Making: Shark Study 18

Review and Practice 20

Connections
Calculator, Data, Estimation, Mental Math, Patterns, Journal

Displaying Data 21

1-4 Tallies, Frequency Charts, and Line Plots 22
Mixed Review and Test Prep

1-5 Scales and Bar Graphs 26
Mixed Review and Test Prep

1-6 Stem-and-Leaf Diagrams 30
Mixed Review and Test Prep

Review and Practice 34

Connections
Data, Estimation, Geography, History, Mental Math, Probability, Science, Social Studies, Time, Journal

Describing Data 35

1-7 Median and Mode 36
Mixed Review and Test Prep

1-8 The Meaning of Mean 40
Mixed Review and Test Prep

Technology Using a Spreadsheet to Find the Median 44

1-9 The Effects of Outliers 46
Mixed Review and Test Prep

Problem Solving Decision Making: Will the Most Valuable Player Please Stand Up? 50

Review and Practice 52

Problem Solving
Make an Organized List

Connections
Consumer, Data, Geography, Health, Measurement, Mental Math, Patterns, Journal

Chapter Resources

Your Choice 53

Ch 1 Review/Test 54

Performance Assessment 55

Math Magazine 56

Ch 1 Cumulative Review 57

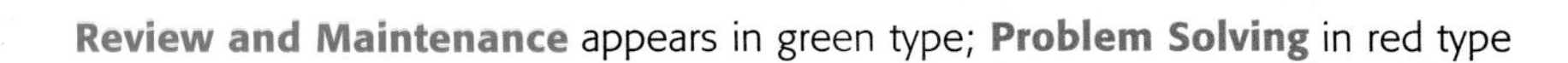

Review and Maintenance appears in green type; **Problem Solving** in red type

CHAPTER 2

Connecting Arithmetic to Algebra 58

Data File 58

Team Project We're Going the Distance! 60

Technology Resources

SECTION A Making Sense of Large Numbers 61

2-1 Reading and Writing Large Numbers 62
Mixed Review and Test Prep

2-2 Rounding Large Numbers 66
Mixed Review and Test Prep

2-3 Comparing and Ordering Numbers 70
Mixed Review and Test Prep

2-4 Exponents 74
Mixed Review and Test Prep

A Review and Practice 78

Problem Solving
Look for a Pattern, Make an Organized List

Connections
Chance, Data, Estimation, Geography, Logic, Measurement, Number Sense, Science, Social Studies, Time, Journal

SECTION B Number Sense and Operation Sense 79

2-5 Mental Math 80
Mixed Review and Test Prep

2-6 Estimating Sums and Differences 84
Mixed Review and Test Prep

2-7 Estimating Products and Quotients 88
Mixed Review and Test Prep

2-8 Order of Operations 92
Mixed Review and Test Prep

STOP Stop and Practice 96

Problem Solving Analyze Word Problems: Finding Unnecessary Information 98

2-9 Numerical Patterns 100
Mixed Review and Test Prep

B Review and Practice 104

Connections
Calculator, Data, Geography, Geometry, Industry, Literature, Logic, Measurement, Mental Math, Money, Patterns, Recreation, Science, Social Science, Journal

SECTION C Introduction to Algebra 105

2-10 Variables and Expressions 106
Mixed Review and Test Prep

2-11 Writing Expressions 110
Mixed Review and Test Prep

2-12 Using Equations 114
Mixed Review and Test Prep

2-13 Solving Equations 118
Mixed Review and Test Prep

Problem Solving Analyze Word Problems: Interpreting Math Phrases 122

Technology Using a Spreadsheet to Guess and Check 124

Problem Solving Decision Making: Journey to the Bottom of the Sea 126

C Review and Practice 128

Problem Solving
Guess and Check, Work Backward

Connections
Calculator, Data, Estimation, Fine Arts, Geography, Health, History, Literature, Science, Journal

Chapter Resources

Your Choice 129

Ch 2 Review/Test 130

Performance Assessment 131

Math Magazine 132

Ch 1–2 Cumulative Review 133

CHAPTER 3

Decimals 134

Data File 134

Team Project Measuring Up 136

Technology Resources

SECTION A

Decimal Concepts 137

3-1 **Decimal Notation** 138
Mixed Review and Test Prep

3-2 **Rounding Decimals** 142
Mixed Review and Test Prep

Technology Using a Spreadsheet and Formatting Decimal Data 146

3-3 **Comparing and Ordering Decimals** 148
Mixed Review and Test Prep

3-4 **Scientific Notation** 152
Mixed Review and Test Prep

A **Review and Practice** 156

Problem Solving
Look for a Pattern

Connections
Data, Estimation, History, Music, Patterns, Science, Social Science, Sports, Time, Journal

SECTION B

Adding and Subtracting with Decimals 157

3-5 **Estimating with Decimals** 158
Mixed Review and Test Prep

3-6 **Adding and Subtracting Decimal Numbers** 162
Mixed Review and Test Prep

STOP **Stop and Practice** 166

3-7 **Solving Decimal Equations: Addition and Subtraction** 168
Mixed Review and Test Prep

Problem Solving Compare Strategies: Work Backward/Guess and Check 172

B **Review and Practice** 174

Problem Solving
Draw a Picture

Connections
Careers, Data, Estimation, Health, Patterns, Social Studies, Journal

SECTION C

Multiplying and Dividing with Decimals 175

3-8 **Multiplying a Whole Number by a Decimal** 176
Mixed Review and Test Prep

Practice Game **Decimal Product Game** 180

3-9 **Multiplying a Decimal by a Decimal** 182
Mixed Review and Test Prep

3-10 **Dividing by a Whole Number** 186
Mixed Review and Test Prep

3-11 **Dividing by a Decimal** 190
Mixed Review and Test Prep

3-12 **Solving Decimal Equations: Multiplication and Division** 194
Mixed Review and Test Prep

Problem Solving Decision Making: Planning a Hike 198

C **Review and Practice** 200

Problem Solving
Draw a Picture

Connections
Algebra, Data, Health, History, Logic, Measurement, Mental Math, Money, Patterns, Journal

Chapter Resources

Your Choice 201

Ch 3 Review/Test 202

Performance Assessment 203

Math Magazine 204

Ch 1–3 Cumulative Review 205

CHAPTER 4

Measurement 206

Data File 206
Team Project Get on Course 208
Technology Resources

SECTION A Units of Measurement 209

4-1 **Perimeter** 210
Mixed Review and Test Prep

4-2 **Converting in the Metric System** 214
Mixed Review and Test Prep

4-3 **Using Conversion Factors** 218
Mixed Review and Test Prep

Problem Solving Analyze Word Problems: Finding Unnecessary Information 222

A Review and Practice 224

Connections
Careers, Data, Estimation, Health, Mental Math, Number Sense, Journal

SECTION B Area of Polygons 225

4-4 **Area of Squares and Rectangles** 226
Mixed Review and Test Prep

4-5 **Area of Parallelograms** 230
Mixed Review and Test Prep

4-6 **Area of Triangles** 234
Mixed Review and Test Prep

Technology Using Dynamic Geometry Software 238

Problem Solving Decision Making: Designing a Shopping Mall 240

B Review and Practice 242

Problem Solving
Look for a Pattern, Make a Table

Connections
Careers, Data, Estimation, Fine Arts, Geography, Geometry, Patterns, Journal

SECTION C Circles 243

4-7 **Discovering Pi** 244
Mixed Review and Test Prep

4-8 **Area of Circles** 248
Mixed Review and Test Prep

4-9 **Area of Irregular Figures** 252
Mixed Review and Test Prep

C Review and Practice 256

Problem Solving
Look for a Pattern, Make a Table

Connections
Data, Geography, Science, Time, Journal

Chapter Resources

Your Choice 257
Ch 4 Review/Test 258
Performance Assessment 259
Math Magazine 260
Ch 1–4 Cumulative Review 261

CHAPTER 5

Patterns and Number Theory 262

Data File 262

Team Project What's Your Number? 264

Technology Resources

SECTION A Number Theory 265

5-1 Divisibility 266
Mixed Review and Test Prep

5-2 Prime Factorization 270
Mixed Review and Test Prep

5-3 Least Common Multiples 274
Mixed Review and Test Prep

Problem Solving Compare Strategies: Solve a Simpler Problem/Make an Organized List 278

A **Review and Practice** 280

Problem Solving
Draw a Picture

Connections
Calculator, Data, History, Math History, Measurement, Money, Patterns, Probability, Social Studies, Time, Journal

SECTION B Connecting Fractions and Decimals 281

5-4 Understanding Fractions 282
Mixed Review and Test Prep

5-5 Fractions in Lowest Terms 286
Mixed Review and Test Prep

5-6 Improper Fractions and Mixed Numbers 290
Mixed Review and Test Prep

STOP **Stop and Practice** 294

5-7 Converting Fractions and Decimals 296
Mixed Review and Test Prep

Technology Using a Spreadsheet to Find Decimal Equivalents for Common Fractions 300

5-8 Comparing and Ordering 302
Mixed Review and Test Prep

B **Review and Practice** 306

Problem Solving
Draw a Picture

Connections
Algebra, Careers, Data, Estimation, Geometry, History, Measurement, Mental Math, Patterns, Journal

Chapter Resources

Your Choice	307
Ch 5 Review/Test	308
Performance Assessment	309
Math Magazine	310
Ch 1–5 Cumulative Review	311

CHAPTER 6 Adding and Subtracting Fractions 312

Data File 312

Team Project Away We Go! 314

Technology Resources

SECTION A Adding and Subtracting Fractions 315

6-1 Adding and Subtracting Fractions with Like Denominators 316
Mixed Review and Test Prep

6-2 Adding and Subtracting Fractions with Unlike Denominators 320
Mixed Review and Test Prep

Stop and Practice 324

Technology Using a Fraction Calculator to Find Fraction Sums and Differences 326

6-3 Solving Fraction Equations: Addition and Subtraction 328
Mixed Review and Test Prep

Problem Solving Analyze Word Problems: Identifying Missing Information 332

A Review and Practice 334

Connections
Data, Estimation, Geography, Logic, Measurement, Mental Math, Money, Patterns, Science, Time, Journal

SECTION B Adding and Subtracting Mixed Numbers 335

6-4 Estimation: Sums and Differences of Mixed Numbers 336
Mixed Review and Test Prep

6-5 Adding Mixed Numbers 340
Mixed Review and Test Prep

6-6 Subtracting Mixed Numbers 344
Mixed Review and Test Prep

Problem Solving Decision Making: Will the River Flood? 348

B Review and Practice 350

Problem Solving
Use Logical Reasoning

Connections
Careers, Logic, Recreation, Journal

Chapter Resources

Your Choice 351

Ch 6 Review/Test 352

Performance Assessment 353

Math Magazine 354

Ch 1–6 Cumulative Review 355

CHAPTER 7

Multiplying and Dividing Fractions 356

Data File 356

Team Project It's Game Time! 358

Technology Resources

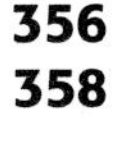

SECTION A Multiplying Fractions 359

7-1 Estimation: Products and Quotients of Fractions 360
Mixed Review and Test Prep

7-2 Multiplying by a Whole Number 364
Mixed Review and Test Prep

7-3 Multiplying by a Fraction 368
Mixed Review and Test Prep

Problem Solving Analyze Word Problems: Identifying Missing Information 372

A Review and Practice 374

Connections
Algebra, Data, Geometry, Health, History, Logic, Measurement, Mental Math, Money, Science, Social Studies, Time, Journal

SECTION B Dividing Fractions 375

7-4 Dividing Whole Numbers by Fractions 376
Mixed Review and Test Prep

7-5 Dividing Fractions by Fractions 380
Mixed Review and Test Prep

Stop and Practice 384

Technology Using a Fraction Calculator to Find Fraction Products and Quotients 386

7-6 Solving Fraction Equations: Multiplication and Division 388
Mixed Review and Test Prep

B Review and Practice 392

Problem Solving
Draw a Picture

Connections
Algebra, Data, Estimation, History, Industry, Measurement, Mental Math, Science, Social Studies, Time, Journal

Chapter Resources

Your Choice 393
Ch 7 Review/Test 394
Performance Assessment 395
Math Magazine 396
Ch 1–7 Cumulative Review 397

CHAPTER 8

The Geometry of Polygons 398

Data File 398
Team Project Here's Looking at Us! 400
Technology Resources

SECTION A Lines and Angles 401

8-1 **Classifying Lines** 402
Mixed Review and Test Prep

8-2 **Classifying Angles** 406
Mixed Review and Test Prep

8-3 **Measuring Angles** 410
Mixed Review and Test Prep

A **Review and Practice** 414

Connections
Estimation, Fine Arts, Measurement, Money, Time, Journal

SECTION B Polygons 415

8-4 **Exploring Angles in a Triangle** 416
Mixed Review and Test Prep

8-5 **Exploring Sides of a Triangle** 420
Mixed Review and Test Prep

8-6 **Polygons** 424
Mixed Review and Test Prep

8-7 **Quadrilaterals** 428
Mixed Review and Test Prep

Technology Using Dynamic Geometry Software to Find Relationships in Triangles 432

Problem Solving Compare Strategies: Logical Reasoning/Draw a Picture 434

B **Review and Practice** 436

Problem Solving
Guess and Check, Look for a Pattern, Make a Table

Connections
Algebra, Data, Geometry, History, Logic, Measurement, Mental Math, Money, Science, Journal

SECTION C Transformations 437

8-8 **Flips and Line Symmetry** 438
Mixed Review and Test Prep

8-9 **Turns and Rotational Symmetry** 442
Mixed Review and Test Prep

8-10 **Slides and Tessellations** 446
Mixed Review and Test Prep

Practice Game Geometry Game 450

C **Review and Practice** 452

Problem Solving
Guess and Check, Look for a Pattern

Connections
Fine Arts, Estimation, Measurement, Money, Science, Journal

Chapter Resources

Your Choice 453
Ch 8 Review/Test 454
Performance Assessment 455
Math Magazine 456
Ch 1–8 Cumulative Review 457

CHAPTER 9

Integers and the Coordinate Plane 458

Data File 458

Team Project Major Mapping 460

Technology Resources

Section A Integers 461

9-1 **Understanding Integers** 462
Mixed Review and Test Prep

9-2 **Adding Integers** 466
Mixed Review and Test Prep

9-3 **Subtracting Integers** 470
Mixed Review and Test Prep

9-4 **Multiplying and Dividing Integers** 474
Mixed Review and Test Prep

Stop and Practice 478

Problem Solving Decision Making: Planning a Dive 480

A Review and Practice 482

Problem Solving
Look for a Pattern, Make an Organized List, Use Logical Reasoning

Connections
Algebra, Careers, Data, Estimation, Measurement, Number Sense, Patterns, Science, Journal

Section B Graphing on the Coordinate Plane 483

9-5 **The Coordinate Plane** 484
Mixed Review and Test Prep

Technology Using Browser Software to Research on the World Wide Web 488

9-6 **Graphing Slides and Flips** 490
Mixed Review and Test Prep

9-7 **Graphing Equations** 494
Mixed Review and Test Prep

Practice Game Hide and Seek Game 498

B Review and Practice 500

Problem Solving
Look for a Pattern

Connections
Data, Geometry, Recreation, Journal

Chapter Resources

Your Choice 501
Ch 9 Review/Test 502
Performance Assessment 503
Math Magazine 504
Ch 1–9 Cumulative Review 505

CHAPTER 10 Ratio, Proportion, and Percent 506

Data File 506
Team Project Finding the Facts 508
Technology Resources

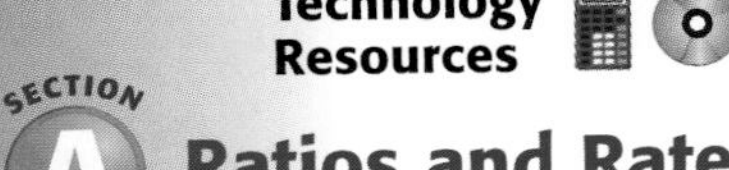

SECTION A Ratios and Rates 509

10-1 **What Is a Ratio?** 510
Mixed Review and Test Prep

10-2 **Equal Ratios** 514
Mixed Review and Test Prep

10-3 **What Is a Rate?** 518
Mixed Review and Test Prep

Problem Solving Decision Making: Fire Alarm 522

A Review and Practice 524

Problem Solving
Make a Table

Connections
Data, Estimation, Geometry, Health, Industry, Patterns, Science, Journal

SECTION B Proportions 525

10-4 **What Is a Proportion?** 526
Mixed Review and Test Prep

10-5 **Solving Proportions Using Cross Products** 530
Mixed Review and Test Prep

10-6 **Solving Proportions Using Unit Rates** 534
Mixed Review and Test Prep

STOP Stop and Practice 538

10-7 **Similar Figures** 540
Mixed Review and Test Prep

Problem Solving Analyze Word Problems: Checking for a Reasonable Answer 544

B Review and Practice 546

Problem Solving
Look for a Pattern

Connections
Consumer, Data, Estimation, Fine Arts, Geography, Geometry, History, Literature, Measurement, Money, Science, Time, Journal

SECTION C Percents 547

10-8 **What Is a Percent?** 548
Mixed Review and Test Prep

10-9 **Estimating Percents** 552
Mixed Review and Test Prep

10-10 **Connecting Percents to Fractions and Decimals** 556
Mixed Review and Test Prep

10-11 **Finding a Percent of a Number** 560
Mixed Review and Test Prep

Technology Using a Spreadsheet to Create a Circle Graph 564

Problem Solving Compare Strategies: Look for a Pattern/Make a Table 566

C Review and Practice 568

Problem Solving
Look for a Pattern

Connections
Algebra, Calculator, Consumer, Data, Estimation, Geography, Health, Industry, Number Sense, Probability, Journal

Chapter Resources

Your Choice 569
Ch 10 Review/Test 570
Performance Assessment 571
Math Magazine 572
Ch 1–10 Cumulative Review 573

CHAPTER 11

Solids and Measurement 574

Data File 574

Team Project Get in the Swim 576

Technology Resources

SECTION A Solids and Surface Area 577

11-1 Classifying Solids 578
Mixed Review and Test Prep

11-2 Exploring Surface Area 582
Mixed Review and Test Prep

11-3 Surface Area Formulas 586
Mixed Review and Test Prep

11-4 Surface Area of a Cylinder 590
Mixed Review and Test Prep

Technology Using a Spreadsheet to Find the Surface Area of a Cylinder 594

A Review and Practice 596

Problem Solving
Draw a Picture

Connections
Calculator, Data, Geometry, History, Industry, Measurement, Money, Patterns, Journal

SECTION B Volume 597

11-5 Three-Dimensional Figures 598
Mixed Review and Test Prep

11-6 Exploring Volume 602
Mixed Review and Test Prep

11-7 Calculating Volume 606
Mixed Review and Test Prep

Problem Solving Decision Making: Building an Aquarium 610

B Review and Practice 612

Problem Solving
Draw a Picture

Connections
Algebra, Consumer, Data, Estimation, Geography, Geometry, Logic, Patterns, Probability, Time, Journal

Chapter Resources

Your Choice 613
Ch 11 Review/Test 614
Performance Assessment 615
Math Magazine 616
Ch 1–11 Cumulative Review 617

CHAPTER 12

Probability 618

Data File 618

Team Project Step Right Up! 620

Technology Resources

SECTION A Introduction to Probability 621

12-1 Probability 622
Mixed Review and Test Prep

12-2 Making Predictions 626
Mixed Review and Test Prep

Problem Solving Analyze Word Problems: Checking for a Reasonable Answer 630

Technology Using a Spreadsheet to Generate Random Numbers 632

12-3 Geometric Models of Probability 634
Mixed Review and Test Prep

A Review and Practice 638

Connections
Calculator, Data, Estimation, History, Logic, Money, Science, Journal

SECTION B Fairness 639

12-4 Tree Diagrams 640
Mixed Review and Test Prep

12-5 Compound Events 644
Mixed Review and Test Prep

Practice Game Probability Game 648

12-6 Fairness and Unfairness 650
Mixed Review and Test Prep

B Review and Practice 654

Problem Solving
Guess and Check

Connections
Algebra, Calculator, Careers, Data, Money, Recreation, Journal

Chapter Resources

Your Choice 655

Ch 12 Review/Test 656

Performance Assessment 657

Math Magazine 658

Ch 1–12 Cumulative Review 659

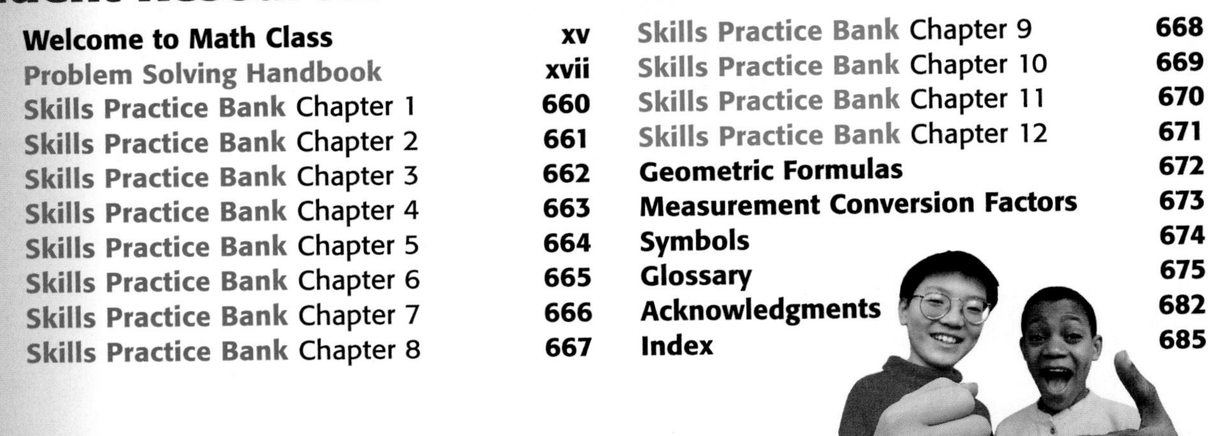

Student Resources

Welcome to Math Class	xv
Problem Solving Handbook	xvii
Skills Practice Bank Chapter 1	660
Skills Practice Bank Chapter 2	661
Skills Practice Bank Chapter 3	662
Skills Practice Bank Chapter 4	663
Skills Practice Bank Chapter 5	664
Skills Practice Bank Chapter 6	665
Skills Practice Bank Chapter 7	666
Skills Practice Bank Chapter 8	667
Skills Practice Bank Chapter 9	668
Skills Practice Bank Chapter 10	669
Skills Practice Bank Chapter 11	670
Skills Practice Bank Chapter 12	671
Geometric Formulas	672
Measurement Conversion Factors	673
Symbols	674
Glossary	675
Acknowledgments	682
Index	685

Welcome to Math Class

Do you recognize me? I'm the **Get Ready** Zoombini. My friends and I can't wait to help out this year in math class.

I'll help you **remember**. You won't forget with me around!

I'm great at giving helpful **math tips!**

I'll help with **problem solving!**

Did you know? I'll let you in on lots of fun facts.

Math is everywhere—not just in math books. We will introduce you to real students who use math every day to help understand the world around them. Have you ever:

- wondered when and where most shark attacks occur?
- compared distances within the solar system?
- planned a backpacking trip?
- discovered number patterns in nature?

- investigated the causes of floods?
- figured out how to build an aquarium for tropical fish?

Reviewing Skills

You already know lots of math!
Let's review some basic facts.

1. $8 + 5$ **2.** $7 + 9$ **3.** $5 + 6$ **4.** $9 + 8$ **5.** $8 + 7$

6. $16 - 8$ **7.** $15 - 9$ **8.** $14 - 5$ **9.** $12 - 7$ **10.** $17 - 8$

11. 7×8 **12.** 9×6 **13.** 8×5 **14.** 7×9 **15.** 8×8

16. $45 \div 5$ **17.** $49 \div 7$ **18.** $72 \div 9$ **19.** $42 \div 6$ **20.** $54 \div 6$

Mental Math Use mental math to find each answer.

21. $42 + 53$ **22.** $57 - 30$ **23.** 31×3 **24.** $78 - 24$ **25.** $84 \div 2$

26. $248 - 48$ **27.** $325 + 75$ **28.** $597 - 50$ **29.** $360 \div 90$ **30.** 600×40

Patterns Complete each pattern.

31. 50, 48, 45, 41, ■, ■, ■ **32.** 3, 9, 27, 81, ■, ■, ■

33. 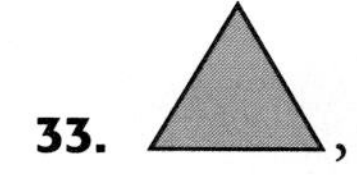, , , ______, ______, ______

Add, subtract, multiply, or divide to solve the riddle. Match each letter to its answer in the blank(s) below. Some letters are not used.

34. $87 \div 3$ [L] **35.** $407 + 329$ [M] **36.** 94×4 [G] **37.** $500 - 268$ [E]

38. $174 + 288$ [A] **39.** 143×3 [H] **40.** $168 \div 7$ [R] **41.** $306 - 154$ [T]

What occurs twice in a moment, once in a minute, but never in forever?

___	___	___
152	429	232

___	___	___	___	___	___		___
29	232	152	152	232	24		736

Problem Solving Handbook

You solve some kinds of problems almost every day, such as when to leave to get to school on time. You solve these problems so often that you don't even have to think to come up with an answer.

Other problems are more difficult to solve. How can you earn enough money to buy a new bicycle? Finding solutions to these kinds of problems requires good problem-solving skills.

Learning mathematics is an excellent way to practice and improve your problem-solving skills. It can help you learn more about how to use data and technology. It also helps you to think in a logical, step-by-step way.

Keep in mind that some problems in math have a "right" answer, but many have more than one answer.

Talk About It

1. What kinds of problems do you solve almost every day?
2. For what kinds of problems do you need to understand and use mathematics?
3. How can a problem have more than one answer?

Problem Solving

The Problem Solving Plan

Learn

You've solved many problems in your previous math classes. Now you'll look more closely at some methods that can help you solve problems.

You need a plan or a strategy to solve any problem. A plan or strategy will help you to understand the problem, to decide on a good approach, to work out a creative solution, and to see if your solution makes sense.

The Plan

Understand

What do you know?

What do you need to find out?

Plan

Have you ever solved a similar problem?

What strategies can you use?

Estimate an answer.

Solve

Do you need to try another strategy?

What is the solution?

Look Back

Did you answer the right question?

Does your answer make sense?

Example

There are 16 teams in a tournament. Each team plays one other team until it loses. How many games are needed to decide the championship?

Understand

What do you know?	There are 16 teams. Each team plays one other team until it loses.
What do you need to find out?	How many games are needed to decide the championship?

Plan

What strategies can you use?	You can draw a diagram.

Solve

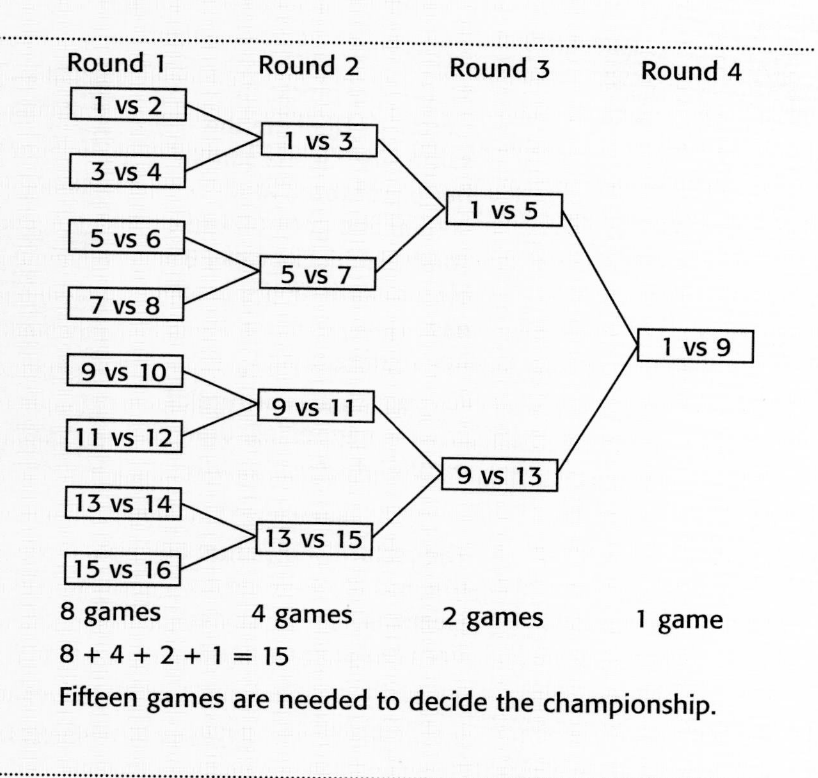

$8 + 4 + 2 + 1 = 15$

Fifteen games are needed to decide the championship.

Look Back

Does you answer make sense?	The right question was answered and the answer makes sense.

Check

1. Solve the problem using a different strategy. Do you get the same answer?
2. Why is it important to have a plan before you begin a solution?

Problem Solving Strategies

- Draw a Picture
- Look for a Pattern
- Guess and Check
- Use Logical Reasoning
- Make an Organized List
- Make a Table
- Solve a Simpler Problem
- Work Backward

Choose a Tool

Draw a Picture

Some problems are visual. They may involve objects, places, or physical situations. To solve such a problem, draw a picture to show relationships among the given data. Then use the relationships to find the answer.

Example

All the city blocks in Gardner's Bluff are the same size. Geena starts her paper route at a corner. She goes 8 blocks south, 13 blocks west, 8 blocks north, and 6 blocks east. How far is she from her starting point?

To get a clearer picture of what is happening, draw a picture of Geena's route.

6 → End — ? → Start
8 ↑ ↓ 8
← 13

The picture shows that at the end of her route, Geena is 13 − 6 blocks from her starting point.

$13 - 6 = 7$

When she finishes, Geena is 7 blocks from her starting point.

Try These

1. A trucker drove 28 miles south of the warehouse to make a delivery. He then made three more deliveries, driving 13 miles west, 43 miles north, and 13 miles east. How far from the warehouse did he make the last delivery?

2. The roots of an elm tree reach 17 feet into the ground. A robin's nest is 13 feet from the top of the tree. From the top of the tree to the tip of the roots, the tree measures 52 feet. How high above the ground is the nest?

Look for a Pattern

Problem Solving Strategies

- Draw a Picture
- Look for a Pattern
- Guess and Check
- Use Logical Reasoning
- Make an Organized List
- Make a Table
- Solve a Simpler Problem
- Work Backward

Choose a Tool

Sometimes the numbers in a problem form a pattern. To solve the problem, find the rule that creates the pattern. Then use the rule to find the answer.

Example

Marsha's hourly wage as a dog groomer increases by a fixed amount each year. She earned \$4.75 per hour her first year on the job and \$5.60 per hour her second year. Find the hourly wage during her fifth year of work.

Second-year wage:	\$5.60
First-year wage:	− 4.75
Wage increase:	\$0.85

The rule is that Marsha's wages increase by \$0.85 each year.

Third-year wage:	\$5.60 + \$0.85 = \$6.45
Fourth-year wage:	\$6.45 + \$0.85 = \$7.30
Fifth-year wage:	\$7.30 + \$0.85 = \$8.15

Marsha's hourly wages during her fifth year of work will be \$8.15.

Try These

1. During the first year of life, swordfish increase in weight at a regular rate. A swordfish weighed 14 pounds at age 1 month and 28 pounds at age 2 months. How much did it weigh at age 6 months?

2. This year, the average price of Concert File CDs went from \$13.95 to \$12.49. If the price continues to change at the same rate, how much will they cost next year?

Problem Solving Strategies

- Draw a Picture
- Look for a Pattern
- Guess and Check
- Use Logical Reasoning
- Make an Organized List
- Make a Table
- Solve a Simpler Problem
- Work Backward

Choose a Tool

Guess and Check

If you're not sure how to solve a problem, make an educated guess at the answer. Check your guess. If you're wrong, use what you've learned in checking your guess to make a better guess. Continue to guess, check, and revise until you find the answer.

Example

Twenty-five dolphins and whales perform at Sea Circus. The circus features 13 more dolphins than whales. How many of each animal perform?

	Dolphins	**Whales**
Guess: Make an educated guess: 15 + 10 = 25	15	10
Check: There should be 13 more dolphins.	15 − 10 = 5	
Think: The difference isn't great enough. I need more dolphins.		
Revise: 20 + 5 = 25	20	5
Check:	20 − 5 = 15	
Think: I'm closer, but now I have too many dolphins.		
Revise: 19 + 6 = 25	19	6
Check:	19 − 6 = 13 √	

There are 19 dolphins and 6 whales.

Try These

1. Before going on vacation, Vanessa bought 21 rolls of film. She bought twice as many rolls of print film as slide film. How many rolls of each type did she buy?
2. One weekend, Allan worked a total of 17 hours helping his uncle paint his cabin. They worked three hours more on Saturday than they worked on Sunday. How many hours did they work each day?

Use Logical Reasoning

To use logical reasoning to solve a problem, decide how the facts of the problem relate to each other. Then work your way step by step from these facts to a sensible solution. Along the way, avoid making false assumptions or unreasonable conclusions.

Problem Solving Strategies

- Draw a Picture
- Look for a Pattern
- Guess and Check
- Use Logical Reasoning
- Make an Organized List
- Make a Table
- Solve a Simpler Problem
- Work Backward

Choose a Tool

Example

Arnie, Becca, and Chad collect coins, rocks, and stamps. Becca is the sister of the rock collector. Chad once had lunch with both the rock collector and the stamp collector. Match each person with his or her hobby.

Take clues one at a time. Use a grid to keep track of your conclusions.

1. Becca is the sister of the rock collector. So she is not the rock collector.

	Stamps	Coins	Rocks
Arnie			
Becca			no
Chad			

2. Chad once had lunch with the rock collector and the stamp collector.

	Stamps	Coins	Rocks
Arnie			
Becca			no
Chad	no		no

That means Chad must collect coins, Becca stamps, and Arnie rocks.

	Stamps	Coins	Rocks
Arnie	no	no	yes
Becca	yes	no	no
Chad	no	yes	no

PROBLEM SOLVING PRACTICE

Try These

1. Tim, Mei, and Jamal are in sixth, seventh, and eighth grades. Mei is not in eighth grade. The sixth grader sings in the chorus with Tim and plays in the band with Mei. Match each student with his or her grade.

2. Sid, Todd, and Maria play soccer, baseball, and tennis. Maria doesn't play tennis. Sid rides the bus with the baseball and tennis players. Match each student with his or her sport.

Problem Solving Strategies

- Draw a Picture
- Look for a Pattern
- Guess and Check
- Use Logical Reasoning
- Make an Organized List
- Make a Table
- Solve a Simpler Problem
- Work Backward

Choose a Tool

Make an Organized List

Sometimes you need to find the number of ways in which something can be done. To solve the problem, make a list of all the ways and count them. It is important to organize your list so that you don't miss any possibilities, or repeat any of them.

Example

At the Healthy Bowl Restaurant, you can order a garden salad with or without dressing, with or without croutons, and with or without bacon bits. If the manager wants to list all the possible combinations in the menu, how many combinations must she list?

One way to organize a list is to pick one item and list all the combinations that include that one item. Then, pick a second item and list all the combinations that include the second item but not the first.

First list the dressing choices:

D
DC
DB
DCB

Now, list the crouton choices without dressing:

C
CB

Now, list the bacon bit choices without dressing or croutons:

B

Finally, list any choices without dressing, croutons, or bacon bits:

no toppings

There are 8 combinations.

Try These

1. There are 5 pitchers and 3 catchers on the Middle School baseball team. How many pitcher-catcher pairs can the coach choose from?
2. Flavor-Filled Ice Cream has four flavors of soft-serve ice cream. How many ways could you choose two different flavors?

Make a Table

Problem Solving Strategies

- Draw a Picture
- Look for a Pattern
- Guess and Check
- Use Logical Reasoning
- Make an Organized List
- Make a Table
- Solve a Simpler Problem
- Work Backward

Choose a Tool

A problem involving a relationship between two sets of numbers can often be solved by making a table. A table helps you organize data so that you can see the numerical relationship among the data and find the answer.

Example

Carl mailed ads for his new craft business to three friends. He asked each friend to mail three copies to friends. Each of these friends was then to mail three ads to friends, and so on. How many ads were sent in the sixth mailing?

Make a table to organize data about the mailings.

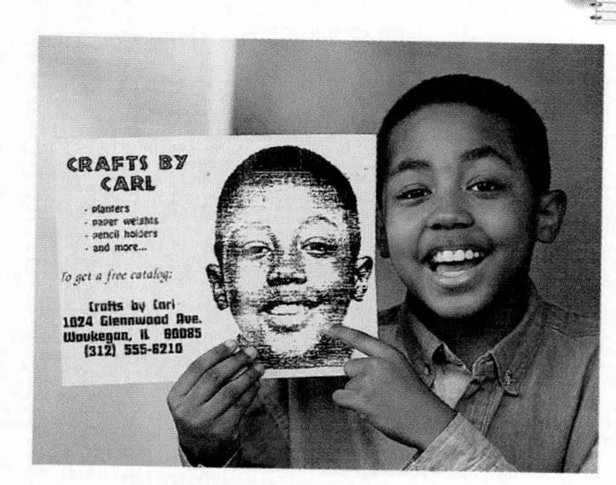

Mailing	1	2	3
Number sent	3	$3 \times 3 = 9$	$3 \times 3 \times 3 = 27$

The table helps you see the relationship between the number of a mailing and the number of ads sent. In mailing **1,** 3 appears **one time** as a factor. In mailing **2,** 3 appears **two times** as a factor. In mailing **3,** 3 appears **three times** as a factor.

So, in mailing **6,** 3 must appear **six times** as a factor.

$3 \times 3 \times 3 \times 3 \times 3 \times 3 = 729$

In the sixth mailing, 729 ads were sent.

Try These

1. Every person is descended from two parents, four grandparents, eight great-grandparents, and so on. Record this information in a table. Then find how many great-great-great-great-great-great-grandparents everyone is descended from.

2. For every two bald eagles seen by visitors to the Audubon Eagle Sanctuary, seven golden eagles are seen. Make a table showing the number of golden eagles seen when two, four, and six bald eagles are seen. Then find the number of bald eagles seen for every 56 golden eagles.

- Draw a Picture
- Look for a Pattern
- Guess and Check
- Use Logical Reasoning
- Make an Organized List
- Make a Table
- Solve a Simpler Problem
- Work Backward

Choose a Tool

Solve a Simpler Problem

A problem may seem very complex. It may contain large numbers or appear to require many steps to solve. Instead of solving the given problem, solve a similar but simpler problem. Look for short cuts, patterns, and relationships. Then use what you've learned to solve the original problem.

Example

A diagonal is a line that connects two points in a figure that are not already connected by a side. For example, you can draw nine diagonals inside a six-sided figure. How many diagonals can you draw inside a nine-sided figure?

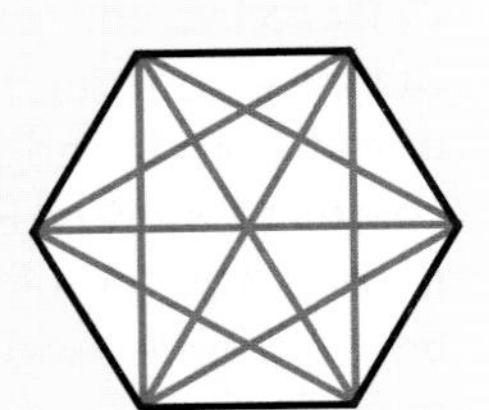

You could draw a nine-sided figure and draw and count the number of diagonals. But that could be very complicated.

Instead, look at some very simple figures.

3-sided figure:
0 diagonals

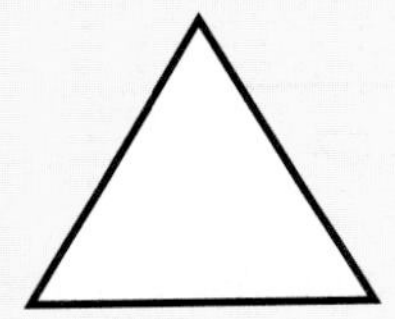

4-sided figure:
2 diagonals

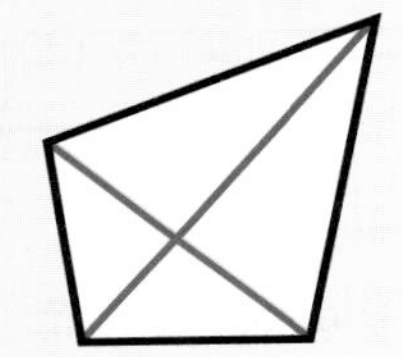

5-sided figure:
5 diagonals

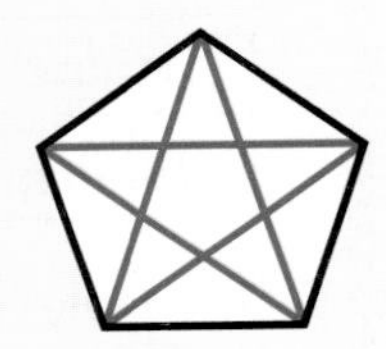

Notice that the four-sided figure has two more diagonals than the three-sided figure. The five-sided figure has three more diagonals than the four-sided figure. The six-sided figure has four more diagonals than the five-sided figure.

A seven-sided figure will have 14 diagonals (9 + 5). An eight-sided figure will have 20 diagonals (14 + 6). A nine-sided figure will have 27 diagonals (20 + 7).

Try These

1. Each side of each triangle is one inch long. If there were 42 triangles in a row, what would be the combined length of all of their sides?

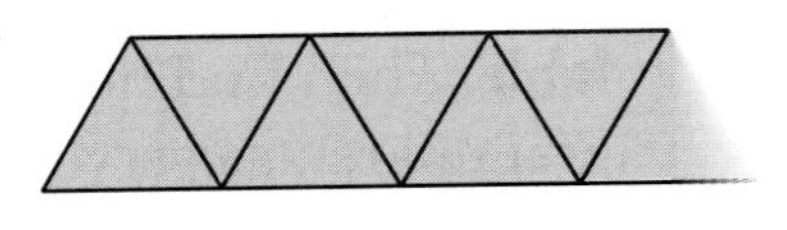

2. A bell rang 22 times. Each ring lasted four seconds. Two seconds elapsed between rings. How long did the ringing last?

Work Backward

A problem may tell you what happened at the end of a series of steps and ask you to find what happened at the beginning. To solve the problem, work backward step by step to the beginning.

Problem Solving Strategies

- Draw a Picture
- Look for a Pattern
- Guess and Check
- Use Logical Reasoning
- Make an Organized List
- Make a Table
- Solve a Simpler Problem
- Work Backward

Choose a Tool

Example

Ed was trying to decide when to get up in the morning. He needed 45 minutes to get ready for school. His bus ride took 25 minutes. He wanted to get to school 20 minutes early to do some library research. If school starts at 8:30, at what time should he get up?

The problem gives you the amounts of time it will take to accomplish three tasks (45 minutes, 25 minutes, 20 minutes). It also tells you the time the last task must end (8:30). To solve the problem, work backward to the beginning.

Task	Amount of Time	Conclusion
3	Ed did research for 20 minutes. Then it was 8:30.	He began his research 20 minutes before 8:30, at 8:10.
2	He rode the bus for 25 minutes. Then it was 8:10.	He got on the bus 25 minutes before 8:10, at 7:45.
1	He spend 45 minutes getting ready. Then it was 7:45.	He began getting ready 45 minutes before 7:45, at 7:00

Ed should get up by 7:00.

Try These

1. One winter night, the temperature fell 14 degrees between midnight and 6 A.M. Between 6 A.M. and 10 A.M., the temperature doubled. By noon it had risen another 11 degrees, to 33°F. Find the midnight temperature.

2. Lake Erie is half as wide as Lake Michigan. Lake Erie is five miles wider than Lake Ontario. Lake Superior is three times as wide as Lake Ontario. Lake Superior is 159 miles wide. How wide is Lake Michigan?

Chapter 1

Statistics—Real-World Use of Whole Numbers

Danger! Shark Attack!

Danger! Shark Attack!
Page 5

Reading and Interpreting Graphs

5

Sharks vary in lengths from 4 inches to 60 feet. Which shark is the longest? Which is the shortest?

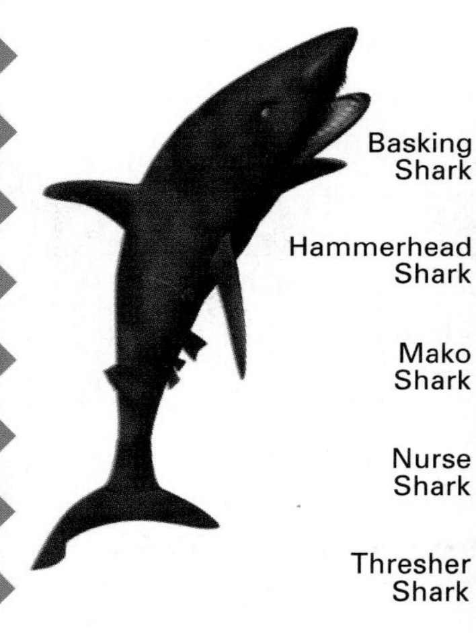

LINKS

Entertainment

227,500,000 homes in China have televisions. The United States has 94,200,000 homes with televisions.

People of the World

Charts and graphs in Japan's *Asahi Shimbun* newspaper are seen by more than 12,500,000 people every day. That's about four times the population of Oklahoma.

Science

If you made a bar graph for the planets' distances from the Sun, Pluto's bar would be 108 times longer than Mercury's.
www.mathsurf.com/6/ch1/science

SECTION B Job Opportunity for Ambitious American

Displaying Data

21

This table gives data on the winners of presidential elections from 1960 to 1996. Whose term in office was the shortest? Who was the oldest president?

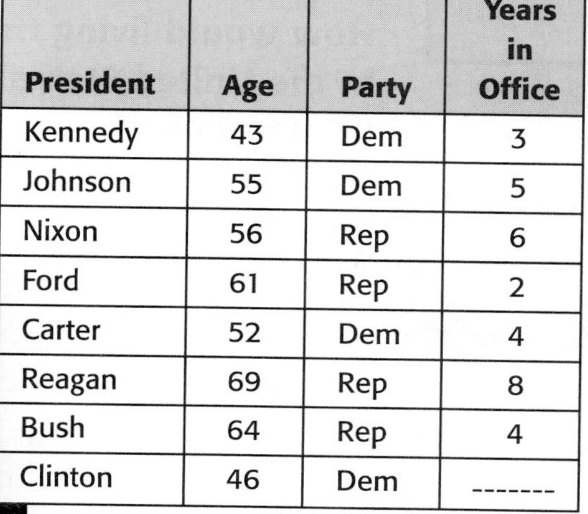

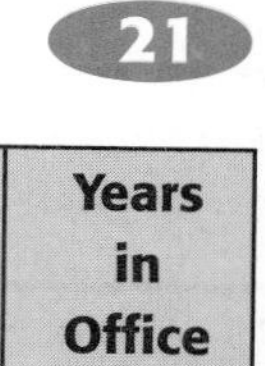

President	Age	Party	Years in Office
Kennedy	43	Dem	3
Johnson	55	Dem	5
Nixon	56	Rep	6
Ford	61	Rep	2
Carter	52	Dem	4
Reagan	69	Rep	8
Bush	64	Rep	4
Clinton	46	Dem	-------

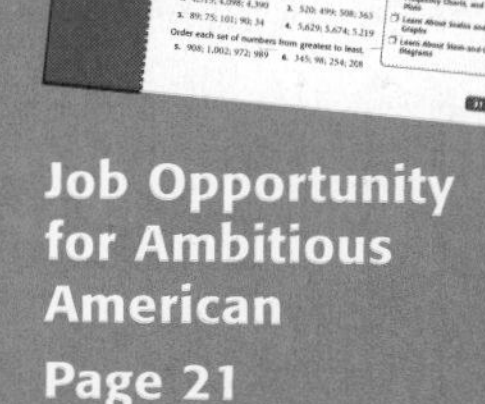

Job Opportunity for Ambitious American
Page 21

SECTION C Will the Real #1 Athlete Please Stand Up?

Describing Data

35

Going, going, gone! How many more home runs did Hank Aaron hit than Harmon Killebrew?

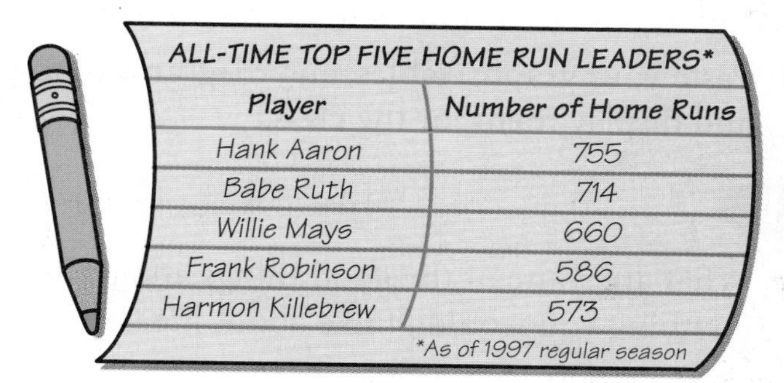

*ALL-TIME TOP FIVE HOME RUN LEADERS**

Player	*Number of Home Runs*
Hank Aaron	755
Babe Ruth	714
Willie Mays	660
Frank Robinson	586
Harmon Killebrew	573

**As of 1997 regular season*

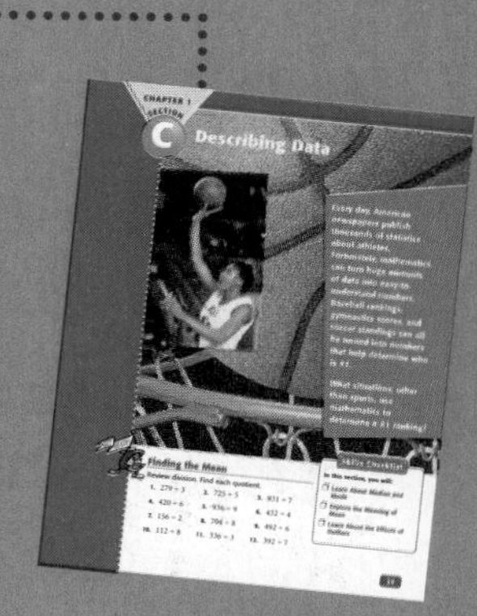

Will the Real #1 Athlete Please Stand Up?
Page 35

Arts & Literature

The letter *e* appears most often in English writings, followed by the letters *t*, *a*, *i*, and *n*.

Social Studies

The mean temperature in Norilsk, Russia, is 12.4°F. Water freezes at temperatures below 32°F.
www.mathsurf.com/6/ch1/social

Materials
posterboard

What is it like to live in another country? How would living there compare to life in the United States? Find out more information about a country your team would like to visit, and present your findings to the class.

Make a Plan

- What country would you like to learn more about?
- How much information will your team need to show others what life is like in another country? Where can you find this information?
- What is the best way to present your data to the class?

Carry It Out

1. Brainstorm a list of all the things you would like to find out about this country.
2. Choose four topics to investigate further.
3. Research your topics. Create bar graphs, tables, or stem-and-leaf diagrams to represent the data you have found.
4. Paste your graphs, tables, and diagrams onto posterboard and display them for the class.

Talk About It

- What are some of the good things about life in this country? Is there anything you wouldn't like about life there?
- How does life in this country compare to your life in the United States? How is it alike? In what ways is it different?

Present the Project

Present your research findings to the class. How does the data on the country you researched compare to the data of the other teams? What else would you like to learn about the places your class explored?

CHAPTER 1

SECTION

A Reading and Interpreting Graphs

Sharks are fascinating but often misunderstood animals. Many more people have been killed by dogs in the last 100 years than by sharks. Out of the 350 species of sharks, only 10 of them are known to have attacked humans.

Why might a graph displaying data about shark attacks be better than a list?

Reading Graphs

Review addition and subtraction. Find each sum or difference.

1. $314 + 56$ **2.** $12 + 233$ **3.** $212 - 71$

4. $149 - 37$ **5.** $566 - 84$ **6.** $108 + 63$

7. $898 - 79$ **8.** $650 + 87$ **9.** $217 + 56$

Skills Checklist

In this section, you will:

- ❒ **Read Graphs**
- ❒ **Learn About Misleading Graphs**
- ❒ **Learn About Scatterplots and Trends**

Chapter 1
Lesson
1

Reading Graphs

You Will Learn

- to read numbers from different types of graphs
- to compare numbers within the same graph

Vocabulary

bar graph

pictograph

line graph

circle graph

Did You Know?

SCUBA is an acronym. It stands for "self-contained underwater breathing apparatus."

Learn

Graphs are a useful way to organize information. A **bar graph** uses vertical or horizontal bars to display numerical information. The length of the bar tells you the number it represents.

Example 1

How much deeper than a free diver can a scuba diver dive?

Look at the bar for the free diver. It represents a depth of about 15 meters. The scuba diver bar represents 50 meters. Since $50 - 15 = 35$, the scuba diver can dive about 35 meters deeper.

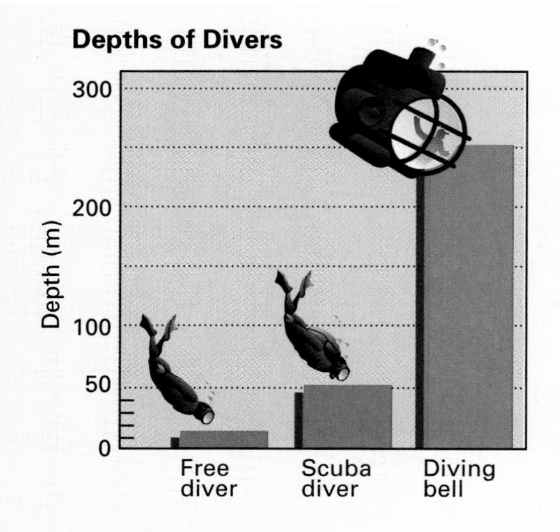

A **pictograph** uses symbols to represent data. Each symbol has the same value. To determine the measure of an item in a pictograph, count the number of symbols and multiply by the value of the symbol.

Example 2

About how many species of animals are there in the San Antonio Zoo?

In the pictograph, the number of species of animals in the San Antonio Zoo is represented by 7 symbols. Each symbol equals 100 species.

$7 \times 100 = 700$

There are about 700 species.

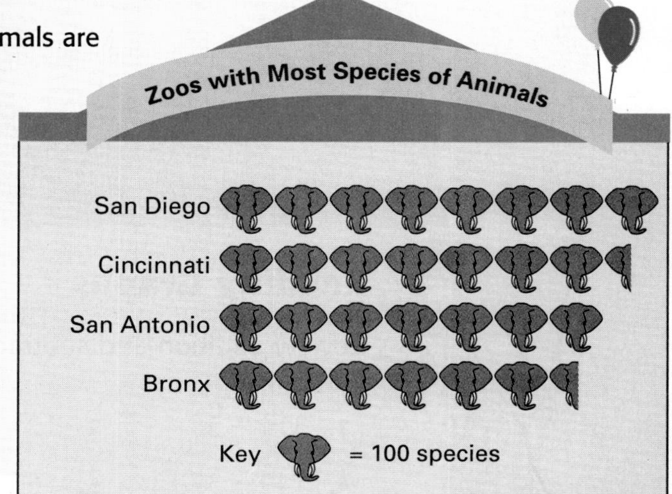

A **line graph** often shows how data changes over time. Each point represents an item of data. The height of the point represents the value of the data. The time is shown by how far to the right the point is.

Example 3

Find the value of a 1980 Rickey Henderson baseball card in 1992.

Find the point above 1992 on the year line. The point is directly to the right of the value 150.

A card was worth $150 in 1992.

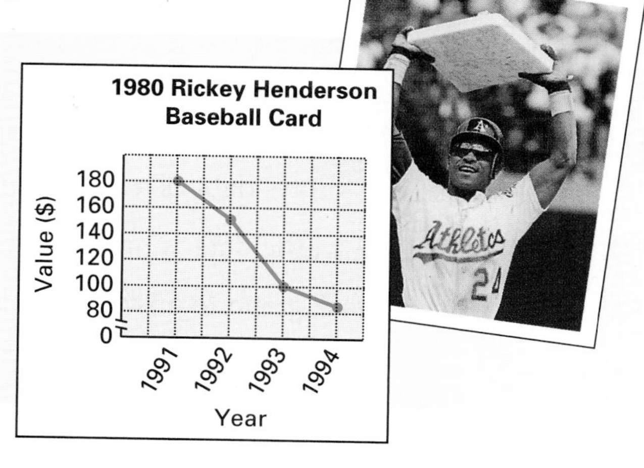

A **circle graph** shows how portions of a set of data compare with the whole set. The greater the value of the data, the wider the wedge that represents the value.

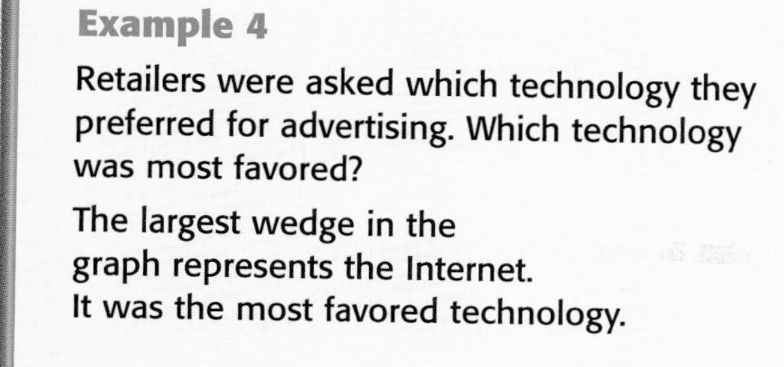

Example 4

Retailers were asked which technology they preferred for advertising. Which technology was most favored?

The largest wedge in the graph represents the Internet. It was the most favored technology.

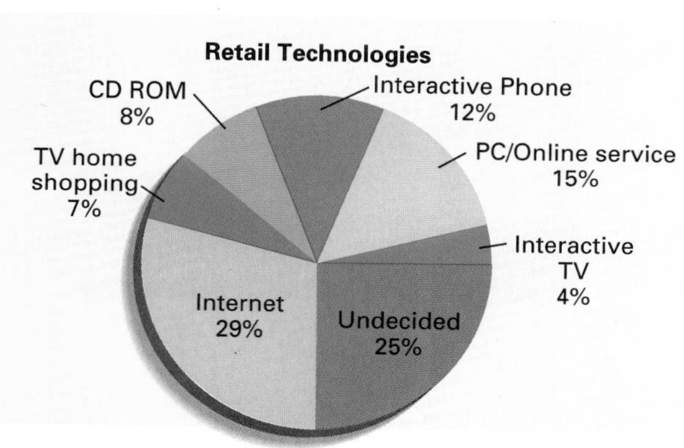

Talk About It

1. How does each type of graph show the value of a data item?
2. For each graph, how can you tell which value is the greatest number? The least number?

Check

1. How much deeper can a diver in a diving bell dive than a scuba diver?
2. About how many species of animals are at the Cincinnati Zoo?
3. In what year was a Rickey Henderson card worth about $100?
4. Which technology was the least preferred for advertising?
5. **Reasoning** On which type of graph is data easiest to interpret? Explain.

Practice

Skills and Reasoning

Fill in each blank with the name of the graph described.

6. A ________ uses symbols to represent data and a key to show the value of each symbol.

7. A ________ shows data as a set of connected points.

8. In a ________, the data is broken into parts of a whole.

Use the Shark Attack graph to answer **9–13.**

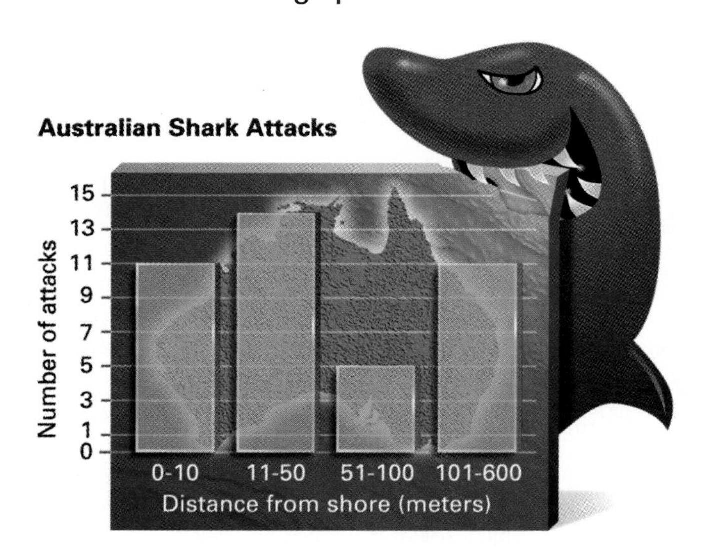

9. What is the total number of shark attacks shown in the data?

10. Which bar represents the most shark attacks? The fewest shark attacks?

11. At what two sets of distances from the shore do the same number of attacks occur?

12. Do more shark attacks take place within 50 m from shore or 51–600 m from shore?

13. **Reasoning** Is swimming close to shore the safest place to swim? Explain.

Use the Cost of Raising a Child graph for **14–19.**

14. What is the cost of transportation?

15. For each \$100 a parent spends on raising a child to age 18, how much more is spent on housing and clothes than on education?

16. **Mental Math** If the cost of housing were $\$33\frac{1}{3}$ instead of \$33, what fraction of the whole would the cost of housing represent?

17. **Mental Math** Which costs are about twice as much as the cost of education? Five times as much? Eleven times as much?

18. Which cost is about the same as the costs of education, clothes, and food combined?

19. **Estimation** For each \$300 spent, estimate how much is spent for food and clothes.

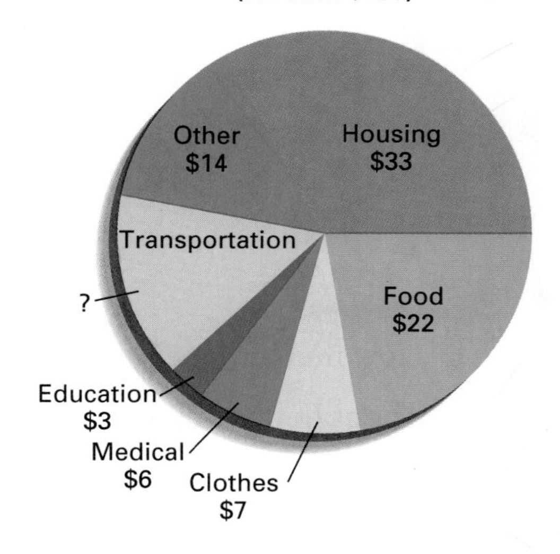

Problem Solving and Applications

Ocean sizes are often measured in square miles. Use this measurement and the graph to answer **20–23.**

20. What is the size of the Arctic Ocean?

21. The total area of the Pacific, Atlantic, and Indian Oceans is 124,000,000 square miles. How many square miles is the Pacific Ocean?

22. Using Data If the Pacific Ocean were included in this pictograph, how many drops of water would be listed after its name?

Ocean Sizes

Atlantic
Indian
Arctic
Key = 4,000,000 sq mi

23. Calculator What is the difference in square miles between the sizes of the Indian Ocean and the Atlantic Ocean?

Use the CD-ROM Sales graph to answer **24–27.**

24. Describe the change(s) in the data overall and from year to year.

25. What's the difference between the number of CD-ROMs sold in 1993 and the number sold in 1994?

26. What year showed the biggest increase in CD-ROM sales?

27. Critical Thinking About how many CD-ROM sales would you expect in the year 2000?

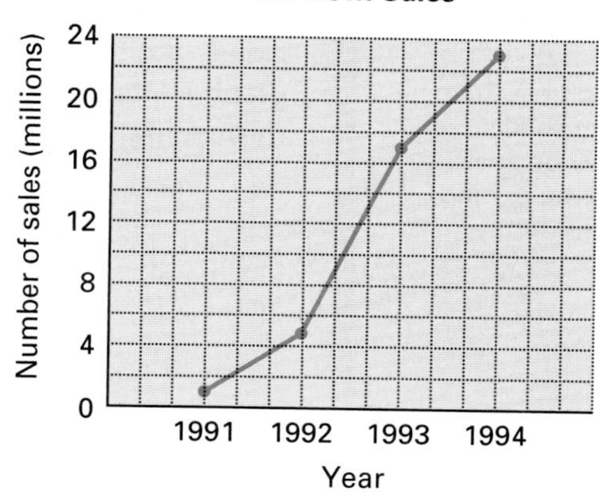

PRACTICE AND APPLY

Mixed Review and Test Prep

STAY SHARP!

Write each number in standard form.

28. five thousand one hundred six

29. eighty thousand twenty-two

30. ten thousand six

31. two thousand four hundred

Add.

32. 23 + 35 **33.** 61 + 29 **34.** 456 + 43 **35.** 712 + 94

36. 888 + 612 **37.** 272 + 422 **38.** 510 + 501 **39.** 348 + 282

40. 643 + 89 **41.** 712 + 280 **42.** 79 + 465 **43.** 811 + 106

44. How much is 257 plus 1,402 plus 1,036?

Ⓐ 2,685 Ⓑ 5,008 Ⓒ 1,795 Ⓓ 2,695

Skills Practice Bank, page 660, Set 1

Chapter 1
Lesson
2

Misleading Graphs

You Will Learn

- to identify common ways that a graph can suggest misleading relationships

Did You Know?

Great white sharks are known to attack humans, but they usually don't eat them. Great white sharks usually prey on seals, sea lions, whales, and other sharks.

Learn

There are many ways to make a graph that can mislead a reader. One way is to start labeling the graph at a number other than zero without indicating that some numbers have been skipped.

Example 1

Is the great white shark twice as long as the mako shark?

In graph A, the top bar is twice as long as the bottom bar. But the value for the great white shark, 16, is not twice the value for the mako shark, 13.

In graph B, the great white shark is clearly not twice as long. When the bar graph starts at 0, the graph is not misleading.

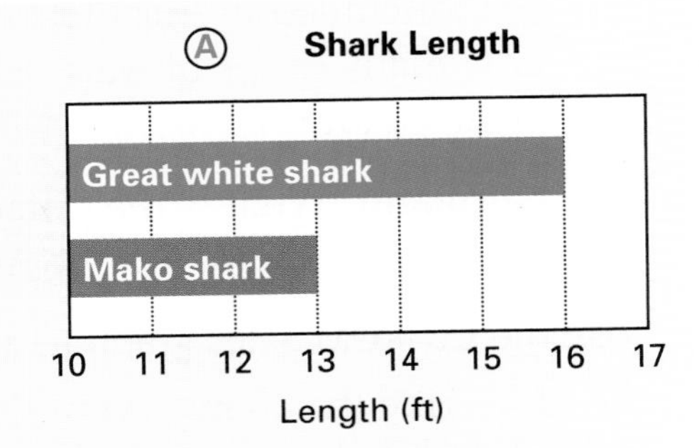

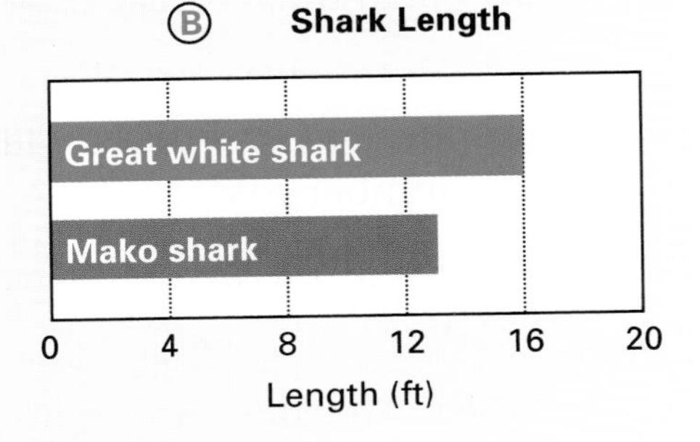

Sometimes the values shown in the vertical scale may not form a consistent pattern.

Example 2

Is the hippo able to hold its breath for twice as long as the sea otter?

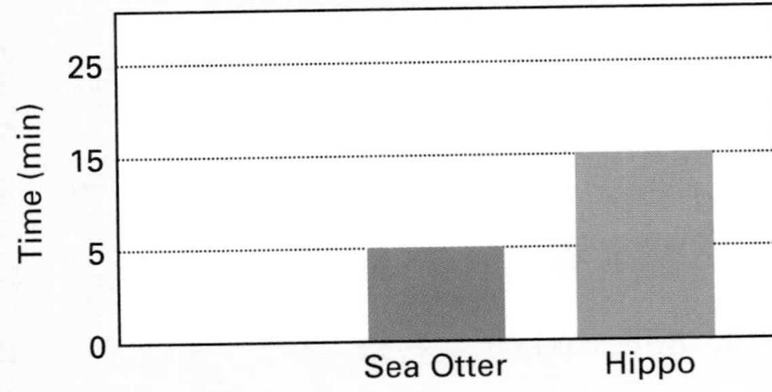

Both bars start at zero, and the hippo bar is twice as tall as the sea otter bar. But the data values show that a sea otter can hold its breath for 5 minutes and the hippo for 15 minutes—three times as long as a sea otter. A misleading impression is created because the 5–15 space covers more values than the 0–5 space, but both spaces have equal heights.

A graph can also lengthen or shorten the spaces between data values in order to mislead readers.

Example 3

Which admission price went up more quickly?

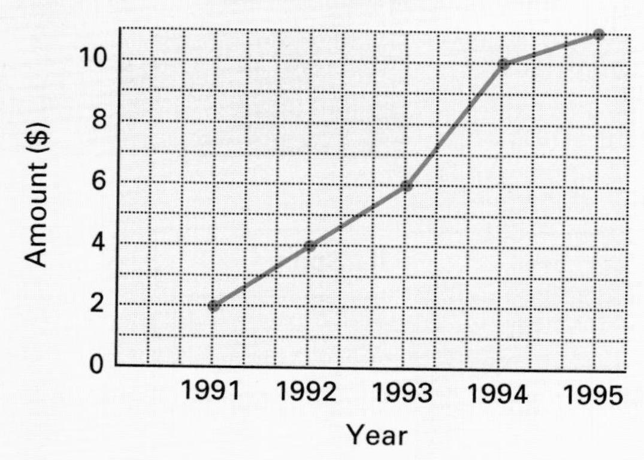

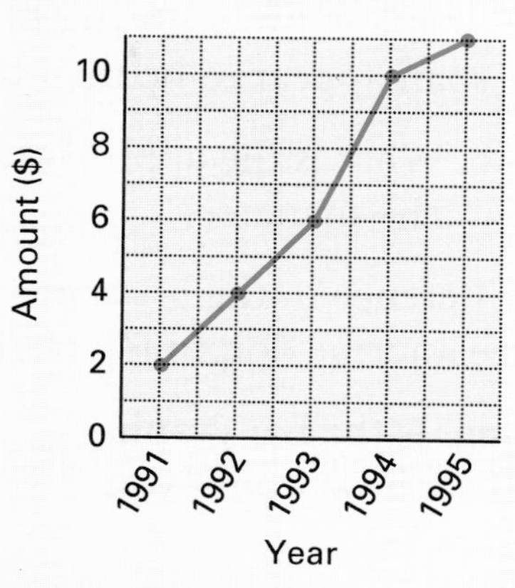

In the graph on the right, the years are much closer together, so the line appears to climb more rapidly. However, both graphs show exactly the same data. Neither admission price went up more quickly.

Math Tip

Many graphs can be misleading because the vertical scale has been drawn incorrectly. When evaluating a graph for misleading impressions, check the vertical scale first.

Talk About It

1. How can a graph's labels be manipulated to mislead the reader?
2. How can the axes of a graph be manipulated to mislead the reader?

Check

Tell how each graph could create a misleading impression.

1.

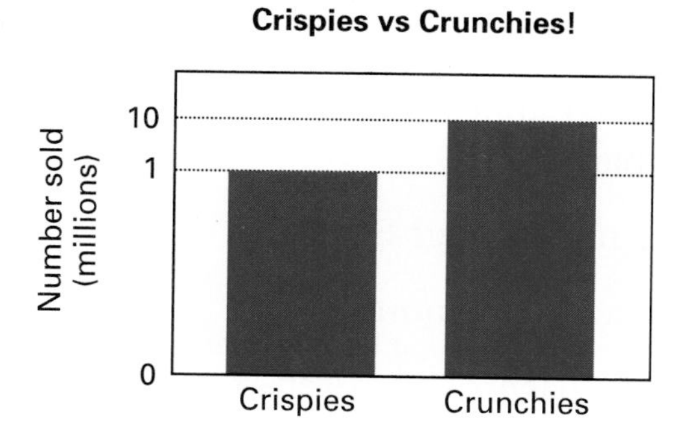

2.

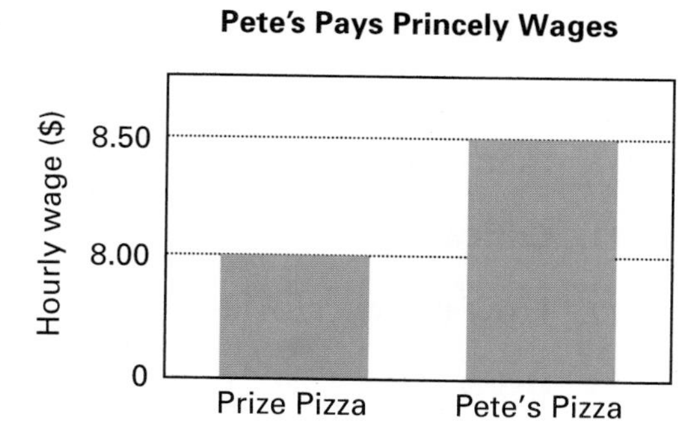

3. **Reasoning** Why might someone want to create a misleading graph? Give examples from everyday life.

Practice

Skills and Reasoning

Use the Life Span graph for **4–8.**

4. What is the information in the graph about?
5. **Estimation** How many times greater does the manatee's life span appear to be than the dolphin's?
6. Read the graph. What is the approximate life span of the dolphin? The manatee?
7. What is the difference in the life spans of the manatee and the dolphin?
8. **Critical Thinking** Is the bar graph misleading? If so, how would you correct the graph?

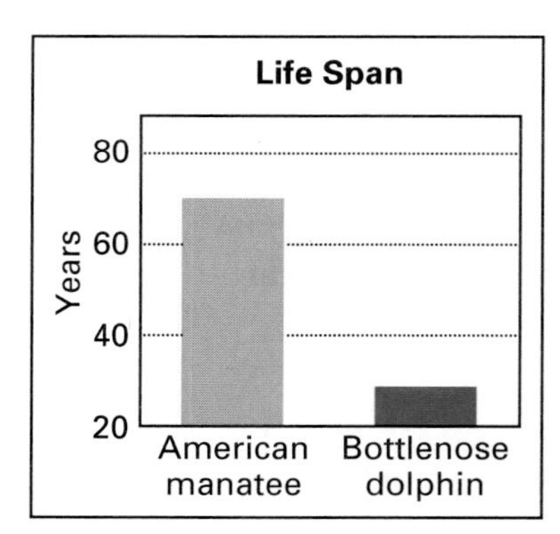

Use the Calories Needed graphs for **9–12.**

Daily Calories Needed

Number of calories

20
15
10
5
0

mouse robin

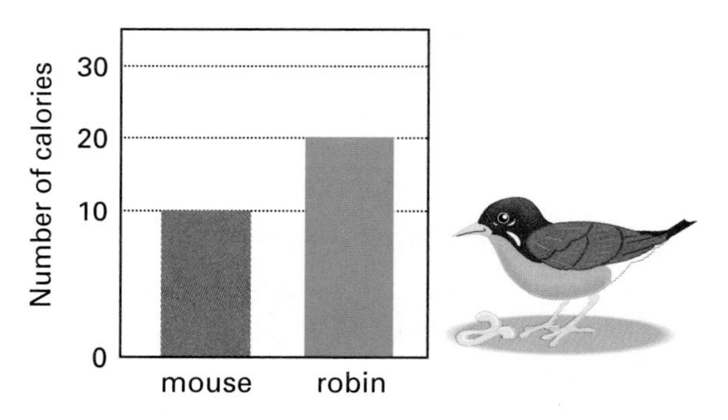

9. **Science** How many calories a day does a mouse need? A robin?
10. **Estimation** For each graph, the robin's calorie bar appears to be how many times greater than the mouse's calorie bar?
11. **Critical Thinking** Do you think either graph is misleading? Explain.
12. How many calories does each animal need in a 30-day month?
13. **Using Data** Use the Lengths of Sharks graph on page 2 to answer each question.
    - **a.** What is the difference in length between the basking shark and the mako shark?
    - **b.** Which shark is one-half the length of the basking shark?

Problem Solving and Applications

Use the population graphs to answer **14–17.**

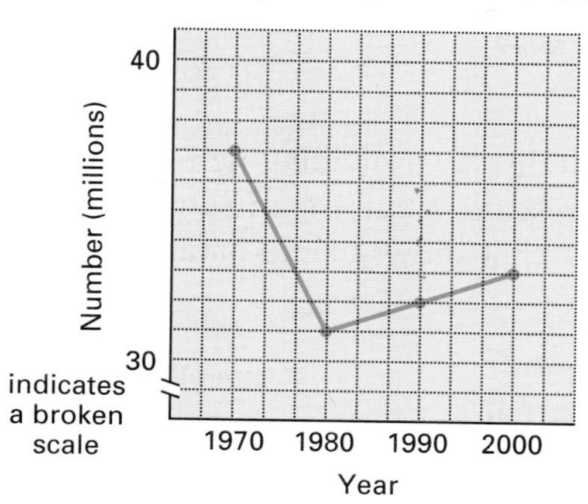

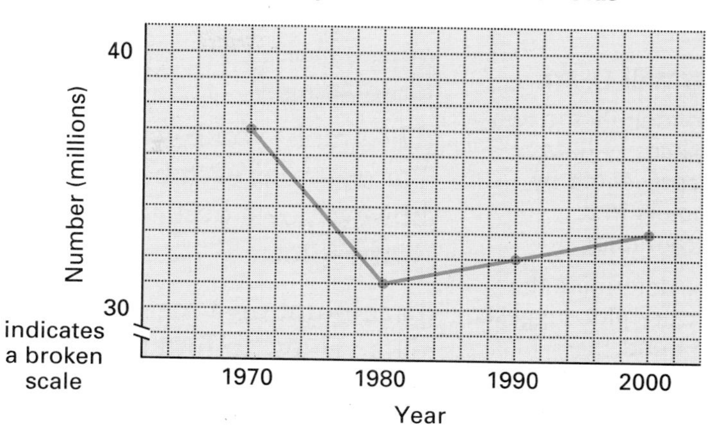

14. Critical Thinking How many more 5–13-year-olds will there be in the year 2000 than there were in the year when their population was the least?

15. Patterns What do you think the population of 5–13-year-olds will be in the year 2010?

16. Reasoning Why might someone want to represent the information with the second graph?

17. Write Your Own Problem Use the population data to write a problem. After solving your problem, exchange it for a classmate's. Then compare answers.

Mixed Review and Test Prep

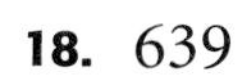

STAY SHARP!

Write each number in words.

18. 639 **19.** 204 **20.** 883 **21.** 913

22. 6,728 **23.** 8,912 **24.** 2,856 **25.** 1,045

Subtract.

26. $239 - 51$ **27.** $681 - 67$ **28.** $714 - 80$ **29.** $809 - 37$

30. $489 - 211$ **31.** $503 - 432$ **32.** $932 - 601$ **33.** $883 - 577$

34. How many times must you rename when you subtract 325 from 4,037?

Ⓐ Zero times Ⓑ One time Ⓒ Three times Ⓓ Four times

Chapter 1
Lesson
3

Scatterplots and Trends

You Will Learn

- to identify the two pieces of data represented by points in a scatterplot
- to determine if a scatterplot suggests a trend

Vocabulary

scatterplot

trend

Did You Know?

The male mako shark usually grows to $6\frac{1}{2}$ feet long. The female shark grows to $8\frac{1}{2}$ feet long. Mako sharks have been known to grow up to 13 feet long.

Learn

The graphs you have studied so far all display individual items of data. For example, each bar in a graph represents one number. Sometimes, however, data occurs in pairs. A graph that shows paired data is called a **scatterplot**.

Each point on a scatterplot represents *two* data values. To find the two values, start at the zero point, or origin, which is in the lower left corner. Find the first value by counting how far *right* you must go until you are under the point. Find the second value by counting how far *up* you must go to reach the point.

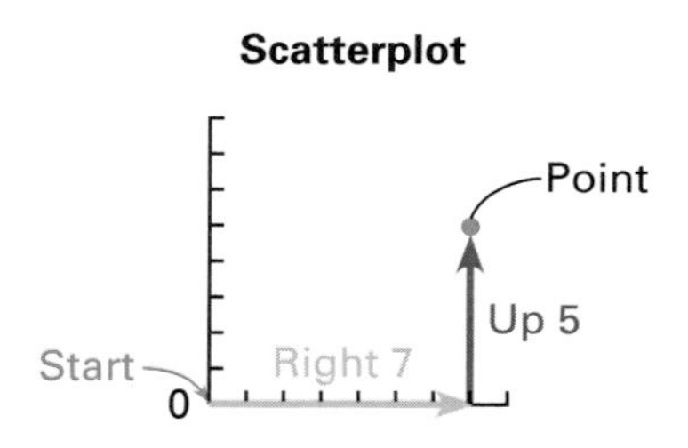

To reach the point shown in this scatterplot, move right 7, then up 5. When describing the position of a point in a scatterplot, always remember to give the horizontal data first and the vertical data second.

Example 1

This scatterplot compares speeds of a mako shark (M) and two blue sharks (B 1 and B 2) to their lengths. Give the length and speed of each shark.

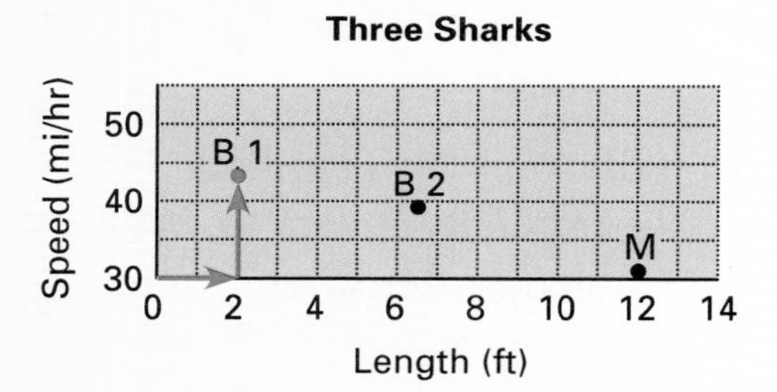

To reach data point B 1, go over to 2 feet and up to about 43 m/hr. This means that the first blue shark was 2 feet long and traveled 43 mi/hr.

Second blue shark:	Length: $6\frac{1}{2}$ feet	Speed: 39 mi/hr
Mako shark:	Length: 12 feet	Speed: 31 mi/hr

Sometimes the points in a scatterplot suggest a relationship between the two measured quantities. Look again at the scatterplot in Example 1. Notice that the farther to the right a point is, the farther down it is. This suggests that for the sharks in the experiment, the longer a shark was, the slower it swam. A relationship between two sets of data that shows a pattern like this is called a **trend**.

Example 2

This scatterplot shows an upward or increasing trend.

Earthquakes and Damaged Houses

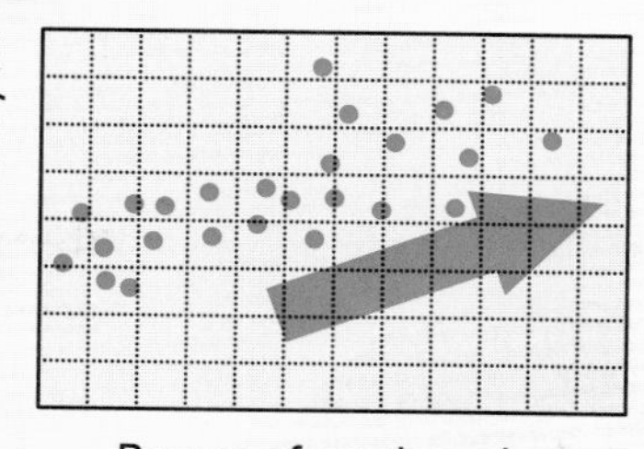

The farther to the right a point is, the farther up it is. This suggests that the greater the power of an earthquake, the greater the number of houses that are destroyed.

Example 3

This scatterplot does not clearly show an increase or a decrease.

Earthquakes and Red Houses

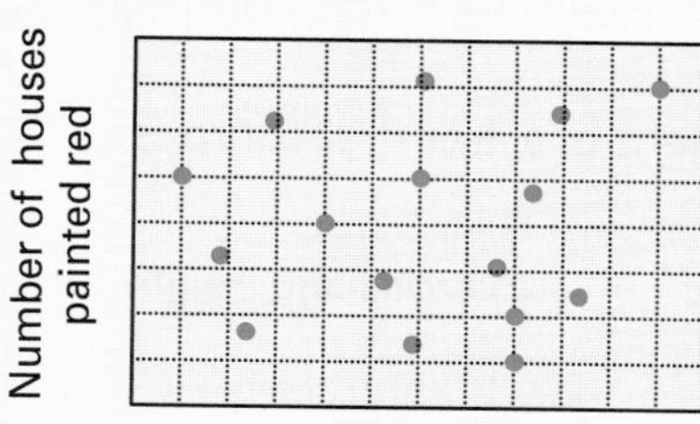

The points don't fall into any particular pattern. This suggests that there is no trend between the power of an earthquake and the number of red houses.

Talk About It

1. In what ways are a line graph and a scatterplot similar? In what ways are they different?
2. How can you determine whether a scatterplot indicates a trend?

Check

1. For each point on the graph, estimate the data represented by the point.

   a. A **b.** B **c.** C **d.** D **e.** E

2. Is there a trend? If so, describe the pattern of the data.
3. **Reasoning** Give an example of two sets of related data that might increase together. Give an example where one increases as the other decreases.

Cordless Phone Sales

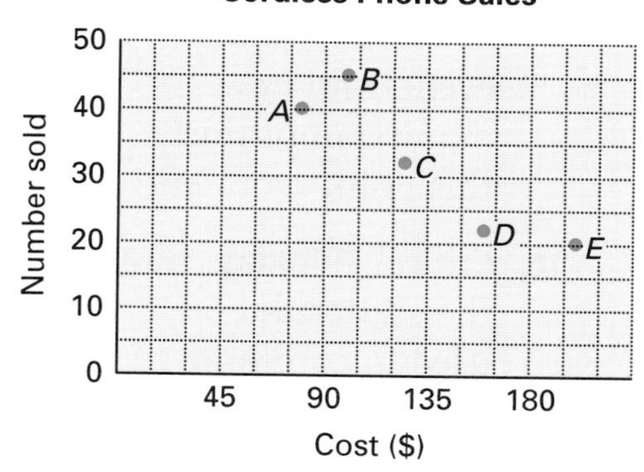

Practice

Skills and Reasoning

For each point on the graph, describe:

4. How far to the right and how far up on the graph it is.

5. The weight and the length each point represents.

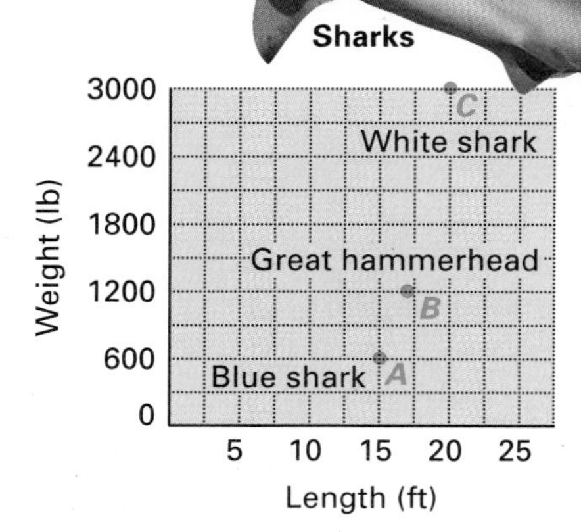

For each scatterplot, determine if there is a trend. If there is, describe the pattern of the data.

6. **Age and Height**

Height

Age

7.

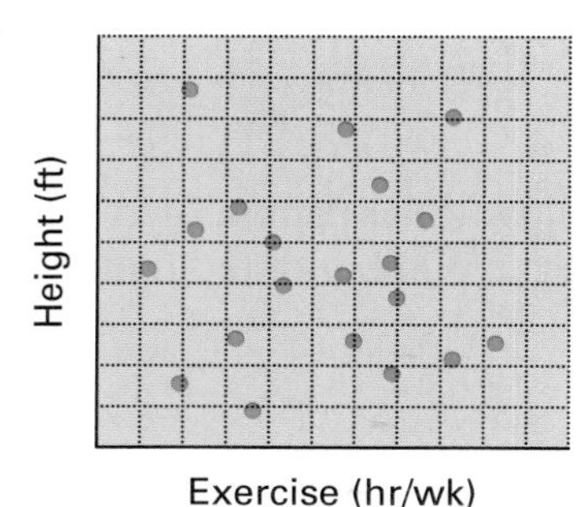

8.

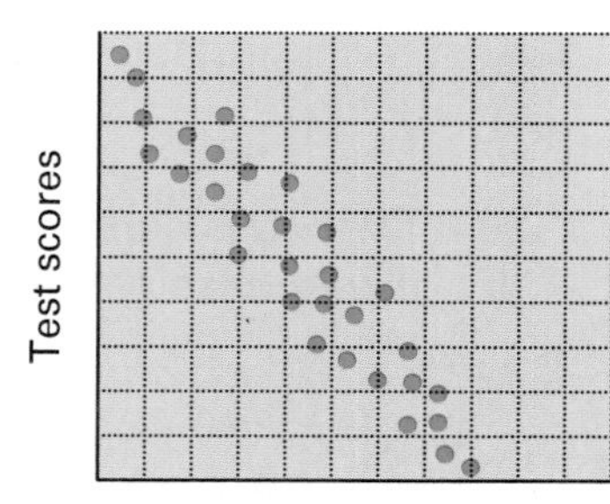

Use the Olympics graph to answer **9** and **10**.

9. **Estimation** Which point represents a number of events that is about four times greater than the number of stamps? About how many events and how many stamps does this point represent?

10. **Critical Thinking** Can the scatterplot be used to compute a mean, or average? Explain.

The Olympics

Number of stamps of events: 0, 5, 10, 15, 20, 25

Number of events: 20, 40, 60

Points: A, B, C, D, E

Problem Solving and Applications

For each situation, describe what the pattern in a scatterplot would look like.

11. The hours people work per week compared to their weekly salary

12. People's ages compared to the amount of sleep needed

13. The number of books you read compared to the scores on your math tests

14. The number of people in a family compared to the amount of money they spend on groceries each week

Use the Calorie Requirements graph for **15–18.**

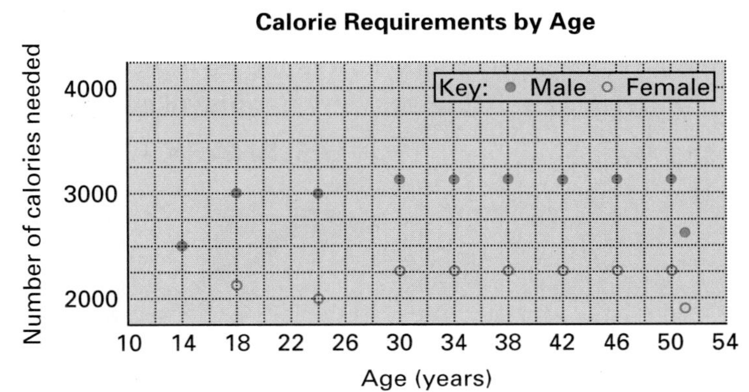

15. At what age(s) do males need the most calories? Females?

16. At what age is the difference in caloric needs the greatest between males and females? The least? How can you tell?

17. **Patterns** What words would you use to describe the pattern that is shown in the data for males? For females? For males and females?

18. **Mental Math** Generally, who needs more calories, males or females?

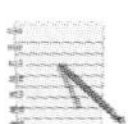

19. **Journal** In your own words, describe and sketch the kinds of patterns you have seen in scatterplots.

Mixed Review and Test Prep

STAY SHARP!

Write each as a number.

20. nine hundred twenty-nine

21. six thousand six hundred six

22. four thousand ninety-eight

23. eight thousand nine hundred

Multiply.

24. 6×425 **25.** 9×481 **26.** 2×804 **27.** 8×236

28. Suppose a line graph displays a negative trend. Which word best describes this situation?

Ⓐ Constant Ⓑ Decreasing Ⓒ Increasing Ⓓ Unchanged

Skills Practice Bank, page 660, Set 2

Chapter 1

Problem Solving

Decision Making: Shark Study

You Will Learn

- to use graphs to make decisions about researching shark attacks

Explore

You want to research sharks and the frequency in which they attack. You must choose either Florida or California for your research and can travel late spring, summer, or early fall.

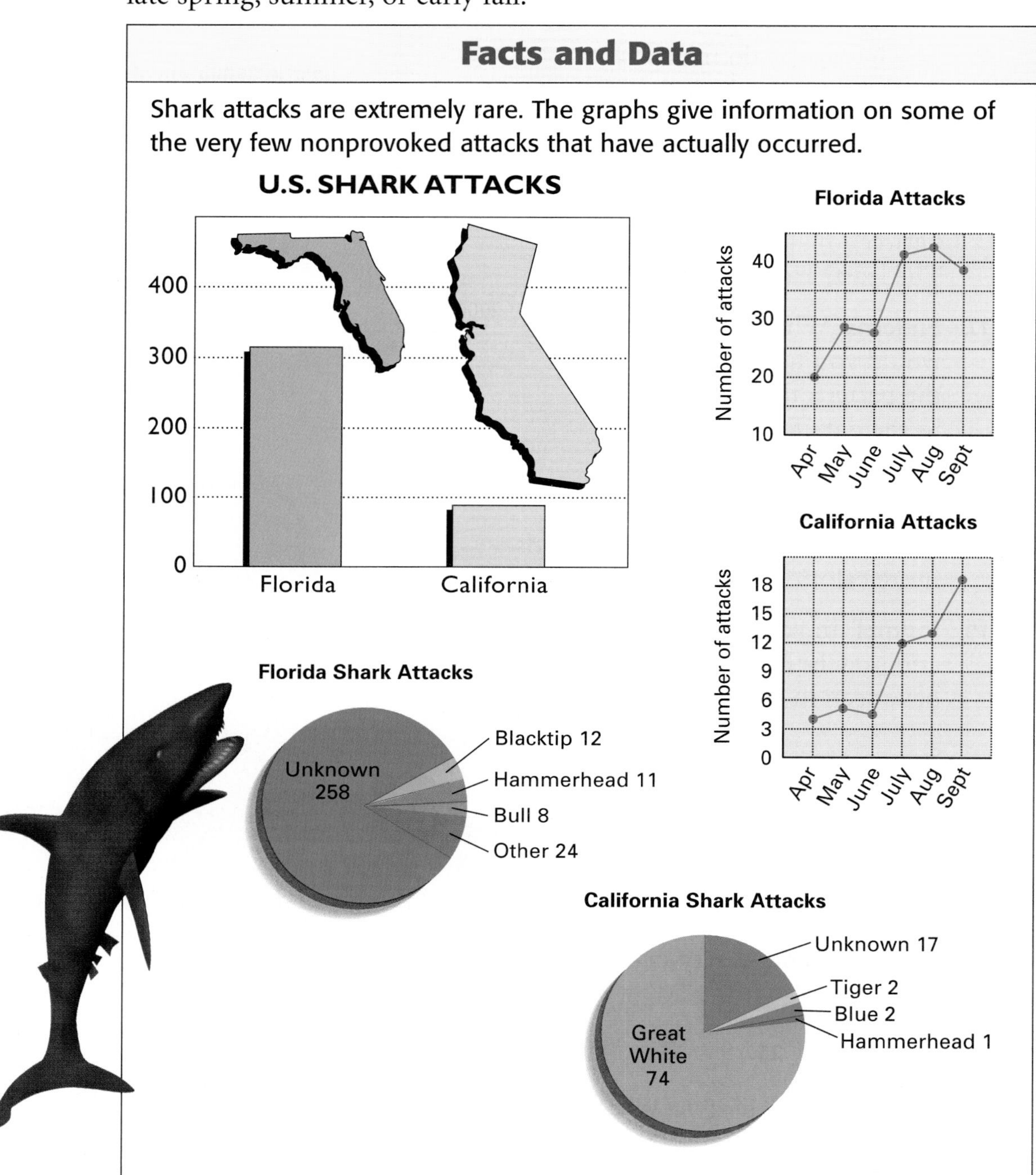

Work Together

Understand

1. What decision are you being asked to make?
2. What kind of information do you have to help you?

Plan and Solve

3. According to the graphs, which state experiences the greatest number of shark attacks?
4. In Florida, during what month(s) is the risk of being attacked by a shark the greatest?
5. In California, during what month(s) is the risk of being attacked by a shark the greatest?
6. In California, which shark appears to be most dangerous?
7. In Florida, which shark appears to attack the least often?
8. Consider all of the information that is provided by the graphs. What specific information is most useful to you?
9. What specific information provided by the graphs is least useful to you?
10. Which of these words—*impossible, not likely, very likely, or certain*—would you choose to describe the chance that a swimmer in California or in Florida will be attacked by a shark? Explain.

Make a Decision

11. When and where did you decide to do your research?
12. What facts and data helped convince you where and when to go?

Present Your Decision

13. Share your decision and the strategies you used with the class.

SECTION A
Review and Practice

(**Lesson 1**) Use the line graphs for **1-3.**

1. In 1980, how much garbage did each person generate in a day? A family of four in a day?
2. Describe the change in data over time.
3. How are the two graphs alike? Different?

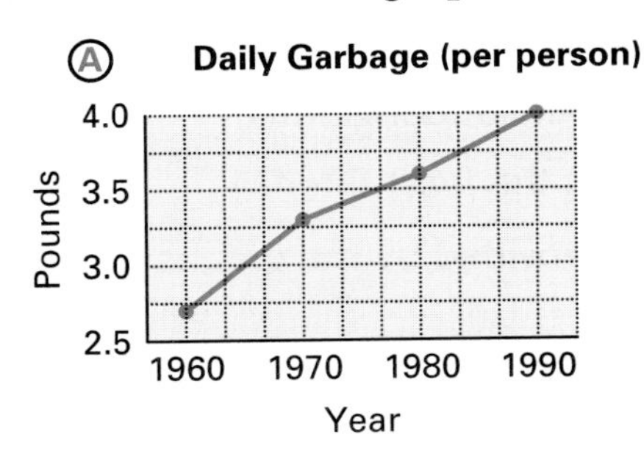

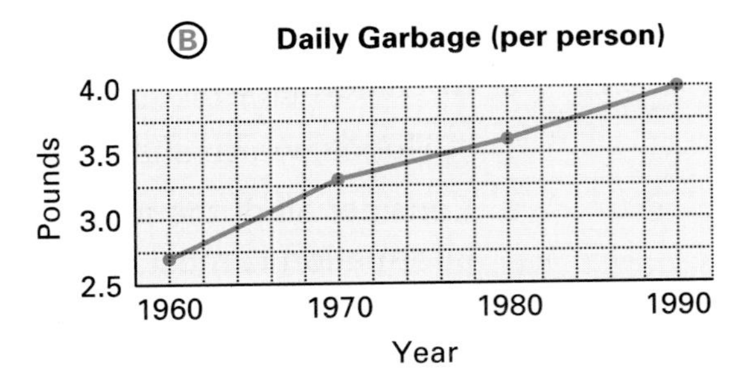

(**Lessons 1 and 2**) Use the bar graph for **4–7.**

4. Which special had the most viewers?
5. How many more viewers watched *The Sharks* than watched *Great Moments?*
6. What was the least-watched show?
7. Could the graph be misleading? Explain.

(**Lessons 2 and 3**) Solve.

8. A group of scientists attached radar tracking devices to two sharks to see how far they would swim in a week. The graph shows the distance traveled by each shark.
   a. How much further did Shark B travel than Shark A?
   b. Is the graph misleading? Explain.

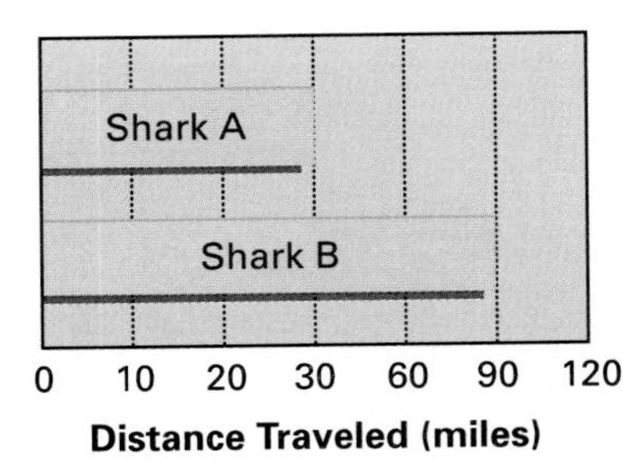

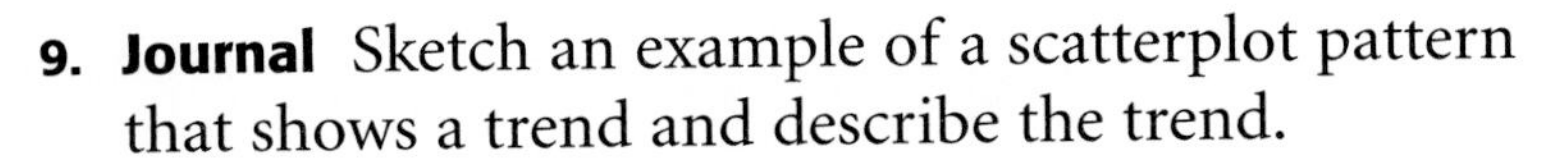

9. **Journal** Sketch an example of a scatterplot pattern that shows a trend and describe the trend.

Skills Checklist

In this section, you have:

- **Read Graphs**
- **Learned About Misleading Graphs**
- **Learned About Scatterplots and Trends**

CHAPTER 1
SECTION
B Displaying Data

Think about what it would be like to have the President's job. Every day, the President of the United States has to organize and interpret vast amounts of information. One way the President can better understand this information is by using mathematics.

Why is it important for numerical data to be organized?

GET READY!

Choosing a Scale

Review ordering numbers. Order each set of numbers from least to greatest.

1. 4,319; 4,098; 4,390 **2.** 520; 499; 508; 365

3. 89; 75; 101; 90; 34 **4.** 5,629; 5,674; 5,219

Order each set of numbers from greatest to least.

5. 908; 1,002; 972; 989 **6.** 345; 98; 254; 208

Skills Checklist

In this section, you will:

- ❒ Learn About Tallies, Frequency Charts, and Line Plots
- ❒ Learn About Scales and Bar Graphs
- ❒ Learn About Stem-and-Leaf Diagrams

Chapter 1
Lesson
4

Tallies, Frequency Charts, and Line Plots

You Will Learn

- to organize data using tallies and frequency charts
- to use a line plot to show the shape of a data set

Vocabulary

tally marks

frequency chart

line plot

Learn

Before data can be displayed, it must be organized. Tallies, frequency charts, and line plots are three ways to organize data.

Tally marks are used to organize large sets of data. Each tally mark indicates one time that the value appears in the data. If a value appears 5 times, or any multiple of 5 times, the fifth tally mark is drawn as a slash to indicate a group of 5.

A **frequency chart** can help you list the data quickly. Each value that appears in the data is followed by the number of times it appeared.

Example 1

Use the data to make a frequency chart. For each age, how many states specify that age in their law?

Ages at Which State Laws Require Children to Be in School									
State	**Age**	**State**	**Age**	**State**	**Age**	**State**	**Age**	**State**	**Age**
CA	6	KS	7	MO	7	NH	6	UT	6
DE	5	MA	6	MT	7	OH	6	VA	5
FL	6	MD	5	NC	7	PA	8	WA	8
ID	7	ME	7	ND	7	TN	7	WI	6
IN	7	MN	7	NE	7	TX	6	WY	7

Math Tip

Some data sets are more easily organized if you put the data into groups. This way, you have fewer categories, and more data per category.

Three states require children to be in school at age 5, eight states at age 6, twelve states at age 7, and two at age 8.

A **line plot** is another way the data can be organized and displayed.

A line plot shows the shape of a set of data. It is similar to a set of tally marks that has been turned onto its side. Instead of tally marks, a line plot uses Xs.

Age	Tally
5	|||
6	~~||||~~ |||
7	~~||||~~ ~~||||~~ ||
8	||

Age 5 6 7 8

Example 2

Make a line plot of the data. What does the line plot show?

Number of Children of 20th-Century Presidents and First Ladies					
2	5	3	3	0	2
2	5	1	1	2	2
2	4	4	2	6	1

The line plot shows that 2 is the most common number of children, 0 and 6 are the least common, and 3, 4, and 5 all appear with the same frequency.

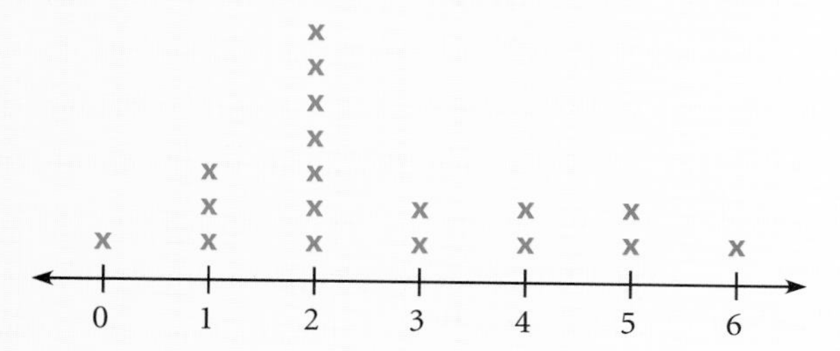

Talk About It

1. How are frequency charts and line plots similar?
2. How are frequency charts different from line plots?

Check

1. Make a tally, a frequency chart, and a line plot of the data in the table.

Average Phone Calls Made (daily)				
2	3	5	2	3
1	0	3	4	2
1	5	3	4	3
2	3	1	4	3

Math Tip
It may be useful to scan the data before you start to tally it. This gives you an idea of how high and how low the numbers will be.

2. **Reasoning** What picture of the data does the line plot show?

Practice

Skills and Reasoning

Record each data set in a tally chart.

3. 5, 4, 1, 3, 3, 6, 10, 4, 7, 3, 1, 1, 2, 1, 4
4. 23, 21, 18, 20, 19, 22, 17, 22, 21, 20, 19, 20, 13, 20
5. 2000, 4000, 5000, 2500, 2000, 1500, 6500, 6000, 4000, 3500

Make a frequency chart for each set of tally marks.

6. Hours spent doing homework each week

Hours	Tally
4	||||
5	𝍸 ||
6	𝍸 𝍸 |||
7	𝍸 ||||
8	𝍸 𝍸 𝍸 |
9	𝍸 𝍸 |
10	𝍸 ||

7. Shoes in your closet

Shoes	Tally
2	𝍸
4	𝍸 |
6	𝍸 ||||
8	𝍸 𝍸 |||
10	𝍸 𝍸 𝍸 |
12	𝍸 𝍸 𝍸 |||

8. Hair length

Length (in.)	Tally
1	|
2	𝍸 |||
3	𝍸 𝍸
4	𝍸
5	|||
6	||
7	|

9. **Geography** Draw a line plot of the number of states bordering each state in the United States.

10. Draw a line plot of the color of students' eyes in your class.

11. **Mental Math** What is the mode of the data in Exercise 9?

12. **History** Draw a line plot of the ages of the first ten Presidents when they took office.

Ages of First Ten Presidents				
51	57	61	54	58
57	61	57	57	68

13. **Reasoning** In which type of graph—tally, frequency chart, or line plot—is the mode easiest to find? Explain.

Problem Solving and HISTORY

If the President signs a bill from the Congress, that bill becomes a law. If the President doesn't think it should become a law, he or she can veto the bill or a portion of the bill. The number of vetoes issued by some early presidents is shown in the table.

President	Number of Vetoes	President	Number of Vetoes
Washington	2	Jackson	12
J. Adams	0	Van Buren	1
Jefferson	0	W. Harrison	0
Madison	7	Tyler	10
Monroe	1	Polk	3
J.Q. Adams	0	Taylor	0

from HERBLOCK: A CARTOONIST'S LIFE (Macmillan Publishing, 1993)

14. Make a frequency chart for the data in the table.

15. Make a line plot for the data in the table.

16. Mental Math What number of vetoes occurred most often?

17. Using Data Which measure—the mean, median, or mode—best describes the number of vetoes the presidents issued?

18. Critical Thinking Does the frequency chart to the right show a data set with mostly even numbers or mostly odd numbers? Explain.

Age	Frequency
5	2
6	5
7	7

19. How does a line plot show the shape of data in a set?

20. Using Data If you were to make a tally of the number of years each president shown on page 3 held office, which president(s) would receive the greatest number of tally marks? The least number?

21. Journal Tell why data should be organized.

Mixed Review and Test Prep

STAY SHARP!

Write each number in words.

22. 217 **23.** 616 **24.** 609 **25.** 2,143 **26.** 9,611

Divide.

27. $98 \div 7$ **28.** $95 \div 5$ **29.** $87 \div 2$ **30.** $74 \div 3$ **31.** $57 \div 1$

32. What is 49 written in expanded form?

Ⓐ $40 + 9$ Ⓑ 49×1 Ⓒ $42 + 7$ Ⓓ forty-nine

Scales and Bar Graphs

You Will Learn

- to make a bar graph

Vocabulary

scale
interval
horizontal axis
vertical axis
range

Learn

A bar graph is a way to visually display and compare numerical data. The **scale** of a bar graph is the "ruler" that measures the heights of the bars. The **interval** is the amount of space between the values on the scale. The lines on which a bar graph is built are the **horizontal axis** and the **vertical axis**.

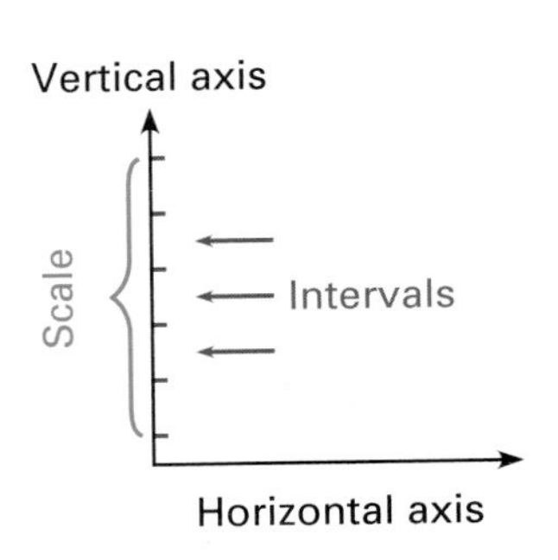

Example 1

The first 42 U.S. Presidents came from five political parties. Use the data to make a bar graph of these parties.

Party	Number of Presidents
Democratic	15
Democratic-Republican	4
Federalist	2
Republican	17
Whig	4

Top value of scale must be greater than 17. Numbers ending in zero are easy to understand and to divide into intervals. Therefore 20 is a good choice for the top of the scale.

20
15
10
5
0

← It is easy to divide 20 into intervals of 5, but you could also use intervals of 2, 4, or 10.

The lowest number in the data is 2. Data is spread fairly evenly across the range from 2 to 17, so zero is a good choice for the bottom of the scale.

Math Tip

The intersection of the vertical and horizontal axes of a bar graph form a 90° or right angle.

Represent each party with vertical bars of the same width. Label the bars and give the graph a title.

Presidents' Political Parties

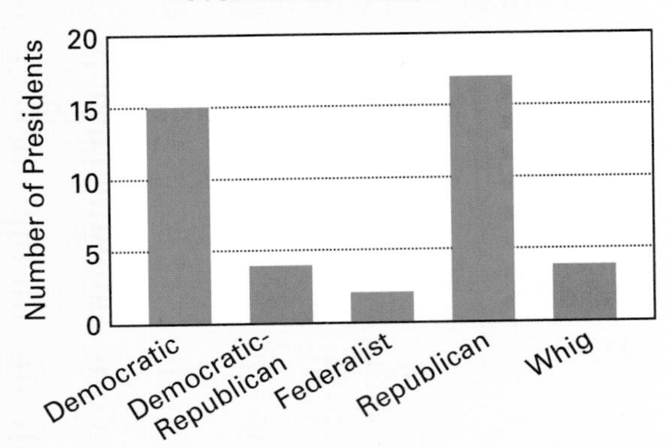

The **range** of a data set refers to the difference between the highest value and the lowest value. For this data set, the highest value is 31, and the lowest is 28. The difference, 31 − 28, is 3. Therefore, the range is 3.

Depending on the range of a set of data, you may sometimes want to "break" the scale of a graph.

Number of Days in Month

31	28	31	30
31	30	31	31
30	31	30	31

Example 2

Make a bar graph of the data.

Lengths of the Great Lakes (through widest point)					
Lake	Erie	Huron	Michigan	Ontario	Superior
Length (mi)	241	206	307	193	350

Since all of the data are 193 or greater, you may want to skip over the values between 0 and 193 by breaking the scale. If you want to show the actual heights of all the bars, however, use the entire scale beginning at 0, as in the right-hand graph.

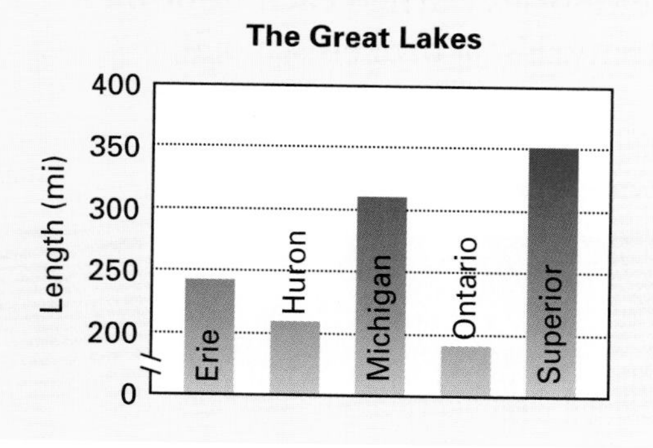

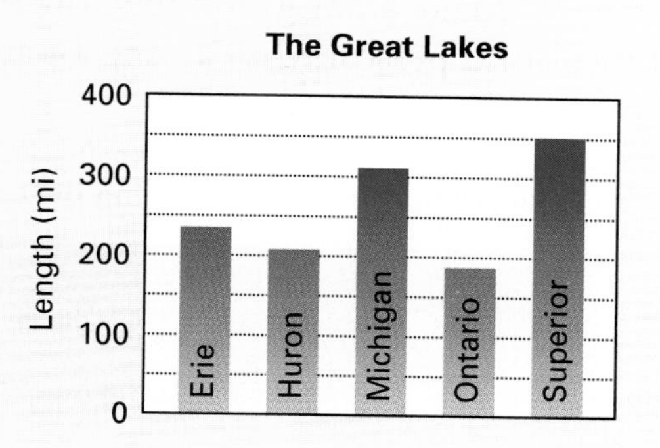

Talk About It

1. How does the range affect the scale and intervals of a bar graph?
2. Is only one scale possible for a given bar graph? Explain.

Check

1. Make a bar graph of the data showing the number of years each female Prime Minister was in office.
2. **Reasoning** When should you use a broken scale on a bar graph? Give an example.

	Meir (Israel)	Ghandi (India)	Thatcher (UK)	Brundtland (Norway)
Years in Office	5	18	11	13

Practice

Skills and Reasoning

For each data set, give the range and choose the better interval to use for a bar graph.

3. Data: 3, 6, 9, 12, 15, 16; interval of 2 or 10?

4. Data: 55, 101, 120, 145; interval of 10 or 25?

5. **Social Studies** Many people consider Presidential burial grounds to be of historical value. The first 20 Presidents were buried in the following states: Illinois (1), Kentucky (1), Massachusetts (2), New Hampshire (1), New York (3), Ohio (3), Pennsylvania (1), Tennessee (3), Vermont (5).

   a. What is the range of values in this set of data?

   b. Make a bar graph of the data.

6. **Science** Make a bar graph to show the calories burned each hour by a 150-pound person while doing an activity. Use a broken scale, if appropriate.

Bicycling

5.5 mi/hr
210 calories

7. **Reasoning** Is only one scale possible for the bar graph you made in Exercise 5? Explain.

8. **Collecting Data** Collect data about the different armspans of your classmates. Round each length to the nearest inch. Make a bar graph of the data.

9. **Mental Math** Suppose the low temperature for a 24-hour period was $-3°$ F and the high temperature was $+2°$ F. What was the range of temperature for that 24-hour period?

10. **Reasoning** Can a broken axis help make a bar graph misleading? Explain.

Problem Solving and Applications

11. Geography The graphs show the average temperatures of two of the coldest and two of the warmest cities in the United States.

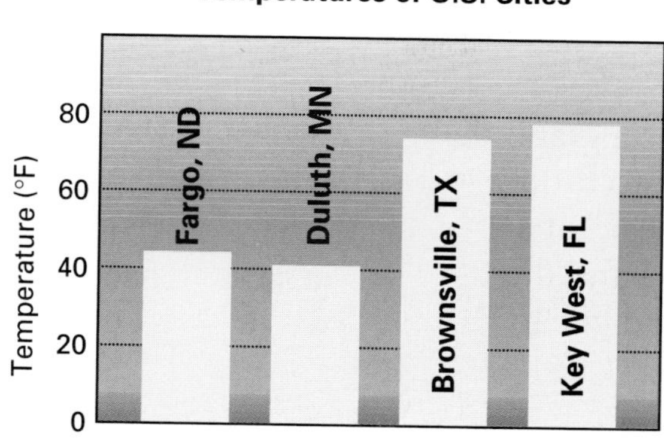

Temperatures of U.S. Cities
Temperature (°F)
0
35
45
55
65
75
85
Fargo, ND
Duluth, MN
Brownsville, TX
Key West, FL

a. For each graph, give the range of values and the interval used on the scale.

b. Critical Thinking Compare the appearance of the two graphs. Could either graph be misleading? Explain.

c. Describe the shape of the data shown in the bar graphs.

12. The bar graph was made from the following data.

a. Which two bars have been drawn incorrectly? What is wrong about them?

b. What would be a better scale for this data?

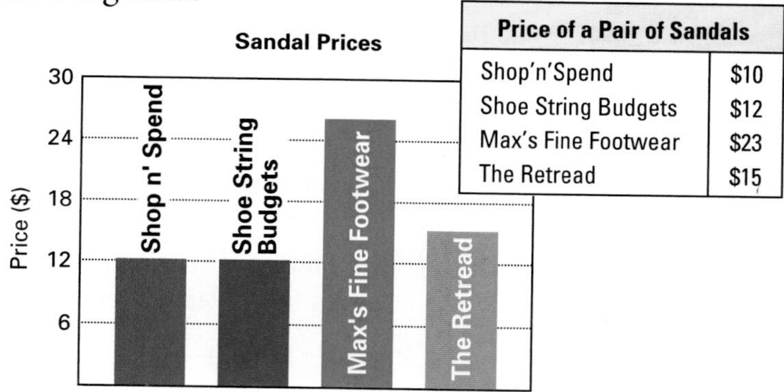

Price of a Pair of Sandals	
Shop'n'Spend	$10
Shoe String Budgets	$12
Max's Fine Footwear	$23
The Retread	$15

Mixed Review and Test Prep

STAY SHARP!

Perform the appropriate operation.

13. 4,678 + 3,909

14. 12,439 + 58,002

15. 536,092 + 182,438

16. 9,346 + 16,724

17. 25,392 + 7,325

18. 36,382 + 945,217

19. 6,329 − 2,735

20. 51,027 − 38,021

21. How many conventions have been held in New York?

Ⓐ 5 Ⓑ 0
Ⓒ 10 Ⓓ 15

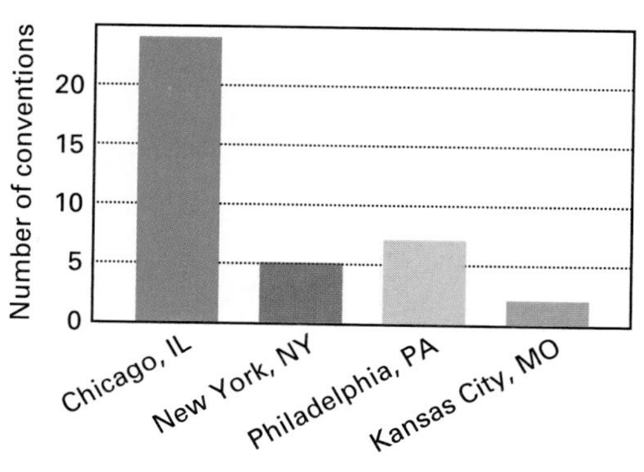

Chapter 1
Lesson
6

Stem-and-Leaf Diagrams

You Will Learn

- to organize large sets of data into stem-and-leaf diagrams

Vocabulary

stem-and-leaf diagram

Learn

A **stem-and-leaf diagram** is a graph that shows the shape of the data according to the data place values. The "leaf" of a number is usually the right-hand digit. The "stem" is the remaining digits to the left.

Number		Stem	Leaf
47	→	4	7
710	→	71	0
8,802	→	880	2
6	→	0	6

Example 1

Analyze the shape of the data in the table by making a stem-and-leaf diagram. Draw two columns, and write the stems in the left column. Since all of the data is in the 40s, 50s, and 60s, you need only three stems: 4, 5, and 6. For every number, write the last digit (the leaf) in the right column on the same line as the matching item.

Ages of 20th-Century Presidents at Inauguration			
42	51	56	55
51	54	51	60
62	43	55	56
61	52	69	64
46			

The diagram shows that the data range from 42 to 69, that the most frequent age is 51, and that most Presidents were in their 50s when they took office.

Stem	Leaf
4	2 3 6
5	1 6 5 1 4 1 5 6 2
6	0 2 1 9 4

Now redraw the diagram, ordering the leaves from least to greatest.

Stem	Leaf
4	2 3 6
5	1 1 1 2 4 5 5 6 6
6	0 1 2 4 9

In this example, note that the data were grouped in intervals of ten: the intervals were 40–49, 50–59, and 60–69. This grouping is different than the grouping you used in other graphs such as bar graphs and tally charts. Those graphs did not group data.

Kennedy was inaugurated at age 43.

Did You Know?

Three presidents have been elected even though they didn't receive the highest number of votes from the people: John Quincy Adams in 1824, Rutherford Hayes in 1876, and Benjamin Harrison in 1888.

The stem-and-leaf diagram in Example 1 shows the data ordered from least to greatest. Ordering the data was the last step that was performed when making the diagram. It can also be the first step.

Example 2

This data shows the age at which our first 20 Presidents died. Display the data in the table in a stem-and-leaf diagram.

Order the data from least to greatest or from greatest to least.

49

53 56

63 64 65 66 67 68

70 71 73 74 77 78 79

80 83 85

90

President	Age	President	Age	President	Age
Washington	67	Van Buren	79	Buchanan	77
J. Adams	90	W. Harrison	68	Lincoln	56
Jefferson	83	Tyler	71	A. Johnson	66
Madison	85	Polk	53	Grant	63
Monroe	73	Taylor	65	Hayes	70
J.Q. Adams	80	Fillmore	74	Garfield	49
Jackson	78	Pierce	64		

Draw two columns. Note the range of the data. Since the data range from 49 to 90 use the 40s, 50s, 60s, 70s, 80s, and 90s as stem intervals. Complete the diagram.

The diagram shows that the data range from 49 to 90, that one President lived for 90 years and another for only 49 years, and that most of our first twenty Presidents died in their 60s or 70s.

Stem	Leaf
4	9
5	3 6
6	3 4 5 6 7 8
7	0 1 3 4 7 8 9
8	0 3 5
9	0

Talk About It

Why is a stem-and-leaf diagram helpful when trying to organize a large set of data?

Check

1. Make a stem-and-leaf diagram of the bowling scores.

130	90	141	128	133	142	113	148	105	93
118	130	133	100	124	146	97	108	126	115
136	144	114	101	93	108	95	143	128	141

2. **Reasoning** Does a stem-and-leaf diagram display organized data? Explain.

3. **Reasoning** Is the median of a stem-and-leaf diagram easy or difficult to find? Explain.

Practice

Skills and Reasoning

4. Follow the steps to make a stem-and-leaf diagram of the data.

   27, 38, 42, 18, 29, 40, 19, 10, 32, 47, 19, 36, 42

   a. Use two columns. Write the stems from least to greatest. Write each leaf to the right of its stem.

   b. Redraw the stem-and-leaf diagram, with the leaves in order from least to greatest.

5. **Science** Make a stem-and-leaf diagram from the data. The ten fastest fish in the world (in miles per hour) include the following: sailfish, 68; blue shark, 43; swordfish, 40; marlin, 50; bluefin tuna, 46; wahoo, 41; tarpon, 35; bonefish, 40; yellowfin tuna, 44; tiger shark, 33.

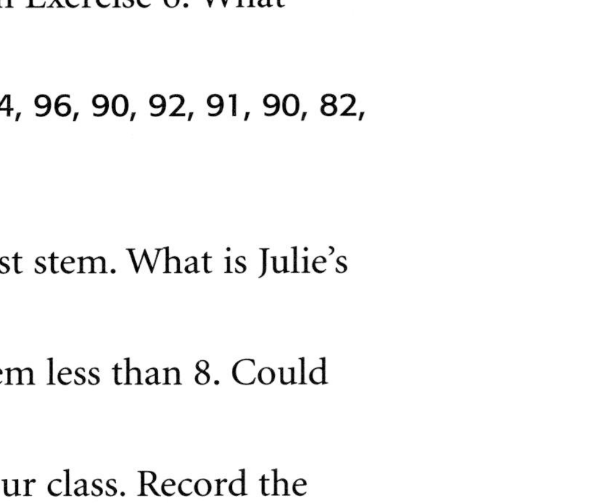

6. **Science** The speed of some animals in the world (in miles per hour) include the following: cheetah, 70; hyena, 40; elephant, 25; domestic rabbit, 35; lion, 50; wart hog, 30; wild turkey, 15; white-tailed deer, 30; squirrel, 12; grizzly bear, 30. Make a stem-and-leaf diagram from the data.

7. **Estimation** Consider the speed of the animals in Exercise 6. What speed do you think a very fast human can run?

This data shows the test scores in Julie's math class: 84, 96, 90, 92, 91, 90, 82, 85, 85, 79, 94, 90, 97, 96. Use the data for **8–10.**

8. Make a stem-and-leaf diagram from the data.

9. Julie's test score is an odd number on the longest stem. What is Julie's score?

10. Michael says his score has 5 as the leaf and a stem less than 8. Could he be correct?

11. Find the height in inches for each student in your class. Record the data in a table. Then make a stem-and-leaf diagram from the data.

Use the stem-and-leaf diagram for **12–14.**

12. What is the range of the values?

13. What value appears most often?

14. What's the largest number in the data that's less than 50?

Stem	Leaf
2	1
4	0 2 2 2 2 3 3
5	0 0 4 4 7 8

Problem Solving and Applications

Use the stem-and-leaf diagram for **15** and **16.**

This stem-and-leaf diagram is based on the available amount of room in cubic feet in the car models of one manufacturer.

Stem	Leaf
0	7 8 8 8
1	3 3 3 3 3 3 3 3 3 3 6 6 7
2	0 0 0
3	3 3 3 3
6	9
8	2
9	1 2 6 6 6 8 8 9 9

15. How many numbers appear three times in the data? How can you tell?

16. Critical Thinking Why is there no 7 in the stem column?

Use the data table in **Exercise 1** for **17–19.**

17. Money Suppose each game shown in the data table cost \$2.50. What was the cost of bowling all of the games shown in the table?

18. Time If each game took 25 minutes to complete, how many hours did it take to complete all of the games?

19. Probability The highest game was 148. Is it *likely* or *unlikely* that the highest game was rolled by the best bowler? Explain.

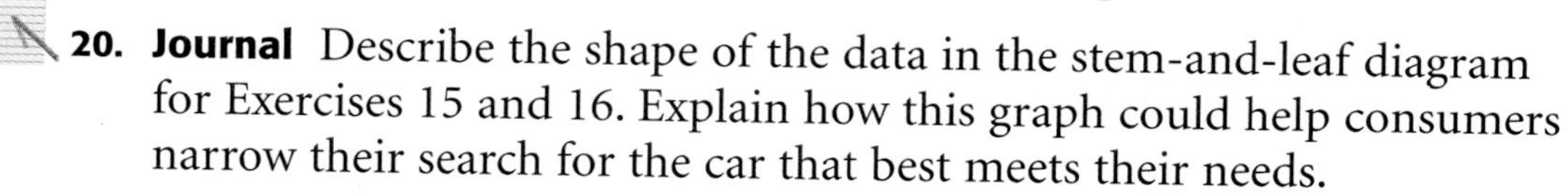

20. Journal Describe the shape of the data in the stem-and-leaf diagram for Exercises 15 and 16. Explain how this graph could help consumers narrow their search for the car that best meets their needs.

Mixed Review and Test Prep

STAY SHARP!

Solve.

21. 16×72 **22.** 35×28 **23.** 68×20 **24.** 44×91

25. $386 \div 2$ **26.** $483 \div 3$ **27.** $790 \div 5$ **28.** $987 \div 7$

Solve for *n*.

29. $n + 6 = 11$ **30.** $n - 7 = 9$ **31.** $n - 4 = 3$ **32.** $n + 5 = 8$

33. $n - 9 = 1$ **34.** $n + 1 = 4$ **35.** $n - 4 = 7$ **36.** $n + 2 = 5$

37. What is the most common value in the line plot?

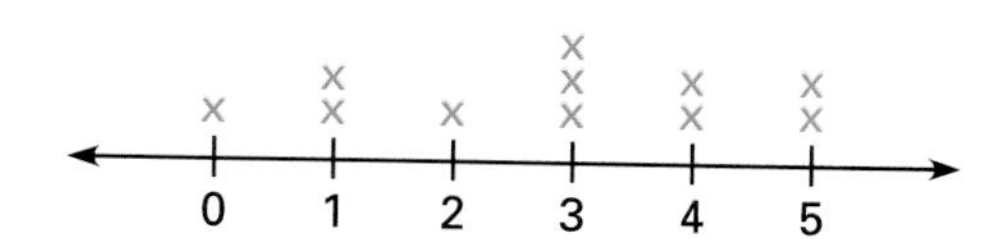

 Ⓐ 4  Ⓑ 1 Ⓒ 3  Ⓓ 5

SECTION B

Review and Practice

Vocabulary Choose the term that best completes each sentence.

1. The difference between the highest and lowest values of a data set is called its (interval, range).
2. Each (tally mark, interval) stands for one time that a value appears in a data set.
3. A graph that shows the shape of data according to place value is called a (frequency chart, stem-and-leaf diagram).

(Lesson 4) Record each data set in a tally chart.

4. 33, 35, 33, 34, 37, 35, 33, 34, 33, 35, 33, 36, 34
5. 545, 540, 544, 544, 543, 545, 545, 543, 542, 540, 541, 545, 543, 543, 545, 545, 543, 541, 545
6. 3,748; 3,744; 3,745; 3,748; 3,744; 3,748; 3,744; 3,749; 3,748; 3,746; 3,749; 3,745; 3,748; 3,744; 3,746; 3,744; 3,748; 3,745; 3,748; 3,748

(Lesson 5) Solve.

7. Matthew collected data on the heights of mountains in the South Pacific. He decided to make this bar graph.
   a. What interval did Matthew use in his bar graph scale?
   b. What is the approximate range of values on the bar graph?

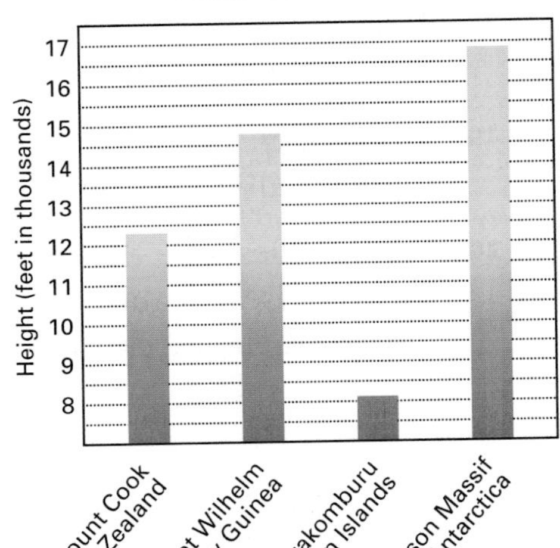

8. As part of her music project, Danya decided to compare the cost of private piano lessons in different places in the United States. Rounding to the nearest dollar, she found that a 30-minute lesson would cost $16.00 in Atlanta, GA, $18.00 in Chicago, IL, $16.00 in Houston, TX, $18.00 in Los Angeles, CA, $19.00 in Miami, FL, and $27.00 in New York, NY. Make a bar graph for this data.

(Lesson 6) Make a stem-and-leaf diagram for each data set.

9. 47, 42, 59, 43, 53, 42, 38, 53, 55, 50, 61, 42, 41, 60, 57
10. 76, 42, 55, 45, 65, 46, 55, 67, 46, 68, 52, 46
11. **Journal** Make a stem-and-leaf diagram for this data: 15, 22, 15, 32, 23, 17, 18, 23, 19, 23, 23, 32, 24. Then describe the shape of the data.

Skills Checklist

In this section, you have:

- ☑ **Learned About Tallies, Frequency Charts, and Line Plots**
- ☑ **Learned About Scales and Bar Graphs**
- ☑ **Learned About Stem-and-Leaf Diagrams**

C Describing Data

Every day, American newspapers publish thousands of statistics about athletes. Fortunately, mathematics can turn huge amounts of data into easy-to-understand numbers. Baseball rankings, gymnastics scores, and soccer standings can all be turned into numbers that help determine who is #1.

What situations, other than sports, use mathematics to determine a #1 ranking?

GET READY!

Finding the Mean

Review division. Find each quotient.

1. $279 \div 3$ **2.** $725 \div 5$ **3.** $931 \div 7$

4. $420 \div 6$ **5.** $936 \div 9$ **6.** $432 \div 4$

7. $156 \div 2$ **8.** $704 \div 8$ **9.** $492 \div 6$

10. $112 \div 8$ **11.** $336 \div 3$ **12.** $392 \div 7$

Skills Checklist

In this section, you will:

- ❒ Learn About Median and Mode
- ❒ Explore the Meaning of Mean
- ❒ Learn About the Effects of Outliers

Chapter 1
Lesson
7

Median and Mode

You Will Learn

- to calculate the median and the mode for a set of data

Vocabulary

median

mode

Learn

The ball's in her court! That's what Alexandra thought when she decided to go out for her school's basketball team.

Alexandra lives in Bloomfield Hills, Michigan.

The **median** of a data set is the middle number when the data are listed from least to greatest. If a set has two middle numbers, the median is the value halfway between the two middle numbers.

Example 1

Find the median number of points Alexandra's team scored this year.

55 45 62 71 74 58 66 58 67 73 71 72 46 62 47

Order the total from least to greatest:

45 46 47 55 58 58 62 62 66 67 71 71 72 73 74

Find the middle number:

45 46 47 55 58 58 62 [62] 66 67 71 71 72 73 74

The median number of points is 62.

Did You Know?

The first National College Athletic Association basketball championship for men was held in 1939. The first national championship for women was held in 1982.

The **mode** of a data set is the item that occurs most often. If all items occur once, there is no mode. If several items occur "most often," each is a mode.

Example 2

Find the median number of wins and the mode number of wins for the Long Beach State women's basketball team.

Long Beach State Win Totals (for 1986–1996)										
29	33	28	30	25	24	21	9	11	13	15

9 11 13 15 21 24 25 28 29 30 33 Order the totals.

9 11 13 15 21 [24] 25 28 29 30 33 Find the middle number.

The median is 24 wins. There is no mode.

In this example, the median was found by ordering the total number of wins from least to greatest. When you order numbers to find a median, you can order from least to greatest or greatest to least.

When data is ordered to find a median, two data values sometimes appear in the middle of a set of data.

Example 3

Twelve Houston babysitters were surveyed to find their hourly rates. Find the median and the mode of the data.

Babysitter Hourly Rates ($)		
4.00	3.30	3.25
3.00	3.75	3.25
3.15	3.50	3.00
3.75	3.75	3.60

To find the median, list the numbers in order.

3.00, 3.00, 3.15, 3.25, 3.25, 3.30, 3.50, 3.60, 3.75, 3.75, 3.75, 4.00

There are two middle numbers, $3.30 and $3.50. The median is the value halfway between, which is $3.40.

The mode is $3.75 because it appears more times than any other number.

Talk About It

1. For any data set, which is greater, the median or the mode?
2. Is the median of a data set always one of the numbers in the set? Is the mode?
3. If a data set has an odd number of values, how would you find the median? How would you find the median if a data set has an even number of values?

Check

Number of Stations on Longest Commuter Rail Systems in the United States								
134	108	18	126	62	101	181	27	158

1. Find the median of the data.
2. Find the mode of the data.
3. What would happen to the median if the data value 181 was eliminated? Explain.
4. In this data set, what would happen to the median if the greatest and least data values in the set (18 and 181) were eliminated?

Practice

Skills and Reasoning

Find the median and the mode for each data set. The data are ordered from least to greatest.

Number of Counties per State

Washington 39
Montana 56
Oregon 36
Idaho 44
Wyoming 23
Nevada 16
Utah 29
Colorado 63
California 58
Arizona 15
New Mexico 33

5. \$1, \$2, \$3, \$4, \$4, \$5, \$10, \$10, \$10

6. 12, 12, 18, 19, 54, 54, 102

7. 82, 82, 84, 85, 87, 88, 95, 98

8. 300, 301, 302, 310, 313, 318

9. Geography Find the median and mode number of counties for the 11 western states shown in the map.

10. Geography Find the median number of counties for the 5 states surrounding Nevada.

11. Geography Find the median number of counties for the 6 states surrounding Utah.

12. Reasoning If the number of counties in Washington and Idaho increased, would your answer for the mode in Exercise 9 change? If so, to what would it change? If not, tell why not.

Find the median and mode.

13.

```
x
x
x  x        x  x  x
x  x  x     x  x  x
10 11 12    13 14 15
```

14.

Stem	Leaf
5	1 2 3
6	5 5 6 7 9
8	1 1 2 2 2 6 6
9	7 7

15.

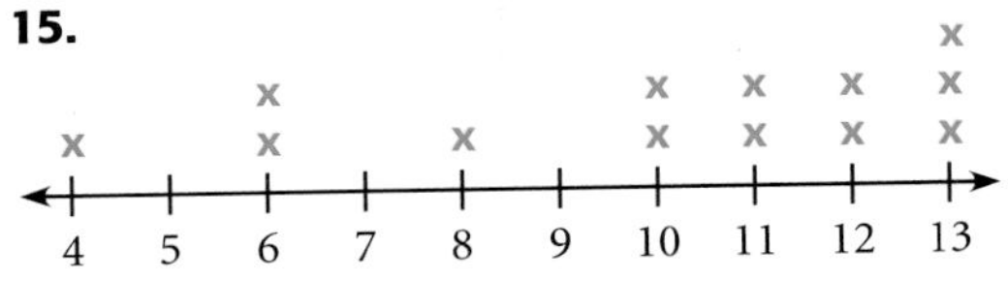

Find the median and mode.

16. 15, 31, 45, 61, 13, 21, 31, 13, 20

17. 25, 26, 24, 21, 25, 21, 23, 21, 26, 21, 20

18. 9, 13, 7, 11, 12, 6, 8, 14

19. 20, 25, 21, 23, 22, 30, 28, 20, 23, 22, 21, 30, 29, 28, 28, 28, 30, 29, 20

20. 72, 88, 92, 34, 48, 62, 62, 88, 62

21. 4, 18, 2, 6, 16, 2, 10, 12

22. 43, 37, 42, 40, 50, 61, 39, 45, 41

Make a line plot for each and then find the median and mode.

23. 6, 11, 12, 5, 7, 11, 6, 6, 10

24. 3, 0, 1, 0, 1, 3, 2, 2, 3, 1, 0, 3

Problem Solving and Applications

25. **Critical Thinking** Create a data set of 10 numbers with a median of 8 and a mode of 10.

26. **Critical Thinking** The following data lists the tennis players with the most Wimbledon titles. Laurence Doherty's data is missing. If the median of the data set is 13 and the modes are 10 and 13, what's the missing data?

Louise Brough	13	Suzanne Longlen	15
Margaret Court	10	Martina Navratilova	18
Laurence Doherty	???	William Renshaw	14
Doris Hart	10	Elizabeth Ryan	19
Billie Jean King	7	Helen Wills-Moody	12

27. **Mental Math** Find the median of a data set that contains two values, 10 and 12.

28. **What If** The mean, median, and mode of a set of data are exactly the same number. What might that data set look like?

29. **Logic** When do you find a mean to find a median?

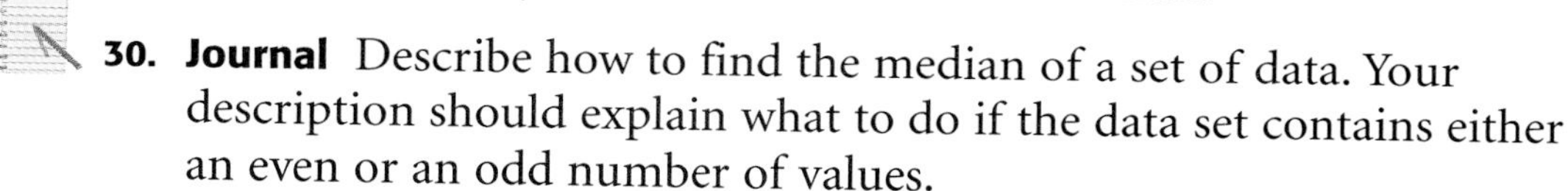

30. **Journal** Describe how to find the median of a set of data. Your description should explain what to do if the data set contains either an even or an odd number of values.

Mixed Review and Test Prep

STAY SHARP!

Multiply.

31. 83×54 32. 29×76 33. 80×32 34. 91×98

Use the graph to answer **35–38**.

35. What's the second highest selling type of shoe?

36. What's the difference between the sales in running shoes and golf shoes?

37. If the total sales equals 100 pairs, what's the number of sales for tennis shoes?

38. If each symbol represented 7 pairs of shoes, how many running shoes would have been sold?

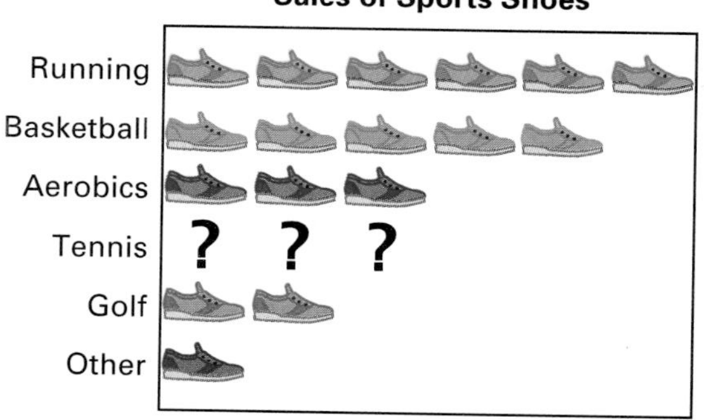

39. This stem-and-leaf plot shows the number of calls made to the public library in 10 days. On how many days were more than 20 calls made?

Ⓐ 3 Ⓑ 4 Ⓒ 5 Ⓓ 7

Stem	Leaf
4	1
3	3 4
2	1 2 5 5
1	0 3 6

The Meaning of Mean

Problem Solving Connection
- Make an Organized List

Materials
- string
- scissors
- meter stick or yard stick

Vocabulary
mean

Explore

A set of numerical data can be described by an average, or mean.

Work Together

Work in a group of at least four students.

1. Choose a member of your group and use string to measure the length of that group member's outstretched arm. Place one end of the string at the tip of the middle finger and measure to the shoulder. Mark the string. Beginning at the mark you made from measuring the first member of your group, measure the length of an outstretched arm of a second group member. Again mark the string. Continue until all arms have been measured on the same string.
2. Cut the string at the last mark. You should now have one length of string that is equal to the combined lengths of all of the arms in your group. Measure and record the entire length of the string.
3. Cut the string into equal-length sections so that there are as many sections as there are members of your group. Measure and record the length of one section. What does the length of one section represent?

Talk About It

4. Does it make a difference which student gets measured first and which student gets measured last?
5. If you add a new person to your group and repeat Steps 1 through 3, will your equal-length section be longer or shorter than your original equal-length section?

Connect and Learn

The **mean** of a data set is sometimes called the *average* of that set. To find a mean, find the sum of the data values in a set and divide by the number of values in that set.

Example 1

The Iditarod dogsled race crosses the Alaskan wilderness from Anchorage to Nome. Susan Butcher has won the race four times. Here are her 1983–1994 finishing positions. (She wasn't in the race in 1985.)
Find the mean of her finishing positions.
9, 2, 1, 1, 1, 2, 1, 3, 2, 4, 10

$9 + 2 + 1 + 1 + 1 + 2 + 1 + 3 + 2 + 4 + 10 = 36$ Add the values.

$36 \div 11 = 3.272727...$ Divide the sum by the number of values.

Susan Butcher's mean finishing position was 3.272727. . . . Sometimes the mean is a decimal value with several digits after the decimal point. Since real-world measurements aren't usually written with many decimal places, it's reasonable to round to the nearest hundredth. Susan Butcher's mean finishing position, rounded to the nearest hundredth, was 3.27.

Check

1. Find the mean number of soccer goals scored: 2, 3, 0, 1, 1, 2, 5, 0, 2, 1, 1, 0.
2. Find the mean temperature for one week in winter: 43°F, 32°F, 40°F, 36°F, 38°F, 42°F, 35°F.
3. Find the mean soccer ball price.

Math Tip

The mean is sometimes referred to as the *equal sharing number.* If all the values in a data set are evened out so that they are all equal to each other and their total is still the same, then each value will be equal to the mean.

Practice

Skills and Reasoning

Find the mean for each set of data.

4. $10, $10, $5, $1, $2, $5, $4, $3

5. 100, 85, 88, 98, 95, 87, 82, 83, 84

6. 5, 5, 5, 5, 5, 5, 5, 5

7. **Health** The data is the number of seconds it took Manuel to run the 100-meter dash. Find his mean time.

   10, 12, 15, 10, 11, 14, 13, 16, 10, 12, 10, 9, 13, 12, 11, 11

8. **Consumer** Find the mean amount of money spent by patrons at theaters.

   $8, $7, $10, $12, $8, $11, $8, $6, $9, $8, $10, $7, $7, $7

Find the mean of each set of data.

9.

Stem	Leaf
1	3 4 5
2	1 2 2 5 6
4	2 4 6 6
5	7 9

10.

```
          x
      x   x   x   x
      x   x   x   x   x
  x   x   x   x   x   x
<-+---+---+---+---+---+->
  1   2   3   4   5   6
```

11. Find the mean, median, and mode for the data below.

NFL Teams That Have Played the Most Post-Season Games (through 1995)			
Team	**Games**	**Team**	**Games**
Cowboys	49	Rams	33
'49ers	33	Raiders	36
Redskins	35		

12. **Reasoning** How is the mean different from the median? The mode?

13. **Reasoning** Is the mean of a data set a member of the set? Explain.

14. **Critical Thinking** Write a data set for which 17 is the mean.

Problem Solving and Applications

15. Critical Thinking Find the mean, median, and mode of the data in the bar graph. Which one best describes the tennis players?

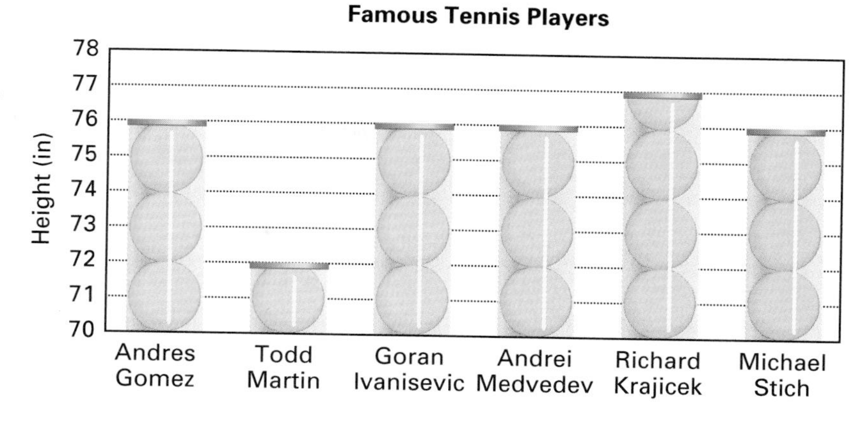

16. Suppose another height was added to the data in the bar graph that made the mean, median, and mode all the same number. What height was added?

17. Critical Thinking Create a data set of five different numbers whose mean is 10. Explain your method.

18. Suppose you have test scores of 92, 85, 86, and 90. What would you need to score on the next test to have a mean score of 90?

19. Critical Thinking How does the mean of a data set change if you add a number to the data that is exactly equal to the mean?

20. Using Data Use the Data File on page 3 to find the mean number of home runs hit by the five all-time home-run leaders.

Mixed Review and Test Prep

STAY SHARP!

21. $275 \div 5$ **22.** $361 \div 7$ **23.** $834 \div 9$ **24.** $709 \div 8$

25. $396 \div 11$ **26.** $522 \div 13$ **27.** $618 \div 15$ **28.** $980 \div 20$

29. $384 \div 24$ **30.** $616 \div 56$ **31.** $996 \div 83$ **32.** $736 \div 32$

33. What is the difference between the weight of a rabbit and the weight of a snake?

34. About how many times taller than the snake bar does the elephant bar appear to be?

35. Do you think the graph is misleading? Explain.

36. Which number is the median for the following data?
6, 7, 7, 7, 6, 4, 4, 7, 7, 2, 4

Ⓐ 7 Ⓑ 5
Ⓒ 6 Ⓓ 50

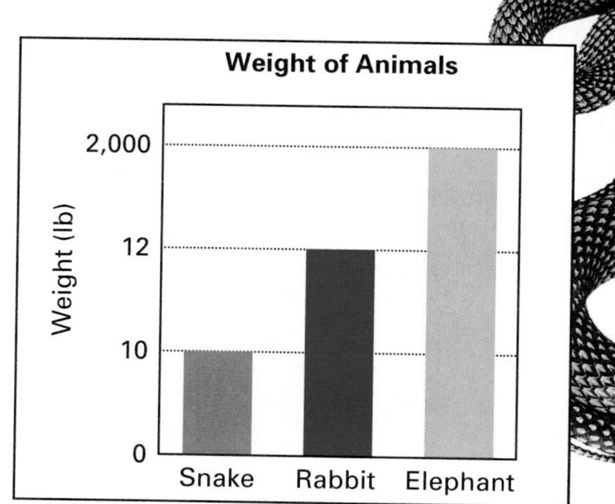

Technology

Using a Spreadsheet to Find the Median

A spreadsheet can help you find the median, especially when you are dealing with large amounts of data. Remember that in order to find the median of a data set, you need to determine the middle number(s) of the set. Instead of sorting the data on your own, a spreadsheet program can do this for you.

Materials

Interactive CD-ROM Spreadsheet/Grapher Tool or other spreadsheet software

This data set shows the scores students received on a test in one class. What is the median of this data set?

Test Scores											
90	80	88	58	78	93	93	93	75	88	90	70
78	95	83	75	78	50	88	78	93	43	93	48
60	93	83	78	48	70	65	73	85	85	88	

Work Together

Use your software to sort the data.

1. Use the spreadsheet software program to create a new spreadsheet of test score data. If you need help creating the sheet, use the Help option in the program.

2. Enter the test score data into column A. Check to make sure you have 35 numbers in the spreadsheet.

	A	B
1	90	
2	80	
3	88	
4	58	
5	78	
6	93	
7	93	
8	93	

3. Use the **Sort** command to arrange the data from least to greatest. To do this, first highlight the data and then select the **Sort** command.

4. Locate the middle number in the data to find the median.

11	75
12	75
13	78
14	78
15	78
16	78
17	78
18	80
19	83
20	83
21	85
22	85
23	88
24	88
25	88

Remember
To find the median of an even number of data, you need to find the number halfway between the two middle numbers in the data set.

Exercises

1. What is the median of the first four columns of data?
2. What is the median of the top two rows of data?
3. Four students were absent the day of the test. Their scores on the make-up test were 89, 92, 77, and 80. Find the new median of the class' scores.

Extensions

4. This data set shows the points scored in one basketball game by each team member on the Roosevelt Rockets. Find the median.

Team Member Scores				
2	12	5	9	6
3	9	11	2	2

5. Use a spreadsheet to find the median number of brothers and sisters your classmates have.
6. How can the sort function of a spreadsheet help you find the mode of a data set?
7. Is it possible to get a wrong answer when using a spreadsheet to find the median? Explain.

Chapter 1
Lesson
9

The Effects of Outliers

You Will Learn

- to determine if an outlier affects the analysis of a data set

Vocabulary

outlier

Learn

Measures such as mean, median, and mode can be affected by data items that are much different from the other items in a set.

An **outlier** is a number in a data set that is very different from the rest of the numbers. Outliers can have a major effect on the mean.

In the last lesson, you saw that the mean of a data set may represent the set well. For example, the mean of the daily high temperatures shown here is 91°F. Because the mean is close to all of the data, it represents the set well.

Daily High Temperatures (°F)	
Monday	88
Tuesday	94
Wednesday	94
Thursday	92
Friday	87

Suppose that on Saturday the temperature plunges to 55°F. Look what happens to the mean:

$88 + 94 + 94 + 92 + 87 + 55 = 510$

$510 \div 6 = 85$

The mean temperature of 85°F is *less than* five of the six data items. It has been pulled downward by the outlier, 55°F.

	Mon–Fri	Mon–Sat
Mean	91	85
Median	92	90
Mode	94	94

The table shows that the median is affected only slightly by the addition of the Saturday outlier. The mode hasn't changed.

You can see that a data set with an outlier is usually better represented by the median or the mode. The mean is often pulled too far toward the outlier to represent the set well.

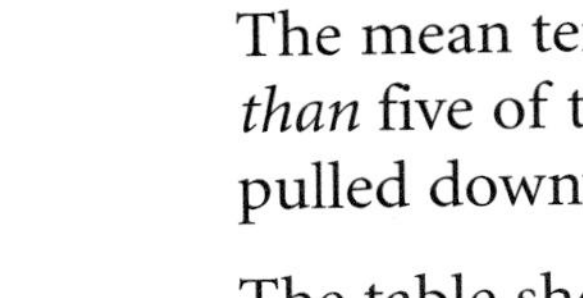

Did You Know?
The highest temperature ever recorded in the United States was 134°F in Death Valley, California, on July 10, 1913.

Example 1

Find the median, mode, and mean of the data with and without the outlier.

Tallest Buildings in Las Vegas	
Building	Height (ft)
Vegas World Tower	1,012
Fitzgerald Hotel	400
Landmark Hotel	356
Las Vegas Hilton	345

Without outlier

Median: 356

No mode

Mean: $400 + 356 + 345 = 1{,}101$

$1{,}101 \div 3 = 367$

With outlier

Median: $400 + 356 = 756$

$756 \div 2 = 378$

No mode

Mean: $400 + 356 + 345 + 1{,}012 = 2{,}113$

$2{,}113 \div 4 = 528.25$

The degree to which an outlier affects the mean is usually significant. Occasionally, it is not.

Example 2

Find the median, mode, and mean of the data with and without the outlier.

Normal January Temperatures in Selected U.S. Cities			
Galveston, TX	53°F	San Francisco, CA	49°F
Mobile, AL	50°F	Savannah, GA	49°F
San Antonio, TX	49°F	Houston, TX	50°F

In this data set, 53°F is the outlier because all of the other temperatures are either 49°F or 50°F.

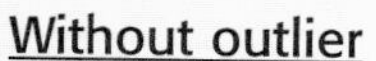

Without outlier

Median: 49°F

Mode: 49°F

Mean: $50 + 49 + 49 + 49 + 50 = 247$

$247 \div 5 = 49.4$°F

With outlier

Median: $49 + 50 = 99$

$99 \div 2 = 49.5$°F

Mode: 49°F

Mean: $53 + 50 + 49 + 49 + 49 + 50 = 300$

$300 \div 6 = 50$°F

When the outlier was included, the mean temperature increased by less than one degree, the median temperature increased by less than one degree, and the mode was unchanged.

Talk About It

1. Why doesn't the mode change when an outlier is added to a data set?
2. Would a high outlier and a low outlier affect a data set differently? If so, how?

Check

1. Find the median, mode, and mean with and without the outlier.

States with Most Indian Reservations								
State	AZ	CA	MN	NV	NM	WA	WI	SD
Number	23	96	14	19	25	27	11	9

2. **Reasoning** What relationship is shared by an outlier and the range of a set of data?

Practice

Skills and Reasoning

Identify the outlier in each data set.

3. 24, 24, 18, 56, 25, 12, 15, 22

4. 34, 28, 31, 34, 2, 29, 21

5. 7, 6, 9, 10, 11, 6, 8, 11, 0, 10, 7, 8

6. 200, 225, 3,000, 500, 325, 311

Identify the outlier in each data set.

7.

Stem	Leaf
0	3
1	0 0 0 1 1 5 8
2	1 3 3 8 9
3	0 0

8.

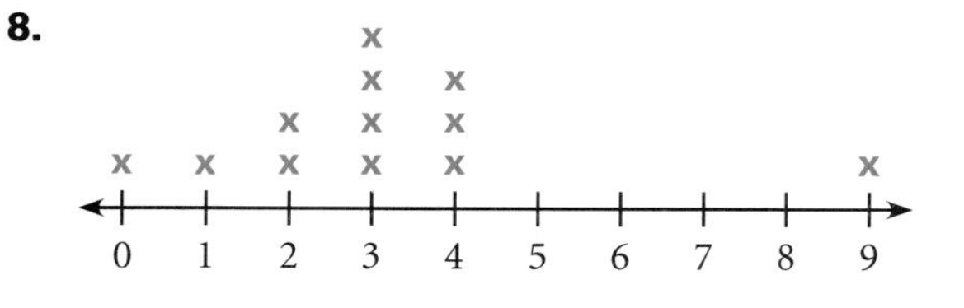

Use the Temperature chart to answer **9.**

9. Find the median, mode, and mean of the temperatures with and without the outlier.

Normal June Temperatures in Corville					
1993	1994	1995	1996	1997	1998
71°F	73°F	72°F	79°F	73°F	73°F

Use the British Open Tournament Scores chart to answer **10** and **11.**

10. Estimation Estimate the mean, median, and mode with and without the outlier, then find them by computing. How did your estimates compare to your computations?

11. Did the outlier affect the mode? The mean? The median? Which did it affect the most?

British Open Tournament Scores (1996)	
John Daly	282
Costantino Rocca	282
Michael Campbell	283
Steven Bottomley	283
Barry Lane	288

Use the Dinah Shore Tournament Scores to answer **12.**

12. a. Find the mean, median, and mode with and without the outlier.

b. Did the outlier affect the mode? The mean? The median? Which did it affect the most?

Dinah Shore Tournament Scores (1996)	
Nanci Bowen	285
Susie Redman	286
Brandie Burton	287
Sherri Turner	287
Meg Mallon	292

13. Critical Thinking Consider the data sets 20, 20, 100 and 450, 450, 460. Without computing, in which set of data will the outlier most affect the mean? Explain.

Problem Solving and Applications

The following table shows the number of games Michael Jordan has played with the Chicago Bulls.

Year	Games Played	Year	Games Played	Year	Games Played
1984–85	82	1988–89	81	1992–93	78
1985–86	???	1989–90	82	1993–94	78
1986–87	82	1990–91	82	1994–95	17
1987–88	82	1991–92	80	1995–96	82

14. Find the mean, median, and mode of the data provided. Ignore the entry for 1985–1986.

15. During the 1985–86 season, Michael had an injury and played only 18 games. Add this outlier to the data and recompute the mean, median, and mode.

16. How do the outliers affect the mean? The median? The mode?

17. **Critical Thinking** Which number (the median, the mode, or the mean) is the best measure to use when describing the number of games Michael played each year? Explain.

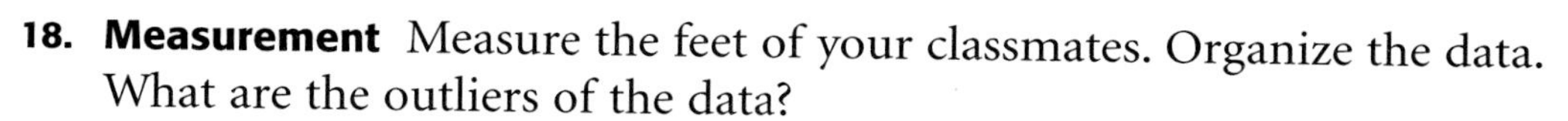

18. **Measurement** Measure the feet of your classmates. Organize the data. What are the outliers of the data?

19. **Patterns** Consider the data in these sets. Look for a pattern.
2, 3, 15   4, 9, 60   8, 27, 240   16, 81, ?
What is the outlier in the fourth set of data?

Mixed Review and Test Prep

STAY SHARP!

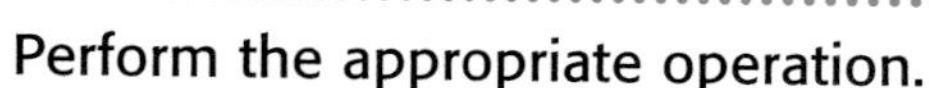

Perform the appropriate operation.

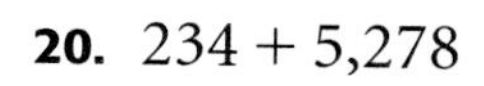

20. $234 + 5{,}278$ **21.** $5{,}678 - 3{,}991$ **22.** 26×52 **23.** $306 \div 9$

24. $43{,}675 + 2{,}344$ **25.** $89{,}021 - 5{,}811$ **26.** 329×86 **27.** $915 \div 30$

28. Does there appear to be a trend in the scatterplot to the right? Explain.

29. Which has the greatest value for the following set of data, the mean, the median, the mode, or the range?
94, 88, 11, 90, 94, 92
Ⓐ Mean Ⓑ Median Ⓒ Mode Ⓓ Range

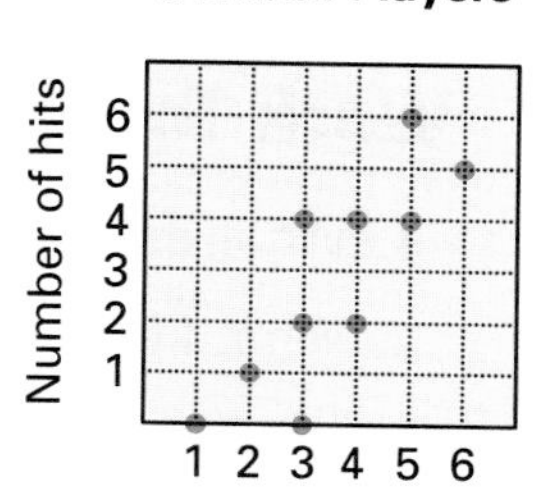

Chapter 1

Problem Solving

Decision Making: Will the Most Valuable Player Please Stand Up?

You Will Learn

- how to use information to make a decision

Explore

Babe Ruth and Hank Aaron are two of baseball's most famous athletes. Both played for different teams and at different times. You want to determine which of these two players was the more valuable hitter. Is it possible to use statistics to determine this?

The following data represent the hits and home runs made by each player during the years he played for the teams shown.

Facts and Data															
Babe Ruth	**New York Yankees (1920–1934)**														
Hits	172	204	128	205	200	104	184	192	173	172	186	199	156	138	105
Home Runs	54	59	35	41	46	25	47	60	54	46	49	46	41	34	22
Hank Aaron	**Milwaukee Braves (1954–1965)**														
Hits	131	189	200	198	196	223	172	197	191	201	187	181			
Home Runs	13	27	26	44	30	39	40	34	45	44	24	32			

Work Together

Understand

1. What decision are you being asked to make?
2. What kind of data have you been given to analyze?
3. How can you analyze the data?
4. How are the mean, median, and mode for a set of data found?

▶ Plan and Solve

5. Copy and complete these data tables for each player.

Number of Hits per Season	
Ruth	**Aaron**
mean = ?	mean = ?
median = ?	median = ?
mode = ?	mode = ?

Number of Home Runs per Season	
Ruth	**Aaron**
mean = ?	mean = ?
median = ?	median = ?
mode = ?	mode = ?

6. How does the mean number of hits and home runs for each player compare?
7. How does the median number of hits and home runs for each player compare?
8. How does the mode number of hits and home runs for each player compare?
9. Subtract the number of home runs from the number of hits for each player. The result shows you the number of non-home run hits for each player. Can you use this data to help make a decision? Explain.

▶ Make a Decision

10. Who did you choose as the more valuable player?
11. What facts and data helped convince you that the player you chose was the most valuable player?

▶ Present Your Decision

12. Write a paragraph explaining your reasoning to the class. Tell about the strategies you used in your paragraph.

SECTION C

Review and Practice

(Lessons 7 and 8) Use the data set to answer **1–3.**

Data Set: 23, 23, 24, 24, 25, 26, 28, 28, 28

1. What is the median of the data set?
2. What is the mode of the data set?
3. What is the mean for the data set?

Find the mean, median, and mode of each set of data.

4. 1, 1, 5, 5, 7, 7, 9, 9, 8, 1, 1, 3, 4, 5, 5, 6

5.

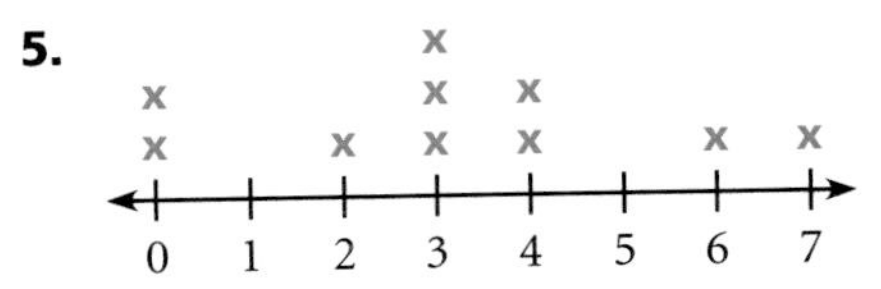

6.

Stem	Leaf
1	0 0 0 1 1 2 2 3 3 4
2	5 5 5

7.

x x x x x x x x x

20 21 22 23 24 25

8.

Stem	Leaf
4	0 0 2 5 6
5	1 2 3 4
6	0 2 2 4 5

9. 12, 15, 22, 14 16, 13, 10, 20, 17, 21

10. Which is the greater value for the following set of data, the median or the mode? Are they equal?

9, 10, 12, 11, 9, 13, 12, 10, 11, 10, 12, 11, 11, 10, 12, 11, 13, 15

(Lesson 9) State whether the data sets for **11–16** have outliers. If so, identify the outlier.

11. 22, 25, 20, 34, 21, 22, 24, 22, 23, 21

12. 572, 572, 568, 570, 571, 572, 569, 570, 571

13. 66, 63, 66, 66, 64, 63, 66, 65, 64, 63, 59, 64, 65, 66

14. 12, 13, 12, 10, 15, 12, 10, 12, 13, 14

15. 612, 650, 609, 607, 610, 612, 615, 616

16. 98, 100, 101, 97, 95, 97, 96, 98, 43, 94

17. In one math class students received the following scores: 78, 86, 86, 94, 96, 98, 83, and 75. In another class students recieved these scores: 93, 97, 78, 86, 84, 80, 79, and 83. Which class had the higher mean score?

18. Create a data set with 5 values that has a median of 20, a mean of 21, and a mode of 20.

19. **Journal** Which measure—the mean, the median, or the mode—can be most affected by an outlier? Why?

Skills Checklist

In this section, you have:

- ☑ **Learned About Median and Mode**
- ☑ **Explored the Meaning of Mean**
- ☑ **Learned About the Effects of Outliers**

REVIEW AND PRACTICE

Choose at least one of the following. Use what you have learned in this chapter.

1 It's My Party

The pictograph shows the number of pizzas a youth group needs for a pizza party. Call or visit a pizza restaurant to find out how much each pizza would cost. Determine the cost for the entire order. Explain how you determined the total cost.

Pizza Party

Large, one topping

Large, two toppings

Medium, one topping

Small, one topping

= 4 pizzas

2 Let's Go Fly a Kite!

Here are the results from the Lakeside Kite Flying Contest:

Contestant	Height (m)	Contestant	Height (m)
Greg	233	Hassan	360
Tyron	212	Bill	274
Ku	272	Cassie	501
Manny	319	Ali	124
Charlene	275	Maria	286

Create a bar graph from this data. List five things that you can learn from the bar graph.

3 State of Recall

At Home Use a watch or clock with a second hand. Ask at least 20 friends, family members, or members of your community to name as many states in the United States as they can in 30 seconds. Count the number of states they identify. Collect and record your data in a table. Make a line plot and a stem-and-leaf diagram of the data. Explain which chart gives a better picture of the data.

OK FL CA TX

4 What's in a Name?

Pick a topic of your choice from **www.mathsurf.com/6/ch1**. Choose a topic that will provide you with a list of people or place names. Make a tally chart of the first letter in each name. Find which letter represents the mode.

CHAPTER 1

Review/Test

(Lessons 1 and 8) Solve.

Favorite sports and the number of millions of people who engaged in them in 1995: Walking, 71; Swimming, 60; Bicycling, 50; and Fishing, 56.

1. Use the data above to draw and label a bar graph. Then find the mean of the data.

(Lesson 2) Use the bar graphs to answer **2** and **3.**

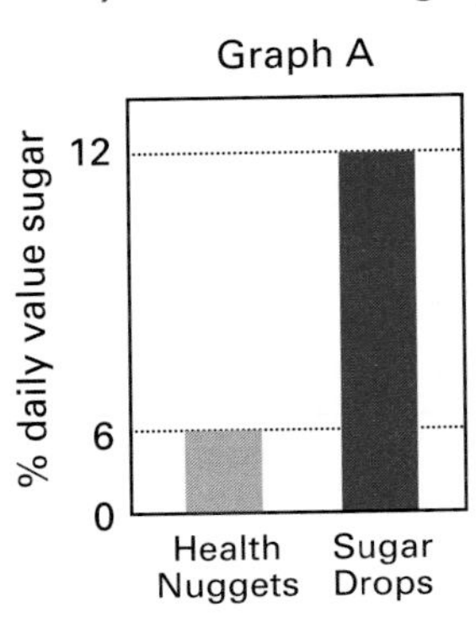

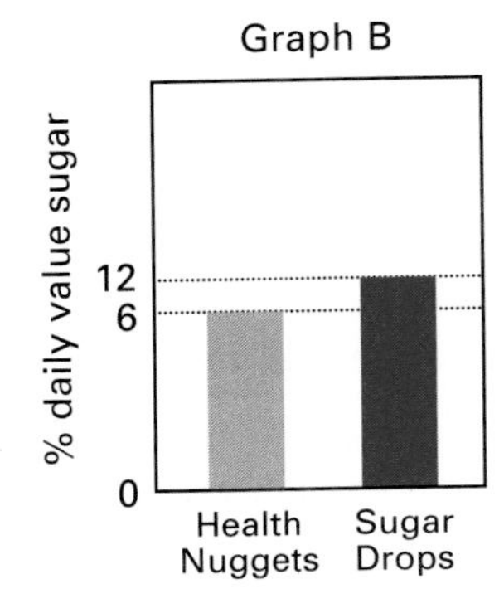

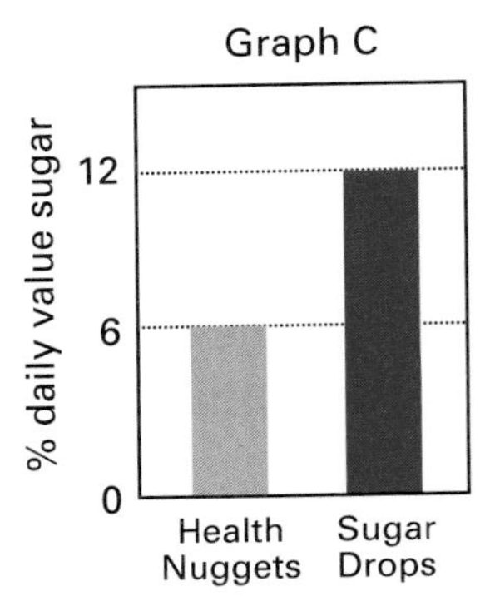

2. Which graph do you think was made by the makers of Sugar Drops? Why?
3. Which graph do you think gives you the best understanding of the data? Why?

(Lesson 4) Use the data shown to answer **4–6.**

books read over the summer: 3, 2, 2, 4, 1, 3, 2, 4, 1, 5, 3, 3, 2, 3, 2, 4, 1, 2, 5, 6, 3, 3

4. Record the number of books read in a tally chart.
5. Make a frequency chart for your set of tally marks.
6. Make a line plot from your tally marks.

(Lessons 1, 3, 5–7, 9) Use the graphs below each pair of questions to answer **7–10.**

7. What is the interval for the distance jumped? The number of jumps?
8. Is there an outlier? If so, where?

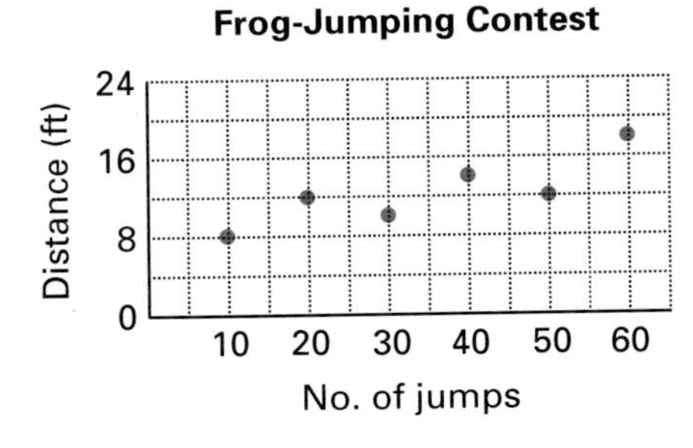

9. What is the value of each symbol?
10. How many cars were washed in all?

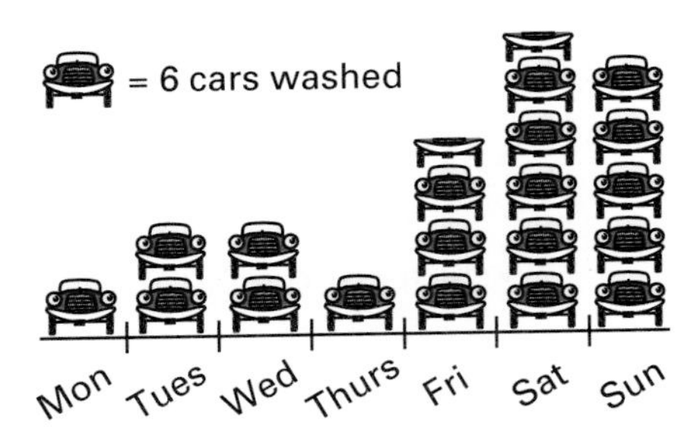

(Lessons 5 and 8) Choose a strategy to solve the problem.

11. Keisha's math test scores are 95, 85, 88, 88, and 92. What is the range of her scores? What does she have to score on her next math test to have a mean of 90?

CHAPTER 1

Performance Assessment

Suppose you notice there is a lot of noise where you live. To convince your community to ban loud noise, you have collected the following information:

- Sound or noise is measured in decibel units. The decibel levels of some common noises are shown in the chart.
- The Environmental Protection Agency proposes an average decibel level of no more than 55 in neighborhoods.
- Too much exposure to loud noise can cause loss of hearing. Eight hours of exposure to 90 decibels of sound can damage a person's hearing. As little as two hours of listening to 100-decibel music can cause damage. Noise at 120 decibels causes damage almost immediately.
- You measure the decibel level of noises outside your window for 2 hours. You gather this data:

Common Noise	Decibel Level
watch ticking	20
suburban street	40
normal conversation	60
noisy restaurant	70
loud music	80
truck	90
rock concert	100
jet engine	110
jackhammer	120

Time/ Duration	Noise	Decibel Level	Time/ Duration	Noise	Decibel Level
4:00–4:20	radio	95	5:30	motorcycle	110
4:20–4:30	jackhammer	120	5:30–5:45	traffic	50
4:30	truck	90	5:45	dog barking	95
4:30–5:10	traffic	50	5:45–5:55	traffic	50
5:10–5:15	car alarm	130	5:55	car horn	100
5:15–5:30	traffic	50	5:55–6:00	traffic	50

Prepare a presentation to help convince your community to ban loud noises. Make at least one graph. Include diagrams and statements.

1. **Decision Making** Analyze the data and decide what type of graph you will include in your presentation.

2. **Recording Data** Make your graphs and diagrams.

3. **Explain Your Thinking** How did you decide which graphs or diagrams to use? Why did you choose one type of display over others?

4. **Critical Thinking** How would you change your presentation if you wanted to convince your community **not** to ban loud noise?

Math Magazine

The Cat's Meow

A box-and-whisker plot will give you a good overview of a set of data.

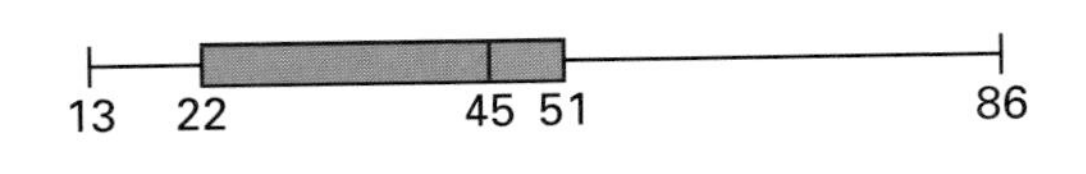

The box shows the median, 45, and the two quartiles at 22 and 51. The "whiskers" extend to the lowest and highest values, 13 and 86.

To make a box-and-whisker plot for the data set 9, 17, 18, 26, 36, 36, 37, 38, 45, and 55, first calculate the median and the quartiles. The median is 36. The quartiles are the medians of the first and second half of the data. They are 18 and 38.

Draw a line and label it with a number scale. Mark the highest and lowest numbers in the data set.

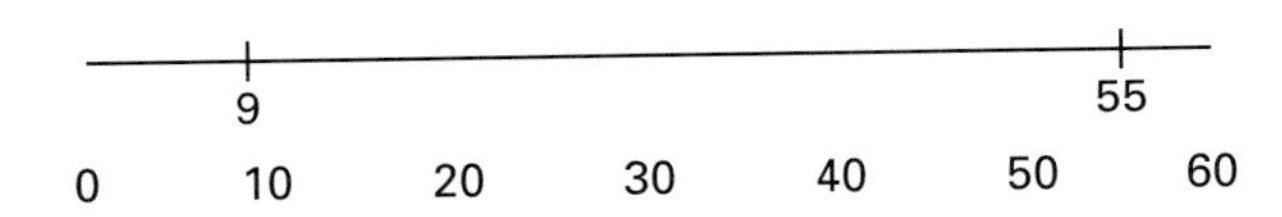

Draw a box using the quartiles as the left and right ends. Label the quartiles and the median.

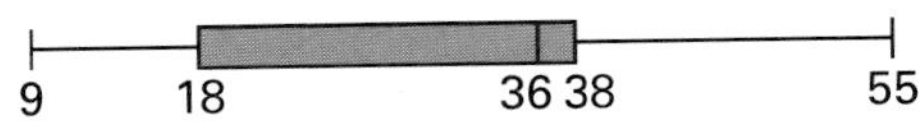

Try These!

1. Draw a box-and-whisker plot for the set of data at the right.
2. If the box in a box-and-whisker plot is shorter than the whiskers, what can you conclude about the data set?
3. Is it possible for the median and a quartile to have the same value? Explain.

CHAPTER 1

Cumulative Review

Test Prep Strategy: Make Smart Choices

Look for Patterns.

What interval would be best to use as a scale for a bar graph with this data: 27, 200, 153, 76, 125?

Ⓐ 2 Ⓑ 35 Ⓒ 25 Ⓓ 100

First examine the data set. Notice that there are large numbers included. You can eliminate choice Ⓐ because the graph would be too big. You can eliminate choice Ⓓ because the graph would be too small. That leaves choices Ⓑ and Ⓒ. Since all the numbers are close to or exactly multiples of 25, choice Ⓒ would be the better choice.

STAY SHARP!

Write the letter of the correct answer.
Choose any strategy.

1. What number in a frequency chart represents this set of tally marks?

卌 卌
卌 ||||

Ⓐ 4 Ⓑ 19 Ⓒ 24 Ⓓ 34

2. What length and height of fish does Point *A* represent?

Ⓐ 1 cm, 1.5 cm

Ⓑ 1.5 cm; 1.5 cm

Ⓒ 1.5 cm; 1 cm

Ⓓ not here

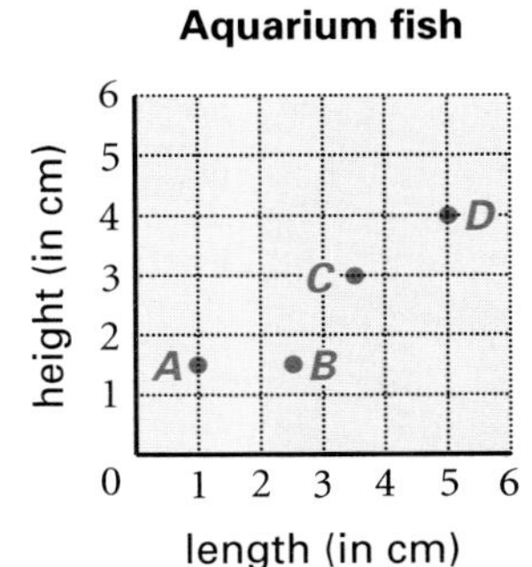

3. Which point represents the length of 3.5 cm and a height of 3 cm?

Ⓐ A Ⓑ B Ⓒ C Ⓓ D

4. These are the numbers of students absent from Mr. Lawson's class every day for two weeks: 0, 0, 0, 1, 1, 1, 2, 2, 2, 2, 3. What is the median number of students absent?

Ⓐ 0 Ⓑ 1 Ⓒ 2 Ⓓ 3

5. What is the mode for the number of students absent?

Ⓐ 0 Ⓑ 1 Ⓒ 2 Ⓓ 3

6. What interval would be best to use as a scale for a bar graph with this data: Jets: 33; Patriots: 24; Broncos: 27; Steelers: 42?

Ⓐ 2 Ⓑ 5 Ⓒ 3 Ⓓ 10

7. Find the mean number of points scored: 10, 24, 42, 35, 14, 17, 24, 26.

Ⓐ 23 Ⓑ 24 Ⓒ 42 Ⓓ not here

Test Prep Strategies

- Read Carefully
- Follow Directions
- Make Smart Choices
- Eliminate Choices
- Work Backward from an Answer

DATA FILE

Chapter 2

Connecting Arithmetic to Algebra

Greetings! from Planet Earth

Greetings! from Planet Earth
Page 61

Making Sense of Large Numbers

61

The nine planets in our solar system constantly orbit around the Sun. Are Mercury and Pluto the same distance from the Sun? Explain.

Planet	Mean Distance from the Sun (mi)
Mercury	36,000,000
Venus	67,000,000
Earth	93,000,000
Mars	141 million
Jupiter	480 million
Saturn	nine hundred million
Uranus	1,800 million
Neptune	2,800 million
Pluto	3,600,000,000

LINKS

Arts & Literature

Vincent van Gogh's *Portrait du Dr. Gachet* sold for $75 million.
www.mathsurf.com/6/ch2/arts

Science

The "flash-to-bang" equation states how far away lightning strikes. The number of seconds between the lightning and the thunder divided by 5 equals the distance in miles.
www.mathsurf.com/6/ch2/science

Entertainment

Billboard uses this formula to rank songs on the Top 40 Chart: (copies sold × 0.4) + (number of radio plays × 0.6) = chart value.

First Class Collectibles

Number Sense and Operation Sense

79

If Christopher Weid were to store his bottles in 6-pack cartons, about how many cartons would he need?

Collector	Item Collected	Amount Collected
Carol McFadden	Pairs of Earrings	18,750
Christopher Weid	Soda Bottles	6,510
Norman W. Bright	Four-Leaf Clovers	7,116
Craig Shergold	Greeting Cards	33,000,000

First Class Collectibles
Page 79

SECTION C

Journey to the Bottom of the Sea

Intoduction to Algebra

105

How would you describe the average depth of the Arctic Ocean as compared to the other three oceans?

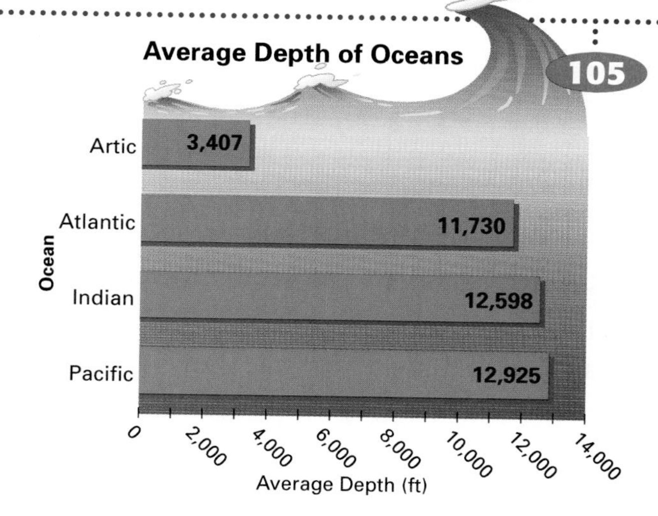

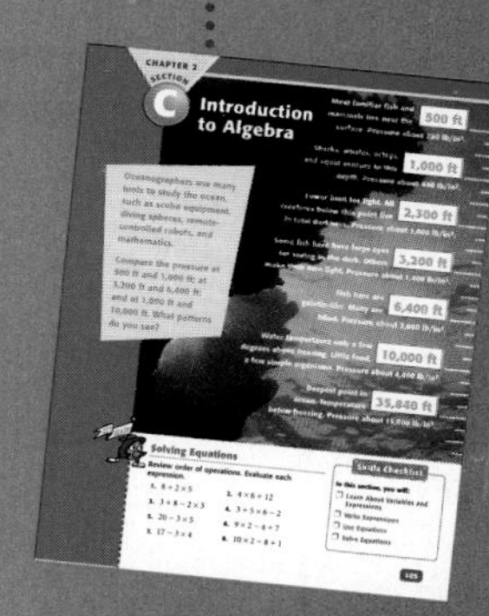

Journey to the Bottom of the Sea
Page 105

Social Studies

The Egyptians used a form of algebra. The Greeks used variables. Arabs contributed the use of the digit 0 to our Hindu-Arabic numeration system.

People of the World

People in China use an *abacus* to calculate numbers. They add, subtract, multiply, and divide by moving beads toward or away from the crossbar.
www.mathsurf.com/6/ch2/people

We're going the distance

Materials
map, posterboard, ruler, markers

If your team could travel anywhere you wished in one 24-hour period, where would you go? What different types of transportation could you use to get there? Plan your trip, then create a map showing the route you would take.

Make a Plan

- What place would you like to visit? Can you get there in 24 hours?
- Do you want to travel far away or stay nearby?
- What information do you need to show the route of the trip?

Carry It Out

1. List all the methods of transportation your team can use.
2. Choose the best type of transportation to get you to your destination.
3. Estimate the distance you would travel. Use your estimate to calculate the average speed you would travel in order to get there within 24 hours.
4. Find or create a map that shows a possible route for your journey. Be sure to include a key that shows the distance you are traveling.
5. Label your route with the average speed necessary to complete your trip on time.

Talk About It

- How did your team find the average speed for your trip?
- If you were to take a different means of transportation, how might your average speed change?

Present the Project

Display the maps of your trip for the class. How does your average speed compare to that of the other groups? Which of the trips would you most like to take?

CHAPTER 2

SECTION

Making Sense of Large Numbers

In order to learn about and describe the universe, people have to use numbers much greater than hundreds, thousands, or even millions. Mathematics provides people with several tools for talking about large numbers conveniently and effectively.

How could you use large numbers to describe things in the universe?

Ordering Numbers

Write the number in standard form.

1. two million, eight hundred two thousand, ninety-nine

Round each number to the underlined place.

2. 5,89<u>9</u>,530   3. 420,0<u>8</u>4   4. <u>7</u>83,256

Skills Checklist

In this section, you will:

- ❒ Read and Write Large Numbers
- ❒ Round Large Numbers
- ❒ Compare and Order Numbers
- ❒ Explore Exponents

Chapter 2
Lesson
1

Reading and Writing Large Numbers

You Will Learn

- the place value of digits in numbers
- to write numbers in standard form, word form, and number word form

Vocabulary

place value

Did You Know?

Pioneer 10 traveled 620,000,000 miles in 1973 to provide the first close-up view of the planet Jupiter.

Learn

You are the commander of a disabled spacecraft. Mission Control in Houston wants to know how far you are from Earth.

Your controls report that you are 45,000,000,000,000 km away. You need to report the distance.

Every digit of a number has a **place value**. The place value tells you how much that digit represents. In 2,364, the digit 3 represents 3 hundreds (or 300) because the 3 is in the hundreds place. In order to use large numbers, you need to know the names of large place values.

Place Value

hundreds	tens	ones	hundreds	tens	ones	hundreds	tens	ones	hundreds	tens	ones	hundreds	tens	ones
	4	5	0	0	0	0	0	0	0	0	0	0	0	0
Trillions			Billions			Millions			Thousands			Ones		

Numbers can be written in different forms.

Standard form: 45,000,000,000,000
Word form: forty-five trillion
Number-word form: 45 trillion

You report to Mission Control, "We are forty-five trillion kilometers from Earth."

Example 1

Find the place value of the 9 in Vega's diameter.

Vega's diameter is 2,5$\boxed{9}$4,200 miles.

The 9 is in the ten-thousands place. It represents 9 ten-thousands, or 90,000.

Diameters of Six Brightest Stars	
Name	**Diameter (mi)**
Sun	864,730
Sirius	1,556,500
Canopus	25,951,900
Alpha Centauri	1,037,700
Arcturus	19,888,800
Vega	2,594,200

Writing numbers in word form helps you know how they are read.

Example 2

Write Alpha Centauri's diameter in word form.

Write each number of trillions, billions, millions, thousands, and ones.

1 million	37 thousands	700 ones
one million	thirty-seven thousand,	seven hundred

Numbers are most commonly seen in standard form.

Example 3

Write seven billion, forty thousand, two in standard form.

billions	millions	thousands	ones
7	000	040	002

7,000,040,002

Number-word form is a combination of word form and standard form.

Example 4

Write 36,000,000,000 in number-word form.

36 is in the billions place.

36,000,000,000 = 36 billion

Astronomers use powerful telescopes to study the heavens.

Is there a name for every number, no matter how large? Explain.

Check

Name the place value position of the given digit in the number 4,017,006,000,000.

1. 4 **2.** 7 **3.** 6 **4.** 1

Write each number in words.

5. 46,000,000 **6.** 105,604,000,000 **7.** 5,014,072 **8.** 26,000,001,000,000

9. Reasoning How is each place value related to the place on the right?

Practice

Skills and Reasoning

Name the place-value position of the given digit in the number 31,480,725.

10. 5 **11.** 7 **12.** 8 **13.** 3

14. 1 **15.** 4 **16.** 0 **17.** 2

Write each number in words.

18. 30,080,705 **19.** 5,111,293,026 **20.** 8,235 **21.** 9,303,946

22. 7,098 **23.** 222 **24.** 56,056,560 **25.** 8,000,969,152,001

Science Write each planet's average distance from Earth in number-word form.

26. Mercury **27.** Venus

28. Saturn **29.** Uranus

30. Neptune **31.** Pluto

Average Distance from Earth	
Name	**Distance (mi)**
Mercury	93,000,000
Venus	141,500,000
Saturn	888,000,000
Uranus	1,779,500,000
Neptune	2,791,000,000
Pluto	3,653,500,000

Write each number in standard form.

32. 52 million **33.** 38 thousand

34. 560 million **35.** 7 trillion

36. 9 thousand **37.** 4 hundred

38. 321 thousand **39.** 26 million

40. forty-two million, six thousand

41. eight hundred four thousand, two

42. nine trillion, twenty billion, thirty

43. four thousand, seven hundred five

44. eighty-one thousand, five hundred

45. three million, nine hundred

Complete in number-word form.

46. 36,000 = 36 ____________

47. ____________ = 42 million

48. 67,000,000,000 = 67 ____________

49. ____________ = 5 trillion

50. Reasoning Explain the difference between the two 7's in the number 737,459.

51. Critical Thinking When the planets are aligned, Earth has an approximate distance of 92,960,000 miles from the sun. Pluto has an approximate distance of 3,573,240,000 miles from the Earth. What is the approximate distance between Pluto and the sun? Explain.

52. Critical Thinking Make a bar graph of a student's budget: $4 for bus, $5 for lunch, $3 for games. Then make a bar graph of a city's budget: $4 million for road maintenance, $5 million for salaries, $3 million for construction. How are the graphs similar? How are they different?

Problem Solving and Applications

Science For each fact, write the number in word form and in number-word form.

53. The Cassini orbiter, designed to carry a probe, science instruments, and fuel into space, weighs 5,655 kg.

54. Scientists can see more than 100,000,000,000 galaxies in the universe.

55. Neptune's mean distance from the sun is 2,798,800,000 miles.

56. Time As of 1995, American astronauts have spent over 17,715 hours in space.

Mixed Review and Test Prep

STAY SHARP!

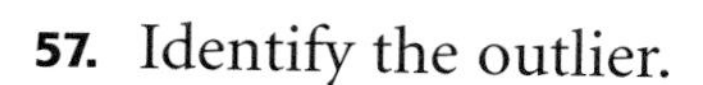

Use the stem-and-leaf diagram for **57** and **58.**

Stem	Leaf
1	4
2	8 8 9
3	2 6 6 7
4	1 2 4 4 4 9

57. Identify the outlier.

58. How many digits are in each number of the data?

59. Find the mean of the data. Round to the nearest tenth. 1, 2, 7, 0, 3, 1, 0, 4, 2, 1, 0

60. Find the mean of this data set: 42, 56, 50, 38, 44.

Ⓐ 18 Ⓑ 38 Ⓒ 44 Ⓓ 46

Skills Practice Bank, page 661, Set 1

Chapter 2
Lesson
2

Rounding Large Numbers

You Will Learn
- to round numbers, and use rounded numbers in real-life situations

Vocabulary
rounding

Learn

Large numbers can be difficult to work with. But you don't always need to use the exact value of large numbers. You can often use numbers that are close to the exact number but easier to work with.

Stay Sharp
Use place value to find the place to which a number is rounded.

Rounding is one way to find a number that's more convenient to work with. Rounding will give you the closest convenient number according to a given place value.

There are four steps involved in the rounding process.

67,683 to thousands		2,341 to hundreds
6[7],683	Find the place value to which you are rounding.	2,[3]41
6[7],683	Look at the digit to the right.	2,[3]41
6[7],683 ↑ Add one	If this digit is 5 or greater, add 1 to the place-value digit. If it's less than 5, leave the place value digit alone.	2,[3]41 ↑ Leave alone
68,000	Change the digits to the right to zeros.	2,300

Example 1

According to the 1990 U.S. Census, there were 45,249,989 people in the 5-to-17 age group. Round the population to the given place.

a. millions 4[5], 2 4 9, 9 8 9 — The digit to the right is less than 5.
45,000,000 — Leave the millions digit unchanged.

b. ten-millions [4]5, 2 4 9, 9 8 9 — The digit to the right is 5 or greater.
50,000,000 — Add 1 to the ten-millions digit.

Sometimes it may make sense to either round up or round down.

Example 2

Danielle thinks her diving tank contains enough air for about a 47-minute dive. Since 47 rounds to 50, can she make a 50-minute dive?

No. Danielle can't afford to run out of air under water. Rounding up gives her a closer number, but common sense says it is safer to round *down* to estimate the length of the dive.

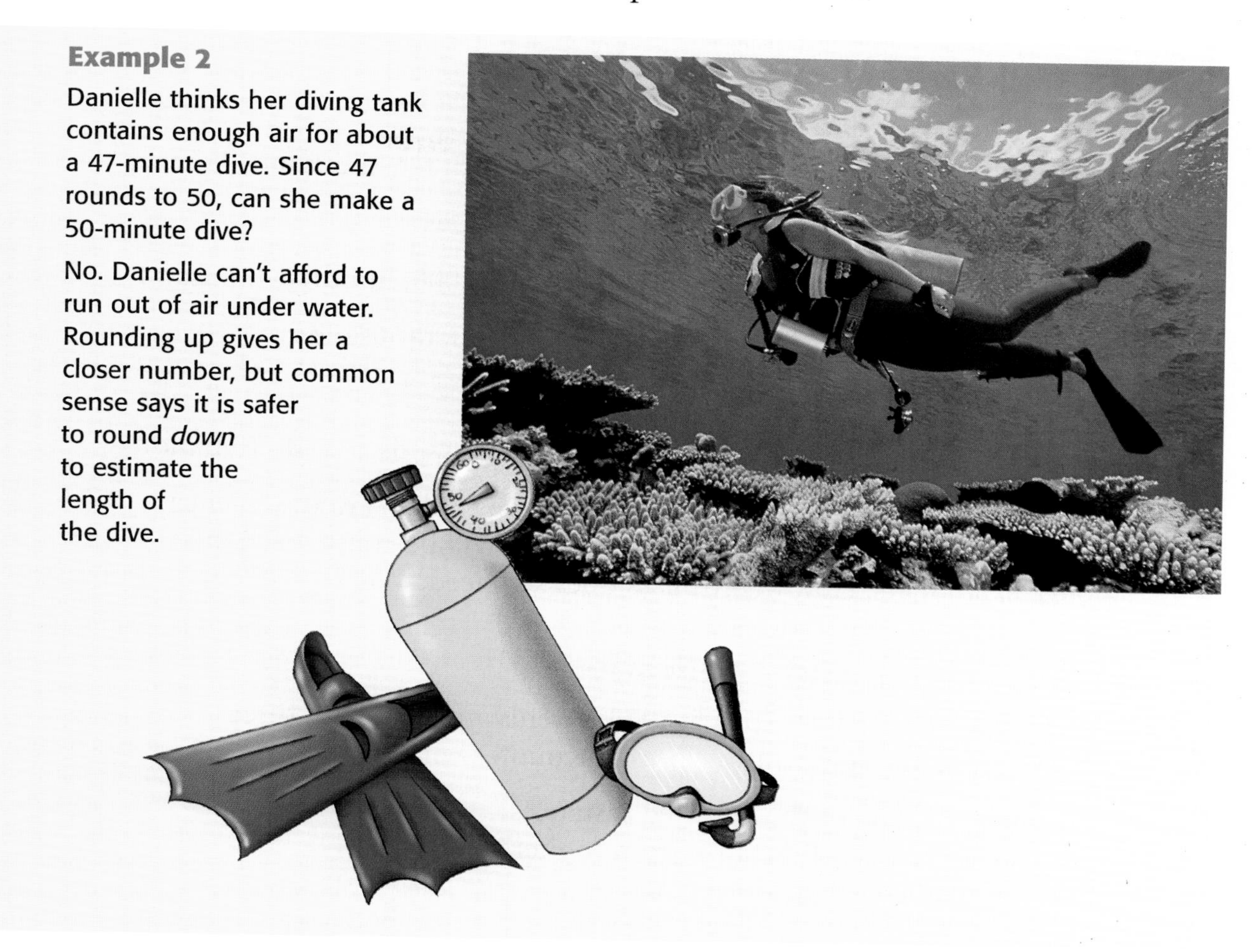

Talk About It

1. Why is a rounded number easier to work with?
2. Describe one situation when you might purposely round up, and one when you might purposely round down.

Check

Round to the given place.

1. 5,427,110; thousands
2. 56,124; ten-thousands
3. 456,145; hundreds
4. 6,741,235; millions
5. 245; tens
6. 1,957,000; hundred-thousands
7. **Reasoning** How many whole numbers less than 1,000 would round to 1,000 when rounding to the nearest hundred? Explain.

Practice

Skills and Reasoning

Round to the given place.

8. 8,702; hundreds

9. 94,655; ten-thousands

10. 1,850,817,349; hundred-millions

11. 738; tens

12. 8,000,000,000; trillions

13. 3,886,000; hundred-thousands

14. 2,790,600,073,521; ten-billions

15. 22,900; thousands

16. Round 84,226,499,391 to the given place.

a. hundreds **b.** 10 thousands **c.** 100 thousands **d.** 10 billions

17. **Reasoning** Claudia must reserve buses to take students to the Science Museum. She thinks that about 263 students will be going. Each bus holds 30 students. How many buses does she need? Why?

Problem Solving and Applications

Pioneer 11 was launched on April 5, 1973. Twenty months later, three reports described the spacecraft's closest encounter with Jupiter.

18. **Reasoning** Do any of the reported distances give *Pioneer 11*'s exact distance from Jupiter? How can you tell?

19. **Critical Thinking** Why do the reports give three different distances?

20. **Reasoning** Earlier in 1973, *Pioneer 10* came within 81,000 miles of Jupiter. To compare *Pioneer 11*'s performance with *Pioneer 10*'s, which of the three reported distances would you use? Explain.

21. **Critical Thinking** A *Pioneer 11* engineer explained why there should be another Jupiter project: "We're getting closer each time. This time we were down to almost 25,000 miles." Why did the engineer use 25,000 miles instead of one of the distances in the reports?

NASA Press Release

Dateline: 12/2/74
Contact: J.P. Richards
NASA Public Relations

Today, December 2, 1974, the space probe Pioneer 11 bypassed Jupiter at an altitude of 26,725 miles.

10A

Pioneer 11 Close to Jupiter

(UPI) — The Planetary explorer Pioneer 11 was nearly 27,000 miles from Jupiter when it flew by yesterday.

Pioneer 11

Late in 1974, Pioneer 11 passed within 30,000 miles of the planet Jupiter.

Problem Solving and SCIENCE

On August 29, 1989, the planetary explorer *Voyager 2* crossed Pluto's orbit and left the solar system. *Voyager 2* was 2,758,530,928 miles from Earth.

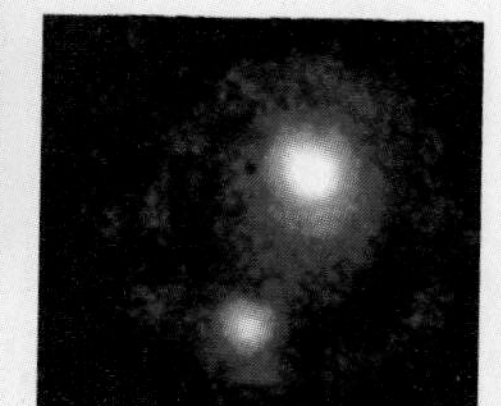

22. Write *Voyager 2*'s distance from Earth in words.

23. Round *Voyager 2*'s distance to the given place.

a. hundred-thousands **b.** ten-millions **c.** hundred-millions **d.** billions

24. Estimation Arnold's car is about to run out of gas. He estimates that the car can go about 25 miles before this happens. The next gas station is 30 miles away. Should he try to make it to the next station? Explain.

25. Critical Thinking While entering 1990 population data into a computer, a census worker mistakenly deleted digits from the populations of two Texas towns.

The worker remembered that both populations rounded to 20,000 to the nearest thousand. What could the two populations be? Explain why.

26. Journal Make a list of everyday situations for which you must use exact numbers. Then make a list of everyday situations when you can use rounded numbers to approximate answers.

Mixed Review and Test Prep

Add.

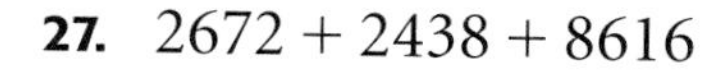

27. 2672 + 2438 + 8616 **28.** 2107 + 596 + 5632 **29.** 759 + 6675 + 3219

Use the data to make a frequency chart and a line plot.

30. 48, 48, 49, 52, 53, 53, 53, 54 **31.** 101, 94, 96, 103, 98, 100, 100

Find the median, mode, and range.

32. 12, 2, 6, 10, 2, 10, 11 **33.** 32, 29, 22, 32, 30, 32

34. What is ninety-five thousand seven hundred in standard form?

Ⓐ 90,570 Ⓑ 95,700 Ⓒ 97,500 Ⓓ 95,070

Comparing and Ordering Numbers

You Will Learn

- to compare and order large numbers

Learn

To compare two numbers with the same number of digits, find the first place-value position that has different digits. The number with the greater digit is the greater number.

The symbols > and < are used to compare numbers. The symbol > means "is greater than," and < means "is less than."

Example 1

Mount Shasta is 14,162 feet tall. Mount Russell is 14,086 feet tall. Compare the heights of these California mountains.

[1]4,162
[1]4,086
The ten-thousands digits are equal. Move to the right.

1[4],162
1[4],086
The thousands digits are equal. Move to the right.

14,[1]62
14,[0]86
In the hundreds place, 1 is greater than 0.

14,162 > 14,086

Mount Shasta is taller than Mount Russell.

Math Tip

If two whole numbers have a different number of digits, the number with more digits is greater.

Sometimes it is helpful to list numbers in order.

Example 2

Order from least to greatest the three craters on the visible side of the moon.

Craters on the Moon	
Name	**Diameter (m)**
Deslandres	234,000
Schickard	227,000
Bailly	303,000

227,000 < 234,000
Schickard < Deslandres
Compare two at a time.

234,000 < 303,000
Deslandres < Bailly
Use the same symbol in the second comparison.

The order is Schickard at 227,000 meters, Deslandres at 234,000 meters, and Bailly at 303,000 meters.

Is it easier to compare greater numbers when they are written in standard form or word form? Why?

Check

Compare the numbers using $>$ or $<$.

1. 462 ● 89 **2.** 56 ● 27 **3.** 842 ● 24 **4.** 3,619 ● 3,610

5. The Belkovich crater is 198,000 meters in diameter. The Janssen crater is 190,000 meters in diameter. Compare the two craters.

6. Order from least to greatest: 138,417; 146,416; 98,419.

7. **Reasoning** Are all five-digit numbers greater than all four-digit numbers?

Practice

Skills and Reasoning

Compare the numbers, using $>$ or $<$.

8. 277 ● 31 **9.** 5,768 ● 924 **10.** 873 ● 2,183 **11.** 327 ● 91

12. 64 ● 65 **13.** 158 ● 185 **14.** 448,119 ● 448,191 **15.** 609 ● 629

Order each group of numbers from least to greatest.

16. 77; 7,777; 777; 77,777

17. 5,678; 5,768; 5,687

18. 57,000; 56,940; 56,490

19. 20,200; 22,000; 20,002

20. 18,962; 18,629; 16,892

21. 4,102; 4,210; 4,010

22. 20 million; 500 thousand; 1 billion

23. 10 hundred; 10 million; 1 trillion

24. 9 hundred; 901; nine

25. 62 thousand; 6 hundred; 29 billion

Order each group of numbers from greatest to least.

26. 582; 502; 525; 528

27. 3,041; 3,401; 3,114

28. 1,014; 1,004; 1,084

29. 9,616; 9,016; 9,916

30. **Measurement** In almost 19 years, *Voyager 1* traveled 11,005,000,000 kilometers, and *Voyager 2* traveled 10,042,000,000 kilometers. Which spacecraft traveled farther?

31. **Reasoning** How many numbers with a 7 in the tens place are less than 260? List the numbers from least to greatest.

32. **Reasoning** The first digit of a number is 7. Is the number greater than another number whose first digit is 6? Explain.

Problem Solving and Applications

North Pole

EQUATOR

South Pole

33. **Logic** Marisela, Luis, and Raymond are comparing heights, Luis is 54 inches tall. Marisela is shorter than Luis but 2 inches taller than Raymond. Order the three students from shortest to tallest.

34. **Geography** The diameter of earth at the equator is 7,926 miles. The diameter from the North Pole to the South Pole is 7,898 miles. Which diameter is greater?

35. **Chance** In the fall raffle at Oakdale Middle School, 4,269 tickets were sold. In the winter raffle, 4,629 were sold. In the spring raffle, 4,962. Rank the raffles from easiest-to-win to hardest-to-win.

36. **Geography** List the cities in order from largest population to smallest: Rio de Janeiro, Brazil: 12,788,000; Buenos Aires, Argentina: 12,232,000; Calcutta, India: 12,885,000.

Elena Kondakova

37. **Science** The two most experienced female astronauts are Shannon Lucid and Elena Kondakova. As of 1996, Lucid had spent 5,354 hours in space. As of 1995, Kondakova had spent 2,033 hours in space. Compare their hours in space, using $>$ or $<$.

38. **Science** Indonesia has 268,356,000 acres of forest. Australia has 261,931,000 acres. Compare the two amounts, using $>$ or $<$.

39. **Critical Thinking** Use the digits 7, 1, 5, 9, and 3 to write the greatest and least possible 5-digit numbers. Each digit must be used exactly once. Use $>$ or $<$ to compare your answers.

Using Data The bar graph shows the five most populated metropolitan areas in the United States, according to the 1990 census. Use the data for **40** and **41.**

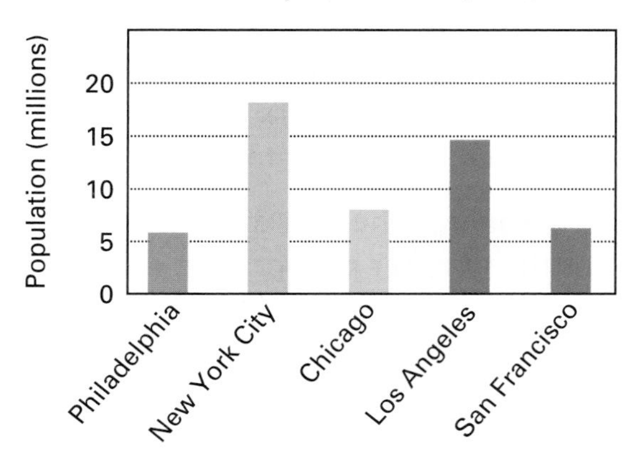

40. **Critical Thinking** The populations of the five areas are 18,087,281; 6,253,311; 14,531,529; 8,065,633; and 5,899,345. Match each area with its population.

41. **Critical Thinking** The population of Jakarta, Indonesia, is greater than that of Chicago. How does Jakarta's population compare with that of San Francisco?

Problem Solving and SCIENCE

The chart lists eight U.S. space probes sent to other planets in our solar system and how far the probes were from the sun when they visited the planets or crossed their orbits.

Probe	Distance (mi)
Mariner 2	sixty-seven million
Pioneer 10	500,000,000
Pioneer 10	4,000,000,000
Pioneer 11	3 billion
Mariner 10	forty million
Viking 1	150 million
Voyager 2	1,700,000,000
Voyager 1	one billion

42. Match each probe and its distance with the planet it visited or the planetary orbit it crossed.

43. Explain how you determined which probe matched up with each planet.

44. Suppose a new planet is discovered between the orbits of Neptune and Pluto. Give its possible distance from the sun.

45. Using Data Use the data on page 58 to check your answers to Exercises 42–44. Explain how the data on page 58 compares with the data shown on this page.

46. Journal Describe at least three situations outside of the classroom when you compare or order numbers.

Mixed Review and Test Prep

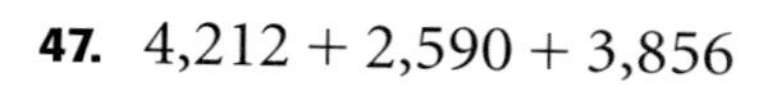

Add.

47. 4,212 + 2,590 + 3,856

48. 22,386 + 6,911

49. 356,093 + 734,035

50. 160,577 + 64,444

51. 454,232 + 711,804

52. 560,380 + 479,120

53. 984,909 + 978,099

54. 328,040 + 288,045

55. 423,371 + 968,195

Find the mean.

56. 40, 34, 50, 39, 61, 34

57. 72, 92, 83, 47, 101

58. 123, 98, 112, 131, 121

59. 204, 342, 267, 412, 383, 439

60. Which number has a 5 in the hundreds place?

Ⓐ 158,028 Ⓑ 13,855 Ⓒ 53,852 Ⓓ 13,555

Chapter 2 Lesson 4

Exponents

Problem Solving Connection

- Look for a Pattern
- Make an Organized List

Materials

scientific calculator

Vocabulary

factor
power
base
exponent
expanded form
standard form
squared
cubed

Did You Know?

The greatest number that can be written with two digits is 9^9. It is equal to 387,420,489.

Explore

You can use your calculator to find certain large numbers.

Work Together

1. Use only the numbers 1, 2, 3, and 4. On your calculator, press this sequence:

   1, 2, 3, or 4 [y^x] 1, 2, 3, or 4 [=]

   Record the numbers you pressed and the answers given by the calculator.

2. Repeat Step 1 as many times as necessary until you understand how the calculator finds the answer. Explain the calculator's method.

3. Predict each result. Then use your calculator to check your prediction.

   a. 2 [y^x] 5 [=] **b.** 6 [y^x] 2 [=] **c.** 10 [y^x] 3 [=]

4. Find 3^5 and 5^3 on your calculator. Are the results the same? Why or why not?

Talk About It

What patterns do you see?

Connect and Learn

When you enter 2 [y^x] 7 into the calculator you are finding 2^7.

You can represent repeated multiplication of the same number by using exponential notation. The **base** is the number to be multiplied. The **exponent** or **power** is the number that tells how many times the base is used as a factor. When you multiply numbers each number is a **factor** of the result.

$$\underbrace{2 \times 2 \times 2 \times 2 \times 2 \times 2 \times 2}_{\text{7 factors}} = 2^7$$

← 7 is the exponent or power

← 2 is the base

Numbers involving exponents can be written in three different forms.

Exponential notation: 2^7

Expanded form: $2 \times 2 \times 2 \times 2 \times 2 \times 2 \times 2 = 2^7$

Standard notation: 128

There are two special powers:

5^2 is 5 to the second power or 5 **squared**.

8^3 is 8 to the third power or 8 **cubed**.

There is also one special base, 10. You can find the value of 10 raised to a power using patterns.

$10^3 = \mathbf{10 \times 10 \times 10 = 1{,}000}$

To find a power of 10 add the same number of zeros as the exponent.

Example 1

Write $8 \times 8 \times 8 \times 8 \times 8 \times 8$ using exponents.

8 is used as a factor 6 times.
Using exponents, you write 8^6.

Example 2

Write 7^4 in expanded form.

The exponent tells you that 7 is used as a factor 4 times.

Using expanded form, you write $7 \times 7 \times 7 \times 7$.

Example 3

Write 5^3 in standard form.

5 is used as a factor 3 times.

$5 \times 5 \times 5 = 125$

Example 4

When the space probe *Mariner 10* passed the planet Mercury in 1972, it was traveling about 19^4 mi/hr. Write 19^4 in standard form.

$19 \times 19 \times 19 \times 19 = 130{,}321$

Check

1. Write $12 \times 12 \times 12 \times 12$ using exponents.
2. Write 5^6 in expanded form.
3. Use mental math to change 9^2 to standard form.
4. **Reasoning** Which is greater, 10^6 or 11^5? Explain.

Practice

Skills and Reasoning

Write using exponents.

5. $5 \times 5 \times 5 \times 5$ **6.** $9 \times 9 \times 9 \times 9 \times 9$ **7.** $24 \times 24 \times 24$ **8.** 79×79

9. $20 \times 20 \times 20$ **10.** $7 \times 7 \times 3 \times 3$ **11.** $8 \times 8 \times 8 \times 4$ **12.** 36

13. $3 \times 3 \times 3$ **14.** $6 \times 6 \times 6 \times 2$ **15.** 12×12 **16.** $4 \times 4 \times 3 \times 3$

Write in expanded form.

17. 4^3 **18.** 25^2 **19.** 11^6 **20.** 200^4 **21.** 13^5 **22.** 7^7

23. 10^{10} **24.** 3^4 **25.** 19^6 **26.** 5^9 **27.** 1^{10} **28.** 9^8

29. 6^5 **30.** 1^4 **31.** 22^2 **32.** 3^7 **33.** 2^5 **34.** 48^3

Write in standard form.

35. 6^2 **36.** 5^3 **37.** 10^4 **38.** 3^5 **39.** 13 squared **40.** 1^{10}

41. 7^5 **42.** 2^8 **43.** 15^4 **44.** 9 cubed **45.** 8^3 **46.** 3^6

47. $\$4.26 + \$32.07 + \$0.52$ **48.** $6.3 + 7.23 + 29.1$ **49.** $50 + 2.852 + 13.6$

Compare, using $<$, $>$, or $=$.

50. 2^3 ● 3^2 **51.** 5^4 ● 5×4 **52.** 1^{12} ● 12^1 **53.** 10^{15} ● 10^{16}

54. 6^4 ● 36^2 **55.** 9^3 ● 13^2 **56.** 4^4 ● 3^5 **57.** 8^2 ● 16×4

Write in standard form.

58. $2^2 \times 3^2$ **59.** $10^4 \times 7$ **60.** $4^8 + 8^4$

61. $10^5 + 10^4$ **62.** $100^6 + 10^8$ **63.** $5^2 + 6^2 + 7^2$

64. $2^5 \times 1^8$ **65.** $100^5 + 10^5 + 1^5$

66. $100^4 \times 10^4 \times 1^4$ **67.** $12^2 \times 12^1 \times 12^3$

68. **Number Sense** Find each number.

a. The number that equals 100 when it is squared.

b. The number that equals 27 when it is cubed.

69. What whole number, when raised to the fourth power, equals 1,296?

70. What is the greatest number that can be written with 3 digits?

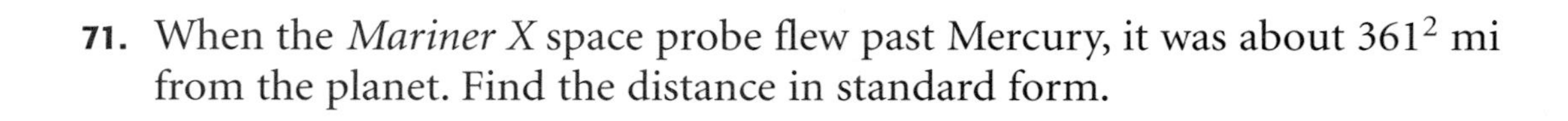

71. When the *Mariner X* space probe flew past Mercury, it was about 361^2 mi from the planet. Find the distance in standard form.

Problem Solving and Applications

72. Critical Thinking The number of bacteria cells in a biology experiment doubles every hour. After one hour there are 2 cells, after 2 hours there are 2×2 (or 4) cells, after 3 hours there are $2 \times 2 \times 2$ (or 8) cells, and so on.

a. Use exponents to write the number of cells after each of the first 10 hours of the experiment.

b. Write an expression in exponential notation for the number of cells after 50 hours.

c. Critical Thinking Would the number of cells after 100 hours be twice the number of cells after 50 hours? Explain.

For each number in exponential notation, identify the base and exponent. Use a calculator and write each number in standard form.

Saturn

73. Science In September of 1979, the space probe *Pioneer 11* approached within 114^2 miles of Saturn. The probe was traveling about 4^8 mi/hr. It collected data showing that Saturn's rings are about 11^5 miles wide.

74. Science Pluto, the planet farthest from the Sun, orbits at a speed of about 8^6 miles per day. At this speed, it takes about 3^5 years to orbit the Sun.

75. Journal Name 2 occupations which might use exponents. Explain.

Mixed Review and Test Prep

Multiply.

76. $2 \times 2 \times 2 \times 2$ **77.** $3 \times 3 \times 3 \times 3$ **78.** $4 \times 4 \times 4 \times 4$

79. $2 \times 3 \times 2 \times 3$ **80.** $2 \times 4 \times 2 \times 4$ **81.** $3 \times 4 \times 3 \times 4$

82. $2 \times 3 \times 4 \times 2$ **83.** $2 \times 3 \times 4 \times 3$ **84.** $2 \times 3 \times 4 \times 4$

Add.

85. \$13,427.00 + \$46,212.00 **86.** \$7,295.63 + \$1,754.89

87. \$824,788 + \$567,673 **88.** \$8,691,288 + \$7,643,841

89. \$372,150 + \$517,720 **90.** \$8,542,505 + \$3,276,023

91. What is 4,382,409 rounded to the nearest hundred thousand?

Ⓐ 4,400,000 Ⓑ 4,000,000 Ⓒ 4,380,000 Ⓓ 4,382,000

SECTION A

Review and Practice

Vocabulary Choose the letter that gives the best answer.

1. Which of the following is 15,983 rounded to the nearest thousands place?
   Ⓐ 15,900 Ⓑ 15,000 Ⓒ 16,000 Ⓓ 15,980

2. Which of the following is the standard form of 2 with an exponent of 5?
   Ⓐ 10 Ⓑ 32 Ⓒ 16 Ⓓ 4

3. What is the place value of 7 in 5,672,501?
   Ⓐ tens Ⓑ hundreds Ⓒ hundred-thousands Ⓓ ten-thousands

(Lesson 1) Write each number in standard form.

4. nine hundred seventy thousand, three hundred fifty
5. eight million, three hundred twenty-one thousand, four hundred twelve
6. 22 billion, thirty-five
7. 422 thousand, three hundred ninety-nine

(Lessons 1 and 4) Solve.

8. The Russian space probe *Venera* measured the surface temperature of Venus as $2^5 \times 3^3$ degrees Fahrenheit. Give the temperature in standard notation.

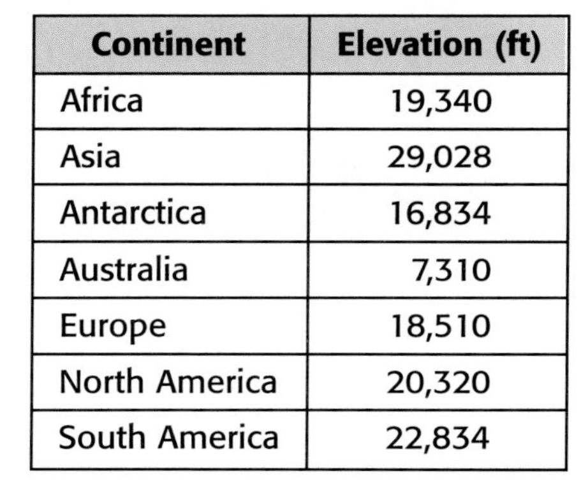

Continent	Elevation (ft)
Africa	19,340
Asia	29,028
Antarctica	16,834
Australia	7,310
Europe	18,510
North America	20,320
South America	22,834

(Lessons 2 and 3) Use the data from the table for **9** and **10.**

9. Round each elevation to the nearest thousand.
10. Order the elevations from least to greatest.

(Lessons 2 and 3) Copy and complete. Use $<$, $>$, or $=$.

11. 9 million ● 9,000,000
12. 2^5 ● 2×5
13. 50,999 ● 51,000
14. 2,080 ● two thousand eight

(Lessons 2 and 4) Write each number in standard form. Then round that number to the place indicated.

15. 4^2; tens
16. 5^3; tens
17. 8^4; thousands
18. 9^2; hundreds
19. **Journal** Compare ordering numbers and putting words in alphabetical order. Describe the similarities and differences between the two processes.

Skills Checklist

In this section, you have:

- ☑ **Read and Written Large Numbers**
- ☑ **Rounded Large Numbers**
- ☑ **Compared and Ordered Numbers**
- ☑ **Explored Exponents**

CHAPTER 2

SECTION

B Number Sense and Operation Sense

People collect everything from autographs to stamps. A good collector uses several skills when trying to assemble the best possible collection for the least amount of money.

How does having a good understanding of mathematics help you build a collection for the least amount of money?

GET READY!

Estimating

Review estimation. Estimate each sum or difference using compatible numbers.

1. $12 + 89$ **2.** $618 - 45$ **3.** $233 + 68$

4. $313 + 62$ **5.** $405 - 39$ **6.** $706 - 53$

7. $99 + 28$ **8.** $478 + 19$ **9.** $107 + 66$

Skills Checklist

In this section, you will:

- ❒ Learn About Mental Math
- ❒ Estimate Sums and Differences
- ❒ Estimate Products and Quotients
- ❒ Learn About the Order of Operations
- ❒ Learn About Numerical Patterns

Chapter 2
Lesson
5

Mental Math

You Will Learn

- to simplify problems mentally using patterns, the Distributive Property, compatible numbers, and compensation

Vocabulary

compatible numbers

compensation

Distributive Property

Remember

The *Commutative Property* states that changing the order of addends or factors does not change the sum or product. For example, $4 \times 7 = 28$, and $7 \times 4 = 28$.

Learn

Loryn lives in Lewisville, TX.

Collecting baseball cards is a popular hobby. Loryn enjoys organizing her card collection by teams. She has 25 San Francisco Giant cards, 18 Cincinnati Reds cards, and 75 Houston Astros cards.

There are several mental math techniques that are helpful when working with numbers.

Compatible Numbers are pairs of numbers that can be computed easily. Combine compatible numbers, and then combine what remains.

Example 1

Use mental math to find the total sum of Loryn's Giants, Reds, and Astros cards.

$25 + 18 + 75$

25 and 75 are compatible because they are easy to add.

$$\begin{aligned} 25 + 18 + 75 &= (25 + 75) + 18 \\ &= 100 + 18 \\ &= 118 \end{aligned}$$

Loryn has 118 cards.

Patterns When multiplying numbers that end in zeros, multiply the non-zero parts and annex one zero to your answer for each zero in the problem. When dividing numbers that end in zeros, subtract the number of zeros in the divisor from the number of zeros in the dividend to find the number in the quotient.

Example 2

Simplify.

20×700

Use patterns:

$2 \times 7 = 14$

1 zero + 2 zeros = 3 zeros

$20 \times 700 = 14{,}000$

Example 3

Simplify.

$5{,}400{,}000 \div 90$

Use patterns:

$54 \div 9 = 6$

5 zeros − 1 zero = 4 zeros

$5{,}400{,}000 \div 90 = 60{,}000$

Compensation Choose a number close to the number in the problem. Then adjust the answer to compensate for the number you chose.

Example 4

Simplify.

58×3

Since 58 is close to 60, you can use compensation:

$58 \times 3 = (60 \times 3) - (2 \times 3)$

$= 180 - 6 = 174$

$58 \times 3 = 174$

Math Tip

The *Associative Property* states that changing the grouping of addends or factors does not change the sum or product.

The Distributive Property Break numbers into smaller numbers. Calculate using the smaller numbers, and then put your answers together.

Example 5

A collector offered to sell five World's Fair posters at $32 apiece. Use the Distributive Property to find the total cost.

$32 \times 5 = (30 + 2) \times 5$	Break 32 into $30 + 2$.
$= (30 \times 5) + (2 \times 5)$	Multiply each by 5.
$= 150 + 10 = 160$	Add.

The total cost is $160.

Talk About It

1. Compatible numbers are numbers that are easy to add or multiply together. What are some pairs of compatible numbers for addition? For multiplication?
2. Why is it useful to be able to do arithmetic in your head?

Check

Simplify.

1. $4{,}000 \times 300$
2. $210{,}000 \div 700$
3. $50 \times 2 \times 13$
4. $296 + 55$
5. 61×3
6. $285 + 47 + 15$
7. 29×6
8. 102×7

Practice

Skills and Reasoning

Simplify.

9. 40×20	**10.** $251 + 314$	**11.** $96 + 117$	**12.** $4 \times 11 \times 25$
13. 24×2	**14.** $240 \div 6$	**15.** $25 + 23 + 75$	**16.** 49×3
17. $198 + 123$	**18.** $2{,}500 \div 50$	**19.** $68 + 31$	**20.** $50 \times 2 \times 9$
21. 30×600	**22.** 31×4	**23.** $750 + 119 + 250$	**24.** 99×7
25. 53×3	**26.** 89×6	**27.** $819 + 120$	**28.** 700×5
29. $147 - 99$	**30.** $250 \times 4 \times 35$	**31.** $90 + 57 + 10$	**32.** $9{,}000 \times 800$
33. $800 + 336 + 200$	**34.** 58×5	**35.** $560{,}000 \div 80$	**36.** $2{,}645 + 213$
37. $5{,}000 \times 18 \times 2$	**38.** $461 - 295$	**39.** 112×4	**40.** $1{,}800{,}000 \div 9{,}000$
41. $12{,}000 \times 300$	**42.** 42×8	**43.** $79 + 98 + 3$	**44.** $550 - 25$
45. $22 + 88$	**46.** $84 - 34$	**47.** $1{,}200{,}000 \times 500$	**48.** 29×6

49. Reasoning How might you use the compensation method to make closer estimates?

50. Patterns Describe a pattern in the sums below that could help you find the sum of \$117.50 and \$227.50 mentally.

\$1.50 + \$2.50 = \$4.00   \$17.50 + \$24.50 = \$42.00

\$46.50 + \$61.50 = \$108.00   \$37.50 + \$19.50 = \$57.00

51. Reasoning Which problem is easier to simplify with mental math, $20 \times 19 \times 5$ or $20 \times 19 \times 6$? Explain your reasoning.

Problem Solving and Applications

52. Geometry Use mental math to find the perimeter of the pentagon.

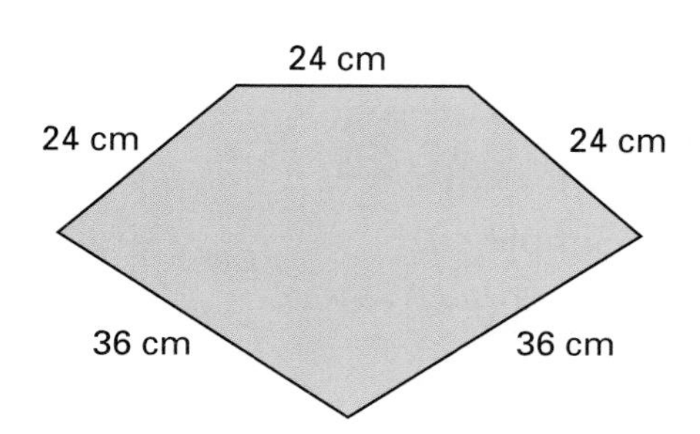

53. Craig earns \$5 per hour at his after-school job. One week he worked 21 hours. Find his total earnings for the week.

Using Data Use the bar graph to answer **54–56.**

54. How many yards did Marcus swim?

55. How much farther did he swim in freestyle than butterfly?

56. How much farther did he swim in freestyle and backstroke than in butterfly and breaststroke?

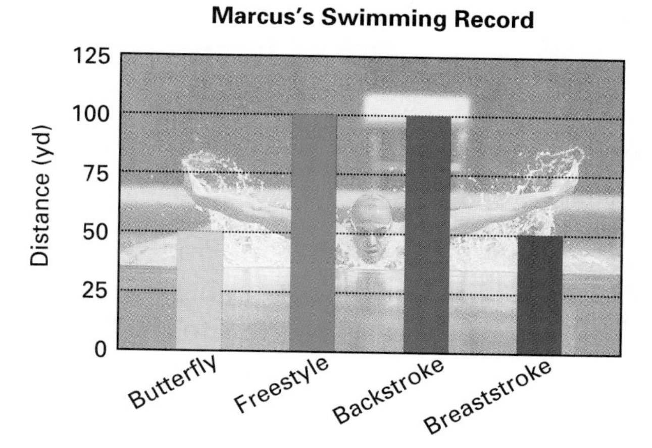

57. Marcie bought a movie poster for $4.45 plus $0.34 sales tax. Find the total cost of the poster.

58. At the Metropolitan Coin Fair, Robbie sold 99 coins from his collection of 876. How many coins did he have left?

59. **Science** The moon is about 240,000 miles from Earth. How long would it take you to fly to the moon at a speed of 40,000 miles per day?

60. **Critical Thinking** Janet has $13.64, and she wants to buy a board game for $15.84. How much more money does she need? If the game goes on sale for $2.00 less, will she have enough money?

61. **Journal** Explain the difference between using compatible numbers and compensation. Give examples to illustrate your answer.

Mixed Review and Test Prep

STAY SHARP!

Write in standard form.

62. six hundred forty-eight million, two hundred twenty-eight thousand, nine hundred seventy-three

63. three hundred thirty-five million, seven hundred twenty-eight thousand, six hundred forty-two

Write in words.

64. 467,987,382 65. 5,976,321,401 66. 5,983 67. 3,093,002

Subtract.

68. 412 − 176 69. 91,233 − 17,974 70. 845,213 − 685,787

71. 6,329,432 − 3,654,987 72. 54,987 − 3,283 73. 94,040 − 32,804

74. 4,931,515 − 34,687 75. 7,237,802 − 5,091,465 76. 111,996 − 22,197

77. What is the place value of 5 in 35,409?

Ⓐ Tens Ⓑ Ones Ⓒ Thousands Ⓓ Hundreds

Chapter 2
Lesson
6

Estimating Sums and Differences

You Will Learn

- to estimate sums and differences using front-end estimation and clustering

Learn

When you don't need an exact answer to a problem, you can estimate. When using *front-end estimation,* add or subtract using only the first digit of each number. Estimate the sum or difference of the remaining digits and add this to the first estimate. For a more accurate estimate, calculate using the first *two* digits.

Example 1

Estimate 982 − 539 using one-digit front-end estimation.

$$\begin{array}{r} \mathbf{9}82 \\ -\mathbf{5}39 \\ \hline \mathbf{4}00 \\ +\ 40 \\ \hline 440 \end{array}$$

Subtract the first digit in each number.
Add 40 because 82 − 39 is about 40.

Example 2

Estimate 23,745 + 54,881 using two-digit front-end estimation.

$$\begin{array}{r} \mathbf{23},745 \\ +\mathbf{54},881 \\ \hline \mathbf{77},000 \\ +\ 1,600 \\ \hline 78,600 \end{array}$$

Add the first two digits in each number.
Add 1,600 because 745 + 881 is about 1,600.

Did You Know?
The most valuable Lincoln-head penny was minted in 1909 in San Francisco. This penny has the initials VDB, which stand for its designer, Victor D. Brenner. Today, a Brenner penny in perfect condition is worth about $750.

When adding several numbers that are approximately equal, use *clustering* to estimate the sum. Replace all of the numbers with a single number close to them that is easy to multiply. Then multiply.

Example 3

A scientist measured four strides of a dinosaur. Estimate the combined length of the four strides.

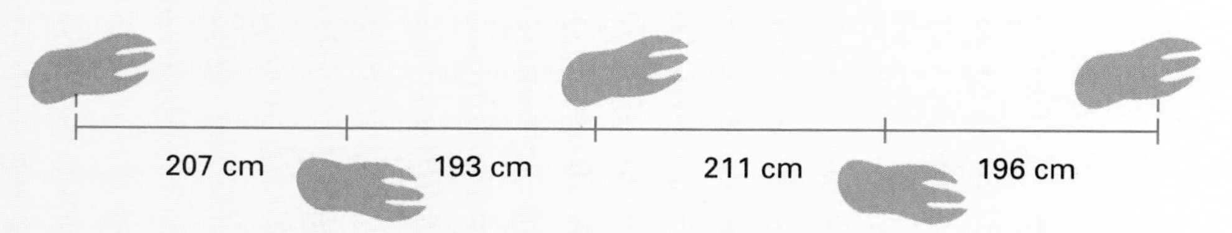

Each distance is approximately 200 cm.

$200 + 200 + 200 + 200 = 4 \times 200 = 800$

The dinosaur walked about 800 cm.

Talk About It

1. Describe some real-life addition and subtraction situations that require exact answers. Describe some where estimates are satisfactory.
2. Is front-end estimation the same as rounding and then adding? Explain.

Check

Estimate.

1. 773 + 848
2. 6,707 − 4,559
3. 307 + 297 + 299
4. **Reasoning** Ron's estimate for 257 + 542 using front-end estimation was 700. What step did he forget? Give a closer estimate for the sum.

Practice

Skills and Reasoning

Estimate.

5. 555 + 429
6. 489 + 495 + 976 + 503 + 515
7. 7,641 − 2,578
8. 98 + 107 + 95 + 97 + 103
9. 53,923,831 + 54,902,756
10. 873 − 549
11. 3,101 + 3,054 + 2,916
12. 5,901,877 − 2,635,392
13. 3,409 + 7,118
14. 257 + 249 + 241 + 259
15. 48,206 + 81,175
16. 443 + 158
17. 1,054 − 928
18. 7,621 + 8,109 + 2,117
19. 14,651 + 23,977
20. 9 + 11 + 13 + 8 + 7 + 12 + 9
21. 15,729 − 7,033
22. 8,715,739 + 9,849,129
23. 891 + 677
24. 1,577 − 1,328
25. **Critical Thinking** Erika estimated the sum of 299 + 298 + 297 as 900. Was her estimate high or low? Explain.

26. **Reasoning** For 86,002 + 17,775, how much more accurate is two-digit front-end estimation than one-digit front-end estimation?
27. **Mental Math** Describe how front-end estimation is similar to compensation when solving problems mentally.

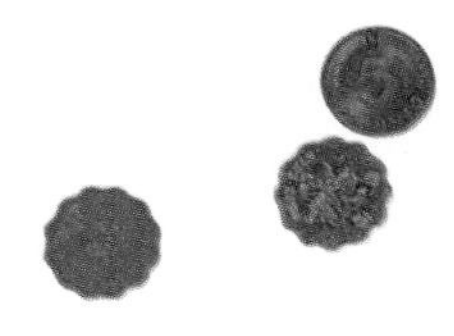

28. How can estimation help you solve problems more efficiently on a calculator?

Problem Solving and Applications

29. **Literature** The letter of the alphabet with the most entries in the *Oxford English Dictionary* is *s*, with 34,556 entries. The next is *c*, with 26,239, and then *p*, with 24,980.
   a. Estimate the number of words in the dictionary that start with either *c* or *p*.
   b. Estimate the difference between the number of words starting with *c* and the number of words starting with *p*.

Using Data Use the table for **30** and **31**.

30. Give one-digit and two-digit front-end estimates for the total number of pennies made at the three mints.

Mint	Number of Pennies Made
Denver	15,804,000
Philadelphia	76,532,352
San Francisco	6,101,000

31. Estimate how much more Philadelphia's total was than Denver's.

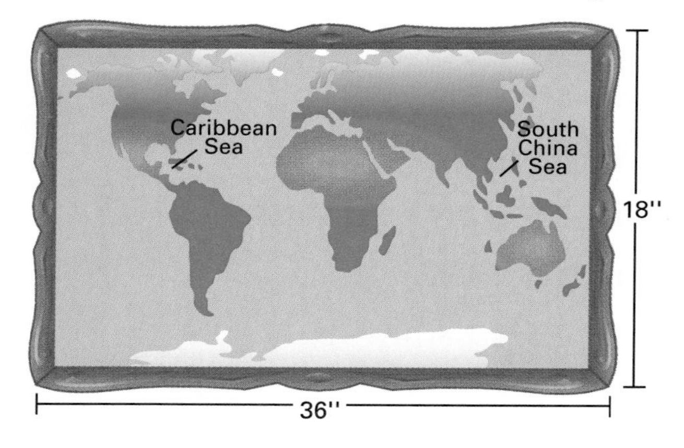

32. **Geography** The average depth of the Caribbean Sea is 8,685 feet. The average depth of the South China Sea is 5,419 feet. About how much deeper is the Caribbean Sea?

33. A picture frame measures 36 in. by 18 in. Estimate the distance around the outside of the frame.

34. **Logic** Maurice estimated the sum of three numbers as 53,300. Pat estimated the same sum as 54,000. If the three numbers were 17,124; 12,652; and 23,507; how could Maurice and Pat have used front-end estimation to get different results?

Using Data Use the data on page 59 to answer **35** and **36**.

35. Suppose the collectors in the table wanted to display their collections. About how many items would be on display?

36. Describe one way you could estimate the space needed to display Craig's greeting cards. How would you set up the display?

Problem Solving and RECREATION

The table gives prices of 1913 Lincoln-head pennies from three mints in five different qualities. Prices are in dollars.

Mint	Good	Very Good	Fine	Very Fine	Extremely Fine
Denver	0.85	1.95	3.79	8.30	16.75
Philadelphia	0.49	0.65	1.19	2.75	9.20
San Francisco	5.15	6.65	7.45	11.19	24.95

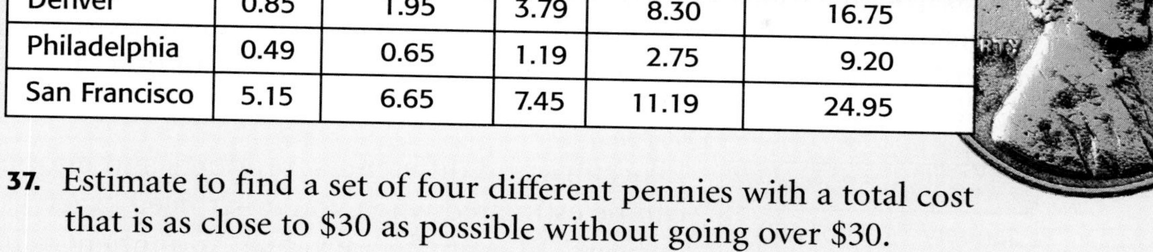

37. Estimate to find a set of four different pennies with a total cost that is as close to $30 as possible without going over $30.

38. Explain how you made your estimates.

39. Find the exact total cost of your four pennies. Compare your results with those of other students.

40. If you round two prices to estimate their sum, how can you be sure that your estimate does not exceed the actual sum?

41. Without using a calculator, how can you tell that the combined cost of the Denver and the San Francisco pennies in fine condition is greater than $11?

42. Journal Explain how to add a group of numbers using clustering. Give an example to illustrate your answer.

Mixed Review and Test Prep

Round to the given place value.

43. 6,967,243; hundred-thousand

44. 42,352,404; hundred

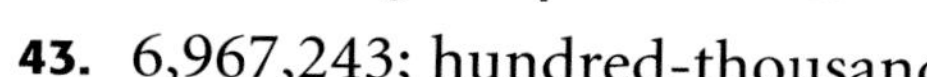

45. 423,855,211; hundred-million

46. 8,788,212,403; thousand

47. 685,490,616; ten-million

48. 16,411,597; ten-thousand

Subtract.

49. $823.44 – $127.58

50. $212,203 – $83,498

51. $62,148.67 – $45,746.23

52. $753,497.62 – $376,032.07

53. $1,029.55 – $734.02

54. $18,229.30 – $12,045.25

55. Give the mean for these test scores.
75, 92, 92, 94, 84, 87, 85

Ⓐ 75 Ⓑ 92 Ⓒ 87 Ⓓ not here

Chapter 2
Lesson
7

Estimating Products and Quotients

You Will Learn
- to estimate products and quotients using rounded and compatible numbers

Learn

The Marbelous Marbles shop sells a rare type of marble known as a Peppermint Swirl. The price of this marble changes each month. If you collected marbles, you may want to estimate the cost of one or several marbles.

Peppermint Swirls	
January	1 for $58
February	3 for $149
March	4 for $149
April	5 for $250
May	2 for $82

Like sums and differences, products and quotients can be estimated when you don't need exact answers. To estimate a product or quotient using *rounding*, round all numbers so that each contains only one nonzero digit. Then multiply or divide.

Remember
The symbol ≈ means "is approximately equal to."

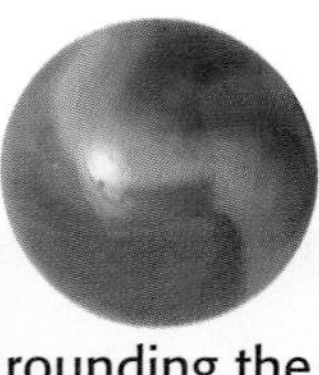

Example 1

a. Estimate using rounding the cost of 21 marbles in January.
$\$58 \times 21 \approx \$60 \times 20$ Round.
$= \$1200$

b. Estimate using rounding the cost of 1 marble in March.
$\$149 \div 4 \approx \$100 \div 4$ Round.
$= \$25$

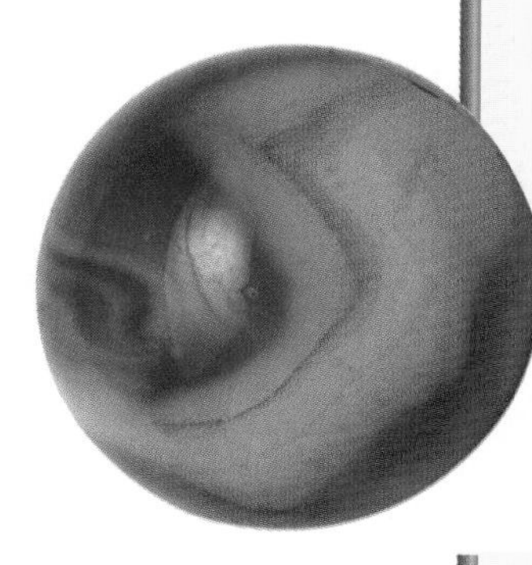

Sometimes closer estimates can be made using *compatible numbers.* To estimate using compatible numbers, rewrite the problem using numbers that go together easily. Then multiply or divide.

Example 2

Estimate using compatible numbers.

a. $\$82 \times 14$
$\$82 \times 14 \approx \$80 \times 15$
$= \$1,200$

b. $\$149 \div 3$
$\$149 \div 3 \approx \$150 \div 3$
$= \$50$

Estimating products and quotients is helpful in many situations.

Example 3

Ted scored 231 points during the 28-game basketball season. Estimate the average number of points he scored each game.

$$231 \div 28 \approx 240 \div 30 = 8$$

He scored about 8 points per game.

How do you know which method to use?
Look at the comparison of the two methods.

Rounding	Compatible Numbers	Actual Solution
$152 \times 34 \approx 200 \times 30 = 6{,}000$	$152 \times 34 \approx 150 \times 30 = 4{,}500$	$152 \times 34 = 5{,}168$
$227 \div 28 \approx 200 \div 30 = 6$ R20	$227 \div 28 \approx 210 \div 30 = 7$	$227 \div 28 = 8$ R3

The rounding method can be simpler for computing multiplication estimates.
The compatible-numbers method can be simpler for computing division estimates, and usually provides a more accurate estimate.

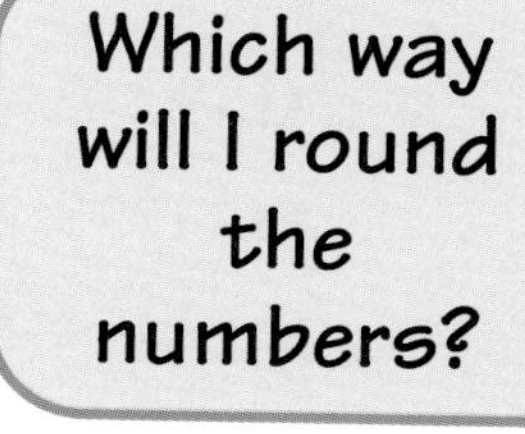

Talk About It

1. Would rounding and compatible numbers be good estimation strategies for addition and subtraction problems? Explain.
2. **a.** Explain two ways you could estimate $3{,}177 \div 45$.

   b. Which method provides the closer estimate?

Check

Estimate using rounding.

1. 84×279 **2.** $7{,}912 \div 43$ **3.** 47×219 **4.** $8{,}160 \div 37$

5. 56×97 **6.** $1{,}200 \times 38$ **7.** $4{,}375 \div 82$ **8.** $212 \div 44$

Estimate using compatible numbers.

9. 22×31 **10.** $553 \div 79$ **11.** 57×91 **12.** $2{,}025 \div 76$

13. $2{,}812 \div 33$ **14.** 69×410 **15.** $2{,}590 \div 63$ **16.** 512×96

17. Reasoning Explain why the compatible-numbers method more often provides a closer estimate than the rounding method.

18. Reasoning In what situations might you choose to use the rounding method rather than the compatible-numbers method?

Practice

Skills and Reasoning

Estimate.

19. $183 \div 21$	**20.** $7{,}111 \times 7{,}888$	**21.** $327 \div 64$	**22.** 448×53
23. $4{,}522 \div 92$	**24.** $9 \times 11 \times 17$	**25.** $11 \times 23 \times 98$	**26.** $777 \div 38$
27. 217×308	**28.** $207 \times 6 \times 15$	**29.** $24{,}111 \div 84$	**30.** 54×82
31. $4{,}270 \div 38$	**32.** $2{,}803 \div 24$	**33.** $1{,}895 \div 463$	**34.** 463×719
35. $5 \times 26 \times 12$	**36.** $175 \div 28$	**37.** $425 \div 59$	**38.** $51 \times 14 \times 19$
39. $6{,}358 \div 7$	**40.** $149 \div 4$	**41.** 29×41	**42.** $19 \times 4 \times 7$
43. $248 \times 5 \times 8$	**44.** $23{,}714 \div 522$	**45.** 185×29	**46.** $200{,}000 \div 720$
47. $2{,}733 \div 71$	**48.** $103 \div 54$	**49.** $3{,}625 \div 581$	**50.** $5 \times 9 \times 2{,}457$
51. $42 \times 27 \times 8$	**52.** $51{,}527 \div 86$	**53.** 296×47	**54.** $561{,}212 \div 687$
55. $94{,}106 \div 11$	**56.** $967 \times 48 \times 12$	**57.** $37 \times 132 \times 6$	**58.** $8 \times 29 \times 492$
59. $106{,}912 \div 100$	**60.** $8{,}346 \div 77$	**61.** $26{,}718 \div 42$	**62.** $1{,}046 \times 58$

63. Reasoning Write five 2-digit by 2-digit multiplication problems that all have a rounding estimate of 2,000.

64. Reasoning Write 5 division problems that all have a compatible-number estimate of 50.

65. Reasoning Why is it important to be able to estimate using mental math?

66. Write Your Own Problem Write a logic puzzle. Give clues to find two or three numbers. One of the clues should be the estimated product and/or quotient of the numbers.

Problem Solving and Applications

67. Critical Thinking You are stacking 105-lb boxes on a freight elevator. A sign on the elevator says, "Do not exceed 1,000 pounds total." What is the maximum number of boxes you can stack on the elevator? Explain your reasoning.

68. Tracy collects old sheet music. In a bin at a flea market, she found 19 songs priced at $4.95 apiece. Estimate the total cost of the music.

69. **Industry** Flight 777 carries 54 passengers, each with 2 suitcases. Each suitcase weighs, on average, 36 pounds. If the airplane was built to carry 5,000 pounds of luggage, is the flight over or under its limit?

70. **Social Science** The *Yomiuri Shimbun* in Japan is the daily newspaper with the highest circulation, at 8,700,000 copies per day. If one day's papers were distributed evenly among Japan's four islands, about how many copies of the paper would be on each island?

71. **Measurement** There are 5,280 feet in a mile and 12 inches in a foot. Estimate the number of inches in a mile.

72. **Choose a Strategy** Leslie won some money in a contest. After spending $12 on a CD, almost $34 on new bicycle tires, and about $16 on a pair of pants, she has about $15 left over. Estimate how much Leslie won. Explain your answer.

73. Carlos has been offered $825 for his collection of 19 model train cabooses. He wants to get an average of at least $40 per caboose. Should he accept the offer? Explain how he can use estimation to decide.

74. **Critical Thinking** You received $50 for your birthday. You are in a music store deciding what to buy. You want 2 CDs that cost $14 each and 1 cassette that costs $10. Can you estimate to see if you have enough money? Explain.

75. **Journal** List two situations where it is better to have an exact answer than an estimate, and explain why.

Mixed Review and Test Prep

Compare. Use > or <.

76. 2,156 ● 2,157
77. 324,265,129 ● 324,264,872
78. 19,667 ● 190,675
79. 3,189 ● 3,891
80. 267 ● 627
81. 134,256 ● 134,265

Order the numbers from least to greatest.

82. 1,023; 10; 356; 1,009; 383
83. 22,456; 122,802; 21,904; 122,501

Multiply.

84. 20×607
85. 50×505
86. 60×304
87. 70×801
88. 14×18
89. 26×21
90. 60×52
91. 83×57
92. 12×12
93. 21×25
94. 63×34
95. 99×99

96. A bank has $2 million. Suppose in one day $1,002,987 is taken out and $2,987,102 is deposited. Which estimate is closest to how much money the bank has at the end of the day?

Ⓐ $1 million Ⓑ $2 million Ⓒ $3 million Ⓓ $4 million

Chapter 2
Lesson
8

Order of Operations

You Will Learn

- to use order of operation rules to solve problems

Vocabulary

order of operations

Learn

David Hicks collects calculators and has a calculator museum on the World Wide Web. One of his calculators is an early HP-01 calculator watch from the 1970s. Another is the HP 9820, one of the first algebraic calculators. Each calculator processed arithmetic problems in a different way.

Sometimes calculators give different answers because they solve different parts of a problem first.

The value of an expression that involves several operations depends on the order in which you perform the operations. Suppose you wanted to simplify $3 + 4 \times 5$.

You could add first or multiply first.

Adding first:	$3 + 4 = 7$
Now multiply:	$7 \times 5 = 35$

Multiplying first:	$4 \times 5 = 20$
Now add:	$3 + 20 = 23$

Math Tip

To find out if your calculator follows order-of-operation rules, press 2 [+] 3 [×] 4 [=]. If the answer is 14, the calculator follows the rules.

So the HP-01 calculator added first. The HP 9820 calculator multiplied first.

Problem	HP-01	HP 9820
$3 + 4 \times 5$	35	23
$2 + 8 \times 6$	60	50
$9 \times 4 - 8$	28	28
$6 + 15 \div 3$	7	11
$20 - 16 \div 4$	1	16
$42 \div 7 + 3$	9	9

Mathematicians use parentheses to show which part of the problem should be done first. But some problems don't have parentheses. To make sure everyone gets the same answer for a problem, mathematicians use a set of rules known as the **order of operations**. Think of the problems that would be caused if we didn't have these rules!

ORDER OF OPERATIONS

1. Simplify inside parentheses.
2. Simplify exponents.
3. Multiply and divide from left to right.
4. Add and subtract from left to right.

Example 1

Simplify.

$7 \times (3 + 2)$

$7 \times (3 + 2) = 7 \times 5$ Simplify inside parentheses first.

$= 35$ Multiply.

Example 2

Simplify.

5×3^2

$5 \times 3^2 = 5 \times 9$ Simplify exponents first.

$= 45$ Multiply.

Example 3

Simplify.

$12 + 5 \times 4$

$12 + 5 \times 4 = 12 + 20$ Multiply first.

$= 32$ Add.

Example 4

Simplify.

$16 \div 2 \times 9$

$16 \div 2 \times 9 = 8 \times 9$ Do left part first.

$= 72$ Do right part.

Talk About It

1. Which calculator follows the order of operations?
2. Why do you need the order of operation rules to compute $20 + 5 \times 3$?

Check

Simplify.

1. $28 - 12 \div 4$
2. $36 \div 12 \div 3$
3. $19 - 4^2$
4. $8 \times (10 - 4)$
5. **Reasoning** If an expression has parentheses, a number with an exponent, and division, which part of the expression is solved first?
6. **Reasoning** Karyn entered $26 + 4 \times 3 - 1$ into a calculator. In what order did the calculator solve the expression if the result was 89?

Practice

Skills and Reasoning

Simplify each expression.

7. $25 - 10 \div 5$ **8.** $14 + 7 \times 6$ **9.** $30 \times 6 + 2$ **10.** $50 \div 5 - 2$

11. $32 \div 8 \div 4$ **12.** $2 \times 4 \times 6$ **13.** $15 \div 3 \times 5$ **14.** $9 \times 6 \div 2$

15. $10 - 8 - 2$ **16.** $(10 - 8) - 2$ **17.** $10 - (8 - 2)$ **18.** $(6^2 \times 4) \times 3$

19. $50 \div 5^2$ **20.** $6^2 - 9$ **21.** $(4 + 5)^2$ **22.** $10^2 \times 3$

23. $6^2 - 2 \times 6$ **24.** $2^3 + 8 \div 4$ **25.** $7^2 - 4^2 \times 3$ **26.** $9 - (4 - 1)^2$

27. $4 \times (5 - 3)$ **28.** $(8 + 7) \div 3$ **29.** $6 \times (9 - 4)^2$ **30.** $(7 + 3)^2 \div 5$

31. $32 - 6 + 5 \times 4$ **32.** $40 + 18 \div 2 - 16$ **33.** $45 \div 9 - 21 \div 7$ **34.** $144 \div 9 \div 8 \div 2$

35. $25 + 2 - 6 \times 2$ **36.** $6 \times (8 - 4) + 2$ **37.** $3 \times 4 \div 6 + 20$ **38.** $3^2 + 2 \times 7 + 3$

Use mental math to evaluate.

39. $30{,}000 - 5{,}000 \times 4$ **40.** $6 + 48{,}000{,}000 \div 800{,}000$ **41.** $60 \times 4 \div 3 + 19$

42. $5{,}000 + 400 \times 8$ **43.** $60 + 60 \div 60$ **44.** $200 - 200 \div 20$

Insert parentheses to make each statement true.

45. $2 \times 3 + 6 = 18$ **46.** $20 \times 15 - 2 = 260$ **47.** $4 + 4^2 \div 5 = 4$ **48.** $2 \times 6^2 - 8 = 56$

49. $6 + 8 \div 2 = 10$ **50.** $12 + 10 \div 11 = 2$ **51.** $5 \times 4 \div 2 = 10$ **52.** $5 + 4 \div 3 = 3$

53. Find an arithmetic expression equal to 9 that contains the following operations.

a. Addition and division

b. Subtraction and division

c. Addition, multiplication, and an exponent

Choose Mental Math, Paper and Pencil, or Calculator. Simplify each expression.

54. $6 \times (25 \times 4) + 7$ **55.** $28 + (64 - 19) \div 3^2$ **56.** $100 \div 5^2 \times (81 + 42)$

57. $600 + 50 \times 6 - 10^2$ **58.** $62 + 57 - 7^2$ **59.** $(8 - 6)^8 + 6 \times 17$

60. $14 + 28 \times 2^3 + 11^5$ **61.** $(37 + 13) \times 5 + 5^3$ **62.** $42 \div (10 - 2^2) + 84$

63. $47 + 3^3 - 52 \div 2^2$ **64.** $8 \times 28 \div 16 + 4^2$ **65.** $235 - (2 \times 10^2) + 114$

66. $(200 + 50) - 100 \times 2$ **67.** $360 \div 6 \times (84 - 26)$ **68.** $(36 - 4^2) \times 6 + (81 + 12)$

69. **Reasoning** Which did you choose to solve Exercise 59—mental math, paper and pencil, or a calculator? Explain the reasoning behind your choice.

Problem Solving and Applications

70. Joy bought four snow globes at \$7.00 each. She used a \$2.00 coupon. After the coupon, the tax came to \$1.96. Joy's father paid half of the final cost. Write an expression that describes the situation and equals the total money Joy paid.

71. The dance committee needs 3 balloons at each of 15 tables. They also need 50 balloons for each of the four walls of the room. For other decorations, they need 35 balloons, and the committee will order 10 extra balloons. Which is the correct order of operations?

a. $3 + 15 + 50 + 4 + 35 + 10$ **b.** $3 \times 15 + 50 \times 4 + 35 + 10$

c. $3 \times 15 + 50 \times 4 + 35 \times 10$ **d.** $3 + 50 \times 15 + 4 + 35 \times 10$

72. Critical Thinking A painter said that a wall measured "twenty plus ten squared" square feet. Explain two possible meanings of the comment. Using the order of operations, what is the correct mathematical meaning of what the painter said?

73. Critical Thinking You order a large pizza, three large drinks, and a bag of apples. You split the cost evenly with three friends. What order of operations would you use to find out how much each person should pay?

74. Write Your Own Problem Write a statement like those in Exercises 45–52 that requires parentheses to make it true. Exchange your statement with another student and solve.

Mixed Review and Test Prep

Simplify.

75. 30^2 **76.** 10^5 **77.** 3^3 **78.** 4^6 **79.** 27^3 **80.** 14^4

Express in exponential notation and then simplify.

81. $8 \times 8 \times 8 \times 8$ **82.** $2 \times 2 \times 2 \times 2 \times 2 \times 2 \times 2$ **83.** $4 \times 4 \times 4 \times 4$

84. $7 \times 7 \times 7 \times 7 \times 7$ **85.** $3 \times 3 \times 3 \times 3 \times 3 \times 3$ **86.** $6 \times 6 \times 6$

Multiply.

87. 127×489 **88.** $856 \times 45{,}625$ **89.** $28{,}598 \times 67{,}204$ **90.** $123{,}087 \times 765{,}294$

91. 305×216 **92.** $502 \times 12{,}337$ **93.** $37{,}205 \times 19{,}631$ **94.** $471{,}213 \times 299{,}808$

95. Choose the best estimate for $5{,}985 \times 89$.

Ⓐ 4,000,000 Ⓑ 450,000 Ⓒ 540,000 Ⓓ 600,000

Skills Practice Bank, page 661, Set 4

STOP and Practice

Write each number in standard form. Then round that number to the place indicated.

1. 5^3; tens **2.** 9^5; hundreds **3.** 7^4; thousands **4.** 12^5; ten-thousands

Compare, using $<$, $>$, or $=$.

5. 500 thousand ● 4,000,000 **6.** 3^6 ● 3×6 **7.** 6^3 ● 36^2

8. 40,000,000 ● 4 million **9.** 7^3 ● 4^5 **10.** 4^4 ● 16^2

Simplify.

11. $3{,}612 + 463$ **12.** 25×11 **13.** $496 \div 8$ **14.** $325 - 176$

15 $5 \times 14 \times 30$ **16.** $1{,}015 \div 5$ **17.** $7{,}900 - 428$ **18.** $73 + 346 + 508 + 912$

19. $5{,}817 - 2{,}450$ **20.** $25 + 175 + 459$ **21.** $675 \div 9$ **22.** $12 \times 9 \times 4$

23. $21{,}072 \div 6$ **24.** $21{,}072 \div 12$ **25.** $35{,}200 \times 2$ **26.** $16{,}800 - 350$

27. $8 + 42{,}094 + 70$ **28.** $104{,}573 - 189$ **29.** $783{,}435 \div 145$ **30.** $2{,}030 \times 62 \times 7$

Use order of operations and simplify.

31. $25 - (15 - 4)$ **32.** $31 - 2 \times 6$ **33.** $20 \div 2 \times 8$ **34.** 7×4^2

35. $15 \times (6 + 3)$ **36.** $4^3 - 3 \times 9$ **37.** $(3 + 5)^2 \div 4$ **38.** $3 \times (7 - 2)^3$

39. $9^2 - 7 \times 2^3$ **40.** $(8^2 - 8) \times 5$ **41.** $4 \times 8 - 18 \div 6$ **42.** $90 + 21 \div 7 - 2$

43. $85 - 72 \div 8$ **44.** $12 + (7 \times 6)$ **45.** $(9 + 6^2) \times 3$ **46.** $7^2 + 8 \times 5$

47. $75 - (10 - 2)^2$ **48.** $3^3 - 2 \times (1 + 5)$ **49.** $(14 - 8)^2 \div 3$ **50.** $4 \times 9 - 8 \div 2$

Error Search

Use order of operations. Find each solution that is not correct.

Write it correctly and explain the error.

51. $25 - 10 \div 5 = 3$ **52.** $6^2 - 4 \times 6 = 192$ **53.** $21 + (6 \div 3) = 9$ **54.** $8 \times 9 \div 4 = 18$

Out of This World!

Simplify. Match each answer to a number below the blanks. Then find the answer to the question. Some letters are not used.

Which landmark space event took place in April 1981?

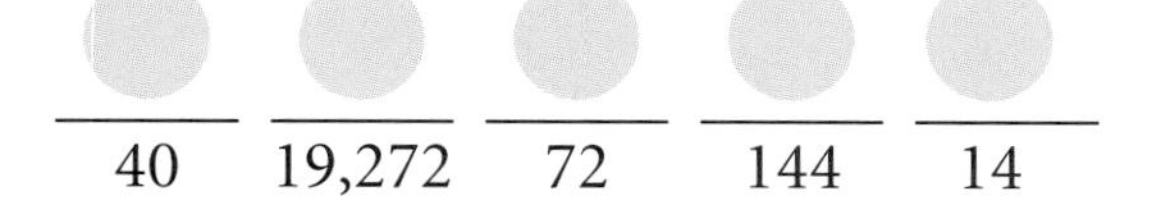

40 19,272 72 144 14

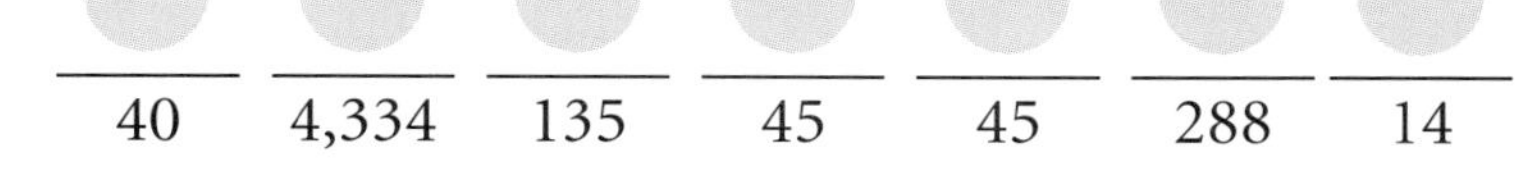

40 4,334 135 45 45 288 14

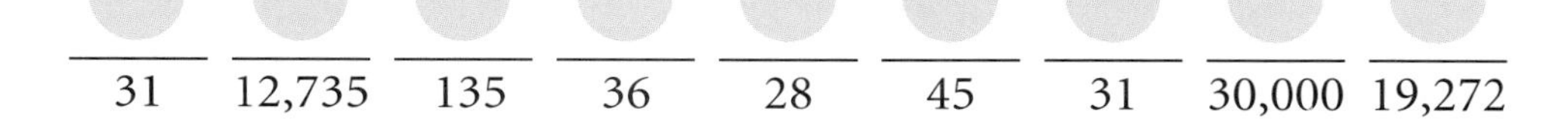

31 12,735 135 36 28 45 31 30,000 19,272

55. $5{,}126 - 792$ (H)
56. 803×24 (P)
57. $3{,}645 \div 27$ (U)
58. $19 + 45 + 267$ (J)
59. $2{,}103 \times 68$ (Y)
60. $12{,}809 - 74$ (O)
61. $360{,}000 \div 12$ (I)
62. $7{,}000 \times 36 \times 2$ (F)
63. $35 - 16 \div 4$ (R)
64. $8 \times (3 + 3)^2$ (L)
65. $570{,}293 \times 3$ (M)
66. $(3 + 1) \times (9 - 5)^2$ (V)
67. $(2 + 4)^2$ (N)
68. $8^2 - 4 \times 9$ (D)
69. $10 + 30 \div 5$ (G)
70. $24 \times 3 + 9 \times 8$ (C)
71. $48 - 9 \div 3$ (T)
72. $7 + 6^2 - 3$ (S)
73. $(9 + 3)^2 \div 2$ (A)
74. $8 \div 4 + 24 \div 2$ (E)

Number Sense Estimation and Reasoning

Copy and complete. Write $>$, $<$, or $=$. Use order of operations, properties, and estimation to help.

75. $2 \times 6 + 10 \bigcirc 9 \times 6 - 10$
76. $8 + 12 \div 3 \bigcirc 12 \div 2^2$
77. $(7 \times 5)^2 \bigcirc (9 \times 6)^2$
78. $32 - 16 + 10 \bigcirc 32 + 10 - 16$
79. $2 + 6 \times 10 \bigcirc 10 \times 6 + 2$
80. $(2 + 6)^3 + 45 \bigcirc 2 + 6^3 + 45$

Chapter 2

Problem Solving

Analyze Word Problems: Finding Unnecessary Information

You Will Learn
- to solve problems with unnecessary information

Learn

The tallest mountain in the United States is Mount McKinley in Alaska. It is 20,320 feet tall. The tallest mountain in the world, Mount Everest, is about 9,000 feet taller. The tallest building in the United States is the Sears Tower in Illinois. It is 1,454 feet tall.

About how many buildings the same size as the Sears Tower would need to be built on top of each other to reach the height of Mount McKinley?

Work Together

▶ Understand

What do you know?

What do you need to find out?

▶ Plan

What information do you need? — Height of Mount McKinley and Sears Tower

What information is unnecessary? — Height of Mount Everest

▶ Solve

To find about how many Sears Towers, estimate. — $20{,}320 \div 1{,}454 \approx 20{,}000 \div 1{,}000 = 20$

Write your answer. — It would take about 20 buildings the size of the Sears Tower to reach the height of Mount McKinley.

▶ Look Back

Is your answer reasonable?

Check

Solve. Identify any unnecessary information.

1. The tallest mountain in the world, Mount Everest, is 29,028 feet high. It is located in Nepal. The second highest mountain, K2, is 778 feet shorter than Mount Everest. The third highest mountain, Kanchenjunga, is 28,208 feet high. What's the difference in elevation between K2 and Kanchenjunga?

Problem Solving Practice

Problem Solving Strategies

- Draw a Picture
- Look for a Pattern
- Guess and Check
- Use Logical Reasoning
- Make an Organized List
- Make a Table
- Solve a Simpler Problem
- Work Backward

Choose a Tool

Solve. Identify any unnecessary information.

2. In Antarctica, there are two mountains higher than 16,000 feet. There are 10 mountains taller than 14,000 feet. There are three mountains whose heights are between 15,000 and 16,000 feet. Their names are Shinn, Gardner, and Epperly. How many mountains are between 14,000 and 15,000 feet?

3. There are 50 tons of garbage on Mount Everest left by people who have climbed the mountain. 17 tons can be found in the South Col area. How many tons can be found on the rest of Mount Everest?

Use the data in the table for **4** and **5**.

	United States	World
Longest River	Mississippi – Missouri 3,710 miles	Nile 4,160 miles
Deepest Lake	Crater Lake 1,932 feet	Lake Baikal 5,315 feet

4. **Measurement** About how many feet long is the longest river in the United States?

5. **Measurement** About how many times as deep is the deepest lake in the world than the deepest lake in the United States?

Chapter 2
Lesson
9

Numerical Patterns

You Will Learn

- to identify and continue numerical patterns based on addition and subtraction

Learn

A numerical pattern is a list of numbers that occur in some predictable way. Numerical patterns can be used to describe real-world things, such as population growth and the decay of materials. They can also be used to generate art such as fractals, which are complex math pictures created by repeating a simple math pattern.

Many patterns use addition and subtraction. To find the pattern, write the number that you need to add or subtract to find the next number in the pattern.

Math Tip

Always calculate the difference between successive numbers in a pattern to help you find the pattern.

Example 1

For each pattern, find the next three numbers.

a. 8, 15, 22, 29, 36,...

8, (+7) 15, (+7) 22, (+7) 29, (+7) 36

Write the number you must add to each number to get the next number.

36, (+7) 43, (+7) 50, (+7) 57

Use the pattern to calculate the next three numbers.

b. 50, 49, 47, 44, 40,...

50, (−1) 49, (−2) 47, (−3) 44, (−4) 40

Write the number you must subtract to get the next number.

40, (−5) 35, (−6) 29, (−7) 22

Use the pattern to calculate the next three numbers.

c. 14, 24, 22, 32, 30,...

14, (+10) 24, (−2) 22, (+10) 32, (−2) 30

Write the number you must add or subtract to get the next number.

30, (+10) 40, (−2) 38, (+10) 48

Use the pattern to calculate the next three numbers.

Patterns are helpful for solving many word problems, too.

Example 2

Ayana bought a stamp for $3. The dealer told her that next year it would be worth $6, the year after that $12, and the year after that $24. If the stamp continues to increase in value this way, what will it be worth in 6 years?

a. 3, 6, 12, 24,...? Write the pattern.

$3 \xrightarrow{+3} 6 \xrightarrow{+6} 12 \xrightarrow{+12} 24,$ Write the number you must add to get the next number.

$24 \xrightarrow{+24} 48 \xrightarrow{+48} 96 \xrightarrow{+96} 192$ Use the pattern to calculate the value 6 years from now.

The stamp will be worth $192 dollars.

Using multiplication can help you solve pattern problems.

Example 3

Skye and Susana are doing an experiment on the growth of mold. The table shows the data they collected. They want to know how long it will take for the mold to weigh at least 1,000 grams.

Day	Weight (g)
1	3
2	7
3	15
4	31
5	63

Addition Method

The pattern is to add twice as much as the number you added before. I'll continue the pattern until I reach 1,000 or more.

$3 \xrightarrow{+4} 7 \xrightarrow{+8} 15 \xrightarrow{+16} 31 \xrightarrow{+32} 63 \xrightarrow{+64} 127 \xrightarrow{+128} 255 \xrightarrow{+256} 511 \xrightarrow{+512} 1{,}023$

It will weigh more than 1,000 grams on Day 9.

Multiplication Method

The pattern is that each number is one more than twice the previous number. I'll continue the pattern until I reach 1,000 or more.

$63 \xrightarrow{\times 2 + 1} 127 \xrightarrow{\times 2 + 1} 255 \xrightarrow{\times 2 + 1} 511 \xrightarrow{\times 2 + 1} 1{,}023$

It will weigh more than 1,000 grams on Day 9.

Talk About It

1. If you had to continue the pattern in Example 3 without using a calculator, which method would you prefer? Explain.
2. Can you describe the pattern in Example 3 in a way that is different from both methods shown? Explain.

Check

Write the number you must add or subtract to get the next number.

1. 3, 9, 15, 21, 27, . . . **2.** 18, 21, 24, 27, 30, . . . **3.** 42, 33, 24, 15, . . .

Find the next three numbers in each pattern.

4. 10, 12, 15, 19, 24, . . . **5.** 30, 26, 22, 18, 14, . . .

6. Reasoning How can you use arithmetic to understand a numerical pattern?

7. Reasoning Does every numerical pattern go up or down by the same number? Explain.

Practice

Skills and Reasoning

Write the number you must add or subtract to get to the next number.

8. 17, 21, 25, 29, 33, . . . **9.** 15, 18, 21, 24, 27, . . . **10.** 7, 7, 7, 7, 7, . . .

11. 22, 35, 48, 61, 74, . . . **12.** 38, 31, 24, 17, 10, . . . **13.** 9, 8, 7, 6, 5, . . .

14. 1,234; 1,244; 1,254; 1,264; 1,274; . . . **15.** 45, 56, 67, 78, 89, . . .

16. 66, 72, 78, 84, 90, . . . **17.** 7,826; 7,797; 7,768; 7,739; 7,710; . . .

18. 299, 267, 235, 203, 171, . . . **19.** 42, 34, 26, 18, 10, . . .

20. 999; 1,002; 1,005; 1,008; 1011; . . . **21.** 29, 44, 59, 74, 89, . . .

22. 101, 91, 81, 71, 61, . . . **23.** 2,158; 2,216; 2,274; 2,332; 2,390; . . .

Find the next three numbers in each pattern.

24. 142, 143, 145, 148, 152, . . . **25.** 299, 293, 288, 282, 277, . . .

26. 480, 492, 486, 498, 492, 504, . . . **27.** 106, 100, 94, 88, 82, . . .

28. 89, 79, 70, 62, 55, . . . **29.** 965, 968, 974, 983, 995, . . .

30. 62, 59, 64, 61, 66, . . . **31.** 6, 8, 7, 9, 8, . . .

32. 43, 44, 46, 49, 53, . . . **33.** 0, 5, 20, 45, 80, . . .

34. 22, 24, 28, 34, 42, . . . **35.** 1,111; 1,115; 1,119; 1,123; 1,127; . . .

36. 15, 21, 27, 33, 39, . . . **37.** 441, 394, 410, 363, 379, . . .

38. Critical Thinking Create a six-number pattern that starts at 2, ends at 2,048, and uses multiplication to get the next number.

39. Reasoning After how many more steps will these patterns have a matching number in them? Explain.

234, 246, 258, 270, . . . and 235, 248, 261, 274, . . .

Problem Solving and Applications

40. Critical Thinking The following pattern is called the *Fibonacci series,* named after the thirteenth-century mathematician who developed it. Describe the pattern and find the next three numbers.

1, 1, 2, 3, 5, 8, 13, 21, . . .

41. Tanya bought a collector's baseball card for $34. She was told that it would be worth $11 more each year. Copy and complete the table to find how much the card will be worth in 10 years.

Start	1	2	3	4	5	6	7	8	9	10
$34	$45	$56								

42. Tanya sold a baseball card for $38. Its value had decreased $4 each of the four years she owned it. How much did she originally pay for it?

43. Science Jeff is conducting a science experiment with a three-rabbit population. Every month, the rabbit population doubles. How many rabbits will he have after 5 months?

44. Social Science In 1965, there were 500 students entering Atherton Middle School. In 1975, there were 450. In 1985, there were 525. In 1995, there were 475. If this pattern continues, how many students will there be in 2005?

45. Money If Samantha earns 2¢ the first day she baby-sits, 4¢ the next day, 8¢ the third day, 16¢ the fourth day, and so on, how much will she have earned altogether after baby-sitting 20 days?

46. Journal How many numbers in a pattern do you need to see to figure out the pattern?

Mixed Review and Test Prep

Simplify mentally.

47. $64 + 102$ **48.** $150 + 157$ **49.** $1762 - 101$ **50.** $22{,}839 - 10{,}838$

51. 41×5 **52.** $236 + 504 + 44$ **53.** $36{,}000 \div 6{,}000$ **54.** $49{,}000 \div 700$

Multiply.

55. $\$2.34 \times 52$ **56.** $\$6.35 \times 365$ **57.** $\$245.75 \times 754$ **58.** $261 \times \$982.20$

59. $\$1.70 \times 14$ **60.** $\$4.87 \times 21$ **61.** $\$66.06 \times 22$ **62.** $11 \times \$34.57$

63. Choose the correct answer for $5^2 - 2 + 8 \times 6$.

Ⓐ 35 Ⓑ 71 Ⓒ 90 Ⓓ Not here

SECTION B

Review and Practice

Vocabulary Copy and complete each sentence with the correct term.

1. When you calculate using numbers that have been broken up into smaller numbers, you are using the ________.
2. Simplifying inside of parentheses is the first step in the ________.

(Lesson 5) Simplify, using mental math. Explain your solution.

3. 300×200
4. $4 \times 3 \times 25$
5. $604 + 275$
6. 19×5
7. $240{,}000 \div 60$
8. Beatrice bought a sandwich for $3.45 and a drink for $0.90. If the sales tax was $0.50, how much did her lunch cost?

(Lessons 6 and 7) Estimate.

9. $3{,}479 + 4{,}625$
10. $488 \div 7$
11. $831 - 546$
12. $503 \times 22 \times 3$
13. 98×230
14. 19×42
15. Antique postcards cost $5 each. Estimate how many you could buy for $547.
16. Angela wanted to send 7 postcards to friends and family living in other parts of the country. How much would she have to spend on 19-cent stamps to mail all her postcards?

(Lesson 8) In **17–21,** match each problem with its solution. Each solution is used exactly once.

17. $(6 - 3) \times (5 + 1 \times 4)$ **a.** 0
18. $5^2 + 7$ **b.** 32
19. $5 + 3 \times 5 + 3 \times 5$ **c.** 27
20. $(100 \div 50 - 2) \times 3$ **d.** 35
21. $8^2 - 2^2 + 4^2$ **e.** 76

(Lesson 9) Find the next three numbers in each pattern.

22. 21, 22, 24, 27, 31…
23. 117, 122, 132, 147, 167…
24. **Journal** An 1856 British Guiana stamp originally sold for 1¢. In 1980, a stamp collector bought it for $935,000. Using any method, compare the 1856 value of the stamp to the 1980 value.

Skills Checklist

In this section, you have:

- **Learned About Mental Math**
- **Estimated Sums and Differences**
- **Estimated Products and Quotients**
- **Learned About the Order of Operations**
- **Learned About Numerical Patterns**

CHAPTER 2

SECTION

Introduction to Algebra

Most familiar fish and mammals live near the surface. Pressure about 220 lb/in².

500 ft

Sharks, whales, octopi, and squid venture to this depth. Pressure about 440 lb/in².

1,000 ft

Lower limit for light. All creatures below this point live in total darkness. Pressure about 1,000 lb/in².

2,300 ft

Some fish here have large eyes for seeing in the dark. Others make their own light. Pressure about 1,400 lb/in².

3,200 ft

Fish here are gelatin-like. Many are blind. Pressure about 2,800 lb/in².

6,400 ft

Water tempertaure only a few degrees above freezing. Little food, a few simple organisms. Pressure about 4,400 lb/in².

10,000 ft

Deepest point in ocean. Temperature below freezing. Pressure about 15,800 lb/in².

35,840 ft

Oceanographers use many tools to study the ocean, such as scuba equipment, diving spheres, remote-controlled robots, and mathematics.

Compare the pressure at 500 ft and 1,000 ft; at 3,200 ft and 6,400 ft; and at 1,000 ft and 10,000 ft. What patterns do you see?

Solving Equations

Review order of operations. Evaluate each expression.

1. $8 + 2 \times 5$

2. $4 \times 6 + 12$

3. $3 + 8 - 2 \times 3$

4. $3 + 5 \times 6 - 2$

5. $20 - 3 \times 5$

6. $9 \times 2 - 4 + 7$

7. $17 - 3 \times 4$

8. $10 \times 2 - 8 + 1$

Skills Checklist

In this section, you will:

- ❒ Learn About Variables and Expressions
- ❒ Write Expressions
- ❒ Use Equations
- ❒ Solve Equations

Chapter 2
Lesson
10

Variables and Expressions

You Will Learn

- the difference between a variable and a constant
- to evaluate expressions

Vocabulary

variable

constant

expression

Did You Know?

x is the letter that mathematicians use most often for a variable, but you can use any letter to represent a variable.

Learn

The ocean is a treasure of dissolved materials. For example, a volume of sea water the size of a 30-story building contains about \$400 worth of dissolved gold. Suppose you have invented a way to recover the gold from a building-size volume of water for \$250. You would want to know how much you could earn with each building-size volume of water. Variables can help you do this.

A **variable** is a quantity that can change or vary. Mathematicians use letters to represent variables. The number of building-size volumes of water you process is a variable. You don't know how much you can process.

A quantity that does not change is a **constant**. \$400 and \$250 are constants. The value of the gold and the cost of recovering it will remain the same.

An **expression** is a mathematical phrase involving constants, variables, and operation symbols. There are different ways to represent different operations.

Addition	Subtraction	Multiplication	Division
$8 + x$	$8 - x$	$8x$	$\frac{8}{x}$

The expression you could use to determine the amount of money you could earn recovering gold from the ocean is:

$$(\$400 - \$250)x$$

where x represents the number of building-size volumes of water you process.

If you know the values of the variable, you can evaluate the expression by replacing the variable with each value. This is known as substituting a value for the variable. If you processed 10 building-size volumes of water, you would replace x with 10.

$$(\$400 - \$250)10 = (\$150)10 = \$1{,}500$$

You would recover \$1,500 worth of gold if you processed 10 building-size volumes of sea water.

Example 1

Evaluate each expression for $x = 1, 2$, and 3.

a.

x	$x + 5$
1	$1 + 5 = 6$
2	$2 + 5 = 7$
3	$3 + 5 = 8$

b.

x	$11 - x$
1	$11 - 1 = 10$
2	$11 - 2 = 9$
3	$11 - 3 = 8$

c.

x	$4x$
1	$4 \times 1 = 4$
2	$4 \times 2 = 8$
3	$4 \times 3 = 12$

d.

x	$\frac{12}{x}$
1	$12 \div 1 = 12$
2	$12 \div 2 = 6$
3	$12 \div 3 = 4$

Evaluating variable expressions is similar to using formulas.

Example 2

Find the value of the gold you could recover if you processed 25, 50, 100 and t building-size volumes of sea water.

Building-size Volumes	Value of Gold Recovered
25	$(\$400 - \$250)25 = \$3,750$
50	$(\$400 - \$250)50 = \$7,500$
100	$(\$400 - \$250)100 = \$15,000$
t	$(\$400 - \$250)t = \$150t$

Talk About It

1. What is the advantage of using a variable to represent a number?
2. Give three examples of constants and three examples of variables. Explain.
3. Describe a real-life situation in which you might use a variable expression.

Check

Evaluate each expression for $x = 3$, 4, and 5.

1. $7x$ **2.** $15 - x$ **3.** $\frac{60}{x}$ **4.** $x + 23$

5. Reasoning State whether the quantity should be represented by a variable or a constant. Explain.

- **a.** Number of days in January
- **b.** Price of a calculator
- **c.** Number of students in a school
- **d.** Number of inches in a foot
- **e.** Number of people in a state
- **f.** Number of giraffes in a herd

JANUARY

S	M	T	W	T	F	S
				1	2	3
4	5	6	7	8	9	10
11	12	13	14	15	16	17
18	19	20	21	22	23	24
25	26	27	28	29	30	31

Practice

Skills and Reasoning

Evaluate each expression for $x = 2$, 3, and 4.

6. $x + 7$ **7.** $12 - x$ **8.** $6x$ **9.** $\frac{24}{x}$ **10.** $12 + x$ **11.** $2x$

12. $8x$ **13.** $x - 1$ **14.** $15 + x$ **15.** $11x$ **16.** $\frac{36}{x}$ **17.** $\frac{x}{1}$

Evaluate each expression for $x = 3$, 5, and 9.

18. $20 - x$ **19.** $9x$ **20.** $\frac{45}{x}$ **21.** $36x$ **22.** $x + 3$ **23.** $x + 12$

24. x **25.** $\frac{135}{x}$ **26.** $x + x$ **27.** $1x$ **28.** x^2 **29.** x^3

Evaluate each expression for $x = 2$, 4, and 7.

30. $\frac{56}{x}$ **31.** $x - 2$ **32.** $3x$ **33.** $\frac{28}{x}$ **34.** $5x$ **35.** $8x$

36. $4x$ **37.** $16 - x$ **38.** $27 + x$ **39.** $39 + x$ **40.** $x + 12$ **41.** $\frac{x}{1}$

Copy and complete the table by evaluating each expression for $x = 1$, 2, and 3.

42.

x	$x + 1$	$2x$	$18 \div x$	
1	$1 + 1 = 2$			$1 - 1 = 0$
2				$2 - 1 = 1$
3				$3 - 1 = 2$

43. Reasoning Which of these expressions will always have the same solution, no matter what you choose for x: $x + 3$, $5 - x$, or $0x$? Explain.

Problem Solving and Applications

Copy and complete each table.

44. History In 1776, there were 13 stars on every United States flag.

Number of Flags	Number of Stars
1	
2	
3	
4	
w	

45. Science Complete the table. An average blue whale eats 9,000 pounds of food each day.

Amount of Food (lb)	Number of Days
63,000	
81,000	
126,000	
f	

46. Critical Thinking Match the situation to the correct expression.

a. Fingers on t hands (including thumbs) **i.** $t - 5$

b. CD price of $\$t$ with a \$5 coupon **ii.** $5t$

c. Price of a $\$t$ sweater with \$5 tax **iii.** $t + 5$

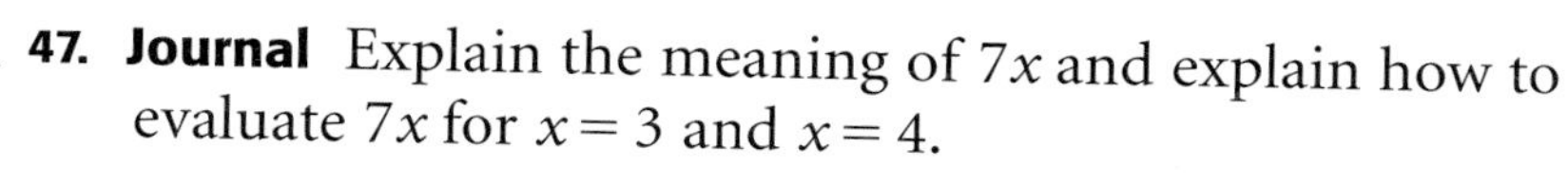

47. Journal Explain the meaning of $7x$ and explain how to evaluate $7x$ for $x = 3$ and $x = 4$.

Mixed Review and Test Prep

Estimate.

48. 1,567 + 5,408 **49.** 21,805 + 79,502 **50.** 45,405 − 9,826

51. 4,305 − 1,875 **52.** 3,615 + 2,778 **53.** 31,618 − 17,611

54. 12,402 + 9,982 **55.** 9,205 − 4,912 **56.** 58,050 + 3,112

Choose the numbers in parentheses that can be divided by each given number with a remainder of 0.

57. 8 (28, 64, 8, 739, 384, 502) **58.** 4 (26, 552, 450, 482, 116, 74)

59. 6 (17, 24, 30, 51, 67, 74) **60.** 9 (21, 37, 45, 55, 82, 93)

59. Use the order of operations to find $6 \times (4 - 2)^2 + 8 \div 4$.

Ⓐ 26 Ⓑ 8 Ⓒ 18 Ⓓ not here

Chapter 2
Lesson
11

Writing Expressions

You Will Learn

- to translate phrases and situations into mathematical expressions

Vocabulary

sum

difference

product

quotient

Learn

You've learned how to evaluate expressions. Now you will learn how to translate word problems into the language of constants, variables, and expressions. Some words in English can be translated into specific mathematical operations.

Word	Definition	Numerical Expression	Variable Expression
Sum	The result of adding numbers	$3 + 5$	$6 + x$
Difference	The result of subtracting numbers	$24 - 8$	$y - 10$
Product	The result of multiplying numbers	2×9	$5b$
Quotient	The result of dividing numbers	$20 \div 5$	$\frac{a}{2}$

Example 1

Write each sentence as an expression.

a. What is the product of 20 and k?

Product means multiplication.

$20k$

b. What is the difference of g and 6?

Difference means subtraction.

$g - 6$

To translate situations that don't use these words, you need to choose an operation that is appropriate for the situation. It may be easier to choose an operation if you first replace the variable with a number.

Remember

The numbers that you multiply together to get a product are called *factors* of the product.

Example 2

Mae bought b bananas and ate 3. How many does she have left?

If Mae bought 10 bananas and ate 3, she'd have 7 bananas, because $10 - 3 = 7$.

The operation to use is subtraction.

$b - 3$

Example 3

Tanisha had a 200-page book about the *Titanic.* She read p pages each day. How many days did it take to read the book?

If Tanisha read 10 pages each day, it would take 20 days, because $200 \div 10 = 20$.
The operation to use is division.

$200 \div p$, or $\frac{200}{p}$

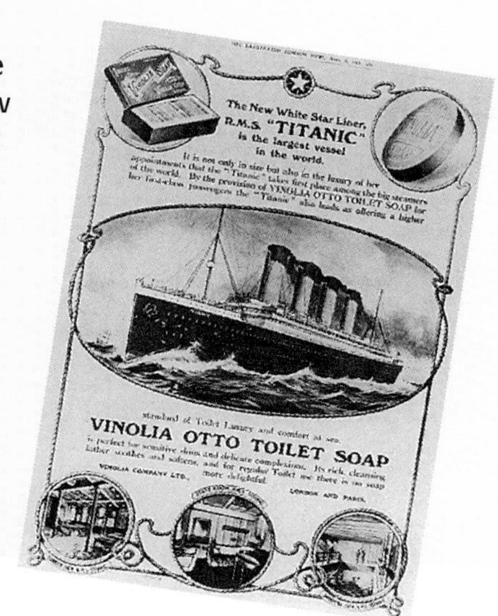

Talk About It

1. Other than *sum, difference, product,* and *quotient,* what words suggest addition? Subtraction? Multiplication? Division?
2. Give a situation suggested by each expression.

   a. $10 - n$ **b.** $\frac{y}{24}$ **c.** $50p$

Check

Write each as an expression.

1. What is the sum of c and 8?
2. What is the quotient of n and 9?
3. Rafael raked r bags of leaves. Nicole raked 5 bags. How many bags were raked altogether?
4. Jake ran x laps every day for 7 days. How many laps did he run?
5. **Reasoning** For the phrase "5 less than y," Darren wrote $5 - y$ and Samantha wrote $y - 5$. Who is correct and why?

6. **Reasoning** Since dividing by a fraction is the same as multiplying by the reciprocal, Cheryl says that $\frac{1}{2}$ of j can be written as $2j$. Is Cheryl correct? Explain.

Practice

Skills and Reasoning

Write each phrase as an expression.

7. q times 10 **8.** half of h **9.** d times 6

10. j and 2 more **11.** s minus 3 **12.** 52 smaller than d

13. v multiplied by 20 **14.** z doubled **15.** y decreased by 3

Write an expression to answer each question.

16. What is the difference of n and 4? **17.** What is 8 more than x?

18. What is the sum of 47 and t? **19.** What is h divided by 20?

20. Reasoning For each expression, write a situation that the expression might describe.

a. $n - 60$ **b.** $60n$ **c.** $\frac{60}{n}$ **d.** $n + 60$

Problem Solving and Applications

Write each problem as an expression.

21. If x students are organized into equal teams of 8, how many teams are there?

22. There are 12 groups with p penguins in each group. How many penguins are there?

23. Science The temperature at the North Pole was 146 degrees Fahrenheit cooler than the temperature in Quito, Ecuador. The temperature in Quito was t degrees. What was the temperature at the North Pole?

24. Literature Author Jules Verne's fictional submarine, the *Nautilus,* traveled 20,000 leagues under the sea. Let m leagues equal 1 mile. How many miles did the *Nautilus* travel?

25. Critical Thinking Write an expression for the distance around each square.

a.

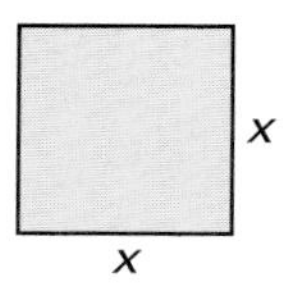

b.

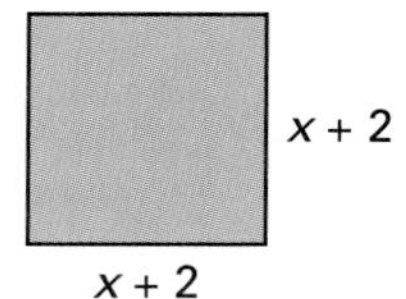

c.

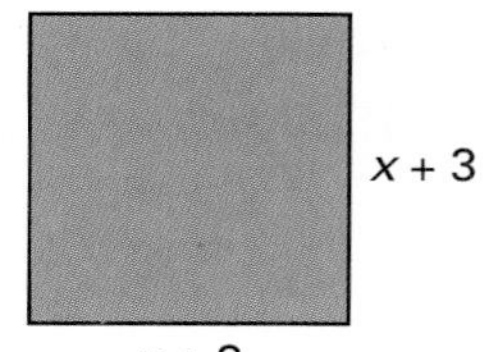

Problem Solving and SCIENCE

In 1922, C. K. Wentworth devised a classification system for sediment found on the ocean floor.

26. Suppose you found the following log written by a scientist during a fact finding expedition. Write a phrase for each expression written describing the samples. Then classify each sample.

Name of Particle	Diameter
boulder	>256 mm
cobble	64–256 mm
pebble	2–64 mm
sand	$\frac{1}{16}$–2 mm
silt	$\frac{1}{256}$–$\frac{1}{16}$ mm
clay	$<\frac{1}{256}$ mm

DATE: AUGUST 24, 1923 LOCATION: CRANBERRY COVE

ON THIS EXPEDITION, I'VE BROUGHT WITH ME AN AVERAGE-SIZE COBBLE (CS) AND A 2MM PIECE OF SAND (SS) FOR COMPARISON. I AM BRINGING THE FOLLOWING SAMPLES OF SEDIMENT BACK TO THE LAB FOR FURTHER RESEARCH. I'VE RECORDED ROUGH ESTIMATES OF THEIR DIAMETERS.

SAMPLE 1 2CS
SAMPLE 2 4CS
SAMPLE 3 CS + 100
SAMPLE 4 CS − 150
SAMPLE 5 $\frac{SS}{4}$
SAMPLE 6 5SS
SAMPLE 7 $\frac{SS}{2}$
SAMPLE 8 SS + 5
SAMPLE 9 $\frac{SS}{16}$
SAMPLE 10 $\frac{SS}{64}$

27. Journal Choose an operation (addition, subtraction, multiplication, or division) and describe three situations that require that operation.

Mixed Review and Test Prep

STAY SHARP!

Estimate.

28. 103×64 **29.** $63{,}880{,}204 \times 80{,}129$ **30.** $8{,}212 \times 779$ **31.** 495×508

32. $52{,}305 \div 4{,}967$ **33.** $112{,}635 \div 52{,}175$ **34.** 633×490 **35.** $123 \div 41$

Divide.

36. $154 \div 7$ **37.** $1{,}464 \div 12$ **38.** $627 \div 33$ **39.** $20{,}097 \div 63$

40. $210 \div 5$ **41.** $624 \div 8$ **42.** $2{,}470 \div 10$ **43.** $56{,}316 \div 13$

44. The pictograph shows the number of pies eaten by 5 contestants in a pie-eating contest. How many more pies did Sonja eat than Bill?

Ⓐ 1 Ⓑ 2 Ⓒ 3 Ⓓ $\frac{1}{2}$

Pie Eating Contest	
Sandy	● ●
Roy	◖
Sonja	● ● ◖
Bill	● ●
Anita	● ◖

● = 2 pies

Chapter 2 Lesson 12

Using Equations

You Will Learn

- what an equation is
- to determine if an equation is true or false

Vocabulary

equation

Learn

On Monday afternoon, four staff members at the Bay City Aquarium made these changes in the central aquarium:

- Leon tripled the number of leather sea stars. Now there are 30.
- Val removed 4 bat rays. Now there are 7.
- Rico added 5 gopher rockfish. Now there are 13.
- Wendy took out half of the wolf eels. Now there are 10.

Did You Know?
Fish that live a mile below sea level have unusual traits that help them survive. These can include flat, uncrushable bodies and glow-in-the-dark skin.

You can use equations to help you determine the number of fish in the aquarium before any changes were made.

An **equation** is a mathematical sentence that uses an equal sign, =, to show that two expressions are equal. An equation can be either true or false.

$5 + 7 = 12$ is true. $16 - 6 = 12$ is false.

$30 \div 5 = 6$ is true. $3 \times 5 = 35$ is false.

An equation with a variable can also be true or false, depending on the value of the variable.

If $x = 5$, $x + 6 = 11$ is true. If $x = 12$, $x + 6 = 11$ is false.

Example 1

Is the equation true for the given value of the variable?

a. $5y = 40$, $y = 8$

$5 \times 8 = 40$ Substitute 8 for y.

$40 = 40$ Multiply.

The equation is true.

b. $r + 20 = 35$, $r = 10$

$10 + 20 = 35$ Substitute 10 for r.

$30 \neq 35$ Add.

Since $10 + 20$ does not equal 35, the equation is false.

Like expressions, equations can be used to model real-world situations.

Example 2

The equation $3s = 30$ describes the change made in the number of starfish in the aquarium. Could $s = 10$?

$3s = 30$, $s = 10$

$3 \times 10 = 30$ Substitute 10 for s.

$30 = 30$ Multiply.

$s = 10$ The equation is true.

There were 10 starfish in the aquarium before the change was made.

Example 3

The equation $5 + g = 13$ describes the change made in the number of rockfish in the aquarium. Could $g = 10$?

$5 + g = 13$, $g = 10$

$5 + 10 = 13$ Substitute 10 for g.

$15 = 13$ Add.

$g \neq 10$ since $15 \neq 13$. The equation is false.

There were not 10 rockfish in the aquarium before the change was made.

Talk About It

1. What are the differences between an equation and an expression?
2. Does every equation have a variable? Explain.
3. Is every equation with a variable true? Explain.

Check

Is each equation true for the given value of the variable?

1. $\frac{30}{z} = 3$, $z = 6$
2. $h - 12 = 24$, $h = 12$
3. $5 + d = 5$, $d = 0$
4. **Reasoning** The equation $b - 4 = 7$ describes the change made in the number of bat rays in the aquarium. Could there have been 8 bat rays in the aquarium before the change was made? Explain.
5. **Reasoning** Is there a number you could use to replace the variable to make the equation $0m = 7$ true? Explain.

Practice

Skills and Reasoning

State if each equation is true for the given value of the variable.

6. $8 + r = 17, r = 9$

7. $16 - x = 7, x = 12$

8. $w - 23 = 2, w = 19$

9. $5h = 25, h = 5$

10. $s + 45 = 52, s = 7$

11. $10y = 30, y = 3$

12. $\frac{15}{q} = 5, q = 5$

13. $22y = 24, y = 2$

14. $\frac{w}{12} = 2, w = 24$

15. $12 \times t = 48, t = 4$

16. $v - 13 = 16, v = 29$

17. $9 \times 3l = 28, l = 3$

18. $\frac{14}{u} = 25, u = 7$

19. $45m = 3, m = 1$

20. $\frac{0}{n} = 0, n = 30$

21. $\frac{e}{3} = 7, e = 21$

22. $\frac{42}{p} = 24, p = 2$

23. $1k = 2, k = 2$

24. $15f = 150, f = 9$

25. $24 + z = 67, z = 32$

26. $b - 11 = 17, b = 7$

27. $\frac{48}{c} = 12, c = 4$

28. $s \div 6 = 17, s = 92$

29. $14 - k = 3, k = 11$

30. $t + 89 = 100, t = 11$

31. $9x = 99, x = 10$

32. $\frac{d}{42} = \frac{1}{2}, d = 21$

33. $a - 47 = 39, a = 77$

34. $52 - g = 7, g = 45$

35. $40m = 120, m = 3$

36. **Reasoning** For an addition equation like $2 + x = 5$, how many values will make the equation true? Explain.

37. **Reasoning** Juan states that $x \times 0 = 4$ will always be false, no matter what value is put in for the variable. Do you agree? Explain.

Problem Solving and Applications

Write an equation for each situation.

38. Mary had f oranges and gave 1 to Byron. She had 3 oranges left.

39. Jarrod bought 12 snacks and shared them equally among p people. Each person got 3 snacks.

40. Nigel has 2 green shirts, b blue shirts, and 3 white shirts. He has a total of 8 shirts.

41. Max washed 3 equal-size loads of towels. Max washed a total of 58 towels, with x towels in each load.

42. **Using Data** Use the Data File on page 59 to write an equation for the following situation. The Atlantic Ocean is 4 times as deep as the Arctic Ocean.

43. Super Sports is selling a Grand Slam baseball bat for \$75. The same bat is on sale at Scoreboard for b. You can save \$26 if you buy the bat at Scoreboard.

44. **Geography** One trail at Takkakaw Falls in Canada is f ft long. Edward walked the trail at a rate of 550 ft/hr. It took him 3 hours.

45. **Geography** King George Falls in Guyana is 1,600 ft high. Angel Falls in Venezuela is x ft higher than King George Falls. Angel Falls is 3,212 ft high.

46. Mona bought \$84 worth of computer supplies and paid d dollars in sales tax. The total came to \$88.

47. Sheena bought r rolls of film at \$4 per roll and paid \$60.

48. Lilla went jogging 20 miles in one week. On Monday, she jogged 2 miles. The rest of the week, she jogged q miles in all.

49. **Choose a Strategy** Franz and Jenna built a rectangular treehouse. The north and south walls were each f feet long. The east and west walls were $f + 2$ feet long. The total distance around the treehouse was 24 feet. Was the north wall 6 feet long? Explain.

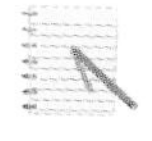

50. **Journal** Explain why an equation is either true or false, but an expression is neither true nor false.

PRACTICE AND APPLY

Mixed Review and Test Prep

STAY SHARP!

Write each multiplication equation as a division equation using the same numbers.

51. $5 \times 111 = 555$
52. $40 \times 30 = 1{,}200$
53. $32 \times 48 = 1{,}536$
54. $77 \times 8 = 616$
55. $42 \times 13 = 546$
56. $31 \times 31 = 961$
57. $23 \times 86 = 1{,}978$
58. $18 \times 98 = 1{,}764$

Write each division equation as a multiplication equation using the same numbers.

59. $64 \div 8 = 8$
60. $2{,}100 \div 700 = 3$
61. $32 \div 4 = 8$
62. $99 \div 9 = 11$
63. $3{,}528 \div 56 = 63$
64. $4{,}402 \div 71 = 62$
65. $1{,}044 \div 12 = 87$
66. $2{,}025 \div 45 = 45$

Evaluate each expression for $x = 1$, 2, and 3.

67. $12 + x$
68. $3x$
69. $\frac{36}{x}$
70. $x - 1$
71. $6x$
72. $7x$
73. $\frac{30}{x}$
74. $8 - x$
75. $x + 7$
76. $5x$

77. What are the next three numbers in the pattern?
20, 35, 30, 45, 40, . . .

Ⓐ 50, 55, 60 Ⓑ 55, 50, 65 Ⓒ 45, 60, 55 Ⓓ 55, 60, 65

Chapter 2
Lesson
13

Solving Equations

Problem Solving Connection
- Guess and Check
- Work Backward

Explore

Evaluating expressions using tables can help you understand how to solve equations.

Work Together

1. Copy the table, and evaluate the expression with the given values.

x	3	5	6	10
$x - 3$				

Math Tip
Notice the operation you use when you work backward.

2. Copy the table, and find the values for the variable that will provide the given values for the expression.

x				
$2x$	6	14	28	42

3. Find the missing expression in the table.

x	1	2	3	4
?	24	12	8	6

4. Explain how you found the values in the table.
5. Find the values that will make each equation true.
   a. $59 + f = 119$
   b. $c - 56 = 121$
   c. $15g = 75$
   d. $\frac{h}{17} = 11$

Talk About It

6. Explain how you found the unknown values. Tell what operations you used.
7. How can you use mental math to help solve an equation?
8. Describe a real-life situation in which you might have to solve an equation with a variable.

Connect and Learn

Number sense can help you to solve equations. Think of equations as questions in which the variable is read as "What number?" For example, $z + 5 = 7$ can be read as "What number plus 5 equals 7?" Use mental math to answer the question.

Example 1

Solve for w.

$w + 13 = 20$	Read as "What number plus 13 equals 20?"
$7 + 13 = 20$	Use mental math.
$20 = 20$	Check to see that the equation is true.
$w = 7$	

Example 2

Solve for x.

$x - 10 = 14$	Read as "What number minus 10 equals 14?"
$24 - 10 = 14$	Use mental math.
$14 = 14$	Check to see that the equation is true.
$x = 24$	

Example 3

Solve for y.

$9y = 180$	Read as "What number times 9 equals 180?"
$9 \times 20 = 180$	Use mental math.
$180 = 180$	Check to see that the equation is true.
$y = 20$	

Example 4

Karen divided her diving time into 25-minute periods. There were 4 periods in all. How many minutes did she spend diving?

$\frac{z}{25} = 4$	Write an equation.
$\frac{z}{25} = 4$	Read as "What number divided by 25 equals 4?"
$\frac{100}{25} = 4$	Use mental math.

She spent 100 minutes diving.

Check

Solve.

1. $a + 7 = 22$ **2.** $b - 12 = 51$ **3.** $5c = 110$ **4.** $\frac{d}{4} = 12$

5. Reasoning Can x have any value in $x + 5$? Can x have any value in $x + 5 = 7$? Explain.

Practice

Find the given value of x that makes each equation true.

6. $x + 7 = 9$ $\quad x = 1, 2, 3, \text{ or } 4$

7. $x - 5 = 4$ $\quad x = 7, 8, 9, \text{ or } 10$

8. $2x = 16$ $\quad x = 2, 4, 6, \text{ or } 8$

9. $x - 3 = 2$ $\quad x = 5, 6, 7, \text{ or } 8$

10. $3 + 5 = x$ $\quad x = 2, 5, 8, \text{ or } 15$

11. $\frac{x}{2} = 6$ $\quad x = 2, 4, 6, \text{ or } 12$

12. $\frac{x}{5} = 2$ $\quad x = 5, 10, 15, \text{ or } 20$

13. $\frac{18}{x} = 3$ $\quad x = 6, 12, 15, \text{ or } 18$

Find the values for the variable that will provide the given values for the expressions.

14.

n	$n - 12$
	10
	14
	19
	31

15.

n	$\frac{n}{12}$
	10
	14
	19
	31

Choose a strategy. Solve each equation.

16. $5j = 30$

17. $12 + l = 18$

18. $9k = 54$

19. $z + 3 = 37$

20. $19 - v = 13$

21. $8b = 64$

22. $\frac{72}{n} = 9$

23. $\frac{m}{4} = 21$

24. $z - 38 = 42$

25. $d + 4 = 37$

26. $\frac{100}{g} = 20$

27. $5p = 150$

28. $21 + k = 30$

29. $w - 30 = 80$

30. $\frac{r}{2} = 84$

31. $37 - x = 15$

32. $6x = 36$

33. $n + 13 = 30$

34. $\frac{z}{4} = 9$

35. $41 - y = 17$

Estimation Estimate to determine if the value of each variable must be greater or less than 6.

36. $r + 5 = 10$

37. $q - 3 = 6$

38. $12 - w = 8$

39. $3r = 6$

40. $6 \times t = 24$

41. $\frac{28}{i} = 7$

42. $p - 16 = 32$

43. $12 + d = 29$

44. $\frac{f}{7} = 14$

45. $g \times 10 = 80$

46. $9 \times y = 81$

47. $13 - q = 8$

48. **Reasoning** Suppose $a + b = 10$. If the value of a increases by 2, how must the value of b change so that the equation is still true?

49. **Reasoning** Hillary says the value of x in $5x = 10$ is 50. Is she correct? If not, explain what she did wrong. Then give the correct answer.

50. Geography The top three gold-producing countries produce 1,171 tonnes (metric tons) of gold. South Africa produces 584 tonnes. Australia produces 256 tonnes. The United States produces u tonnes. How many tonnes does the United States produce?

51. The French submarine *Nautile* can dive to 20,000 ft. Diving at x ft/hr, it takes 20 hours to reach the maximum depth. How fast must the *Nautile* dive to reach that depth?

52. Geography The largest desert in the world is the Sahara Desert, which covers 3,500,000 square miles. The second largest desert, the Australian Desert, is d square miles, 2,030,000 less than the Sahara. What area does the Australian Desert cover?

53. Critical Thinking If the average depth of the Arctic Ocean were tripled, the result would be 114 meters more than 3,000 meters. The equation $3x - 114 = 3{,}000$ models this situation. Find the average depth of the Arctic Ocean.

54. Calculator Jamie wanted to use her calculator to find the value of x that makes $56x + 716 = 5{,}140$. Describe how to do it.

55. Collecting Data Research to find more data on the ocean. This data can be anything from ocean depths and temperatures to types of fish and mammals. Use the data to write your own problem similar to Exercises 50–52.

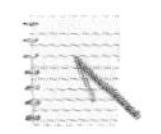

56. Journal Describe at least three methods you can use to solve equations. Give one example for each method.

Mixed Review and Test Prep

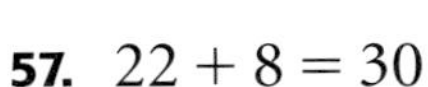

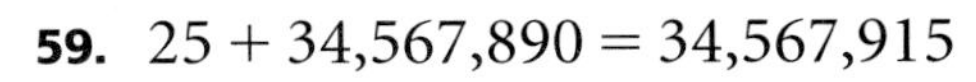

Write each addition equation as a subtraction equation with the same numbers.

57. $22 + 8 = 30$ **58.** $49 + 151 = 200$ **59.** $25 + 34{,}567{,}890 = 34{,}567{,}915$

Write each subtraction equation as an addition equation with the same numbers.

60. $53 - 10 = 43$ **61.** $163 - 57 = 106$ **62.** $180{,}000 - 21{,}000 = 159{,}000$

63. Evaluate the expression $12x$ for $x = 10$.

Ⓐ 12 Ⓑ 120 Ⓒ 2 Ⓓ 22

Chapter 2

Problem Solving

Analyze Word Problems: Interpreting Math Phrases

You Will Learn

- to interpret math phrases in order to help you solve problems

Learn

Hinda has an aquarium with 7 neon tetras. She has twice as many head-and-tail-light tetras. How many head-and-tail-light tetras does Hinda have?

Work Together

Understand

What information do you have?

What are you trying to find?

Plan

What math phrases are in this problem?

7 neon tetras
Twice as many head-and-tail-light tetras

What does the phrase "twice as many" mean?

Two times as many

Solve

How many head-and-tail-light tetras does Hinda have?

Twice as many as neon tetras
$2 \times 7 = 14$

Hinda has 14 head-and-tail-light tetras.

Look Back

Is your answer reasonable?

1. Make a list of math phrases. Look through the problems in previous lessons to help you. Then interpret each phrase.
2. How can interpreting math phrases help you solve problems?

Check

1. David had seven butterflies in his insect collection. Jennifer had eight more butterflies than David. How many butterflies did Jennifer have?
   a. Write the math phrases in this problem.
   b. Interpret each math phrase.
   c. How many butterflies did Jennifer have?

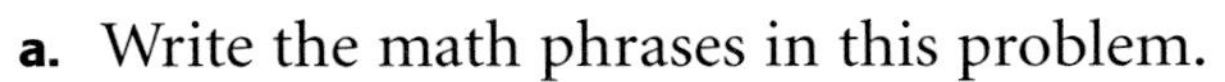

For each problem, write down the answer and the arithmetic you did to find the answer. For example, if you added 5 and 7 to get 12, write "5 + 7 = 12".

2. Patty had twelve crickets. Lila had four crickets less than Patty. How many crickets did Lila have?
3. Camille had twenty grasshoppers. Barbara had half as many grasshoppers as Camille. How many grasshoppers did Barbara have?
4. Richard had three dragonflies. Phoebe had three times as many dragonflies as Richard. How many did Phoebe have?
5. Ada had ten more ladybugs than Mark. Mark had fourteen ladybugs. How many did Ada have?
6. Jack had twice as many beetles as Lois. Jack had six beetles. How many did Lois have?
7. Kristen had half as many bees as Terri. Kristen had seven bees. How many did Terri have?

- Draw a Picture
- Look for a Pattern
- Guess and Check
- Use Logical Reasoning
- Make an Organized List
- Make a Table
- Solve a Simpler Problem
- Work Backward

Choose a Tool

Using a Spreadsheet to Guess and Check

A spreadsheet can help you solve two equations at the same time. Use the spreadsheet to help you "guess and check" to solve a problem. Each time you make a new guess, the spreadsheet will solve the equations for you.

> **Materials**
>
> *Interactive CD-ROM Spreadsheet/Grapher Tool* or other spreadsheet software

What values for x and y will make these two equations true at the same time?

$x - y = 25$ and $xy = 150$

Work Together

Use your spreadsheet software to set up two formulas, one for each equation.

1. Create a new spreadsheet in the software program. Enter the information into the spreadsheet as shown.

2. In cell B4, enter the formula $=B1-B2$. This formula will find the difference between x and y. In cell B5, enter the formula $=B1*B2$. This formula will find the product of x and y.

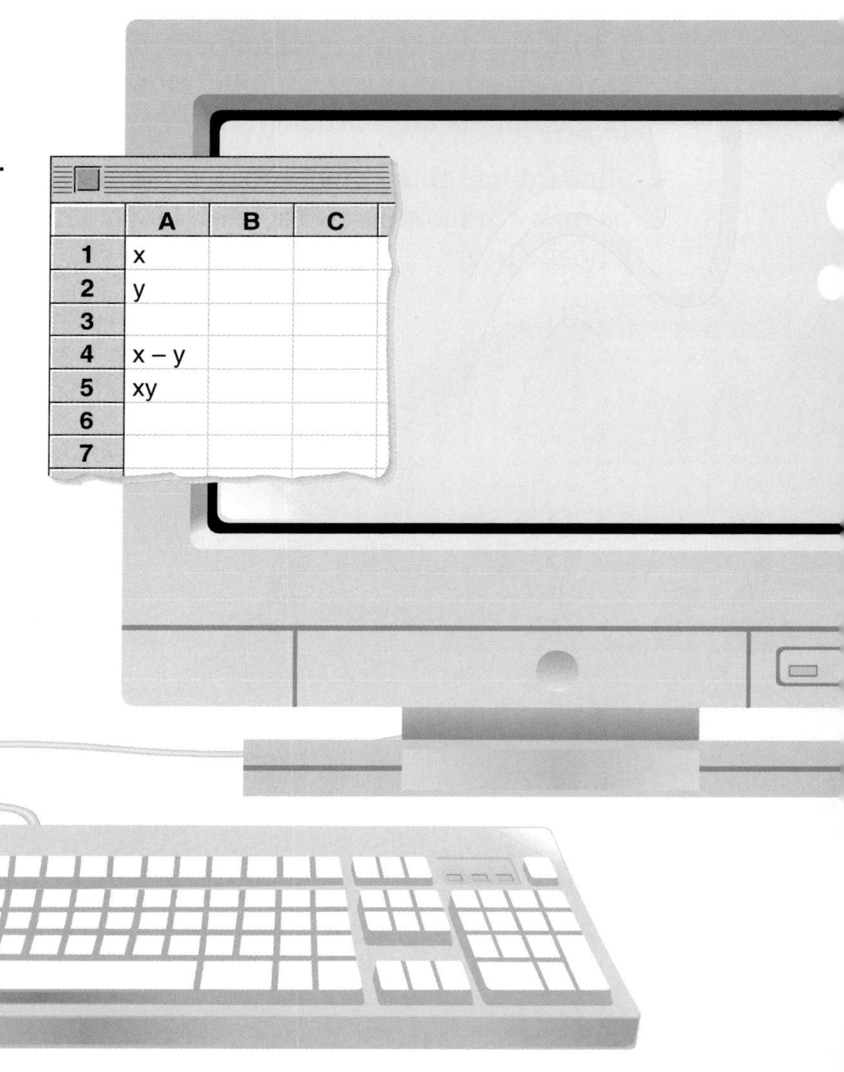

3. Enter values into cell B1 for x and cell B2 for y. Start with values you know are true for the equation $x - y = 25$.

	A	B	C
1	x	40	
2	y	15	
3			
4	x – y	25	
5	xy	600	
6			
7			

4. Check your guess by seeing whether the values for $x - y = 25$ are also true for $xy = 150$. If the answer for xy is too high, choose lesser values for x and y. If the answer for xy is too low, choose greater values for x and y.

	A	B	C
1	x	30	
2	y	5	
3			
4	x – y	25	
5	xy	150	
6			
7			

Exercises

Use a spreadsheet to help you guess and check the values of x and y.

1. Find a solution for $x + y = 36$ and $\frac{x}{y} = 5$.
2. Find a solution for $x - y = 9$ and $xy = 90$.
3. Find a solution for $xy = 24$ and $\frac{x}{y} = 24$.
4. The sum of two numbers is 30 and their product is 209. What are the two numbers?

Extensions

5. Find a solution for $x + y = 20$, $x - y = 6$, and $xy = 91$.
6. When going from a bad guess to a better guess, why is it important to change the values for both x and y?
7. Is it faster to find a solution for x and y with a spreadsheet or without a spreadsheet? Explain.
8. Work with a partner. Each of you should come up with two equations using x and y as variables. Work backward using whole numbers, and then substitute x and y to represent the two values. Exchange your equations and solve them using spreadsheets to help you guess and check.

Problem Solving

Decision Making: Journey to the Bottom of the Sea

You Will Learn

- how to use data to solve problems to make a decision

Explore

On January 23, 1960, Jacques Piccard and Donald Walsh used a diving vessel called a bathyscaphe to descend nearly 7 miles into the deepest part of the Pacific Ocean. Their descent was the deepest ever made by humans. Such adventures are dangerous and costly. However, much of today's deep-sea research is done by robots called ROVs, or "remote operated vehicles."

The fearsome angler fish makes its home in the ocean at a depth of around 3,000 feet. An oceanography research team wants to rent an ROV and try to get photos of an angler fish. The price for renting ROV-1 is $1 per minute plus $545. The price for renting ROV-2 is $5 per minute. The team has limited funds and must find the best possible deal.

Work Together

Understand

1. What are you asked to do?
2. What kind of information do you have to help you?

Plan and Solve

3. If the team wants to use an ROV for 5 hours, what would it cost to rent ROV-1? ROV-2?
4. For each ROV, write an expression you can use to determine the total rental cost for x minutes.
5. Make a table showing the total cost of each ROV for 30 minutes, 60 minutes, 90 minutes, and so on up to 240 minutes (4 hours).
6. In general, when is it cheaper to rent ROV-1? When is it cheaper to rent ROV-2?

Make a Decision

7. Suppose the team had exactly $3,000 to spend on ROV rental. For how long could they rent each ROV?
8. Which ROV should the team rent? Explain your reasoning.

Present Your Decision

9. How did you make your decision?
10. Prepare a presentation to show the class how you made your decision. Use graphs, tables, models, or other visuals to help you.

SECTION C
Review and Practice

(Lesson 10) State whether each quantity should be represented by a variable or a constant.

1. The height of Mount McKinley
2. The value of an old comic book
3. The length of your pet dog
4. The outside temperature
5. The number of cookies in a dozen

(Lesson 11) Write each situation as an expression.

6. d divided by 4
7. 16 less than g
8. m times 16
9. 4 added to h
10. The Carson family evenly distributed d dollars to 17 different charities.
11. Kyle began his deep-water dive at y ft. He dove down 25 ft.
12. k snorkels less the number 30 distributed to students in the scuba-diving class.

(Lesson 12) Is the equation true for the given value of each variable?

13. $\frac{14}{q} = 2, q = 7$
14. $9y = 24, y = 2$
15. $w - 1 = 13, w = 13$

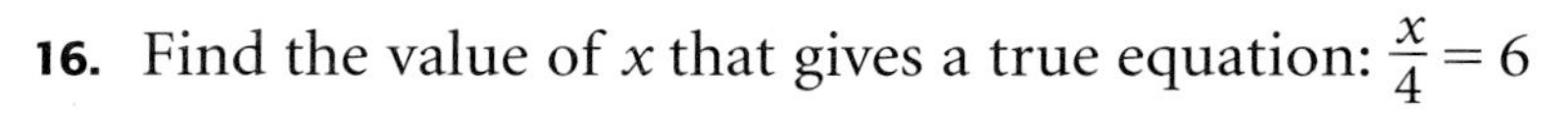

16. Find the value of x that gives a true equation: $\frac{x}{4} = 6$

(Lesson 13) Solve.

17. $6 + x = 28$
18. $\frac{x}{5} = 15$
19. $9x = 45$
20. $x - 3 = 27$
21. Jamal's scuba-diving class has 30 students. Jane's class has d students, 19 less than Jamal's class. How big is Jane's class?
22. In Tom's scuba diving class there are 3 times as many girls as boys. If there are 24 students in the class, how many students are boys?
23. **Journal** Describe the numbers that will make the following equation true. Explain your thinking.
$1 \times d = d$

Skills Checklist

In this section, you have:

- ☑ **Learned About Variables and Expressions**
- ☑ **Written Expressions**
- ☑ **Used Equations**
- ☑ **Solved Equations**

Choose at least one of the following. Use what you have learned in this chapter.

1 Pleasing Patterns

Work with a partner. Create a number pattern on a hundred chart, then make a list of all the numbers to be filled in. Trade lists with your partner, and re-create his or her chart. What number patterns can you identify in each of your charts?

A	B	C	D	E	F	G	H	I	J
1	2	3	4	5	6	7	8	9	10
11	12	13	14	15	16	17	18	19	20
21	22	23	24	25	26	27	28	29	30
31	32	33	34	35	36	37	38	39	40
41	42	43	44	45	46	47	48	49	50
51	52	53	54	55	56	57	58	59	60
61	62	63	64	65	66	67	68	69	70
71	72	73	74	75	76	77	78	79	80
81	82	83	84	85	86	87	88	89	90
91	92	93	94	95	96	97	98	99	100

List A: 1, 11, 41, 51, 81, 91
List B: 2, 12, 32, 42, 52, 62, 82, 92
List C: 23, 33, 63, 73
List D: 14, 24, 44, 54, 74, 84
List E: 5, 15, 35, 65, 85, 95
List F: 6, 16, 36, 66, 86, 96
List G: 17, 27, 47, 57, 77, 87
List H: 28, 38, 68, 78
List I: 9, 19, 39, 49, 59, 69, 89, 99
List J: 10, 20, 50, 60, 90, 100

2 Massive Math 

Go online to **www.mathsurf.com/6/ch2** to find five numbers which can be rounded to the place values listed in the chart below. Challenge yourself to write each rounded number as a power of 10.

Data Found	Number	Rounds to	Power of 10
		100 thousands	
		1 millions	
		10 millions	
		100 millions	
		1 billions	

3 Going the Distance

At Home Ask three family members or friends to first estimate how far he or she can jump from a standing position; then jump. Mark and measure the distance with a yardstick. Have each person repeat this two more times. Do the estimates get closer to the actual jumps?

38 in.

4 Elegant Estimates

Write a short poem to help you remember how to estimate sums, differences, products, or quotients.

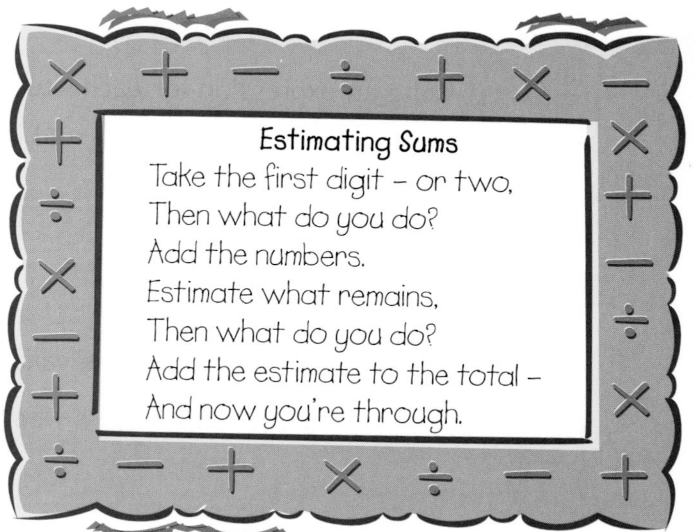

REVIEW AND PRACTICE

CHAPTER 2

Review/Test

(Lessons 1 and 4) Write each number in standard form.

1. seventy-five thousand, three hundred
2. two billion, five million, one
3. 10^5
4. 3^3
5. 7^4
6. 5^5

(Lesson 2) Round to the given place.

7. 34,578; hundreds
8. 436; tens
9. 3,521,337; hundred thousands

(Lesson 3) Use $>$, $<$, or $=$ to compare the numbers in **10–12.**

10. Dallas's 1990 census of 1,006,877 to Detroit's census of 1,027,974
11. Anna's fundraising total of $251.59 to Kalil's total of $257.09
12. Michael's 2^2 mile bike ride to Gita's 2^3 mile ride

(Lesson 5) Explain how you would solve each problem using mental math.

13. 49×2
14. $4{,}800 \div 60$
15. $76 + 17 - 6$
16. 4×206

(Lessons 6 and 7) Estimate each answer.

17. A stamp collector counted 31 New Zealand, 36 Canadian, 33 French, and 28 British stamps. What was the total number of stamps he had?
18. 286×43
19. $35{,}782 \div 3{,}939$
20. $426 \div 69$

(Lesson 8) Solve the problems using order of operations.

21. 35×10^3
22. $3^3 - 7 \times 2$
23. $7 \times (8 + 12)$
24. $(5 + 2)^2 - 40$

(Lesson 9) For each pattern, find the next three numbers.

25. 6, 8, 12, 18, 26, . . .
26. 10, 7, 4, 9, 6, 3, 8, . . .

(Lesson 10) Evaluate each expression for $x = 5, 6, 7$.

27. $2x$
28. $x - 2$
29. $x + 19$

(Lesson 11) Write an expression for each situation.

30. The distance around the box.

31. Submarine A dove 1,600 ft less than submarine B. How deep did submarine A dive?

(Lessons 12 and 13) Find the value of the variable that makes the equation true.

32. $\frac{d}{6} = 20$
33. $c + 32 = 37$
34. $9y = 108$
35. $y - 7 = 42$

REVIEW/TEST

CHAPTER 2

Performance Assessment

You have decided to open a muffin shop. You know the price of the ingredients needed to make a dozen muffins. You need to find out how much it costs to make each muffin and how much to charge for each muffin in order to make a profit.

1. **Decision Making** How much profit do you want to make on each muffin? How much will you need to charge to make this profit? If c is the cost to make each muffin and p is the profit, write an equation to show the price, m, you should charge for each muffin.

2. **Explain Your Thinking** How will you use the total cost of the ingredients for a dozen muffins to determine the cost of ingredients per muffin?

3. **Critical Thinking** Suppose you want to make a profit on each muffin that is twice the cost of its ingredients. Write an equation to show your profit.

4. **Critical Thinking** Suppose you want to sell each muffin for a price that covers the cost of its ingredients and a profit of twice that cost. Write an equation that shows the price (m) you should charge. Then solve the equation using the cost you found in Exercise 2 above.

Math Magazine

One, three, six, and ten dots can be arranged in triangle shapes. For this reason, 1, 3, 6, and 10 are called triangular numbers.

1 3 6 10

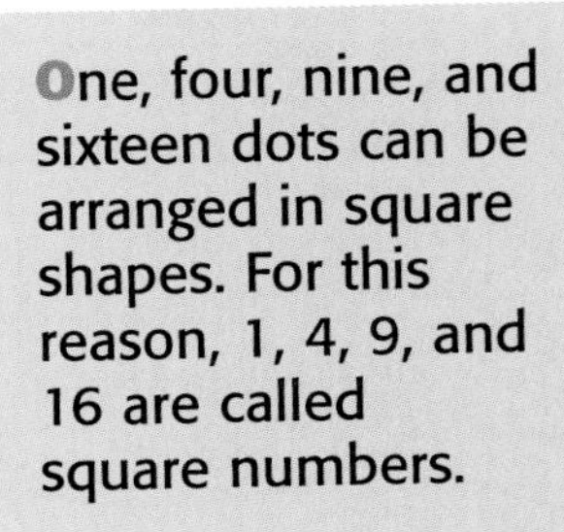
One, four, nine, and sixteen dots can be arranged in square shapes. For this reason, 1, 4, 9, and 16 are called square numbers.

Try These!

1. What are the next two triangular numbers? Sketch them.
2. What are the next two square numbers? Sketch them.
3. The number 1 can be shown as both a triangular and square number. Name the next smallest number that can be shown both ways.
4. Describe a pattern for determining the first ten triangular numbers, without using a drawing.
5. Describe a pattern for determining the first ten square numbers, without using a drawing.

CHAPTERS 1–2

Cumulative Review

Test Prep Strategy: Work Backward from an Answer

What number gives a quotient of 73 when divided into 1,898?

Ⓐ 18 Ⓑ 24 Ⓒ 26 Ⓓ 27

Sometimes working backward from an answer can help you solve a problem. You know the answer, or quotient, is 73, and the dividend is 1,898. Replace the missing divisor with each possible answer, then check to see if it is correct.

$73 \times 18 = 1{,}314$ – no

$73 \times 24 = 1{,}752$ – no

$73 \times 26 = 1{,}898$ – yes

The correct answer is choice Ⓒ.

STAY SHARP!

Write the letter of the correct answer. Choose any strategy.

1. Choose the greatest number.

   Ⓐ 7,135,528 Ⓑ 8,105,528 Ⓒ 8,130,528 Ⓓ 7,150,528

2. For the data 25, 22, 24, 20, 29, 36, 23, 25, which has the lowest value, the mean, the median, the mode, or the outlier?

   Ⓐ mean Ⓑ median Ⓒ mode Ⓓ outlier

3. Jessie has started doing sit-ups. If she does 2 the first day and each day does 2 times as many as the day before, how many will she do on the third day?

   Ⓐ 2^6 Ⓑ 2^3 Ⓒ 2^5 Ⓓ 3^2

4. Choose the next number in the pattern. 180, 173, 184, 177, 188, . . .

   Ⓐ 200 Ⓑ 181 Ⓒ 196 Ⓓ 234

5. Choose the best estimate for $4{,}235 + 9{,}608 + 9{,}342$.

   Ⓐ 13,800 Ⓑ 22,400 Ⓒ 20,700 Ⓓ 23,000

6. Simplify $14 + (9 - 3)\,2 \div 2$.

   Ⓐ 32 Ⓑ 25 Ⓒ 17 Ⓓ not here

7. Round three million, six hundred eighty-four to the nearest thousand.

   Ⓐ 3,684,000 Ⓑ 3,006,840 Ⓒ 3,001,000 Ⓓ 3,000,684

8. Manuel's dog has a litter of puppies. He gives three puppies away and has two left. Choose the correct equation to model the problem.

   Ⓐ $p = 3 - 2$ Ⓑ $2 - p = 3$ Ⓒ $p - 3 = 2$ Ⓓ $3 - p = 2$

9. In a pictograph, each fish symbol represents 5 million fish. How many millions of fish do 7 symbols represent?

   Ⓐ 7.5 million Ⓑ 35 million Ⓒ 12 million Ⓓ not here

10. Evaluate the expression $\frac{144}{x}$ for $x = 2$, 3, and 4.

    Ⓐ 146, 147, 148 Ⓑ 72, 46, 36 Ⓒ 142, 141, 140 Ⓓ 72, 48, 36

Test Prep Strategies

- Read Carefully
- Follow Directions
- Make Smart Choices
- Eliminate Choices
- Work Backward from an Answer

REVIEW AND PRACTICE

DATA FILE

Chapter 3
Decimals

A Bouquet of Spiders

A Bouquet of Spiders
Page 137

Decimal Concepts

137

This table lists information on four types of orb weaver spiders found in North America. Orb weavers spin spiraling orb webs on support lines that stretch out from the center of the web. Which of the male spiders has the greatest body length? Which of the female spiders has the shortest body length?

Name of Spider	Habitat	Length of Male Body (cm)	Length of Female Body (cm)
Barn spider	Barns, caves, mines	3.81	4.445
Garden spider	Gardens	2.413	3.175
Marbled orb weaver	Meadows, shrubs	2.405	3.558
Golden-silk spider	Shaded woods, swamps	1.143	3.56

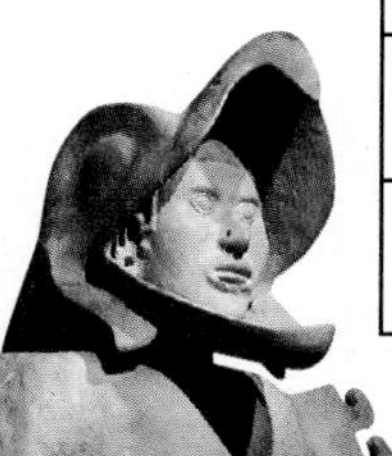

LINKS

Social Studies

The Aztecs are credited as one of the first cultures to use the number 0.
www.mathsurf.com/6/ch3/social

Entertainment

In 1988, Carl Lewis won the Olympic gold medal for the 100-meter dash by completing the race in 9.92 seconds.
www.mathsurf.com/6/ch3/ent

SECTION B Getting Your Money's Worth

Adding and Subtracting with Decimals

157

This table shows the exchange rates for a few countries. Which country's currency has the greatest value in U.S. dollars?

Country	Basic Unit	Value of One Unit in U.S. Dollars ($)	Number of Units One U.S. Dollar Will Buy
Belgium	Franc	0.03258	30.693
China	Yuan	0.12038	8.3071
India	Rupee	0.02802	35.695

Getting Your Money's Worth
Page 157

SECTION C Trials and Trails

Multiplying and Dividing with Decimals

This map shows one recommended biking tour in Pennsylvania. It begins at the same spot where General George Washington crossed the Delaware River. Which leg of the tour is longer: from Washington Crossing Park to New Hope or from New Hope to Bowman's Hill Tower?

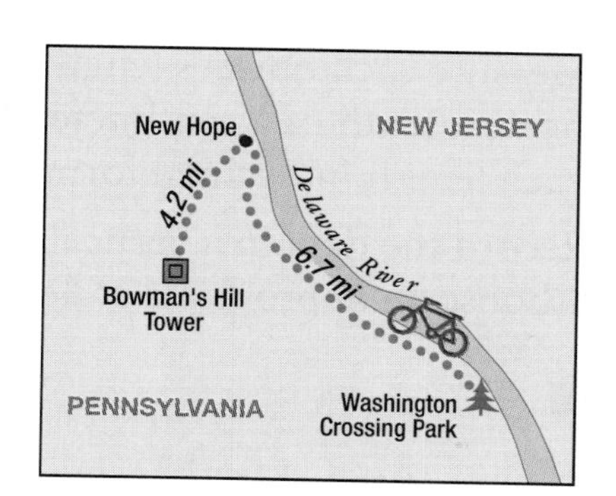

Trials and Trails
Page 175

Science

The Richter scale measures earthquake magnitude. A 1.3 earthquake is recorded but not felt.

www.mathsurf.com/6/ch3/science

People of the World

In Europe, a comma is used in the place of a decimal point.

Arts & Literature

In *The Gift of the Magi*, O. Henry stated "One dollar and eighty-seven cents. That was all. And sixty cents of it was in pennies."

Materials

centimeter ruler, graph paper or graphing software

What are the lengths of the objects you use every day in your classroom? Choose five objects and measure their length to the nearest tenth of a centimeter. Then make a bar graph to compare the data.

Make a Plan

- What objects will you measure?
- How will you measure their length?
- How will you organize your data?
- How will you divide tasks among team members?

Carry It Out

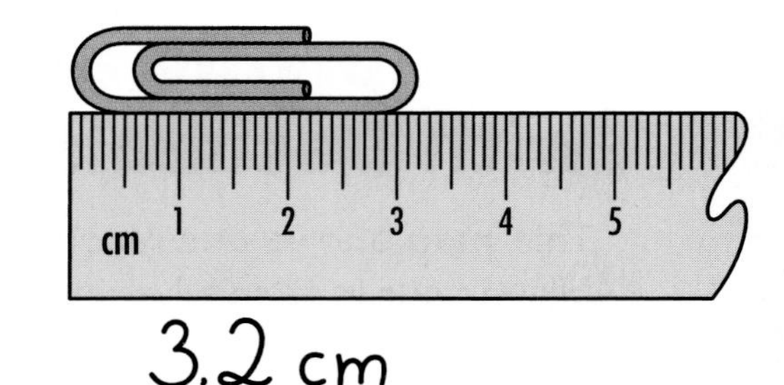

1. Choose five objects in your classroom to measure.
2. Measure each object's length to the nearest tenth of a centimeter. Record each length in decimal form.
3. Record the data in a vertical bar graph. Choose an appropriate scale for the vertical axis.

Talk About It

- Which of the objects you measured is the longest? The shortest?
- What is the difference in length between the longest and shortest objects?
- What is the average length of the five objects? How could you decrease the average length?

Present the Project

Present your bar graph to the class. How did your team decide on a scale for your bar graph? How does the bar graph help you compare the lengths of the objects you measured?

CHAPTER 3

SECTION

A Decimal Concepts

"Hello? Yes, I'd like to get three Chilean roses at $15 each, two Peruvian pinktoes at $35 each, a Togo starburst for $16, and a common bluebloom for $75." Believe it or not, this wasn't an order for flowers. It was an order for tarantulas! While some people find spiders fearsome creatures, arachnologists (a-rak-NAH-luh-jists) spend thousands of dollars and hours studying these eight-legged wonders.

Why would arachnologists use small numbers when studying spiders?

GET READY!

Comparing and Ordering Decimals

Review comparing and ordering numbers. Copy and complete each expression. Write >, <, or =.

1. 47 ● 45 **2.** 606 ● 613 **3.** 4,291 ● 4,991

Order each group of numbers from least to greatest.

4. 23,819; 23,911; 22,018

5. 180,544; 180,555; 108,622

Skills Checklist

In this section, you will:

- ❒ Learn About Decimal Notation
- ❒ Round Decimals
- ❒ Compare and Order Decimals
- ❒ Learn About Scientific Notation

Chapter 3 Lesson 1

Decimal Notation

You Will Learn

- how to write numbers in decimal notation
- how to represent numbers using a grid model

Learn

Sometimes when you measure an object or a distance, the measure isn't a whole number.

Decimal numbers are used to describe measures that are in between whole numbers.

A desert tarantula measures 6.94 cm in length.

Did You Know?
Desert tarantulas seldom bite people. Their venom is usually no more dangerous than a bee sting.

The place-value system of ones, tens, hundreds, thousands, and so on, allows you to write any whole numbers using the digits 0 to 9. You can write numbers that are in between whole numbers by using a decimal point and place values that are less than ones.

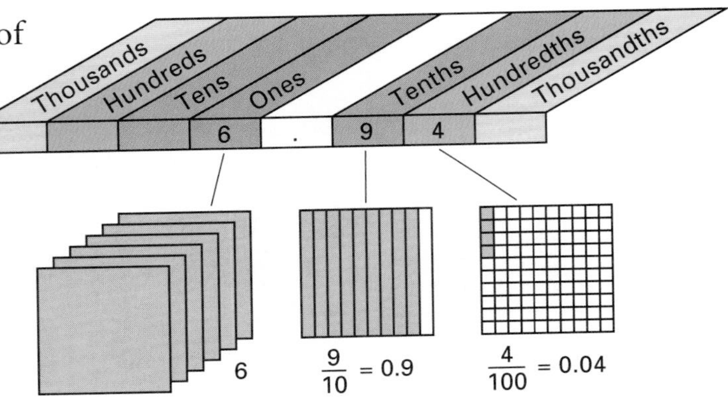

Example 1

What decimal number does the grid represent?

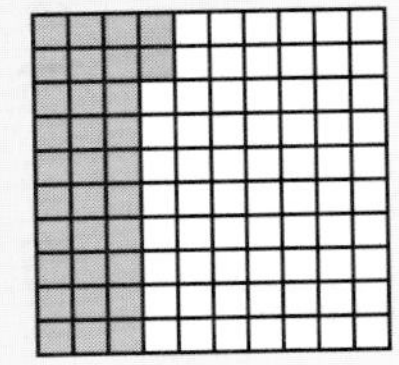

The grid represents 0.32.

Example 2

Draw a grid to represent 0.8.

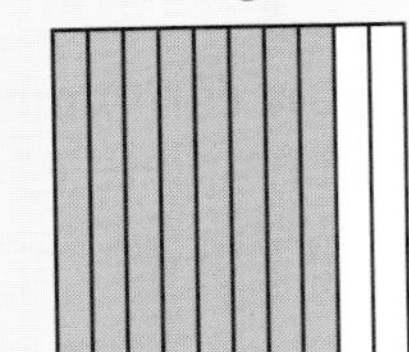

You can write decimals in *word form* or in *decimal form.*

Example 3

Write 6.94 in word form.

6.94 = six and ninety-four hundredths

Example 4

Write one and twenty-one thousandths in decimal form.

one and twenty-one thousandths = 1.021

ones	tenths	hundredths	thousandths
1	.0	2	1

Talk About It

1. How many tenths are in a whole? How many hundredths? How many thousandths?
2. How many hundredths are in a tenth?
3. How many thousandths are in a tenth?
4. Why is the United States money system referred to as a decimal system?

Math Tip

All the place values less than one have names that end in *ths.*

Check

What decimal numbers does each grid represent?

1. 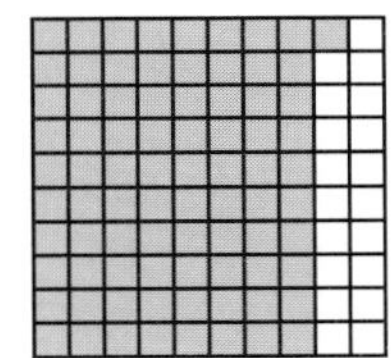

2. 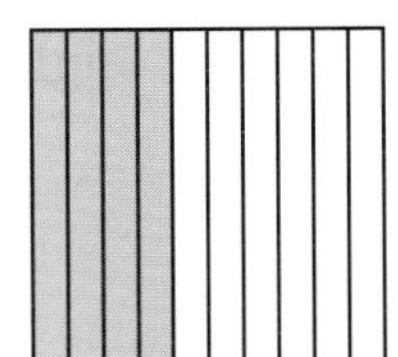

3. 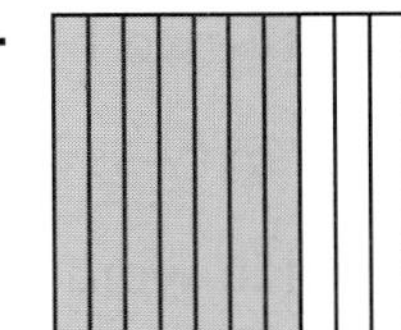

Draw a grid to represent each decimal.

4. 0.2
5. 0.13
6. 0.37
7. 1.35
8. 0.09
9. 0.1
10. 0.4
11. 0.57

Write in word form.

12. 3.051
13. 0.171
14. 0.47
15. 8.1
16. 0.08
17. 0.63
18. 1.02
19. 2.9

Write in standard form.

20. nine hundredths
21. two and one hundred one thousandths
22. seventy-eight hundredths
23. six and four tenths
24. **Reasoning** How many decimal numbers are there between 1 and 2? Explain.

Practice

Skills and Reasoning

Write each fraction as a decimal.

25. $\frac{6}{10}$ **26.** $\frac{43}{100}$ **27.** $\frac{312}{1,000}$ **28.** $\frac{9}{10}$ **29.** $\frac{97}{1,000}$ **30.** $\frac{8}{100}$

What decimal number does each grid or set of grids represent?

31. 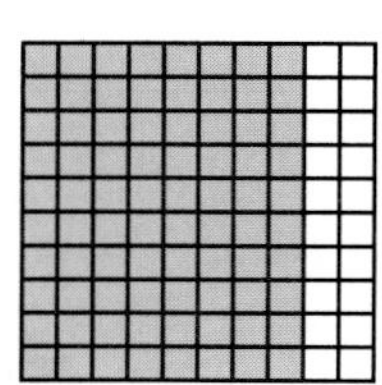

32. 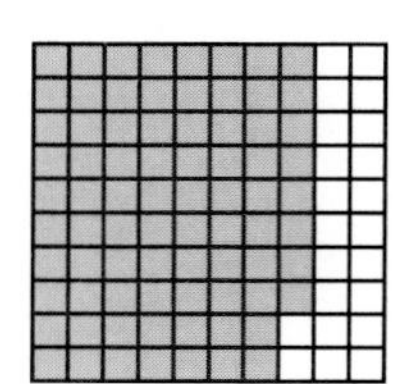

33. 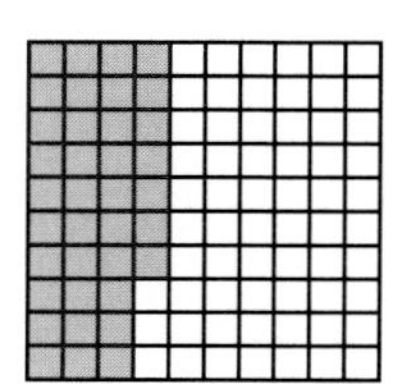

34. 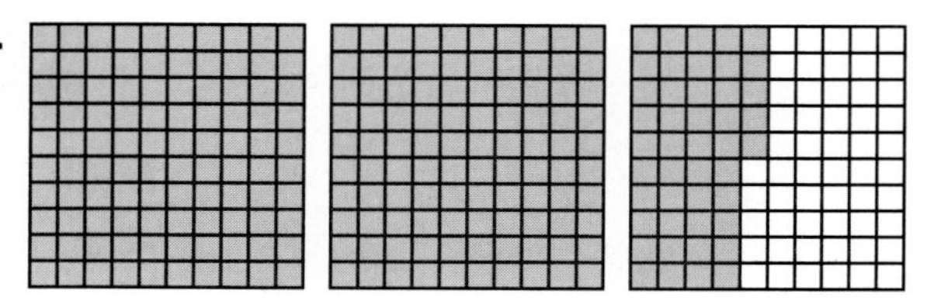

Draw a grid to represent each decimal.

35. 0.7 **36.** 0.18 **37.** 0.5 **38.** 0.99 **39.** 0.67 **40.** 0.07

For **41–46,** write each number as a decimal.

41. fifty-one hundredths

42. one and sixty-seven thousandths

43. three and forty-two hundredths

44. eight hundredths

45. one hundred sixty-seven thousandths

46. two tenths

Write each decimal in word form.

47. 0.67 **48.** 0.075 **49.** 8.611

50. 5.09 **51.** 12.006 **52.** 0.4

Use a calculator and your knowledge of patterns to complete the table.

	Hundreds	Tens	Ones		
Arithmetic Form	100 ÷ 1	10 ÷ 1	1 ÷ 1	1 ÷ 10	1 ÷ 100
53. Fraction Form	$\frac{100}{1}$				
54. Calculator Form					

55. Patterns How are the columns to the right of the "Ones" similar to the columns to the left of the "Ones"? How are they different?

56. Reasoning How many numbers are there between 1.01 and 1.10? Explain.

Problem Solving and Applications

Solve each of the following.

57. **Science** The average body length of a dust mite is fifteen thousandths of an inch. Write this number as a decimal.

58. **History** The ancient Greeks discovered that a person's height from the floor to the waist is about sixty-two hundredths of the total height. Write this number as a decimal.

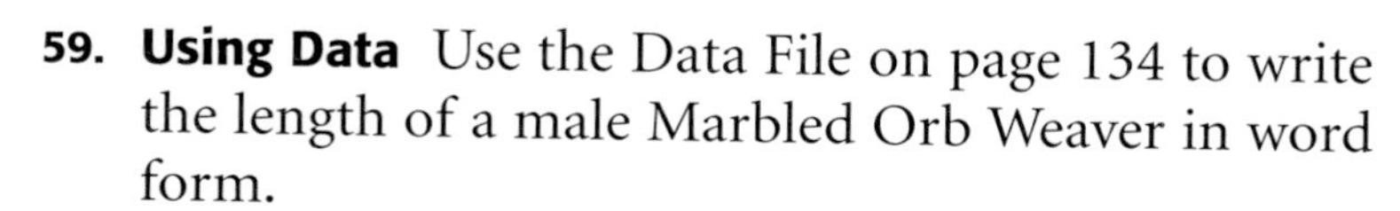

59. **Using Data** Use the Data File on page 134 to write the length of a male Marbled Orb Weaver in word form.

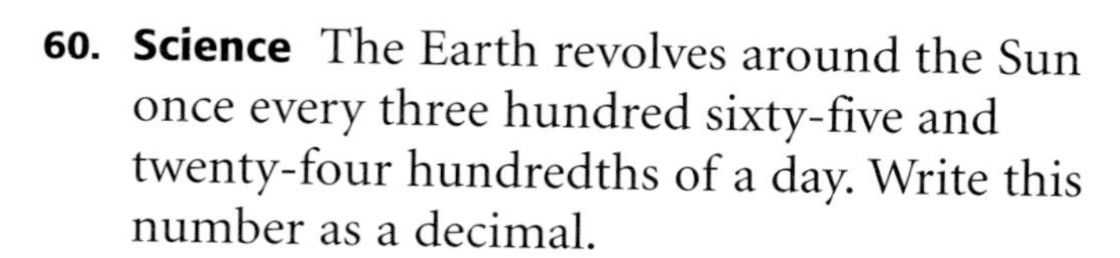

60. **Science** The Earth revolves around the Sun once every three hundred sixty-five and twenty-four hundredths of a day. Write this number as a decimal.

61. **Sports** In 1988, Florence Griffith-Joyner broke the women's world record in the 100-meter dash with a time of 10.49 seconds. Write her time in word form.

62. **Critical Thinking** Jarvis made a four-digit number with 0, 3, 6, and 8. The number was less than 5 but greater than 1. What could his number be? Explain.

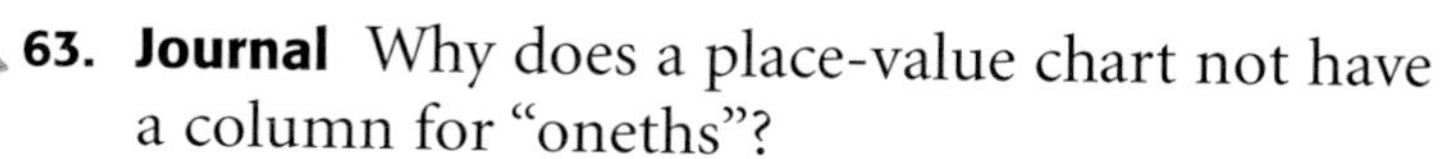

63. **Journal** Why does a place-value chart not have a column for "oneths"?

Mixed Review and Test Prep

For each data set, make a frequency chart and a line plot.

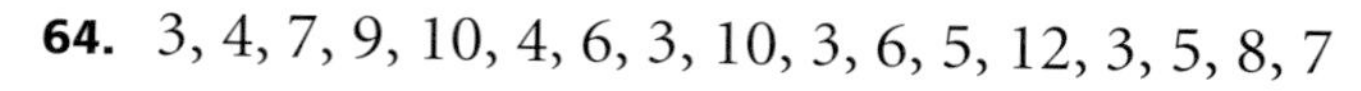

64. 3, 4, 7, 9, 10, 4, 6, 3, 10, 3, 6, 5, 12, 3, 5, 8, 7

65. 20, 50, 70, 80, 40, 100, 30, 60, 70, 70, 70, 80, 30, 20, 50, 10, 50

Evaluate each expression for the given values of the variable.

66. $g + 13$; $g = 2, 3, 4$
67. $d - 10$; $d = 21, 18, 15$
68. $3k$; $k = 4, 6, 10$
69. $\frac{r}{2}$; $r = 2, 16, 22$
70. $5p$; $p = 2, 6, 7$
71. $20 - b$; $b = 3, 5, 19$

Simplify.

72. $286 + 312$
73. $618 - 202$
74. 200×317
75. $606 \div 202$

76. Choose the number form for two hundred twenty-nine thousand.

Ⓐ 20,029 Ⓑ 229 Ⓒ 2,029 Ⓓ 229,000

Chapter 3
Lesson
2

Rounding Decimals

You Will Learn
- how to round decimal numbers
- how to measure length with a metric ruler

Materials
metric rulers

Learn

A scale on a microscopic slide allows a biologist to estimate lengths to the nearest hundredth of a centimeter. A spider egg measures 0.1347 cm in length.

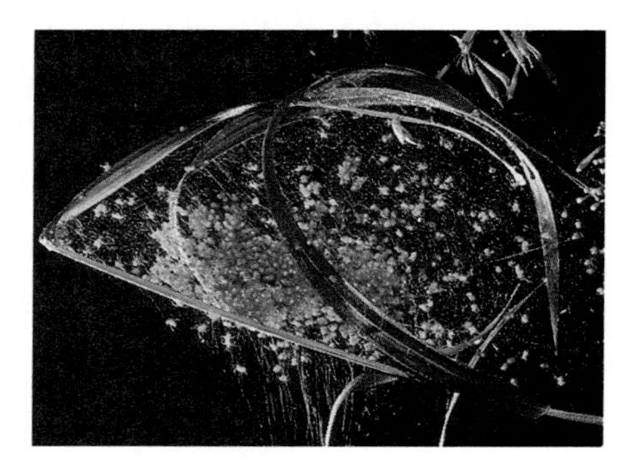

You can *round* numbers when you want to estimate an answer, or when you don't need as precise a measurement as the one you are given.

Example 1

Estimate the length of the spider egg to the nearest hundredth.

0.1[3]67	Find the hundredths place value.
0.1[3]67	Look at the digit to the right. If it is 5 or greater, add 1 to the hundredths place. If it is less than 5, leave the digit alone and drop the digits to the right.
0.14	Add 1 to the hundredths place.

0.1367 rounds to 0.14.

Did You Know?
Spiders are not insects, although they also are invertebrates, or animals without spines. They belong to a separate class of arthropods called *Arachnida.*

Example 2

A spitting spider can squirt a sticky substance on a prey that is up to 1.905 cm away. What is this distance rounded to the nearest tenth?

1.[9]05	This is the tenths place.
	The digit to the right is less than 5.
1.9	Drop the digits to the right of the tenths place.

The distance to the nearest tenth is 1.9 cm.

Rounding decimals is useful when you are measuring lengths. Three units often used to measure length are the meter, the centimeter, and the millimeter. The meter (m) is about the distance from the floor to a doorknob. A centimeter (cm) is $\frac{1}{100}$ of a meter. A millimeter (mm) is $\frac{1}{1000}$ of a meter.

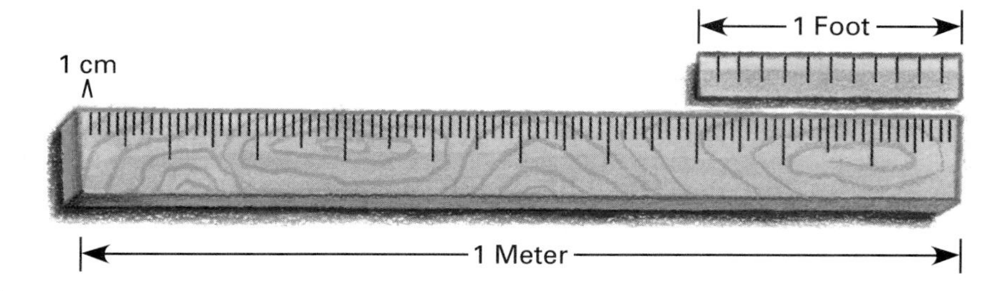

You can use a metric ruler to measure the length of an object in centimeters. No measurement is exact, so centimeter measurements are usually rounded to the nearest centimeter, or the nearest tenth of a centimeter.

Example 3

Estimate the length of the pencil to the nearest centimeter and then measure to the nearest tenth of a centimeter.

The tip of the pencil is between the 10 mark and the 11 mark, and it is closer to the 11 mark.

To the nearest centimeter, the pencil is 11 cm long.

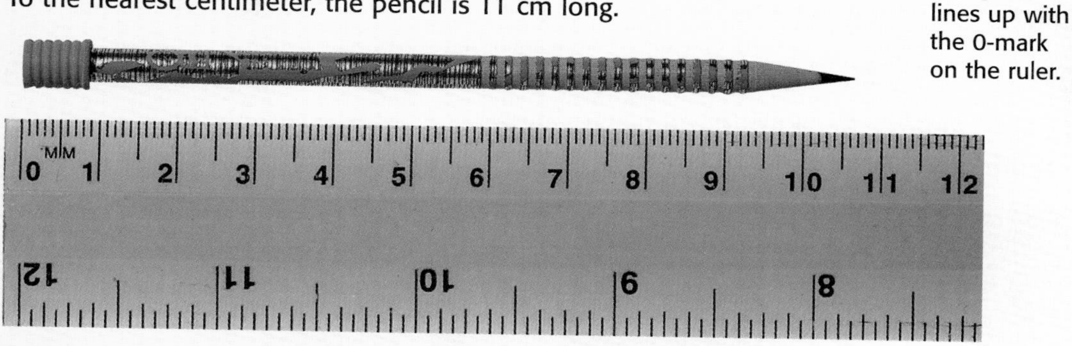

On a metric ruler, each centimeter is divided into ten sections. Each section is one tenth of a centimeter. The tip of the pencil is between the 10.6 mark and the 10.7 mark, but closer to the 10.7 mark.

To the nearest tenth of a centimeter, the pencil is 10.7 cm long.

Remember

When measuring with a ruler, make sure one edge of the object being measured lines up with the 0-mark on the ruler.

1. How is estimating to the nearest centimeter like rounding?
2. How is rounding to thousands similar to rounding to thousandths?

Check

1. Estimate the length of the spider's body to the nearest centimeter and measure to the nearest tenth of a centimeter.
2. Estimate the length of the photo to the nearest centimeter and measure to the nearest tenth of a centimeter.
3. **Reasoning** How can 0.5, 0.51, and 0.513 all be estimates for 0.5128?

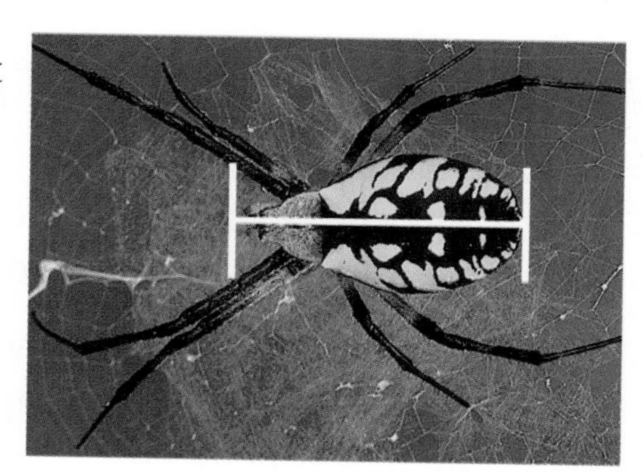

Practice

Skills and Reasoning

Round to the nearest whole number.

4. 0.78 **5.** 2.65 **6.** 3.34 **7.** 0.11 **8.** 1.49 **9.** 2.22

Round to the underlined place value.

10. $10.6\underline{7}4$ **11.** $5.\underline{8}1$ **12.** $56.0\underline{9}8$ **13.** $0.47\underline{1}5$

14. $1\underline{1}.99$ **15.** $4.\underline{3}54$ **16.** $904.\underline{8}46$ **17.** $0.10\underline{0}2$

18. $0.28\underline{0}2$ **19.** $33.\underline{4}56$ **20.** $8.9\underline{2}8$ **21.** $16.1\underline{2}87$

22. $4.\underline{0}02$ **23.** $7.3\underline{0}06$ **24.** $26.9\underline{0}3$ **25.** $8\underline{8}.3$

Estimate each object's height to the nearest centimeter and measure to the nearest tenth of a centimeter.

26.

27.

28.

29.

30.

31. Wendell and Terry both rounded the number 3.462. Wendell says that he rounded the number to a greater number. Terry says that he rounded the number to a lesser number. To what place value might the number have been rounded by Wendell? By Terry? Explain.

Problem Solving and Applications

32. Science The largest sea spider ever found was 75 cm long from leg to leg. The smallest sea spider measures only 0.1 cm. Round the length of the smallest sea spider to the nearest centimeter.

33. Estimation Jonathan has discovered a trail of ants on his porch. Each ant is about 0.93 cm long, and he guesses there are almost 100 of them. Estimate how long the ant trail is.

34. Critical Thinking Form a decimal out of the digits 1, 2, 4, 6, and 8, so that the decimal will round up if rounded to the nearest tenth, but stay the same if rounded to the nearest hundredth. You do not need to use all five digits.

Problem Solving and SCIENCE

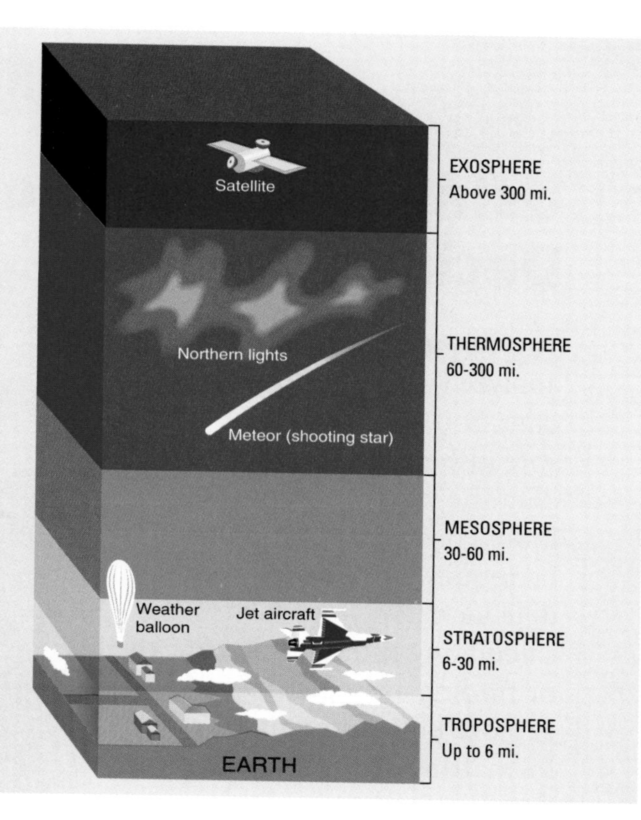

The troposphere is the first layer of the atmosphere around the Earth. It contains all the Earth's weather, and all life on Earth. It is composed of gases.

35. The percent, by volume, of nitrogen in the troposphere is 78.08. What is 78.08 to the nearest tenth?

36. Oxygen is 20.95 percent, by volume, of the troposphere. What is 20.95 to the nearest whole number and tenth?

37. At a research center, Chelsea estimated the percent, by volume, of neon in the troposphere to be 0.0018. She wanted to record her estimate to the nearest hundredth but decided to record it to the nearest thousandth. Explain why she changed her mind.

38. Reasoning Which number would give the most accurate measurement: 0.8, 0.83, or 0.834? Explain.

39. Journal Explain why a measurement is always an estimate.

Mixed Review and Test Prep

STAY SHARP!

For each set of data, draw a bar graph.

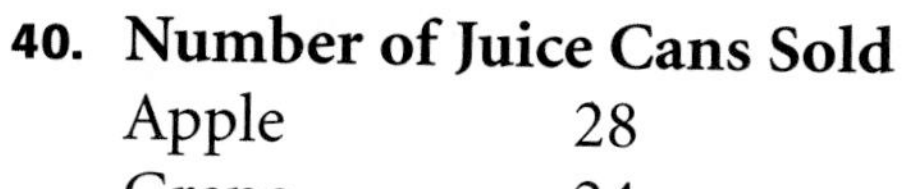

40. Number of Juice Cans Sold

Apple	28
Grape	24
Orange	37
Cranberry	21

41. Number of Telephones in House

None	1
One	4
Two	12
Three or more	6

For each situation, write an algebraic expression.

42. Elaine ate 12 crackers, and then she ate k more. How many crackers did Elaine eat?

43. Carlos worked for five days. He earned w dollars each day. How many dollars did Carlos earn?

44. Sandy is 60 inches tall. His sister is n inches shorter. How tall is Sandy's sister?

45. Choose the number form for six and thirty-six hundredths.

Ⓐ 6.36 Ⓑ 6,360 Ⓒ 636.00 Ⓓ 6.036

Technology

Using a Spreadsheet to Format Decimal Data

Materials

Interactive CD-ROM Spreadsheet/Grapher Tool or other spreadsheet software

You can use spreadsheets to analyze large amounts of data. You also can use spreadsheets to format the data the way you want it to look. For instance, you may be required to format decimal data a certain way when calculating money amounts or finding averages. You will explore how different types of formatting are appropriate for different types of data.

Given the data below, what's the average number of customers per day rounded to the nearest whole number?

Work Together

Use your software to organize this data.

1. Create a spreadsheet like the one shown. Enter the information about the number of customers served at a hotdog stand into the spreadsheet.

	A	B	C	D	E	F	G
1		Mon	Tue	Wed	Thu	Fri	
2	8:00 – 10:00	23	36	67	90	35	
3	10:00 – 12:00	25	4	78	21	47	
4	12:00 – 2:00	79	67	89	87	14	
5	2:00 – 4:00	2	43	55	43	56	
6	4:00 – 6:00	15	56	90	53	23	
7	6:00 – 8:00	45	32	66	14	23	
8							
9	Average						
10							

2. In cell B9, enter the formula = *average(B2:B7)*. This will calculate the Monday average.

3. Copy the formula across the row to column F.

4. Use the format command to format the averages to show no places after the decimal. This will round all averages to the nearest whole number.

Format
- Number...
- Alignment...
- Font...
- Border...
- Patterns...
- Cell Protection...
- Style...
- AutoFormat...
- Row Height...
- Column Width...
- Justify ⌘J
- Bring to Front
- Send to Back
- Group
- Object Properties...

	A	B	C	D	E	F	G
1		Mon	Tue	Wed	Thu	Fri	
2	8:00 – 10:00	23	36	67	90	35	
3	10:00 – 12:00	25	4	78	21	47	
4	12:00 – 2:00	79	67	89	87	14	
5	2:00 – 4:00	2	43	55	43	56	
6	4:00 – 6:00	15	56	90	53	23	
7	6:00 – 8:00	45	32	66	14	23	
8							
9	Average	32	40	74	51	33	
10							

Exercises

1. If the data was about ounces of ketchup used, you might want to see the data to the nearest tenth. Format the averages to show tenths.

2. If the data was about money collected, you might want to see the data to nearest hundredth. Format the averages to show hundredths.

Extensions

3. Name a situation where it might make sense to round a number to the nearest thousandth.

4. If a number in a spreadsheet is 700, can you tell how many places it's been rounded to?

5. What other ways can you format numbers in a spreadsheet?

Chapter 3
Lesson
3

Comparing and Ordering Decimals

You Will Learn

- how to compare and order decimals

Learn

Every spider leg is made of seven segments.

This table shows the lengths of the segments in a golden huntsman spider.

Segment Length (cm)		
0.9	0.881	0.804
0.892	0.87	
0.85	0.876	

You can compare and order these decimals on a number line.

A golden huntsman spider

On a number line, the farther to the right a number is, the greater it is. The farther to the left a number is, the less it is.

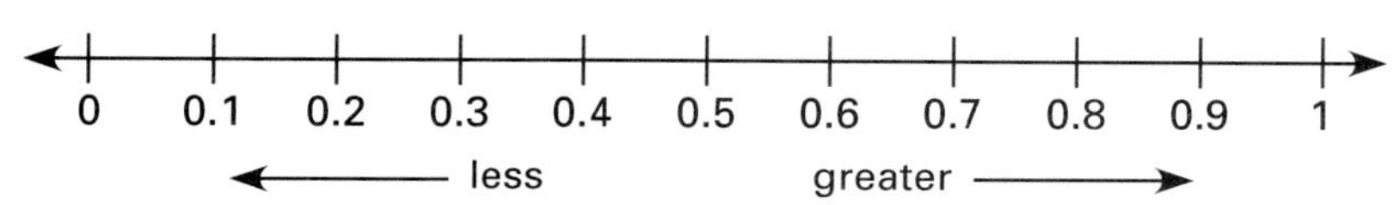

On a number line, the interval from 0 to 1 can be divided into tenths, hundredths, and (if needed) thousandths. Then, each decimal value can be located on the number line.

Did You Know?

Unlike most spiders, the golden huntsman does not spin an organized web. Instead, it walks in slow search of its prey.

Example 1

Order the segment lengths from least to greatest.

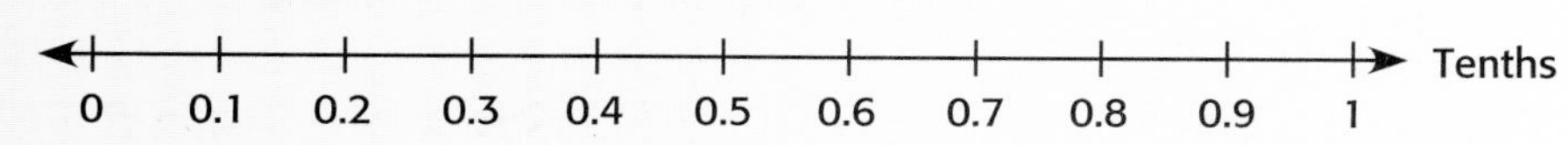

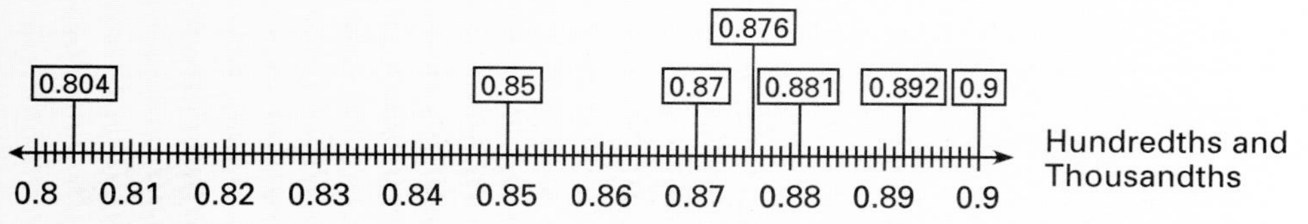

The segment lengths from least to greatest are 0.804, 0.85, 0.87, 0.876, 0.881, 0.892, and 0.9.

You can compare and order decimals without using a number line when the decimals have the same number of digits after the decimal point.

Annexing zeros can help you do this.

When you *annex* zeros to the right of a decimal number, you do not change the value of the number.

$4.37 = 4.370 = 4.3700 = 4.37000$

Example 2

Compare 0.5 and 0.07.

0.5**0** ● 0.07 Annex zeros.

Compare the decimals using the same place value.

50 hundredths is greater than 7 hundredths.

$0.5 > 0.07$

Example 3

Compare 32.207 and 32.3.

32.207 ● 32.3**00** Annex zeros.

Compare the decimals using the same place value.

207 thousandths is less than 300 thousandths.

$32.207 < 32.3$

Talk About It

1. If 35 is greater than 4, why is 0.4 greater than 0.35?
2. Name two numbers between 1.52 and 1.53.
3. You are given two decimal numbers, and you need to decide which one is greater. Which part of the number should you look at first? Why?
4. Which method of comparing and ordering decimals would you prefer to use? Why?

Check

Use the data in the table for **1a** and **1b.**

1. Rank the earthquakes in order of their measure on the Richter scale.

   a. Locate the measurements on a number line like the one shown.

   8 8.1 8.2 8.3 8.4 8.5 8.6 8.7 8.8 8.9 9

   b. Annex zeros and compare the numbers.

Earthquakes		
1755	Lisbon, Portugal	8.75
1906	San Francisco, USA	8.3
1950	Assam, India	8.7
1977	Indonesia	8
1985	Mexico City, Mexico	8.1

2. **Reasoning** Maritess says 8.3 is to the left of 8.27 on the number line. Explain why Maritess' statement is incorrect.

Practice

Skills and Reasoning

Annex zeros so that the numbers have the same number of digits after the decimal point.

3. 0.276 and 0.28 **4.** 1.45 and 1.3942 **5.** 1.67 and 1.679 **6.** 0.3 and 0.4783

Use >, <, or = to compare each pair of numbers.

7. 0.193 ○ 0.187 **8.** 7.32 ○ 7.320 **9.** 52.1 ○ 52.16 **10.** 2.1 ○ 1.94

11. 5.07 ○ 5.16 **12.** 8.600 ○ 8.6 **13.** 21.7 ○ 21.07 **14.** 3.04 ○ 3.1

15. 66.77 ○ 67.77 **16.** 34.21 ○ 35.19 **17.** 98.23 ○ 98.3 **18.** 6.9 ○ 6.96

19. 4.6 ○ 4.60 **20.** 5.03 ○ 5.30 **21.** 30.1 ○ 30.11 **22.** 0.02 ○ 0.20

Order from least to greatest.

23. 27.948, 27.939, 27.946 **24.** 0.53, 0.534, 0.538 **25.** 1.23, 2.64, 1.5

26. 11.066, 11.0666, 11.66 **27.** 2.96, 2.84, 3.02 **28.** 0.1147, 0.217, 0.1146

29. 31.7, 31.07, 3.107, 30.17, 310.7 **30.** 2.12, 2.22, 1.22, 1.21, 2.21, 1.11

31. Reasoning Joel says 7.49 is greater than 7.6 because 49 is greater than 6. Explain why Joel's statement is incorrect.

32. Critical Thinking Write a number that has a thousandths place and is between 8.75 and 8.739. Explain how you chose the number.

Problem Solving and Applications

Use the graph for **33–35.** The lengths of the spiders, in no particular order, are 0.872, 0.989, 0.83, 0.746, and 0.675 inches.

33. How long is the golden-silk spider?

34. How long is the turret spider?

35. How long is the wolf spider?

Marbled Orb Weaver

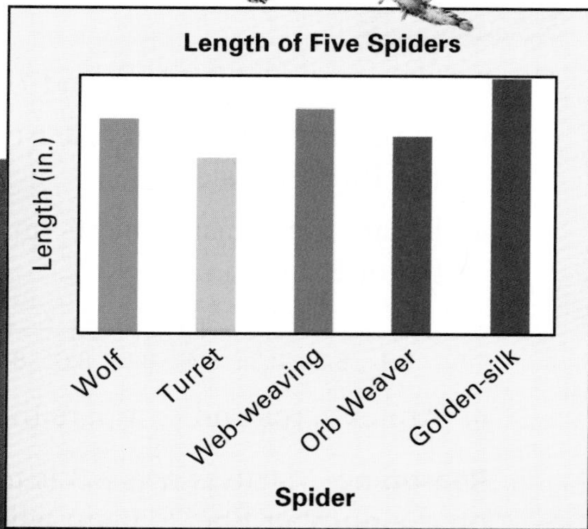

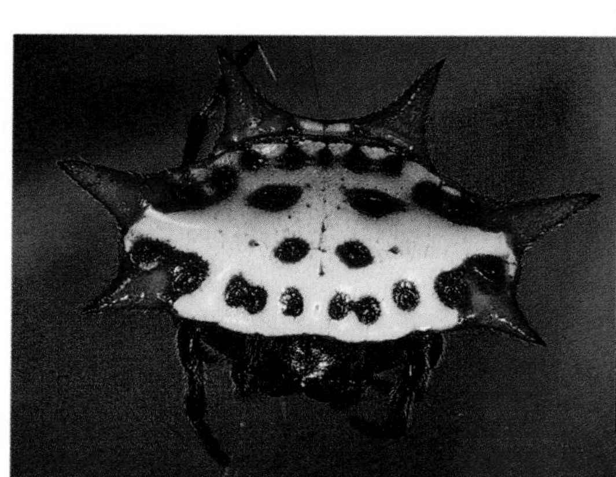

Web-Weaving Spider

36. The chart shows the finishing times for a swimming race. Who came in first, second, and third?

Swimmer	Time (sec)
Gabe	32.10
Raul	31.84
Josh	31.92

37. The track coach measured the running strides of her distance runners. Sue's stride was 1.34 m, Angela's was 1.41 m, and Temeca's was 1.4 m. The coach chose the two runners with the longest strides to run the 800-meter race. Whom did she choose?

38. Critical Thinking Letti's time in the 50-m freestyle was clocked to the thousandths place but rounded to 25.69 seconds. Give a possible slower time that would round to 25.69. Give a possible faster time that would round to 25.69. Explain.

39. Collecting Data Many libraries use the Dewey decimal system to arrange nonfiction books. Books are arranged in order of the Dewey decimal numbers. Go to the library and pick five books. List their Dewey decimal numbers in order from least to greatest.

40. Journal Explain how annexing zeros to decimal numbers helps you to compare and order them.

Mixed Review and Test Prep

For the given data, make a stem-and-leaf diagram.

41. 51, 42, 68, 32, 60, 61, 36, 49, 30, 47, 48, 61, 32, 44, 50, 52, 63, 51

42. 7, 9, 10, 13, 12, 11, 6, 4, 7, 3, 6, 10, 13, 16, 13, 11, 10, 7, 11, 8, 4, 11, 19

43. 16, 20, 23, 21, 21, 14, 21, 22, 22, 23, 18, 18, 21, 20, 19

State whether each equation is true for the given value.

44. $4x = 28$; $x = 7$ **45.** $25 - y = 20$; $y = 15$ **46.** $12 + p = 20$; $p = 16$

47. $16 - z = 9$; $z = 6$ **48.** $10x = 120$; $x = 12$ **49.** $b + 19 = 44$; $b = 25$

50. $46x = 0$; $x = 0$ **51.** $y - 12 = 30$; $y = 52$ **52.** $33 \div z = 11$; $z = 11$

53. Choose the group of numbers where the second number shows the first number rounded to the nearest hundredth.

Ⓐ 0.532, 0.52 Ⓑ 6.839, 6.9 Ⓒ 153.8, 200 Ⓓ 0.162, 0.16

Chapter 3 Lesson 4

Scientific Notation

Problem Solving Connection
- Look For a Pattern

Materials
scientific calculator

Vocabulary
scientific notation

Explore

According to scientists, spiders first appeared on Earth 350,000,000 years ago.

Numbers like 350,000,000 can be hard to work with because they have so many zeros. Scientists use **scientific notation** as an easier way to write these numbers.

A number in scientific notation is written as the product of a decimal number and a power of 10.

Work Together

1. Copy the table below. Continue the table for even exponents of 10 from 2 to 16. Use [y^x] to find how the calculator displays numbers given in exponent form. Example: To find 10^2, use 10 [y^x] 2 [=].

Exponent Form	Number of Factors of 10	Calculator Display	Number of Zeros in Standard Form
10^2	2	100	2
10^4	4	10000	4

Remember
An *exponent* tells how many times a number, the *base*, has been used as a factor.

$8 \times 8 \times 8 \times 8 \times 8$

8^5 ← exponent
↑
base

Read: 8 to the 5th power.

2. Describe any patterns you see in the table.
3. How does the number of zeros compare with the exponent?
4. In your own words, write a rule for evaluating 10 raised to any power.

Talk About It

5. Why doesn't the calculator display 1,000,000,000,000 for 10^{12}?
6. How would a calculator display 100,000,000,000,000,000,000?
7. Why do you think people use scientific notation when writing large numbers?

Connect and Learn

You can convert a number from standard form to scientific notation and from scientific notation to standard form.

Example 1

Convert 350,000,000 from standard form to scientific notation.

The first factor is a number greater than or equal to 1 but less than 10. Use the same digits as in the original number.

3.5 is the first factor.

The second factor is a power of 10 in exponent form. The exponent equals the number of places the decimal point moves to the left.

3.50000000 It moves 8 places.

10^8 is the second factor.

Standard Form		**Scientific Notation**
350,000,000	=	3.5×10^8

Example 2

Convert 5.2×10^7 from scientific notation to standard form.

Move the decimal point to the right the same number of places as the power.

Scientific Notation		**Standard Form**
5.2×10^7	=	52,000,000

Check

Write in standard form.

1. 3×10^4 **2.** 9.062×10^{10}

3. 6.8×10^3 **4.** 5.1087×10^9

Write in scientific notation.

5. 52,000 **6.** 1,740,000,000

7. 302,000 **8.** 18,052,000,000

9. Reasoning If you write 361,000 in scientific notation, will you write 3.61×10^5 or 361×10^3? Explain.

Practice

Skills and Reasoning

Write the missing exponent.

10. $47{,}000 = 4.7 \times 10^{■}$ **11.** $800{,}000 = 8 \times 10^{■}$ **12.** $5{,}380 = 5.38 \times 10^{■}$

13. $12{,}000 = 1.2 \times 10^{■}$ **14.** $4{,}500{,}000 = 4.5 \times 10^{■}$ **15.** $960 = 9.6 \times 10^{■}$

Write each number in standard form.

16. 8.3×10^3 **17.** 7.5×10^4 **18.** 6.7×10^6 **19.** 2×10^5

20. 6.89×10^4 **21.** 8.89×10^6 **22.** 2.3×10^2 **23.** 2.549×10^{12}

24. 1.02×10^2 **25.** 4.456×10^{11} **26.** 2.405×10^{14} **27.** 6.9×10^9

28. 7×10^{12} **29.** 3.7×10^5 **30.** 2.33×10^4 **31.** 5.7×10^7

Write each number in scientific notation.

32. 5,000 **33.** 3,200 **34.** 160,000 **35.** 4,700,000

36. 7,900,000,000 **37.** 99,000,000,000 **38.** 51 million **39.** 3 billion

40. 6 trillion **41.** 47,000 **42.** 500 **43.** 32,000,000

44. Complete the table.

Planet	km from Sun in Scientific Notation	km from Sun in Standard Form	km from Sun in Number-Word Form
Mercury	5.8×10^7		
Venus		110,000,000	
Earth			150 million
Mars	2.3×10^8		

Math Tip

Many calculators have an "EE" button that lets you put numbers in scientific notation.

45. **Science** The adult human body contains 5×10^{13} cells. Write this number in standard form.

46. **Science** Scientists believe there may be 3.5×10^4 kinds of spiders. Write this number in standard form.

47. **Science** Large female spiders can lay more than 2×10^3 eggs at one time. Write this number in standard form.

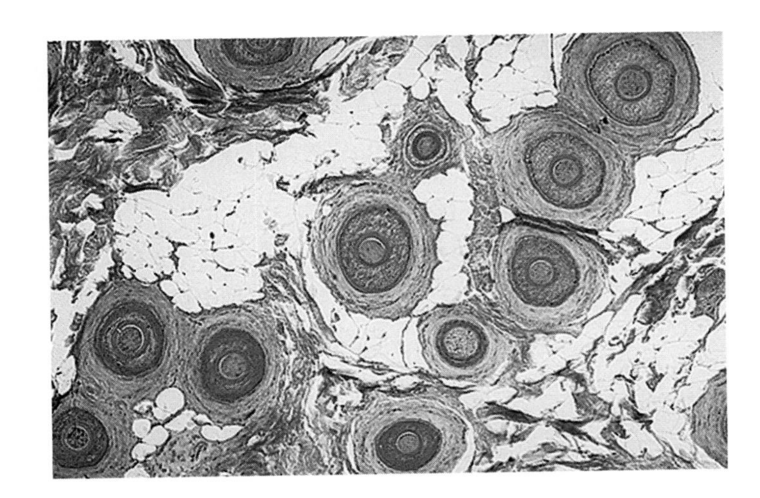

Problem Solving and Applications

48. Science In some species, newborn spiders travel to other areas by making parachutes out of their silk thread. Sailors more than 12,000,000 feet out at sea have seen these "flying" spiders. Write the number in scientific notation.

49. Time There are 6.048×10^5 seconds in one week. Write this number in standard form.

50. Social Science According to the *World Almanac*, there were 5.7 billion people on Earth in 1995. Write this number in scientific notation.

51. What If Scientists decide scientific notation should always have the second factor be 10^5. How would you write 2,600,000 in scientific notation?

52. Music In 1993, the U.S. Post Office released a large number of stamps picturing Elvis Presley. In scientific notation, the exponent is 8. The decimal factor has three digits, all of them odd. It's greater than 5.13, less than 5.19, and all the digits are different. How many Elvis Presley stamps were issued in 1993?

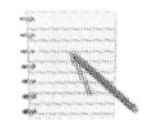

53. Journal How is the number of zeros at the end of 45,000,000,000 related to the exponent in 4.5×10^{10}?

Mixed Review and Test Prep

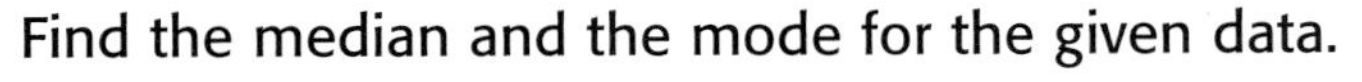

Find the median and the mode for the given data.

54. Number of minutes spent brushing teeth: 5, 7, 5, 3, 12, 8, 6, 8, 10, 11, 7

55. Number of left-handed students in each class: 3, 0, 2, 1, 1, 0, 2, 2, 0, 2

Solve.

56. $5h = 50$ **57.** $m - 13 = 20$ **58.** $20 + p = 32$ **59.** $\frac{36}{b} = 6$

60. Choose the group of decimal numbers that is in order from least to greatest.

Ⓐ 0.34, 0.35, 0.306 Ⓑ 1.2, 2.4, 3.1 Ⓒ 10.21, 10.124, 10.209

SECTION A

Review and Practice

Vocabulary

1. Which of the following is an example of scientific notation?

   Ⓐ 8.6 Ⓑ 8.6×10^4 Ⓒ 86,000 Ⓓ eighty-six thousand

(Lesson 1) Write each as a decimal.

2. $\frac{7}{10}$ 3. $\frac{49}{100}$ 4. twenty-six and five-tenths 5. sixty-three hundredths

(Lesson 2) Measure each length to the nearest centimeter.

6. 

7. 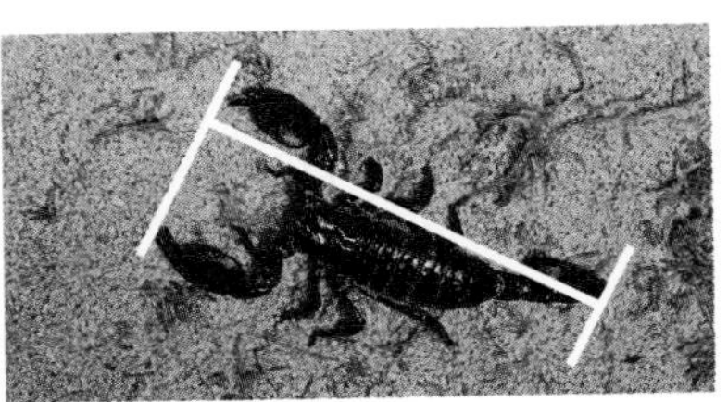

Round to the underlined place value.

8. $0.\underline{1}4$ 9. $0.3\underline{5}1$ 10. $2.4\underline{1}7$ 11. $0.08\underline{1}3$ 12. $6.\underline{9}68$ 13. $1.98\underline{2}7$

(Lesson 3) Use >, <, or = to compare each pair of numbers.

14. 0.507 ● 0.57 15. 17.802 ● 17.8 16. 1.09 ● 1.090 17. 0.029 ● 0.091

Order from least to greatest.

18. 12.6, 12.68, 13.2, 12.08 19. 0.78, 0.078, 0.708 20. 4.09, 5.0, 4.99, 4.80

21. In a potato-sack race, Tina crossed the finish line in 51.8 seconds, Luis finished in 51.9 seconds, and Nona finished in 50.3 seconds. List the racers in order from fastest to slowest.

(Lesson 4) Write each number in standard form.

22. 7×10^3 23. 1.2×10^8

24. 2.92×10^5 25. 5.6×10^5

Write each number in scientific notation.

26. 45 billion 27. 480,000

28. 6,780,000 29. 63 trillion

30. 4,500 31. 32 million

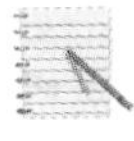

32. **Journal** Explain how you would round 5.96 to the nearest tenth.

Skills Checklist

In this section, you have:

- ☑ **Learned About Decimal Notation**
- ☑ **Rounded Decimal Numbers**
- ☑ **Compared and Ordered Decimals**
- ☑ **Learned About Scientific Notation**

REVIEW AND PRACTICE

CHAPTER 3

SECTION

B Adding and Subtracting with Decimals

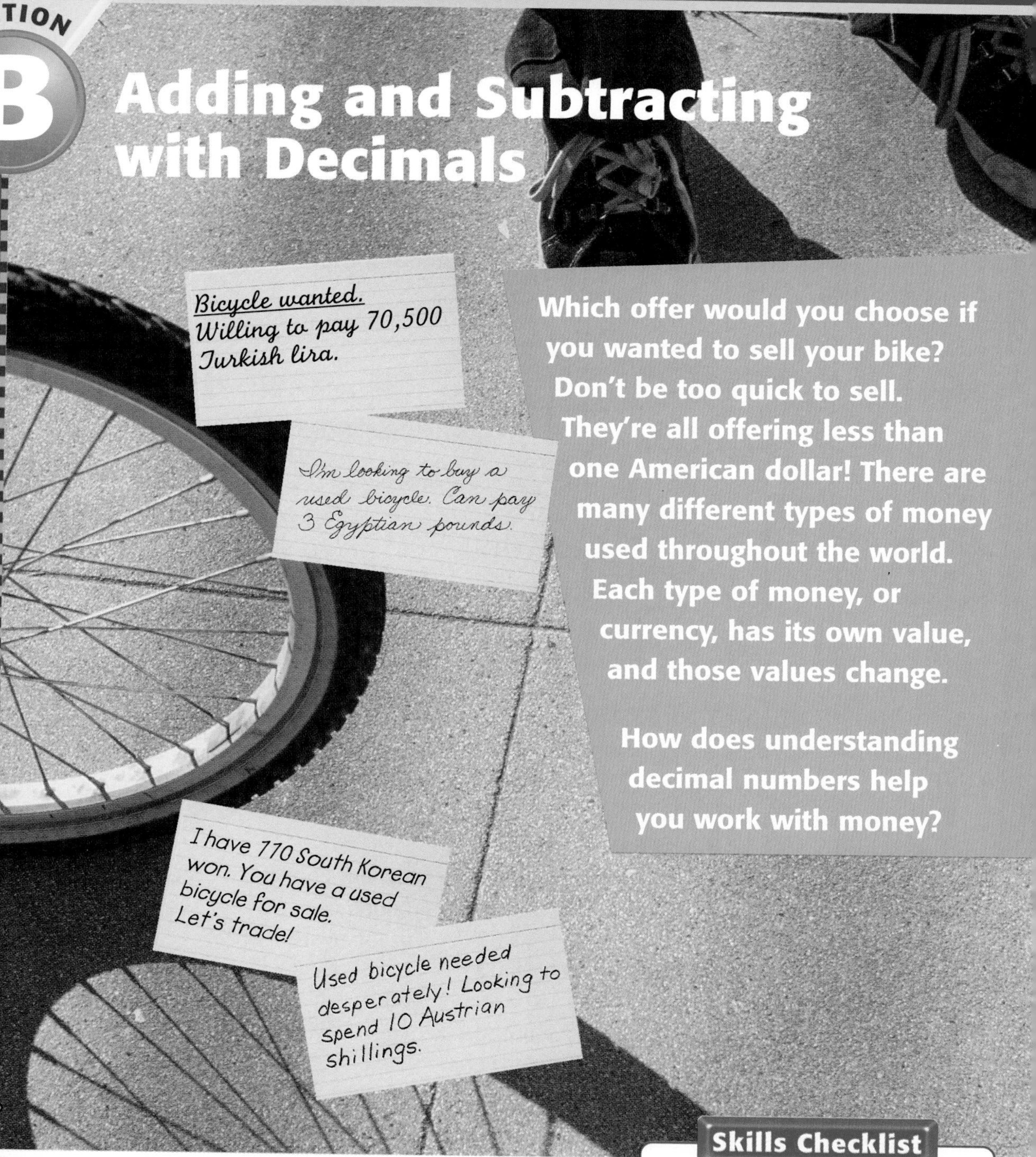

Bicycle wanted. Willing to pay 70,500 Turkish lira.

I'm looking to buy a used bicycle. Can pay 3 Egyptian pounds.

I have 770 South Korean won. You have a used bicycle for sale. Let's trade!

Used bicycle needed desperately! Looking to spend 10 Austrian shillings.

Which offer would you choose if you wanted to sell your bike? Don't be too quick to sell. They're all offering less than one American dollar! There are many different types of money used throughout the world. Each type of money, or currency, has its own value, and those values change.

How does understanding decimal numbers help you work with money?

GET READY!

Estimating

Review estimating. Estimate each sum or difference.

1. $567 + 317$
2. $4{,}262 - 2{,}189$
3. $12{,}356 + 18{,}703 + 14{,}491$
4. $679 - 223$
5. $17 + 9 + 12 + 16 + 6 + 7$
6. $303 - 144$
7. $65{,}158 + 22{,}834$
8. $7{,}263 - 2{,}271$

Skills Checklist

In this section, you will:

- ❒ Estimate Sums, Differences, Products, and Quotients with Decimals
- ❒ Add and Subtract Decimal Numbers
- ❒ Solve Decimal Equations: Addition and Subtraction

You Will Learn

- how to estimate sums, differences, products, and quotients with decimals

Learn

Here's the menu for International Night at the Buena Vista School. How can you estimate if certain combinations of foods from the menu could be purchased?

You can use rounding to estimate sums and differences with decimals.

Did You Know?

Many countries use a unit of currency called the *dollar.* They include Australia, Canada, Jamaica, New Zealand, Singapore, Taiwan, and the United States.

Example 1

Tanya wants to try miso soup, dal, and lasagna. She has $10. Is this enough?

$2.95	→	$3.00	Round each number
$0.89	→	$1.00	to the nearest dollar.
$5.75	→	$6.00	
		$10.00	Add.

The cost is about $10.00. Since Tanya rounded up, the actual sum is less than the estimate. Tanya has enough money to buy the soup, dal, and lasagna.

You can also use rounding to estimate a decimal product or quotient.

Example 2

Estimate $34.95 \div 7.39$.

$$\begin{array}{ccccc} 34.95 & \div & 7.39 & = & ? \\ \downarrow & & \downarrow & & \\ 35 & \div & 7 & = & 5 \end{array}$$

So, $34.95 \div 7.39 \approx 5$.

Rounded numbers may not always be easier to use than the original numbers. *Compatible numbers* often work better for estimating decimal products and quotients.

Remember
Compatible numbers are numbers that can be computed easily, such as $75 + 25$ or 4×100.

Example 3

Estimate 9.38×23.15.

$9.38 \rightarrow 10$ Choose numbers compatible for multiplying.

$23.15 \rightarrow 23$

$10 \times 23 = 230$

So, $9.38 \times 23.15 \approx 230$.

Example 4

Estimate \$158.75 ÷ \$28.95.

\$158.75 → \$150 Choose numbers compatible for dividing.

\$28.95 → \$30

\$150 ÷ \$30 = \$5

So, \$158.75 ÷ \$28.95 ≈ \$5.

Talk About It

1. How can you decide whether a decimal estimate is high or low?
2. Some problems involving decimals require an exact answer. For others, an estimate is good enough. Give an example of each.
3. How do basic facts help you when estimating decimal products and quotients?

Check

Choose the better estimate.

1. 3.125×2.56; 6 or 9
2. $365.1 \div 6.2$; 60 or 70
3. $2.18 + 6.95 + 8.2$; 16 or 17
4. $93.1 - 34.061$; 60 or 70

Estimate each sum, difference, product or quotient.

5. \$14.63 + \$19.26
6. $58.37 - 22.84$
7. 67.52×9.18
8. $47.13 \div 6.4$
9. 42.83×11.3
10. $16.8 + 19.53$
11. $19.75 \div 3.8$
12. $62.44 - 12.02$
13. **Reasoning** Selina thinks 70 is a better estimate for 9.45×7.8. Luis thinks 80 is a better estimate. Which do you think is a better estimate? Explain.

Practice

Skills and Reasoning

Choose the better estimate.

14. 5.714×8.53; 40 or 50

15. $124.93 \div 5.17$; 20 or 25

16. $39.76 - 30.02$; 10 or 15

17. $0.35 + 3.8029$; 4 or 5

Estimate each sum, difference, product, or quotient.

18. $\$31.27 + \$18.52$ **19.** $\$5.93 - \$3.68$ **20.** $\$4.98 \times 9$ **21.** $39.43 \div 8$

22. $10.581 - 1.203$ **23.** $6.53 + 2.48$ **24.** $15.391 - 8.67$ **25.** 62.3×4.9

26. 27.32×4.09 **27.** $\$7.84 \times 28$ **28.** $30.49 \div 4.7$ **29.** $31.23 \div 5.1$

30. $35.617 + 0.816$ **31.** $89.632 - 47.32$ **32.** 14.32×2.26 **33.** $36.26 + 36.7$

34. $\$8.47 - \$1.26$ **35.** 1.628×82.09 **36.** $23.42 + 89.67$ **37.** 27.83×62.9

38. $65.298 + 14.83$ **39.** $\$102.36 \div 48.2$ **40.** $63.501 - 3.999$ **41.** $37.32 \div 5.99$

42. $0.756 + 63.5$ **43.** 93.278×86.059 **44.** $12.89 - 10.432$ **45.** 45.01×16.3

46. To estimate $70.69 \div 8.51$, would you round the numbers or use compatible numbers? Explain.

Problem Solving and Applications

Use the picture for **47** and **48**.

47. Estimation About how many CDs could you buy with $40? With $20?

48. Estimation One week the music store sold 35 copies of the more expensive CD. Estimate how much money the store collected from those sales.

49. Health Carlos's dad uses a pedometer to determine how far he walks. He walked 16.4 km in 5 days. Estimate how far he walked each day.

50. Critical Thinking You bought four pairs of pants at the same price. Based on rounding, your estimate of the total cost was $40 before tax.

a. If you rounded to the nearest dollar, what is the maximum price for each pair? Explain.

b. If you rounded to the nearest dollar, what is the minimum price? Explain.

Problem Solving and CAREERS

Fabric designers purchase supplies, such as paints and inks, and fabrics, such as silk, cotton, and wool. They often use estimates when purchasing these supplies.

51. If natural silk costs \$4.75 a square yd, about how much will it cost for 30 square yd?

52. A designer chooses to use a silk-screen printing process to produce 300 yards of fabric. About how much black ink will be needed if 0.18 gal is needed for each yard?

53. To produce fabric for a dress, a designer spends \$18.87 for fabric and \$6.35 for inks. Estimate the cost to the nearest dollar to produce the fabric for the dress.

54. **Using Data** Myron has \$20.75 in U.S. dollars to spend on fabric while in India. Use the Data File on page 135 to determine if he has enough money to purchase a bolt of fabric on sale for 600 rupees.

55. **Journal** Describe a situation involving money where it makes more sense to estimate high. Then describe a situation where it makes more sense to estimate low.

Mixed Review and Test Prep

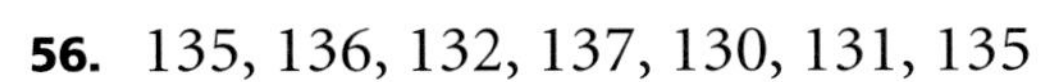

STAY SHARP!

Find the mean of each set of data.

56. 135, 136, 132, 137, 130, 131, 135 **57.** 72, 68, 55, 62, 70, 57, 72

Write each fraction as a decimal.

58. $\frac{78}{100}$ **59.** $\frac{32}{100}$ **60.** $\frac{3}{10}$ **61.** $\frac{789}{1000}$ **62.** $\frac{560}{100}$

Insert parentheses to make each statement true.

63. $3 \times 4 - 2 = 6$ **64.** $3 + 3^2 \div 3 = 4$ **65.** $16 - 5 \times 2 = 6$ **66.** $40 \div 40 + 40 = 41$

Solve each equation.

67. $4d = 32$ **68.** $8 + m = 21$ **69.** $35 - x = 14$ **70.** $\frac{81}{x} = 27$

71. Choose the best estimate for $676 + 20$.

Ⓐ 675 Ⓑ 690 Ⓒ 700 Ⓓ 725

Chapter 3
Lesson
6

Adding and Subtracting Decimal Numbers

Problem Solving Connection
- Draw a Picture

Materials
- 10×10 grids
- colored pencils

Explore

Adding and subtracting decimals is similar to adding and subtracting whole numbers.

Work Together

1. Use a 10×10 grid to find $0.14 + 0.67$.
   - **a.** Shade the tenths for the first number.
   - **b.** Use a different color to shade the tenths for the second number.
   - **c.** Shade the hundredths for the first number.
   - **d.** Use a different color to shade the hundredths for the second number.
   - **e.** Describe the number shown in the grid.

$$\begin{array}{r} 0.14 \\ +\ 0.67 \\ \hline 0.81 \end{array}$$

2. Use grids to find each sum.
   a. $0.35 + 0.42$ **b.** $0.63 + 0.20$ **c.** $0.16 + 0.77$ **d.** $0.03 + 0.07$
3. Use a 10×10 grid to find $0.75 - 0.36$.
   - **a.** Shade the first number.
   - **b.** Cross out the second number from the first number.
   - **c.** Describe the amount left in the grid.

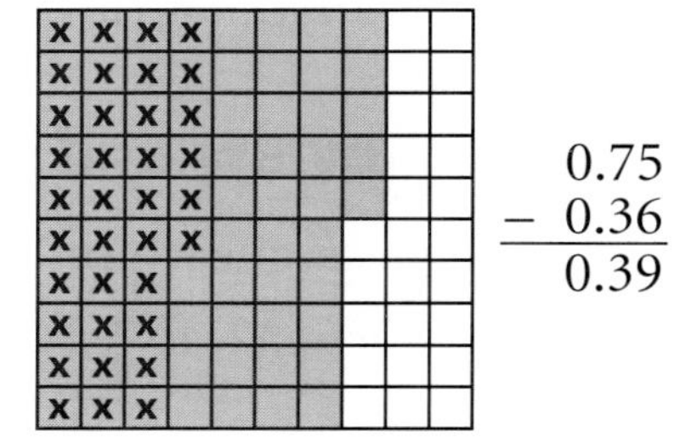

4. Use grids to find each difference.
   a. $0.68 - 0.27$ **b.** $0.93 - 0.40$ **c.** $0.52 - 0.08$ **d.** $0.88 - 0.49$

Talk About It

5. In the problem $0.03 + 0.07$, both addends have hundredths. When you add, are there any hundredths in the answer? Explain.
6. In the problem $0.52 - 0.08$, how can you take eight hundredths away from the first number when the first number only has two hundredths?
7. Could you use the grids to find $0.6 + 0.3$? Explain.
8. Could you use the grids to find $0.006 - 0.003$? Explain.

Connect and Learn

When you add, you must make sure you're adding tenths to tenths, hundredths to hundredths, and so on. To do this, make sure to line up the decimal points. Then add as if you were adding whole numbers.

Example 1

Add 1.7 and 2.49.

$$\begin{array}{r} 1.7 \\ +\ 2.49 \\ \hline 4.19 \end{array}$$

Line up the decimal points.

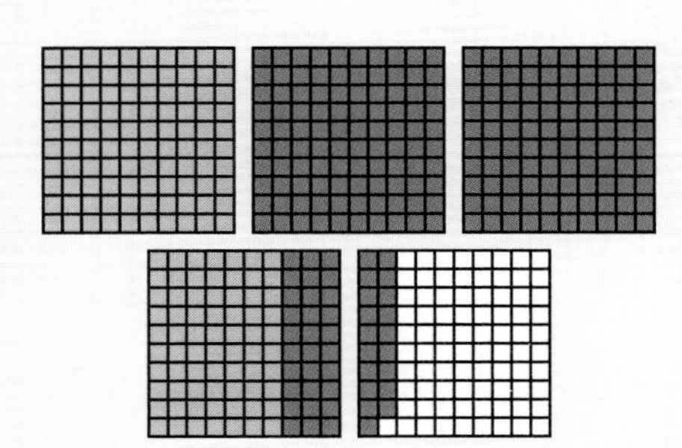

Estimate: $2 + 2 = 4$

Since 4.19 is close to the estimate of 4, the answer is reasonable.

Use the same plan when subtracting decimals. Line up the decimal points and then subtract as if you were subtracting whole numbers. Annex zeros if the second number has more digits after the decimal point than the first.

Remember

Annexing zeros to the right of a decimal number does not change the value of the number.

Example 2

The United Kingdom uses a decimal currency based on the pound (£). Paul has £1.8. Edmund has only £1.38. How many more pounds does Paul have?

Subtract to find the difference.

$$\begin{array}{r} 1.8\mathbf{0} \\ -\ 1.38 \\ \hline 0.42 \end{array}$$

Line up the decimal points.
Annex zeros.

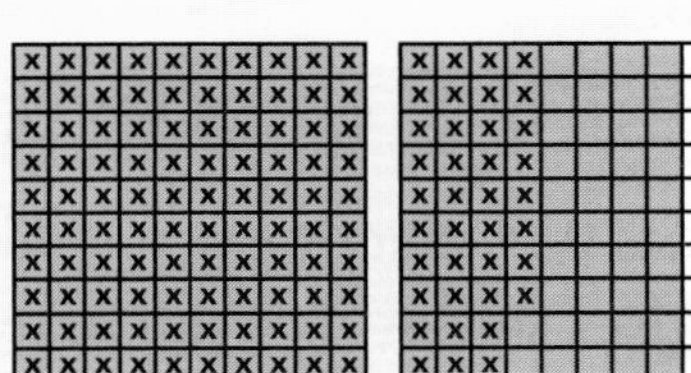

Paul has £0.42 more than Edmund.

Estimate to tenths: $1.8 - 1.4 = 0.4$

Since 0.42 is close to 0.4, the answer is reasonable.

Check

Find each sum or difference.

1. $4.631 + 3.986$
2. $8.592 - 4.635$
3. $5.6 + 1.973$
4. $7.3 - 4.45$
5. $0.04 + 18.6$
6. $9.72 - 1.80$
7. $2.5 - 0.25$
8. $0.198 + 1.18$
9. **Reasoning** Will drew this grid to model $0.4 + 0.25$. Is he correct? Explain.

Practice

Skills and Reasoning

Choose the equation that each grid models.

10.

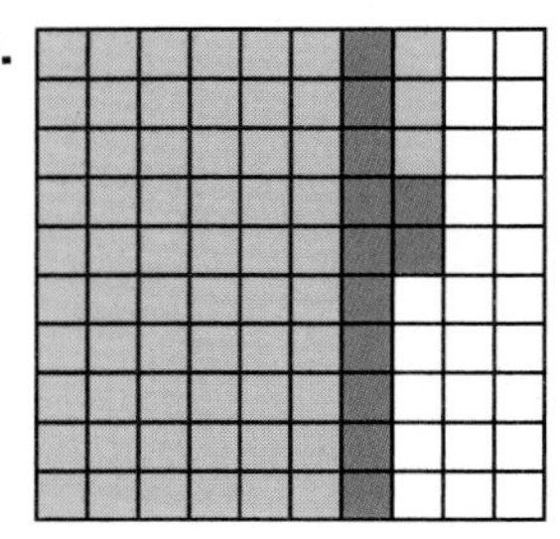

a. $0.63 + 0.12 = 0.75$

b. $0.63 + 0.21 = 0.51$

11.

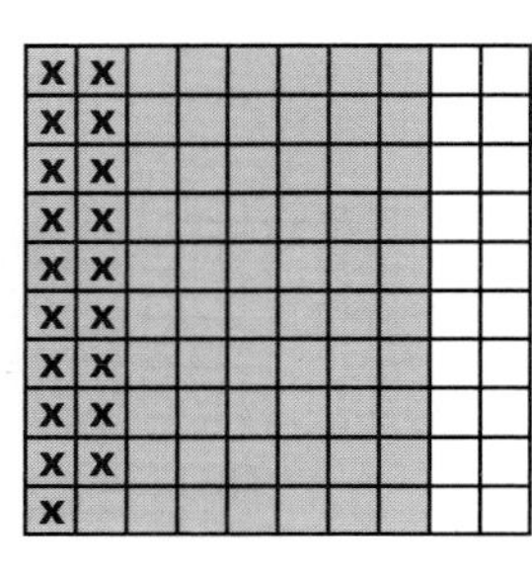

a. $0.80 - 0.28 = 0.99$

b. $0.80 - 0.19 = 0.61$

12.

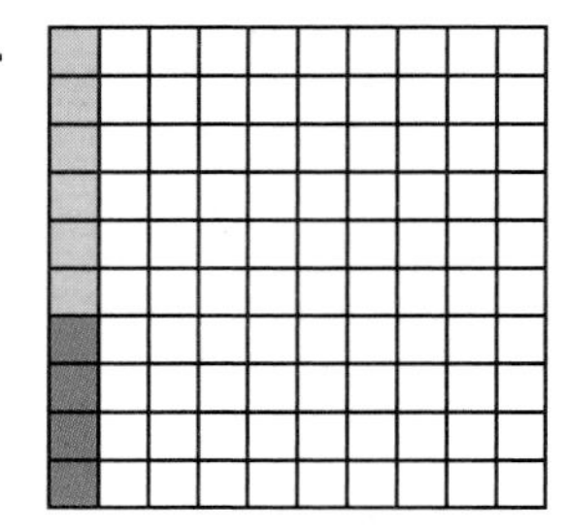

a. $0.06 + 0.04 = 0.10$

b. $0.05 + 0.04 = 1.00$

Simplify.

13. $3.56 + 8.75$ **14.** $94.716 - 47.81$ **15.** $34.982 - 8.52$ **16.** $8.2 + 0.2$

17. $7.5 - 0.492$ **18.** $\$25 - \$13.75$ **19.** $23.05 + 67.06$ **20.** $12.904 + 13$

21. $3.05 + 4.902$ **22.** $78.234 - 12.0056$ **23.** $14 - 7.95$ **24.** $0.001 + 0.06$

25. $3.2 - 1.2$ **26.** $\$38 - \$27.99$ **27.** $74.008 + 1.021$ **28.** $11.6 + 2.78$

29. $54.81 + 54.81$ **30.** $506 - 63.8178$ **31.** $60.49 - 44.72$ **32.** $34.8 + 6.89$

33. $\$4.26 + \$32.07 + \$0.52$ **34.** $6.3 + 7.23 + 29.1$ **35.** $50 + 2.852 + 13.6$

36. $\$72.61 + \$1.45 + \$2.51$ **37.** $4.5 + 2.78 + 30.01$ **38.** $7.8 + 80 + 16.87$

39. Use each of the digits 0–9 exactly once. Make two decimal numbers whose sum is close to 2 and whose difference is close to 1.

Problem Solving and Applications

40. Critical Thinking You and your friend won a radio contest and get to be DJs for part of a day. You must put together a 15-minute segment of consecutive songs chosen from the list. No more than 2 minutes can be left at the end of the set.

a. Which songs would you pick?

b. How much time would the songs use?

c. How much time would you have left at the end of your segment?

d. What is the maximum number of songs that you could choose to fill 15 minutes?

SONGS	TIME
Born in the USA (Bruce Springsteen)	4.65 min
On Bended Knee (Boyz II Men)	5.48 min
Old Time Rock and Roll (Bob Seger)	3.21 min
I Only Want To Be With You (Hootie and the Blowfish)	3.76 min
Are You Ready For This? (B2 Unlimited)	3.77 min
YMCA (Village People)	3.48 min

Problem Solving and SOCIAL STUDIES

The exchange rates of foreign currency can change on a daily basis. These rates are based on international demand for different currencies. For instance, if American consumers buy more British products, the U.S. demand for the British pound increases and the pound rises in value against the U.S. dollar.

41. One day, 1 Japanese yen was worth 0.0098 U.S. dollars. The same day, a Swedish krona was worth 0.1297 U.S. dollars.

a. How much more was the krona worth than the yen that day?

b. On the same day, 1 Thai baht was worth 0.0398 U.S. dollars. How much U.S. money equals one baht plus one yen?

42. One day, one U.S. dollar was worth 149.149 Spanish pesetas. How many Spanish pesetas would two U.S. dollars be worth?

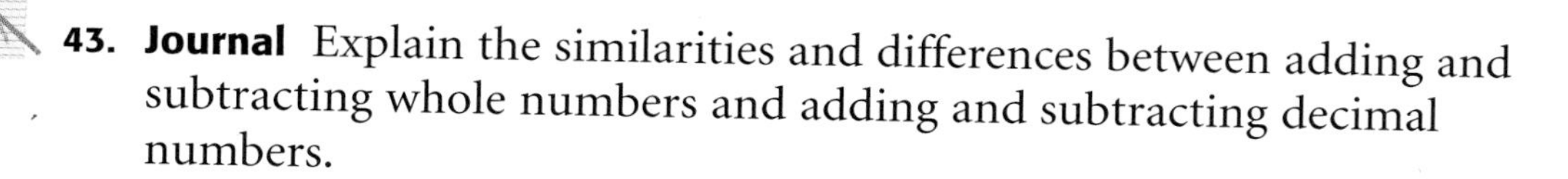

43. Journal Explain the similarities and differences between adding and subtracting whole numbers and adding and subtracting decimal numbers.

PRACTICE AND APPLY

Mixed Review and Test Prep

STAY SHARP!

Find the mean, median, and modes with and without the outlier. Then describe how the outlier affects the mean.

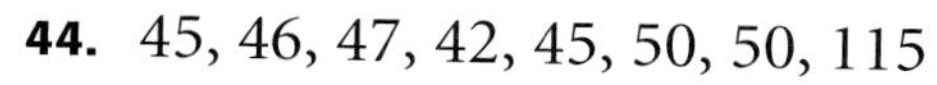

44. 45, 46, 47, 42, 45, 50, 50, 115

45. 23, 68, 19, 22, 20, 21, 20

46. 10, 10, 10, 12, 12, 11, 11, 11, 18

47. 42, 38, 39, 40, 41, 37, 2, 35, 35

Round to the given place value.

48. 0.273, hundredths

49. 5.998, thousandths

50. 62.73, tenths

51. 34.5, ones

52. 2.006, hundredths

53. 0.156, tenths

Simplify each expression.

54. $4 + (12 - 6) \times 2$

55. $50 \div 5 - (2 + 2)$

56. $64 \div 8 + 2 \times 7$

57. Jamie is 62 in. tall. He is 8 in. taller than Crystal. Which of the following equations would you solve to find Crystal's height?

Ⓐ $62 + n = 8$ Ⓑ $n - 8 = 62$ Ⓒ $8n = 62$ Ⓓ $62 - n = 8$

and Practice

Write each as a decimal.

1. $\frac{38}{100}$ **2.** $\frac{5}{10}$ **3.** six and four-tenths **4.** ninety-two hundredths

Round to the underlined place value.

5. $0.\underline{2}8$ **6.** $0.7\underline{4}3$ **7.** $3.4\underline{5}2$ **8.** $0.09\underline{4}8$ **9.** $5.\underline{8}74$ **10.** $2.7\underline{6}14$

Use $>$, $<$, or $=$ to compare each pair of numbers.

11. 0.468 ● 0.472 **12.** 0.248 ● 0.24 **13.** 1.34 ● 1.340 **14.** 35.8 ● 35.08

Simplify.

15. $2.83 + 5.16$ **16.** $12.25 - 10.73$ **17.** $5.2 + 0.9$ **18.** $24.982 - 5.64$

19. $15 + 18.96$ **20.** $11.5 - 0.863$ **21.** $29.405 - 5.83$ **22.** $10.5 + .5$

23. \$25 − \$9.78 **24.** $3{,}125 + 0.78$ **25.** $704 - 62.35$ **26.** $3.04 + 7.168$

27. \$83 + \$15.59 **28.** $50.24 - 31.67$ **29.** $18 - 6.32$ **30.** $58.341 - 14.0072$

31. $0.08 + 42.094$ **32.** \$10.57 − \$1.89 **33.** $1.03 + 491.6$ **34.** $0.92 - 0.03$

35. $0.806 - 0.3$ **36.** $3.1 - 0.04$ **37.** \$19.04 + \$5.50 **38.** $1.7 + 60.3$

39. $15 + 230.09$ **40.** $62.843 - 57.009$ **41.** $8.3 + 9.47$ **42.** $29 - 0.42$

43. \$1,025 − \$28.65 **44.** $26.08 - 0.5$ **45.** $0.08 - 0.013$ **46.** $19.308 + 4.07$

47. $70 + 1.384 + 29.6$ **48.** $0.89 + 7 + 64.5$ **49.** $159.6 + 0.04 + 35.801$

50. $0.85 + 1.53 + 0.29$ **51.** $1.02 + 0.70 + 100$ **52.** \$15.76 + \$6.49 + \$0.38

Error Search

Find each sum or difference that is not correct. Write it correctly and explain the error.

53. $1.78 + 32.5 = 5.03$ **54.** \$54 − \$1.26 = \$52.74 **55.** $54.02 - 1.013 = 43.89$

56. $12.6 + 30.4 = 43$ **57.** $1.09 + 21.11 = 2.22$ **58.** \$23.79 − \$14.89 = \$8.90

Get to the Point!

Simplify. Match each answer to a number below the blanks. Then find the answer to the question. Some letters are not used.

___	___	___	___	___	___	___	___
18.78	0.17	$11.25	91.645	0.17	7,039	91.645	18.78

___	___	___	___	___	___
1.866	56.95	48.7	1.866	180.09	18.78

___	___	___	___	___
1.866	68.11	91.645	1.866	18.79

59. $3.7 + 15.09$ (D) **60.** $19.5 - 0.72$ (S) **61.** $9.45 - 0.92$ (C) **62.** $7{,}010.5 + 28.5$ (N)

63. $54 + 126.09$ (Y) **64.** $11.5 - 0.863$ (U) **65.** $49.15 + 7.8$ (L) **66.** $38.5 + 9.5 + 0.7$ (W)

67. \$74 − \$68.96 (R) **68.** $0.92 + 0.946$ (A) **69.** $0.45 - 0.28$ (O) **70.** $51.007 - 3.049$ (I)

71. \$12 − \$0.75 (M) **72.** $1.05 - 0.13$ (B) **73.** $2.3 + 65.81$ (H) **74.** $2.615 + 89.03$ (E)

Number Sense Estimation and Reasoning

Copy and complete. Write $>$, $<$, or $=$. Use properties and estimation to help.

75. $2.902 + 10$ ● $29.02 + 10$ **76.** $8 - 0.76$ ● $8 - 0.92$

77. $35.46 - 1.7$ ● $35.46 - 1.8$ **78.** $0.58 - 0.06$ ● $0.68 - 0.06$

79. $1.75 + 1.25$ ● $1.45 + 1.55$ **80.** $1.68 + 20.76$ ● $16.8 + 2.076$

81. $0.0563 + 1$ ● $0.563 + 1$ **82.** $67.8 - 2.46$ ● $67.03 - 0.01$

Chapter 3
Lesson
7

Solving Decimal Equations: Addition and Subtraction

You Will Learn

- how to solve equations that involve adding and subtracting decimals

Learn

William is busy! He lives where the sun shines and the plants grow . . . all year round! This is quite an asset for his lawn-maintenance business. As with any business, William has to keep an accurate record of his expenses and income. This month his expenses were \$8.50. He collected \$96.75 from his clients.

William lives in Orlando, Florida.

You can solve addition and subtraction equations involving decimals by using subtraction to work backward.

Did You Know?

Grass is classified into six main groups. Grasses used to cover lawns, playgrounds, parks, and fields are known as turfgrasses.

Example 1

What was William's profit this month?

Let x = William's profit.

$\$8.50 + x = \$96.75$ Read as "What number plus \$8.50 equals \$96.75?"

$x = \$96.75 - \$8.50$ Use subtraction to work backward.

$x = \$88.25$

$\$8.50 + \$88.25 = \$96.75$ Substitute \$88.25 for x.

$\$96.75 = \$96.75$ Check to see that the equation is true.

William's profit was \$88.25.

You can also use mental math to solve equations.

Example 2

Solve $x - 2.3 = 3.4$ Read "What number minus 2.3 equals 3.4?

$5.7 - 2.3 = 3.4$ Use mental math.

$3.4 = 3.4$ Check to see that the equation is true.

The value of x is 5.7.

Sometimes you need to add before you can use mental math or work backward to solve equations.

Example 3

This diagram shows the measurements of two sides of a triangle. The total distance around the triangle is also given. Find the length of the unknown side.

Let $x =$ the length of the unknown side.

Distance = 19.8 cm

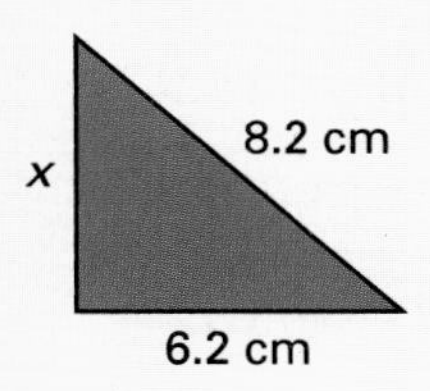

$x + 8.2 + 6.2 = 19.8$	Add 8.2 and 6.2
$x + 14.4 = 19.8$	
$5.4 + 14.4 = 19.8$	Use mental math.
$19.8 = 19.8$	Check to see that the equation is true.

The length of the unknown side is 5.4 cm.

Talk About It

1. How can you decide whether to use mental math or to work backward?
2. Could a subtraction problem be used to describe the length of the unknown side in Example 3?

Check

Solve each equation.

1. $x + 9.4 = 19.5$
2. $n - 0.5 = 10.1$
3. $j + 7.1 = 12.2$
4. $p - 2.0 = 0.2$
5. $8.6 - p = 3.7$
6. $4.2 + x = 6.3$
7. $y - 3.5 = 6$
8. $n + 0.7 = 19.2$
9. $2.7 + r = 9.1$
10. $6.1 - c = 3.3$
11. $7.5 + z = 10.1$
12. $14.8 - a = 3.7$

Given the distance around each shape, find the length of the unknown side.

13. **Distance = 14.7 m**

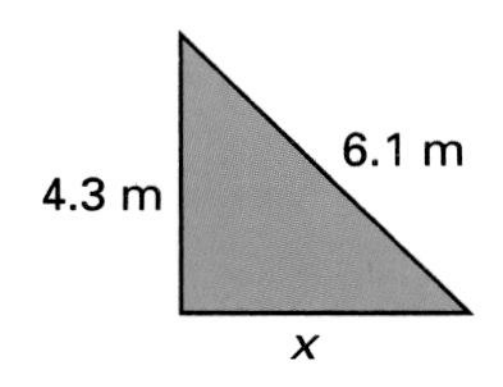

14. **Distance = 23.3 ft**

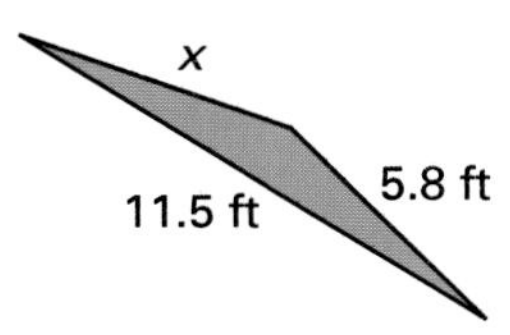

15. **Reasoning** Would you solve $4.3 + x = 7.7$ the same way you would solve $x + 4.3 = 7.7$?

Practice

Skills and Reasoning

State if each equation is true or false for $h = 1.4$.

16. $h - 1.3 = 0.1$ **17.** $h + 2.4 = 4.0$ **18.** $0.6 + h = 2.0$ **19.** $5.8 - h = 3.4$

Solve.

20. $11.6 - b = 8.3$ **21.** $0.12 + d = 0.52$ **22.** $\$75.40 + n = \$100$

23. $x + 5.7 = 13.8$ **24.** $y - 10.1 = 60$ **25.** $u + \$12.60 = \$14.97$

26. $25.001 - n = 24$ **27.** $w + 7.4 = 35.6$ **28.** $p - 4.01 = 15.08$

29. $1.12 + a = 2.34$ **30.** $0.06 - v = 0.02$ **31.** $c + 14.99 = 15.01$

32. $e + 4.35 = 10.5$ **33.** $\$16.75 + f = \$20$ **34.** $g + 8.7 = 10.1$

35. $i - 42.7 = 45$ **36.** $j + 0.088 = 0.099$ **37.** $m - 0.035 = 0.053$

38. $r + 32.45 = 62.78$ **39.** $3.43 - w = 1.11$ **40.** $k + \$66.45 = \$76.90$

41. $100.7 - z = 40.7$ **42.** $l - 682 = 0.251$ **43.** $t + 1.33 = 2$

Given the distance around each shape, find the length of the unknown side.

44.

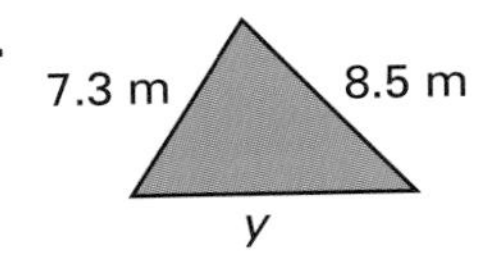

Distance = 25.5 m

45.

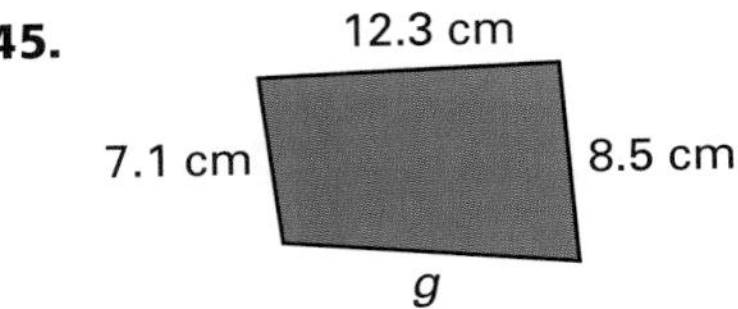

Distance = 40 cm

46. Critical Thinking Maurice has 30 m of fence to make a rectangular dog run. The width can only be 3.75 m because of the shape of his yard. What is the maximum length of the dog run?

47. Reasoning Would $2.3 + 4.1 + x = 10$ result in the same value for x as $6.4 + x = 10$? Explain.

48. Samantha said that the value of x in the equation $8.6 + x = 12.8$ was 21.4. Is she correct? Explain.

49. Write Your Own Problem Write a word problem modeled by $2.2 + 2.2 + 3.1 + x = 12.8$. Then draw a diagram for your word problem. Include a solution to the problem. Exchange problems with a classmate and solve.

Problem Solving and Applications

Write and solve an equation for each situation.

50. A store owner obtained a jacket for \$46.25 and sold it for \$66.75. What was the profit?

51. A pair of tennis shoes cost the owner \$26.49. She wants to make a profit of \$18.50. What should the selling price be?

Problem Solving Hint

When a store buys something at one price and then sells it at a higher price, the difference in prices is called the *profit*.

52. Critical Thinking In West Lafayette, the fine for a speeding ticket in dollars is \$32.62 + x, where x is the miles per hour over the speed limit.

a. What is the fine for going 38.6 mi/hr in a 25 mi/hr school zone?

b. Ed was fined \$50.50 for speeding in this school zone. How fast was he traveling?

53. Jorge won a cash prize in a contest. He donated half of the money to his Boy Scout troop. Then he spent \$19.49 on a computer game and put the rest, \$30.51, into his savings account. How much money did he win?

54. Patterns Study the pattern:

$x + 3.2 = 9.2$

$x + 6.4 = 12.4$

$x + 9.6 = 15.6$

a. What is the value of x?

b. What are the next three equations in this pattern?

55. Journal Change one digit in $x + 2.3 = 8.6$ so that the value of x is 6.1.

Mixed Review and Test Prep

STAY SHARP!

Order from least to greatest

56. 4.65, 4.663, 4.664 **57.** 0.123, 1.784, 0.672 **58.** 32.5, 32.67, 32.495

Write each number in word form.

59. 560,326,700,000 **60.** 4,983,229 **61.** 2,892,000,362,421 **62.** 763,218

63. Choose the correct value for x: $x + 311 = 423$.

Ⓐ 112 Ⓑ 734 Ⓒ 188 Ⓓ not here

Chapter 3

Problem Solving

Compare Strategies: Work Backward/Guess & Check

You Will Learn

- when to use the Work Backward and the Guess and Check strategies

Learn

Christopher and Erin are numismatists. (*Numismatists* study or collect coins or paper money.) They have two buffalo-head nickels in their collection. The value of one coin is $15 higher than that of the other. The sum of their values is $115. Erin and Christopher determine the value of each coin.

Christopher's Way

Guess and Check

Guess: $75 - 60 = 15$

Check: Their sum should be 115. $75 + 60 = 135$

Think: The sum is too great. I need to decrease the numbers.

Revise: Try $60 - 45 = 15$

Check: $60 + 45 = 105$

Think: Now the sum is not enough. I need values between my two guesses.

Revise: Try $65 - 50 = 15$

Check: $65 + 50 = 115$

Erin's Way

Work Backward

There are two facts:

1. Value of one coin is $15 higher than the other
2. Sum is $115

Subtract the amount you know from the total:

$115 - 15 = 100$

There are two coins.
$100 \div 2 = 50$

One coin is worth $50. The other coin is worth $15 more, so its value is $\$50 + \$15 = \$65$.

Check: $\$50 + \$65 = \$115$

The value of one nickel is $50. The other nickel is worth $65.

Did You Know?
In 1979, $25,235,360 was paid for a collection of U.S. and colonial coins.

Talk About It

1. Why is it valuable to use each guess to help you make your next guess?
2. When do you think Work Backward is a good strategy to use?

Check

Use any strategy to solve.

1. **Money** Gracie bought two coins for her collection. One coin cost \$3.25 more than the other. According to her receipt, the two coins cost a total of \$14.05. How much was each coin?

Problem Solving Practice

Use any strategy to solve each problem.

2. **Measurement** The largest paper money ever issued was the 1-guam note of the Chinese Ming Dynasty in 1368. Its length was 4 inches more than its width. Its area was 117 square inches. Find the dimensions of the 1-guam note.

3. **Money** At a sale, coin holders were marked down \$3. Janice bought 5 holders. A sales tax of \$0.50 was added to her bill, bringing the total to \$10.50. Find the price of the coin holders before the sale.

Problem Solving Strategies

- Draw a Picture
- Look for a Pattern
- Guess and Check
- Use Logical Reasoning
- Make an Organized List
- Make a Table
- Solve a Simpler Problem
- Work Backward

Choose a Tool

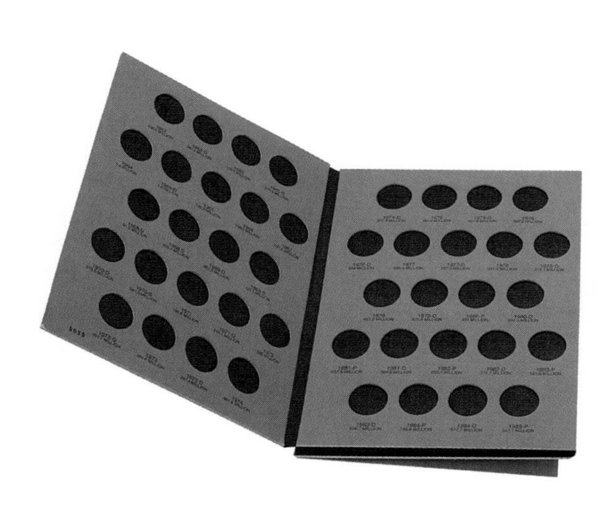

4. **Money** Betty wants to buy 2 CDs at \$8 each and a pack of batteries at \$5.75. She has \$20. Can she buy the CDs and the batteries?

5. **Time** Ms. Fraser must catch the 8:15 A.M. train. It usually takes her 25 minutes to get to the station. A stop at the bakery for coffee and donuts adds 15 minutes less than twice the usual time to her total time. What time must she have left home to be on time for the train?

6. The 8:15 A.M. train usually takes 28 minutes to arrive at New City. Today it arrived at 8:47 A.M. How late was the train?

SECTION B

Review and Practice

(Lesson 5) Estimate each sum, difference, product, or quotient.

1. $7.16 + 2.82$
2. $\$12.30 - \$5.99$
3. 5.62×9.7
4. $40.99 \div 6.1$
5. $20.48 - 8.75$
6. 8.8×7.8
7. $\$64.25 \div 8.32$
8. $0.88 + 23.5$
9. Lily lives 1.78 mi from school. About how many miles does she travel to and from school in 4 days? Explain your thinking.
10. A class of 42 students had $237.50 to spend on souvenirs during a class trip to the art museum. About how much could each student equally spend on souvenirs? Explain your thinking.

(Lesson 6) Find each sum or difference.

11. $4.5 + 23.9$
12. $8.65 - 4.2$
13. $3.05 + 2.111$
14. $6.01 - 2.222$
15. $14.89 - 3.9$
16. $7.055 + 12.35$
17. $22.013 + 4.09$
18. $18.07 - 5.79$

Find the distance around each figure.

19.

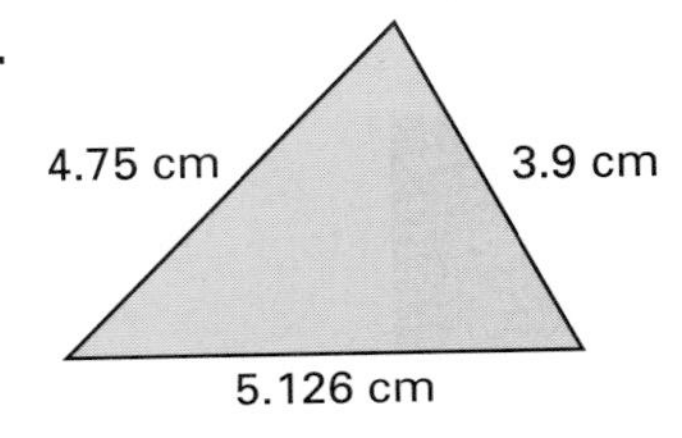

20.

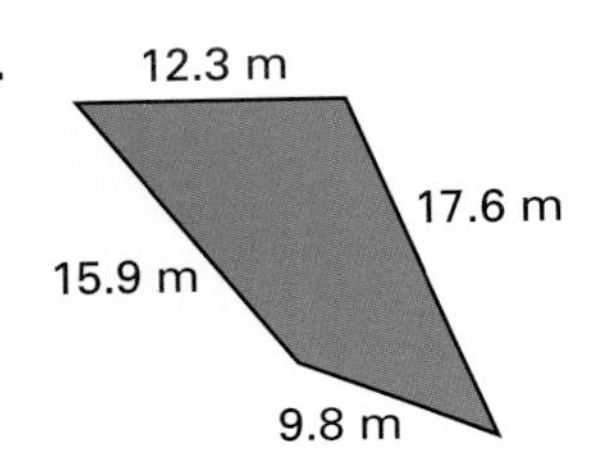

21.

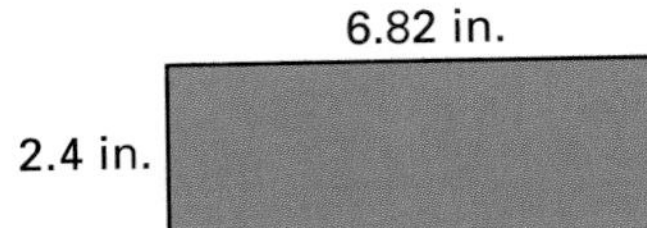

(Lesson 7) Solve each equation.

22. $x - 7.2 = 16.85$
23. $y + 12.52 = 19.37$
24. $9.8 + n = 27.3$
25. $7.22 - x = 5.13$
26. $y + 12.73 = 15.69$
27. $8.02 - n = 1.15$
28. $x - 0.05 = 1.23$
29. $23.7 + x = 28.9$
30. Susan had $32.50. She gave some money to her sister. After she bought a CD for $12.99, she had $10.39 left over. How much money did she give to her sister?
31. Cedric built a small rectangular fence in his backyard for his dog. The short side of the fence is 9.6 m and the long side is 14.2 m. What is the total distance around the fence?

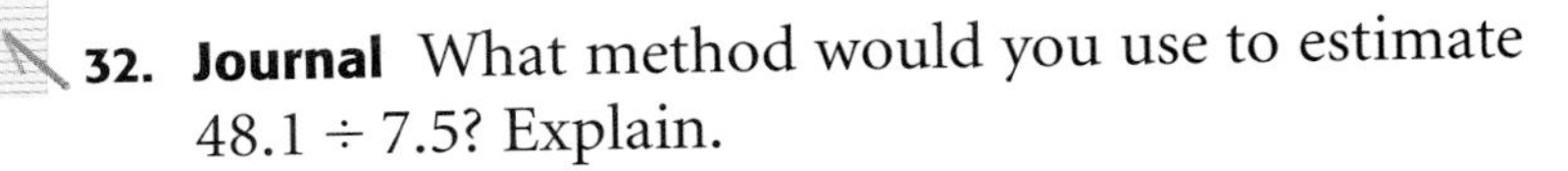

32. **Journal** What method would you use to estimate $48.1 \div 7.5$? Explain.

Skills Checklist

In this section, you have:

- **Estimated Sums, Differences, Products, and Quotients with Decimals**
- **Added and Subtracted Decimal Numbers**
- **Solved Decimal Equations: Addition and Subtraction**

CHAPTER 3

SECTION

C Multiplying and Dividing with Decimals

What is the longest trip you've ever taken? How long did it take? Imagine life as a pioneer on the Oregon Trail. In the 1800s, more than a quarter-million people endured the 2,000-mile journey riding or walking alongside their covered wagons.

How could mathematics help pioneers in the 1800s?

GET READY!

Multiplying and Dividing Decimals

Review estimating. Estimate each product or quotient.

1. 461×22

2. $319 \div 8$

3. 728×47

4. $625 \div 73$

5. $12{,}093 \times 5 \times 4$

6. $8{,}637 \div 32$

7. $52 \times 36 \times 19$

8. $5{,}531 \div 86$

Skills Checklist

In this section, you will:

- ❒ Multiply a Whole Number by a Decimal
- ❒ Multiply a Decimal by a Decimal
- ❒ Divide by a Whole Number
- ❒ Divide by a Decimal Number
- ❒ Solve Decimal Equations: Multiplication and Division

Chapter 3
Lesson
8

Multiplying a Whole Number by a Decimal

You Will Learn

- to multiply a whole number by a decimal

Learn

It took almost six months for the first wagon train to complete the 2,000-mile journey west on the Oregon Trail.

A wagon on the Oregon Trail could travel about 2.5 mi/hr on flat ground. About how many miles could it travel in 3 hours?

You can use repeated addition to find the product of a whole number and a decimal.

Math Tip

You can also use the Distributive Property. Add the whole numbers three times: $2 + 2 + 2 = 6$. Add the decimal parts three times: $0.5 + 0.5 + 0.5 = 1.5$. Add 6 and 1.5 to get 7.5.

Example 1

Multiply 2.5×3.

Add 2.5 three times:

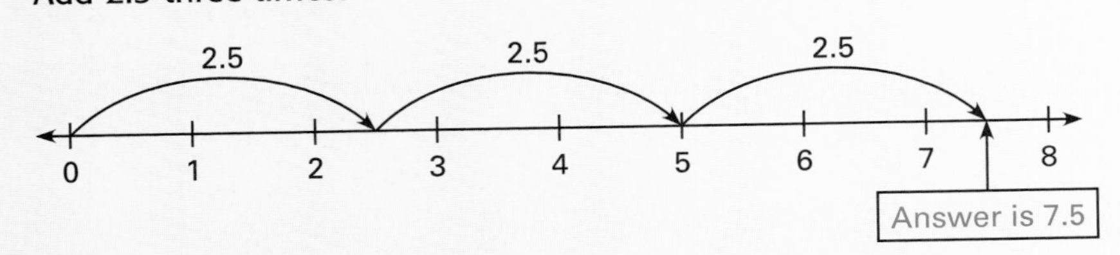

$2.5 + 2.5 + 2.5 = 7.5$

$2.5 \times 3 = 7.5$

A wagon on the Oregon Trail could travel about 7.5 miles in 3 hours.

You can use arithmetic to multiply a whole number by a decimal. Multiply as though you were multiplying two whole numbers. Then count the number of digits after the decimal in the decimal factor. Place the decimal in the answer so that the answer has the same number of digits after the decimal.

$$\begin{array}{r} 43 \\ \times 0.27 \\ \hline 3\,01 \\ 8\,6 \\ \hline 11.61 \end{array}$$

You can also model multiplication problems using grids.

Example 2

Multiply: 0.41×3

Color the tenths for the decimal number. Do this as many times as the whole number.

Color the hundredths for the decimal number. Do this as many times as the whole number.

Describe the number modeled in the grid.

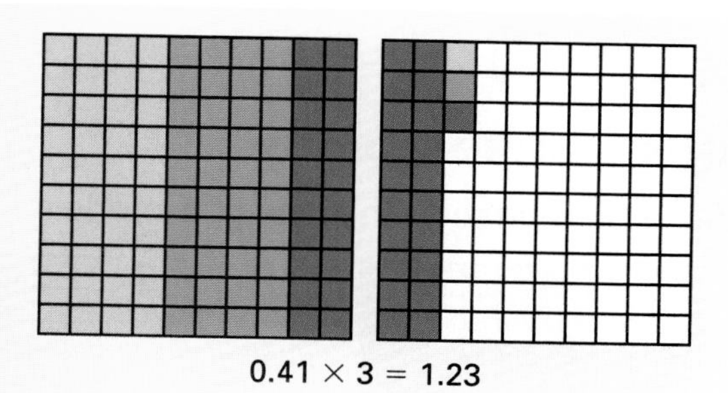

$0.41 \times 3 = 1.23$

Use these shortcuts to multiply a number by 10, 100, or 1,000:

- To multiply by 10, move the decimal point one place to the right.
- To multiply by 100, move the decimal point two places to the right.
- To multiply by 1,000, move the decimal point three places to the right.

Example 3

$0.81 \times 1{,}000 = ?$

Annex a zero so you can move the decimal point.

$0.810 = 810$

Move the decimal point three places to the right.

The product is 810.

Remember

If you annex zeros to the end of a decimal, you do not change its value.

Talk About It

1. How is multiplication of a whole number by a decimal the same as multiplication of whole numbers?
2. When you multiply a whole number by a decimal less than one with tenths and no hundredths, does your answer have tenths? Hundredths?
3. When you multiply a whole number by a decimal less than one with hundredths and no tenths, does your answer have tenths? Hundredths?
4. When you multiply a decimal and a whole number, is your answer greater or less than the whole number? Explain.

Check

Multiply.

1. 1.2×4 **2.** 0.6×7 **3.** 9.813×12 **4.** 0.62×100

5. **Reasoning** Which is greater, 5×0.03 or 5×0.003? Explain.

Practice

Skills and Reasoning

Choose the equation that the grid models.

6. 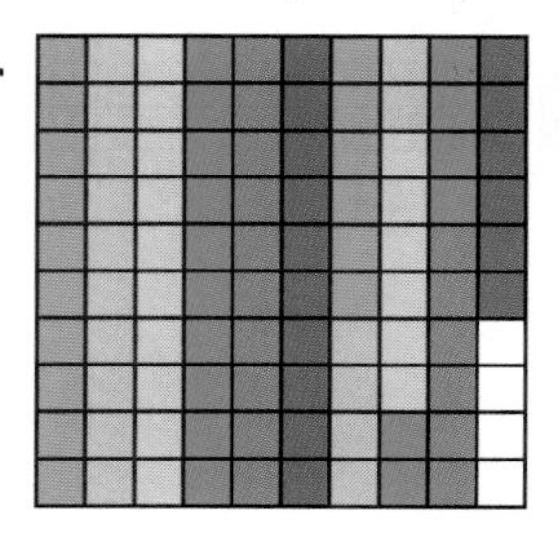

a. $6 \times 0.16 = 0.96$

b. $5 \times 0.16 = 0.80$

7. 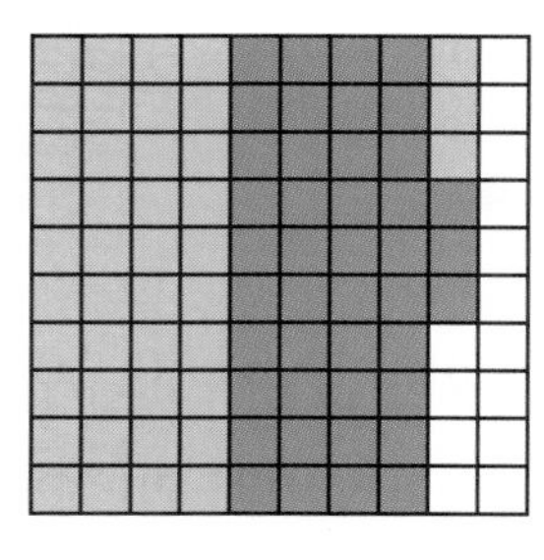

a. $2 \times 0.19 = 0.38$

b. $2 \times 0.43 = 0.86$

8. 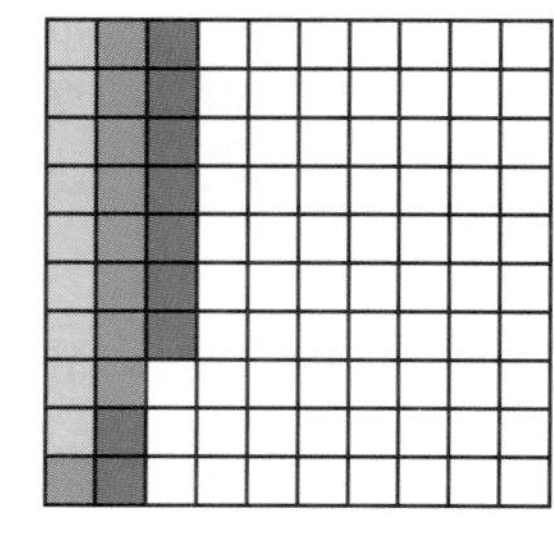

a. $3 \times 0.09 = 0.27$

b. $6 \times 0.03 = 0.18$

Insert a decimal in each answer to make the equation true.

9. $76.89 \times 23 = 176847$ **10.** $4 \times 8.53 = 3412$ **11.** $5.6 \times 72 = 4032$

12. $3.004 \times 8 = 24032$ **13.** $9 \times 3.33 = 2997$ **14.** $14 \times 62.345 = 87283$

Multiply.

15. 10×3.578 **16.** 100×3.578 **17.** $1{,}000 \times 3.578$ **18.** 8.7×6

19. 13.9×7 **20.** 143×6.1 **21.** 448×0.2 **22.** $\$86.15 \times 7$

23. $\$6.85 \times 19$ **24.** 415×0.031 **25.** 5.283×46 **26.** 8.07×10

27. 100×74.4 **28.** $3.85 \times 1{,}000$ **29.** 10×0.059 **30.** $\$25.39 \times 100$

31. **Reasoning** Compare the products of 231×6, 23.1×6, and 2.31×6. Explain where the decimal is in each answer.

Problem Solving and Applications

Use the Data File on page 135 to answer **32** and **33**.

32. Each weekend for 6 weeks Mark and Ann have taken a bike tour from Washington Crossing Park to New Hope and back. How many miles has each logged?

33. The nine members of the Kinkley family enjoy riding bike trails together. One weekend they all rode from Bowman's Hill Tower to New Hope and back. How many miles did the Kinkley family log in all?

34. History Salt was a valuable possession to the travelers of the Oregon Trail. It improved the taste of the food and took little space to store. According to the graph, how much salt did the Olsen family use on July 4?

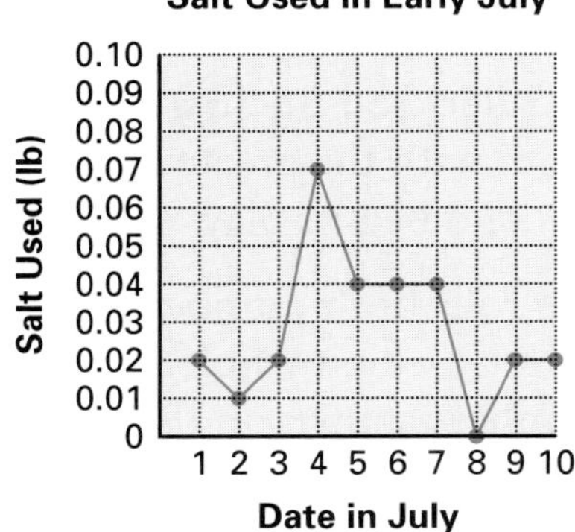

35. Pony Express riders carried mail in leather saddle bags called mochilas. A rider normally carried about 1,000 letters, each weighing 0.6 oz. Find the weight of the mail in a mochila.

36. Andrea drinks 54.3 ounces of milk each week. She also drinks a 6-ounce can of orange juice and 8 glasses of water every day. If she drinks 544.3 ounces of liquid in a week and every glass of water is the same size, how big is each glass of water?

37. Critical Thinking Jamie wants to buy 5.4 feet of wood for a bookshelf. The wood costs \$3 a foot, and Jamie has \$17.50. Does he have enough for all the wood he wants? Explain.

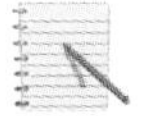

38. Journal You meet someone who never learned how to multiply. He wants to buy 6 things from you that each cost \$2.75. How would you explain to him that $6 \times \$2.75 = \$16.50$?

Mixed Review and Test Prep

STAY SHARP!

Order each group of numbers from least to greatest.

39. 34,890,000; 34,891,000; 34,790,001

40. 784,983; 784,982; 785,984

41. 12,590; 12,509; 12,059

42. 402,960; 40,296; 402,690

Write each number in standard form.

43. 5.54×10^3

44. 7.92×10^7

45. 1.42×10^4

46. 9.28×10^5

47. 7×10^{12}

48. 1.932×10^6

49. 2.54×10^8

50. 3.6×10^1

51. Choose the best estimate for 569×29.

Ⓐ 1,500 Ⓑ 10,000 Ⓒ 1,800 Ⓓ 18,000

Players

3–4 teams, 2–4 players each

Materials

2 number cubes marked as follows:

1: 1, 2, 3, 4, 5, 6

2: 0, 2, 3, 4, 5, 6

gameboard

scratch paper

pencils

Object

The object of the game is to get a total score as close to 1,000 as possible without going over.

How to Play

1. Team leaders roll the first number cube. The team with the greater number is Team A and begins play.
2. Team A rolls both number cubes and creates a two-digit whole number from the numbers shown on the cubes.
3. Team members then choose a decimal number from the gameboard. They multiply the decimal by the two-digit whole number. Then they record the product on scratch paper.

   Example:

$$\begin{array}{r} 1.29 \\ \times \quad 41 \\ \hline 52.89 \end{array}$$

0.21	1.06	4.04	2.79	0.15
2.45	0.91	3.17	1.29	0.69
3.66	0.89	2.49	0.68	3.22
1.72	2.07	6.21	3.82	0.34
3.59	2.96	1.69	0.81	4.82

4. Team B then rolls the number cubes, chooses a decimal, multiplies, and records the product of its multiplication problem. Play continues so that each team has a turn.

5. Each time a team creates a new multiplication problem, it adds the new product to the previous one.

6. Play continues as teams near the 1,000 limit. Any team that gets more than 1,000 is eliminated from play. Any team may elect to stop rolling and 'hold' with its total. The team closest to 1,000 wins the game.

Talk About It

1. How did play change during the game?

2. What strategy did you use to get the product you wanted?

More Ways to Play

- Use an extra number cube to create problems with a three-digit whole number.

- Play as before, except the object is to be the first team to go beyond 1,000.

Reasoning

1. Is it always to your team's advantage to choose the largest two-digit number from the number cubes?

2. Suppose you rolled a 6 and a 4 and you need an answer with a small product. What two-digit number would you choose?

3. How would your strategy change if you were trying to go beyond 1,000 first?

Chapter 3
Lesson
9

Multiplying a Decimal by a Decimal

You Will Learn
- to multiply a decimal by a decimal

Learn

German settlers arriving in Cincinnati, Ohio, in 1838 faced a long and hard trip north to purchase land. The completion of the Erie Canal provided less expensive and quicker transportation. Land travel took more than twice the time needed to travel the same distance by canal!

You can multiply a decimal by a decimal using the same method for multiplying a whole number by a decimal. The product of a decimal-multiplication problem has the same number of decimal places as the number of decimal places in both factors.

Example 1

The Romer family traveled 19.5 hours by canal to reach New Bremen, Ohio. The Mayer family took 2.3 times as long to travel the same distance over land. How many hours did it take the Mayer family?

Multiply: 19.5×2.3

$$\begin{array}{r l} 19.5 & \text{1 decimal place} \\ \times\ 2.3 & \text{1 decimal place} \\ \hline 585 & \\ 390 & \\ \hline 44.85 & \text{2 decimal places} \end{array}$$

Estimate $20 \times 2 = 40$.
The answer is reasonable.

The Mayers traveled 44.85 hours over land.

Math Tip
During a test or quiz, estimating the answer can help you determine if the answer is reasonable.

When you multiply two decimal numbers between zero and one, their product is less than both factors.

Example 2

Multiply: 0.644×0.7

0.644	3 decimal places	Estimate $0.6 \times 1 = 0.6$
$\times$ 0.7	1 decimal place	The answer is reasonable.
0.4508	4 decimal places	0.4508 is less than both 0.644 and 0.7

Use these shortcuts to multiply a number by 0.1, 0.01, or 0.001.

- To multiply by 0.1, move the decimal point one place to the left.
- To multiply by 0.01, move the decimal point two places to the left.
- To multiply by 0.001, move the decimal point three places to the left.

Example 3

Multiply: 21×0.1

$21 \times 0.1 = 2.1$ Move the decimal point one place to the left.

Example 4

Multiply: 5.47×0.001

$5.47 \times 0.001 = 0.00547$ Move the decimal point three places to the left.

Talk About It

1. When you multiply a number by 0.1, will the result be greater or less than that number? Explain.
2. How is multiplying a decimal by a decimal similar to multiplying two whole numbers?

Check

Multiply.

1. In the grid, which colors show the factors and the product for $0.3 \times 0.4 = 0.12$?

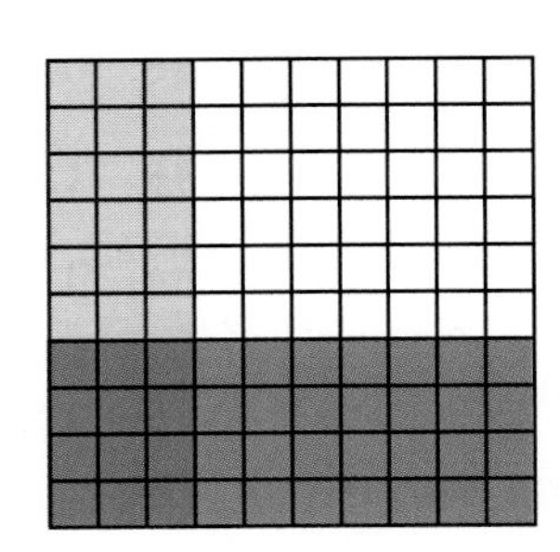

2. 0.4×23.6
3. 52.4×2.8
4. 0.009×4.1
5. $5{,}677 \times 0.01$
6. 210×0.001
7. 6×0.1
8. 3.2×0.001
9. 0.82×0.06
10. 8.3×0.1
11. **Reasoning** Which is greater, 6.2×0.4 or 6.2×0.04? Explain.

Practice

Skills and Reasoning

Choose the equation that the grid models.

12. 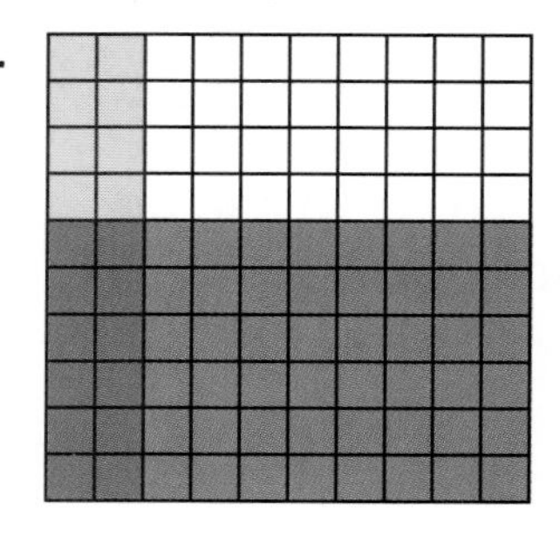

a. $0.2 \times 0.6 = 0.12$

b. $0.3 \times 0.5 = 0.15$

c. $0.2 \times 1.02 = 6.204$

13. 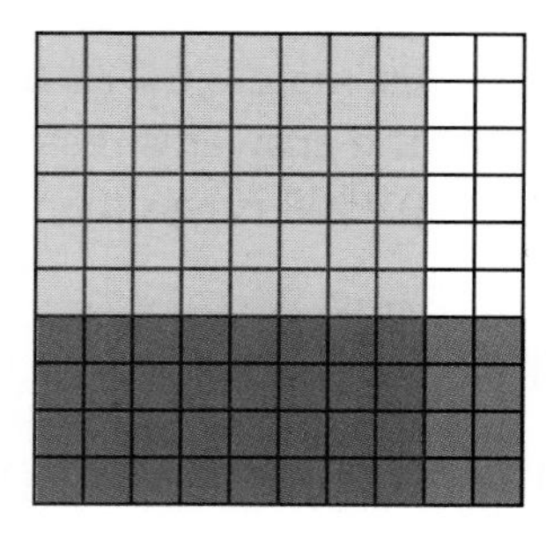

a. $8 \times 0.4 = 3.2$

b. $0.8 \times 0.4 = 0.032$

c. $0.8 \times 0.4 = 0.32$

14. 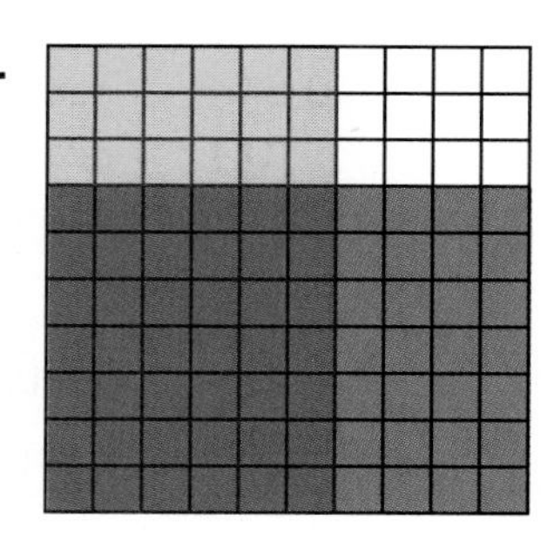

a. $0.6 \times 0.7 = 4.2$

b. $0.6 \times 0.7 = 0.42$

c. $0.06 \times 0.7 = 0.042$

Insert a decimal in each answer to make the equation true.

15. $0.57 \times 0.102 = 05814$ **16.** $4.17 \times 0.23 = 09591$ **17.** $1.9 \times 13.2 = 2508$

18. $1.567 \times 5.23 = 819541$ **19.** $4.09 \times 1.2 = 4908$ **20.** $65.1 \times 65.1 = 423801$

Multiply.

21. 0.1×75.4 **22.** 0.01×6.8 **23.** 0.001×265.3 **24.** 0.65×0.01

25. 97.8×0.1 **26.** 4.25×0.001 **27.** 4.2×6.3 **28.** 5.8×6.7

29. 9.7×0.6 **30.** 5.4×4.3 **31.** 0.29×0.4 **32.** 1.3×0.42

33. 2.07×0.03 **34.** 6.24×8.7 **35.** 0.08×6.5 **36.** 9.37×0.08

37. 10.2×0.4 **38.** 0.31×2.5 **39.** 0.4×0.18 **40.** 0.92×4.6

41. 100.3×0.01 **42.** 0.04×0.028 **43.** 0.38×4.1 **44.** 0.78×5.4

Compare using $<$, $>$, or $=$.

45. 79.1×0.1 ● 79.1×0.01 **46.** 0.001×12.5 ● 0.01×12.5

47. 2.4×0.134 ● 0.24×0.134 **48.** 15.2×0.38 ● 1.52×3.8

49. 6.1×0.001 ● 0.061×0.1 **50.** 3.4×0.88 ● 0.34×0.88

51. **Critical Thinking** Explain why $0.4 \times 0.2 \neq 0.8$.

52. **Critical Thinking** Is it possible to write 3.75×8.12 with only two numbers to the right of the decimal point? Explain your answer.

53. **Reasoning** Explain why multiplying numbers by 1,000 moves the decimal point to the right, and multiplying by 0.001 moves the decimal to the left.

Problem Solving and Applications

Estimate. Then solve.

54. Measurement Joel decided that his wrapping string should be 42.6 times as long as the piece shown here. How long should his string be?

55. In 1863, at Fort Kearny, Nebraska, gingham cloth sold for $0.25 a yard. Mrs. Parks bought 16.5 yards to make clothes for her family. How much did she spend on cloth?

56. In 1863, emigrants could buy rice for $0.11 per pound in Chimney Rock, Nebraska. The Wilsons' barrel could hold 19.25 pounds. How much did it cost to fill the barrel?

57. Health Ava read on the wrapper that a candy bar had 12.5 g of fat. One gram of fat gives you 9.4 calories. How many calories from fat are in the candy bar?

58. History The population of Ohio in 1800 was about 42,000. By 1810 the population was more than 230,000. The increase was largely due to the building of the canal system. Write both of these numbers in scientific notation.

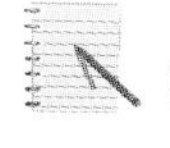

59. Journal Imagine you are on the Oregon Trail in 1845. Write a problem that you might encounter on the trail that you can solve by multiplying two decimals.

Mixed Review and Test Prep

STAY SHARP!

Simplify each expression, using the correct order of operations.

60. $50 - 10 \div 2$ **61.** $72 \div 9 - 1$ **62.** $6 \times 5 \times 3$ **63.** $42 \times 2 - 3$

64. $3 \times (8 - 6)$ **65.** $4 \div 2 - 0^6$ **66.** $50 \div 10 \times 4$ **67.** $(3 \times 4)^2 - 1$

Estimate each sum, difference, product, or quotient.

68. $65.79 + 12.56$ **69.** $7.67 - 5.33$ **70.** 7.87×10.06 **71.** $12.29 \div 4.47$

72. $72.59 + 3.07$ **73.** $21.09 - 11.06$ **74.** $55.88 \div 10.48$ **75.** 9.5×3.667

76. Choose the correct product of 385×0.17.

Ⓐ 654.5 Ⓑ 6.545 Ⓒ 65.45 Ⓓ not here

Chapter 3
Lesson
10

Dividing by a Whole Number

You Will Learn

- to divide a decimal number by a whole number

Learn

The Pony Express mail route was exhausting and extremely hazardous. In May 1860, "Pony Bob" Haslam used four horses to make a run of 162 miles.

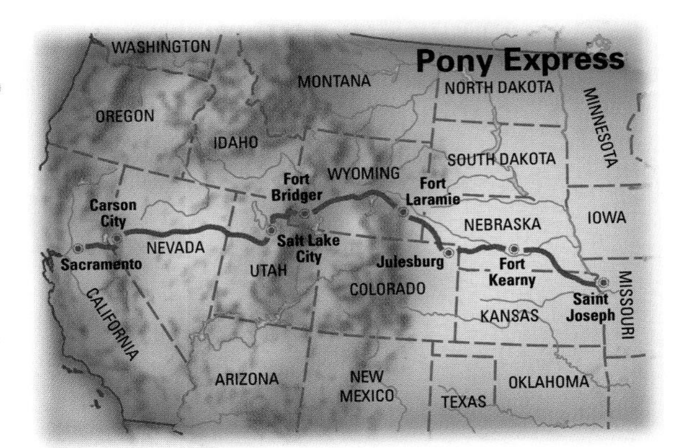

Example 1

Find the average distance run by each horse. Average = 162 ÷ 4

Step 1

Divide as usual.

```
   40
4)162
 -16
   02
   -0
    2
```

Estimate: 160 ÷ 4 = 40

Step 2

Place the decimal. Annex a zero.

```
   40.5
4)162.0
 -16
   02
   -0
    20
   -20
     0
```

Remember

The number being divided is the dividend. The number you divide by is the divisor. The answer is the quotient.

Dividend		Divisor		Quotient
12	÷	3	=	4

The average distance run by each horse was 40.5 miles.

When you have a decimal dividend place a decimal point in the quotient directly above the decimal point in the dividend.

Example 2

Divide: 153.92 ÷ 32

```
     4.81
32)153.92
  -128
    259
   -256
     32
    -32
      0
```

Estimate: 150 ÷ 30 = 5

153.92 ÷ 32 = 4.81

Example 3

Divide: 427.5 ÷ 6

```
   71.25
6)427.50  ← Annex a zero
 -42
   07
   -6
    15
   -12
     30
    -30
      0
```

Estimate: 420 ÷ 6 = 70

427.5 ÷ 6 = 71.25

Use these shortcuts to divide a number by 10, 100, or 1,000:

- To divide by 10, move the decimal point one place to the left.
- To divide by 100, move the decimal point two places to the left.
- To divide by 1,000, move the decimal point three places to the left.

Math Tip

Sometimes a decimal quotient is so long that the calculator cannot show the entire number. In that case, the calculator may round the quotient to a shorter number.

Example 4

The table gives the estimated world population at two times 100 years apart.

What is the average increase in population per year?

$$\begin{array}{r} 6{,}261{,}000{,}000 \\ -1{,}600{,}000{,}000 \\ \hline 4{,}661{,}000{,}000 \end{array}$$

The total increase in 100 years is about 4,661,000,000.

To find the average increase per year, divide by 100:

$4{,}661{,}000{,}000 \div 100 = 46{,}610{,}000.00$

The average annual population increase is about 46,610,000.

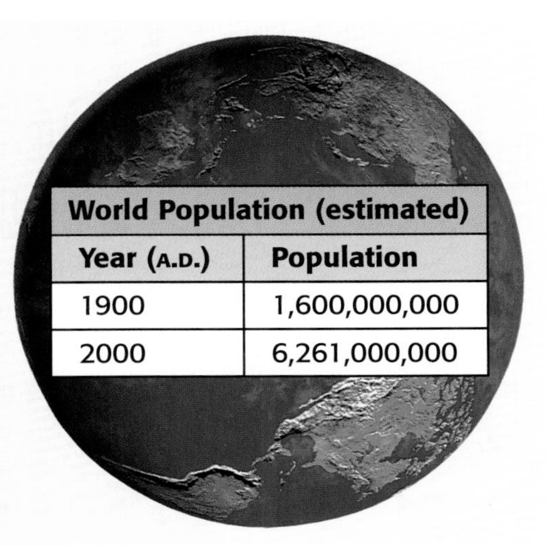

World Population (estimated)	
Year (A.D.)	**Population**
1900	1,600,000,000
2000	6,261,000,000

Talk About It

1. Dividing by 10 is the same as multiplying by 0.1. Give two other pairs of numbers for which dividing by one of them is the same as multiplying by the other. Explain.
2. How can you use multiplication to check a quotient?

Check

Choose the equation that the grid models.

1. **a.** $4.8 \div 6 = 0.8$

   b. $48 \div 6 = 8$

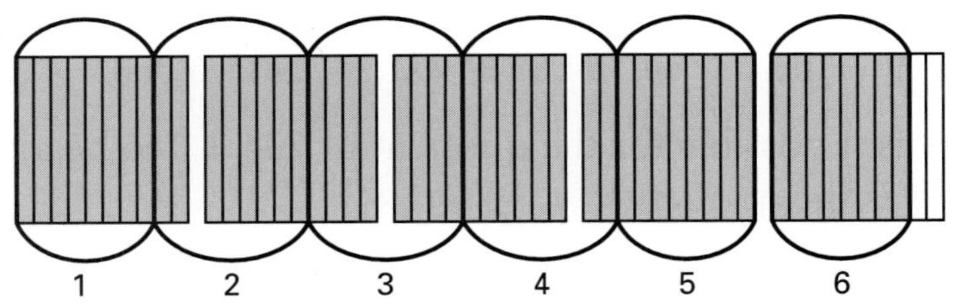

Divide.

2. $154.4 \div 8$
3. $20.47 \div 23$
4. $8.029 \div 74$
5. $26.2 \div 100$
6. $3.012 \div 1{,}000$
7. $45 \div 10$
8. **Reasoning** How is $15.8 \div 2$ similar to $158 \div 2$?

Practice

Skills and Reasoning

Choose the equation that the grid models.

9.

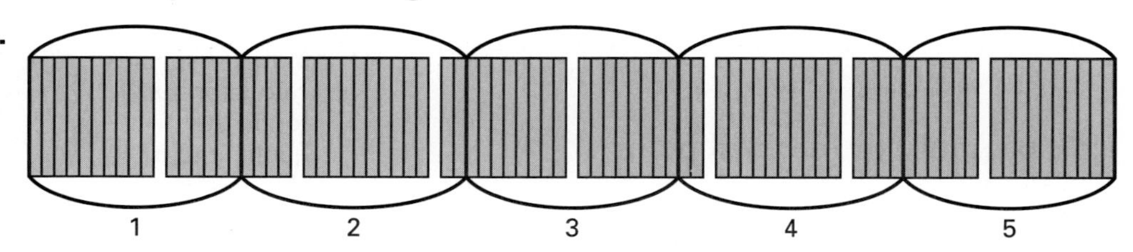

a. $8 \div 5 = 1.6$ **b.** $80 \div 5 = 16$

10.

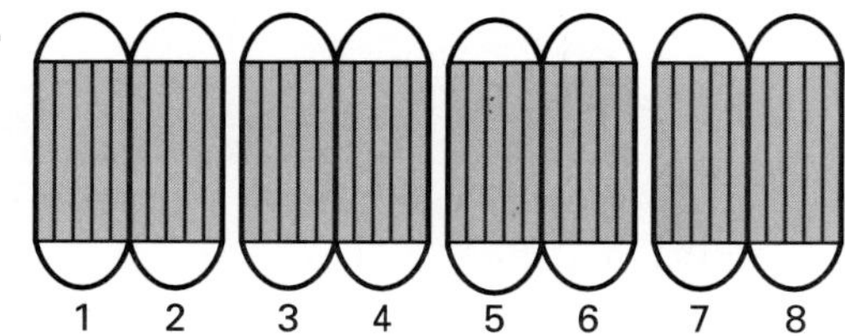

a. $4 \div 8 = 0.5$ **b.** $40 \div 8 = 5$

11.

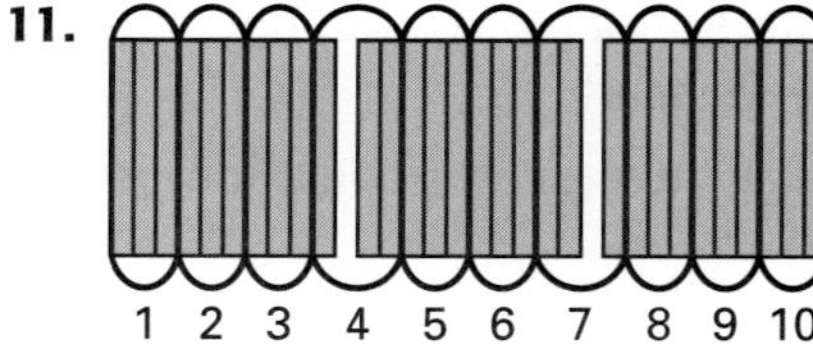

a. $3 \div 10 = 0.3$ **b.** $30 \div 10 = 3$

Insert a decimal in each answer to make the equation true.

12. $24.36 \div 6 = 406$ **13.** $287.63 \div 49 = 587$ **14.** $0.475 \div 5 = 095$

15. $99.4 \div 100 = 994$ **16.** $4.96 \div 10 = 0496$ **17.** $25.8 \div 1{,}000 = 0258$

Divide.

18. $27 \div 6$ **19.** $13.932 \div 9$ **20.** $987.6 \div 12$

21. $133.414 \div 41$ **22.** $49.92 \div 16$ **23.** $0.104 \div 8$

24. $341.6 \div 56$ **25.** $2.856 \div 34$ **26.** $15.25 \div 61$

27. $9.92 \div 8$ **28.** $615.34 \div 10$ **29.** $945.25 \div 19$

30. $40.24 \div 8$ **31.** $382.092 \div 17$ **32.** $0.126 \div 7$

33. $56.88 \div 3$ **34.** $3.534 \div 6$ **35.** $2.035 \div 5$

36. $37.5 \div 3$ **37.** $4.69 \div 7$ **38.** $76.2 \div 6$

Mental Math Find each quotient mentally.

39. $378.19 \div 10$ **40.** $54.89 \div 100$ **41.** $6.003 \div 10$ **42.** $8{,}265.987 \div 1000$

43. How is it possible for the quotient of $234 \div 5$ to be a decimal number? What is the quotient?

44. **Reasoning** Does $2.4 \div 3$ have the same answer as $3 \div 2.4$? Explain.

45. You know that $63.2 \div 8$ is about 8. Is the exact quotient greater than or less than the estimate? Find estimates for $6.32 \div 8$, $0.632 \div 8$, and $0.0632 \div 8$.

Problem Solving and Applications

46. Along the Oregon Trail, the trader's post in Fort Laramie, Wyoming, sold a 16-pound box of beef jerky for $5.92. What was the cost per pound?

47. **Health** The emigrants used lard for their cooking oil. 15 grams of lard have 141 calories. How many calories are in 1 gram?

48. **Measurement** The distance between Fort Boise, Idaho, and Oregon City is 413 mi. On the emigrant's map, the distance was 3 in. How many miles does an inch on the map represent?

49. Maria spent $13.50 buying her class 30 ice cream bars. How much did each bar cost?

50. **Critical Thinking** In a whole-number division problem, both divisor and dividend are whole numbers. What kind of whole-number division problems have whole-number answers, and what kind of whole-number problems have decimal answers?

51. **Critical Thinking** In a gymnastic competition, Dominique scored 9.5, 9.6, 9.5, 9.4, 9.7, and 9.6. Kim scored 9.5, 9.4, 9.6, 9.7, 9.7, and 9.5. Who had the highest average score? Explain.

52. **Write Your Own Problem** Suppose you are on the Oregon trail in 1848. Invent a problem you would solve by dividing a decimal by a whole number.

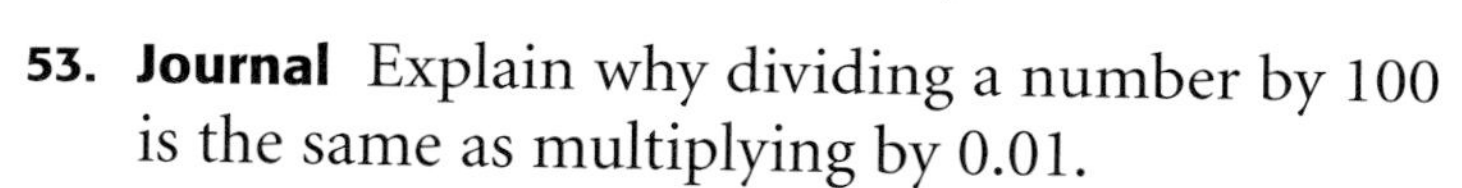

53. **Journal** Explain why dividing a number by 100 is the same as multiplying by 0.01.

Mixed Review and Test Prep

Find the next three numbers in each pattern.

54. 55, 60, 61, 66, 67, 72, ...
55. 2, 4, 8, 16, 32, ...
56. 38, 37, 35, 32, 28, ...

Simplify.

57. $49.02 + 3.05$
58. $56.75 - 46.25$
59. $0.267 - 0.26$
60. $19.31 + 21.4$
61. $6.98 - 3.45$
62. $\$23.40 - \$16.22$
63. $5.847 + 1.152$
64. $14.23 + 6.28$

Find the mean.

65. 305, 115, 313, 284, 228
66. 28, 36, 42, 30

67. Which type of graph shows how portions of a set of data compare with the whole set?

Ⓐ Line graph Ⓑ Bar graph Ⓒ Circle graph Ⓓ not here

Chapter 3
Lesson
11

Dividing by a Decimal

Problem Solving Connection
- Draw a Picture

Materials
- tenths grids
- colored pencils

Explore

Dividing by a decimal is like dividing by a whole number. When you divide by a decimal, you break the dividend into equal groups or groups of equal size. You can use tenths grids to help you divide by a decimal. This model shows that there are 3 equal-sized groups of 0.8 in 2.4.

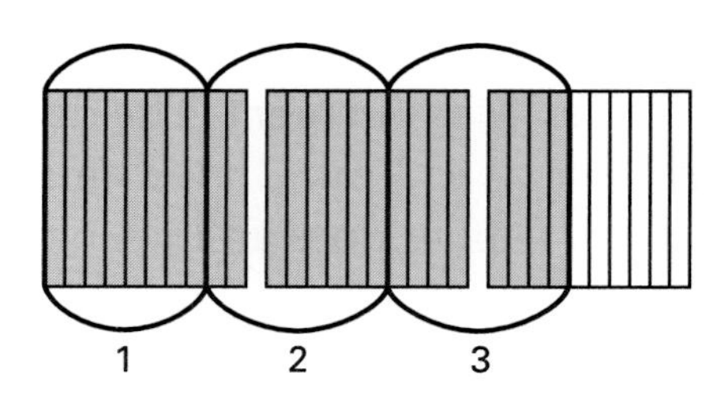

Work Together

Did You Know?
Pioneers who couldn't complete the Oregon Trail before winter would often die from the harsh weather and lack of food.

1. Use a tenths grid to divide by a decimal. Find $2.8 \div 0.7$.

a. Color the first number.

b. Break the first number down into groups. Each group should be as large as the second number.

c. Describe the number of groups in the grid.

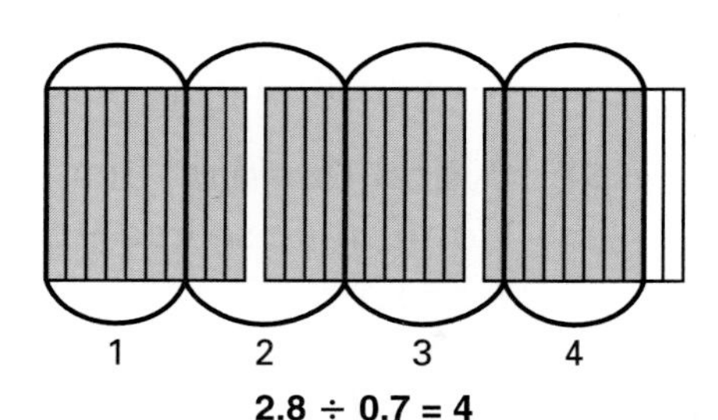

$2.8 \div 0.7 = 4$

2. Use grids to find each quotient.

a. $3.0 \div 0.3$	**b.** $4.5 \div 0.9$	**c.** $4.2 \div 0.7$	**d.** $3.6 \div 0.6$
e. $2.4 \div 0.8$	**f.** $2.5 \div 0.5$	**g.** $2.6 \div 0.1$	**h.** $1.2 \div 0.1$

Talk About It

3. When you divide a number by a decimal less than 1, is your answer less or greater than the number you started with?

4. In the problem $3.0 \div 0.6 = 5.0$, which number represents the number of groups? Which number represents the size of the groups? Which number represents the size of the groups all together?

5. What kind of grid would you need to use to solve $3.0 \div 0.03$? Explain.

6. Look back at Exercise 2. Do you see a pattern in the quotients? Explain.

Connect and Learn

A problem with a decimal divisor can be changed to one without a decimal divisor.

Multiply both divisor and dividend by a power of 10 that will make the divisor a whole number.

Dividend Divisor

$2.618 \div 0.34 = 261.8 \div 34.$

$\times 100 \quad \times 100$

Math Tip

To multiply a number by 100 move the decimal two places to the right.

Example 1

Find the quotient $5.832 \div 1.62$

$5.832 \div 1.62 = 583.2 \div 162.$ — Multiply dividend and divisor by 100 to make the divisor a whole number.

Divide.

$$\begin{array}{r} 3.6 \\ 162\overline{)583.2} \\ -486 \\ \hline 97\,2 \\ -97\,2 \\ \hline 0 \end{array}$$

The quotient is 3.6

Check

Choose the equation that the grid models.

1. a. $2.5 \div 5 = 5$

   b. $2.5 \div 0.5 = 5$

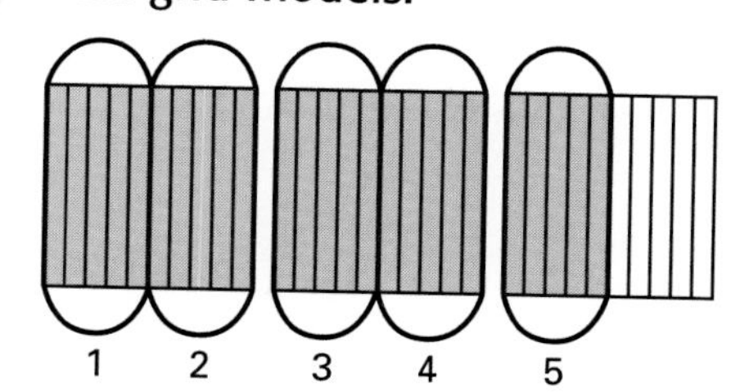

Insert a decimal in each answer to make the equation true. Insert zeros, if necessary.

2. $4.2 \div 1.2 = 35$
3. $0.0006 \div 0.2 = 3$
4. $14.552 \div 6.8 = 214$
5. $8.5 \div 0.5 = 17$
6. $24.6 \div 1.2 = 205$
7. $0.5 \div 0.2 = 25$

Divide.

8. $3.248 \div 2.03$
9. $8.1 \div 0.09$
10. $2.75 \div 1.25$
11. $0.13 \div 6.5$
12. **Reasoning** What do $6 \div 2$, $60 \div 20$, and $6{,}000 \div 2{,}000$ have in common? Explain.
13. **Reasoning** Emily solved $1.25 \div 2.5$. She said the answer was 5. Is she correct? Explain.

Practice

Skills and Reasoning

Choose the equation that the grid models.

14.

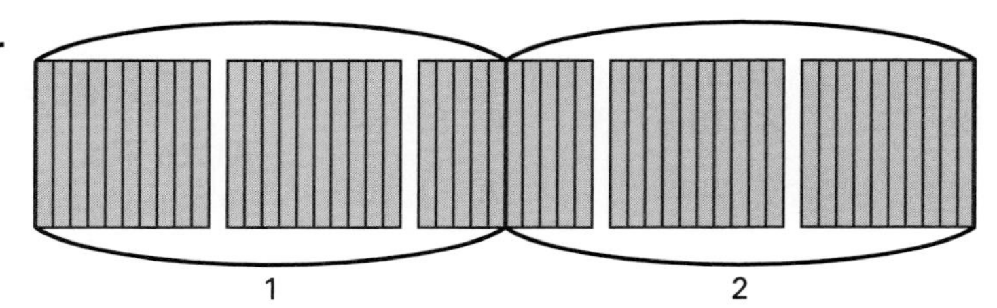

a. $50 \div 25 = 2$

b. $5 \div 2.5 = 2$

15.

5 10 15 20 25 30

a. $60 \div 20 = 30$

b. $6 \div 0.2 = 30$

16.

1 2 3 4

a. $4.4 \div 1.1 = 4$

b. $44 \div 11 = 33$

Insert a decimal in each answer to make the equation true. Insert zeros, if necessary.

17. $10.58 \div 2.3 = 46$

18. $2.24 \div 0.8 = 28$

19. $6.12 \div 1.8 = 34$

20. $0.0036 \div 0.009 = 4$

21. $98.6 \div 2.9 = 340$

22. $45.505 \div 9.5 = 479$

Divide.

23. $0.685 \div 2.74$

24. $9.483 \div 8.7$

25. $0.8449 \div 0.71$

26. $2.4 \div 0.3$

27. $0.104 \div 0.08$

28. $0.427 \div 6.1$

29. $0.804 \div 0.4$

30. $5.49 \div 0.9$

31. $422.1 \div 60.3$

32. $69.09 \div 7$

33. $126.28 \div 8.2$

34. $13.3666 \div 6.89$

35. $0.3321 \div 4.1$

36. $50.4 \div 1.2$

37. $6.89 \div 1.3$

38. $2.59 \div 0.7$

39. $6.684 \div 0.06$

40. $3.48 \div 5.8$

41. $87.4 \div 0.38$

42. $2.5 \div 0.005$

43. Patterns Find the next equation in the pattern, and explain what the pattern is.

$8 \div 2 = 4 \quad 80 \div 20 = 4 \quad 800 \div 200 = 4$

44. Reasoning Estimate the quotient for $13.65 \div 2.1$. Will the actual quotient be greater or less than the estimate? Explain.

45. Algebra Readiness What would you need to divide 2.4 by to get a quotient of 120?

Problem Solving and Applications

46. **Critical Thinking** In Fort Hall, Idaho, people could buy 10 pounds of candles for \$2.50 or 100 pounds of sugar for \$12.50. Which item costs less per pound?

47. The Smith's wagon train was about 98.98 feet long. Each wagon was about 9.8 feet long. If the wagons traveled end to end, how many wagons were in the train?

48. **Money** Peter and Sonia wanted to buy 30 ounces of trail mix for a 3-day hike. Trail mix sells for \$0.26 per ounce, or 32.5 ounce packages for \$7.15. Which is the better buy?

49. Find the next three numbers in the pattern, and explain what the pattern is:

    32, 16, 8, 4, 2, 1, 0.5, 0.25, 0.125 . . .

50. **Logic** Remember that multiplying by 0.1, 0.01, and 0.001 moves the decimal to the left. Explain what dividing by 0.1, 0.01, and 0.001 does. Show an example of each.

51. **Choose a Strategy** Manuel was counting the lights on parade floats. Each float was 36.4 feet long, and they ran bumper to bumper for 5,314.4 feet. If there were 150 lights on each float, how many lights did he count?

52. **Journal** Explain what numbers you can divide by to get a quotient smaller than the dividend and what numbers you can divide by to get a quotient larger than the dividend.

Mixed Review and Test Prep

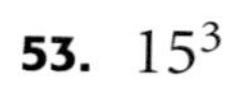
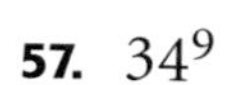

Write each number in expanded form.

53. 15^3	**54.** $8^3 \times 2^4$	**55.** $7^3 \times 8^2$	**56.** 29^2	**57.** 34^9
58. 1^{15}	**59.** 2^5	**60.** 3^6	**61.** $4^8 \times 6^7$	**62.** 10^9
63. 6^3	**64.** $2^2 \times 3^8$	**65.** $4^1 \times 8^2$	**66.** $1^3 \times 5^2$	**67.** 9^4

Solve.

68. $e + 4.5 = 12.6$	**69.** $\$20 + f = \$22.55$	**70.** $3.9 = g + 2.7$
71. $i - 98.6 = 38.3$	**72.** $j + 0.5 = 1.8$	**73.** $m - 0.056 = 0.077$
74. $x - 28.2 = 17.5$	**75.** $6.9 + y = 18.4$	**76.** $49.7 - q = 24.6$

77. Which problem has the same product as 13.7×8.16?

    Ⓐ 137×816 Ⓑ 13.7×81.6 Ⓒ 1.37×8.16 Ⓓ 1.37×81.6

Skills Practice Bank, page 662, Set 4

Chapter 3
Lesson
12

Solving Decimal Equations: Multiplication and Division

You Will Learn

- to solve decimal equations with multiplication and division

Learn

Traveling the Oregon Trail was expensive. Few poor people made the journey because they could not afford the supplies.

The table lists prices of items that pioneers could buy in 1850 in Independence, Missouri, before setting out on the Oregon Trail.

ITEM	COST ($)
Beans	1.50/bushel
Blanket	1.70
Bucket	0.30
Cloth	0.25/yard
Corn Meal	0.17/lb
Flour	3.00/sack
Lard	0.10/lb
Rice	0.15/lb
Salt	0.02/lb
Tent	15.00
Tools	4.50/set

You can solve multiplication equations with decimals using mental math and number sense. Use mental math to determine the digits in the answer. Then use number sense to determine where the decimal should be placed.

Did You Know?
Sailors use decimal equations to determine how fast to travel to reach a given port on a given day.

Example 1

Narcissa Whitman, a pioneer on the Oregon Trail, paid \$0.75 for rice. How many pounds of rice did she buy?

Let x = the number of pounds she bought.

$\$0.15x = \$0.75 \rightarrow 15x = 75$ Think of the numbers as whole numbers. Read as "What number times 15 equals 75?"

$15 \times 5 = 75$ Use mental math.

$\$0.15 \times 5 = \$0.75$ Since there are two decimal places in 0.15 and two in 0.75, there should be no decimal places in 5.

Narcissa purchased 5 pounds of rice.

You can also solve division equations with decimals using mental math and number sense.

Example 2

$\frac{x}{3} = 0.5$. Solve for x. Think of the numbers as whole numbers. Read as "What number divided by 3 equals 5?"

$\frac{15}{3} = 5$ Use mental math.

$\frac{1.5}{3} = 0.5$ Since there is one digit after the decimal in 0.5, there should be one digit after the decimal in 1.5.

$x = 1.5$

When mental math isn't convenient, you can solve multiplication and division equations by working backward.

Example 3

Solve: $n \times 0.6 = 3.48$

$3.48 \div 0.6 = n$ — Work backward using division.

$34.8 \div 6 = n$ — Change to division with a whole number.

Divide.

$$\begin{array}{r} 5.8 \\ 6\overline{)34.8} \\ -30 \\ \hline 48 \\ -48 \\ \hline 0 \end{array}$$

$n = 5.8$

Example 4

Solve: $x \div 2.1 = 7.89$

$x = 7.89 \times 2.1$ — Work backward using multiplication.

Multiply.

$$\begin{array}{r} 7.89 \\ \times\ 2.1 \\ \hline 789 \\ 15\ 78 \\ \hline 16.569 \end{array}$$

$x = 16.569$

Talk About It

1. How does number sense help you to solve decimal equations?
2. Give a real-world problem modeled by $0.5x = 3.5$.
3. Would you solve $x \div 3.1 = 8.01$ the same way you would solve $\frac{x}{3.1} = 8.01$?

"Pilgrims on the plains" sketched by Theo. R. Davis

Check

Solve each equation.

1. $3j = 2.1$
2. $0.4w = 2.4$
3. $\frac{t}{5} = 1.1$
4. $\frac{f}{0.7} = 0.7$
5. $0.3x = 0.9$
6. $5q = 4$
7. $\frac{m}{0.2} = 9$
8. $\frac{r}{0.5} = 0.3$
9. $1.2y = 3.6$
10. $0.18n = 5.4$
11. $x \div 3.2 = 0.8$
12. $0.11n = 0.275$
13. $4.2t = 4.62$
14. $\frac{m}{1.1} = 8.8$
15. $\frac{h}{0.91} = 0.3$
16. $\frac{k}{0.17} = 0.17$
17. $y \div 2.9 = 1.03$
18. $54p = 8.1$
19. $\frac{z}{1.06} = 6$
20. $t \div 2.6 = 0.5$
21. **Reasoning** Why is it easier to solve $8.73n = 31.428$ by working backward than by using mental math?

Practice

Skills and Reasoning

For each equation, determine which of the given values of x will make the equation true.

22. $0.024x = 24$; 0.001 or 1,000

23. $\frac{450}{x} = 4.5$; 100 or 1,000

24. $8.5 \div x = 8.5$; 0.1 or 10

25. $78.34x = 7.834$; 1 or 0.1

Solve. Use mental math or work backward.

26. $0.5d = 0.045$

27. $\frac{e}{3} = 0.07$

28. $\frac{t}{9} = 0.07$

29. $0.7r = 35$

30. $0.9g = 72$

31. $1.6w = 0.032$

32. $\frac{p}{0.02} = 4.4$

33. $\frac{s}{1.07} = 107$

34. $9b = 8.1$

35. $\frac{u}{1.5} = 30$

36. $0.09k = 0.063$

37. $\frac{q}{5} = 0.5$

38. $\frac{p}{0.3} = 11$

39. $0.6h = 3.6$

40. $0.4m = 0.004$

41. $0.8n = 0.056$

42. $\frac{s}{0.07} = 0.4$

43. $\frac{v}{6} = 0.3$

44. $1.2z = 0.144$

45. $8k = 0.64$

46. $1.1a = 0.066$

47. $\frac{j}{0.7} = 0.2$

48. $\frac{f}{10} = 1.13$

49. $\frac{u}{0.4} = 0.05$

50. $14.8y = 75.628$

51. $\frac{t}{3.99} = 6.8$

52. $\frac{m}{8.3} = 73.1$

53. $0.08r = 68$

54. $g \div 5.4 = 6.2$

55. $30.24 = 9.6n$

56. $12 = 8x$

57. $w \div 15 = 7.42$

58. **Reasoning** Would it be easier to solve $g \div 3.8 = 4.9$ using mental math or working backward? Explain.

59. Marcia solved $1.39x = 9.313$ for x. Marshal solved $9.313 \div 1.39 = x$ for x. What can you tell about x in each equation? Explain.

60. How can you be sure 2.18 is the value of y in $3y = 6.54$?

Problem Solving and Applications

For **61–64,** set up an equation and solve.

61. Sarah York said "I bought 3 of the same item for \$9. The price for each item was v."

62. Henderson Luelling said "I bought 2 of the same item for \$3.40. The price for each item was w."

63. Peter Burnett said "I bought 100 of the same item for \$15. The price for each item was y."

64. Randolph Marcy said, "I paid \$18 for z yards of cloth."

65. Along the Oregon Trail, the Spikle family left Fort Boise with 36 kilograms (kg) of flour. They divided it into bags of 0.6 kg. How many bags did they have?

66. The Carlson family spent several days hiking through the Rocky Mountains. Every day, they hiked 8.3 miles. At the end of the vacation, they had hiked a total of 83 miles. How many days did they hike?

67. A wagon weighs 165.3 kg. Carrying riders, the wagon weighs 465 kg. What is the weight of the riders?

68. Helen put several stamps on a large envelope. She placed 6 stamps of equal value on the envelope. The stamps together were worth $0.90. How much was each stamp worth?

69. A chemist conducting an experiment took a package of salt and split the contents into nine even groups. Each group weighed 0.08 kilograms. How much salt was in the original package?

70. Traders used the Santa Fe Trail to take manufactured goods from Kansas City to Santa Fe and return with gold, silver, furs, and wool. The wagons averaged 6.5 miles per hour over the 800 mile trail. They could travel 7 hours per day. How many days would it take the traders to make a round trip from Kansas City?

71. Write an equation involving decimal multiplication or division where the answer is 12.

72. **Journal** Explain the difference between the expression $0.3x$ and $0.3x = 2.1$.

Mixed Review and Test Prep

STAY SHARP!

Use the Calories in a Meal graph to answer each question.

73. What is the total number of calories for this meal?

74. Which part of the meal has the most calories?

75. How many combined calories are in the shake and the dessert?

Calories in a Meal

Chocolate éclair 245
Mango colada shake 140
Chicken sausage link 123
Greek pasta salad 280
Snap beans 35

Multiply.

76. 1.45×6 **77.** 4.07×3 **78.** 5×4.36

79. 83×1.2 **80.** 51×1.06 **81.** 73.8×5

82. What is $13.05 \div 0.9$?

Ⓐ 145 Ⓑ 14.5 Ⓒ 1.45 Ⓓ 0.145

Skills Practice Bank, page 662, Set 5

Chapter 3

Problem Solving

Decision Making: Planning A Hike

You Will Learn

- to calculate the time involved when hiking on a trail

Explore

You and some friends are planning a 3-day backpacking trip on the John Muir Trail. This means you will be eating, sleeping, and enjoying the great outdoors. You want to hike one of the two trail sections shown in these "profiles."

Dollar Lake to Lake Marjorie

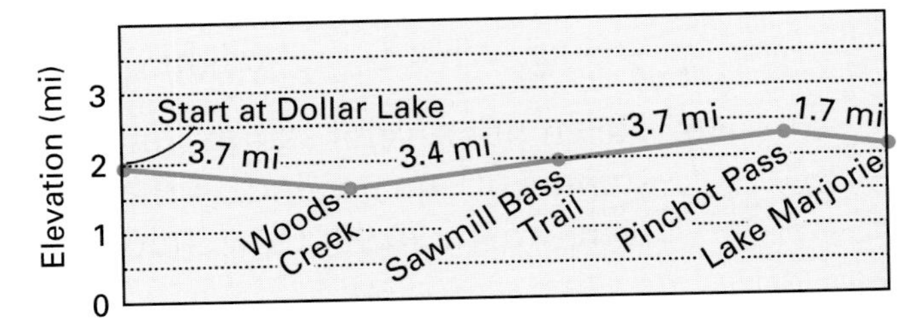

Lower Trinity Lake to Lyell Pass

Facts and Data

- You need to choose one of the sections to hike.
- You must decide if you will hike the entire section.
- You must allow time for eating, sleeping, setting up camp, and breaking down camp.
- Each mile uphill adds 2.5 hr on to your time.
- Each mile downhill adds 1.5 hr on to your time.
- Resting on average will be 0.25 hr for every hour of hiking.
- You will be hiking for 3 days.

Work Together

Understand

1. What are you asked to do?
2. What information is shown on each map?
3. What information do you have to help you decide which section to take?

Plan and Solve

4. What do you need to consider when making your decision?
5. How might estimation help you make your choices?
6. How long will it take you to hike each section if you average 2.4 mi/hr?
7. How long will it take you to hike each section if you figure in the extra time needed for uphill and downhill mileage?
8. How long will it take you to hike each section if you add rest time?

Make a Decision

9. What factors do you need to consider when planning how long your hike will take?
10. What other factors should be a part of your plans?
11. Make a schedule for your 3-day hike. Start with the time you begin a trail until you end it 3 days later.

Present Your Decision

12. Present your decision to your class.
13. Share your strategies for making your decisions with your class.

SECTION C

Review and Practice

Vocabulary Match each term with a number in the equation shown.

1. quotient
2. divisor $\qquad 56 \div 8 = 7$
3. dividend

(Lesson 8) Multiply.

4. 5.07×10
5. 82×2.9
6. $\$42.75 \times 5$
7. 7×0.902
8. 7.05×23
9. 100×4.387
10. 54.1×11
11. $\$12.99 \times 10$

(Lesson 9) Multiply.

12. 0.2×12.9
13. 6.04×6.4
14. 10.9×0.08
15. 45.6×1.02
16. 3.12×0.2
17. 13.6×2.8
18. 0.05×10.7
19. 5.08×11.8

(Lesson 10) Divide.

20. $74.4 \div 12$
21. $3.612 \div 14$
22. $27.18 \div 6$
23. $73.44 \div 4$
24. $57.8 \div 10$
25. $39.84 \div 40$
26. $37.046 \div 2$
27. $141.75 \div 45$
28. Students at the Washington School formed a hiking club. On Saturdays, they hiked 9.1 km, 8.3 km, 12.4 km, 9.6 km, and 14.5 km. What was the mean length of a hike for the club?

(Lesson 11) Divide.

29. $2.1335 \div 42.67$
30. $3.68 \div 0.08$
31. $0.264 \div 0.24$
32. $61.02 \div 22.6$
33. $73.593 \div 5.661$
34. $0.52 \div 6.5$
35. $18.05 \div 0.1$
36. $406.4 \div 50.8$

(Lesson 12) Solve.

37. $1.2t = 3.6$
38. $\frac{u}{6} = 23.7$
39. $0.02b = 0.4$
40. $0.11n = 5.5$
41. $\frac{w}{5.7} = 14.8$
42. $0.2s = 16.4$
43. $\frac{t}{0.08} = 18.9$
44. $0.01v = 8.3$

Set up an equation and solve.

45. If a wagon wheel travels 0.02 km in one revolution, how many times will the wheel revolve in 23.8 km?

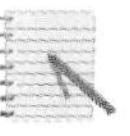

46. **Journal** Which of the following has a greater quotient: $208.4 \div 0.1$ or $208.4 \div 0.01$? Explain.

Skills Checklist

In this section, you have:

- ☑ Multiplied a Whole Number by a Decimal
- ☑ Multiplied a Decimal by a Decimal
- ☑ Divided by a Whole Number
- ☑ Divided by a Decimal Number
- ☑ Solved Decimal Equations: Multiplication and Division

Choose at least one of the following. Use what you have learned in this chapter.

1 Kangaroo Patterns

In the grid, the numbers in every row form decimal patterns. To 'hop' from one number to the next, you must always add or subtract the same number. The numbers in every column also form decimal patterns. Copy the grid, then find the patterns and fill in the missing values.

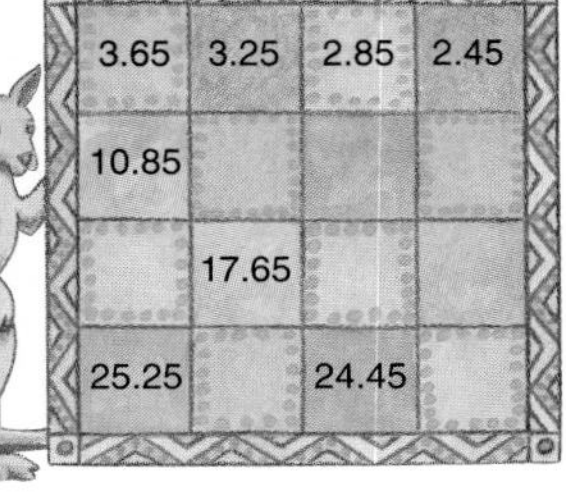

2 Earthquakes

Go online to learn more about how earthquakes are measured at **www.mathsurf.com/6/ch3/science**.

1996 Earthquakes		
Date	**Location**	**Magnitude**
Jan. 1	Indonesia	7.7
Feb. 25	Mexico	6.8
Apr. 29	Solomon Islands	7.5
June 11	Philippines	7.0
June 17	Indonesia	7.5

Use the data in the table to construct a graph comparing the magnitude of the earthquakes. Then write a paragraph explaining why the type of graph you chose is the best for comparing the data.

3 Photo Possibilities

At Home Choose two of the photos shown. Work with a family member to write a word problem for each. One problem must use decimals. Each problem must be related to the subject of the photo. Write equations for each problem and solve them.

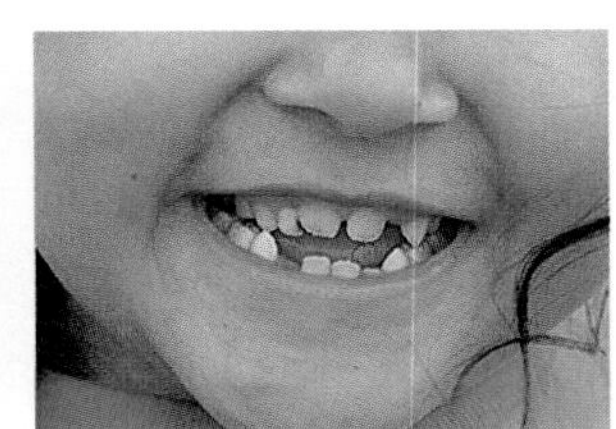

4 An Exponential Challenge

Write each of the numbers and expressions shown as a single number in standard form. If you add the numbers in each row, which row will have the greatest sum?

Team	Round 1	Round 2	Round 3
A	23×10^2	$6^2 - 3 + 5^3$	0.547×10^4
B	$15^3 + 5^2$	0.03×10^5	$3^3 - 4^2 + 24^1$
C	$7^6 \div$ 7 cubed	7 squared	0.007×10^6

CHAPTER 3

Review/Test

Vocabulary Copy and complete each sentence with a term from the word list.

Word List
scientific notation
dividend
divisor
quotient

1. In the expression $45.6 \div 3$, 45.6 is the ________.
2. 2.5×10^6 is an example of ________.
3. In the equation $16.38 \div 3.9 = 4.2$, the ________ is 4.2.
4. The number by which you are dividing is called the ________.

(Lessons 1–4)

5. What place value is to the left of the hundred-thousandths place?
6. Write three hundred and thirty-six hundredths in number form.
7. One way nails are sized is by their gauge, or thickness. Order these nails from least to greatest according to their gauge in millimeters: 3.76, 3.05, 3.43, 3.33.
8. Name two numbers between 2.007 and 2.009.
9. There are an estimated 103,000 species of bees and wasps. Write this number in scientific notation.

(Lesson 5) Estimate. Then find each sum, difference, product, or quotient.

10. $\$17.32 - \$5.76$
11. $4.9967 + 3.021$
12. $382.8 \div 8.7$
13. 2.8×0.93

(Lesson 6) Solve.

14. **Measurement** One kind of scale measures in units called Kelvins. The boiling point of gold is at 1,074 K, and the boiling point of water is 700.852 K lower. Find the boiling point of water in Kelvins.

(Lessons 8–11) Find each product or quotient.

15. 3.45×0.001
16. 0.87×5
17. $18.41 \div 7$
18. $75.36 \div 1.2$
19. $33.36 \div 8$
20. $27.5 \div 4.4$
21. 6.18×1.1
22. 13.4×0.07

(Lessons 7, 12) Solve each equation.

23. $m + 4.2 = 6.9$
24. $\frac{x}{100} = 10{,}000$
25. $12.3a = 36.9$
26. $y - 14.8 = 6.2$
27. $r - 1.8 = 17.6$
28. $w + 2.9 = 31.1$
29. $\frac{v}{40} = 35$
30. $3.2p = 22.4$

(Lessons 6, 9) Write an equation for each exercise and solve it.

31. What is the difference in size between a wheel 52.52 mm across and one 42.5 mm across?
32. A sonora blue butterfly measures 2.1 cm in length. A waved sphinx moth measures 8.4 cm long. How many times longer is the moth than the butterfly?

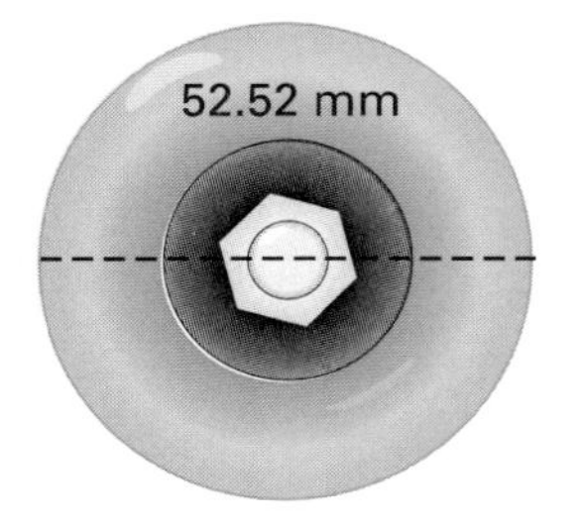

CHAPTER 3

Performance Assessment

You've won a trip to three different nations and have $600 U.S. to spend! Choose three nations from the table that you would like to visit. You will be given $200 U.S. to use as spending money in each country.

1. **Decision Making** Decide which countries you will visit.

2. **Estimate** Estimate the amount of each country's money you will get in exchange for your $200 U.S.

Country	Estimated Amount in Exchange for $200 U.S.	Actual Amount in Exchange for $200 U.S.

EXCHANGE

THURSDAY, SEPTEMBER 11, 1997

Country	Basic Unit	Value of One Unit in U.S. Dollars ($)	Number of Units One U.S. Dollar Will Buy
Chile	Peso	0.00243	410.80
Colombia	Peso	0.00096	1046.50
Indonesia	Rupiah	0.00043	2340.70
Nigeria	Naira	0.01264	79.10
Pakistan	Rupee	0.02807	35.6189

3. **Record Your Data** Make a table like the one above. Record your estimates and the actual amounts for exchanging $200 U.S.

4. **Explain Your Thinking** How did you decide which countries to visit? Did the exchange rates affect your decision making? What estimation strategies did you use? How did you find the actual amounts?

5. **Extend Your Thinking** Suppose that after your trip, you have 3 units of each country's money left to exchange to U.S. dollars. Make a new table to show how much 3 units of each currency are worth in U.S. dollars. Round to the nearest cent. How much of your $600 did you spend?

Math Magazine

As Easy as 1, 10, 11!

The Hindu-Arabic Numeration system we use is also called the base 10 system. There are ten digits in it: 0, 1, 2, 3, 4, 5, 6, 7, 8, and 9. Every place represents a power of 10.

Computers don't use the base 10 system to make calculations. Instead, they use the base 2 system, which is also called the binary system. In the binary system, there are only two digits: 0 and 1. Every place is a power of 2.

2^3	2^2	2^1	2^0	← Power of 2
8	4	2	1	← Value

$9 = 8 + 0 + 0 + 1$

$9 = 1 \quad 0 \quad 0 \quad 1$

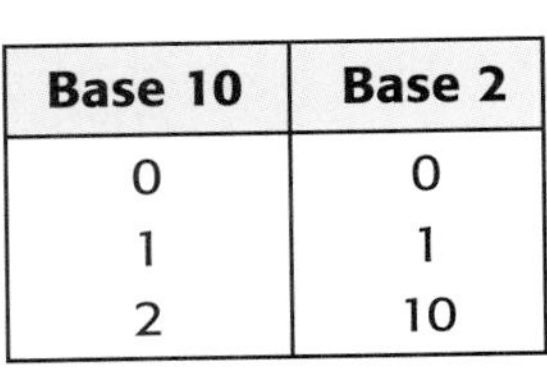

Base 10	Base 2
0	0
1	1
2	10

Base 10	Base 2
3	11
4	100
5	101

Base 10	Base 2
6	110
7	111
8	1000

Try These!

1. What are the binary numbers for the base 10 numbers 10 through 16?
2. What are the base 10 numbers for the following binary numbers?

   a. 10001 **b.** 10100 **c.** 10111 **d.** 11111
3. In base 10, the first nine powers of 2 are 1, 2, 4, 8, 16, 32, 64, 128, and 256. How do you write the first nine powers of 2 in the binary system?
4. In base 10, the number 0.1 means one-tenth. In the binary system, what do you think 0.1 means? Explain.

CHAPTERS 1–3

Cumulative Review

Test Prep Strategy: Eliminate Choices

What is the product when 207 is multiplied by 0.7?

Ⓐ 1,449 Ⓑ 351.9 Ⓒ 145.6 Ⓓ 144.9

Because 0.7 is less than 1, the product will be less than 207. This eliminates choices Ⓐ and Ⓑ. Because $7 \times 7 = 49$, the final digit in the product will be 9. This eliminates choice Ⓒ. Choice Ⓓ is the only remaining answer.

STAY SHARP!

Write the letter of the correct answer. Choose any strategy.

1. Simplify the expression 7^4.

Ⓐ 2,401 Ⓑ 28 Ⓒ 70,000 Ⓓ 16,384

2. Simplify the expression $5^2 + 2^3 \times 7$.

Ⓐ 39 Ⓑ 52 Ⓒ 231 Ⓓ 81

3. Which expression means "8 less than j"?

Ⓐ $8 - j$ Ⓑ $j - 8$ Ⓒ $j/8$ Ⓓ not here

4. Choose the equation that describes the following situation: Paul had to drive for 2 hours after spending t hours on the train. He spent 5 hours travelling all together.

Ⓐ $5 + 2 = t$ Ⓑ $\frac{t}{2} = 5$ Ⓒ $t + 2 = 5$ Ⓓ $2t = 5$

5. Solve the equation $7r = 63$.

Ⓐ $r = 6$ Ⓑ $r = 7$ Ⓒ $r = 8$ Ⓓ $r = 9$

6. Write the number four hundred five million, eighty thousand, five hundred one in standard form.

Ⓐ 450,080, 510 Ⓑ 405,800,510

Ⓒ 405,080,501 Ⓓ 450,800,501

7. Find the mean of this data set: 8, 11, 4, 7, 7, 3, 6, 2.

Ⓐ 6 Ⓑ 7 Ⓒ 8 Ⓓ 48

8. Write the following in scientific notation: 40,001,000.

Ⓐ 4.1×10^7 Ⓑ 40.001×10^6

Ⓒ 4.001×10^7 Ⓓ 4.0001×10^7

9. Simplify the following: $21.78 + 11.81$.

Ⓐ 32.59 Ⓑ 22.59 Ⓒ 33.59 Ⓓ 33.61

10. Divide: $68.8 \div 0.4$.

Ⓐ 17.2 Ⓑ 172 Ⓒ 1.72 Ⓓ 1,720

Test Prep Strategies

- Read Carefully
- Follow Directions
- Make Smart Choices
- Eliminate Choices
- Work Backward from an Answer

DATA FILE

Chapter 4

Measurement

One Person's Trash is Another Person's . . .

One Person's Trash is Another Person's . . .

Page 209

Units of Measurement

209

What trends does the timeline show about the amount of waste generated and the amount of materials recovered?

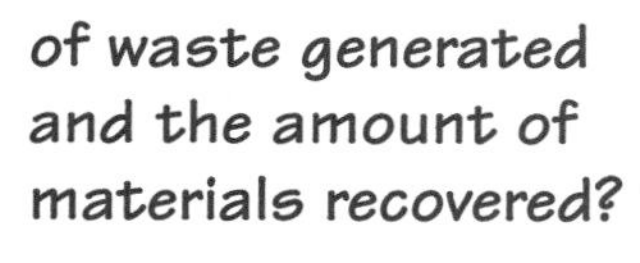

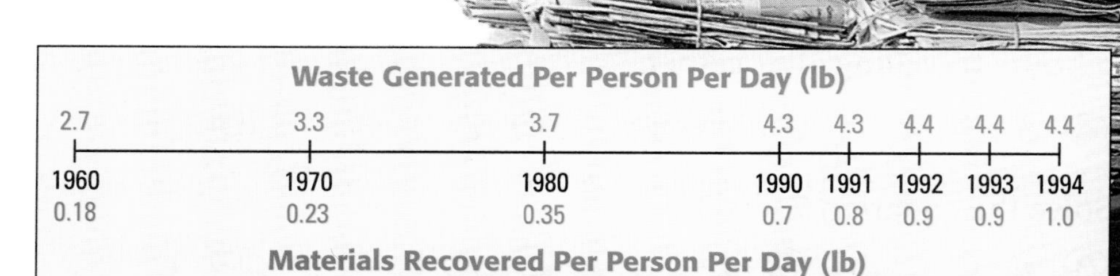

	1960	1970	1980	1990	1991	1992	1993	1994
Waste Generated Per Person Per Day (lb)	2.7	3.3	3.7	4.3	4.3	4.4	4.4	4.4
Materials Recovered Per Person Per Day (lb)	0.18	0.23	0.35	0.7	0.8	0.9	0.9	1.0

LINKS

Social Studies

The ancient Incas used knotted rope called *quipus* to determine how large fields were, and how much tax to charge for them.

www.mathsurf.com/6/ch4/social

Arts & Literature

Jules Verne stated in *20,000 Leagues Under the Sea,* ". . . the temperature dropped below 5° Celsius or 23° Fahrenheit . . ." However, 5° Celsius is 41° Fahrenheit.

www.mathsurf.com/6/ch4/arts

Science

A meter was originally known as $\frac{1}{10,000,000}$ the distance from Earth's equator to the North Pole.

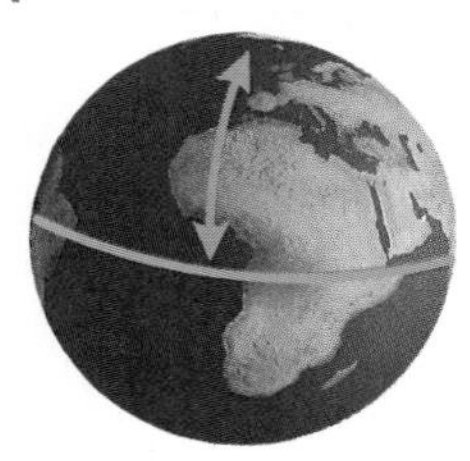

The Monster That Ate Minnesota

Area of Polygons

225

There were only about 10 shopping centers before World War II. By 1994, there were more than 40,000 centers. According to the table, the greatest increase in the number of shopping centers took place for which area size? Why do you think more shopping centers of this size were built?

Number of U.S. Shopping Centers by Area			
Year	400,001–800,000 ft^2	800,001–1,000,000 ft^2	More than 1 million ft^2
1990	1,102	288	357
1992	1,170	294	371
1993	1,194	295	374
1994	1,210	297	376

Invention-al Wisdom

Circles

243

The High-Wheeler, a bicycle invented in the 1870s, had a large front wheel that was 5 ft in diameter. This table shows the wheel diameters of some other remarkable cycles. Which cycle do you think would travel the farthest with one rotation of the wheel? Explain.

Type of Cycle	Wheel Diameter
Smallest bicycle	0.76 in.
Largest bicycle	10 ft
Largest tricycle	11 ft
Smallest unicyle	1 in.

People of the World

The great wall of China covers so much area that it is visible from outer space.

www.mathsurf.com/6/ch4/people

Entertainment

The area of a standard football field is 57,600 ft^2. A football field can hold about 7 baseball diamonds, 20 tennis courts, or 1,280 table-tennis tables.

The Monster That Ate Minnesota
Page 225

Invention-al Wisdom
Page 243

Materials
ruler, graph paper

Design your own miniature golf course. Begin by thinking about the sorts of shapes and kinds of obstacles you want to put in your golf course.

Make a Plan

- How much does your group know about miniature golf?
- How many holes will your course have? Will the length vary from hole to hole?
- What kinds of measurements will you use in your design?

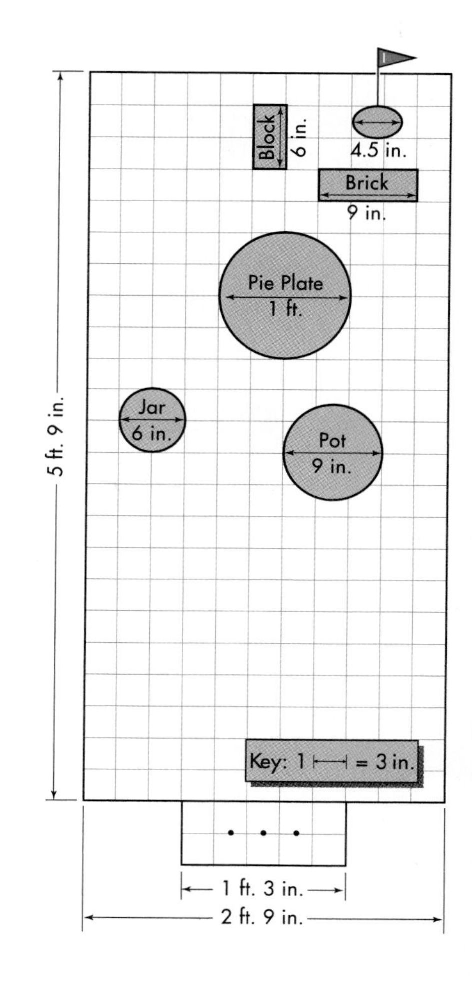

Carry It Out

1. Make a list of the type of shapes and objects for your golf course.
2. Estimate the length of each hole.
3. Draw a sketch on a sheet of graph paper for each hole in your golf course. Provide a key that indicates the length of each square in the grid.
4. Label your sketches.

Talk About It

- How did your team decide on the shapes and objects to use in the course?
- Explain how your group decided on the length and width of each hole.

Present the Project

Compare your golf course plans with another team's plans. Choose the most difficult holes from each to plan one "Super Course."

CHAPTER 4

SECTION

A Units of Measurement

Every day, the world produces tons of trash. But for some, garbage isn't something to throw away. The Museum of International Folk Art in Santa Fe, New Mexico, examines how people take garbage and recycle it into something useful, pleasant, or fun. How do you think mathematics is used in the management of garbage and recycling?

Converting Measurement

Review multiplying by powers of ten. Find each product.

1. $23 \times 1{,}000$
2. $1{,}890 \times 0.1$
3. 320×10
4. 102×0.01
5. 12×100
6. 35×0.1
7. 783×100
8. 98×0.1
9. 100×0.001

Skills Checklist

In this section, you will:

- ❒ Learn About Perimeter
- ❒ Convert in the Metric System
- ❒ Use Conversion Factors

Chapter 4
Lesson
1

Perimeter

Learn

You Will Learn

- to find the perimeter of a geometric figure

Vocabulary

perimeter

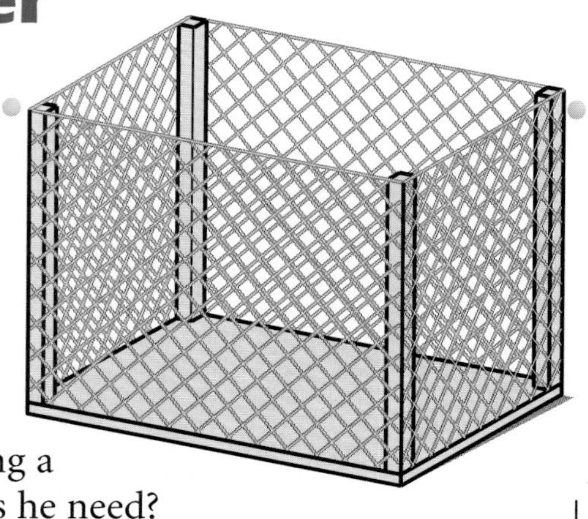

Antwon wants to build a composter out of wire mesh. He wants it to be a 4-ft by 3-ft rectangle. How long a piece of mesh does he need?

The distance around the outside of a figure is the **perimeter**. Here are two ways to find the perimeter of the composter.

Did You Know?
Composting allows organic garbage such as peels and grass to break down quickly and naturally. This leaves more room in landfills to store the garbage that cannot be recycled or broken down quickly.

One Way

Add the lengths of all four sides.

Perimeter = length + width + length + width

$= 4\text{ ft} + 3\text{ ft} + 4\text{ ft} + 3\text{ ft}$

$= 14\text{ ft}$

Antwon needs a 14-ft-long piece of wire mesh.

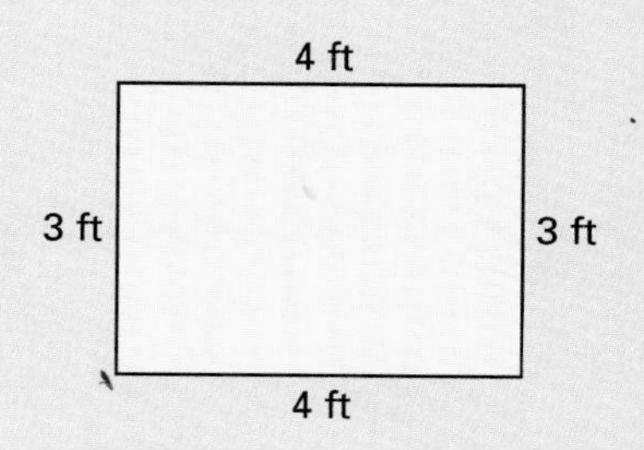

Another Way

Add the length and width of the rectangle. Since there are two lengths and two widths, multiply the sum by 2 to find the perimeter. Remember that opposite sides of a rectangle are the same length.

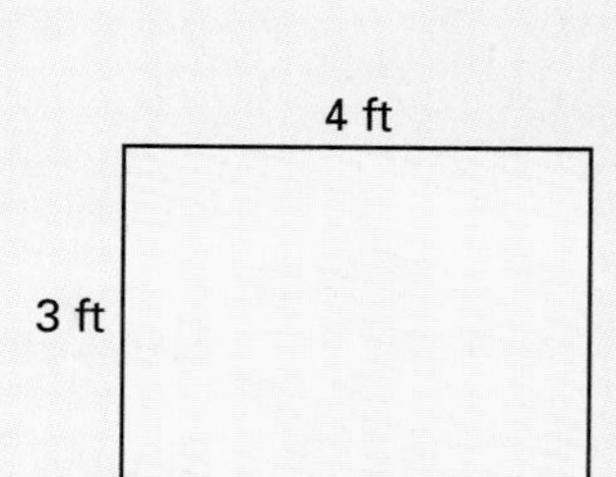

Perimeter $= 2 \times (\text{length} + \text{width})$

$= 2 \times (4\text{ ft} + 3\text{ ft})$

$= 2 \times (7\text{ ft})$

$= 14\text{ ft}$

Example 1

Find the perimeter.

Add the lengths of all four sides.

$P = 18.3 + 12.5 + 18.3 + 12.5$
$= 61.6$ cm

or

Add the length and width and multiply the sum by 2.

$P = 2 \times (18.3 + 12.5)$
$= 61.6$ cm

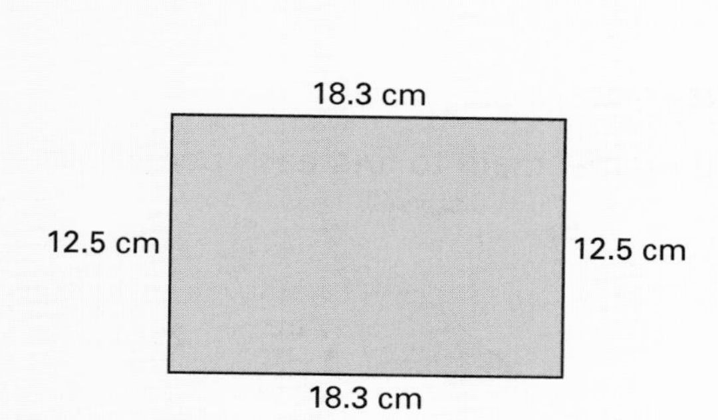

Remember
When adding decimals, line up the decimal points. This helps you to be sure that you are adding digits with the same place value.

Sometimes, a figure does not give all the side lengths. You can often determine the length of an unlabeled side by looking at the opposite side.

Example 2

Find the perimeter.

The bottom is equal to the top two sides. Since the top two sides are 8 in. and 15 in., the bottom is 23 in.

The shortest side plus 7 in. is equal to 10 in. The shortest side is therefore $10 - 7$, or 3 in.

Perimeter $= 15 + 3 + 8 + 10 + 23 + 7$, or 66 in.

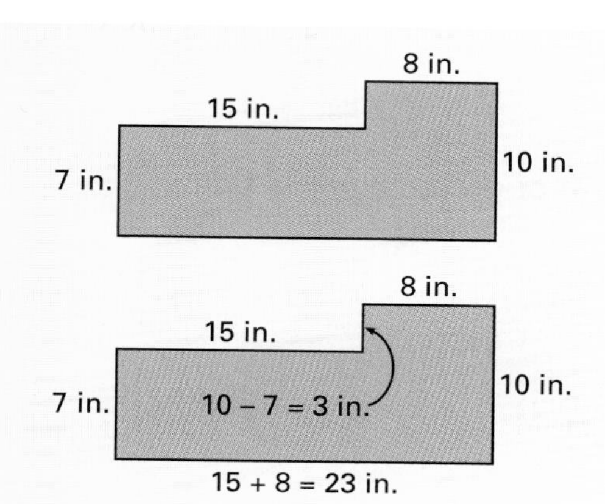

Talk About It

1. How are the two methods for finding perimeter the same? How are they different?
2. If you know the length of one side of a square, how can you use multiplication to find the perimeter? Explain.

Check

Find each perimeter.

1.
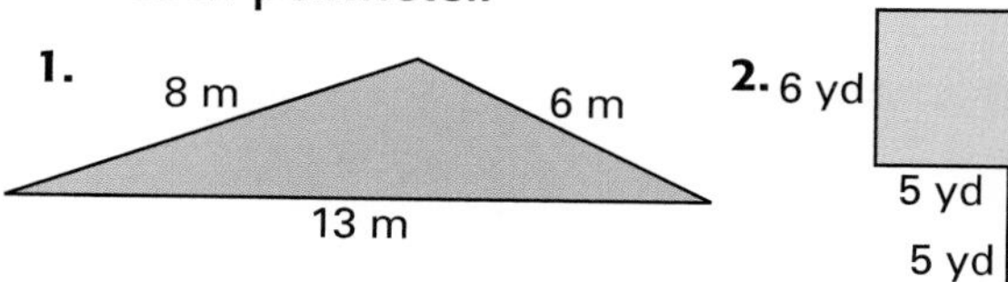

2.
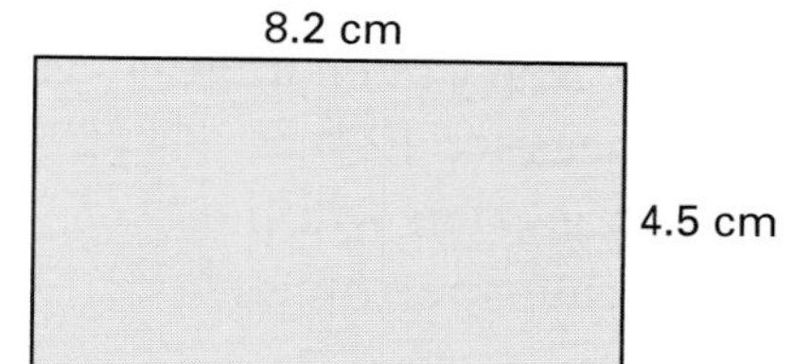

3.

4. **Reasoning** Larry planted a garden with a perimeter of 70 feet. Catherine planted a garden with a perimeter of 64 feet. Must Larry's garden have more sides than Catherine's garden? Explain.

Practice

Skills and Reasoning

Mental Math Use mental math to find each perimeter.

5.

40 cm
50 cm
50 cm
40 cm

6.

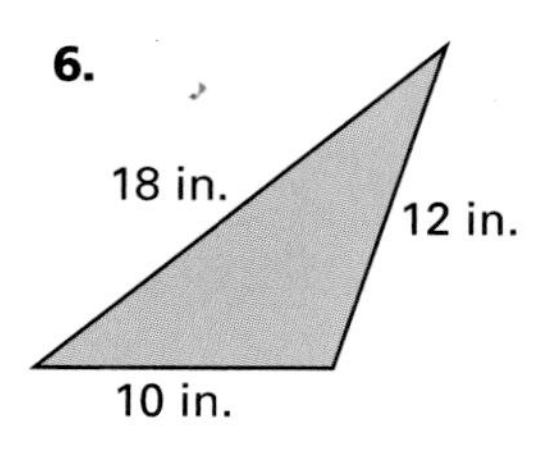

7.

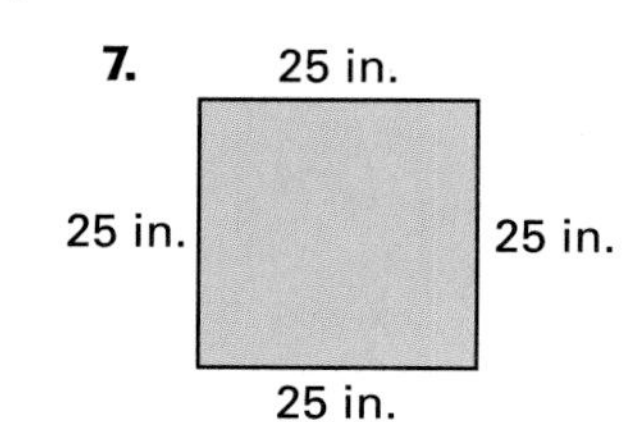

8.

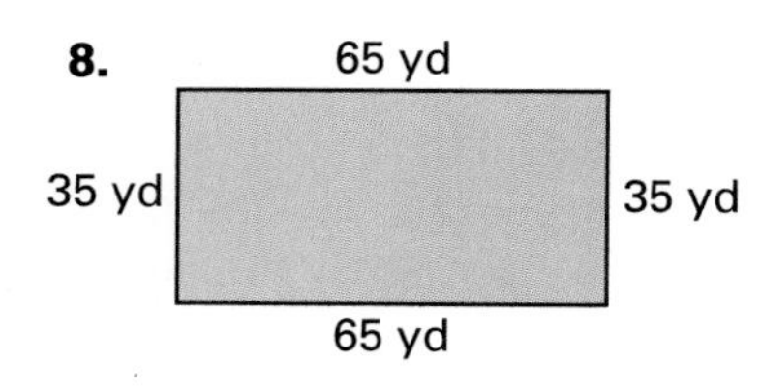

Find each perimeter.

9.

2 cm
2 cm

10.

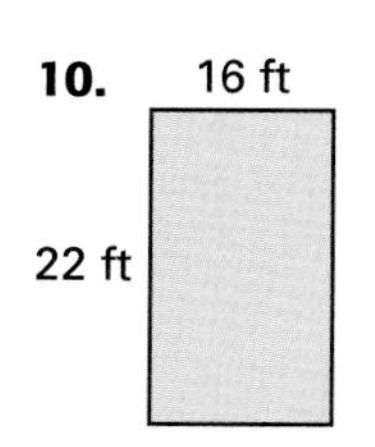

11.

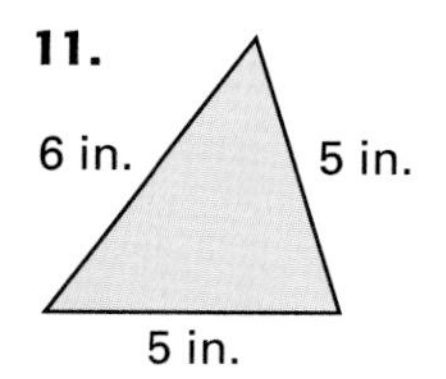

12.

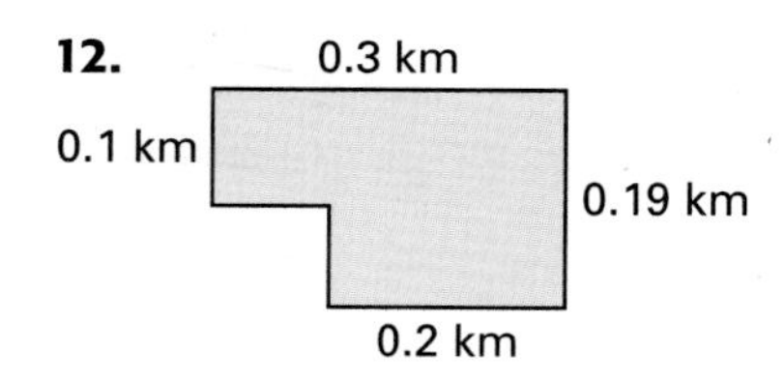

Find the length of each unknown side.

13.

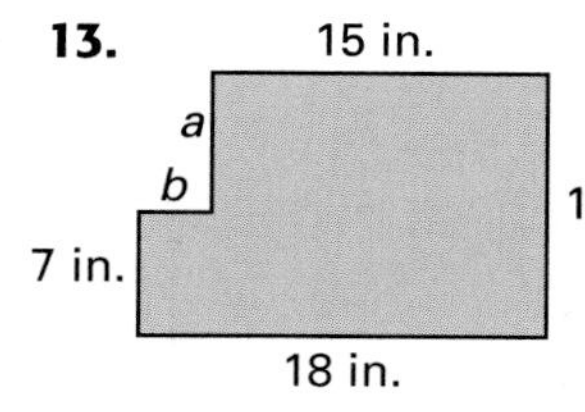

14.

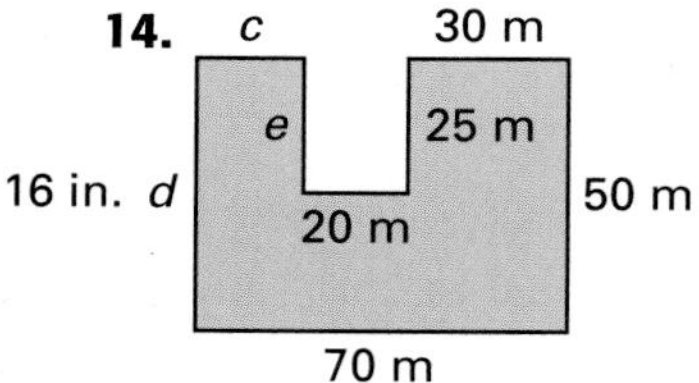

15.

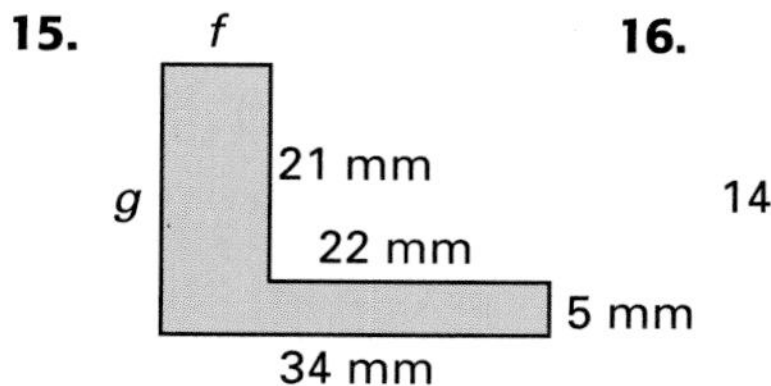

16.

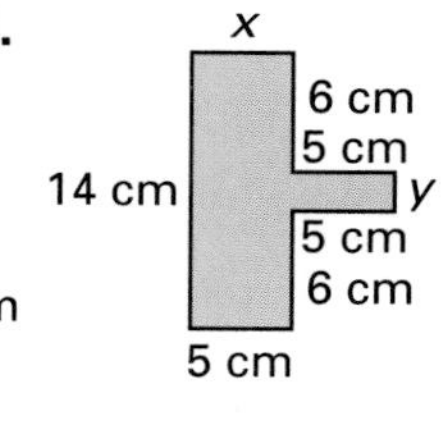

17. Kristin wants to put organic garbage in a compost pile. She staked out a triangular area on the ground. The triangle she created has two sides of 6 and 8 feet. If the perimeter of the area is 21 feet, how long is the third side?

18. Both Pang and Mary decided to create gardens. One side of Pang's square garden will measure 12 feet. A short side of Mary's rectangular garden will also measure 12 feet. Which garden will have the greater perimeter? Explain.

Problem Solving and Applications

19. Using Data Use the drawings of the baseball diamonds to find the difference in running distance for a home run.

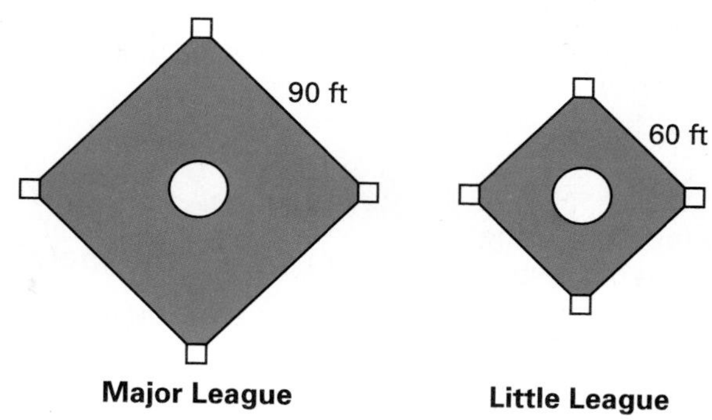

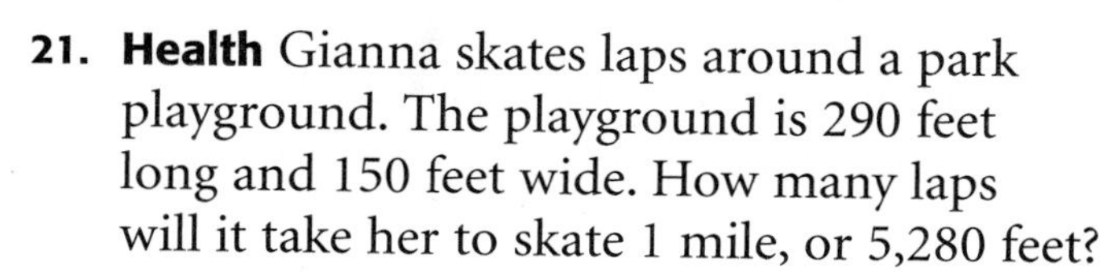

20. Critical Thinking The students of Twin Creeks Middle School planted a rectangular garden. Thirty-six feet of decorative material was used for the border. Make a 2-column table showing the lengths and widths for at least four possible gardens.

21. Health Gianna skates laps around a park playground. The playground is 290 feet long and 150 feet wide. How many laps will it take her to skate 1 mile, or 5,280 feet?

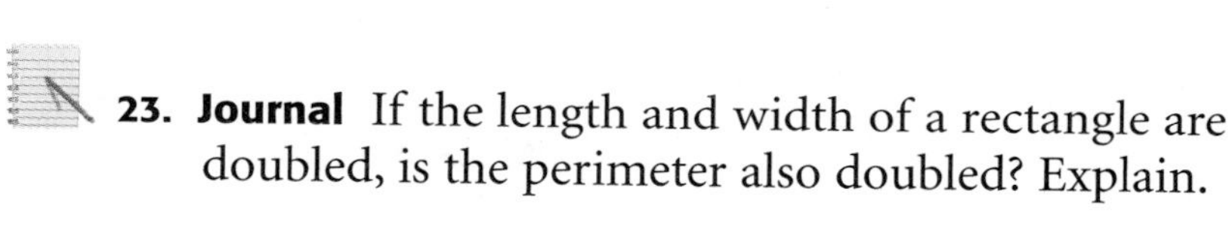

22. Explain the steps needed to find the unknown side of a triangle if the other two sides are 7 inches and 9 inches, and the perimeter is 30 inches.

23. Journal If the length and width of a rectangle are doubled, is the perimeter also doubled? Explain.

Mixed Review and Test Prep

Using Data Use the Reaction Time graph to answer **24–26.**

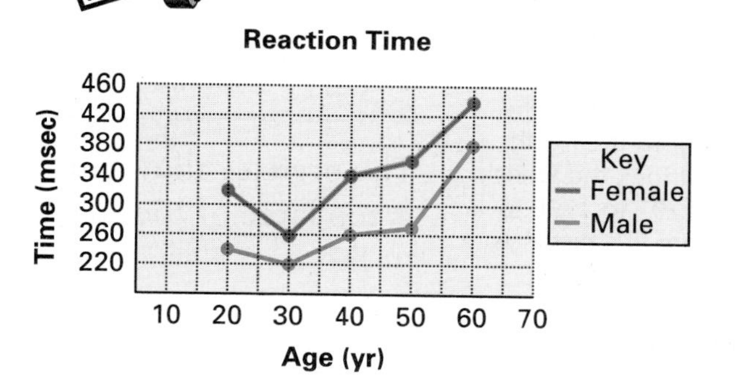

24. At what age is the reaction time slowest for females? Slowest for males?

25. What is the difference between male and female reaction at age 50?

26. What do you think the reaction times for 70-year-old females will be?

Write in scientific notation.

27. 56,000 **28.** 72,300,000 **29.** 2 trillion **30.** 6 thousand

31. 1,600 **32.** 48 billion **33.** 94,560,000 **34.** 874,870,000,000

35. The mass of Object A is 3.1 times as great as the mass of Object B. The mass of Object B is 77.5 grams. Choose the correct equation, where x is the mass of Object A.

Ⓐ $3.1x = 77.5$ Ⓑ $77.5x = 3.1$ Ⓒ $\frac{3.1}{x} = 77.5$ Ⓓ not here

Chapter 4
Lesson
2

Converting in the Metric System

You Will Learn

- to measure using the metric system and to convert units within that system

Vocabulary

metric system
meter
gram
liter
kilo-
centi-
milli-

Learn

You can use the **metric system** to describe an object's length, mass, or volume. The base unit for measuring length is the **meter**. The base unit for measuring mass is the **gram**. The base unit for measuring volume is the **liter**.

The metric system also uses prefixes to describe amounts that are larger or smaller than the base unit. The most common prefixes are **kilo-**, meaning 1,000; **centi-**, meaning $\frac{1}{100}$; and **milli-**, meaning $\frac{1}{1,000}$.

	Name	Abbreviation	Number of Base Units	Approximate Comparison
Length	**Kilo**meter	km	1,000	9 football fields
Length	Meter	m	1	Half the height of a door
Length	**Centi**meter	cm	$\frac{1}{100}$	Length of a raisin
Length	**Milli**meter	mm	$\frac{1}{1,000}$	Width of a period at the end of a sentence
Mass	**Kilo**gram	kg	1,000	Mass of a cantaloupe
Mass	Gram	g	1	Mass of a raisin
Volume	Liter	L	1	Half a large bottle of soda
Volume	**Milli**liter	mL	$\frac{1}{1,000}$	Half an eyedropper

Did You Know?

The meter was originally defined as $\frac{1}{10,000,000}$ of the distance from the equator to the North Pole. It took the French from 1792 to 1798 to measure this distance. Today's satellites confirm that their measurements were only off by 0.2 mm.

The prefixes allow you to choose a convenient unit when something is too large or too small to be easily measured in meters, grams, or liters.

Example 1

Complete. Use the abbreviation for the most appropriate metric unit.

Height of a single-serving soda bottle: 17 ______

Since length (height) is being measured, the base unit should be the meter. Since a bottle is about 17 raisins tall, the appropriate unit is centimeters, abbreviated as cm.

The height is 17 cm.

To convert a unit in the metric system, you multiply or divide by a power of 10. The table below lists the powers of 10 to use when converting.

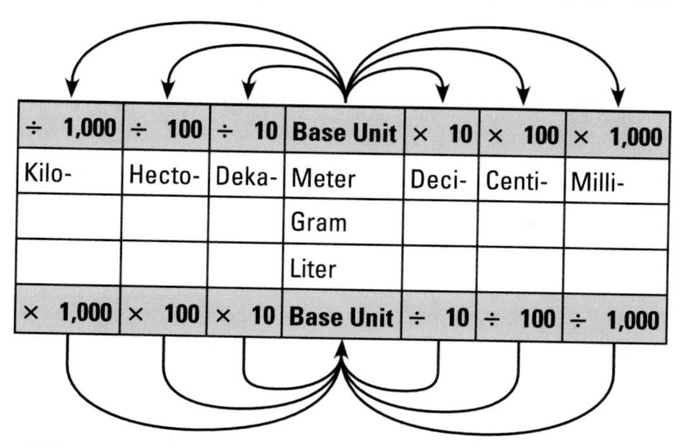

÷ 1,000	÷ 100	÷ 10	**Base Unit**	× 10	× 100	× 1,000
Kilo-	Hecto-	Deka-	Meter	Deci-	Centi-	Milli-
			Gram			
			Liter			
× 1,000	× 100	× 10	**Base Unit**	÷ 10	÷ 100	÷ 1,000

Remember

A shortcut for multiplying by 1,000 is to move the decimal point three places to the right. A shortcut for dividing by 1,000 is to move the decimal point three places to the left.

Example 2

The Danville Stroller Derby is 5 km long. How many meters is that?

The first unit is given in kilometers. To convert from kilometers to meters, you multiply by 1,000.

5 km × 1,000 = 5,000 m

Example 3

60,000 cm = ■ km

To convert from centimeters to meters, you divide by 100. Then to convert from meters to kilometers, you divide by 1,000.

60,000 cm ÷ 100 = 600 m

600 m ÷ 1,000 = 0.6 km

Talk About It

1. How are kilograms and kilometers similar? How are they different?
2. Can any measurement in milliliters be converted to liters? Can any measurement in milligrams be converted to meters? Explain.

Check

Complete. Use the abbreviation for the most appropriate metric unit.

1. Length of a marathon route: 42 _____
2. Amount of water in a small fishbowl: 2 _____
3. Mass of a dog: 15 _____
4. Width of a thumbnail: 1.5 _____

Convert.

5. 7.36 km = ■ m
6. 0.008 L = ■ mL
7. 325 g = ■ kg
8. **Reasoning** Is the length of the bar 370 cm or 3.7 cm? Explain.

37 mm

Practice

Skills and Reasoning

For each pair of measurements, choose the larger.

9. 1 meter, 1 kilometer **10.** 1 kilogram, 1 gram **11.** 1 centimeter, 1 meter

12. 1 liter, 1 milliliter **13.** 1 centimeter, 1 millimeter **14.** 1 kilometer, 1 millimeter

For **15–20,** name an appropriate unit of measure.

15. Weight of a 6th grader

16. Amount of water in a swimming pool

17. Distance from New York to Washington, DC

18. Amount of water in a raindrop

19. Weight of an aluminum can

20. Height of a stack of daily newspapers read in one month

Convert.

21. 90 g = ■ kg **22.** 32.6 mm = ■ m

23. 0.1 L = ■ mL **24.** 5.3 m = ■ mm

25. 7.88 mL = ■ L **26.** 1 m = ■ cm

27. 0.0042 kg = ■ g **28.** 3 L = ■ mL

29. 5 g = ■ kg **30.** 25 kg = ■ g

31. 13.1 cm = ■ mm **32.** 8 mL = ■ L

33. 2.67 km = ■ cm **34.** 18 cm = ■ m **35.** 42.9 kg = ■ g

36. Every year, a person creates 163,300 grams of food and yard waste. Convert this amount to kilograms

37. Newspapers make up the largest part of the trash in landfills. A 30.48 cm stack of newspapers has a mass of about 15.87 kg. Would it be appropriate to say that a 3 m stack of newspapers has a mass of about 16 kg? Explain.

Problem Solving and Applications

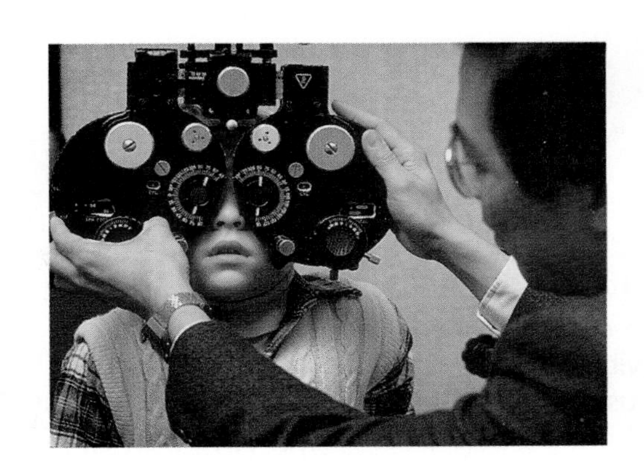

38. Careers Which measurement unit, millimeters or meters, would an optometrist use when measuring patients' eyes?

39. Estimation A person should drink eight glasses of water every day. Estimate if this is more or less than 1 liter.

40. Give the perimeter in millimeters, centimeters, and meters of a square whose sides are each 12 cm.

Problem Solving Hint
Draw a diagram.

41. Critical Thinking Robert and his granddaughter Bailey built a playhouse. The foundation of the playhouse was a 1.86 m-by-95 cm rectangle. What was the perimeter of Bailey's playhouse? Explain.

42. Using Data As part of a statistics experiment, seven students measured the approximate distance around a bus token. Find the average measurement rounded to the nearest hundredth of a centimeter. Explain your reasoning.

Jon	3.6 cm
Diane	34.2 mm
Wu-Lin	3.4 cm
Shelly	3.8 cm
Truc	37.5 mm
Mary	32.1 cm
Jason	3.5 cm

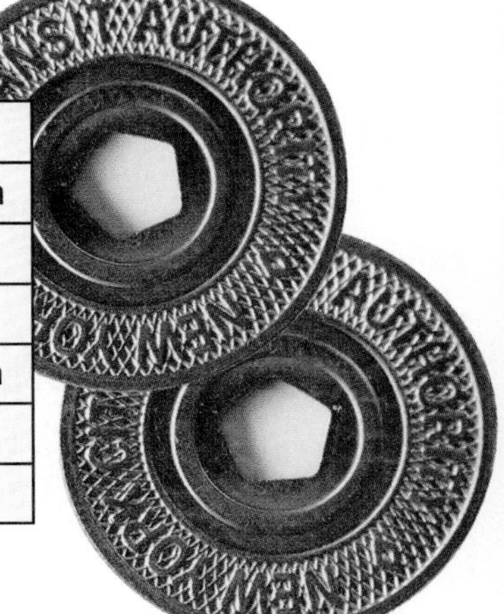

43. Journal Describe a situation in which you would use liters and one in which you would use milliliters. Explain why each measurement is appropriate.

Mixed Review and Test Prep

STAY SHARP!

Write in standard form.

44. one hundred three **45.** 8 trillion **46.** 45 billion **47.** two thousand, five

48. forty-five thousand, six hundred twelve **49.** one million, sixty-one thousand, twenty-two

Write each fraction as a decimal.

50. $\frac{55}{100}$ **51.** $\frac{2}{10}$ **52.** $\frac{67}{1,000}$ **53.** $\frac{532}{1,000}$ **54.** $\frac{4}{10}$

55. $\frac{9}{10}$ **56.** $\frac{2}{100}$ **57.** $\frac{10}{10}$ **58.** $\frac{8}{1,000}$ **59.** $\frac{99}{100}$

60. What is the sum of 16.82 and 8.09?

Ⓐ 8.73 Ⓑ 24.91 Ⓒ 136.0738 Ⓓ not here

Chapter 4
Lesson
3

Using Conversion Factors

You Will Learn

- to convert units within the customary system of measurement

Vocabulary

inch
foot
yard
mile
ounce
pound
quart
gallon
conversion factor

Did You Know?

In the 1300s, the standard for the foot was often the length of the king's foot. This length was usually copied inaccurately, and so the foot varied from village to village.

Learn

Tinoka is a "Trash Buster." Every spring for the past 3 years, Tinoka and other students at her school have volunteered to clean up their town.

Tinoka Dean lives in Evanston, Illinois.

The customary system is another system of measurement used in the United States to describe how long, how heavy, or how big something is. **Inch**, **foot**, **yard**, and **mile** are units for measuring length. **Ounce** and **pound** are units for measuring weight. **Quart** and **gallon** are units for measuring volume.

The customary system does not use a base unit and prefixes. Each unit has a separate name.

	Name	Abbreviation	Approximate Comparison
Length	Inch	in.	Length of half a thumb
	Foot	ft	Length of adult male foot
	Yard	yd	Length from nose to outstretched fingertip
	Mile	mi	Length of 14 football fields
Mass	Ounce	oz	Weight of greeting card
	Pound	lb	Weight of three apples
Volume	Quart	qt	Amount in a medium container of milk
	Gallon	gal	Amount in a small bucket

Inches can be abbreviated with quotation marks: 15" means 15 inches. Feet can be abbreviated with an apostrophe: 21' means 21 feet.

You can use the **customary system** to describe an object's length, weight, or volume.

Example 1

Some Trash Busters find bottles like this one. Use the abbreviation for the most appropriate customary unit.

Height of a plastic water bottle: 11 ______

Since length is being measured, the customary unit should be inches, feet, yards, or miles. Since a bottle is about 11 half-thumbs, the appropriate unit is inches, which is abbreviated "in."

The customary system is not based on powers of 10. In order to convert from one unit to another, you need to know the **conversion factor**, or the number of units that another unit is equal to.

Length	Weight	Liquid Capacity
1 foot = 12 inches	1 pound = 16 ounces	1 gallon = 4 quarts
1 yard = 3 feet		
1 mile = 5,280 feet		

Example 2

The average adult in the United States generates 8 pounds of newspaper garbage in a month. How many ounces is this?

One pound equals 16 ounces.

To convert pounds to lesser units, you multiply by the conversion factor, 16.

$8 \times 16 = 128$ ounces

Example 3

An oil company can re-refine 62 gallons of new oil from every 400 quarts of recycled oil. 400 quarts is equal to how many gallons?

One gallon equals 4 quarts.

To convert quarts to greater units, you divide by the conversion factor, 4.

$400 \div 4 = 100$ gallons

When converting, how can you tell when to multiply and when to divide?

Check

Convert.

1. 7 gal = ▒ qt
2. 64 oz = ▒ lb
3. 2 mi = ▒ ft
4. 4 ft = ▒ in.
5. **Reasoning** Which package weight is greatest: 48 ounces, 4 pounds, or 60 ounces? Explain.

Practice

Skills and Reasoning

Convert.

6. 496 ounces = ■ pounds

7. 252 inches = ■ feet

8. 15 pounds = ■ ounces

9. 36 feet = ■ yards

10. 4 feet = ■ inches

11. 2 pounds = ■ ounces

12. 48 quarts = ■ gallons

13. 12 yards = ■ feet

14. 10,560 feet = ■ miles

15. 24 pounds = ■ ounces

16. 9 gallons = ■ quarts

17. 4 miles = ■ feet

18. 192 inches = ■ feet

19. 21,120 feet = ■ yards

20. 44 quarts = ■ gallons

21. Many people recycle aluminum cans. An ordinary paper grocery bag holds about 1.5 pounds of crushed aluminum cans. How many ounces is that?

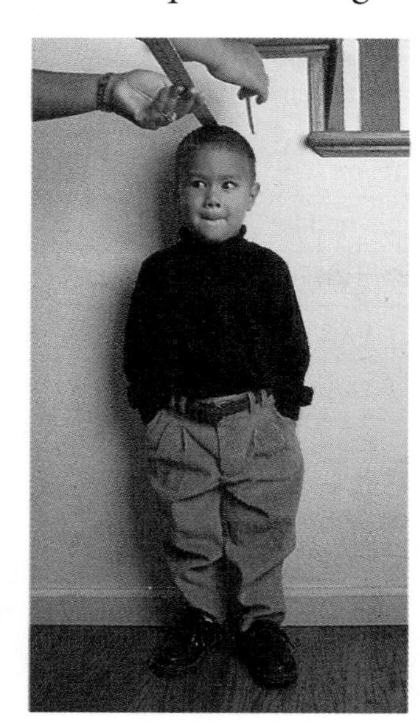

22. **Number Sense** You can double the height of a 2-year-old child to get an estimate of how tall he or she will be as an adult. Grant is 2 years old and 36 inches tall. How tall will he be as an adult? Give the answer in feet and in inches.

23. Patti made this drawing to help her remember the conversion factor for quarts and gallons.

a. How many quarts are in a gallon?

b. How many quarts are in 4 gallons?

c. How many gallons are in 32 quarts?

24. To perform well on the balance beam, a gymnast must always be aware of the length of the beam. The length of the balance beam at the Olympic Games is 96 inches, and it is 4 inches wide. How many feet long is the balance beam?

25. Order the following distances from least to greatest distance: 2 miles; 15,840 feet; 63,360 inches; 7,040 yards.

26. Carla is 48 in. tall. Her brother is 5 ft tall. Who is taller? Explain.

Problem Solving and Applications

Estimation Use the table to answer **27** and **28.**

27. Estimate how many heights in the table are between 5 and 6 feet.

28. Convert the heights in the table to feet. How close was your estimate?

Name	Height (in.)
Alison	53
Clive	57
Alberto	60
Maurice	63
Tanya	72

Using Data Use the Data File on page 206 to solve **29** and **30.**

29. Compare the waste generated in 1960 to 1990. How many more ounces of waste were generated per person per day?

30. Suppose the waste generated per person per day is the same today as in 1994.

a. About how many days would it take for one person to generate one ton of waste? Hint: One ton equals 2,000 pounds.

b. About how many years would it take for one person to generate one ton of waste?

31. **Critical Thinking** There are 16 ounces in a pound. You can use the equation $16x = y$ to convert ounces to pounds or pounds to ounces. Which variable is ounces and which is pounds? Explain.

32. **Journal** Is it easier to convert in the metric system or the customary system? Why?

Mixed Review and Test Prep

Using Data Use the scatterplot to answer **33–35.**

33. What was the highest score? Who received it?

34. What was the age of person B?

35. If another person, G, scored a 45, between which two scores was that score?

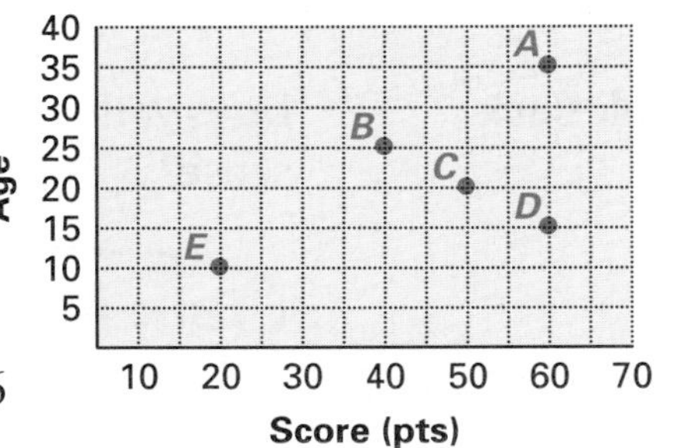

Order from least to greatest.

36. 0.77, 0.7777, 1.77, 0.777

37. 1.34, 1.06, 1.36, 1.66

38. 55.64, 0.564, 5.64, 5.06

39. 0.678, 0.0349, 0.982, 0.56

40. 3.005, 3.011, 3.002, 3.01

41. 67.1, 68.3, 66.3, 67.4, 67.5

42. What is the product of 2.8×0.6?

Ⓐ 16.8 Ⓑ 3.4 Ⓒ 1.68 Ⓓ 0.168

Chapter 4

Problem Solving

Analyze Word Problems: Finding Unnecessary Information

You Will Learn

- to find out whether a problem has unnecessary information and, if so, which information is not needed

Learn

In 1961, Yuri Gagarin became the first person in space when he orbited Earth once. Gherman Titov orbited Earth 17 times in the *Vostok II*. John Glenn was the first American to orbit Earth. He did so three times in 1962. Altogether, how many orbits did these three astronauts make?

Work Together

▶ Understand

What do you know?

What do you need to find out?

▶ Plan

What information do you need? — Number of orbits each astronaut made

Is there any unnecessary information? — The dates

Problem Solving Hint

Once you decide what information you need, ignore the other information.

▶ Solve

To find the total, add. — $1 + 17 + 3 = 21$

Write your answer. — Altogether, the first three astronauts made 21 orbits.

▶ Look Back

Does your answer make sense?

How do you know if you have unnecessary information?

Check

For each problem, state which numerical information is necessary and which is unnecessary. A problem may not have any unnecessary information. Then solve it.

1. The Grimaldi Crater has a diameter of 138 miles, or 222 kilometers, The Janssen Crater has a diameter of 118 miles, or 190 kilometers. What's the difference in miles between the diameters of these two craters?

2. The first artificial satellite, *Sputnik 1,* was launched on October 4, 1957. The second, *Sputnik 2,* was launched November 3, 1957. How many days later was *Sputnik 2* launched?

Problem Solving Strategies

- Draw a Picture
- Look for a Pattern
- Guess and Check
- Use Logical Reasoning
- Make an Organized List
- Make a Table
- Solve a Simpler Problem
- Work Backward

Choose a Tool

For each problem, state which numerical information is necessary and which is unnecessary. A problem may not have any unnecessary information. Then solve it.

3. On September 29, 1988, the U.S. space shuttle began flying after a $2\frac{1}{2}$ year delay. The next day, 7,122 human-made objects were being tracked in space. Of these, only 1,734 were satellites. The rest were junk—broken rocket parts and trash. About how many pieces of space junk large enough to track were in space?

4. *Skylab,* the first U.S. space station, was launched in 1973. Before it fell from orbit in 1979, three crews carried out missions lasting 28 days, 59 days, and 84 days. How long was *Skylab* in space?

Using Data Use the table to answer **5** and **6.**

HISTORICAL U.S. LAUNCH VEHICLES		
Launch Vehicle	**Height (ft)**	**Significant Launch**
Jupiter C	68	First U.S. satellite in 1958
Mercury-Redstone	83	First U.S. manned space flight in 1961
Saturn 5	363	First person to walk on moon in 1969
Space shuttle	184	First U.S. woman in space in 1983

5. What is the mean height of the launch vehicles?

6. How many years after the United States launched an astronaut into space did it launch its first female astronaut?

SECTION A

Review and Practice

(Lesson 1) Find the perimeter in **1–4.** Give the answer in centimeters.

1.

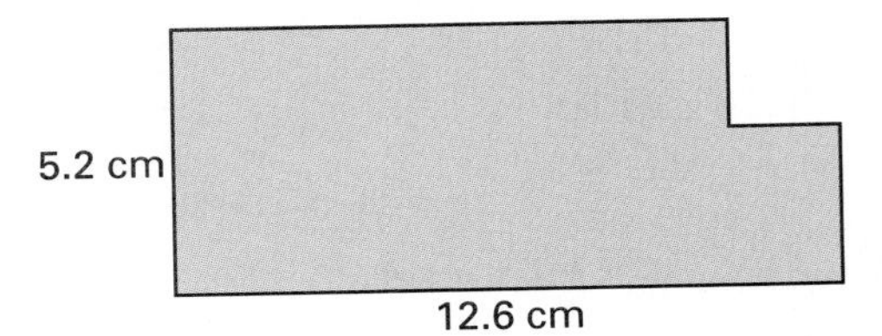

2.

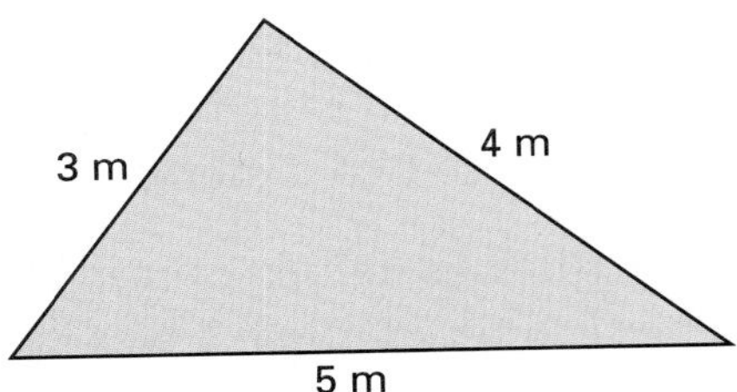

3. A square with a side length of 7.8 meters

4. A 6-sided figure with all sides 6.8 mm long

Find the perimeter in **5–9.** Give the answer in feet.

5.

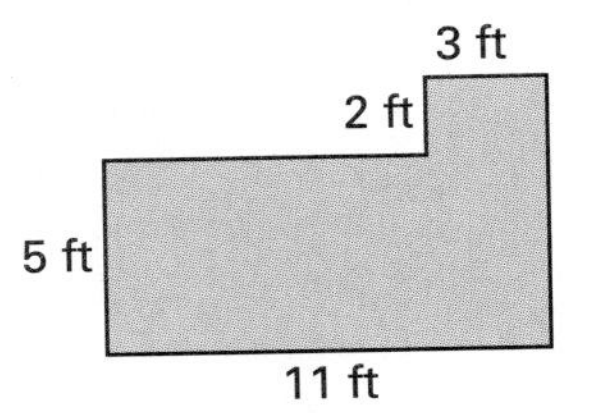

6.

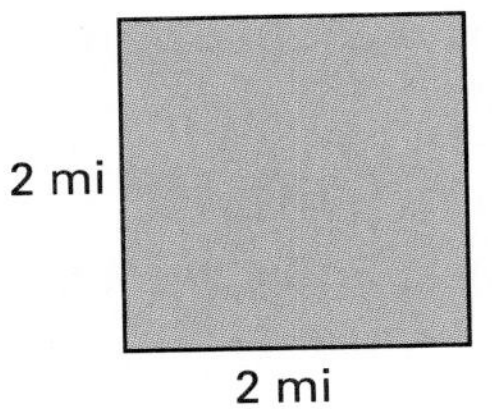

7. A triangle with sides of 6, 8, and 8 feet

8. A square with 5-yard sides

9. Sayaka's parents decided to build a wall around their rectangular garden. Two sides are 25 feet long and the other sides are 18 feet long. What is the perimeter of their garden?

(Lessons 2 and 3) Convert.

10. 8 L = ▒ mL **11.** 1,963.7 g = ▒ kg **12.** 38 km = ▒ mm

13. The school recycling drive collected 3 bags of 2-liter bottles. If each bag holds 50 bottles, how many liters can the collected bottles hold? How many milliliters can the collected bottles hold?

14. 128 ounces = ▒ pounds **15.** 116 quarts = ▒ gallons **16.** 180 feet = ▒ inches

17. The school recycling drive also collected 4 bags of quart cans. If each bag contains 75 cans, what is the total number of quart cans collected? How many gallons can the cans hold?

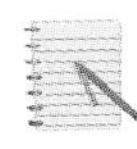

18. Journal Describe a situation in which you might need to convert from a larger measurement to a smaller one and from a smaller to a larger one.

Skills Checklist

In this section, you have:

- ☑ **Learned About Perimeter**
- ☑ **Converted in the Metric System**
- ☑ **Used Conversion Factors**

REVIEW AND PRACTICE

CHAPTER 4

SECTION B

Area of Polygons

It's bigger than a T-Rex! It attracts more than 100,000 people every day! It stretches over 4.2 million square feet! It's the Mall of America in Bloomington, Minnesota. This monster of a mall is the largest mall in the United States. Geometry helps designers and architects determine the area of objects, such as malls. Why do you think it's important to know the size of a building's rooms before you start building it?

GET READY!

Finding the Area of Polygons

Review multiplication. Find each product.

1.	312×13	**2.**	108×22	**3.**	275×15
4.	300×20	**5.**	420×11	**6.**	762×10
7.	522×30	**8.**	118×65	**9.**	305×50
10.	190×20	**11.**	219×17	**12.**	520×21

In this section, you will:

- ❒ **Explore the Area of Squares and Rectangles**
- ❒ **Learn About the Area of Parallelograms**
- ❒ **Learn About the Area of Triangles**

Chapter 4
Lesson
4

Area of Squares and Rectangles

Problem Solving Connection
- Look for a Pattern
- Make a Table

Materials
transparent 10×10 grids

Vocabulary
area
square inch
square centimeter
base
height
right angle

Explore

You have calculated the distance around the outside of squares and rectangles. How can you calculate the amount of surface they cover?

Work Together

1. The grid contains 100 small squares. Estimate the number of small squares it takes to cover each gray figure.

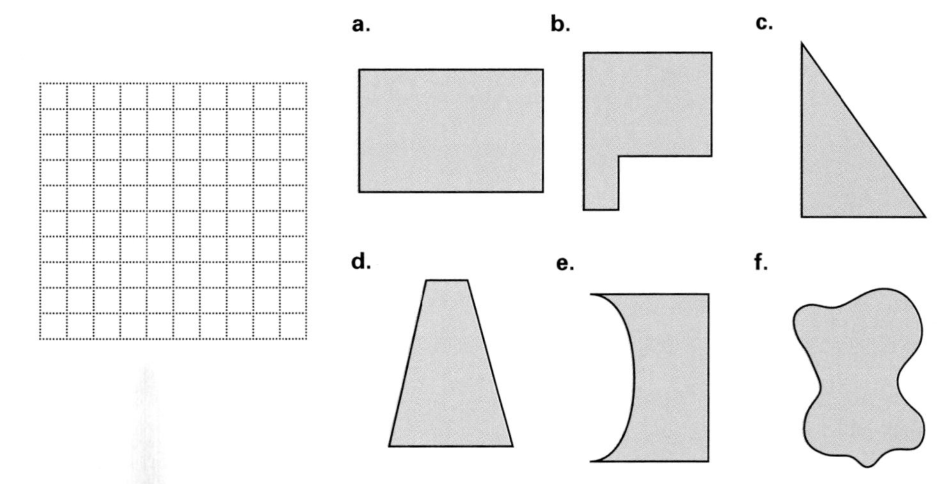

2. Place a transparent grid on top of each figure. Record the actual number of squares needed to cover the figure. For some figures, you may still need to estimate.
3. Record your findings in a table.

Figure	Squares Needed to Cover Figure (Estimate)	Squares Needed to Cover Figure (Actual)

Talk About It

4. For which figure was your estimate closest to the actual measurement? Why was your estimate so accurate?
5. For which figure was your estimate furthest from the actual measurement? Why was your estimate so inaccurate?
6. Why were some of your measurements with the grids still estimates?

Connect and Learn

The **area** of a figure is the amount of surface it covers. Area is measured by the number of unit squares of the same size that fit into the figure.

Example 1

Which rectangle has the greater area?

The first rectangle contains 28 squares. It has an area of 28 square units.

The second rectangle contains 27 squares. It has an area of 27 square units.

The first rectangle has a greater area.

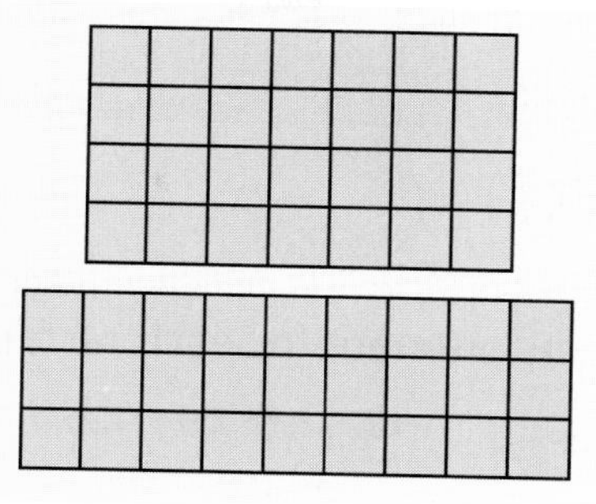

If a figure is labeled with inches, the area is expressed in **square inches** (in^2). A square inch is a square whose sides measure 1 inch. A **square centimeter** (cm^2) is a square whose sides measure 1 centimeter. A figure without labels is measured in square units ($units^2$).

You can find the area of a square or rectangle without counting the squares inside by using a formula.

The **base** of a square or rectangle is the distance across the bottom. The **height** is the distance along a side. A **right angle** is an angle as wide as the corner of a page. The height of a shape always forms a right angle with the base.

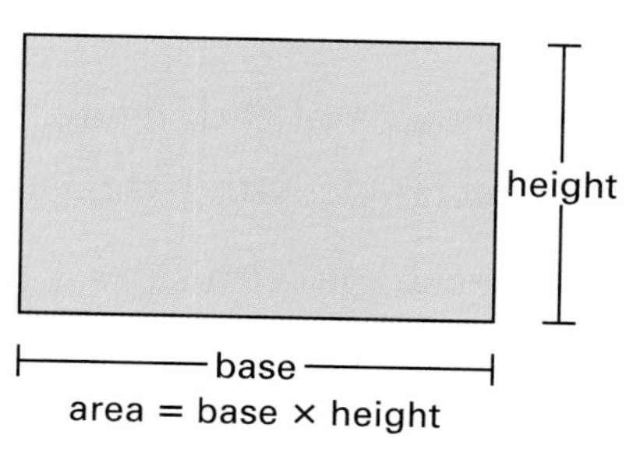

Example 2

Karen is designing the layout for the customer area of her clothing store. The area is a square. Each side is 21 ft long. How big is the customer area?

The base and height of the customer area are both 21 feet.

$A = bh$

$= 21 \times 21 = 441 \text{ ft}^2$

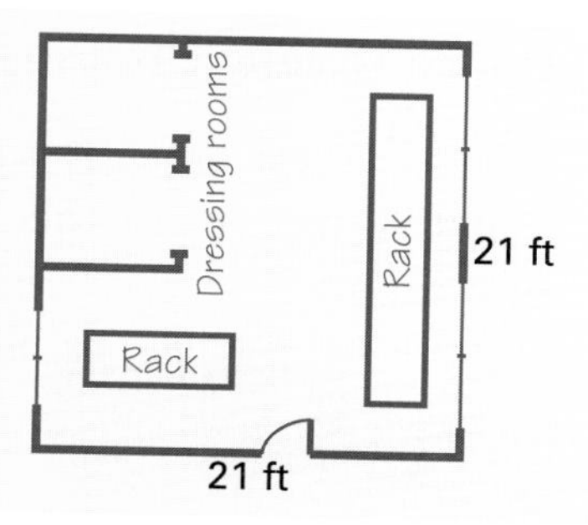

Check

Find each area.

1. 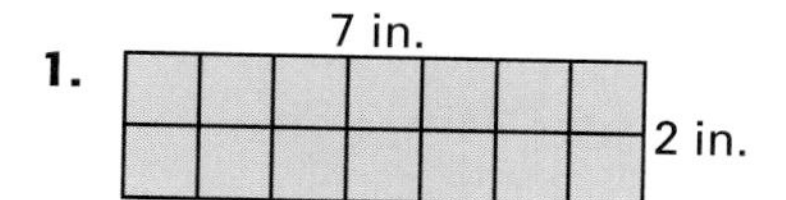

2. 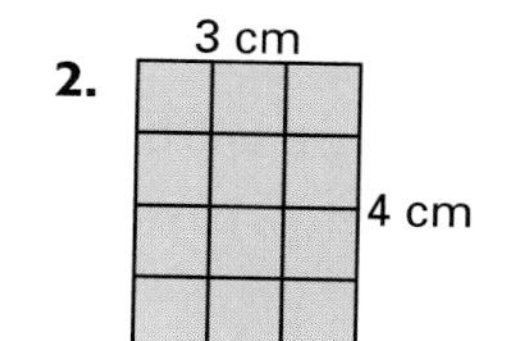

3. 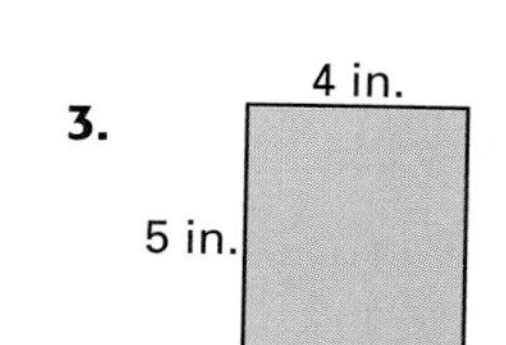

4. 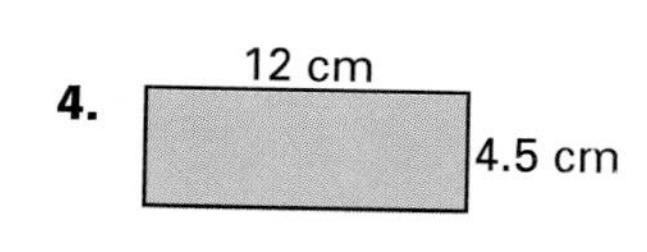

Practice

Find each area.

5. 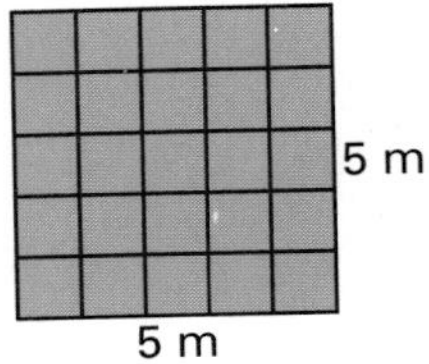

6. 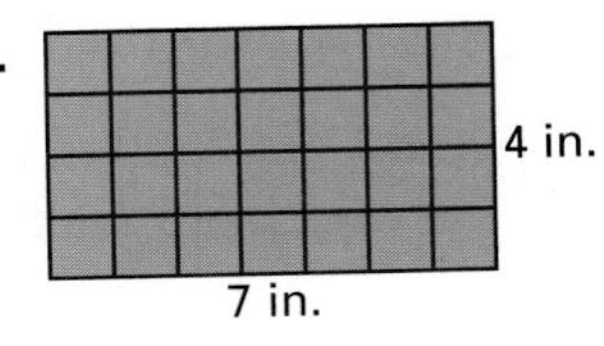

7. 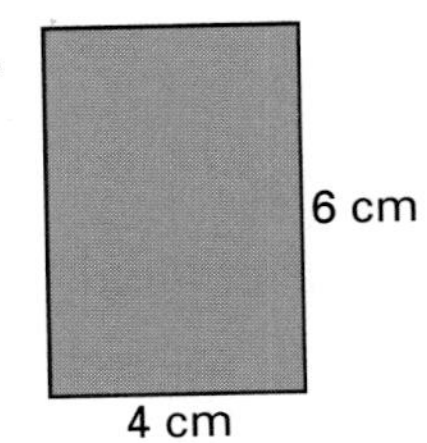

8. 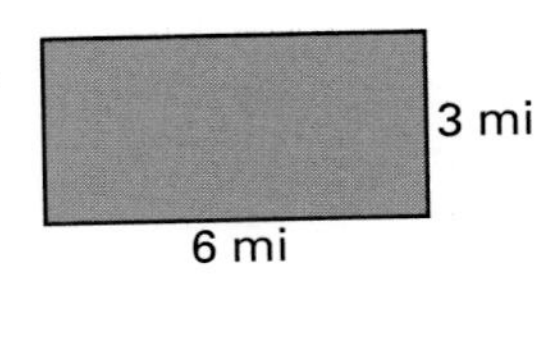

Find the missing measurement for each rectangle.

9. Area = 48 cm^2
Base = 2 cm
Height = ?

10. Area = 12.96 ft^2
Base = ?
Height = 7.2 ft

11. Area = ?
Base = 3 ft
Height = 9 ft

12. Area = 28.8 in^2
Base = ?
Height = 9.6 in.

13. $A = ?$
$b = 0.8$ km
$h = 1.5$ km

14. $A = 33$ yd^2
$b = 6$ yd
$h = ?$

15. $A = ?$
$b = 12$ mm
$h = 11$ mm

16. $A = 300$ in^2
$b = 30$ in.
$h = ?$

17. $A = 95.2$ ft^2
$b = 6.8$ ft
$h = ?$

Find the area of each figure.

18. Rectangle with base 3 and height 6

19. Square with side 2 cm

20. Rectangle with sides 4 in. and 12 in.

21. Square centimeter

Using Data Use the scatterplot to answer **22–24**.

22. What is the area of each rectangle?

23. Which rectangle is also a square? How can you tell?

24. What is the area of the rectangle with a height of 3 inches?

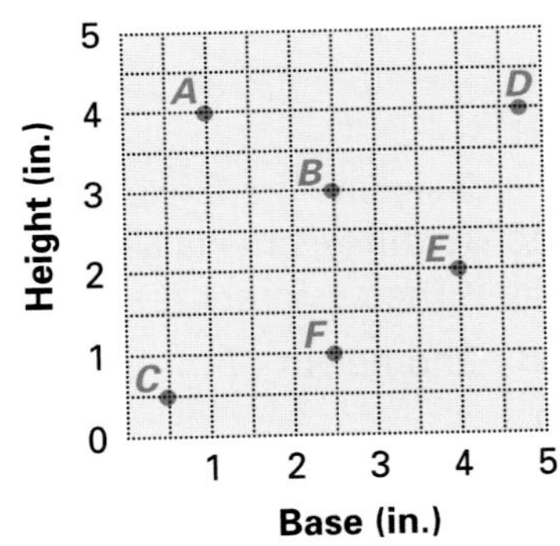

Johnson, William H., "Man in Vest" 1939-40. National Museum of American Art, Smithsonian Institute, Gift of Harmon Foundation.

25. Fine Arts *Young Man in a Vest,* painted by William H. Johnson, is 30 inches tall and 24 inches wide. Find the area of the painting.

26. Geometry For the dance fundraiser, Janet and Paul need a piece of tarp to cover and protect the gym floor. The floor is 90 feet by 100 feet. What size rectangular tarp is needed?

Problem Solving and CAREERS

Mall developers plan the location and layout of malls. They also encourage a variety of stores to locate in malls and set rents based on the space occupied by stores.

Using Data Use the map of the shopping mall to answer **27** and **28.**

27. What is the area of the largest store? Explain.

28. Critical Thinking The annual rent for each store is $35 per square foot. Find the range of rental costs. Explain your method.

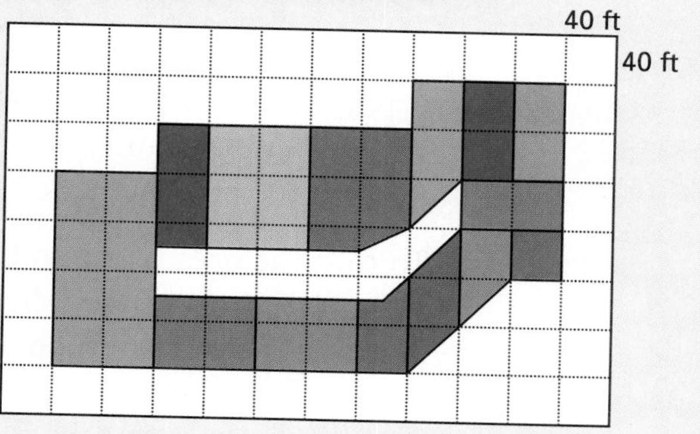

29. The perimeter of a rectangular bookstore is 220 ft, and its length is 50 ft. What is the annual rent for the bookstore if the rent is $20 per square foot each year? Explain.

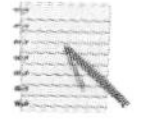

30. Journal For a given rectangle, if you switch the numbers for base and height, do you get a different area? Explain.

Mixed Review and Test Prep

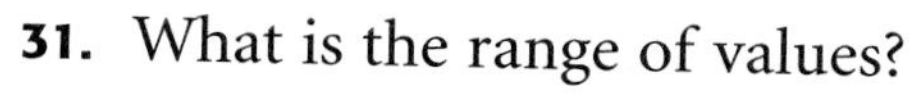

Use the stem-and-leaf diagram to answer **31–33.**

31. What is the range of values?

32. Is the median or the mean of the data greater? Explain.

33. What is the greatest number in the data that is less than 25?

Stem	Leaf
0	9
1	2 5 6 6 7 9
2	1 1 2 3 5 7 7 8 8
4	0 0 1

Estimate each sum, difference, product, or quotient.

34. $67.29 + 3.01$ **35.** $14.76 \div 6.12$ **36.** 13.546×1.68 **37.** $0.886 - 0.324$

38. $52{,}395 \div 9{,}546$ **39.** $\$16.34 - \$5.49$ **40.** $87.003 + 56.31$ **41.** 23.3×4.37

42. Cristina's painting is 2 feet tall. What else must she know to calculate how much wood she will need to build a frame for it?

Ⓐ The number of paintings on the wall
Ⓑ The length of the room
Ⓒ The width of the painting
Ⓓ The height of the ceiling

Chapter 4
Lesson
5

Area of Parallelograms

You Will Learn
- to find the area of parallelograms

Vocabulary
parallelogram

Learn

A parallelogram is a four-sided figure whose opposite sides are parallel.

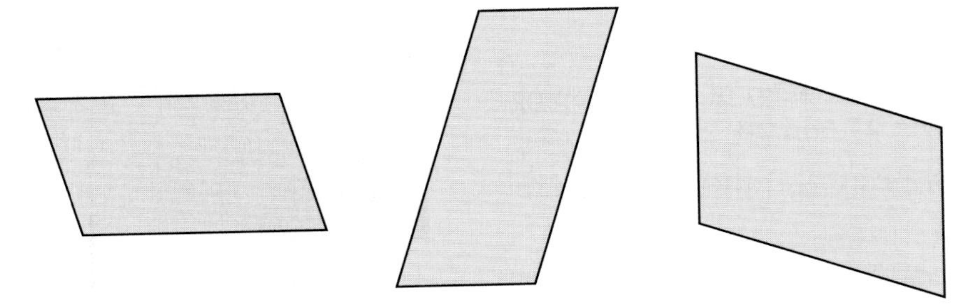

A parallelogram has the same area as a rectangle of equal base and height. You can cut a triangle-shaped piece from one side of a parallelogram and move it to the other side to form a rectangle.

To find the area of a parallelogram, use the same formula for the area of a rectangle: area = base × height, or $A = bh$. The height of a parallelogram is always a measure perpendicular to the base, not a slanted measure. It is usually shown as a dashed line.

Remember
Parallel lines are straight lines that never meet, just like the two l's in the word parallel.

Slide ΔJRK to ΔMSL.
Area of rectangle $RKLS = bh$
$9 \times 3 = 27 \text{ cm}^2$

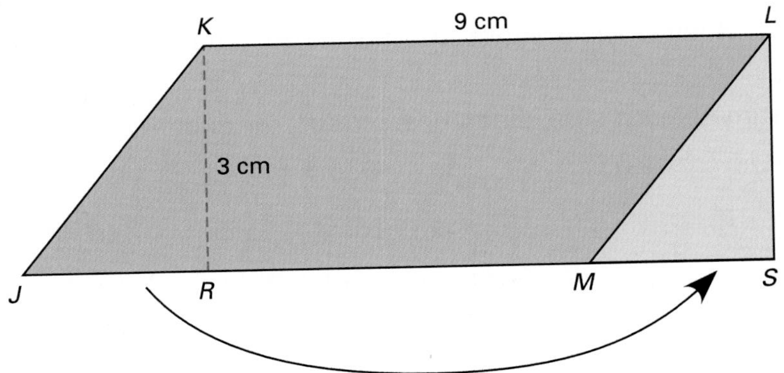

Example 1

Find the area.

There are 6 squares across the base.

The height is 2 squares.

$A = bh$

$= 6 \times 2 = 12$ units^2

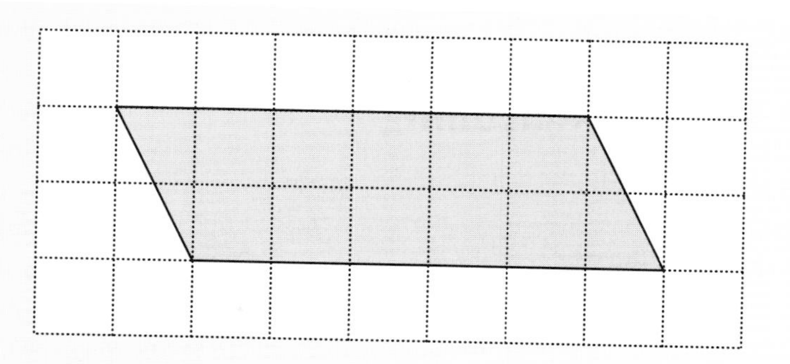

Example 2

Find the area.

$A = bh$

$= 7 \times 4 = 28$ in^2

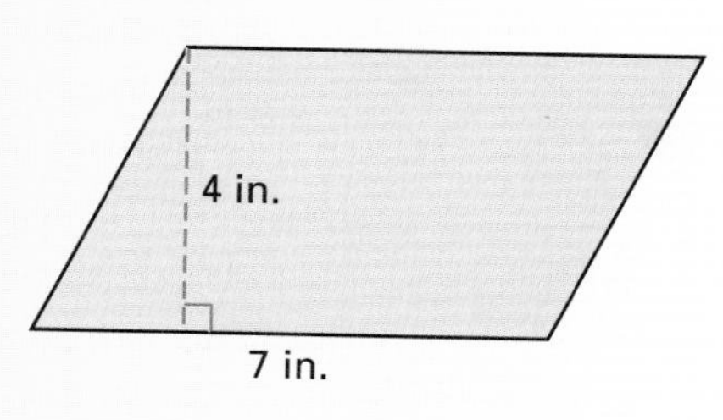

Example 3

Find the area.

$A = bh$

$= 8 \times 6.4 = 51.2$ cm^2

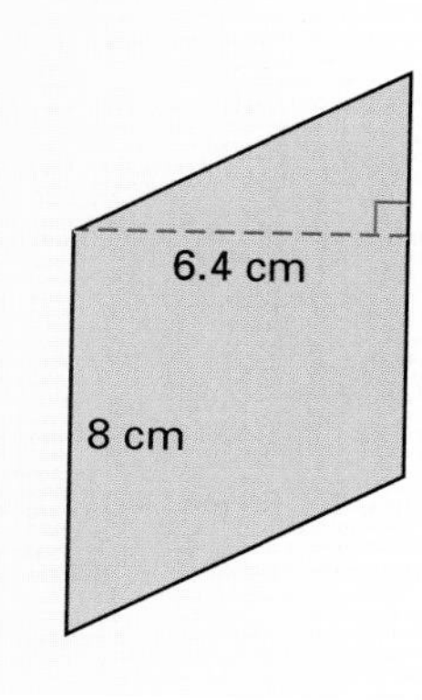

Talk About It

1. Can every parallelogram be changed into a rectangle by moving a section? Explain.
2. Can you use the formula for the area of a rectangle for any four-side figure? Explain.

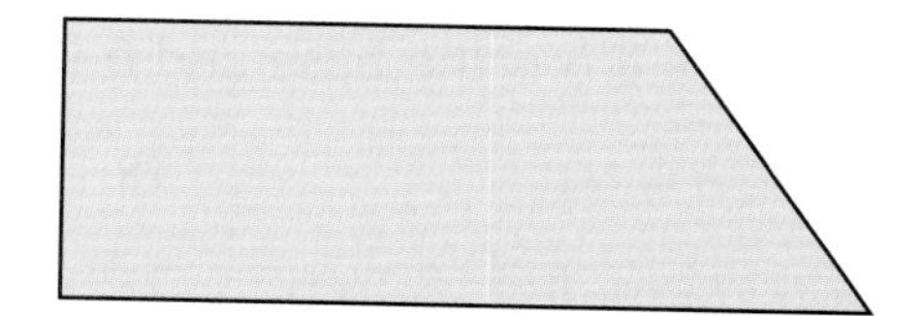

Check

Find the area.

1. 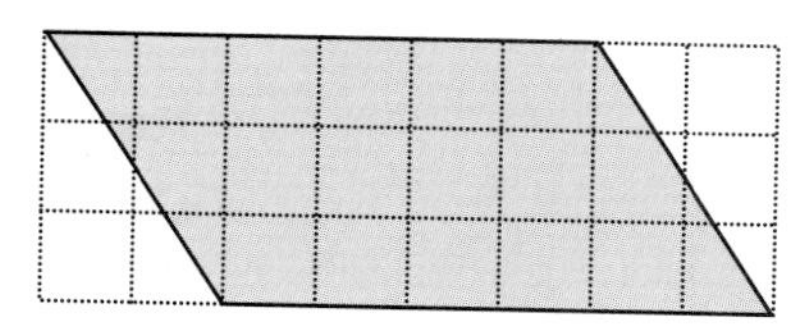

2. 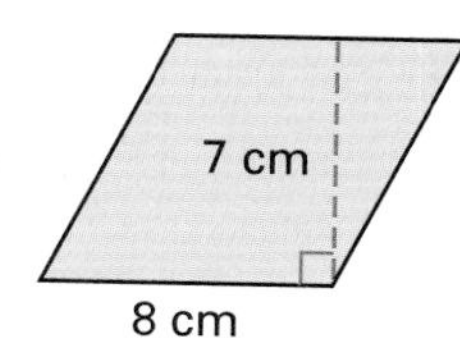

3. 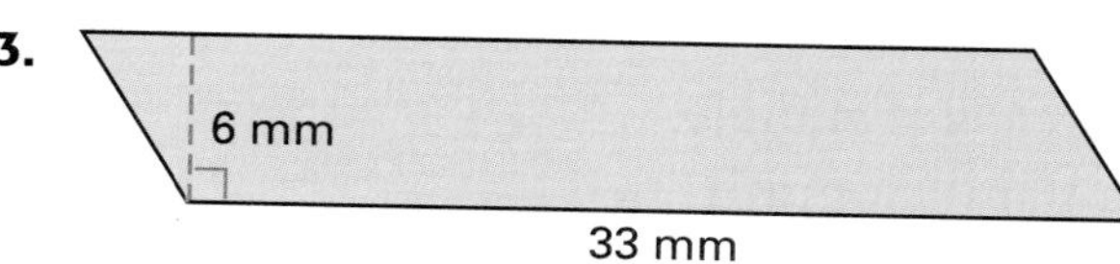

4. 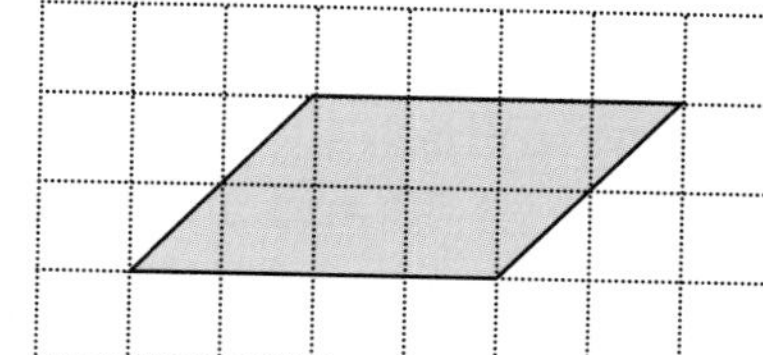

5. **Reasoning** Which figure has the greater area, a parallelogram with a base of 14 cm and a height of 5 cm or a parallelogram with a base of 14 cm and a slanted side of 5 cm? Explain.

Practice

Skills and Reasoning

Find each area.

6. 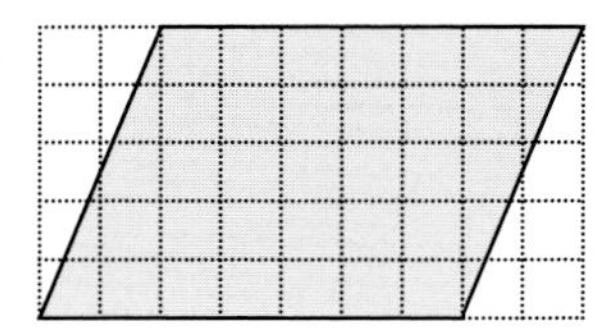

7. 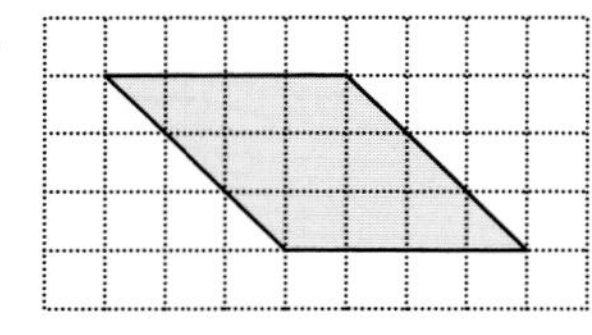

8. 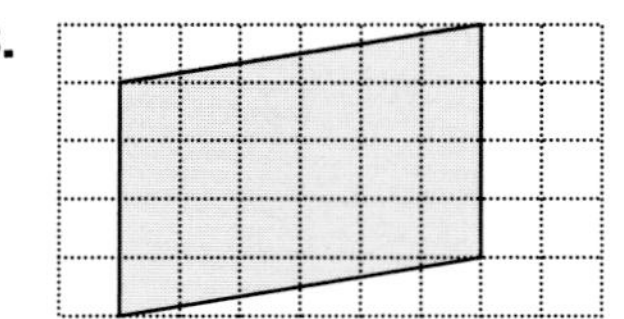

9. 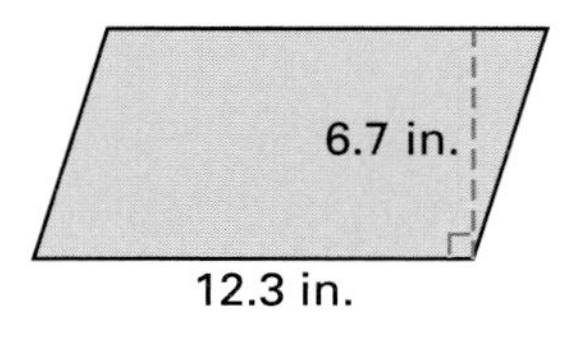

10. 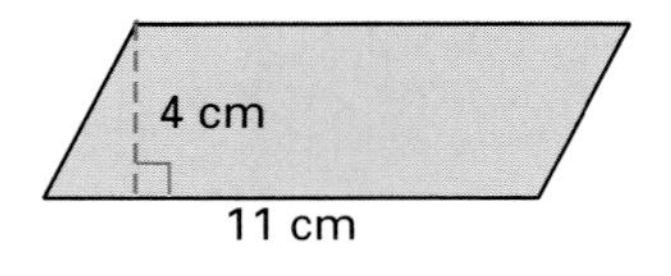

11. 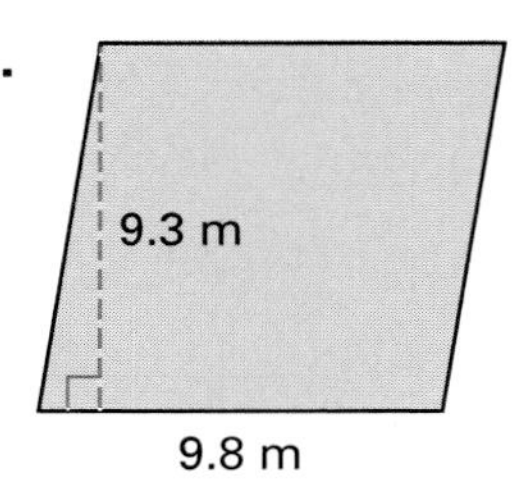

12. 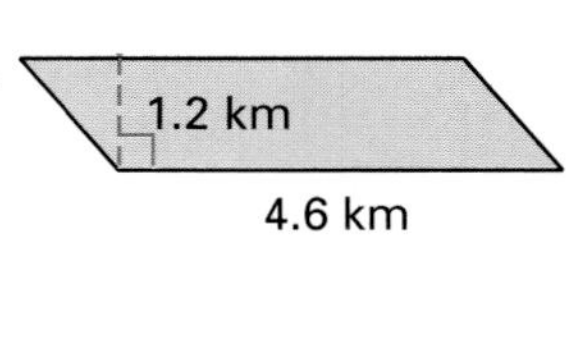

13. 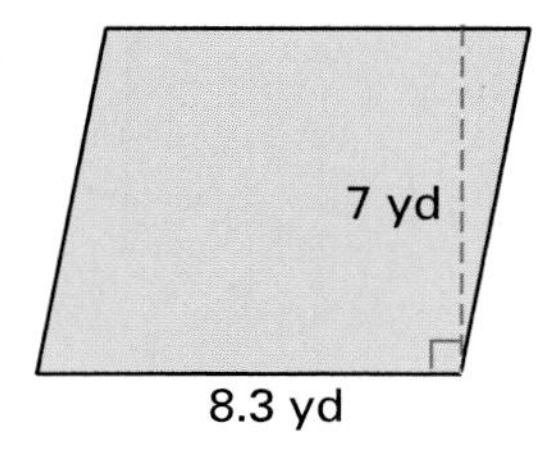

14. 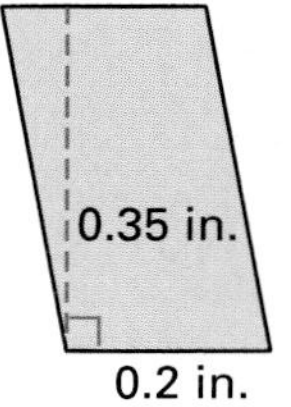

15. 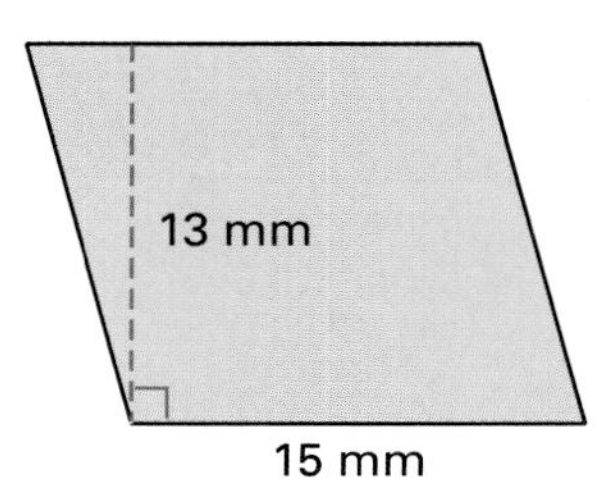

16. 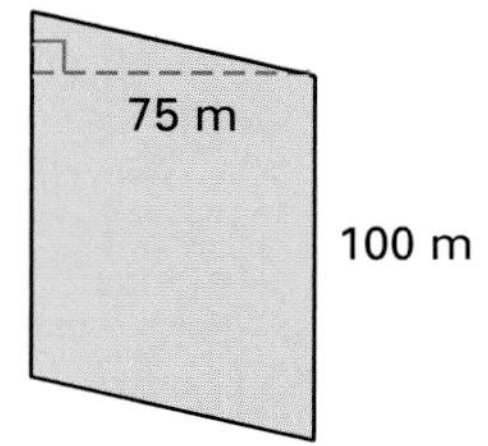

Find each area if b is the base and h is the height of a parallelogram.

17. $b = 20$, $h = 6$
18. $b = 12$ yd, $h = 7$ yd
19. $h = 25$ ft, $b = 25$ ft
20. $h = 14.7$ cm, $b = 18.1$ cm
21. $h = 13.2$ m, $b = 0.5$ m
22. $b = 1{,}000$ km, $h = 1{,}000$ km

23. 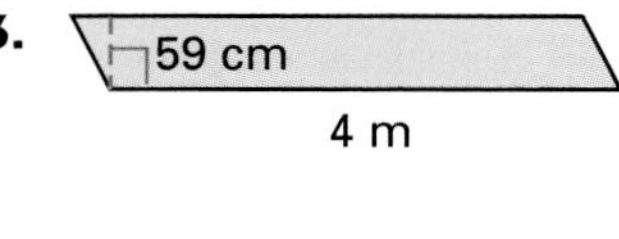

24. 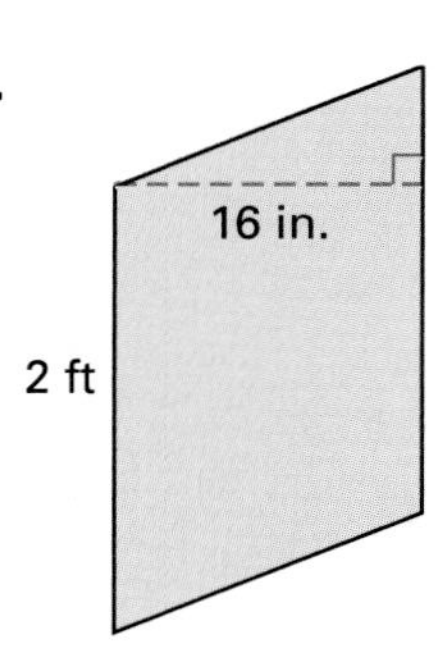

25. 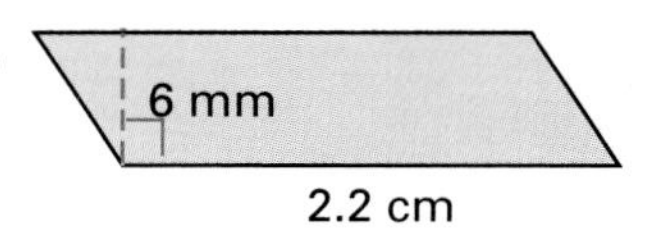

Remember
Convert to one unit of measure before multiplying.

26. **Reasoning** Which figure has the greater area, a rectangle with a base of 50 and a height of 20, or a parallelogram with a base of 50 and a slanted side of 20? Explain.

Problem Solving and Applications

27. Geometry At some malls, parking spots are shaped like parallelograms. If a spot is 3.1 meters wide and 4.7 meters long, what is its area?

28. Estimation The state of Tennessee is shaped roughly like a parallelogram. Its northern border is about 442 miles long and the shortest distance between the northern and southern borders is about 115 miles. Estimate the area of Tennessee.

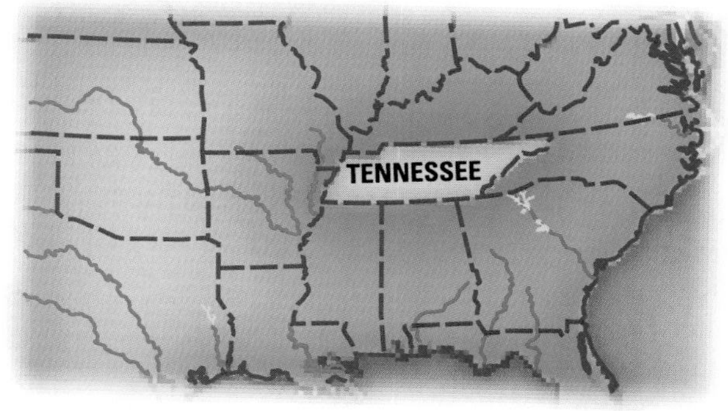

29. Patterns Jaspar drew a parallelogram with a base of 2 cm and a height of 2 cm. He drew another with base 2 cm and height 4 cm and a third with base 2 cm and height 8 cm. If Jaspar continues drawing parallelograms in this pattern, what will the area of the sixth shape be?

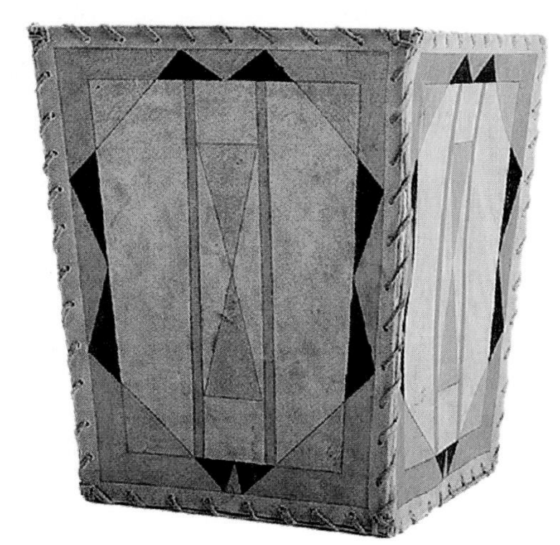

30. Fine Arts Violet wants to add parallelograms to the design of her Native American drum. Each parallelogram should be about 36 square inches. If she wants the height to be four times as long as the base, what should the height of each parallelogram be?

Mixed Review and Test Prep

STAY SHARP!

Write in standard form.

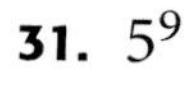

31. 5^9 **32.** 3^4 **33.** 9^5 **34.** 12^2 **35.** 2^6 **36.** 4^3

37. 10^{13} **38.** 1^9 **39.** 6^1 **40.** 8^7 **41.** 20^2 **42.** 7^8

Simplify.

43. $108.93 - 72.41$ **44.** $0.5678 + 1.3452$ **45.** $6.25 + 7.36$ **46.** $238.14 - 5.67$

47. $32.08 - 5.99$ **48.** $1.5 + 0.5$ **49.** $2.3 + 4.5$ **50.** $87.003 - 56.31$

51. Choose the correct unit for the area of a figure.

Ⓐ Centimeter Ⓑ Meter Ⓒ Square centimeter Ⓓ Foot

Chapter 4
Lesson
6

Area of Triangles

You Will Learn

- to find the area of a triangle

Did You Know?

Many kites are made of one or more triangles. Kites are the oldest form of aircraft.

Learn

Sonia and Aaron are building the set for a play about ancient Egypt. They need to paint a large cardboard triangle to look like an Egyptian pyramid. The triangle measures 14 ft wide by 8 ft high. They have enough paint for about 60 square feet of cardboard. Do they have enough paint?

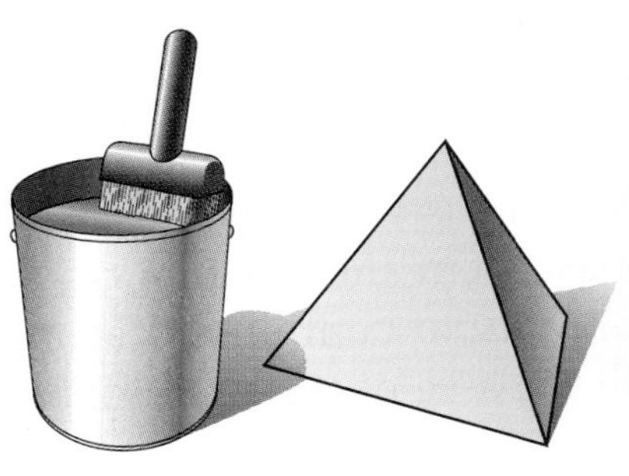

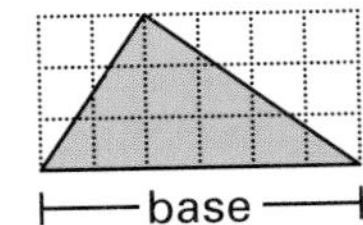

The area of a triangle equals half the area of a rectangle whose base and height are the same as the triangle's.

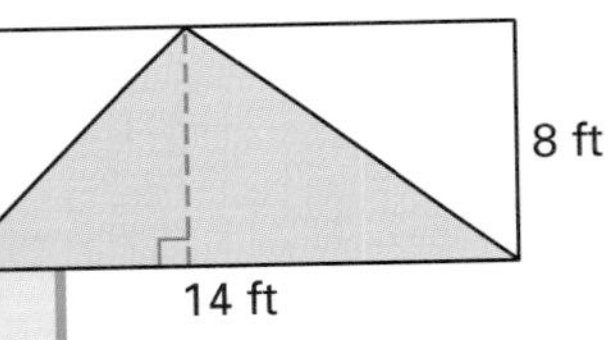

Sonia thinks...

I'll imagine there's a rectangle around the triangle.

I'll find the area of the rectangle and cut it in half.

$A = bh$

$= 14 \text{ ft} \times 8 \text{ ft}$

$= 112 \text{ ft}^2$

Half of 112 is 56. The cardboard is 56 square feet, so we have enough paint.

Aaron thinks...

I'll use the area formula for a triangle.

$A = \frac{1}{2}bh$

$= \frac{1}{2} \times 14 \text{ ft} \times 8 \text{ ft}$

$= 56 \text{ ft}^2$

The area is 56 ft^2. We have enough paint.

Example 1

Find the area.

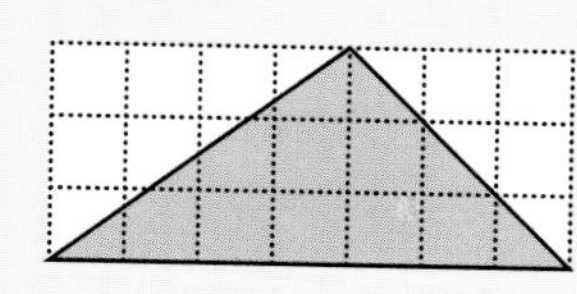

Area of a rectangle $= bh$
$= 7 \times 3$
$= 21$ units^2
Half of 21 is 10.5 units^2.

Area of a triangle $= \frac{1}{2}bh$
$= \frac{1}{2} \times 7 \times 3$
$= 10.5$ units^2

The height of a triangle is always perpendicular to the base.

Example 2

Find the area.

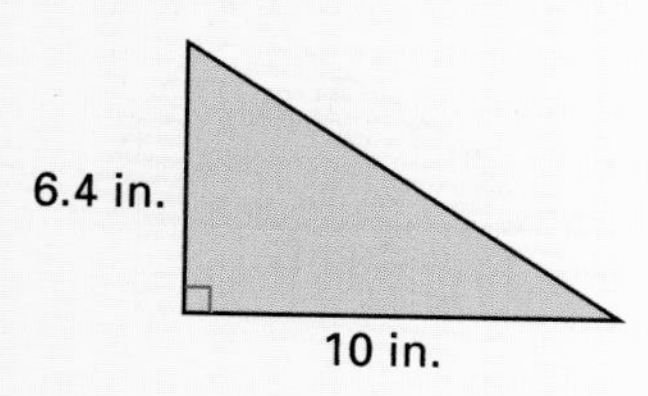

area $= \frac{1}{2} \times$ base $\times$ height
$= \frac{1}{2} \times 10$ in. $\times 6.4$ in.
$= 32$ in^2

Example 3

Devon has a triangular kite that is 5 ft wide and has an area of 10 ft^2. How tall is the kite?

$A = \frac{1}{2}bh$

$10 = \frac{1}{2} \times 5 \times h$

$10 = \frac{5}{2}h$

$20 = 5h$

$4 = h$

5 ft

The kite is 4 ft tall.

Math Tip

If you are given the area of a triangle and either its base or height, you can still find the missing measure using the formula for the area of a triangle.

1. Why isn't division shown in Sonia's way on page 234?
2. Why do you need to multiply by $\frac{1}{2}$ when finding the area of a triangle?

Check

Find each area.

1. 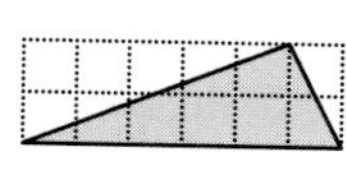

2. 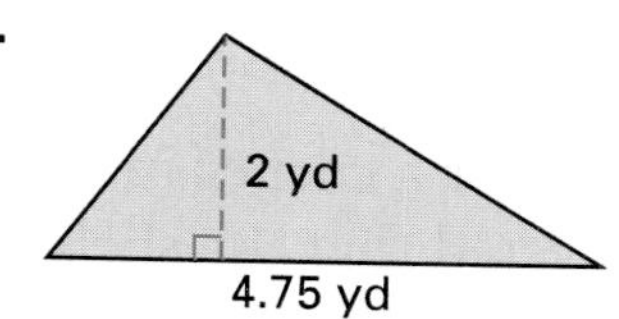

3. 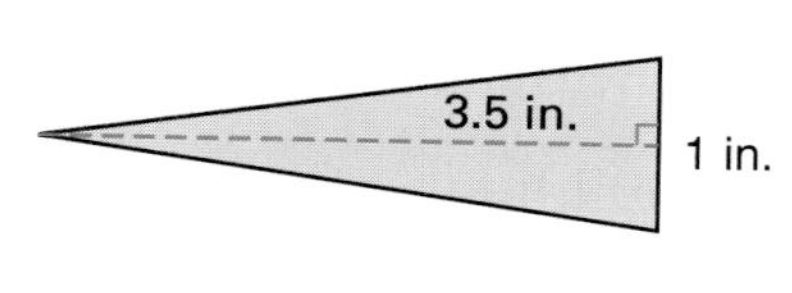

4. **Reasoning** Two triangular sails are each 16 feet tall. Do they both have the same area? Explain.

Practice

Skills and Reasoning

Find the area of each triangle.

5. 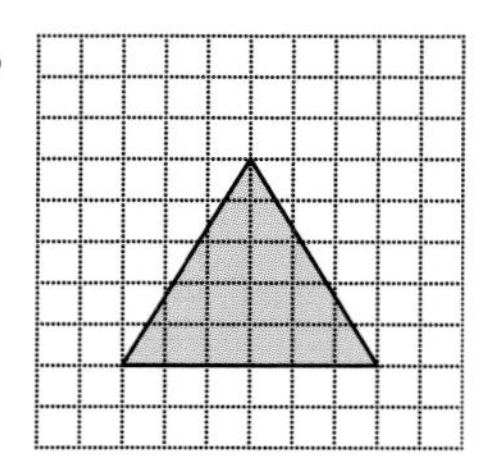

6. 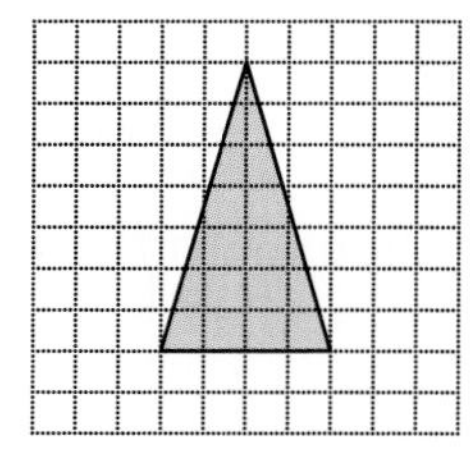

7. 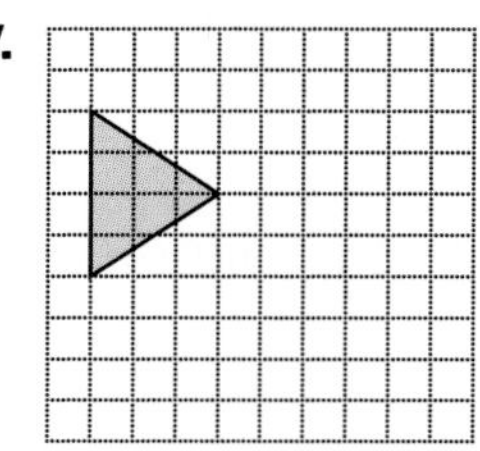

8. 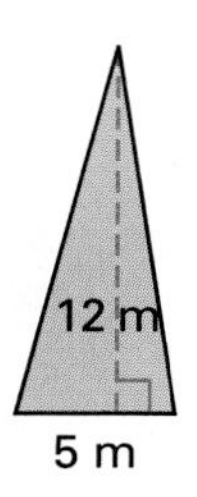

9. 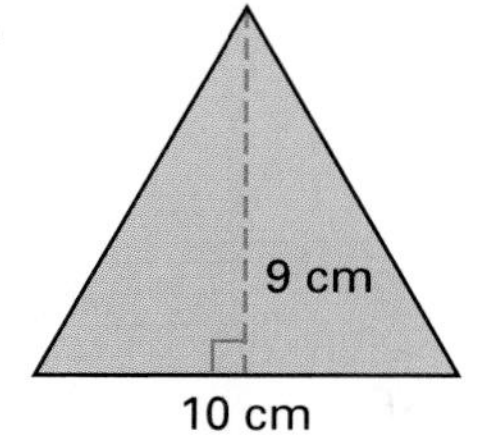

10. 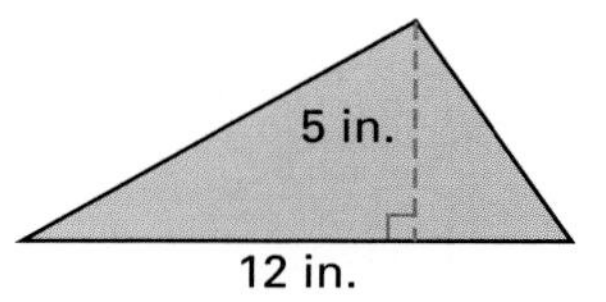

11. 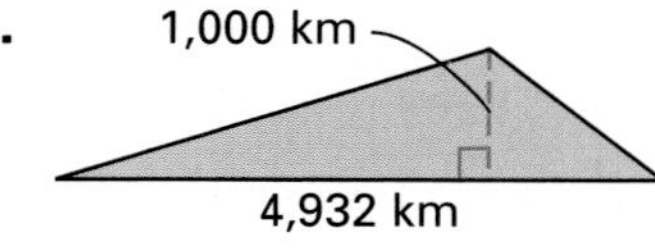

12. 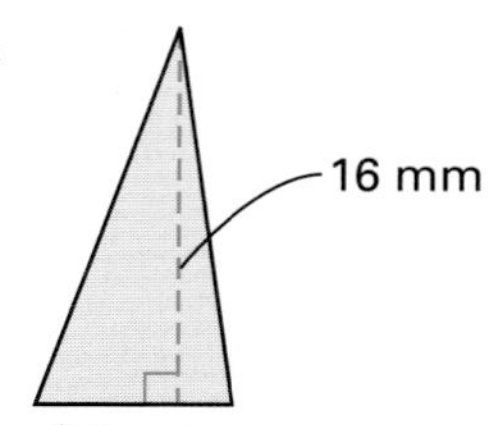

13. 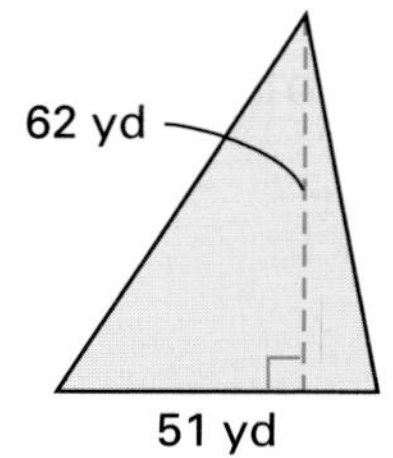

14. 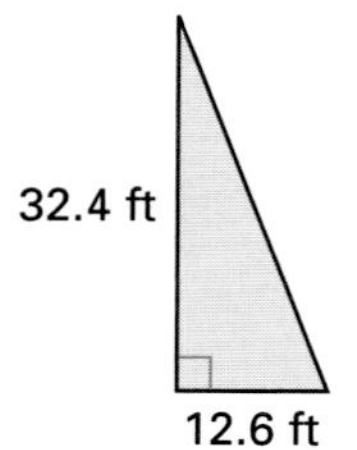

15. 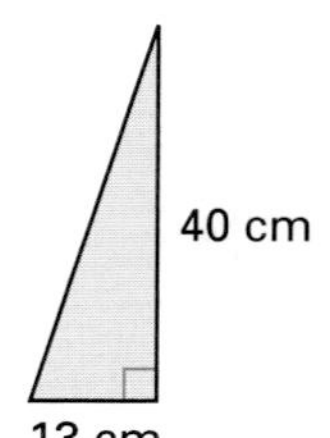

16. 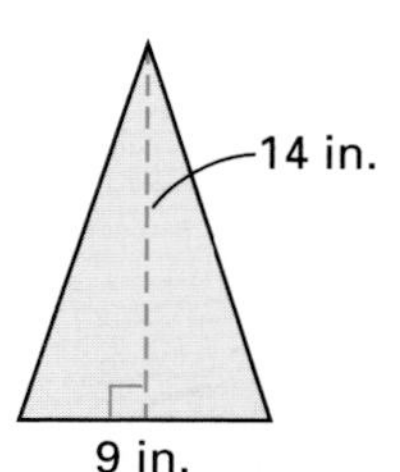

Find the height of each triangle if b is the base and A is the area.

17. $b = 6$ in., $A = 54$ in^2
18. $b = 62$ ft, $A = 186$ ft^2
19. $b = 9$ in., $A = 63$ in^2

20. A rectangular plot of ground and a triangular plot of ground have the same area. The rectangular plot is 2 miles by 4 miles. The triangular plot has a base of 2 miles. What is the triangle's height? Explain.

21. Which has the greater area: a triangle with a height of 20 and a base of 3 or one with a height of 3 and a base of 20? Explain.

22. Tina is building a set of triangular shelves for a corner in her bedroom. She sketched this plan, but she has discovered that the shelves need to be 3 in. shorter than she planned. What will the area of each new shelf be?

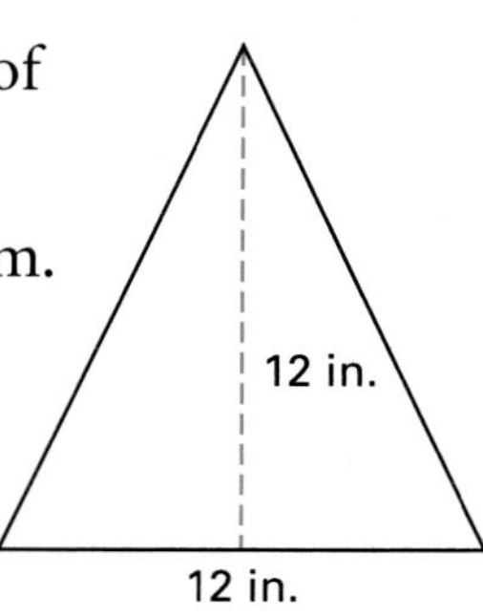

Problem Solving and Applications

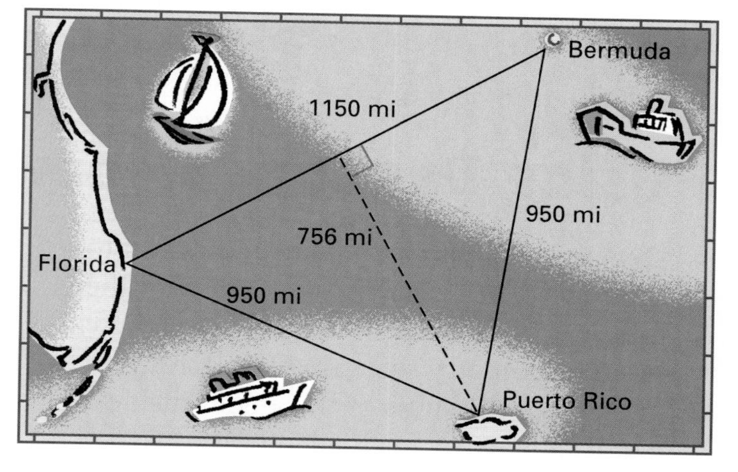

23. **Geography** The Bermuda Triangle is a region in the Atlantic Ocean where ships and airplanes are reported to have mysteriously disappeared since the 1940s. Use the diagram to find the area of the Bermuda Triangle.

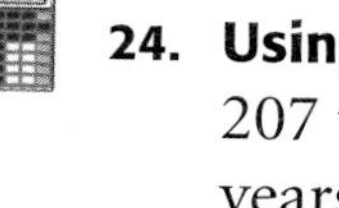

24. **Using Data** Use the table on page 207 to find between which two years the greatest increase in the number of shopping centers occurred.

25. **Critical Thinking** The central plaza of a shopping mall has four triangular flower beds. Each bed has a base of 60 inches and a height of 48 inches. If one plant can be planted every 4 square inches, how many are needed to fill the flower beds? Explain.

26. **Journal** A triangular plot of land has a base of 1 mile and an area of 1 square mile. Explain how both can have a measure of 1 unit.

Mixed Review and Test Prep

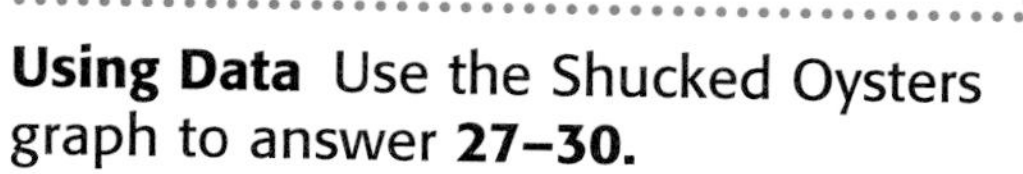

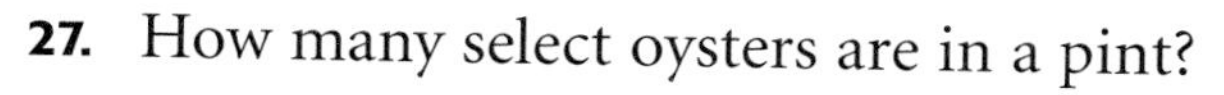

Using Data Use the Shucked Oysters graph to answer **27–30.**

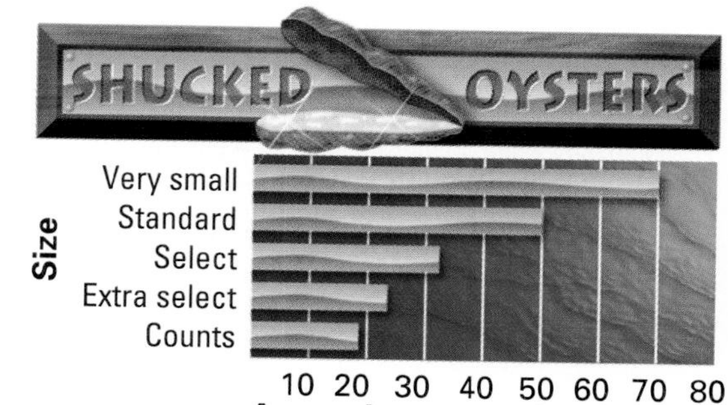

27. How many select oysters are in a pint?

28. How many more very small oysters than counts oysters are there in a pint?

29. Which size oyster gives the greatest number per pint?

30. Which size oyster gives about twice as many oysters per pint as extra select?

Write each expression using exponents.

31. $6 \times 6 \times 6 \times 6 \times 6$

32. $435 \times 435 \times 435$

33. $7 \times 7 \times 7 \times 7$

34. $5 \times 5 \times 9 \times 9 \times 9$

35. $10 \times 10 \times 10 \times 10$

36. $1 \times 1 \times 1 \times 1 \times 1 \times 1$

37. What is 2,482,698,212 rounded to the nearest ten million?

Ⓐ 2,500,000,000 Ⓑ 2,482,700,000 Ⓒ 2,480,000,000 Ⓓ 2,482,698,000

Technology

Using Dynamic Geometry Software

Dynamic geometry software allows you to draw geometric figures and work with them in a variety of ways. In this activity, you will use the geometry software to look for patterns in the sums of the angles inside quadrilaterals, or four-sided polygons.

Materials

Interactive CD-ROM Geometry Tool or other geometry software

How can you use the geometry software to determine the sum of the interior angles in a quadrilateral?

Work Together

Use your geometry software.

1. Draw a quadrilateral. Make sure you draw only a convex polygon. Do **not** draw a figure with a "dent" in it, like this one.

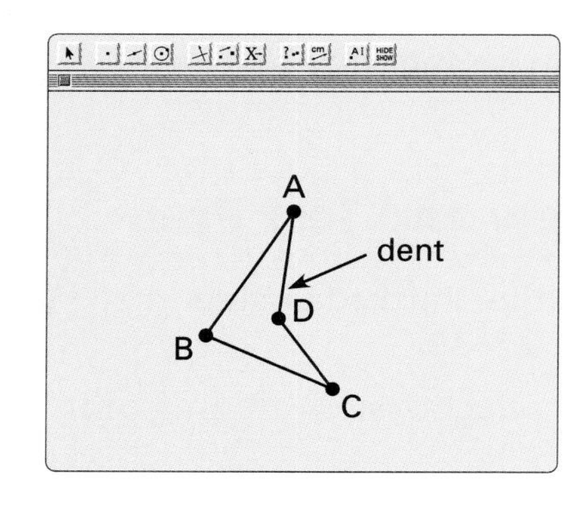

2. Use the measure tool to measure the interior angles in your quadrilateral.

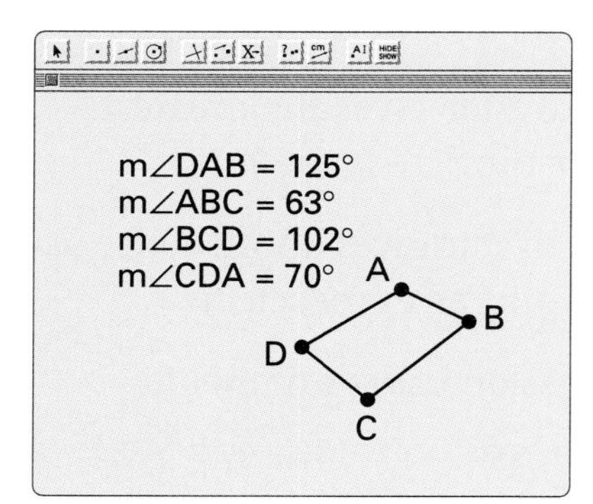

3. Use the calculator feature of the software to find the sum of the measures of the angles.

4. Without creating a dent, change the shape and size of the quadrilateral. You can do this by clicking on any of the points in your figure and dragging it to a new location.

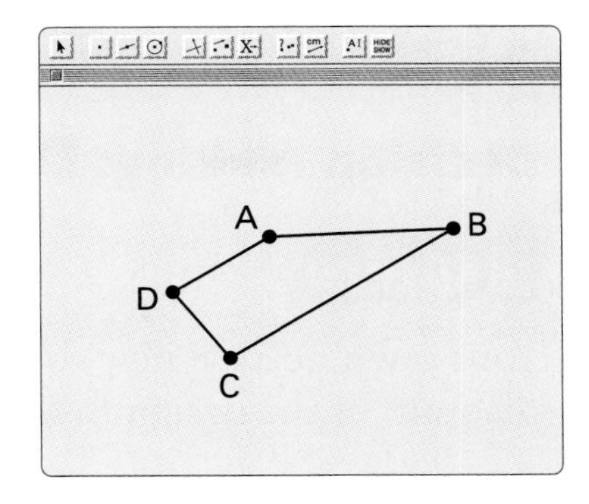

5. Measure the angles of the new quadrilateral and determine if the sum of the angles changes.

6. Repeat steps 4 and 5. What generalization can you make about the sum of the interior angles in any quadrilateral.

Exercises

Use your geometry software to answer **1** and **2.**

1. Find the sum of the interior angles in a five-sided polygon.
2. Find the sum of the interior angles in a six-sided polygon.

Extensions

3. Predict the sum of the interior angles in a seven-sided polygon. Explain your prediction. Draw a seven-sided polygon with the software and check to see if your prediction is correct.
4. Write a rule or formula for the sum of the interior angles in any polygon, no matter how many sides it has. Explain your thinking.
5. Draw a four-sided concave polygon—a polygon with a "dent" in it. Is the sum of the interior angles different for this type of polygon? Explain.

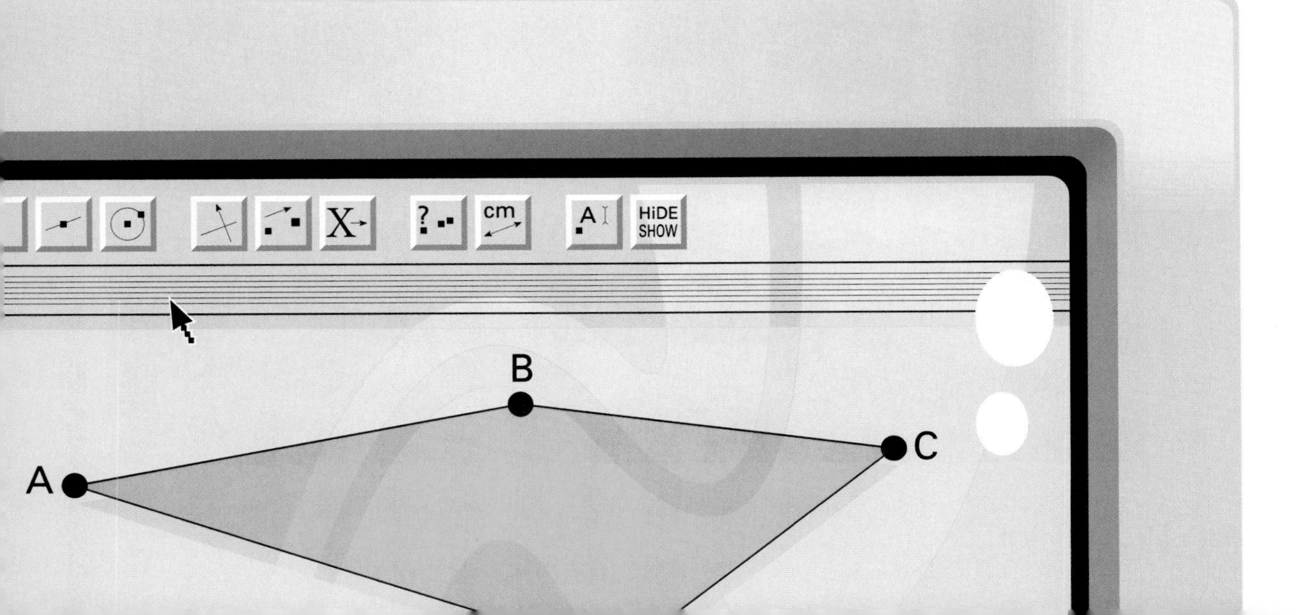

Chapter 4

Problem Solving

Decision Making: Designing a Shopping Mall

You Will Learn

- how to use what you know about area to make decisions

Materials

- centimeter ruler
- colored markers or pencils

Explore

Your town needs a new shopping mall. Design a mini-mall and present a diagram of the design to the city council.

Facts and Data
• The mall must have at least six stores.
• The mall must have a central area with benches and a fountain.
• Customers can walk through the area from store to store.
• The mall must have restrooms and an elevator to a restaurant on the roof.
• The mall's area must be at least 1,800 m^2.
• You do not need to include the restaurant or its area in your design, because it is on another floor.

To make your diagram easy to read, you plan to:

- use one color to label the length of each line in centimeters.
- use another color to label the length that each wall will actually be.
- write the area for each store, the central area, the restrooms, and the elevator on the diagram.

Work Together

Understand

1. What are you asked to do?
2. What kind of information do you have to help you?
3. What other things are important to you in designing the mall?
4. How can you use you knowledge of area to help you make your design?

Plan and Solve

5. What stores will you have in your mall?
6. Where will each store, the central area, the restrooms, and the elevator be located?
7. How long will each wall actually be?
8. How long will each wall be on your diagram?
9. What is the area of each store, the central area, the restrooms, and the elevator?

Make a Decision

10. How did you decide what stores to have in your mall and where to put them?
11. How did you decide how large to make each store, the central area, the restrooms and the elevator?

Present Your Decision

12. Share your design with others. Explain how you made your design decisions.

SECTION B

Review and Practice

(Lesson 4) Find the area of each rectangle or square.

1.

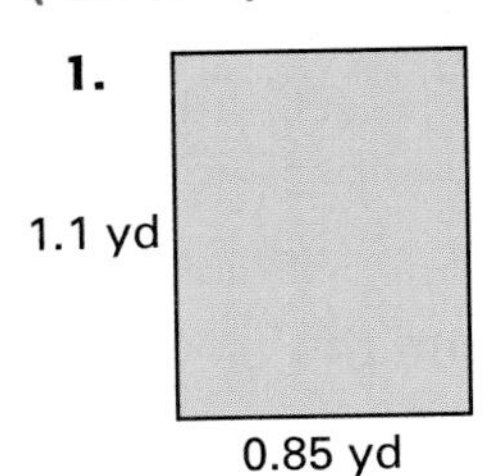

2.

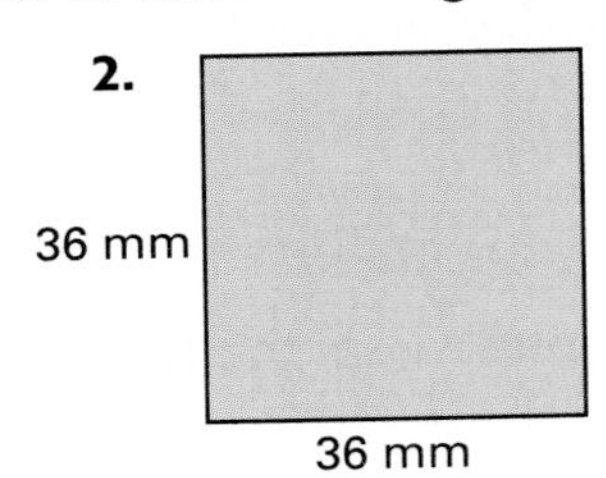

3.

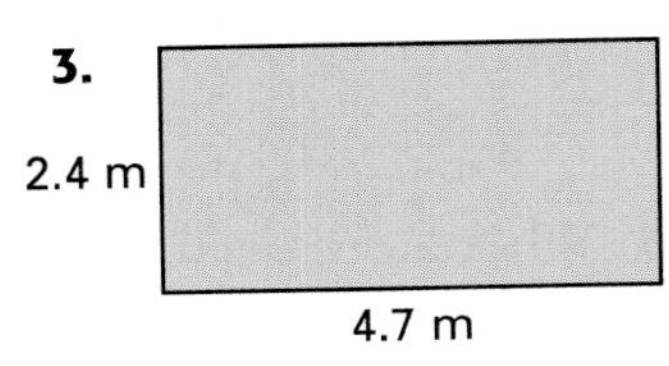

4.

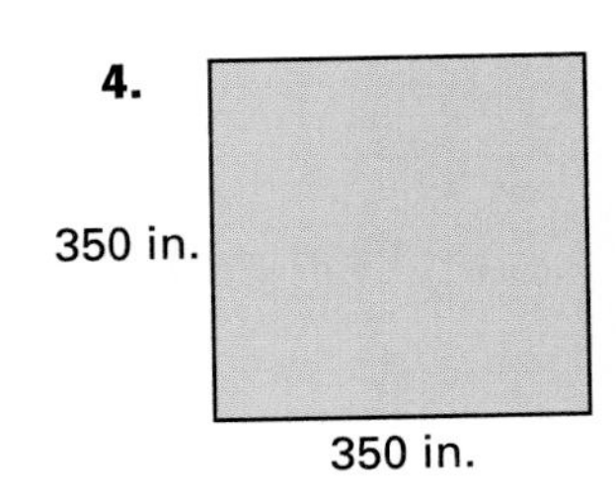

5. Bob wants to cover the floor of his patio with tiles. The floor measures 14.5 by 10.5 ft. If Bob has 150 tiles that each measures 1 ft by 1 ft, does he have enough to cover the patio?

6. Furry Friends Pet Store is going to expand to the space next door. The new space is the same length as shown in this figure but its width is 5 meters less. What is the area of the new space?

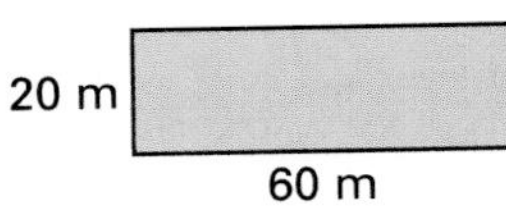

(Lessons 5 and 6) Find the area of each figure.

7.

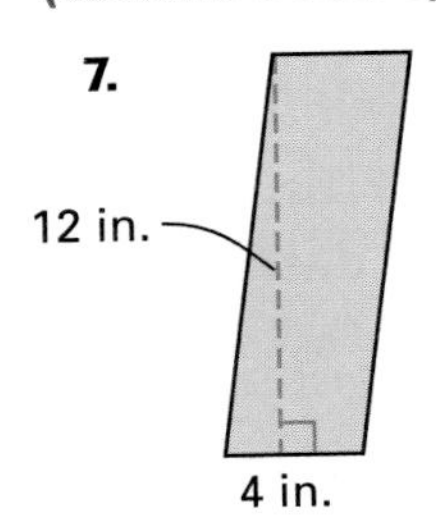

8.

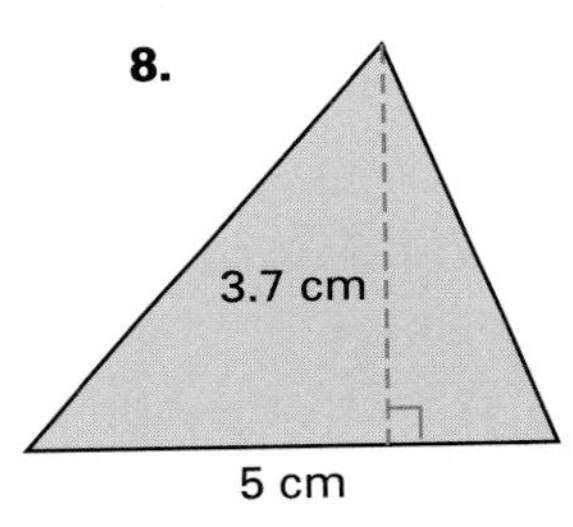

9.

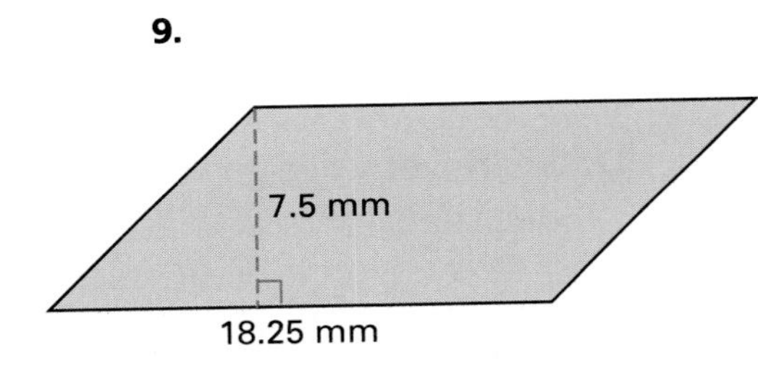

10.

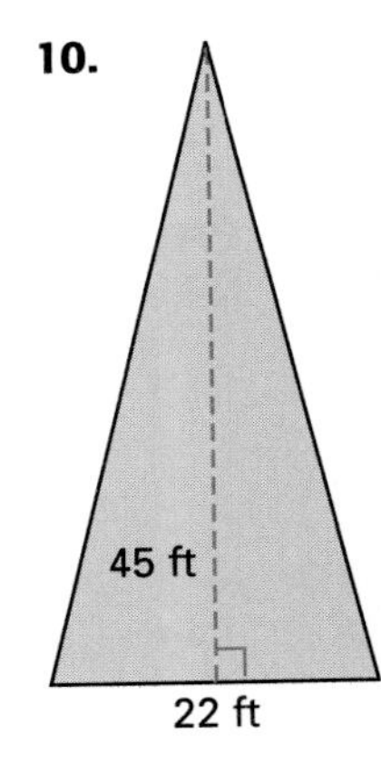

11. The game of shuffleboard started as a small board game in which coins were shoved onto a scoring pattern. Cruise ships enlarged the game into a deck game for passengers. What is the area of the large triangle on a single shuffleboard court?

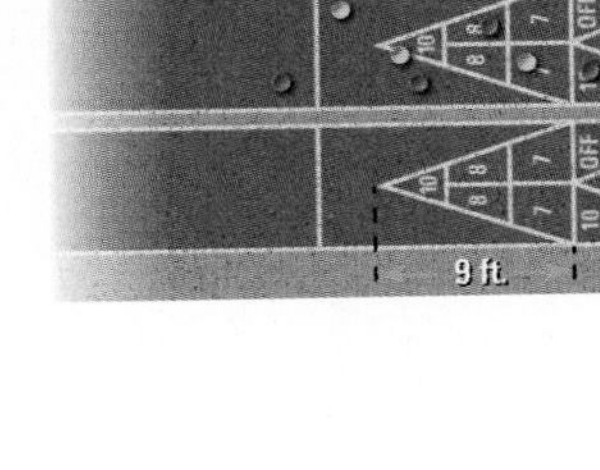

12. **Journal** When might you need to calculate the area of a triangle?

Skills Checklist

In this section, you have:

- ☑ **Explored the Area of Squares and Rectangles**
- ☑ **Learned About the Area of Parallelograms**
- ☑ **Learned About the Area of Triangles**

CHAPTER 4

SECTION

C Circles

For thousands of years, people have been designing and creating inventions to make their work easier. The design of virtually every complex invention requires an understanding of mathematics. Why is an understanding of mathematics important when designing an invention?

GET READY!

Discovering Pi

Review multiplying decimals. Find each product.

1. 12×0.15 **2.** 4.1×1.08 **3.** 10×2.89

4. 34×0.03 **5.** 9×4.77 **6.** 2.6×0.61

7. 52×0.90 **8.** 12.5×2.46 **9.** 70×3.06

10. 1.8×0.6 **11.** 22.6×5 **12.** 0.4×16

Skills Checklist

In this section, you will:

- ❐ Explore Discovering Pi
- ❐ Explore the Area of Circles
- ❐ Learn About the Area of Irregular Figures

Chapter 4
Lesson
7

Discovering Pi

Problem Solving Connection
- Look for a Pattern
- Make a Table

Materials
- five circular objects
- metric tape measure
- calculator

Vocabulary
radius
diameter
circumference
pi

Explore

You have found the distance around shapes that have straight sides. How can you find the distance around circles?

Work Together

1. Gather five circular objects.
2. Use a tape measure to measure the distance around the outside of each object. Measure to the nearest centimeter.
3. Measure the distance across the middle of each object to the nearest centimeter.
4. Using a calculator, divide the distance around the outside by the distance across the middle. Round the result to two decimal places.

5. Record your findings in a table.

Object	Distance Around Outside	Distance Across Middle	Distance Around Outside ÷ Distance Across Middle

Talk About It

6. Describe any patterns you see in the values in the last column of your table.
7. Suppose you ordered a pizza that was 14 inches across the middle. About how many inches around would you expect the pizza to be? Explain.

Connect and Learn

The **radius** of a circle is any line from the center to any point on the circle.

The **diameter** of a circle is any line from one point on the circle to another point on the circle that passes through the center.

The **circumference** of a circle is the distance around the circle.

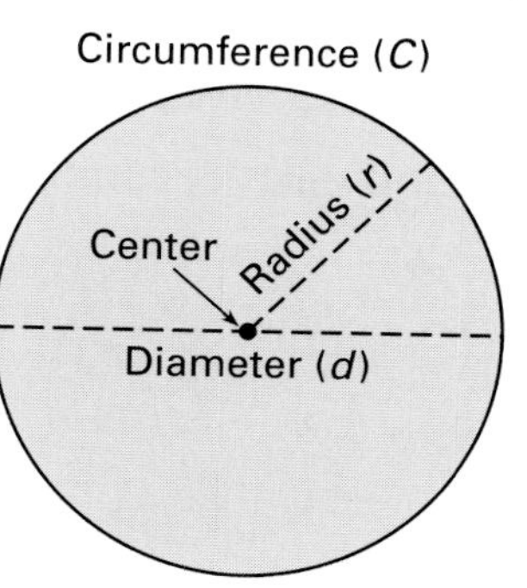

For any circle, the circumference divided by the diameter always equals 3.14159265.... This value is called **pi** and is represented by the Greek letter π. Because the digits in π go on forever, the number 3.14 is used as an approximation.

If you know the diameter or the radius of a circle, you can use π to find the circumference.

Example 1

Find the circumference.

Circumference = $\pi \times$ diameter

$C = \pi \times d$

$= 3.14 \times 5$ cm

$= 15.7$ cm

5 cm

Example 2

Find the circumference.

Circumference = $2 \times \pi \times r$

$C = 2 \times \pi \times r$

$= 2 \times 3.14 \times 8$ in.

$= 50.24$ in.

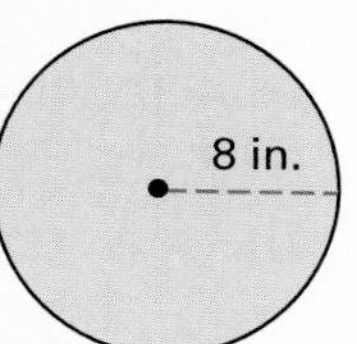

If you know the circumference of a circle, you can use π to find the diameter or radius.

Example 3

Find the diameter and radius of a merry-go-round with a circumference of 75 feet. Round to the nearest hundredth.

Circumference $\div \pi$ = Diameter

$C \div \pi = d$

75 ft $\div 3.14 = 23.89$ ft

The radius is half of the diameter, or 11.95 ft.

Math Tip

Some calculators have a button that enters an approximation for π. If a circle has a diameter of 5, entering $5 \times \pi =$ will give you the circumference.

Check

1. Find the circumference.

2. Find the diameter.

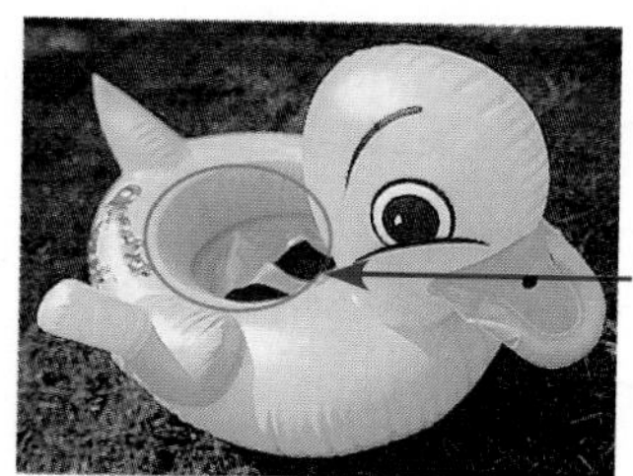

79 cm

3. **Reasoning** Write an equation to show how you would find the radius of a compact disc if you were given its circumference.

Practice

Skills and Reasoning

Find each circumference. Use 3.14 for π.

4.

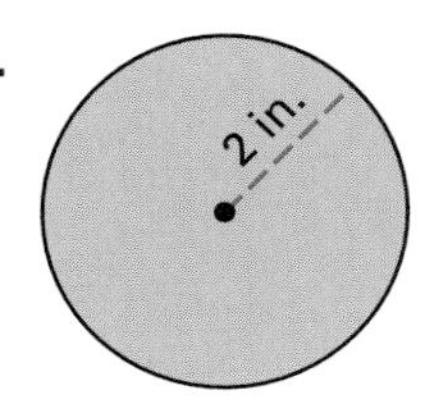

5.

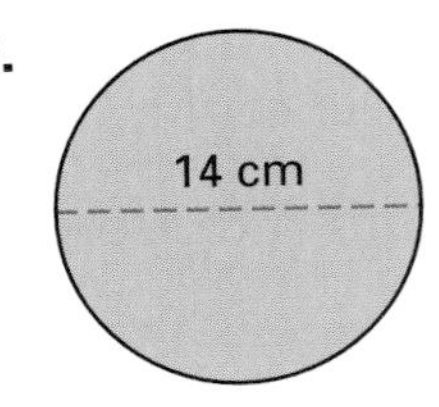

6.

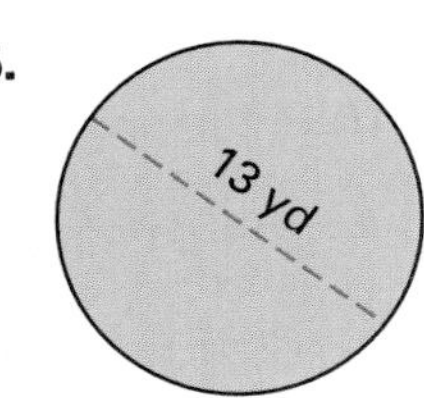

7.

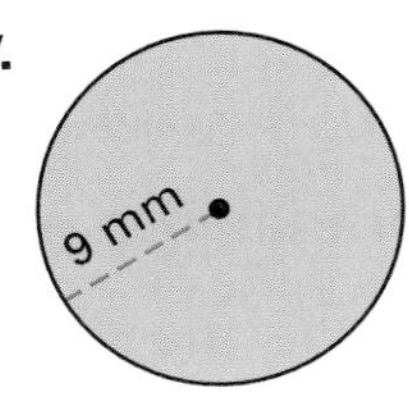

Find the missing measurements for each circle, where r = radius, d = diameter, and C = circumference. Round to the nearest hundredth.

8. $r = 3$ mm, $d = 6$ mm, $C =$ ■

9. $r = 4.5$ ft, $d =$ ■, $C = 28.26$ ft

10. $r = 0.62$ in., $d =$ ■ in., $C =$ ■

11. $r =$ ■, $d =$ ■, $C = 47.1$ yd

12. $r =$ ■, $d = 17.2$ yd, $C =$ ■

13. $r =$ ■, $d = 11$ m, $C =$ ■

14. $r =$ ■, $d =$ ■ km, $C = 0.942$ km

15. $r =$ ■, $d = 18.6$ in., $C = 58.404$ in.

16. Kartek is making a pencil holder. The bottom of the holder is a circle with a diameter of 7 cm. How long must the felt strip be to go around the bottom?

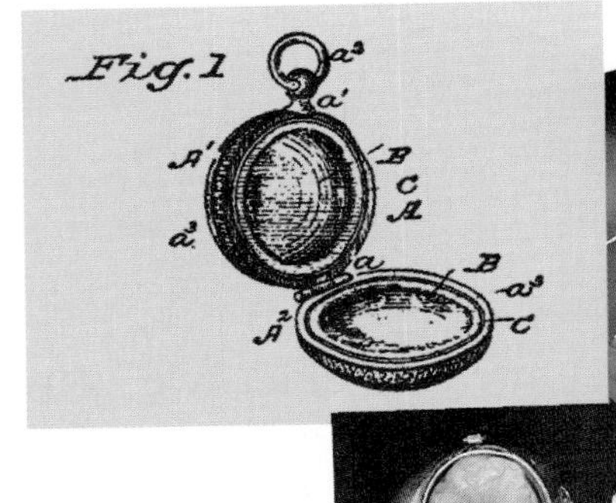

17. Using Data The drawing shows a chewing gum locket. The opening measures 2 cm across. What is its circumference ?

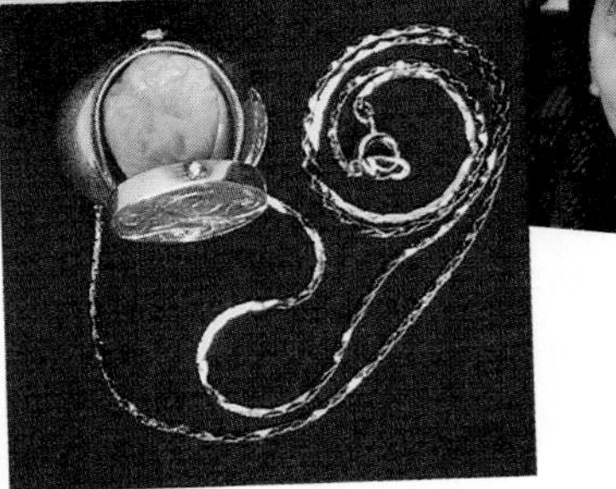

18. Hula hoops were popular during the 1960s and are still used today. A hula hoop is made by bending 2.6 meters of plastic tubing to form a circle. Find the diameter of the hula hoop, rounded to hundredths of a meter.

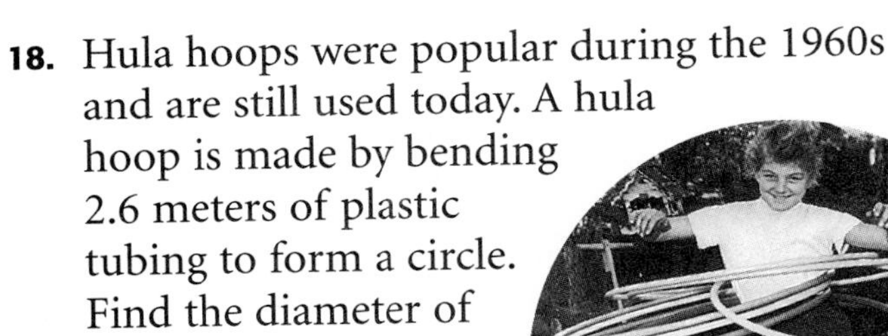

Problem Solving and Applications

19. Using Data Use the table on page 207 to find how far each type of cycle will travel with one rotation of the wheel. Round your distances to the nearest hundredth unit.

20. Critical Thinking Pat's bicycle has a wheel with a radius of 13 inches. If she rides the bicycle 1 mile (63,360 inches), how many times has the wheel rotated? Explain.

21. In an experiment, Abel measured a circle but separated the data from the labels. The data is 6.8, 21.352, 3.14, and 3.4. The labels are Radius, Diameter, Circumference, and Pi. Match the data items with the correct labels.

22. A grass fire is burning a circular region with a radius of 65 feet. How many firefighters are needed to surround the fire if they stand 10 feet apart from each other and 2 feet from the fire?

23. An ice skater is following a path of two circles shaped like a figure 8. One loop has a diameter of 8 meters, and the other loop has a diameter of 10 meters. How far does the skater travel in one complete figure 8?

24. Journal When you multiply the diameter of a circle by π to get the circumference, why is the answer never exact?

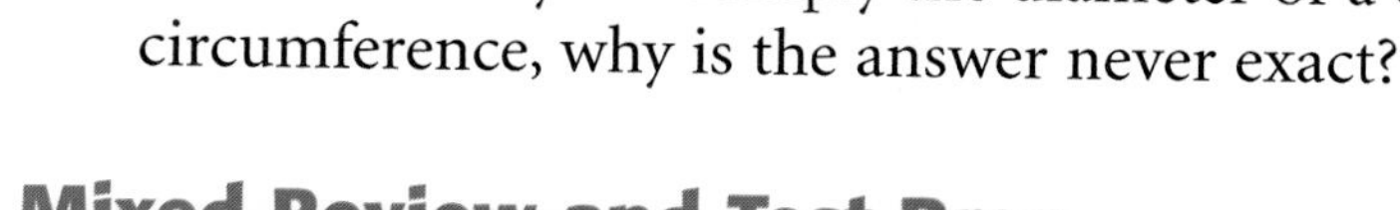

Mixed Review and Test Prep

STAY SHARP!

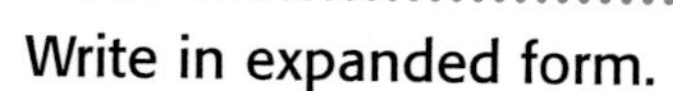

Write in expanded form.

25. $11{,}658^1$ **26.** 28^4 **27.** 3^5 **28.** 56^2

29. 9^6 **30.** 7^3 **31.** 12^5 **32.** 36^8

33. 6^3 **34.** 41^7 **35.** 13^{11} **36.** 8^5

Estimate each sum or difference.

37. $567 + 324$ **38.** $49 + 52 + 53 + 50$ **39.** $23 - 12$ **40.** $227 + 225 + 224$

41. $452 - 262$ **42.** $9{,}324 + 675$ **43.** $\$16 - \$9$ **44.** $6{,}218 - 3{,}281$

45. What is the value of x for $\frac{2.6}{x} = 0.5$?

Ⓐ 5.2 Ⓑ 1.15 Ⓒ 13.52 Ⓓ 2.1

Chapter 4
Lesson
8

Area of Circles

Problem Solving Connection
- Look for a Pattern
- Make a Table

Materials
- grid paper
- compass
- scissors

Did You Know?
The person who holds the most U.S. patents is Thomas Edison, inventor of the light bulb and the phonograph. He received 1,093 patents from the U.S. Patent Office.

Explore

You know how to find the distance around the outside of a circle. How can you find the area inside a circle?

Work Together

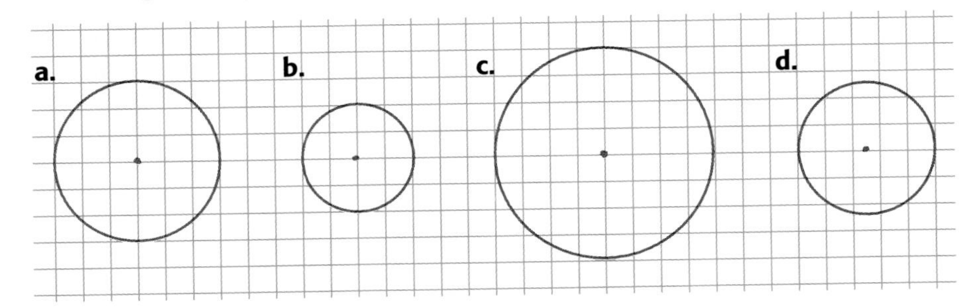

1. Use a compass to copy each circle on grid paper.
2. Count squares to estimate the area of each circle.
3. For each circle, make a radius square.
   a. Draw a square whose sides are as long as the radius of the circle.
   b. Cut out the square. Then find the area of the square.
4. For each circle, use the radius square to estimate the area of the circle.
   a. Estimate the number of radius squares that would fit inside the circle.
   b. Multiply the number of radius squares by the area of one square.
5. Record your findings in a table.

Circle	Estimated Area (square units)	Area of Radius Square (square units)	Number of Radius Squares that Fit Inside Circle	Number of Radius Squares × Area of Radius Square (square units)

Talk About It

6. How do the estimates you made counting grid squares compare to the estimates you made using a radius square?
7. Describe any patterns you see in the number of radius squares that fit inside a circle.

Connect and Learn

The circumference and the diameter of a circle are related by the number π. The radius and the area of a circle are also related by the number π. If you know the radius of a circle, you can use π to find the area.

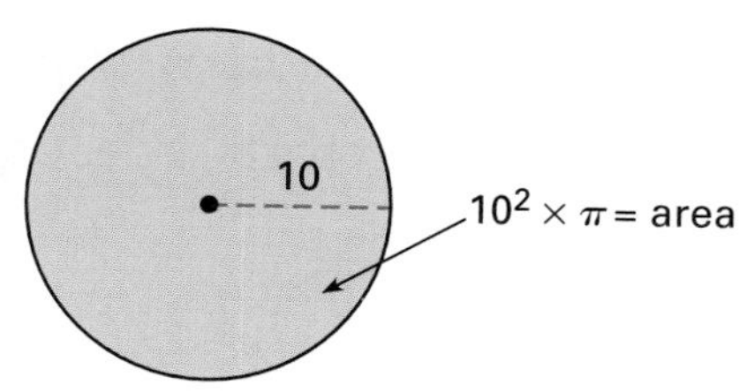

This can also be described by the formula:

Area $= \pi \times r^2$, or $A = \pi r^2$, where r is the radius.

Example 1

Find the area.

Area $= \pi r^2$

$= 3.14 \times 7^2$

$= 3.14 \times 49$

$= 153.86 \text{ in}^2$

7 in.

Remember

To square a number means to use it as a factor two times.

$5^2 = 5 \times 5$

If you know the diameter of a circle, you can still use the formula to find the area of the circle.

Example 2

The Combined Grocer's Package, Grater, Slicer, and Mouse and Fly Trap has a lid with a 4-inch diameter. What is the area of the lid?

$A = \pi r^2$

$= 3.14 \times 2^2$ Since the diameter is 4 in., the radius is 2 in.

$= 3.14 \times 4$

$= 12.56 \text{ in}^2$

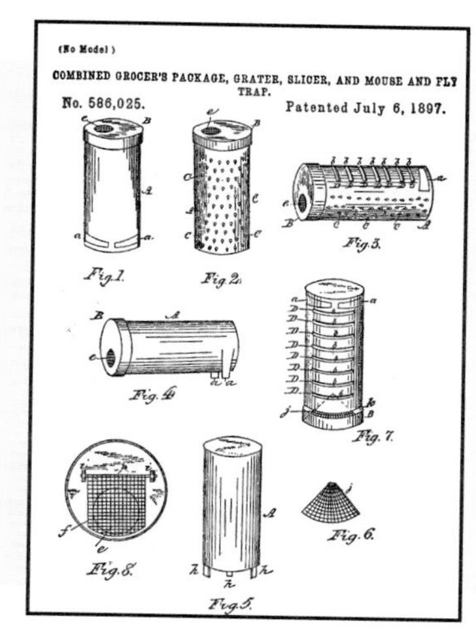

Check

Find each area. Use 3.14 for π.

1.

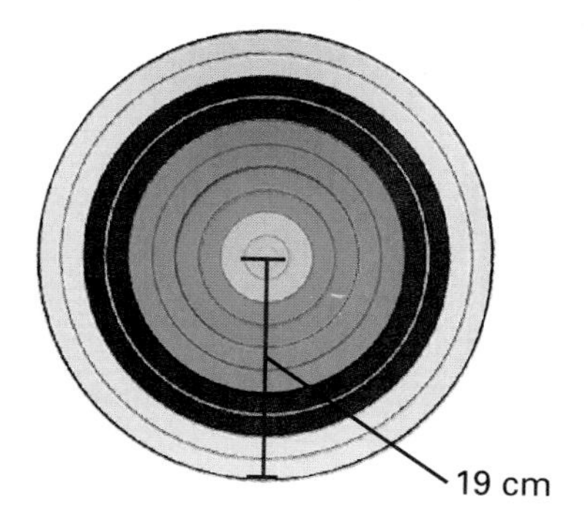

2.

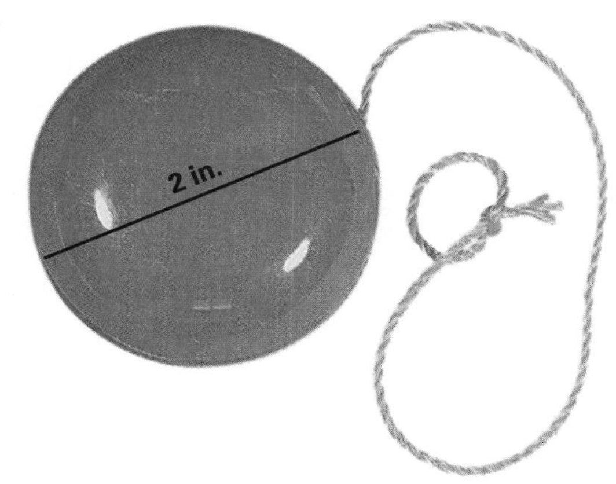

Practice

Skills and Reasoning

Find the area of each circle. Use 3.14 for π.

3.
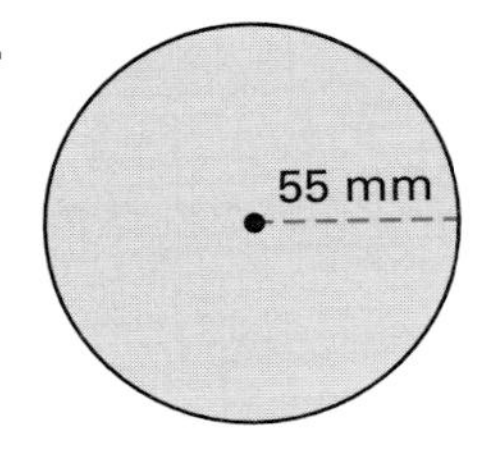

4.
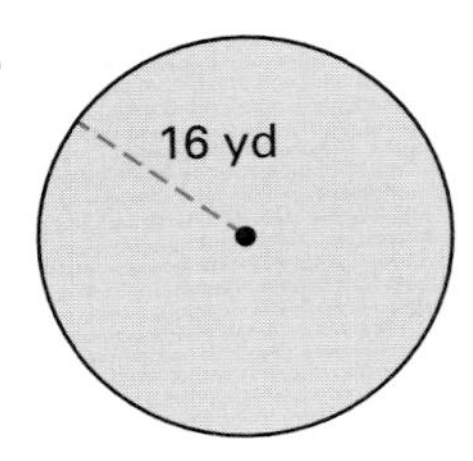

5.
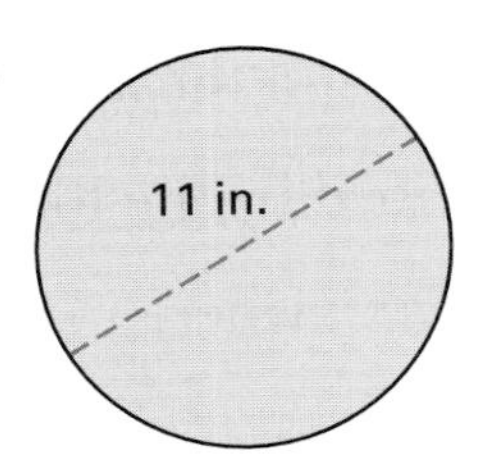

6.
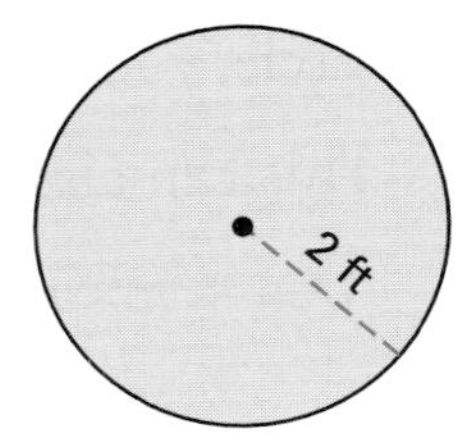

Given the radius or diameter of each circle, find its area.

7. $r = 4$ cm **8.** $d = 12.8$ feet **9.** $d = 62$ cm **10.** $r = 17$ feet

11. $r = 10$ inches **12.** $r = 50$ mm **13.** $d = 16$ yards **14.** $r = 0.6$ miles

Given the circumference of each circle, find its radius and area rounded to the nearest tenth.

15. $C = 12$ feet **16.** $C = 8.2$ km **17.** $C = 63$ cm **18.** $C = 3.14$ mm

19. $C = 7$ inches **20.** $C = 1.33$ miles **21.** $C = 21$ yards **22.** $C = 18$ meters

23. Science A sand dollar is an animal that lives slightly buried in the sand of shallow coastal waters. Its thin, circular body is about 2 to 4 inches wide. What are the smallest and largest areas of sand dollars?

24. This 1879 invention allowed people to land safely if they had to jump from a window to escape a fire. If the opened and flattened parachute is a circle with a diameter of 1.3 yards, what is its area?

Use the Carpet Comparison scatterplot for **25–27.** All of the carpets are circular.

25. How much does the carpet with a diameter of 3 feet cost?

26. Which carpet costs the most per square feet?

27. Which carpet has the greatest circumference?

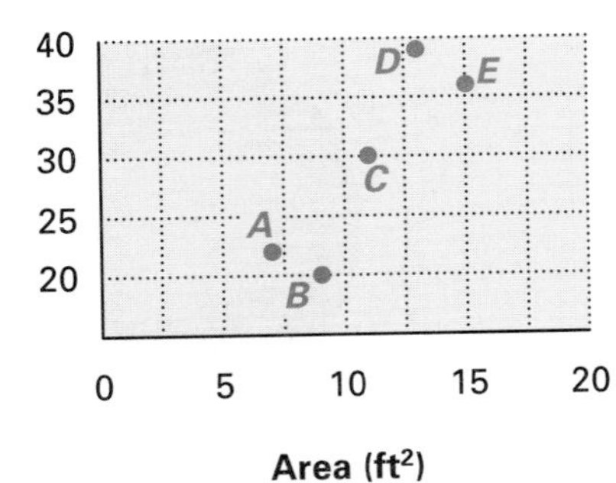

Problem Solving and SOCIAL STUDIES

Stonehenge is a circular grouping of immense stones in southwestern England. Archaeologists believe Stonehenge may have been used to determine when certain astronomical events would occur.

28. Time Archaeologists found that Stonehenge was built in three parts from 2800 B.C. to 1500 B.C. About how long ago was Stonehenge built?

29. The outer ring of stones is 30 m in diameter. What are the area and circumference of this ring?

30. The outer ring originally consisted of 30 stones averaging 25 metric tons each. A metric ton is the same as 1,000 kilograms. What was the total weight in kilograms of the stones in this ring?

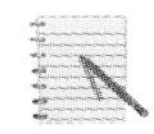

31. Journal Is the area of a circle with a diameter of 2 inches larger than or smaller than the area of a 2-inch square? Explain without using numbers.

Mixed Review and Test Prep

STAY SHARP!

For each scatterplot, determine whether there is a trend. If there is, describe the trend.

32.

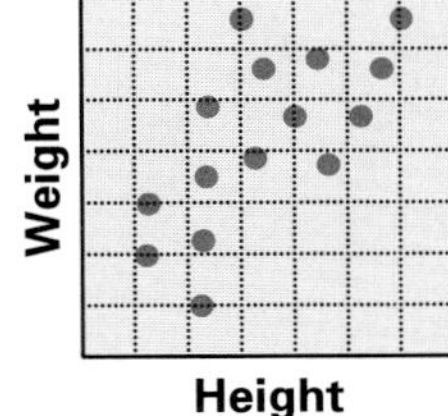

33.

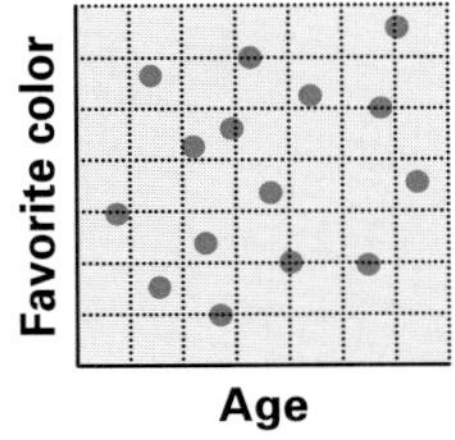

34.

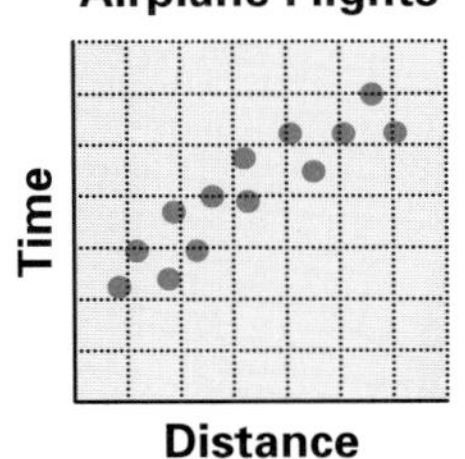

Estimate each product or quotient.

35. 26×3 **36.** $\$92 \div 31$ **37.** 78×3 **38.** $565 \div 53$

39. 82×16 **40.** $678 \div 35$ **41.** $20{,}654 \times 39$ **42.** $729 \div 96$

43. On a water ride at the amusement park, a rotating valve sprays water for 15 feet in all directions. What is the circumference of the circular wet patch it creates?

Ⓐ 706.5 ft Ⓑ 31.4 ft Ⓒ 94.2 ft Ⓓ 2,220.7 ft

Chapter 4
Lesson
9

Area of Irregular Figures

You Will Learn

- to find the area of irregular figures

Did You Know?
The prefix semi-means "half." A semiannual event happens once every half year.

Learn

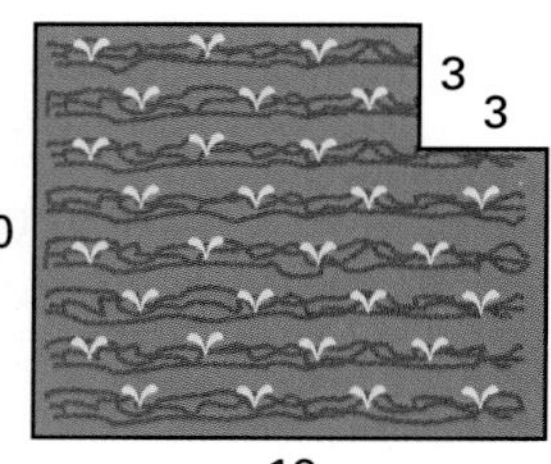

Ricardo and Peggy are planning how to plant their garden. The sketch shows the shape of the garden. All of the measurements are in feet. What is the area of the garden?

Figures are not always perfect rectangles, triangles, or circles. To find the area of an irregular figure, you may need to break it down into smaller familiar figures. Then you can find the area of each smaller figure.

Ricardo thinks . . .

12 – 3 = 9
3
3
10
10 – 3 = 7
12

I'll divide the garden into two rectangles. I'll find the missing measurements, and the area of each rectangle. Then I'll add the areas together.

The area of the top rectangle equals 3 x 9, or 27.

The area of the bottom equal 12 x 7, or 84.

The total area is 27 + 84, which is 111 ft^2.

Peggy thinks . . .

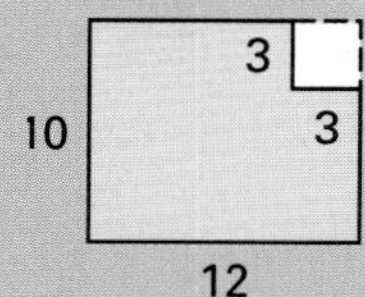

The garden looks like a rectangle with a missing piece. I'll find the area of the rectangle, and then subtract the area of the piece missing from the top corner.

The area of the whole rectangle is 10 x 12 = 120.

The area of the missing piece is 3 x 3 = 9.

The total area is 120 – 9, or 111 ft^2.

Example 1

Find the area of the figure.

The figure can be divided into a triangle and a square.

The square has a base of 8 and a height of 8.
The area is bh, or 8×8, which is 64 units^2.

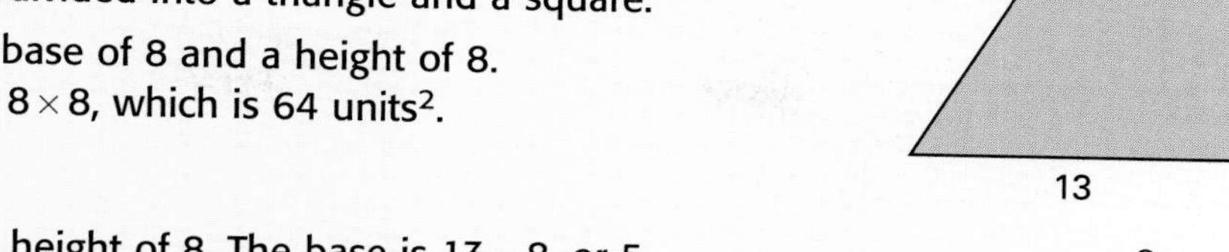

The triangle has a height of 8. The base is $13 - 8$, or 5.
The area is $\frac{1}{2}\,bh$, or $\frac{1}{2} \times 8 \times 5$, which is 20 units^2.

The total area is $64 + 20$, or 84 units^2.

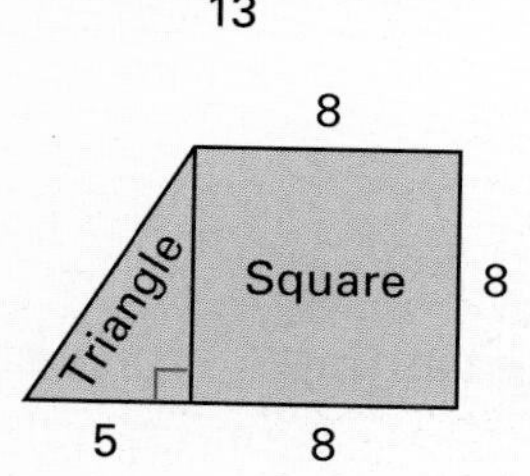

Example 2

Find the area of the figure.

The figure is made up of 2 triangles.

$$\text{The area of each triangle} = \frac{1}{2}\,bh$$
$$= \frac{1}{2} \times 4 \text{ in.} \times 8 \text{ in.}$$
$$= 16 \text{ in}^2$$

The total area is 16 in^2 + 16 in^2, or 32 in^2.

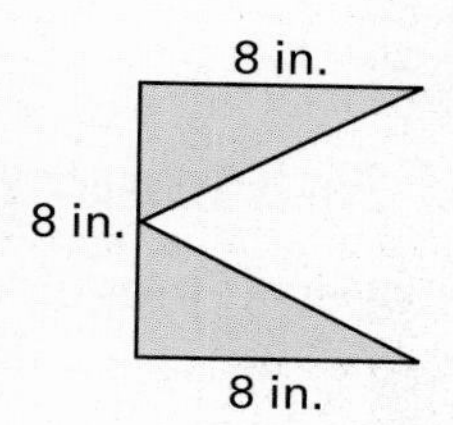

Example 3

What is the area of the candy part of the "candy pin"?

The top part of the badge is a semicircle with a radius of 0.8 cm.

$$\text{Area of circle} = \pi r^2$$
$$= 3.14 \times 0.8^2$$
$$= 2.0096 \text{ cm}^2$$

Since the figure is only a semicircle, you must divide the area in half.

Area of semicircle $= 2.0096 \div 2$, or 1.0048 cm^2.

The bottom part is a triangle with a base of 1.6 cm and a height of 2 cm.

$$\text{Area of triangle} = \frac{1}{2}\,bh$$
$$= \frac{1}{2} \times 1.6 \times 2$$
$$= 1.6 \text{ cm}^2$$

The total area = 1.0048 cm^2 + 1.6 cm^2, or 2.6048 cm^2.

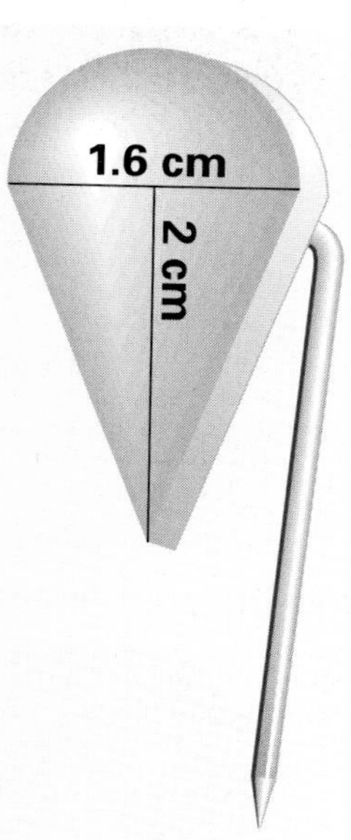

Talk About It

1. Could Ricardo have split the garden into two rectangles in a different way? Would he get a different answer? Explain.
2. How could you use Peggy's method to find the area in example 1?
3. Can every figure be broken down into smaller figures? Explain.

Check

Find the area of each figure.

1.

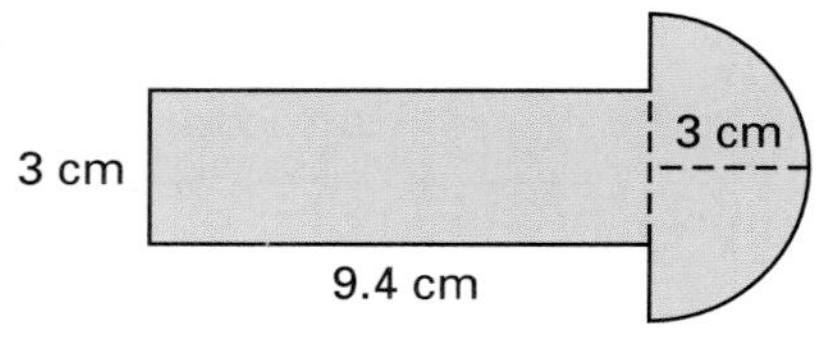

2.

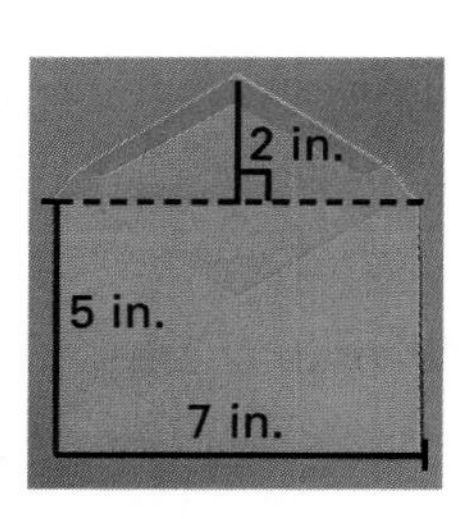

3. **Reasoning** Which has a greater area: a semicircle with a radius of 4 inches or a rectangle with sides of 4 inches and 8 inches? Explain.

Practice

Skills and Reasoning

Find the area of each irregular figure. Round to the nearest hundredth.

4.

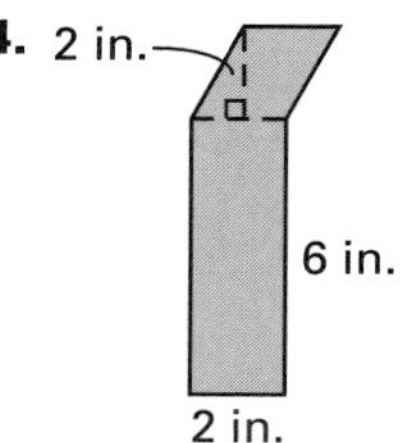

5.

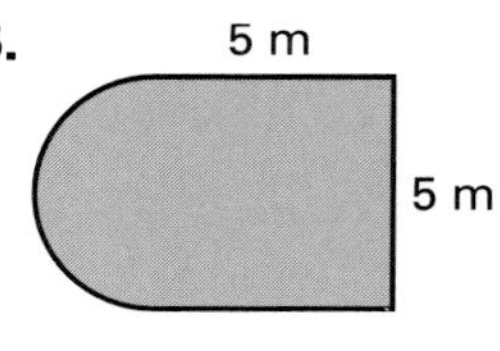

6.

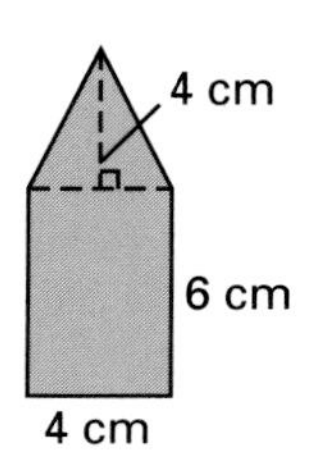

7.

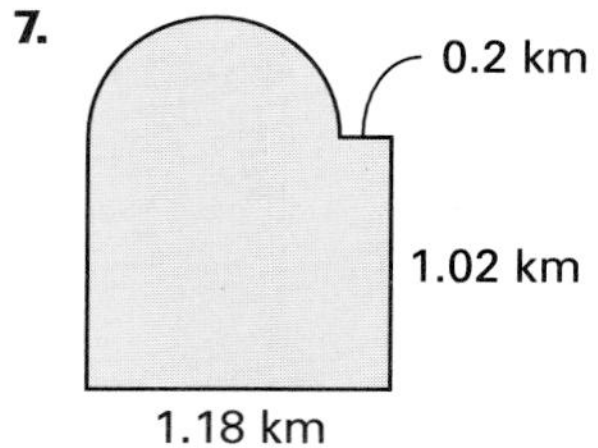

8.

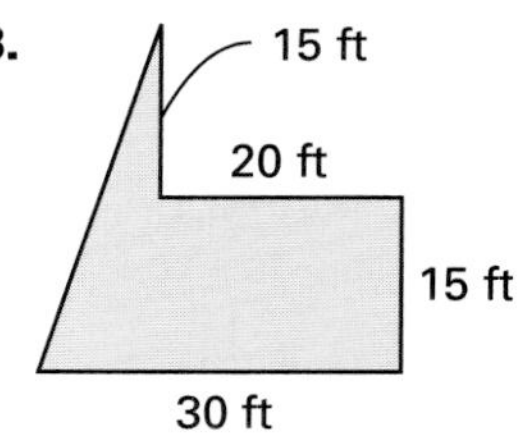

9.

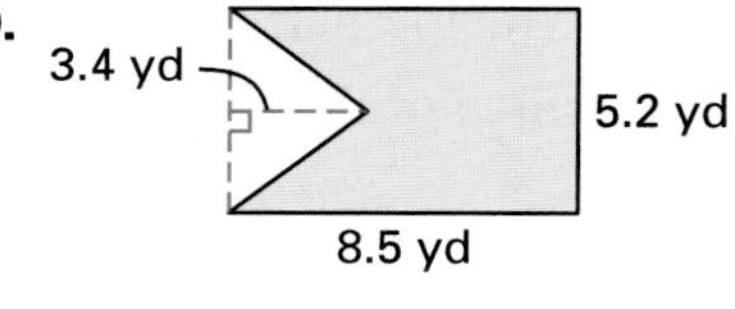

Find the area of each object.

10.

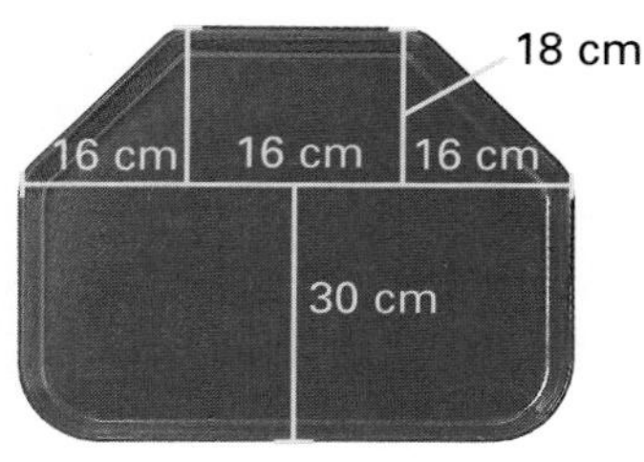

11.

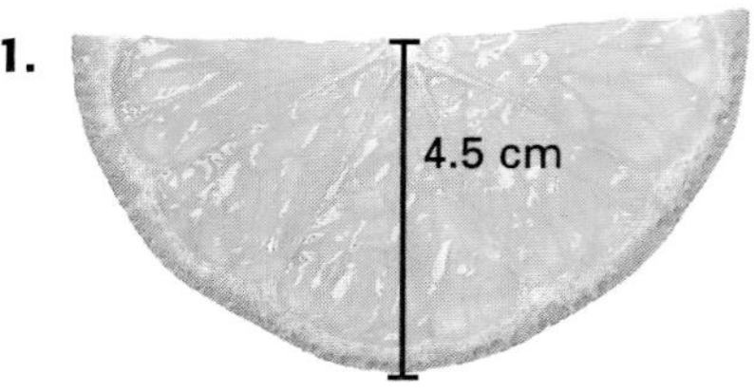

12. Order the following figures from least area to greatest area: a circle with a diameter of 8 in., a semicircle with a diameter of 16 in., a quarter circle with a diameter of 12 in.

13. **Reasoning** Which figure has the greatest area: a semicircle with a diameter of 7 m or a square with sides of 3.3 m?

Problem Solving and Applications

14. Geography Find the approximate area of South Australia. All distances are in miles.

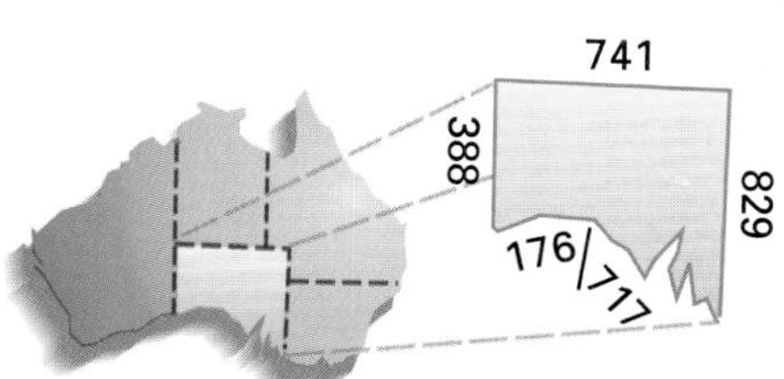

15. Find the area of the combined clothes brush, bottle, and drinking cup.

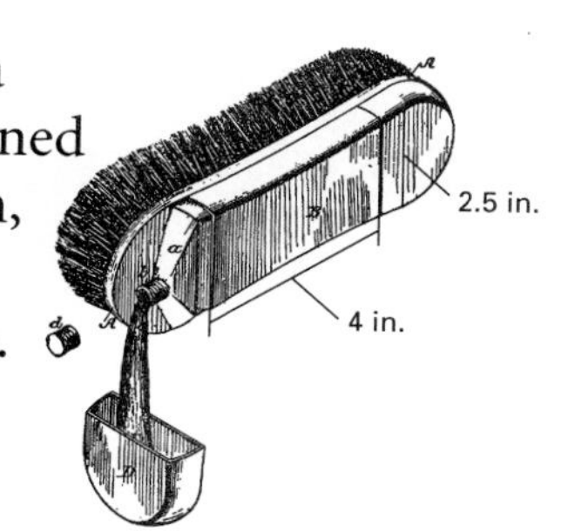

16. Caitlin is making a tablecloth for a circular table. The circumference of the table is 13.8 feet. She has a square piece of cloth that is 4.5 feet on each side. If she cuts out the largest possible circle from the cloth, will it be big enough to cover the table? Explain.

17. Using Data Sheetal is painting a cardboard cutout for her school's annual play. The cardboard is a triangle 7 feet tall and 7 feet wide. It has a square opening as shown in the drawing. How many square feet does Sheetal need to paint?

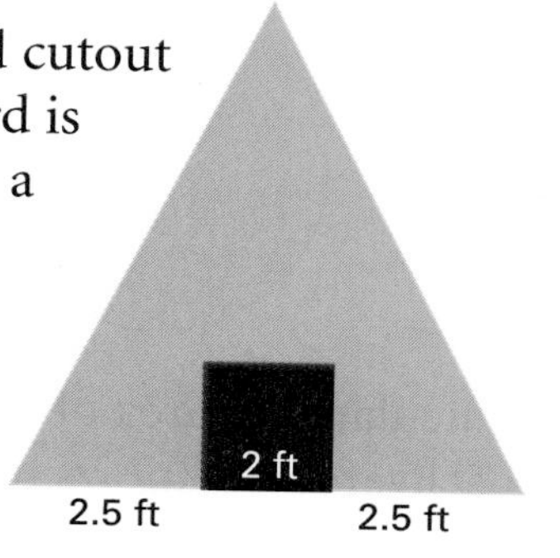

18. Using Data Joe and his dad are redoing the tile in the kitchen and living room. According to the picture, how many square feet do they have to retile?

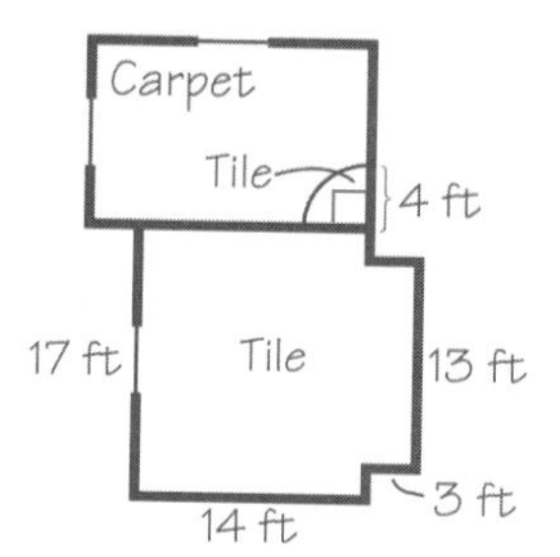

19. Journal A spinner is divided into six equal sections. The radius of the spinner is 10 cm. What is the area of each section? Explain.

Mixed Review and Test Prep

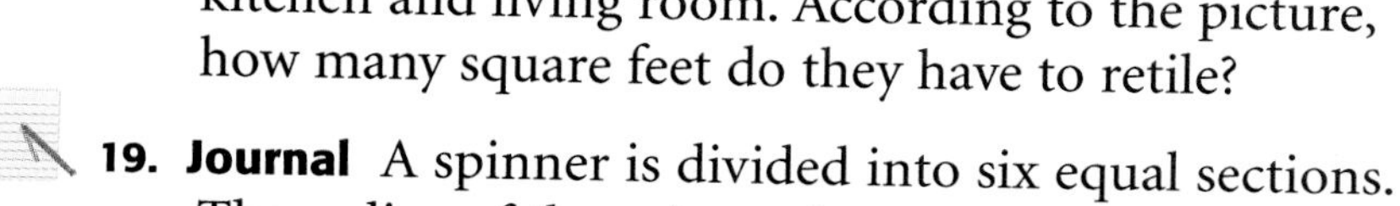

Simplify.

20. $14 + 10 - 3$ **21.** $62 \div (1 + 1)$ **22.** $28 \div 2 + 6$ **23.** $5 \times 6 - 25$

24. $18 + 18 \div 3$ **25.** $2 \times 10 - 4 \div 2$ **26.** $2 \times (10 - 4) \div 2$ **27.** $8 + 33 \times 4$

Solve.

28. $16.1 - f = 9.1$ **29.** $r + 25.3 = 50.73$ **30.** $56.04 + k = 64.06$ **31.** $m - 7.25 = 19.75$

32. $e - 86.5 = 76$ **33.** $86.8 + q = 100.9$ **34.** $47.34 - g = 42.04$ **35.** $z + 0.13 = 6.68$

36. To the nearest hundredth, what is diameter of a circle whose circumference is 14.6 in.?

Ⓐ 4.65 in. Ⓑ 45.84 in. Ⓒ 0.22 in. Ⓓ 11.46 in.

SECTION C

Review and Practice

(Lessons 7–9) Find the area of each figure and the circumference of each circle.

1.

2.

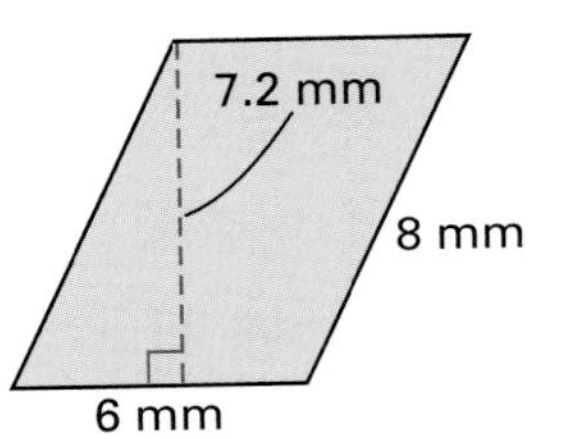

3.

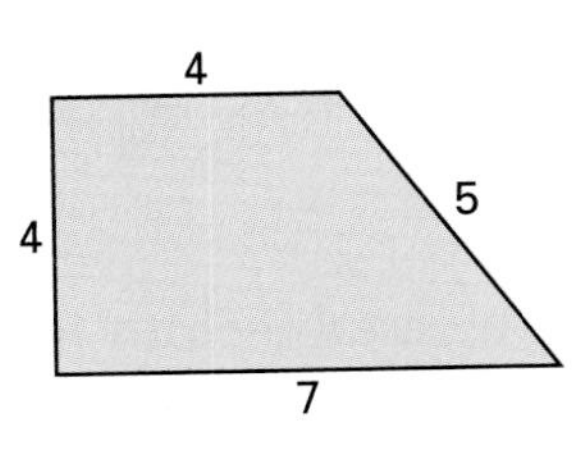

4.

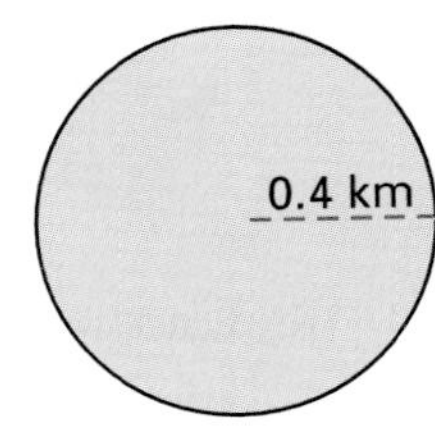

5.

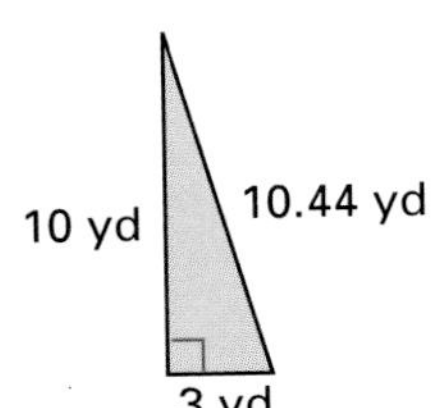

6.

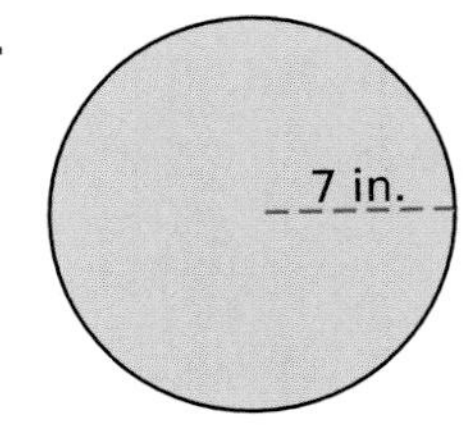

7.

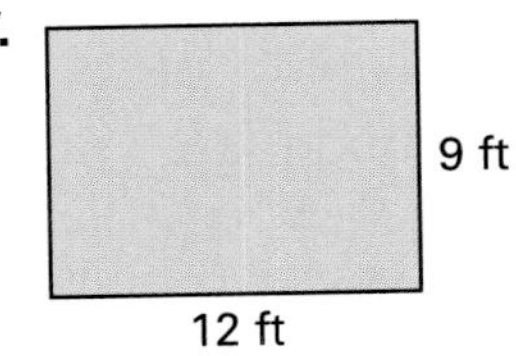

8.

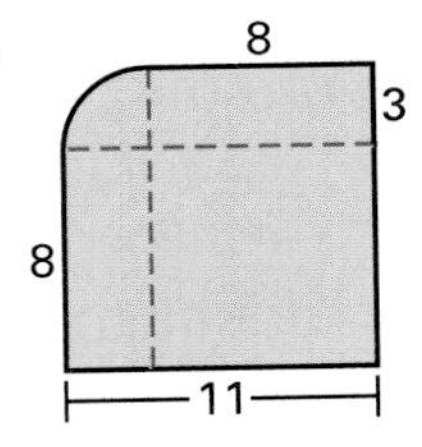

9. Scott wants to calculate the area of the circular pool in his grandparents' backyard. He knows that the diameter of the pool is 15 ft. What is the area of the pool?

10. Tawana swims in a pool that is 15 ft by 15 ft. What is the area of that pool?

11. The chocolate chip cookie was invented in 1933 by Ruth Wakefield of Massachusetts. If she made a giant cookie with a radius of 9 inches, what would be the cookie's circumference? What would be its area?

(Lesson 9) Find the area of each figure.

12.

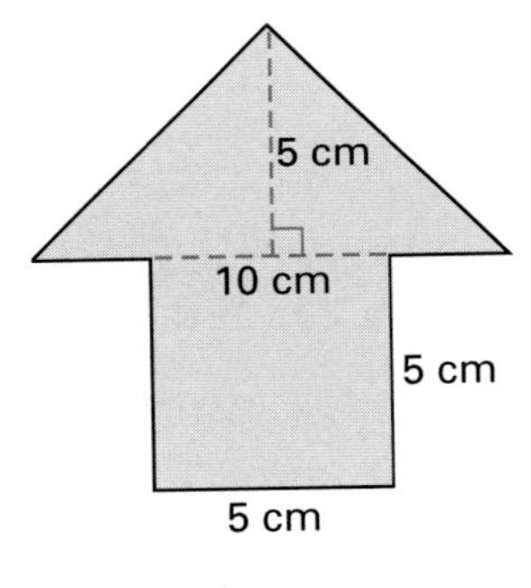

13.

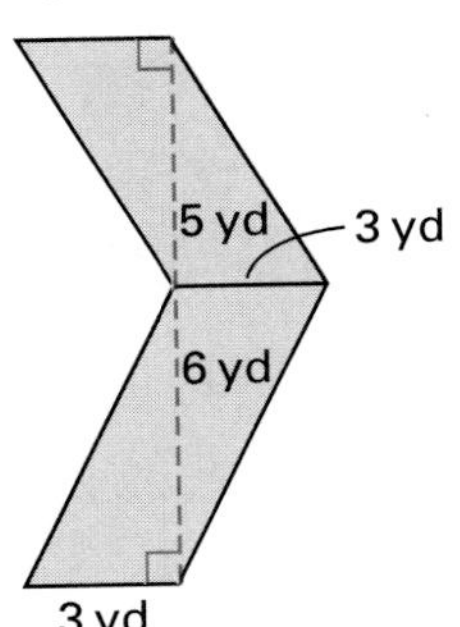

14.

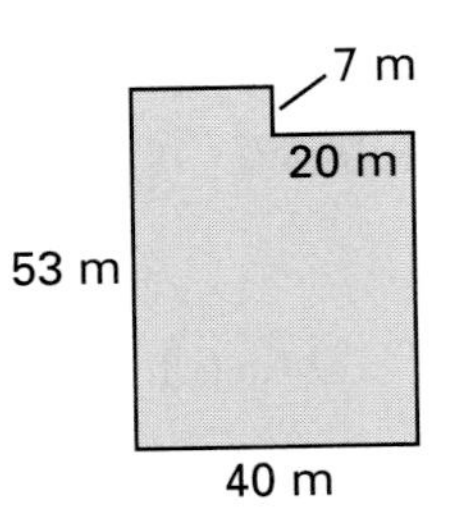

15. Journal Explain an easy way to estimate the area and circumference of a circle if you know the radius or diameter.

Skills Checklist

In this section, you have:

- **Explored Discovering Pi**
- **Explored the Area of Circles**
- **Learned About the Area of Irregular Figures**

Choose at least one of the following. Use what you have learned in this chapter.

1 There's No Place Like Home

At Home Ask a family member to help you create a floor plan for one room in your house or apartment. Measure the base of each wall and record the length. Sketch the room and find the area and perimeter.

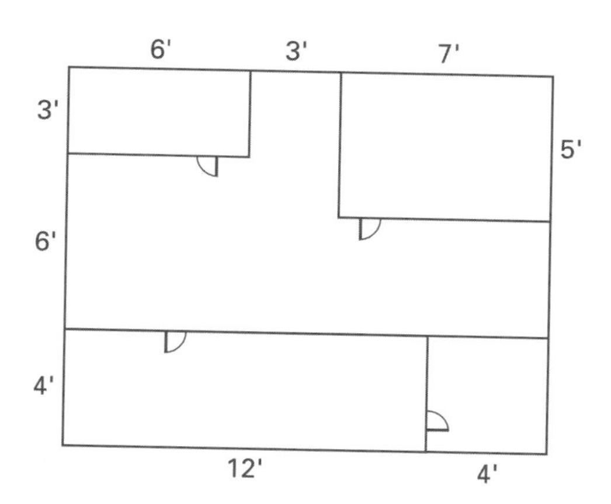

2 Metric Metamorphosis

Surf a topic of your choice from **www.mathsurf.com/6**. Choose a topic that will give you data expressed in meters. Write and solve a problem with your data. Challenge yourself to express the answer as kilometers, centimeters, and millimeters.

3 Fancy Footwork

At one time, the unit of measure we now call a "foot" varied depending on the size of the real foot of the king or queen ruling England. Work with five of your classmates to use your own feet to measure the length of a classroom wall. Make a bar graph illustrating the results. Discuss what your results tell you about standard measurement.

4 We're Not Foolin' Around

Select 7 objects from your house with circular bases. Trace each base on a sheet of paper, and use a ruler to find the diameter and radius of each circle in cm. Label your circles. Then cut them out and arrange them into an animal or plant shape.

CHAPTER 4

Review/Test

Vocabulary Supply the missing word in each sentence.

Word List
perimeter
metric
radius
diameter
conversion factor
area

1. The distance from the center of a circle to any point on the circle is called the ________.
2. The value of the symbol π is the circumference of any circle divided by its ________.
3. Powers of 10 are used to convert from one related measure to another in the ________ system.
4. ________ is measured in square units.
5. The distance around a figure is known as the ________.
6. The ________ is used when changing measurements from one unit to another.

(Lessons 1, 4–6) For each figure, find its perimeter and area.

7.

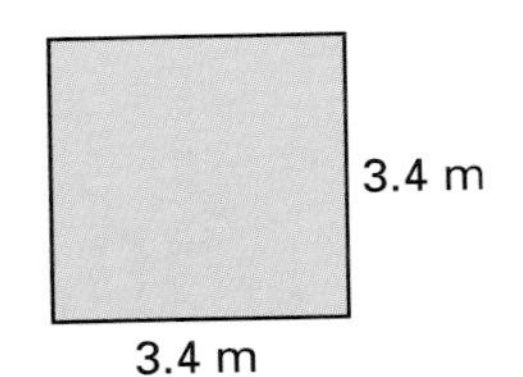

8.

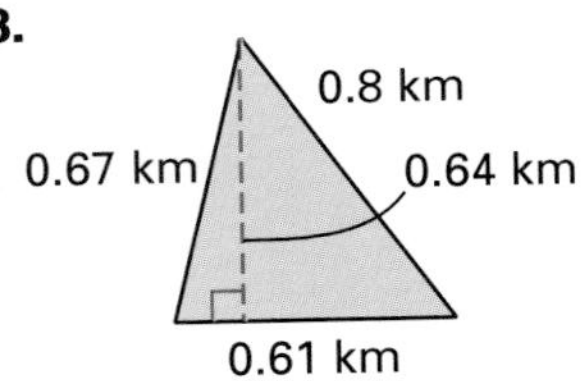

9.

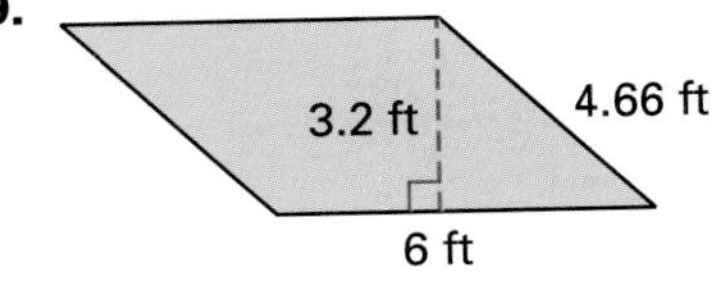

(Lessons 2, 3) Use powers of 10 or conversion factors to find each measure.

10. 12 yd = ________ ft
11. 75 mm = ________ cm
12. 1 km = ________ m

(Lessons 7–9) Use the information provided to find the missing measurements.

13. What is the diameter of the circle?

Circumference = 28.26 mi

14. What is the area of the circle to the nearest tenth?

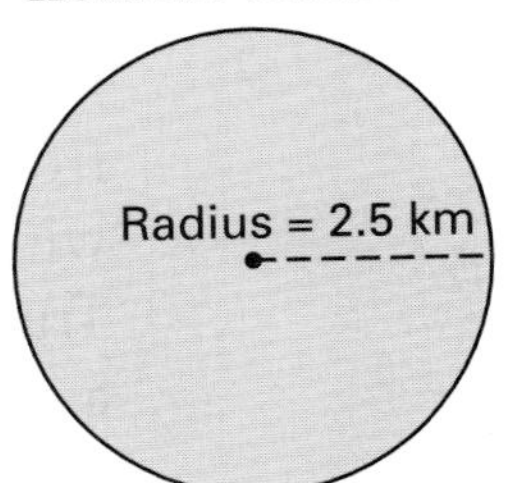

15. **a.** What is the diameter of the semicircle?
    b. What is its radius?
    c. What is the perimeter of the semicircle?
    d. What is its area?

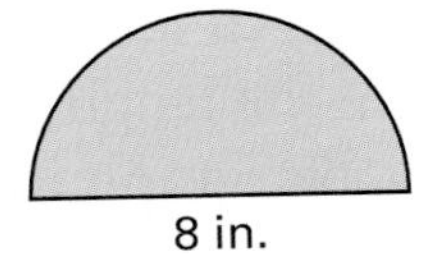

(Lesson 9) Find the area of each irregular figure.

16.

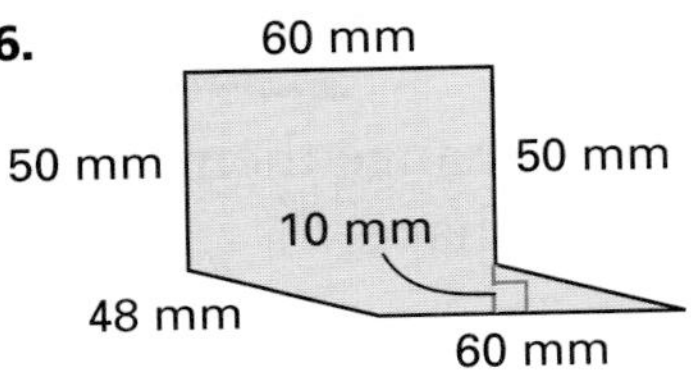

17.

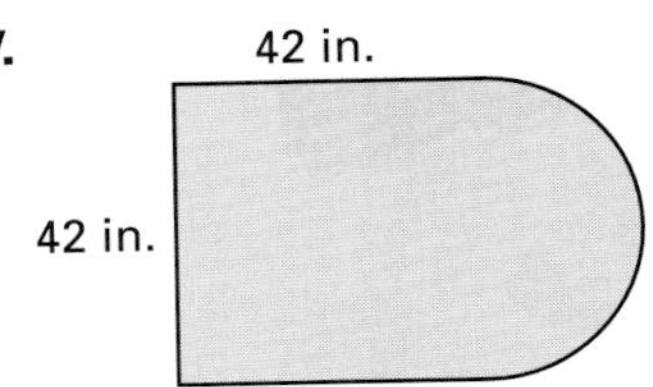

REVIEW/TEST

CHAPTER 4

Performance Assessment

Suppose you want to design a new size of basketball court. You need to decide on the lengths of each line segment in the diagram, labeled a to e. You will also need to find the perimeter and area of your court.

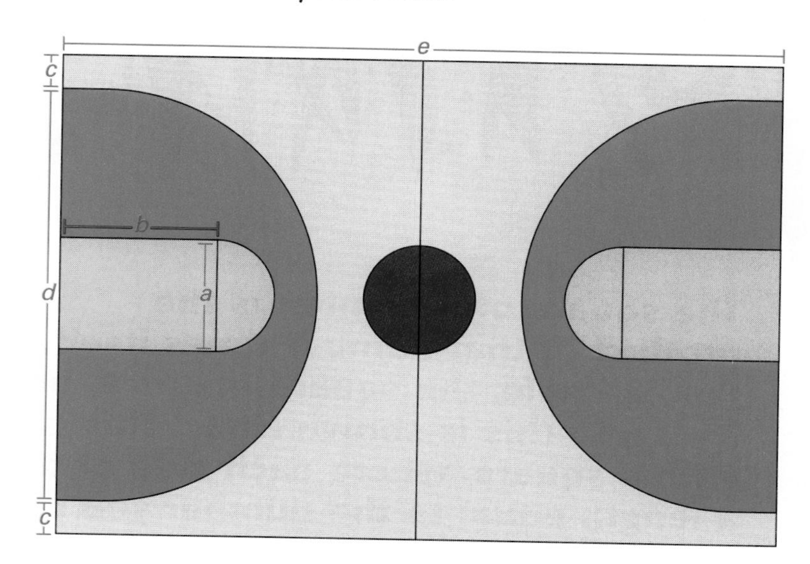

1. **Decision Making** Analyze the diagram. Choose lengths for a to e that are close in proportion to the lengths shown in the diagram.

2. **Recording Data** Make a table listing each of the line segments and your chosen lengths. Explain how you decided on your lengths and how they relate to the segments shown in the diagram.

3. **Critical Thinking** Use your chosen lengths to find the area of the entire court (outside rectangle). Show how you found the area. Then use your chosen measurements to find the perimeter of the outside rectangle. Show how you found the perimeter.

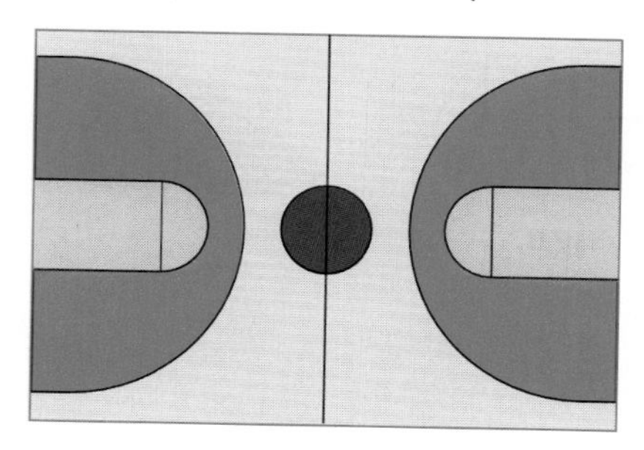

4. **Critical Thinking** The rim of a basketball hoop has a circular shape. Give the circumference and area for this basketball hoop.

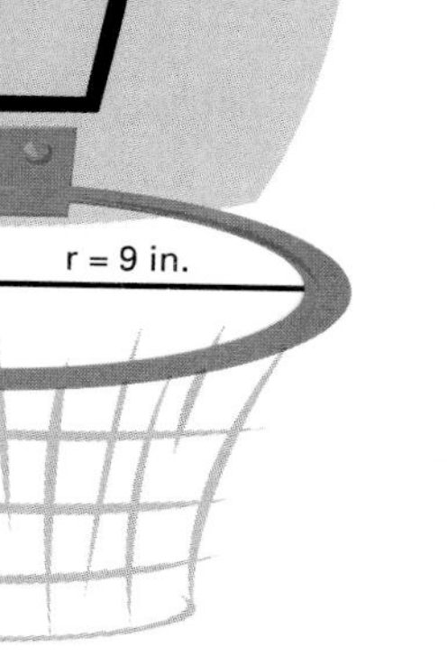

5. **Decision Making** Suppose you have been asked to design a court for a new type of game. Plan and draw your new court design. Make sure you include one circular figure and one triangle in your design. Make a table listing the measures for your design. Find and record the area and perimeter of the entire court. Also find and record the area of the other parts of your court.

Math Magazine

The Root of the Problem

The square of a number is the product of that number times itself. For example, the square of 3 is 9, because $3 \times 3 = 9$. This is shown as 3^2. This can be modeled with a square, where each side of the square has a length equal to the number you start with. The number squared is the area.

The opposite of squaring a number is finding the **square root**. The square root answers the question, "What number times itself equals the number I started with?" For example, the square root of 16 is 4. This can be modeled by a square whose area is equal to the number you started with, 16. The square root is the length of one side, 4.

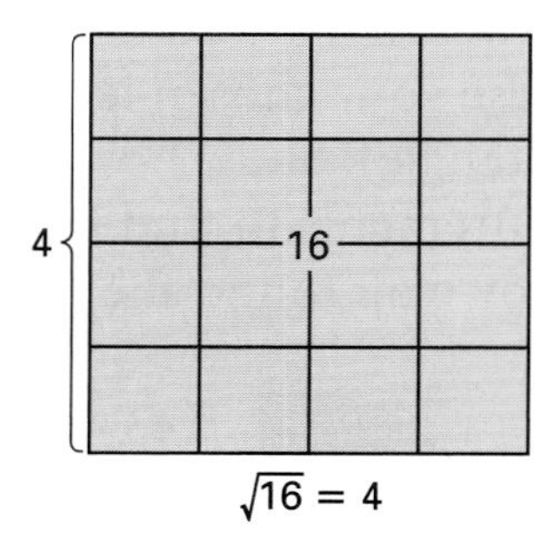

The symbol for square root is $\sqrt{\ }$. It is called a **radical sign**.

Try These!

Find the square root of each number by sketching a square with the given area. What is the length of one side?

1. 4 **2.** 36 **3.** 81 **4.** 25 **5.** 49 **6.** 100

Use number sense to find the square roots.

7. $\sqrt{400}$ **8.** $\sqrt{144}$ **9.** $\sqrt{64}$

10. $\sqrt{169}$ **11.** $\sqrt{324}$ **12.** $\sqrt{121}$

CHAPTERS 1–4

Cumulative Review

Test Prep Strategy: Read Carefully

Watch for tricky problems.

Which number is the least?

Ⓐ 307.852 Ⓑ 307.421 Ⓒ 308.01 Ⓓ 307.4018

Compare the numbers on the left of the decimal point. This eliminates choice Ⓒ because 308 > 307. Then look at the tenths place. Choice Ⓐ is eliminated because 8 > 4. In the hundredths place, choice Ⓑ is eliminated because 2 > 0. The answer is choice Ⓓ.

STAY SHARP!

Write the letter of the correct answer. Choose any strategy.

1. Which of the following would make you think a bar graph might be misleading?

   Ⓐ All bar heights start from zero.

   Ⓑ The values on the scale are not equally spaced.

   Ⓒ A broken graph symbol showing a break in the values

   Ⓓ Not here

2. What number in a frequency chart represents this set of tally marks?

   Ⓐ 12 Ⓑ 10 Ⓒ 2 Ⓓ not here

3. What is the place value of the digit 7 in 31,076,123?

   Ⓐ millions Ⓑ thousands Ⓒ ten-thousands Ⓓ not here

4. Use the order of operations to evaluate the expression $(18 + 9) \div 3$.

   Ⓐ 9 Ⓑ 33 Ⓒ 45 Ⓓ 243

5. There are m marbles arranged in 7 equal groups. Write an expression to show the number of marbles in each group.

   Ⓐ $m + 7$ Ⓑ $m - 7$ Ⓒ $7m$ Ⓓ $\frac{m}{7}$

6. Solve for x if $x + 41.5 = 43.2$.

   Ⓐ 1.7 Ⓑ 2.7 Ⓒ 2.8 Ⓓ not here

7. Simplify: 3.76×0.08.

   Ⓐ 0.2968 Ⓑ 0.3008 Ⓒ 2.968 Ⓓ 3.008

8. Find the area of the triangle.

   4 m

   12 m

   Ⓐ 24 m² Ⓑ 14 m² Ⓒ 12 m² Ⓓ 10 m²

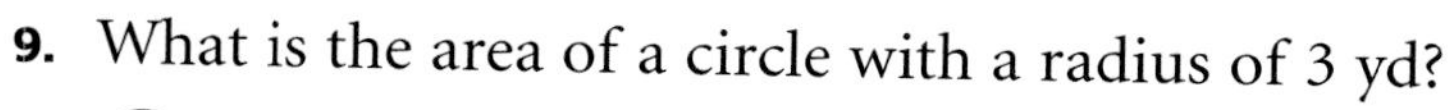

9. What is the area of a circle with a radius of 3 yd?

   Ⓐ 28.26 yd² Ⓑ 18.84 yd² Ⓒ 9.42 yd² Ⓓ not here

Test Prep Strategies

- Read Carefully
- Follow Directions
- Make Smart Choices
- Eliminate Choices
- Work Backward from an Answer

DATA FILE

Chapter 5

Patterns and Number Theory

SECTION A: A Switch in Time . . .

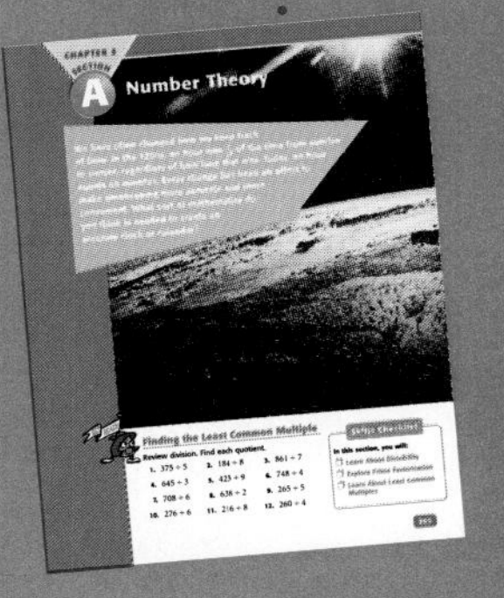

A Switch in Time . . .
Page 265

Number Theory

265

Our calendar year of 12 months is based on the time it takes Earth to complete one orbit around the Sun. What kind of calendar year do you think you would have if you lived on another planet? Explain your thinking.

Planet	Time It Takes to Orbit Around the Sun
Mercury	88 days
Venus	225 days
Earth	365 days
Mars	687 days

LINKS

Entertainment

On an average day, $\frac{16}{100}$ of the people listening to the radio are listening to news or talk stations. $\frac{9}{100}$ of the people are listening to Top 40 stations.
www.mathsurf.com/6/ch5/ent

Arts & Literature

A Japanese haiku poem contains 3 lines. The first line has 5 syllables, the next has 7, and the last has 5.
www.mathsurf.com/6/ch5/arts

People of the World

About $\frac{1}{3}$ of the people in the world eat with a fork and a knife. About $\frac{1}{3}$ eat with chopsticks. About $\frac{1}{3}$ eat with their hands.

SECTION B

Meanwhile, Back at the Wrench

Connecting Fractions and Decimals

281

An adjustable wrench like the one shown allows you to change the size of the wrench's grip. Other wrenches are made with preset sizes in fractions of inches or in millimeters. Which of the wrench sizes shown do you think would have the widest grip?

Common Wrench Sizes (in.)	$\frac{1}{4}$	$\frac{5}{16}$	$\frac{3}{8}$	$\frac{7}{16}$	$\frac{1}{2}$	$\frac{9}{16}$

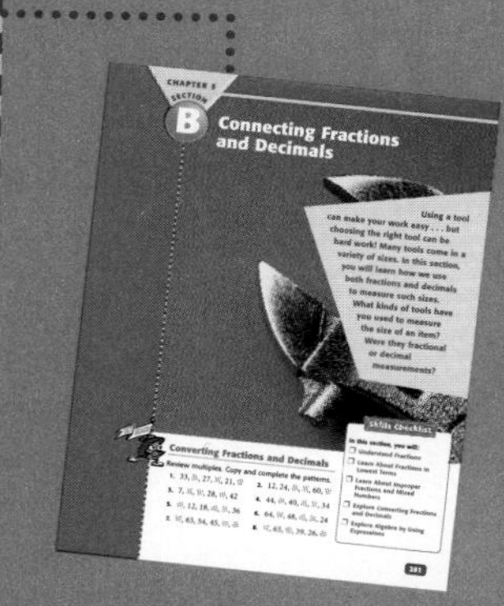

Meanwhile, Back at the Wrench
Page 281

Social Studies

Angel Falls, in Venezuela, is 3,212 ft high. It has the longest single drop of any waterfall in the world, 2,684 ft. This is more than $\frac{3}{4}$ of the entire waterfall.
www.mathsurf.com/6/ch5/social

Science

The Fibonacci number pattern, 1, 1, 2, 3, 5, 8, . . . , describes many things in nature, including how tree branches grow and what the surface of a pineapple looks like.
www.mathsurf.com/6/ch5/science

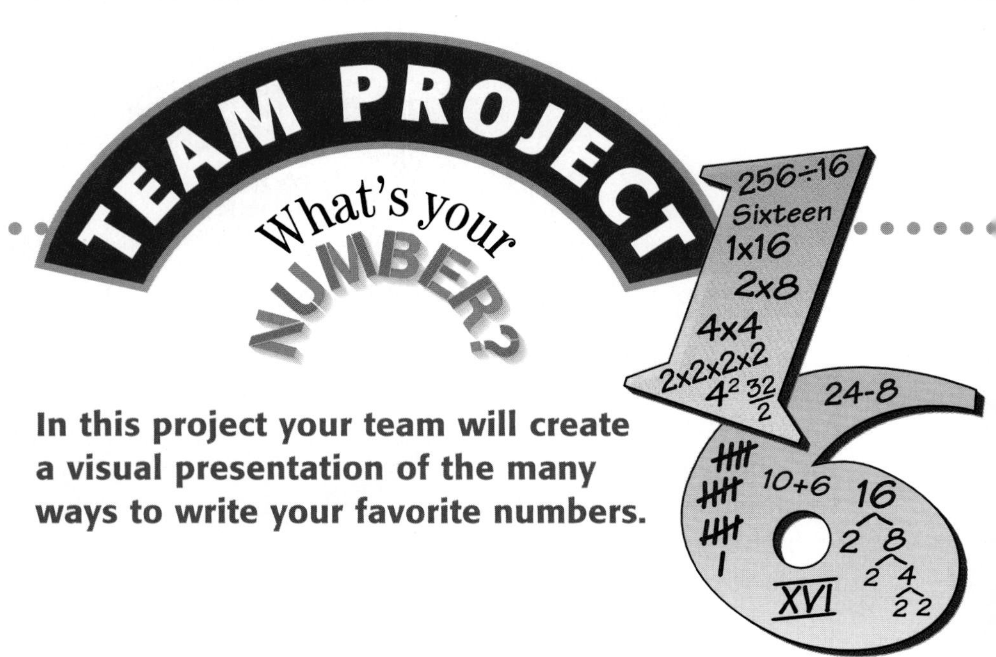

Materials

colored construction paper, scissors, markers, glue, posterboard

In this project your team will create a visual presentation of the many ways to write your favorite numbers.

Make a Plan

- How many ways can your team think of to write a single number?
- Are your favorite numbers one digit or more than one digit?
- How many prime factors are there in your numbers? How many least common multiples do pairs of your numbers have?

Carry It Out

1. Make a list of each team member's favorite number. Indicate which numbers are prime numbers and which are composite numbers.
2. Draw and cut out your favorite number from a sheet of construction paper.
3. Think of one way to write your favorite number. Use a marker to write this way on the cut-out of your favorite number.
4. Exchange your cut-out numbers with the whole group and find other ways to write your favorite numbers.
5. Paste your cut-out numbers onto posterboard.

Talk About It

- Did your group have more ways of writing prime numbers or composite numbers? Why do you think this is so?

Present the Project

Look at all the different ways other teams decided to show their favorite numbers. Are there more ways that another group could have shown their numbers? Did the way another team presented their numbers give you ideas about writing your own numbers? If you could add numbers to your poster, what ways of writing the numbers would you add?

CHAPTER 5

Number Theory

We have often changed how we keep track of time. In the 1200s, an hour was $\frac{1}{12}$ of the time from sunrise to sunset, regardless of how long that was. Today, an hour equals 60 minutes. Every change has been an effort to make timekeeping more accurate and more convenient. What sort of mathematics do you think is needed to create an accurate clock or calendar?

GET READY!

Finding the Least Common Multiple

Review division. Find each quotient.

1. $375 \div 5$
2. $184 \div 8$
3. $861 \div 7$
4. $645 \div 3$
5. $423 \div 9$
6. $748 \div 4$
7. $708 \div 6$
8. $638 \div 2$
9. $265 \div 5$
10. $276 \div 6$
11. $216 \div 8$
12. $260 \div 4$

Skills Checklist

In this section, you will:

- ❒ Learn About Divisibility
- ❒ Explore Prime Factorization
- ❒ Learn About Least Common Multiples

Chapter 5 Lesson 1

Divisibility

You Will Learn
- the rules of divisibility

Materials
calculator

Vocabulary
divisible

Learn

A television news producer has to have perfect timing. For a 30-minute newscast, there are about 24 minutes to fill with different news "segments."

Suppose a news producer has several 4-minute segments to use in the program. Can the producer use 4-minute segments to fill the entire 24 minute newscast? Can he use only 5-minute segments?

A whole number is **divisible** by another number if you can divide the first number by the second without leaving a remainder.

Example 1

Is 24 divisible by 4?

$4\overline{)24}$ = 6 — 24 is divisible by 4.

Is 24 divisible by 5?

$5\overline{)24}$ = 4 R4 — 24 is **not** divisible by 5.

The producer can use 4-minute segments to fill the newscast.

Remember
An *even* number ends in 0, 2, 4, 6, or 8. An *odd* number ends in 1, 3, 5, 7, or 9.

For any number, you can list all the numbers that are divisible by that number. Sometimes, you will see patterns that can help you determine if a number is divisible by another number without actually needing to divide.

Some patterns depend on the ones digit in the number.

Divisibility Rules	
A whole number is divisible by	Examples
• 2 if the ones digit is even.	2, 4, 6, 8, 10, . . .
• 5 if the ones digit is 5 or 0.	5, 10, 15, 20, 25, . . .
• 10 if the ones digit is 0.	10, 20, 30, 40, 50, . . .

Example 2

Is 28 divisible by 2, 5, or 10?

2? Yes; The ones digit is even.

5? No; The ones digit is neither 5 nor 0.

10? No; The ones digit is not 0.

Some patterns depend on the sum of the digits.

A whole number is divisible by	Examples
• 3 if the sum of its digits is divisible by 3.	3, 6, 9, 12, 15, . . .
• 9 if the sum if its digits is divisible by 9.	9, 18, 27, 36, 45, . . .

Some patterns depend upon other patterns.

A whole number is divisible by	Examples
• 6 if it is divisible by both 2 and 3.	6, 12, 18, 24, 30, 42, . . .

Example 3

Test 945 for divisibility by 2, 3, 5, 6, 9, and 10.

2? No; The ones digit is not even.

3? Yes; $9 + 4 + 5 = 18$, which is divisible by 3.

5? Yes; The ones digit is 5.

6? No; 945 is divisible by 3, but not by 2.

9? Yes; $9 + 4 + 5 = 18$, which is divisible by 9.

10? No; The ones digit is not 0.

Example 4

Test 792 for divisibility by 2, 3, 5, 6, 9, and 10.

2? Yes; The ones digit is even.

3? Yes; $7 + 9 + 2 = 18$, which is divisible by 3.

5? No; The ones digit is not 5 or 0.

6? Yes; 792 is divisible by both 2 and 3.

9? Yes; $7 + 9 + 2 = 18$, which is divisible by 9.

10? No; The ones digit is not 0.

Talk About It

1. What are the advantages of knowing divisibility rules?
2. Which divisibility rules do you think are easiest to use? Explain.

Check

Tell whether each number is divisible by 2, 3, 5, 6, 9, or 10.

1. 141 **2.** 455 **3.** 684 **4.** 555 **5.** 2,700

6. **Reasoning** Juanita teaches a dance class of 24 dancers. She wants to arrange the class into equal groups. Which ways can she group the dancers? Explain.

Practice

Skills and Reasoning

Tell whether each number is divisible by 2, 5, or 10.

7. 66 **8.** 228 **9.** 45 **10.** 120 **11.** 985 **12.** 30

Tell whether each number is divisible by 2, 3, 5, 6, 9, or 10.

13. 63 **14.** 55 **15.** 117 **16.** 81 **17.** 621

18. 1,360 **19.** 35 **20.** 42 **21.** 104 **22.** 4,320

23. 10 **24.** 90 **25.** 27 **26.** 68 **27.** 180

28. 135 **29.** 282 **30.** 56 **31.** 5,555 **32.** 48

33. 362 **34.** 1,110 **35.** 9 **36.** 24 **37.** 66

38. 75 **39.** 85 **40.** 695 **41.** 588 **42.** 96

Tell whether the first number is divisible by the second.

43. 33, 3 **44.** 132, 11 **45.** 41, 5 **46.** 105, 8 **47.** 63, 4

48. 92, 9 **49.** 65, 10 **50.** 99, 11 **51.** 78, 6 **52.** 60, 4

53. 93, 2 **54.** 115, 5 **55.** 171, 9 **56.** 109, 7 **57.** 52, 6

58. 160, 8 **59.** 54, 7 **60.** 30, 4 **61.** 52, 11 **62.** 58, 8

63. 84, 7 **64.** 76, 2 **65.** 30, 10 **66.** 120, 12 **67.** 37, 3

68. **Reasoning** A year that ends in two zeros must be divisible by 400 to be a leap year. Would the year 1900 be a leap year? Explain.

Problem Solving and Applications

69. There are approximately 52 weeks in a year. Is this number divisible by 12? Why would it be important for you to know this? Explain.

70. **History** Abraham Lincoln's Gettysburg Address begins "Four score and seven years ago . . ." A score is 20 years, so "four score and seven" is 87 years. A score is divisible by what numbers?

71. Determine if the number of years in each of the following is divisible by 2, 3, 5, 6, 9, or 10.

a. A decade (10 years)

b. A century (100 years)

c. A millennium (1,000 years)

72. **Using Data** Use the data in Exercise 68 to name three years that were or will be leap years.

73. **Critical Thinking** Marvel Models produces 53,716 model cars each month. They want to design shipping cartons that hold more than 3 but fewer than 10 models each. They want to pack each month's cars in the cartons, with no cars left over. What are their choices? Explain.

74. **History** The solar calendar of the Aztec people had 365 days, which was 18 months of 20 days and 5 "unlucky" extra days. How could the Aztecs have rearranged their calendar so that each month had the same number of days and no "unlucky" days? Explain.

75. **Critical Thinking** If a number is divisible by both 2 and 3, it is divisible by 6. If a number is divisible by 2 and 5, by what other number is it divisible? Explain.

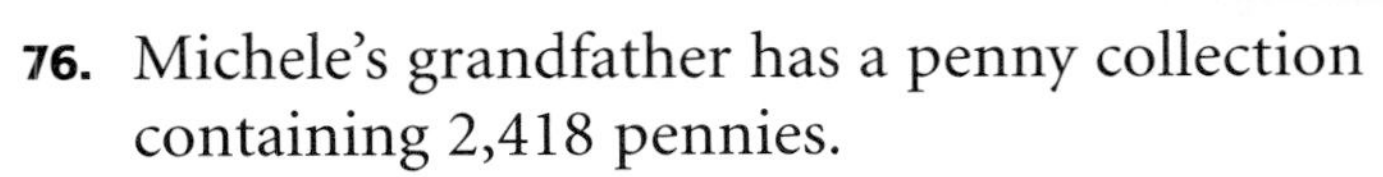

76. Michele's grandfather has a penny collection containing 2,418 pennies.
    a. Can Michele and her two sisters split the collection evenly? Explain.
    b. If Michele's brother and parents also wanted to share the collection evenly with Michele and her sisters, would this be possible? Explain.

77. **Journal** Find the year that you will graduate from high school. Is that year divisible by 2, 3, 4, 5, 6, 7, 8, or 9? Explain.

Mixed Review and Test Prep

STAY SHARP!

Write each number in word form.

78. 54,007 **79.** 500,200 **80.** 101,110 **81.** 2,345

Multiply.

82. 32×0.5 **83.** 15×0.9 **84.** 8.1×0.6 **85.** 5.5×1.4

86. 17×0.4 **87.** 21×0.3 **88.** 68×0.2 **89.** 51×1.2

90. What is the circumference of a circle whose radius is 6 cm?

Ⓐ 3.82 cm Ⓑ 18.84 cm Ⓒ 37.68 cm Ⓓ 113.04 cm

Chapter 5
Lesson
2

Prime Factorization

Problem Solving Connection
- Draw a Picture

Materials
graph paper

Vocabulary
prime number
composite number
prime factorization

Explore

Any number of squares can be arranged into a rectangle. Some can be arranged into only one rectangle, and some can be arranged into several different rectangles.

Work Together

1. On a sheet of graph paper, copy and complete the following table down to 20 squares. Two rectangles are the same if one can be turned to look like the other.

Number of Squares	Number of Rectangles	Sketches
1	1	
2	1	
3	1	
4	2	

2. Make a list of the numbers for which you could draw only one rectangle. Make a second list of the numbers for which you could draw more than one.

3. How many factors does each number in your first list have? How many does each number in your second list have?

Did You Know?
Computer programmers use prime numbers when developing security programs that make it difficult to read information from other people's computers.

Talk About It

4. What can you conclude about the numbers that can be made into only one rectangle?

5. Is there a number of squares that cannot be arranged into a rectangle? Explain.

Connect and Learn

Every whole number greater than 1 is either a **prime number** or a **composite number**. A prime number has exactly two factors, 1 and itself. A composite number has more than two factors. The least number that is either composite or prime is 2. Mathematicians consider 0 and 1 to be neither prime nor composite.

	4	7	10	25	29
Factors	1, 2, 4	1, 7	1, 2, 5, 10	1, 5, 25	1, 29
Type	composite	prime	composite	composite	prime

Every human being has a unique fingerprint. Similarly, every composite number has a unique "factorprint." It is called the **prime factorization**. It's the set of prime numbers whose product equals the number.

You can use a "factor tree" to find a prime factorization. Find two numbers whose product equals the original number and write them below. If a number is prime, circle it. If a number is composite, continue to break it apart until you only have prime numbers left. Rewrite the prime factors at the bottom from least to greatest.

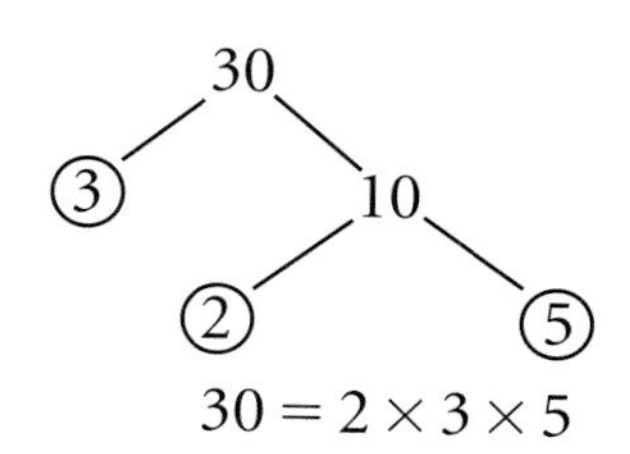

Example

Find the prime factorization of 630.

Use the divisibility rules to find factors and draw "branches."

630 ends in 0, so it's divisible by 10.
$630 \div 10 = 63$

Circle prime factors when you find them.

Stop when the "leaves" at ends of branches are all circled.

The prime factorization is $2 \times 3 \times 3 \times 5 \times 7$, or $2 \times 3^2 \times 5 \times 7$.

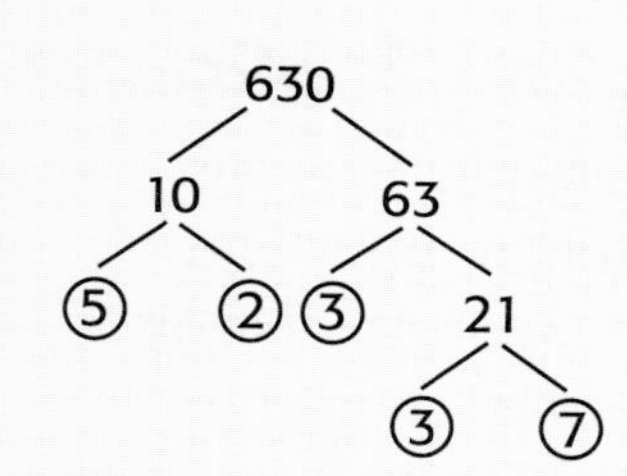

Remember

3^2 is in exponential notation. It means 3×3. The exponent, in this case 2, tells you how many times the base, in this case 3, is used as a factor.

Check

Find the prime factorization of each number.

1. 12 **2.** 20 **3.** 36 **4.** 45 **5.** 210

6. Reasoning Rachel says 121 is prime, since it is odd and she can't find a number that divides into it without a remainder. Is she right? Explain.

Practice

Skills and Reasoning

Use mental math to find the prime factorization.

7. 15 **8.** 33 **9.** 14 **10.** 21 **11.** 6

Given the number and its factors, tell whether it is prime or composite.

12. 45: 1, 3, 5, 9, 15, 45 **13.** 67: 1, 67 **14.** 37: 1, 37 **15.** 26: 1, 2, 13, 26

16. 53: 1, 53 **17.** 65: 1, 5, 13, 65 **18.** 11: 1, 11 **19.** 9: 1, 3, 9

Find the prime factorization.

20. 58 **21.** 25 **22.** 26 **23.** 95 **24.** 405

25. 125 **26.** 56 **27.** 6 **28.** 27 **29.** 60

30. 32 **31.** 105 **32.** 96 **33.** 48 **34.** 13

35. 85 **36.** 297 **37.** 162 **38.** 5,670 **39.** 165

40. 693 **41.** 468 **42.** 10 **43.** 42 **44.** 29

45. The prime factorization of a number is $2 \times 3 \times 5 \times 5 \times 7 \times 13 \times 29$. What is the number?

46. What is the least composite number that has all of the first 5 prime numbers as factors? Explain.

Problem Solving and Applications

47. Mr. Arnold has 36 students in his math class. He wants to put them into groups of the same size. He also wants the number in each group to be a prime factor of 36. What are his choices?

48. Three of Olivia's friends live in her apartment building. One day she noticed that they all had apartment numbers that were three-digit prime numbers less than 110. If everyone lived in a different apartment, what were the four apartment numbers?

49. **Write Your Own Problem** Choose any four-digit number. Write clues to help a friend guess your number. At least one of your clues should involve prime numbers.

50. Probability Bryan dropped a marker on the board. Was it more likely to fall on a prime number or on a composite number? Explain.

51. Money Samuel wants to save $8.50 in nickels. Can this be done? Explain.

APRIL

S	M	T	W	T	F	S
			1	2	3	4
5	6	7	8	9	10	11
12	13	14	15	16	17	18
19	20	21	22	23	24	25
26	27	28	29	30		

Johnson, William H., Untitled (Soapbox Racing), 1939-40. National Museum of American Art, Smithsonian Institute. Washington, D.C.

52. Measurement An April calendar shows 30 days, labeled 1 through 30. How many days have a prime number date? How many have a composite number date?

53. What portion of people born in April have a prime number birth date?

54. Math History Eratosthenes designed a method, called the Sieve of Eratosthenes, to find prime numbers. Between the numbers 40 and 80, he found 10 prime numbers. What are they?

55. Using Data Use the Data File on page 262. Which planet orbits the sun in a number of days that is divisible by a prime number? Explain.

56. Which number(s) appears more than once in the prime factorization of 100?

57. Critical Thinking Find two numbers with prime factorizations that use the same prime factors.

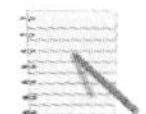

58. Journal A prime number is any whole number with exactly two factors, itself and 1. Explain why 1 isn't a prime number.

Mixed Review and Test Prep

Round each number to the given place value.

59. 456,892; thousands

60. 5,678,022; hundred-thousands

61. 923,894; hundreds

62. 5,890,324,331; millions

Divide.

63. $10 \div 6$ **64.** $12 \div 10$ **65.** $4 \div 8$ **66.** $14 \div 56$

67. $1 \div 5$ **68.** $1 \div 4$ **69.** $1 \div 10$ **70.** $1 \div 2$

71. What is the sum of 2.69 and 0.98?

Ⓐ 1.71 Ⓑ 3.67 Ⓒ 36.7 Ⓓ 367

Chapter 5
Lesson
3

Least Common Multiples

You Will Learn
- to find the least common multiple for two numbers

Vocabulary
multiple
common multiple
least common multiple (LCM)

Did You Know?
Astronomers use least common multiples to determine when celestial objects will pass Earth at the same time.

Learn

Mercury and Venus are closer than the Earth to the Sun. The Earth takes 365 days (12 months) to orbit the Sun. Mercury makes a complete orbit around the Sun in 88 days (about 3 months on Earth). Venus travels around the Sun in 225 days (about 7 months on Earth).

A **multiple** of a number is the product of the number and a whole number.

Multiples of 3: 3, 6, 9, 12, 15, 18, **21**, 24, 27, 30, 33, 36, 39, **42**, . . .

Multiples of 7: 7, 14, **21**, 28, 35, **42**, 49, 56, 63, 70, 77, . . .

Numbers that appear on both lists are **common multiples**. The **least common multiple (LCM)** of two numbers is the *smallest* common multiple of the numbers.

One way to find the LCM of two numbers is to list multiples of both numbers. Then choose the smallest multiple that appears on both lists.

Suppose Mercury's orbit places it directly between Venus and the Sun. How many months will pass before both planets are in the same place again?

Find the least common multiple of 3 and 7.

Look at the lists for 3 and 7 above.

21 is the smallest multiple on both lists, so Mercury and Venus will be in the same position in 21 months.

Example 1

Find the first two common multiples of 10 and 12.

Multiples of 10: 10, 20, 30, 40, 50, **60,** 70, 80, 90, 100, 110, **120**, . . .

Multiples of 12: 12, 24, 36, 48, **60,** 72, 84, 96, 108, **120**, . . .

The first two common multiples of 10 and 12 are 60 and 120.

Example 2

Find the least common multiple of 6 and 8.

Multiples of 6: 6, 12, 18, **24**, 30, 36, . . .

Multiples of 8: 8, 16, **24**, . . .

The least common multiple of 6 and 8 is 24.

You can use multiples to help you solve problems.

Example 3

A U.S. president is elected every 4 years. A U.S. senator is elected every 6 years. If a senator is elected the same year as the president, how many years will it be until the senator could run for reelection during a presidential campaign?

Multiples of 4: 4, 8, **12,** 16, 20, 24, 28, 32, . . .

Multiples of 6: 6, **12,** 18, 24, 30, 36, . . .

The senator will run for reelection during a presidential campaign in another 12 years.

Did You Know?

According to the U.S. Constitution, a person can be elected to serve only two 4-year terms as president. There are no term limits for senators. There is no limit to the number of times a person can be elected to serve as a senator.

Talk About It

1. For any pair of numbers, is the least common multiple always greater than either number? Explain.
2. What's the difference between a factor and a multiple?
3. How many factors does 8 have? How many multiples?

"When I said, 'term limits,' I was speaking in dog years."

Check

Find the LCM of each pair of numbers.

1. 5, 7 **2.** 3, 10 **3.** 20, 25 **4.** 1,297; 1 **5.** 8, 2

6. **Reasoning** Terence believes that the least common multiple of two prime numbers is always the product of those numbers. Do you think Terence is correct? Explain.

Practice

Skills and Reasoning

List the first five multiples of each number.

7. 3 **8.** 10 **9.** 8 **10.** 11 **11.** 4

List the first three common multiples of each pair of numbers.

12. 4, 6 **13.** 1, 5 **14.** 6, 2 **15.** 12, 5 **16.** 3, 9

17. 6, 7 **18.** 8, 11 **19.** 8, 4 **20.** 10, 15 **21.** 16, 4

Find the LCM of each pair.

22. 7, 11 **23.** 3, 33 **24.** 8, 16 **25.** 5, 13 **26.** 2, 15

27. 10, 5 **28.** 15, 7 **29.** 4, 3 **30.** 6, 9 **31.** 14, 21

32. 4, 6 **33.** 6, 7 **34.** 6, 8 **35.** 10, 20 **36.** 3, 11

37. 7, 2 **38.** 88, 4 **39.** 15, 3

40. Victoria wears jeans every 2 days. She wears her jogging shoes every 3 days. If she wears jeans with jogging shoes on June 1, what are the next three dates on which she will wear both jeans and jogging shoes?

41. The Blue Line bus arrives at Chesapeake Parkway every 20 minutes. The Express Shuttle arrives at the same stop every 3 minutes. How often do both busses arrive at the same time?

42. **Calculator** Use your calculator to find the LCM of two numbers. Try 12 and 15. Enter [ON/AC] [+] 12 [=] [=] and so on. List the multiples. Do the same for 15. The first multiple that is a multiple of both is the LCM.

43. **Reasoning** Compare the LCM of 3 and 7 with the LCM of 7 and 21. What do you notice? Explain.

44. In a middle school, the principal plans to hide prizes in the new lockers for the students. The principal plans to put a binder in every 10th locker, a school tee shirt in every 15th locker, and a new backpack in every 50th locker. If she starts counting at locker number 1, what is the number of the first locker in which the principal will put all three prizes?

Problem Solving and HISTORY

The clepsydra (KLEP-suh-druh), or water clock, and the hourglass were among the first clocks. In a clepsydra, water pours from one container into another at the regular rate to mark the passage of time. In an hour glass, sand flows from the top container to the bottom one.

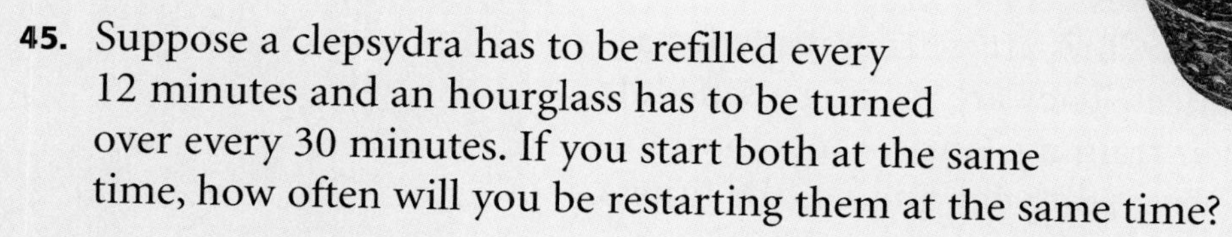

45. Suppose a clepsydra has to be refilled every 12 minutes and an hourglass has to be turned over every 30 minutes. If you start both at the same time, how often will you be restarting them at the same time?

46. In ancient times, clepsydras were used in courts of law. Sometimes corrupt lawyers would bribe the timekeepers to put muddy water in the clepsydra. This water would flow more slowly, and the lawyer would have more time to talk. Suppose a clepsydra filled with muddy water had to be refilled every 24 minutes and one filled with clear water had to be filled every 14 minutes. How many times would each clepsydra need to be refilled before they both measure the exact same amount of time?

47. Kyle and Treva made their own clepsydras to use as bathroom clocks. They put small holes in the bottom of plastic cups and hung them in their showers. Kyle determined that 8 oz of water in his clock would drip for 12 minutes. Treva determined that 12 oz of water in her clock would drip for 18 minutes. How long does it take before both clocks need to be refilled at the same time?

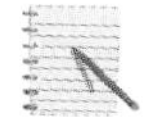

48. Journal Explain how you would find the LCM of 24 and 18.

Mixed Review and Test Prep

STAY SHARP!

Compare, using > or <.

49. 23,301 ● 23,103 **50.** 7,377 ● 73,777 **51.** 501,501 ● 501,105

52. 16,010 ● 16,001 **53.** 414,141 ● 414,414 **54.** 19,989 ● 19,991

Divide.

55. $42 \div 0.7$ **56.** $100 \div 0.05$ **57.** $6.32 \div 0.01$

58. $500 \div 0.02$ **59.** $16 \div 1.6$ **60.** $1.25 \div 0.8$

61. Round 1.495 to the nearest whole number. Choose the correct answer.

Ⓐ 0 Ⓑ 1 Ⓒ 2 Ⓓ 14

Skills Practice Bank, page 664, Set 2

Chapter 5

Problem Solving

Compare Strategies: Solve a Simpler Problem/Make an Organized List

You Will Learn

- to solve problems by solving a simpler problem and making an organized list

Learn

Sean and Chris are getting ready for a track meet. They are making a schedule for their training. Chris wants to run a mile every other day and use the fitness equipment every third day. Sean wants to run 2 miles every 3 days and use the fitness equipment every other day. They want to know what days they will both be using the fitness equipment during March if they both start their training March 1st.

Emily and Paul used two different strategies to solve the problem.

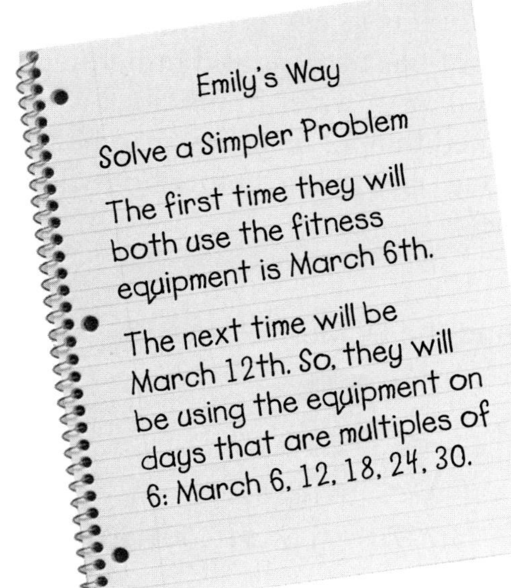

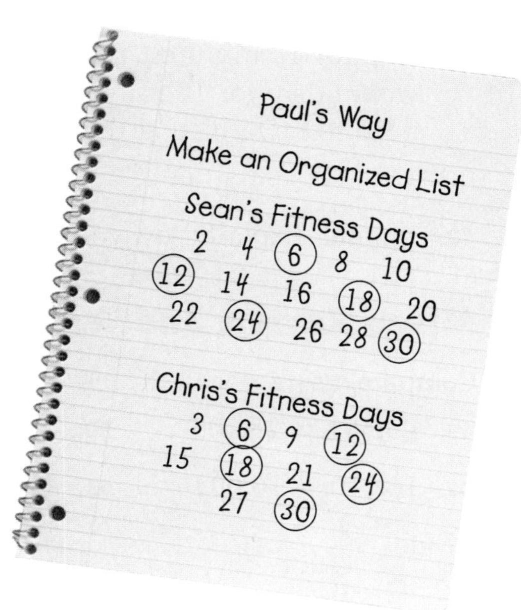

Talk About It

1. Which way of solving the problem do you think has more chances for making a mistake? Why?
2. Which method do you like better? Explain.

Check

Use Solve a Simpler Problem or Make an Organized List to solve.

1. Sean and Chris want to know how far they will run in a month and who will run the farthest.
   a. Describe how you can use the Solve a Simpler Problem method to find out how far Sean will run in March.
   b. Describe how you can use the Make an Organized List method to find out how far Chris will run in March.
   c. Who will run farther? How much farther?

Problem Solving Practice

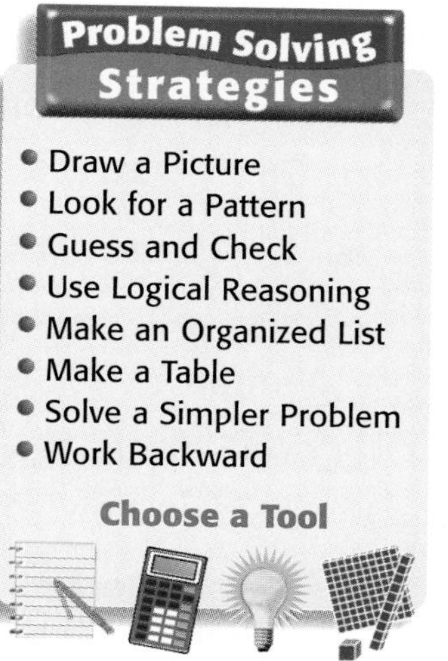

Use any strategy to solve each problem.

2. Venus begins a new year every 225 days. Earth begins a new year every 365 days. Suppose both planets begin a new year on the same day.
   a. How many days will pass before that happens again?
   b. How many years is that on Earth?
   c. How many years is that on Venus?
3. **Time** Sean was born in February. He says he was born on a prime number day. February has 28 days except during leap year when it has 29 days.
   a. How many days in February could be Sean's birthday?
   b. If you guessed one of the prime number days, what is the probability that you would guess Sean's birthday?
4. Jodi waters her tomatoes every other day. She waters the ivy every 3 days. If she waters both on May 8th, what are the next three dates on which she will water both?
5. **Patterns** Jayne is making a beaded necklace. Every third bead is red, every fifth bead is blue. When she needs a bead to be both red and blue, she uses a purple bead. The rest of the beads are yellow. Jayne is making a necklace of 30 beads. How many of each color bead will Jayne need?

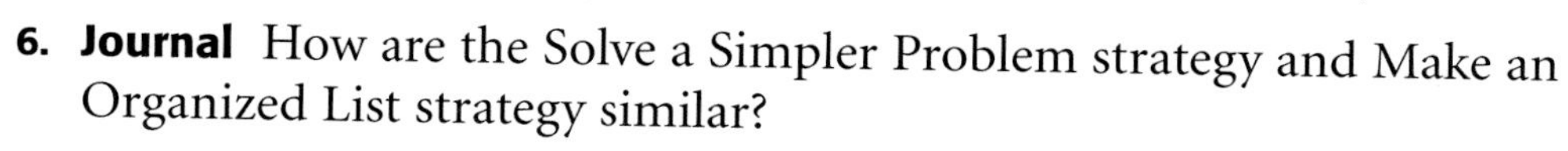

6. **Journal** How are the Solve a Simpler Problem strategy and Make an Organized List strategy similar?

PROBLEM SOLVING PRACTICE

SECTION A

Review and Practice

(Lesson 1) Write whether the first number is divisible by the second.

1. 6, 4 **2.** 31, 7 **3.** 48, 2 **4.** 63, 9 **5.** 48, 6

6. 22, 6 **7.** 80, 10 **8.** 175, 5 **9.** 882, 9 **10.** 13, 3

Write whether each number is divisible by 2, 5, or 10.

11. 25 **12.** 1,500 **13.** 2,972 **14.** 1,112 **15.** 750

16. 918 **17.** 777 **18.** 10,450 **19.** 4,025 **20.** 40

(Lesson 2) Find the prime factorization.

21. 76 **22.** 24 **23.** 22 **24.** 59 **25.** 47

26. 12 **27.** 44 **28.** 114 **29.** 243 **30.** 62

31. The prime factorization of a number is $3 \times 3 \times 5 \times 13$. What is the number?

32. What is the least number that is divisible by 2, 3, 4, 5, 6, 9, and 10? Explain how you found your answer.

33. If you choose a two-digit number at random, is it more likely that the number will be divisible by 5 or by 7? Explain.

(Lesson 3) List the first seven multiples of each number.

34. 2 **35.** 6 **36.** 7

37. 9 **38.** 0 **39.** 12

Find the LCM of each pair.

40. 3, 6 **41.** 5, 15 **42.** 6, 9

43. 8, 12 **44.** 10, 20 **45.** 9, 2

46. 12, 26 **47.** 2, 8 **48.** 6, 22

Solve.

49. Social Studies Members of the House of Representatives are elected in years divisible by 2. Which years between 1996 and 2006 will have congressional elections?

50. Journal How can you use the rules of divisibility to help determine if a number is prime or composite? Give an example.

Skills Checklist

In this section, you have:

- **Learned About Divisibility**
- **Explored Prime Factorization**
- **Learned About Least Common Multiples**

CHAPTER 5

SECTION

B Connecting Fractions and Decimals

Using a tool can make your work easy . . . but choosing the right tool can be hard work! Many tools come in a variety of sizes. In this section, you will learn how we use both fractions and decimals to measure such sizes. What kinds of tools have you used to measure the size of an item? Were they fractional or decimal measurements?

Skills Checklist

In this section, you will:

- ❒ Understand Fractions
- ❒ Learn About Fractions in Lowest Terms
- ❒ Learn About Improper Fractions and Mixed Numbers
- ❒ Explore Converting Fractions and Decimals
- ❒ Explore Algebra by Using Expressions

GET READY!

Converting Fractions and Decimals

Review multiples. Copy and complete the patterns.

1. 33, ■, 27, ■, 21, ■
2. 12, 24, ■, ■, 60, ■
3. 7, ■, ■, 28, ■, 42
4. 44, ■, 40, ■, ■, 34
5. ■, 12, 18, ■, ■, 36
6. 64, ■, 48, ■, ■, 24
7. ■, 63, 54, 45, ■, ■
8. ■, 65, ■, 39, 26, ■

Chapter 5
Lesson
4

Understanding Fractions

You Will Learn

- to represent values between whole numbers as fractions

Vocabulary

fraction

denominator

numerator

equivalent fractions

Learn

Gerald likes to build things such as birdhouses. He is saving to purchase a set of screwdrivers. The set he hopes to buy has 12 screwdrivers, 5 Phillips and 7 standard.

Gerald lives in Lubbock, Texas.

You can use a **fraction** to describe a part of a whole. The bottom number, called the **denominator**, gives the number of parts in the whole. The top number, the **numerator**, tells how many of the parts are being named.

Example 1

What fraction of all the screwdrivers in the set are standard screwdrivers? What fraction are Phillips screwdrivers?

There are **12** screwdrivers in the whole set.

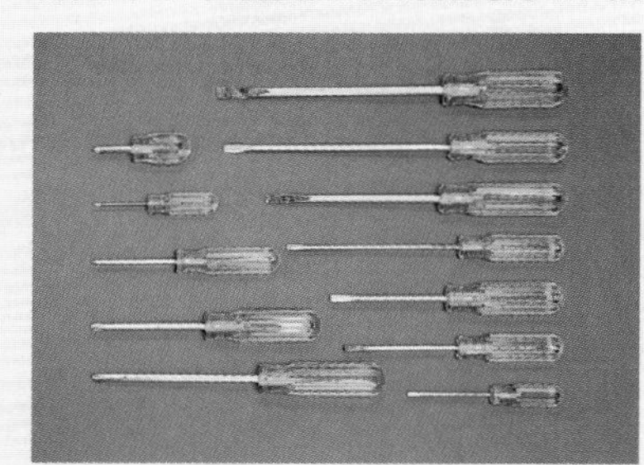

$\frac{\mathbf{7}}{\mathbf{12}}$ ⟵ are standard (numerator)
⟵ in all (denominator)

$\frac{7}{12}$ are standard.

$\frac{\mathbf{5}}{\mathbf{12}}$ ⟵ are Phillips (numerator)
⟵ in all (denominator)

$\frac{5}{12}$ are Phillips.

You can read the fraction $\frac{5}{12}$ two ways: "five twelfths," or "five out of twelve."

Did You Know?

A standard screwdriver has an end that looks like −. A Phillips screwdriver has a head that looks like a +.

You can use a fraction to describe a portion of something that has been divided into equal parts.

Example 2

What part of each rectangle is shaded?

All of the parts are equal.

2 out of 3 parts, or $\frac{2}{3}$, are shaded.

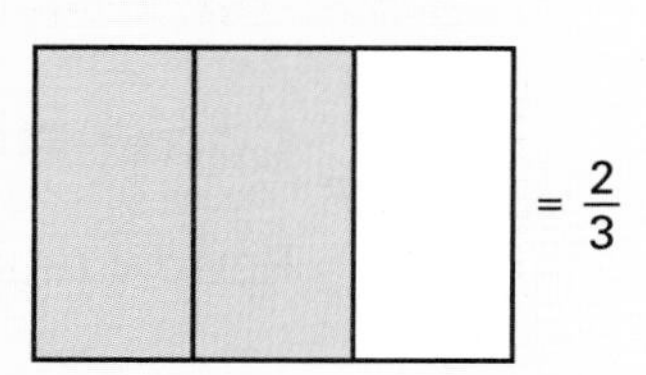

$= \frac{2}{3}$

In the second one, all of the parts are equal.

6 out of 6 parts, or $\frac{6}{6}$, are shaded.

The numerator and the denominator are the same number.

$\frac{6}{6}$ = one whole = 1

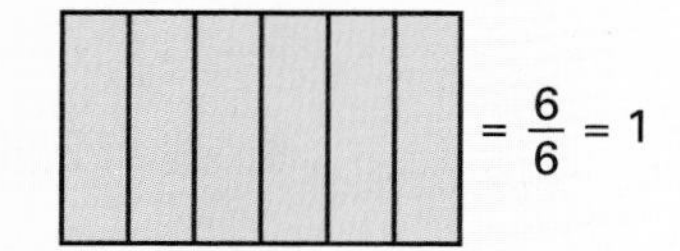

$= \frac{6}{6} = 1$

Two fractions that name the same amount are called **equivalent fractions**.

Example 3

$\frac{3}{5}$ of the rectangle has been shaded.
Name a fraction equivalent to $\frac{3}{5}$.

You can draw a line across the rectangle, cutting it into 10 equal pieces. Then 6 pieces are shaded. $\frac{3}{5} = \frac{6}{10}$

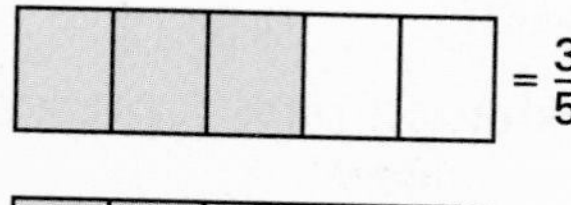

$= \frac{3}{5}$

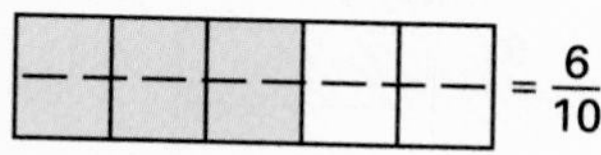

$= \frac{6}{10}$

You can name more than one equivalent fraction for a fraction.

Example 4

Jake measured the tack to be $\frac{1}{2}$ inch. Jay said it is $\frac{2}{4}$ inch. Marsha said it is $\frac{4}{8}$ inch. Who is correct?

They all are.

$\frac{1}{2}$, $\frac{2}{4}$, and $\frac{4}{8}$ are equivalent fractions.

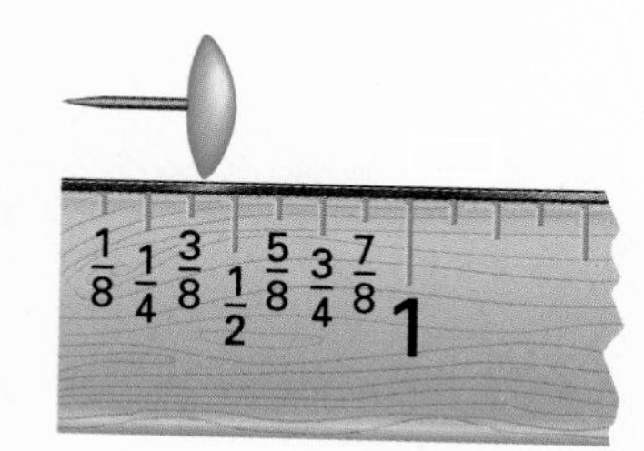

Talk About It

1. How are the numerator and denominator of a fraction different?
2. Describe patterns you see in fractions that are equivalent to $\frac{1}{2}$.
3. How many fractions can you use to describe one inch? Explain.

Check

1. What fraction of the jalapeño peppers are red?
2. What fraction of the peppers are not red?
3. What fraction does the shaded part of the rectangle represent?

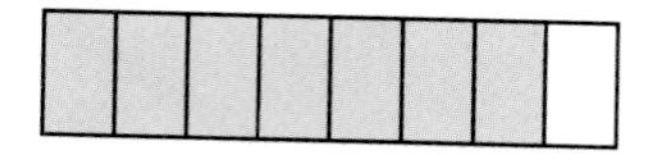

4. Name an equivalent fraction for your answer to 3.
5. Draw a model for $\frac{3}{4}$. Use your model to show and name 2 more equivalent fractions.
6. **Reasoning** How can the numerator and denominator of a fraction increase and yet name the same part of a whole?

Practice

Skills and Reasoning

What fraction does the shaded part represent?

7. 

8. 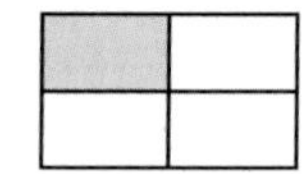

9. 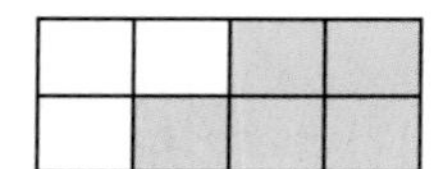

10. 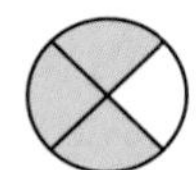

For each fraction, draw a model and name an equivalent fraction.

11. $\frac{3}{4}$	**12.** $\frac{7}{9}$	**13.** $\frac{1}{2}$	**14.** $\frac{12}{17}$	**15.** $\frac{5}{8}$
16. $\frac{2}{3}$	**17.** $\frac{12}{12}$	**18.** $\frac{8}{16}$	**19.** $\frac{11}{11}$	**20.** $\frac{4}{10}$
21. $\frac{6}{7}$	**22.** $\frac{3}{8}$	**23.** $\frac{1}{9}$	**24.** $\frac{6}{8}$	**25.** $\frac{2}{7}$
26. $\frac{2}{4}$	**27.** $\frac{8}{11}$	**28.** $\frac{9}{10}$	**29.** $\frac{1}{5}$	**30.** $\frac{1}{6}$

Geometry Use the shapes pictured to answer **31–33.**

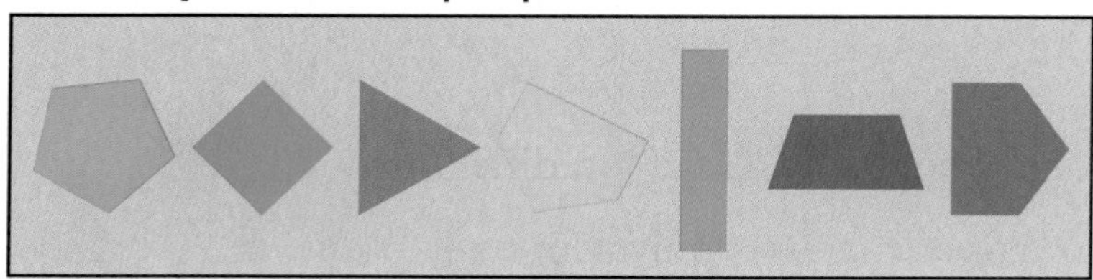

31. What fraction of the shapes shown have five sides?

32. What fraction of the shapes do not have exactly three sides?

33. Which fraction is larger, the fraction of the shapes with four sides or the fraction of the shapes with five sides?

34. Reasoning $\frac{5}{20}$ and $\frac{1}{4}$ are equivalent fractions. If you ate $\frac{1}{4}$ of a pizza and your friend ate $\frac{8}{20}$ of a pizza, who would have eaten more? Explain.

Problem Solving and Applications

Use the drill-bit size chart for **35** and **36**.

35. Patterns The bit sizes increase according to a mathematical pattern. What will the size of the #10 drill be?

36. What number bit would you need to drill a $\frac{3}{4}$-inch hole?

Number	Bit Size
#4	$\frac{1}{4}$ inch
#5	$\frac{5}{16}$ inch
#6	$\frac{6}{16}$ inch
#7	$\frac{7}{16}$ inch
#8	$\frac{2}{4}$ inch

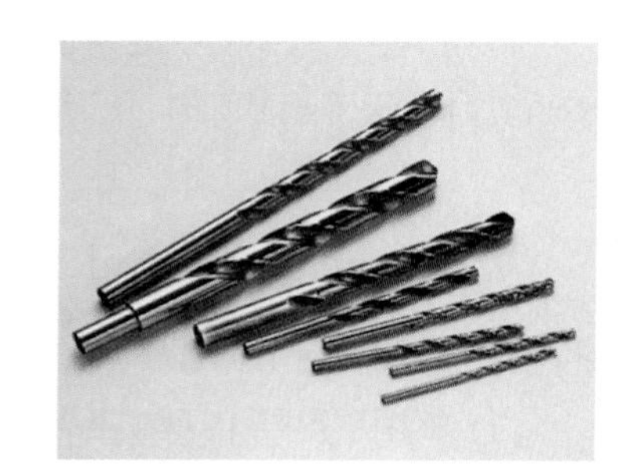

37. Chinese chopsticks are 10 inches long with flat ends. Japanese chopsticks are 7 to 8 inches long with pointed ends. What fraction of the individual chopsticks are Chinese? Give two equivalent fractions for your answer.

Use the illustration for **38–40.** The window shown has equal-size sections made of both stained glass and clear glass.

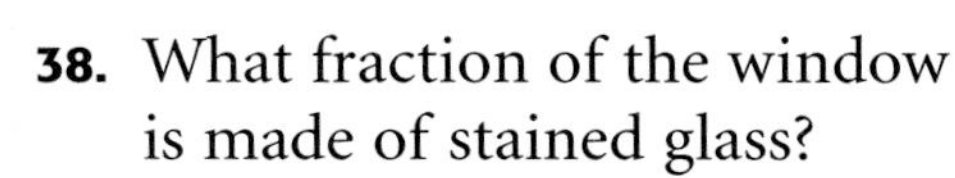

38. What fraction of the window is made of stained glass?

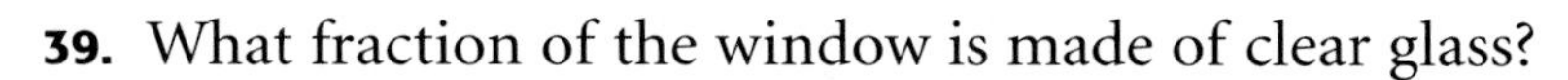

39. What fraction of the window is made of clear glass?

40. Suppose three sections of the window need to be replaced. Name two fractions that describe this amount

41. **Using Data** Use the Data File on page 262. Write two equivalent fractions for the fraction of people listening to news or talk shows on the radio on an average day.

42. Celia needs 20 nails and 8 screws to build a bookshelf. What fraction of the hardware she needs are screws?

43. Name two fractions that describe the number of square picture frames. Identify the numerators and denominators.

44. Sandra went shopping and bought 4 bananas, 2 oranges, 3 red peppers, 2 onions, and 2 apples. What fraction of these items are fruit? Vegetables?

45. **Journal** Explain what happens to the value of a fraction when the numerator gets bigger and the denominator stays the same. What happens when the denominator gets bigger and the numerator doesn't change?

Mixed Review and Test Prep

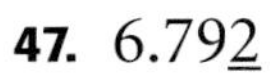

Round to the underlined place value.

46. $101.\underline{9}3$ **47.** $6.79\underline{2}$ **48.** $48.\underline{2}5$ **49.** $\underline{0}.672$ **50.** $\underline{8}.7$ **51.** $12.\underline{7}02$

Solve.

52. $92.4n = 9{,}240$ **53.** $p \div 0.05 = 5$ **54.** $x \div 0.12 = 1.2$

55. $1.45h = 2.9$ **56.** $w \div 3 = 333.3$ **57.** $8.1m = 810$

58. Which appears more than once in the prime factorization of 200?

Ⓐ 2 and 5 Ⓑ only 2 Ⓒ only 5 Ⓓ there are no repeated factors

Chapter 5
Lesson
5

Fractions in Lowest Terms

You Will Learn

- to write a fraction in lowest terms

Vocabulary

common factor

lowest terms

greatest common factor (GCF)

Did You Know?

Alexis Soyer, a French chef, developed recipes for inexpensive, nutritious soups for the working class. In 1847 he opened soup kitchens in Ireland to feed those who were starving as a result of the Potato Famine.

Learn

When does a spider not have eight legs? When it's a long-handled tool used to remove solids from soups. The disk at the end of some spiders have a mesh with holes as fine as $\frac{4}{32}$ of an inch apart. Some have even finer meshes.

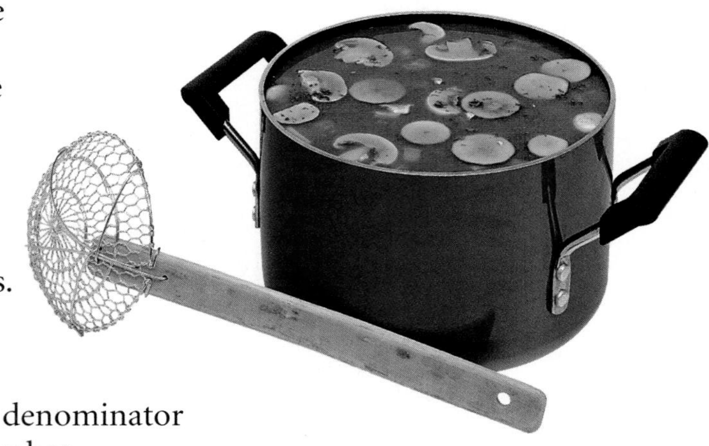

You can find equivalent fractions by multiplying or dividing the numerator and denominator of a fraction by the same number.

Example 1

Find two fractions equivalent to $\frac{4}{32}$.

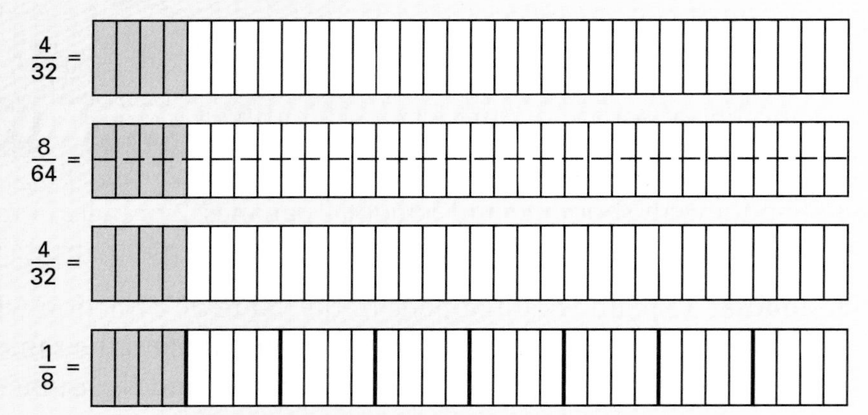

$\frac{4 \times 2}{32 \times 2} = \frac{8}{64}$ Multiply numerator and denominator by 2.

$\frac{4 \div 4}{32 \div 4} = \frac{1}{8}$ Divide numerator and denominator by 4.

Two equivalent fractions for $\frac{4}{32}$ are $\frac{8}{64}$ and $\frac{1}{8}$.

When you divide, you use a **common factor**, a whole number that will divide both the numerator and denominator. A fraction is in **lowest terms** when there is no common factor.

Example 2

A size 15 knitting needle measures about $\frac{24}{60}$ of an inch. What is this fraction in lowest terms?

$\frac{24 \div 4}{60 \div 4} = \frac{6}{15}$ Divide numerator and denominator by 4.

$\frac{6 \div 3}{15 \div 3} = \frac{2}{5}$ Divide numerator and denominator by 3.

There is no common factor for 2 and 5, other than 1.

$\frac{24}{60}$ in lowest terms is $\frac{2}{5}$.

The greatest whole number that divides two numbers is called the **greatest common factor (GCF)**. You can use the greatest common factor to write a fraction in lowest terms.

Example 3

Find the GCF of 36 and 90.

Factors of 36: $\boxed{1}$, $\boxed{2}$, $\boxed{3}$, 4, $\boxed{6}$, $\boxed{9}$, 12, $\boxed{18}$, 36

Factors of 90: $\boxed{1}$, $\boxed{2}$, $\boxed{3}$, 5, $\boxed{6}$, $\boxed{9}$, 10, 15, $\boxed{18}$, 30, 45, 90

The common factors of 36 and 90 are 1, 2, 3, 6, 9, and 18.

The *greatest* common factor is 18.

Example 4

Find the GCF of 24 and 30, and use it to simplify $\frac{24}{30}$.

Factors of 24: $\boxed{1}$, $\boxed{2}$, $\boxed{3}$, 4, $\boxed{6}$, 8, 12, 24

Factors of 30: $\boxed{1}$, $\boxed{2}$, $\boxed{3}$, 5, $\boxed{6}$, 10, 15, 30

The common factors of 24 and 30 are 1, 2, 3, and 6.

The *greatest* common factor is 6.

$\frac{24 \div 6}{30 \div 6} = \frac{4}{5}$

$\frac{24}{30}$ in lowest terms is $\frac{4}{5}$.

Talk About It

How can you use the GCF when simplifying a fraction to lowest terms?

Check

Find two fractions equivalent to each fraction.

1. $\frac{6}{10}$ **2.** $\frac{12}{15}$ **3.** $\frac{7}{21}$ **4.** $\frac{5}{7}$

Find the GCF of each pair.

5. 15, 20 **6.** 10, 12 **7.** 18, 45 **8.** 11, 66

Write in lowest terms.

9. $\frac{8}{10}$ **10.** $\frac{21}{28}$ **11.** $\frac{36}{54}$ **12.** $\frac{12}{18}$ **13.** $\frac{18}{30}$

14. Reasoning Explain why fractions whose numerators are one less than their denominators are in lowest terms.

Practice

Skills and Reasoning

Find two fractions equivalent to each fraction.

15. $\frac{3}{5}$ **16.** $\frac{6}{18}$ **17.** $\frac{5}{20}$ **18.** $\frac{1}{6}$ **19.** $\frac{2}{7}$

20. $\frac{9}{21}$ **21.** $\frac{12}{24}$ **22.** $\frac{10}{25}$ **23.** $\frac{21}{35}$ **24.** $\frac{11}{33}$

25. $\frac{7}{11}$ **26.** $\frac{4}{9}$ **27.** $\frac{1}{3}$ **28.** $\frac{3}{8}$ **29.** $\frac{17}{20}$

Find the GCF of each pair.

30. 4, 8 **31.** 15, 25 **32.** 12, 15 **33.** 6, 8 **34.** 3, 7

35. 2, 5 **36.** 18, 27 **37.** 16, 24 **38.** 11, 23 **39.** 10, 100

40. 35, 24 **41.** 36, 16 **42.** 22, 66 **43.** 27, 72 **44.** 64, 32

45. 48, 28 **46.** 11, 17 **47.** 3, 105 **48.** 19, 12 **49.** 50, 4

Write in lowest terms.

50. $\frac{7}{14}$ **51.** $\frac{5}{25}$ **52.** $\frac{20}{30}$ **53.** $\frac{6}{18}$ **54.** $\frac{12}{36}$

55. $\frac{8}{10}$ **56.** $\frac{6}{8}$ **57.** $\frac{9}{15}$ **58.** $\frac{3}{21}$ **59.** $\frac{4}{24}$

60. $\frac{21}{35}$ **61.** $\frac{6}{9}$ **62.** $\frac{10}{12}$ **63.** $\frac{11}{44}$ **64.** $\frac{2}{8}$

65. $\frac{5}{30}$ **66.** $\frac{8}{36}$ **67.** $\frac{3}{18}$ **68.** $\frac{9}{21}$ **69.** $\frac{14}{38}$

70. **Reasoning** Marilee says that if a fraction's numerator and denominator are both prime numbers, then the fraction is in lowest terms. Gerry says she is wrong. Why?

71. **What If** Add 5 to both the numerator and the denominator of $\frac{4}{8}$. Can it still be simplified to $\frac{1}{2}$? Explain.

72. **Critical Thinking** Explain why $\frac{2}{17}$, $\frac{11}{13}$, $\frac{2}{3}$, and $\frac{5}{7}$ cannot be written in lower terms. What do the numbers making up the fractions have in common?

73. What is the GCF of 1 and x? Explain.

Problem Solving and Applications

74. **History** Medieval carpenters used tools with narrow cutting edges, called gouges, to shape their work. The width of one paring gouge was about $\frac{4}{16}$ in. Write the width in lowest terms.

75. Marlyn sold $\frac{3}{6}$ of the raffle tickets at a carnival. Darren sold $\frac{2}{8}$ of them. Jamelya sold the rest. Who sold more tickets, Marilyn by herself, or Darren and Jamelya together? Explain.

76. **Mental Math** Use mental math to write $\frac{20}{70}$, $\frac{200}{700}$, and $\frac{2{,}000}{7{,}000}$ in lowest terms.

77. **Collecting Data** Look in your silverware drawer at home. Use the number of forks as your numerator and the number of spoons as your denominator. Write this fraction. Simplify it if you can. If not, write an equivalent fraction for this fraction.

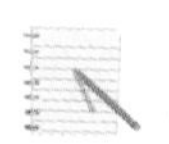

78. **Algebra Readiness** Freda wrote a fraction for the number of forks to spoons in her silverware drawer. It was $\frac{8}{15}$. Her friend, Henry, said his fraction for forks to spoons was equivalent to Freda's. Henry has 45 spoons. How many forks does Henry have?

79. The head of a sledgehammer is shaped like a barrel. What fraction in lowest terms describes the number of hammers that are sledgehammers?

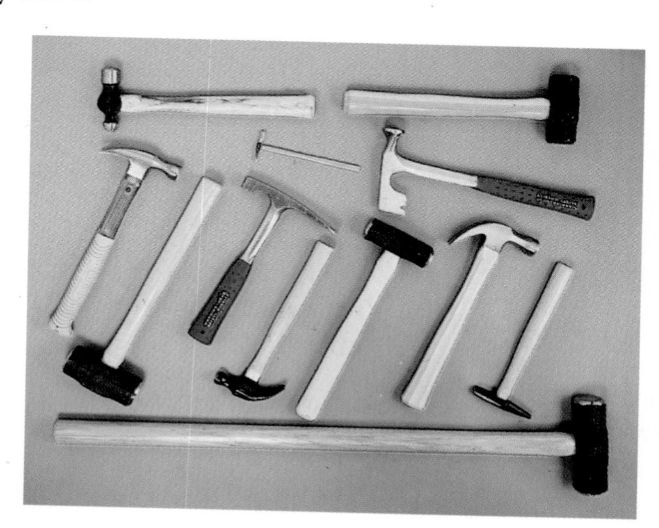

80. What fraction in lowest terms describes the number of hammers that don't have blue handles?

81. **Journal** Explain the difference between LCM and GCF. Can the LCM and GCF of two numbers ever be equal? Explain.

Mixed Review and Test Prep

82. For each point in the graph, approximate the data represented by the point.

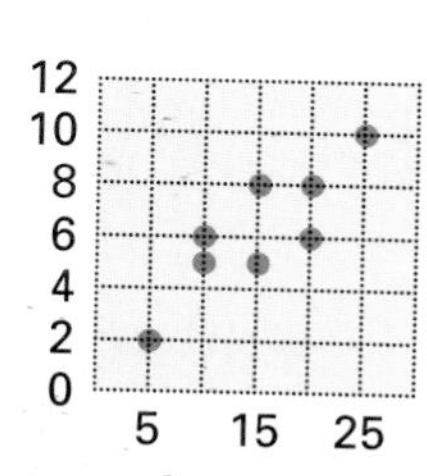

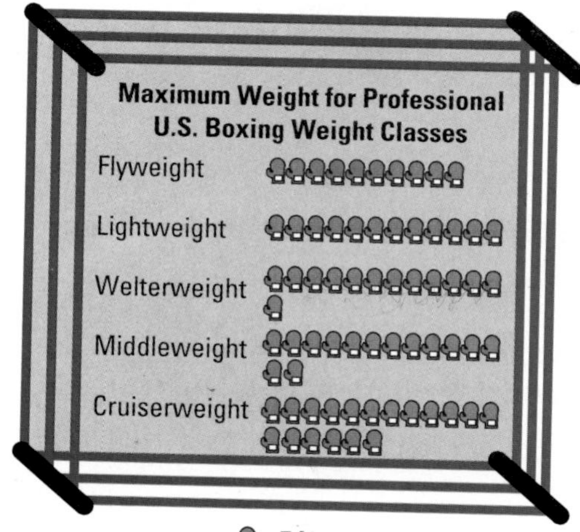

Use the Maximum Weight graph for **83** and **84.**

83. What is the maximum weight for a flyweight boxer?

84. Tony weighs 76 kg. What weight class is he in?

85. What is the difference in the maximum weights for the cruiserweight and the welterweight?

Ⓐ 20 kg Ⓑ 25 kg
Ⓒ 95 kg Ⓓ 100 kg

Chapter 5
Lesson
6

Improper Fractions and Mixed Numbers

Learn

You Will Learn

- to convert between improper fractions and mixed numbers

Vocabulary

improper fraction

mixed number

Water, water everywhere! Do we have a drop to spare? Wasting water can be expensive, whether it comes in a bottle or out of a tap. An average person can easily use $85\frac{3}{4}$ gallons of water daily. Little things we do daily, like brushing our teeth with the water running, could use at least $\frac{7}{4}$ gallons in only a few minutes. Drink a glass of water, $\frac{1}{16}$ gallon, several times a day. It all adds up!

A proper fraction has a value less than or equal to 1. $\frac{2}{3}$

An **improper fraction** has a numerator that is greater than its denominator. $\frac{8}{5}$

A **mixed number** combines a whole number and a fraction. $16\frac{3}{4}$

Did You Know?
Manufacturers of new cars use about 39.090 gallons of water per car.

Example 1

Use the data from the first paragraph above. Tell which number is the proper fraction, the improper fraction, and the mixed number. Explain.

Proper fraction:	$\frac{1}{16}$	$\frac{1}{16}$ is less than 1.
Improper fraction:	$\frac{7}{4}$	7 is greater than 4.
Mixed number:	$85\frac{3}{4}$	85 is a whole number and $\frac{3}{4}$ is a fraction.

Improper fractions can be written as mixed numbers by dividing the numerator by the denominator.

Example 2

Flushing a toilet can easily use $\frac{23}{4}$ gallons of water. Write $\frac{23}{4}$ as a mixed number.

$\frac{23}{4} = 23 \div 4$ Divide the numerator by the denominator.

$4\overline{)23}$ = **5R3** The quotient is the whole number. The remainder is the numerator of the fraction part.

$\frac{23}{4} = \mathbf{5\frac{3}{4}}$ The denominator stays the same.

Sometimes, mixed numbers are written as improper fractions. In order to change a mixed number to an improper fraction, multiply the fraction's denominator by the whole number. Then add the mixed number's numerator. Write this amount over the same denominator.

Example 3

A running faucet uses $3\frac{7}{8}$ gallons of water every minute.
Write $3\frac{7}{8}$ as an improper fraction.

$3\frac{7}{8} = \frac{(8 \times 3) + 7}{8}$ Multiply the denominator by the whole number and then add the numerator.

$3\frac{7}{8} = \frac{31}{8}$ Use the same denominator.

Remember
Use the rules for order of operations when you have to perform more than one operation to solve a problem.

Talk About It

1. Can any improper fraction be written as a mixed number? Explain.
2. Can any mixed number be written as an improper fraction? Explain.
3. What kind of number do you get when you simplify a proper fraction whose numerator and denominator are equal? Will you always get that kind of number? Explain.

Check

Identify each fraction as proper or improper.

1. $\frac{1}{5}$ **2.** $\frac{3}{10}$ **3.** $\frac{15}{7}$ **4.** $\frac{14}{3}$ **5.** $\frac{10}{17}$ **6.** $\frac{21}{4}$

Write each mixed number as an improper fraction.

7. $1\frac{5}{6}$ **8.** $4\frac{1}{8}$ **9.** $2\frac{3}{5}$ **10.** $11\frac{6}{7}$

11. $7\frac{2}{9}$ **12.** $4\frac{1}{11}$ **13.** $3\frac{4}{5}$ **14.** $7\frac{1}{7}$

Write each improper fraction as a mixed number.

15. $\frac{14}{3}$ **16.** $\frac{26}{9}$ **17.** $\frac{35}{4}$ **18.** $\frac{18}{7}$

19. $\frac{38}{3}$ **20.** $\frac{17}{5}$ **21.** $\frac{31}{8}$ **22.** $\frac{47}{6}$

23. **Reasoning** Inga thinks $23\frac{5}{6}$ is equivalent to $\frac{143}{5}$. Is she correct? Explain.

Practice

Skills and Reasoning

Identify each fraction as proper or improper.

24. $\frac{9}{10}$ **25.** $\frac{12}{3}$ **26.** $\frac{3}{2}$ **27.** $\frac{4}{6}$ **28.** $\frac{17}{8}$ **29.** $\frac{8}{2}$

Write each mixed number as an improper fraction.

30. $1\frac{1}{8}$ **31.** $1\frac{9}{5}$ **32.** $1\frac{6}{3}$ **33.** $3\frac{1}{3}$ **34.** $4\frac{9}{8}$ **35.** $2\frac{6}{4}$

36. $1\frac{2}{5}$ **37.** $2\frac{4}{5}$ **38.** $1\frac{1}{4}$ **39.** $3\frac{1}{10}$ **40.** $5\frac{4}{5}$ **41.** $2\frac{9}{12}$

Write each improper fraction as a mixed number.

42. $\frac{10}{3}$ **43.** $\frac{14}{5}$ **44.** $\frac{15}{8}$ **45.** $\frac{11}{2}$ **46.** $\frac{14}{3}$ **47.** $\frac{23}{8}$

48. $\frac{50}{7}$ **49.** $\frac{99}{10}$ **50.** $\frac{201}{2}$ **51.** $\frac{805}{8}$ **52.** $\frac{40}{9}$ **53.** $\frac{29}{11}$

54. Reasoning Kara says that if you simplify an improper fraction whose numerator is a multiple of the denominator you get a whole number. Is she correct? Explain.

55. Algebra Readiness $\frac{47}{8} = 5\,\frac{x}{8}$. What is the value of x?

56. Estimation Is $\frac{4{,}478}{5}$ closer to 900 or 800?

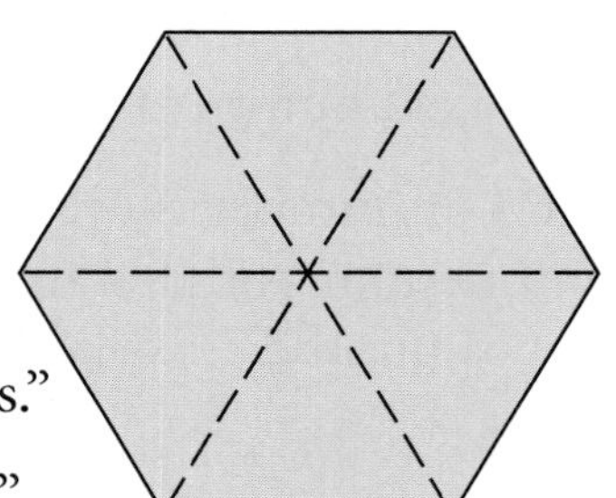

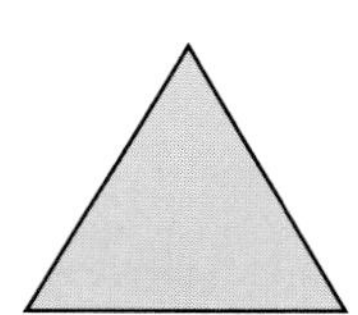

Use the figure to the right to answer **57–59.**

57. Write the fraction naming one "part".

58. Write the improper fraction that describes "all parts."

59. Write the mixed number that describes "all parts."

Problem Solving and Applications

Using Data Use the data in the Learn section on page 290 to answer **60** and **61.**

60. Write the number of gallons of water a person uses daily as an improper fraction.

61. Write the number of gallons used while brushing teeth as a mixed number.

62. Measurement Cesar has a tool box that is $15\frac{3}{4}$ in. long. His hammer is $\frac{45}{4}$ in. long. Will the hammer fit in the tool box?

63. **Critical Thinking** Darrell needs to measure a board about 6 feet long. He can't find his ruler, but he knows his hand is $\frac{1}{2}$ a foot long. How many hand-lengths will he have to mark to get the length he needs?

64. **Careers** A carpenter is installing a counter top in a kitchen. The counter top measures $61\frac{2}{3}$ inches. What is that length written as an improper fraction?

65. Which is more, $\frac{9}{4}$ slices of cantaloupe or $1\frac{1}{2}$ slices? Explain your answer.

66. **Critical Thinking** The picture models a number greater than one. Write the value it represents as a mixed number and as an improper fraction. Explain.

67. A typical 10-minute shower can use about $\frac{303}{4}$ gallons of water. Is this more or less than 75 gallons?

68. Eileen needs $\frac{115}{3}$ yards of nylon fabric to make a tent. Write the length as a mixed number.

69. **Critical Thinking** Sari wants to plug a computer into a socket $\frac{27}{4}$ feet away. The computer's power cord is $5\frac{3}{4}$ feet long. Will she need an extension cord?

70. **Journal** Tell how $2\frac{3}{4}$ and $\frac{11}{4}$ can each be written as the other.

Mixed Review and Test Prep

STAY SHARP!

Find the mean, median, and mode with and without the outlier. Which does the outlier affect the most?

71. 20, 31, 32, 34, 35, 35, 35, 36, 37

72. 7, 4, 3, 6, 20, 7, 7, 4, 5, 2, 2, 1, 2

73. Make a line plot of the data in Exercise 71. Do not include the outlier.

74. Make a line plot of the data in Exercise 72. Do not include the outlier.

Convert.

75. 2 mi = ▒ feet
76. 60 in. = ▒ feet
77. 27 ft = ▒ yards
78. 3 lb = ▒ oz
79. 5 mi = ▒ ft
80. 108 in. = ▒ ft
81. 90 ft = ▒ yd
82. 7 lb = ▒ oz

83. Which fraction expresses one out of seven equal pieces?

Ⓐ $\frac{7}{1}$ Ⓑ $\frac{1}{7}$ Ⓒ $\frac{7}{7}$ Ⓓ not here

Skills Practice Bank, page 664, Set 4

STOP and Practice

Decide whether the first number is divisible by the second. Then find the prime factorization of the first number.

1. 54, 9 **2.** 104, 8 **3.** 45, 4 **4.** 35, 7 **5.** 78, 6

Determine what fraction each shaded part represents. Identify the numerator and denominator of each fraction.

6. 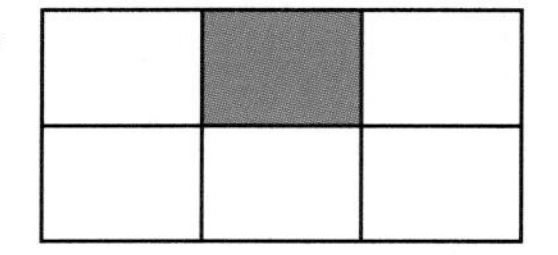 **7.** 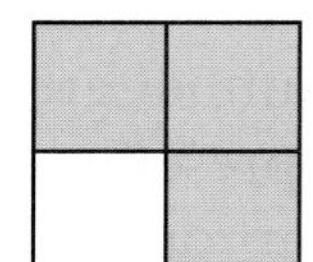 **8.** 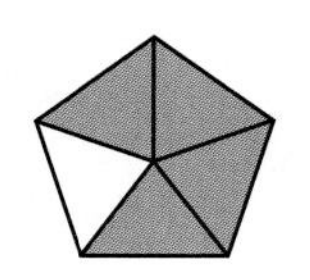 **9.** 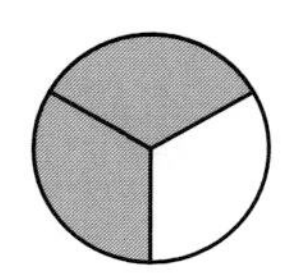

Write each fraction in lowest terms.

10. $\frac{6}{10}$ **11.** $\frac{45}{50}$ **12.** $\frac{2}{16}$ **13.** $\frac{16}{100}$ **14.** $\frac{16}{56}$ **15.** $\frac{3}{12}$

16. $\frac{6}{36}$ **17.** $\frac{36}{48}$ **18.** $\frac{24}{54}$ **19.** $\frac{12}{15}$ **20.** $\frac{16}{18}$ **21.** $\frac{10}{20}$

22. $\frac{18}{42}$ **23.** $\frac{60}{96}$ **24.** $\frac{2}{6}$ **25.** $\frac{14}{21}$ **26.** $\frac{8}{36}$ **27.** $\frac{14}{40}$

Write each mixed number as an improper fraction and each improper fraction as a mixed number. Write mixed numbers in lowest terms.

28. $3\frac{2}{5}$ **29.** $\frac{42}{8}$ **30.** $9\frac{2}{3}$ **31.** $\frac{16}{5}$ **32.** $\frac{29}{3}$ **33.** $1\frac{3}{7}$

34. $\frac{6}{4}$ **35.** $8\frac{7}{6}$ **36.** $\frac{22}{7}$ **37.** $\frac{38}{9}$ **38.** $4\frac{5}{11}$ **39.** $3\frac{5}{12}$

40. $\frac{6}{2}$ **41.** $\frac{45}{10}$ **42.** $3\frac{3}{8}$ **43.** $2\frac{5}{6}$ **44.** $\frac{48}{9}$ **45.** $\frac{39}{4}$

46. $7\frac{6}{7}$ **47.** $\frac{45}{9}$ **48.** $12\frac{2}{5}$ **49.** $\frac{20}{8}$ **50.** $1\frac{1}{6}$ **51.** $10\frac{2}{3}$

52. $\frac{37}{8}$ **53.** $\frac{32}{6}$ **54.** $7\frac{1}{4}$ **55.** $\frac{51}{12}$ **56.** $\frac{51}{2}$ **57.** $5\frac{9}{7}$

Error Search

Find each fraction not written in lowest terms correctly. Write it correctly and explain the error.

58. $\frac{6}{10}=\frac{2}{5}$ **59.** $\frac{27}{54}=\frac{1}{2}$ **60.** $\frac{8}{24}=\frac{1}{8}$ **61.** $\frac{12}{14}=\frac{3}{7}$ **62.** $\frac{9}{18}=\frac{1}{2}$

63. $\frac{14}{36}=\frac{7}{9}$ **64.** $\frac{18}{32}=\frac{9}{16}$ **65.** $\frac{15}{40}=\frac{3}{8}$ **66.** $\frac{20}{25}=\frac{2}{5}$ **67.** $\frac{7}{42}=\frac{1}{6}$

All or None!

Write each improper fraction as a mixed number in lowest terms. Match each answer to a number below the blanks. Then find the answer to the question. Some letters are not used.

From what can you take away the whole and still have some left?

___ ___ ___   ___ ___ ___ ___

$3\frac{2}{5}$ $4\frac{1}{2}$ $9\frac{1}{2}$ $3\frac{3}{4}$ $8\frac{1}{3}$ $5\frac{1}{2}$ $3\frac{3}{7}$

___ ___ ___ ___ ___ ___ ___ ___ ___

$3\frac{3}{4}$ $4\frac{1}{2}$ $8\frac{1}{3}$ $9\frac{4}{5}$ $9\frac{1}{2}$ $7\frac{1}{4}$ $8\frac{1}{3}$ $3\frac{1}{2}$ $9\frac{1}{2}$

68. $\frac{58}{8}$ (S) **69.** $\frac{33}{6}$ (R) **70.** $\frac{42}{10}$ (N) **71.** $\frac{115}{100}$ (A)

72. $\frac{19}{2}$ (E) **73.** $\frac{50}{4}$ (B) **74.** $\frac{75}{9}$ (O) **75.** $\frac{14}{4}$ (M)

76. $\frac{10}{3}$ (G) **77.** $\frac{72}{16}$ (H) **78.** $\frac{26}{12}$ (I) **79.** $\frac{49}{5}$ (L)

80. $\frac{85}{25}$ (T) **81.** $\frac{24}{7}$ (D) **82.** $\frac{46}{6}$ (K) **83.** $\frac{30}{8}$ (W)

Number Sense Estimation and Reasoning

Compare using <, >, or =. Use estimation to help.

84. $\frac{5}{8}$ ● $\frac{1}{2}$ **85.** $\frac{9}{12}$ ● $\frac{3}{4}$ **86.** $\frac{5}{12}$ ● $\frac{2}{3}$

87. $\frac{5}{14}$ ● $\frac{4}{7}$ **88.** $\frac{2}{3}$ ● $\frac{8}{9}$ **89.** $\frac{3}{16}$ ● $\frac{1}{4}$

90. $\frac{4}{7}$ ● $\frac{5}{8}$ **91.** $\frac{11}{12}$ ● $\frac{5}{9}$ **92.** $\frac{6}{13}$ ● $\frac{3}{4}$

Chapter 5
Lesson
7

Converting Fractions and Decimals

Problem Solving Connection
- Draw a Picture

Materials
- tenths grids
- hundredths grids
- colored pencils

Vocabulary

terminating decimal

repeating decimal

Explore

Fractions and decimals are two different ways of describing numbers between whole numbers. A fraction and a decimal can represent the same value.

Work Together

1. Use a tenths grid to convert $\frac{3}{5}$ to a decimal.
   a. Divide the strips into a number of groups equal to the denominator. Each group should have the same number of strips.
   b. Color in as many groups as the numerator.
   c. Describe the number modeled in the grid as a fraction and as a decimal.

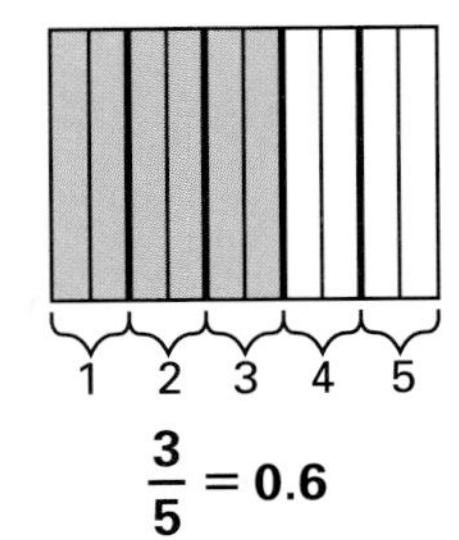

$\frac{3}{5} = 0.6$

2. Use tenths grids to convert each fraction to a decimal.

   a. $\frac{1}{2}$ b. $\frac{2}{5}$ c. $\frac{7}{10}$ d. $\frac{4}{5}$

3. Use a hundredths grid to convert $\frac{3}{4}$ to a decimal.
   a. Divide the squares into a number of groups equal to the denominator. Each group should have the same number of squares.
   b. Color in as many groups as the numerator.
   c. Describe the number modeled in the grid as a fraction and as a decimal.

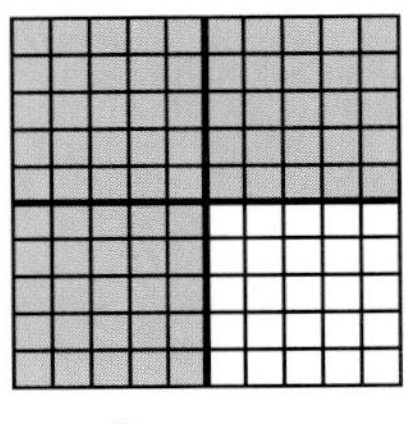

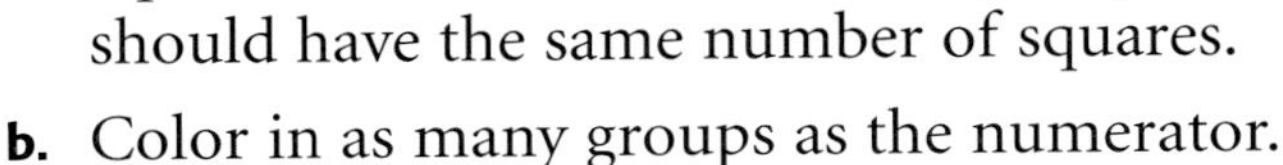

$\frac{3}{4} = 0.75$

4. Use hundredths grids to convert each fraction to a decimal.

   a. $\frac{4}{10}$ b. $\frac{1}{4}$ c. $\frac{3}{20}$ d. $\frac{13}{50}$

5. Use a hundredths grid to convert 0.55 to a fraction.
   a. Shade the number of hundredths in the number.
   b. The number shaded is the numerator.
   c. The denominator is the size of the grid.
   d. Describe the number modeled in the grid as a fraction in lowest terms.

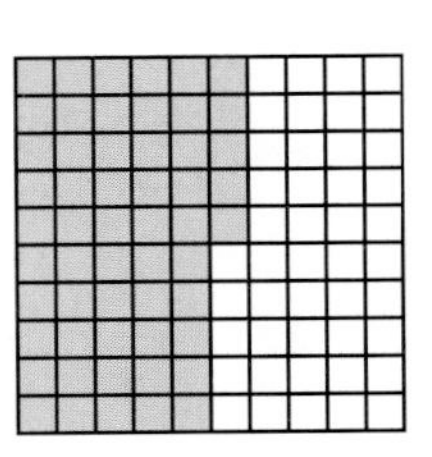

$0.55 = \frac{55}{100} = \frac{11}{20}$

6. Can you use a tenths grid to change $\frac{1}{3}$ to a decimal? A hundredths grid?

Connect and Learn

To convert a decimal to a fraction, write the place value of the decimal as the denominator. Write the digits of the decimal as the numerator.

$0.9 = \text{nine tenths} = \frac{9}{10}$

$0.013 = \text{thirteen thousandths} = \frac{13}{1{,}000}$

To convert a fraction to a decimal, divide the numerator by the denominator. You may need to annex zeros to the dividend.

$$\frac{3}{4} = 4\overline{)3.00} = 0.75$$

Annex 2 zeros.

$$\begin{array}{r} 0.75 \\ 4\overline{)3.00} \\ \underline{28} \\ 20 \\ \underline{20} \\ 0 \end{array}$$

When you convert a fraction to a decimal, you can end up with a **terminating decimal** or a **repeating decimal**.

A **terminating decimal** ends:

$$\frac{5}{8} = \begin{array}{r} 0.625 \\ 8\overline{)5.000} \\ \underline{48} \\ 20 \\ \underline{16} \\ 40 \\ \underline{40} \\ 0 \end{array}$$

$\frac{5}{8} = 0.625$. The decimal ends.

A **repeating decimal** repeats a pattern of digits continuously:

$$\frac{4}{11} = \begin{array}{r} 0.363636\ldots \\ 11\overline{)4.000000} \\ \underline{33} \\ 70 \\ \underline{66} \\ 40 \\ \underline{33} \\ 7 \end{array}$$

$\frac{4}{11} = 0.3636\ldots$ The decimal repeats.

To show a repeating decimal, draw a bar over the repeating digits. $\frac{4}{11} = 0.\overline{36}$.

Check

Rewrite using bar notation.

1. 0.66666666 **2.** 0.63636363 **3.** 0.73333333 **4.** 0.409090909

Write each decimal as a fraction in lowest terms.

5. 0.9 **6.** 0.19 **7.** 0.26 **8.** 0.555

Write each fraction as a decimal. State whether the decimal terminates or repeats.

9. $\frac{1}{5}$ **10.** $\frac{13}{20}$ **11.** $\frac{12}{33}$ **12.** $\frac{1}{9}$

13. Reasoning How can you tell if a fraction names an amount greater than or less than 0.6?

Practice

Skills and Reasoning

Rewrite using bar notation.

14. 0.33333333 . . . **15.** 0.14141414 . . . **16.** 0.827272727 . . . **17.** 1.345345 . . .

Write each decimal as a fraction in lowest terms.

18. 0.25 **19.** 0.4 **20.** 0.75 **21.** 0.44 **22.** 0.3 **23.** 0.67

24. 0.168 **25.** 0.35 **26.** 0.64 **27.** 0.52 **28.** 0.332 **29.** 0.192

30. 0.6 **31.** 0.7 **32.** 0.36 **33.** 0.128 **34.** 0.28 **35.** 0.88

Write each fraction as a decimal. State whether the decimal terminates or repeats.

36. $\frac{2}{5}$ **37.** $\frac{2}{11}$ **38.** $\frac{7}{10}$ **39.** $\frac{9}{20}$ **40.** $\frac{2}{22}$ **41.** $\frac{7}{25}$

42. $\frac{17}{20}$ **43.** $\frac{4}{6}$ **44.** $\frac{11}{6}$ **45.** $\frac{5}{2}$ **46.** $\frac{62}{62}$ **47.** $\frac{5}{4}$

48. $\frac{7}{9}$ **49.** $\frac{72}{100}$ **50.** $\frac{5}{8}$ **51.** $\frac{3}{4}$ **52.** $\frac{5}{6}$ **53.** $\frac{4}{8}$

54. Reasoning Is $\frac{2}{3}$ closer to 0.67 or 0.667? Explain.

Problem Solving and Applications

55. Measurement Chi is using a set of measuring cups that contains these measures: $\frac{1}{4}$ cup, $\frac{1}{3}$ cup, $\frac{1}{2}$ cup, and 1 cup. Write the decimal name for each measure.

56. Measurement Melissa is using a set of wrenches that come in these sizes: 0.125 in., 0.25 in., 0.375 in., 0.5 in., 0.625 in., 0.75 in., and 0.875 in. Write each wrench size as a fraction in lowest terms.

57. Jane needs to drill a hole at least 0.7 in. wide. Her hand drill has a #10 auger bit, which is $\frac{5}{8}$ in. wide. Is the auger bit big enough? Explain.

Problem Solving and CAREERS

Some paleontologists work in the field, carefully chipping fossil deposits out of the rocks. Others work in the laboratory, delicately removing the remaining rock that clings to the fossils. Paleontologists arrange fossils and reconstruct organisms as they appeared in life.

58. Paleontologists use calipers to measure the width of solid objects. A paleontologist measures two bones as $\frac{2}{9}$ in. and $\frac{3}{32}$ in. Write these measures as decimals. Which value is greater?

59. Jim spent most of his first day as a paleontologist chipping away $\frac{11}{12}$ in. of rock from a dinosaur bone. Write this number as a decimal. Round to the nearest thousandth.

60. Jesse's job in the laboratory was to use a dentist's tool to carefully remove 0.012 in. of rock from a shellfish fossil. Write this number as a fraction in lowest terms.

61. Journal Explain the difference between a terminating decimal and a repeating decimal.

Mixed Review and Test Prep

Simplify mentally.

62. 60×10 **63.** $175 + 425$ **64.** $86 + 24$ **65.** $3 \times 68 \times 10$

66. $8{,}000 \div 200$ **67.** 300×50 **68.** $17 + 70 + 30$ **69.** 34×3

70. Make a bar graph of the data.

Mass of U.S. Coins (grams)				
Penny	Nickel	Dime	Quarter	Half Dollar
2.60	5.14	2.26	5.47	10.99

Draw a model for each of the fractions.

71. $\frac{1}{3}$ **72.** $\frac{2}{5}$ **73.** $\frac{3}{7}$ **74.** $\frac{9}{10}$ **75.** $\frac{3}{12}$ **76.** $\frac{1}{4}$

77. Choose the mixed number equivalent to $\frac{10}{6}$.

Ⓐ $\frac{5}{3}$ Ⓑ $\frac{6}{10}$ Ⓒ $1\frac{4}{6}$ Ⓓ $2\frac{2}{6}$

Skills Practice Bank, page 664, Set 5

Technology

Using a Spreadsheet to Find Decimal Equivalents for Common Fractions

You can build a table in a spreadsheet to show decimal forms for different fractions. The spreadsheet will quickly calculate the decimal equivalents for the fractions you enter.

> **Materials**
>
> *Interactive CD-ROM Spreadsheet/Grapher Tool* or other spreadsheet software

What patterns can you find in decimal equivalents for fifths?

Work Together

Use your spreadsheet software to calculate the decimal equivalents.

1. Create a new spreadsheet in the software program. Enter the information into the spreadsheet as shown.

	A	B	C	D	E	F	G
1	Numerator	1	2	3	4	5	
2	Denominator	5	5	5	5	5	
3							
4	Decimal						
5							

2. In cell B4, enter the formula $=B1/B2$. This formula will find the decimal form of each fraction by dividing the fraction's numerator by its denominator.

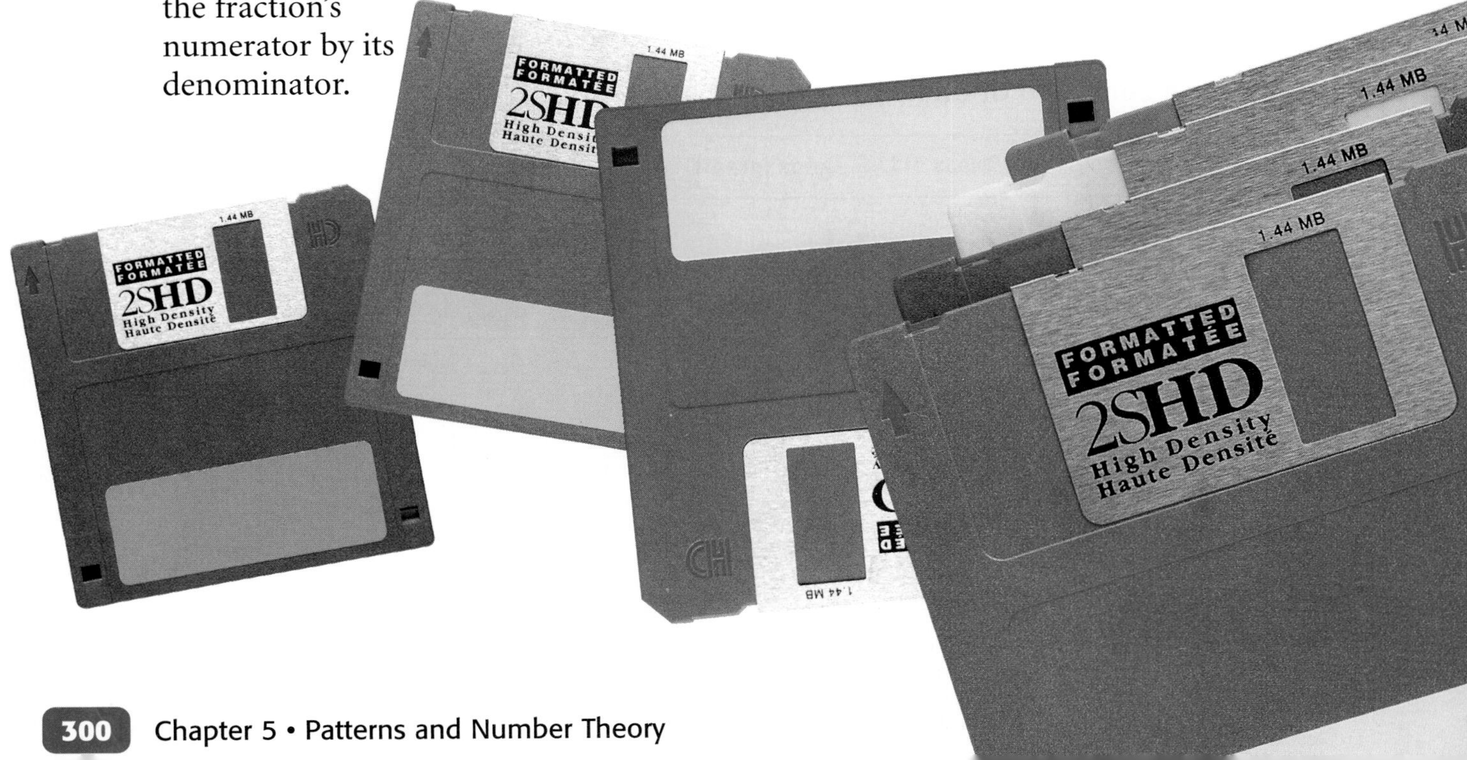

3. Copy the formula across the row to column F. You may need to format row 4 to see all the numbers after the decimal place.

4. Describe the pattern you see in the decimal numbers.

	A	B	C	D	E	F	G
1	Numerator	1	2	3	4	5	
2	Denominator	5	5	5	5	5	
3							
4	Decimal	0.2	0.4	0.6	0.8	1.0	
5							

Exercises

Use your spreadsheet software to answer **1–3.**

1. Find a decimal pattern for ninths.
2. Find a decimal pattern for eighths.
3. Find a decimal pattern for sevenths.

Extensions

4. Is the decimal value in C4 always twice as big as the decimal value in B4? Explain.
5. When converting a fraction pattern with an even denominator into decimals, the number 0.5 always appears as one of the decimals. Explain why.
6. Shauna created the spreadsheet below to find decimal equivalents for fourths. What mistake did she make?

Workbook1

	A	B	C	D	E	F
1	Numerator	1	2	3	4	
2	Denominator	4	4	4	4	
3						
4	Decimal	4	2	1.33333333	1	
5						
6						

Chapter 5
Lesson
8

Comparing and Ordering

You Will Learn

- to compare and order fractions

Vocabulary

common denominator

Did You Know?

Aluminum is used in the U.S. principally in transportation, packaging, and building.

Learn

For a report on recycling, Peggy and Zack read that 8 out of every 21 aluminum cans were recycled in 1990. In 1993, 5 out of every 14 aluminum cans were recycled.

You can compare fractions by renaming each of them with an equivalent fraction with the same denominator. Then compare the numerators. When two fractions have the same denominator, it is called a **common denominator**.

You can use the least common multiple of the two denominators as a common denominator.

Example 1

Peggy and Zack wanted to know whether the fraction of cans recycled increased or decreased from 1990 to 1993. Compare $\frac{8}{21}$ and $\frac{5}{14}$.

Multiples of 14: 14, 28, $\boxed{42}$, . . . Find the LCM of 14 and 21.

Multiples of 21: 21, $\boxed{42}$, . . .

$\frac{8 \times 2}{21 \times 2} = \frac{16}{42}$ Multiply the numerator and the denominator by the factor (2) that will make the denominator 42.

$\frac{5 \times 3}{14 \times 3} = \frac{15}{42}$ Multiply the numerator and the denominator by the factor (3) that will make the denominator 42.

Since $\frac{16}{42} > \frac{15}{42}$, $\frac{8}{21} > \frac{5}{14}$.

The fraction of cans recycled decreased from 1990 to 1993.

You can get a common denominator by multiplying the two denominators together. Then write an equivalent fraction for each using that common denominator.

Example 2

Compare $\frac{5}{6}$ and $\frac{7}{8}$.

$\frac{5}{6} = \frac{5 \times 8}{6 \times 8} = \frac{40}{48}$ Multiply the numerator and denominator by the denominator of the *other* fraction.

$\frac{7}{8} = \frac{7 \times 6}{8 \times 6} = \frac{42}{48}$

Since $\frac{42}{48} > \frac{40}{48}$, $\frac{7}{8} > \frac{5}{6}$.

You can also compare fractions by rewriting them as decimals. Then compare the decimals.

Example 3

Clay needs $\frac{4}{5}$ yd of vinyl fabric to make a cover for his tennis racket. He found a piece marked $\frac{7}{8}$ yd. Should he buy it?

7 [÷] 8 [=] 0.875

4 [÷] 5 [=] 0.8

Use a calculator to write the fractions as decimals.

$0.875 > 0.800$, so $\frac{7}{8} > \frac{4}{5}$.

Clay should buy the fabric.

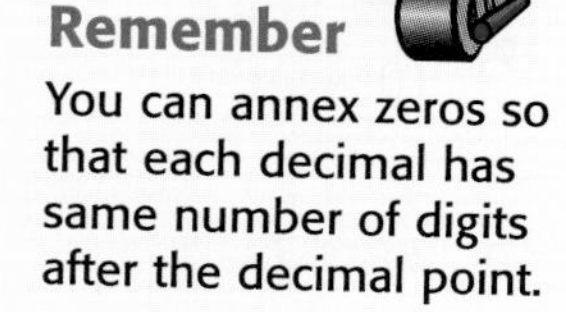

Remember

You can annex zeros so that each decimal has same number of digits after the decimal point.

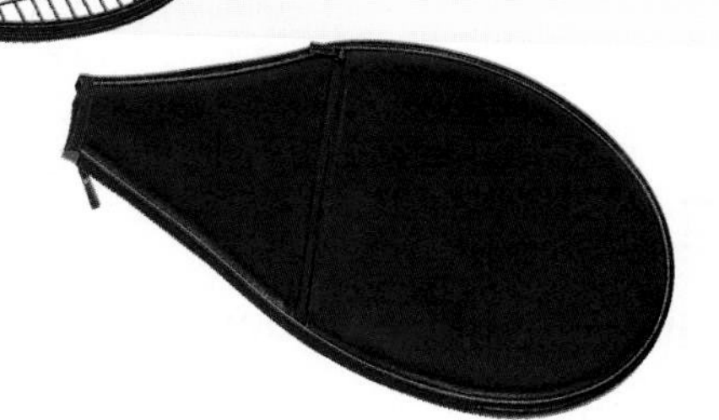

Talk About It

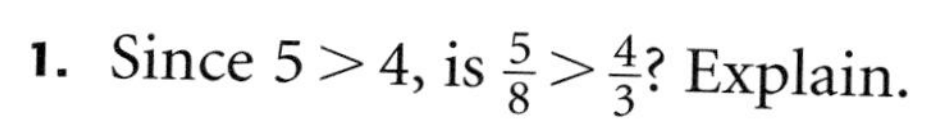

1. Since $5 > 4$, is $\frac{5}{8} > \frac{4}{3}$? Explain.
2. Two fractions have the same numerator. How can you use the denominator to compare fractions?

Check

Compare using <, >, or =.

1. $\frac{3}{8}$ ● $\frac{7}{16}$
2. $\frac{3}{4}$ ● $\frac{5}{6}$
3. $\frac{8}{11}$ ● $\frac{5}{7}$
4. $\frac{5}{6}$ ● $\frac{9}{10}$

Order from least to greatest.

5. $\frac{2}{6}, \frac{2}{9}, \frac{1}{12}$
6. $\frac{5}{6}, 0.75, \frac{8}{9}$
7. $\frac{1}{2}, \frac{3}{8}, \frac{4}{9}$
8. $\frac{1}{8}, \frac{8}{10}, \frac{3}{5}$
9. **Reasoning** Nancy says that $\frac{16}{17}$ is greater than $\frac{2}{3}$. Is she correct? Explain.

Practice

Skills and Reasoning

Compare using <, >, or =.

10. $\frac{1}{5}$ ● $\frac{2}{5}$ **11.** $\frac{3}{7}$ ● $\frac{2}{7}$ **12.** $\frac{3}{8}$ ● $\frac{9}{8}$ **13.** $\frac{16}{20}$ ● $\frac{7}{20}$

14. $\frac{7}{12}$ ● $\frac{11}{12}$ **15.** $\frac{5}{2}$ ● $\frac{8}{2}$ **16.** $\frac{4}{3}$ ● $\frac{8}{3}$ **17.** $\frac{5}{9}$ ● $\frac{7}{9}$

Give the least common denominator that could be used to compare each pair of fractions. Then compare using <, >, or =.

18. $\frac{2}{3}$ ● $\frac{8}{2}$ **19.** $\frac{5}{6}$ ● $\frac{5}{8}$ **20.** $\frac{1}{4}$ ● $\frac{5}{12}$ **21.** $\frac{3}{6}$ ● $\frac{6}{9}$

22. $\frac{4}{10}$ ● $\frac{6}{15}$ **23.** $\frac{3}{4}$ ● $\frac{6}{8}$ **24.** $\frac{5}{8}$ ● $\frac{10}{24}$ **25.** $\frac{1}{11}$ ● $\frac{3}{12}$

26. $\frac{3}{7}$ ● $\frac{6}{3}$ **27.** $\frac{7}{11}$ ● $\frac{2}{3}$ **28.** $\frac{9}{15}$ ● $\frac{3}{5}$ **29.** $\frac{5}{10}$ ● $\frac{7}{14}$

Order from least to greatest.

30. $\frac{2}{3}, \frac{2}{6}, \frac{4}{9}$ **31.** $\frac{7}{9}, \frac{5}{6}, \frac{4}{8}$ **32.** $\frac{18}{4}, \frac{16}{5}, \frac{19}{20}$ **33.** $\frac{3}{11}, \frac{11}{3}, \frac{11}{11}$

34. $\frac{9}{12}, \frac{3}{6}, \frac{15}{18}$ **35.** $\frac{4}{5}, \frac{4}{6}, \frac{4}{7}$ **36.** $\frac{32}{10}, \frac{25}{100}, \frac{16}{1}$ **37.** $\frac{3}{5}, \frac{2}{7}, \frac{3}{8}$

38. $\frac{1}{2}, \frac{1}{4}, \frac{1}{3}$ **39.** $\frac{3}{22}, \frac{10}{11}, \frac{2}{33}$ **40.** $\frac{4}{10}, \frac{3}{5}, \frac{6}{7}$ **41.** $\frac{7}{36}, \frac{13}{4}, \frac{1}{6}$

Critical Thinking Order from least to greatest.

42. 0.34, $\frac{2}{3}$, 0.145 **43.** $\frac{1}{2}$, 0.23, $\frac{2}{3}$, 0.4 **44.** $\frac{3}{4}$, 0.77, $\frac{1}{7}$ **45.** $\frac{4}{9}, \frac{3}{8}$, 0.6, 0.15

46. Reasoning Kerry says that fractions like $\frac{5}{7}$ and $\frac{3}{7}$ are easy to compare. Peter says that fractions like $\frac{1}{17}$ and $\frac{1}{7}$ are even easier to compare. What patterns are they using to make their comparisons easy?

Problem Solving and Applications

47. $\frac{3}{5}$ of the tourists who visit Florida come during the summer. $\frac{3}{10}$ travel to Florida during the winter. During which season does Florida get more tourists?

48. On a recent test, Renaldo got $\frac{5}{6}$ of the problems correct and Julius got $\frac{7}{9}$ of them correct. All the problems were worth the same amount. Who got the higher grade?

49. Mayra has drill bits measuring $\frac{5}{32}$ in, $\frac{3}{16}$ in., and $\frac{1}{8}$ in. She wants to use the largest bit. Which one should she use?

50. Zoe is planning a conference. Here is the schedule: meeting, snack, meeting, lunch, meeting, break, meeting. The four meetings will be $\frac{1}{2}$, $\frac{4}{2}$, $\frac{45}{30}$, and $\frac{9}{12}$ hr long. The longest meeting should be after the snack and the second-longest right after lunch. The shortest meeting should be after the break. How long is the first meeting? The second? the third? The fourth?

51. Measurement Flannery has $3\frac{5}{8}$ yards of ribbon. Does she have enough to complete a project that calls for $3\frac{1}{2}$ yards?

52. Order the wood screw lengths, in inches, from longest to shortest: $\frac{1}{4}$, $\frac{3}{8}$, $\frac{10}{32}$, $\frac{10}{16}$, $\frac{7}{8}$, $\frac{2}{16}$.

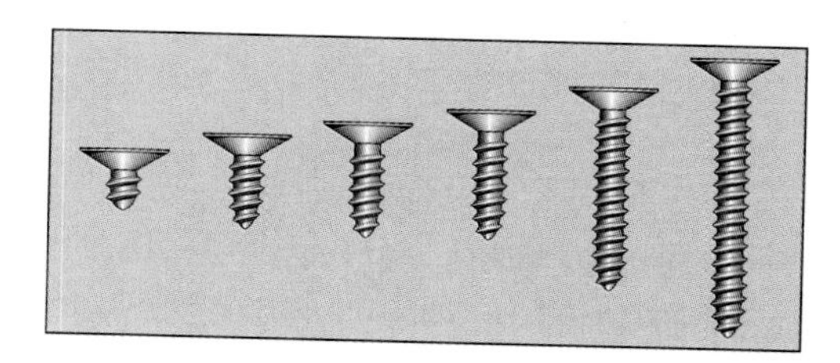

53. Journal Can you always tell by looking at a calculator display if a decimal terminates or repeats? Explain your answer.

Mixed Review and Test Prep

STAY SHARP!

Evaluate each expression for $x = 5$, 9, and 11.

54. $\frac{495}{x}$ **55.** $x - 5$ **56.** $8x$ **57.** $\frac{990}{x}$ **58.** $5x$

59. $7x$ **60.** $x + 10$ **61.** $13 - x$ **62.** $x + 101$ **63.** $\frac{x}{1}$

Make a stem-and-leaf diagram of the data.

64. 1, 4, 4, 5, 7, 11, 11, 12, 12, 13, 14

65. 101, 102, 105, 105, 108, 111, 112

66. 31, 31, 32, 30, 27, 28, 26, 33, 28, 31

67. Choose the equivalent decimal for $\frac{5}{6}$.

Ⓐ 0.3333 Ⓑ $0.\overline{3}$ Ⓒ 0.8 Ⓓ $0.8\overline{3}$

Skills Practice Bank, page 664, Set 6

SECTION B

Review and Practice

(Lesson 4) Name the fraction represented by the shaded part and provide two equivalent fractions.

1. 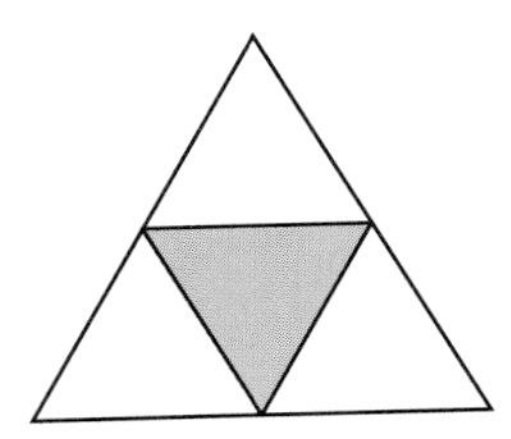

2. 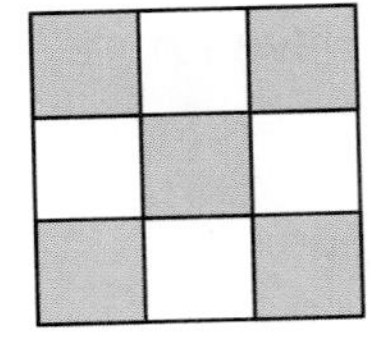

3. 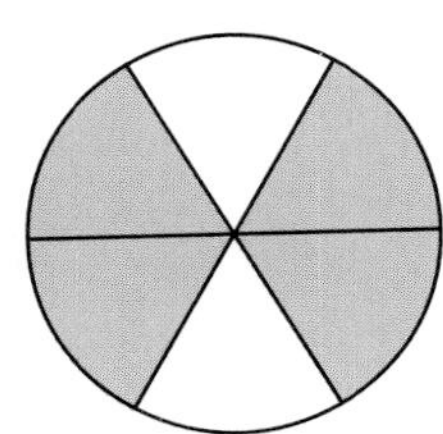

4. 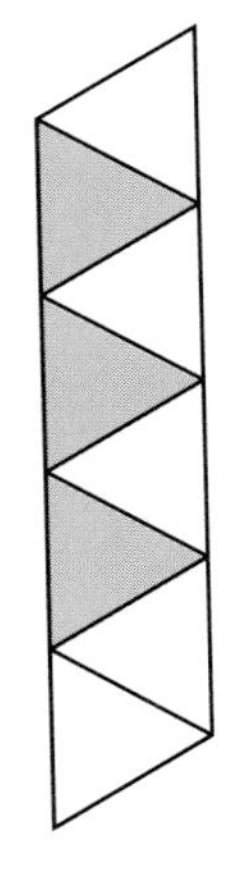

Determine what fraction each shaded part represents. Identify the numerator and denominator of each fraction.

5. 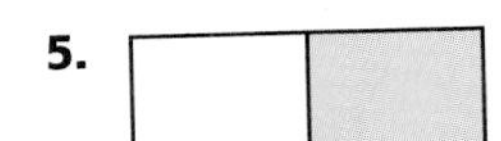

6. 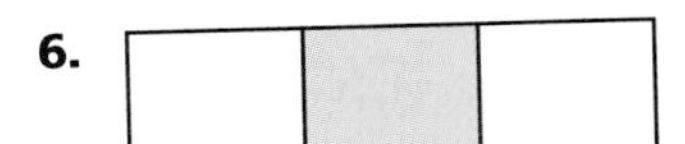

7. 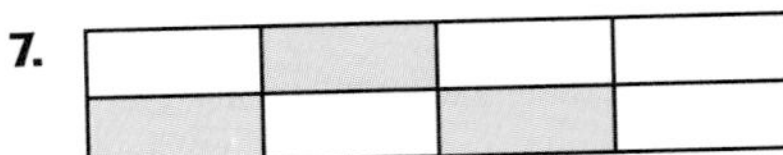

(Lesson 6) Write each mixed number as an improper fraction and each improper fraction as a mixed number. Write your answer in lowest terms.

8. $4\frac{1}{7}$ **9.** $\frac{32}{10}$ **10.** $\frac{99}{11}$ **11.** $4\frac{5}{8}$ **12.** $\frac{29}{3}$

13. $7\frac{4}{5}$ **14.** $12\frac{7}{8}$ **15.** $\frac{42}{5}$ **16.** $\frac{62}{12}$ **17.** $5\frac{4}{5}$

(Lessons 5 and 7) Write each fraction in lowest terms and as a decimal to the nearest tenth.

18. $\frac{4}{6}$ **19.** $\frac{18}{24}$ **20.** $\frac{2}{8}$ **21.** $\frac{12}{16}$

22. $\frac{5}{15}$ **23.** $\frac{8}{12}$ **24.** $\frac{12}{24}$ **25.** $\frac{21}{24}$

(Lesson 8) Solve.

26. Reiko and her friends are building a set of bookshelves. While working, they use $\frac{7}{12}$ of the supply of hammers and $\frac{5}{9}$ of the supply of screwdrivers. If there were an equal number of tools, which one was used more?

27. Journal Explain which is greater, $\frac{3}{5}$ or 0.75. How do you know?

Skills Checklist

In this section, you have:

- ☑ Understood Fractions
- ☑ Learned About Fractions in Lowest Terms
- ☑ Learned About Improper Fractions and Mixed Numbers
- ☑ Explored Converting Fractions and Decimals
- ☑ Explored Algebra by Using Expressions

Choose at least one of the following. Use what you have learned in this chapter.

1 Stop and Go Patterns

Create a three-column table. Write these fractions in the first column: $\frac{1}{2}$, $\frac{1}{3}$, $\frac{1}{4}$, $\frac{1}{5}$, $\frac{1}{6}$, $\frac{1}{7}$, $\frac{1}{8}$, $\frac{1}{9}$, $\frac{1}{10}$, $\frac{1}{11}$, $\frac{1}{12}$, $\frac{1}{15}$, $\frac{1}{16}$, $\frac{1}{18}$, $\frac{1}{20}$. Use a calculator to fill in the second column with the decimal value equivalent to each fraction. In the third column, mark each decimal with an **R** if it repeats and with a **T** if it doesn't.

Fraction	Decimal	T or R?
$\frac{1}{2}$	0.5	T
⋮		
$\frac{1}{20}$		

2 Area Breakdown

At Home
Measure and record the floor area of up to five rooms in your home.

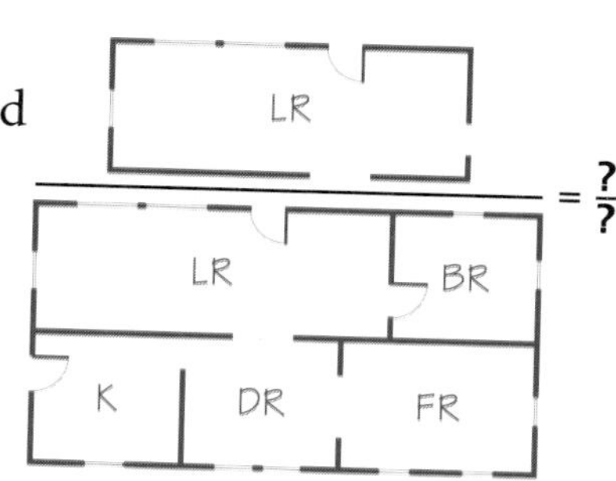

Find the total of the areas you measured. What fractional part is each floor area of the total area you measured? What kind of graph would be used to show this data? Explain.

3 Prime Time

Find the prime factorization of these pairs of numbers: 30 and 35, and 18 and 45. Then find the LCM of the pair of numbers and the prime factorization of the LCM.

How can the prime factorization of each pair of numbers help you find the LCM? Explain.

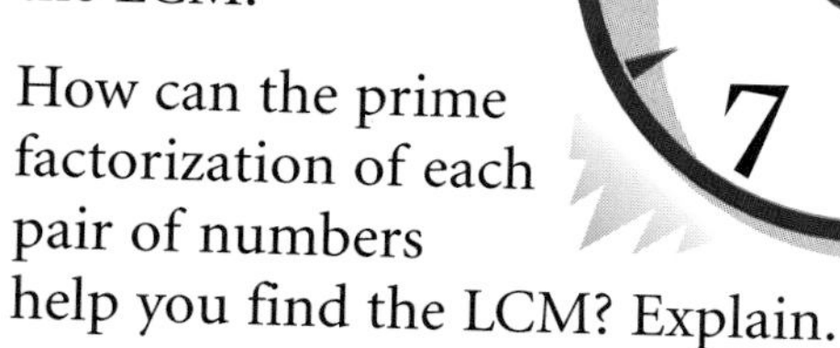

4 Number Strain

Use a 10×10 grid numbered from left to right from 1 to 100. Follow these steps:

- Cross out 1.
- Cross out multiples of 2 (except 2 itself) and 3 (except 3 itself).
- Cross out multiples of 5 (except 5 itself) and 7 (except 7 itself).

What are the numbers that have not been crossed out called?

Explain why there were no steps listed for crossing out the multiples of 4, 6, 8, or 9.

REVIEW AND PRACTICE

CHAPTER 5

Review/Test

(Lesson 1) Tell whether each number is divisible by 2, 3, 5, 6, 9, and 10.

1. 3,447 **2.** 485 **3.** 2,400 **4.** 6,775 **5.** 3,662

(Lesson 2) Identify each number as prime or composite.

6. $2 \times 2 \times 2 \times 2 \times 2 \times 2$ **7.** 1×47 **8.** 3×109 **9.** 51×2

(Lessons 2–4) Solve **10–15.** Choose any strategy.

10. Find the prime factorization of 234.

11. Find the least common multiple of 9 and 12.

12. If John walks to the park every third day, and Sue walks to the park every fourth day, when will they walk to the park on the same day?

13. a. Identify the numerator and denominator of the fraction $\frac{5}{8}$.

b. Write $\frac{5}{8}$ as a decimal number.

14. The prime factorization of a number is $2 \times 2 \times 3 \times 7$. What is the number?

15. A pet store owner wants to arrange 30 cages in equal groups. How many ways can she do this?

(Lesson 5) Write each fraction in lowest terms.

16. $\frac{16}{56}$ **17.** $\frac{120}{360}$ **18.** $\frac{25}{60}$ **19.** $\frac{3}{27}$

20. $\frac{32}{60}$ **21.** $\frac{150}{200}$ **22.** $\frac{68}{120}$ **23.** $\frac{14}{49}$

Find the GCF of each pair of numbers.

24. 30, 50 **25.** 42, 70 **26.** 15, 25 **27.** 16, 24

(Lesson 6) Write each improper fraction as a mixed number and each mixed number as a improper fraction.

28. $5\frac{3}{8}$ **29.** $\frac{17}{4}$ **30.** $\frac{37}{5}$ **31.** $8\frac{4}{5}$

(Lesson 7) Write each fraction as a decimal and each decimal as a fraction.

32. $\frac{3}{8}$ **33.** 0.44 **34.** 0.65 **35.** $\frac{5}{8}$

(Lesson 8) Solve the following problems by comparing numbers.

36. $\frac{2}{8}$ of the students in Mrs. Bright's math class have pet cats. $\frac{8}{16}$ of the students have dogs for pets. Only $\frac{1}{4}$ of the class have fish for pets.

a. Which group of students has the most pets?

b. Are there more cat owners than fish owners? Explain.

37. During the last spelling bee, Julia spelled $\frac{6}{9}$ of the words correctly and Hee-Jean spelled $\frac{5}{6}$ correctly. Who spelled more words correctly?

CHAPTER 5

Performance Assessment

Suppose you wish to buy and sell stocks. Stocks are shares of a compan
U.S. stock exchanges now use a system of fractions of a dollar for the va
stocks. In the near future the stock exchanges plan to convert to a decimal system.

1. **Analyze Data** Analyze the stock data in the chart below. Suppose you want to buy two stocks from the list. You want to buy only stocks with a value of less than \$10 and that have increased in value by at least $1\frac{1}{2}$. Which two stocks would you buy? Evaluate the data in the table. Eliminate stocks that do not fit your criteria. Which stocks can you choose from?

Name of company → Symbol

Value of one share in dollars today → Last

The amount that the value has changed in dollars since the previous day of exchanging → Change

Symbol	Last	Change
BJP	8 3/4	+1 1/8
CYI	11 1/4	+1 7/8
DZN	9 3/8	+1 5/8
EPD	7 1/8	+1 3/8
IHQ	6 3/4	−1 7/8
JCT	5 1/4	+1 3/4
LFA	8 1/2	−1 1/2
NVW	12 7/8	+1 3/8
VYB	6 1/8	+2

A − sign means the value has decreased.

A + sign means the value has increased.

2. **Explain Your Thinking** Write the price of one share of each stock that met the criteria in Exercise 1. Which is the more valuable stock?

3. **Decision Making** Choose the two stocks you would purchase.

4. **Critical Thinking** Suppose you want to buy a total of 600 shares of stock from the two companies you chose in Exercise 3. How many shares would you buy from each company? How much would the shares cost altogether?

Math Magazine

Loop the Group

A Venn diagram is one or more loops that show how groups of items are related. Every loop has a rule. Only items that follow the rule can be inside the loop.

In this Venn diagram, all the words in the loop start with the letter "b." None of the words outside the loop start with "b."

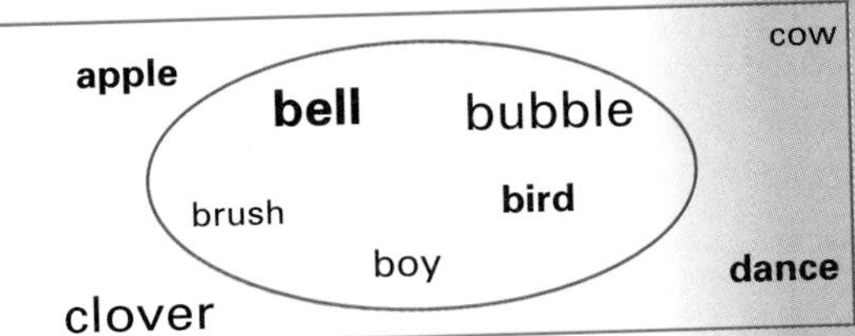

A Venn diagram may have more than one loop. Things that follow one rule go in one loop but not the other. Things that follow both rules go in the part of the loops that overlap.

The numbers in the red loop are divisible by 2. The numbers in the blue loop are divisible by 3. The numbers in both loops are divisible by 2 and by 3.

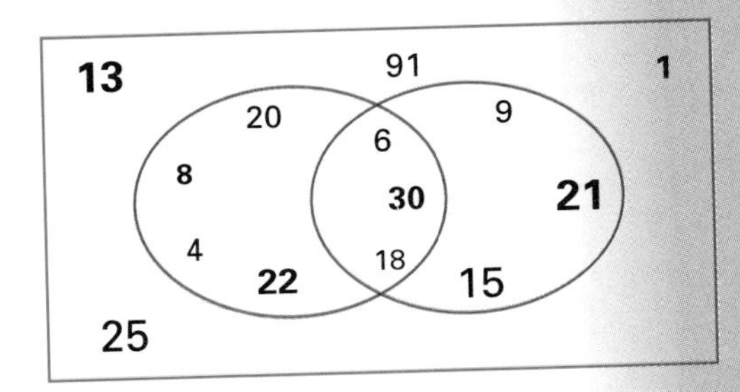

Try These!

1. Draw a Venn diagram with one loop where all the shapes inside the loop are triangles. There should be at least three shapes inside the loop and three shapes outside the loop.

2. Draw a Venn diagram with two loops, where one loop represents numbers greater than 20 and the other loop represents odd numbers. Put at least twelve numbers in the diagram. Three numbers should be in both loops.

3. Draw a Venn diagram with two loops. One loop should have numbers divisible by 5. The other should have numbers divisible by 10. Put at least 9 numbers in the diagram.

CHAPTERS 1–5

Cumulative Review

Test Prep Strategy: Work Backward from an Answer

What is the height of a parallelogram whose base is 14 ft and whose area is 252 ft²?

Ⓐ 12 ft Ⓑ 14 ft Ⓒ 16 ft Ⓓ 18 ft

You know the formula for finding the area of a parallelogram is *base × height = area.* You know the base and area of this parallelogram, so 14 ft × height = 252 ft². Replace the missing height with each choice, then check to see if it is correct.

$14 \times 12 = 168$ – no

$14 \times 14 = 196$ – no

$14 \times 16 = 224$ – no

$14 \times 18 = 252$ – yes

The answer is choice Ⓓ.

Write the letter of the correct answer. Choose any strategy.

1. Find the mean of this data set: 58, 67, 46, 85, 71, 65, 70, 58.
   Ⓐ 65 Ⓑ 46 Ⓒ 58 Ⓓ 85
2. Estimate using compatible numbers: $562 \div 47$.
   Ⓐ 12 Ⓑ 11.9 Ⓒ 12.9 Ⓓ 11
3. Simplify: $6^2 + (8 - 2)^2$.
   Ⓐ 40 Ⓑ 42 Ⓒ 96 Ⓓ 72
4. Round 346.8273 to the nearest hundredth.
   Ⓐ 300 Ⓑ 346.83 Ⓒ 346.8 Ⓓ 346.9
5. Multiply: 7.483×259.
   Ⓐ 193.8097 Ⓑ 19380.97 Ⓒ 1938.097 Ⓓ 1,938,097
6. What is the base of a rectangle whose area is 16.96 ft² and whose height is 5.3 ft?.
   Ⓐ 3.2 ft Ⓑ 3.32 ft Ⓒ 3.12 ft Ⓓ 3.3 ft
7. Which improper fraction can be written as $3\frac{3}{8}$?
   Ⓐ $\frac{24}{8}$ Ⓑ $\frac{27}{8}$ Ⓒ $\frac{6}{8}$ Ⓓ $\frac{9}{8}$
8. Find the area of the triangle.
   Ⓐ 4.64 cm² Ⓑ 5.27 cm² Ⓒ 9.28 cm² Ⓓ 9.7 cm²

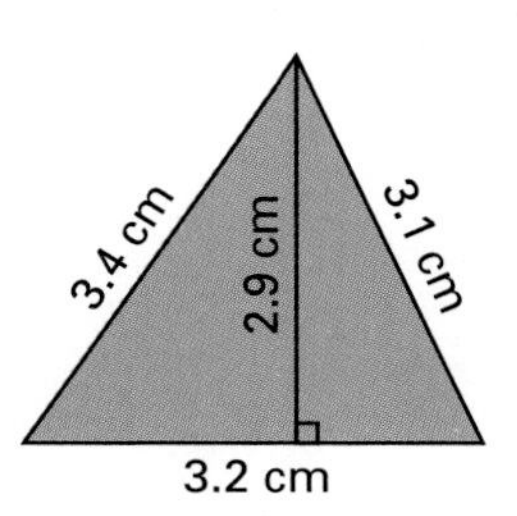

9. Which fraction is equivalent to a repeating decimal?
   Ⓐ $\frac{2}{30}$ Ⓑ $\frac{12}{30}$ Ⓒ $\frac{15}{30}$ Ⓓ $\frac{27}{30}$
10. What is the least common multiple of 6 and 15?
    Ⓐ 3 Ⓑ 5 Ⓒ 30 Ⓓ 60
11. Which fraction is not written in lowest terms?
    Ⓐ $\frac{2}{21}$ Ⓑ $\frac{3}{21}$ Ⓒ $\frac{4}{21}$ Ⓓ $\frac{5}{21}$

Test Prep Strategies

- Read Carefully
- Follow Directions
- Make Smart Choices
- Eliminate Choices
- Work Backward from an Answer

Chapter 6
Adding and Subtracting Fractions

DATA FILE

SECTION A What's Your Type?

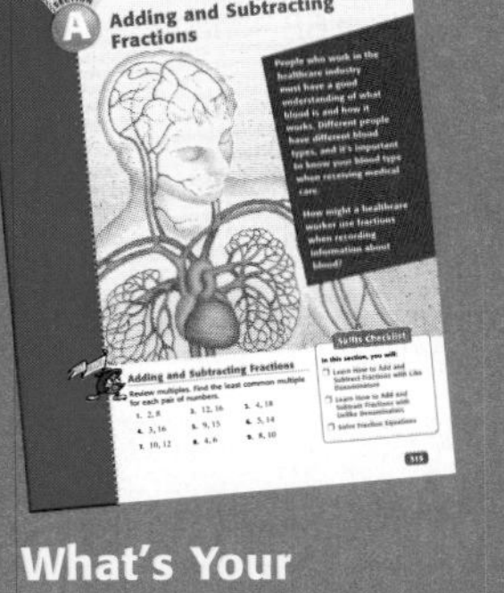

What's Your Type?
Page 315

Adding and Subtracting Fractions

315

Each person has one of eight blood types. This table shows what fraction of the population has each blood type. Which blood type is the most common? Least common?

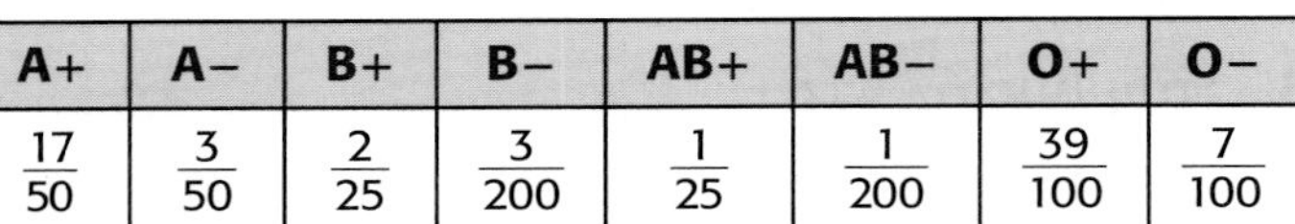

A+	A−	B+	B−	AB+	AB−	O+	O−
$\frac{17}{50}$	$\frac{3}{50}$	$\frac{2}{25}$	$\frac{3}{200}$	$\frac{1}{25}$	$\frac{1}{200}$	$\frac{39}{100}$	$\frac{7}{100}$

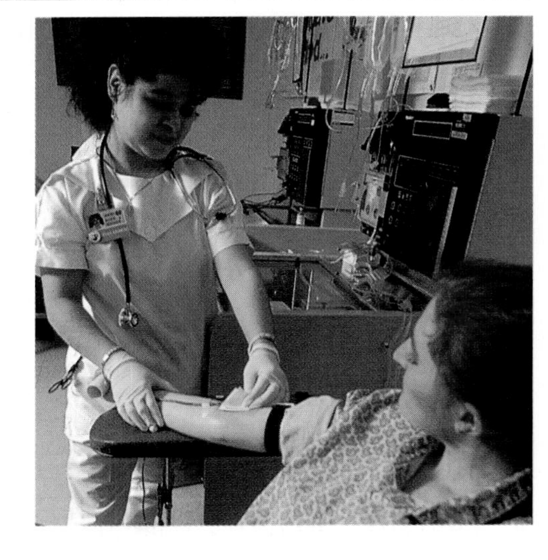

LINKS

Social Studies

If the World Trade Center Towers in New York City were stacked one on top of the other, the combined height would be more than $\frac{1}{2}$ mile high.

People of the World

Sweden has the most telephones per person. If evenly distributed, $\frac{17}{25}$ of Sweden's total population would have a telephone.

Science

A male California sea lion grows to between $6\frac{1}{2}$ and $8\frac{1}{6}$ feet tall and weighs between 400 and 660 pounds.
www.mathsurf.com/6/ch6/science

Deep Waters Still Run

Adding and Subtracting Mixed Numbers

335

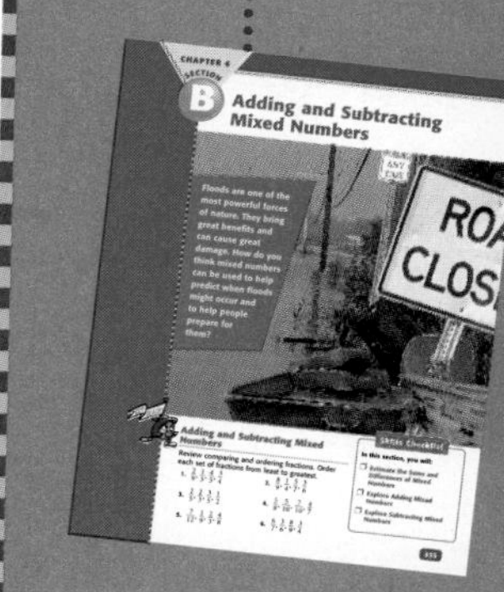

Deep Waters Still Run
Page 335

Tides are the result of the gravitational pull of the Sun and the Moon combined. Round the tides to the nearest foot. Which cities have tides with about the same average rise and fall?

Average Rise and Fall of the Tides (ft)			
Eastport, ME	$19\frac{1}{3}$	Portland, ME	$9\frac{11}{12}$
Seattle, WA	$11\frac{1}{3}$	Ft. Pulaski, GA	$7\frac{1}{2}$
Vancouver, B.C.	$10\frac{1}{2}$	Philadelphia, PA	$6\frac{3}{4}$
Boston, MA	$10\frac{1}{3}$	San Francisco, CA	$5\frac{5}{6}$

Arts & Literature

In 15th century Italy, church buildings were designed so that heights of the walls were either $\frac{1}{2}$, $\frac{2}{3}$, or $\frac{3}{4}$ the distance across the church.

Entertainment

$\frac{1}{3}$ of the money spent on newly published comic books goes to Marvel Comics, the publishers of *The X-Men* and *Spider-Man.* $\frac{1}{5}$ goes to DC Comics, the publishers of *Batman* and *Superman.*
www.mathsurf.com/6/ch6/ent

Materials
paper, pencils, rulers, atlas

Your team is going on a trip. You can travel between any of the cities on the map, but you cannot travel further than the distances shown in the chart.

Day	Distance Allowed (in.)
Monday	$6\frac{1}{3}$
Tuesday	4
Wednesday	$5\frac{7}{8}$
Thursday	$3\frac{3}{8}$
Friday	$6\frac{1}{2}$
Saturday	$5\frac{2}{3}$
Sunday	$4\frac{3}{4}$

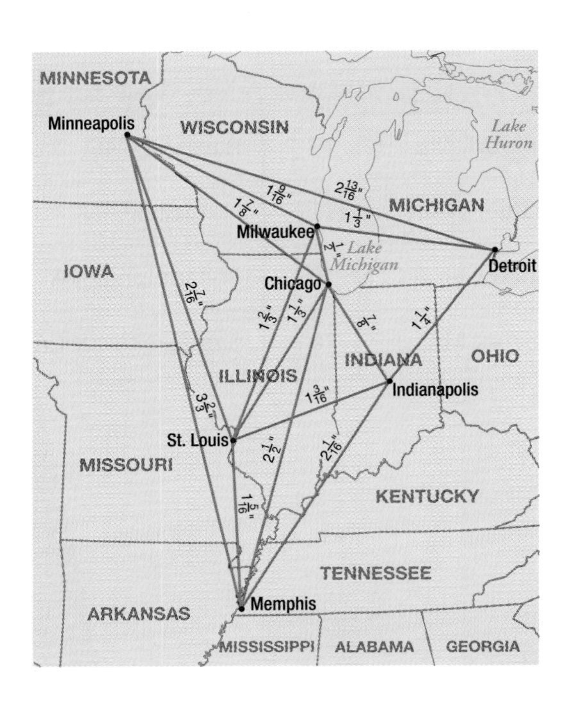

Make a Plan

- Which city will be your starting point? Which cities will you visit?
- How will you keep track of the distances you travel each day?

Carry It Out

1. Record the cities you will visit and the daily distances you will travel.
2. Find the planned total distance and compare it to the distance you are allowed to travel each day.
3. If possible, tell how many more inches you could have gone each day.

Talk About It

- How did your team decide which cities to visit?

Present the Project

Present your team's travel trip to the class.

CHAPTER 6

Adding and Subtracting Fractions

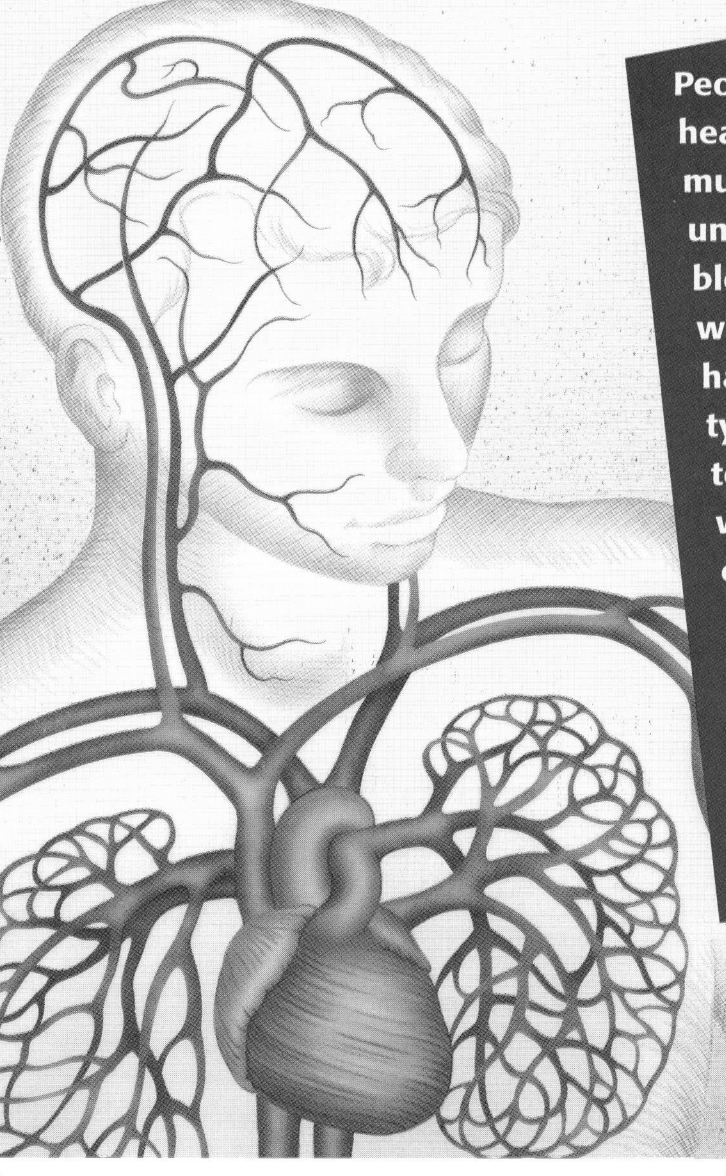

People who work in the healthcare industry must have a good understanding of what blood is and how it works. Different people have different blood types, and it's important to know your blood type when receiving medical care.

How might a healthcare worker use fractions when recording information about blood?

GET READY!

Adding and Subtracting Fractions

Review multiples. Find the least common multiple for each pair of numbers.

1. 2, 8	**2.** 12, 16	**3.** 4, 18
4. 3, 16	**5.** 9, 15	**6.** 5, 14
7. 10, 12	**8.** 4, 6	**9.** 8, 10

Skills Checklist

In this section, you will:

- ❒ Learn How to Add and Subtract Fractions with Like Denominators
- ❒ Learn How to Add and Subtract Fractions with Unlike Denominators
- ❒ Solve Fraction Equations

Chapter 6
Lesson
1

Adding and Subtracting Fractions with Like Denominators

You Will Learn

- to add and subtract fractions with like denominators

Vocabulary

like denominators

Learn

David is from Durham, North Carolina.

David lives near the Museum of Life and Science, which has a very popular hands-on exhibit of the circulatory system. David is planning to see the entire museum in one week.

Two fractions with the same denominator have **like denominators**.
When you add and subtract fractions with like denominators, the denominator acts as a label. It tells you what size pieces you're using. The numerators tell the number of pieces you add or subtract.

Example 1

By Tuesday, David had been through $\frac{2}{7}$ of the museum. By Saturday, he had been through another $\frac{4}{7}$ of the museum. How much of the museum has David seen so far?

Add: $\frac{2}{7} + \frac{4}{7}$

$\frac{2}{7} + \frac{4}{7} = \frac{2+4}{7}$ Add numerators only.

$\frac{2}{7} + \frac{4}{7} = \frac{6}{7}$ Denominators do not change.

Remember

Like denominators are also known as common denominators.

Example 2

Subtract: $\frac{4}{8} - \frac{1}{8}$

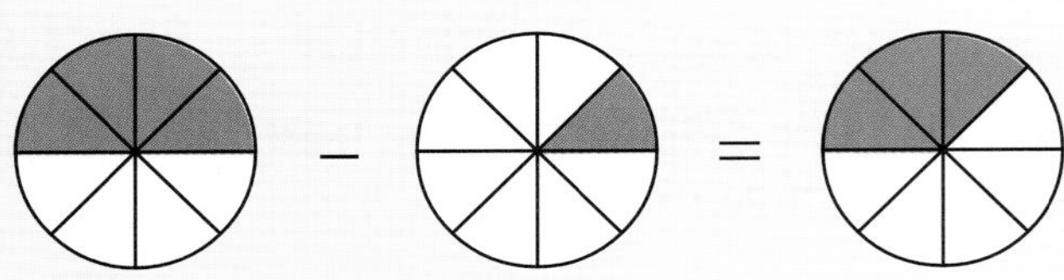

$\frac{4}{8} - \frac{1}{8} = \frac{4-1}{8}$ Subtract numerators only.

$\frac{4}{8} - \frac{1}{8} = \frac{3}{8}$ Denominators do not change.

You can add and subtract improper fractions with like denominators. Write the answer as a mixed number.

Example 3

In 1940, Charles Drew revolutionized the way doctors cared for patients by devising a blood bank plan for adequate storage of blood.

When an adult man donates blood to a blood bank, he donates about $\frac{1}{2}$ of a quart. The body of an average man contains about 5, or $\frac{10}{2}$, quarts of blood. How much blood is in his body after the donation?

$$\frac{10}{2} - \frac{1}{2} = \frac{10-1}{2}$$

$$= \frac{9}{2} = 4\frac{1}{2}$$

There are $\frac{9}{2}$, or $4\frac{1}{2}$ quarts, left in his body.

When adding and subtracting fractions, write the sum or difference in lowest terms.

Example 4

Add: $\frac{5}{16} + \frac{3}{16}$

$$\frac{5}{16} + \frac{3}{16} = \frac{5+3}{16}$$

$$= \frac{8}{16} = \frac{2}{4} = \frac{1}{2}$$

$\frac{5}{16} + \frac{3}{16} = \frac{1}{2}$

Example 5

Subtract: $\frac{7}{8} - \frac{1}{8}$

$$\frac{7}{8} - \frac{1}{8} = \frac{7-1}{8}$$

$$= \frac{6}{8} = \frac{3}{4}$$

$\frac{7}{8} - \frac{1}{8} = \frac{3}{4}$

Talk About It

1. When you add or subtract fractions with like denominators, why doesn't the denominator change?
2. What values can n have to make the equation $\frac{3}{n} + \frac{5}{n} = \frac{8}{n}$ true?

Check

Simplify. Write each answer in lowest terms.

1. $\frac{3}{10} + \frac{4}{10}$
2. $\frac{5}{7} - \frac{3}{7}$
3. $\frac{8}{2} + \frac{9}{2}$
4. $\frac{4}{9} - \frac{4}{9}$
5. $\frac{3}{4} - \frac{2}{4}$
6. $\frac{5}{3} - \frac{2}{3}$
7. $\frac{1}{6} + \frac{7}{6}$
8. $\frac{1}{5} + \frac{1}{5}$
9. $\frac{6}{8} - \frac{2}{8}$
10. $\frac{11}{12} + \frac{10}{12}$
11. **Reasoning** How is adding fractions with like denominators similar to subtracting fractions with like denominators?

Practice

Skills and Reasoning

Simplify. Write each answer in lowest terms.

12. $\frac{3}{5}+\frac{1}{5}$ **13.** $\frac{9}{10}-\frac{8}{10}$ **14.** $\frac{7}{8}+\frac{5}{8}$ **15.** $\frac{4}{3}+\frac{2}{3}$ **16.** $\frac{12}{5}-\frac{6}{5}$

17. $\frac{4}{3}-\frac{3}{3}$ **18.** $\frac{98}{10}+\frac{2}{10}$ **19.** $\frac{3}{4}-\frac{1}{4}$ **20.** $\frac{4}{11}+\frac{3}{11}$ **21.** $\frac{12}{18}-\frac{9}{18}$

22. $\frac{15}{19}+\frac{5}{19}$ **23.** $\frac{7}{9}-\frac{3}{9}$ **24.** $\frac{6}{8}-\frac{4}{8}$ **25.** $\frac{5}{13}+\frac{1}{13}$ **26.** $\frac{34}{12}-\frac{30}{12}$

State whether the answer is greater than, less than, or equal to 1.

27. $\frac{7}{9}+\frac{2}{9}$ **28.** $\frac{1}{2}+\frac{3}{2}$ **29.** $\frac{2}{7}+\frac{6}{7}$ **30.** $\frac{3}{4}-\frac{2}{4}$

31. $\frac{9}{5}-\frac{4}{5}$ **32.** $\frac{7}{12}+\frac{7}{12}$ **33.** $\frac{1}{10}-\frac{1}{10}$ **34.** $\frac{16}{13}+\frac{4}{13}$

Tillie's volleyball team had a picnic. Team members brought food or games. The bar graph represents the players who brought an item of food. Use the graph for **35–41.**

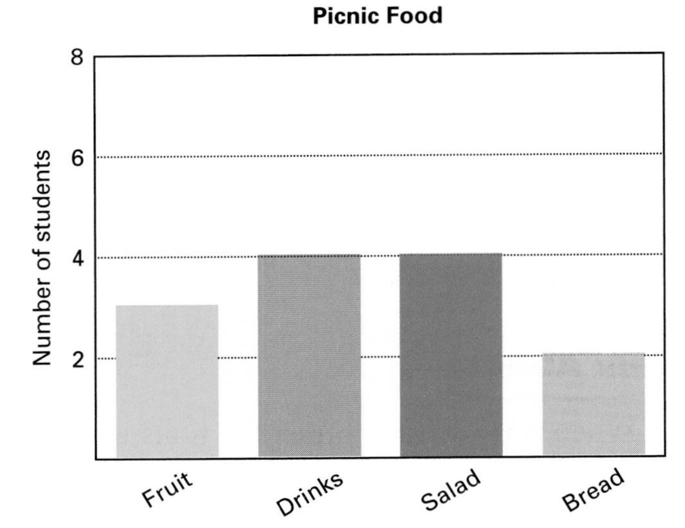

35. What fraction of the students shown in the graph brought fruit or drinks?

36. What is the difference between the fraction of students who brought drinks and the fraction who brought fruit?

37. What fraction of the students shown in the graph brought fruit, drinks, or salad?

38. If 15 students attended the picnic, how many did not bring fruit, drinks, salad, or bread?

39. What is the difference between the fraction of students who brought fruit or bread and the fraction who brought salad?

40. Two more students attended the picnic at the last minute and both brought bread. What would the new fraction of students bringing bread be?

41. **Critical Thinking** Which two foods represent over $\frac{1}{2}$ of the foods brought to the picnic?

Problem Solving and Applications

42. **Geography** About $\frac{3}{50}$ of the earth's surface is covered with land that can be farmed. $\frac{12}{50}$ is desert, ice or mountains. $\frac{35}{50}$ is liquid. What fraction of the earth's surface is not liquid?

43. Sandra makes bracelets, necklaces, and chokers using leather string. A bracelet requires $\frac{7}{12}$ ft of string, and a necklace requires $\frac{22}{12}$ ft. She has $\frac{81}{12}$ ft, which is exactly enough to make 3 bracelets, 2 necklaces, and 1 choker. How much string does each choker require? Explain.

44. The sum of 2 fractions is $\frac{11}{12}$. If one fraction is $\frac{4}{12}$, what is the other fraction?

45. **Logic** For the equation $\frac{3}{11} + \frac{x}{y} = \frac{10}{11}$, name two values for both x and y that will make the equation true. Explain your reasoning.

Using Data Use the Data File on page 312 to answer **46** and **47.**

46. What fraction of the population has an A+ or A− blood type?

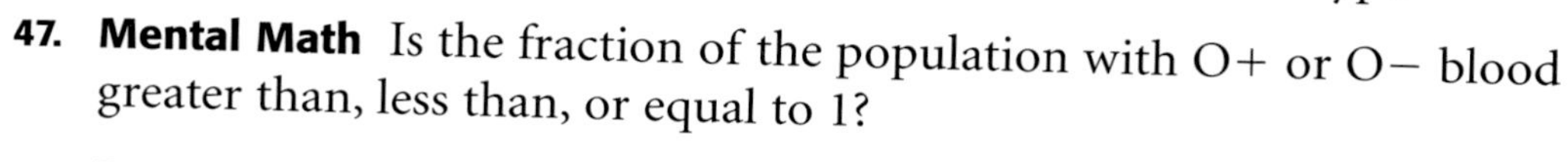

47. **Mental Math** Is the fraction of the population with O+ or O− blood greater than, less than, or equal to 1?

48. **Patterns** In this pattern, what fraction is next?
$\frac{4}{1}, \frac{16}{1}, \frac{64}{1}, \frac{256}{1}, ?$

49. **Collecting Data** What fraction of your class is male? What fraction is female? What is the sum of the fractions?

Mixed Review and Test Prep

Find the least common multiple of each pair of numbers.

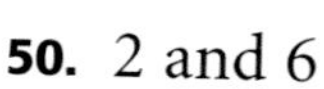

50. 2 and 6 **51.** 5 and 20 **52.** 4 and 9 **53.** 10 and 12

54. 15 and 60 **55.** 7 and 8 **56.** 2 and 11 **57.** 3 and 4

58. One side of an equilateral triangle measures 4.25 cm. What is the perimeter of the triangle?

59. Sylvia wants to buy a 6-pack of juice drink. The store only sells single cans for $0.83. If Sylvia has $5, does she have enough to buy what she wants? Explain.

60. What is the area of a triangle with a base of 7 in. and a height of 12 in.?

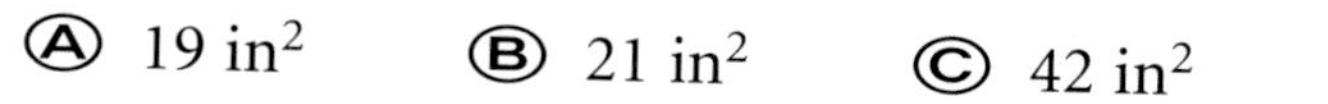

Ⓐ 19 in^2 Ⓑ 21 in^2 Ⓒ 42 in^2 Ⓓ 84 in^2

Adding and Subtracting Fractions with Unlike Denominators

You Will Learn

- to add and subtract fractions with unlike denominators

Vocabulary

unlike denominators
least common denominator (LCD)

Did You Know?

In 1897, Bram Stoker wrote *Dracula,* the story of a vampire who drank human blood to survive.

Learn

Fractions with like denominators are easy to add and subtract because they represent parts of the same size. Fractions with different denominators, or **unlike denominators**, are not as easy to work with because they represent parts of different sizes.

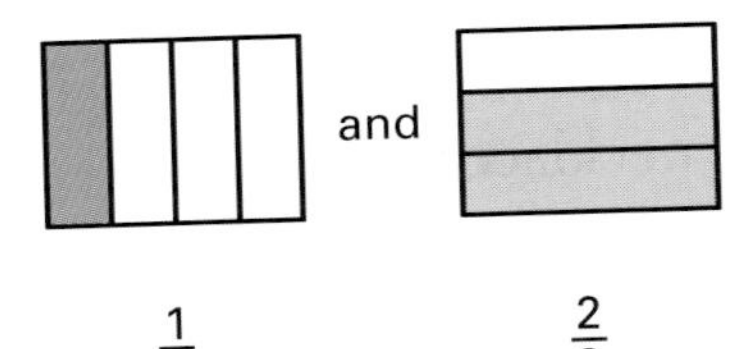

$\frac{1}{4}$ $\frac{2}{3}$

In order to add or subtract fractions with unlike denominators, you need to change them to equivalent fractions with the same denominator. One way to do this is to multiply the numerator and the denominator of each fraction by the denominator of the other fraction.

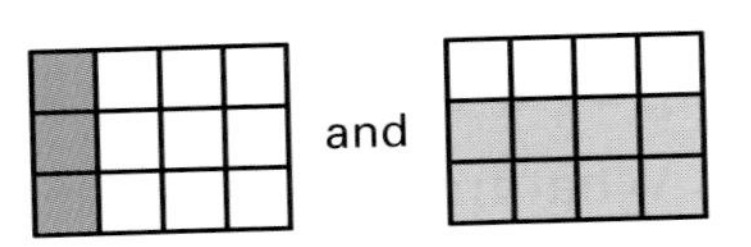

$\frac{1 \times \mathbf{3}}{4 \times \mathbf{3}} = \frac{3}{12}$ $\frac{2 \times \mathbf{4}}{3 \times \mathbf{4}} = \frac{8}{12}$

Example 1

Dwayne is playing Count Dracula in the school production of *Dracula*. He still has to memorize $\frac{3}{4}$ of all of his lines. If he memorizes $\frac{1}{3}$ of all of his lines today, what fraction of all of his lines will he have left to memorize?

$\frac{3}{4} - \frac{1}{3}$ Write an expression for the problem.

$\frac{3}{4} = \frac{3 \times 3}{4 \times 3} = \frac{9}{12}$ For $\frac{3}{4}$, multiply the numerator and denominator by 3.

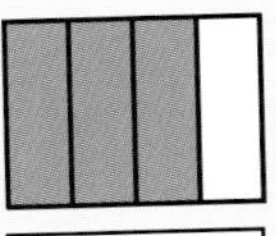

$\frac{1}{3} = \frac{1 \times 4}{3 \times 4} = \frac{4}{12}$ For $\frac{1}{3}$, multiply the numerator and denominator by 4.

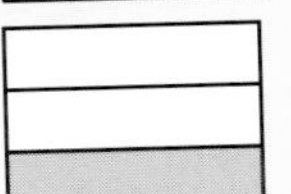

$\frac{3}{4} - \frac{1}{3} = \frac{9}{12} - \frac{4}{12}$ Rewrite the expression using equivalent fractions.

$\frac{9 - 4}{12} = \frac{5}{12}$ Subtract.

He will have $\frac{5}{12}$ of his lines left to memorize.

Sometimes it is easier to find the least common multiple of the two denominators and convert both fractions to that denominator. In fractions, this number is known as the **least common denominator**.

Example 2

There are eight human blood types: A+, A−, B+, B−, AB+, AB−, O+, and O−. There are three cat blood types: A, B, and AB. $\frac{73}{100}$ of all cats have type A blood. $\frac{13}{50}$ have type B blood. What fraction of all cats have either type A blood or type B blood?

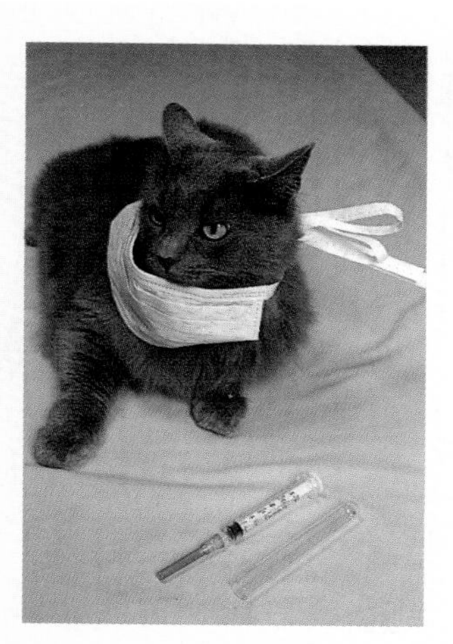

Add: $\frac{73}{100} + \frac{13}{50}$ — The least common denominator of 50 and 100 is 100. Only the second fraction needs to be changed to an equivalent fraction.

$\frac{13}{50} = \frac{13 \times 2}{50 \times 2} = \frac{26}{100}$ — Multiply the numerator and denominator by 2.

$\frac{73}{100} + \frac{26}{100} = \frac{73 + 26}{100} = \frac{99}{100}$ — Add.

$\frac{99}{100}$ of all cats have either type A or type B blood.

In some cases, both fractions need to be changed to an equivalent fraction.

Example 3

What is $\frac{3}{10} - \frac{1}{4}$?

The least common multiple of 10 and 4 is 20.

$\frac{3}{10} = \frac{3 \times 2}{10 \times 2} = \frac{6}{20}$ — Multiply $\frac{3}{10}$ by 2 to get an equivalent fraction with a denominator of 20.

$\frac{1}{4} = \frac{1 \times 5}{4 \times 5} = \frac{5}{20}$ — Multiply $\frac{1}{4}$ by 5 to get an equivalent fraction with a denominator of 20.

$\frac{6}{20} - \frac{5}{20} = \frac{6 - 5}{20}$ — Subtract.

$\frac{6}{20} - \frac{5}{20} = \frac{1}{20}$

Talk About It

Why is it necessary for fractions to have like denominators before you add or subtract?

Check

Simplify. Write each answer in lowest terms.

1. $\frac{3}{4} - \frac{1}{2}$ **2.** $\frac{1}{3} + \frac{2}{6}$ **3.** $\frac{5}{6} - \frac{2}{15}$ **4.** $\frac{5}{9} + \frac{1}{6}$ **5.** $\frac{3}{8} + \frac{1}{6}$

6. Reasoning Why should you use the least common denominator instead of any common denominator?

Practice

Skills and Reasoning

Simplify. Write each answer in lowest terms.

7. $\frac{3}{5} + \frac{1}{4}$
8. $\frac{5}{12} - \frac{1}{6}$
9. $\frac{1}{2} + \frac{1}{3}$
10. $\frac{3}{4} - \frac{7}{12}$
11. $\frac{9}{10} - \frac{1}{2}$
12. $\frac{3}{4} + \frac{1}{2}$
13. $\frac{7}{8} - \frac{5}{6}$
14. $\frac{1}{4} + \frac{5}{7}$
15. $\frac{4}{11} + \frac{4}{44}$
16. $\frac{7}{6} - \frac{3}{5}$
17. $\frac{5}{8} + \frac{3}{4}$
18. $\frac{3}{10} + \frac{3}{4}$
19. $\frac{3}{9} + \frac{3}{2}$
20. $\frac{19}{25} - \frac{3}{5}$
21. $\frac{9}{13} - \frac{9}{26}$
22. $\frac{5}{7} + \frac{1}{4}$
23. $\frac{1}{12} + \frac{5}{6}$
24. $\frac{8}{9} - \frac{1}{3}$
25. $\frac{1}{2} - \frac{3}{8}$
26. $\frac{4}{10} + \frac{3}{5}$
27. $\frac{1}{8} + \frac{2}{16}$
28. $\frac{7}{9} - \frac{1}{2}$
29. $\frac{6}{11} - \frac{1}{3}$
30. $\frac{3}{4} + \frac{1}{8}$
31. $\frac{2}{5} + \frac{2}{6}$

Find each missing numerator.

32. $\frac{2}{5} + \frac{7}{10} = \frac{■}{10} + \frac{■}{10}$
33. $\frac{3}{4} + \frac{5}{6} = \frac{■}{12} + \frac{■}{12}$
34. $\frac{5}{8} - \frac{1}{6} = \frac{■}{24} - \frac{■}{24}$
35. $\frac{3}{8} + \frac{1}{2} = \frac{■}{8} + \frac{■}{8}$
36. $\frac{4}{9} - \frac{1}{3} = \frac{■}{9} - \frac{■}{9}$
37. $\frac{3}{4} - \frac{1}{3} = \frac{■}{36} - \frac{■}{36}$
38. $\frac{4}{7} + \frac{1}{3} = \frac{■}{21} + \frac{■}{21}$
39. $\frac{5}{8} - \frac{1}{16} = \frac{■}{16} - \frac{■}{16}$
40. $\frac{2}{5} + \frac{3}{7} = \frac{■}{35} + \frac{■}{35}$

41. **Science** Most of the cells in your blood are either red blood cells, white blood cells, or platelets. When you cut yourself, blood platelets help the blood to clot so that you don't bleed to death. Platelets can survive for $\frac{10}{14}$ of a week. White blood cells can survive for more than $\frac{126}{21}$ weeks. How much longer is the life span of a white blood cell?

White blood cell

42. **Money** Choose two different U.S. coins. Express each as a fraction of one dollar. Together, the coins represent what fraction of one dollar?

43. **Reasoning** Will finding the product of the denominators of two fractions always give you the least common denominator? Explain.

44. **Mental Math** What is the least common denominator for 2 and 5?

Problem Solving and Applications

45. **Time** Suppose you studied $\frac{3}{4}$ of an hour for a quiz and your friend studied $\frac{5}{6}$ of an hour. Who studied more? How many minutes more?

46. **Critical Thinking** A recipe for fruit punch calls for $\frac{3}{8}$ of a quart of lemon drink, $\frac{3}{2}$ of a quart of orange juice, $\frac{1}{10}$ of a quart of cranberry juice, and $\frac{3}{4}$ of a quart of soda water. How large a container is needed for the punch? Explain.

47. **Choose a Strategy** Denzel had walked $\frac{1}{3}$ of the way to school when he realized he had dropped a book. He turned around, and had covered $\frac{1}{4}$ of the distance between home and school before finding it. What fraction of the total distance between home and school did Denzel now have to walk? Explain.

48. **Critical Thinking** Four people are sharing a pizza. Ana would like to eat $\frac{1}{8}$, Jon wants $\frac{1}{4}$, Yi wants $\frac{1}{3}$, and Lisa would like $\frac{1}{6}$. What is the least number of slices of the same size that must be cut for each person to get what he or she wants? How much pizza is left over? Explain.

Mixed Review and Test Prep

Find the area of each shape.

49. Rectangle: 14 ft by 5 ft

50. 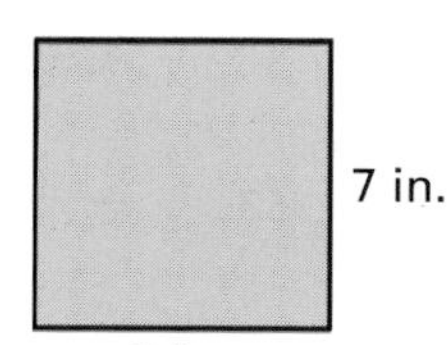

51. Rectangle: 12 yd by 0.5 yd

Write an expression to describe each situation.

52. Henri had h hens. Each laid 4 eggs. How many eggs did Henri have?

53. Julia read b books last week and 2 books this week. How many books did Julia read?

54. Jake had x pairs of shoes. If he lost three shoes, how many shoes does he have left?

55. Sam has a science test on Thursday. On Monday, he studied $\frac{2}{9}$ of the material. On Tuesday, he studied $\frac{5}{9}$ more. How much material has he already reviewed?

Ⓐ $\frac{3}{12}$　　Ⓑ $\frac{5}{9}$　　Ⓒ $\frac{7}{9}$　　Ⓓ $\frac{3}{3}$

and Practice

Simplify. Write each answer in lowest terms.

1. $\frac{2}{9}+\frac{4}{9}$ **2.** $\frac{8}{12}-\frac{5}{12}$ **3.** $\frac{5}{4}+\frac{3}{4}$ **4.** $\frac{2}{3}-\frac{1}{3}$ **5.** $\frac{6}{15}+\frac{4}{15}$

6. $\frac{8}{6}-\frac{3}{6}$ **7.** $\frac{17}{8}+\frac{7}{8}$ **8.** $\frac{6}{7}-\frac{2}{7}$ **9.** $\frac{36}{5}+\frac{9}{5}$ **10.** $\frac{30}{20}-\frac{18}{20}$

11. $\frac{6}{10}-\frac{1}{10}$ **12.** $\frac{14}{11}-\frac{8}{11}$ **13.** $\frac{7}{3}+\frac{11}{3}$ **14.** $\frac{2}{12}+\frac{6}{12}$ **15.** $\frac{13}{6}-\frac{11}{6}$

16. $\frac{7}{16}+\frac{5}{16}$ **17.** $\frac{12}{13}-\frac{9}{13}$ **18.** $\frac{16}{18}-\frac{7}{18}$ **19.** $\frac{8}{9}-\frac{5}{9}$ **20.** $\frac{2}{12}+\frac{7}{12}$

21. $\frac{2}{5}+\frac{1}{9}$ **22.** $\frac{2}{3}-\frac{1}{2}$ **23.** $\frac{3}{4}-\frac{2}{3}$ **24.** $\frac{5}{6}-\frac{1}{2}$ **25.** $\frac{5}{9}+\frac{1}{3}$

26. $\frac{1}{2}+\frac{3}{8}$ **27.** $\frac{3}{5}+\frac{2}{6}$ **28.** $\frac{5}{8}-\frac{1}{3}$ **29.** $\frac{5}{10}+\frac{1}{4}$ **30.** $\frac{12}{24}-\frac{1}{6}$

31. $\frac{2}{3}-\frac{1}{5}$ **32.** $\frac{2}{6}-\frac{1}{7}$ **33.** $\frac{4}{12}+\frac{2}{4}$ **34.** $\frac{4}{5}-\frac{14}{20}$ **35.** $\frac{5}{7}-\frac{2}{9}$

36. $\frac{2}{4}-\frac{3}{7}$ **37.** $\frac{1}{2}-\frac{3}{9}$ **38.** $\frac{1}{5}-\frac{1}{8}$ **39.** $\frac{7}{18}+\frac{3}{6}$ **40.** $\frac{7}{8}-\frac{1}{6}$

41. $\frac{1}{2}+\frac{1}{8}$ **42.** $\frac{1}{5}+\frac{7}{10}$ **43.** $\frac{3}{4}-\frac{2}{3}$ **44.** $\frac{6}{7}-\frac{1}{7}$ **45.** $\frac{1}{9}+\frac{1}{3}$

46. $\frac{9}{10}+\frac{1}{10}$ **47.** $\frac{4}{5}+\frac{1}{9}$ **48.** $\frac{5}{8}-\frac{2}{6}$ **49.** $\frac{9}{20}-\frac{3}{10}$ **50.** $\frac{1}{12}+\frac{3}{6}$

51. $\frac{3}{8}-\frac{2}{40}$ **52.** $\frac{1}{16}+\frac{3}{4}$ **53.** $\frac{5}{12}-\frac{1}{3}$ **54.** $\frac{2}{15}+\frac{4}{5}$ **55.** $\frac{1}{3}+\frac{1}{2}$

56. $\frac{9}{12}-\frac{5}{12}$ **57.** $\frac{2}{8}+\frac{1}{5}$ **58.** $\frac{1}{4}+\frac{3}{5}$ **59.** $\frac{9}{10}-\frac{2}{5}$ **60.** $\frac{1}{2}-\frac{3}{8}$

61. $\frac{3}{13}+\frac{10}{13}$ **62.** $\frac{7}{9}-\frac{1}{3}$ **63.** $\frac{2}{5}+\frac{1}{9}$ **64.** $\frac{10}{11}-\frac{4}{11}$ **65.** $\frac{9}{12}-\frac{2}{3}$

66. $\frac{4}{5}+\frac{1}{6}$ **67.** $\frac{11}{12}-\frac{5}{12}$ **68.** $\frac{3}{20}+\frac{3}{4}$ **69.** $\frac{3}{8}+\frac{5}{8}$ **70.** $\frac{2}{3}-\frac{1}{9}$

71. $\frac{3}{4}+\frac{1}{4}$ **72.** $\frac{1}{3}+\frac{1}{8}$ **73.** $\frac{5}{9}+\frac{2}{5}$ **74.** $\frac{5}{3}-\frac{2}{3}$ **75.** $\frac{4}{6}+\frac{1}{4}$

76. $\frac{2}{3}-\frac{2}{5}$ **77.** $\frac{1}{4}+\frac{3}{10}$ **78.** $\frac{7}{6}-\frac{4}{6}$ **79.** $\frac{1}{2}-\frac{2}{5}$ **80.** $\frac{8}{13}+\frac{2}{13}$

Error Search

Find each sum or difference that is not correct. Write it correctly and explain the error.

81. $\frac{2}{5}+\frac{3}{8}=1$ **82.** $\frac{5}{9}-\frac{1}{5}=\frac{4}{5}$ **83.** $\frac{2}{3}-\frac{2}{5}=\frac{4}{15}$ **84.** $\frac{1}{4}+\frac{6}{16}=\frac{22}{16}$

85. $\frac{5}{8}-\frac{1}{4}=\frac{3}{8}$ **86.** $\frac{5}{6}-\frac{1}{4}=\frac{13}{12}$ **87.** $\frac{2}{6}+\frac{2}{7}=\frac{13}{21}$ **88.** $\frac{7}{12}+\frac{1}{3}=\frac{11}{12}$

It Just Doesn't Add Up!

Simplify. Write each answer in lowest terms. Match each answer to a number below the blanks. Then find the answer to the question. Some letters are not used.

Where does 9 plus 4 equal 1?

___	___	___
$\frac{17}{42}$	$\frac{7}{36}$	$\frac{5}{6}$

___	___	___	___	___	___	___	___	___
$\frac{11}{30}$	2	$\frac{17}{42}$	$\frac{11}{30}$	$\frac{5}{7}$	$\frac{9}{28}$	$\frac{5}{6}$	$\frac{11}{30}$	$\frac{9}{10}$

89. $\frac{3}{7} + \frac{2}{7}$ (K)

90. $\frac{14}{25} + \frac{8}{25}$ (D)

91. $\frac{15}{16} - \frac{7}{16}$ (S)

92. $\frac{5}{8} + \frac{11}{8}$ (L)

93. $\frac{1}{3} + \frac{4}{8}$ (A)

94. $\frac{2}{3} - \frac{3}{5}$ (T)

95. $\frac{4}{7} - \frac{1}{4}$ (F)

96. $\frac{3}{4} - \frac{5}{9}$ (N)

97. $\frac{2}{4} + \frac{2}{5}$ (E)

98. $\frac{5}{6} - \frac{3}{7}$ (O)

99. $\frac{4}{5} - \frac{3}{6}$ (R)

100. $\frac{7}{10} - \frac{1}{3}$ (C)

Number Sense Estimation and Reasoning

Compare using <, >, or =. Use estimation or mental math to help.

101. $\frac{5}{8} + \frac{2}{8} \bigcirc \frac{1}{6} + \frac{2}{6}$

102. $\frac{3}{4} - \frac{1}{4} \bigcirc \frac{9}{10} - \frac{2}{10}$

103. $\frac{2}{4} + \frac{1}{4} \bigcirc \frac{2}{8} + \frac{4}{8}$

104. $\frac{5}{12} - \frac{1}{12} \bigcirc \frac{15}{16} - \frac{2}{16}$

105. $\frac{2}{3} + \frac{1}{3} \bigcirc \frac{4}{7} + \frac{3}{7}$

106. $\frac{3}{6} - \frac{1}{4} \bigcirc \frac{1}{4} - \frac{1}{8}$

107. $\frac{3}{10} + \frac{6}{10} \bigcirc \frac{2}{9} + \frac{1}{3}$

108. $\frac{5}{6} - \frac{2}{3} \bigcirc \frac{4}{5} - \frac{2}{5}$

109. $\frac{9}{4} - \frac{7}{4} \bigcirc \frac{14}{16} - \frac{1}{4}$

Technology

Using a Fraction Calculator to Find Fraction Sums and Differences

Sometimes adding or subtracting fractions involves numbers that are not easy to work with mentally. A fraction calculator can help you in these situations.

Materials
Fraction calculator

What is the sum of $\frac{7}{17}$ and $\frac{16}{29}$?

Work Together

Use a calculator to find the sum.

1. Enter the numerator of the first fraction, then press the [/] key. [7] [/]
2. Enter the denominator of the first fraction, then press the [+] key. [1] [7] [+]
3. Enter the numerator of the second fraction, then press the [/] key. [1] [6] [/]
4. Enter the denominator of the second fraction, then press the [=] key. [2] [9] [=]
5. What is the sum of $\frac{7}{17}$ and $\frac{16}{29}$?
6. The process is the same to find the difference of two fractions.

$\frac{11}{15} - \frac{24}{41}$ 11 [/] 15 [−] 24 [/] 41 [=] 91/615

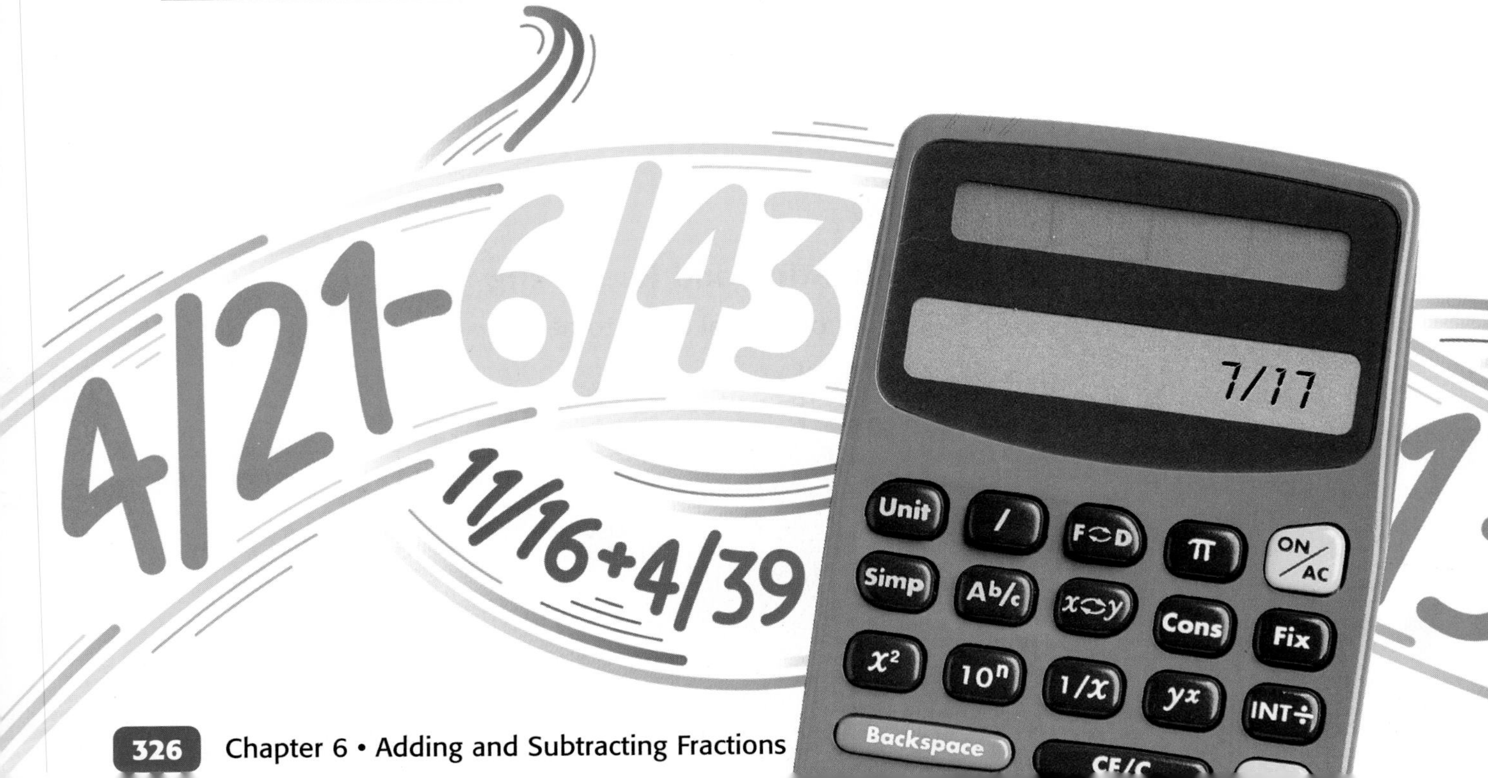

Exercises

Use your calculator to find each sum or difference.

1. $\frac{5}{23} + \frac{14}{37}$
2. $\frac{8}{21} - \frac{4}{41}$
3. $\frac{13}{33} + \frac{9}{30}$
4. $\frac{17}{21} - \frac{6}{19}$
5. $\frac{27}{28} - \frac{14}{15}$
6. $\frac{16}{29} + \frac{9}{34}$
7. $\frac{4}{19} - \frac{5}{31}$
8. $\frac{5}{19} + \frac{7}{51}$
9. $\frac{4}{21} - \frac{6}{43}$
10. $\frac{11}{18} + \frac{9}{39}$
11. $\frac{14}{19} + \frac{6}{23}$
12. $\frac{15}{32} - \frac{4}{11}$
13. $\frac{2}{17} + \frac{9}{16}$
14. $\frac{11}{18} - \frac{29}{60}$
15. $\frac{19}{45} + \frac{7}{20}$
16. $\frac{14}{17} - \frac{21}{31}$
17. What is the sum of $\frac{12}{25}$ and $\frac{7}{19}$?
18. What is the difference of $\frac{18}{33}$ and $\frac{7}{18}$?

Extensions

19. Alexis used her calculator to find the sum of two fractions. The sum of the two fractions was $\frac{9}{19}$. If one fraction was $\frac{1}{30}$, what was the other fraction?
20. Would you use a calculator or pencil and paper to find the sum of $\frac{9}{12}$ and $\frac{3}{48}$? Explain.
21. Find the sum of $\frac{6}{13}$ and $\frac{20}{21}$. What does the calculator display show when the sum of two fractions is greater than 1?
22. The sum of $\frac{45}{51} + \frac{67}{91}$ has a denominator greater than 1,000. What does the calculator do when the answer has a four-digit denominator?
23. How can you find the sum of two fractions with a non-fraction calculator?

Chapter 6
Lesson
3

Solving Fraction Equations: Addition and Subtraction

You Will Learn

- to solve equations by adding and subtracting fractions

Learn

When the body is at rest, blood is distributed throughout the capillaries, heart, lungs, systemic arteries, and systemic veins.

A cardiologist added together the blood found in two different organs. Unfortunately, some of the data was accidentally deleted.

Organ 1, Fraction of blood	Organ 2, Fraction of blood	Total
Heart, $\frac{1}{10}$	Lungs, ???	$\frac{2}{10}$

When the denominators are the same, you can solve addition or subtraction equations using mental math.

Problem Solving Hint

Since all of the denominators are the same, you can rewrite this as a simpler problem: $x - 2 = 5$.

Example 1

How much blood is in the lungs when the body is at rest?

$\frac{1}{10} + x = \frac{2}{10}$ Read as "$\frac{1}{10}$ plus what number equals $\frac{2}{10}$?"

$\frac{1}{10} + \mathbf{\frac{1}{10}} = \frac{2}{10}$ Use mental math.

$\frac{2}{10} = \frac{2}{10}$ Check to see that the equation is true.

$\frac{1}{10}$ of the body's blood is in the lungs when the body is at rest.

You can also rewrite an addition or subtraction equation as a simpler problem when the denominators are the same.

Example 2

Kevin had to write a report about the human eye. He completed $\frac{5}{8}$ of the report in two nights. On the second night of work, Kevin completed $\frac{3}{8}$ of the report. How much did he complete on the first night?

$\frac{5}{8} - x = \frac{3}{8}$ Read as "$\frac{5}{8}$ minus what number equals $\frac{3}{8}$?"

$5 - x = 3, x = 2$ Rewrite it as a simpler problem.

$\frac{5}{8} - \mathbf{\frac{2}{8}} = \frac{3}{8}$ Replace x with $\frac{2}{8}$.

$\frac{3}{8} = \frac{3}{8}$ Check to see that the equation is true.

He completed $\frac{2}{8}$, or $\frac{1}{4}$, on the first night.

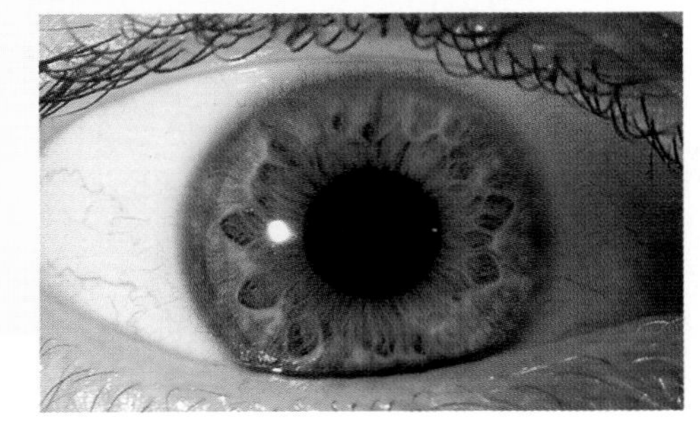

To solve equations using fractions with unlike denominators, you need to change the fractions to equivalent fractions with like denominators.

Example 3

$\frac{43}{100}$ of your blood is made up of only red blood cells. $\frac{9}{20}$ of your blood is made up of red and white blood cells. What fraction of your blood is made up of only white blood cells?

Solve: $\frac{x+43}{100}=\frac{9}{20}$

$\frac{9}{20}=\frac{9\times5}{20\times5}=\frac{45}{100}$ Change to an equivalent fraction.

$\frac{x+43}{100}=\frac{45}{100}$ Read as "What number plus $\frac{43}{100}$ equals $\frac{45}{100}$?"

$\mathbf{\frac{2}{100}}+\frac{43}{100}=\frac{45}{100}$ Use mental math or rewrite it as a simpler problem.

$\frac{2}{100}$, or $\frac{1}{50}$, of your blood is made up of only white blood cells.

Sometimes you need to find equivalent fractions for both fractions.

Example 4

Solve: $\frac{x-5}{6}=\frac{1}{15}$

$\frac{5}{6}=\frac{5\times5}{6\times5}=\frac{25}{30}$ The least common denominator of 6 and 15 is 30.

$\frac{1}{15}=\frac{1\times2}{15\times2}=\frac{2}{30}$ Change to equivalent fractions.

$\frac{x-25}{30}=\frac{2}{30}$ Read as "What number minus $\frac{25}{30}$ equals $\frac{2}{30}$?"

$\mathbf{\frac{27}{30}}-\frac{25}{30}=\frac{2}{30}$ Use mental math or rewrite it as a simpler problem.

$x=\frac{27}{30}$, or $\frac{9}{10}$

Talk About It

1. When solving equations, how can you check to see that the answer is correct?
2. Will multiplying the denominators of any two fractions with unlike denominators together always give you their LCD? Explain.

Check

Solve. Write each answer in lowest terms.

1. $\frac{1}{5}+n=\frac{4}{5}$ **2.** $x-\frac{2}{3}=\frac{5}{6}$ **3.** $b+\frac{1}{10}=\frac{3}{4}$ **4.** $\frac{1}{3}-y=\frac{1}{8}$

5. $z+\frac{2}{9}=\frac{8}{9}$ **6.** $\frac{7}{12}+c=\frac{5}{6}$ **7.** $\frac{4}{50}+f=\frac{12}{25}$ **8.** $\frac{1}{3}-v=\frac{1}{21}$

9. Reasoning How are the x in $\frac{2}{3}-x$ and the x in $\frac{2}{3}-x=\frac{1}{3}$ different?

Practice

Skills and Reasoning

Solve. Write each answer in lowest terms.

10. $\frac{2}{5} + p = \frac{7}{5}$

11. $\frac{3}{7} - k = \frac{1}{7}$

12. $w + \frac{4}{9} = \frac{9}{9}$

13. $r - \frac{9}{10} = \frac{3}{10}$

14. $\frac{1}{3} + j = \frac{5}{6}$

15. $r + \frac{2}{5} = \frac{7}{10}$

16. $t - \frac{4}{5} = \frac{1}{10}$

17. $v - \frac{1}{2} = \frac{3}{8}$

18. $d + \frac{7}{9} = \frac{8}{9}$

19. $\frac{80}{5} - x = 12$

20. $q - \frac{1}{8} = \frac{3}{4}$

21. $4 - b = \frac{3}{7}$

22. $\frac{17}{100} + a = \frac{67}{100}$

23. $\frac{11}{12} - h = \frac{3}{4}$

24. $g + \frac{1}{8} = \frac{1}{6}$

25. $f - \frac{4}{9} = \frac{6}{3}$

26. $e + \frac{5}{28} = \frac{5}{14}$

27. $\frac{15}{22} - z = \frac{1}{2}$

28. $x - \frac{23}{4} = \frac{24}{3}$

29. $3 + y = \frac{10}{3}$

Write a true equation for each set of fractions.

30. $\frac{1}{3}, \frac{2}{3}, 1$

31. $\frac{3}{4}, \frac{1}{2}, \frac{1}{4}$

32. $\frac{5}{6}, \frac{1}{3}, \frac{1}{2}$

33. $\frac{7}{12}, \frac{1}{6}, \frac{5}{12}$

34. $\frac{51}{36}, \frac{5}{6}, \frac{7}{12}$

35. $\frac{14}{18}, \frac{1}{3}, \frac{90}{81}$

36. $\frac{3}{11}, \frac{8}{11}, \frac{5}{11}$

37. $\frac{2}{12}, \frac{13}{15}, \frac{7}{10}$

38. Reasoning Explain the difference in the use of x in $\frac{1}{3} + x = \frac{4}{5}$ and in $\frac{1}{3} + \frac{x}{5} = \frac{4}{5}$.

Write and solve an equation for each situation.

39. Marilyn collected $\frac{3}{4}$ of a pound of seashells. She used some to decorate a picture frame, and she had $\frac{1}{6}$ of a pound left. How many pounds of shells did she use to decorate the frame?

40. Measurement Pam had $\frac{35}{36}$ of a yard of string. After she cut the string once, she had $\frac{1}{2}$ of a yard left. In inches, what was the length of string that Pam cut?

41. Critical Thinking The perimeter of the lid to Janice's rectangular jewelry box is $\frac{10}{4}$ of a yard. If the longer sides are $\frac{3}{4}$ of a yard, how long are the shorter sides? Explain.

42. Write Your Own Problem Write a problem that could be solved with the equation $\frac{7}{10} + y = \frac{26}{20}$. Explain how you created the problem and solve it.

43. Andrea is making tuna salad. She had $\frac{3}{4}$ lb of tuna fish before she made the salad. When she was done, she had $\frac{5}{12}$ lb left. How much tuna did she use in the salad?

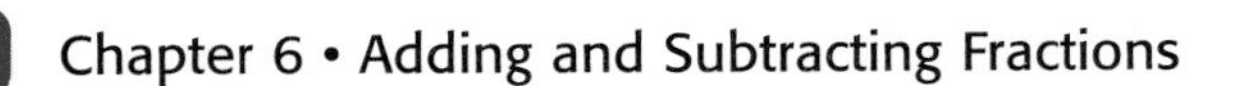

Problem Solving and SCIENCE

The table shows how blood is distributed when the body is at rest.

Organ	Fraction of Blood	Organ	Fraction of Blood
Capillaries	$\frac{1}{20}$	Systemic arteries	$\frac{1}{10}$
Heart	$\frac{1}{10}$	Systemic veins	$\frac{13}{20}$
Lungs	$\frac{1}{10}$		

44. A doctor used the table to calculate the amount of blood in the arteries, veins, and one other organ. The total amount is $\frac{16}{20}$. Which other organ did the doctor use in her calculations?

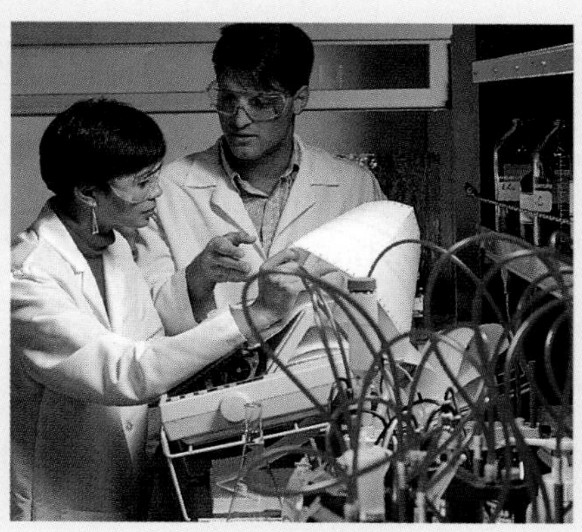

45. About $\frac{11}{20}$ of the blood in your body is made up of plasma, a straw-colored fluid. What fraction of the blood in your body is not made up of plasma?

46. Estimation The typical human body contains 4 to 6 liters of blood. Estimate the weight of one liter of blood, then estimate the fraction of your body mass that is made up of blood.

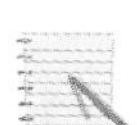

47. Journal Write an equation using unlike denominators that you can solve using mental math. Explain how you would use mental math to solve it.

Mixed Review and Test Prep

Find the area of each parallelogram.

48.

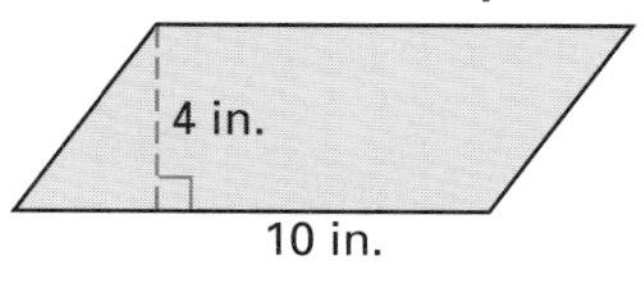

49.

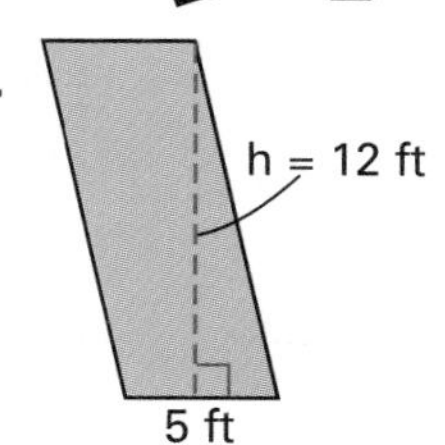

50.

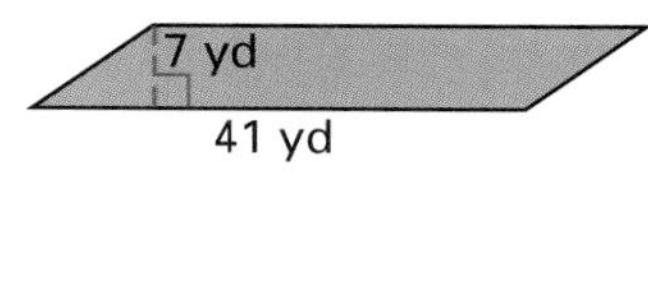

State if the equation is true for the given value of the variable.

51. $x + 17 = 50; x = 43$ **52.** $5j = 60; j = 14$ **53.** $21 - k = 14; k = 7$

54. At the Sierra Road Inn, $\frac{7}{11}$ of the parking lot was full. How much of the parking lot was empty?

Ⓐ $\frac{3}{11}$ Ⓑ $\frac{4}{11}$ Ⓒ $\frac{7}{11}$ Ⓓ $\frac{9}{11}$

Chapter 6

Problem Solving

Analyze Word Problems: Identifying Missing Information

You Will Learn

- how to recognize if information you need to solve the problem is missing

Learn

This table lists the types of blood that each blood type can receive.

Patient Type	Can RECEIVE types...	Patient Type	Can RECEIVE types...
A+	A+, A−, O+, O−	AB+	A+, A−, B+, B−, AB+, AB−, O+, O−
A−	A−, O−	AB−	A−, B−, AB−, O−
B+	B+, B−, O+, O−	O+	O+, O−
B−	B−, O−	O−	O−

What fraction of the population can give blood to a person who has type A− blood?

Work Together

Understand

What question are you being asked to answer?

Plan

What information is given? — The types of blood a person with A− blood can receive

What information do you need to answer the question? — The fractions of the population who have A− or O− blood

Is there any missing information? Where can you find it? — Yes; In the Data File on page 312

Solve

Find the fractions for the population who have A− or O− blood and add them.

A− $\frac{3}{50}$ O− $\frac{7}{100}$

$\frac{3}{50} + \frac{7}{100} = \frac{6}{100} + \frac{7}{100} = \frac{13}{100}$

$\frac{13}{100}$ of the population can give blood to a person with A− blood.

Look Back

Is your answer sensible? — Yes; More people can give to someone who has A− blood than have A− blood.

How did you decide what information was needed to solve the problem?

Check

Solve each problem. If information is missing, write what is needed to solve.

1. What fraction of the population has type O+ or type O– blood?
2. What fraction of the students in your school have type A+ blood?

Problem Solving Practice

- Draw a Picture
- Look for a Pattern
- Guess and Check
- Use Logical Reasoning
- Make an Organized List
- Make a Table
- Solve a Simpler Problem
- Work Backward

Choose a Tool

If possible, solve each problem. If information is missing and you can find it, write where you found it before solving the problem.

3. Determine the fraction of the population from which each patient type can receive blood.
4. If a person can receive a great number of blood types, can that person receive blood from a greater fraction of the population? Explain.
5. In Kelly's school, $\frac{2}{5}$ of the students have O+ blood. How many students have this blood type?
6. A "universal recipient" is a person who can receive blood from anyone, regardless of blood type. What fraction of the population are universal recipients? Explain?
7. A "universal donor" can give blood successfully to all blood types. Use the table on page 332 to decide which blood type is a universal donor. Explain.
8. Look at the charts on page 312 and page 332. Which blood type do you think would have the most trouble finding a donor? Explain.
9. Which two blood types does about $\frac{3}{4}$ of the population have? Explain.

SECTION A

Review and Practice

Vocabulary Copy and complete each sentence with the best term.

1. When you add or subtract fractions with ________________, you add or subtract the numerators and keep the denominators the same.
2. When you add or subtract fractions with ________________, you must first change them to equivalent fractions with the same denominators.
3. When you convert the denominators of two fractions to their least common denominator, the number that results is called the ________________.

(Lessons 1 and 2) Simplify. Write each answer in lowest terms.

4. $\frac{3}{11}+\frac{5}{11}$ **5.** $\frac{3}{5}-\frac{1}{5}$ **6.** $\frac{1}{8}+\frac{3}{8}$ **7.** $\frac{9}{10}-\frac{6}{10}$

8. $\frac{7}{9}+\frac{5}{9}$ **9.** $\frac{1}{2}+\frac{4}{2}$ **10.** $\frac{7}{16}-\frac{3}{16}$ **11.** $\frac{14}{15}-\frac{4}{15}$

12. $\frac{3}{4}+\frac{3}{5}$ **13.** $\frac{5}{8}+\frac{2}{5}$ **14.** $\frac{1}{4}+\frac{1}{6}$ **15.** $\frac{4}{5}-\frac{1}{4}$

16. Newspaper ads are available in sizes that are a fraction of a page: $\frac{1}{8}$, $\frac{1}{4}$, $\frac{1}{2}$, and $\frac{3}{4}$. Find a combination of ads that will take up a whole page. Explain your reasoning.

BLOOD DRIVE!
PLEASE GIVE!
Our local hospitals and blood banks need your donations. Come to the Spruce Street School on Saturday from 10am to 3pm.

(Lesson 3) Solve. Write each answer in lowest terms.

17. $\frac{5}{9}-x=\frac{11}{36}$ **18.** $j+\frac{1}{3}=\frac{7}{12}$ **19.** $\frac{7}{10}+w=\frac{9}{10}$ **20.** $t-\frac{1}{2}=\frac{1}{4}$

21. $y+\frac{1}{10}=\frac{4}{5}$ **22.** $\frac{3}{4}-z=\frac{1}{12}$ **23.** $r-\frac{1}{3}=\frac{4}{15}$ **24.** $\frac{5}{6}+p=\frac{29}{24}$

25. When counting the amount of blood at the hospital blood bank, Christine determined that about $\frac{2}{5}$ of the blood was type O and about $\frac{1}{4}$ of the blood was type A. What fraction of the blood is neither type O nor type A?

Skills Checklist

In this section, you have:

- **Learned How to Add and Subtract Fractions with Like Denominators**
- **Learned How to Add and Subtract Fractions with Unlike Denominators**
- **Solved Fraction Equations**

26. Journal Explain the difference in the use of y in $\frac{1}{y}+\frac{2}{3}=\frac{17}{21}$ and in $\frac{1}{7}+\frac{2}{3}=y$.

REVIEW AND PRACTICE

Adding and Subtracting Mixed Numbers

Floods are one of the most powerful forces of nature. They can cause great damage. How do you think mixed numbers can be used to help predict when floods might occur and to help people prepare for them?

Adding and Subtracting Mixed Numbers

Review comparing and ordering fractions. Order each set of fractions from least to greatest.

1. $\frac{2}{9}, \frac{1}{3}, \frac{4}{5}, \frac{3}{4}$
2. $\frac{8}{9}, \frac{1}{4}, \frac{5}{7}, \frac{3}{6}$
3. $\frac{2}{5}, \frac{2}{3}, \frac{3}{5}, \frac{1}{2}$
4. $\frac{5}{8}, \frac{5}{10}, \frac{7}{10}, \frac{4}{7}$
5. $\frac{7}{12}, \frac{1}{9}, \frac{2}{3}, \frac{4}{8}$
6. $\frac{6}{7}, \frac{3}{6}, \frac{8}{9}, \frac{3}{4}$

Skills Checklist

In this section, you will:

- ❒ Estimate the Sums and Differences of Mixed Numbers
- ❒ Explore Adding Mixed Numbers
- ❒ Explore Subtracting Mixed Numbers

Chapter 6
Lesson
4

Estimation: Sums and Differences of Mixed Numbers

You Will Learn
- to estimate sums and differences of mixed numbers

Learn

Just as rounding can be used to estimate sums and differences of whole numbers and fractions, it can also be used to estimate sums and differences of mixed numbers.

Recall that a *mixed number* contains a whole number and a fraction. You can estimate sums and differences of mixed numbers by rounding each number to the nearest whole number.

Math Tip
A fraction is less than $\frac{1}{2}$ if the numerator is less than half of the denominator.

To round a mixed number, look at the fractional part of the mixed number.

Drop the fraction and leave the whole number unchanged if the fractional part is less than $\frac{1}{2}$. $2\frac{1}{3} \rightarrow 2$

Round to the next whole number if the fractional part is $\frac{1}{2}$ or greater. $2\frac{2}{3} \rightarrow 3$

One way to round mixed numbers is to draw and use a number line.

Example 1

In 1974, the Mississippi River near New Orleans measured $8\frac{9}{10}$ feet above its normal level. To the nearest foot, how far above its normal level was the river?

Draw a number line that shows the whole number less than $8\frac{9}{10}$, the whole number greater than $8\frac{9}{10}$, and the mixed number itself.

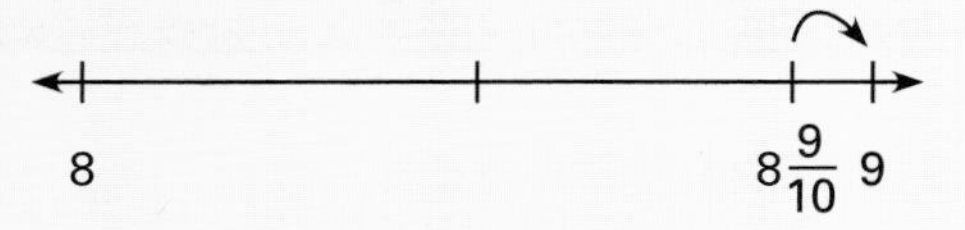

Since $8\frac{9}{10}$ is greater than $8\frac{1}{2}$, and it is nearer to 9 than it is to 8, the mixed number $8\frac{9}{10}$ rounds to 9.

To the nearest foot, the river was 9 feet above its normal level.

You can also round mixed numbers by comparing the numerator of the fractional part to its denominator.

Example 2

The mean annual rainfall amount in Lagos, Nigeria is $72\frac{3}{8}$ in. Round this to the nearest inch.

The numerator of the fraction, 3, is less than half the denominator, 8. Therefore, $\frac{3}{8} < \frac{1}{2}$.

$72\frac{3}{8}$ rounds to 72.

Example 3

The mean annual rainfall amount in Athens, Greece is $17\frac{13}{16}$ in. Round this to the nearest inch.

The numerator of the fraction, 13, is more than half the denominator, 16. Therefore, $\frac{13}{16} > \frac{1}{2}$.

$17\frac{13}{16}$ rounds to 18.

In order to estimate sums and differences of mixed numbers, round each mixed number to the nearest whole number and find the sum or difference of the numbers.

Example 4

Estimate: $4\frac{1}{3} + 6\frac{3}{4}$

Round: $4\frac{1}{3} \rightarrow 4$

$6\frac{3}{4} \rightarrow 7$

Estimate: $4 + 7 = 11$

Example 5

Estimate: $9\frac{1}{2} - 4\frac{7}{10}$

Round: $9\frac{1}{2} \rightarrow 10$

$4\frac{7}{10} \rightarrow 5$

Estimate: $10 - 5 = 5$

Talk About It

1. How is rounding mixed numbers like rounding fractions?
2. Describe methods you can use to tell if a fraction is greater than, equal to, or less than $\frac{1}{2}$.

Check

Round to the nearest whole number.

1. $6\frac{2}{7}$
2. $1\frac{1}{2}$
3. $3\frac{5}{8}$
4. $2\frac{7}{16}$
5. $4\frac{9}{11}$
6. Estimate the sum of $3\frac{1}{2}$ and $11\frac{7}{8}$.
7. Estimate the difference between $8\frac{2}{3}$ and $1\frac{4}{9}$.
8. Estimate the sum of $9\frac{5}{6}$ and $10\frac{1}{10}$.
9. Estimate the difference between $5\frac{9}{16}$ and $2\frac{7}{8}$.
10. **Reasoning** Describe a situation where it might be a good idea to round a mixed number up to the next whole number, even if the number would normally be rounded down.

Practice

Skills and Reasoning

Round to the nearest whole number.

11. $4\frac{3}{8}$ **12.** $3\frac{1}{9}$ **13.** $4\frac{7}{10}$ **14.** $12\frac{1}{5}$ **15.** $25\frac{3}{5}$

16. $1\frac{6}{12}$ **17.** $33\frac{4}{8}$ **18.** $11\frac{7}{9}$ **19.** $8\frac{4}{9}$ **20.** $65\frac{5}{10}$

21. $6\frac{2}{3}$ **22.** $5\frac{1}{5}$ **23.** $2\frac{2}{7}$ **24.** $7\frac{12}{96}$ **25.** $18\frac{34}{101}$

Estimate.

26. $10\frac{11}{20} - 3\frac{6}{25}$ **27.** $1\frac{2}{9} + 8\frac{1}{4}$ **28.** $7\frac{5}{6} - 5\frac{12}{13}$ **29.** $4\frac{3}{7} + 3\frac{2}{5}$

30. $4\frac{1}{3} + 7\frac{3}{4} + 2\frac{8}{9}$ **31.** $11\frac{5}{8} - 4\frac{1}{6}$ **32.** $3\frac{1}{9} + 4\frac{1}{8} + 7\frac{1}{5}$ **33.** $7\frac{5}{8} - 2\frac{4}{5}$

34. $9\frac{1}{9} - 3\frac{1}{3}$ **35.** $12\frac{1}{2} + 7\frac{3}{7} + 5\frac{5}{8}$ **36.** $8\frac{7}{10} - 1\frac{1}{2}$ **37.** $3\frac{2}{5} + 12\frac{1}{6}$

38. $10\frac{3}{5} + 5\frac{2}{3}$ **39.** $22\frac{5}{12} - 2\frac{3}{5}$ **40.** $13\frac{1}{10} + 8\frac{1}{8}$ **41.** $\frac{1}{10} + 7\frac{2}{13}$

42. Dimitri lives near the Colorado River. He should evacuate his home when the river reaches 28 feet. The river is now at $21\frac{7}{10}$ feet and is predicted to rise another $6\frac{1}{2}$ feet this evening. Will Dimitri need to evacuate?

43. At noon, the Colorado River measured a depth of 26 feet. By midnight, the river had fallen by $5\frac{3}{8}$ feet. About how deep was the river at midnight?

44. Mental Math Estimate the mean of $5\frac{11}{12}$, $6\frac{1}{10}$, $6\frac{2}{15}$, and $5\frac{7}{8}$.

45. Reasoning Suppose the fuel gauge of an automobile you were riding in showed the gasoline tank to be $\frac{1}{4}$ full. Is the tank closer to full or closer to empty? When should you stop to purchase more gasoline?

Problem Solving and Applications

46. Patterns The numbers in this set form a pattern. What mixed number is the next term in the set? $0, \frac{5}{8}, 1\frac{1}{4}, 1\frac{7}{8}, 2\frac{1}{2}, 3\frac{1}{8}, 3\frac{3}{4}, ?$

47. Estimation In the equation $7\frac{1}{4} + x = 10\frac{1}{5}$, estimate the value of x. Explain what you did.

48. Critical Thinking Compare rounding mixed numbers by rounding to the nearest whole number with rounding mixed numbers by always rounding up. Which is easier? Which is more accurate? Explain.

49. Critical Thinking At the county fair, Brian entered his frog Horton in the frog jumping contest. Horton's first jump was $10\frac{7}{8}$ feet. His second was $11\frac{1}{5}$ feet, and his third was $9\frac{4}{5}$ feet. Estimate the average length of Horton's jumps. Explain.

Using Data Use the Data File on page 313 to answer **50** and **51.**

50. Which city has the greatest average rise and fall of tides? Which city has the least? Estimate the sum and difference of the tides in these cities.

51. A difference of about 12 ft exists between the average tides in which two cities?

52. Journal Describe how you would estimate the median of $5\frac{3}{4}, 5\frac{1}{3}, 3\frac{1}{4}, 1\frac{7}{8}, 6\frac{1}{10}, 1\frac{1}{5}, 7\frac{1}{9}$, and $3\frac{8}{9}$.

Mixed Review and Test Prep

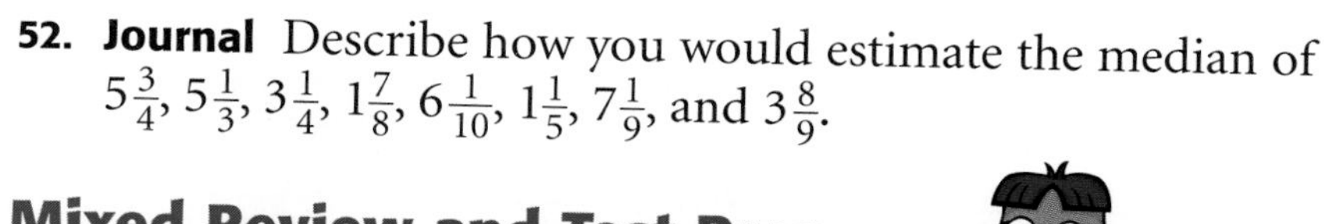

Find the area of each figure.

53.

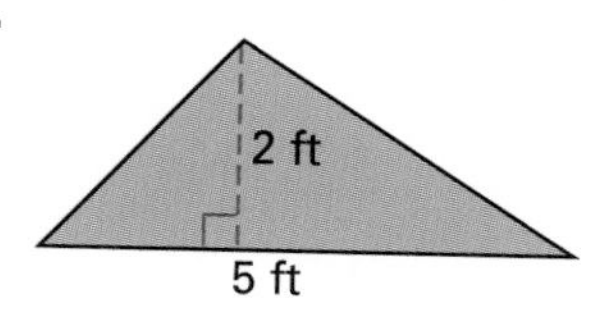

54.

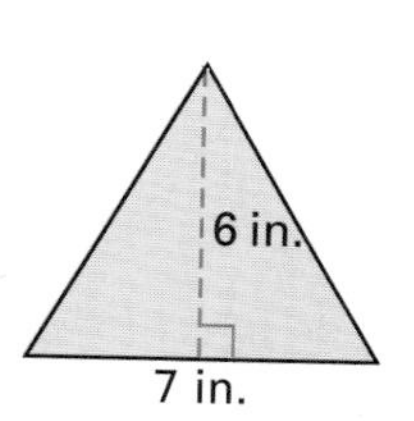

55.

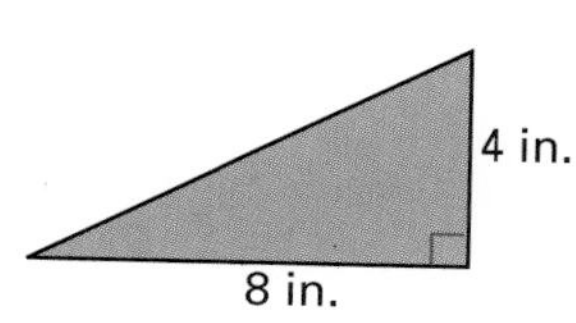

Solve.

56. $m + 22 = 43$ **57.** $n - 11 = 10$ **58.** $15 + v = 27$ **59.** $44 - x = 12$

60. $12b = 36$ **61.** $\frac{x}{2} = 4$ **62.** $3c = 15$ **63.** $\frac{e}{11} = 2$

64. $5z = 35$ **65.** $j + 7 = 13$ **66.** $14 - f = 10$ **67.** $\frac{40}{x} = 8$

68. To change 16 quarts into gallons, you should

Ⓐ multiply by 2. Ⓑ multiply by 4. Ⓒ divide by 2. Ⓓ divide by 4.

Chapter 6
Lesson
5

Adding Mixed Numbers

Problem Solving Connection
- Use Logical Reasoning

Materials
Fraction Bars®

Explore

Just as you can find exact sums of fractions with like and unlike denominators, you also can find exact sums of mixed numbers. You can use fraction bars to help you add mixed numbers.

Work Together

Find the sum of $1\frac{3}{4}$ and $1\frac{1}{2}$.

1. Use fraction bars to model the whole number for the first mixed number.
2. Next to that, use fraction bars to model the fraction for the first mixed number.
3. Next to that, use fraction bars to model the whole number for the second mixed number.
4. Next to that, use fraction bars to model the fraction for the second mixed number.
5. Using a whole number and a fraction less than 1, describe the model.
   $1\frac{3}{4} + 1\frac{1}{2} = 3\frac{1}{4}$

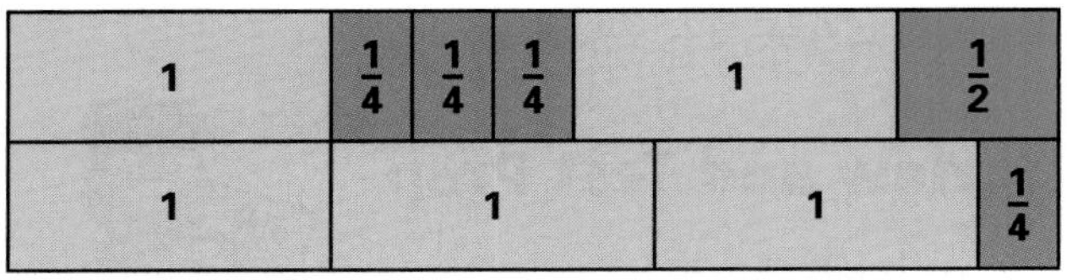

1	$\frac{1}{4}$	$\frac{1}{4}$	$\frac{1}{4}$	1	$\frac{1}{2}$
1	1			1	$\frac{1}{4}$

6. Use fraction bars to find each sum.

   a. $1\frac{1}{4} + 2\frac{1}{2}$ **b.** $1\frac{2}{3} + 1\frac{3}{6}$ **c.** $1\frac{3}{8} + 2\frac{1}{8}$ **d.** $1\frac{3}{6} + 2\frac{1}{2}$

   e. $2\frac{1}{3} + 1\frac{5}{6}$ **f.** $1\frac{1}{2} + 1\frac{1}{4}$ **g.** $2\frac{5}{6} + 1\frac{1}{6}$ **h.** $1\frac{1}{8} + 2\frac{5}{8}$

Talk About It

7. Does the whole number in the answer always equal the sum of the two whole numbers in the problem? Tell why or why not.
8. Is the sum of two mixed numbers always a mixed number? Tell why or why not.
9. How is adding mixed numbers like adding fractions?
   How is it different?

Connect and Learn

To add mixed numbers: $5\frac{2}{3} + 1\frac{1}{4}$

1. Add the whole numbers. $5 + 1 = 6$
2. Add the fractions. $\frac{2}{3} + \frac{1}{4} = \frac{8+3}{12} = \frac{11}{12}$
3. Put the two parts together. $= 6\frac{11}{12}$

Remember to estimate each time you add mixed numbers.

Example 1

Add: $1\frac{1}{3} + 2\frac{1}{2}$

$1\frac{1}{3} = 1\frac{2}{6}$ $2\frac{1}{2} = 2\frac{3}{6}$ Rewrite the fractions using the LCD of 6.

$1 + 2 = 3$ $\frac{2}{6} + \frac{3}{6} = \frac{5}{6}$ Add whole numbers and add fractions.

$3\frac{5}{6}$

Estimate: $1 + 3 = 4$. $3\frac{5}{6}$ is close to 4. The answer is reasonable.

If the sum of the fractions is an improper fraction, you may need to rewrite it as a mixed number, and add the whole number parts together.

Example 2

During the 1993 flood, the Mississippi River rose to $27\frac{9}{10}$ feet. Then it rose another $3\frac{3}{5}$ feet. Find the river's final height.

$27\frac{9}{10} = 27\frac{9}{10}$ $3\frac{3}{5} = 3\frac{6}{10}$ Rewrite the fractions using the LCD of 10.

$27 + 3 = 30$ $\frac{9}{10} + \frac{6}{10} = \frac{15}{10}$ Add whole numbers and add fractions.

$30\frac{15}{10} = 31\frac{5}{10}$ Rewrite the improper fraction as a mixed number.

$31\frac{5}{10} = 31\frac{1}{2}$ Add and write in lowest terms.

The final height was $31\frac{1}{2}$ feet. Estimate: $28 + 4 = 32$. The answer is reasonable.

Check

Add. Write each answer as a whole or mixed number in lowest terms.

1. $6 + 2\frac{3}{4}$
2. $1\frac{1}{2} + 3\frac{1}{4}$
3. $3\frac{7}{8} + 2\frac{5}{8}$
4. $4\frac{7}{12} + 2\frac{5}{6}$
5. **Reasoning** When adding the fractional parts of mixed numbers, why do you sometimes need to rewrite the fraction sum?

Practice

Add. Write each answer as a whole or mixed number in lowest terms.

6. $6 + 5\frac{2}{3}$ **7.** $8 + 7\frac{3}{8}$ **8.** $4\frac{1}{2} + 2$ **9.** $3\frac{6}{7} + 9$

10. $5\frac{1}{3} + 4\frac{2}{6}$ **11.** $6\frac{1}{2} + 2\frac{5}{6}$ **12.** $35 + 27\frac{3}{4}$ **13.** $47\frac{1}{2} + 49\frac{3}{7}$

14. $8\frac{2}{4} + 2\frac{1}{2}$ **15.** $12\frac{3}{5} + 3\frac{4}{5}$ **16.** $1\frac{7}{8} + 3\frac{5}{6}$ **17.** $9\frac{3}{7} + 1\frac{2}{7}$

18. $1\frac{3}{5} + 5\frac{1}{5}$ **19.** $3\frac{4}{5} + 15$ **20.** $8\frac{2}{9} + 7\frac{2}{3}$ **21.** $22\frac{3}{4} + 19\frac{2}{5}$

22. $7\frac{4}{9} + 5\frac{2}{3}$ **23.** $45\frac{3}{4} + 21\frac{7}{8}$ **24.** $1\frac{3}{10} + 12\frac{4}{5}$ **25.** $2\frac{4}{5} + 3\frac{1}{2}$

26. $9\frac{3}{7} + 12\frac{1}{3}$ **27.** $12\frac{2}{3} + 7\frac{5}{8}$ **28.** $3\frac{3}{8} + 4\frac{5}{8}$ **29.** $8\frac{2}{3} + 8\frac{3}{4}$

30. $9\frac{7}{9} + 32$ **31.** $7\frac{1}{3} + 2\frac{2}{3}$ **32.** $42\frac{1}{6} + 9\frac{11}{12}$ **33.** $93\frac{1}{12} + 7$

34. Careers The U.S. Geological Survey measured the depth of a Rio Grande River channel during flooding. The difference between the highest and lowest depths was $9\frac{3}{4}$ feet. If the lowest reading was $28\frac{1}{2}$ feet, what was the highest reading?

35. Reasoning What estimate would you make when adding $3\frac{5}{12}$ and $10\frac{7}{12}$? Explain.

36. Reasoning Explain how you could estimate the sum $5\frac{15}{32} + 5\frac{7}{16}$ using only whole numbers.

Problem Solving and Applications

37. Describe a situation where you use addition and would want to write $7\frac{5}{3}$ as $8\frac{2}{3}$.

38. **Choose a Strategy** The combined area of Shapes A and B is $4\frac{2}{3}$ m². The area of Shape B is $1\frac{1}{3}$ m² more than the area of shape A. Find the areas of both shapes.

39. **Logic** Explain how you could use a calculator to add mixed numbers.

40. **Choose a Strategy** Mario walks each day for exercise. These facts describe his walk yesterday. How many miles altogether did Mario walk? How far from home was he at the end of his walk?

Began at home and walked $2\frac{1}{8}$ miles north.

Turned and walked $1\frac{1}{2}$ miles west.

Turned and walked $1\frac{3}{4}$ miles south.

Turned and walked $1\frac{1}{2}$ miles east.

Turned and walked $\frac{3}{8}$ miles south.

41. **Journal** Describe some similarities and differences between adding whole numbers and adding mixed numbers.

Mixed Review and Test Prep

42. Find the circumference of each object.

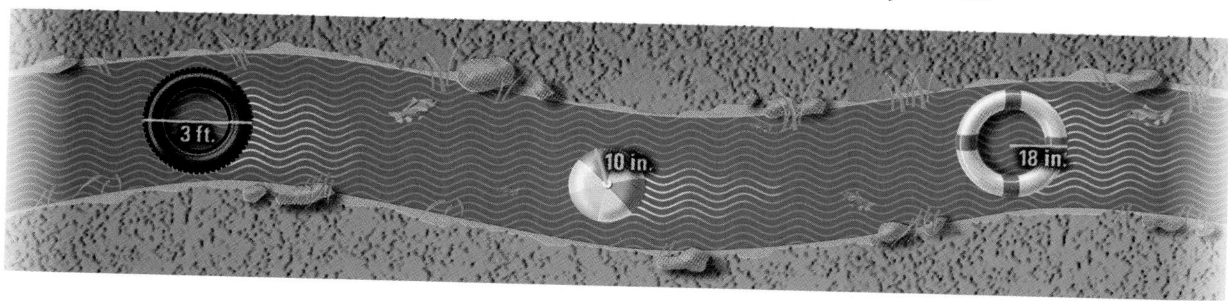

Write in standard form.

43. 3.1×10^3 **44.** 4.27×10^5 **45.** 5.45×10^7 **46.** 1.124×10^6

47. Samantha ran her part of a 1,600-meter relay in 1.5 minutes. Juana ran in 1.34 minutes, Anna in 1.4 minutes, and Adrienne in 1.25 minutes. How long did it take their team to run the race?

Ⓐ 4.49 min Ⓑ 5.49 min Ⓒ 5.55 min Ⓓ 6 min

Chapter 6 Lesson 6

Subtracting Mixed Numbers

Problem Solving Connection

- Use Logical Reasoning

Materials

Fraction Bars®

Explore

Subtracting mixed numbers is similar to adding mixed numbers. You've seen that regrouping may be necessary when you add mixed numbers. You may also need to regroup when you subtract mixed numbers.

Work Together

Find $2\frac{1}{4} - 1\frac{1}{2}$.

1. Model the whole number for the first mixed number.
2. Next to that, model the fraction for the first mixed number.
3. Below the first whole number, model the whole number for the second mixed number.
4. Next to that, model the fraction for the second mixed number.
5. Next to the second mixed number, model the difference between the first and second model. What does this represent?
6. Use fraction bars to find each difference.

1	1	$\frac{1}{4}$		
1	$\frac{1}{2}$	$\frac{1}{4}$	$\frac{1}{4}$	$\frac{1}{4}$

$2\frac{1}{4} - 1\frac{1}{2} = \frac{3}{4}$

a. $2\frac{3}{4} - 1\frac{1}{4}$ **b.** $3\frac{2}{3} - 1\frac{1}{6}$ **c.** $2 - \frac{3}{4}$

d. $4\frac{1}{4} - 1\frac{1}{2}$ **e.** $4\frac{3}{8} - 3\frac{3}{4}$ **f.** $5\frac{3}{4} - 3\frac{5}{8}$

Talk About It

7. Can you subtract two mixed numbers if the fraction in the second mixed number is greater than the fraction in the first mixed number? If you can, tell how.
8. If one mixed number is subtracted from another mixed number, is the difference always a mixed number? Explain. Use an example in your explanation.

Connect and Learn

When subtracting whole numbers, sometimes a digit in the second number is greater than the digit in the same place in the first number. To subtract, you need to regroup the first number.

$$\begin{array}{r} \overset{6}{\cancel{7}}\overset{12}{\cancel{2}} \\ -18 \\ \hline 54 \end{array}$$

You can use a similar process to subtract two mixed numbers.

1. Remove 1 from the whole number.	$9\frac{1}{5} - 4\frac{4}{5}$	$7 - 2\frac{1}{3}$
	$8\frac{1}{5} + 1$	$6 + 1$
2. Rename the 1 as a fraction with the same numerator and denominator.	$8\frac{1}{5} + \frac{5}{5}$	$6 + \frac{3}{3}$
3. Rewrite the mixed number in its new form. Subtract.	$8\frac{6}{5} - 4\frac{4}{5} = 4\frac{2}{5}$	$6\frac{3}{3} - 2\frac{1}{3} = 4\frac{2}{3}$

Example 1

Find $7\frac{2}{9} - 3\frac{2}{3}$.

$7\frac{2}{9} = 6\frac{2}{9} + 1 = 6\frac{2}{9} + \frac{9}{9} = 6\frac{11}{9}$ Remove 1 from the whole number.

$3\frac{2}{3} = 3\frac{6}{9}$ Rename the second fraction with a common denominator.

$6\frac{11}{9} - 3\frac{6}{9} = 3\frac{5}{9}$ Subtract.

You can also use this process when subtracting a mixed number from a fraction.

Example 2

Find $3 - 1\frac{5}{12}$.

$3 \rightarrow 2\frac{12}{12}$ Regroup 3 as $2\frac{12}{12}$.

$2\frac{12}{12} - 1\frac{5}{12} = 1\frac{7}{12}$ Subtract.

Check

Subtract. Write each as a whole or mixed number in lowest terms.

1. $6\frac{1}{5} - 2\frac{4}{5}$ **2.** $8\frac{1}{2} - 3\frac{2}{3}$ **3.** $12 - 9\frac{5}{9}$ **4.** $5\frac{1}{4} - 3\frac{3}{4}$

5. Reasoning In a subtraction problem, when might you need to convert a whole number into a mixed number?

Practice

Skills and Reasoning

Subtract. Write each answer as a whole or mixed number in lowest terms.

6. $6\frac{3}{4} - 4$ **7.** $7\frac{7}{8} - 2$ **8.** $12\frac{1}{2} - 10$ **9.** $3\frac{4}{5} - 2$

10. $7\frac{1}{2} - 6\frac{1}{4}$ **11.** $7\frac{2}{9} - 6\frac{1}{3}$ **12.** $2\frac{1}{4} - 1\frac{3}{4}$ **13.** $9\frac{1}{6} - 4\frac{2}{3}$

14. $1\frac{1}{3} - \frac{2}{3}$ **15.** $4\frac{5}{6} - 2\frac{1}{6}$ **16.** $2\frac{1}{6} - 1\frac{1}{8}$ **17.** $5\frac{1}{5} - 3\frac{2}{3}$

18. $9\frac{7}{8} - 1\frac{6}{8}$ **19.** $4\frac{1}{3} - 3\frac{1}{4}$ **20.** $7\frac{3}{5} - 4\frac{2}{5}$ **21.** $10\frac{7}{10} - 4\frac{4}{5}$

22. $6\frac{3}{4} - 2\frac{1}{5}$ **23.** $3\frac{2}{3} - \frac{2}{3}$ **24.** $1\frac{1}{4} - \frac{1}{2}$ **25.** $2\frac{1}{6} - 1\frac{1}{2}$

26. $6\frac{4}{5} - 3\frac{1}{5}$ **27.** $7\frac{1}{2} - 1\frac{3}{4}$ **28.** $8\frac{5}{7} - 2\frac{1}{4}$ **29.** $4\frac{1}{8} - 1\frac{5}{9}$

Problem Solving and Applications

30. Helen and Joe expected the stream near their house to rise to 9 feet when the snow melted. It only rose to $7\frac{4}{5}$ feet. By how much was their prediction off?

31. A large financial institution trading on the New York Stock Exchange listed its highest selling price in the last year at $80\frac{3}{8}$ points. The difference between its highest and lowest prices was $26\frac{1}{2}$ points. Write and solve an equation to find the lowest selling price.

32. **Critical Thinking** $5\frac{x}{11} - 2\frac{y}{11}$ equals a whole number. List three possible values for x and y. Explain.

33. **Reasoning** Why is it helpful to compare an exact answer with an estimate?

Problem Solving and RECREATION

The circle graph shows the number of hours Kente spends playing sports. Use the graph for **34** and **35.**

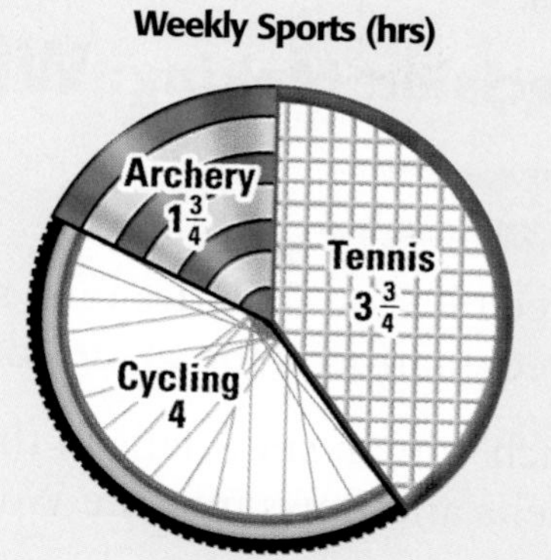

34. How many more hours did Kente spend cycling than practicing archery?

35. Kente predicted that he would play tennis for 7 hours during the week. By how much was his prediction off?

36. Wahn has a box of macaroni and cheese that contains 6 servings. He plans to eat $1\frac{1}{3}$ servings. How many servings will be left?

37. Critical Thinking If you change one of the digits in $3\frac{1}{4} + 2\frac{5}{8}$ to a 9, and you want to get the smallest possible answer, which digit should you change?

38. Measure the length of your desk and your textbook to the nearest $\frac{1}{4}$ of an inch. Which is longer? By how much?

39. Patterns Write the next three numbers in the pattern. Then tell what rule was used to make the pattern. $13\frac{1}{8}, 11\frac{3}{4}, 10\frac{3}{8}, \ldots$

40. Journal Describe some similarities and differences between subtracting with whole numbers and subtracting with mixed numbers.

Mixed Review and Test Prep

STAY SHARP!

Find the area of each shape.

41.

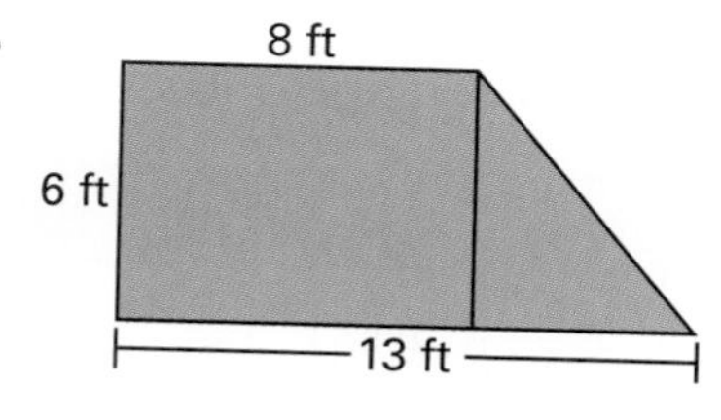

42.

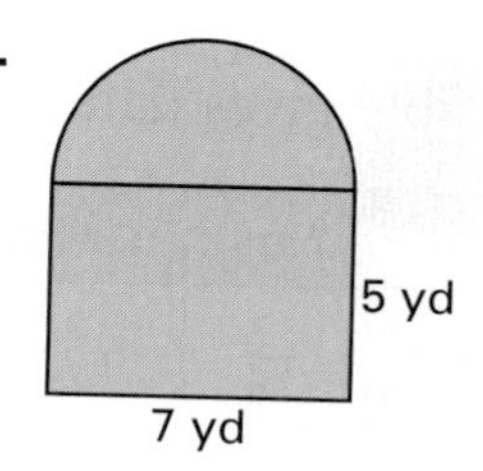

43.

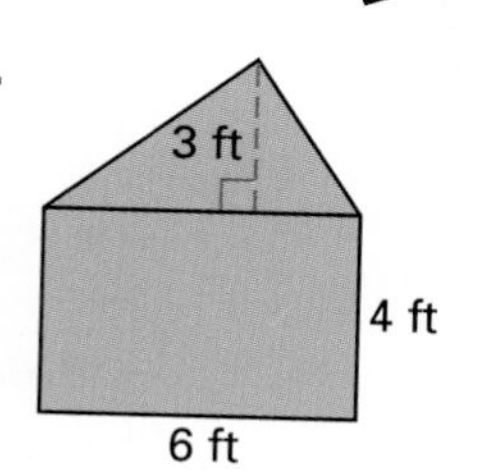

Write each number in scientific notation.

44. 340,000 **45.** 47,500 **46.** 5,000,000 **47.** 4,000 **48.** 6,200,000

49. What is the sum of $1\frac{1}{6}$ and $4\frac{3}{8}$?

Ⓐ $5\frac{4}{14}$ Ⓑ $3\frac{7}{10}$ Ⓒ $5\frac{13}{24}$ Ⓓ $4\frac{13}{24}$

Chapter 6

Problem Solving

Decision Making: Will the River Flood?

You Will Learn

- to use information to make a prediction

Explore

Precipitation includes rain, snow, sleet, or hail. If the amount of precipitation is too great, some areas of the earth experience flooding.

Each winter, snow falls in the Sunset Mountains. Each spring, the snow melts and flows into the Wolverine River. The Wolverine River will flood in July if *both* of the following conditions are met:

a. The total amount of precipitation during December, January, February, and March is greater than 30 inches.

b. The number of days during April, May, and June in which the air temperature exceeds 90°F must be greater than $11\frac{1}{2}$.

The following table gives data for November 1994 to June 1995.

	Nov	Dec	Jan	Feb	Mar	Apr	May	Jun
Precipitation (in.)	$3\frac{3}{4}$	$6\frac{1}{2}$	$8\frac{3}{4}$	$9\frac{5}{6}$	$6\frac{2}{3}$	$1\frac{1}{2}$	$1\frac{5}{12}$	$\frac{5}{58}$
Days over 90°F	0	0	0	0	$1\frac{3}{5}$	$2\frac{4}{5}$	$3\frac{3}{10}$	$4\frac{1}{2}$

Based on this data, should the town begin flood preparations for the month of July?

Work Together

▶ **Understand**

1. What decision are you being asked to make?
2. What information will you use in making a decision?

▶ **Plan and Solve**

3. What conditions need to be met in order for the river to flood?
4. What computations will you perform to help you make your decision?
5. How might estimation help you make your decision?
6. Find the amount of precipitation from December through March.
7. Find the number of days over 90°F from April through June.

▶ **Make a Decision**

8. Do your computations indicate that the river will flood in July?
9. Will it be necessary to begin flood preparations for July? Explain.

▶ **Present Your Decision**

10. Write a summary describing your decision, and on what information your decision was based.
11. Name another factor, aside from temperature and precipitation, that can contribute to flooding.

SECTION B

Review and Practice

(Lesson 4) Round each mixed number to the nearest whole number.

1. $2\frac{1}{3}$ **2.** $11\frac{5}{7}$ **3.** $14\frac{1}{2}$ **4.** $5\frac{2}{5}$ **5.** $7\frac{3}{9}$

Estimate each sum or difference.

6. $4\frac{1}{2} + 1\frac{1}{3}$ **7.** $2\frac{3}{5} + 2\frac{1}{5}$ **8.** $7\frac{2}{3} - 5\frac{3}{7}$ **9.** $16\frac{5}{9} - 5\frac{1}{5}$

10. Steve plans to do chores for $1\frac{1}{2}$ hours, do homework for $2\frac{1}{4}$ hours, and play baseball for $2\frac{3}{4}$ hours. Estimate the amount of time this will take.

11. Carmelo spent his summer learning how to kayak on the Hudson River in New York City. He kept a log of how many hours he spent on the river every time he kayaked. In one week he kayaked $4\frac{1}{2}$ hours and $5\frac{1}{8}$ hours. Estimate how much time he spent kayaking that week.

(Lessons 5 and 6) Simplify. Write each answer in lowest terms.

12. $4\frac{1}{4} - 2\frac{3}{5}$ **13.** $15 + 7\frac{4}{7}$ **14.** $2\frac{7}{9} - 1\frac{2}{5}$ **15.** $12\frac{7}{8} - 8\frac{3}{8}$

16. $6\frac{1}{3} - 2\frac{7}{9}$ **17.** $3\frac{9}{11} + 2\frac{6}{11}$ **18.** $33\frac{1}{3} + 78\frac{1}{8}$ **19.** $1\frac{4}{5} - \frac{1}{8}$

20. $2\frac{1}{3} + 3\frac{5}{3}$ **21.** $6\frac{5}{6} - 4\frac{2}{3}$ **22.** $20 - 3\frac{1}{2}$ **23.** $11\frac{7}{8} - 8\frac{5}{8}$

24. $2\frac{4}{18} - 2\frac{3}{18}$ **25.** $3\frac{4}{5} + 10\frac{1}{2}$ **26.** $6\frac{3}{4} - 3\frac{1}{2}$ **27.** $1\frac{5}{8} + 2\frac{7}{24}$

28. During the 1973 Mississippi River flood, the Fifth Army Corps of Engineers used a number of vehicles to help with the disaster. $\frac{5}{7}$ were jeeps. $\frac{5}{21}$ were tank trucks. What fraction were neither jeeps nor tank trucks?

29. Rob and Thomas Lin and Helena and Sara Seleca spent an afternoon painting a house. Rob used $3\frac{1}{3}$ gallons of paint. Sara used $4\frac{1}{4}$. Thomas used $5\frac{3}{5}$. Helena used $4\frac{4}{5}$. Did the Lins or the Selecas use more paint? How much more?

30. Robyn ran $2\frac{2}{3}$ miles in the morning and $3\frac{1}{4}$ miles after school. How many miles did she run altogether?

31. **Journal** When might you want to convert a whole number into a mixed number in a subtraction problem?

Skills Checklist

In this section, you have:

- ☑ **Estimated the Sums and Differences of Mixed Numbers**
- ☑ **Explored Adding Mixed Numbers**
- ☑ **Explored Subtracting Mixed Numbers**

Choose at least one of the following. Use what you have learned in this chapter.

1 Braille Basics

Braille is a system of raised dots of smaller and larger sizes which enable the visually impaired to "read" with their fingers. Use the chart to find the equivalent of the Braille numbers. Subtract the fractions and write your answer in lowest terms.

1 2 3 4 5 6 7 8 9 0

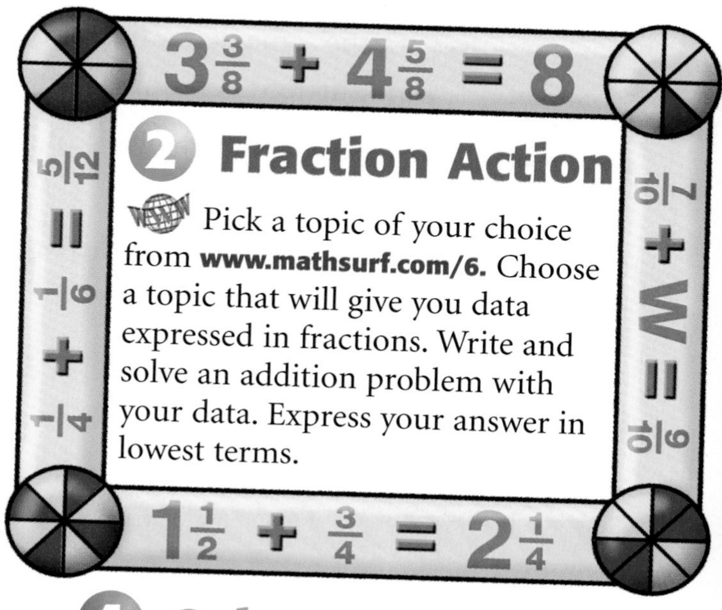

2 Fraction Action

Pick a topic of your choice from **www.mathsurf.com/6.** Choose a topic that will give you data expressed in fractions. Write and solve an addition problem with your data. Express your answer in lowest terms.

3 Dollar Dimensions

All money printed in the United States measures $6\frac{1}{8}$ inches wide and $2\frac{5}{8}$ inches long. Use paper money to estimate the length and width of your desk. What is the perimeter of the desk? Check your estimate with a ruler.

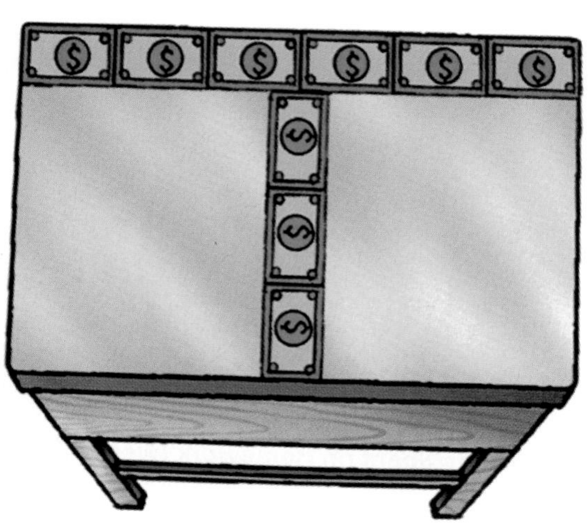

4 Color My World

At Home Ask at least 20 friends, family members, or members of your community to name their favorite color. What fraction of those surveyed chose red or blue as their favorite color? Record your data in a circle graph and share it with the people you surveyed.

CHAPTER 6

Review/Test

Vocabulary For **1–3**, match each description with a vocabulary word.

1. The least multiple two denominators have in common
2. Fractions with the same denominators have
3. Fractions with different denominators have

a. least common denominator
b. like denominators
c. mixed number
d. unlike denominators

(Lesson 2) Find the least common multiple of each number pair.

4. 5, 6
5. 12, 15
6. 5, 20
7. 30, 35

(Lessons 1 and 2) Add or subtract. Write each answer in lowest terms.

8. $\frac{8}{9}-\frac{2}{9}$
9. $\frac{4}{17}+\frac{7}{17}$
10. $\frac{6}{11}+\frac{8}{11}$
11. $\frac{3}{8}-\frac{1}{8}$
12. $\frac{5}{6}+\frac{5}{6}$
13. $\frac{10}{12}-\frac{3}{6}$
14. $\frac{1}{3}+\frac{1}{2}$
15. $\frac{1}{2}+\frac{1}{7}$

(Lesson 3) Solve each equation.

16. $\frac{7}{15}+w=\frac{9}{15}$
17. $k-\frac{1}{5}=\frac{3}{10}$
18. $x+\frac{1}{4}=\frac{5}{7}$
19. $\frac{49}{63}-t=\frac{1}{3}$

20. Amad and Phoebe sorted $\frac{5}{6}$ of the donations for their school's Used-Clothing Drive. If Phoebe sorted $\frac{1}{3}$ of the donations, how many did Amad sort?

(Lessons 4 and 5) Estimate each sum or difference.

21. $3\frac{1}{3}+6\frac{7}{11}$
22. $11\frac{1}{2}-7\frac{3}{5}$
23. $8\frac{10}{21}-2\frac{1}{19}$
24. $5\frac{4}{5}-5\frac{4}{10}$

(Lessons 5 and 6) Simplify each expression.

25. $2\frac{1}{5}+5\frac{3}{5}$
26. $8\frac{1}{8}+7\frac{1}{10}$
27. $6\frac{6}{8}-3\frac{5}{8}$
28. $11\frac{10}{13}-6\frac{4}{13}$
29. Find the sum of $9\frac{3}{5}$ and $4\frac{4}{5}$.
30. Find the sum of $2\frac{2}{3}$ and $3\frac{2}{3}$.

(Lesson 6) Use the data from the circle graph to answer **31** and **32.**

31. What is the total number of hours that Jason spends on his homework each week?
32. How many more hours does Jason spend on his math homework than he does on his science homework?

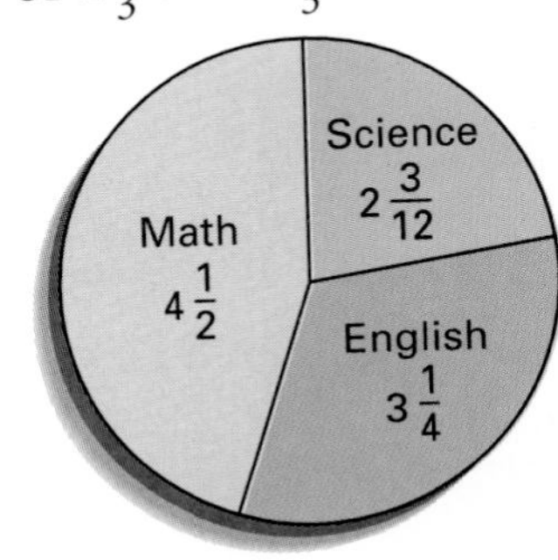

Hours Spent on Homework (weekly)

Performance Assessment

Suppose you are the owner of a small baking business. You have decided to change the packaging for some of your special biscuits and cookies. The chart below shows how many ounces each of the packages holds and your planned changes.

COOKIES

Pack	Now Hold (oz.)	Change (oz.)
A	$8\frac{3}{4}$	$-\frac{1}{8}$
B	$7\frac{7}{8}$	$-\frac{7}{8}$
C	$8\frac{5}{8}$	$+\frac{3}{4}$
D	8	$-\frac{5}{8}$
E	$7\frac{5}{8}$	$+\frac{5}{8}$
F	$8\frac{1}{8}$	$-\frac{1}{2}$

1. **Explain Your Thinking** Which of the following packs now holds more? How much more? How did you find your answers?
   a. A or B
   b. B or C
   c. E or F
2. **Critical Thinking** Which of the packs above now hold more than $\frac{1}{2}$ lb? Remember 1 lb = 16 oz. Which packs will hold more than $\frac{1}{2}$ lb after the change in packaging?
3. **Decision Making** You decide to put the contents of 2 packs you have now into a 1 lb box. Which two packs can you put together to make exactly 1 lb?
4. **Recording Data** Make a chart to show how much each pack holds after you make the change shown in the table above.
5. **Critical Thinking** Suppose you decide each of your packs should hold exactly 8 oz. Make a chart to show the change you will need to make to both your old and new packs.

Math Magazine

Are We There Yet?

When you subtract whole numbers, you sometimes have to regroup tens as tens and ones to be able to subtract the ones. The same thing can happen when you subtract time. You may need to regroup the hour part if the minute part isn't great enough.

The bus leaves Allentown at 3:46 P.M. and arrives at Weslaco at 5:17 P.M. How long does the trip take?

$$\begin{array}{r} 5{:}17 \\ -3{:}46 \\ \hline \end{array}$$

You can subtract the 6 minutes from the 7 minutes, but you can't subtract 40 minutes from 10 minutes. You need to regroup 5 hours as 4 hours and 60 minutes.

$$\begin{array}{r} \overset{4}{\cancel{5}}{:}\overset{7}{\cancel{1}}7 \\ -3{:}46 \\ \hline 1{:}31 \end{array}$$

When you regroup, remember that 1 hour equals 60 minutes, not 100 minutes. Only add 6 to the ten-minutes place.

The ride takes 1 hour and 31 minutes.

To find an arrival time, add the length of the trip to the start time.

HEDULE

ille	Allentown	Danford	Weslaco
	2:11	3:06	3:42
	3:46	4:41	5:17
	5:05	6:00	6:36
	6:05	7:00	7:36
	7:10	8:05	8:41

Try These!

Find the length of time for each trip.

1. Leaves 6:05 A.M., arrives 7:15 A.M.
2. Leaves 9:15 P.M., arrives 11:26 P.M.
3. Leaves 8:36 A.M., arrives at noon.

Find each arrival time.

4. Leaves 4:00 P.M., trip takes 3 hours, 15 minutes.
5. Leaves 1:15 A.M., trip takes 6 hours 36 minutes.

CHAPTERS 1–6
Cumulative Review

Test Prep Strategy: Follow Directions

Answer the question asked.

Tea bought three computer games for $9.95 each. She gave the sales clerk $40.00. How much change did Tea receive?

Ⓐ $10.15 Ⓑ $49.95 Ⓒ $30.05 Ⓓ $29.85

Did you notice that Tea bought *three* games? You have to multiply the price of each game by 3, then subtract that amount from $40.00.
$3 \times \$9.95 = \$29.85$.
$\$40.00 - \$29.85 = \$10.15$.
The answer is choice Ⓐ.

STAY SHARP!

Write the letter of the correct answer. Choose any strategy.

1. What age and height does point B represent in the scatterplot?
   Ⓐ 3 yr, 35 in. Ⓑ 3 yr, 40 in. Ⓒ 4 yr, 40 in. Ⓓ not here

Age and Height

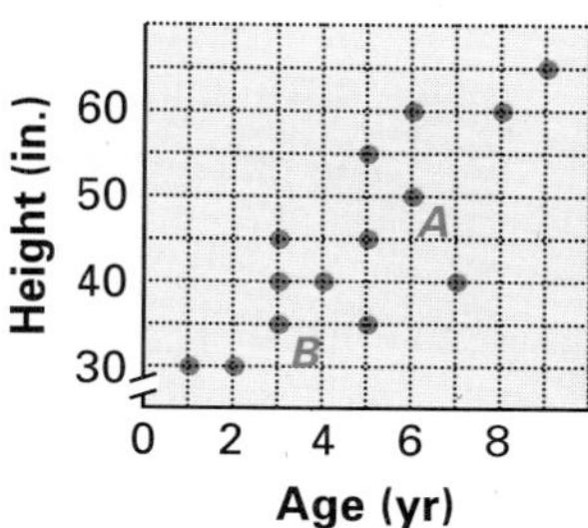

2. Which of the following would you represent with a variable?
   Ⓐ number of feet in a mile Ⓑ number of dimes in a dollar
   Ⓒ number of letters in your first name Ⓓ number of jackets sold each day
3. Which expression represents 4,500,000 in scientific notation?
   Ⓐ 4.5×10^5 Ⓑ 4.5×10^6 Ⓒ 45×10^5 Ⓓ 45×10^6
4. Find the median of the data in the stem-and-leaf diagram.
   Ⓐ 1 Ⓑ 36 Ⓒ 39 Ⓓ not here

Stem	Leaf
2	2 3 6
3	4 4 8 9 9
4	1 1 1 3 7

5. Joyce cut $1\frac{3}{4}$ inches off the end of a cord $7\frac{1}{2}$ inches long. What length of cord was left?
   Ⓐ $6\frac{3}{4}$ in. Ⓑ $9\frac{1}{4}$ in. Ⓒ 6 in. Ⓓ $5\frac{3}{4}$ in.
6. Simplify: $67.5 \div 0.25$.
   Ⓐ 23 Ⓑ 27 Ⓒ 230 Ⓓ 270
7. What is the area of a rectangle 3 ft long and 7 ft wide?
   Ⓐ 10 ft Ⓑ 10 ft^2 Ⓒ 21 ft Ⓓ 21 ft^2
8. Find the prime factorization of 78.
   Ⓐ 2×34 Ⓑ $70 + 8$ Ⓒ $2 \times 3 \times 13$ Ⓓ 2×39
9. Add $4\frac{1}{3}$ and $2\frac{5}{12}$.
   Ⓐ $6\frac{6}{12}$ Ⓑ $6\frac{3}{4}$ Ⓒ $6\frac{4}{11}$ Ⓓ not here
10. Write $10\frac{3}{5}$ as a decimal.
   Ⓐ 106 Ⓑ 50.3 Ⓒ 10.6 Ⓓ 10.06

Test Prep Strategies

- Read Carefully
- Follow Directions
- Make Smart Choices
- Eliminate Choices
- Work Backward from an Answer

DATA FILE

Chapter 7

Multiplying and Dividing Fractions

A Taste from the North Pacific

A Taste from the North Pacific
Page 359

Multiplying Fractions

359

About $\frac{2}{3}$ of the world's commercial catch of seafood comes from the Pacific Ocean. About how much comes from the Atlantic Ocean?

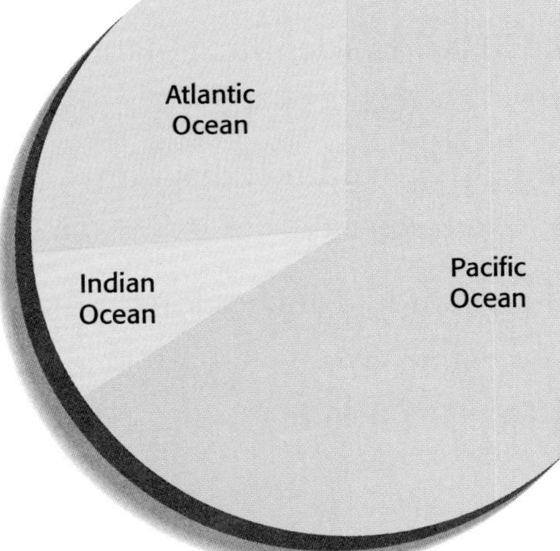

World's Commercial Catch of Seafood

LINKS

People of the World

With a world population of about 5,800,000,000, there are about 900,000,000 people living in India. This means that about 1 out of every 6 people in the world lives in India.

Entertainment

Naim Suleymanoglu of Turkey won the 1996 Olympic Gold Medal in the 141-lb division by lifting 413 lb, more than $2\frac{3}{4}$ times his own body weight.

www.mathsurf.com/6/ch7/ent

364.4 Smoots and One Ear

Dividing Fractions

375

364.4 Smoots and One Ear

Page 375

There are many different ways to measure the number, weight, length, or capacity of items. For instance, how many sheets of paper would you have if you had $2\frac{1}{4}$ reams of paper?

Unit of Measure	Is Equal to . . .
A baker's dozen	13
A last of fish	20,000
A firkin of butter	56 lb (in England)
A bale of cotton	500 lb
A cran of herring	47 gal
A ream of paper	500 sheets
A fortnight	2 weeks

Arts & Literature

Upon completion, the statue of Chief Crazy Horse at Thunderhead Mountain, South Dakota, will be 563 ft tall. The model of the statue on display is $\frac{1}{34}$ the size of the final statue.

www.mathsurf.com/6/ch7/arts

Science

Carbon 14 is radioactive. It takes 5,730 years for $\frac{1}{2}$ of the radioactive material to decay.

www.mathsurf.com/6/ch7/science

Social Studies

Louis XIV, king of France from 1643 to 1715, had the longest documented reign of any monarch. Franklin D. Roosevelt, U.S. President from 1933 to 1945, served as U.S. President the longest. His presidency lasted $\frac{1}{6}$ of the reign of Louis XIV.

Materials

posterboard, construction paper, markers, and other art materials as needed

Work with members of your team to create a game that involves multiplying or dividing fractions.

Make a Plan

- What will be the object of your game?
- What materials will you need to make the game?
- What are the rules for playing the game?
- How will you incorporate multiplying and dividing fractions into the game?

Carry It Out

1. Generate a list of possible games and pick one to design.
2. Determine the object of the game, the materials you will need to make the game, and the rules for playing the game.
3. Make sure your team tests the game by playing a few rounds. Make any changes to the game as necessary.

Talk About It

- How did your team decide how to use multiplying and dividing fractions in the game?
- What was the easiest part of designing the game? The most difficult part?

Present the Project

Exchange your game with another team. Record any problems you may encounter while playing the game so the other team can make adjustments.

CHAPTER 7

SECTION

A Multiplying Fractions

Sweet and Sour Porcupine
Legs of porcupine
2 sliced onions
1 cup cider vinegar
3/4 cup brown sugar
1/2 teaspoon nutmeg
Fat

Wallpaper Paste
4 cups flour
1 cup sugar
1 gallon warm water
1 quart cold water

Chicken-Fried Muskrat
Dressed muskrat
Marinade:
1 quart of water plus
1 tablespoon salt
Salt, pepper, paprika
to taste
Flour
Bacon fat
1 cup sour cream

Eskimo Ice Cream (Akutaq)
2 cups seal oil
Bowl of loose snow
1 1/2 pounds of reindeer fat
Wild berries

These are all authentic recipes from the North Pacific. One of the four is different from the other three. Can you tell which recipe it is? Why might you multiply fractions when using a recipe?

GET READY!

Multiplying Fractions

Review fractions. Decide whether each fraction is greater than, less than, or equal to $\frac{1}{2}$.

1. $\frac{1}{8}$ **2.** $\frac{2}{3}$ **3.** $\frac{5}{6}$ **4.** $\frac{5}{10}$

Write the multiplication problem each model represents.

5.

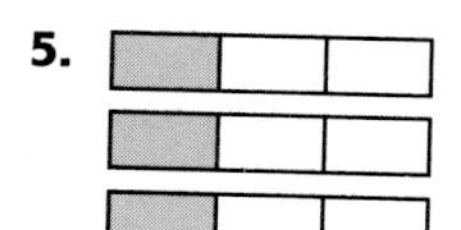

6.

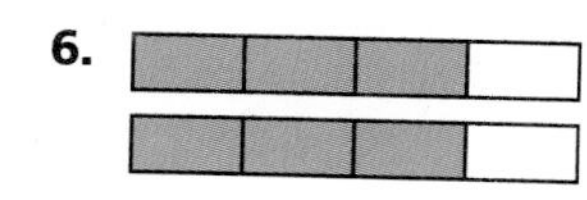

Skills Checklist

In this section, you will:

- ❒ Estimate Products and Quotients of Fractions
- ❒ Multiply Fractions by a Whole Number
- ❒ Multiply Fractions by a Fraction

Chapter 7
Lesson
1

Estimation: Products and Quotients of Fractions

You Will Learn

- to estimate products and quotients of fraction problems

Math Tip

When finding a product, if you round *one or both numbers up,* your result will be an *over*estimate. When finding a quotient, if you round the *divisor down,* you will get an *over*estimate. If you round the *divisor up* you will get an *under*estimate.

Learn

Homemade creations add a personal touch to gift giving. They make unique gifts for teachers, neighbors and friends. The Ringles family uses this recipe to make bread dough snowflakes.

Ornaments

$3\frac{1}{4}$ cups flour

1 cup salt

$1\frac{1}{2}$ cups water

Makes 25 snowflake ornaments

You can use rounding to estimate products of fractions and mixed numbers.

Example 1

Ramon plans to use the recipe to make snowflakes for his school fair. About how much flour will Ramon need if he makes $2\frac{1}{3}$ times the recipe?

Estimate: $3\frac{1}{4} \times 2\frac{1}{3}$

To be sure there is enough flour, you should overestimate.

Round $3\frac{1}{4}$ up to 4.

$\frac{1}{3} < \frac{1}{2}$, so $2\frac{1}{3}$ rounds down to 2.

Estimate: $4 \times 2 = 8$

Ramon will need about 8 cups of flour.

You can also use rounding to estimate quotients of fractions and mixed numbers.

Example 2

A gardener wants to build a 36-ft fence using $3\frac{1}{2}$ ft planks. About how many planks should she buy to be sure there are enough?

Estimate: $36 \div 3\frac{1}{2}$

To be sure there is enough wood, you should overestimate.

$3\frac{1}{2}$ is the divisor.

Round $3\frac{1}{2}$ down to 3.

Estimate: $36 \div 3 = 12$

The gardener should buy 12 planks.

You can use compatible numbers to estimate quotients of fractions and mixed numbers.

Example 3

Estimate: $8\frac{2}{3} \div 3\frac{1}{5}$

$\frac{1}{5} < \frac{1}{2}$, so $3\frac{1}{5}$ rounds down to 3.

9 is compatible with 3, so round $8\frac{2}{3}$ up to 9.

Estimate: $9 \div 3 = 3$

Round the divisor first, and then round the dividend to the nearest compatible number.

Remember

Compatible numbers are numbers that can be computed easily, such as $75 \div 5$ or $100 \div 4$.

You can use compatible numbers to estimate products of fractions and mixed numbers.

Example 4

Estimate: $30\frac{3}{4} \times 19\frac{1}{8}$

$\frac{3}{4} > \frac{1}{2}$, so round $30\frac{3}{4}$ to 31.

20 is easier to multiply by than 19, so round $19\frac{1}{8}$ to 20.

Estimate: $31 \times 20 = 620$

Choose numbers compatible for multiplying. 31×20 is easier to multiply mentally than 31×19.

Talk About It

1. When rounding fractions to the closest whole number, when do you round up?
2. Give a real-world situation with fractions where you would overestimate.
3. Why does rounding the divisor up result in an underestimate?

Check

Round each mixed number to the nearest whole number.

1. $4\frac{7}{9}$ lb of grapes
2. $1\frac{1}{3}$ yd of fabric
3. $3\frac{1}{8}$ cups of juice
4. $14\frac{5}{6}$ mi car trip
5. $19\frac{2}{7}$ oz of juice
6. $28\frac{2}{3}$ yd of ribbon

Estimate.

7. $4\frac{3}{4} \times 3\frac{1}{6}$
8. $1\frac{1}{3} \times 2\frac{1}{2}$
9. $5\frac{2}{3} \div 1\frac{4}{5}$
10. $1\frac{1}{3} \div \frac{3}{4}$
11. $18\frac{5}{8} \div 5\frac{1}{3}$
12. $\frac{3}{5} \times 23$
13. $51\frac{4}{5} \div 4\frac{3}{4}$
14. $5\frac{3}{5} \times 4\frac{1}{9}$
15. **Reasoning** Rachel thinks 14 is a better estimate for $2\frac{1}{3} \times 6\frac{4}{5}$. Lena thinks 12 is a better estimate. Which do you think is a better estimate? Explain.

Practice

Skills and Reasoning

Round each mixed number to the nearest whole number.

16. $4\frac{2}{3}$ **17.** $3\frac{3}{7}$ **18.** $6\frac{1}{8}$ **19.** $5\frac{7}{10}$ **20.** $8\frac{1}{2}$ **21.** $8\frac{4}{8}$

Estimate.

22. $3\frac{1}{5} \times 4\frac{7}{8}$ **23.** $12\frac{1}{8} \div 6\frac{1}{3}$ **24.** $9\frac{1}{2} \times 4\frac{7}{8}$ **25.** $15\frac{1}{7} \div 2\frac{9}{10}$

26. $2\frac{2}{3} \times 3\frac{6}{7}$ **27.** $12\frac{9}{10} \div 6\frac{7}{8}$ **28.** $8\frac{3}{5} \times 7\frac{3}{4}$ **29.** $10\frac{2}{5} \div 5\frac{4}{13}$

30. $6\frac{3}{8} \times 10\frac{2}{5}$ **31.** $10\frac{4}{7} \div 5\frac{1}{2}$ **32.** $6\frac{8}{10} \times 5\frac{3}{9}$ **33.** $13\frac{4}{7} \div 3\frac{2}{7}$

34. $4\frac{1}{4} \times 7\frac{3}{13}$ **35.** $12\frac{2}{6} \div 4\frac{1}{3}$ **36.** $2\frac{1}{2} \times 4\frac{1}{9}$ **37.** $17\frac{5}{11} \div 3\frac{3}{10}$

38. $5\frac{2}{11} \times 8\frac{1}{10}$ **39.** $8\frac{5}{10} \div 3\frac{5}{6}$ **40.** $10\frac{2}{7} \times 3\frac{4}{9}$ **41.** $14\frac{6}{9} \div 6\frac{3}{8}$

42. $\frac{95}{9} \times 2\frac{2}{9}$ **43.** $7\frac{5}{8} \div 2\frac{1}{4}$ **44.** $6\frac{1}{3} \times 1\frac{3}{11}$ **45.** $3\frac{2}{3} \div 1\frac{2}{4}$

46. $8\frac{4}{7} \times 11\frac{3}{7}$ **47.** $10\frac{3}{8} \div 4\frac{2}{3}$ **48.** $3\frac{2}{5} \times 6\frac{1}{2}$ **49.** $11\frac{1}{8} \div 3\frac{1}{10}$

50. Reasoning To estimate $13\frac{1}{4} \div 2\frac{1}{8}$, would you round the numbers or use compatible numbers? Explain.

51. Reasoning In $7\frac{2}{3} \div 2\frac{1}{4}$, if you round only the first number up, will you get an overestimate or an underestimate? Explain.

Problem Solving and Applications

52. Social Studies The population of Massachusetts in 1890 was $2\frac{1}{4}$ million. The population in 1990 was $6\frac{1}{6}$ million. About how many times as great was the population in 1990?

53. **Using Data** Use the Data File on page 356 to estimate what $3\frac{1}{2}$ times Naim Suleymanoglu's weight division would be.

54. **History** Native Americans and the early European settlers used every part of the common swamp cattail as food. A recipe for cattail pancakes calls for $2\frac{2}{3}$ cups of cattail pollen. You have 6 cups of cattail pollen. Do you have enough to triple the recipe?

55. A plumber needs 15 pieces of pipe, each $4\frac{1}{4}$ feet long. Will 58 feet of pipe be enough?

56. **Critical Thinking** Use estimation to complete the table. Explain your reasoning.

Full Price	$3.73	$4.65	$6.99	$8.23
$\frac{1}{2}$ Price				
$\frac{3}{4}$ Price				

57. **Critical Thinking** Give five pairs of values for x and y so that $5\frac{x}{y}$ will round to 6 when rounded to the nearest whole number. What do all of your pairs of numbers have in common?

58. **Algebra Readiness** Name two fractions that would make this statement true: $4\frac{6}{7} \times F$ is about 15.

59. **Geometry Readiness** The height of a wall is $12\frac{1}{3}$ feet. Its length is $6\frac{1}{8}$ feet. Will there be enough paint to cover the wall if the can of paint covers about 72 square feet? Explain.

60. **What If** Ramon decided to make 150 snowflake ornaments using his bread dough recipe. About how much flour would he need?

61. **Journal** Describe a situation involving a recipe where it makes more sense to overestimate. Then describe a situation where it makes more sense to underestimate.

Mixed Review and Test Prep

STAY SHARP!

Convert.

62. 8 m = ▒ cm   63. 126 L = ▒ mL   64. 976 mm = ▒ cm

Tell whether the first number is divisible by the second.

65. 34, 9   66. 55, 5   67. 62, 4   68. 88, 11

69. Choose the best estimate for $13.57 + $19.12.

Ⓐ $24   Ⓑ $32   Ⓒ $33   Ⓓ $34

Skills Practice Bank, page 666, Set 1

Chapter 7 Lesson 2

Multiplying by a Whole Number

You Will Learn

- to multiply whole numbers by fractions

Learn

Because the hummingbird has a rapid metabolism, it must consume a tremendous amount of calories. If a hummingbird were the size of a human, it would need to consume 155,000 calories each day, the equivalent of 80 gallons of yogurt.

Hummingbirds can be seen hovering midair over flowers as they feed. Some bird watchers say the recipe for attracting them to your yard is to grow bright red flowers. Others say to mix up a batch of nectar to attract the hummers!

Remember

To change a mixed number to an improper fraction, multiply the fraction denominator by the whole number, then add the numerator.

You can multiply a fraction or mixed number by a whole number by writing both factors as fractions.

Example 1

A recipe for hummingbird food calls for $1\frac{5}{8}$ cups of sugar. How much sugar should you use to triple the recipe?

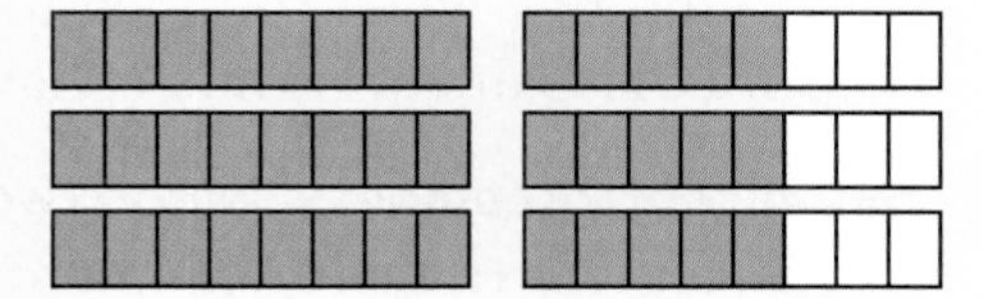

Multiply: $3 \times 1\frac{5}{8}$

$3 \times 1\frac{5}{8} = \frac{3}{1} \times \frac{13}{8}$ Write the factors as fractions.

$= \frac{3 \times 13}{1 \times 8}$ Multiply the numerators. Multiply the denominators.

$= \frac{39}{8}$, or $4\frac{7}{8}$ Simplify.

You should use $4\frac{7}{8}$ cups of sugar.

Some problems ask you to find the fractional part of a whole number.

Example 2

About $\frac{2}{3}$ of the 360 students at Kensington Middle School belong to an after-school club or activity. How many students is this?

Multiply: $360 \times \frac{2}{3}$

$360 \times \frac{2}{3} = \frac{360}{1} \times \frac{2}{3}$ Write the factors as fractions.

$= \frac{360 \times 2}{1 \times 3}$ Multiply the numerators, then the denominators.

$= \frac{720}{3}$, or 240 Simplify.

240 students participate in a club or activity.

You can use the Distributive Property to multiply a mixed number by a whole number.

Example 3

Lauren and Skye are making wallpaper paste. They have $2\frac{3}{4}$ cups of sugar, and they want to adjust the recipe to use all of it. They need to determine how much flour to use in the adjusted recipe.

Wallpaper Paste

4 cups flour
1 cup sugar
1 gallon warm water
1 quart cold water

Multiply: $4 \times 2\frac{3}{4}$ — Use the Distributive Property.

$4 \times 2 = \mathbf{8}$ — Multiply 4 times the whole number.

$4 \times \frac{3}{4} = \frac{\overset{1}{\cancel{4}} \times 3}{1 \times \underset{1}{\cancel{4}}} = \frac{1 \times 3}{1 \times 1} = \mathbf{3}$ — Multiply 4 times the fraction.

$\mathbf{8} + \mathbf{3} = 11$ — Add the results. $4 \times 2\frac{3}{4} = 11$

They need 11 cups of flour.

Talk About It

1. Is the product of a whole number and a fraction always greater than either number? Explain.
2. Are the products $12 \times \frac{3}{5}$ and $\frac{3}{5} \times 12$ equal? Explain.
3. When multiplying a mixed number or fraction by a whole number how do you know which method to use: the Distributive Property or writing both factors as fraction?

Check

Choose the multiplication problem the model represents.

1.

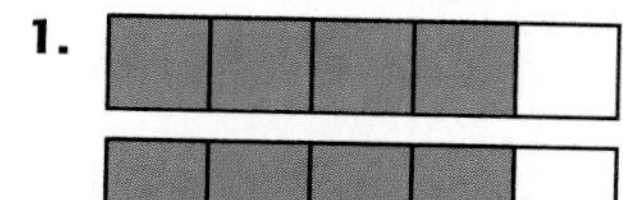

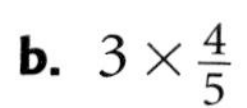

a. $4 \times \frac{3}{5}$

b. $3 \times \frac{4}{5}$

2.

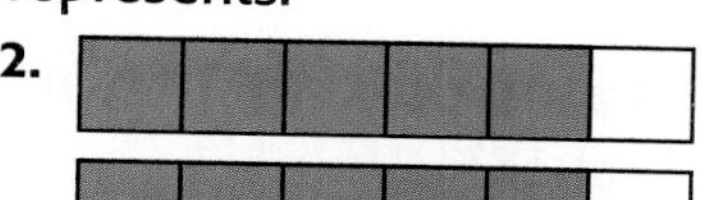

a. $2 \times \frac{5}{6}$

b. $5 \times \frac{1}{3}$

Simplify.

3. $4 \times \frac{2}{3}$ **4.** $3 \times 1\frac{3}{4}$ **5.** $\frac{1}{2}$ of 16 **6.** $\frac{5}{6}$ of 30

7. $\frac{1}{9}$ of 450 **8.** $12 \times 3\frac{1}{2}$ **9.** $6 \times 1\frac{5}{12}$ **10.** $3 \times 1\frac{7}{12}$

11. What is the product of 14 and $\frac{2}{7}$?

12. What is the product of $2\frac{1}{3}$ and 6?

13. Reasoning Wendell said that the product of $6\frac{1}{4}$ and 12 was 300. Is he correct? Explain.

14. Reasoning Without multiplying, what can you tell about the product of $\frac{2}{3} \times 5$?

Practice

Skills and Reasoning

Write the multiplication problem each model represents.

15. 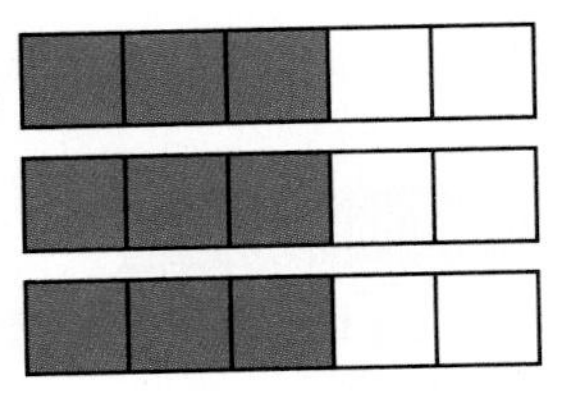

16. 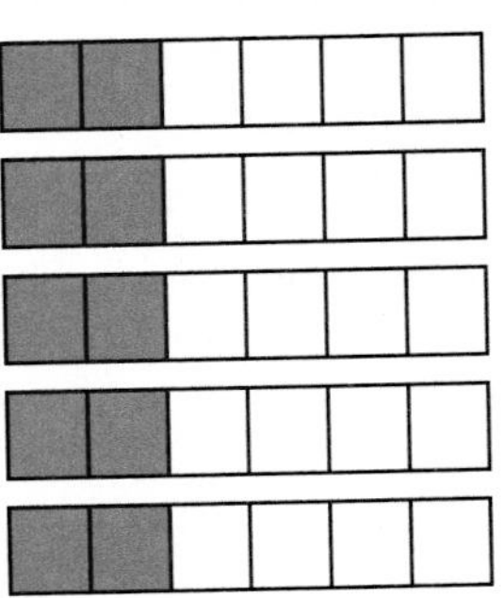

17. 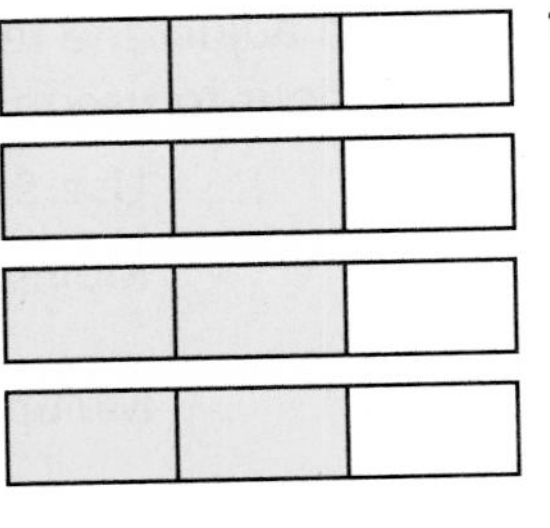

18. 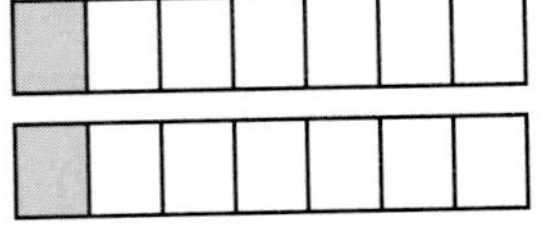

Simplify.

19. $\frac{1}{3} \times 2$ **20.** $\frac{1}{6} \times 8$ **21.** $2 \times \frac{3}{10}$ **22.** $3\frac{3}{8} \times 5$ **23.** $1\frac{2}{5} \times 25$

24. $10 \times \frac{2}{3}$ **25.** $\frac{2}{7} \times 7$ **26.** $\frac{2}{3} \times 3$ **27.** $4 \times \frac{5}{7}$ **28.** $8 \times \frac{7}{8}$

29. $\frac{1}{4} \times 6$ **30.** $3 \times \frac{3}{11}$ **31.** $\frac{3}{5} \times 11$ **32.** $\frac{4}{8} \times 6$ **33.** $3\frac{3}{7} \times 2$

34. $5 \times \frac{4}{9}$ **35.** $\frac{3}{7} \times 9$ **36.** $9 \times \frac{6}{10}$ **37.** $1 \times \frac{11}{12}$ **38.** $2\frac{1}{2} \times 5$

39. $3 \times \frac{17}{12}$ **40.** $4\frac{5}{9} \times 12$ **41.** $7 \times 1\frac{5}{6}$ **42.** $12 \times 2\frac{10}{11}$ **43.** $\frac{9}{10} \times 4$

44. $2\frac{2}{5} \times 4$ **45.** $6 \times \frac{3}{7}$ **46.** $8 \times 8\frac{3}{8}$ **47.** $5\frac{2}{7} \times 10$ **48.** $2 \times 1\frac{1}{4}$

49. Find $\frac{2}{3}$ of 45. **50.** What is $\frac{3}{4}$ of 36?

51. What is $\frac{2}{5}$ of 50? **52.** Find $\frac{5}{8}$ of 64.

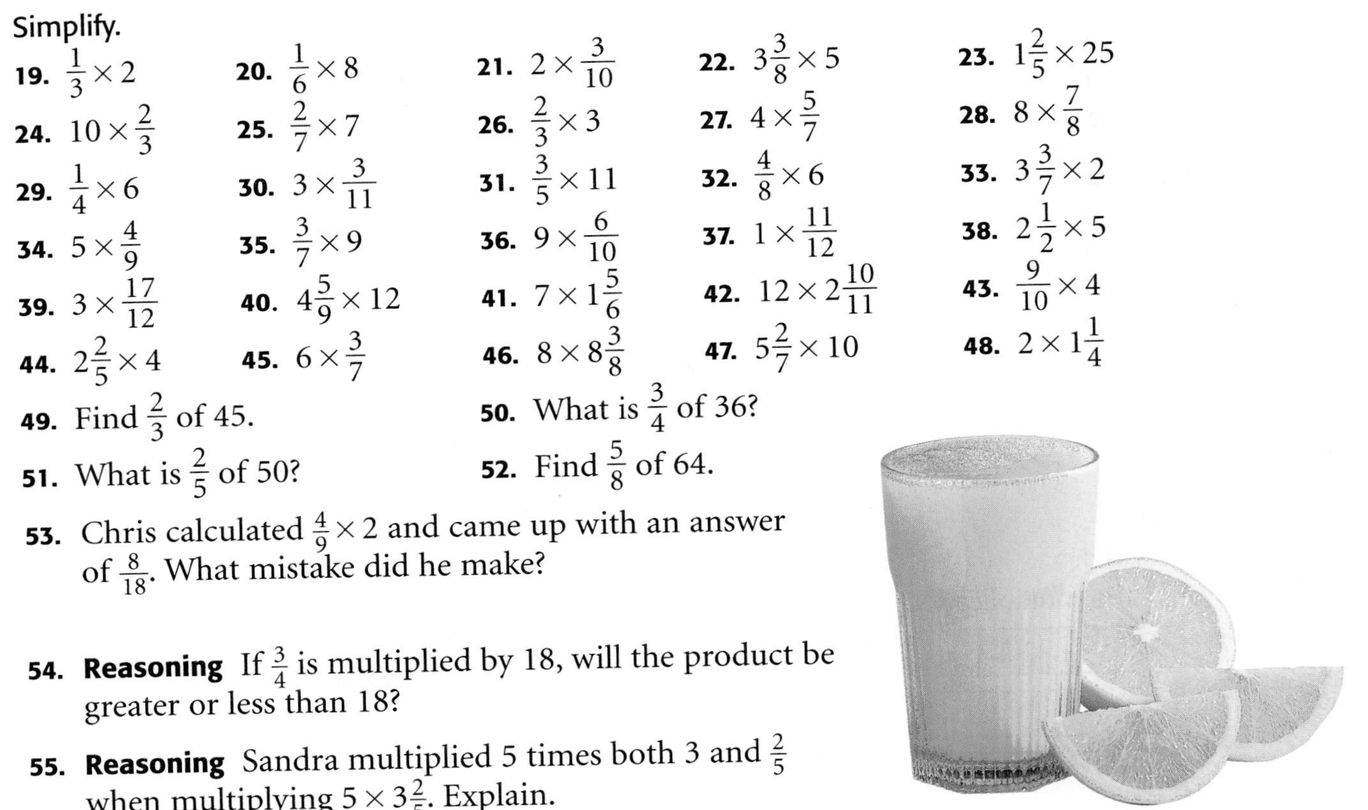

53. Chris calculated $\frac{4}{9} \times 2$ and came up with an answer of $\frac{8}{18}$. What mistake did he make?

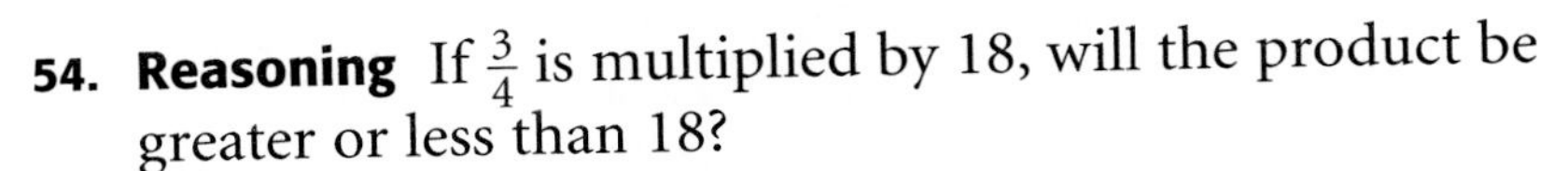

54. Reasoning If $\frac{3}{4}$ is multiplied by 18, will the product be greater or less than 18?

55. Reasoning Sandra multiplied 5 times both 3 and $\frac{2}{5}$ when multiplying $5 \times 3\frac{2}{5}$. Explain.

56. Health Complete the table for calories in orange juice.

Servings	$\frac{1}{4}$	$\frac{1}{2}$	$\frac{3}{4}$	1	$1\frac{1}{2}$	2
Ounces				8		
Calories				110		

57. Algebra Readiness $\frac{4}{9}$ of what number is 32?

58. Logic $\frac{1}{3}$ of a number is 33. $\frac{2}{3}$ of the same number is 66. What is $\frac{3}{3}$ of that number?

Problem Solving and Applications

Science Use the Life Span graph for **59** and **60**.

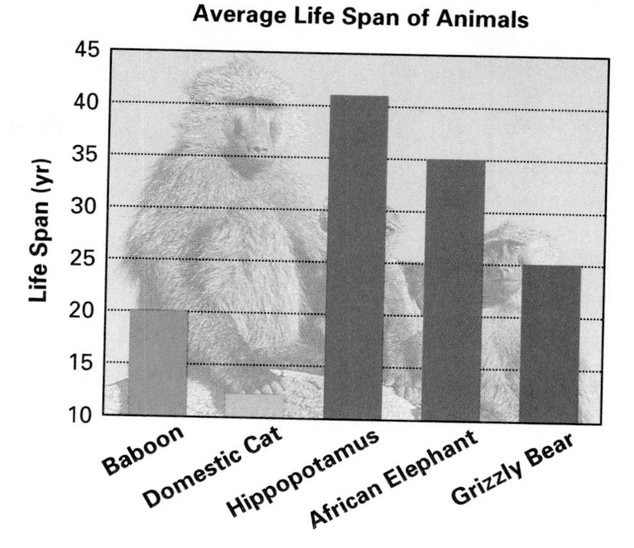

59. The maximum recorded life span for a baboon is $2\frac{1}{4}$ times the average life span. What is the maximum recorded life span?

60. The maximum recorded life span of a domestic cat is $2\frac{1}{3}$ times the average life span. What is the maximum recorded life span?

61. **History** In colonial times, houses in New England were often painted with a glazed whitewash. One gallon of whitewash includes $\frac{3}{4}$ lb rice and $\frac{1}{2}$ lb sugar. How much of these ingredients are needed for 3 gallons of whitewash?

62. **Critical Thinking** Castile soap is named for the kingdom of Castile in Spain where the soap was first produced. To make about 36 bars, 1 pound 9 ounces of olive oil is needed. If a pound of olive oil costs $8.00, how much does the olive oil for this recipe cost? Explain.

63. **Mental Math** A human-sized hummingbird would need to consume 155,000 calories, or 80 gallons of yogurt each day. Without calculating, which would have more calories: $\frac{2}{3}$ of the calories a human-sized hummingbird would need, or 40 gallons of yogurt? Explain.

64. **Measurement** If about $\frac{2}{5}$ of 1 inch equals 1 cm, how many inches equal 15 centimeters?

65. **Journal** Explain how you can tell without multiplying if the product of $\frac{9}{10}$ and 15 is more than 15 or less than 15.

Mixed Review and Test Prep

Convert.

66. 1,176 inches = ■ feet **67.** 38 feet = ■ inches **68.** 96 inches = ■ feet

Find the prime factorization.

69. 63 **70.** 1,060 **71.** 17 **72.** 99 **73.** 57 **74.** 34

75. Andrew has read 0.75 of his 304-page book. How many pages has he read?

Ⓐ 76 Ⓑ 152 Ⓒ 228 Ⓓ not here

Chapter 7 Lesson 3

Multiplying by a Fraction

You Will Learn
- to multiply a fraction by another fraction

Learn

Many different colors of dye can be made from common plants. The bark of the American black oak tree can be used to make bright yellow. The flowers and stems from Queen Anne's lace can be used to make pale green.

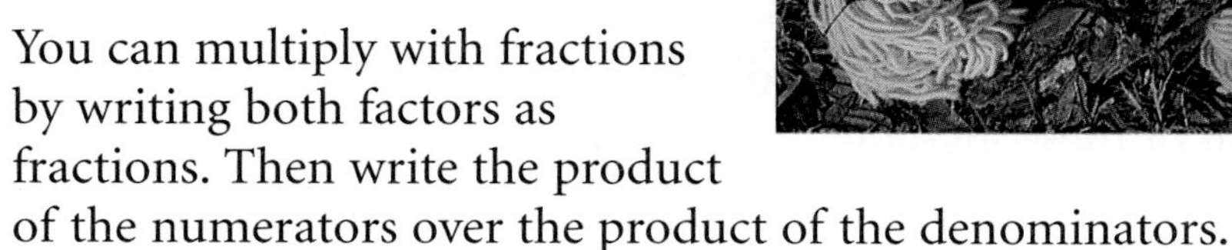

You can multiply with fractions by writing both factors as fractions. Then write the product of the numerators over the product of the denominators.

Did You Know?
In 1856, seventeen-year-old William Perkin was the first person to produce an effective synthetic dye. His discovery brought the pleasure of color within everyone's grasp.

Example 1

A recipe for dyeing wool calls for $\frac{1}{4}$ pound of tea leaves for each pound of wool. Find the amount of leaves needed to dye $\frac{2}{3}$ pound of wool.

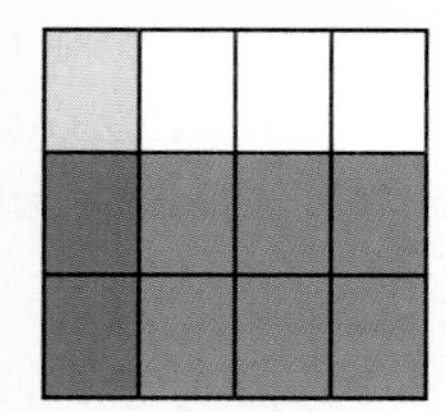

$\frac{1}{4} \times \frac{2}{3} = \frac{1 \times 2}{4 \times 3}$ Multiply the numerators. Multiply the denominators.

$= \frac{2}{12}$ or $\frac{1}{6}$ Simplify.

You need $\frac{1}{6}$ pound of tea leaves.

If the numerator and the denominator have a common factor, you can simplify before you multiply.

Example 2

Multiply: $\frac{3}{8} \times \frac{4}{7}$

$\frac{3}{8} \times \frac{4}{7} = \frac{3 \times 4}{8 \times 7}$ Write the factors as one fraction.

$= \frac{3 \times \overset{1}{\cancel{4}}}{\underset{2}{\cancel{8}} \times 7}$ Divide common factors.

$= \frac{3}{14}$ Multiply the numerators, then the denominators.

$\frac{3}{8} \times \frac{4}{7} = \frac{3}{14}$

Some problems may ask you to find a fractional part of a fraction. You can use multiplication to solve these problems.

Example 3

Mr. Hamilton bought $2\frac{1}{2}$ gallons of milk. He used half of it to make ice cream. How much did he use?

$2\frac{1}{2} \times \frac{1}{2} = \frac{5}{2} \times \frac{1}{2}$ — Write the mixed number as an improper fraction.

$= \frac{5 \times 1}{2 \times 2}$ — Multiply the numerators. Multiply the denominators.

$= \frac{5}{4}$, or $1\frac{1}{4}$ — Simplify.

He used $1\frac{1}{4}$ gallons of milk.

Talk About It

1. How is multiplying two fractions different from adding two fractions?
2. Is the product of two fractions greater or less than both of the fractions you started with?
3. How is dividing the common factors in $\frac{3}{4} \times \frac{4}{7}$ like dividing by 1?

Check

Choose the multiplication problem the model represents.

1. 

   a. $\frac{2}{5} \times \frac{3}{4}$ b. $\frac{4}{5} \times \frac{2}{3}$

2. 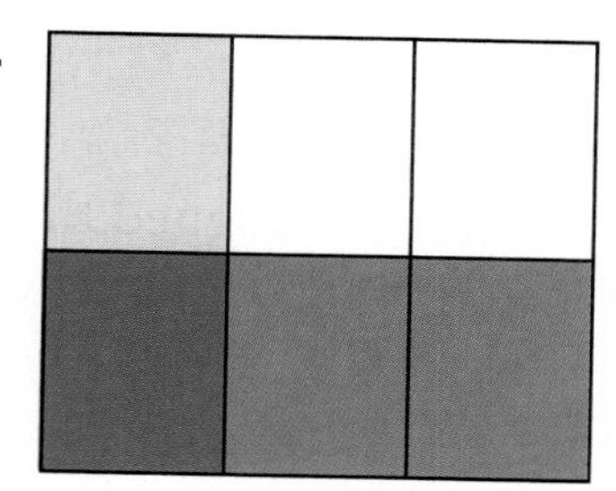

   a. $\frac{1}{3} \times \frac{1}{2}$ b. $\frac{1}{6} \times \frac{1}{3}$

Find each product.

3. $\frac{4}{5} \times \frac{3}{7}$
4. $\frac{8}{9}$ of $1\frac{1}{2}$
5. $1\frac{2}{3} \times 1\frac{3}{7}$
6. $\frac{1}{9}$ of $\frac{2}{5}$
7. $1\frac{1}{5} \times \frac{3}{5}$
8. $\frac{4}{5}$ of $2\frac{1}{2}$
9. $\frac{6}{7} \times \frac{7}{12}$
10. $1\frac{1}{4} \times \frac{1}{6}$
11. What is $\frac{4}{7} \times 1\frac{1}{5}$?
12. Find $\frac{1}{3} \times \frac{7}{8}$.
13. Find $3\frac{3}{4} \times \frac{6}{11}$.
14. What is $\frac{5}{9} \times \frac{4}{5}$?
15. **Reasoning** Victor said that $\frac{4}{9} \times \frac{1}{9} = \frac{4}{1}$. George said that the product is $\frac{4}{81}$. Who is correct? Explain.

Practice

Skills and Reasoning

Write the multiplication problem each model represents.

16. 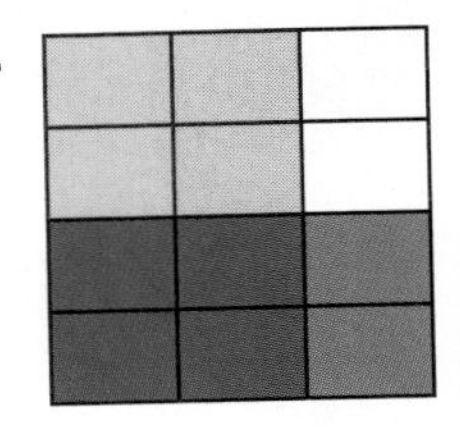

17. 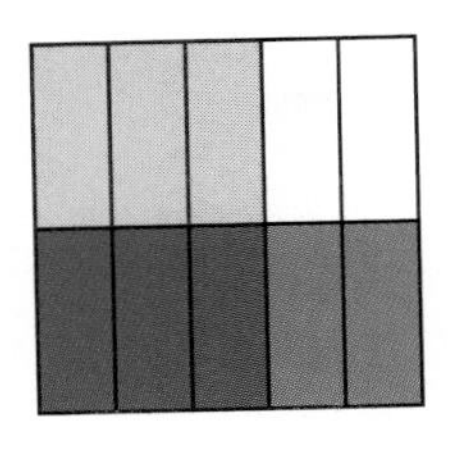

18. 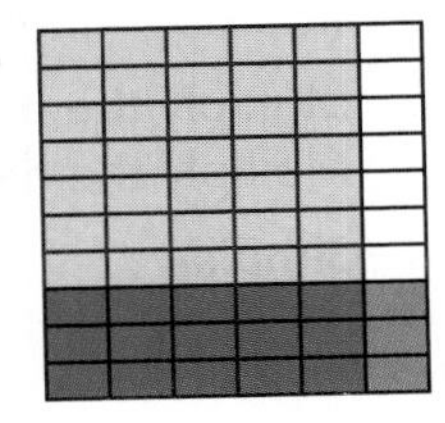

19. 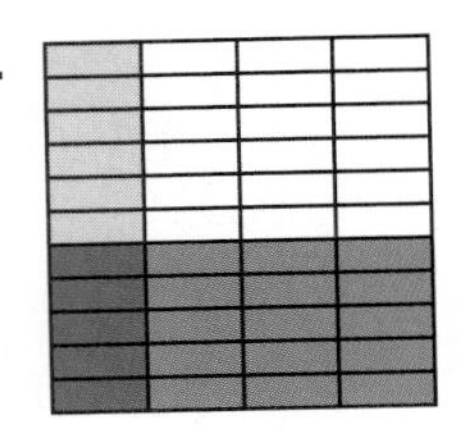

Find each product.

20. $\frac{3}{7} \times \frac{2}{3}$ **21.** $\frac{5}{9} \times \frac{1}{2}$ **22.** $\frac{3}{4} \times \frac{7}{10}$ **23.** $\frac{1}{5} \times \frac{1}{5}$

24. $\frac{11}{15} \times 4\frac{6}{7}$ **25.** $7\frac{1}{3} \times \frac{7}{9}$ **26.** $\frac{13}{17} \times \frac{6}{11}$ **27.** $\frac{1}{9} \times \frac{7}{13}$

28. $\frac{4}{5} \times 10\frac{3}{8}$ **29.** $6\frac{2}{5} \times \frac{9}{11}$ **30.** $\frac{13}{20} \times \frac{1}{3}$ **31.** $\frac{2}{5} \times \frac{10}{11}$

32. $\frac{9}{13} \times 2\frac{9}{13}$ **33.** $\frac{2}{5} \times \frac{7}{10}$ **34.** $\frac{4}{7} \times 2\frac{3}{8}$ **35.** $5\frac{5}{7} \times 5\frac{8}{9}$

36. $\frac{11}{21} \times \frac{1}{2}$ **37.** $9\frac{2}{9} \times 3\frac{4}{9}$ **38.** $\frac{1}{8} \times \frac{3}{8}$ **39.** $\frac{4}{5} \times \frac{3}{8}$

40. $\frac{6}{11} \times \frac{6}{11}$ **41.** $8\frac{2}{5} \times \frac{3}{7}$ **42.** $\frac{4}{7} \times 4\frac{9}{14}$ **43.** $\frac{5}{8} \times \frac{8}{9}$

44. Reasoning When Felicia was assigned the problem $\frac{4}{5} \times \frac{2}{3}$, she said that she had forgotten how to find the common denominator. What would you tell her?

45. Reasoning Which expression has the greater product: $\frac{4}{5} \times 4$ or $\frac{4}{5} \times \frac{4}{5}$?

Problem Solving and Applications

46. Science An alligator is $12\frac{1}{2}$ feet long. Its tail is half as long as its total length. How long is the alligator's tail?

47. Choose a Strategy To make $\frac{3}{4}$ cup of powdered-milk paint, you mix $\frac{1}{2}$ cup of powdered nonfat milk and $\frac{1}{2}$ cup of water. Adjust this recipe to make one whole cup of paint. Explain your method.

Problem Solving and HEALTH

Ultra-violet rays can be harmful even in the shade. Sunscreens absorb the shorter, most harmful rays. The best sunscreens contain PABA (para-aminobenzoic acid) and are rated SPF 10 or above.

48. To find out how long a sunscreen's protection is supposed to last, multiply the SPF by the amount of time in hours in which a burn would ordinarily occur without protection. So if a burn occurs in $\frac{1}{2}$ hr, a sunscreen with an SPF of 10 should protect for $\frac{1}{2} \times 10$, or 5 hours. How long would a sunscreen with an SPF of 25 protect?

49. Collecting Data Look at the products in your home that contain sunscreen: lotion, lip balm, make-up, etc. Determine how many hours of protection are provided if a burn usually occurs after $\frac{1}{4}$ hour in the sun.

50. Time Chuck works odd jobs to earn extra money. He usually burns after $\frac{3}{4}$ hour in the sun. Today he forgot his sunscreen. He worked $\frac{3}{5}$ of his $2\frac{1}{2}$ hours indoors, out of the sun. If today was a hot sunny day, did Chuck get a sunburn? Explain.

51. Trisha bought $8\frac{3}{4}$ ounces of sunscreen. She used $\frac{4}{5}$ of it on her vacation to the beach. How many ounces did she use?

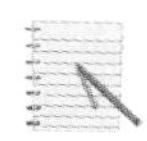

52. Journal Describe how you multiply $\frac{2}{3}$ by $\frac{5}{6}$. Use pictures.

Mixed Review and Test Prep

STAY SHARP!

Convert.

53. 1 mile = ▮ feet

54. 10,560 feet = ▮ inches

55. 6 miles = ▮ feet

56. 15,840 feet = ▮ inches

57. 10 miles = ▮ feet

58. 5280 feet = ▮ inches

Simplify. Write each answer in lowest terms.

59. $5\frac{1}{3} - 2\frac{2}{9}$

60. $2\frac{1}{4} + 3\frac{1}{2}$

61. $1\frac{5}{8} - \frac{3}{8}$

62. Choose the best estimate for $4\frac{1}{5} + 6\frac{6}{11}$.

Ⓐ 11 Ⓑ 10 Ⓒ 17 Ⓓ $10\frac{7}{16}$

Chapter 7

Problem Solving

Analyzing Word Problems: Identifying Missing Information

You Will Learn

- to determine whether any additional information is needed to solve a problem

Learn

Mr. and Mrs. Halloran and their children, David and Jennie, are planning to drive to Arches National Park. Mrs. Halloran suggests that they drive 400 miles each day. At this rate, how long will it take them to get there?

Work Together

Understand

What do you know?

What do you need to find out?

Plan

What information do you need?	The distance to Arches National Park

Solve

To find a rate, divide.	Total number of miles ÷ 400 miles per day = time needed to get to Arches National Park
Write your answer.	The problem does not give enough information to solve it.

Look Back

How can you be certain that the information is missing?	Reread the problem and compare it to the plan for solving it.

Talk About It

1. Can you think of a real-life problem that does not give enough information to solve it?
2. Would there ever be a problem with too little information that you could solve? If so, give an example and tell how you could solve it.

Check

Write whether each problem gives enough information to solve it. Solve, if possible, or write what is needed to solve.

1. The Hallorans stopped at a restaurant to eat shrimp. Mrs. Halloran had twice as much shrimp as David. Jennie had three more pieces than Mr. Halloran. Who ate the most shrimp?

2. David had to write a 500-word report. He wrote half of the report at the park, and half of what was left on the way home. How many words did he have to write to finish the report?

Practice

Write whether each problem gives enough information to solve. Solve if possible, or write what is needed to solve. Use any strategy.

3. **Patterns** Maryanne cut a piece of paper in half. Then she cut one of the halves in half again. If she continues to do this, how many cuts will she make before getting a piece of paper that is $\frac{1}{32}$ the size of the original?

4. **Using Data** Use the Data File on page 356. In 1993, Texas fishermen landed a total of 84,716,200 pounds of shellfish. Give the ratio of the pounds of shellfish landed by Texans to the pounds landed from the Pacific Ocean.

5. **Money** At the park, Jennie bought a souvenir map for \$2.25, three postcards at \$0.50 each, and a key ring for \$1.00. If she gave the clerk a \$10.00 bill, what change did she receive?

Problem Solving Strategies

- Draw a Picture
- Look for a Pattern
- Guess and Check
- Use Logical Reasoning
- Make an Organized List
- Make a Table
- Solve a Simpler Problem
- Work Backward

Choose a Tool

Science Use the data in the table for **6** and **7.**

6. The Junior Florist Group needs to have at least 50 pumpkin seeds to germinate. How many packets should they purchase?

7. A packet of tomato seeds cost \$1.49 and a packet of zinnia seeds cost \$0.99. Which plant has the better germination rate?

8. The sixth graders decided to sell plants to raise money for a trip to a zoo in a nearby town. They charged \$1.25 for 4-inch plants and \$2 for 6-inch plants. How much money did they make on the plant sale?

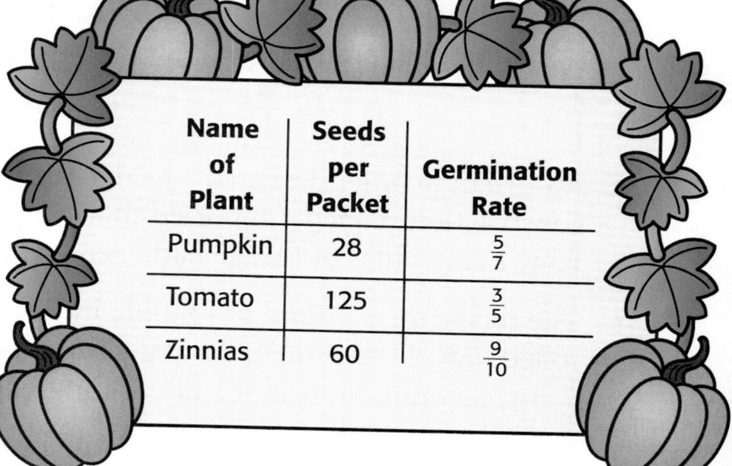

Name of Plant	Seeds per Packet	Germination Rate
Pumpkin	28	$\frac{5}{7}$
Tomato	125	$\frac{3}{5}$
Zinnias	60	$\frac{9}{10}$

SECTION A

Review and Practice

(Lesson 1) Estimate each product or quotient.

1. $8\frac{7}{8} \div 3\frac{1}{3}$ **2.** $8\frac{9}{10} \times 2\frac{7}{8}$ **3.** $9\frac{3}{5} \times 2\frac{7}{8}$ **4.** $15\frac{1}{7} \div 2\frac{9}{10}$

5. A recipe for pasta salad calls for $2\frac{2}{3}$ cups of cooked pasta. Alberto has 5 cups of cooked pasta. Does Alberto have enough pasta to double the recipe?

(Lesson 2) Write the multiplication problem each model represents.

6. 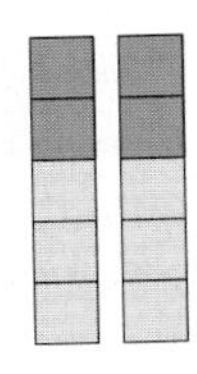

7. 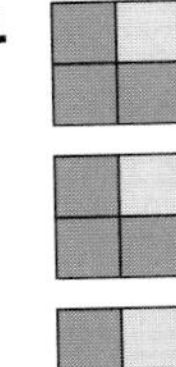

8. 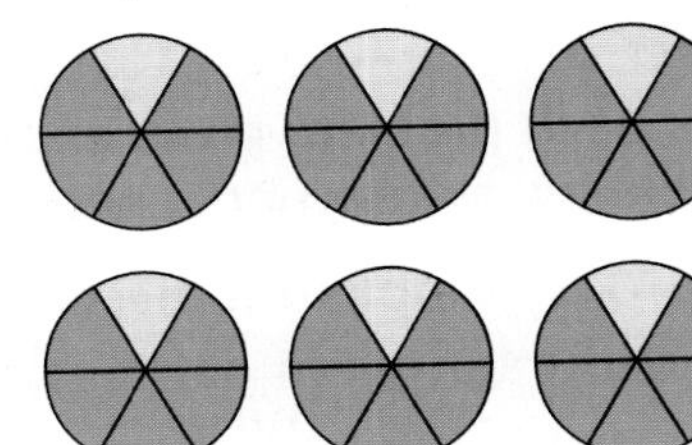

For **9** and **10**, use the cold cream recipe.

9. For each ingredient, find the amount you would use to triple the cold cream recipe.

10. For each ingredient, find the amount you would use to make 6 times as much cold cream.

Homemade Cold Cream

1 ounce bowstring wax*
$6\frac{1}{2}$ tablespoons mineral oil
3 tablespoons water
$\frac{1}{4}$ teaspoon borax

***Used for archery. Found in sports specialty stores.**

(Lesson 3) Find each product.

11. $\frac{4}{7} \times \frac{3}{4}$ **12.** $\frac{3}{5} \times \frac{8}{12}$ **13.** $1\frac{1}{5} \times 2\frac{2}{5}$ **14.** $5\frac{4}{9} \times 2\frac{2}{9}$

15. An urban planner designed a bridge that was $3\frac{1}{3}$ miles long. The construction manager reported that $\frac{1}{2}$ of the bridge was complete. How many miles of bridge had been completed?

16. The recipe for a pound of granola includes $2\frac{3}{4}$ cups rolled oats, $1\frac{1}{2}$ cups mixed nuts, $\frac{3}{4}$ cup raisins, and $\frac{1}{4}$ cup coconut. How much of each ingredient is needed to make $\frac{1}{2}$ pound granola?

17. Journal When you multiply a whole number and a fraction, will the product be equal to, greater, or less than the fraction if the whole number is 1? Greater than 1?

Skills Checklist

In this section, you have:

- **Estimated Products and Quotients of Fractions**
- **Multiplied Fractions by a Whole Number**
- **Multiplied Fractions by a Fraction**

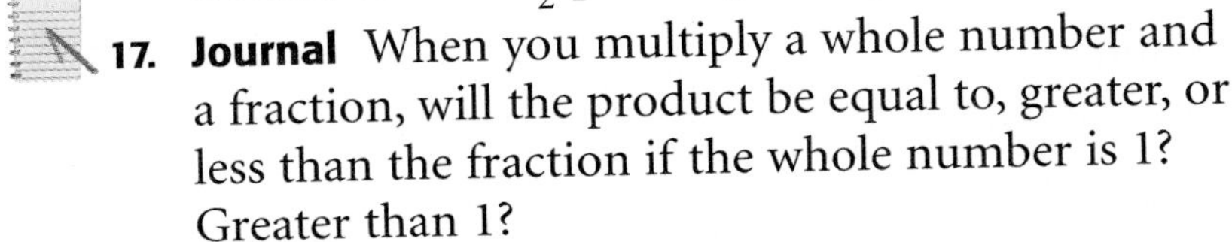

CHAPTER 7

SECTION

B Dividing Fractions

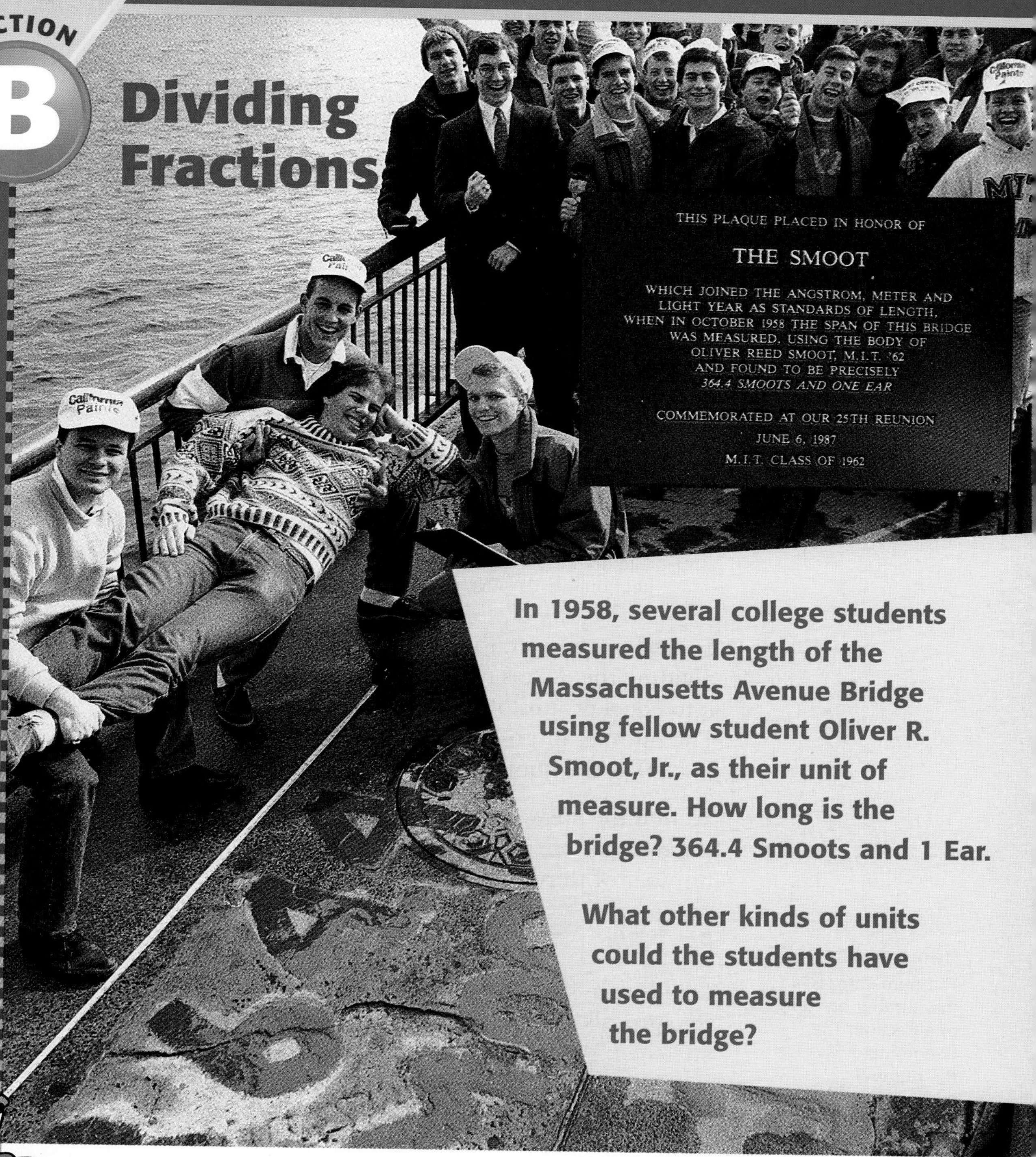

THIS PLAQUE PLACED IN HONOR OF

THE SMOOT

WHICH JOINED THE ANGSTROM, METER AND LIGHT YEAR AS STANDARDS OF LENGTH, WHEN IN OCTOBER 1958 THE SPAN OF THIS BRIDGE WAS MEASURED, USING THE BODY OF OLIVER REED SMOOT, M.I.T. '62 AND FOUND TO BE PRECISELY *364.4 SMOOTS AND ONE EAR*

COMMEMORATED AT OUR 25TH REUNION JUNE 6, 1987 M.I.T. CLASS OF 1962

In 1958, several college students measured the length of the Massachusetts Avenue Bridge using fellow student Oliver R. Smoot, Jr., as their unit of measure. How long is the bridge? 364.4 Smoots and 1 Ear.

What other kinds of units could the students have used to measure the bridge?

GET READY!

Dividing Fractions

Review multiplying with fractions. Find each product.

1. $\frac{2}{3} \times \frac{3}{5}$ **2.** $\frac{3}{8} \times \frac{5}{6}$ **3.** $\frac{5}{7} \times 2\frac{1}{3}$

4. $3\frac{1}{4} \times 2\frac{2}{9}$ **5.** $1\frac{3}{5} \times 3\frac{3}{8}$ **6.** $2\frac{1}{2} \times 1\frac{3}{7}$

Review dividing. Find each quotient.

7. $1,470 \div 42$ **8.** $3,420 \div 36$ **9.** $2,013 \div 3$

Skills Checklist

In this section, you will:

- ❒ Divide Whole Numbers by Fractions
- ❒ Divide Fractions by Fractions
- ❒ Solve Fraction Equations

Chapter 7
Lesson
4

Dividing Whole Numbers by Fractions

You Will Learn

- to divide a whole number by a fraction

Vocabulary

reciprocal

Learn

Danielle enjoys trying out new recipes and sharing what she makes with family and friends. Suppose Danielle has a recipe that makes 6 cups of pasta sauce, and she wants to know how many $\frac{2}{3}$-cup servings this recipe will make.

Danielle does most of her cooking from her home in West Nyack, New York.

To find the answer, think of dividing the 6 cups of sauce into equal groups of $\frac{2}{3}$, or $6 \div \frac{2}{3}$. The number of groups you have, 9, is the quotient.

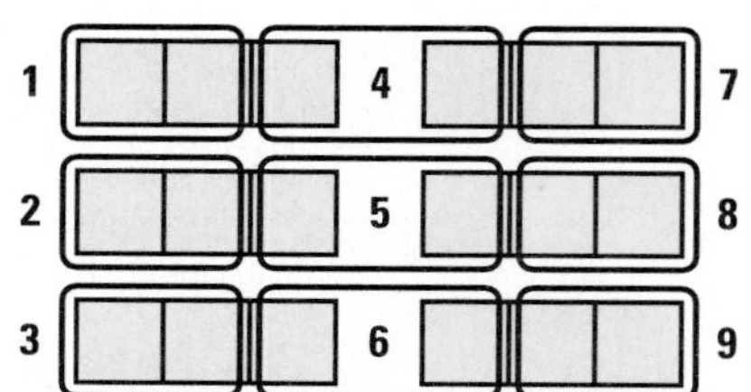

To find the answer, you first found the number of thirds by multiplying the number of cups, 6, by the denominator, 3. Then you divided the number of thirds by the numerator, 2.

$$6 \div \frac{2}{3} = 6 \times 3 \div 2 = 9$$

Remember

The numerator is the number on top of a fraction. The denominator is the number on the bottom.

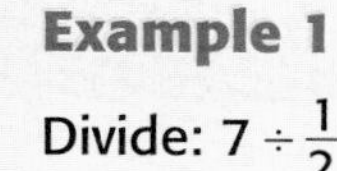

Dividing by a fraction is the same as multiplying by its **reciprocal**. Reciprocals are numbers whose numerators and denominators have been switched. When two numbers are reciprocals, their product is 1.

Example 1

Divide: $7 \div \frac{1}{2}$

$7 \div \frac{1}{2} = \frac{7}{1} \times \frac{2}{1}$ — Multiply by the reciprocal.

$= \frac{7 \times 2}{1 \times 1}$

$= \frac{14}{1}$, or 14 — Simplify.

The reciprocal of $\frac{1}{2}$ is $\frac{2}{1}$ because $\frac{1}{2} \times \frac{2}{1} = 1$.

To divide with mixed numbers, rewrite the mixed numbers as improper fractions. Then multiply by the reciprocal of the divisor.

Example 2

Three measurements used primarily for cloth include the *nail,* the *finger,* and the *span*. A *finger* is equal to $4\frac{1}{2}$ inches. A *span* is equal to 9 inches. 1 *nail* $= 2\frac{1}{4}$ inches of cloth. Find the length of 5 inches of cloth in nails.

Divide: $5 \div 2\frac{1}{4}$

$5 \div 2\frac{1}{4} = \frac{5}{1} \div \frac{9}{4}$ — Rewrite $2\frac{1}{4}$ as an improper fraction.

$= \frac{5}{1} \times \frac{4}{9}$ — Multiply by the reciprocal of the divisor.

$= \frac{5 \times 4}{1 \times 9}$

$= \frac{20}{9}$, or $2\frac{2}{9}$ — Simplify.

A 5-inch piece of cloth is $2\frac{2}{9}$ nails long.

Talk About It

1. When you divide a whole number by a fraction less than 1, is the quotient greater or less than the original whole number? Why?
2. How is dividing 3 by $\frac{2}{5}$ different from multiplying 3 by $\frac{2}{5}$?
3. How can you use the "reciprocal rule" for dividing by a fraction to find $25 \div 5$?
4. How can you find the reciprocal of a mixed number?

Check

State the reciprocal of each fraction.

1. $\frac{2}{3}$ **2.** $\frac{12}{45}$ **3.** $\frac{3}{8}$ **4.** $2\frac{3}{4}$ **5.** $\frac{23}{55}$

Simplify.

6. $4 \div \frac{3}{5}$ **7.** $1 \div \frac{4}{7}$ **8.** $10 \div \frac{17}{4}$ **9.** $3 \div \frac{3}{5}$

10. $8 \div 2\frac{1}{4}$ **11.** $15 \div 1\frac{2}{3}$ **12.** $2 \div 3\frac{1}{5}$ **13.** $12 \div 2\frac{2}{5}$

14. Reasoning Will $3 \div \frac{2}{5}$ have a whole number answer? Explain.

Practice

Skills and Reasoning

State the reciprocal of each fraction

15. $\frac{5}{7}$ **16.** $\frac{1}{2}$ **17.** $\frac{2}{9}$ **18.** $\frac{10}{14}$ **19.** $\frac{1}{4}$ **20.** $\frac{4}{5}$

Simplify.

21. $6 \div \frac{1}{3}$ **22.** $2 \div \frac{3}{5}$ **23.** $3 \div \frac{6}{7}$ **24.** $1 \div \frac{3}{4}$

25. $9 \div \frac{4}{5}$ **26.** $7 \div \frac{6}{5}$ **27.** $4 \div 3\frac{5}{8}$ **28.** $5 \div \frac{1}{4}$

29. $10 \div 7\frac{2}{3}$ **30.** $8 \div 8\frac{7}{8}$ **31.** $3 \div \frac{10}{11}$ **32.** $5 \div \frac{9}{2}$

33. $16 \div \frac{2}{5}$ **34.** $7 \div 6\frac{3}{4}$ **35.** $8 \div 2\frac{1}{6}$ **36.** $2 \div 4\frac{2}{7}$

37. Algebra Readiness What number divided by $\frac{2}{3}$ is 24?

38. Write Your Own Problem Write a division equation using $\frac{3}{8}$, 2, and $5\frac{1}{3}$.

39. Reasoning How could you rearrange the numbers in $2 \div \frac{5}{18}$ so that the quotient is a whole number?

Problem Solving and Applications

40. Measurement Use your calculator to convert 8°C to Fahrenheit. To convert from Celsius to Fahrenheit, divide by $\frac{5}{9}$, then add 32.

41. Collecting Data Use a strip of paper 3 feet long. Record the "hands" length it is for 10 different people.

Use the Data File on page 357 for **42** and **43**.

42. How many $\frac{2}{3}$ lb of butter could you get from a firkin of butter?

43. A *quire* of paper is $\frac{1}{20}$ of a ream. Monique wanted to know how many sheets of paper were in a quire. She calculated and decided that a quire of paper was 10,000 sheets. Is her answer reasonable? Explain?

44. Using Data Use the data about measuring cloth on page 377 to find the length of 36 inches in fingers.

45. Time A certain brand of candle burns evenly. If one candle lasts for $\frac{4}{5}$ of an hour, how many candles will you need to keep time for a day?

46. **Critical Thinking** This recipe makes 1 batch of cookies. About how many batches can you make if you change the recipe to include the following? Explain your answers.

a. A 2-pound bag of flour? (1 cup $= \frac{1}{4}$ pound)

b. A pound of margarine? (1 cup $= \frac{1}{2}$ pound)

c. A 4-pound bag of white sugar? (1 cup $= \frac{1}{2}$ pound)

PRACTICE AND APPLY

47. **Science** $\frac{4}{5}$ of a cubic foot of copper weighs 440 pounds. What is the weight of 1 cubic foot of copper?

48. **Social Studies** Pennsylvania has 21 seats in the House of Representatives. This is $\frac{7}{10}$ as many seats as Texas has. How many seats does Texas have?

49. A faucet drips every $\frac{2}{15}$ of a minute. How many drips would drop in 30 minutes?

50. **Journal** Explain how you can tell if two numbers are reciprocals of each other.

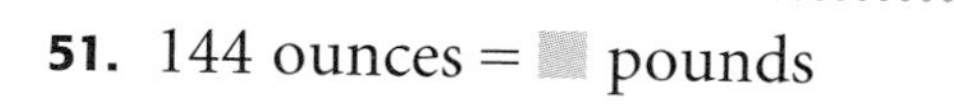

Mixed Review and Test Prep

51. 144 ounces = ▒ pounds

52. 56 pounds = ▒ ounces

53. 80 ounces = ▒ pounds

54. 100 gallons = ▒ quarts

55. 64 quarts = ▒ gallons

56. 40 gallons = ▒ quarts

For each fraction, draw a model.

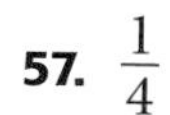

57. $\frac{1}{4}$ 58. $\frac{7}{8}$ 59. $\frac{4}{7}$ 60. $\frac{80}{100}$ 61. $\frac{9}{15}$ 62. $\frac{5}{7}$

63. Which two expressions have the same product as $2\frac{3}{4} \times 4\frac{3}{9}$?

I. $\frac{11}{4} \times \frac{39}{9}$ II. $\frac{11}{3} \times \frac{39}{3}$ III. $8 \times \frac{9}{36}$ IV. $\frac{11}{4} \times \frac{13}{3}$

Ⓐ I and II Ⓑ I and IV Ⓒ III and II Ⓓ III and IV

Chapter 7
Lesson
5

Dividing Fractions by Fractions

Problem Solving Connection
- Draw a Picture

Materials
Fraction Bars®

Explore

When you divide a whole number by a fraction, you get the same result as if you had multiplied the whole number by the fraction's reciprocal. This is also true when you divide a fraction by a fraction.

Work Together

1. Use fraction bars to find $\frac{2}{3} \div \frac{1}{12}$.
   a. Line up the fraction bars for the first fraction.
   b. Line up fraction bars for the second fraction.
   c. Describe the number of times the second fraction is placed below the first fraction bar.

$\frac{1}{3}$ $\frac{1}{3}$

$\frac{1}{12}$

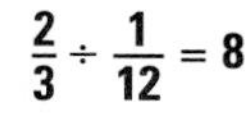
$\frac{2}{3} \div \frac{1}{12} = 8$

2. Use fraction bars to find each quotient.

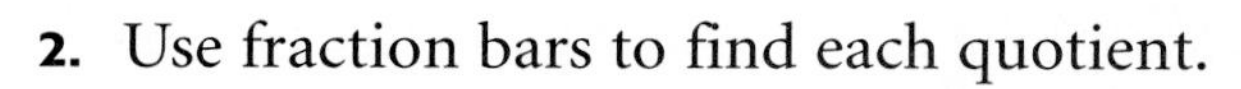

   a. $\frac{3}{6} \div \frac{1}{12}$ **b.** $\frac{1}{2} \div \frac{1}{4}$ **c.** $\frac{2}{3} \div \frac{1}{6}$ **d.** $\frac{2}{4} \div \frac{2}{12}$

Did You Know?
The term *furlong* originated in the Middle Ages. The furlong was originally a "furrow long," the length of a plowed strip of land on a standard-size field.

Dividing fractions by mixed numbers is similar to dividing whole numbers by mixed fractions.

3. Use fraction strips to find $\frac{1}{2} \div 1\frac{1}{2}$.
   a. Line up the fraction bars for the first fraction.
   b. Line up fraction bars for the second fraction.
   c. Describe the part of the second fraction that is below the first fraction bar.

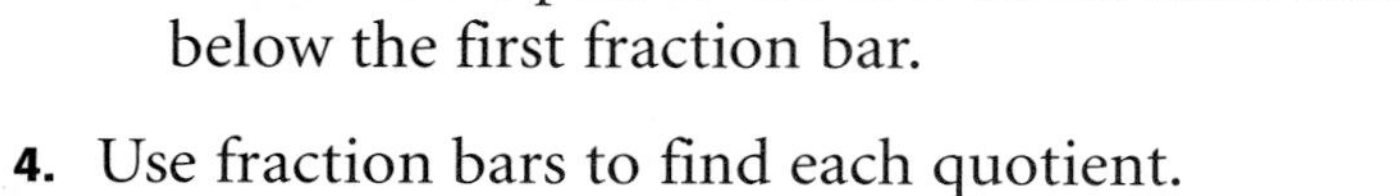

$\frac{1}{2}$

$1\frac{1}{2}$

$\frac{1}{3}$ of $1\frac{1}{2}$

4. Use fraction bars to find each quotient.

   a. $\frac{2}{3} \div 2\frac{2}{3}$ **b.** $\frac{1}{2} \div 1\frac{1}{3}$ **c.** $\frac{5}{8} \div 1\frac{1}{4}$ **d.** $\frac{1}{4} \div 1\frac{1}{4}$

Talk About It

5. When you divide a fraction by a fraction less than 1, why is the answer greater than the fraction you started with?
6. When you divide a fraction by a mixed number, why is the answer less than the fraction you started with?
7. How is dividing a fraction by a fraction similar to dividing a whole number by a fraction?

Connect and Learn

Dividing a whole number or a fraction by a fraction is the same as multiplying the whole number by the fraction's reciprocal.

Example 1

Horse races are measured in *furlongs* (1 furlong $= \frac{1}{8}$ mi). The Kentucky Derby is $1\frac{1}{4}$ mi long. How long is it in furlongs?

$1\frac{1}{4} \div \frac{1}{8} = \frac{5}{4} \div \frac{1}{8}$ Write the numbers as fractions.

$= \frac{5}{4} \times \frac{8}{1}$ Multiply by the reciprocal.

$= \frac{40}{4}$, or 10 Simplify.

The Kentucky Derby is 10 furlongs long.

When dividing by a mixed number, write it as an improper fraction.

Example 2

What is $\frac{2}{5} \div 3\frac{1}{4}$?

$\frac{2}{5} \div 3\frac{1}{4} = \frac{2}{5} \div \frac{13}{4}$ Write the mixed number as an improper fraction.

$= \frac{2}{5} \times \frac{4}{13}$ Multiply by the reciprocal of $\frac{13}{4}$.

$= \frac{8}{65}$ Simplify.

When dividing by a whole number, write it as a fraction with a denominator of 1.

Example 3

What is $\frac{3}{5} \div 6$?

$\frac{3}{5} \div 6 = \frac{3}{5} \div \frac{6}{1}$ Rewrite the whole number.

$= \frac{3}{5} \times \frac{1}{6}$ Multiply by the reciprocal of $\frac{6}{1}$.

$= \frac{3}{30}$, or $\frac{1}{10}$ Simplify.

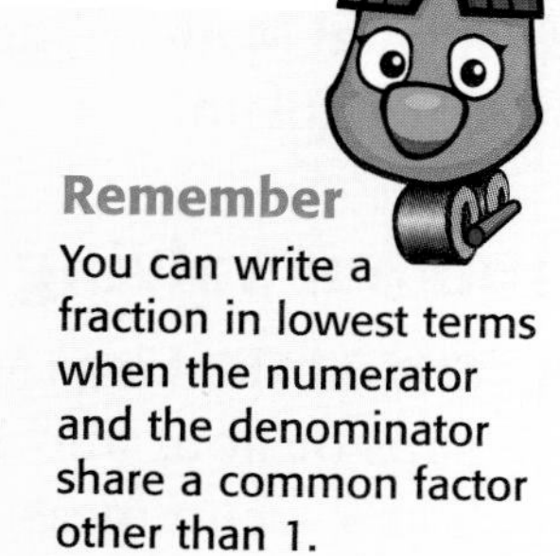

Remember

You can write a fraction in lowest terms when the numerator and the denominator share a common factor other than 1.

Check

Divide.

1. $\frac{4}{5} \div \frac{5}{8}$ **2.** $\frac{3}{7} \div \frac{2}{7}$ **3.** $\frac{1}{5} \div 2$ **4.** $\frac{2}{5} \div 4\frac{3}{5}$

5. Reasoning $\frac{1}{2} \times \frac{1}{4} = \frac{1}{4} \times \frac{1}{2}$. Does $\frac{1}{2} \div \frac{1}{4} = \frac{1}{4} \div \frac{1}{2}$? Explain.

Practice

Skills and Reasoning

Write the division problem that each model represents.

6. $\frac{1}{3}$ $\frac{1}{3}$ / $\frac{1}{6}$ $\frac{1}{6}$ $\frac{1}{6}$ $\frac{1}{6}$

7. 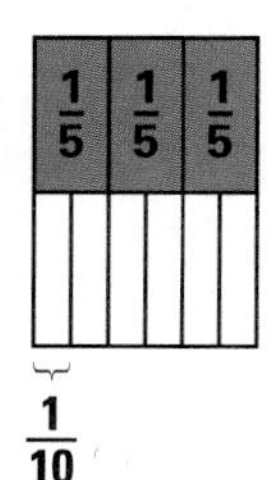

8. 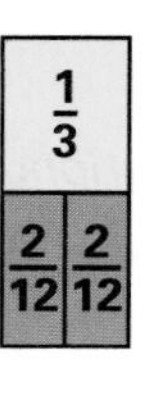

9. $\frac{1}{4}$ $\frac{1}{4}$ / $\frac{1}{6}$ $\frac{1}{6}$ $\frac{1}{6}$

Divide.

10. $\frac{6}{15} \div \frac{3}{3}$
11. $\frac{1}{3} \div 6$
12. $\frac{7}{8} \div \frac{1}{8}$
13. $\frac{6}{7} \div \frac{2}{7}$
14. $\frac{15}{16} \div \frac{3}{4}$
15. $\frac{1}{4} \div \frac{1}{2}$
16. $\frac{5}{7} \div 6\frac{3}{4}$
17. $\frac{1}{2} \div \frac{2}{3}$
18. $\frac{2}{3} \div 9\frac{4}{3}$
19. $1\frac{1}{2} \div \frac{1}{2}$
20. $2\frac{1}{2} \div 8$
21. $2\frac{7}{8} \div 1\frac{1}{12}$
22. $2\frac{1}{2} \div \frac{1}{4}$
23. $4\frac{1}{3} \div 3$
24. $2\frac{2}{3} \div \frac{1}{3}$
25. $\frac{1}{2} \div 3\frac{3}{4}$
26. $\frac{4}{5} \div 5$
27. $\frac{9}{14} \div \frac{3}{7}$
28. $3\frac{4}{5} \div 8\frac{1}{5}$
29. $\frac{11}{13} \div \frac{13}{11}$
30. **Reasoning** If $5 \div \frac{x}{3} = 5 \times \frac{x}{3}$, what is the value of x? Explain.
31. **Estimation** Use rounding to estimate the quotient of $3\frac{5}{6}$ and $1\frac{7}{8}$. Compare your estimate to the exact quotient.
32. Which expression has the lesser quotient: $6\frac{1}{2} \div \frac{1}{2}$ or $6\frac{1}{2} \div 3\frac{1}{2}$?

33. **Mental Math** Which numbers are evenly divisible by $\frac{1}{2}$: 12, 13, 23, and 31? Explain.

Problem Solving and Applications

34. **Critical Thinking** A popover recipe calls for $1\frac{1}{4}$ cups of flour and $1\frac{1}{4}$ cups of milk. If you only had a $\frac{1}{2}$-cup measure, how could you use it to complete the recipe?
35. **Measurement** A developer plans to subdivide 15 acres of land into $1\frac{1}{2}$-acre building sites. How many building sites will there be?
36. **Write Your Own Problem** Choose 2 fractions of your own. Find their quotient. Interchange the dividend and divisor and find their quotient. What do you notice?

37. Industry The size of letters in printed material such as newspapers or books is measured in points. One point equals $\frac{1}{72}$ of an inch.

a. What is the point size of type that is $\frac{1}{8}$ of an inch high?

b. What is the point size of type that is $1\frac{1}{2}$ inches high?

PRACTICE AND APPLY

38. Measurement Caroline received a letter from England telling her about the birth of a new baby. The baby weighed $\frac{1}{2}$ stone. One pound equals $\frac{1}{14}$ stone. How many pounds did the baby weigh?

39. One peck equals $\frac{1}{2}$ bushel. If Peter Piper had picked a half-bushel of pickled peppers, how many pecks of pickled peppers would Peter Piper have picked?

40. Use a calculator to determine x in the following equation.

$$6\frac{1}{2} \div \frac{7}{x} = \frac{286}{14}$$

41. Collecting Data Measure the length of a pencil and a pen to the nearest $\frac{1}{8}$ inch. Divide each length by $\frac{2}{3}$. Which is greater? By how much?

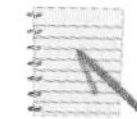

42. Journal Explain why $5\frac{1}{2} \div \frac{1}{2}$ has a larger quotient than $5\frac{1}{2} \div 2\frac{1}{2}$.

Mixed Review and Test Prep

Find the missing measurements for each circle, where r = radius, d = diameter, and C = circumference. Use 3.14 for π.

43. $r = ▒$, $d = 1.4$ km, $C = ▒$

44. $r = ▒$, $d = ▒$, $C = 50.24$ cm

45. $r = 4.2$ m, $d = ▒$, $C = ▒$

46. $r = ▒$, $d = ▒$, $C = 25.12$ mm

What fraction does each shaded part represent?

47. 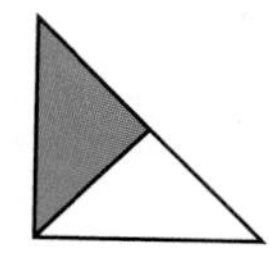

48. 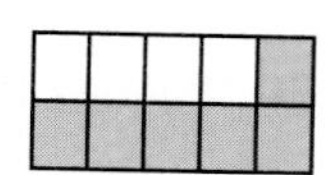

49. 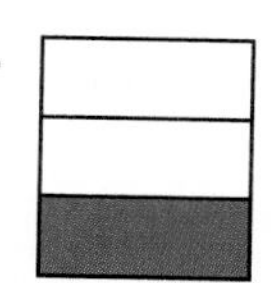

50. 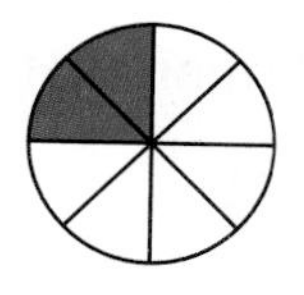

51. Choose the expression with the greatest product.

Ⓐ $4\frac{1}{3} \times 2$ Ⓑ $4\frac{1}{3} \times \frac{1}{2}$ Ⓒ $2 \times 4\frac{1}{3}$ Ⓓ $4 \times 3\frac{1}{2}$

and Practice

Simplify.

1. $3 \times \frac{4}{5}$
2. $\frac{2}{5} \times 7$
3. $9 \div \frac{8}{13}$
4. $1 \div \frac{1}{8}$
5. $5 \times \frac{1}{4}$
6. $10 \div 3\frac{5}{6}$
7. $\frac{6}{7} \div \frac{1}{3}$
8. $\frac{1}{6} \times 4$
9. $8 \div 4\frac{5}{8}$
10. $2\frac{1}{3} \times 4$
11. $\frac{11}{15} \div \frac{5}{9}$
12. $7 \times 4\frac{2}{3}$
13. $4 \div \frac{6}{2}$
14. $2 \div \frac{12}{3}$
15. $\frac{7}{10} \times \frac{1}{8}$
16. $11 \div 5\frac{1}{2}$
17. $\frac{3}{8} \times 2\frac{2}{5}$
18. $4\frac{1}{2} \div 8$
19. $3\frac{7}{8} \div 1\frac{1}{4}$
20. $\frac{2}{3} \times \frac{2}{3}$
21. $7 \div \frac{10}{9}$
22. $1\frac{3}{4} \times \frac{5}{13}$
23. $\frac{7}{8} \div \frac{9}{8}$
24. $3\frac{1}{3} \times 2\frac{2}{5}$
25. $4\frac{1}{3} \div \frac{5}{7}$
26. $\frac{19}{10} \div \frac{4}{4}$
27. $3\frac{1}{6} \times \frac{10}{11}$
28. $\frac{2}{9} \times 6\frac{3}{7}$
29. $\frac{12}{17} \times \frac{1}{3}$
30. $2\frac{4}{15} \times \frac{1}{2}$
31. $\frac{11}{14} \div \frac{1}{4}$
32. $\frac{5}{6} \div 1\frac{2}{13}$
33. $\frac{5}{13} \times 6$
34. $3\frac{4}{9} \div 10$
35. $\frac{11}{18} \div \frac{4}{3}$
36. $\frac{6}{15} \times \frac{3}{5}$
37. $1\frac{1}{8} \times 1\frac{1}{10}$
38. $5 \div 2\frac{7}{10}$
39. $9\frac{1}{2} \div \frac{1}{2}$
40. $1\frac{3}{4} \times 2\frac{3}{8}$
41. $1\frac{1}{8} \times \frac{2}{5}$
42. $\frac{6}{7} \times 2\frac{1}{2}$
43. $14 \div \frac{3}{4}$
44. $\frac{5}{9} \times 1\frac{1}{5}$
45. $2\frac{3}{5} \div \frac{5}{6}$
46. $\frac{3}{12} \times 3\frac{2}{3}$
47. $1\frac{4}{7} \div \frac{2}{3}$
48. $\frac{5}{12} \times \frac{1}{2}$
49. $2\frac{1}{4} \times \frac{7}{12}$
50. $\frac{6}{10} \div \frac{1}{5}$
51. $2\frac{2}{7} \times \frac{6}{9}$
52. $2\frac{2}{9} \div \frac{5}{8}$
53. $\frac{4}{7} \times 2\frac{8}{9}$
54. $\frac{6}{13} \times \frac{2}{3}$
55. $3\frac{1}{3} \div \frac{4}{9}$
56. $12 \div 2\frac{7}{8}$

Error Search

Find each solution that is not correct. Write it correctly and explain the error.

57. $4 \div 3\frac{1}{3} = 13\frac{1}{3}$
58. $1\frac{3}{8} \times \frac{5}{8} = 6\frac{7}{8}$
59. $\frac{5}{6} \times \frac{4}{7} = 1\frac{11}{24}$
60. $2 \div 4\frac{1}{10} = 8\frac{1}{5}$
61. $\frac{5}{4} \div \frac{4}{5} = \frac{9}{20}$
62. $2\frac{2}{8} \div 2 = 1\frac{1}{8}$

Funny Moon-ey!

Simplify. Match each answer to a number below the blanks. Then find the answer to the question. Some letters are not used.

Why is the moon like a dollar?

___ $\frac{27}{40}$ ___ $15\frac{1}{5}$ ___ $3\frac{2}{7}$ ___ $11\frac{4}{7}$ ___ 35 ___ $\frac{8}{21}$ ___ $1\frac{3}{5}$ ___ $\frac{1}{6}$ ___ $\frac{12}{91}$

___ $3\frac{7}{8}$ ___ $\frac{1}{6}$ ___ $11\frac{4}{7}$ ___ $\frac{12}{91}$ ___ $15\frac{1}{5}$ ___ $1\frac{8}{13}$ ___ $\frac{12}{91}$ ___ 35

63. $5 \div \frac{1}{7}$ (S) **64.** $\frac{1}{5} \times 8$ (O) **65.** $4 \div 2\frac{1}{9}$ (N) **66.** $1\frac{2}{7} \times 9$ (A)

67. $8 \times \frac{7}{9}$ (L) **68.** $3 \div \frac{13}{7}$ (E) **69.** $\frac{8}{9} \div \frac{2}{3}$ (M) **70.** $2 \times 7\frac{3}{5}$ (T)

71. $\frac{3}{7} \div 3\frac{1}{4}$ (R) **72.** $\frac{2}{9} \times \frac{3}{4}$ (U) **73.** $\frac{3}{8} \times 1\frac{4}{5}$ (I) **74.** $2\frac{4}{7} \times \frac{1}{5}$ (C)

75. $\frac{4}{9} \times \frac{6}{7}$ (F) **76.** $1\frac{5}{9} \times 2\frac{2}{7}$ (D) **77.** $\frac{5}{7} \times 4\frac{3}{5}$ (H) **78.** $5\frac{1}{6} \div 1\frac{1}{3}$ (Q)

Number Sense Estimation and Reasoning

Compare using <, >, or =. Use properties to help.

79. $6 \times \frac{1}{5}$ ● $6 \times \frac{1}{10}$ **80.** $12 \div \frac{1}{9}$ ● $12 \div \frac{7}{9}$ **81.** $\frac{1}{12} \times 20$ ● $20 \times \frac{1}{12}$

82. $\frac{8}{15} \div 4$ ● $4 \div \frac{8}{15}$ **83.** $12 \div \frac{1}{3}$ ● $9 \div \frac{1}{4}$ **84.** $\frac{1}{2} \times \frac{6}{7}$ ● $\frac{1}{4} \times \frac{6}{7}$

Technology

Using a Fraction Calculator to Find Fraction Products and Quotients

Materials
Fraction calculator

What would you do if you had to find $\frac{4}{70} \div \frac{14}{51}$? You can use a fraction calculator to help you work with large numbers. A fraction calculator can help you multiply or divide fractions.

What is the quotient of $\frac{4}{70} \div \frac{14}{51}$?

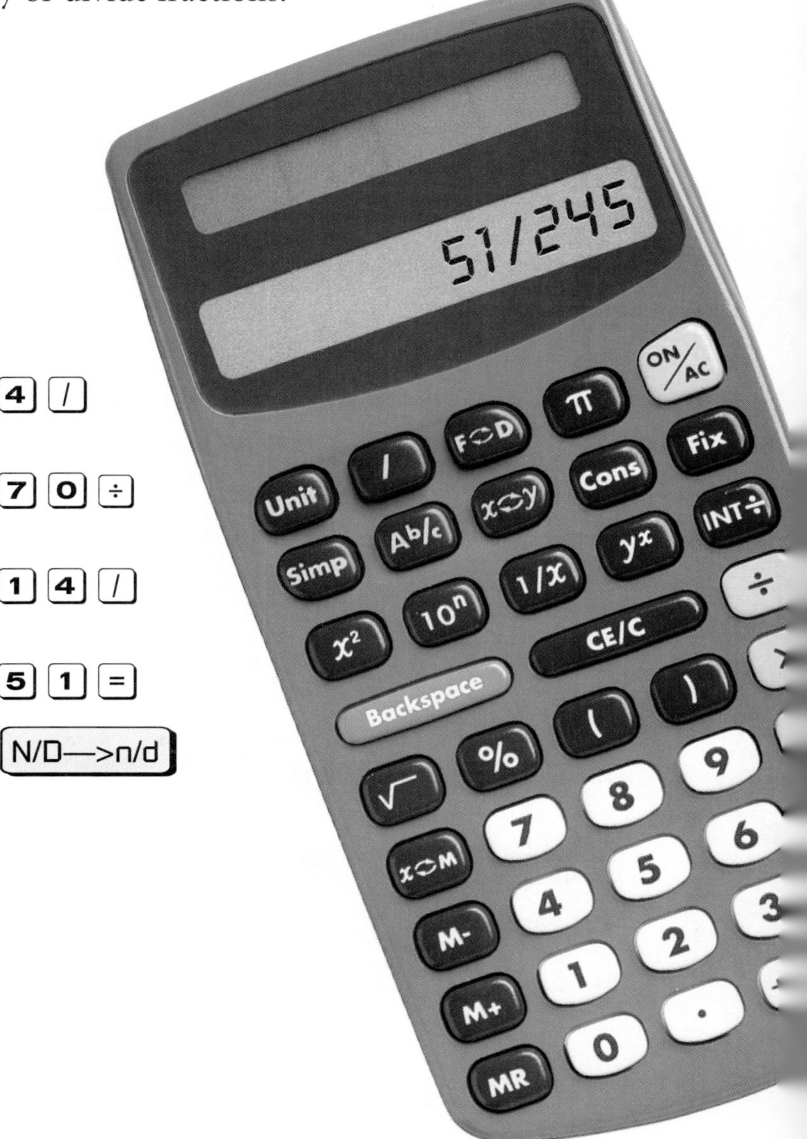

Work Together

Use a calculator to find the quotient.

1. Enter the numerator of the first fraction, then press the [/] key. — [4] [/]
2. Enter the denominator of the first fraction, then press the [÷] key. — [7] [0] [÷]
3. Enter the numerator of the second fraction, then press the [/] key. — [1] [4] [/]
4. Enter the denominator of the second fraction, press the [=] key. — [5] [1] [=]
5. Your calculator may indicate that the answer is not in lowest terms by showing N/D—>n/d in the display. Press the [Simp] key and then the [=] key to simplify the fraction. You may need to do this more than once to get the fraction in lowest terms. — N/D—>n/d
6. What is the quotient of $\frac{4}{70} \div \frac{14}{51}$?

Exercises

Use your calculator to find each product or quotient.

1. $\frac{7}{25} \times \frac{18}{31}$
2. $\frac{6}{37} \div \frac{10}{19}$
3. $\frac{12}{19} \times \frac{9}{25}$
4. $\frac{11}{27} \times \frac{4}{35}$
5. $\frac{3}{41} \div \frac{13}{22}$
6. $\frac{21}{76} \div \frac{6}{15}$
7. $\frac{8}{39} \times \frac{10}{21}$
8. $\frac{1}{25} \div \frac{13}{24}$
9. $\frac{4}{33} \times \frac{9}{17}$
10. $\frac{14}{21} \times \frac{7}{15}$
11. $\frac{13}{33} \times \frac{6}{19}$
12. $\frac{8}{23} \div \frac{17}{31}$
13. What is $\frac{5}{56} \times \frac{12}{13}$?
14. What is $\frac{6}{37} \times \frac{11}{20}$?
15. What is $\frac{2}{43} \div \frac{19}{20}$?
16. What is $\frac{2}{57} \div \frac{13}{18}$?

Extensions

If the quotient of two fractions is larger than 1, the calculator will display the answer as an improper fraction. However, you can use your calculator to change an improper fraction to a mixed number.

Display

The [Ab/c] key will convert the improper fraction into a mixed number. The **u** in the display tells you it is a mixed number: $1\frac{224}{364}$. Remember, you may still need to reduce the answer to lowest terms by using the [Simp] and [=] keys first. $1\frac{224}{364}$ simplifies to $1\frac{8}{13}$.

Use your calculator to find each quotient. Convert all improper fractions to mixed numbers with your calculator.

17. $\frac{11}{24} \div \frac{13}{32}$
18. $\frac{19}{29} \div \frac{5}{16}$
19. $\frac{14}{17} \div \frac{4}{27}$
20. $\frac{9}{11} \div \frac{20}{31}$
21. $\frac{18}{23} \div \frac{29}{42}$
22. $\frac{20}{29} \div \frac{4}{31}$
23. $\frac{9}{17} \div \frac{5}{32}$
24. $\frac{11}{20} \div \frac{16}{41}$
25. When multiplying or dividing fractions, is using a fraction calculator always the fastest way to find the answer? Explain.

Chapter 7
Lesson
6

Solving Fraction Equations: Multiplication and Division

Learn

What's the missing link? Surveyors often measure distances in *chains*. They use a special chain that is divided into 100 equal units, called *links*.

You Will Learn

- to solve multiplication and division equations containing fractions

You can use mental math to solve multiplication equations involving fractions.

Example 1

Solve: $\frac{2}{3}x = \frac{8}{15}$

$\frac{2}{3}x = \frac{8}{15}$	Read as "What number times $\frac{2}{3}$ equals $\frac{8}{15}$?"
$\frac{2}{3} \times \frac{4}{?} = \frac{8}{15}$	Using mental math, find the numerator.
$\frac{2}{3} \times \frac{4}{5} = \frac{8}{15}$	Using mental math, find the denominator.
$\frac{8}{15} = \frac{8}{15}$	Check to see that the equation is true.

x is equal to $\frac{4}{5}$.

If the equation includes whole numbers or mixed numbers, you can rewrite these numbers as fractions.

Did You Know?

The surveyor's chain is also known as Gunter's chain, after its inventor, the English mathematician Edmund Gunter. Each link is $7\frac{23}{25}$ in. long.

Example 2

A field 33 yards long measured $1\frac{1}{2}$ chains. How many yards are in a chain?

Let x = the number of yards in a chain.

$1\frac{1}{2}x = 33$	Read as "What number times $1\frac{1}{2}$ equals 33?"
$\frac{3}{2}x = 33$	Write the mixed number as an improper fraction.
$\frac{3}{2}x = \frac{66}{2}$	Write the whole number as a fraction with the same denominator.
$\frac{3}{2} \times \frac{22}{1} = \frac{66}{2}$	Use mental math.

1 chain equals 22 yards.

You can use mental math to solve division equations involving fractions. Rewrite the equations as a multiplication equation by using the reciprocal of the divisor.

Example 3

Solve: $y \div \frac{2}{3} = \frac{9}{10}$

$y \times \frac{3}{2} = \frac{9}{10}$ Rewrite as a multiplication equation.

$\frac{3}{5} \times \frac{3}{2} = \frac{9}{10}$ Use mental math.

$\frac{9}{10} = \frac{9}{10}$ Check to see that the equation is true.

y is equal to $\frac{3}{5}$.

You can rewrite the equations as a multiplication equation even if the unknown is the divisor. Your final answer will be the reciprocal of the answer to the multiplication equation.

Example 4

Solve: $\frac{4}{5} \div z = \frac{12}{25}$

$\frac{4}{5} \times ? = \frac{12}{25}$ Rewrite as a multiplication equation.

$\frac{4}{5} \times \frac{3}{5} = \frac{12}{25}$ Use mental math to solve the multiplication equation.

$z = \frac{5}{3}$ Use the reciprocal for the answer to the original equation.

Talk About It

1. Why is it sometimes a good idea to rewrite a division equation as a multiplication equation?
2. If fractions in a multiplication equation have unlike denominators, do you need to change them to fractions with like denominators? Explain.
3. When the unknown in a division equation is the divisor, why is the final answer the reciprocal of the answer to the multiplication equation?

Check

Solve for x.

1. $\frac{1}{2}x = 3$
2. $\frac{3}{4}x = \frac{15}{16}$
3. $1\frac{1}{4}\,x = 15$
4. $5x = 3$
5. $\frac{7}{3} \div x = 1\frac{1}{6}$
6. $\frac{4}{3} \div x = \frac{8}{12}$
7. $x \div 2\frac{2}{3} = \frac{9}{16}$
8. $x \div \frac{2}{3} = 6$
9. **Reasoning** Explain why the solution of $\frac{7}{8}\,x = 43$ is greater than 43.

Practice

Skills and Reasoning

For each equation, state if the given value will make the equation true.

10. $\frac{3}{5}x = \frac{9}{10}$; $x = \frac{2}{3}$ **11.** $\frac{1}{3}x = \frac{1}{15}$; $x = \frac{1}{4}$ **12.** $z \div \frac{4}{5} = \frac{10}{16}$; $z = \frac{4}{2}$

Solve.

13. $\frac{1}{2}g = 6$ **14.** $2k = \frac{4}{7}$ **15.** $\frac{8}{9} \div r = \frac{16}{18}$ **16.** $p \div \frac{5}{4} = 12$

17. $e \div \frac{6}{7} = \frac{1}{3}$ **18.** $\frac{4}{5}w = \frac{3}{5}$ **19.** $\frac{5}{6}t = 30$ **20.** $a \div 2\frac{2}{3} = \frac{3}{4}$

21. $q \div \frac{10}{3} = \frac{3}{4}$ **22.** $s \div 1\frac{1}{5} = 3\frac{1}{3}$ **23.** $\frac{5}{9}d = \frac{15}{27}$ **24.** $\frac{5}{7}f = 1\frac{4}{21}$

25. $7g = \frac{5}{8}$ **26.** $j \div 16 = 1\frac{3}{32}$ **27.** $\frac{3}{8}z = 1\frac{1}{8}$ **28.** $\frac{9}{2} \div c = 3\frac{3}{8}$

29. $\frac{5}{4} \div v = \frac{10}{16}$ **30.** $\frac{2}{3} \div b = \frac{16}{30}$ **31.** $6\frac{4}{5}m = 3\frac{2}{5}$ **32.** $i \div 8 = \frac{6}{7}$

33. **Reasoning** David says that $m = 8$ in $\frac{2}{3} \div m = \frac{1}{12}$. Jonathan says it is $\frac{1}{8}$. Who is correct? Explain.

34. Irene needs $\frac{1}{2}$ yard of ribbon for each wreath she makes. She is making 33 wreaths. If she has 20 yards of ribbon, does she have enough? Explain.

Problem Solving and Applications

Use the circle graph for **35–37.**

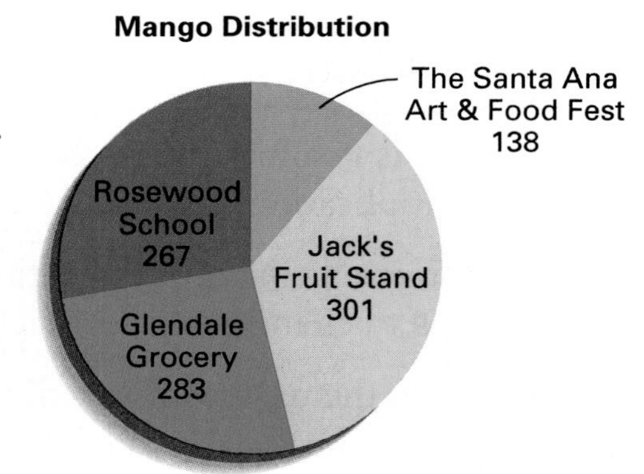

35. What fraction of the total number of mangoes went to Jack's Fruit Stand? Explain your reasoning.

36. Which place received about $\frac{3}{10}$ of the total mangoes? Explain how you can use estimation skills to determine this.

37. What fraction of the total number of mangoes went to either Glendale Grocery or the Rosewood School?

38. **History** Length was once measured in palms and spans. One inch equaled $\frac{1}{3}$ of a palm and $\frac{1}{9}$ of a span.

a. Which equation could you use to find the number of palms in 12 inches?

$p \div \frac{1}{3} = 12$ $\frac{1}{3}p = 12$

b. How many palms are in 12 inches?

c. Write and solve an equation to find the number of spans in 18 inches.

Problem Solving and SCIENCE

Use the data in the table to answer **39–43.**

The Avoirdupois [a-VWA-du-PWA] system of weight measurement is the part of the customary system used to measure most things in everyday life, such as food, cars, or people. The Troy system measures the weight of precious metals and jewels. One Avoirdupois grain equals one Troy grain.

Avoirdupois Weight	Troy Weight
$27\frac{11}{32}$ grains = 1 drachma	24 grains = 1 pennyweight
16 drachmas = 1 ounce	20 pennyweights = 1 ounce
16 ounces = 1 pound	12 ounces = 1 pound

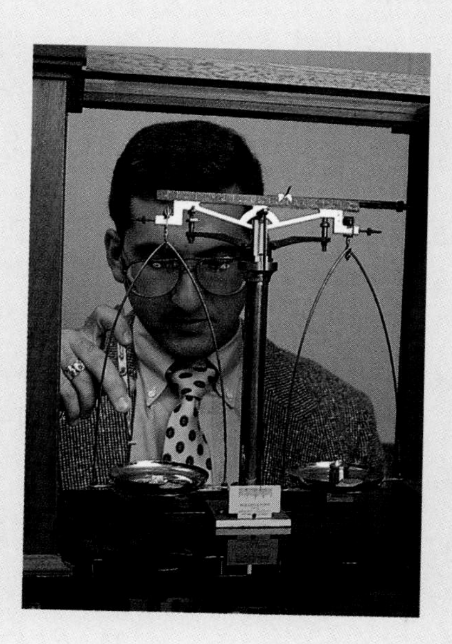

39. How many drachmas are in an Avoirdupois pound?

40. How many grains are in an Avoirdupois pound?

41. How many pennyweights are in a Troy pound?

42. How many grains are in a Troy pound?

43. The equation $x\frac{5760}{7000} = y$ can be used to convert from one type of pound to the other. Which variable represents an Avoirdupois pound? Which variable represents the Troy pound? Explain your reasoning.

44. A long ton in the Avoirdupois system equals $1\frac{3}{25}$ short tons. How many short tons would $3\frac{3}{4}$ long tons equal?

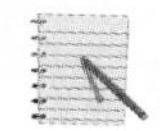

45. Journal Shaun said, "I'm thinking of a fraction. If I divide it by $\frac{1}{2}$, I get $\frac{7}{12}$." Describe how you would determine what fraction Shaun was thinking of.

Mixed Review and Test Prep

STAY SHARP!

Name two equivalent fractions for each.

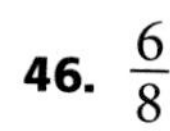

46. $\frac{6}{8}$ **47.** $\frac{3}{8}$ **48.** $\frac{2}{5}$ **49.** $\frac{10}{20}$ **50.** $\frac{6}{24}$ **51.** $\frac{11}{14}$

Find the GCF of each pair.

52. 4, 8 **53.** 3, 27 **54.** 18, 96 **55.** 7, 15 **56.** 33, 66

Solve.

57. $\frac{2}{3} + 1\frac{5}{9}$ **58.** $4\frac{3}{5} - 2\frac{7}{8}$ **59.** $8\frac{1}{3} + 3\frac{4}{11}$ **60.** $\frac{4}{9} - \frac{7}{81}$

61. Choose the expression with the greatest quotient.

Ⓐ $5\frac{1}{2} \div \frac{1}{4}$ Ⓑ $3\frac{1}{3} \div \frac{1}{4}$ Ⓒ $7 \div \frac{1}{4}$ Ⓓ $\frac{1}{10} \div \frac{1}{4}$

SECTION B

Review and Practice

1. Which of the following is the reciprocal for $2\frac{1}{3}$?

   Ⓐ $\frac{2}{3}$ Ⓑ $\frac{3}{7}$ Ⓒ $\frac{1}{6}$ Ⓓ $1\frac{1}{2}$

(Lesson 4) State the reciprocal of each fraction.

2. $\frac{4}{5}$
3. $1\frac{1}{2}$
4. $\frac{1}{6}$
5. $\frac{5}{6}$
6. $1\frac{3}{5}$

(Lessons 4 and 5) Simplify.

7. $4 \div \frac{1}{2}$
8. $\frac{2}{3} \div 12$
9. $2\frac{1}{2} \div 3$
10. $\frac{9}{4} \div \frac{1}{4}$
11. $\frac{6}{7} \div \frac{1}{3}$
12. $\frac{5}{4} \div \frac{6}{7}$
13. $2\frac{8}{11} \div 2$
14. $\frac{9}{10} \div \frac{4}{5}$
15. Ellen needs to take 2 teaspoons of medicine. She has only a $\frac{1}{2}$ teaspoon measure. How many $\frac{1}{2}$ teaspoons should she take? Explain whether Ellen should use an exact answer or an estimate.
16. The rod was once used to measure distance. There are $5\frac{1}{2}$ yd in 1 rod. How many rods equal 11 yd?

(Lesson 6) Solve.

17. $\frac{1}{2}v = 16$
18. $\frac{3}{5} \div k = 2\frac{1}{2}$
19. $x \div 6 = \frac{1}{3}$
20. $\frac{1}{3}w = 2\frac{2}{3}$
21. $2p = \frac{4}{5}$
22. $\frac{9}{5} \div e = 5$
23. $\frac{1}{2}u = \frac{4}{5}$
24. $c \div 4\frac{1}{3} = \frac{1}{3}$
25. $4z = \frac{1}{2}$
26. A Shetland pony is 11 hands high. One inch $= \frac{1}{4}$ hand. Explain how you can use either multiplication or division to find this pony's height in inches.
27. Write and solve an equation to find the number of centimeters in 5 inches. (1 inch $\approx 2\frac{1}{2}$ centimeters)
28. Write and solve an equation to find the number of gallons in 12 quarts. (1 quart $= \frac{1}{4}$ gallon)
29. Write and solve an equation to find the number of pints in $1\frac{1}{2}$ cups. (1 cup $= \frac{1}{2}$ pint)

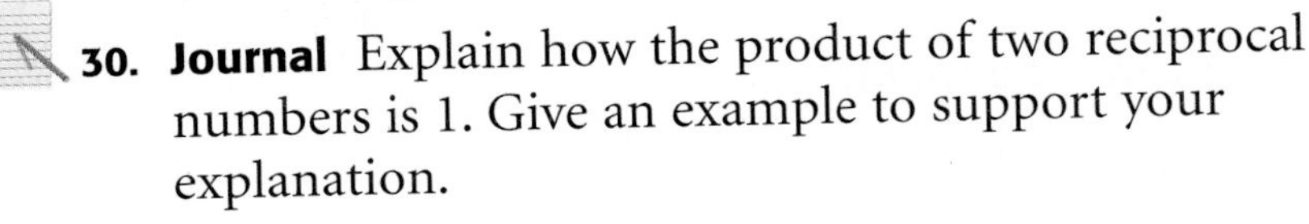

30. **Journal** Explain how the product of two reciprocal numbers is 1. Give an example to support your explanation.

Skills Checklist

In this section, you have:

- ☑ **Divided Whole Numbers by Fractions**
- ☑ **Divided Fractions by Fractions**
- ☑ **Solved Fraction Equations**

Choose at least one of the following. Use what you have learned in this chapter.

1 The 2-3-4-5 Scramble

You can form 24 mixed numbers using three of the digits 2, 3, 4, and 5 without repeating any digits. $2\frac{3}{5}$ and $4\frac{2}{3}$ are two possibilities. $2\frac{2}{3}$ is not a possibility because it repeats the digit 2.

Find the 24 possible mixed numbers and their decimal equivalents.

3 Horsing Around

The table lists the range of height, in hands, of several breeds of draft horses.

Horse	Height (in hands)	Colors
Belgian	15.3 to 17.0	chestnut, roan
Percheron	16.0 to 17.0	gray, black
Clydesdale	16.0 to 16.2	bay, brown
Shire	17.0 to 17.1	black, bay, brown, roan
German Coach	15.2 to 16.3	black
Suffolk	15.2 to 16.2	chestnut

One inch equals $\frac{1}{4}$ of a hand. Rewrite the chart to show the range of height in inches.

2 Recipes of Data

Collect copies of at least eight cake recipes. Each recipe should call for a specific amount of flour and either milk or water. Compile two lists, one for the amount of flour called for, and one for the amount of milk or water called for. (For example, if the recipe calls for $4\frac{1}{2}$ cups of flour, you would write $4\frac{1}{2}$ on your flour list.) For each list of amounts: What fraction of the total number of items on the lists are fractions? What is the mode? Is the mode a fraction?

4 High Bars

At Home Measure the heights of seven people, including yourself. Draw a bar graph of the data. Find the mean height. Which person is closest to having the mean height? Find the median height. Are there more people shorter than the median height, or taller than the median height? Why?

CHAPTER 7

Review/Test

Vocabulary Copy and complete the sentence by choosing the correct definition from the list.

1. A reciprocal is
   a. a number combining a whole number and a fraction
   b. the bottom number in a fraction
   c. a fraction whose numerator and denominator have been switched

(Lesson 1) Estimate.

2. $5\frac{2}{5} \times 2\frac{6}{8}$
3. $7\frac{3}{9} \times 10\frac{1}{4}$
4. $11\frac{1}{3} \div 1\frac{5}{6}$
5. $8\frac{4}{5} \div 3\frac{8}{11}$

(Lessons 2–4) Write the problem that each model represents.

6.
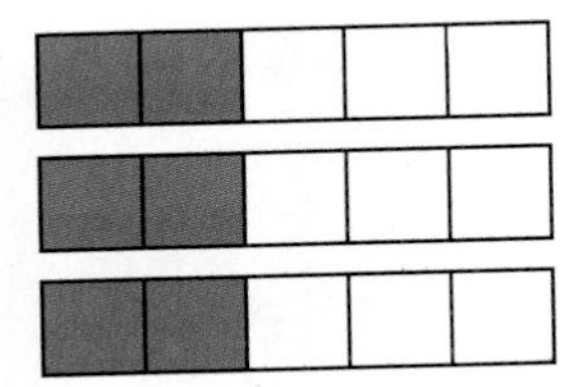

7.
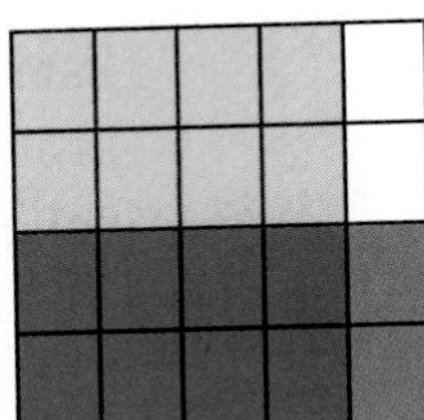

8.
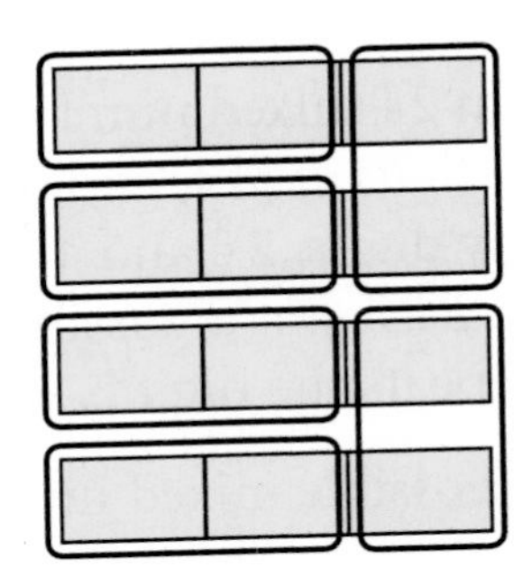

(Lessons 2–5) Simplify.

9. $3 \times \frac{4}{9}$
10. $6 \times 3\frac{3}{7}$
11. $\frac{1}{4} \times \frac{7}{8}$
12. $8\frac{4}{5} \times \frac{4}{7}$
13. $4 \times \frac{3}{11}$
14. $6 \times \frac{2}{5}$
15. $7 \times \frac{3}{10}$
16. $\frac{7}{10} \times \frac{1}{5}$
17. $9\frac{1}{2} \times \frac{7}{11}$
18. $7\frac{2}{5} \times \frac{7}{11}$
19. $9 \div \frac{2}{5}$
20. $8 \div 1\frac{1}{9}$
21. $8 \div \frac{2}{4}$
22. $4\frac{2}{3} \div 7$
23. $\frac{1}{7} \div \frac{2}{8}$
24. $\frac{5}{12} \div \frac{3}{4}$
25. $6\frac{1}{5} \div \frac{1}{9}$
26. $\frac{3}{8} \div \frac{5}{9}$
27. $2\frac{1}{2} \div \frac{1}{2}$
28. $2\frac{3}{5} \div \frac{2}{3}$

(Lesson 4) State the reciprocal.

29. $\frac{5}{9}$
30. $\frac{6}{11}$
31. 4
32. $4\frac{1}{3}$
33. $6\frac{4}{7}$

(Lesson 6) For each equation, state if the given value will make the equation true.

34. $\frac{1}{3}g = 10;\ g = 2$
35. $\frac{4}{7}w = \frac{12}{49};\ w = \frac{3}{7}$
36. $p \div \frac{1}{4} = 2;\ p = \frac{1}{8}$
37. $\frac{2}{9} \div r = \frac{2}{9};\ r = \frac{2}{9}$

(Lesson 6) Solve.

38. $\frac{2}{5}g = 8$
39. $\frac{3}{11}w = \frac{15}{88}$
40. $p \div \frac{3}{2} = \frac{2}{15}$
41. $\frac{5}{7} \div r = \frac{20}{21}$

42. Morgan made 10 cups of hot cocoa. Using a $1\frac{1}{4}$-cup ladle, she divided it among her after-school activity group so that each person received an equal serving. How many students are in Morgan's group?

REVIEW/TEST

CHAPTER 7

Performance Assessment

You and your friends are planning a camping trip. You are in charge of making and bringing enough trail mix. The trail mix needs to provide each person with one serving for each of the day of the trip. Here is the recipe for the trail mix:

1. **Analyzing the Data** How many cups in all does the recipe make? If one serving is $\frac{1}{2}$ cup, how many servings does the recipe make?

2. **Critical Thinking** Suppose 12 people go on the camping trip for 3 days. How many cups in all should you make? How much of each ingredient should you use to make enough trail mix for each person to have a $\frac{1}{2}$-cup serving on each day?

3. **Critical Thinking** Suppose 3 people are going on the camping trip for 3 days and each serving of trail mix is $\frac{1}{4}$ cup. How many cups in all should you make? How much of each ingredient should you use?

4. **Decision Making** Choose the number of people who will go on your camping trip, the number of days of the trip, and the amount of each serving of trail mix. List each of the ingredients and the amount you should use for your chosen situation. Include how many cups in all you should make.

5. **Explain Your Thinking** How did you decide on the amount of each ingredient? What information did you use?

Math Magazine

Left-Overs Again?

In the customary system of measurement, you can often convert from a small unit to a larger unit and get a whole number answer. For example, you can convert 24 inches to 2 feet. Sometimes, however, the answer does not work out evenly, and you have some of the smaller units left over.

When this happens, find the number of times the smaller units can be equally converted into the larger unit. Write the remainder in the smaller unit.

$$\begin{array}{r} 2\text{ R }7 \\ 12\overline{)31} \\ \underline{24} \\ 7 \end{array} =$$

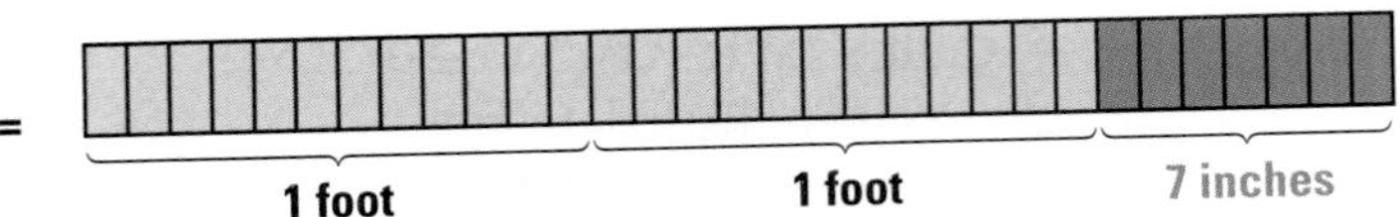

You know there are 12 inches in 1 foot. If you are converting 31 inches into feet, divide 31 by 12. You get 2 with a remainder of 7. So 31 inches equals 2 feet 7 inches.

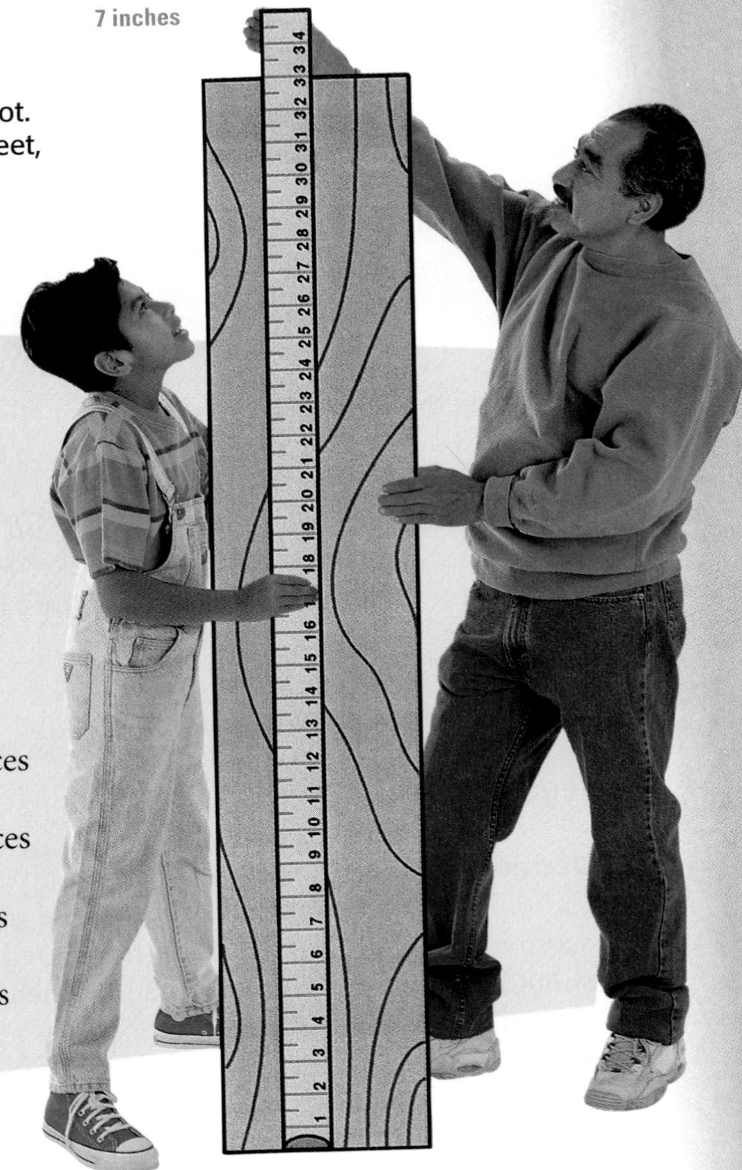

Try These!

Convert each measurement.

1. 40 inches = ■ feet ■ inches
2. 79 inches = ■ feet ■ inches
3. 13 feet = ■ yards ■ feet
4. 53 feet = ■ yards ■ feet
5. 50 ounces = ■ pounds ■ ounces
6. 91 ounces = ■ pounds ■ ounces
7. 11 quarts = ■ gallons ■ quarts
8. 31 quarts = ■ gallons ■ quarts

CHAPTERS 1–7

Cumulative Review

Test Prep Strategy: Eliminate Choices

Lawry has 30 yd of plastic to cover plants on cold nights. If he uses $\frac{3}{4}$ yd for each plant, how many plants can he cover?

Ⓐ 30 Ⓑ 75 Ⓒ 40 Ⓓ $22\frac{1}{2}$

Dividing a whole number by a fraction less than 1 will give a quotient larger than the whole number. This eliminates choices Ⓐ and Ⓓ. $30 \div \frac{3}{4} = 30 \times \frac{4}{3}$. This gives the answer $\frac{120}{3}$ or 40. Ⓒ is the correct choice.

Write the letter of the correct answer. Choose any strategy.

1. Choose the greatest number.
   Ⓐ 15,804 Ⓑ 158,040 Ⓒ 158,400 Ⓓ 158,004
2. Choose the best estimate for the product of 42.07 and 9.843.
   Ⓐ 400 Ⓑ 500 Ⓒ 360 Ⓓ 420
3. Calculate 5.38×6.46.
   Ⓐ 34.7 Ⓑ 34.75 Ⓒ 34.754 Ⓓ 34.7548
4. A circle's radius is 7 mm. What is its circumference?
   Ⓐ 14 mm Ⓑ 21.98 mm Ⓒ 43.96 mm Ⓓ not here
5. Which mixed number could be written as the improper fraction $\frac{13}{3}$?
   Ⓐ $4\frac{1}{3}$ Ⓑ $3\frac{1}{3}$ Ⓒ $4\frac{2}{3}$ Ⓓ $3\frac{2}{3}$
6. Simplify: $\frac{6}{13} + \frac{8}{13}$.
   Ⓐ $\frac{48}{13}$ Ⓑ $\frac{2}{13}$ Ⓒ $\frac{13}{14}$ Ⓓ not here
7. Estimate: $6\frac{5}{8} + 12\frac{3}{10}$.
   Ⓐ 19 Ⓑ 18 Ⓒ 20 Ⓓ 21
8. Estimate the data for point C on the graph.
   Ⓐ (15,4) Ⓑ (12, 12) Ⓒ (6, 7) Ⓓ (10, 10)

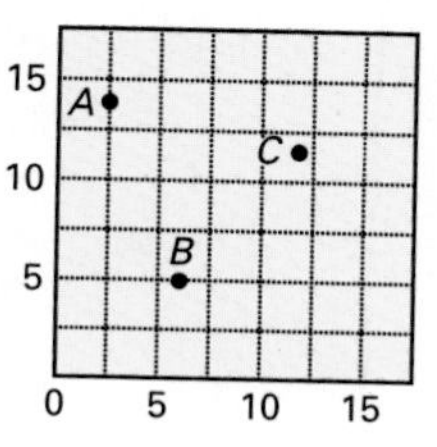

9. What is the sum of $4\frac{3}{4}$ and $7\frac{11}{12}$?
   Ⓐ $12\frac{4}{6}$ Ⓑ $12\frac{8}{12}$ Ⓒ $12\frac{2}{3}$ Ⓓ $11\frac{2}{3}$

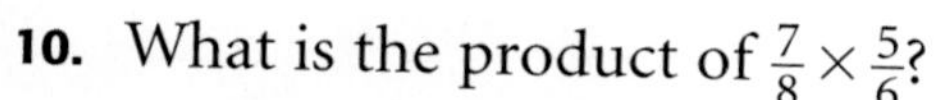

10. What is the product of $\frac{7}{8} \times \frac{5}{6}$?
   Ⓐ $\frac{5}{7}$ Ⓑ $\frac{35}{48}$ Ⓒ $\frac{35}{40}$ Ⓓ $\frac{8}{9}$
11. A factory used 24 yd of ribbon to decorate some hats. Each hat used $\frac{2}{3}$ yd of ribbon. Which equation shows the number of hats decorated?
   Ⓐ $\frac{2}{3} \div h = 24$ Ⓑ $24 \div h = \frac{2}{3}$ Ⓒ $24h = \frac{2}{3}$ Ⓓ $h \div \frac{2}{3} = 24$

Test Prep Strategies

- Read Carefully
- Follow Directions
- Make Smart Choices
- Eliminate Choices
- Work Backward from an Answer

DATA FILE

Chapter 8

The Geometry of Polygons

SECTION A The Tale of the Magic Paper

The Tale of the Magic Paper
Page 401

401

Lines and Angles

These figures show the first two steps to make an origami cup. *Origami,* a Japanese word that means "the folding of paper," was once used only for ceremonial purposes, but it now is practiced widely by both children and adults. What shapes would you get before and after folding the paper on the dashed lines?

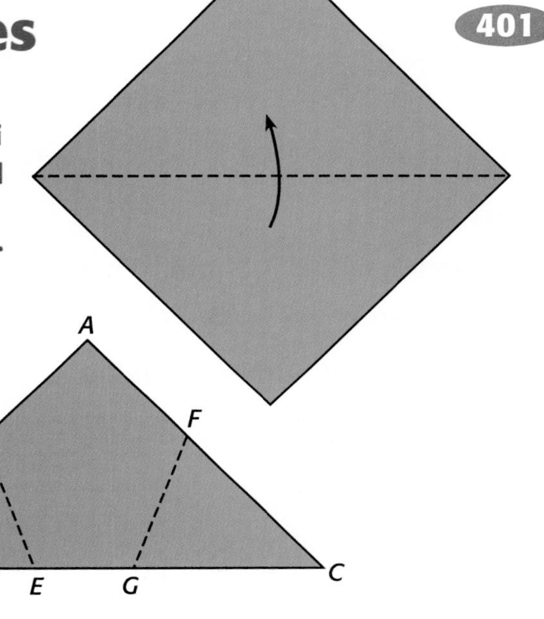

LINKS

Social Studies

The Pentagon is the headquarters for the U.S. Department of Defense. The building is shaped like a regular pentagon with each side 921 ft long.
www.mathsurf.com/6/ch8/social

Science

Some bees communicate using the "waggle dance." The angle formed by the bee's motion and the Sun indicates the location of pollen.
www.mathsurf.com/6/ch8/science

The Geometry of Gems

Polygons

415

This diagram shows an unusual diamond pattern called the "cross-rose." Each polygon is a face that has been ground into the crystal by the diamond cutter. Why do you think this pattern is called the cross-rose?

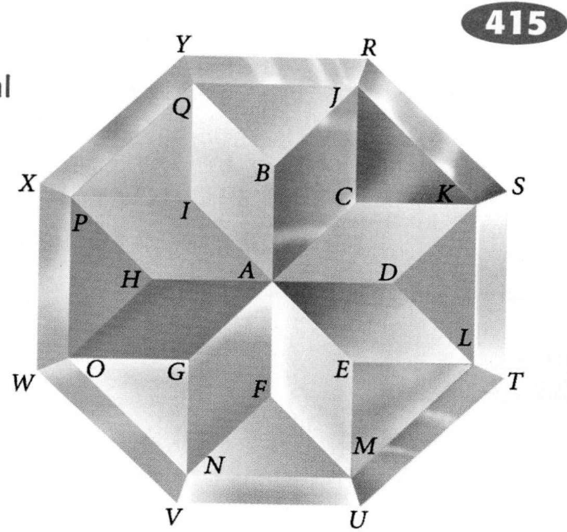

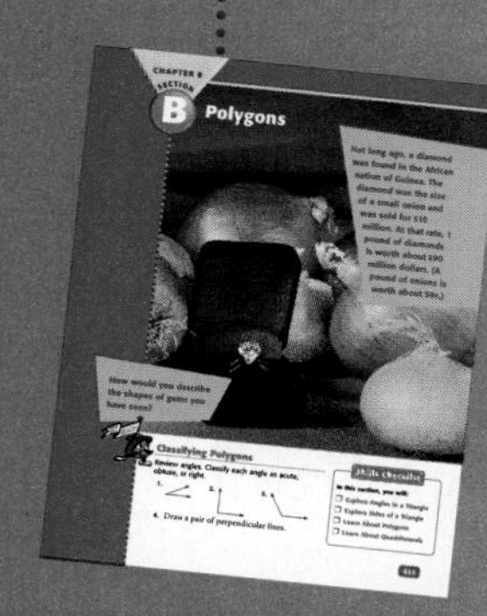

The Geometry of Gems
Page 415

Artistic Solutions

Transformations

437

A tessellation is a design created by repeating a shape that fits together with no space in between. M. C. Escher (1898–1972) is an artist who is perhaps best known for his tessellations. Describe the pattern that is repeated in this work by Escher.

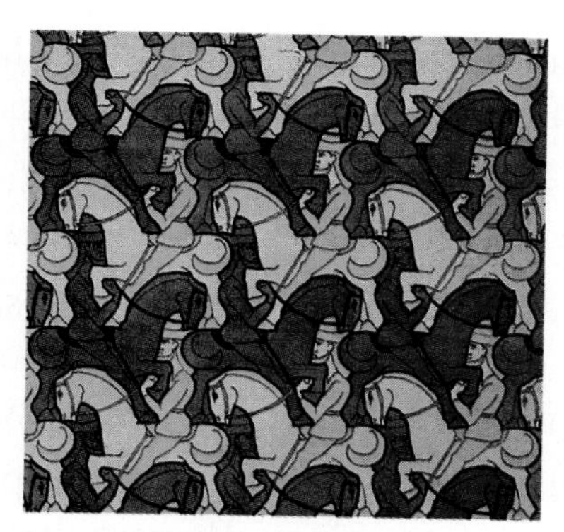

Symmetry Drawing E67 by M. C. Escher.

Artistic Solutions
Page 437

Entertainment

During floor exercises, gymnasts perform tumbling routines on a square mat with sides 12 m long.

People of the World

The astrolabe was a device used by early Islamic astronomers to help them determine the time of day.
www.mathsurf.com/6/ch8/people

Materials
markers, rulers, construction paper or posterboard

In this project, you will create a team logo. How can your logo reflect the individual interests of each person and the team as a whole?

Make a Plan

- Are there any logos that your team already likes to give you some ideas on how to get started?
- Will the logo be divided up into sections for each member, or will the logo be more unified in design?
- What colors, objects, activities, or symbols does your team want to use into the logo?

Carry It Out

1. Make a list of names that would be good for your team.
2. Decide on a shape for your logo. Make sure that your logo includes several different polygons.
3. Discuss the colors, objects, activities and/or symbols your group wants to incorporate into your team logo.
4. Have each team member make a sketch of the logo, incorporating as many of the ideas you talked about as possible. Compare your teammate's sketches, and decide which one you like the best.
5. On a large sheet of construction paper or posterboard, draw the outlines of your logo. Be sure that each person is involved in coloring in and completing the logo. Share your logo with the class.

Talk About It

- Can you name all of the polygons that were used in making your logo?
- What shapes in your logo have either line or rotational symmetry?

Present the Project

Present your logo to the other teams. Are the other teams able to identify all of the polygons used in creating your logo?

CHAPTER 8

SECTION

A Lines and Angles

Long ago, a woman made lunch for a samurai. To thank her, the samurai took a piece of magic paper and folded it in strange and wonderful ways. Before her eyes, the paper turned into a fish! This is a story of *origami,* the ancient Japanese art of paper folding.

Why would an understanding of geometry help you create an interesting origami figure?

Classifying Lines and Angles

Review patterns. Copy and continue each pattern.

1. 11, 22, 33, ▒, ▒, ▒

2. 675, 625, 575, 525, ▒, ▒, ▒

3.

 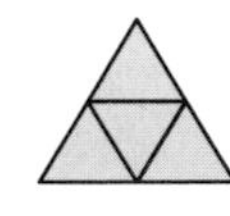 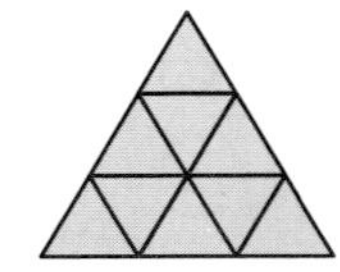 ____________

Skills Checklist

In this section, you will:

- ❒ Classify Lines
- ❒ Classify Angles
- ❒ Measure Angles

Chapter 8
Lesson
1

Classifying Lines

You Will Learn

- to describe different kinds of lines

Vocabulary

line
segment
endpoint
ray
intersect
perpendicular
parallel

Did You Know?

John Smith developed the Origami Instructional Language, which converts instructions into a compact list of numbers and symbols.

Learn

Wassily Kandinsky used lines and shapes in much of his work. Geometry is the branch of mathematics that studies shapes and figures. In order to describe shapes exactly, mathematicians use words with precise meanings. One class of word describes the different kinds of lines used to make figures.

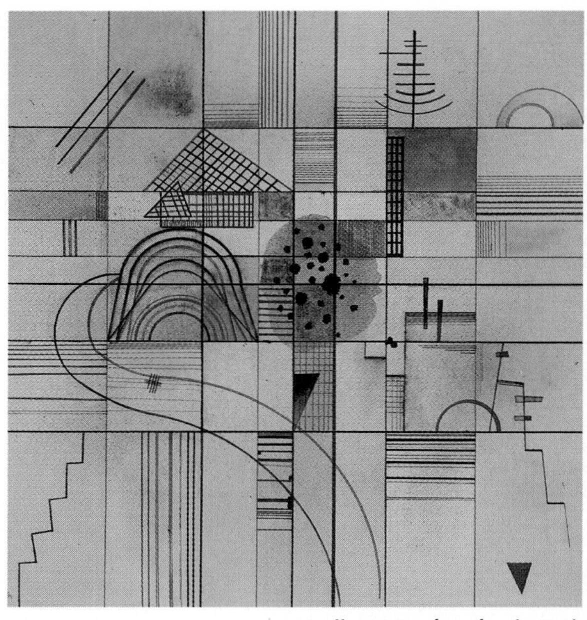

Variierte Rechtecke (1929)

A **line** extends forever in both directions. To show that a figure is a line, draw an arrow at each end.

A line **segment** has two **endpoints**. The segment does not extend beyond these endpoints. To show that a figure is a segment, draw the endpoints.

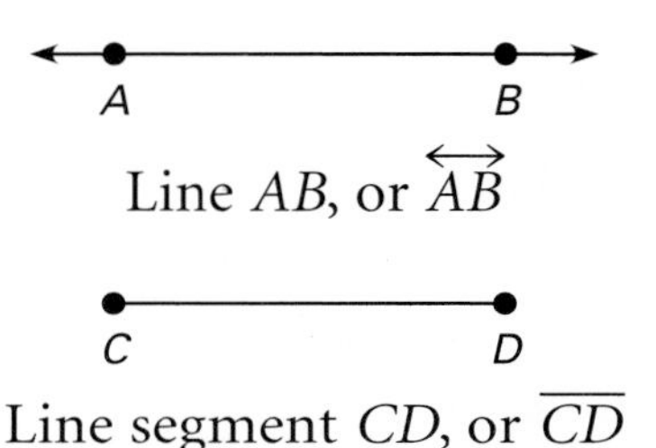

Line AB, or $\overleftrightarrow{AB}$

Line segment CD, or $\overline{CD}$

A **ray** has one endpoint, and extends forever in the opposite direction. To show that a figure is a ray, use an endpoint on one end and an arrow through a point on the other.

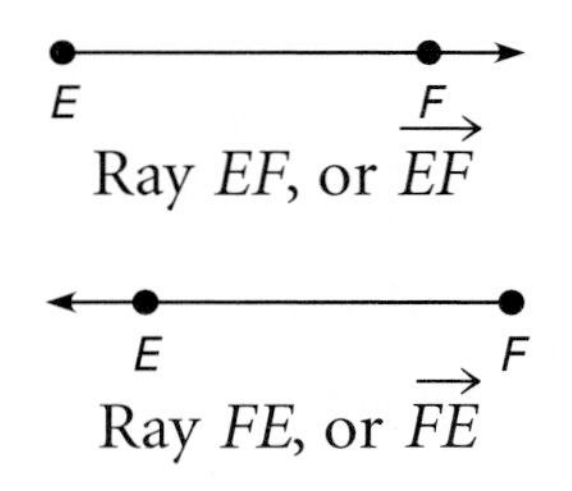

Ray EF, or $\overrightarrow{EF}$

Ray FE, or $\overrightarrow{FE}$

If lines cross at a point, they **intersect**.

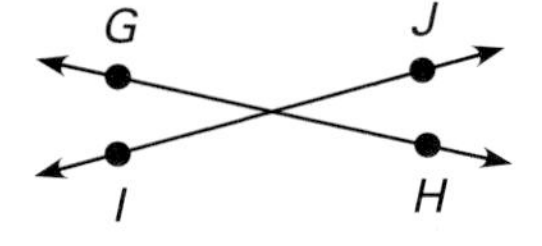

GH and *IJ* are intersecting.

If lines intersect at right angles, they are **perpendicular**.

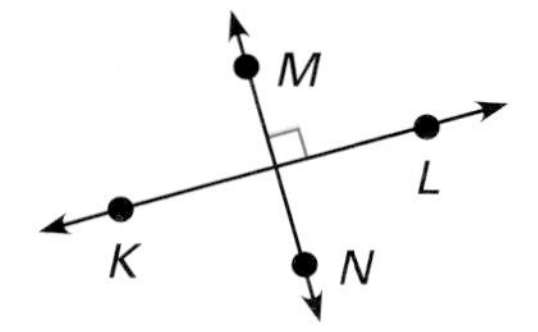

KL and *MN* are perpendicular.

If lines do not intersect no matter how far they are extended, they are **parallel**.

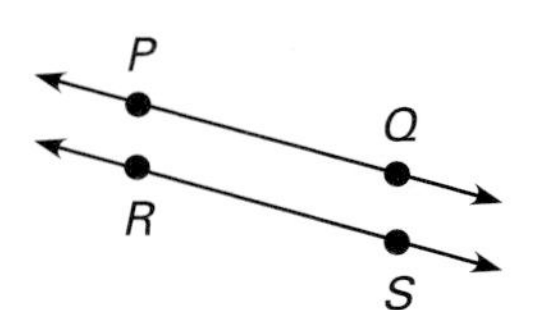

PQ and *RS* are parallel.

Example 1

Describe the relationship between the lines.

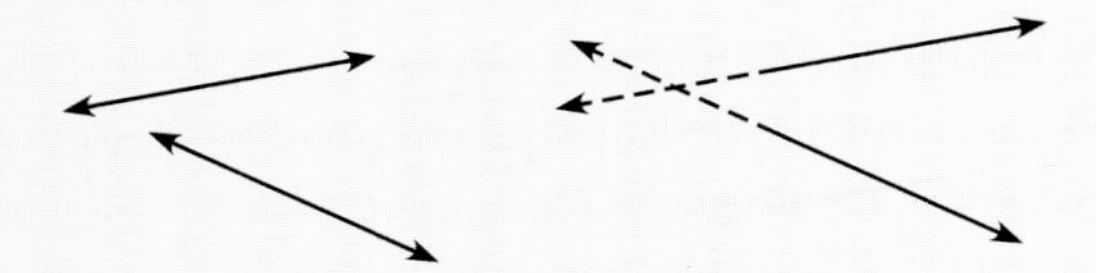

When the lines are extended, they cross at a point, so they are intersecting.

Rays and segments can also intersect, be perpendicular, or be parallel.

Example 2

The origami angelfish has been labeled with several points. Describe the relationships between $\overline{AE}$ and $\overline{BE}$, $\overline{BE}$ and $\overline{CE}$, and $\overline{AD}$ and $\overline{BC}$.

$\overline{AE}$ and $\overline{BE}$ are intersecting line segments. $\overline{BE}$ and $\overline{CE}$ are perpendicular line segments. $\overline{AD}$ and $\overline{BC}$ are parallel line segments.

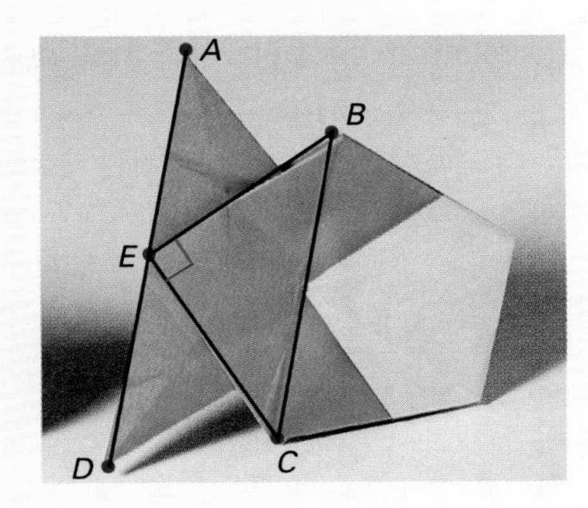

Talk About It

1. Which is longer, a segment or a line? How much longer?
2. If two segments do not intersect, does that mean that they are parallel? Explain.

Check

Draw an example of each.

1. $\overline{YZ}$ 2. $\overrightarrow{YZ}$ 3. $\overleftrightarrow{YZ}$

Describe the relationship between the lines, rays, or segments.

4. 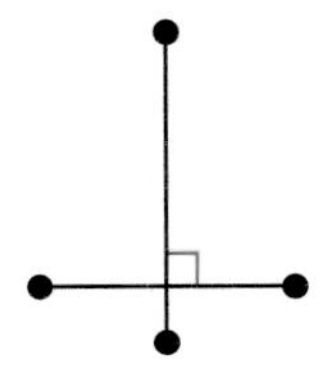

5. 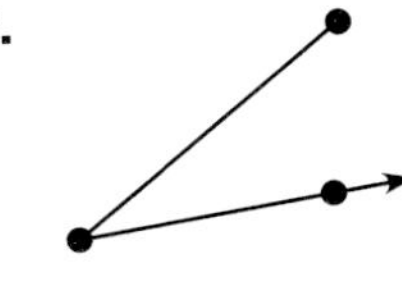

6. **Reasoning** Dustin walked 200 feet south and Kim walked 200 feet west before they met each other. What is the relationship of the streets on which they are walking?

Practice

Skills and Reasoning

Write the name for each.

7. 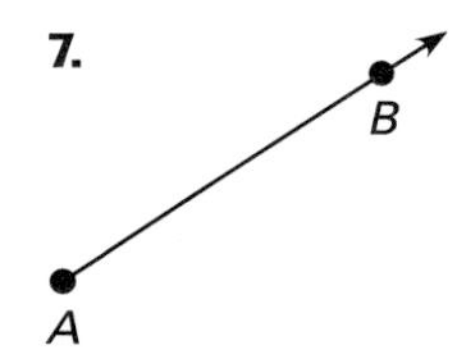

8. **9.** 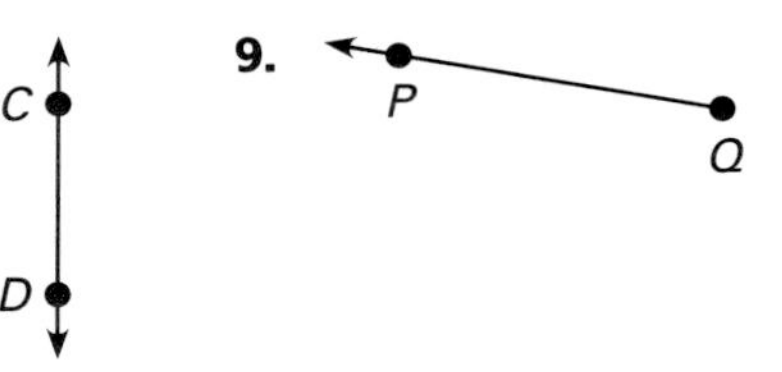

10. 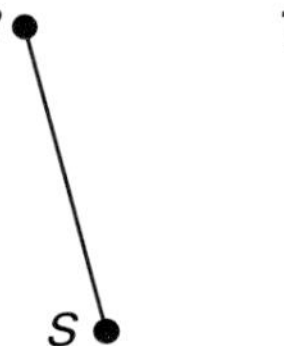

11. 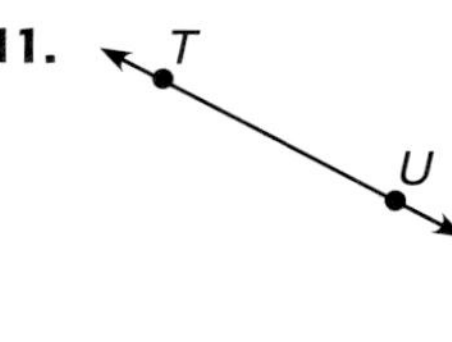

Draw an example of each.

12. $\overline{AB}$ **13.** $\overleftrightarrow{AB}$ **14.** $\overrightarrow{AB}$ **15.** $\overline{JK}$ **16.** $\overleftrightarrow{JK}$ **17.** $\overrightarrow{JK}$

Describe the relationship between the lines, rays, or segments.

18. 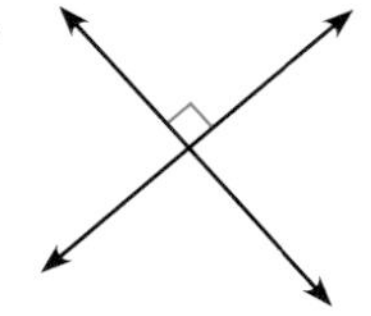

19. 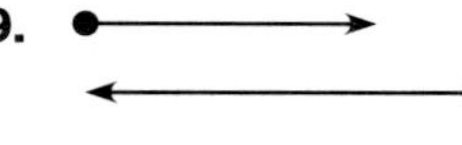

20. 

21. 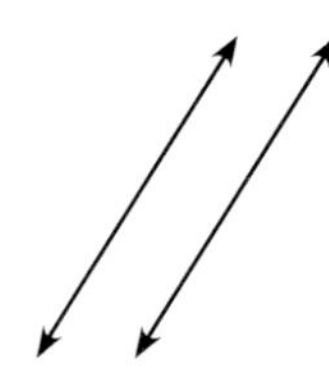

22. 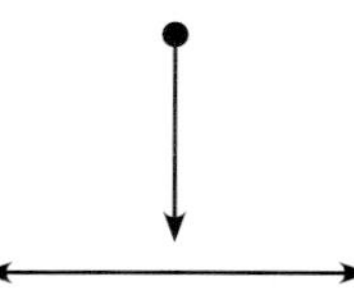

23. 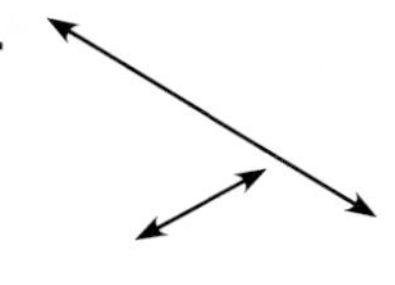

24. 

25. 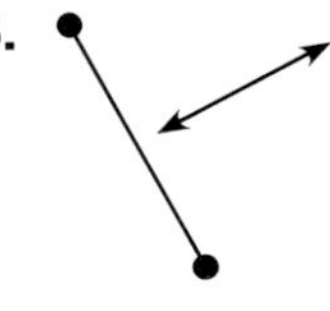

Write whether each statement is always, sometimes, or never true.

26. The rails on a set of train tracks are parallel.

27. Two intersecting streets are perpendicular.

28. The paths of two airplanes flying above Texas will intersect.

29. A line is longer than a segment.

30. Miranda and Hien are walking along parallel streets in a neighborhood. If the girls are 150 feet apart when they start walking, how long will they have to walk until their paths cross?

31. Choose the lines that are parallel.

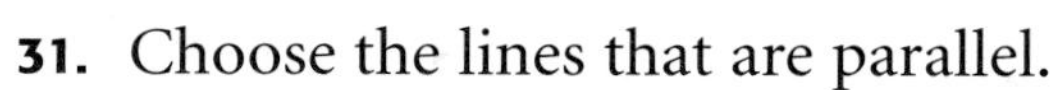

Ⓐ A and D Ⓑ C and E

Ⓒ A and C Ⓓ E and D

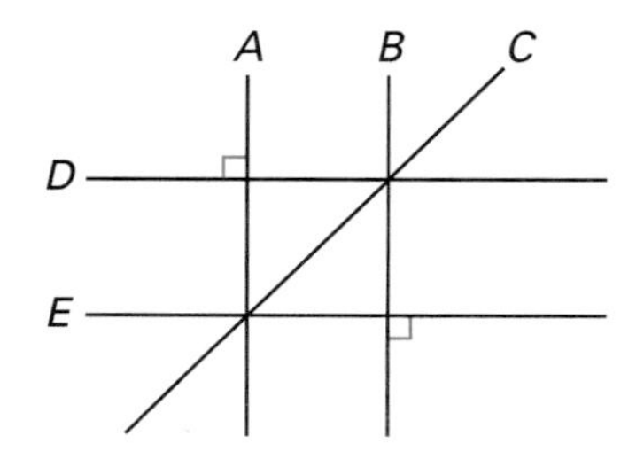

Problem Solving and Applications

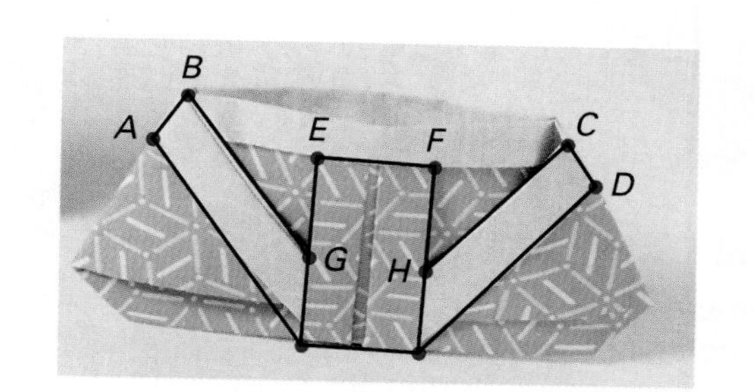

32. Fine Arts The photo shows a completed origami figure.

a. Name three pairs of parallel segments.

b. Name two segments that intersect but are not perpendicular.

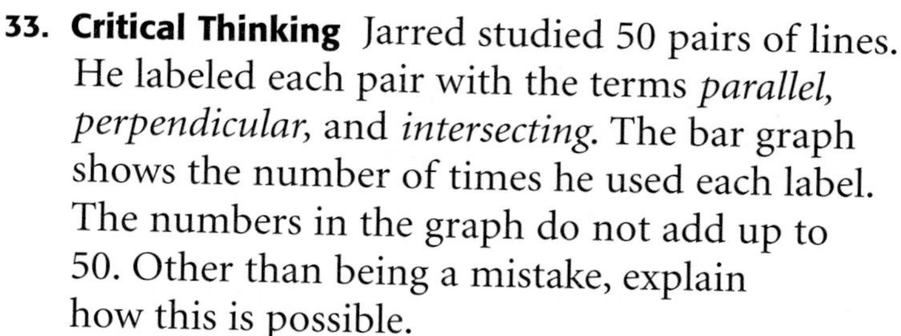

33. Critical Thinking Jarred studied 50 pairs of lines. He labeled each pair with the terms *parallel, perpendicular,* and *intersecting.* The bar graph shows the number of times he used each label. The numbers in the graph do not add up to 50. Other than being a mistake, explain how this is possible.

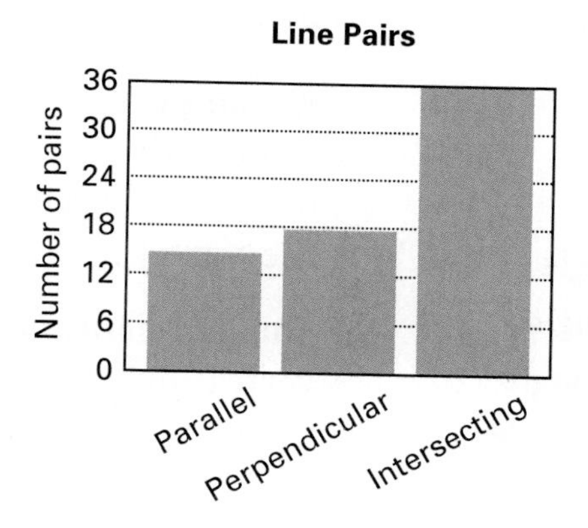

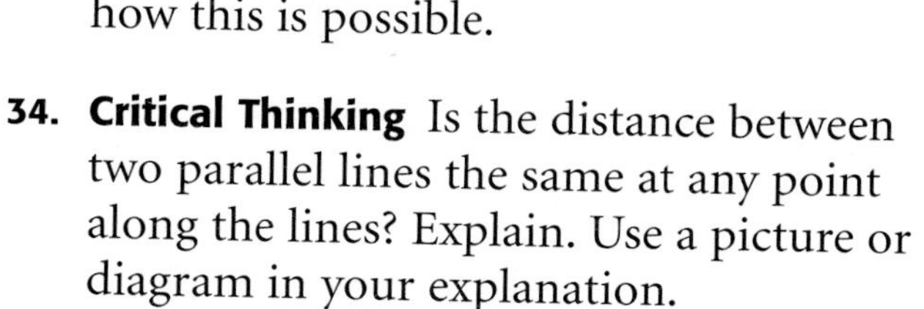

34. Critical Thinking Is the distance between two parallel lines the same at any point along the lines? Explain. Use a picture or diagram in your explanation.

35. Journal List three real-world situations that involve parallel lines. Do the situations also involve perpendicular lines? Explain.

Mixed Review and Test Prep

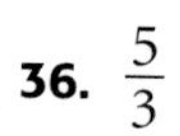

Write each fraction as a mixed number.

36. $\frac{5}{3}$ **37.** $\frac{3}{2}$ **38.** $\frac{7}{3}$ **39.** $\frac{9}{4}$ **40.** $\frac{12}{8}$ **41.** $\frac{9}{8}$

42. $\frac{7}{2}$ **43.** $\frac{14}{6}$ **44.** $\frac{9}{5}$ **45.** $\frac{18}{4}$ **46.** $\frac{13}{5}$ **47.** $\frac{22}{4}$

48. $\frac{6}{4}$ **49.** $\frac{10}{7}$ **50.** $\frac{12}{5}$ **51.** $\frac{8}{3}$ **52.** $\frac{17}{6}$ **53.** $\frac{5}{2}$

Simplify.

54. $\frac{2}{7}+\frac{5}{7}$ **55.** $\frac{4}{5}-\frac{1}{5}$ **56.** $\frac{7}{10}+\frac{9}{10}$ **57.** $\frac{55}{100}+\frac{46}{100}$ **58.** $\frac{8}{4}-\frac{3}{4}$

59. $\frac{4}{3}-\frac{1}{3}$ **60.** $\frac{12}{15}+\frac{13}{15}$ **61.** $\frac{7}{8}-\frac{4}{8}$ **62.** $\frac{9}{12}+\frac{3}{12}$ **63.** $\frac{3}{5}-\frac{1}{5}$

64. $\frac{18}{25}-\frac{9}{25}$ **65.** $\frac{1}{6}+\frac{4}{6}$ **66.** $\frac{5}{9}-\frac{1}{9}$ **67.** $\frac{9}{13}+\frac{1}{13}$ **68.** $\frac{10}{42}+\frac{11}{42}$

69. Choose the mixed number that is equivalent to $\frac{109}{8}$.

Ⓐ $12\frac{3}{8}$ Ⓑ $13\frac{5}{8}$ Ⓒ $11\frac{7}{8}$ Ⓓ $13\frac{3}{8}$

Chapter 8
Lesson
2

Classifying Angles

You Will Learn

- to name and describe angles

Vocabulary

angle
side
vertex
right angle
acute angle
obtuse angle
straight angle

Learn

In the last lesson, you learned that lines, rays and segments are basic elements in geometry. Now you'll learn about a simple figure made up of these parts—the angle.

An **angle** is formed by two rays with the same endpoint. The rays are the **sides** of the angle. The common endpoint is the **vertex**.

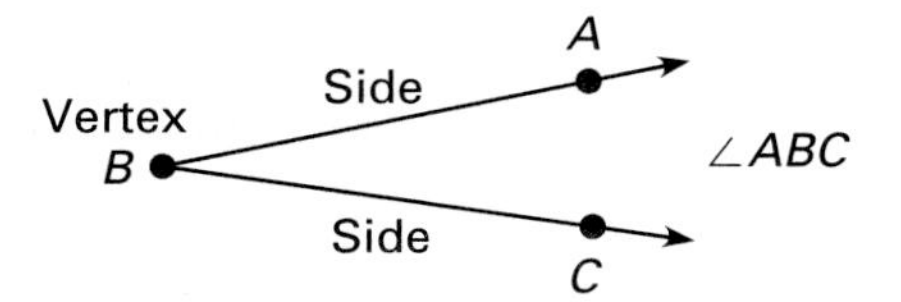

You can name an angle using a point on each side and the vertex. The vertex must appear as the middle letter. When it is not confusing, you can name an angle using the vertex alone.

Did You Know?
Some words have a non-mathematical meaning that is similar to their mathematical meaning. The word *acute* can also mean "having a sharp point." The word *obtuse* can also mean "blunt, not sharp."

Example 1

Name the angle in three ways.

The points on each side are P and R and the vertex is Q, so the angle can be called $\angle PQR$, read "angle PQR," or $\angle RQP$. Using the vertex only, the angle can also be called $\angle Q$.

Angles can be classified by their size.

An **acute angle** is smaller than a right angle.

A **right angle** is like the corner of an index card.

An **obtuse angle** is greater than a right angle but smaller than a straight angle.

A **straight angle** forms a line.

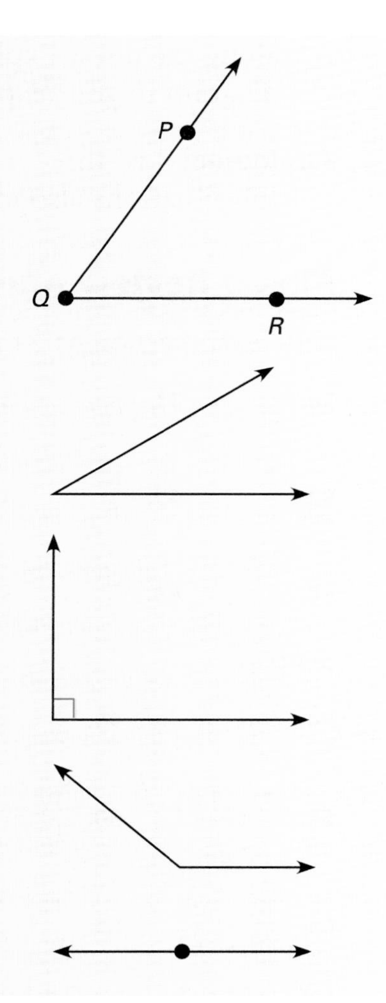

Example 2

Classify each angle as acute, right, obtuse, or straight.

a.

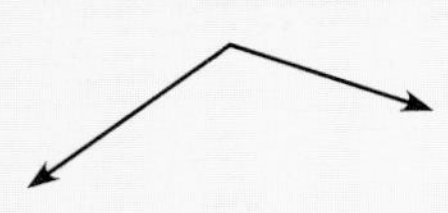

The angle is obtuse.

b.

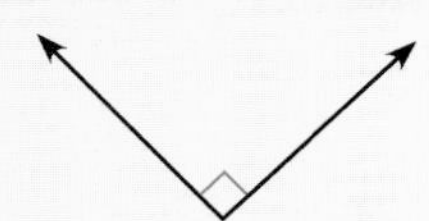

The angle is a right angle.

c.

The angle is acute.

Talk About It

1. Find an example of each type of angle in your classroom.
2. Why do mathematicians sometimes use three letters to name an angle instead of just using the vertex?

Check

Name each angle in three ways.

1.

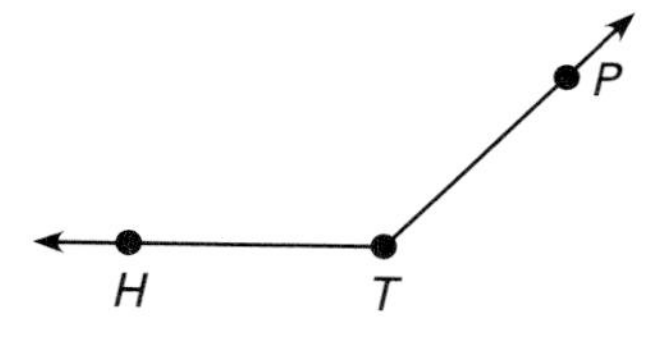

2.

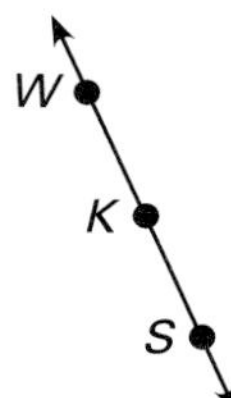

3.

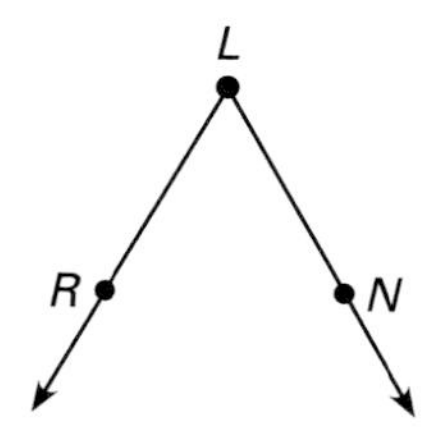

Classify each angle as acute, right, obtuse, or straight.

4.

5.

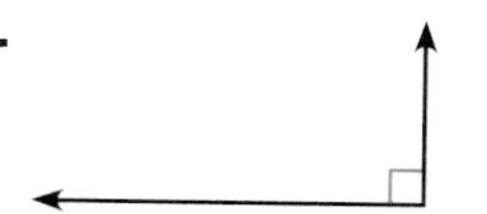

6.

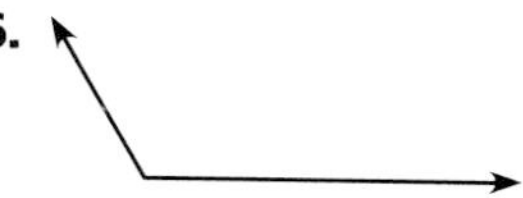

7.

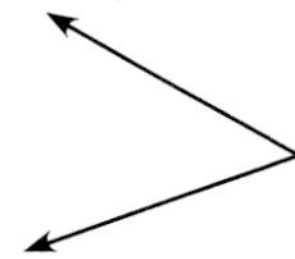

8. You can find angles in real-life objects, such as the corner of a door or window. Find two examples each of acute, right, obtuse, and straight angles in this picture and sketch them.

9. **Reasoning** Sarah drew angle *CAP*. She said the angle is made of rays *CA* and *AP*. Is she correct? Explain.

Practice

Skills and Reasoning

Name each angle in three ways.

10.

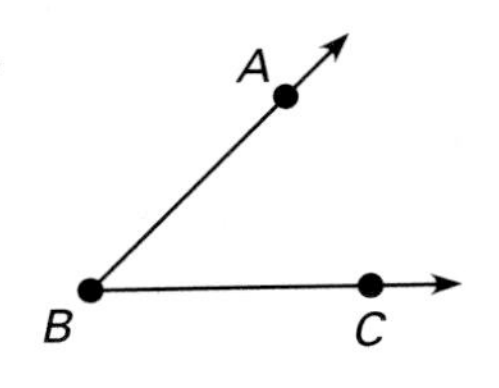

11.

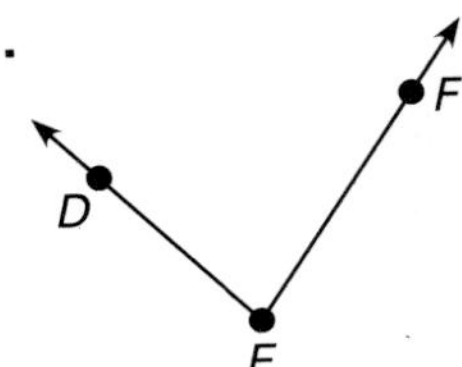

12.

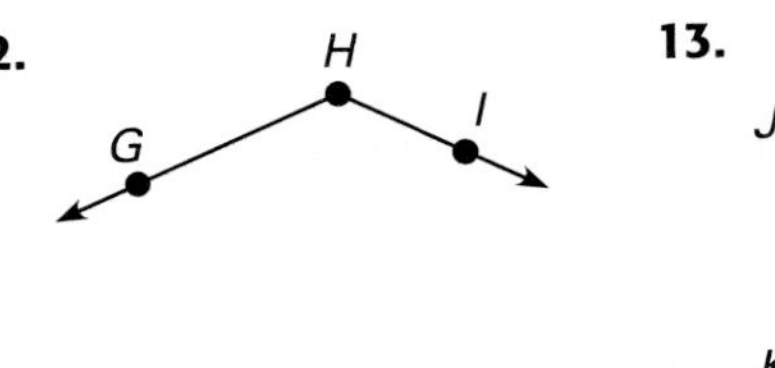

13.

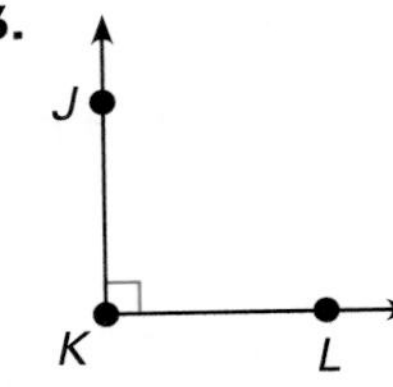

Classify each angle as acute, right, obtuse, or straight.

14.

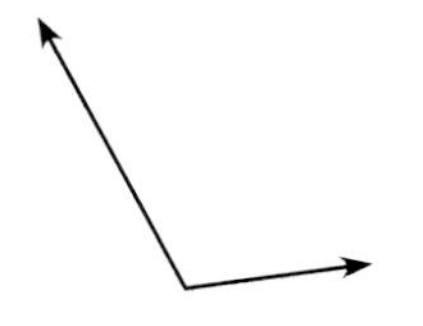

15.

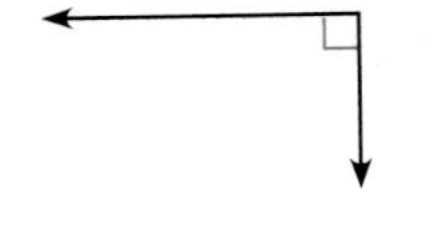

16.

17.

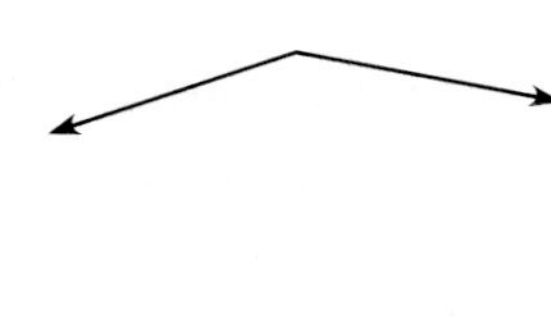

18.

19.

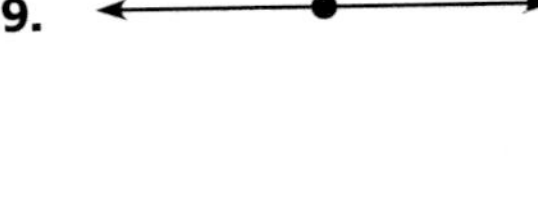

20.

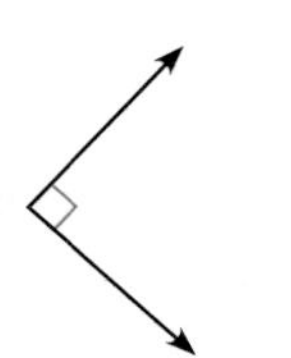

21.

Classify each angle shown in the origami figure in the Data File on page 398.

22. $\angle DEB$ **23.** $\angle AFG$ **24.** $\angle BAC$ **25.** $\angle DEG$ **26.** $\angle FCG$ **27.** $\angle AFC$

Tell whether each statement is always, sometimes, or never true.

28. Two acute angles of the same size form a right angle.

29. A right angle and an acute angle form an obtuse angle.

30. An angle consists of two endpoints, a vertex, and a ray.

Problem Solving and Applications

31. Describe the angle that is formed by the corner of this page.

Time Classify the angle made by the hands of a clock at each time.

32. 3:00 **33.** 7:15 **34.** 2:45 **35.** 6:00 **36.** 1:00 **37.** 10:00

38.

New York City, USA

39.

London, England

40.

Moscow, Russia

Fine Arts Use the unfolded pattern of the inside reverse fold for **41–43.**

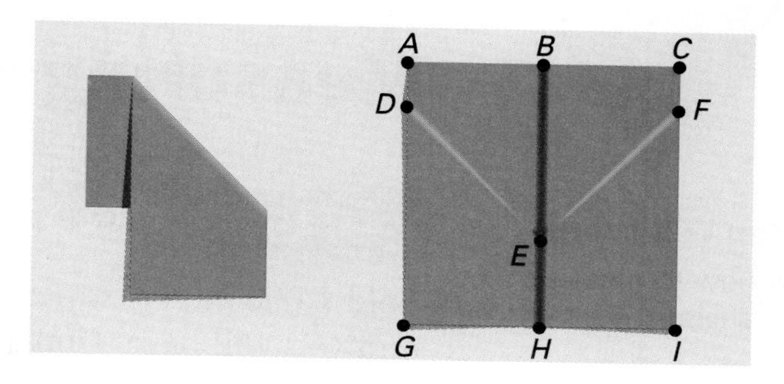

41. Name five angles and classify each as acute, right, or obtuse.

42. Name and classify two angles which make up a straight angle.

43. Suppose AB measures 2.5 cm, BC measures 2.5 cm, CF measures 1.5 cm, and FI measures 5 cm.

a. Find the perimeter of the largest rectangle.

b. Find the area of the largest rectangle.

44. Critical Thinking Two angles placed together make a straight line. If one is an obtuse angle, what is the other? Explain.

45. Critical Thinking Draw two rays that don't make an angle. Explain your drawing.

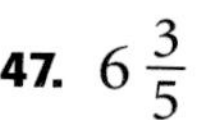

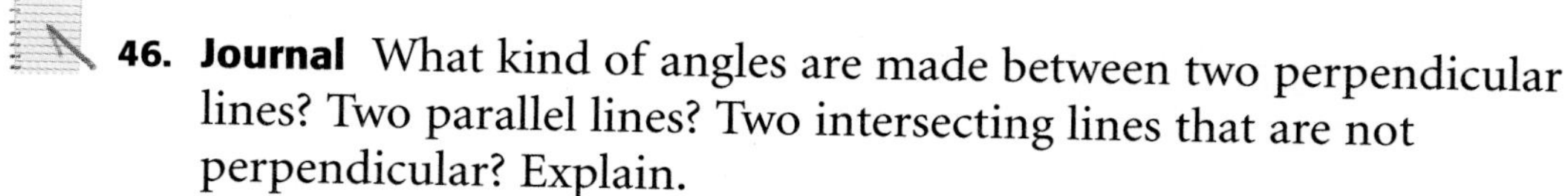

46. Journal What kind of angles are made between two perpendicular lines? Two parallel lines? Two intersecting lines that are not perpendicular? Explain.

Mixed Review and Test Prep

Write each mixed number as an improper fraction.

47. $6\frac{3}{5}$ **48.** $12\frac{2}{3}$ **49.** $3\frac{1}{2}$ **50.** $2\frac{4}{5}$ **51.** $6\frac{1}{8}$ **52.** $7\frac{4}{5}$

53. $10\frac{9}{11}$ **54.** $4\frac{1}{4}$ **55.** $9\frac{3}{4}$ **56.** $5\frac{2}{5}$ **57.** $5\frac{7}{8}$ **58.** $1\frac{6}{7}$

59. $2\frac{1}{6}$ **60.** $6\frac{2}{3}$ **61.** $3\frac{6}{7}$ **62.** $7\frac{3}{5}$ **63.** $10\frac{3}{4}$ **64.** $8\frac{1}{9}$

Simplify.

65. $\frac{7}{9}+\frac{3}{4}$ **66.** $\frac{6}{12}-\frac{2}{6}$ **67.** $\frac{2}{3}+\frac{6}{9}$ **68.** $\frac{3}{4}-\frac{5}{8}$ **69.** $\frac{1}{2}-\frac{1}{8}$

70. $\frac{12}{18}+\frac{5}{9}$ **71.** $\frac{9}{10}-\frac{2}{5}$ **72.** $\frac{2}{3}+\frac{3}{8}$ **73.** $\frac{6}{11}+\frac{6}{22}$ **74.** $\frac{4}{5}-\frac{3}{4}$

75. Which number is **not** the mean, median, or mode for the following data?

6, 7, 7, 7, 6, 4, 4, 7, 2, 0

Ⓐ 7 Ⓑ 5 Ⓒ 6 Ⓓ 50

Chapter 8
Lesson
3

Measuring Angles

You Will Learn
- how to measure angles

Materials
protractor

Vocabulary
degree
protractor
complementary angles
supplementary angles

Learn

Fold 1,000 paper cranes and you will have a long and peaceful life. That's what a Japanese legend says. And that's just what Ellen and China did.

Ellen and China live in South Bend, Indiana.

Angles are measured in units called **degrees**.
The symbol ° indicates degrees. A complete circle measures 360°.
A 1° angle is $\frac{1}{360}$ of a circle.

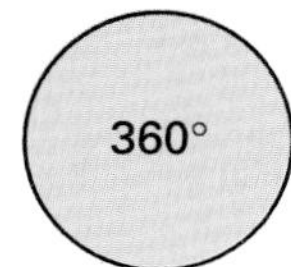

= 1°

A **protractor** is a tool that measures angles.

An acute angle measures more than 0° and less than 90°.

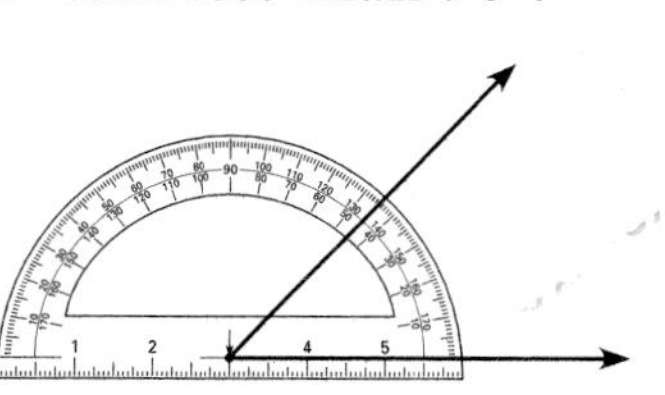

A right angle measures exactly 90°.

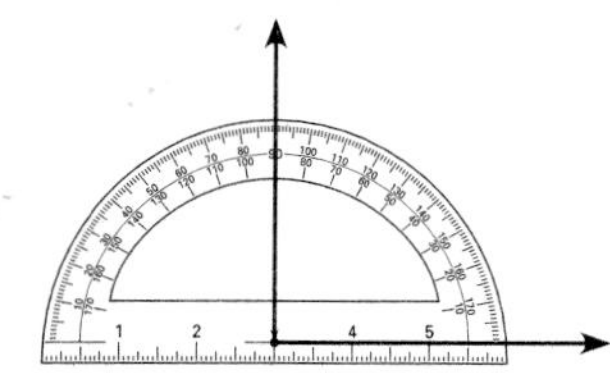

An obtuse angle measures more than 90° and less than 180°.

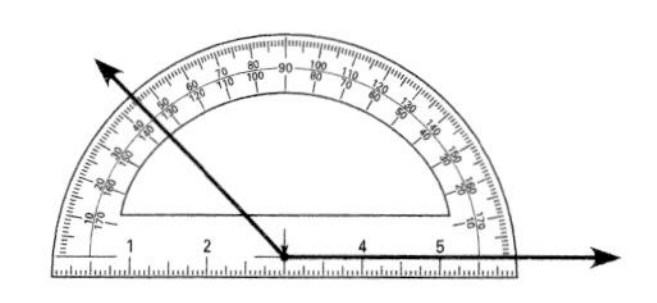

Did You Know?
In 1995, some Japanese citizens folded a paper crane $52\frac{1}{2}$ ft tall with a wingspan of 117 ft 2 in.

Example 1

Part way through folding a crane, the paper looks like this.

Measure and classify $\angle ABC$.

Place the protractor so that the middle of its bottom edge is over the vertex, *B*, and one side of the bottom edge is over one side of the angle. Read the pair of numbers where the other side of the angle, $\overrightarrow{BC}$, passes underneath the protractor. If the angle is an acute angle, use the smaller number in the pair. If the angle is obtuse, use the larger number.
$\angle ABC$ measures 45°.

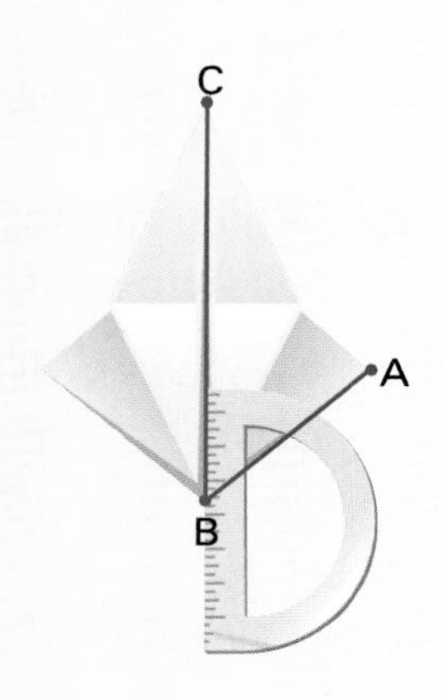

Two angles are **complementary** angles if the sum of their measures equals 90°. Two angles are **supplementary** angles if the sum of their measures equals 180°.

Example 2

State the angle measures that are complementary and supplementary to $\angle DAE$.

$90° - 40° = 50°$, so the angle measure complementary to $\angle DAE$ is 50°

$180° - 40° = 140°$; so the angle measure supplementary to $\angle DAE$ is 140°.

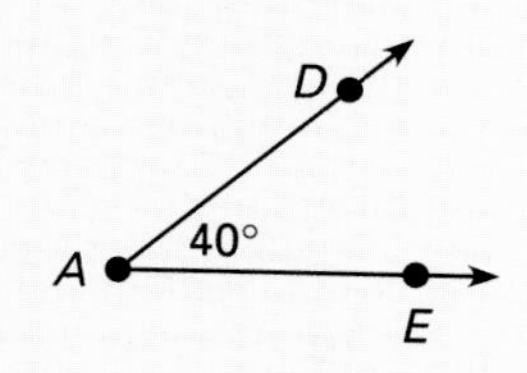

To draw an angle, you can use a protractor.

Example 3

Draw an angle that measures 60°.

Draw a ray. Place the protractor so that the middle of its bottom edge is over the endpoint of the ray. Place a point at 60°. Starting at the endpoint of the first ray, draw another ray through the point at 60°.

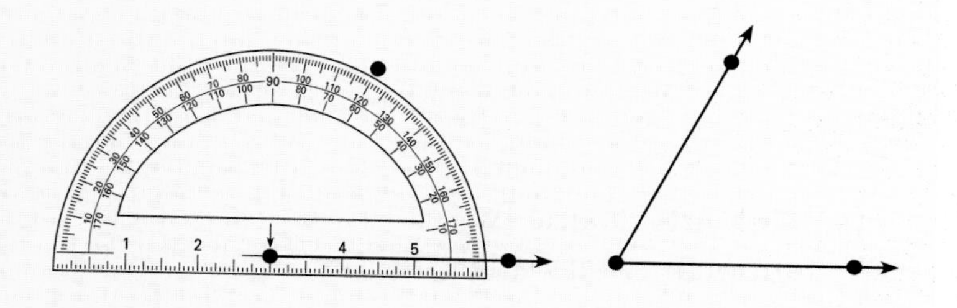

Talk About It

1. The protractor in Example 3 has two sets of numbers. It does not show the number 45. How do you know that an angle measures 45°?
2. If someone tells you the measure of an angle, how can you tell if the angle is an acute angle, a right angle, or an obtuse angle?

Check

Measure each angle with a protractor.

1. 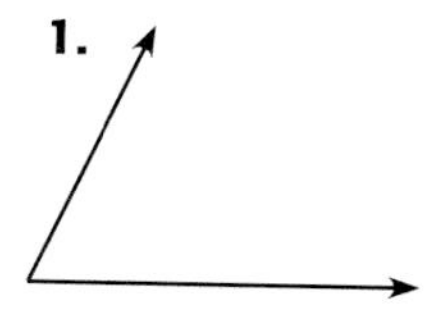

2. 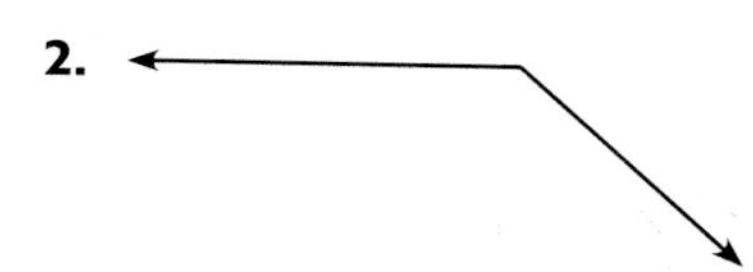

Draw the angle for each measure. Then classify each as acute, obtuse, or right.

3. 150°

4. 43°

5. **Reasoning** What kind of angle is formed by two complementary angles? By two supplementary angles? Explain.

Practice

Skills and Reasoning

Estimation Estimate the measure of each angle. Then measure each with a protractor.

Math Tip
To measure an angle, you may need to trace it and extend its sides.

6. 

7. 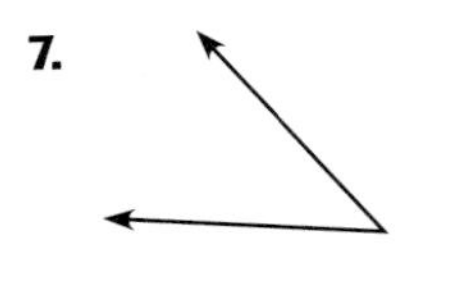

8.

9. 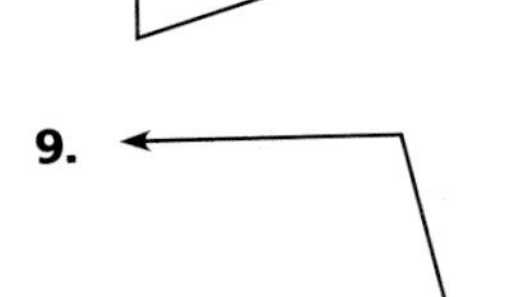

10. 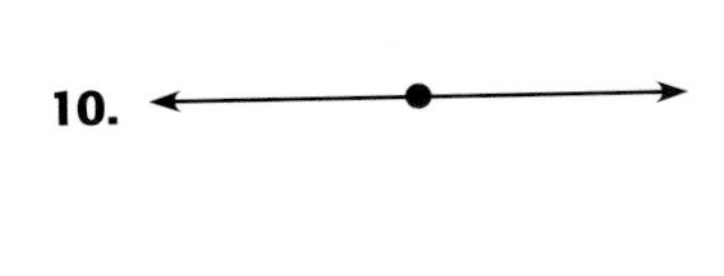

11. 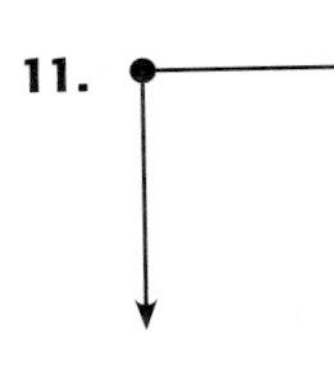

12. 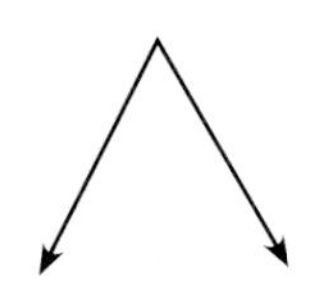

13. 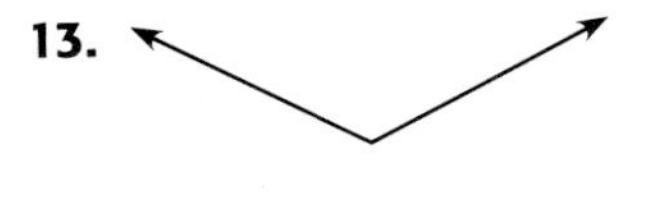

14. 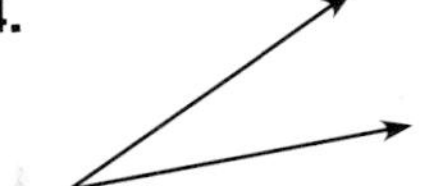

15. **Fine Arts** Name two supplementary angles in the origami photo.

Draw the angle for each measure. Then classify each as acute, obtuse, or right.

16. 50° **17.** 140° **18.** 70° **19.** 110°

State the angle measure that is complementary to the given angle.

20. 23° **21.** 79° **22.** 62° **23.** 3°

State the angle measure that is supplementary to the given angle.

24. 127° **25.** 52° **26.** 60° **27.** 90°

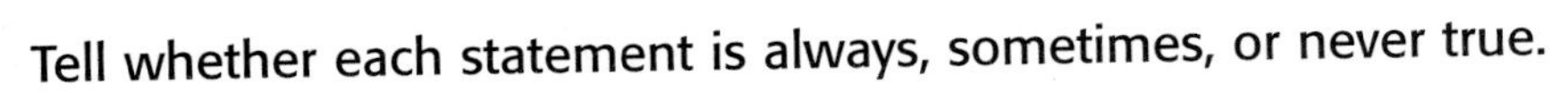

Tell whether each statement is always, sometimes, or never true.

28. Degrees are used to measure the sides of angles.

29. Two angles whose measures are 45° and 45° are complementary.

30. Two obtuse angles are supplementary.

31. **Time** A clock face is divided into 360°. About how long does it take the hour hand to travel 720°? 270°? Explain.

32. Which measure is the measurement of an obtuse angle?

Ⓐ 45° Ⓑ 135° Ⓒ 90° Ⓓ 270°

Problem Solving and SOCIAL STUDIES

In 1791, Washington, DC. was chosen as the capital of the United States. The map shows the area around the United States Capitol.

33. Measurement Tell whether each pair of streets is parallel, perpendicular, or intersecting.

a. Pennsylvania Ave. and Constitution Ave.

b. Constitution Ave. and Independence Ave.

34. Describe the angles formed by each intersection as acute, right, obtuse, or straight.

a. Delaware Ave. and Constitution Ave.

b. Louisiana Ave and New Jersey Ave.

35. Find the angles formed by the intersection of Louisiana and Constitution Avenues.

a. What are their measures?

b. Are the angles complementary or supplementary? Explain.

36. Money An airline is offering a special rate of $99 each way to fly from Indianapolis to Washington, DC. What is the total cost for a family of four to fly round trip between Indianapolis and Washington, DC?

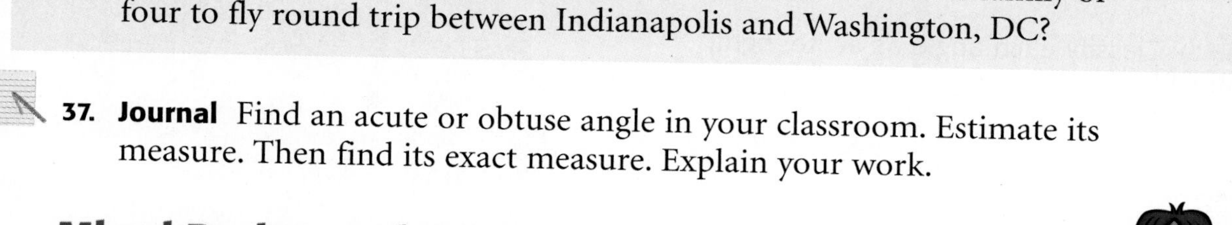

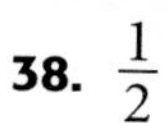

37. Journal Find an acute or obtuse angle in your classroom. Estimate its measure. Then find its exact measure. Explain your work.

Mixed Review and Test Prep

Write each fraction as a decimal. Round all repeating decimals to the nearest hundredth.

38. $\frac{1}{2}$ **39.** $\frac{2}{3}$ **40.** $\frac{1}{4}$ **41.** $\frac{3}{4}$ **42.** $\frac{1}{3}$ **43.** $\frac{5}{6}$

44. $\frac{4}{9}$ **45.** $\frac{3}{5}$ **46.** $\frac{12}{22}$ **47.** $\frac{7}{8}$ **48.** $\frac{673}{673}$ **49.** $\frac{5}{8}$

Solve.

50. $\frac{5}{6} + w = \frac{7}{8}$ **51.** $t + \frac{4}{9} = \frac{3}{4}$ **52.** $p - \frac{5}{6} = \frac{6}{11}$ **53.** $n - \frac{3}{4} = \frac{1}{2}$

54. $a + \frac{3}{8} = \frac{4}{9}$ **55.** $\frac{60}{10} - j = 5$ **56.** $b - \frac{4}{5} = \frac{1}{10}$ **57.** $4 - m = \frac{3}{5}$

58. Choose the correct answer for: $5\frac{1}{3} + 4\frac{5}{6}$.

Ⓐ $10\frac{1}{6}$ Ⓑ $11\frac{5}{6}$ Ⓒ $9\frac{5}{6}$ Ⓓ $11\frac{1}{6}$

SECTION A

Review and Practice

Vocabulary Circle the term that best completes each sentence.

1. A (right angle, straight angle) is also a line.
2. A(n) (right angle, acute angle) measures 90°.
3. If lines do not intersect, no matter how far they extend, they are (parallel, perpendicular).

(Lesson 1) Describe the relationship between the lines, rays, or segments.

4. 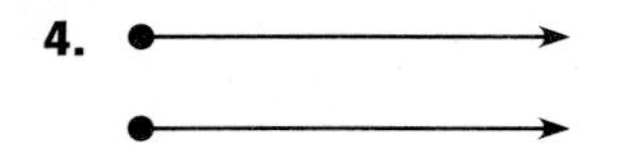

5.

6. 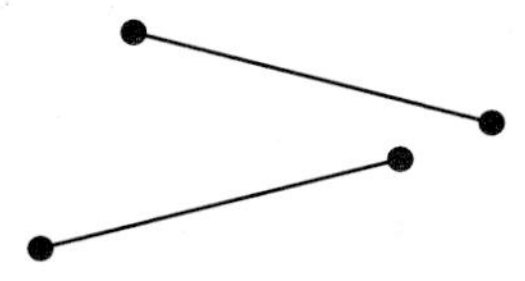

7. 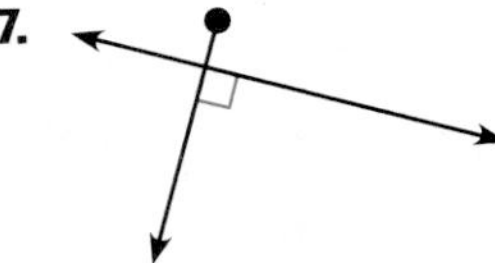

8. Zack walks east along Horn Street and Marisa walks north on Flatbush. Are their routes perpendicular or parallel? If Zack turns north on Baltimore, are their routes then perpendicular or parallel?

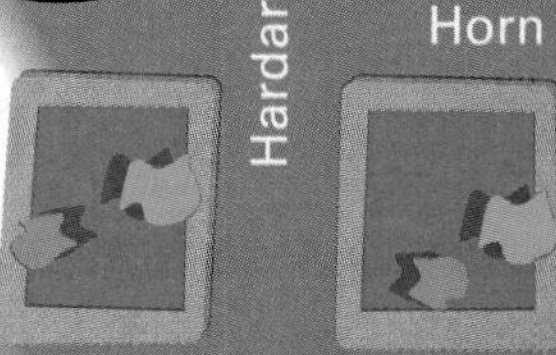

(Lesson 2) Classify each angle as acute, right, or obtuse.

9. 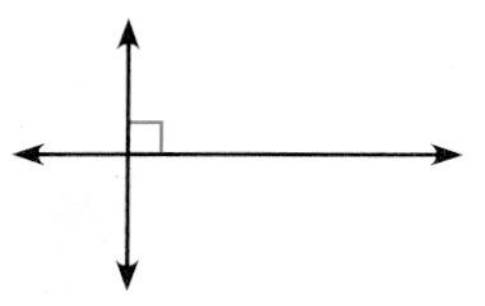

10. 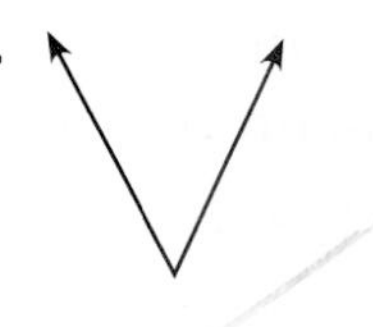

11. 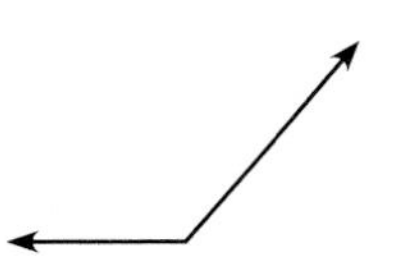

12. 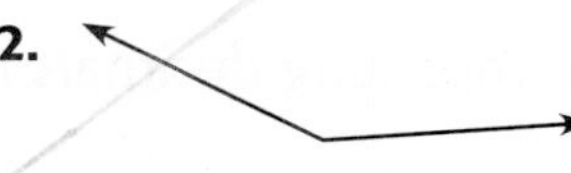

(Lesson 3) Trace each angle. Then measure it and find its complement and supplement.

13. 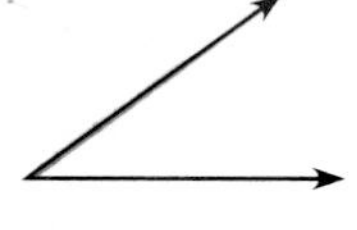

14. 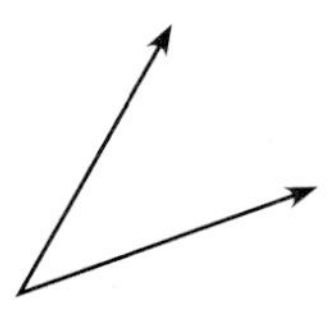

15. **Journal** Why are all perpendicular lines intersecting but not all intersecting lines perpendicular?

Skills Checklist

In this section, you have:

- ☑ **Classified Lines**
- ☑ **Classified Angles**
- ☑ **Measured Angles**

REVIEW AND PRACTICE

CHAPTER 8

SECTION

B Polygons

Not long ago, a diamond was found in the African nation of Guinea. The diamond was the size of a small onion and was sold for $10 million. At that rate, 1 pound of diamonds is worth about $90 million dollars. (A pound of onions is worth about 59¢.)

How would you describe the shapes of gems you have seen?

GET READY!

Classifying Polygons

Review angles. Classify each angle as acute, obtuse, or right.

1.

2. 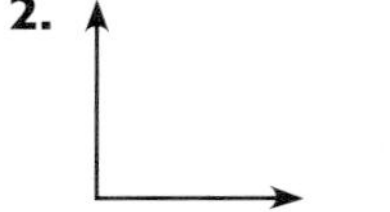

3. 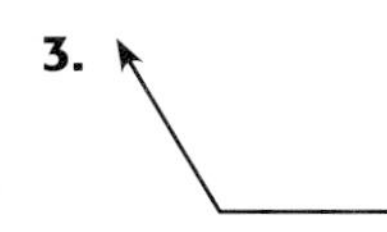

4. Draw a pair of perpendicular lines.

Skills Checklist

In this section, you will:

- ❒ Explore Angles in a Triangle
- ❒ Explore Sides of a Triangle
- ❒ Learn About Polygons
- ❒ Learn About Quadrilaterals

Chapter 8
Lesson
4

Exploring Angles in a Triangle

Problem Solving Connection
- Look for a Pattern
- Make a Table

Materials
- ruler
- scissors
- protractor

Vocabulary
triangle
acute triangle
right triangle
obtuse triangle

Explore

A **triangle** is a closed figure made from three line segments.

Work Together

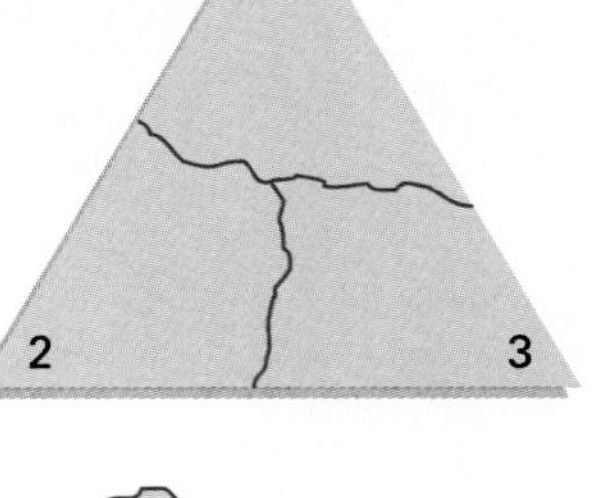

1. Draw and cut out a large triangle. Label the angles 1, 2, and 3.
2. Tear the triangle into three pieces as shown. Each piece should have one and only one labeled angle.
3. Put the three pieces together so that the labeled angles are touching.

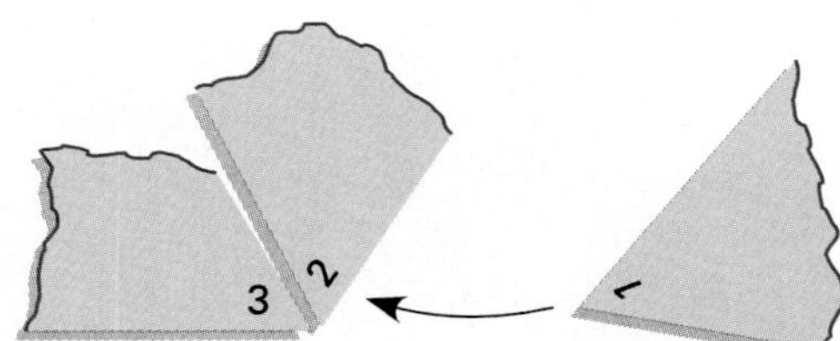

4. Estimate the sum of the three angle measures of your triangle.
5. Use a protractor to find the measure of each angle.
6. Calculate the sum of the angle measures. How does the sum compare to your estimate?
7. Repeat steps 1–6 with two more triangles.
8. Record your findings in a table. Compare the sums of the angles for your three triangles. Describe any patterns you see in the sums.

Remember
A closed figure has all sides connected.

Triangle	Estimated Sum of Angle Measures	Angle Measures	Actual Sum of Angle Measures

Talk About It

9. How did you estimate the sum of the angle measures?
10. Describe any patterns you see in your table.

Connect and Learn

Triangles can be classified using the terms *acute, right,* and *obtuse.*

An **acute triangle** has three acute angles.

57°
61° 62°

A **right triangle** has exactly one right angle.

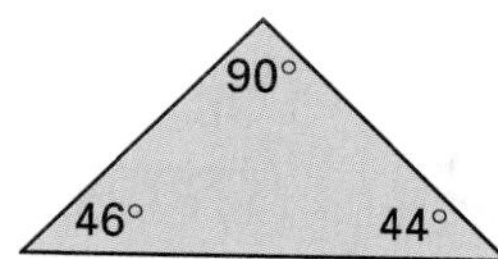

An **obtuse triangle** has exactly one obtuse angle.

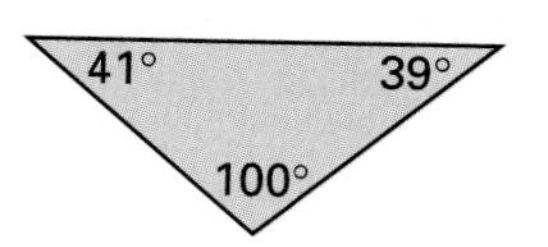

Example 1

Classify each triangle as acute, right, or obtuse.

a.

The face has one obtuse angle, so the triangle is obtuse.

b.

The face has three acute angles, so the triangle is acute.

c.

The face has a right angle, so the triangle is a right triangle.

The sum of the angles of any triangle is always equal to 180°.

Example 2

Find the measure of the missing angle in each triangle.

a.

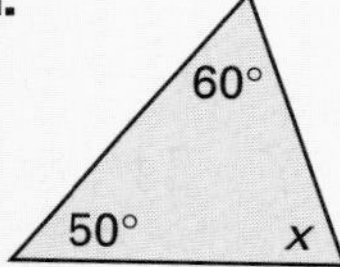

$50° + 60 + x = 180°$

$110° + x = 180°$

$110° + \mathbf{70}° = 180°$

The angle measures 70°.

b.

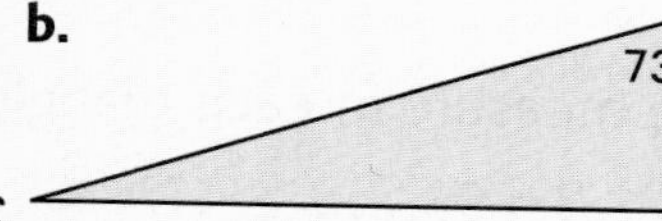

$90° + 73° + y = 180°$

$163° + y = 180°$

$163° + \mathbf{17}° = 180°$

$m\angle C = 17°$ (Read as "Measure of angle *C* equals 17°.")

Check

Classify each triangle as acute, right, or obtuse.

1.

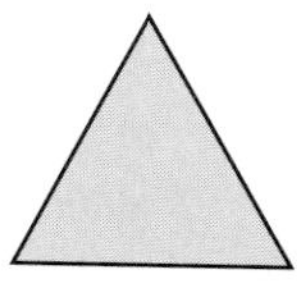

2.

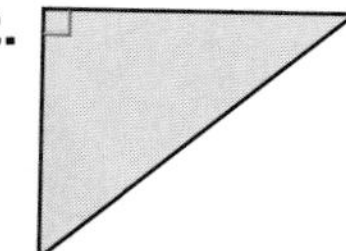

3.

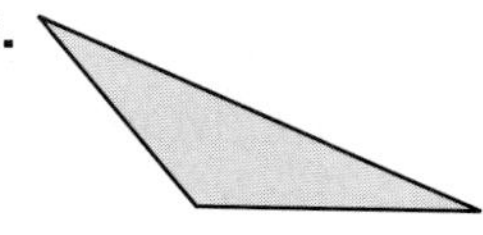

4.

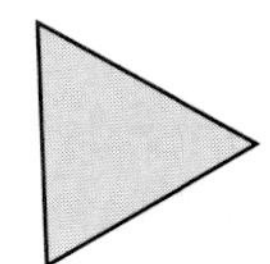

Find the missing angle measure in each triangle.

5.

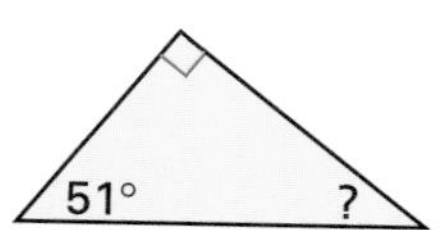

6.

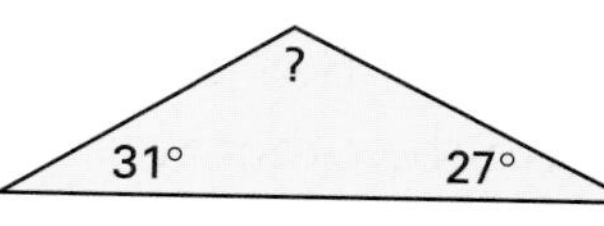

7. Reasoning Can any three angles form a triangle? Explain.

Practice

Mental Math Given the measures of two angles of a triangle, find the measure of the third angle.

8. 100°, 40° **9.** 60°, 60° **10.** 80°, 20° **11.** 50°, 50° **12.** 30°, 50° **13.** 80°, 90°

For **14–21,** classify each triangle as acute, right, or obtuse.

14.

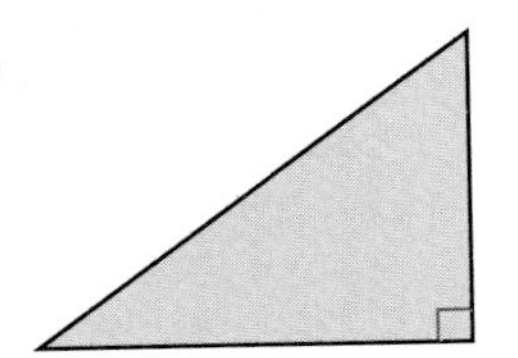

15.

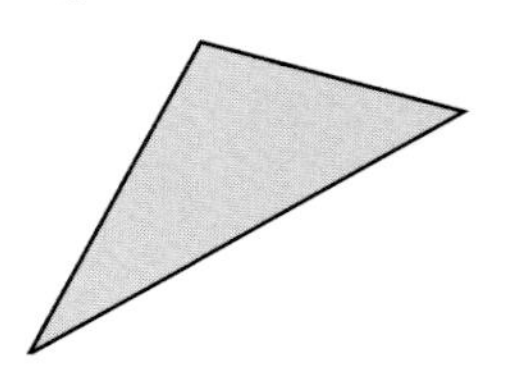

16.

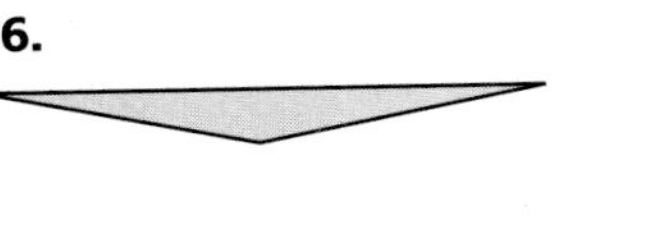

17.

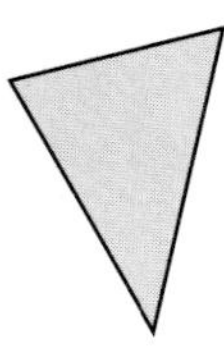

18. $m\angle T = 67°$, $m\angle H = 34°$, $m\angle W = 79°$

19. $m\angle S = 124°$, $m\angle D = 50°$, $m\angle P = 6°$

20. $m\angle V = 30°$, $m\angle R = 60°$, $m\angle F = 90°$

21. $m\angle E = 60°$, $m\angle J = 60°$, $m\angle B = 60°$

Use a protractor to determine the measure of all angles in each triangle.

22.

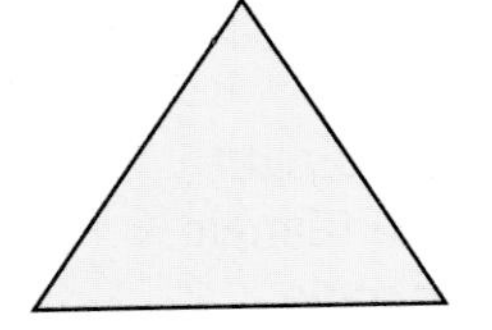

23.

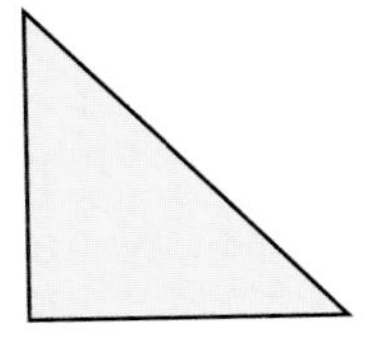

24.

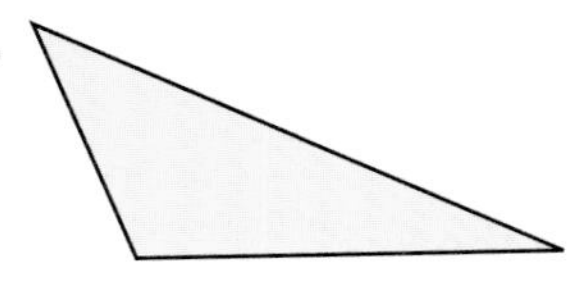

25.

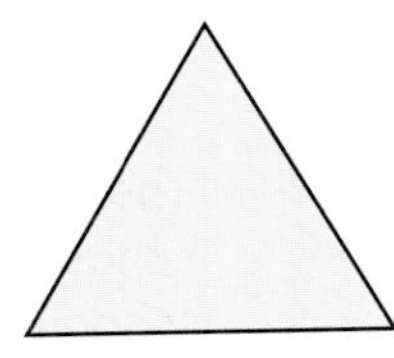

26.

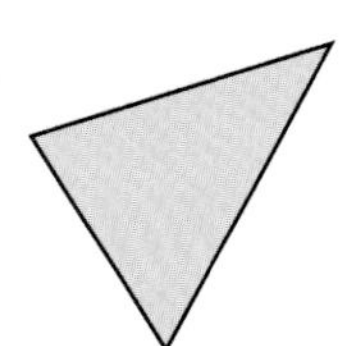

27.

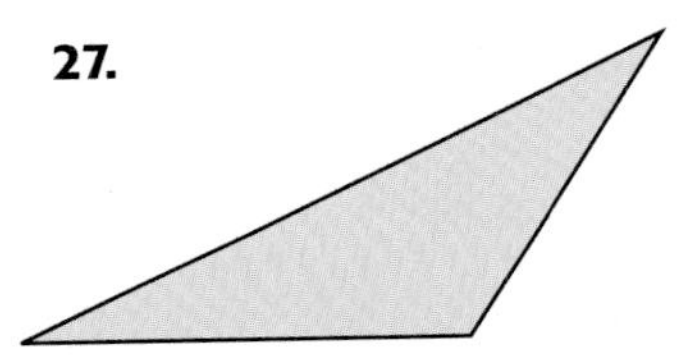

28.

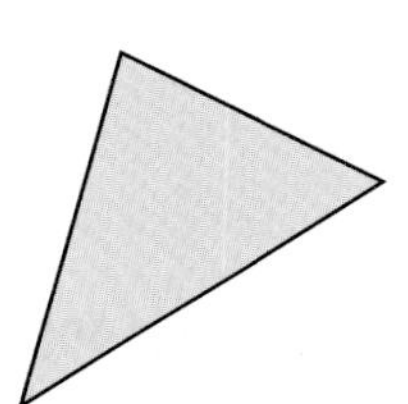

29.

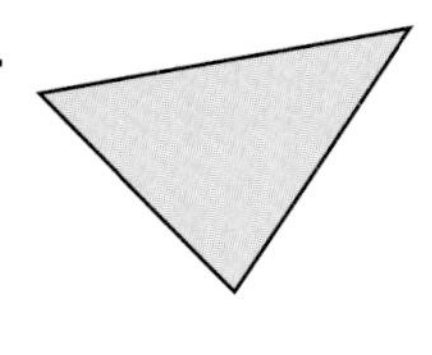

Find the missing angle measure in each triangle.

30. $m\angle A = 56°$, $m\angle B = 93°$, $m\angle C =$ ■

31. $m\angle X = 115°$, $m\angle Y = 34°$, $m\angle Z =$ ■

32. $m\angle L = 170°$, $m\angle M = 5°$, $m\angle N =$ ■

33. $m\angle R = 48°$, $m\angle S = 63°$, $m\angle T =$ ■

34. $m\angle I = 78°$, $m\angle J = 12°$, $m\angle K =$ ■

35. $m\angle D = 25°$, $m\angle G = 80°$, $m\angle P =$ ■

Geometry For **36–39,** decide whether a triangle can be formed with the angle measurements given. If a triangle can be formed, draw and classify it.

36. 35°, 65°, 80° **37.** 45°, 45°, 90° **38.** 95°, 45°, 40° **39.** 55°, 50°, 50°

40. **Science** Magnetite is one of only two common minerals that are magnetic. Magnetite was used in early versions of modern-day compasses. What are the angle measures for the magnetic crystal shown?

41. Angela drew a triangle and measured two of the angles. One angle was 75°and the other was 89°. What is the measure of the third angle?

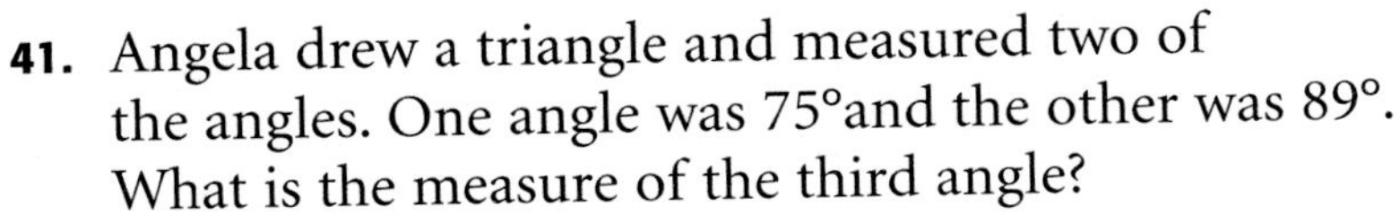

Problem Solving and Applications

42. Using Data Classify the triangles shown on the cross-rose pattern in the Data File on page 399.

43. Critical Thinking What is the measure of $\angle ABC$ in the figure to the right?

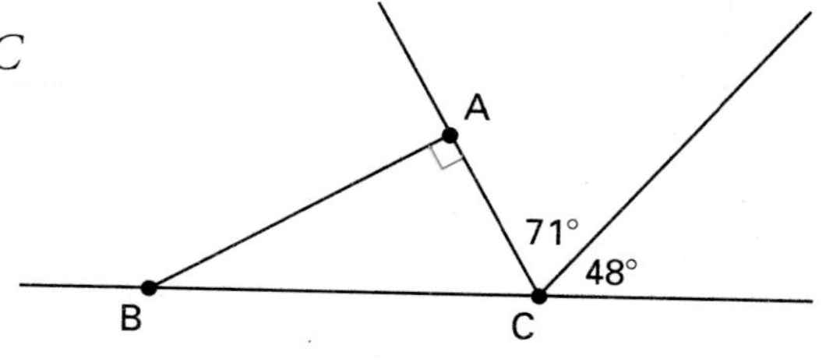

44. Algebra Readiness The measures of two angles of a triangle are 45° and 55°. Write an equation using the variable n to show that the sum of the measures of the angles of the triangle equals 180°.

45. Critical Thinking Is the shadow of a right triangle always a right triangle?

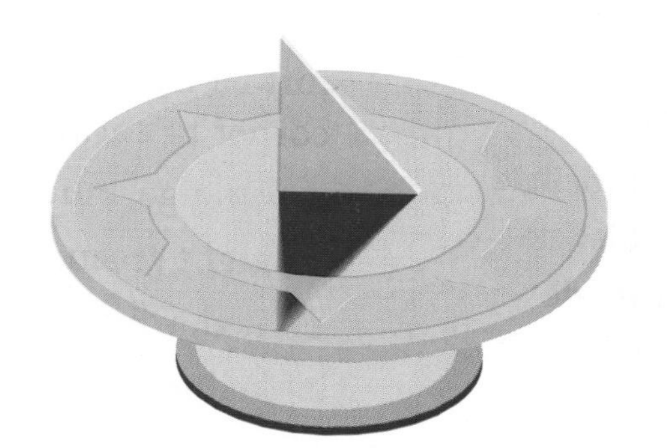

46. Critical Thinking A triangle has angles A, B, and C. The complement of $\angle A$ is 58°, and the supplement of $\angle B$ is 60°. What is the measure of $\angle C$?

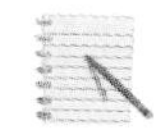

47. Journal Why can't a triangle have more than one obtuse angle?

Mixed Review and Test Prep

Write each decimal as a fraction in lowest terms.

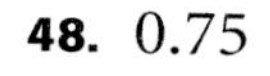

48. 0.75 **49.** 0.78 **50.** 0.596 **51.** 0.9 **52.** 0.38

53. 0.72 **54.** 0.55 **55.** 0.138 **56.** 0.7 **57.** 0.375

58. 0.2 **59.** 0.999 **60.** 0.16 **61.** 0.33 **62.** 0.05

63. 0.125 **64.** 0.88 **65.** 0.9 **66.** 0.48 **67.** 0.68

Estimate.

68. $5\frac{1}{2} - 4\frac{6}{8}$ **69.** $2\frac{6}{7} - 2\frac{1}{9}$ **70.** $4\frac{8}{9} - 2\frac{1}{3}$ **71.** $9\frac{5}{6} + 5\frac{3}{4}$

72. $6\frac{2}{7} + 9\frac{3}{7}$ **73.** $8\frac{9}{14} - 3\frac{5}{6}$ **74.** $7\frac{5}{7} + 7\frac{5}{7}$ **75.** $9\frac{4}{8} - 4\frac{3}{6}$

76. $7\frac{3}{4} - 2\frac{1}{9}$ **77.** $9\frac{11}{17} - 5\frac{1}{8}$ **78.** $3\frac{2}{3} + 4\frac{3}{4}$ **79.** $6\frac{2}{5} - 4\frac{1}{3}$

80. What is the area of this figure?

Ⓐ 30 in^2 Ⓑ 60 in^2

Ⓒ 120 in^2 Ⓓ 240 in^2

Chapter 8
Lesson
5

Exploring Sides of a Triangle

Problem Solving Connection
- Look for a Pattern
- Guess and Check

Materials
Cuisenaire rods®

Vocabulary
equilateral triangle
isosceles triangle
scalene triangle

Explore

You have investigated classifying triangles by their angles. In this activity, you will investigate classifying triangles by the lengths of their sides.

Work Together

1. For each set of rods, determine if the rods can be placed together to form a triangle. In order to count as a triangle, every rod must touch corner to corner.
   a. Orange, blue, dark green
   b. Light green, yellow, dark green
   c. Red, white, black
   d. Yellow, brown, light green
   e. Dark green, yellow, red
   f. Purple, dark green, white
   g. Orange, blue, white
   h. Black, dark green, red
2. Find five new sets of three rods that can form a triangle.
3. Find five new sets of three rods that cannot form a triangle.

Talk About It

4. Without actually putting them together, how can you tell whether or not three rods will form a triangle?
5. Could you form a triangle with two rods of one color and one rod of another color? With three rods of the same color? Explain.

Connect and Learn

An **equilateral triangle** has three sides of the same length.

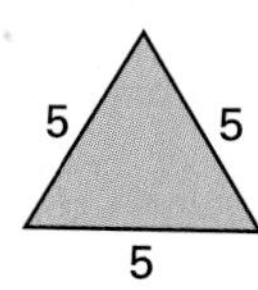

An **isosceles triangle** has two sides of the same length.

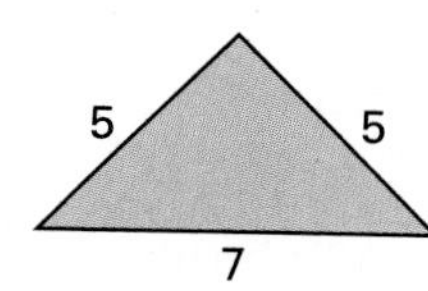

A **scalene triangle** has no sides of the same length.

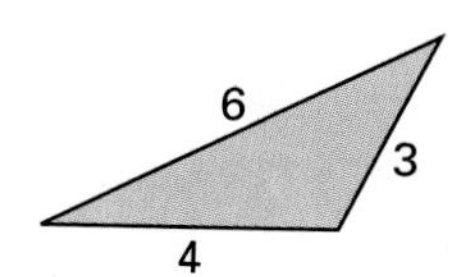

Example 1

The diamond is cut in the "American brilliant" style. Classify the triangles as shown that form facets *a*, *b*, and *c*.

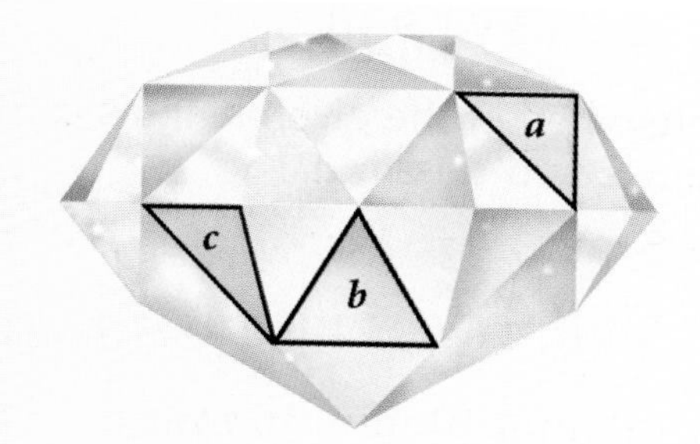

Triangle *a* has 2 equal sides, so it is isosceles.
Triangle *b* has 3 equal sides, so it is equilateral.
Triangle *c* has no equal sides, so it is scalene.

In order for three lengths to form a triangle, the sum of the two shortest lengths must be greater than the longest length.

In the first cabin, the sum of the heights of the walls is *greater than* the length of the floor.

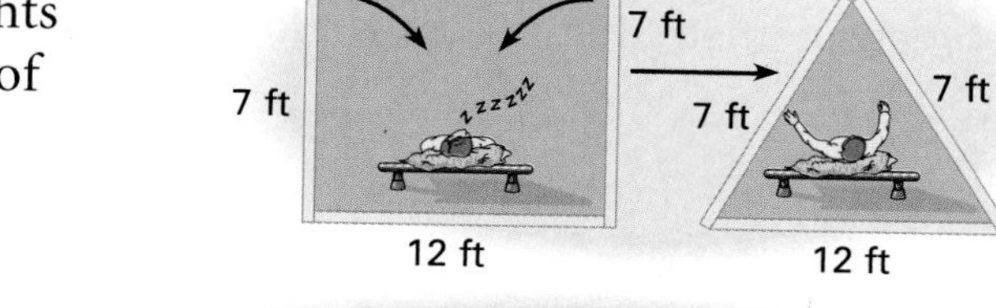

In the second cabin, the sum of the heights of the walls is *less than* the length of the floor.

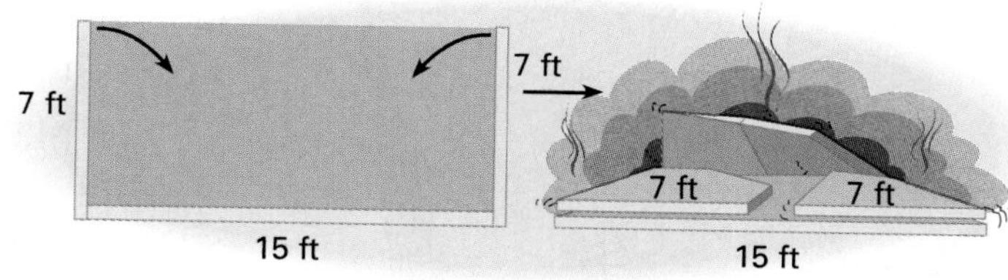

Example 2

State whether the given lengths can form a triangle.

a. 5 in., 9 in., 13 in.

$5 + 9 > 13$

A triangle can be formed.

b. 10 cm, 14 cm, 25 cm.

$10 + 14 < 25$

A triangle cannot be formed.

Check

Classify each triangle as scalene, equilateral, or isosceles.

1. 1 cm, 1 cm, 1 cm

2.

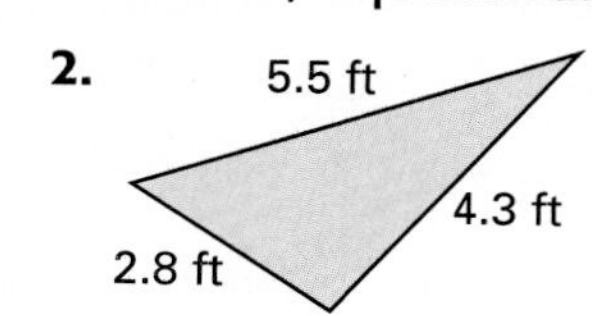

3.

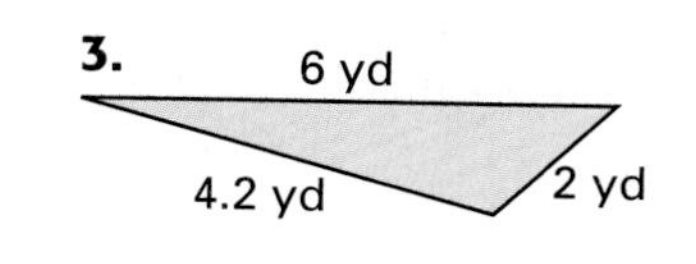

4.

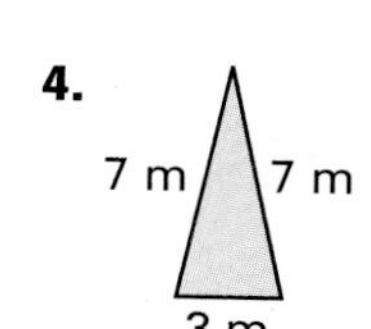

Practice

Classify each triangle as scalene, equilateral, or isosceles.

5.

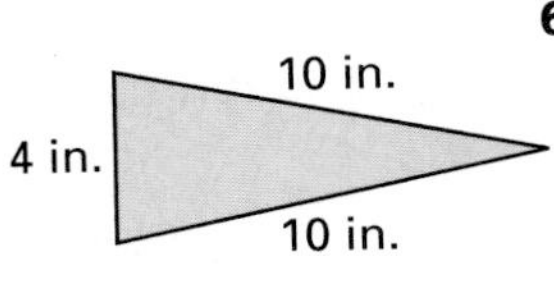

6.

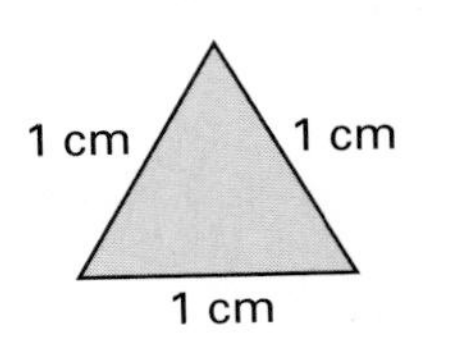

7

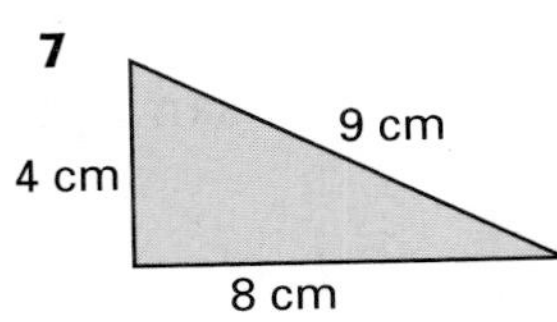

8.

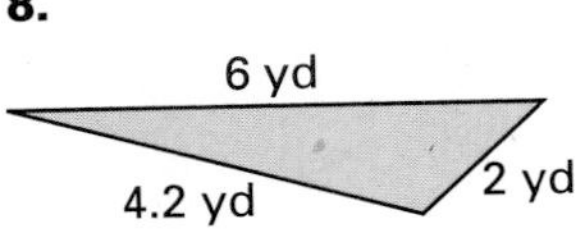

9. Sides: 40 cm, 55 cm, 45 cm

10. Sides: 1.67 in., 1.53 in., 0.28 in.

11. Sides: 3 yd, 9 yd, 3 yd

12. Sides: 6 in., 6 in., 6 in.

State whether the given lengths can form a triangle. If they can, draw the triangle and classify it.

13. 5 cm, 3 cm, 2 cm

14. 3 in., 6 in., 8 in.

15. 7 m, 7 m, 10 m

16. 2.1 ft, 4.6 ft, 3.1 ft

17. 15 cm, 7 cm, 7 cm

18. 3 in., 6 in., 9 in.

19. 10 mm, 10 mm, 10 mm

20. 9.6 yd, 9.4 yd, 9.3 yd

21. 2 yd, 14 yd, 7 yd

Problem Solving and Applications

Logic Given the lengths of two sides of a triangle, state the greatest whole-number measurement that is possible for the third.

22. 1 m, 4 m

23. 2 in., 6 in.

24. 10 ft, 11 ft

25. 4 cm, 6 cm

26. 5 yd, 5 yd

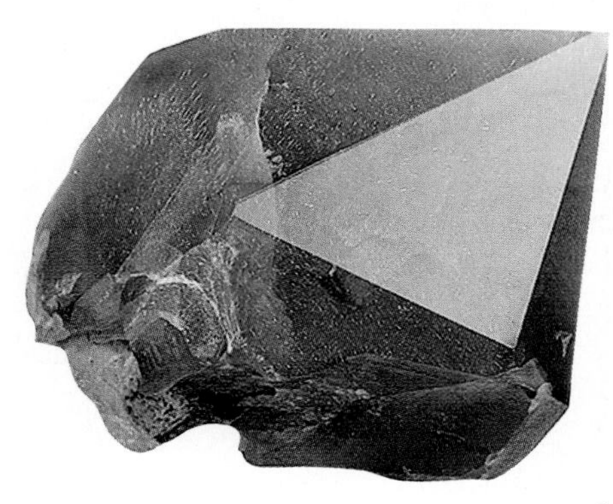

27. History In ancient times it was thought that rock crystal was ice that had frozen so hard it would never melt. We know now that it is formed by other molecules, like silicon dioxide. Classify the triangular face of the smoky quartz rock crystal shown by the lengths of its sides.

28. Geometry Jeremy has two poles for the end of his tent. They are each 4 feet long.

a. Can he form the triangular end of his tent if he puts two ends together and places the other ends 9 feet apart?

b. What is the greatest whole number of feet apart Jeremy can place the poles to form a triangle?

29. **Using Data** Classify the triangles shown in the cross-rose pattern in the Data File on page 399 by the lengths of their sides.

Critical Thinking Classify each triangle as acute, right, or obtuse, and also as equilateral, isosceles, or scalene.

30. 4 cm, 4 cm, 6 cm

31. 3 m, 5 m, 4 m

32. 1 cm, 10 cm, 10 cm

33.

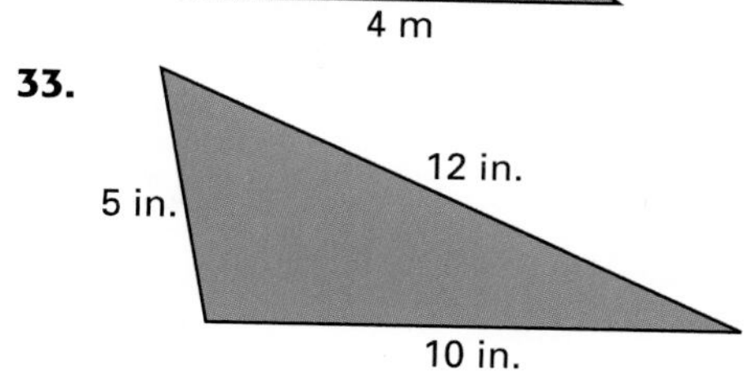

Critical Thinking Explain whether it is possible to draw each triangle. If it is possible, draw the triangle.

34. An obtuse right triangle
35. A scalene acute triangle
36. An isosceles right triangle

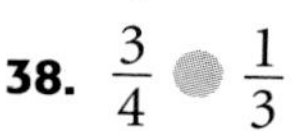

37. **Journal** If you fold an equilateral triangle in half, what kind of triangles are the smaller two triangles? Explain.

Mixed Review and Test Prep

STAY SHARP!

Compare using >, <, or =.

38. $\frac{3}{4} \bigcirc \frac{1}{3}$
39. $\frac{7}{8} \bigcirc \frac{6}{7}$
40. $\frac{5}{9} \bigcirc \frac{7}{10}$
41. $\frac{1}{8} \bigcirc \frac{2}{17}$
42. $\frac{2}{4} \bigcirc \frac{9}{18}$
43. $\frac{20}{10} \bigcirc \frac{15}{3}$
44. $\frac{12}{18} \bigcirc \frac{26}{39}$
45. $\frac{3}{19} \bigcirc \frac{6}{38}$

Find each sum. Simplify.

46. $4\frac{3}{5} + 6\frac{2}{3}$
47. $3\frac{1}{4} + 4\frac{3}{7}$
48. $10 + 13\frac{4}{8}$
49. $62\frac{3}{4} + 3\frac{5}{9}$
50. $6\frac{1}{5} + 5\frac{2}{7}$
51. $8\frac{4}{7} + 9\frac{10}{14}$
52. $5\frac{6}{7} + 1\frac{4}{5}$
53. $7\frac{2}{7} + 4\frac{6}{9}$

54. Classify the triangle by its angles.

Ⓐ acute
Ⓑ right
Ⓒ obtuse
Ⓓ not here

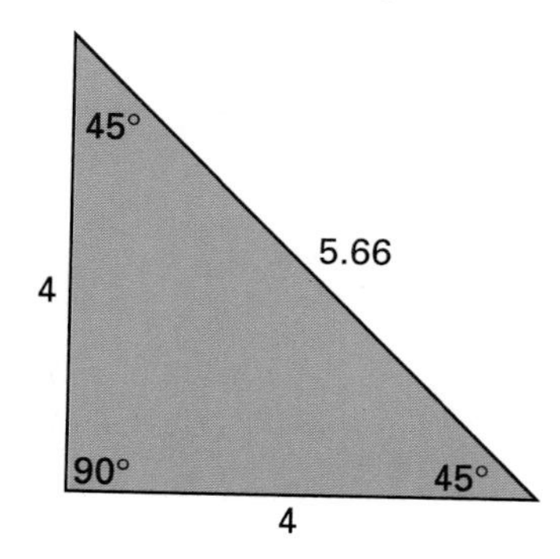

Chapter 8
Lesson
6

Polygons

You Will Learn

- to classify polygons

Vocabulary

polygon
quadrilateral
pentagon
hexagon
octagon
regular polygon

Learn

A **polygon** is a closed figure made of line segments. The word *polygon* comes from Greek and means "many angled."

All figures shown to the right are polygons.

Polygons are named by their number of sides.

Just as triangles can be classified by the length of their sides and the measures of their angles, so can polygons. In a **regular polygon**, all the sides and all the angles have the same measures. Of the twelve polygons, 1, 8, and 10 are regular polygons. The remaining polygons are irregular polygons.

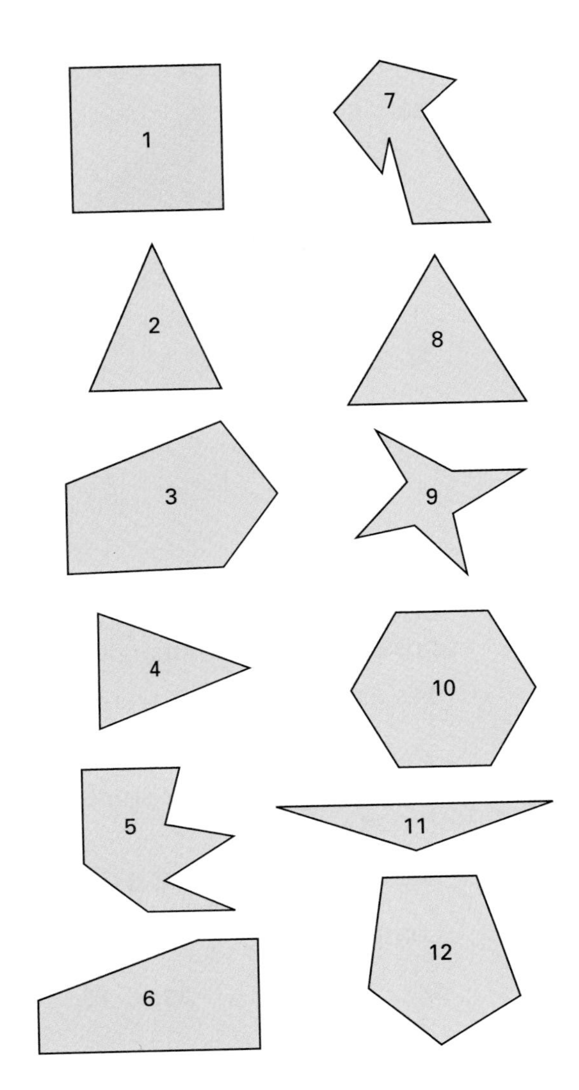

Polygons Shown	Number of Sides	Polygon Name
2, 4, 8, 11	3	triangle
1	4	quadrilateral
3, 6, 12	5	pentagon
10	6	hexagon
5, 7, 9	8	octagon

Example 1

All the figures shown are regular polygons. Name each polygon.

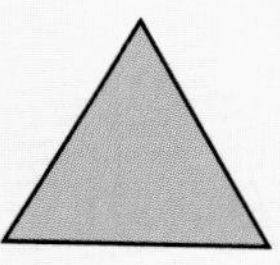

3 sides
triangle

4 sides
quadrilateral

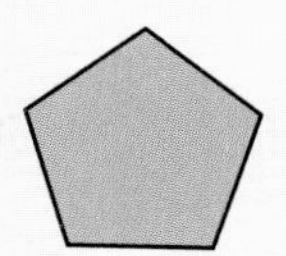

5 sides
pentagon

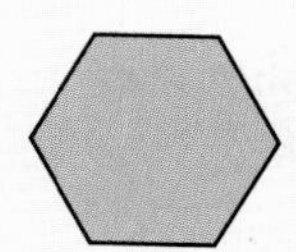

6 sides
hexagon

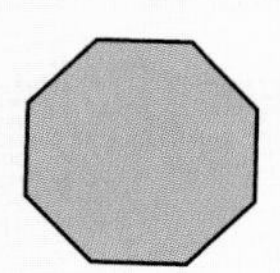

8 sides
octagon

To give a better description of a polygon, the polygon's name can be preceded by *regular* or *irregular*.

Example 2

Name each polygon and tell if it appears to be regular or irregular.

a.

Regular triangle

The figure is a triangle. Its sides and angles are equal, so it is regular.

b.

Irregular quadrilateral

The figure is a quadrilateral. Neither its sides nor its angles are equal, so it is irregular.

c.

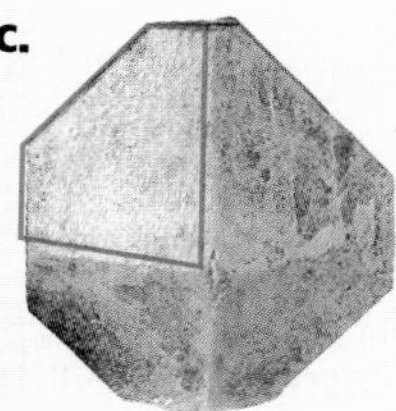

Irregular pentagon

The figure is a pentagon. Neither its sides nor its angles are equal, so it is irregular.

Talk About It

Name something that is the shape of a quadrilateral, a pentagon, a hexagon, and an octagon. Explain.

Check

Name each polygon and tell if it appears to be regular or irregular.

1.

2.

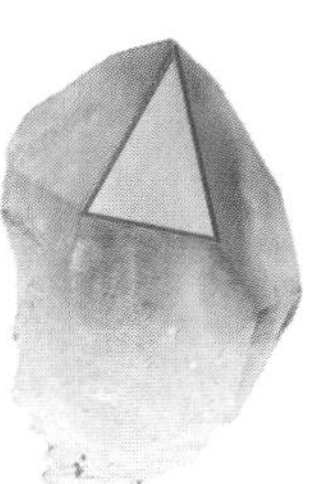

3.

4. **Reasoning** A polygon has four sides of 6 cm each, two angles of 70° each, and two angles of 110° each. What kind of polygon is it? Explain.

Practice

Skills and Reasoning

State why each figure is not a polygon.

5. 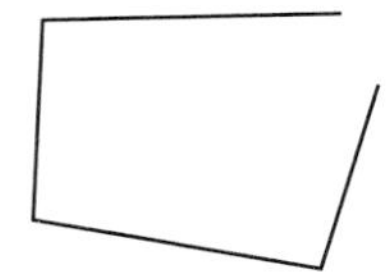

6. 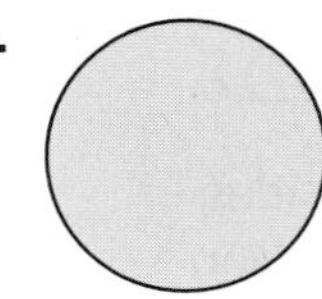

7. 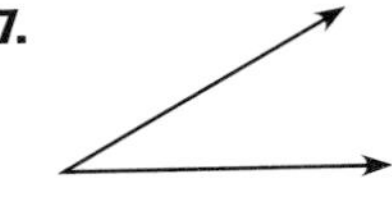

8. 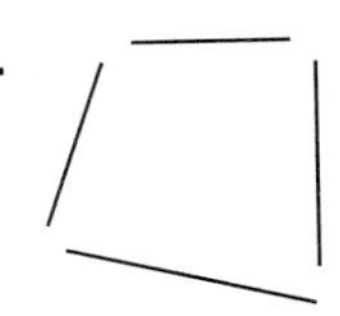

Name each polygon and tell if it appears to be regular or irregular.

9. 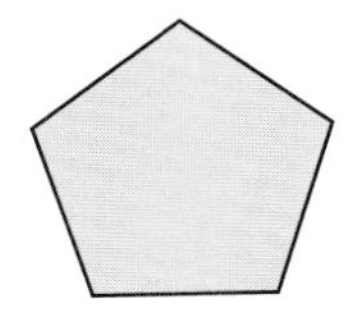

10. 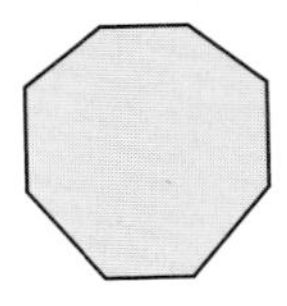

11. 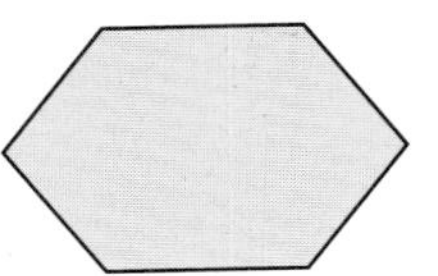

12. 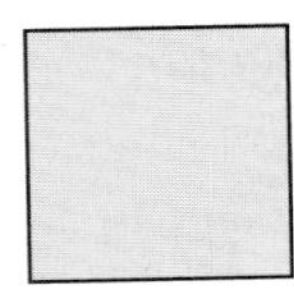

13. 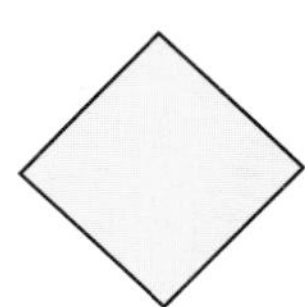

14. 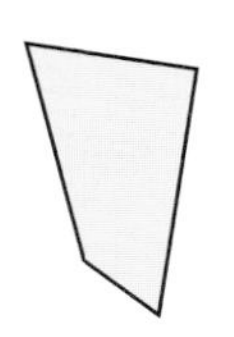

15. 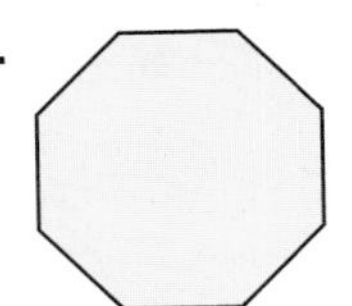

16. 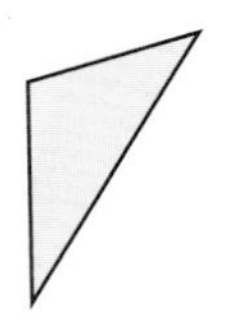

Draw an example of each figure and classify each of the angles in your drawing.

17. Irregular quadrilateral
18. Regular pentagon
19. Regular hexagon
20. Irregular octagon
21. Regular triangle
22. Irregular pentagon
23. **Science** Rays are relatives of sharks. Their fins are greatly enlarged and flap like wings when they swim. What polygon can the shape of the ray shown be most closely classified as?

State the shape of each crystal.

24. 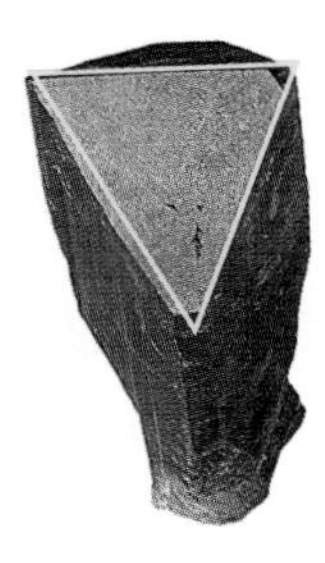

25. 

26. 

27. The floor of a ballroom in a large hotel is shaped like an octagon. How many walls does the room have?
28. The lengths of the sides of a quadrilateral are 3.5 ft, $\frac{7}{2}$ ft, $3\frac{1}{2}$ ft, and $2\frac{3}{2}$ ft. Is the quadrilateral regular or irregular? Explain.

Problem Solving and CAREERS

Police officers must enforce traffic laws among other duties. Different traffic signals are posted on signs with distinctive colors and shapes. These characteristics make it easy for drivers to recognize and obey the signs' messages immediately.

What kind of polygon is each sign? Is the polygon regular or irregular?

29.

30.

31.

32.

33. Money In one state, speeders are fined \$55 for speeding, and \$2 for each mile over the speed limit they traveled. Use the sign in Problem 32. How much would a person be fined driving a car at 78 miles per hour?

34. Journal Classify acute, right, obtuse, equilateral, isosceles, and scalene triangles as regular or irregular polygons. Explain your reasoning.

Mixed Review and Test Prep

Order from least to greatest.

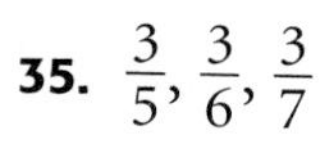

35. $\frac{3}{5}, \frac{3}{6}, \frac{3}{7}$ **36.** $\frac{8}{9}, \frac{4}{5}, \frac{7}{8}$ **37.** $\frac{13}{2}, \frac{12}{3}, \frac{14}{15}$ **38.** $\frac{6}{9}, \frac{9}{6}, \frac{6}{6}$

39. $\frac{24}{3}, \frac{24}{8}, \frac{24}{6}$ **40.** $\frac{1}{2}, \frac{1}{3}, \frac{1}{4}$ **41.** $\frac{4}{6}, \frac{6}{8}, \frac{8}{10}$ **42.** $\frac{6}{7}, \frac{7}{6}, \frac{9}{8}$

Simplify.

43. $3\frac{3}{4} - 1\frac{2}{3}$ **44.** $5\frac{4}{7} - 3\frac{4}{5}$ **45.** $6\frac{1}{3} - 3\frac{2}{6}$ **46.** $4\frac{3}{8} - 4\frac{1}{4}$ **47.** $8\frac{5}{6} - 7\frac{1}{3}$

48. $12\frac{5}{8} - 9\frac{3}{7}$ **49.** $9\frac{2}{5} - 4\frac{6}{7}$ **50.** $7\frac{1}{3} - \frac{8}{9}$ **51.** $3\frac{3}{4} - 1\frac{3}{8}$ **52.** $6\frac{4}{7} - 2\frac{1}{4}$

53. What is 1,700 written in scientific notation?

Ⓐ 17×10^3 Ⓑ 1.7×10^4 Ⓒ 1.7×10^3 Ⓓ 170×10^2

Quadrilaterals

You Will Learn
- to classify quadrilaterals

Vocabulary
trapezoid
parallelogram
rhombus
rectangle
square

Learn

Yoko, Janelle, Lucas, and Andrew classified groups of quadrilaterals.

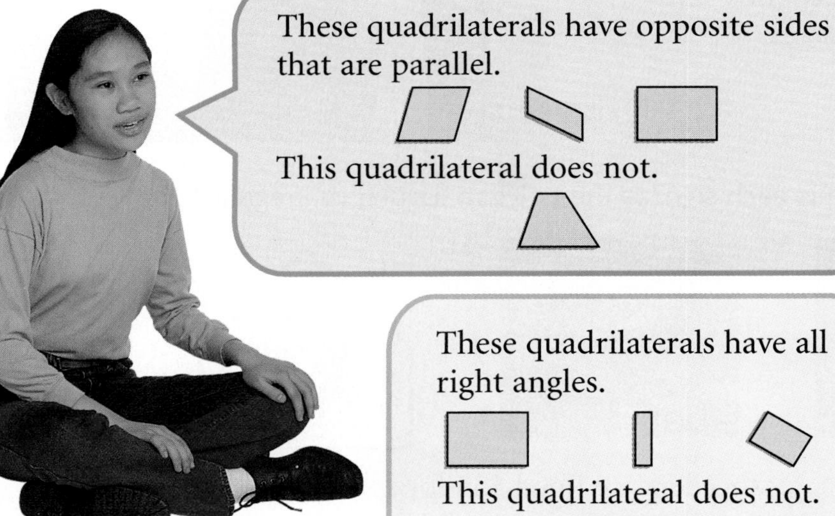

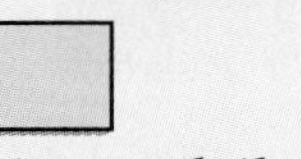

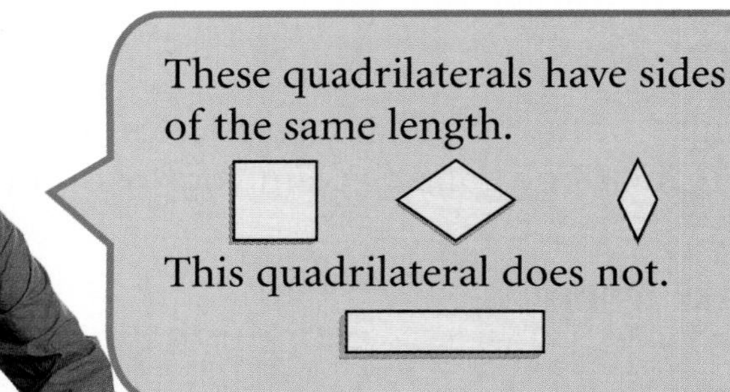

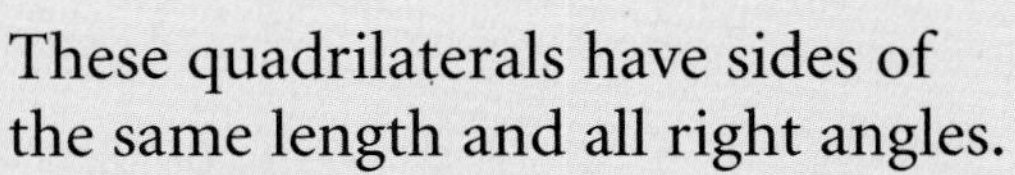

Any polygon with four sides is a quadrilateral. There are five special types of quadrilaterals: **trapezoid**, **parallelogram**, **rhombus**, **rectangle**, and **square**.

Each has different features, and some can be classified in different ways.

Definitions of Quadrilaterals

Quadrilateral
- Four sides

Trapezoid
- Exactly two sides parallel

Parallelogram
- Opposite sides same length
- Opposite sides parallel

Rectangle
- Opposite sides same length
- All angles 90°

Rhombus
- All sides same length
- Opposite sides parallel

Square
- All sides same length
- All angles 90°

Example 1

True or false: A square is a rectangle.

A square has opposite sides of the same length, and all angles are 90°.

A square is a rectangle.

The statement is true.

The chart above can help you find all the classifications for a figure.

Example 2

Classify the figure in as many ways as possible.

The figure is a rhombus.

In the chart, "rhombus" points to "parallelogram," which points to "quadrilateral."

So, any rhombus is also a parallelogram and also a quadrilateral.

Talk About It

1. A geometry book said that a square is a "rectangular rhombus." Do you agree? Explain your reasoning.
2. How are trapezoids and parallelograms alike? How are they different?
3. Quadrilaterals can be classified based on whether or not their opposite sides are parallel. Can triangles also be classified in this way? Explain.

Check

Answer true or false.

1. A rhombus is a trapezoid.
2. A rectangle is a parallelogram.
3. Classify the figure in as many ways as possible.

4. **Reasoning** A quadrilateral has sides of 2 in. and 6 in. and two 40° angles. Classify the quadrilateral.

Practice

Skills and Reasoning

For each figure, state how many pairs of opposite sides are parallel.

5. 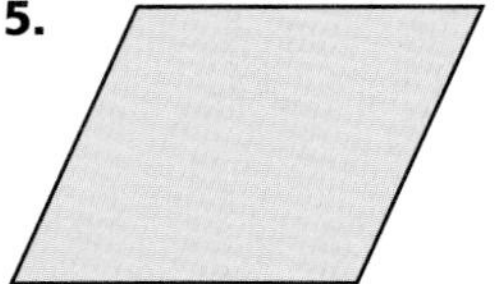

6. 

7. 

8. 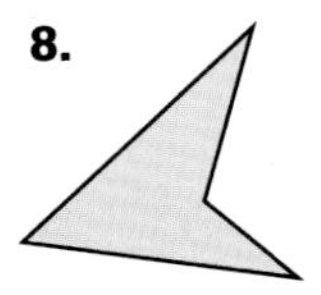

Classify each figure in as many ways as possible.

9. 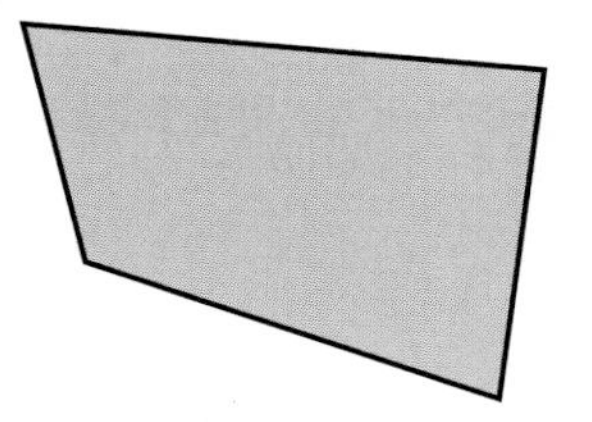

10. 

11. 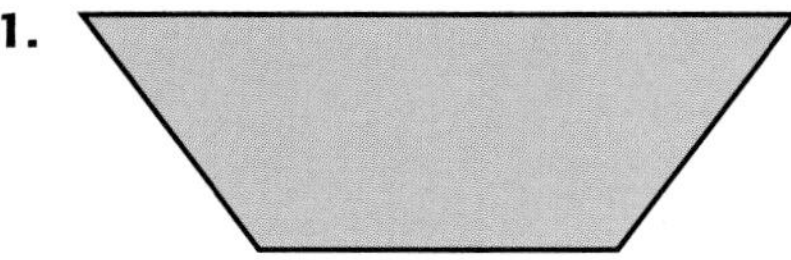

12. 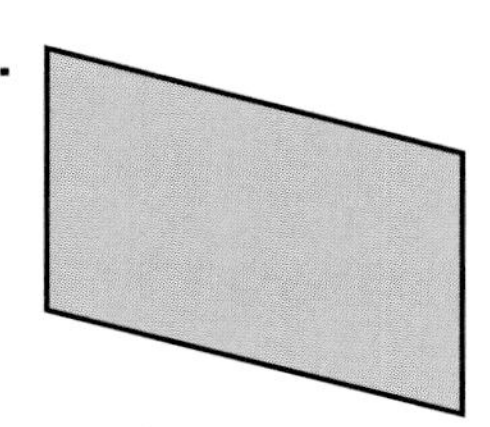

13. 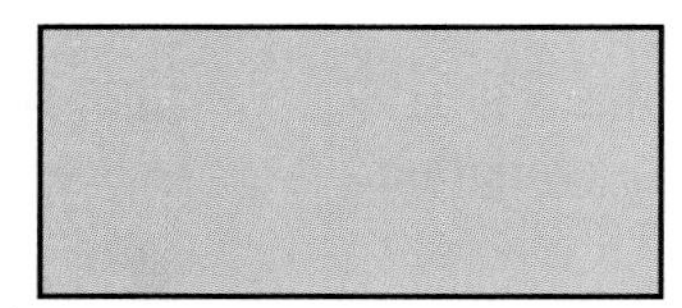

14. 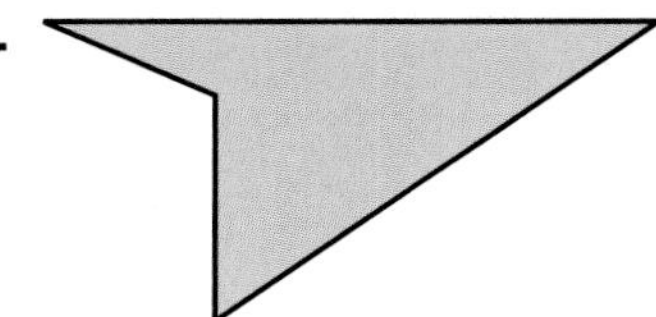

15. 

16. 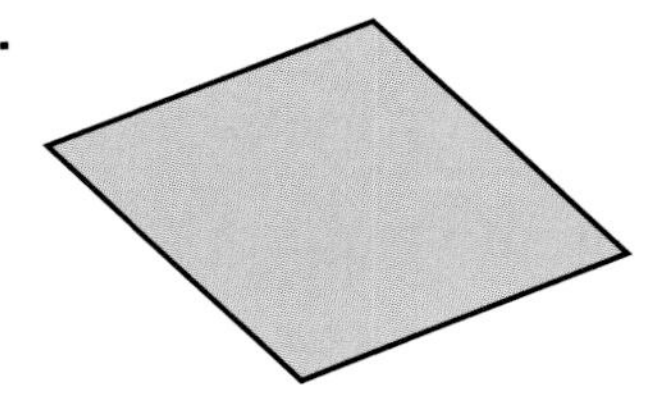

Draw an example of each figure. Classify each of the angles in your drawing.

17. Trapezoid **18.** Parallelogram **19.** Rhombus

20. Rectangle **21.** Square **22.** Quadrilateral

Tell whether each statement is true or false.

23. Every four-sided figure can be classified as more than one type of quadrilateral.

24. A square is a parallelogram.

25. A trapezoid is never a rectangle.

Problem Solving and Applications

26. History In 1851, the Crystal Palace was built in London as an exhibition hall. The roof and outer walls were built of almost 300,000 panes of glass. Are any windows parallelograms?

Measurement Given the information, can you determine the lengths of each figure's sides for **27–29**? If so, give the lengths.

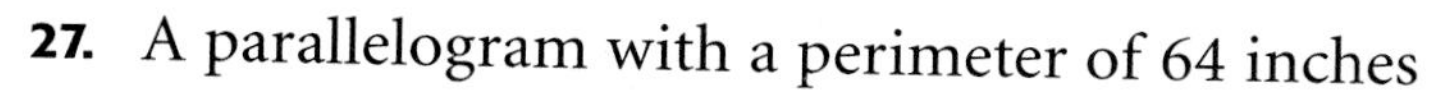

27. A parallelogram with a perimeter of 64 inches

28. A rhombus with a perimeter of 8 feet

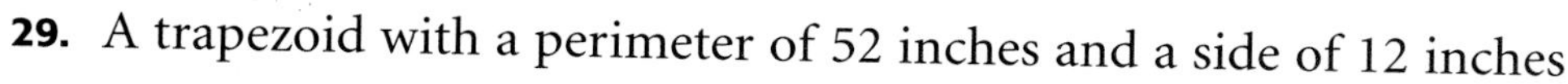

29. A trapezoid with a perimeter of 52 inches and a side of 12 inches

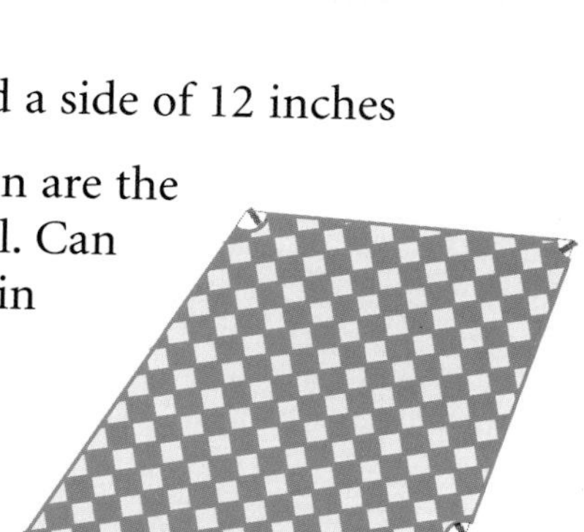

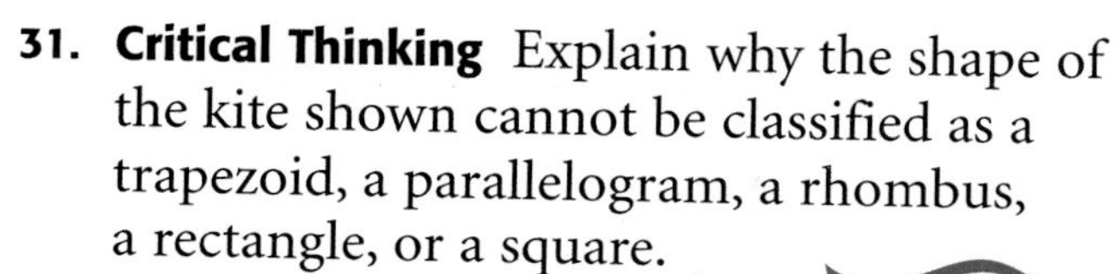

30. Critical Thinking The sides of a regular octagon are the same length, and all opposite sides are parallel. Can the octagon be classified as a rhombus? Explain your reasoning.

31. Critical Thinking Explain why the shape of the kite shown cannot be classified as a trapezoid, a parallelogram, a rhombus, a rectangle, or a square.

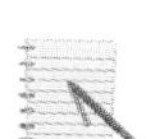

32. Journal Every square is also a rectangle, but every rectangle is not necessarily a square. Explain.

Mixed Review and Test Prep

Compare using >, <, or =.

33. $\frac{1}{2}$ ● 0.54 **34.** $\frac{3}{4}$ ● 0.65 **35.** $\frac{2}{9}$ ● 0.4 **36.** $\frac{5}{6}$ ● 0.83

37. $\frac{2}{3}$ ● 0.67 **38.** $\frac{4}{5}$ ● 0.8 **39.** $\frac{5}{8}$ ● 0.652 **40.** $\frac{1}{7}$ ● 0.2

41. $\frac{2}{5}$ ● 0.4 **42.** $\frac{11}{22}$ ● 0.5 **43.** $\frac{6}{9}$ ● 0.75 **44.** $\frac{2}{6}$ ● 0.25

Multiply.

45. 5×6.27 **46.** 12×2.45 **47.** 3×0.151 **48.** 56.7×4

49. 34.56×100 **50.** 6.89×7 **51.** $\$34 \times 1.4$ **52.** 0.004×10

53. Which is the correct product for 6.507×14?

Ⓐ 91.098 Ⓑ 71.098 Ⓒ 20.507 Ⓓ 26.028

Technology

Using Dynamic Geometry Software to Find Relationships in Triangles

You can tell a great deal about a triangle just by looking at it, but there is more to a triangle than meets the eye. You can use geometry software to stretch and shrink triangles and to change from one type of triangle to another.

Materials

Interactive CD-ROM Geometry Tool or other geometry software

What figures can you form by stretching or shrinking the sides of a scalene triangle?

Work Together

Use your geometry software to create, stretch, and shrink a triangle.

1. Draw a scalene triangle with sides measuring 8, 12, and 15 cm.

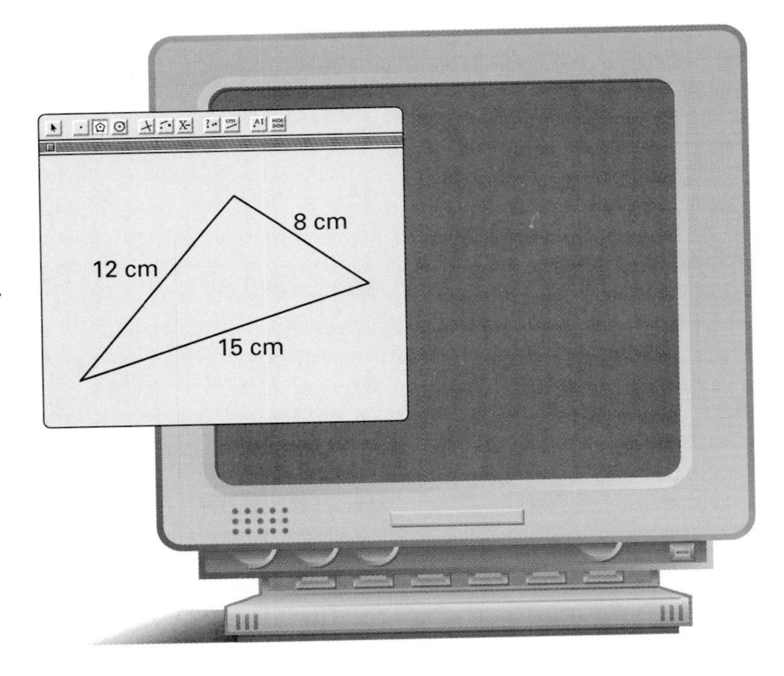

2. Drag one endpoint of the shortest side so that the side stretches to 12 cm, but the lengths of the other sides are unchanged. Record the type of triangle you have formed.

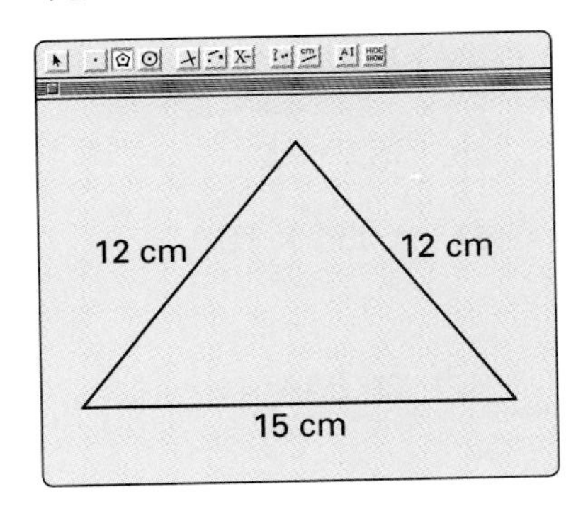

3. Drag one of the endpoints of the 15 cm side so that the side shrinks to 12 cm but the other sides remain the same. Record the type of triangle you have formed.

4. Draw other scalene triangles. Stretch or shrink the sides of each to create other triangles. Classify your triangles.

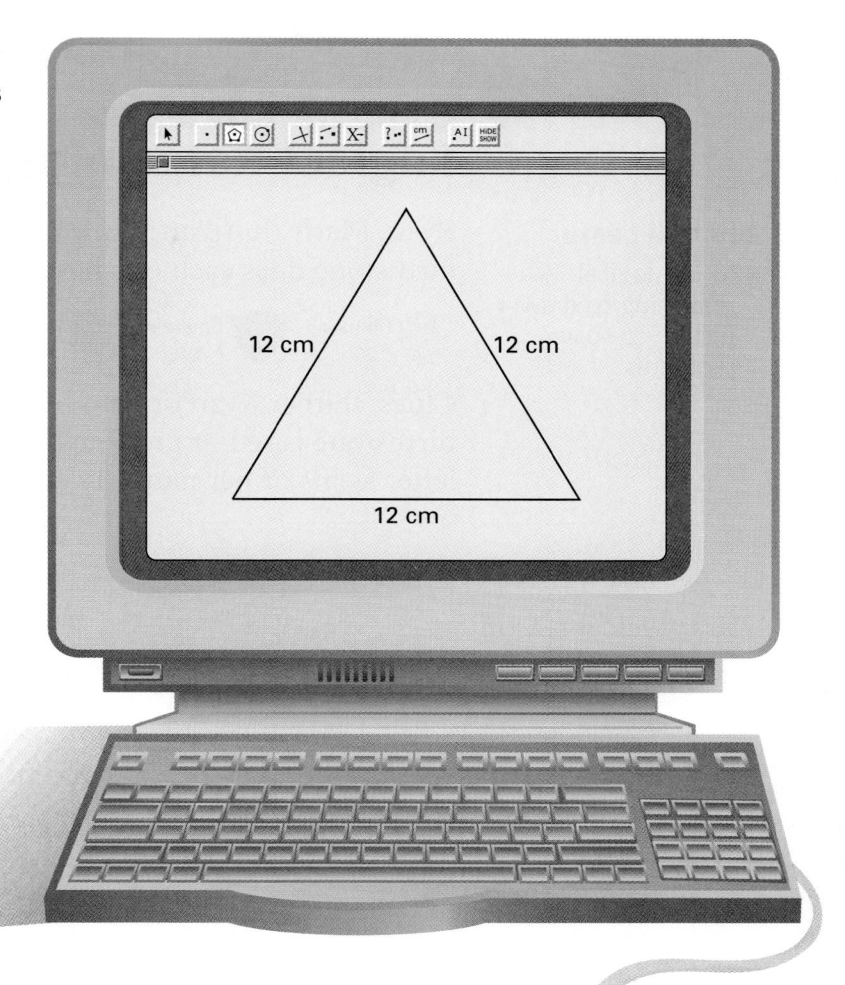

Exercises

Use your geometry software to stretch and shrink other figures.

1. Draw a square. Stretch or shrink one or more sides to form a trapezoid. Describe your method.
2. Draw a rectangle that is not a square. Find two ways to stretch or shrink sides of the rectangle to form a square. Describe your methods.

Extensions

3. Name a figure that cannot be formed by stretching or shrinking the sides of a scalene triangle. Explain why it cannot be formed.
4. If you stretch one side of a square, what must you do to the other sides of the new figure to form a rhombus?
5. When investigating triangles, is it easier to create examples on paper or with geometry software? Why?

Chapter 8

Problem Solving

Compare Strategies: Logical Reasoning/ Draw a Picture

You Will Learn

- to use logical reasoning or draw a picture to solve problems

Ryan, Marie, Julie, and Sam were born in different months. What birthstone does each one have?

Diamond April

Emerald May

Ruby July

Sapphire September

Clues: Either Ryan or Sam has a diamond for his birthstone. Julie's birthstone is red or green. No one has a birthstone starting with the same letter as his or her name. Ryan was born in May.

One Way

Use logical reasoning.

	Ryan	Marie	Julie	Sam
diamond	no	no	no	yes
emerald	yes	no	no	no
ruby	no	no	yes	no
sapphire	no	yes	no	no

1. Ryan or Sam has the diamond. Write *no* for diamond under Marie and Julie.
2. Julie's birthstone is either an emerald or a ruby. Write *no* for sapphire under Julie.
3. Ryan cannot have a ruby, so write *no* under Ryan. Sam cannot have a sapphire, so write *no* under Sam.
4. Ryan's birthstone is an emerald. Write *yes* under Ryan. Then write *no* for emerald for everyone else and *no* for diamond and sapphire under Ryan.

Julie must have the ruby. That leaves Marie with the sapphire and Sam with the diamond.

Another Way

Draw colored arrows, red for *yes* and blue for *no.*

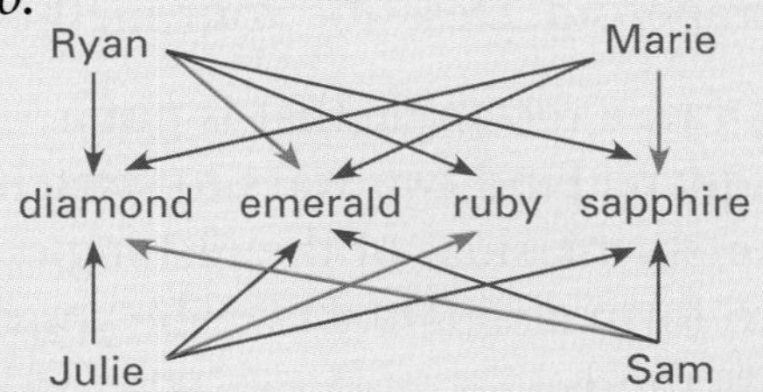

1. Draw blue arrows from Marie and Julie to diamond.
2. Draw a blue arrow from Julie to sapphire.
3. Draw a blue arrow from Ryan to ruby and from Sam to sapphire.
4. Draw a red arrow from Ryan to emerald.

Draw blue arrows from everyone else to emerald and from Ryan to all other stones. Draw a red arrow from Julie to ruby. Marie must have a red arrow to sapphire and Sam a red arrow to diamond.

How are these problem-solving strategies the same? How are they different?

Check

Copy and complete the table.

1. Jay, Lisa, Hector, and Tina each have a different collection: rocks, insects, stamps, and baseball cards. Jay collects rocks or insects. Hector's friends collect rocks and stamps. The objects in Tina's collection were once alive. What collection does each person have?

	Rocks	Insects	Stamps	Baseball Cards
Jay				
Lisa				
Hector				
Tina				

Problem Solving Practice

Problem Solving Strategies

- Draw a Picture
- Look for a Pattern
- Guess and Check
- Use Logical Reasoning
- Make an Organized List
- Make a Table
- Solve a Simpler Problem
- Work Backward

Choose a Tool

Use logical reasoning, draw a picture, or use any strategy to solve each problem.

2. Molly, Tony, Jason, and Kim are artists in four different fields: pottery, painting, woodworking, and basketry. Molly doesn't like to paint. Jason always admires the baskets and bowls his friends make. Kim likes to paint or make vases. Tony often uses a saw. Which artist practices which art?

3. Mark made a design in which one rectangle was surrounded by six squares. He changed the design to show two rectangles and ten squares, and then three rectangles and 14 squares. If he continues this way, how many squares will he use in a design with seven rectangles?

4. Dan, Rachel, Anna, and Paco each designed a new logo for their school using a different shape: a square, a trapezoid, a hexagon, and an octagon. Rachel did not use a quadrilateral. Anna's shape had fewer sides than Dan's. Paco's shape was not a regular polygon. Dan used a shape with twice as many sides as Paco's. Which shape did each person use?

5. **Write Your Own Problem** Write a problem using the table.

6. **Journal** When you can use either logical reasoning or draw a picture, which do you prefer? Explain.

	Jo	Harry	Bart	Kara
Catcher	no	no	no	yes
First Baseman	yes	no	no	no
Pitcher	no	no	yes	no
Shortstop	no	yes	no	no

PROBLEM SOLVING PRACTICE

SECTION B

Review and Practice

Vocabulary Match each description with a vocabulary word.

1. A closed figure with 4 sides and 1 pair of opposite sides parallel
2. A closed figure with all the sides the same length
3. A triangle with two sides of the same length
4. A closed figure made from 5 line segments
5. A closed figure made from 3 line segments

- **a.** right triangle
- **b.** triangle
- **c.** trapezoid
- **d.** pentagon
- **e.** regular polygon
- **f.** isosceles

(Lessons 4 and 5) Classify each triangle by its sides. Find the measure of each missing angle.

6. 61° 62°

7. 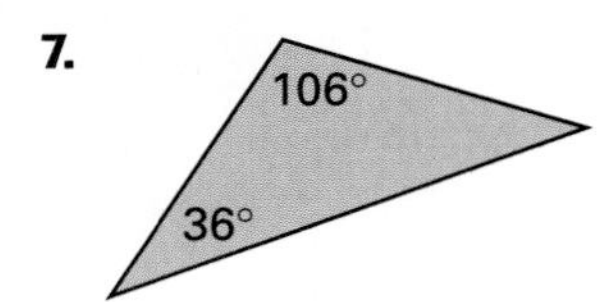

8. 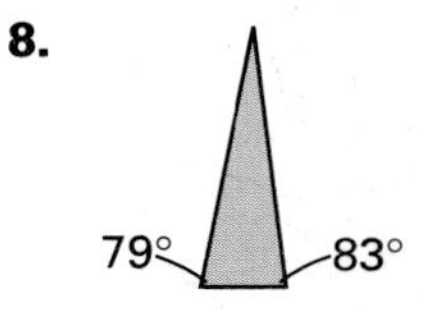

9. 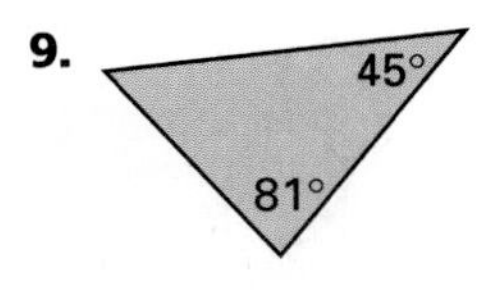

(Lesson 6) Draw an example of each figure.

10. Regular quadrilateral **11.** Regular octagon **12.** Irregular hexagon

State the shape of each figure.

13. 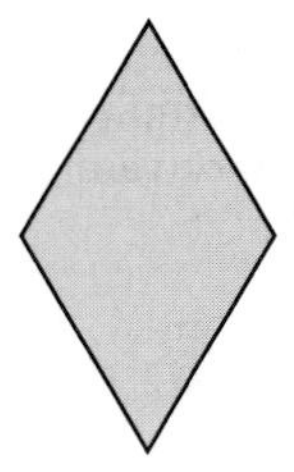

14. 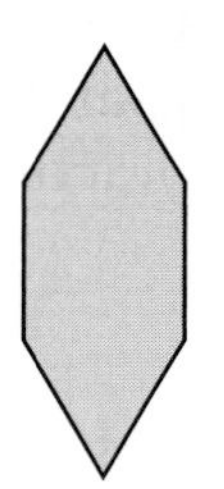

15. 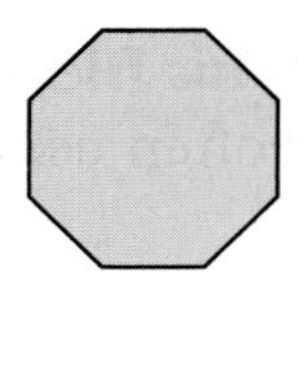

16. Sasha's classroom is a regular quadrilateral with one wall measuring 15 ft. What is the perimeter of the room?

(Lesson 7) Classify each figure in as many ways as possible.

17. 

18. 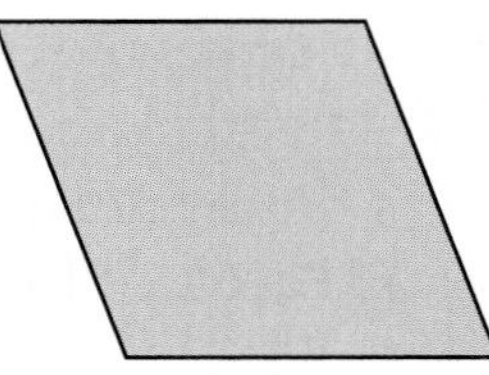

19. 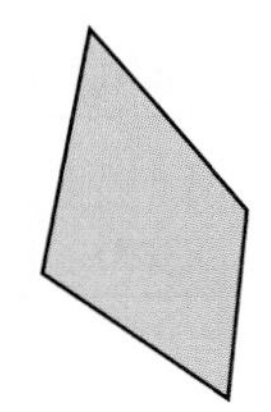

20. 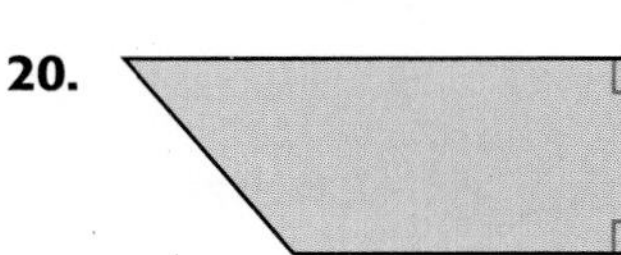

21. Journal Explain why all rectangles are parallelograms, but not all parallelograms are rectangles.

Skills Checklist

In this section, you have:

- Explored Angles in a Triangle
- Explored Sides of a Triangle
- Learned About Polygons
- Learned About Quadrilaterals

REVIEW AND PRACTICE

CHAPTER 8

SECTION C

Transformations

Early Islamic artisans of the 600s faced a challenge in designing their artwork. Their religion did not allow for art to include images of humans or animals. Instead, they used repeating and interlocking geometric patterns to create art that is both beautiful and mathematically complex.

How can geometric patterns be used to decorate things?

GET READY!

Exploring Flips, Slides, Turns, and Symmetry

Review congruent figures. Decide whether each pair of figures is congruent.

1. 

2. 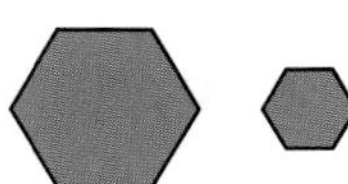

3. 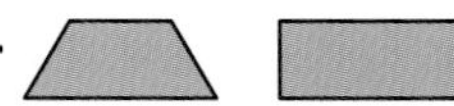

4. 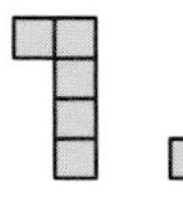

Skills Checklist

In this section, you will:

- ❒ Explore Flips and Lines of Symmetry
- ❒ Explore Turns and Rotational Symmetry
- ❒ Explore Slides and Tessellations

Chapter 8 Lesson 8

Flips and Line Symmetry

Problem Solving Connection
- Guess and Check
- Look for a Pattern

Materials
- unlined paper
- scissors

Vocabulary
congruent
line symmetry
reflection

Explore

Some geometric figures involve repeating patterns.

Work Together

1. Fold a sheet of paper in half. Draw a polygon with one side *along the fold.*

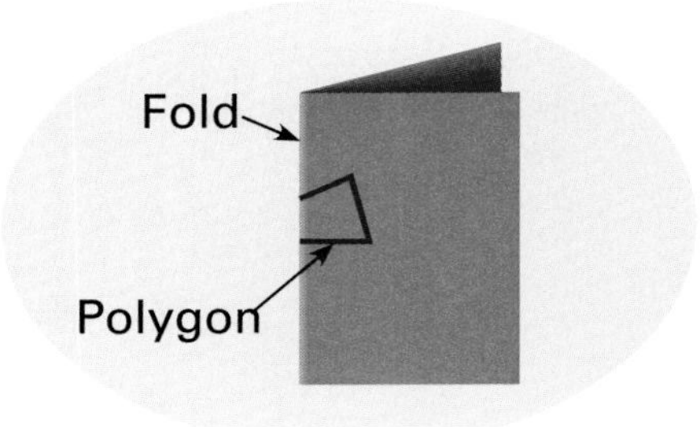

2. Cut out the figure. Do not cut through the fold. Sketch the shape you think it will have. Open the cutout and compare it with the one you predicted.

3. Fold a sheet from left to right, then top to bottom. With the paper as shown, draw 2 or 3 line segments from the top fold to the left fold. Repeat Step 2.

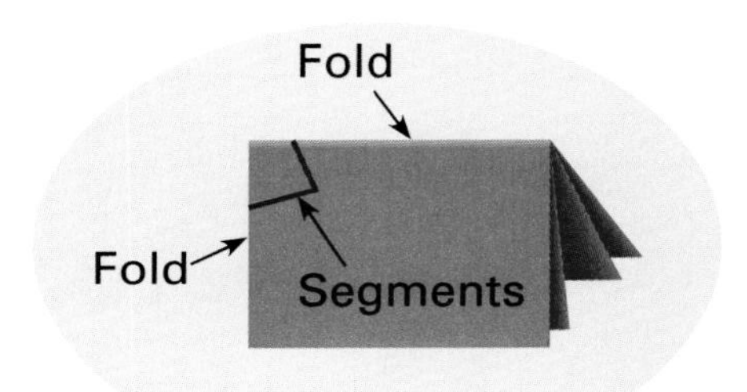

4. Fold a sheet "accordion-style" with three folds. Draw a polygon with one side along the top fold. Repeat Step 2, cutting through all four layers.

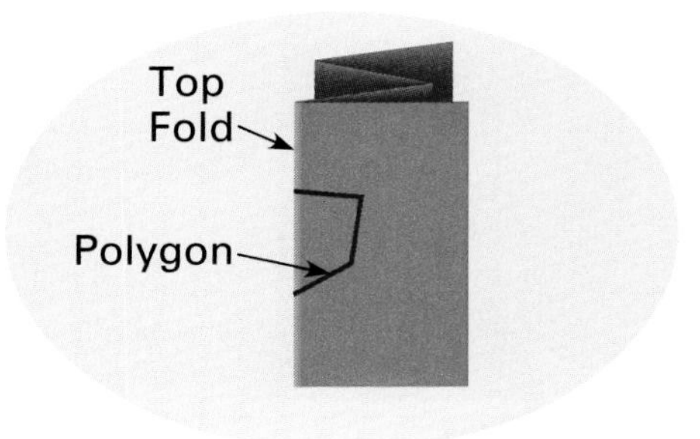

Talk About It

5. How did you predict the shape of each cutout?
6. A fold line divides each of your cutouts in half. How do the halves of each figure compare to each other?

Connect and Learn

Two figures are **congruent** if they have the same size and shape.

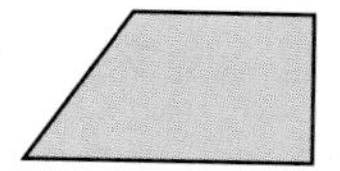 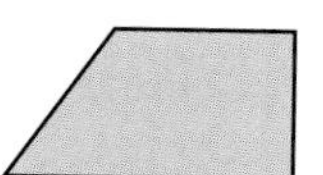

A figure that can be folded into congruent halves has **line symmetry**.

Example 1

This Islamic design is an illuminated page of Nasta'liq script by Mir'Ali Haravi from the early 16th-century Safavid dynasty in Iran. Early Islamic artists believed that the universe had a natural order to it. They chose to make their designs symmetrical as a representation of this natural order. Does the figure below have line symmetry?

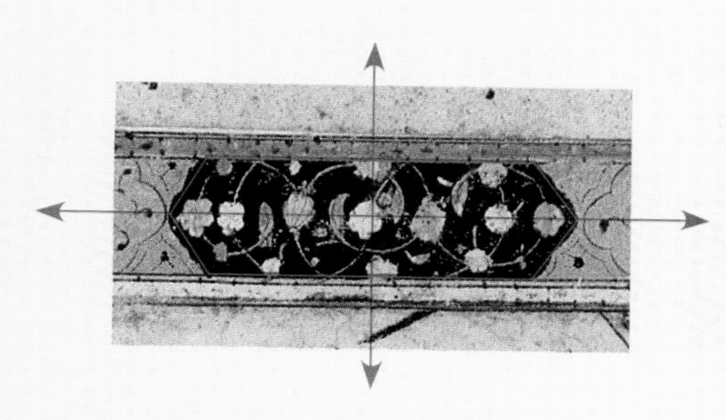

Yes. The figure has two lines of symmetry.

Ink and color on paper. Gift of the Todd G. Williams Memorial Fund and the Society for Asian Art. The Asian Art Museum of San Francisco. B87-D6.

A **reflection** is the mirror image of a figure that has been "flipped" over a line.

Example 2

Draw the reflection of the figure over the line.

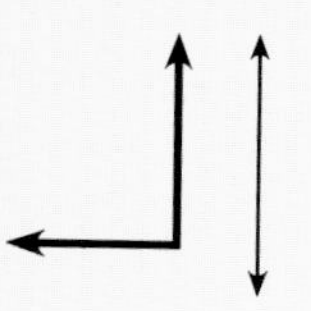

Imagine how the figure would look if you flipped it over.

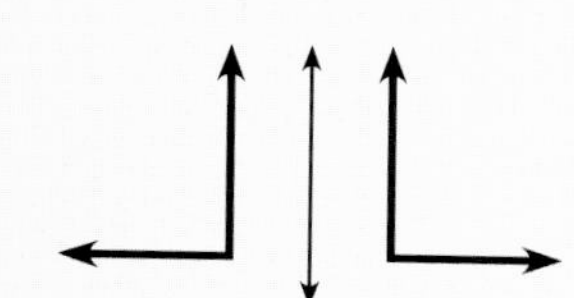

Check

Tell whether each figure has line symmetry. If it does, draw its line(s) of symmetry.

1. 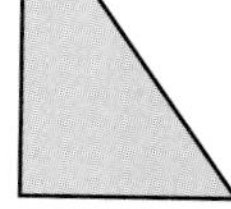

2. 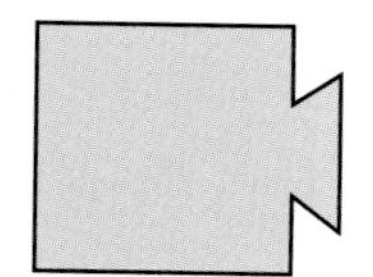

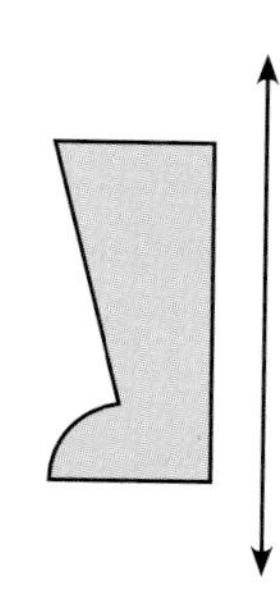

3. Trace the figure and draw its reflection over the line.

4. **Reasoning** B is the reflection of A. Are A and B congruent? Explain.

Practice

Skills and Reasoning

Trace each figure and draw its reflection over the line.

5. 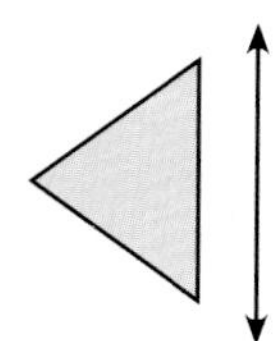

6. 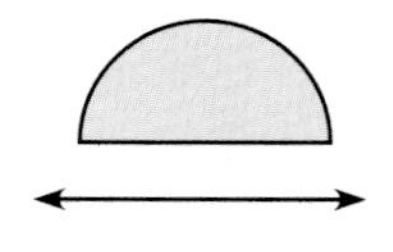

7. 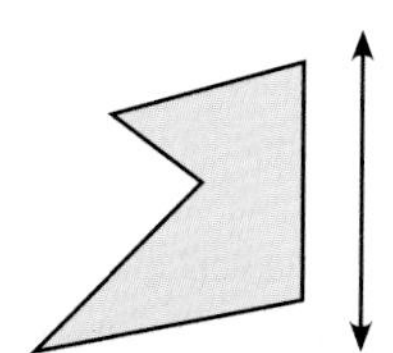

8. 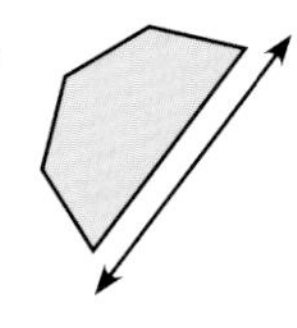

Tell if each photo has line symmetry. If it does, tell how many lines of symmetry it has.

9. 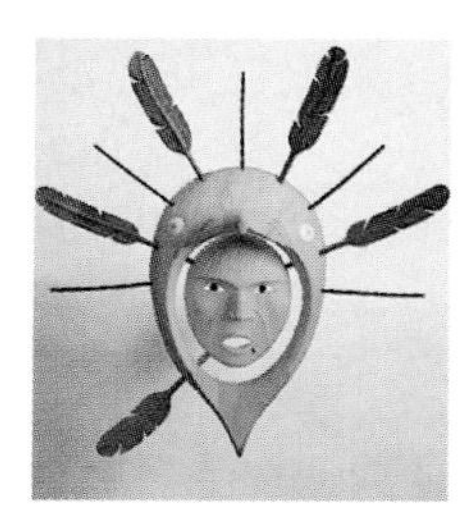

10. 

11. 

12. 

Tell if each is a line of symmetry.

13. 

14. 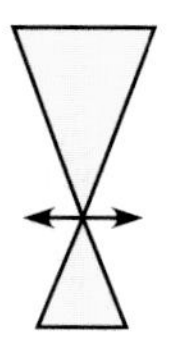

15. 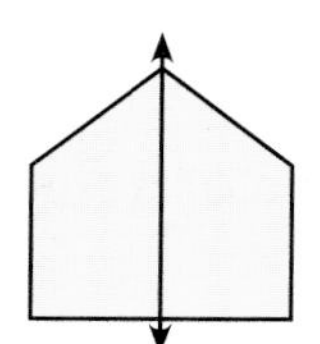

16. 

Tell if each pair of figures is congruent. If not, draw a figure that is congruent to each.

17. 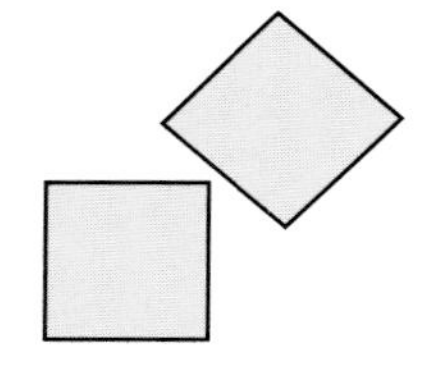

18. 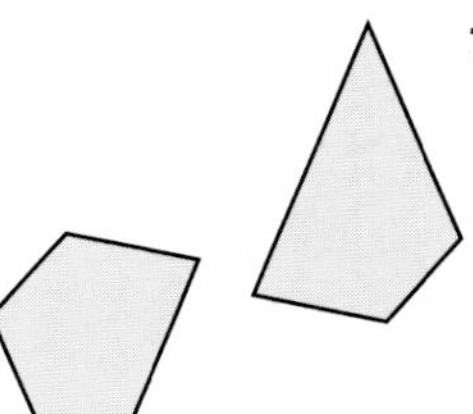

19. 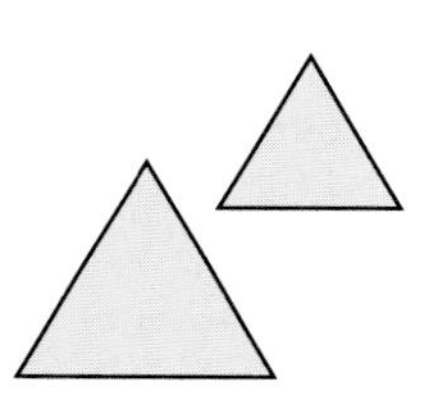

Problem Solving and Applications

20. Fine Arts This window is from the Dome of the Rock mosque in Jerusalem, Israel. Describe the lines of symmetry in the window's design.

Fine Arts The front wall of the Islamic palace of Mshatta was built around 743. Use the design on the wall for **21** and **22.**

21. Sketch a pair of congruent figures in the design.

22. Determine the number of lines of symmetry that the design has.

23. **Critical Thinking** Draw a regular octagon, a regular hexagon, and a regular pentagon. Which polygon has the most lines of symmetry? Explain.

24. **Critical Thinking** A triangle has one angle of 40°. The other angles are congruent to each other. What are the measurements of the other two angles? Explain.

25. **Journal** List five objects in your classroom or home that have line symmetry. Explain why and describe the line(s) of symmetry.

Mixed Review and Test Prep

Order from least to greatest.

26. $\frac{5}{6}$, 0.5, $\frac{1}{3}$
27. $\frac{7}{9}$, $\frac{2}{3}$, 0.75
28. $\frac{14}{7}$, $\frac{7}{7}$, 2.12
29. 1.1, $\frac{7}{6}$, 1.167

30. 2.2, 2.22, $\frac{2}{22}$
31. $\frac{1}{3}$, $\frac{3}{1}$, 1.3
32. $\frac{1}{10}$, 1.10, 10.1
33. 2.5, $\frac{2}{5}$, 0.25

Multiply.

34. 4.6×8.2
35. 9.54×3.2
36. 0.06×3.29
37. 0.92×4.76

38. 3.1×3.1
39. 1.9×9.1
40. 0.4×0.44
41. 6.6×0.6

42. 1.4×4.1
43. 3.5×0.3
44. 2.7×0.27
45. 0.3×0.45

46. 5.6×1.3
47. 2.5×0.6
48. 7.1×5.5
49. 0.03×1.9

50. Look at the shape to the right. Choose the shape that is a reflection of this shape.

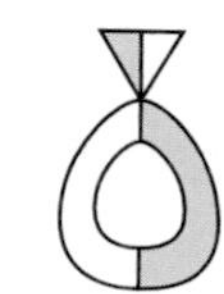

Ⓐ 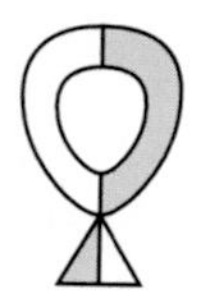
Ⓑ 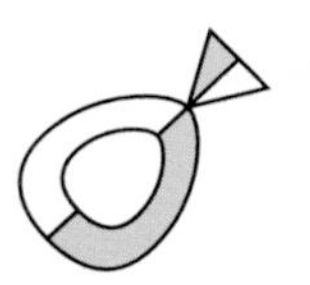
Ⓒ 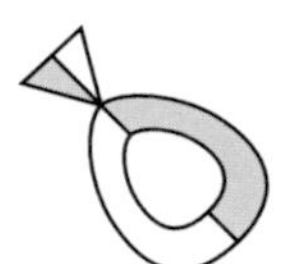
Ⓓ 

Chapter 8
Lesson
9

Turns and Rotational Symmetry

Problem Solving Connection
- Guess and Check

Materials
tracing paper

Vocabulary
rotation
clockwise
counterclockwise
rotational symmetry

Explore

In the last lesson, you saw what happens when a figure is flipped over a line. Now you'll look at what happens when a figure is turned like a wheel.

Work Together

The 15 shapes below include 7 pairs of identical shapes. One shape has no match.

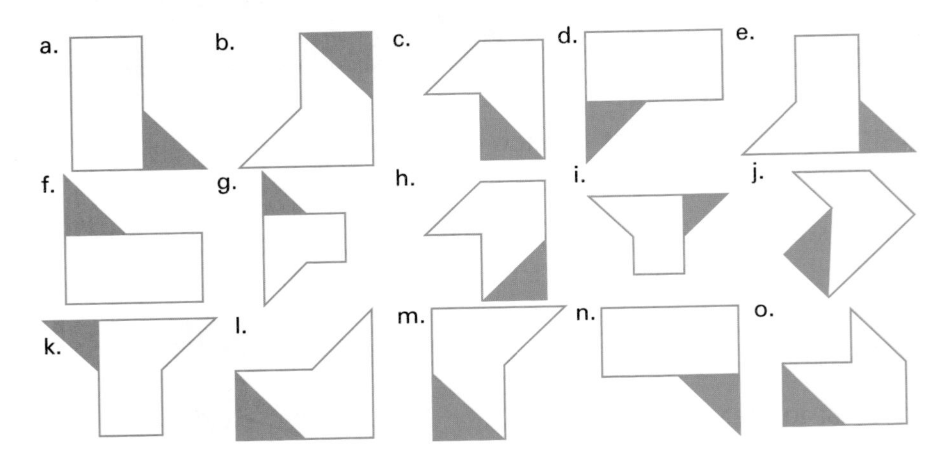

1. For each shape, find its match. To help, you may trace the shapes.
2. For the leftover shape, draw a match that is facing in a different direction.

Talk About It

3. How did you find the matching shapes?
4. How can you prove that the shape you drew matches the leftover shape?

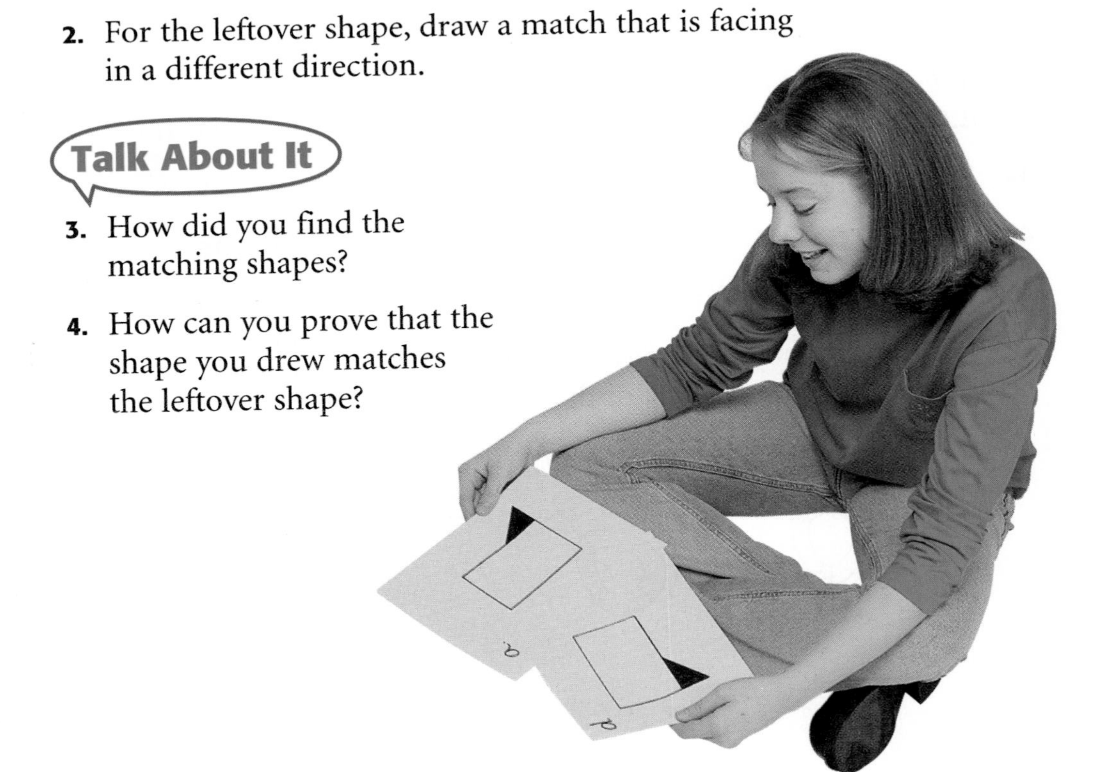

Connect and Learn

A **rotation** is the image of a figure that has been turned, as if it were on a wheel. When the top of a figure turns to the right, it is turned **clockwise**. When the top turns to the left, it is turned **counterclockwise**.

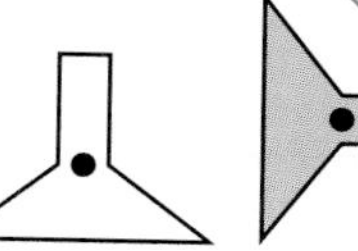

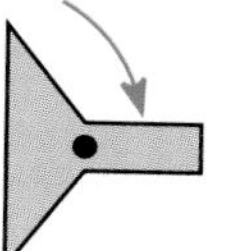

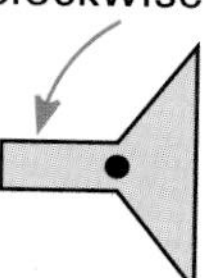

If a figure can be rotated less than a full circle, and the rotation exactly matches the original image, then the figure has **rotational symmetry**.

Example 1

Does each figure have rotational symmetry? What is the least rotation that will land the figure on top of itself?

a.

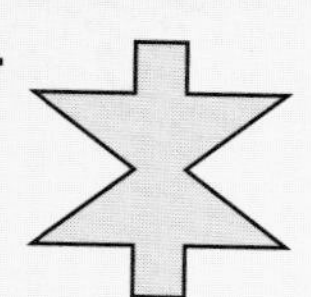

This figure has rotational symmetry. It must be turned at least 180° to land on itself.

b.

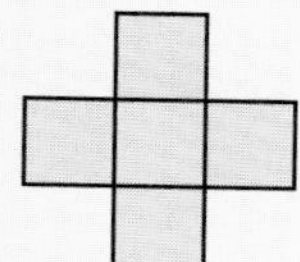

This figure has rotational symmetry. It must be turned at least 90° to land on itself.

c.

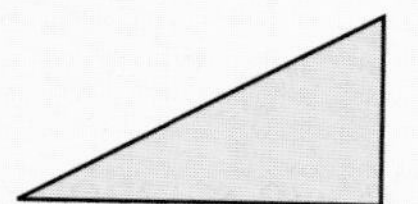

This figure does not have rotational symmetry. It must be turned at least 360° to land on itself.

Remember

A circle has 360°, so a $\frac{1}{4}$ turn is 90°, a $\frac{1}{2}$ turn is 180°, and a $\frac{3}{4}$ turn is 270°.

During a 360° rotation, some figures will land on themselves more than once.

Example 2

If the figure is rotated 360°, how many times will it land on itself?

The figure will land on itself three times.

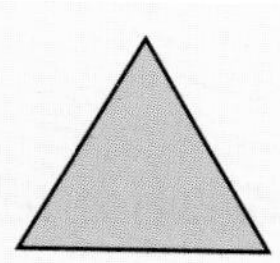

Check

1. Give the number of degrees and the direction the figure has rotated.

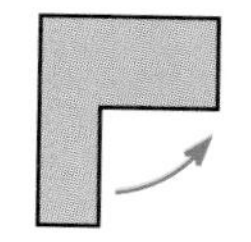

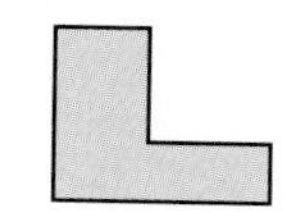

2. Draw a 270° clockwise rotation of the figure.

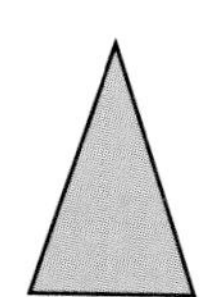

3. If the figure is rotated 360°, how many times will it land on itself?

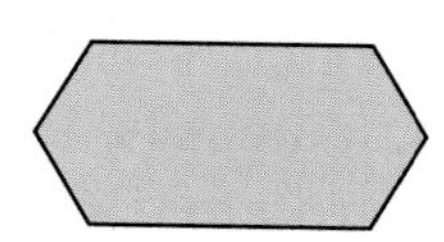

4. What is the least rotation that will land the figure in Exercise 3 on top of itself?

Practice

Skills and Reasoning

What is the least number of degrees and the direction that each figure has been rotated?

5. 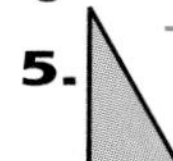 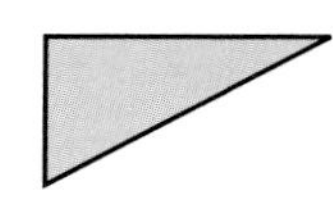

6. 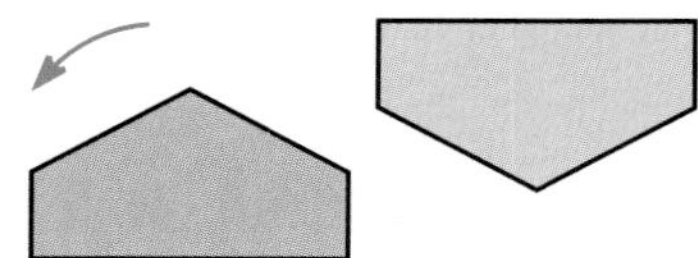

What is the least rotation that will land the figure on top of itself?

7. 

8. 

9. 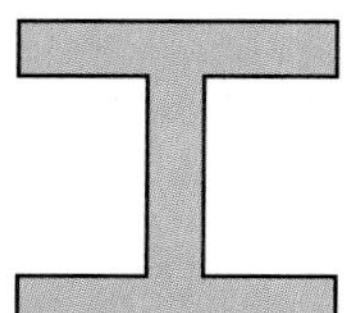

10. 

Draw a 90° counterclockwise rotation of each figure.

11. 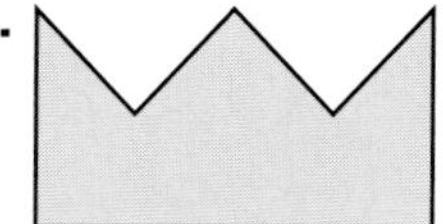

12. 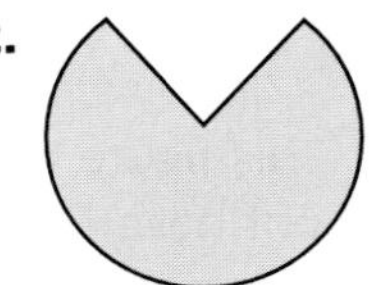

13. 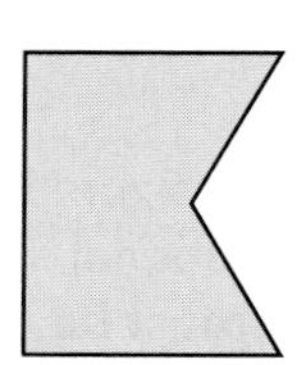

14. 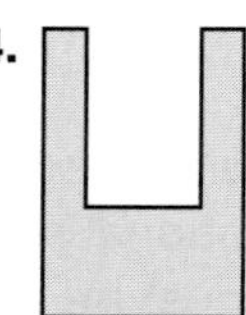

Draw a 45° clockwise rotation of each figure.

15. 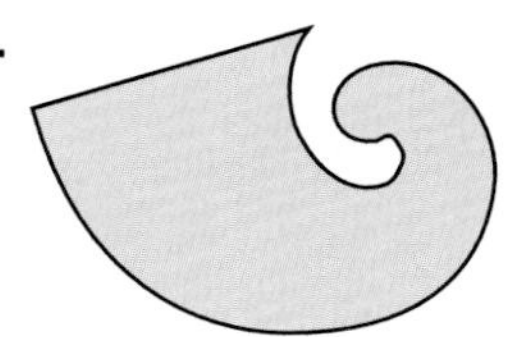

16. 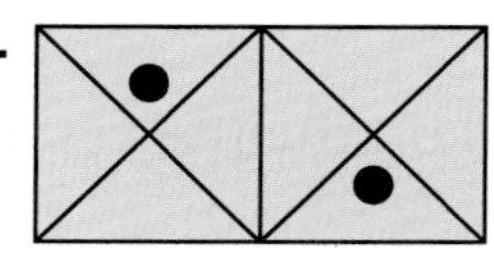

17. 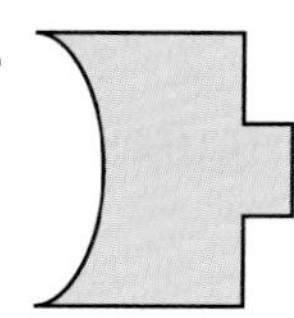

18. 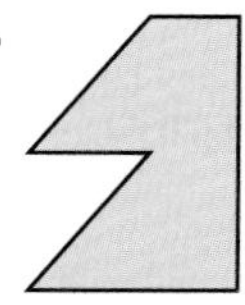

Draw a 180° clockwise rotation of each figure.

19. 

20. 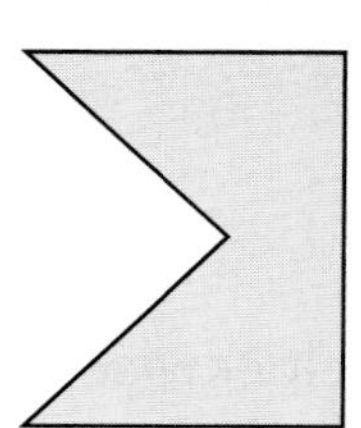

21. 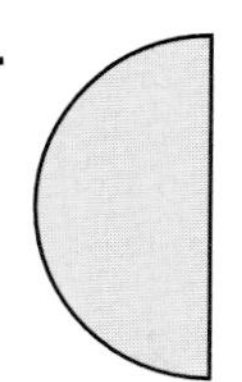

22. 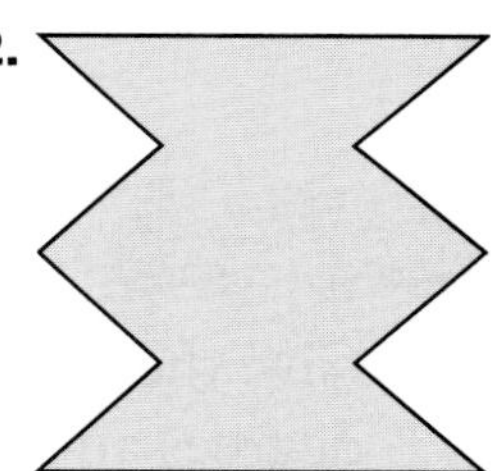

Problem Solving and Applications

23. Fine Arts If the outline of this design is rotated 360°, how many times will it land on itself?

Il-Khanid Star Shaped Tile, 1293. Earthenware with lustre decoration. The Avery Brundage Collection. The Asian Art Museum of San Francisco. B60 P2148

Estimation Estimate the number of degrees that each figure has been rotated.

24.

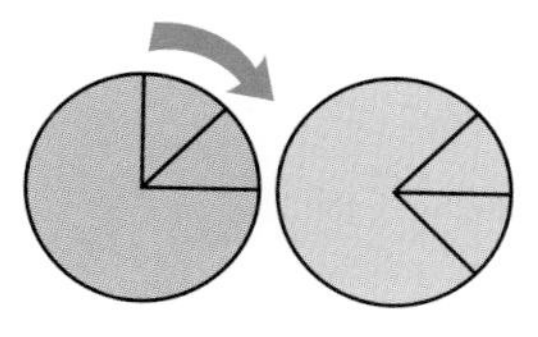

25.

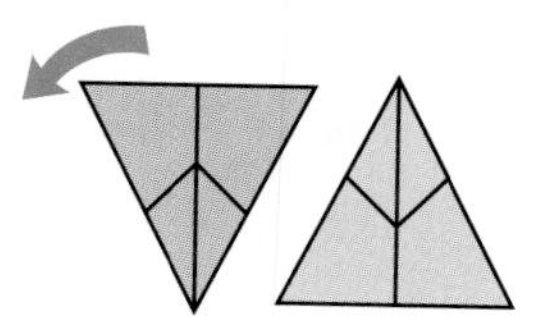

26.

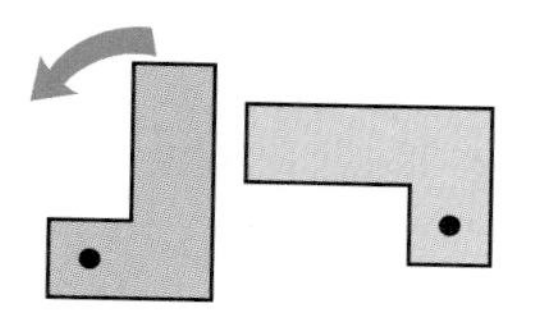

27.

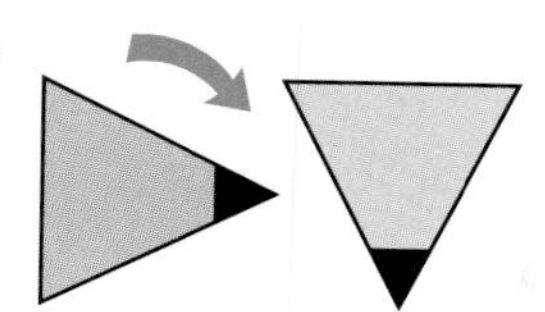

Fine Arts Use the floral pattern for **28–29.**

28. If one of the flowers is rotated 360°, how many times will it land on itself?

29. What is the least number of degrees of rotation that will land a flower on top of itself?

Using Data Use the description of the mat used by gymnasts on page 399 to answer **30–33.**

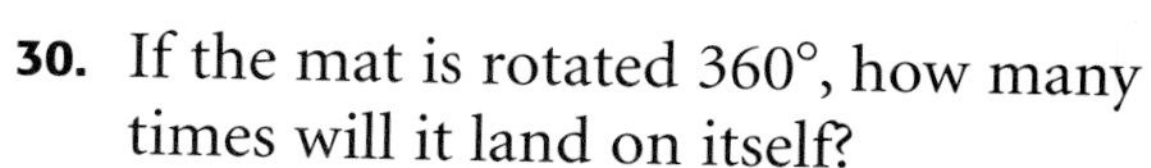

30. If the mat is rotated 360°, how many times will it land on itself?

31. What is the least rotation that will land the mat on top of itself?

32. How many lines of symmetry does the mat have?

33. **Measurement** What is the perimeter of the mat? The area?

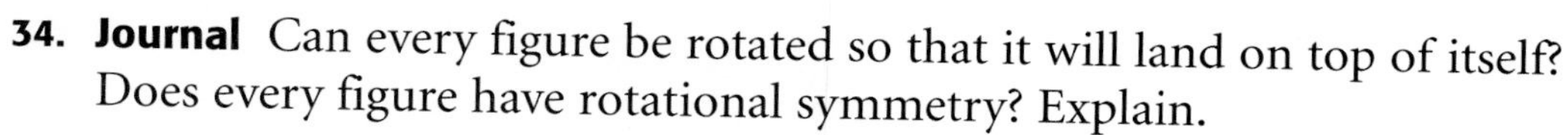

34. **Journal** Can every figure be rotated so that it will land on top of itself? Does every figure have rotational symmetry? Explain.

Mixed Review and Test Prep

Divide. Round each quotient to the nearest hundredth.

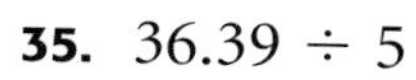

35. 36.39 ÷ 5	**36.** 14.2 ÷ 4	**37.** 1.89 ÷ 10	**38.** 2.86 ÷ 22
39. 25.5 ÷ 5	**40.** 0.65 ÷ 11	**41.** 0.79 ÷ 8	**42.** 7.111 ÷ 3
43. 13.26 ÷ 0.6	**44.** 98.28 ÷ 5.4	**45.** 16.324 ÷ 1.54	**46.** 57.2 ÷ 21.3
47. 37.97 ÷ 0.78	**48.** 100.82 ÷ 7.1	**49.** 0.75 ÷ 0.25	**50.** 39.2 ÷ 5.6

51. Convert 462.8 meters to kilometers.

Ⓐ 4,628 km Ⓑ 0.4628 km Ⓒ 462,800 km Ⓓ 4.628 km

Chapter 8
Lesson
10

Slides and Tessellations

Problem Solving Connection
- Look for a Pattern

Materials
- tracing paper

Vocabulary
translation
tessellation

Explore

You know what happens to a figure when you flip it or turn it. What happens when you slide a figure to a new position?

Work Together

These figures are regular polygons.

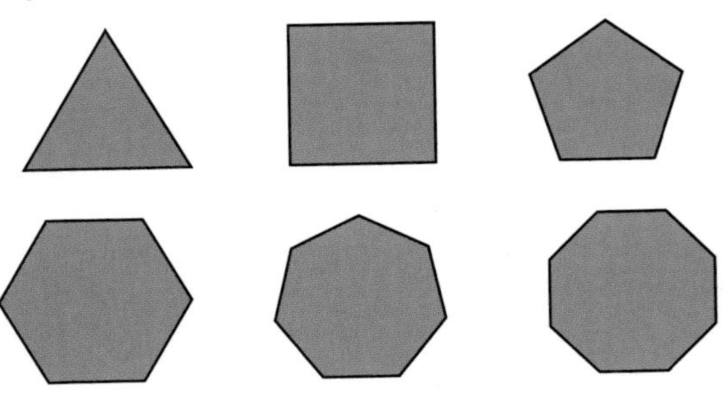

Math Tip
A 7-sided polygon is a heptagon.

1. Copy the triangle onto tracing paper several times. Place the triangles as close together as possible without overlaps. Could you cover a sheet of paper with the triangles without overlapping or leaving space between the shapes?
2. Repeat Step 1 for the other polygons. Which of these could cover a sheet of paper without overlapping or leaving space between the shapes?
3. Draw a polygon that does not appear above that could be used to cover a sheet of paper without any overlaps or spaces in between.

Talk About It

4. Without using tracing paper, what patterns do you see that could help you determine if a polygon would cover a sheet of paper without any overlaps or spaces in between?

Connect and Learn

When a figure is slid to a new position without flipping or turning, the new image is called a slide, or a **translation**.

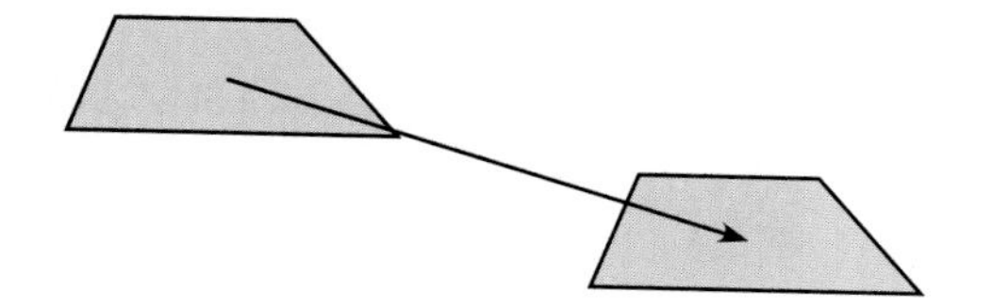

In Islamic art, the design of a mosaic wall sometimes consists of a single figure translated to every possible position on the wall. As a result, the wall is completely covered by the figure.

A pattern of congruent shapes like the one above, with no gaps or overlaps, is called a **tessellation**. There are 17 basic tessellation patterns. Every tessellation can be broken down into one of these 17 patterns.

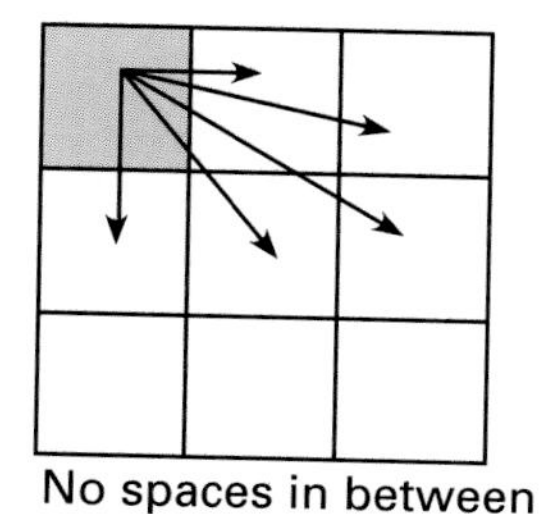

A square tessellates.

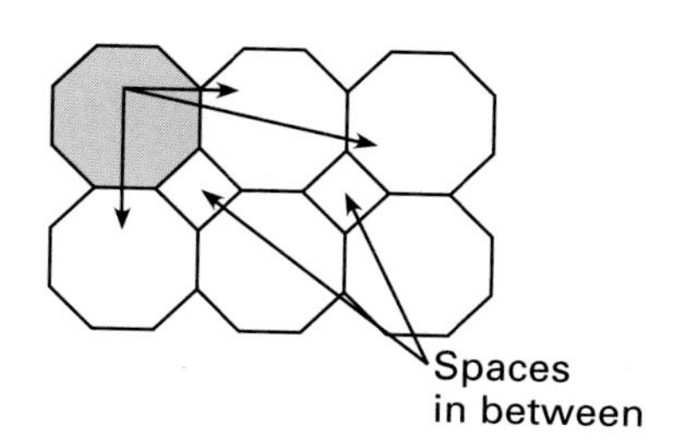

A regular octagon does not tessellate.

Example

Does the figure tessellate? Make a drawing to show your answer.

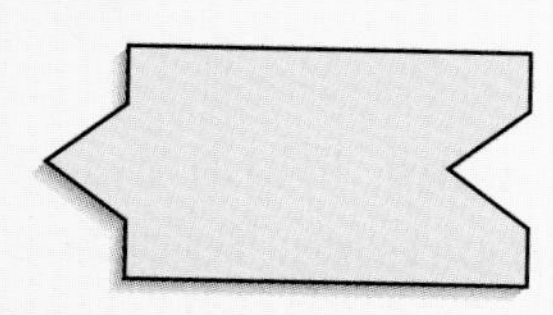

Yes, the figure tessellates.

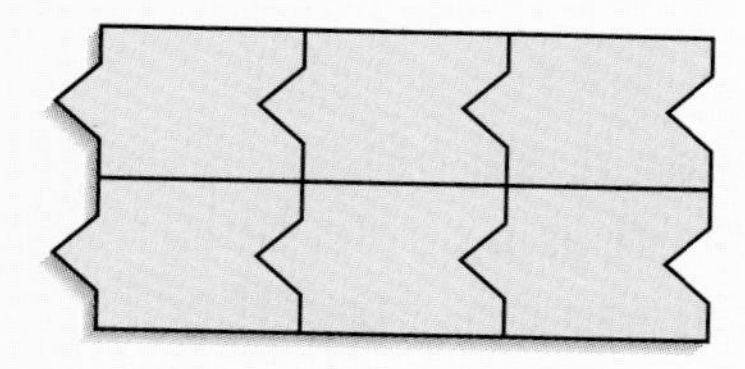

Check

1. Is one figure a translation of the other?

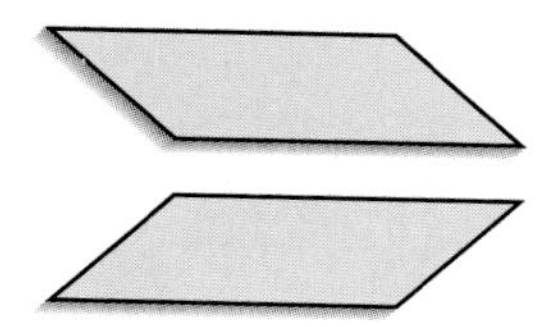

2. Does the figure tessellate? Make a drawing to show your answer.

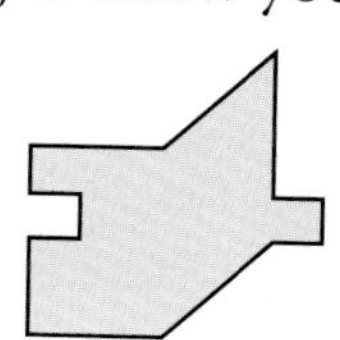

3. **Reasoning** Does a figure that tessellates have line symmetry? Rotational symmetry? Explain.

Practice

Skills and Reasoning

These designs can be found on the Dome of the Rock in Jerusalem, the oldest Islamic monument standing. Name the polygon that is tessellated in each design.

4. 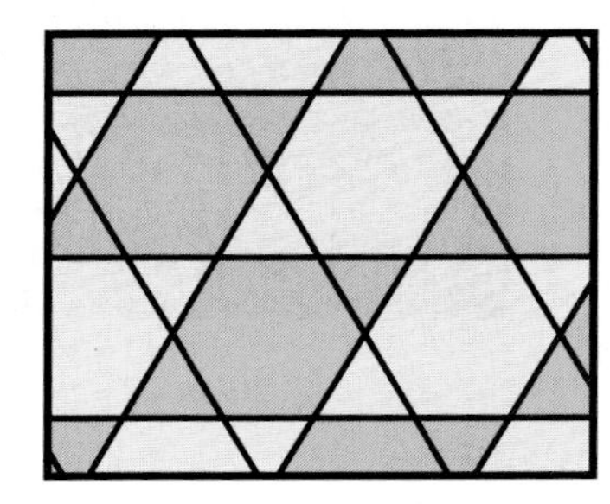

5. 

State if the figure tessellates. Make a drawing to show your answer.

6. 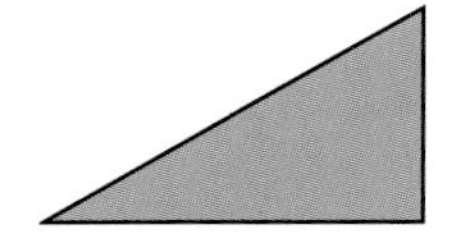

7. 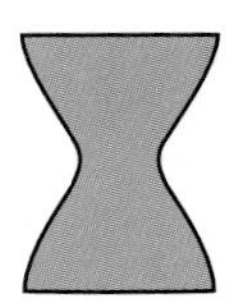

8. 

9. 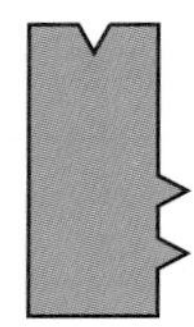

10. 

11. 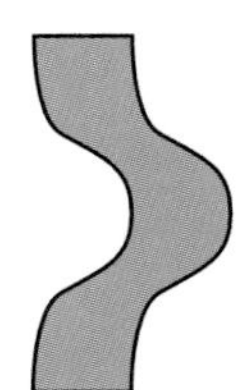

12. 

13. 

14. **Science** An individual cell of honeycomb starts off as a circle, but because the cells are so close together, the circles flatten out. The result is a tessellation. What polygon is tessellated in a honeycomb?

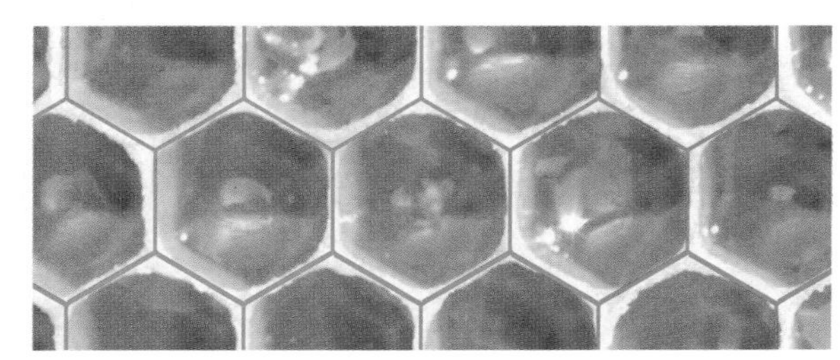

15. **Critical Thinking** Ralph made this tessellation pattern. To create the tessellated figure, Ralph started with a square. Describe how Ralph changed the square to produce the figure.

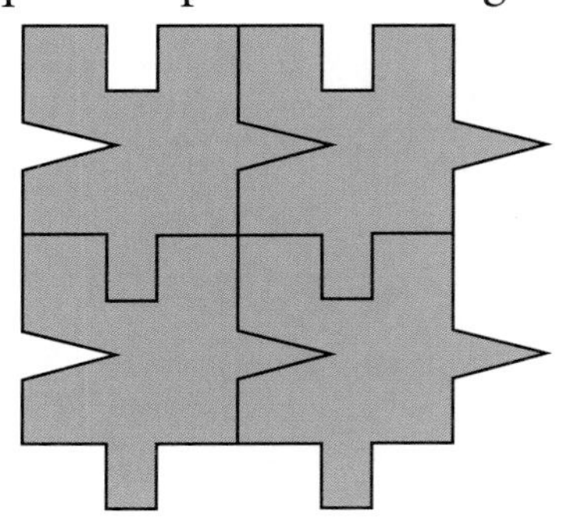

16. Draw a tessellation that does not use a polygon as the figure tessellated. Explain your tessellation.

Problem Solving and Applications

Interior designers help people select wall and floor coverings for their homes. They must be able to figure out how much tile is needed to cover a floor without overlapping or leaving any space between tiles.

Using Data Use the drawing of the entry hall to answer **17–19.**

17. A homeowner wants to cover the hall floor with one shape of tile. Which shapes should the interior designer recommend?

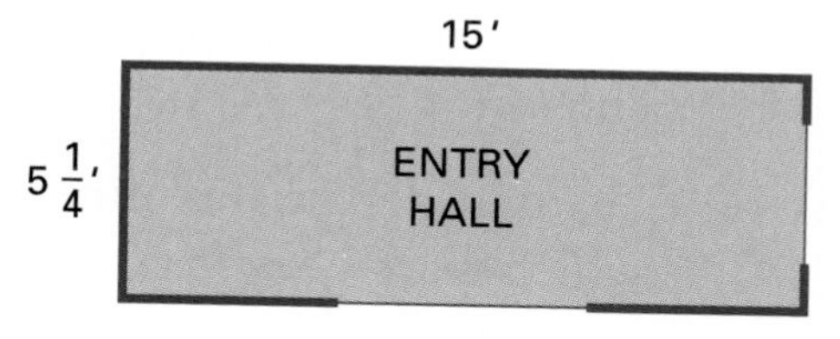

a.  **b.** 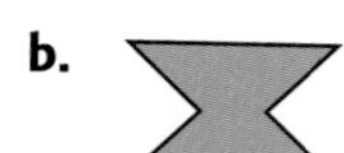 **c.**  **d.** 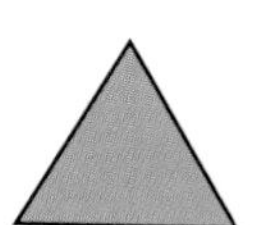 **e.** 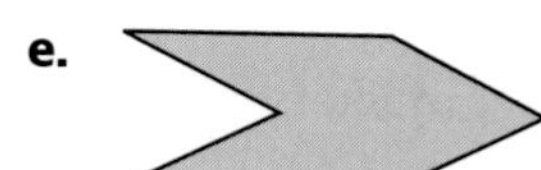

18. The homeowner selects 9-inch square tiles priced at \$2.75 each.

a. How many tiles are needed to make one row across the short edge of the hall?

b. How many rows are needed?

c. How many tiles are needed in all?

d. **Money** What is the total cost of the tiles?

19. What if you could design a tile shape to cover the hall? Make a sketch of it, including dimensions. Tell how many tiles you would need in all. You may cut tiles at the edges of the hall to form straight lines.

20. **Journal** Do all squares, rectangles, and parallelograms tessellate? Explain.

Mixed Review and Test Prep

Find the perimeter of each figure.

21.

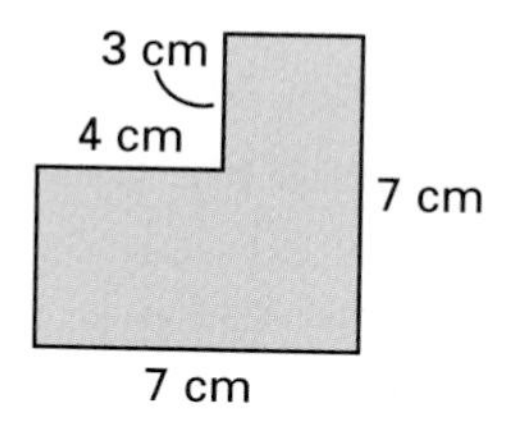

22.

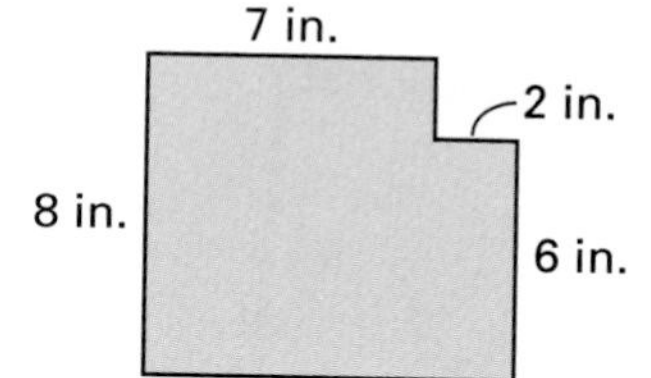

23.

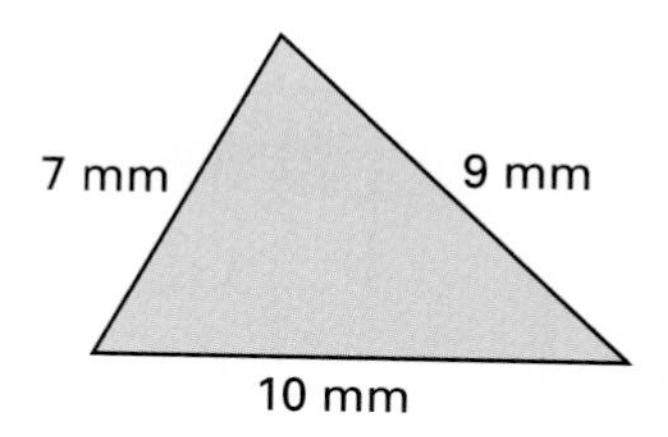

Convert.

24. 6 kg = ■ g **25.** 3.1 m = ■ mm **26.** 650 mL = ■ L

27. Choose the correct value for m if $7m = 749$.

Ⓐ 100 Ⓑ 700 Ⓒ 701 Ⓓ 107

GEOMETRY GAME

Players
2 teams of 2 players

Materials
2 number cubes (1–6)
counter for each team
gameboard
paper
markers

Object
The object of the game is to complete the game sheet by drawing an accurate example for each category given.

Geometry Game
Game Sheet
Team ______

Line	Angle	Triangle	Polygon
Congruence	**Line Symmetry**	**Reflection**	**Rotation**
Rotational Symmetry	**Translation**	**Tessellation**	

How to Play

1. Players make one gameboard as shown. Each team also makes a game sheet as shown.
2. Team leaders toss a number cube to see which team goes first. The team that tosses the greater number goes first.
3. Team A and B place counters on opposite corners of the gameboard. Team A tosses the two number cubes and decides whether to add or subtract the numbers tossed to get the number of spaces to move on the board. Teams can move in any direction along the board.
4. Team A moves its counter to the appropriate space and makes a drawing on its game sheet to match the description in the space. If both teams determine the drawing is accurate, Team A has completed the drawing for that category. If a team lands on a space and has already completed the category, the team does nothing and play continues with the other team.
5. Play alternates until one team has completed all categories on its game sheet except the Tessellation category, which is to be completed only as the last category. To reach it, teams must land on the space with an exact number.
6. The first team that completes all categories wins.

Talk About It

1. How does the work on your game sheet help you decide whether to add or subtract the numbers tossed during the game?
2. How did you decide in which direction to move your counter during the game?

More Ways to Play

- Move only in a clockwise direction.
- Decide whether to add, subtract, multiply, or divide the numbers tossed to get the number of spaces to move.

Reasoning

1. Suppose you needed the Regular Polygon category and your counter was on the Congruent Figures space. What two numbers would you hope to toss?
2. Suppose you needed the Tessellation category and your counter was on the Quadrilateral space. You roll 6 and 4. Can you complete the Tessellation category?
3. Suppose Team A drew this figure for its Reflection category. Is the drawing accurate? Explain.

Congruent Figures	Right Angle	Ray	A Figure and Its Clockwise Rotation	Right Triangle	Perpendicular Lines	Pentagon	A Figure that has Line Symmetry
Regular Polygon							Obtuse Triangle
Acute Triangle							Hexagon
Quadrilateral			A Figure that Tessellates and Its Tessellation Pattern				A Figure and Its Counter-clockwise Rotation
Acute Angle							Obtuse Angle
Isosceles Triangle							Scalene Triangle
Line Segment							Line
A Figure that has Rotational Symmetry	Equilateral Triangle	Parallel Lines	A Figure and Its Translation	Octagon	Lines that Intersect	Straight Angle	A Figure and Its Reflection

SECTION C

Review and Practice

Vocabulary Tell whether each transformation is a reflection, a rotation, or a translation.

1. 

2. 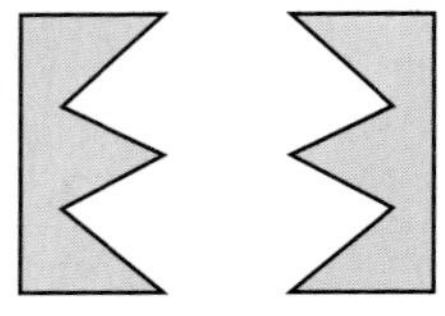

3. 

(Lesson 8) The Alcázar in Seville, Spain, was built in the 14th century by Spain's Pedro I, who wanted it to resemble a Moorish palace. Use the design from one of its walls to answer **4** and **5.**

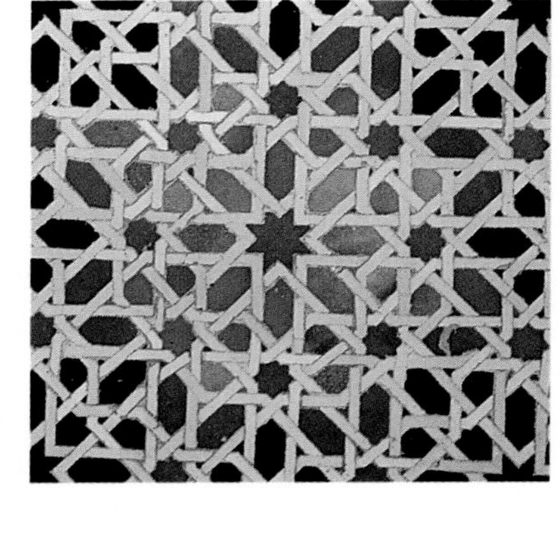

4. Locate and sketch a pair of congruent figures in the design.

5. How many lines of symmetry can you find in the design?

(Lessons 8 and 9) Name each polygon and tell if it has line symmetry. If it does, tell how many lines of symmetry it has.

6. 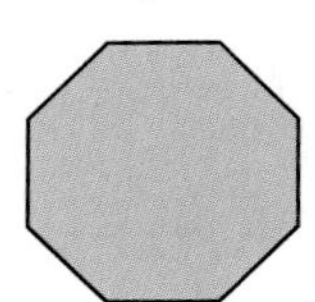

7. 

8. 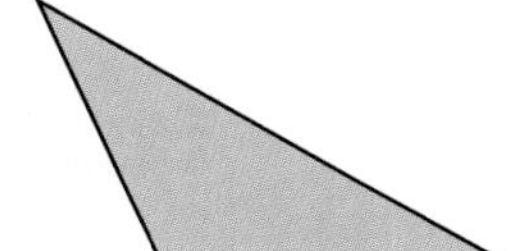

9. 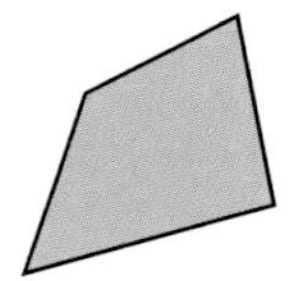

10. Which of the figures from Exercises 6–9 has rotational symmetry? Explain.

(Lesson 10) State if each figure will tessellate. Draw a diagram to show your answer.

11. 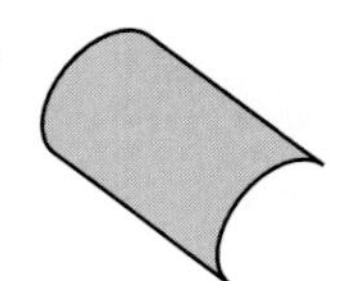

12. 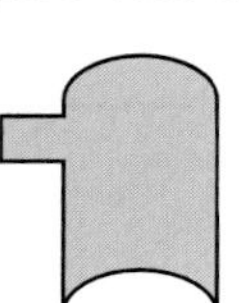

13. 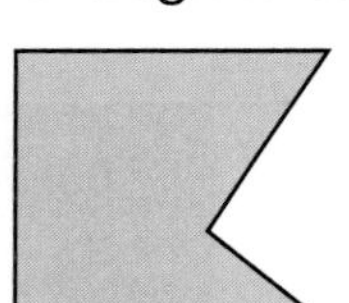

14. 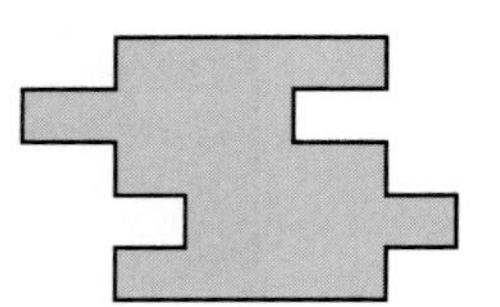

15. The Mezquita in Córdoba, Spain was originally built as an Islamic mosque around A.D. 785. It was turned into a cathedral about 1236, and its architecture shows the influence of both functions. Is the design of this portion of its roof a tessellation?

16. Journal Does a figure that translates also tessellate? Explain.

Skills Checklist

In this section, you have:

- **Explored Flips and Lines of Symmetry**
- **Explored Turns and Rotational Symmetry**
- **Explored Slides and Tessellations**

Choose at least one of the following. Use what you have learned in this chapter.

1 Neighborhood Navigation

At Home

Accompanied by a parent or guardian, walk or drive five blocks in each direction from your home. Use your trip as the basis for a map of your neighborhood. Identify the streets that are perpendicular, parallel, intersecting, and nonintersecting. Share your map with the adult who helped you tour your neighborhood.

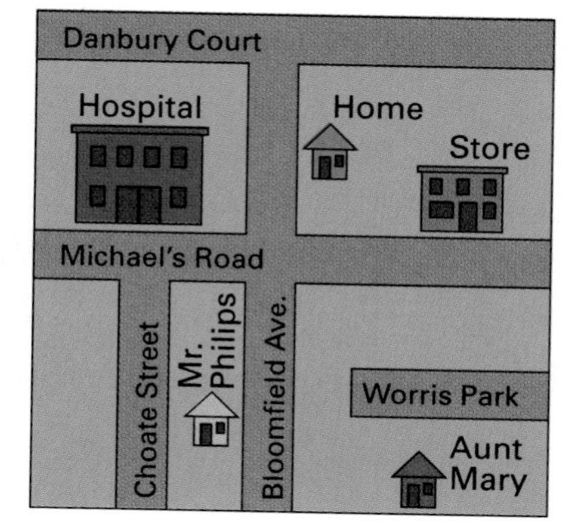

2 Shape Up!

Get in shape at **www.mathsurf.com/6**. Choose data which is illustrated by many different types of shapes. State which figures are polygons, then identify them by name.

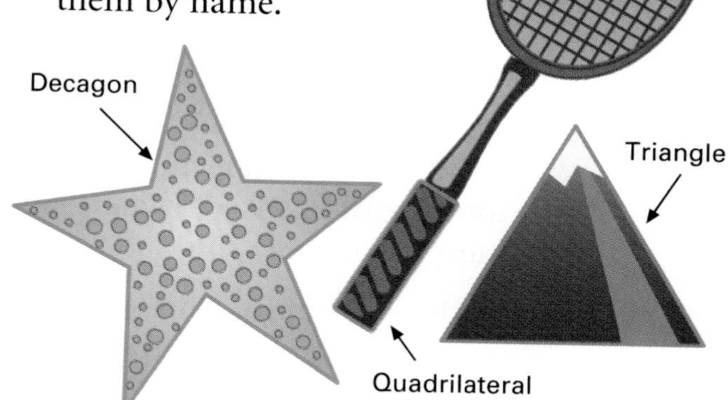

3 Shape Search

Choose a partner. Challenge another pair of students to find as many types of polygons in the same room as possible. Indicate whether the shapes you found are regular or irregular. The team to find the most examples wins.

4 Angular American Adventure

Locate the following groups of cities on a map which shows U.S. state capitals. Use a ruler to form angles between the cities. Identify the angles as acute, right, or obtuse. Check your answers with a protractor.

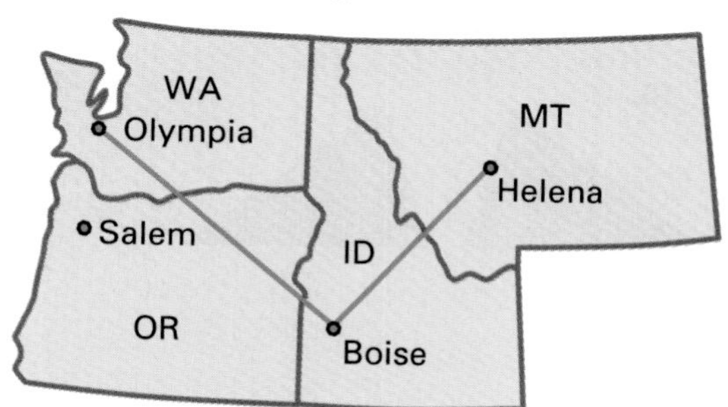

CHAPTER 8

Review/Test

(Lesson 1) For each group, describe the figures and their relationship.

1. 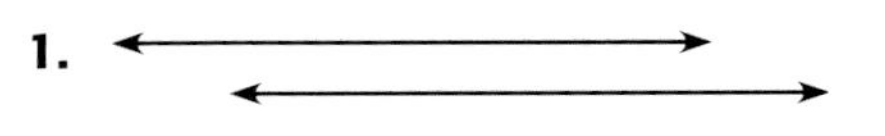

2. 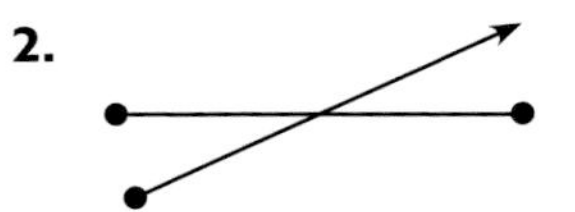

3. 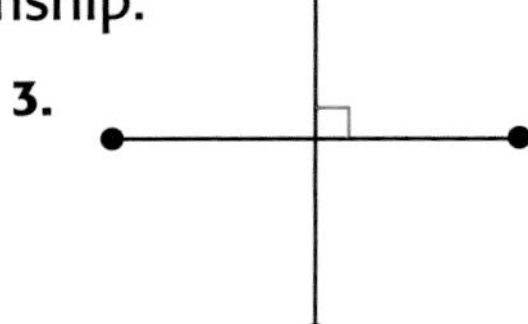

(Lessons 2–7) Solve.

4. Classify the triangle whose angles measure 82°, 90°, and 8°.

5. Can you measure the length of a line? A line segment? A ray? Explain.

Use the diagram to answer **6** and **7**.

6. Name the vertex of the angle.

7. Name the angle in three ways.

8. The sum of two angles of a triangle is 85°. What is the measure of the third angle?

9. Can the lengths of 4 m, 8 m, and 10 m form a triangle? If so, draw the triangle and classify it.

10. Angles A and B are complements. If the measure of $\angle A$ is 37°, what is the measure of $\angle B$?

11. Classify the triangle whose sides each measure 6 feet.

12. Can you draw a triangle whose angles measure 62°, 63°, and 65°? Explain.

13. Classify the figure in as many ways as possible.

14. Louis designed a garden in his backyard in the shape of a rhombus. If the perimeter of the garden is 16 feet, what is the length of one of the sides?

(Lesson 6) Name each polygon and tell if it is regular or irregular.

15. 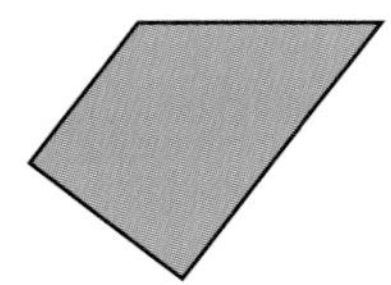

16. 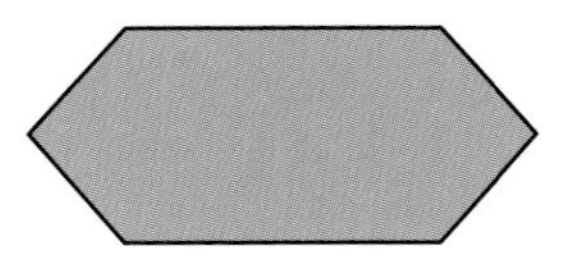

17. 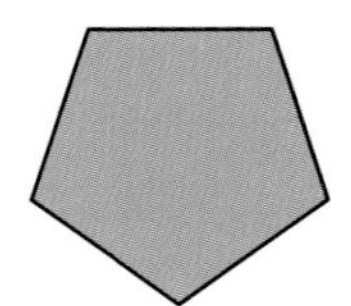

(Lessons 8–10) Tell whether the second figure is a reflection, translation, or rotation of the first.

18. 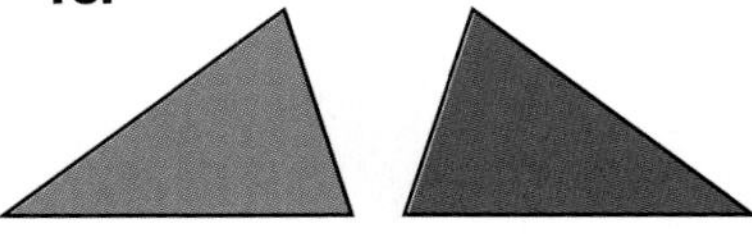

19. 

20. 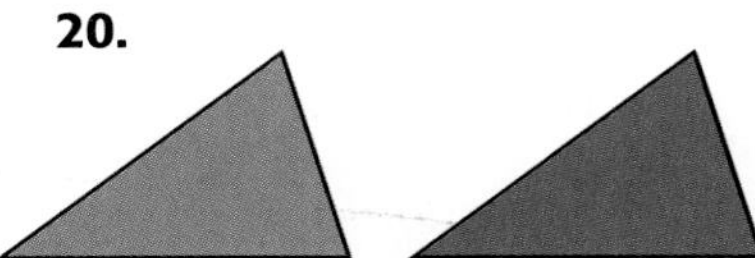

REVIEW/TEST

CHAPTER 8

Performance Assessment

Native American rugs often are made up of lines, angles, and polygons in designs that are examples of reflections, rotations, translations, and tessellations.

Use what you have learned in this chapter to create your own design for a rug.

Your rug design must include:

- at least one set of intersecting, perpendicular, or parallel lines
- at least two of the following angles: acute, right, obtuse
- two of the following types of triangles: scalene, isosceles, equilateral

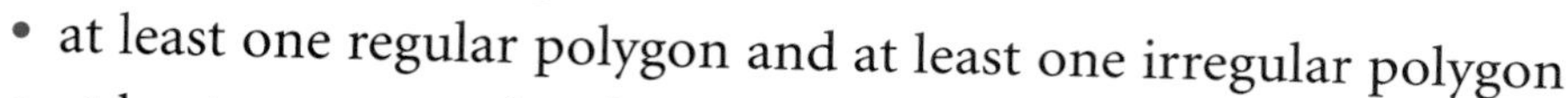

- at least one regular polygon and at least one irregular polygon
- at least one example of a figure and its reflection
- at least one example of a figure and its rotation
- at least one example of a figure and its translation
- at least one example of a figure that tessellates and its tessellation pattern

1. **Decision Making** Decide which lines, angles, figures, and transformations will meet the requirements. Decide how you will position the lines, angles, and figures in your rug design. What tools might you need to draw your design? You may want to draw your design on grid paper.

2. **Critical Thinking** Which element do you think will be the most difficult to include in your design? How will you make sure to include it in your design? What part of creating the design will be the easiest?

3. **Explain Your Thinking** How did you decide on the elements that you chose for your design? How did you decide on how to place the elements in the space of your rug?

Math Magazine

Half for You, Half for Me . . .

A construction is a drawing of a geometric figure made using a compass and a straightedge. Bisecting is a construction that divides a figure into two congruent parts.

Bisecting a Line

1. Open the compass more than half the length of the segment. Place the compass point on *A* and draw an arc.

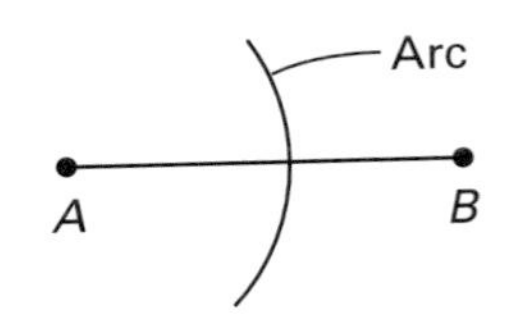

2. Without changing the opening of the compass, place the point on *B* and draw an arc.

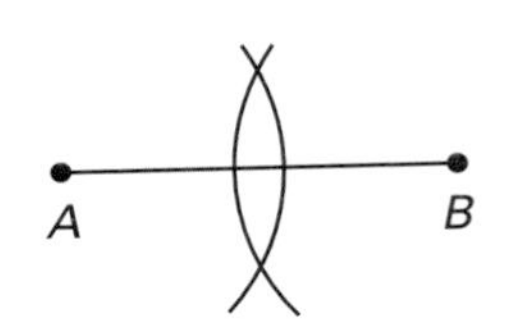

3. Use the straightedge to draw a line through the two points where the arcs intersect. This line bisects the original segment *AB*.

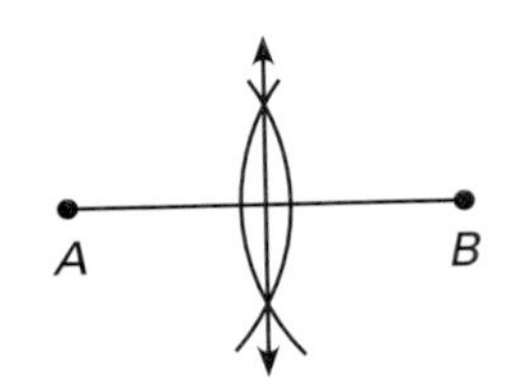

Bisecting an Angle

1. Place the compass point on the vertex and draw an arc. Label the points where the arc crosses the angle as *D* and *E*.

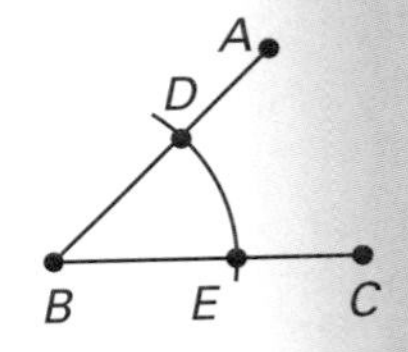

2. Using a smaller opening, place the point on *D* and draw an arc. Place the point on *E* and draw an arc.

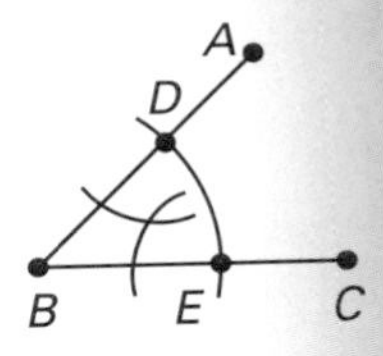

3. Draw a line through the point of intersection of the two new arcs and the vertex. This line bisects $\angle ABC$.

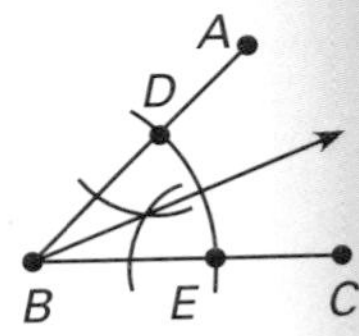

Try These!

Trace and bisect each figure.

1.

2.

CHAPTERS 1–8

Cumulative Review

Test Prep Strategy: Make Smart Choices

Multiply: 1.6×3.23.

Ⓐ 5.168 Ⓑ 4.7 Ⓒ 6.268 Ⓓ 5.38

The product of two decimals will have as many decimal places as the total of those in both factors. Since 1.6 has one decimal place and 3.23 has two, the product will have three decimal places. This eliminates choices Ⓑ and Ⓓ. $1.6 \times 3.23 = 5.168$, choice Ⓐ.

Write the letter of the correct answer. Choose any strategy.

1. Which graph uses wedge-shaped pieces to represent data?
   Ⓐ bar Ⓑ circle Ⓒ line Ⓓ scatterplot
2. One business plan calls for a change in employees of 2^5. A second plan calls for a change that is twice as large as 2^5. What is the change in employees for the second plan?
   Ⓐ 2^6 Ⓑ 2^7 Ⓒ 2^{10} Ⓓ 4^5
3. What is the decimal form for seven and twenty-nine thousandths?
   Ⓐ 7029.0 Ⓑ 7.029 Ⓒ 7.0029 Ⓓ 0.7029
4. Find the product of 0.01×32.
   Ⓐ 32,000 Ⓑ 320 Ⓒ 0.32 Ⓓ 0.0032
5. What is the area of a rectangle 4 ft long and 6 ft wide?
   Ⓐ 20 ft Ⓑ 24 ft Ⓒ 20 ft^2 Ⓓ 24 ft^2
6. Write $\frac{29}{9}$ as a mixed number.
   Ⓐ $20\frac{1}{9}$ Ⓑ $4\frac{2}{9}$ Ⓒ $3\frac{2}{9}$ Ⓓ $3\frac{1}{9}$
7. Simplify: $3\frac{2}{3} + 1\frac{3}{4}$.
   Ⓐ $4\frac{5}{7}$ Ⓑ $5\frac{5}{12}$ Ⓒ $5\frac{7}{12}$ Ⓓ not here
8. Simplify: $32 \times 1\frac{1}{2}$.
   Ⓐ 16 Ⓑ 32.5 Ⓒ 48 Ⓓ not here
9. Solve for x, if $x \div \frac{3}{4} = \frac{8}{9}$.
   Ⓐ $\frac{3}{2}$ Ⓑ $\frac{27}{32}$ Ⓒ $\frac{2}{3}$ Ⓓ not here
10. What kind of a triangle has exactly two equal sides?
    Ⓐ isosceles Ⓑ obtuse Ⓒ right Ⓓ scalene

Test Prep Strategies

- Read Carefully
- Follow Directions
- Make Smart Choices
- Eliminate Choices
- Work Backward from an Answer

DATA FILE

Chapter 9
Integers and the Coordinate Plane

SECTION A The Third Sphere From the Sun

461

Integers

Which state had the record lowest temperature? The record highest temperature?

Record Temperatures by State Through 1995		
State	**Lowest °F**	**Highest °F**
Alaska	−80	100
California	−45	134
Indiana	−36	116
Michigan	−51	112
North Carolina	−34	110
Texas	−23	120
Utah	−69	117

The Third Sphere From the Sun

Page 461

LINKS

Arts & Literature

Some photographs use the spaces in between objects to create interesting shapes. Photographers say these kinds of shapes create "negative space."

Social Studies

The location of any place in the world can be described using the lines of longitude and latitude. Washington, DC, is located at 38° North, 77° West.

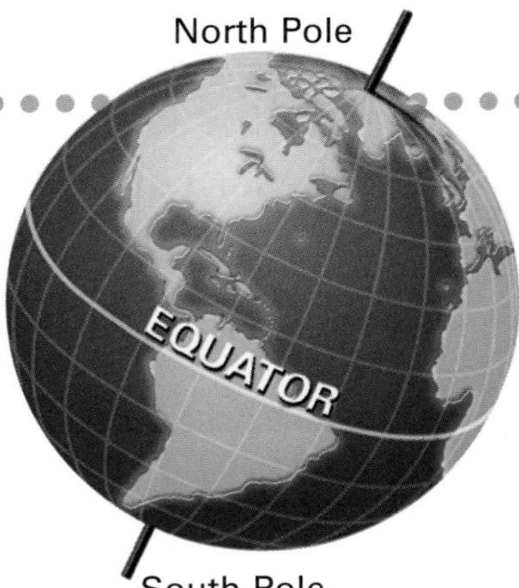

SECTION B

A Hunting We Will Go . . .

Graphing on the Coordinate Plane

483

Wichita County is a county in north central Texas that borders Oklahoma. According to the coordinate grid, where is Burkburnett located?

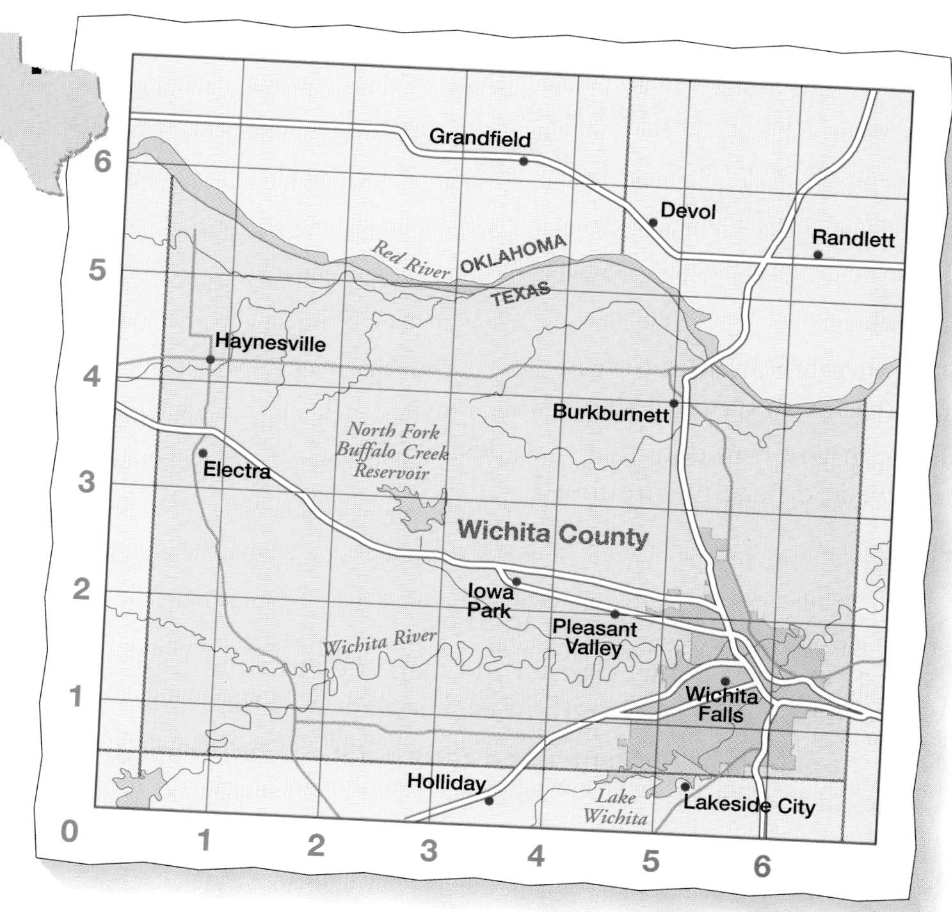

A Hunting We Will Go . . .
Page 483

Entertainment

Par refers to the number of golf strokes that are expected to sink the ball in a particular hole.
www.mathsurf.com/6/ch9/ent

People of the World

In the Netherlands, Amsterdam has an elevation of −22 feet. Since the city is below sea level, it is lined with canals and dikes to prevent flooding.
www.mathsurf.com/6/ch9/people

Science

As you walk across a carpeted floor, you collect electrons and develop a negative charge. Touching something with a positive charge may cause the electrons to create a shock.

Materials
atlas, graph paper, ruler

In this project, you will create a drawing of a real country on a coordinate plane and find facts that use positive and negative numbers.

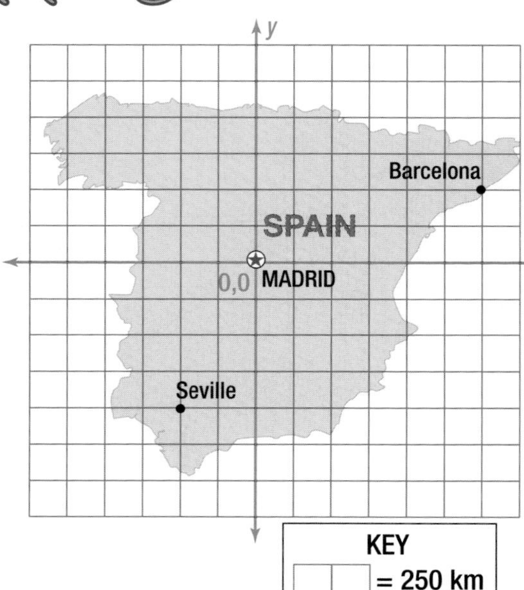

Make a Plan

- Look through an atlas to find countries with unusual shapes.
- How can you find data that includes positive and negative numbers?

Carry It Out

1. Decide on a country you want to draw.
2. Using a ruler as a guide, transfer the map's key to your graph paper. What distance does the length of each square represent?
3. Using the capital as the center and zero-point of your map, draw the borders of the country.
4. Find out facts about this country that include both positive and negative numbers.
5. Display your map and data. Include coordinates for locations of a few major cities.

Talk About It

- How did using a coordinate grid make your map more accurate?
- What types of data are represented with positive numbers? With negative numbers?

Present the Project

Examine the maps of the other teams. Compare how each team made its map.

CHAPTER 9

SECTION

A Integers

Have you ever wondered how the heights of mountains are measured? Whom would you ask to find out? Earth scientists are people who study the earth. This group includes zoologists, who study animals; botanists, who study plants; geologists, who study rocks; and many other types of scientists.

Besides mountain heights, what else could you measure about the Earth?

GET READY!

Understanding Integers

Review finding temperatures. Decide whether each temperature is above, below, or equal to 0°F.

1. °F 10 0 −10

2. °F

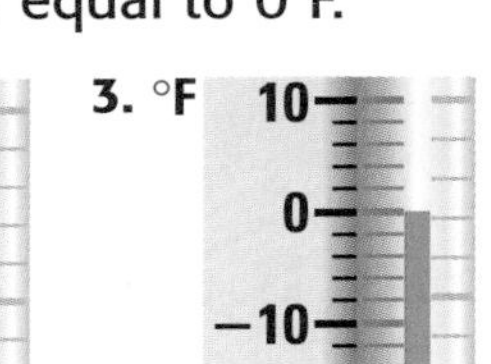

3. °F 10 0 −10

Skills Checklist

In this section, you will:

- ❐ **Explore Integers**
- ❐ **Add Integers**
- ❐ **Subtract Integers**
- ❐ **Multiply and Divide Integers**

Chapter 9
Lesson
1

Understanding Integers

You Will Learn
- to order integers

Vocabulary

positive numbers

negative numbers

integers

Explore

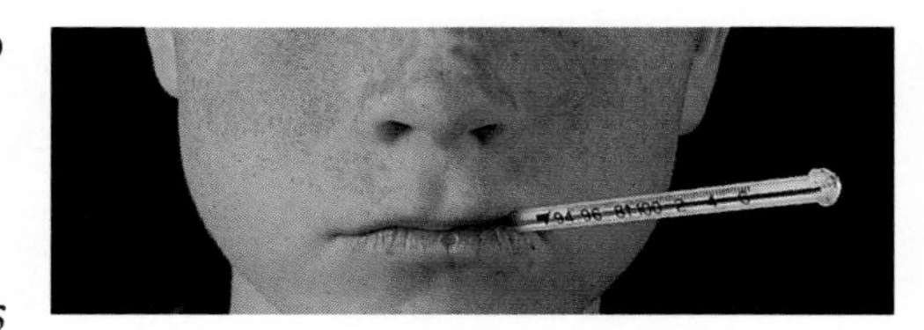

Most of the numbers you have seen so far have been greater than or equal to 0. Numbers greater than zero are known as **positive numbers**. There is another set of numbers that are all *less than 0.* These are known as **negative numbers**.

Work Together

1. Determine how much money each person will have or how much they will owe when all the monies owed have been paid.
2. Rank the five friends from who has the most money to who owes the most money.
3. Copy this number line and indicate where each person is.

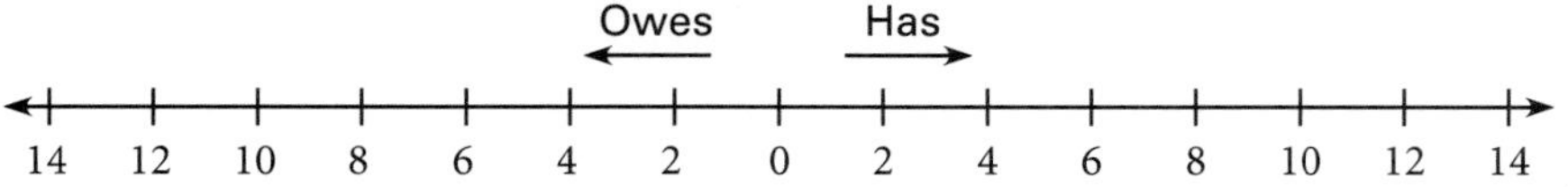

4. Without using words, how could you indicate if an answer of "6" meant "has 6 dollars" or "owes 6 dollars?"

Talk About It

5. Is a negative number always less than a positive number? Explain.

Connect and Learn

The number line shows positive and negative numbers.

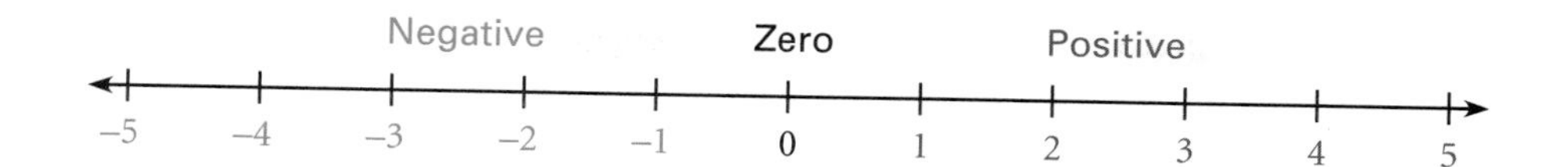

Negative numbers are used to keep track of values below a certain mark. They are used to describe debts, depths below sea level, and temperature in degrees Celsius below freezing.

Negative numbers are always shown with a minus (−) sign. Positive numbers may or may not have a plus (+) sign. Whole numbers (0, 1, 2, 3, . . .) and their negative counterparts (−1, −2, −3, . . .) are known as **integers**. On a number line, the further to the right a number is, the greater it is. The further to the left it is, the less it is.

Math Tip

You can remember the difference between $>$ and $<$ by recalling that the wider end always faces the greater amount.

Example 1

Order the integers from least to greatest: 1, −2, 4, −5, 0.

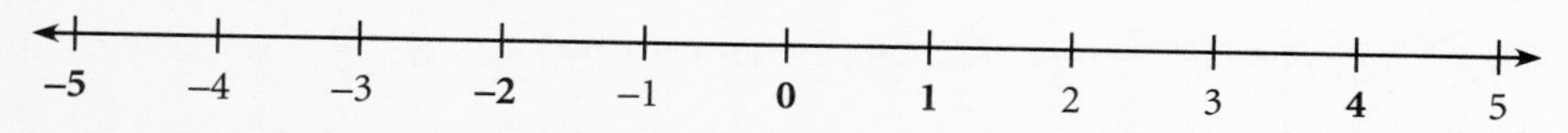

Locate the numbers on the number line.

$-5 < -2$ $-2 < 0$ $0 < 1$ $1 < 4$

The integers from least to greatest are −5, −2, 0, 1, 4

Example 2

Order the integers from greatest to least: −3, 5, −4, 4, −1.

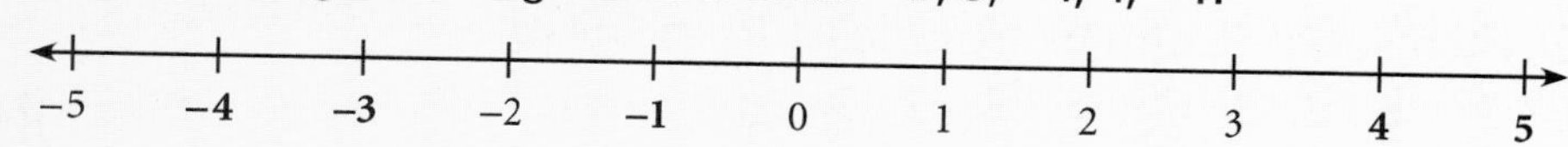

Locate the numbers on the number line.

$5 > 4$ $4 > -1$ $-1 > -3$ $-3 > -4$

The integers from greatest to least are 5, 4, −1, −3, −4.

Check

Draw a number line. Locate each integer on the number line.

1. −3 **2.** 0 **3.** 4 **4.** −5 **5.** 2 **6.** −1

7. Order the integers from least to greatest: 1, −3, −10, 7, 10, 0.

8. What kinds of numbers are integers?

Practice

Skills and Reasoning

Draw a number line. Locate each integer on the number line.

9. -5 **10.** 2 **11.** 0 **12.** -4 **13.** 3 **14.** -2

15. -1 **16.** 4 **17.** -6 **18.** 9 **19.** 5 **20.** -8

Compare using $>$ or $<$.

21. -8 ● -10 **22.** -6 ● 5 **23.** -1 ● 1 **24.** 12 ● -42 **25.** -66 ● -68

26. -45 ● -49 **27.** -16 ● -26 **28.** -24 ● -18 **29.** 5 ● -5 **30.** -55 ● 32

31. 12 ● 21 **32.** -15 ● 19 **33.** -14 ● -21 **34.** -20 ● -15 **35.** -4 ● 4

Order from greatest to least. You may use a number line if you wish.

36. $3, -4, -5, 2$ **37.** $-45, 67, -67, 45$ **38.** $-78, 13, -16, -56$

39. $-2, -42, -24, -4$ **40.** $16, -10, 12, 0$ **41.** $-45, -32, -59, -14$

42. $16, 17, -18, 19$ **43.** $-99, -100, -89, -47$ **44.** $0, 5, -10, 15$

45. $-42, 19, -21, 27$ **46.** $12, -19, -11, -5$ **47.** $-21, -25, 5, -10$

48. $16, 32, 4, -9, -16, 5, -1$ **49.** $28, 36, -10, -12, 42, -19, -22$

50. $-10, -8, -5, -1, 0, -4, -6$ **51.** $52, 39, -5, 14, -17, -21, -19$

Reasoning Tell if each number is an integer. If it is not, explain why.

52. -78 **53.** $\frac{1}{2}$ **54.** 56 **55.** -54.7 **56.** 0 **57.** $+33$

58. Reasoning Is $\frac{1}{2}$ an integer? Is $-\frac{1}{2}$? Explain your reasoning.

59. Algebra Readiness Like integers, decimals can be either positive or negative. Order each set of decimals from least to greatest.

a. $1.6, -2.7, -5.6$ **b.** $-7.3, -2.5, -5.8$ **c.** $-0.25, 0.5, -0.75$ **d.** $-0.3, -0.5, -0.4$

60. Critical Thinking Order $-5, -26, 8, 19$, and -20 from least to greatest. Then order these same numbers from closest to zero to farthest from zero. Explain the similarities and differences between your two lists.

Problem Solving and Applications

Write each number as an integer.

61. Ethanol freezes at 114°C below zero.

62. Measurement Lori is 62 inches tall.

63. Measurement Todd lost 7 pounds.

64. Kay took five dives to these depths below sea level: $-107, -52, -213, -211, -76$. Order these integers from least to greatest.

65. At the Spring Carnival Go-Fish booth, the 6th-grade class had expenses of \$12. They took in \$22. Write the money amounts as integers.

Write each amount as an integer.

66. Bryan has a debt of \$49.

67. **Measurement** The picture is 37 in. wide.

68. **Measurement** Chelsea hopped 5 ft backwards.

69. Byron is making up a board game. He wants to write the following on the board spaces: Go back two spaces; Move ahead four spaces; Move ahead three spaces; Go back five spaces; Move ahead one space. If he writes these instructions using integers, will he have more negative numbers or more positive numbers?

70. **Career** Before a space shuttle takes off, astronauts count the time remaining in negative numbers. Order these takeoff times from earliest to latest: −4 minutes, −15 minutes, −3 minutes, −20 minutes, −5 minutes, −1 minute, −2 minutes.

71. **Journal** What is the greatest positive integer? The greatest negative integer? Explain your reasoning.

Mixed Review and Test Prep

Estimate.

72. $6\frac{2}{3} \times 2\frac{1}{3}$ **73.** $11\frac{3}{4} \div 3\frac{5}{8}$ **74.** $2\frac{6}{7} \times \frac{1}{2}$ **75.** $15\frac{3}{7} \div 3\frac{1}{3}$

76. $4\frac{1}{4} \times 10\frac{4}{5}$ **77.** $9\frac{8}{9} \div 1\frac{7}{8}$ **78.** $20\frac{2}{5} \times 8\frac{5}{6}$ **79.** $5\frac{7}{8} \div 2\frac{8}{9}$

Describe the relationship between the lines, rays, or segments.

80.

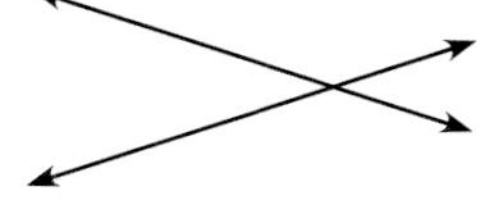

81.

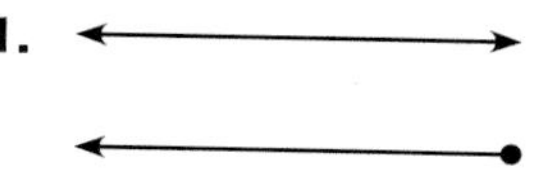

82.

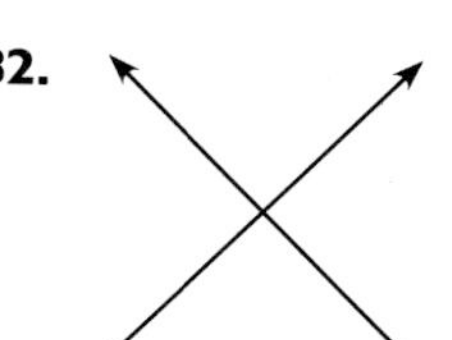

83.

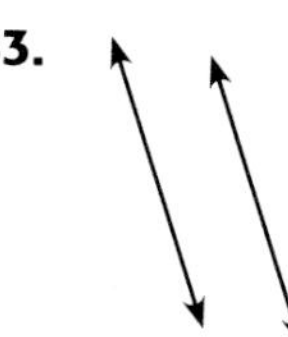

84.

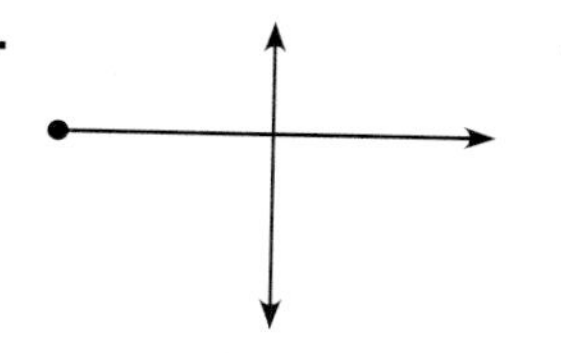

85.

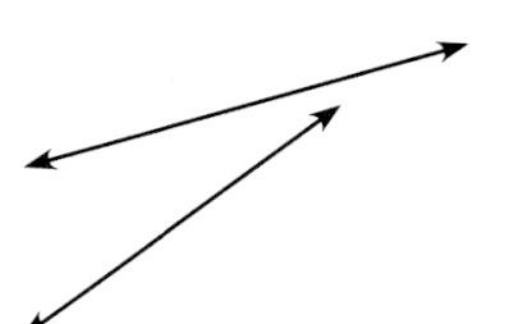

86.

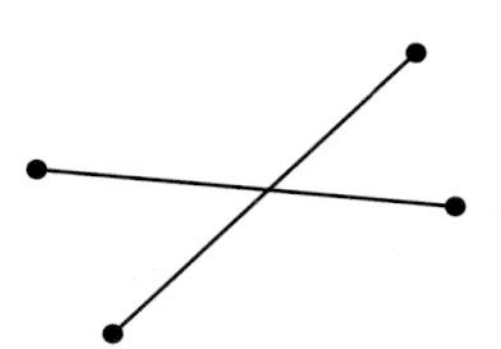

87.

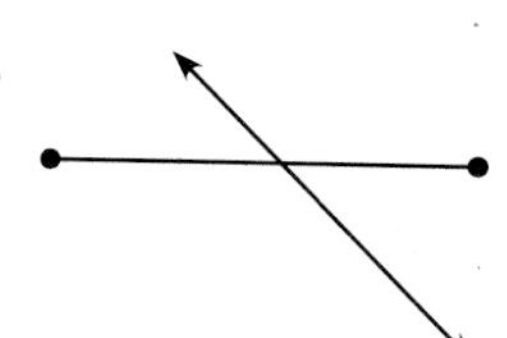

88. What is the sum of $6\frac{1}{2}$ and $3\frac{4}{5}$?

Ⓐ $2\frac{7}{10}$ Ⓑ $10\frac{3}{10}$ Ⓒ $9\frac{5}{7}$ Ⓓ $9\frac{9}{10}$

Chapter 9
Lesson
2

Adding Integers

Problem Solving Connection
- Look for a Pattern

Materials
2-color counters

Vocabulary
opposite

Explore

The **opposite** of an integer is the integer on the opposite side of zero but at the same distance from zero. 8 and −8 are the same distance from zero, so they are opposites.

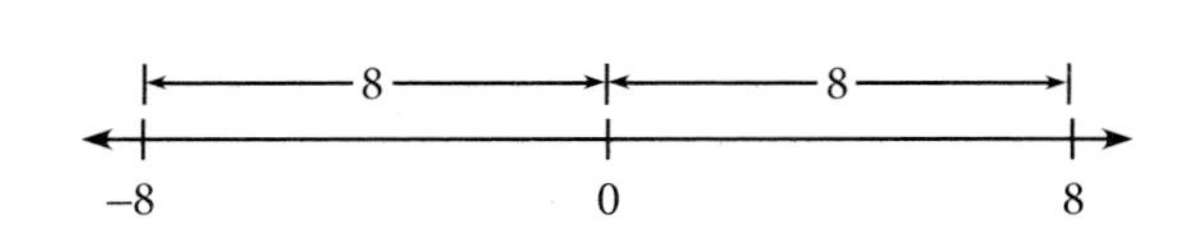

The sum of an integer and its opposite will always equal 0.

Work Together

- Count out enough counters to represent the first number. If the number is positive, put the yellow sides up. If it is negative, put the red sides up.
- Repeat the first step for the second number.
- Make as many opposite pairs of one yellow and one red counter as possible. Since each pair equals 0 when added together, remove each pair.
- Describe the number and color of the counters left over.

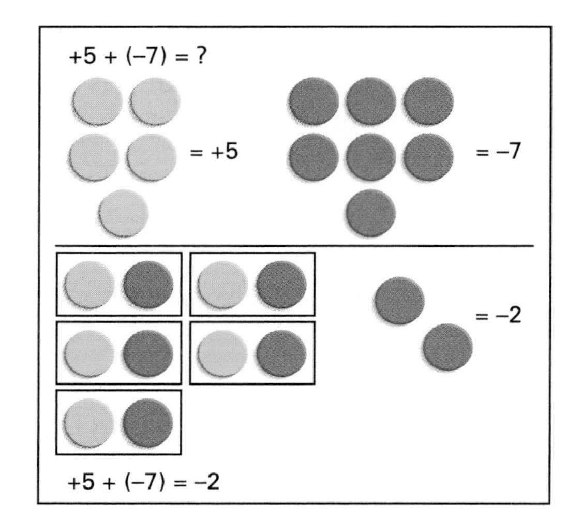

Math Tip
To enter a negative number into a calculator, enter the number and then press the +/− key.

1. Use counters to model each addition expression. Give the answer.

   a. $10 + (-7)$ **b.** $-6 + 5$ **c.** $4 + (-12)$ **d.** $-5 + 0$

   e. $-3 + (-8)$ **f.** $6 + 2$ **g.** $-4 + 4$ **h.** $-7 + 7$

Talk About It

2. Is the sum positive or negative when you add two positive integers? Two negative integers? Explain.
3. How can you predict the sign of the sum when you add a positive integer to a negative integer?

Connect and Learn

You can add integers using a number line.

Find the first number on the line. Move *right* to add a positive number. Move *left* to add a negative number.

Example 1

Add: $-3 + 5$

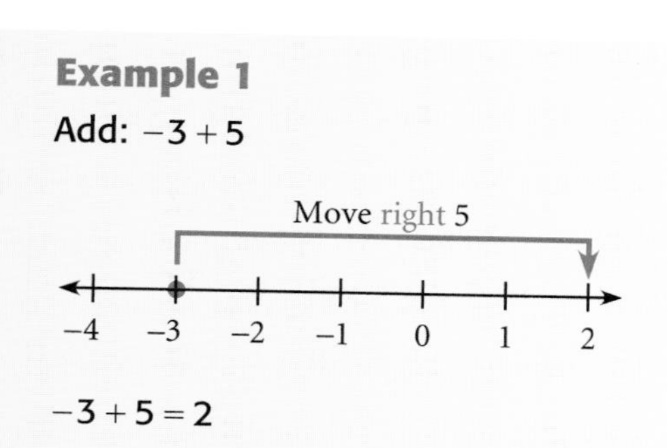

$-3 + 5 = 2$

Example 2

Add: $2 + (-4)$

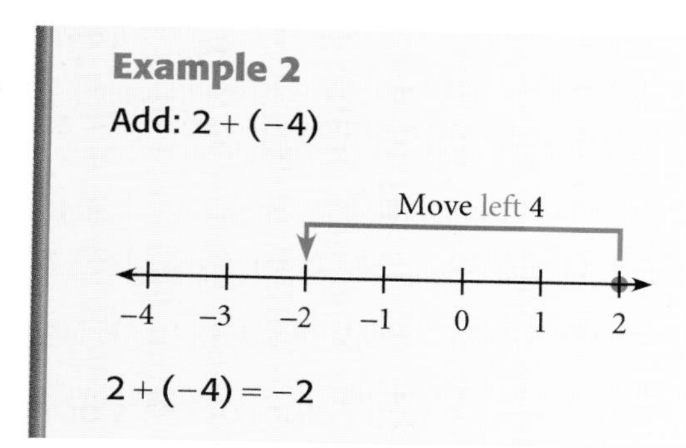

$2 + (-4) = -2$

You can also use integers to model real-life situations.

Example 3

A geologist removed a rock sample from 12 ft below sea level. She then climbed 31 ft and removed another rock sample. From what height was the second rock sample removed?

$-12 + 31$ Write an expression.

$-12 + 31 = 19$ Add.

The second rock sample was 19 ft above sea level.

Check

Add. You may use two-color counters or number lines to help.

1. $6 + -4$ **2.** $-3 + (-5)$ **3.** $-7 + 8$ **4.** $2 + (-2)$

5. $10 + -3$ **6.** $-6 + 12$ **7.** $5 + (-2)$ **8.** $5 + (-8)$

9. Reasoning If you add a positive integer to a negative integer, will the sum be positive or negative? Explain.

10. Reasoning Which is closer to zero, the sum of -5 and 2 or the sum of -4 and 3? Explain.

Practice

Skills and Reasoning

State each number's opposite.

11. 6 **12.** 12 **13.** -35 **14.** -40 **15.** 0 **16.** $-1,589$

17. 56 **18.** 27 **19.** -522 **20.** 266 **21.** -89 **22.** -128

State if the sum is positive, negative, or zero.

23. $10 + 4$ **24.** $-7 + (-3)$ **25.** $-8 + 2$ **26.** $-3 + 7$ **27.** $5 + (-3)$

28. $21 + (-21)$ **29.** $63 + (-32)$ **30.** $-47 + 35$ **31.** $-15 + 15$ **32.** $-6 + (-22)$

33. $4 + 9$ **34.** $-4 + (-23)$ **35.** $89 + (-91)$ **36.** $-18 + 56$ **37.** $-47 + 47$

Add. You may use two-color counters or number lines to help.

38. $2 + (-6)$ **39.** $-8 + (-4)$ **40.** $-2 + 19$ **41.** $2 + (-4)$ **42.** $4 + (-4)$

43. $7 + (-1)$ **44.** $-7 + (-1)$ **45.** $-7 + (-5)$ **46.** $7 + (-5)$ **47.** $-14 + (-3)$

48. $-10 + (-2)$ **49.** $-6 + 7$ **50.** $-9 + 4$ **51.** $-10 + 12$ **52.** $5 + (-7)$

53. $-13 + 7$ **54.** $6 + (-3)$ **55.** $16 + (-3)$ **56.** $-17 + (-5)$ **57.** $-20 + 6$

58. $-8 + 9$ **59.** $11 + (-2)$ **60.** $18 + (-12)$ **61.** $-4 + 3$ **62.** $-5 + 2$

63. $-16 + (-15)$ **64.** $-13 + 16$ **65.** $-5 + (-9)$ **66.** $-6 + (-6)$ **67.** $8 + (-8)$

68. Number Sense Which depth is lower, -157 ft or the opposite of 211 ft?

69. Measurement Which number is farther from zero, -5 or the opposite of $+3$?

Problem Solving and Applications

70. During a football game the ball is advanced 4 yd, returned 6 yd, advanced 21 yd, and returned 5 yd. Altogether, how far has the ball advanced or returned?

71. Leona runs a lemonade stand. One week she spent \$7 on ingredients and sold \$12 worth of lemonade. What was Leona's profit?

Using Data Use the line graph for **72** and **73.**

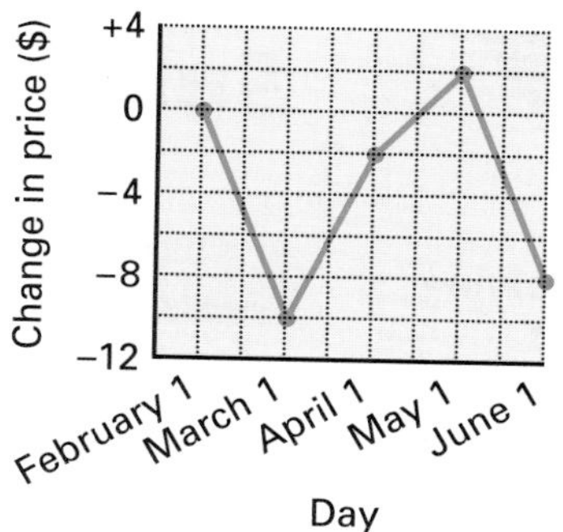

72. Sam wanted to buy a video game system. He recorded the change in price over several months on a line graph. How did the original price compare to the final price? Use numbers in your answer.

73. In what month did the price go up the most?

74. **Critical Thinking** Jamie earns money by conducting nature hikes. She earned and spent the following dollar amounts: -3, $+4$, -3, $+6$, -2, $+5$, $+12$. How could you use number sense to determine if Jamie made money or lost money?

75. **Critical Thinking** Leon had the following test scores to average: 87, 91, 88, 95, and 89. He said, "I guess my average is about 90. My scores are off that by -3, $+1$, -2, $+5$, and -1. When I add those numbers they add to zero. So I must be right." Do you agree with Leon? Explain.

76. **Journal** Does $-5 + 3$ equal $3 + (-5)$? Use number lines to explain your answer.

Mixed Review and Test Prep

Simplify.

77. $5\frac{3}{4} \times 6$ **78.** $\frac{3}{7} \times 7$ **79.** $2 \times \frac{1}{2}$ **80.** $10 \times \frac{17}{19}$

81. $\frac{5}{6} \times 8$ **82.** $3\frac{2}{3} \times 6$ **83.** $8 \times 6\frac{1}{4}$ **84.** $6 \times \frac{5}{6}$

Classify each angle as acute, right, obtuse, or straight.

85.

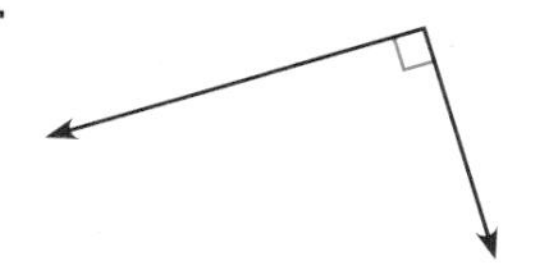

86.

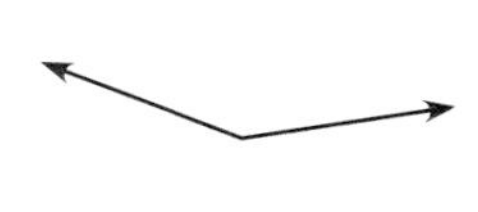

87.

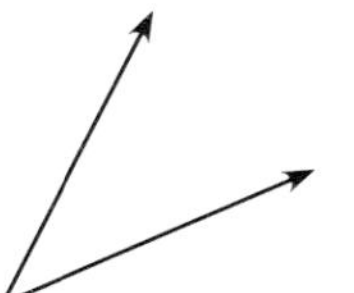

88.

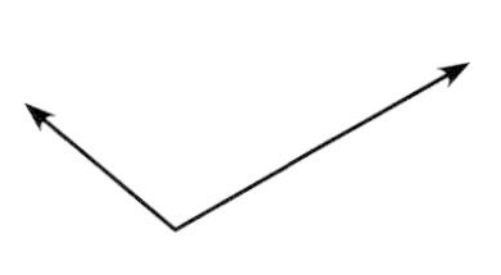

89. Which of the following shows these integers ordered from least to greatest: 0, 7, -5, -3?

Ⓐ $-5, -3, 0, 7$ Ⓑ $7, 0, -3, -5$ Ⓒ $0, -3, -5, 7$ Ⓓ $7, -5, -3, 0$

Chapter 9 Lesson 3

Subtracting Integers

Problem Solving Connection
- Look for a Pattern
- Use Logical Reasoning

Materials

2-color counters

Remember

The opposite of a number is the same number with the opposite sign, as in 4 and −4. The sum of two opposites is always 0.

Explore

Addition and subtraction are opposite operations. When you take a number and add a negative number to it, the results get less. So when you take a number and *subtract* a negative number, the results get greater.

Work Together

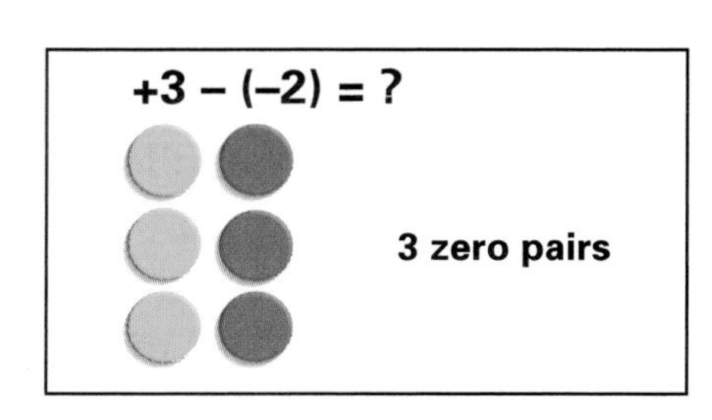

- Count out the same number of zero pairs as the greatest number in the problem.
- Count out counters to represent the first number. Put the yellow side up for a positive number and the red side up for a negative number.

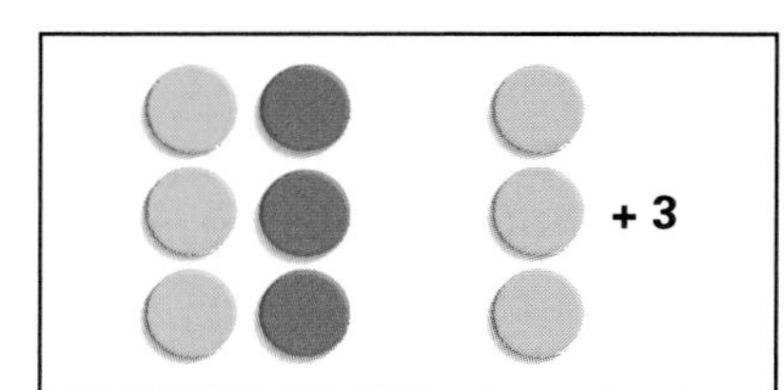

- Take away enough counters to represent the second number. (Since it is (-2) take 2 red counters.)
- Remove any zero pairs left.
- Describe the number and color of the counters left.

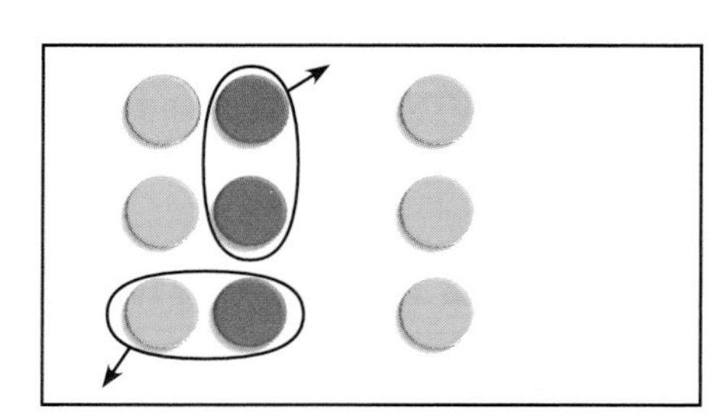

1. Model each problem using 2-color counters. Follow the directions above.

   a. $+4-(-1)$ **b.** $-5-(+3)$ **c.** $+2-(-2)$ **d.** $0-(-5)$

   e. $-4-(-1)$ **f.** $+5-(+3)$ **g.** $-7-(-7)$ **h.** $-7-(+7)$

Talk About It

2. When you subtract a positive number, is the difference greater or less than the original number?
3. When you subtract a negative number, is the difference greater or less than the original number?
4. How is subtraction of integers like addition of integers?

Connect and Learn

You can subtract integers on a number line by reversing the procedure you used for addition. Find the first number on the line. Move *left* to subtract positive numbers. Move *right* to subtract negative numbers.

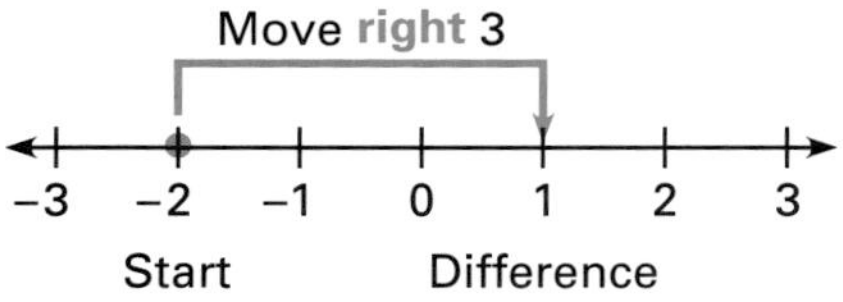

$-2 - (-3) = 1$

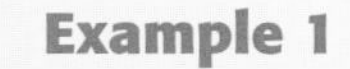

Example 1

Subtract: $-1 - (-4)$

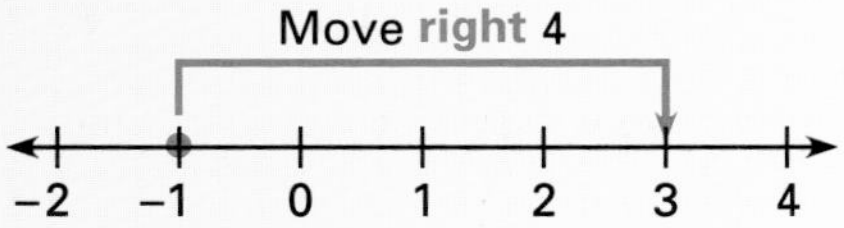

$-1 - (-4) = 3$

Example 2

Subtract: $1 - 3$

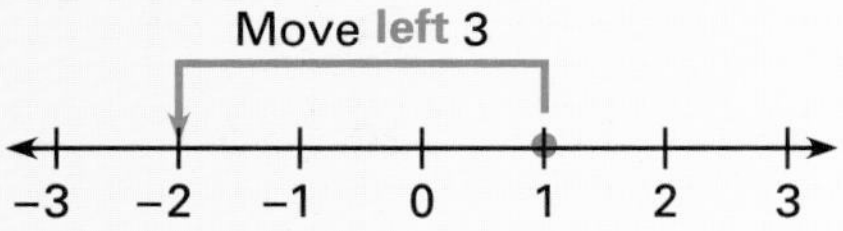

$1 - 3 = -2$

You can subtract an integer by adding its opposite.

Example 3

Jennifer earned $14 working in a hydroponics garden. She spent $16 buying shoes and gloves for the job. Find the amount of money she earned or lost.

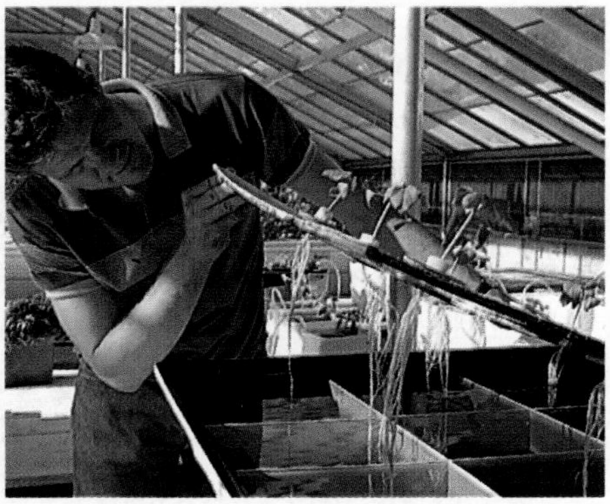

$14 - 16$	Write an expression.
$14 + (-16)$	Rewrite the expression by adding the opposite.
$14 + (-16) = -2$	Add.

She had a $2 loss.

Check

1. Write a subtraction equation that shows the difference between S and T on the number line.

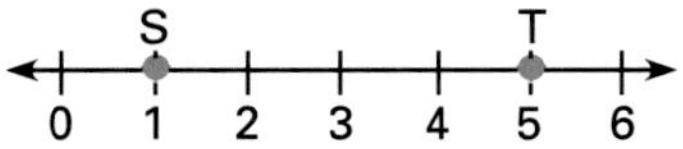

Subtract. You may use two-color counters or number lines to help.

2. $5 - (-12)$ **3.** $-8 - (-13)$ **4.** $10 - (-16)$ **5.** $-24 - (-13)$

6. $-4 - (-2)$ **7.** $9 - (-11)$ **8.** $-23 - (-4)$ **9.** $15 - (-10)$

10. Reasoning When you subtract a negative number, why is the result greater than the original number?

Practice

Skills and Reasoning

Write a subtraction equation that shows the difference between *P* and *Q* on each number line.

11. 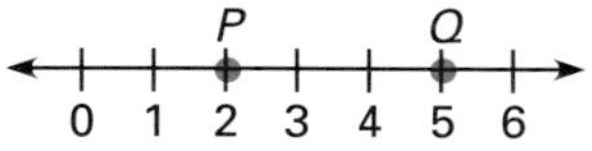

12. 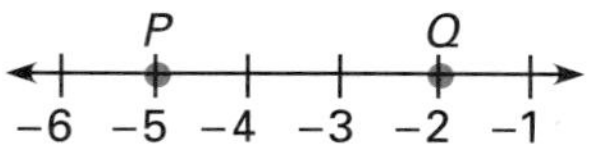

13. 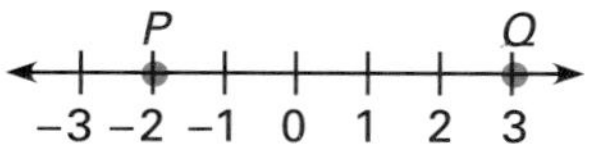

Subtract. You may use two-color counters or number lines to help.

14. $-7 - 2$	**15.** $-7 - (-2)$	**16.** $7 - (-2)$	**17.** $-9 - 11$	**18.** $4 - (-8)$
19. $6 - (-3)$	**20.** $-3 - (-5)$	**21.** $7 - (-4)$	**22.** $-8 - 3$	**23.** $-9 - 7$
24. $14 - (-5)$	**25.** $10 - (-9)$	**26.** $-8 - 12$	**27.** $16 - (-1)$	**28.** $-13 - (-2)$
29. $-2 - 1$	**30.** $-5 - 3$	**31.** $-4 - (-6)$	**32.** $8 - (-5)$	**33.** $6 - (-12)$
34. $-9 - (-4)$	**35.** $0 - (-8)$	**36.** $9 - (-11)$	**37.** $-17 - (-2)$	**38.** $-5 - 8$
39. $-9 - 0$	**40.** $16 - (-6)$	**41.** $-3 - 1$	**42.** $2 - (-9)$	**43.** $8 - (-9)$

44. Reasoning Which is greater, the difference between 6 and 9 or 6 and −9?

Problem Solving and Applications

45. Critical Thinking Nicki visited her dad at work and got lost in the building. She started on the first floor. She rode the elevator up 4 floors, then down 2 floors, then up 6 more floors, then down another floor.

a. Write an expression to represent this situation.

b. If Nicki started on the first floor, which floor did she end up on?

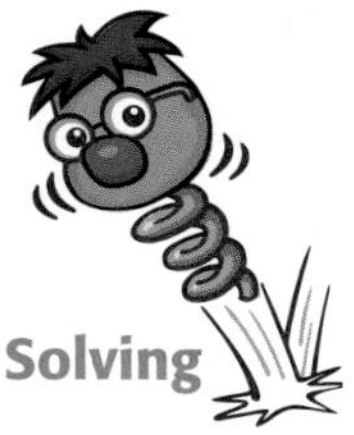

Problem Solving Hint

Try using the strategy Draw a Diagram to help you solve Exercise 45.

46. Using Data Use the data on page 458 to solve this problem. What is the difference between the record-highest and record-lowest temperatures shown in the table?

47. Estimation The lowest elevation on Earth is on the shore of the Dead Sea, 1,310 ft below sea level. The highest elevation on Earth is Mt. Everest in the Himalayas at 29,028 ft. Estimate the difference.

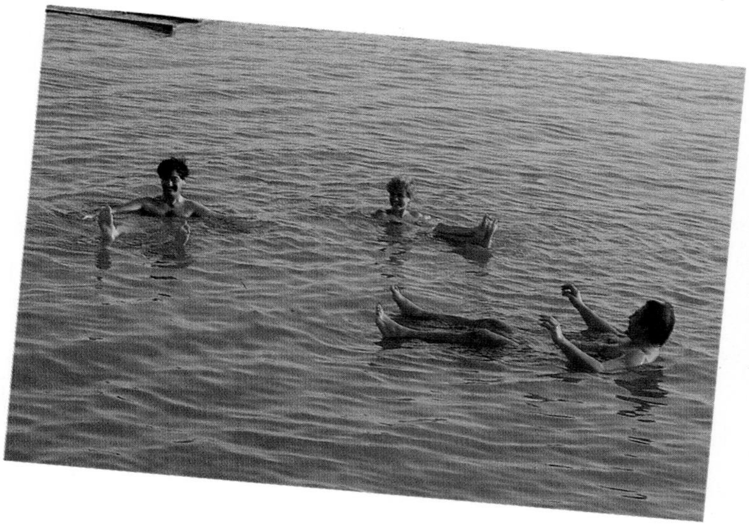

48. Write Your Own Problem Write a word problem that uses real-life data involving integers. Make sure the problem requires subtraction to solve. Exchange your problem with a classmate and solve.

Using Data Use the diagram for **49** and **50.**

49. What is the distance from the bottom of the ship to the deck?

50. How many feet of the ship are under water?

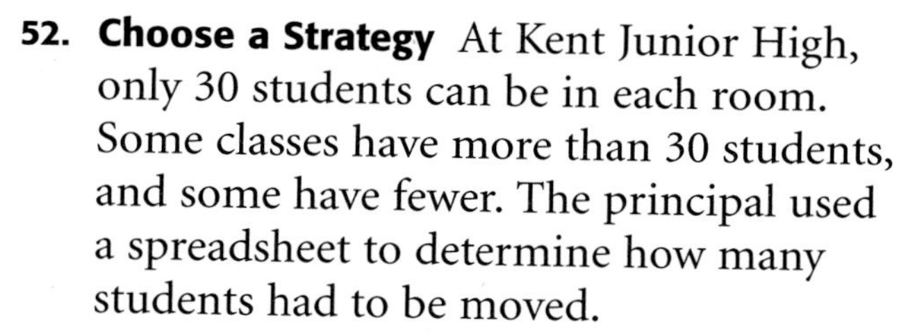

51. Science In a magazine, John read that the average temperature on the surface of Earth is 15°C. The average temperature on the surface of Mars is -50°C. What is the difference between the two temperatures?

52. Choose a Strategy At Kent Junior High, only 30 students can be in each room. Some classes have more than 30 students, and some have fewer. The principal used a spreadsheet to determine how many students had to be moved.

a. How many students need to be moved in Rooms 12 and 13? What integers should be in the Adjustment column? Explain.

b. How many students are currently in Rooms 14 and 15? Explain.

	A	B	C
	Room No.	Students	Adjustment
1	10	31	-1
2	11	25	$+5$
3	12	27	
4	13	34	
5	14		-3
6	15		$+4$

Mixed Review and Test Prep

Estimate the measure of each angle. Then measure each with a protractor.

53.

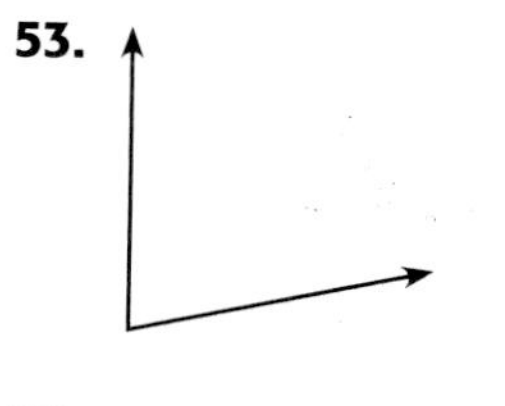

54.

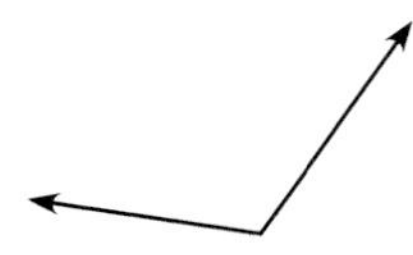

55.

56.

Multiply.

57. $4\frac{1}{3} \times 7\frac{9}{10}$ **58.** $\frac{4}{5} \times 5\frac{3}{4}$ **59.** $1\frac{2}{7} \times 3\frac{4}{7}$ **60.** $10\frac{3}{8} \times \frac{1}{5}$

61. The temperature outside at sunset yesterday was -2°C. It rose 5° overnight. What was the temperature this morning?

Ⓐ -7°C Ⓑ -3°C Ⓒ 3°C Ⓓ 7°C

Skills Practice Bank, page 668, Set 2

Chapter 9
Lesson
4

Multiplying and Dividing Integers

Problem Solving Connections
- Look for a Pattern
- Make an Organized List

Materials
spreadsheet software
red counters

Explore

Recall that multiplication is repeated addition. $2 \times 3 = 2 + 2 + 2$

This can help you find the product of a positive integer and a negative integer.

$(-2) \times 3 = (-2) + (-2) + (-2) = -6$

Work Together

1. You can use a spreadsheet to create a multiplication table for positive and negative numbers. Enter the following information on a blank spreadsheet.

	A	B	C	D	E	F	G	H
1		−3	−2	−1	0	1	2	3
2	−4	=A2*B1	=A2*C1	=A2*D1	=A2*E1	=A2*F1	=A2*G1	=A2*H1
3	−3							
4	−2							
5	−1							
6	0							
7	1							
8	2							
9	3							
10	4							

Math Tip
Multiplication is repeated addition. Division can be thought of as repeated subtraction.

2. In each column, copy the formula from row 2 down to row 10.
3. Study the signs of the products in the spreadsheet. Describe any patterns that you see.
4. Predict the sign of the product of two integers having the following signs.
   - **a.** Positive, positive
   - **b.** Positive, negative
   - **c.** Negative, positive
   - **d.** Negative, negative

5. Do you think the product of $(-3) \times (-3) \times (-3)$ will be a positive number or a negative number? Explain your reasoning.

Connect and Learn

You can multiply and divide integers.

Example 1

When two integers have like signs, the product or quotient will be positive. When two integers have unlike signs, the product or quotient will be negative.

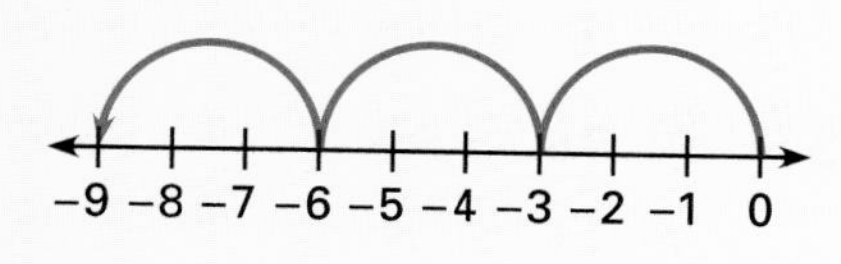

$3 \times 3 = 9$

$3 \times (-3) = -9$

$-9 \div 3 = -3$

$-9 \div (-3) = 3$

Example 2

Multiply: $-7 \times (-9)$

The signs are alike, so the product is positive.

$-7 \times (-9) = 63$

Example 3

Divide: $72 \div (-9)$

The signs are different, so the quotient is negative.

$72 \div (-9) = -8$

Some problems can be solved using integers.

Example 4

Over four consecutive hours, the temperature dropped from 0°F to −56°F. If the temperature dropped the same amount each hour, how much did the temperature change each hour?

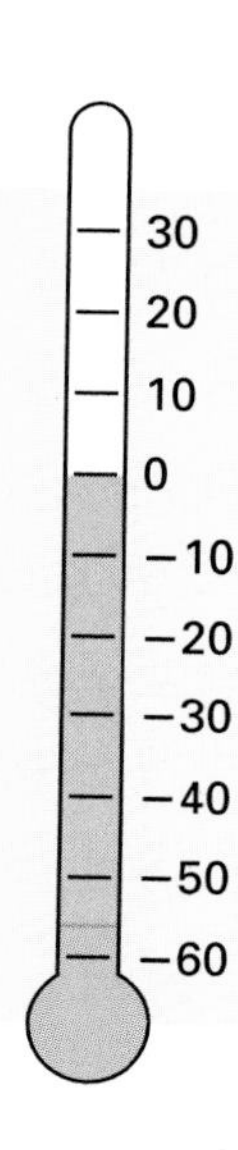

$-56 \div 4$	Write an expression.
$-56 \div 4 = ?14$	Determine the numerical value of the quotient.
$-56 \div 4 = -14$	Determine the sign of the quotient.

The temperature dropped 14 degrees each hour.

Check

Multiply.

1. $4 \times (-8)$ **2.** $-15 \times (-6)$ **3.** 12×5 **4.** -10×1

Divide.

5. $-12 \div 3$ **6.** $24 \div 8$ **7.** $30 \div (-6)$ **8.** $-9 \div (-3)$

9. Reasoning What do you know about the signs of two integers if their product is positive? If their quotient is negative?

Practice

Skills and Reasoning

Multiply. You may use counters or number lines to help.

10. $5 \times (-4)$ **11.** $-9 \times (-1)$ **12.** $-6 \times (-7)$ **13.** $-20 \times (-5)$ **14.** -5×8

15. $4 \times (-3)$ **16.** -9×9 **17.** $-2 \times (-9)$ **18.** $6 \times (-12)$ **19.** -10×2

20. -7×10 **21.** $8 \times (-6)$ **22.** $5 \times (-3)$ **23.** -8×4 **24.** $20 \times (-3)$

25. 4×9 **26.** $-6 \times (-6)$ **27.** $-15 \times (-6)$ **28.** -5×12 **29.** 1×10

30. -20×4 **31.** -9×4 **32.** $18 \times (-5)$ **33.** $-7 \times (-7)$ **34.** 14×10

35. $-4 \times (-8)$ **36.** $10 \times (-6)$ **37.** $-17 \times (-2)$ **38.** 41×6 **39.** -27×3

40. -16×4 **41.** $-15 \times (-10)$ **42.** $12 \times (-12)$ **43.** -11×5 **44.** -21×6

Divide. You may use counters or number lines to help.

45. $-6 \div 3$ **46.** $12 \div (-4)$ **47.** $8 \div (-2)$ **48.** $-16 \div (-4)$ **49.** $-21 \div 3$

50. $-14 \div (-2)$ **51.** $-60 \div 3$ **52.** $9 \div (-3)$ **53.** $4 \div (-2)$ **54.** $-18 \div (-9)$

55. $21 \div (-3)$ **56.** $-24 \div (-6)$ **57.** $-72 \div 9$ **58.** $-30 \div 10$ **59.** $-9 \div (-3)$

60. $-12 \div 3$ **61.** $24 \div 8$ **62.** $30 \div (-6)$ **63.** $-30 \div (-5)$ **64.** $28 \div (-7)$

65. $-39 \div (-3)$ **66.** $-81 \div (-9)$ **67.** $-27 \div 9$ **68.** $-21 \div 7$ **69.** $-36 \div (-4)$

70. $-48 \div (-4)$ **71.** $-90 \div 3$ **72.** $100 \div (-10)$ **73.** $144 \div 12$ **74.** $36 \div (-3)$

75. $60 \div (-5)$ **76.** $-42 \div (-7)$ **77.** $56 \div (-7)$ **78.** $63 \div 3$ **79.** $66 \div (-6)$

Patterns Copy and complete each pattern.

80.
$6 \div (-2) = -3$
$4 \div \blacksquare = -2$
$2 \div (-2) = \blacksquare$
$0 \div (-2) = \blacksquare$
$-2 \div \blacksquare = 1$
$-4 \div \blacksquare = \blacksquare$
$\blacksquare \div \blacksquare = \blacksquare$

81.
$-4 \times 3 = \blacksquare$
$-4 \times \blacksquare = -8$
$-4 \times 1 = -4$
$-4 \times 0 = \blacksquare$
$\blacksquare \times -1 = 4$
$-4 \times \blacksquare = 8$
$\blacksquare \times \blacksquare = \blacksquare$

82.
$(-2)^1 = -2$
$(-2)^2 = 4$
$(-2)^3 = -8$
$(-2)^4 = \blacksquare$
$(-2)^5 = \blacksquare$
$(-2)^6 = \blacksquare$
$(-2)^7 = \blacksquare$

83.
$-9 \div 3 = -3$
$-6 \div 3 = \blacksquare$
$\blacksquare \div 3 = -1$
$\blacksquare \div 3 = 0$
$\blacksquare \div \blacksquare = 1$
$6 \div \blacksquare = \blacksquare$
$\blacksquare \div \blacksquare = \blacksquare$

84. Reasoning Can you use the patterns you found when adding and subtracting integers to help you determine the signs on products or quotients?

85. Reasoning Use a number line to show $-12 \div 2$.

86. Reasoning Write two different equations that could be modeled with the counters shown.

Problem Solving and Applications

87. Write Your Own Problem Write a problem involving products or quotients of integers.

88. Ryan spent $5.00 for lunch 5 days in a row. Write an integer multiplication sentence to find the amount of money Ryan spent on lunch.

89. In 4 hours, the temperature dropped steadily from 0°C to -20°C. Using at least one negative integer, write an equation that shows how much the temperature dropped in 1 hour.

90. Critical Thinking Toby's game scores were -5, -10, 5, -20, and 15. Toby guessed his average score to be -5. State the difference between his guessed average and his actual average. Explain your reasoning.

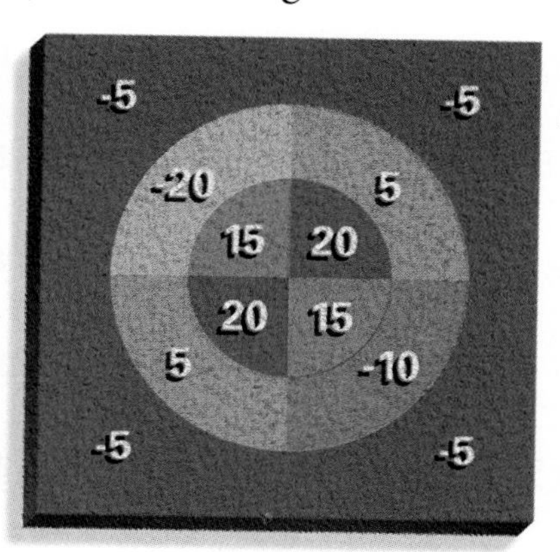

91. Sal's business currently has expenses of $4 million and sales of $9 million. Sal wants to triple the size of his business. Express the new expenses, sales, and profit as integers.

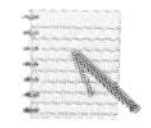

92. Journal Does -6×4 equal $4 \times (-6)$? Use number lines to explain your answer.

Mixed Review and Test Prep

Divide.

93. $4 \div \frac{6}{7}$ **94.** $1 \div 10\frac{1}{2}$ **95.** $7 \div \frac{3}{4}$ **96.** $9 \div 4\frac{3}{5}$

97. $8 \div \frac{2}{7}$ **98.** $3 \div \frac{7}{8}$ **99.** $5 \div 2\frac{4}{9}$ **100.** $6 \div \frac{5}{8}$

Find the measure of the missing angle in each triangle.

101. $m\angle S = 35°$, $m\angle D = 72°$, $m\angle F = $ ■ **102.** $m\angle J = 90°$, $m\angle C = 45°$, $m\angle M = $ ■

103. $m\angle D = 117°$, $m\angle G = 52°$, $m\angle H = $ ■ **104.** $m\angle B = 19°$, $m\angle N = 24°$, $m\angle M = $ ■

105. Which equations are correct?

I. $-10 + -5 = 15$ **II.** $-10 - (-5) = -5$ **III.** $10 + -5 = -5$ **IV.** $10 - (-5) = 15$

Ⓐ Only I Ⓑ Only II and III Ⓒ Only IV Ⓓ Only II and IV

STOP and Practice

Simplify.

1. $-7+(-8)$
2. $-1-9$
3. $4\div(-2)$
4. $2\times(-6)$
5. $-9+(-16)$
6. $5\times(-8)$
7. $-6+(-2)$
8. $-3-8$
9. $6\div(-2)$
10. $-7-5$
11. $8\div(-4)$
12. $-6-1$
13. $7\times(-4)$
14. $-13+(-10)$
15. $6\div(-3)$
16. $-5-(-9)$
17. $8\times(-20)$
18. $-23+(-34)$
19. $18\div(-3)$
20. $9\times(-11)$
21. $-18+(-1)$
22. $21\div(-7)$
23. $10\times(-3)$
24. $-4-(-2)$
25. $-3+(-2)$
26. $0-(-3)$
27. $-17+(-3)$
28. $15\div(-5)$
29. $-31+(-14)$
30. $15\times(-9)$
31. $-9\div 3$
32. $-8-(-6)$
33. $-8\div 2$
34. $-4-(-1)$
35. $-3\times(-3)$
36. $-15+(-25)$
37. $-4\times(-7)$
38. $-8\div 4$
39. $-5\times(-2)$
40. $-11-(-7)$
41. $-6\times(-11)$
42. $-6\div 2$
43. $-10-1$
44. $1-(-8)$
45. $-11+(-37)$
46. $-7\times(-15)$
47. $5+(-9)$
48. $3+(-1)$
49. $-12\div 3$
50. $-20\times(-4)$
51. $2-(-5)$
52. $-14\div 7$
53. $-12\times(-5)$
54. $7-(-2)$
55. $12+(-12)$
56. $-24\div 3$
57. -5×9
58. $6-(-3)$
59. $8-(-6)$
60. $-4\div(-2)$
61. $19+(-16)$
62. $3+(-4)$
63. -7×7
64. $-6\div(-3)$
65. $-8\div(-4)$
66. $5-(-4)$
67. $-9\div(-3)$
68. $9+(-14)$
69. -9×3
70. $4-(-10)$
71. -2×15
72. $8+(-4)$
73. -3×12
74. $4-(-11)$
75. $-36\div(-4)$
76. $-16\div(-2)$
77. $14+(-14)$
78. $-28\div(-4)$
79. -10×4
80. $-13\times(-4)$

Error Search

Find each solution that is not correct. Write it correctly and explain the error.

81. $-11+(-4)=-7$
82. $-8-(-4)=-12$
83. $10-(-2)=8$
84. $7+(-1)=6$
85. $-5\times(-9)=-45$
86. $-24\div(-3)=-8$

Scrambled, Please!

This code gives each of these five integers a different letter.

−3 (N) −5 (A) −2 (O) 9 (T) −7 (I)

Use the letters to make as many two-letter words as you can. Use the order of letters in each of your words to make up expressions. Make up one addition expression and one subtraction expression for each word. Simplify.

Word	Addition Expression	Subtraction Expression
87. *ON*	$-2+(-3)=-5$	$-2-(-3)=1$
88.		
89.		
90.		
91.		
92.		

Now simplify the expression underneath each blank below. Match each solution to an integer and letter from the code above. Then find the answer to the question.

93. When is the best time to travel backwards and arrive at the same time, again?

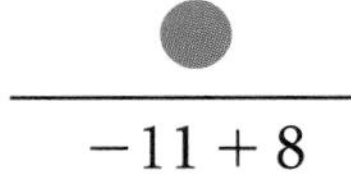

______	______	______	______
$-11+8$	$6+(-8)$	$-12-(-10)$	$6+(-9)$

Number Sense Reasoning

Write whether each statement is true or false. Explain your answer.

94. $-10+6=4$

95. $-9\times-7=63$

96. $9-(-4)=-13$

97. $11+(-4)=-7$

98. $-3\times4=12$

99. $-8-2=-10$

Chapter 9

Problem Solving

Decision Making: Planning a Dive

You Will Learn

- to use integers to make a decision

Explore

Let's go below 0! Below sea level, that is. That's what Langston and his dad do each time they scuba dive. With a breathing device, a diver can go to a depth of no more than 250 ft.

Langston is from Los Altos, CA. He enjoys photographing ocean life.

You and your family have almost completed a one-week vacation. On June 13 you began scuba diving training. During vacation, you kept a journal of the dives you made.

Here is the data of your dives so far.

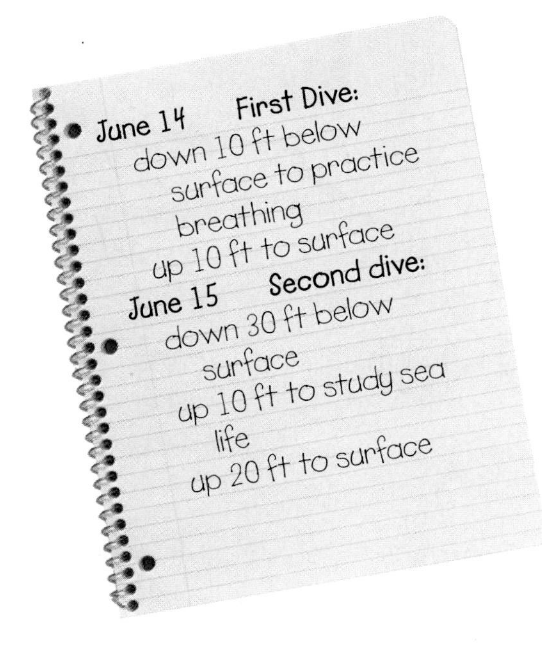

June 14 First Dive:
down 10 ft below surface to practice breathing
up 10 ft to surface
June 15 Second dive:
down 30 ft below surface
up 10 ft to study sea life
up 20 ft to surface

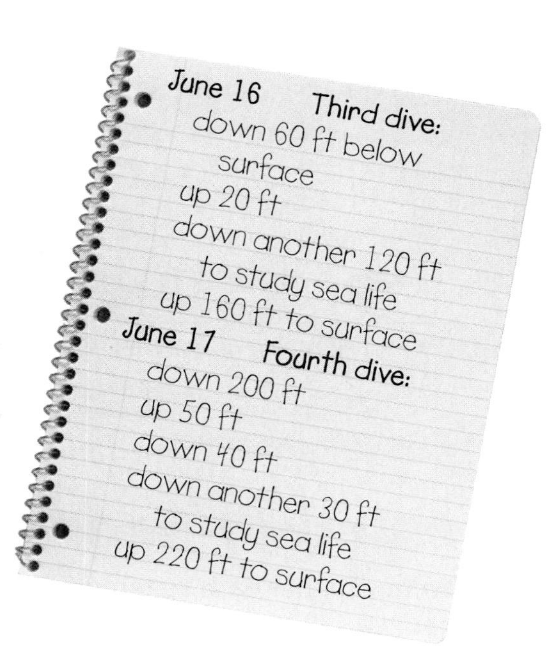

June 16 Third dive:
down 60 ft below surface
up 20 ft
down another 120 ft to study sea life
up 160 ft to surface
June 17 Fourth dive:
down 200 ft
up 50 ft
down 40 ft
down another 30 ft to study sea life
up 220 ft to surface

Plan your fifth dive so that the total depth of all dives equals –790 ft.

Work Together

▶ Understand

1. What are you asked to do?
2. What information is given in the journal about the first four dives?
3. What information do you have to help you plan the fifth dive?

▶ Plan and Solve

4. What is the total depth already dived?
5. How might estimation help you plan your fifth dive?
6. Will you need to go to a depth and then come up some feet and then go down again? Explain.

▶ Make a Decision

7. List the first four dives, using +/− signs to indicate the feet dived and surfaced.
8. Write a description of your fifth dive. Use the journal format shown on the previous page.

▶ Present Your Decision

9. Present your journal to your class. Use the overhead or the chalkboard to show how your dives total 790 ft.

PROBLEM SOLVING PRACTICE

SECTION A

Review and Practice

(Lesson 1) Order from greatest to least.

1. $-3, -5, 0, 2, 1, -1$
2. $-10, 11, 12, 0, -1, -13$
3. $100, -99, 99, -100, 101, -1, 77$

Write each number as an integer.

4. Kelly owes John 5 dollars.
5. Helen gained 6 pounds.
6. The mountain is 2,555 ft above sea level.
7. The canyon trail descended 534 ft.
8. Keiko dove 50 ft below the surface of the water.
9. Whenever Jill buys new books, she sells back old ones. For each book returned, Jill gets a $2 refund. She pays $3 for every book she buys. How many books could Jill have bought if her bill was $4 after the refund?
10. On the second day of her descent, a mountain climber started at 12,500 ft above sea level. By the end of the day, she had gone down 2,500 ft. How far above sea level was she at the end of the day?

(Lessons 2–4) Simplify.

11. -9×7
12. $25 \times (-4)$
13. $-6 - (-5)$
14. $12 + (-3)$
15. $16 \div (-4)$
16. $-7 + 2$
17. $-2 - (-4)$
18. $-2 \times (-1)$
19. $45 \div (-5)$
20. $-32 \div (-2)$
21. $7 \times (-6)$
22. $7 - (-6)$
23. $-7 + 6$
24. $-7 - (-6)$
25. $-16 \div 8$
26. $8 \times (-5)$
27. $40 \div (-5)$
28. $-6 \times (-4)$
29. $24 \div (-4)$
30. $23 \div (-1)$

For **31–33,** solve each problem, state the operation you used, and explain your answer.

31. Ryan spent $12 to go to a baseball game. He earned $8 the next day. What was the overall change in money for the two days?
32. On 4 plays, the Cardinals lost 10 yd. If they gained 2 yd on the first play, how many did they gain or lose on the other 3 plays?
33. In 3 hours, the temperature dropped steadily from 0°C to -12°C. How much did the temperature drop in one hour?

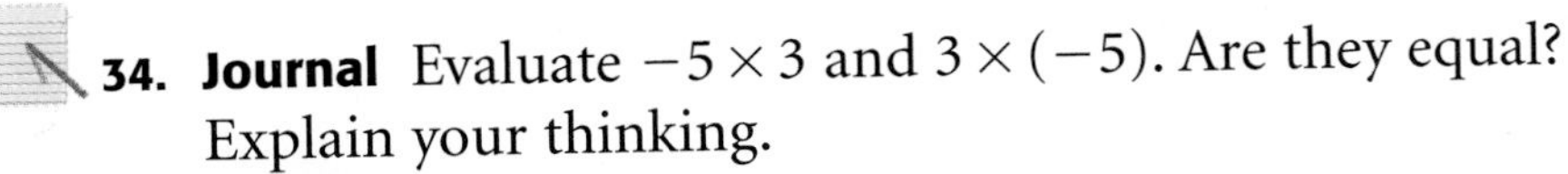

34. **Journal** Evaluate -5×3 and $3 \times (-5)$. Are they equal? Explain your thinking.

Skills Checklist

In this section, you have:

- ☑ **Explored Integers**
- ☑ **Added Integers**
- ☑ **Subtracted Integers**
- ☑ **Multiplied and Divided Integers**

CHAPTER 9

SECTION

B Graphing on the Coordinate Plane

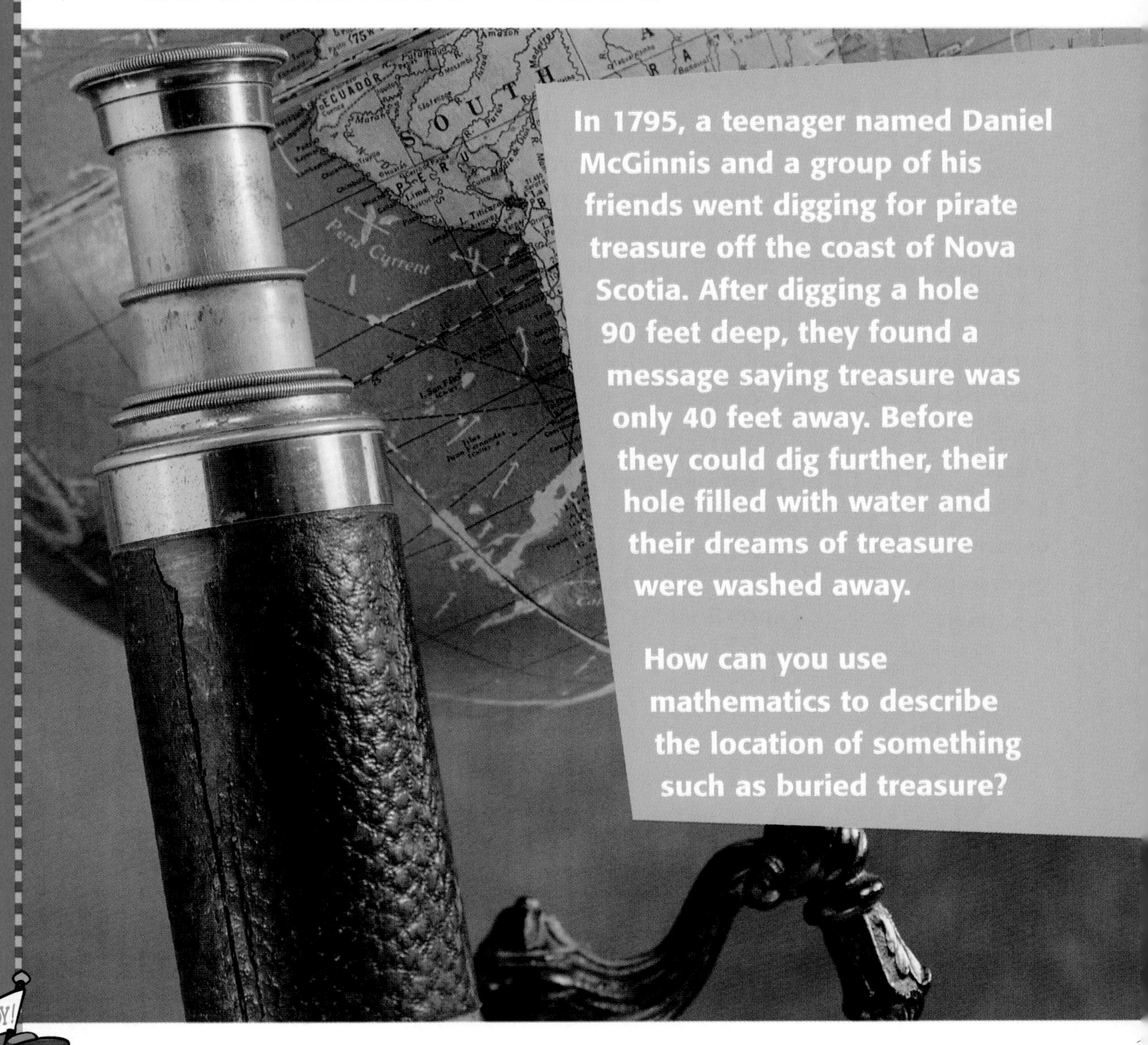

In 1795, a teenager named Daniel McGinnis and a group of his friends went digging for pirate treasure off the coast of Nova Scotia. After digging a hole 90 feet deep, they found a message saying treasure was only 40 feet away. Before they could dig further, their hole filled with water and their dreams of treasure were washed away.

How can you use mathematics to describe the location of something such as buried treasure?

GET READY!

Graphing

Review number lines. Identify each point on the number line shown.

1. Point A
2. Point B
3. Point C
4. Write an expression to show the move from Point D to Point E.

Skills Checklist

In this section, you will:

- ❒ Learn About the Coordinate Plane
- ❒ Graph Slides and Flips
- ❒ Graph Equations

Chapter 9
Lesson
5

The Coordinate Plane

You Will Learn
- to plot points on a coordinate plane
- to read the coordinates of points on a coordinate plane

Materials
graph paper or coordinate grids

Vocabulary
coordinate plane
***x*-axis**
***y*-axis**
origin
quadrant
ordered pair
coordinate

Learn

Forest rangers use the **coordinate plane** to map locations of forest fires.

You can use a coordinate plane to locate points. The ***x*-axis** and the ***y*-axis** are number lines. They intersect at right angles at their zero points, the **origin**. The two axes divide the plane into 4 **quadrants**, numbered I, II, III, and IV.

Any point can be located using an **ordered pair**. The first **coordinate** tells you how far to move on the *x*-axis from the origin. The second coordinate tells you how far to move on the *y*-axis from the origin.

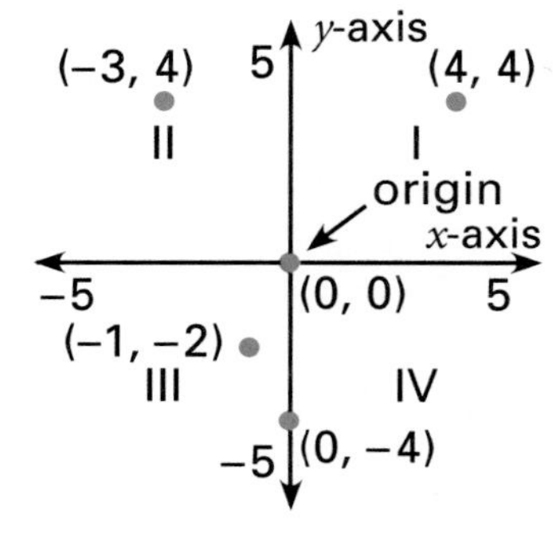

Math Tip
You can remember that the second coordinate in an ordered pair is the *y*-coordinate by remembering that, in the alphabet, *y* comes after *x*.

Example 1

Give the coordinates of the points.

Starting at the origin, go right (+) or left (−) along the *x*-axis until you're above or below the point. Then, go up (+) or down (−) along the *y*-axis to the point.

Coordinates: *A* (4, 1), *B* (1, 4), *C* (−3, −5), *D* (0, −2), *E* (−3, 0), *F* (2, −4), *G* $(3\frac{1}{2}, 4\frac{1}{2})$

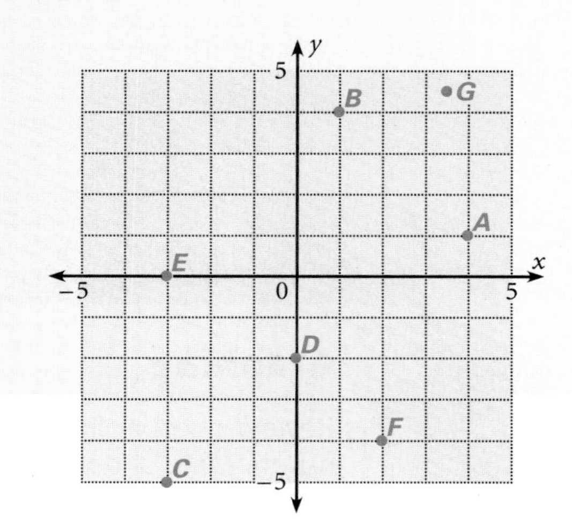

When given a coordinate, you can find its place on the coordinate plane.

Example 2

On the map, plot the points $M(-2, 5)$ and $N(3, -3)$.

For M, start at the origin. Go left (−) 2 units. Go up (+) 5 units. Mark the point.

For N, start at the origin. Go right (+) 3 units. Go down (−) 3 units. Mark the point.

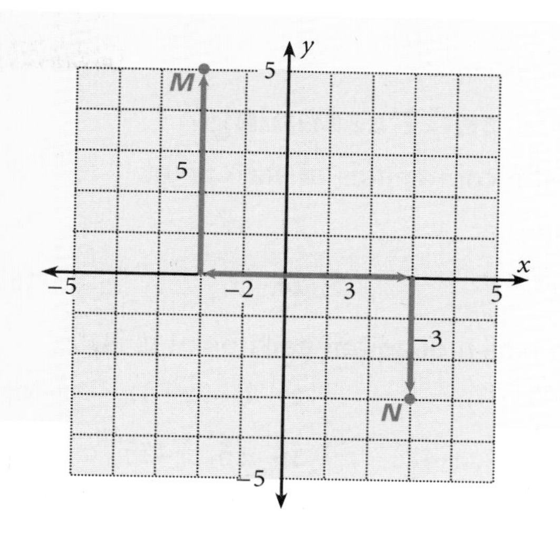

Talk About It

1. How can you use the signs of the coordinates of a point to predict which quadrant the point is in?
2. Why do you need two coordinates to locate a point in the plane?
3. Are the points (2, 3) and (3, 2) the same? Explain.

Check

Give the coordinates of each point.

1. A 2. B
3. C 4. D
5. E 6. F
7. G 8. Origin

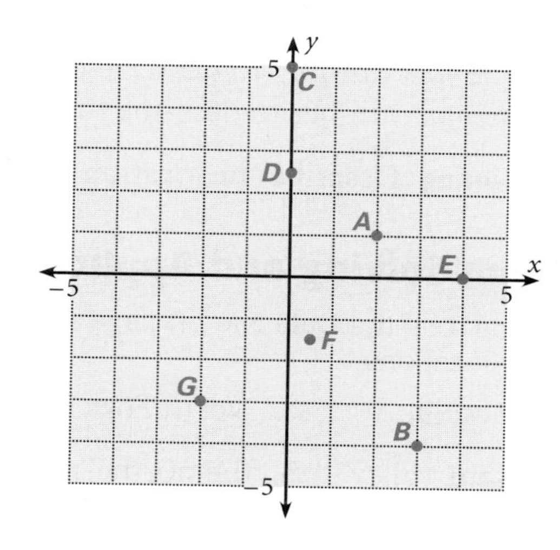

Plot and label each point on graph paper.

9. $H(-2, 2)$ 10. $I(5, 3)$ 11. $J(4, -3)$
12. $K(0, 1)$ 13. $L(-1, -5)$ 14. $M(5, 0)$
15. $N(-3.5, 4)$ 16. $O(2.5, 1.5)$ 17. $P(3, -3)$
18. **Reasoning** If a point lies in Quadrant IV, what are the signs on the x and y coordinates?
19. **Reasoning** Why is the order of the numbers in a coordinate pair important?

Practice

Skills and Reasoning

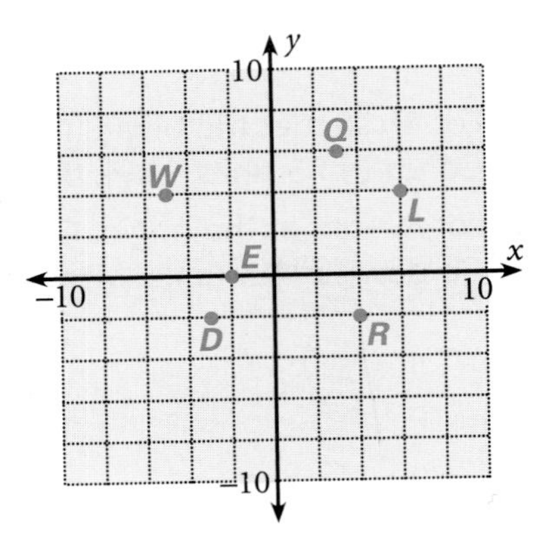

Give the coordinates of each point.

20. Q **21.** W **22.** E

23. D **24.** R **25.** L

State which quadrant each point is in.

26. $(4, 10)$ **27.** $(-7, 18)$ **28.** $(32, -18)$

29. $(-52, -48)$ **30.** $(6, -45)$ **31.** $(-13, 17)$

Plot and label each point.

32. $M(4, 6)$ **33.** $R(0, 6)$ **34.** $K(3, 0)$ **35.** $N(-3, 7)$

36. $T(2, -5)$ **37.** $S(-4, -5)$ **38.** $J(0, -2)$ **39.** $Q(-6, -2)$

40. $P(0, 0)$ **41.** $H(5, 4)$ **42.** $V(6, -6)$ **43.** $L(-8, 2)$

Describe how to locate each point.

44. $(-35, -18)$ **45.** $(0, -3)$ **46.** $(4, 10)$

47. $(-52, 63)$ **48.** $(88, -23)$ **49.** $(-19, 0)$

50. Reasoning When plotting an ordered pair, why is it important to always use the *first* number to describe the left/right location of the point and the *second* number to describe the up/down location of the point?

51. Reasoning Describe the location of the point $(x, 0)$.

Problem Solving and Applications

Using Data Use the Data File on page 459 to give the coordinates of the following locations.

52. Haynesville **53.** North Fork Buffalo Creek Reservoir

54. Pleasant Valley **55.** the northernmost point of Red River

56. Critical Thinking Use the map and directions given to find the coordinates of the Smallville School. The school and the marketplace have the same y-coordinate. The x-coordinate of the school is twice the difference between the y-coordinate of the marketplace and the y-coordinate of the gas station.

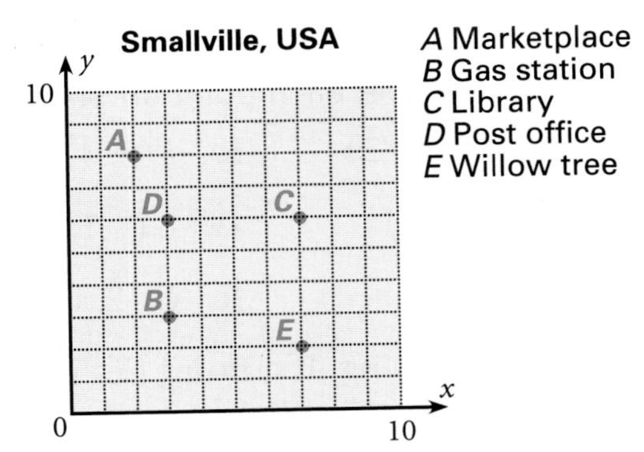

57. Geometry Plot these points: $(4, 3)$, $(-2, 3)$, $(6, -2)$, and $(-4, -2)$.

a. Connect the points to form a quadrilateral.

b. Classify the quadrilateral in as many ways as possible.

Problem Solving and RECREATION

Battleship is a game that requires the use of ordered pairs. Imagine you are locating buried treasure rather than ships and submarines.

You have a map to the 9 treasures of Apple Island. You're at the apple tree in the middle of the island.

58. Give the coordinates of each buried item.

a. treasure chest
b. bag of gold
c. necklace
d. telescope
e. gold coins
f. vase
g. white diamond
h. red ruby
i. crown

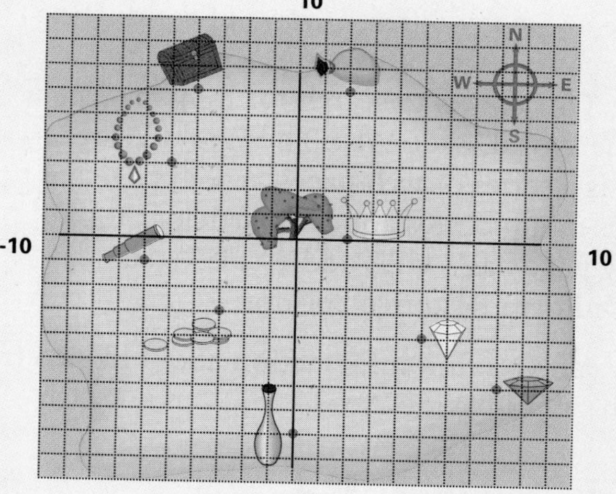

59. Draw your own map of buried treasure. Choose three items to bury and plot their positions on the map. Play a game with a partner. Take turns giving each other clues for finding your buried treasure. Clues could describe the quadrant in which the treasure lies, the sign on one of the coordinates, or anything that describes the ordered pairs of the location of the treasure. After giving a clue, have your partner guess the location of the treasure. Continue until each player has found the three buried items.

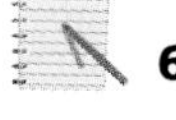

60. Journal What are the signs of each of the coordinates of any point in the first quadrant? The second quadrant? The third quadrant? The fourth quadrant? Explain.

Mixed Review and Test Prep

State whether the given lengths can form a triangle.

61. 7 m, 8 m, 14 m **62.** 12 cm, 12 cm, 36 cm **63.** 3 yd, 4 yd, 5 yd

64. Which of the following shows an obtuse angle?

Technology

Using Browser Software to Research on the World Wide Web

There are many different ways of conducting research to learn more about a particular topic. One way is to search for information on the World Wide Web. The World Wide Web is a series of web pages. A web page has words and pictures about a particular topic. Every page has a URL address. URL stands for Uniform Resource Locator.

Materials

Computer with access to the World Wide Web

How can you find information about buried treasure on the World Wide Web?

Work Together

Use your browser software to research on the World Wide Web.

1. If you know the URL address for a page you want to visit, you can type it into your browser and press the return key. The software will try to connect you to that page. Sometimes, a page cannot be reached because the computer connected to that page isn't working, or the page no longer exists.

2 You can also use a *search engine* to find pages on a particular topic. The search engine will ask you for a key word or groups of words related to your topic. For instance, if you were looking for information about buried treasure, you might type in the key word *treasure.* Your browser will list descriptions of the pages related to the key word. You can click on a description to go to that page.

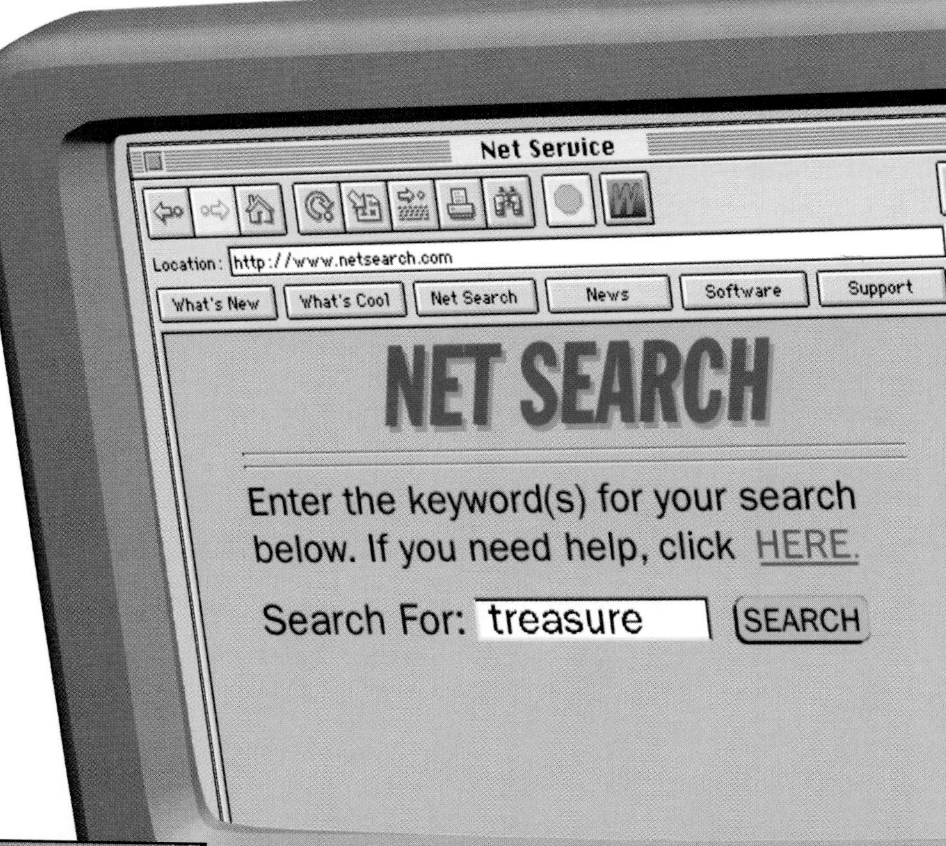

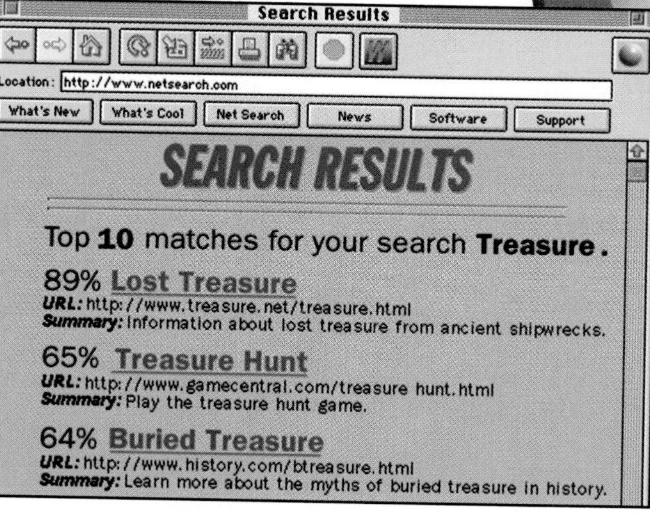

3 Many pages have *links* to other pages with related information. A link often appears as an underlined word or phrase, and it is usually in a different color. You can go to these other pages by clicking on the link.

Exercises

1. Try to find information about one of the following topics: pirates, explorers, archaeology, Antarctica.
2. Use the World Wide Web to research a topic of your own choice.

Extensions

3. What do you think are some of the benefits of researching on the World Wide Web?

Graphing Slides and Flips

You Will Learn

- to graph translations and reflections on the coordinate plane

Materials

graph paper or coordinate grids

Learn

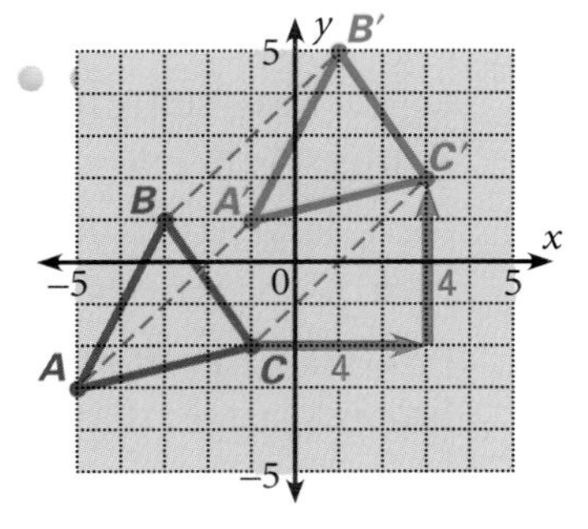

A *translation* slides a figure to a new position without rotating the figure. You can graph translations on a coordinate grid. To translate $\triangle ABC$, move each vertex right 4 units and up 4 units. The new triangle is $\triangle A'B'C'$, read as "triangle A prime B prime C prime."

Example 1

Create $\triangle A'B'C'$ by translating $\triangle ABC$ 5 units left and 3 units up. Give the coordinates of A', B', and C'. Describe any patterns you find.

$\triangle ABC$ has coordinates A (0, −2), B (3, −3), and C (4, −1).

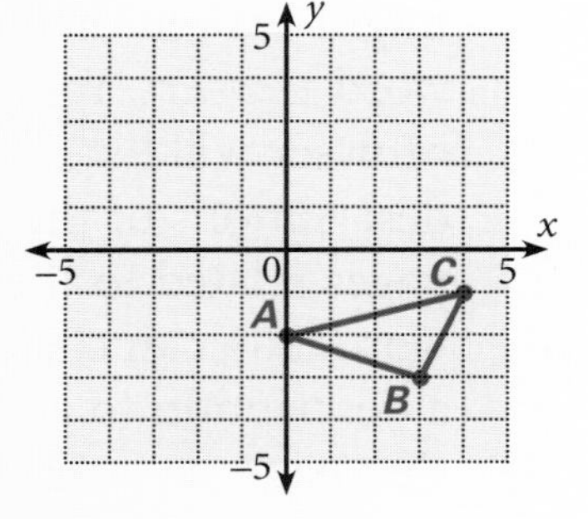

left 5 ↓ up 3 ↓

$A\ (0, -2) \longrightarrow A'\ (0 - 5, -2 + 3) = A'\ (-5, 1)$

$B\ (3, -3) \longrightarrow B'\ (3 - 5, -3 + 3) = B'\ (-2, 0)$

$C\ (4, -1) \longrightarrow C'\ (4 - 5, -1 + 3) = C'\ (-1, 2)$

$\triangle A'B'C'$ has coordinates A' (−5, 1), B' (−2, 0), and C' (−1, 2).

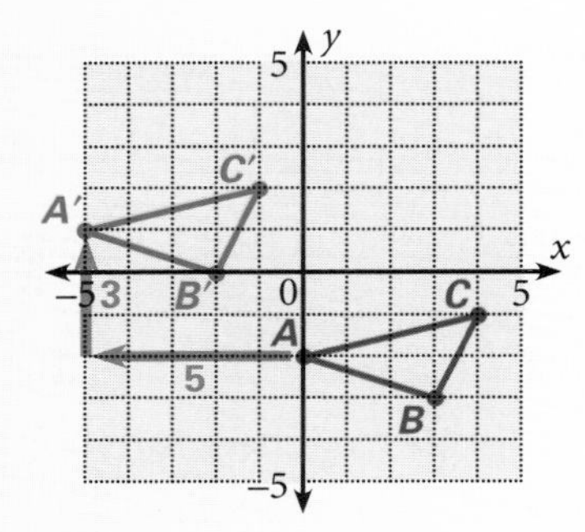

Notice that in Example 1, the x-coordinates of $\triangle A'B'C'$ are 5 *less than* the x-coordinates of $\triangle ABC$. That's because $\triangle ABC$ was translated 5 units *left* (−).

The y-coordinates of $\triangle A'B'C'$ are 3 *more than* the y-coordinates of $\triangle ABC$. That's because $\triangle ABC$ was translated 3 units *up* (+).

A *reflection* "flips" a shape over a line of symmetry. $\triangle A$ in the figure has been reflected across the y-axis to give $\triangle B$. The y-axis is the line of symmetry. $\triangle A$ and $\triangle B$ are reflections of each other.

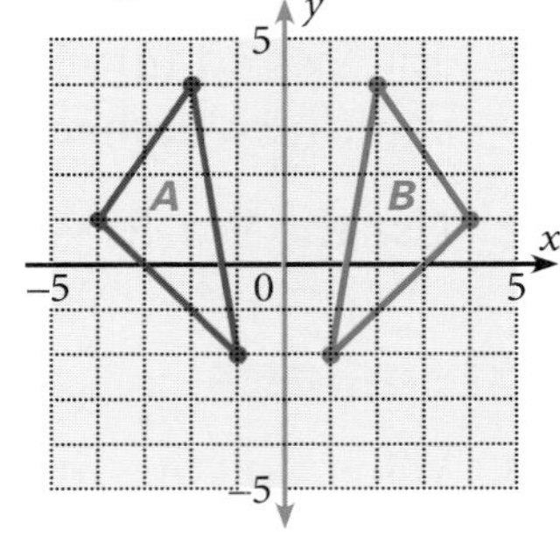

Example 2

Create $\triangle R'S'T'$ by reflecting $\triangle RST$ across the x-axis. Give the coordinates of R', S', and T'. Describe any patterns you find.

$\triangle RST$ has coordinates $R\ (-3, 1)$, $S\ (-1, 4)$, and $T\ (3, 2)$.

$\triangle R'S'T'$ has coordinates $R'(-3, -1)$, $S'\ (-1, -4)$, and $T'(3, -2)$.

Notice that the x-coordinates of $\triangle RST$ are the same as the x-coordinates of $\triangle R'S'T'$. That's because a reflection across the x-axis does not move the triangle left or right.

Reflections across the x-axis change each y-coordinate into its *opposite.*

$R\ (-3, \mathbf{1}) \longrightarrow R'(-3, \mathbf{-1})$

opposite

$S\ (-1, \mathbf{4}) \longrightarrow S'\ (-1, \mathbf{-4})$

opposite

$T\ (3, \mathbf{2}) \longrightarrow T'\ (3, \mathbf{-2})$

opposite

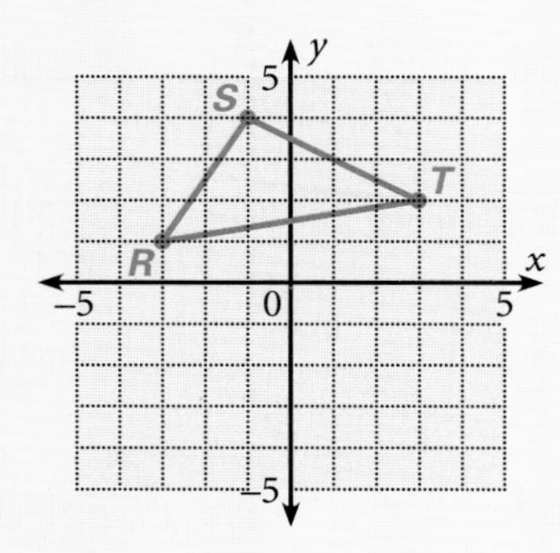

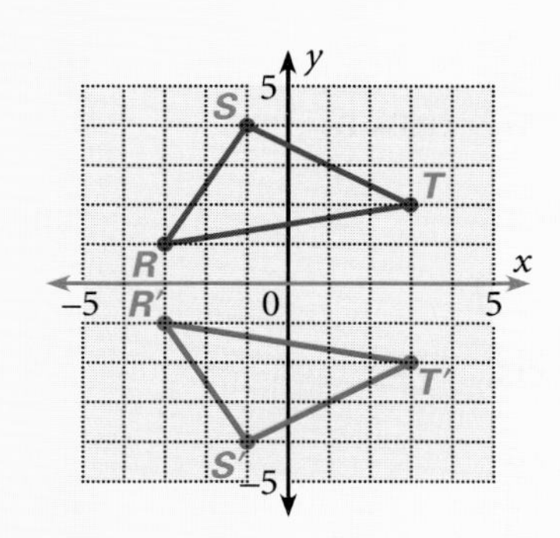

Talk About It

1. How are the coordinates of a point changed if the point is translated up or down?
2. How are the coordinates of a point changed if the point is translated right or left?
3. How are the coordinates of a point changed if the point is reflected across the x-axis?
4. How are the coordinates of a point changed if the point is reflected across the y-axis?

Check

Plot the image of $\triangle LMN$.

1. Translate 6 units right and 4 units down.
2. Reflect $\triangle LMN$ over the y-axis.

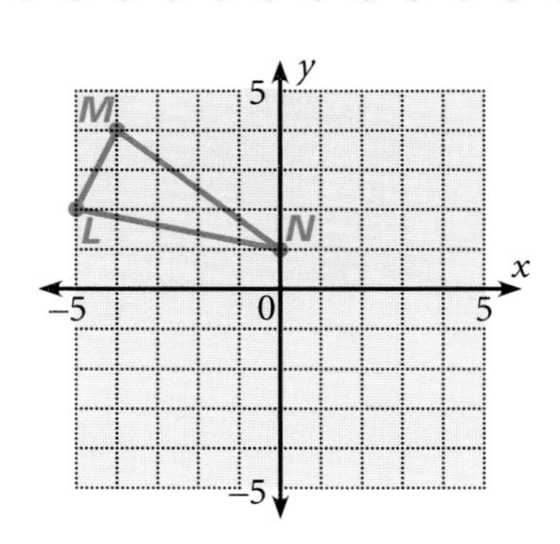

Practice

Skills and Reasoning

For **3–8,** use the point $P(2, 3)$ to plot and label P'.

3. Slide P to the right 3 units.

4. Reflect P across the y-axis.

5. Slide P 1 unit right and 2 units up.

6. Slide P to the left 2 units and down 3 units.

7. Slide P 2 units down and 1 unit up.

8. Slide P 3 units right and 3 units left.

For **9–12,** plot the image of quadrilateral $G'H'I'J'$.

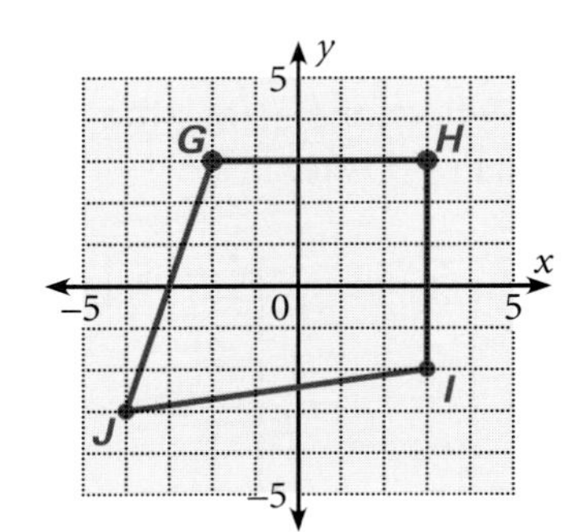

9. Translate $GHIJ$ 3 units up, 4 units right.

10. Slide $GHIJ$ 2 units left, 5 units up.

11. Slide $GHIJ$ 2 units right, 3 units down.

12. Translate $GHIJ$ 5 units down.

For **13–16,** refer to the graph of $\triangle RST$.

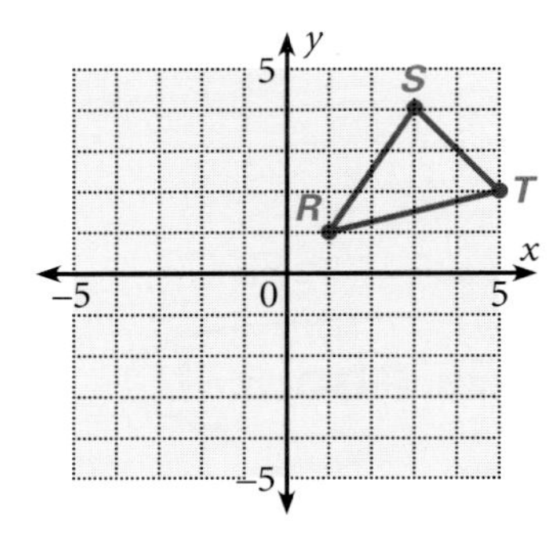

13. Reflect $\triangle RST$ across the x-axis.

14. Reflect $\triangle RST$ across the y-axis.

15. Plot a point at $(3, -1)$. Label it V. Reflect $\triangle RVT$ across the y-axis.

16. Plot a point at $(-3, 3)$. Label it W. Reflect $\triangle RWS$ across the x-axis.

17. Reasoning Can a reflection of a figure and a translation of the same figure be the same shape and have the same coordinates on a coordinate grid? Explain.

18. Reasoning If the coordinates of the vertices of a figure are integers, will the translation or reflection always have integers as coordinates of the vertices?

Problem Solving and Applications

19. Geometry $\triangle RST$ has vertices at $R(-1, 1)$, $S(1, 3)$, and $T(4, -1)$.

a. Draw the graph of $\triangle RST$.

b. Create $\triangle R'S'T'$ by translating $\triangle RST$ 3 units right and 2 units up.

c. State the coordinates of the vertices of $\triangle R'S'T'$.

20. One item that Cheryl had to find on a treasure hunt was located at the point (3, 4) on the map. When Cheryl got there, she realized she had the map upside down. How many units left, right, up, and down on the map should Cheryl walk to find the correct location?

21. Geometry $\triangle XYZ$ has vertices at $X(-4, 2)$, $Y(4, 3)$, and $Z(2, 1)$.

a. Draw the graph of $\triangle XYZ$.

b. Create $\triangle X'Y'Z'$ by reflecting $\triangle XYZ$ across the x-axis.

c. Give the coordinates of the vertices of $\triangle X'Y'Z'$.

22. Critical Thinking A polygon has vertices at $A(2, 5)$, $B(5, 5)$, $C(5, -1)$, and $D(2, -1)$. Reflect the polygon across the y-axis. Then translate the image 4 units to the right and 2 units down. Give the coordinates of the vertices of the new image. Explain your reasoning.

Mixed Review and Test Prep

STAY SHARP!

Solve.

23. $t \div \frac{2}{3} = \frac{9}{16}$ **24.** $\frac{1}{2}p = 2\frac{1}{5}$ **25.** $\frac{12}{15} \div j = \frac{4}{5}$ **26.** $\frac{8}{9}e = 1$

Name each polygon and tell if it is regular or irregular.

27. 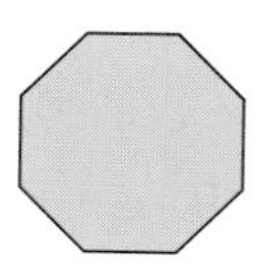

28. 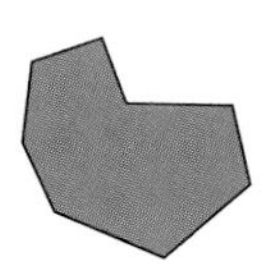

29. 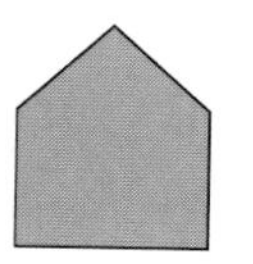

30. 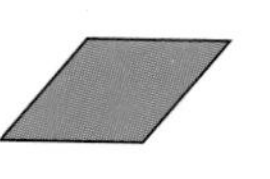

Estimate.

31. $6\frac{2}{3} + 5\frac{1}{4}$ **32.** $4\frac{2}{7} - 1\frac{3}{5}$ **33.** $9\frac{4}{5} \times 2\frac{3}{8}$ **34.** $16\frac{1}{4} \div 3\frac{7}{9}$

35. Morgan knows that a certain number is divisible by 24. What other numbers must also be able to divide the number evenly?

I. 2, 5, and 10 **II.** 2, 3, and 4 **III.** 6 and 8 **IV.** 1 and 12

Ⓐ I only Ⓑ II, III, and IV only Ⓒ all choices Ⓓ not here

Skills Practice Bank, page 668, Set 5

Chapter 9
Lesson
7

Graphing Equations

Problem Solving Connection
- Look for a Pattern

Materials
graph paper

Vocabulary
T-table

Explore

The algebraic equations you have seen so far have had one variable, as in $x + 3 = 7$. The coordinate plane uses two variables, x for the first coordinate and y for the second. You can use the coordinate plane to draw a picture of an equation.

Work Together

In 1705, the pirate ship *Silver Legend* sank in the Atlantic Ocean at the point $(-5, -9)$ on the map. Every year, the Gulf Stream current moves the ship 1 unit east and 2 units north.

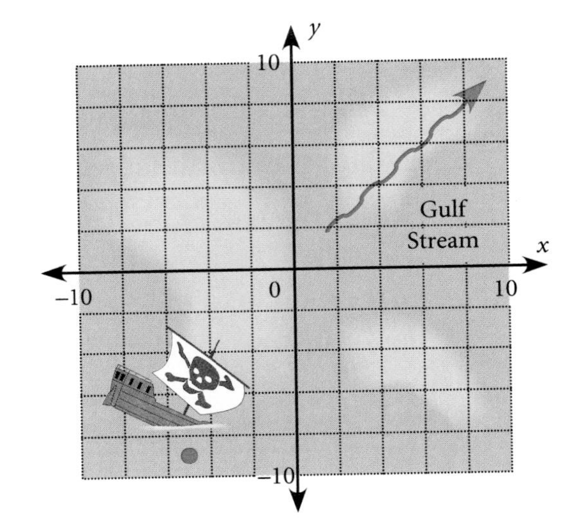

1. Draw a coordinate plane.
2. Mark where the ship sank.
3. Draw the ship's location one year later, two years later, and three years later.
4. Explain how you determined the location for each year.
5. Draw the ship's location $1\frac{1}{2}$ years after it sank.
6. Explain how you determined the ship's location at that time.
7. Draw a line indicating the path the ship will travel over the years.
8. Explain how you determined where this line should be.
9. The year 2005 is 300 years after the sinking. Estimate the coordinates of the ship's location in 2005. Explain how you could determine the exact coordinates of the ship's location in 2005.

Talk About It

10. Name the coordinates of the location four years after the ship sank.
11. How many years after the ship sank will the ship be found at $(5, 11)$?

Connect and Learn

To draw the graph of an equation:

1. Make a T-table like the one here. List three or four values for x. Choose easy numbers to work with, such as -1, 0 and 1.
2. For each value of x, use the equation to determine a value for y.
3. Plot the point for each pair of (x, y) values on a coordinate plane.
4. Draw a line connecting the points. This line represents all the other values you could have chosen for x, and the matching y values.

$y = x + 1$

x	y
−1	0
0	1
1	2
2	3

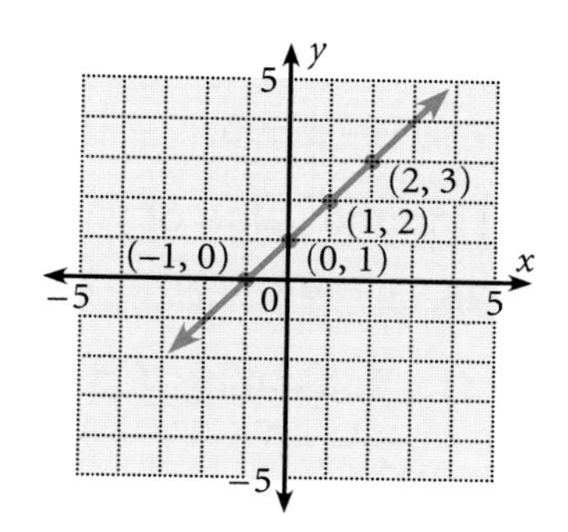

Example 1

Graph the equation $y = x - 4$.

$y = x - 4$

x	y
−1	−5
0	−4
1	−3
2	−2

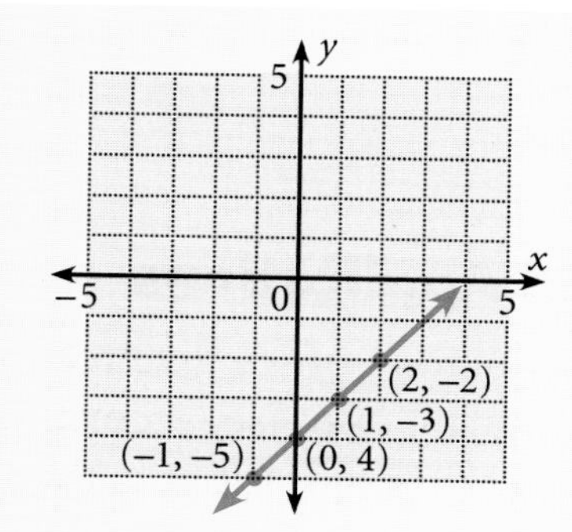

Example 2

Graph the equation $y = -2x$.

$y = -2x$.

x	y
−1	2
0	0
1	−2
2	−4

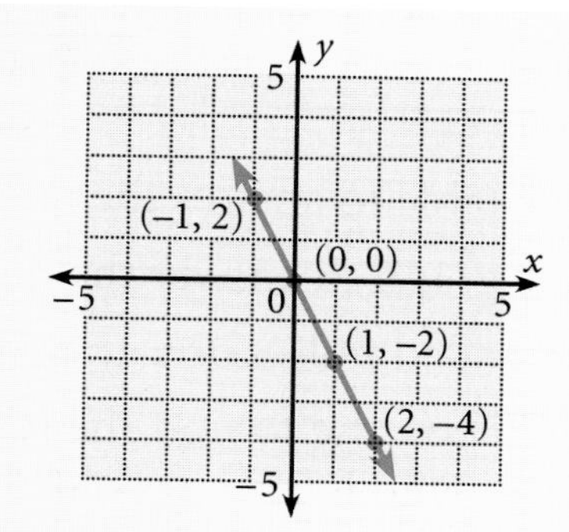

Check

Graph each equation.

1. $y = x + 5$ 2. $y = 2x$ 3. $y = 8 - x$ 4. $y = -14$
5. **Reasoning** Is the point (1, 3) on the graph of $y = x + 3$? Explain.

Practice

Skills and Reasoning

For **6–10,** make a T-table with five (x, y) pairs for each.

6. $y = x - 53$ **7.** $y = x + 27$ **8.** $y = x - 106$ **9.** $y = -50x$ **10.** $y = 12x$

Graph each equation.

11. $y = x + 1$ **12.** $y = 1 + x$ **13.** $y = -5x$ **14.** $y = 3x$ **15.** $y = 3 + x$

16. $y = x$ **17.** $y = -1x$ **18.** $y = x - 3$ **19.** $y = 2 + x$ **20.** $y = 2x$

21. $y = x + 6$ **22.** $y = -2x$ **23.** $y = x - 4$ **24.** $y = 0x$ **25.** $y = 9$

Find the value of y when $x = 4$.

26. $y = 47 - x$ **27.** $y = 1 - x$ **28.** $y = -3 - x$ **29.** $y = x + 33$ **30.** $y = -2$

31. Reasoning Complete the T-table.

$y = -3x + 7$

x	y
0	■
−1	■
■	19
■	−2

32. Reasoning Describe how you found the x values in Exercise 31.

Problem Solving and Applications

33. A table and graph in a doctor's office give recommended maximum pulse rates during exercise, according to age. Susana and Larry are 15 years old. What is their recommended pulse rate?

Age (years)	10	20	30	40	50
Rates (beats/min)	152	144	136	128	120

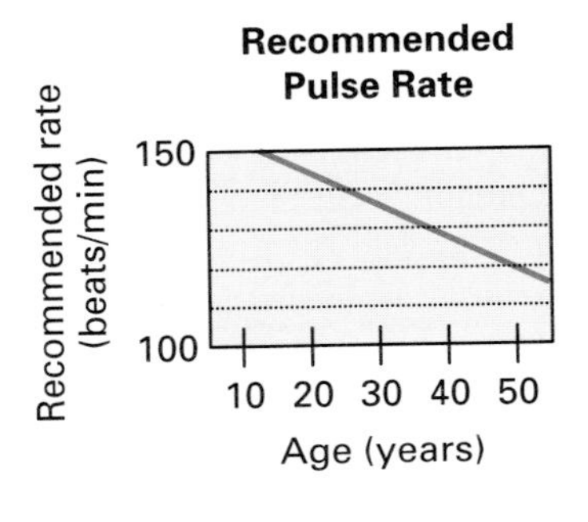

a. How can you use the table to answer the question?

b. How can you use the graph to answer the question?

c. What is the recommended pulse for a 15-year-old?

d. Which method would you use to find the recommended pulse rate for a person who is 32 years old? Explain.

34. Critical Thinking Graph the equations $y = x + 3$ and $y = x + (-3)$ on the same coordinate plane. Describe the relationship between the lines.

35. The equation that models the ship's movement in the Explore activity is $y = 2x + 1$. Add 5 to the x value to determine the number of years since the ship sank. Copy and complete the table.

Years Since Ship Sank	Position	
	x	y
5	0	■
15	■	21
■	−2	−3
■	25	■

36. Critical Thinking Shelley earns money bathing dogs. This month, her expenses were only $12. She collected x dollars from her customers.

a. Write an equation for Shelley's profit. Use y for the money she made and x for the money she collected from her customers.

b. Graph the equation.

c. Using the graph, how could you predict what Shelley's profit would be if she collected $25 from her customers?

d. Using the equation, how could you predict what Shelley's profit would be if she collected $25 from her customers?

37. Critical Thinking Graph the equations $y = 3x$ and $y = 5x$. Which line is steeper? Explain why you think this happens.

38. Journal Explain how you can determine from an equation if the line will pass through the origin.

Mixed Review and Text Prep

STAY SHARP!

Convert.

39. 72 feet = ▒ inches **40.** 94 inches = ▒ feet **41.** 3 feet = ▒ inches

42. 52 inches = ▒ feet **43.** 0.75 feet = ▒ inches **44.** 0.5 feet = ▒ inches

Draw an example of each.

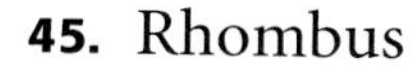

45. Rhombus **46.** Parallelogram **47.** Trapezoid **48.** Square

Classify each figure in as many ways as possible.

49.

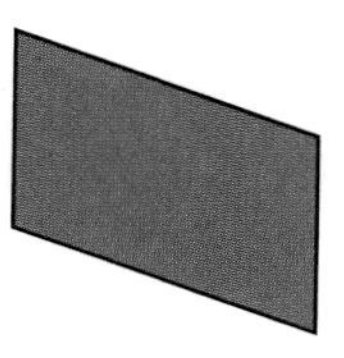

50.

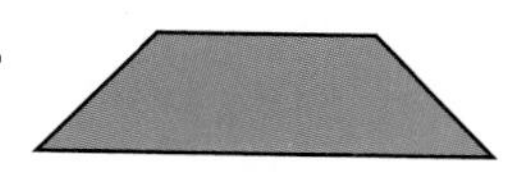

51.

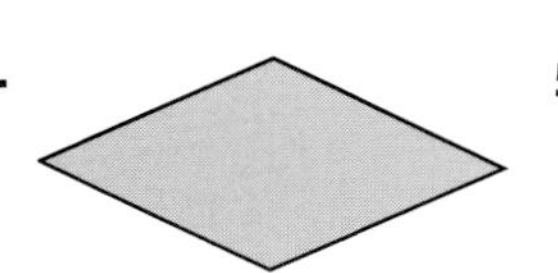

52.

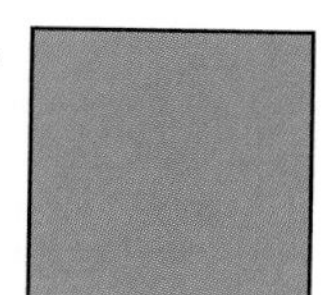

53. Choose the graph that shows $\overrightarrow{KL}$ translated 3 units right and 1 unit down.

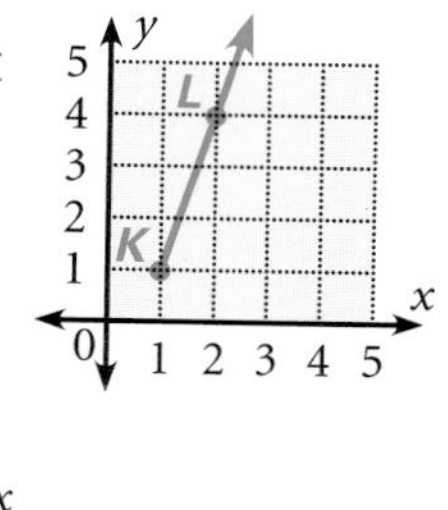

Ⓐ

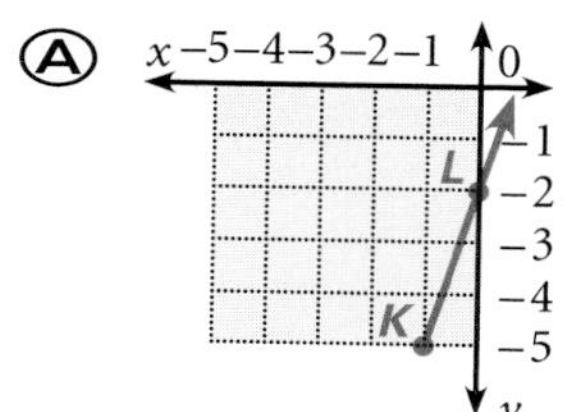

Ⓑ

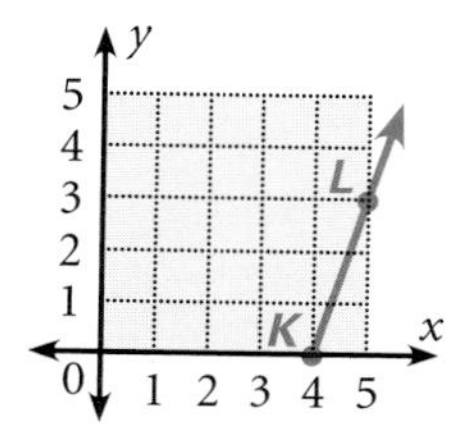

Ⓒ

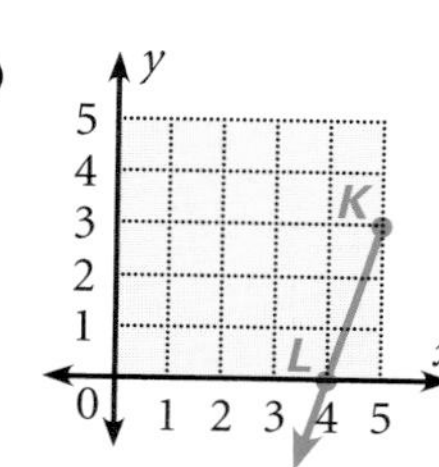

The Hide and Seek Game

Players
2 players

Materials
graph paper
book or other object to serve as a screen

Object
The object of the game is to graph the opponent's "hidden" triangle.

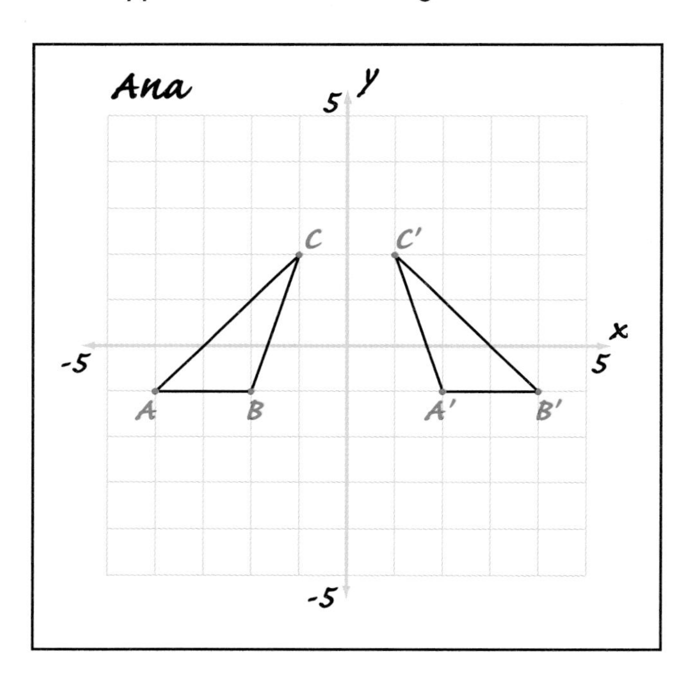

How to Play

1. Each player creates a coordinate plane on graph paper. Each player also draws a triangle on the coordinate plane, labeling the vertices *A*, *B*, *C*, and writing the coordinates at the bottom of the paper. On another sheet of graph paper, each player makes a copy of the coordinate plane and triangle.
2. Players give each other their copies of the coordinate plane and triangle.
3. Players set up a screen between each other using a book or other object. Players then "hide" their triangles by making a translation or reflection of their triangles on their own copy of the coordinate plane and labeling the vertices *A*′, *B*′, *C*′.
4. Players take turns guessing the coordinates of each vertex of the opponent's hidden triangle. Opponents respond to guesses by stating "yes" or "no." Players can keep track of their guesses by marking the coordinates on their sheets.
5. The first player who guesses all three vertex coordinates of the opponent's hidden triangle wins.

Talk About It

1. How did you decide where to hide your triangle?

2. How did you choose which coordinates to guess when looking for your opponent's hidden triangle?

More Ways to Play

- Make a quadrilateral instead of a triangle.
- Hide the original triangle and have your opponent try to find the original triangle and its translation or reflection.
- Hide your triangle by making a translation **and** a reflection.

Reasoning

1. Suppose you have found the coordinates for two of your opponent's hidden vertices.

$\triangle ABC$:	A (3, 1)
	B (3, 4)
	C (0, 1)
$\triangle A'B'C'$:	Vertex (3, –1)
	Vertex (3, –4)

   What might your next guess be? Explain.

2. Suppose your guess shows that the hidden triangle in the above example is not a reflection. What other guess might you make?

SECTION B

Review and Practice

Vocabulary Copy and complete each sentence with the best term.

1. A coordinate plane is divided into 4 ________.
2. A coordinate plane is divided by 2 axes, the ________ and the ________.
3. The axes intersect at their zero points, the ________.
4. Any point on a coordinate plane can be located by using an ________ made up of two ________.

(Lessons 5 and 6) For **5–9,** use the coordinate grid.

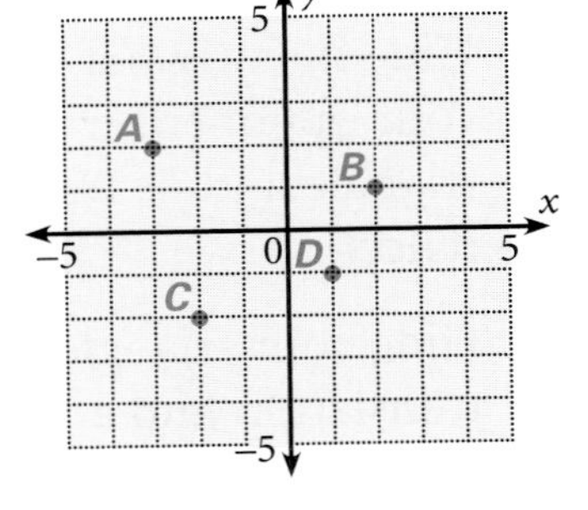

5. What are the coordinates of each point?
6. If Point A were translated left 1 space and up 3 spaces, what would be the coordinates of A'?
7. If Point B were reflected across the y-axis, what would be the coordinates of B'?
8. If Point C were reflected across the y-axis and translated 3 points to the right and 2 points down, what would be the coordinates of its image?
9. If Point D were translated 3 spaces to the right and 5 spaces up, what would be the coordinates of its image?
10. Brooke learns that on a coordinate plane, numbers above the x-axis and numbers to the right of the y-axis are always positive.

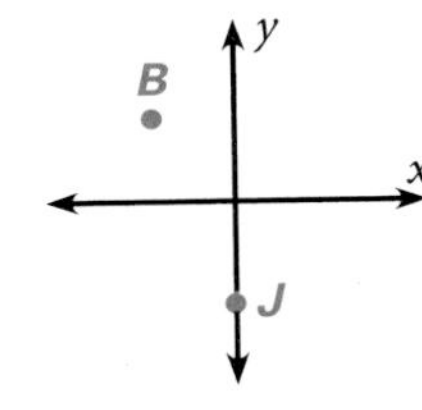

a. What would be a possible ordered pair for point B?

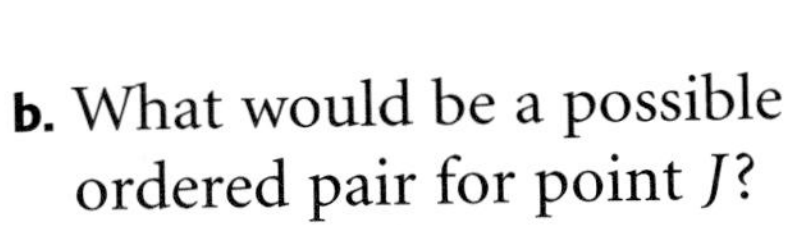

b. What would be a possible ordered pair for point J?

(Lesson 7) Graph each equation.

11. $y = 2x$
12. $y = 6 + x$
13. $y = x - 2$
14. $y = x + (-2)$
15. $y = 7$
16. $y = x - 1$
17. Jason graphed the equation $y = 3 + x$. He then graphed the equation $y = 2x$ on the same coordinate plane. He said that the two lines were parallel. Is he correct? Explain.

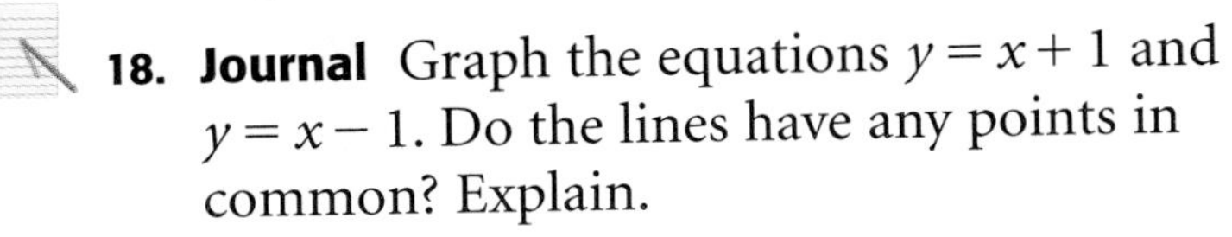

18. **Journal** Graph the equations $y = x + 1$ and $y = x - 1$. Do the lines have any points in common? Explain.

Skills Checklist

In this section, you have:

- ☑ **Learned About the Coordinate Plane**
- ☑ **Graphed Slides and Flips**
- ☑ **Graphed Equations**

REVIEW AND PRACTICE

Choose at least one of the following. Use what you have learned in this chapter.

1 Ups and Downs

At Home Bar graphs can show negative as well as positive values.

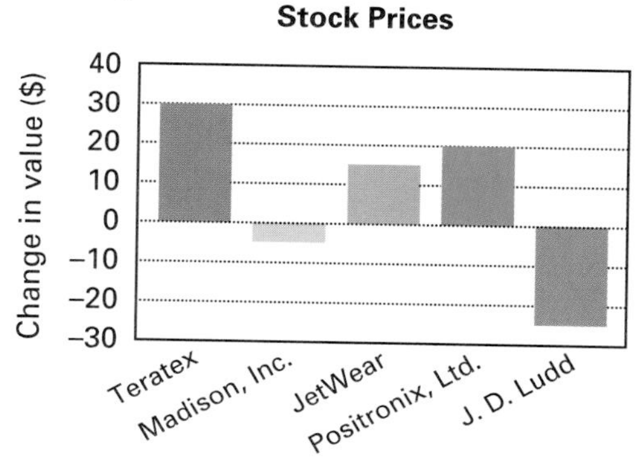

Read the weather page in your newspaper or search the World Wide Web and find the temperatures for five cities on the same day. At least two must be positive, and at least two must be negative. Graph the five temperatures on a bar graph.

2 The Powers of Negative Numbers

Make a table that shows the values of 2^2, 2^3, 2^4, $\ldots$ 2^{10}. In another table, show the values for $(-2)^2$, $(-2)^3$, $(-2)^4$, $\ldots$ $(-2)^{10}$. Describe any patterns you see.

3 Decimal Delights

An ice cream store specializes in making very long sundaes for large groups. A plain, 1-scoop sundae with chocolate topping costs \$1.40. Each additional scoop costs an additional \$1.40. Write an equation that represents the situation and graph it. How much would a 25-scoop sundae cost? A 40-scoop sundae?

4 Point Me in the Right Direction

Graph the points (4, 3) and (4, −2) on a coordinate grid. Then state the coordinates of two points which could be connected to (4, 3) and (4, −2) to form each figure.

a. Trapezoid

b. Nonrectangular parallelogram

c. Rectangle

d. Quadrilateral that cannot be classified as a trapezoid or a parallelogram.

CHAPTER 9

Review/Test

Vocabulary Fill in each blank with the correct word.

Word List
coordinate
negative
quadrants
origin
T-table
opposite
y-axis

1. The sum of an integer and its ________ is zero.
2. Numbers less than 0 are called ________ numbers.
3. To draw a graph of an equation, start by making a ________.
4. The vertical axis in a coordinate plane is the ________.
5. The x- and y-axes of a coordinate grid divide a plane into four ________.
6. The point (0, 0) on a coordinate grid is called the ________.
7. The number –6 is the first ________ of the ordered pair $(-6, 7)$.

(Lesson 1) Order the integers from greatest to least.

8. $15, 25, -3, -45, 1$
9. $-65, 47, -47, 65$
10. $-1, 2, -3, 4, -5$
11. $-108, -55, -113, -199$

(Lessons 2–4) Simplify.

12. $-10 + 7$
13. $4 - (-6)$
14. $8 \times (-6)$
15. $-6 \div 6$
16. $-4 \times (-2)$
17. $-5 + 5$
18. $-5 - (-5)$
19. $-21 \div (-21)$

(Lessons 3 and 5) Solve.

20. It was 36°F at noon in Des Moines. Over the next 7 hours the temperature fell 48°. What integer would you use to represent the new temperature?
21. Kayla's class is on a scavenger hunt. The location of each of the hints is mapped out. Each student starts at the origin and has to go to the three different points for clues.

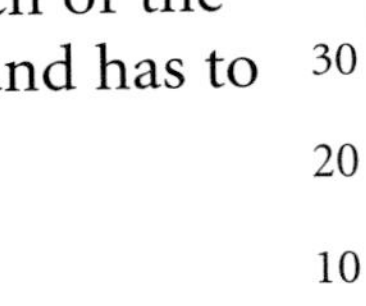

   a. What are the coordinates for hint #2?
   b. What are the coordinates for hint #1?
   c. What are the coordinates for hint #3?

(Lessons 5–7)

22. Create $\triangle D'E'F'$ by reflecting $\triangle DEF$ across the y-axis. Give the coordinates of D', E', and F'.

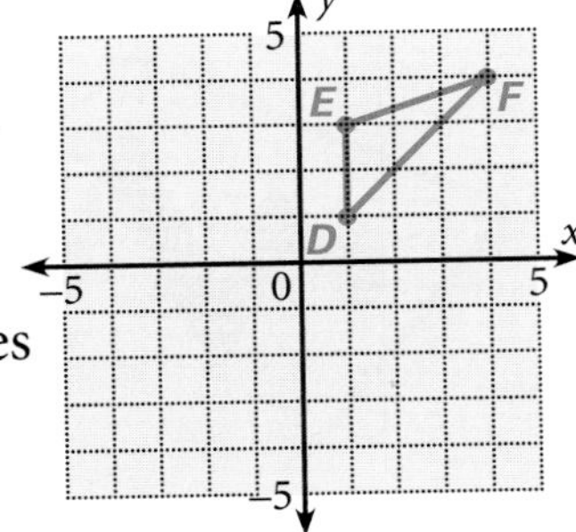

23. Translate $\triangle RST$ 3 units to the right and 4 units down. Give the coordinates of R', S', and T'.

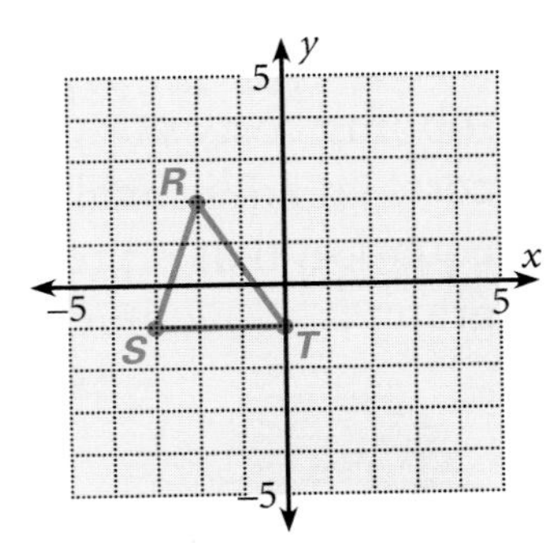

24. Use a T-table and graph the equation $y = -2x$.

CHAPTER 9

Performance Assessment

You are conducting a science experiment which involves cooling a gelatin liquid. You want to know whether using a cold water bath will cool the liquid more quickly than using an ice bath.

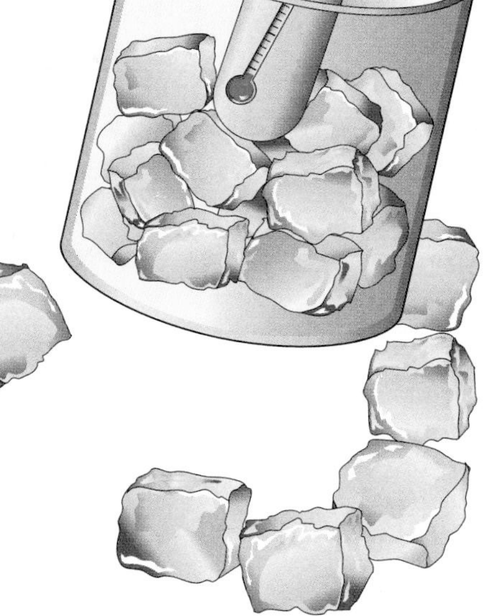

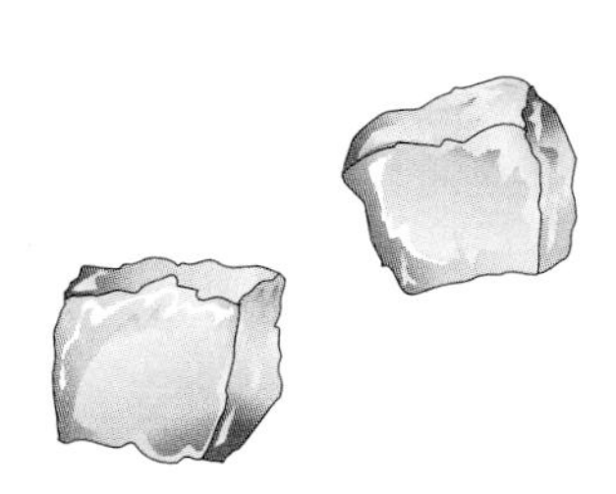

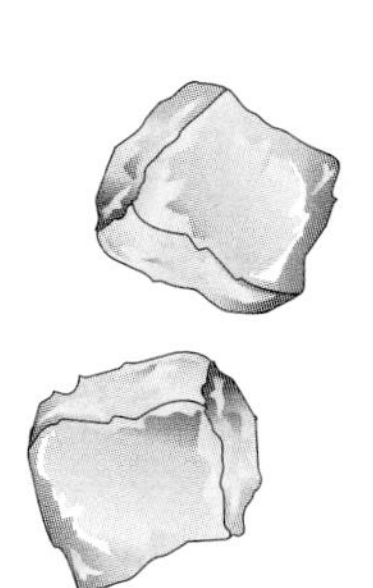

1. **Analyzing and Recording** You measure the temperature of the gelatin liquid and use cold water to decrease its temperature. You start a stopwatch as soon as you place the liquid into the water. The gelatin liquid is 24°C. You examine the liquid each time its temperature decreases by 3°C and record the time. Graph the data and connect the points to form a line.

Time	Temperature
0 min	24°C
5 min	21°C
10 min	18°C
15 min	15°C
20 min	12°C

2. **Analyzing** Describe patterns you see in the data. Then use the pattern to find the temperature of the liquid at the following times:

   25 min   35 min   50 min

3. **Problem Solving** You discover that the liquid becomes a gel at −6°C. How long will it take for the liquid to become a gel if the starting temperature is 30°C?

4. **Decision Making** Now you use ice to cool the liquid. You record the time each time the temperature drops 5°C. Graph the data and connect the points to form a line. Write about the relationship between the two lines.

Time	Temperature
0 min	24°C
5 min	19°C
10 min	14°C
15 min	9°C

5. **Critical Thinking** Find how long it will take for the liquid to cool to a gel using ice. What happens to the amount of time needed as the temperature decrease becomes greater? What happens to the amount of time needed as the temperature decrease becomes lesser? Explain.

Math Magazine

Dot's Moving the Other Way! You can write large numbers using scientific notation. A number in scientific notation is a number between 1 and 10 multiplied by a power of 10. The exponent of the 10 tells you how many places to move the decimal point to write the number in standard form.

A large number written in scientific notation has a positive exponent.

$2.4 \times 10^5 = 240{,}000$

10^5 means move the decimal point 5 places to the right.

To write a large number in scientific notation, write the non-zero part as a decimal number between 1 and 10 and a power of 10. The number of places the decimal moves to the right will be the positive exponent.

$37{,}000 = 3.7 \times 10^{\square}$

$37{,}000 = 3.7 \times 10^4$

A small number written in scientific notation has a negative exponent.

$2.4 \times 10^{-5} = 0.000024$

10^{-5} means move the decimal point 5 places to the left.

To write a small number in scientific notation, write the non-zero part as a decimal number between 1 and 10 and a power of 10. The number of places the decimal moves to the left will be the negative exponent.

$0.00037 = 3.7 \times 10^{\square}$

$0.00037 = 3.7 \times 10^{-4}$

Try These!

Write the following numbers in standard form.

1. 5.6×10^{-3} **2.** 4.9×10^5 **3.** 2.8×10^{-2} **4.** 1.7×10^{-6}

5. 6.63×10^4 **6.** 5.14×10^{-5} **7.** 2.22×10^7 **8.** 8.35×10^{-4}

Write the following numbers in scientific notation.

9. 0.000056 **10.** 0.0000071 **11.** 43,000 **12.** 0.067

13. 64,500 **14.** 0.00891 **15.** 340,000,000 **16.** 0.00000022

CHAPTERS 1–9

Cumulative Review

Test Prep Strategy: Read Carefully

Which measure is the equivalent of 7.8 kg?

Ⓐ 7,800 g Ⓑ 780 g Ⓒ 78 g Ⓓ 0.0078 g

When comparing units of measure, read carefully to see which units are being compared. This question compares kilograms to grams. Since 1 kilogram is equal to 1,000 grams, 7.8 kilograms is equal to more than 7,000 grams. The correct answer is choice Ⓐ.

STAY SHARP!

Write the letter of the correct answer. Choose any strategy.

1. In a pictograph, one whale symbol represents 50 whales. How many whales are represented by 8 symbols?

   Ⓐ 40 Ⓑ 400 Ⓒ 50 Ⓓ 58

2. Simplify: $(15 + 10) \times 3$.

   Ⓐ 55 Ⓑ 75 Ⓒ 30 Ⓓ 750

3. Solve: $t + 3.05 = 12.62$.

   Ⓐ $t = 9.57$ Ⓑ $t = 15.67$ Ⓒ $t = 38.49$ Ⓓ $t = 4.15$

4. What is the perimeter of this figure?

   Ⓐ 10.9 yd Ⓑ 13.8 yd

   Ⓒ 12.9 yd Ⓓ 17.8 yd

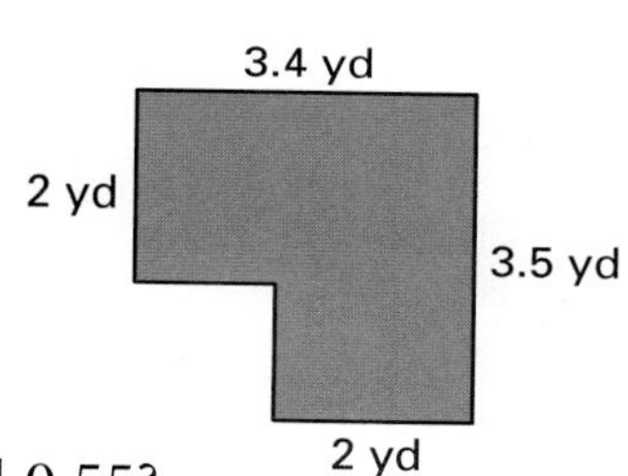

5. Which fraction is equivalent to the decimal 0.55?

   Ⓐ $\frac{5}{10}$ Ⓑ $\frac{5}{11}$ Ⓒ $\frac{11}{25}$ Ⓓ $\frac{11}{20}$

6. At the grocery store, $\frac{3}{7}$ of the parking lot is being repaved. Choose the equation that shows how much of the lot was available for parking.

   Ⓐ $1 - \frac{3}{7} = x$ Ⓑ $\frac{3}{7} - x = 1$ Ⓒ $x + 1 = \frac{3}{7}$ Ⓓ $\frac{3}{7} + 1 = x$

7. Choose the expression with the least quotient.

   Ⓐ $3\frac{1}{4} \div \frac{1}{3}$ Ⓑ $2\frac{5}{8} \div \frac{2}{5}$ Ⓒ $6 \div \frac{1}{9}$ Ⓓ $5 \div \frac{2}{7}$

8. Which term correctly describes this angle?

   Ⓐ acute Ⓑ right Ⓒ obtuse Ⓓ not here

9. Find the sum: $-4 + (-4)$.

   Ⓐ 0 Ⓑ 8 Ⓒ 4 Ⓓ -8

10. Find the product: $-8 \times (-5)$.

    Ⓐ -3 Ⓑ 40 Ⓒ 13 Ⓓ -40

Test Prep Strategies

- Read Carefully
- Follow Directions
- Make Smart Choices
- Eliminate Choices
- Work Backward from an Answer

REVIEW AND PRACTICE

Chapter 10

Ratio, Proportion, and Percent

Fire Alarm

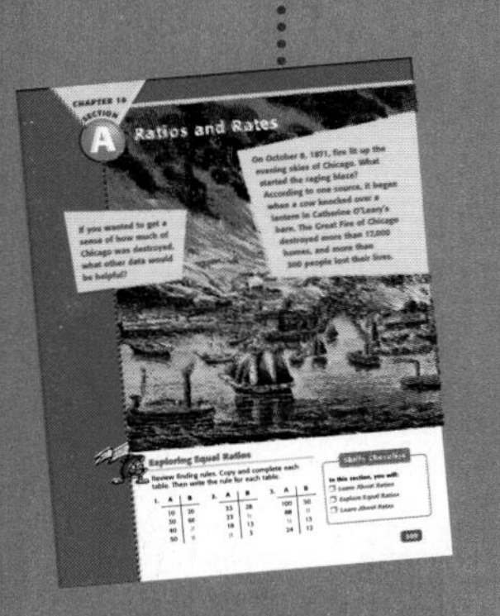

Fire Alarm
Page 509

Ratios and Rates

509

In 1995, almost 3 out of every 4 structure fires happened in people's homes. Which type of fires occurred most often in 1995?

U.S. Fires, 1995	
Total fires	**1,965,500**
Structure fires	573,500
Vehicle fires	406,500
Fires in outside properties (includes storage, crops, and timber)	985,500

LINKS

Entertainment

In 1930, less than 1% of the cars sold in the United States had a radio. By 1970, over 90% of them had a radio.

Social Studies

New Jersey has a population density of 1,042 people per square mile. Alaska's population density is 1 person per square mile.

Arts & Literature

A harp string that is twice as long as another string will play the same note one octave lower. A string that is half as long as another string will play the same note one octave higher.
www.mathsurf.com/6/ch10/arts

SECTION B A Monumental Story

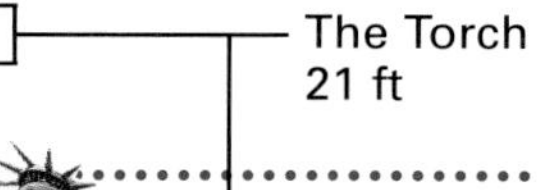

Proportions

How tall is the Statue of Liberty from the base of the pedestal to the top of the torch?

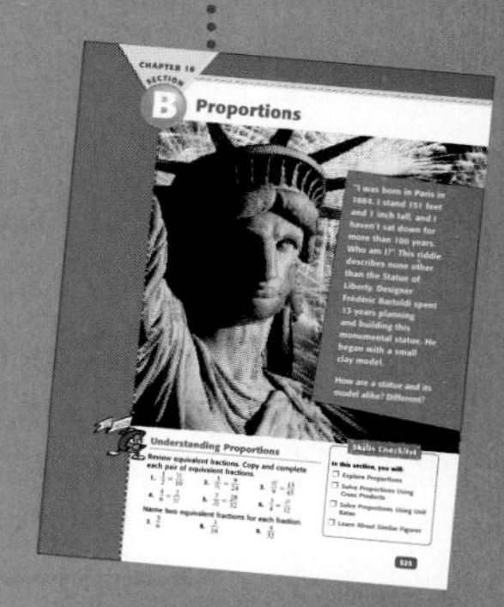

A Monumental Story
Page 525

SECTION C Touring the Rain Forest

Percents

547

What comparative statement(s) could you make about tropical rain forests and nontropical areas based on the data from the table?

Interesting Facts About . . .	Tropical Rain Forests	Nontropical Areas
Area and Species of Plants	Tropical Costa Rica: Area of 20,000 mi^2 and 8,000 species of plants	Great Britain: Area of 94,000 mi^2 and 1,600 species of plants
Area and Species of Birds	La Selva Rain Forest: Area of 3 mi^2 and 394 species of birds	Pennsylvania: Area of 45,000 mi^2 and 197 species of birds
Inches of Rain Per Year	Most Tropical Rain Forests: About 200 in. of rain per year	Northern Alaska: 50 in. of rain per year

Touring the Rain Forest
Page 547

Science

The speed of a rotating object is often recorded in revolutions per minute (rpm) or revolutions per second (rps).

www.mathsurf.com/6/ch10/science

People of the World

The Parthenon, built in Athens in the 400s B.C., incorporated the Greek's ideal "Golden Ratio," which is approximately 1.618 to 1.

www.mathsurf.com/6/ch10/people

Finding the Facts

Materials

construction paper, markers, rulers, graph paper or graphing software

Every sport uses its own ratios, proportions, and percents, whether it be for keeping score, keeping time, or ranking its members. What kinds of quantities are compared in your favorite sport?

Make a Plan

- What are some of the sports that members of your team enjoy? What facts and figures does your team know about these sports?
- How can you find out more information about these sports?
- What type of sports data is most likely to be expressed as ratios, proportions, or percents?

Carry It Out

1. Choose one sport you would like to learn more about.
2. Have each member of your team research more information about this sport. What resources can your team use to search for additional data?
3. Copy your data onto individual sheets of paper. On the back of each sheet, identify the data as ratios, proportions, or percents. How can you use graphs, charts, and tables to best illustrate the data?

Talk About It

- Why do you think sports data uses ratios, proportions, and percents?
- Which types of the data you found are represented with ratios? With proportions? With percents?

Present the Project

Share your results with the class. How did your choice of a sport affect the type of data that your team found?

CHAPTER 10

SECTION

A Ratios and Rates

On October 8, 1871, fire lit up the evening skies of Chicago. What started the raging blaze? According to one source, it began when a cow knocked over a lantern in Catherine O'Leary's barn. The Great Fire of Chicago destroyed more than 17,000 homes, and more than 300 people lost their lives.

If you wanted to get a sense of how much of Chicago was destroyed, what other data would be helpful?

Exploring Equal Ratios

Review finding rules. Copy and complete each table. Then write the rule for each table.

1.

A	B
10	20
30	60
40	■
50	■

2.

A	B
33	28
23	■
18	13
■	3

3.

A	B
100	50
88	■
■	13
24	12

Skills Checklist

In this section, you will:

- ❒ Learn About Ratios
- ❒ Explore Equal Ratios
- ❒ Learn About Rates

Chapter 10
Lesson
1

What Is a Ratio?

You Will Learn
- to express two quantities as a ratio

Vocabulary
ratio

Learn

A **ratio** is a comparison of two quantities. For example, there are six girls and four boys in the drawing. The ratio of girls to boys is 6 to 4.

Ratios can be written in three different ways. 6 to 4, 6:4, and $\frac{6}{4}$ are all the same ratio.

Example 1

Give a ratio comparing the number of presents to the number of people at the party.

There are 14 presents and 10 people. The ratio is 14 to 10, 14:10, or $\frac{14}{10}$.

Example 2

Give a ratio comparing the number of hats to scarves.

There are 5 hats and 8 scarves.

The ratio is 5 to 8, 5:8, or $\frac{5}{8}$.

Just like fractions, ratios should be written in lowest terms.

Example 3

It is recommended that the batteries in a smoke detector should be tested once a month, and replaced at least once a year. Six out of ten fire deaths occur in homes without smoke detectors. Write this ratio in lowest terms.

$\frac{6}{10} = \frac{6 \div 2}{10 \div 2}$ Divide numerator and denominator by the same number.

$= \frac{3}{5}$ Simplify.

In lowest terms, the ratio is 3 to 5, 3:5, or $\frac{3}{5}$.

Example 4

Give a ratio comparing the number of male soccer players to the total number of players in lowest terms.

$\frac{\text{number of male players}}{\text{number of players}} = \frac{2}{6} = \frac{1}{3}$

The ratio is 1 to 3, 1:3, or $\frac{1}{3}$.

1. How is a ratio like a fraction? How is it different?
2. Give an example of a ratio that compares a part to the whole. Give an example of a ratio that compares a part to a part.

Check

Give a ratio comparing the quantities in lowest terms.

1. Number of triangles and number of squares
2. Number of squares and number of figures

Use the picture on page 510 to answer **3–6.** Give each ratio in lowest terms.

3. Number of candles and number of presents
4. Number of pizza slices and number of pizzas
5. Number of jeans and number of girls
6. Number of people and number of pizza slices
7. **Reasoning** Are 4:10 and 2 to 5 the same ratio? Explain.
8. **Reasoning** Explain why it is important to write ratios and fractions in lowest terms.

Practice

Skills and Reasoning

Geometry For **9–12,** use the shapes pictured.

9. What is the ratio of squares to hexagons?

10. Give the ratio of hexagons to squares.

11. What is the ratio of triangles to circles?

12. Give the ratio of hexagons to the whole group.

A bag contains 3 red marbles, 8 blue marbles, and 10 yellow marbles. Give each ratio in three ways.

13. Red marbles to blue marbles

14. Yellow marbles to blue marbles

15. Red marbles to all marbles

16. Blue marbles to all marbles

17. At Midtown School, 24 out of the 49 sixth graders are in one of Ms. Campbell's classes. Write this as a ratio.

18. Mrs. Ng has 12 boys and 15 girls in her science class. Give each ratio.

a. Boys to girls **b.** Girls to boys **c.** Boys to students **d.** Girls to students

For **19–21,** refer to the animals pictured.

19. The ratio of which animal to the whole group is 3:14?

20. The ratio of which animal to the whole group is 2:7?

21. Which two animals are compared in a ratio of 3:4?

22. **Reasoning** In the picture on page 510, is the ratio of girls to total number of guests 3 to 5? Explain.

Reasoning State if each is a ratio. If not, explain why.

23. 6:13 **24.** 6×13 **25.** $\frac{6}{13}$ **26.** 13 to 6 **27.** $6 + 13$ **28.** $6 - 13$

Problem Solving and Applications

Using Data Use the Data File on page 506 to solve **29–31.**

29. Write the ratio of vehicle fires to structure fires.

30. What is the ratio of fires in outside properties to total fires?

31. Which is greater, the number of fires in outside properties, or the number of structure and vehicle fires?

32. Industry Fire engines carry fire hoses. Fire trucks carry mainly ladders and fire-fighting equipment other than hoses. At one point, the city of San Francisco had 40 fire engines and 18 fire trucks.

a. Give the ratio of fire engines to fire trucks in lowest terms.

b. Give the ratio of fire trucks to total fire vehicles in lowest terms.

c. If each fire engine carried six fire hoses, what is the ratio of fire engines to fire hoses?

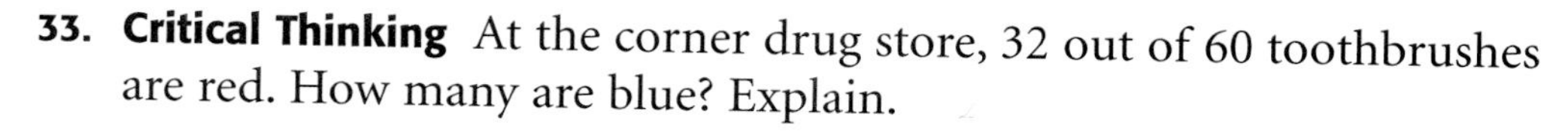

33. Critical Thinking At the corner drug store, 32 out of 60 toothbrushes are red. How many are blue? Explain.

34. Patterns Susan has noted that every time the Bentley Park Club gets together, the ratio of girls to boys is 4 to 5. Draw pictures to show the number of people at a meeting with:

a. 8 girls **b.** 15 boys **c.** 36 people

35. Journal How is writing a ratio in lowest terms like writing a fraction in lowest terms?

Mixed Review and Test Prep

STAY SHARP!

Write if each line is a line of symmetry.

36.

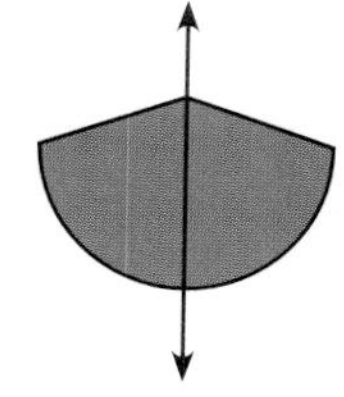

37.

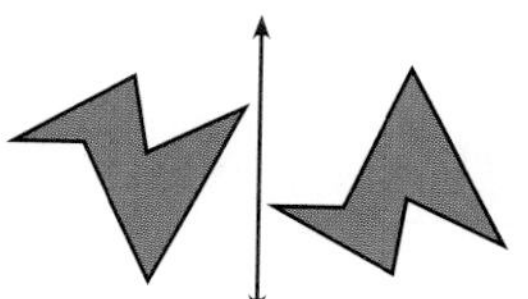

38.

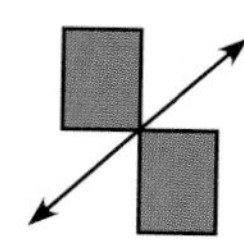

39.

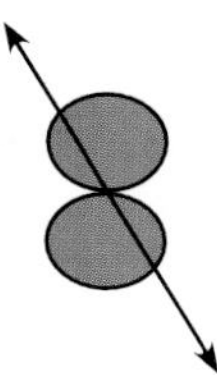

Find the missing measurement for each rectangle.

40. Area = 72 in^2
base = 8 in.
height = ■

41. Area = ■
base = 6.4 mm
height = 2.3 mm

42. Area = 27.2 km^2
base = ■
height = 13.6 km

43. Area = ■
base = 5 cm
height = 12 cm

44. Area = 92.7 ft^2
base = ■
height = 9 ft

45. Area = 14.5 m^2
base = 5 m
height = ■

46. What is $-10 \times (-12)$?

Ⓐ -120 Ⓑ -22 Ⓒ 2 Ⓓ 120

Chapter 10
Lesson
2

Equal Ratios

Problem Solving Connection
- Make a Table

Explore

Sometimes you need to find ratios that are equal to a known ratio. You can create equal ratios by multiplying both quantities of the ratio by the same non-zero amount. A table can help organize the information.

Work Together

1. Copy and complete the table based on your own classroom. For the last two lines, choose your own items and count them.

Item	Number	Item	Number
Boys		Doors	
Girls		Windows	
Teachers		Pencil sharpeners	
Desks		Your choice #1	
Chairs		Your choice #2	

Remember
You can use either multiplication or division to find fractions equal to a given fraction.

2. Write the following ratios.
   a. Boys to girls
   b. Teachers to students
   c. Desks to chairs
   d. Doors to windows
   e. Doors to people
   f. People to pencil sharpeners
3. Write three ratios of your own. State the items being compared.
4. Find two quantities in your classroom whose ratio is about 2:1. How do you know the ratio is about 2:1? Repeat using 5:1 and 10:1.

Which ratios in Step 2 are important to people outside your class? Who might want to know these ratios? Why?

Connect and Learn

You can find equivalent ratios using either multiplication or division.

In Erica and Jamar's homeroom, 24 out of 32 students want to go to Hillsdale Park for the school picnic. Erica and Jamar both found equal ratios using different methods.

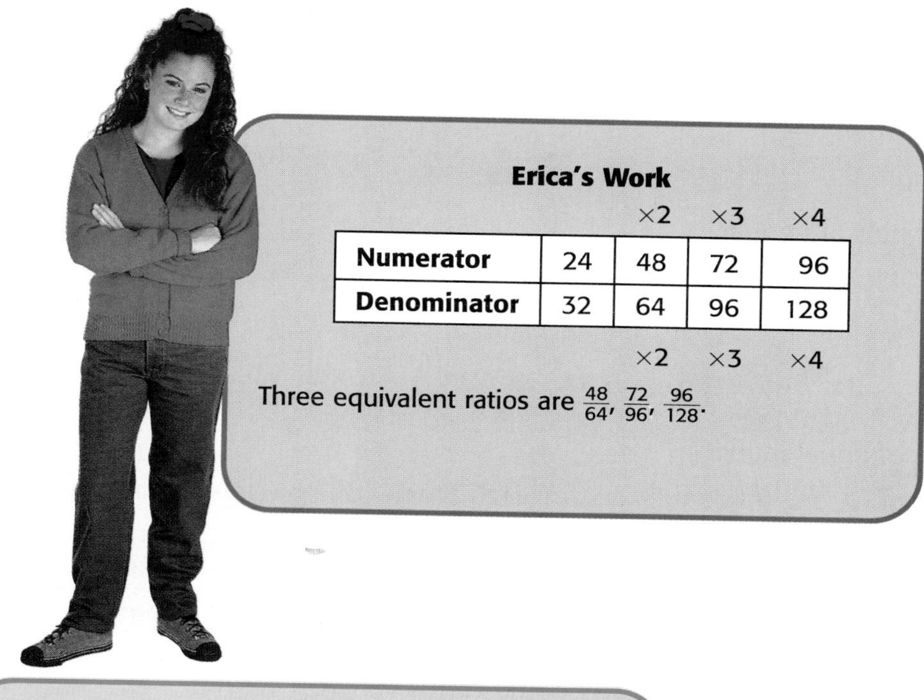

Erica's Work

		×2	×3	×4
Numerator	24	48	72	96
Denominator	32	64	96	128
		×2	×3	×4

Three equivalent ratios are $\frac{48}{64}$, $\frac{72}{96}$, $\frac{96}{128}$.

Jamar's Work

		÷2	÷4	÷8
Numerator	24	12	6	3
Denominator	32	16	8	4
		÷2	÷4	÷8

Three equivalent ratios are $\frac{12}{16}$, $\frac{6}{8}$, and $\frac{3}{4}$.

Problem Solving Hint

When using division, try to choose numbers that are easy to divide by. Use rules of divisibility to help you.

Check

Give two ratios equal to each given ratio.

1. 1:3 **2.** 2 to 5 **3.** $\frac{4}{7}$ **4.** 8:9 **5.** $\frac{8}{3}$ **6.** 1 to 4

7. **Reasoning** If Erica and Jamar wanted to convince their teacher to have the picnic at Hillsdale Park, which ratio do you think would be more convincing? Explain your reasoning.

Practice

Skills and Reasoning

Give two ratios equal to each given ratio.

8. 4 to 5 **9.** $\frac{10}{20}$ **10.** 12:8 **11.** $\frac{25}{40}$ **12.** $\frac{4}{6}$ **13.** 3:7

14. $\frac{4}{8}$ **15.** 7 to 1 **16.** $\frac{1}{8}$ **17.** 5:10 **18.** $\frac{3}{4}$ **19.** 2.1 to 4.2

20. 2 to 9 **21.** $\frac{7}{8}$ **22.** 1:7 **23.** $\frac{5}{15}$ **24.** 21 to 28 **25.** 3.2 to 3.6

State if each pair of ratios are equal.

26. 7 to 21; 1 to 3 **27.** 6:9; 3:2 **28.** $\frac{5}{4}$; 10:8 **29.** 1 to 10; $\frac{2}{5}$

30. 8 to 64; $\frac{1}{8}$ **31.** 16:24; 4:6 **32.** 19:21; $\frac{18}{20}$ **33.** 60 to 40; 2:3

Complete each table of equal ratios.

34. 8 men to 10 women

Men	4			16
Women		10	15	20

35. 5 fire fighters for each truck

Fire fighters				
Trucks	1	2	3	4

36. 6 triangles out of 15 figures

Triangles			6	8
Figures	5	10		

37. **Reasoning** For a given ratio, how many equal ratios can you create?

38. **Reasoning** Is it possible to find a ratio that is equal to $\frac{2}{5}$, 2:5, and 2 to 5? Explain.

39. How many whole-number ratios equal to 40:100 can you find using division? Explain your method.

40. The ratios 1 to 2, 2 to 4, and 3 to 6 are equal ratios.

a. Graph the ratios on the same coordinate grid. Use the first number in the ratio as the x-coordinate and the second as the y-coordinate.

b. Draw a straight line that connects the points.

c. Repeat steps **a** and **b** using the ratios 2 to 3, 4 to 6, and 6 to 9.

d. Do you think every set of equal ratios can be graphed as a straight line? Explain.

Problem Solving and Applications

41. The circle graph shows the number of colored beads used in a hand-beaded bracelet. Carole wants to make a smaller bracelet using the same ratios of colors. Draw a circle graph that shows how many beads of each color Carole could use.

Colored Beads

42. **Estimation** Mary jogs 5 laps in 7 minutes. Rikki jogs 11 laps in 15 minutes. Do Mary and Rikki jog at about the same speed?

PRACTICE AND APPLY

For **43–45,** give three equal ratios.

43. **Science** In Oregon in 1995, for every forest fire caused by lightning, about 3 forest fires were caused by humans.

44. Seven out of ten calls to the fire department are for medical purposes.

45. A college residence hall has 7 students for every 2 bathrooms.

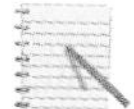

46. **Journal** Describe the steps you would follow to find equal ratios for 6:7.

Mixed Review and Test Prep

STAY SHARP!

What is the least rotation that will land the figure on top of itself?

47. 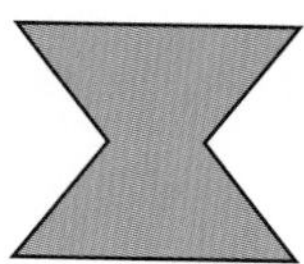

48. 

49. 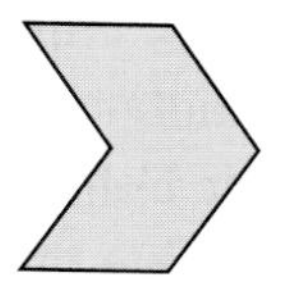

50. 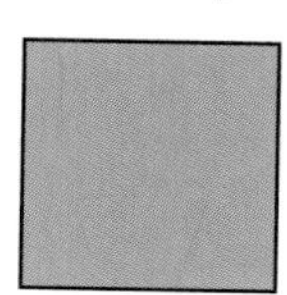

Find the area of each parallelogram. Base (b) and height (h) are given.

51. $b = 4, h = 5$

52. $b = 6$ in., $h = 3$ in.

53. $h = 12$ cm, $b = 3$ cm

54. $h = 10$ ft, b = 88 ft

55. $h = 10.5$ m, $b = 1.5$ m

56. $b = 67$ mm, $h = 100$ mm

57. Choose the graph of $y = 3x$.

Ⓐ 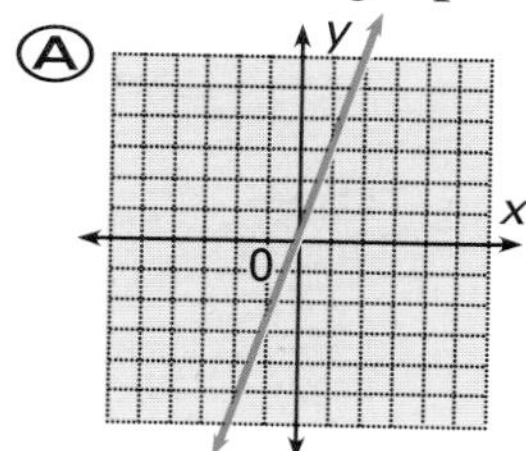

Ⓑ 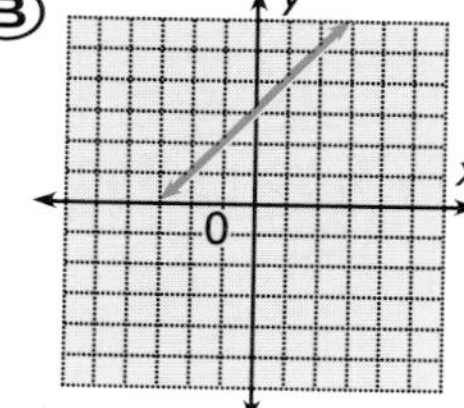

Ⓒ 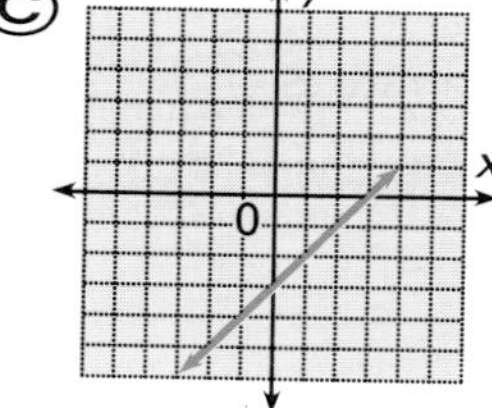

Ⓓ 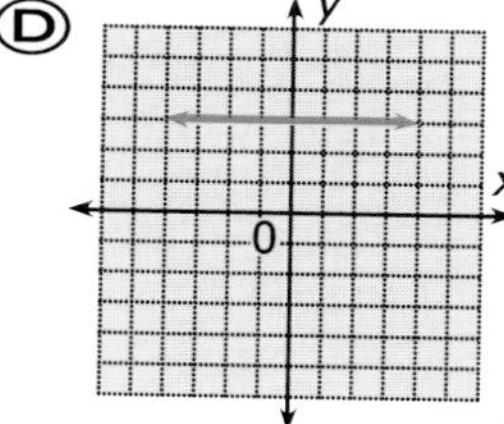

Chapter 10
Lesson
3

What Is a Rate?

You Will Learn

- to express two quantities with different units as a rate

Vocabulary

rate

unit rate

Learn

Some ratios are known as **rates**. A rate is a comparison of two quantities with different units of measure.

The average Dalmatian can run 15,400 feet in 5 minutes. The rate $\frac{15{,}400 \text{ feet}}{5 \text{ minutes}}$ compares the number of *feet* to the number of *minutes*. This can be read "15,400 feet *per* 5 minutes."

If the comparison is to 1 unit, the rate is called a **unit rate**.

$$\frac{15{,}400 \text{ feet} \div 5}{5 \text{ minutes} \div 5} = \frac{3{,}080 \text{ feet}}{1 \text{ minute}} \longleftarrow 1 \text{ unit}$$

The unit rate is **3,080** feet per minute.

Did You Know?

Dalmatians were first used by firemen because the dogs developed a strong attachment to the firemen's horses. The dogs would bark if any thieves tried to steal the horses.

Example 1

A typical fire engine can hold 500 gallons of water. This water is used up in 10 minutes of continuous spraying. What is the rate of gallons per minute?

The rate that compares 500 gallons with 10 minutes is $\frac{500 \text{ gallons}}{10 \text{ minutes}}$.
If you divide both numbers by 10, you get the unit rate of $\frac{50 \text{ gallons}}{1 \text{ minute}}$.

Example 2

A pretzel-making machine in a factory can produce 10 boxes of pretzels in 5 minutes. What is the rate of boxes to minutes?

The rate is $\frac{10 \text{ boxes}}{5 \text{ minutes}}$.
If you divide both numbers by 5, you get the unit rate of $\frac{2 \text{ boxes}}{1 \text{ minute}}$.

Using a table can help you find many equivalent rates.

Example 3

Every 3 hours, Henry's hamster eats 4 ounces of food. Use a table to find four rates describing this situation.

Since a rate is a ratio, you can find equal rates the same way you found equal ratios. Multiply both quantities by the same number.

$\times 2 \quad \times 3 \quad \times 4$

Ounces of food	4	8	12	16
Number of hours	3	6	9	12

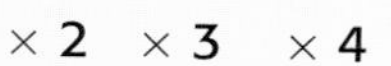

Four rates that describe this situation are $\frac{4 \text{ oz}}{3 \text{ hr}}$, $\frac{8 \text{ oz}}{6 \text{ hr}}$, $\frac{12 \text{ oz}}{9 \text{ hr}}$, and $\frac{16 \text{ oz}}{12 \text{ hr}}$.

Example 4

Dani is making home-made greeting cards to send to her family and friends. She can make 24 cards in 80 minutes. Use a table to find three rates describing this situation.

Divide both quantities by the same number.

$\div 2 \quad \div 4 \quad \div 8$

Number of cards	24	12	6	3
Minutes	80	40	20	10

$\div 2 \quad \div 4 \quad \div 8$

Three rates that describe this situation are $\frac{12 \text{ cards}}{40 \text{ minutes}}$, $\frac{6 \text{ cards}}{20 \text{ minutes}}$, and $\frac{3 \text{ cards}}{10 \text{ minutes}}$.

Talk About It

1. Give an example of a ratio that is not a rate. Why isn't it a rate?
2. How can you tell if a rate is a unit rate?
3. A race car went 200 miles an hour. Is this a ratio? Is it a rate?

Check

For each situation, give two equal rates.

1. Maggie read 3 books in 2 days.
2. Milo ran 1 mile in 5 minutes.
3. Marietta did 12 chin-ups in 1 minute.

Practice

Skills and Reasoning

State if the ratio is a unit rate.

4. $\frac{9 \text{ ft}}{1 \text{ hour}}$ **5.** $\frac{6 \text{ red marbles}}{9 \text{ green marbles}}$ **6.** $\frac{5 \text{ books}}{5 \text{ days}}$ **7.** $\frac{19 \text{ apples}}{1 \text{ meal}}$

8. $\frac{3 \text{ in.}}{1 \text{ year}}$ **9.** $\frac{5 \text{ apples}}{7 \text{ oranges}}$ **10.** $\frac{3 \text{ inches}}{1 \text{ inch}}$ **11.** $\frac{5 \text{ dollars}}{1 \text{ pound}}$

For each situation, give two equal rates.

12. Margaret rode her bicycle 14 miles in 2 hours.

13. Randy bought fabric with a pattern of 5 shapes in every 3 feet.

14. Justen did 30 jumping jacks in 40 seconds.

For **15–17,** use the bar graph.

15. Give three different rates that describe the speed of the cheetah.

16. Give a rate that uses the number 10.

17. Give a rate that compares a distance to $\frac{1}{2}$ hour.

18. Communicate Describe how you could change a rate of meters per second to meters per minute.

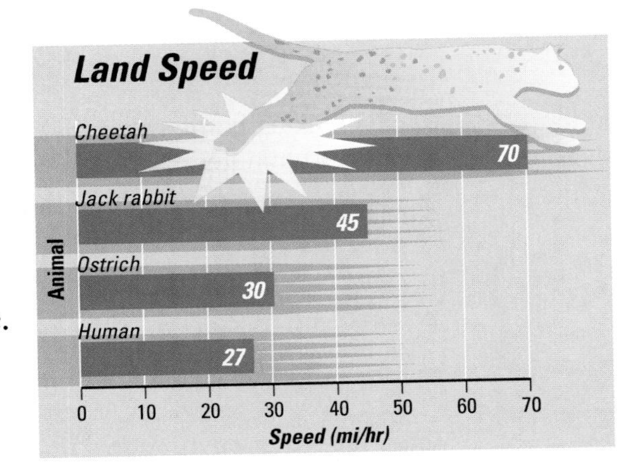

Problem Solving and Applications

Use the table for **19** and **20.**

Color	Rate (L/min)
Green	5,677
Orange	3,784
Red	1,892

19. Industry The table shows the maximum rate of water flow from fire hydrants of different colors. The rates are written in liters per minute. How many liters of water flow from each fire hydrant in five minutes?

20. Industry If a fire hydrant pumped 227,040 liters in 60 minutes, what color would the fire hydrant be?

21. Health Raul checked his pulse, and counted 27 beats in 15 seconds. At that rate, how many beats would he have counted in 45 seconds?

22. Critical Thinking Cameron is making decorations for "Back to School Night." He can make 2 posters in an hour. At this rate, how long will it take him to make 5 posters? Explain.

23. In 1987, Australian Greg Mutton paddled a bathtub 36 miles in 82 minutes, a world record. Use a table to find four rates describing this situation.

Problem Solving and RECREATION

Four students are in the Bookworm Club. They want to know who reads the fastest.

- Kevin reads 2 books every week.
- Joanna reads 7 books a month.
- Carlo reads 113 books a year.
- Noriko reads $\frac{1}{4}$ of a book each day.

24. Write a rate to describe each student's reading.

25. How many books does Kevin read each month if there are 4 weeks in a month?

26. How many books does Joanna read each year?

27. Calculate the number of books each student reads per week. When necessary, round to the nearest whole book.

28. Is it possible to find the number of books read per day? Per decade? Per any length of time? Explain.

29. **Critical Thinking** Do you think the rate of books read per year would be accurate for each student? Explain.

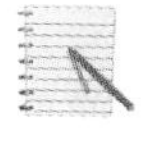

30. **Journal** Describe the similarities and differences between ratios and rates.

Mixed Review and Test Prep

State if each figure will tessellate. If it tessellates, make a sketch to show how.

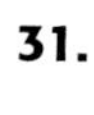

31. 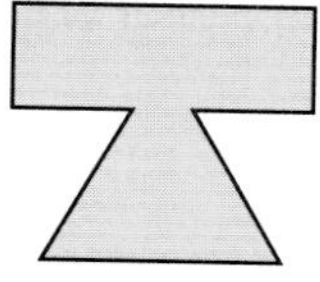

32. 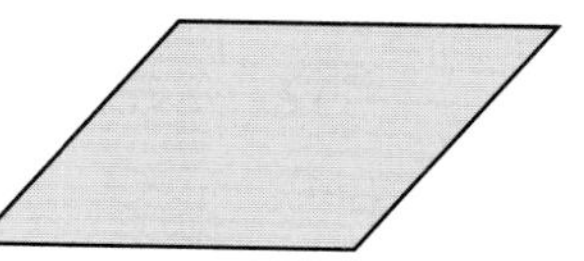

33. 

34. 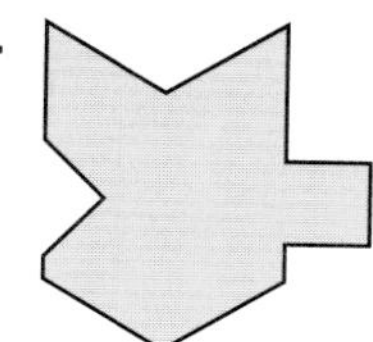

Find the area of the triangle if b is the base and h is the height.

35. $b = 7$ ft, $h = 6$ ft **36.** $b = 1.6$ m, $h = 3$ m **37.** $h = 5$ in., $b = 50$ in.

38. $h = 0.3$ cm, $b = 0.8$ cm **39.** $h = 12$ yd, $b = 3$ yd **40.** $b = 600$ mi, $h = 400$ mi

41. Sylvia has two square pieces of fabric that she wants to sew together to make a rectangular tablecloth. If one piece of fabric is $2\frac{5}{8}$ ft long and the other is $2\frac{3}{4}$ ft long, how long will the finished tablecloth be?

Ⓐ $\frac{1}{8}$ ft Ⓑ $7\frac{7}{32}$ ft Ⓒ $3\frac{3}{8}$ ft Ⓓ $5\frac{3}{8}$ ft

Skills Practice Bank, page 669, Set 2

Chapter 10

Problem Solving

Decision Making: Fire Alarm

You Will Learn

- how to make plans for emergency evacuations

Materials

- watch with second hand
- yardstick or meter stick

Explore

What are the fire safety rules in your school building? Jared is interested in fire prevention and safety. He knows that if rooms are too crowded, everyone might not be able to leave quickly. The maximum occupancy of a room is the number of people that can be evacuated safely in 1 minute.

Jared lives in Logan, West Virginia.

Do you know the maximum occupancy of your classroom or other rooms in your school? You can determine the maximum safe occupancy of your classroom or your cafeteria.

Work Together

▶ Understand

1. What is it you are trying to determine?
2. How could you determine if people can leave your classroom or cafeteria safely?
3. What information do you need to help you make a decision?

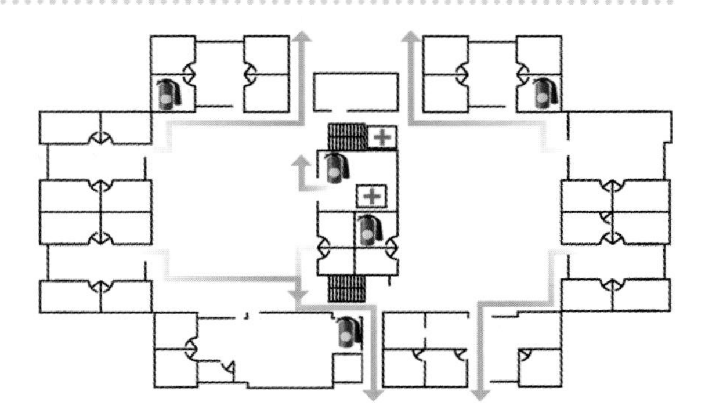

▶ Plan and Solve

4. Have everyone in your class exit through one classroom door in an orderly fashion. Time how long this takes.
5. Write a rate giving the number of people that can exit through the door per minute.
6. Estimate the rate at which people can exit the cafeteria through the doors.
7. Check the number and size of the other cafeteria doors. Then estimate the rate at which people can exit the cafeteria through all its doors.
8. Estimate the maximum occupancy of your classroom and the cafeteria.

▶ Make a Decision

9. Can your class safely evacuate your classroom? Explain.
10. Estimate the number of students in the cafeteria at lunch. Could the students safely evacuate the cafeteria?

▶ Present Your Decision

11. Write a report to the principal evaluating your classroom or cafeteria in terms of emergency evacuation. Is the maximum occupancy you calculated a good recommendation? Could your classroom or cafeteria be improved to allow for a faster evacuation?

SECTION A

Review and Practice

1. Which of the following shows the ratio of 10 firefighters for every fire truck?

   Ⓐ $\frac{1}{10}$ Ⓑ 10:1 Ⓒ 1:10 Ⓓ 10

2. Which rate is equivalent to 27 pounds in 12 hours?

   Ⓐ 8 pounds/18 hours Ⓑ 8 hours/18 minutes

   Ⓒ 27 ounces/12 minutes Ⓓ 9 pounds/4 hours

(Lessons 1 and 2) Find the ratios for **3–7.**

3. 23,000 of the 30,000 fire departments in the United States are staffed by volunteers. Write this ratio in lowest terms.

4. Last month the County Fire Department responded to 8 home fires and 6 brush fires. Give each ratio in lowest terms.

   a. Home fires to brush fires **b.** Brush fires to home fires

   c. Home fires to all fires **d.** Brush fires to all fires

5. Tamara has 3 red marbles, 5 blue marbles, and 4 green marbles. Give 5 ratios in lowest terms to describe the situation.

6. Complete each table of equal ratios.

Squares	3	6		12
Circles	5		15	

Binders	3	9	27	300
Books			18	

7. Give three ratios equal to 6:16.

For **8–10,** use the stones pictured.

8. Give the ratio of metallic stones to red stones.

9. What is the ratio of purple and blue stones to green stones?

10. Write a ratio which compares something to the total number of stones.

(Lesson 3) Find the unit rate for each ratio.

11. 51 people/142 ft^2 12. \$39/60 min

13. 59 pretzels/10 servings 14. 18 commercials/30 min

15. **Journal** Explain why a rate is always a ratio, but a ratio is not always a rate.

Skills Checklist

In this section, you have:

- ☑ **Learned About Ratios**
- ☑ **Explored Equal Ratios**
- ☑ **Learned About Rates**

REVIEW AND PRACTICE

CHAPTER 10

SECTION

B Proportions

"I was born in Paris in 1884. I stand 151 feet and 1 inch tall, and I haven't sat down for more than 100 years. Who am I?" This riddle describes none other than the Statue of Liberty. Designer Frédéric Bartoldi spent 13 years planning and building this monumental statue. He began with a small clay model.

How are a statue and its model alike? Different?

GET READY!

Understanding Proportions

Review equivalent fractions. Copy and complete each pair of equivalent fractions.

1. $\frac{1}{2} = \frac{\blacksquare}{10}$ **2.** $\frac{3}{\blacksquare} = \frac{9}{24}$ **3.** $\frac{\blacksquare}{9} = \frac{15}{45}$

4. $\frac{4}{6} = \frac{2}{\blacksquare}$ **5.** $\frac{7}{\blacksquare} = \frac{28}{32}$ **6.** $\frac{3}{4} = \frac{\blacksquare}{12}$

Name two equivalent fractions for each fraction.

7. $\frac{5}{6}$ **8.** $\frac{3}{16}$ **9.** $\frac{4}{32}$

Skills Checklist

In this section, you will:

- ❒ Explore Proportions
- ❒ Solve Proportions Using Cross Products
- ❒ Solve Proportions Using Unit Rates
- ❒ Learn About Similar Figures

What Is a Proportion?

Problem Solving Connection
- Look for a Pattern

Vocabulary
cross product
proportion

Explore

A **proportion** is a pair of equal ratios.

Proportions often include different units of measurement. Units must be the same across the top and bottom *or* down the left and right sides. If the units only match diagonally, then the ratios do not form a proportion.

Work Together

Each "four-square" below represents a pair of equal ratios using four sets of shapes arranged in a particular order. One set of shapes in each four-square is missing.

A.

▲	●
▲▲	? ?

B.

▲▲	▲▲▲▲
●●	? ?

C.

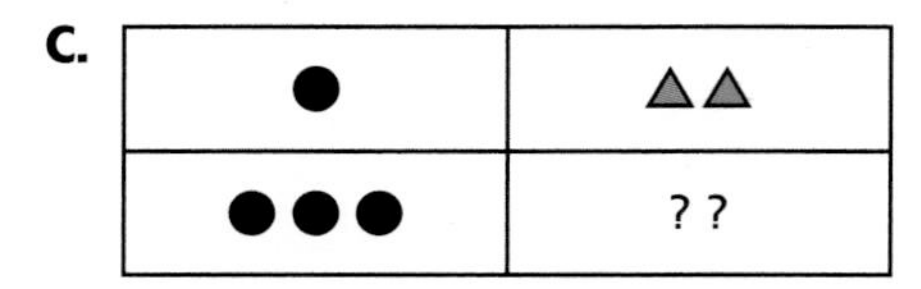

D.

●●	●●●●
▲▲▲▲	? ?

1. These are the missing shapes from the four-squares. Determine where each set of shapes belongs. Explain your answers.

   a. ▲▲▲▲▲▲ **b.**  **c.**  **d.** 

2. For the four-squares above, can the shape in the upper left corner match the shape below it? Can it match the shape to the right of it? Can it match the shape diagonal to it? Explain.
3. Create three four-square patterns of your own like the ones above.
4. Share your patterns with a friend. Try to solve your friend's four-square patterns.
5. Describe the patterns you see in your four-square patterns.
6. Replace each set of shapes with a number that describes the number of shapes. Write the patterns as ratios. For example, the four-square pattern for B would become $\frac{2}{2} = \frac{4}{4}$.
   Make this change in the four-square patterns shown as well as your own.

How can you tell if two ratios form a proportion? Give an example.

Connect and Learn

For two ratios, a **cross product** is the result of multiplying the top value in one ratio by the bottom value in the other. In a proportion, the cross products of the two ratios are equal.

Example 1

Decide if the ratios form a proportion.

a. $\frac{6 \text{ ft}}{10 \text{ sec}} \stackrel{?}{=} \frac{9 \text{ ft}}{15 \text{ sec}}$

The units are the same across the top and bottom.

$6 \times 15 = 90$

$10 \times 9 = 90$

The cross products are equal. It is a proportion.

b. $\frac{4 \text{ ft}}{6 \text{ ft}} \stackrel{?}{=} \frac{12 \text{ sec}}{18 \text{ sec}}$

The units are the same down the left and right sides.

$4 \times 18 = 72$

$6 \times 12 = 72$

The cross products are equal. It is a proportion.

c. $\frac{5 \text{ ft}}{10 \text{ sec}} \stackrel{?}{=} \frac{4 \text{ sec}}{8 \text{ ft}}$

The units are not the same across or down.

It is not a proportion.

Example 2

The Golden Gate Bridge is 6,480 ft long, with 756-ft towers. The model of the bridge used in *Superman* was 60 ft long with 7-ft towers. Was the model proportional to the actual bridge?

$\frac{60}{7} \stackrel{?}{=} \frac{6{,}480}{756}$ ⟵ bridge length ⟵ tower height

Write terms of the ratios in the same order. Determine the cross products.

$60 \times 756 = 45{,}360$

$7 \times 6{,}480 = 45{,}360$

The cross products are equal, so the ratios form a proportion. The model was proportional.

Check

State whether or not each pair of ratios forms a proportion.

1. $\frac{4}{3}; \frac{12}{9}$ **2.** $\frac{8}{5}; \frac{11}{7}$ **3.** $\frac{8}{3}; \frac{32}{12}$ **4.** $\frac{27}{4}; \frac{20}{3}$ **5.** $\frac{45}{81}; \frac{5}{9}$

6. What does it mean to say that quantities are “proportional”?

Practice

Skills and Reasoning

State whether or not each pair of ratios forms a proportion.

7. $\frac{6}{25}; \frac{4}{117}$
8. $\frac{7}{2}; \frac{21}{6}$
9. $\frac{3}{23}; \frac{6}{50}$
10. $\frac{3}{16}; \frac{5}{30}$
11. $\frac{29}{4}; \frac{24}{6}$
12. $\frac{5}{6}; \frac{2}{3}$
13. $\frac{15}{17}; \frac{30}{34}$
14. $\frac{8}{9}; \frac{12}{13}$
15. $\frac{5}{3}; \frac{5}{3}$
16. $\frac{2}{3}; \frac{8}{12}$
17. $\frac{8}{13}; \frac{2}{3}$
18. $\frac{14}{10}; \frac{70}{50}$
19. $\frac{1}{8}; \frac{4}{32}$
20. $\frac{26}{20}; \frac{39}{30}$
21. $\frac{1}{7}; \frac{7}{49}$
22. $\frac{2 \text{ tsp}}{1 \text{ oz}}; \frac{4 \text{ oz}}{8 \text{ tsp}}$
23. $\frac{75 \text{ mi}}{3 \text{ hr}}; \frac{125 \text{ mi}}{5 \text{ hr}}$
24. $\frac{6 \text{ acres}}{10 \text{ acres}}; \frac{15 \text{ ft}}{25 \text{ ft}}$
25. $\frac{6 \text{ ft}}{10 \text{ sec}}; \frac{9 \text{ ft}}{15 \text{ sec}}$
26. $\frac{4 \text{ ft}}{6 \text{ ft}}; \frac{12 \text{ sec}}{18 \text{ sec}}$
27. $\frac{5 \text{ m}}{8 \text{ sec}}; \frac{10 \text{ sec}}{16 \text{ m}}$

For **28** and **29**, choose the proportion that is written correctly.

28. **a.** $\frac{1 \text{ cat}}{2 \text{ dogs}} = \frac{4 \text{ dogs}}{8 \text{ cats}}$

b. $\frac{1 \text{ cat}}{2 \text{ dogs}} = \frac{4 \text{ cats}}{8 \text{ dogs}}$

c. $\frac{1 \text{ cat}}{8 \text{ cats}} = \frac{4 \text{ dogs}}{2 \text{ dogs}}$

29. **a.** $\frac{24 \text{ inches}}{2 \text{ feet}} = \frac{48 \text{ inches}}{4 \text{ feet}}$

b. $\frac{24 \text{ inches}}{2 \text{ feet}} = \frac{48 \text{ feet}}{4 \text{ inches}}$

c. $\frac{24 \text{ inches}}{2 \text{ feet}} = \frac{4 \text{ feet}}{48 \text{ inches}}$

30. **Reasoning** How do you use multiplication to determine if two ratios are proportional?

31. **Reasoning** The following ratios do not form a proportion: $\frac{3}{8}$ and $\frac{6}{9.5}$. How can you determine this without actually finding the cross products?

32. Explain why the following is not a proportion:

$\frac{\$0.25}{1 \text{ lb of apples}}$ and $\frac{3 \text{ lb of apples}}{\$0.75}$

Problem Solving and Applications

33. **a.** Write the next two fractions to continue the pattern.

$\frac{5}{15}, \frac{3}{9}, \frac{9}{27}, \frac{7}{21}, \ldots$

b. Describe the pattern. How can you use proportions to check your answer?

34. **Fine Arts** Here is a picture of the *Motherland* in Volgograd, Russia. In the photo, 1 cm is about 19 feet. Approximately how tall is the actual statue?

35. Cedrick earned $209 for 38 hours of work last week. This week he earned $176 for 32 hours of work. Do these rates form a proportion?

Use the bar graph for **36–39**.

36. For which two classes are the ratios of boys to girls proportional?

37. For which two classes are the ratios of girls to total students proportional?

38. Last year Ms. Lee's class had the same ratio of boys to girls. There were 20 boys in her class. How many students were in her class last year?

39. **Write Your Own Problem** Write a ratio using the data in the graph.

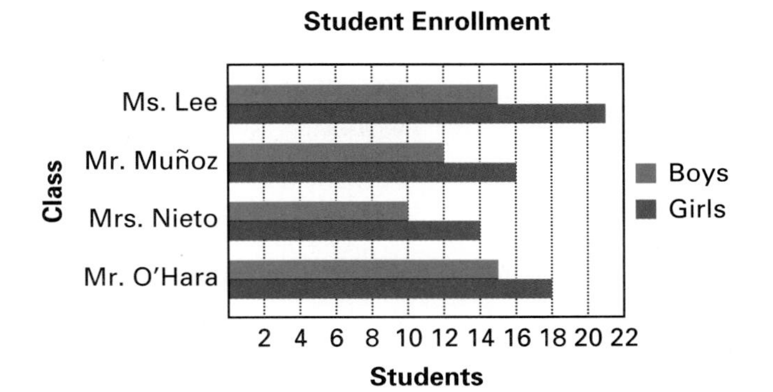

40. **Consumer** A 16-oz drink at Tito's Sandwich Shop costs 99¢. A 20-oz drink costs $1.19. Are these prices proportional?

41. Janice can run 100 meters in 12 seconds. Carlos can run 500 meters in 48 seconds. Susan runs at a rate of 10 meters per second. Philip can run 200 meters in 24 seconds. Which two students run at the same rate? Explain how you found your answer.

Mixed Review and Test Prep

STAY SHARP!

Order from greatest to least.

42. 4, −7, −2, −9 **43.** 31, −55, 55, −13 **44.** 2, 22, −22, −222 **45.** −17, −53, −31, −9

46. 18, 0, −5, 22 **47.** 41, −14, −41, 44 **48.** 26, −6, −2, 62 **49.** −178, 133, 0, −100

Find the missing measurement(s) for each circle, given that r = radius, d = diameter, and C = circumference. Use 3.14 for π.

50. $r = 4$ mm, $d = 8$ mm, $C \approx$ ▒ **51.** $r = 2.1$, $d =$ ▒, $C \approx 13.188$

52. $r = 1.1$ in., $d =$ ▒, $C \approx$ ▒ **53.** $r =$ ▒, $d =$ ▒, $C \approx 27.632$ yd

54. Which of the following are factors of 36?
I. 1 and 36 II. 5 III. 18 IV. 9

Ⓐ only I Ⓑ only I and IV Ⓒ I, II, III, and IV Ⓓ only I, III, and IV

Chapter 10 Lesson 5

Solving Proportions Using Cross Products

You Will Learn

- to solve proportions using cross products

Learn

People use proportions to determine the value of an unknown measurement.

You can use a proportion to determine an unknown quantity if only one of the ratios has an unknown. You can use what you already know about multiplication and division to help you solve proportions.

Math Tip

Since the denominator in the first fraction is three times as great as the denominator in the second fraction, the numerator must also be three times as great.

Example 1

Use cross products to solve the proportion $\frac{x}{15} = \frac{3}{5}$.

$5x = 15 \times 3$	Write the cross products.
$5x = 45$	Multiply.
$x = 9$	Think: What number times 5 equals 45?

If the numbers in a proportion are so complex that you can't use mental math to determine the value of a variable, you can use division. Division is the inverse operation for multiplication, so it can be used to undo multiplication.

Example 2

Use cross products to solve the proportion $\frac{t}{27} = \frac{8}{35}$.

$35t = 8 \times 27$	Write the cross products.
$35t = 216$	Multiply.
$\frac{35t}{35} = \frac{216}{35}$	Use division to undo multiplication.
$t = 6.17$	Round to the nearest hundredth.

Proportions are also helpful when solving real-world problems.

Example 3

A 24-ft statue of the Sioux chief Sitting Bull, in Denmark, is made entirely of LEGO® blocks. If the real Sitting Bull stood 6 ft and his head was 0.875 ft, find the height of the statue's head.

Let h be the height of the statue's head.

$\frac{\text{head height}}{\text{total height}} \longrightarrow \frac{h}{24} = \frac{0.875}{6}$ Write a proportion.

$6h = 24 \times 0.875$ Write the cross products.

$6h = 21$ Multiply.

$h = 21 \div \mathbf{6}$ Use division to undo multiplication.

$h = 3.5$

The statue's head is 3.5 ft tall.

Remember

For decimal multiplication, the number of digits after the decimal point in the product should be the same as the total number of digits after the decimal points in the factors.

Example 4

Suppose you want to build a model of a building. Your model is going to be 5 ft tall and 3 ft wide. The building is actually 1,000 ft tall. How wide is the actual building?

Let w be the width of the building.

$\frac{\text{height}}{\text{width}} \longrightarrow \frac{5 \text{ ft}}{3 \text{ ft}} = \frac{1{,}000 \text{ ft}}{w \text{ ft}}$

$5w = 3 \times 1{,}000 = 3{,}000$

$w = 600$

The building is 600 ft wide.

Talk About It

1. If all the numbers are different, how many numbers do you need in a proportion to be able to solve it using cross products? Why?
2. Can you solve a proportion without using cross products? Explain.

Check

Solve each proportion.

1. $\frac{8}{12} = \frac{6}{x}$ **2.** $\frac{4}{x} = \frac{6}{15}$ **3.** $\frac{5}{20} = \frac{x}{6}$ **4.** $\frac{4}{x} = \frac{10}{18}$

5. Reasoning Describe how you used cross products to solve one of the exercises above.

Practice

Skills and Reasoning

Solve each proportion. Round to the nearest hundredth as needed.

6. $\frac{6}{8} = \frac{x}{12}$ **7.** $\frac{x}{8} = \frac{21}{14}$ **8.** $\frac{45}{m} = \frac{5}{3}$ **9.** $\frac{10}{14} = \frac{c}{35}$ **10.** $\frac{15}{14} = \frac{210}{l}$

11. $\frac{6}{11} = \frac{9}{x}$ **12.** $\frac{a}{7} = \frac{5}{3}$ **13.** $\frac{2.4}{4.5} = \frac{u}{1.8}$ **14.** $\frac{8.4}{y} = \frac{11.2}{6.8}$ **15.** $\frac{m}{3} = \frac{10}{5}$

16. $\frac{5}{6} = \frac{3}{a}$ **17.** $\frac{6}{16} = \frac{w}{12}$ **18.** $\frac{5}{22} = \frac{35}{m}$ **19.** $\frac{p}{12} = \frac{5}{15}$ **20.** $\frac{12}{20} = \frac{14}{x}$

21. Reasoning In the proportion $\frac{-4}{10} = \frac{z}{-20}$, will the value of z be greater than or less than 0? Explain.

Problem Solving and Applications

22. Yesterday Stu earned $31.50 for 5 hours of work. Today he worked for 7 hours at the same pay rate. How much did he earn today?

23. Measurement If the rectangles shown are proportional to each other, what are the lengths of the unknown sides?

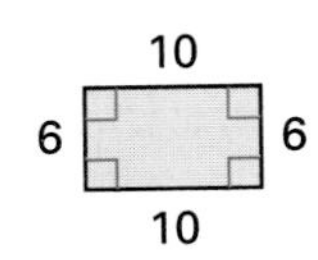

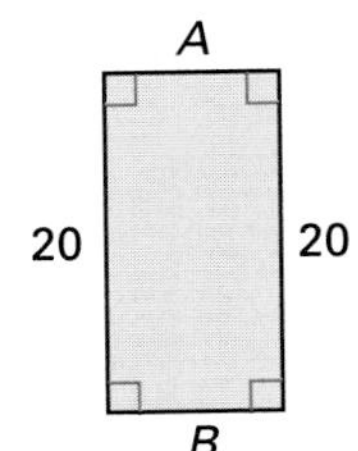

24. History In 1885, U.S. citizens living in Paris gave France a model of the Statue of Liberty. The model now stands on an island in the Seine River in Paris. The Statue of Liberty is about 150 feet tall, and the model in Paris is about 40 feet tall. If the torch of the taller statue measures about 20 feet and the statues are proportional to each other, how tall is the model's torch?

Using Data Use the Data File on page 507 to solve **25** and **26.**

25. Find the height of the model's pedestal to the nearest hundredth of a foot.

26. Find the height of the model's observation deck to the nearest hundredth of a foot.

27. Darius thought that you could solve proportions only when three of the values are given, and one value is missing. Then he saw the proportion $\frac{4}{x} = \frac{x}{9}$, where two values are given and two are missing. Darius was able to solve the problem. What is the value of x? Explain your method.

Problem Solving and GEOGRAPHY

Proportions are helpful not only when building models, but also when reading or making maps. The scale of the map is a ratio. Every 1 cm of distance on the map represents 200 m of actual distance.

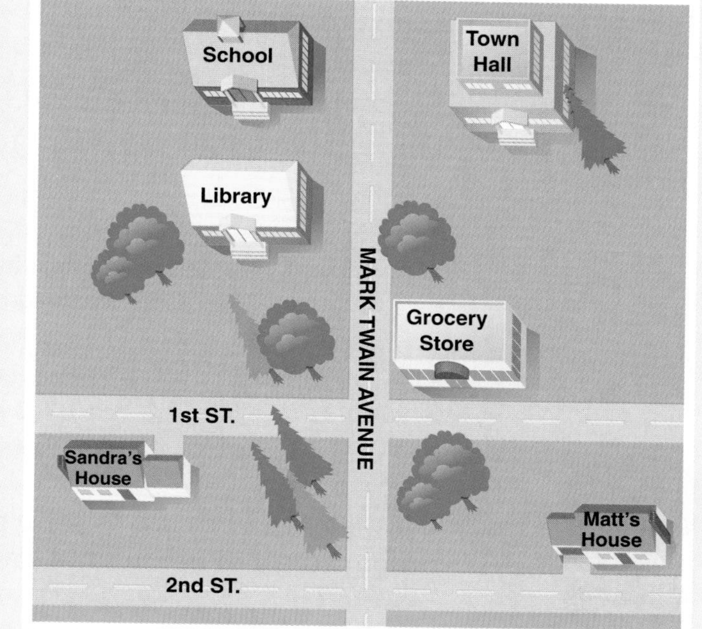

28. Use a ruler to measure the distance from the school to Sandra's house. Write a proportion to find the actual distance from the school to Sandra's house.

29. Find the actual distance from the school to Matt's house.

30. Find the actual distance from Sandra's house to Matt's house.

31. If Theo lives 5 km from the school, how far from the school should his house be on the map?

32. Collecting Data Draw a map of your town. Find actual distances and choose an appropriate scale so your drawing will easily fit on a sheet of paper. Show your school, the neighborhood, or some other area near where you live.

33. Journal Explain how to find the missing value in a proportion.

Mixed Review and Test Prep

STAY SHARP!

Add.

34. $4 + (-7)$ **35.** $-8 + (-10)$ **36.** $-12 + 11$ **37.** $3 + (-9)$ **38.** $6 + (-2)$

Find the area of each circle, where r = radius and d = diameter. Use 3.14 for π. Round to the nearest hundredth.

39. $r = 2$ cm **40.** $d = 6.6$ feet **41.** $d = 14$ cm **42.** $r = 11$ feet

43. $r = 12$ inches **44.** $r = 40$ mm **45.** $d = 9.1$ yards **46.** $r = 0.4$ miles

47. Maria designs flags and banners. She always makes the ratio of the width of a flag to the height of the flagpole from which it hangs the same. If one flag is 6 feet wide and its pole is 24 feet tall, which measure below shows the width of a flag Maria would design for a 20-foot pole?

Ⓐ 5 feet Ⓑ 8 feet Ⓒ 50 feet Ⓓ 80 feet

Chapter 10
Lesson
6

Solving Proportions Using Unit Rates

You Will Learn

- to solve proportions using unit rates

Learn

Recall that a unit ratio is a ratio where one quantity is compared to exactly one unit of another quantity. You can find the unit rate by using division.

Example 1

Market Supreme sells granola by the pound. Tammy's granola weighed 8 pounds. The cashier charged her $12. What was the price per pound?

$\frac{\$12}{8 \text{ pounds}} = \frac{\$12 \div 8}{8 \text{ pounds} \div 8}$ Write a ratio. Divide by the unit quantity.

$= \frac{\$1.50}{1 \text{ pound.}}$

Math Tip

You can also use a calculator to find a unit rate by entering numerator [÷] denominator [=].

Unit rates can be used to solve proportions. Find the unit rate of the given proportion, and use multiplication to find the unknown value.

Example 2

The *Tian Tan* (Temple of Heaven) *Buddha* on Lantau Island, Hong Kong, weighs 275 tons and cost $9,000,000 to build. At 112 feet tall, it is one of the tallest free-standing statues in the world. If the cost of the statue is proportional to the weight, how much would the statue have cost if it weighed 300 tons?

$\frac{\$9,000,000}{275 \text{ tons}} \frac{\div 275 \text{ tons}}{\div 275 \text{ tons}} = \frac{\$32,727.27}{1 \text{ ton}}$

Find the unit rate.

The statue cost about $32,727.27 per ton. Now, multiply by the new number of tons.

300 tons × $32,727.27 per ton = $9,818,181.82

It would have cost about $9,818,182.

You can use unit rates and proportions to solve the same problem.

Example 3

Show how you can use unit rates and proportions to solve this problem.

Lauren wants to read *The Lion, the Witch, and the Wardrobe.* The book is 216 pages long. Yesterday she read the first 12 pages in about 18 minutes. How long will it take Lauren to read the entire book?

Unit Rate Method

$\frac{18 \text{ minutes}}{12 \text{ pages}} = \frac{18 \text{ minutes} \div 12}{12 \text{ pages} \div 12}$

Lauren reads at a rate of about 1.5 minutes per page.

216 pages × 1.5 minutes per page = 324 minutes

Proportion Method

$\frac{18 \text{ minutes}}{12 \text{ pages}} = \frac{x \text{ minutes}}{216 \text{ pages}}$

$\frac{3{,}888}{12} = \frac{12x}{12}$

$324 = x$

It will take 324 minutes, or about $5\frac{1}{2}$ hours, to read the book.

Talk About It

1. How does solving a proportion by unit rates differ from solving by cross products?
2. Which method do you prefer? Why?

Check

1. A zebra can run 420 ft in 7 seconds. Find the zebra's rate of speed per minute.
2. Keith walks 870 yd to school in 15 min. Find Keith's rate of speed per minute.
3. Veronica bought 20 pencils for $1.60. At that rate, how much would 35 pencils cost?
4. **Reasoning** Do you use both multiplication and division when solving problems with either method? Explain.

5. **Reasoning** Give an example of how shoppers use unit rates.

Practice

Skills and Reasoning

Find the unit rate for each. Round to the nearest hundredth as needed.

6. $\frac{6\text{ mi}}{12\text{ sec}}$ **7.** $\frac{10\text{ houses}}{5\text{ mi}}$ **8.** $\frac{12\text{ pencils}}{3\text{ boxes}}$ **9.** $\frac{62\text{ holes}}{12\text{ in}^2}$

10. $\frac{\$18}{4\text{ lb}}$ **11.** $\frac{6\text{ waves}}{10\text{ sec}}$ **12.** $\frac{17\text{ people}}{37\text{ ft}^2}$ **13.** $\frac{9\text{ slices}}{3\text{ people}}$

14. $\frac{7\text{ in. rain}}{3\text{ days}}$ **15.** $\frac{6\text{ m}}{18\text{ hr}}$ **16.** $\frac{14\text{ kg}}{3\text{ bags}}$ **17.** $\frac{11\text{ cups}}{22\text{ servings}}$

18. $\frac{16\text{ shapes}}{5\text{ boxes}}$ **19.** $\frac{13\text{ turtles}}{2\text{ mi}^2}$ **20.** $\frac{62\text{ lines}}{1\text{ sheet}}$ **21.** $\frac{15\text{ m}}{2\text{ sec}}$

Solve each proportion using unit rates.

22. $\frac{24\text{ lb}}{12\text{ ft}} = \frac{?}{28\text{ ft}}$ **23.** $\frac{?}{6\text{ hr}} = \frac{210\text{ mi}}{5\text{ hr}}$ **24.** $\frac{?}{3\text{ lb}} = \frac{\$3.50}{7\text{ lb}}$ **25.** $\frac{6.6\text{ points}}{3\text{ games}} = \frac{?}{1\text{ game}}$

26. $\frac{62\text{m}}{20\text{ sec}} = \frac{?}{32\text{ sec}}$ **27.** $\frac{?}{3\text{ sec}} = \frac{21\text{ drops}}{7\text{ sec}}$ **28.** $\frac{?}{9\text{ m}} = \frac{16\text{ kites}}{0.25\text{ m}}$ **29.** $\frac{3\text{ apples}}{5\text{ lunches}} = \frac{?}{2\text{ lunches}}$

Choose mental math, paper and pencil, or a calculator to solve each proportion.

30. $\frac{46}{12} = \frac{t}{30}$ **31.** $\frac{16}{x} = \frac{12}{3}$ **32.** $\frac{65}{4} = \frac{13}{y}$ **33.** $\frac{28}{m} = \frac{238}{102}$

34. $\frac{12}{62} = \frac{24}{s}$ **35.** $\frac{v}{2} = \frac{12}{24}$ **36.** $\frac{p}{12} = \frac{63}{108}$ **37.** $\frac{21}{17} = \frac{b}{51}$

38. Reasoning If 7 square feet of carpet cost $4.50, how can you find the rate of square feet per dollar? How can you find the rate of dollars per square foot? If you were carpeting a room, which rate would be the most sensible rate to use?

39. Reasoning Name five unit rates that people use every day. For example, there are 60 minutes in 1 hour.

40. Science The speed of sound through water is $\frac{1{,}460\text{ m}}{\text{sec}}$. Is this a unit rate? How far does sound travel through water in 2 seconds?

41. Money Which is a better value, 2 pounds of bananas for 50¢ or 3 pounds of bananas for 72¢?

Problem Solving and Applications

42. Geography The *Colossi of Memnon* in Karnak, Egypt, are 21 meters tall. They also measure 70 feet tall. Using these measurements, find the number of meters in a foot.

43. Estimation Emma estimates that she collected about 70 apples from the orchard and put an equal number of apples into each of 6 baskets. Mrs. Sanders wants 3 baskets of apples. Set up and solve a proportion to determine about how many apples Mrs. Sanders would receive.

44. Literature Janet wants to make a wooden carving of Artemis, Greek goddess of the hunt. She imagines that Artemis is 7 feet tall. If her carving is 12 inches tall, how many feet does 1 inch represent?

45. Critical Thinking Fiona is filming a 6-inch lizard to represent a 48-foot monster. The lizard moves at a rate of 5 inches per second.

a. If Fiona films a 20-inch-tall movie set, how tall does the set look in the movie? Explain.

b. How long will it take for the small lizard to move 35 inches? Explain how you found your answer.

c. Is there any numerical information in the problem that isn't needed to answer the first two questions? Explain.

46. Journal Describe a situation where you could use mental math to find the unit rate of a ratio.

Mixed Review and Test Prep

Find the area of the irregular shape. Round to the nearest hundredth.

47.

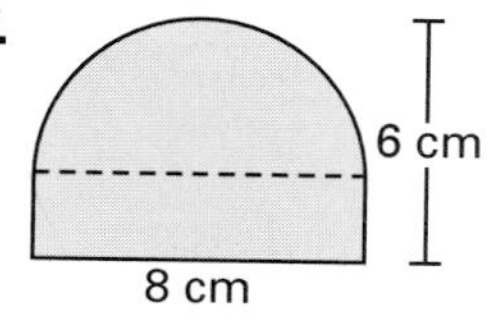

48.

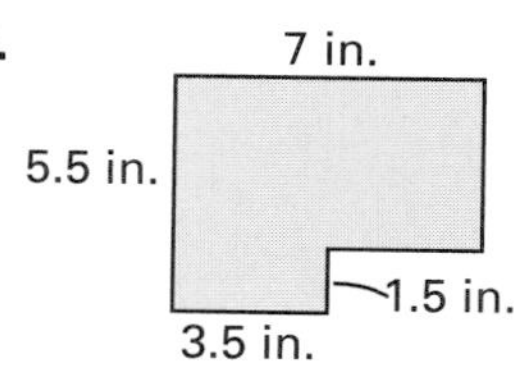

49.

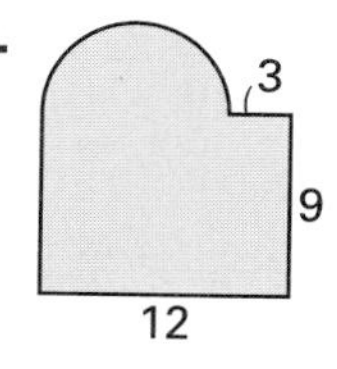

50.

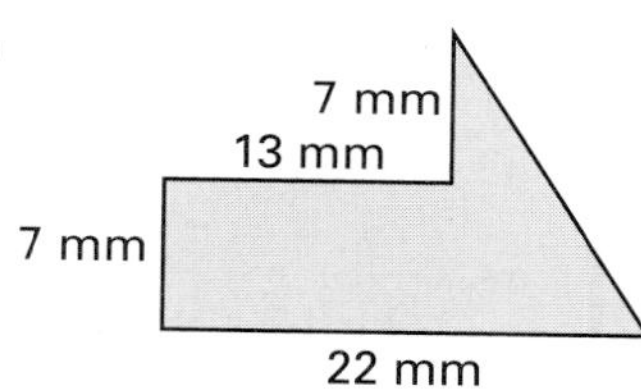

Subtract.

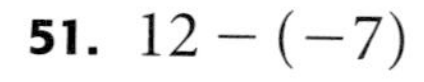

51. $12 - (-7)$ **52.** $-8 - 9$ **53.** $-16 - 10$ **54.** $11 - (-3)$

55. $-5 - (-9)$ **56.** $-4 - (-1)$ **57.** $0 - (-13)$ **58.** $2 - (-4)$

59. Which animal is moving the fastest?

Ⓐ A cat at 660 ft per 15 sec

Ⓑ A greyhound at 616 ft per 12 sec

Ⓒ A zebra at 645 ft per 11 sec

Ⓓ An elephant at 1,100 ft per 30 sec

and Practice

Solve each proportion.

1. $\frac{4}{14} = \frac{x}{35}$
2. $\frac{8}{12} = \frac{12}{n}$
3. $\frac{16}{24} = \frac{28}{m}$
4. $\frac{c}{70} = \frac{2}{5}$
5. $\frac{9}{15} = \frac{u}{35}$
6. $\frac{18}{g} = \frac{30}{15}$
7. $\frac{v}{16} = \frac{18}{24}$
8. $\frac{6}{9} = \frac{q}{21}$
9. $\frac{i}{7} = \frac{9}{17.5}$
10. $\frac{4.5}{5.4} = \frac{1.5}{w}$
11. $\frac{b}{9} = \frac{6}{13.5}$
12. $\frac{6.6}{z} = \frac{8.8}{9.6}$
13. $\frac{d}{24} = \frac{7}{12}$
14. $\frac{6}{16} = \frac{e}{24}$
15. $\frac{20}{30} = \frac{j}{34.5}$
16. $\frac{18}{24} = \frac{q}{28}$
17. $\frac{4}{10} = \frac{30}{p}$
18. $\frac{2.2}{8} = \frac{1.65}{t}$
19. $\frac{f}{20} = \frac{3}{15}$
20. $\frac{2}{p} = \frac{14}{91}$
21. $\frac{20}{16} = \frac{25}{c}$
22. $\frac{11}{33} = \frac{x}{120}$
23. $\frac{a}{12} = \frac{2}{8}$
24. $\frac{39.75}{150} = \frac{r}{20}$
25. $\frac{9}{24} = \frac{3}{n}$
26. $\frac{54 \text{ ft}}{3 \text{ sec}} = \frac{v}{13 \text{ sec}}$
27. $\frac{y}{3 \text{ lb}} = \frac{\$3.44}{4 \text{ lb}}$
28. $\frac{126 \text{ mi}}{9 \text{ hr}} = \frac{70 \text{ mi}}{x}$
29. $\frac{n}{15 \text{ sec}} = \frac{120 \text{ m}}{24 \text{ sec}}$
30. $\frac{91 \text{ gal}}{7 \text{ min}} = \frac{k}{2 \text{ min}}$
31. $\frac{\$12.50}{5 \text{ doz}} = \frac{\$20.00}{i}$
32. $\frac{948 \text{ mi}}{p} = \frac{790 \text{ mi}}{5 \text{ hr}}$
33. $\frac{13.6 \text{ in}}{8 \text{ sec}} = \frac{z}{9 \text{ sec}}$
34. $\frac{t}{0.5 \text{ m}} = \frac{48 \text{ pt}}{4 \text{ m}}$
35. $\frac{58¢}{a} = \frac{87¢}{3 \text{ lb}}$
36. $\frac{42 \text{ lb}}{20 \text{ sec}} = \frac{x}{15 \text{ sec}}$
37. $\frac{260 \text{ mi}}{4 \text{ wk}} = \frac{650 \text{ mi}}{b}$
38. $\frac{\$9.06}{2 \text{ wk}} = \frac{\$22.65}{m}$
39. $\frac{8 \text{ lb}}{6 \text{ wk}} = \frac{q}{2 \text{ wk}}$
40. $\frac{y}{7 \text{ hr}} = \frac{\$420}{35 \text{ hr}}$
41. $\frac{9 \text{ lb}}{k} = \frac{10.5 \text{ lb}}{7 \text{ doz}}$
42. $\frac{72 \text{ mi}}{j} = \frac{168 \text{ mi}}{7 \text{ gal}}$
43. $\frac{t}{2 \text{ mi}} = \frac{115 \text{ laps}}{5 \text{ mi}}$
44. $\frac{52 \text{ ft}}{4 \text{ min}} = \frac{x}{10 \text{ min}}$
45. $\frac{h}{6 \text{ hr}} = \frac{150 \text{ ft}}{10 \text{ hr}}$
46. $\frac{y}{8 \text{ hr}} = \frac{\$240}{40 \text{ hr}}$
47. $\frac{270 \text{ cans}}{15 \text{ boxes}} = \frac{x}{4 \text{ boxes}}$
48. $\frac{\$64}{4 \text{ wk}} = \frac{\$96}{z}$
49. $\frac{196 \text{ mi}}{4 \text{ days}} = \frac{d}{7 \text{ days}}$

Error Search

Find each solution that is not correct. Write it correctly and explain the error.

50. $\frac{312 \text{ mi}}{12 \text{ gal}} = \frac{x}{5 \text{ gal}}$
    $x = 125$ mi
51. $\frac{y}{14 \text{ hr}} = \frac{\$189}{21 \text{ hr}}$
    $y = \$126$
52. $\frac{24 \text{ gal}}{3 \text{ min}} = \frac{16 \text{ gal}}{k}$
    $k = 8$ min
53. $\frac{13 \text{ cars}}{0.25 \text{ mi}} = \frac{z}{2 \text{ mi}}$
    $z = 10.4$ cars

Pie Try!

Solve each proportion. Match each solution to a number below the blanks. Then find the answer to the question. Some letters are not used.

It took each of four contestants eight minutes to eat eight pies. How long did it take one contestant to eat eight pies?

  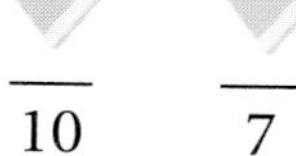

___ ___ ___ ___ ___
7 3.6 16 8 10

___ ___ ___ ___ ___ ___ ___
15 3.6 28 21 10 7 6

54. $\frac{2}{5} = \frac{z}{15}$ (S) **55.** $\frac{18}{6} = \frac{27}{y}$ (O) **56.** $\frac{3}{14} = \frac{6}{x}$ (N) **57.** $\frac{w}{15} = \frac{9}{3}$ (A)

58. $\frac{24}{v} = \frac{42}{28}$ (G) **59.** $\frac{q}{3} = \frac{10}{2}$ (M) **60.** $\frac{20}{9} = \frac{8}{p}$ (I) **61.** $\frac{28}{4} = \frac{k}{3}$ (U)

62. $\frac{6}{5} = \frac{j}{25}$ (F) **63.** $\frac{10.5}{7} = \frac{12}{d}$ (H) **64.** $\frac{3}{c} = \frac{7.5}{25}$ (T) **65.** $\frac{b}{20} = \frac{5.6}{16}$ (E)

Number Sense Reasoning

Write whether each statement is true or false. Explain your answer.

66. $\frac{5}{10} = \frac{x}{21}$ The value of x is greater than 15.

67. $\frac{4}{9} = \frac{2}{y}$ The value of y is less than 9.

68. $\frac{3}{z} = \frac{6}{14}$ The value of z is equal to 14.

69. $\frac{v}{8} = \frac{2}{3}$ The value of v is greater than 2.

Similar Figures

Problem Solving Connection
- Look for a Pattern

Materials
- centimeter ruler
- protractor

Vocabulary
similar

Explore

Recall that figures with the same size and shape are congruent. The symbol $\cong$ means "is congruent to."

Figures that have the same shape but not necessarily the same size are **similar** figures. The symbol $\sim$ means "is similar to."

The objects pictured are similar because their shapes are the same, even though their sizes may be different.

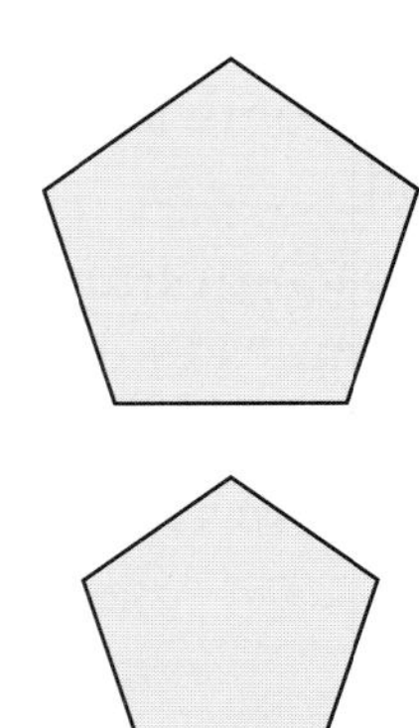

Work Together

Remember
Congruent triangles have corresponding sides of the same length and corresponding angles of the same size. They have the same size and shape.

1. Draw a large triangle, $\triangle A$, with three unequal sides. Measure and label the length of each side and the width of each angle.
2. Draw a smaller triangle whose angles have the same measures as the angles of $\triangle A$. Call the new triangle $\triangle B$. Measure and label the length of each side.
3. Find these ratios:
   a. $\frac{\text{longest side of } \triangle A}{\text{longest side of } \triangle B}$
   b. $\frac{\text{mid-length side of } \triangle A}{\text{mid-length side of } \triangle B}$
   c. $\frac{\text{shortest side of } \triangle A}{\text{shortest side of } \triangle B}$
4. Are the longest sides proportional to the shortest sides? Explain.
5. Are the longest sides proportional to the mid-length sides? Explain.
6. Are the mid-length sides proportional to the shortest sides? Explain.

Talk About It

7. How are similar figures and congruent figures alike?
8. How are similar figures and congruent figures different?
9. If two figures are congruent, are they similar? Explain.

Connect and Learn

If two figures are similar, their corresponding angles have the same measure and their corresponding sides are proportional.

$\triangle A \sim \triangle B$

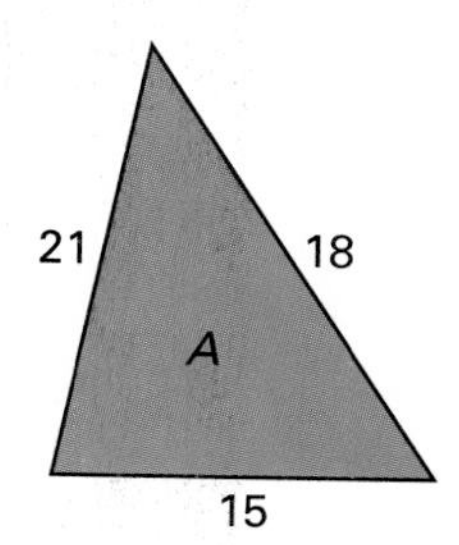

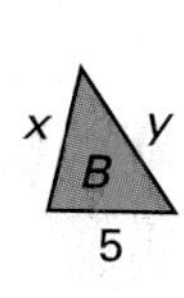

The triangles are similar, so the matching sides are proportional. Find the length of x in $\triangle B$.

$\frac{21}{x} = \frac{15}{5}$	To find the length of the side labeled x, write a proportion using the sides that match each other.
$15x = 21 \times 5$	Write the cross products.
$15x = 105$	Multiply. Think: What number times 15 equals 105?
$x = 105 \div 15$	Use division to undo multiplication.
$x = 7$	The length of x in $\triangle B$ is 7 units.

Problem Solving Hint

Some problems give you information that isn't needed to solve the problem. In this example, you don't need to know that the length of the right side of $\triangle A$ is 18.

Check

Find the missing side lengths in each pair of similar or congruent figures.

1.

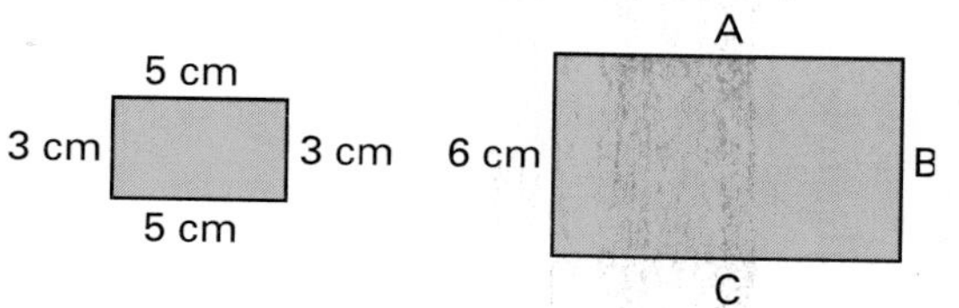

2.

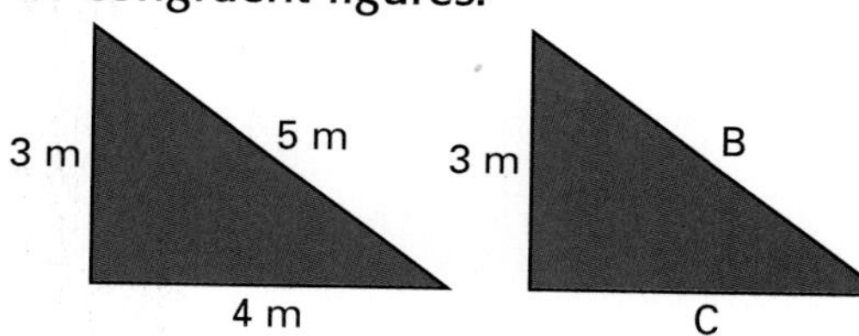

3.

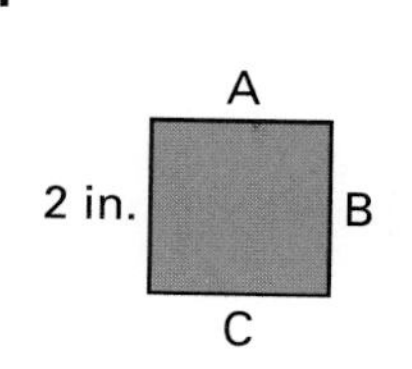

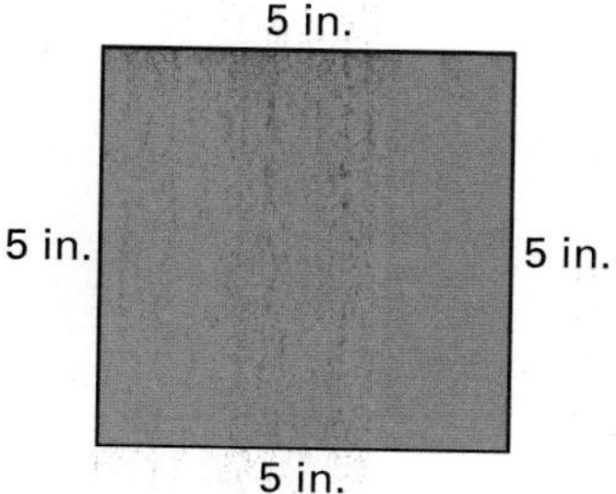

4.

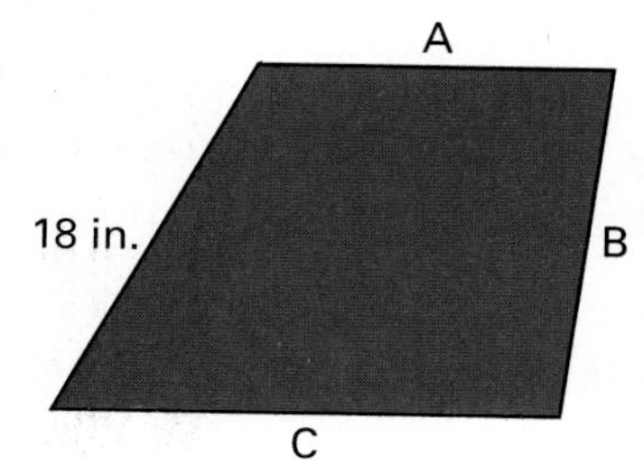

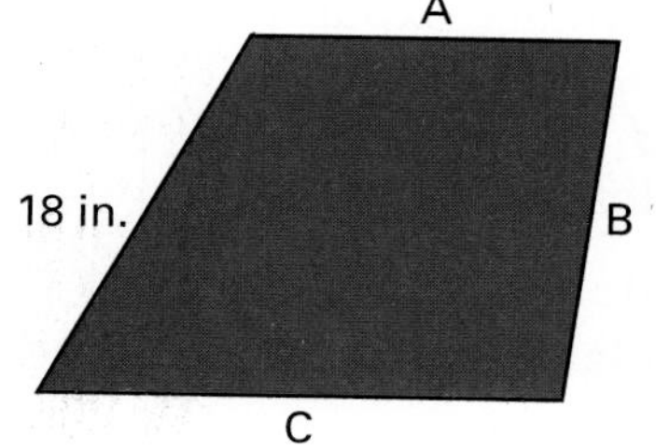

3 in.
3 in. 2 in.
4 in.

Practice

Skills and Reasoning

Find the missing side lengths in each pair of similar figures.

5.

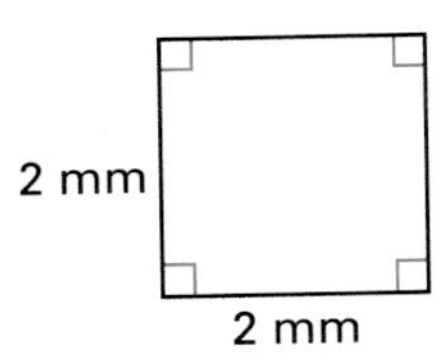

1 mm, C, A, B

6.

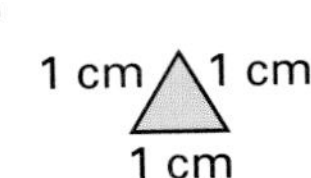

A, 3.5 cm, B

7.

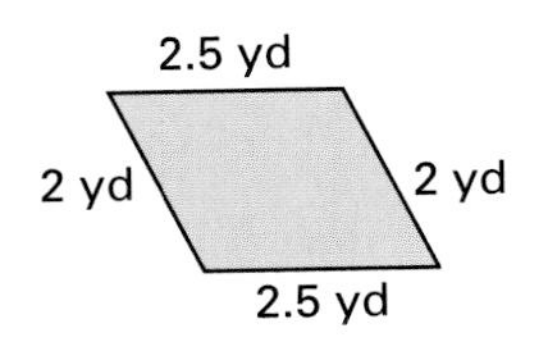

A, B, 0.5 yd, C

8.

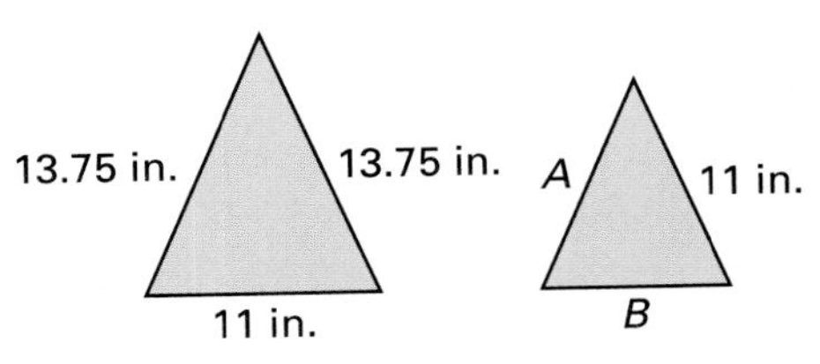

The statues shown in **9** and **10** are proportional with their drawings, so these are similar figures. Find the missing lengths.

9.

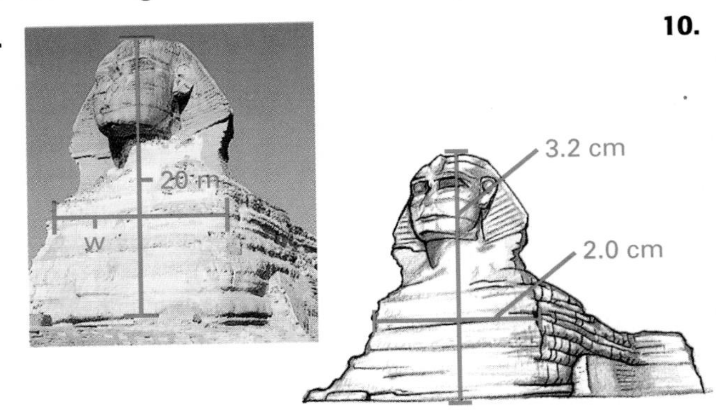

10.

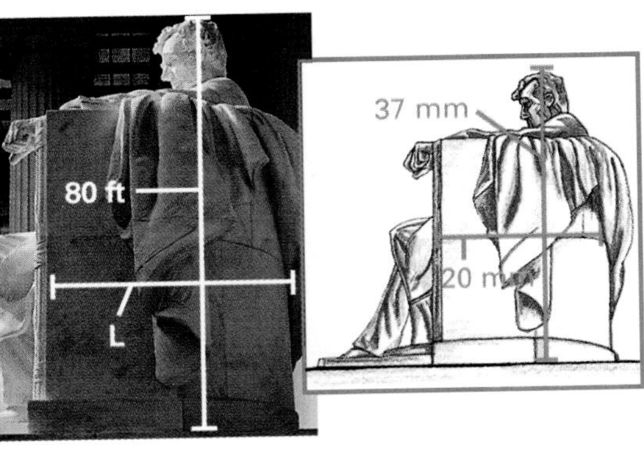

Reasoning State whether the polygons are congruent, similar, or neither.

11.

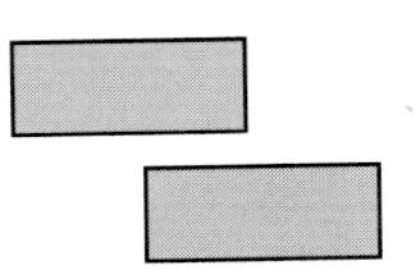

12.

13.

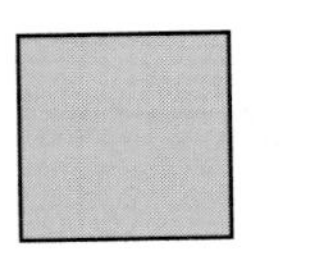

14.

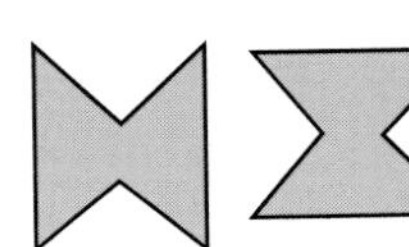

15. Reasoning Is every pair of similar figures congruent? Is every pair of congruent figures similar? Explain.

16. Reasoning If two triangles are equilateral, are they similar? Explain.

17. Geography On the map, 1 inch equals 190 actual miles.

a. Estimate the actual distances of the triangular flight plan indicated on the map.

b. Are the triangle shown on the map and the life-size triangle similar figures?

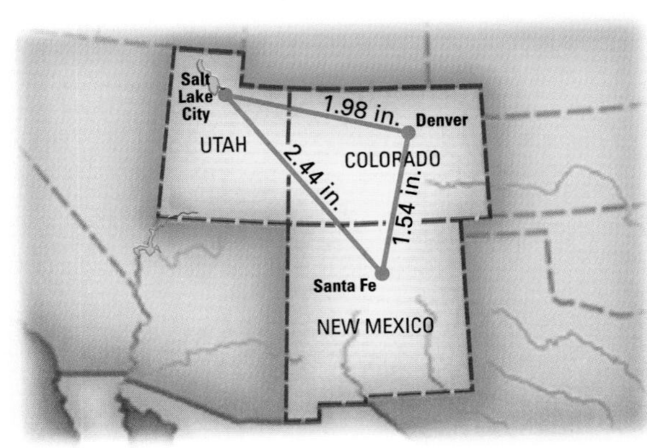

18. **Geometry** A rectangle has sides of 5 ft and 8 ft. A similar rectangle has two sides of 40 feet. There are two possible answers for the length of the other side of the larger rectangle. What are they?

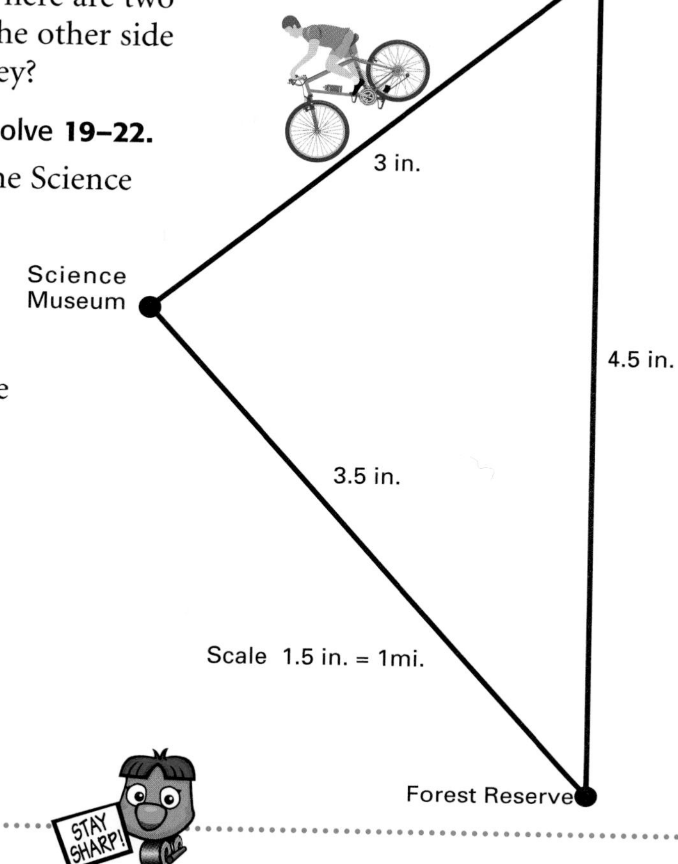

Using Data Use the data on the map to solve **19–22.**

19. Michelle rode from Cody Park to the Science Museum. What was the actual distance she rode?

20. **Time** Michelle's ride from Cody Park to the Science Museum took 24 minutes. How long should it take Michelle to ride from the Science Museum to the Forest Reserve?

21. **Time** If Michelle can maintain the same speed, how long should it take her to ride the entire path?

22. What is the distance of the entire path?

Mixed Review and Test Prep

STAY SHARP!

Simplify.

23. $7 \times (-3)$ **24.** $18 \div (-9)$ **25.** $-8 \times (-2)$ **26.** $-22 \div 11$ **27.** -10×7

28. $-14 \div 7$ **29.** $-2 \times (-13)$ **30.** $6 \div (-3)$ **31.** $-36 \div (-3)$ **32.** $-25 \times (-4)$

Tell whether the first number is divisible by the second.

33. 65, 5 **34.** 33, 11 **35.** 57, 6 **36.** 106, 10 **37.** 882, 9 **38.** 116, 2

39. 36, 4 **40.** 59, 3 **41.** 49, 7 **42.** 81, 8 **43.** 100, 25 **44.** 1,265, 5

45. The blueprint for Gigi's house is drawn to scale. Her house is shaped like a rectangle. On the blueprint, the base and height of the rectangle are 4 inches and 5 inches. If the shorter side of her house is 40 feet, what is the perimeter?

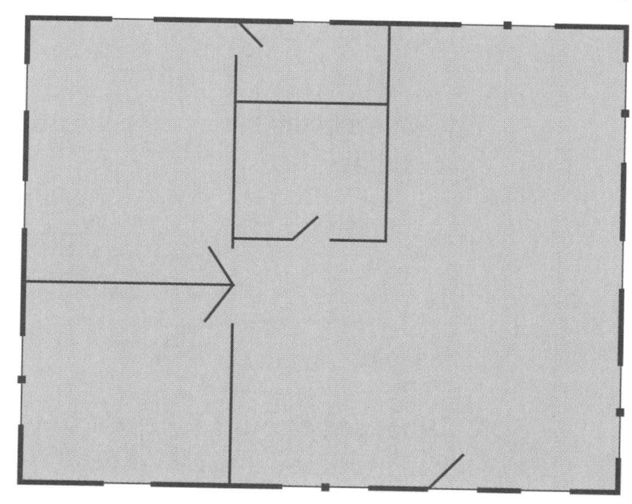

Ⓐ 90 ft Ⓑ 144 ft Ⓒ 180 ft Ⓓ 99 ft

Skills Practice Bank, page 669, Set 4

Chapter 10

Problem Solving

Analyze Word Problems: Checking for a Reasonable Answer

You Will Learn
- to check for a reasonable answer

Learn

Kate is building a model of the Gateway Arch. This structure is 192 meters tall. The scale she wants to use for the model is 1 meter for every 100 meters. She's estimated the height and says she shouldn't have any problem getting her model through a 1.65 m tall doorway. Is Kate's estimate reasonable?

Work Together

Understand

What do you know?

What do you need to find out?

Plan

What will you do to find the answer? Compare the height of the model to the height of the doorway

Solve

What is a good estimate for the height of Kate's model? The Gateway Arch is almost 200 m tall. Using a scale of 1 m to 100 m, the model will be just under 2 m tall.

Look Back

Is Kate's estimate reasonable? The doorway is just over 1.5 m tall. The model is almost 2 m tall. The model will not fit through the doorway.

Talk About It

What scale could Kate use to make her model so she could get it through the doorway?

Check

The population of Amherst is 36,000. In a recent election, $\frac{3}{4}$ of the population voted.

1. Todd estimated that 20,000 residents voted. Is his estimate too high, too low, or about right?

2. Karyn estimated that 25,000 residents voted. Is her estimate too high, too low, or about right?

Problem Solving Practice

Problem Solving Strategies

- Draw a Picture
- Look for a Pattern
- Guess and Check
- Use Logical Reasoning
- Make an Organized List
- Make a Table
- Solve a Simpler Problem
- Work Backward

Choose a Tool

Each of these problems has an estimate as an answer, but some estimates are not good estimates. State if the answer is too low, too high, or close enough, and explain why.

3. A community garden is being designed for a vacant lot. The entire lot measures 127 feet by 160 feet. What is the area of the lot? *20,000 ft²*

4. On the first day of planting, 144 people volunteered to help with the planting. One-fourth of the volunteers tilled the soil. How many of the volunteers tilled the soil? *45*

5. The garden committee will build a fence around the lot. They will plant ivy to grow along the sides of the fence. How much fencing will they need for the 127- by 160-foot lot? *385 feet*

6. A space in the shape of a hexagon is set aside to be planted with marigolds. The perimeter of the hexagon will have a border of square tiles. Each side of the hexagon is $5\frac{1}{2}$ feet. Each tile is 1 square foot. How many tiles will the committee need? *36*

SECTION B

Review and Practice

(Lesson 4) State whether or not each pair of ratios forms a proportion.

1. $\frac{2}{5}$ $\frac{12}{30}$ **2.** $\frac{7}{10}$ $\frac{14}{5}$ **3.** $\frac{9}{3}$ $\frac{45}{15}$ **4.** $\frac{14}{6}$ $\frac{42}{18}$

(Lessons 5 and 6) Solve each proportion.

5. $\frac{2}{7} = \frac{\blacksquare}{14}$ **6.** $\frac{\blacksquare}{28} = \frac{3}{6}$ **7.** $\frac{35}{\blacksquare} = \frac{14}{4}$ **8.** $\frac{63}{20} = \frac{\blacksquare}{40}$ **9.** $\frac{1}{2} = \frac{600}{\blacksquare}$

10. The statue shown is a 14-ft statue of King Kamehameha. It stands outside Aliiolani Hale, the state supreme court building, in Honolulu, Hawaii. The base of the statue is 6 feet tall, and the statue itself is 8 feet tall. If the statue and base together were 20 feet tall, how tall would each part be? Round your answer to the nearest tenth of a foot.

11. If Danielle can wash 2 cars in 24 minutes, how many cars can she wash in an hour?

12. Hector bought 6 pounds of cornmeal. If he was charged \$11.10, what was the price per pound?

13. Which is a better value, 3 pounds of cornmeal for \$4.00 or 4 pounds of cornmeal for \$5.00?

(Lesson 7) Find the missing side lengths in each pair of similar figures.

14.

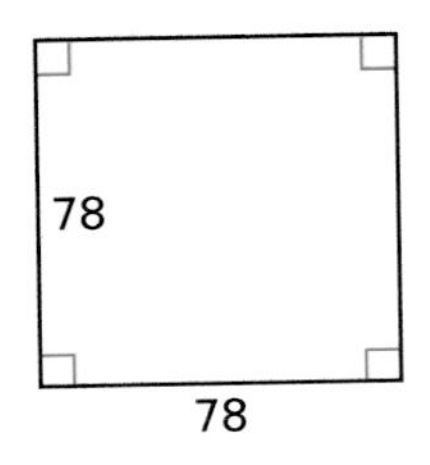

B
A C
26

15.

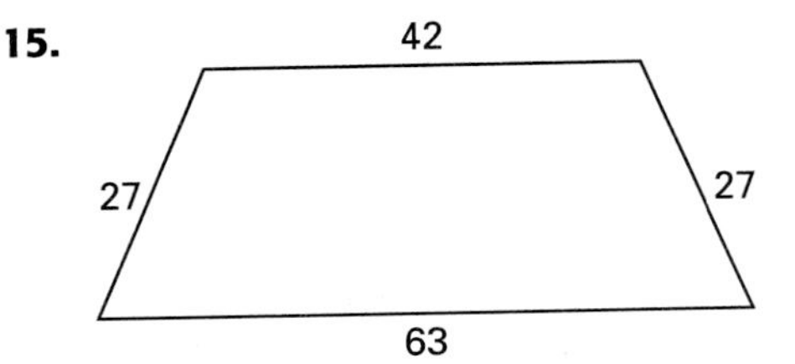

A
3 B
C

16.

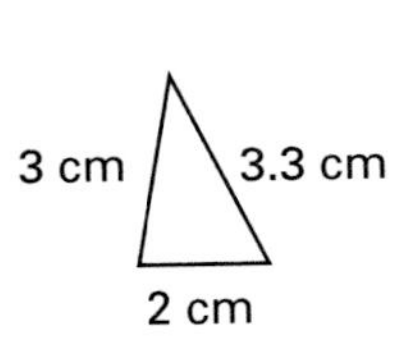

A B
3 cm

17.

B
A C
0.3 in.

18. Journal Why are some figures similar but not congruent?

Skills Checklist

In this section, you have:

- **Explored Proportions**
- **Solved Proportions Using Cross Products**
- **Solved Proportions Using Unit Rates**
- **Learned About Similar Figures**

REVIEW AND PRACTICE

CHAPTER 10

SECTION

C Percents

Rain forests are teeming with life—both plant and animal. In the rain forests of the Malay Archipelago, 25,000 plant species have been identified. These include orchids (4,000 species), large trees (2,500 species), heathers (700 species), and figs (500 species).

How could you use percents to describe the data about the plant species?

GET READY!

Understanding Percents

Review estimating with fractions. Estimate the fraction that is shaded for each figure.

1.

2. 

3. 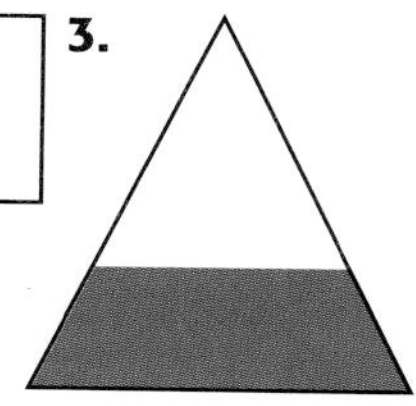

Skills Checklist

In this section, you will:

- ❑ Learn About Percents
- ❑ Estimate Percents
- ❑ Connect Percents to Fractions and Decimals

Chapter 10
Lesson
8

What Is a Percent?

You Will Learn

- to express a quantity as a percent

Vocabulary

percent

Learn

A **percent** is a ratio that compares a part to a whole using the number 100. The percent is the number of hundredths that represents the part.

Mrs. Roberts says her favorite football team wins 100% of the time. Do you think she is exaggerating?

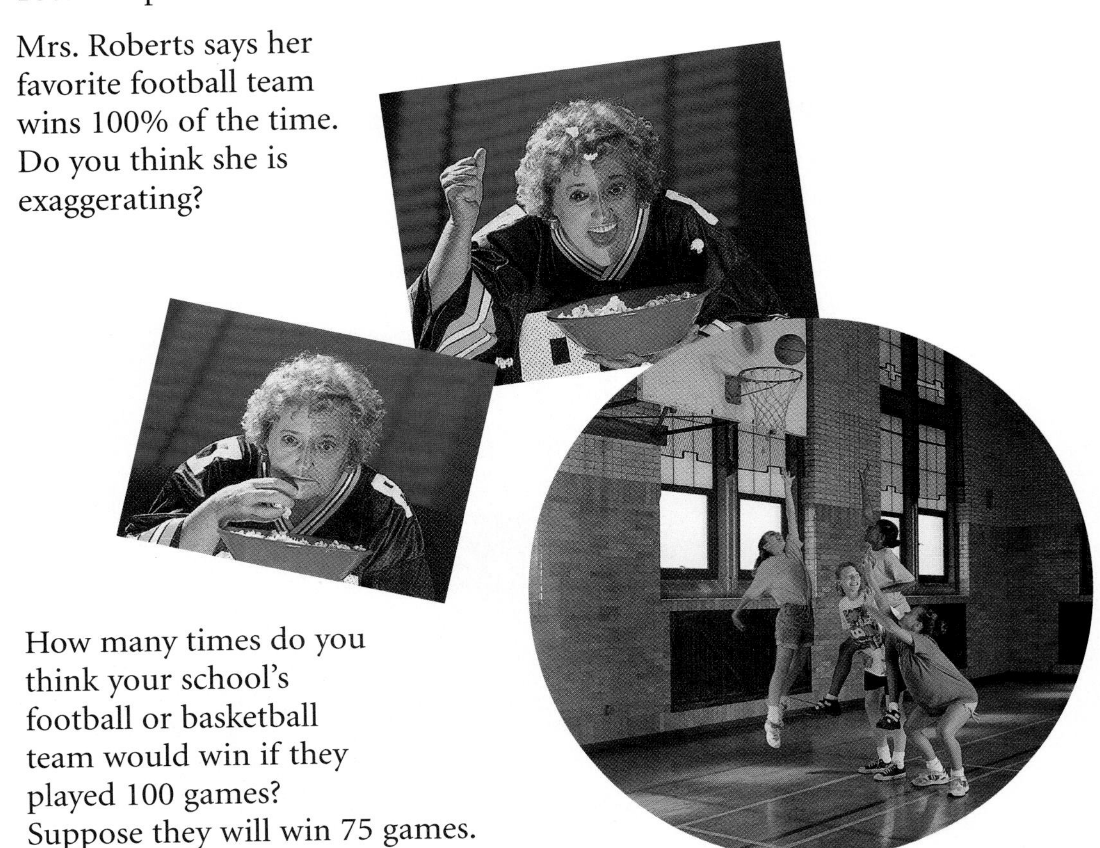

How many times do you think your school's football or basketball team would win if they played 100 games?
Suppose they will win 75 games.

$$\frac{\text{Number of wins}}{\text{Number of games}} \quad \frac{75 \text{ wins}}{100 \text{ games}} = 75\%$$

Your team wins 75% of its games.

Remember

$\frac{1}{10}$ of $100 = \frac{1}{10} \times 100 = 10$

$\frac{1}{4}$ of $100 = \frac{1}{4} \times 100 = 25$

$\frac{1}{2}$ of $100 = \frac{1}{2} \times 100 = 50$

$\frac{3}{4}$ of $100 = \frac{3}{4} \times 100 = 75$

If a quantity is broken into 100 pieces, it is easy to describe using percents. It is also easy to use percents when working with fourths or tenths.

$\frac{1}{10} = \frac{10}{100}$, or 10%

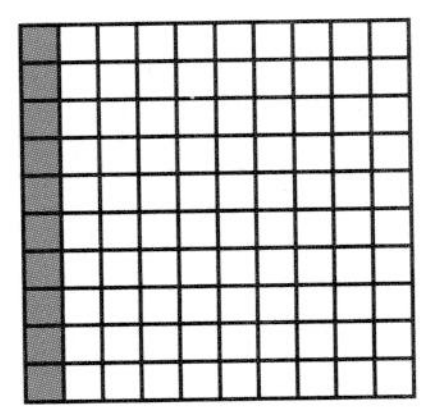

$\frac{1}{4} = \frac{25}{100}$, or 25%

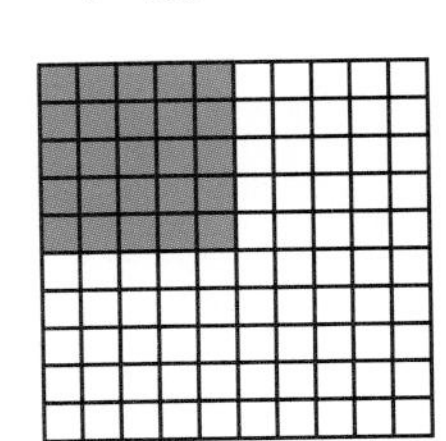

$\frac{1}{2} = \frac{50}{100}$, or 50%

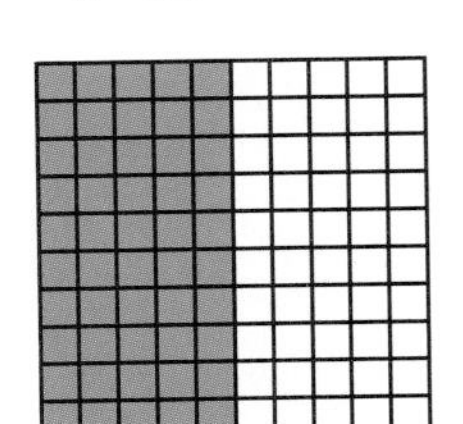

$\frac{3}{4} = \frac{75}{100}$, or 75%

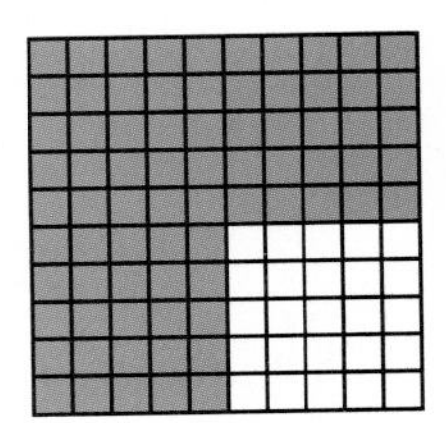

Example 1

Give the percent for the portion of each figure that is shaded.

a.

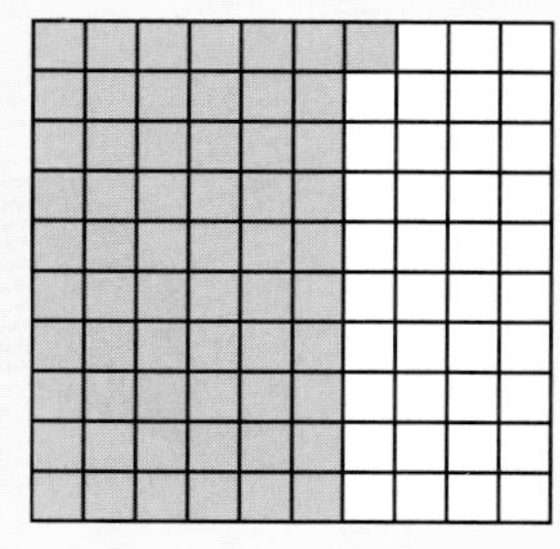

61 of the 100 squares are shaded.

$\frac{61}{100} = 61\%$

b.

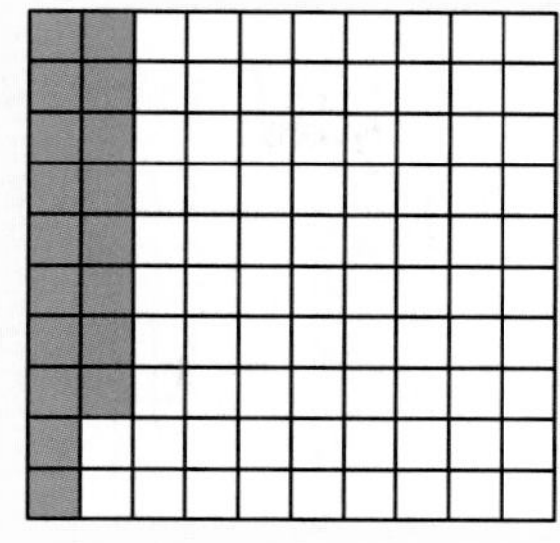

18 of the 100 squares are shaded.

$\frac{18}{100} = 18\%$

Percents are very helpful in solving real-world problems. Percents make it easier to visualize a portion of a group.

Example 2

The shaded portion of the figure represents the portion of the world's bird species that live in rain forests. What percent of bird species live in rain forests?

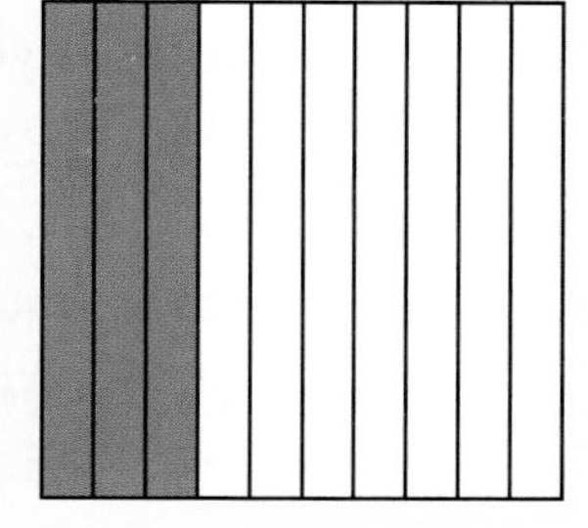

Each shaded section is $\frac{1}{10}$ of the figure. Three sections, or $\frac{3}{10}$, are shaded.

$\frac{3}{10} = \frac{x}{100}$

Think: $10 \times 10 = 100$

So, $3 \times 10 = 30$

$\frac{3}{10} = \frac{30}{100} = 30\%$

Talk About It

1. What is 100% of something? What is 0% of something?
2. Can a quantity be *more than* 100% of another quantity?

Check

Give the percent of each figure that is shaded.

1. 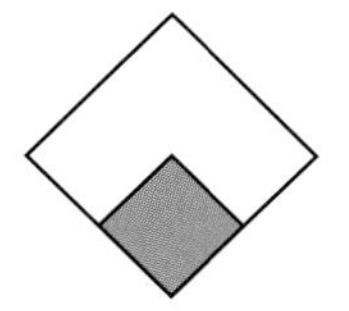

2. 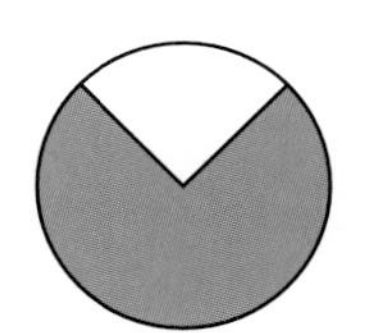

3. Can 25% of something be greater than 50% of something else? Explain?

Practice

Skills and Reasoning

Give the percent of each figure that is shaded.

4. 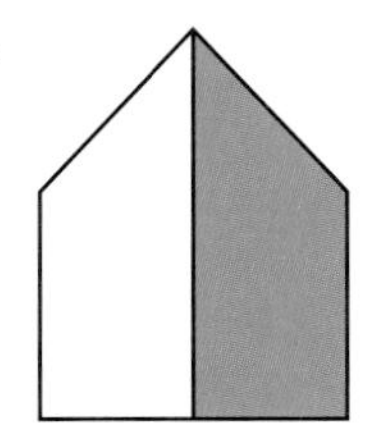

5. 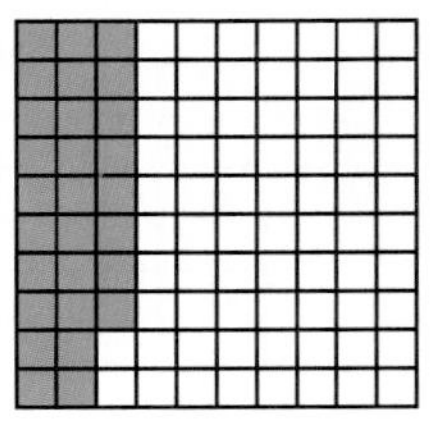

6. 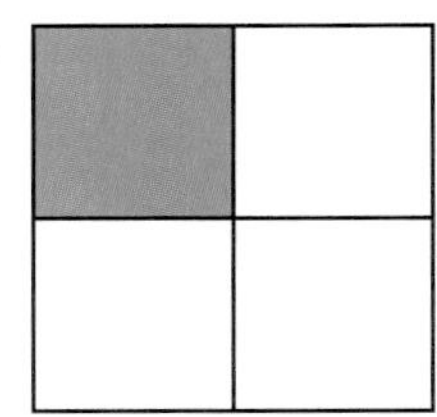

7. 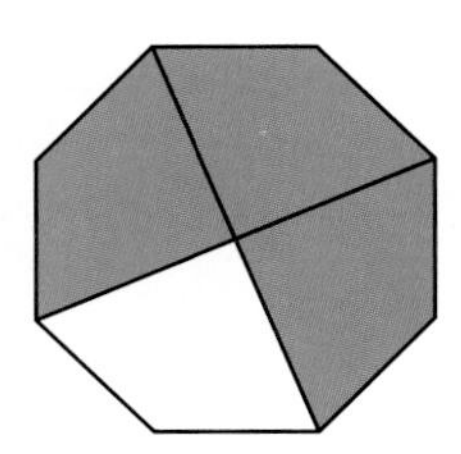

8. 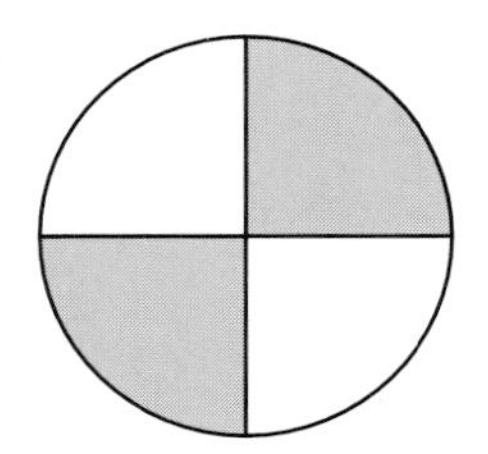

9. 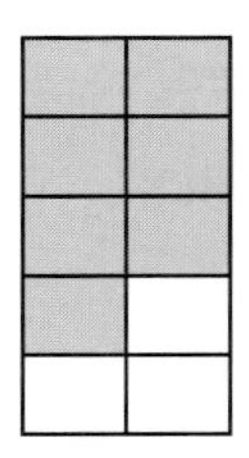

10. 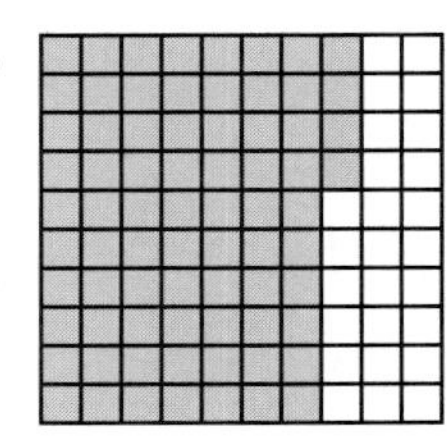

11. 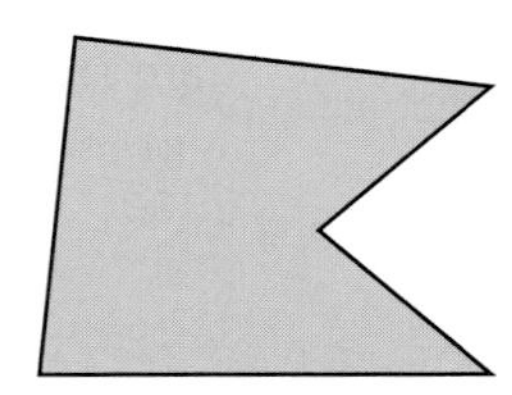

Reasoning Write whether each ratio is greater or less than 50%.

12. $\frac{56}{100}$ **13.** $\frac{23}{100}$ **14.** $\frac{5}{100}$ **15.** $\frac{80}{100}$ **16.** $\frac{45}{100}$ **17.** $\frac{98}{100}$

18. **Reasoning** Do you think every ratio can be written as a percent? Explain your reasoning.

Geography The circle graph shows the percent of Asia's rain forest that is located in each country. Use the graph for **19–21**.

19. About what percent of Asia's rain forest is located in Myanmar? Outside of Myanmar?

20. Which country has the highest percent of Asia's rain forest? Estimate the percent.

21. What three parts of the graph combined account for about 50% of Asia's rain forest?

Asia's Rain Forests

Malaysia
India
Indonesia
Other
Myanmar

22. **Geometry** What percent of the shapes are quadrilaterals?

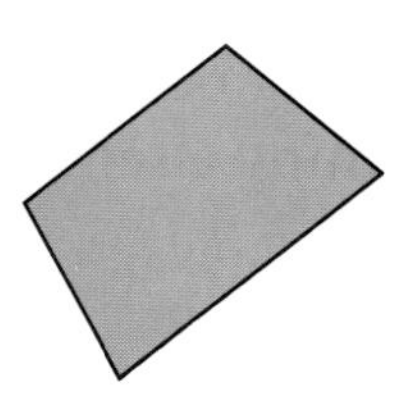

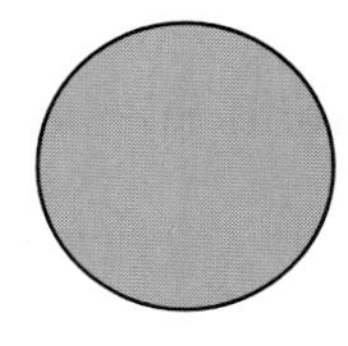

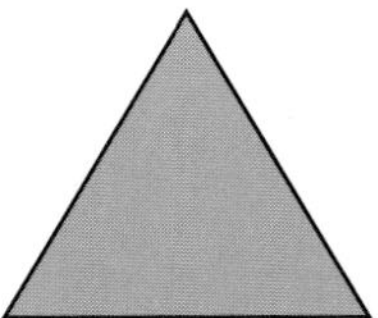

23. **Number Sense** Kwi and Park are building a model out of sugar cubes. Each has half of a box. If Kwi has used half of his sugar cubes, what percent of the whole box has he used?

24. Crista's end-of-the-year math test had 100 problems.

   a. If she got 89 of them correct, what percent of the problems did she get correct?

   b. Is it possible for her to get 113% of the problems correct?

25. **Communicate** A corporation says that its 1997 earnings were 120% of its 1996 earnings. Explain how this percent can be greater than 100%.

Critical Thinking Tell if the situations in **26–28** are possible or not. Explain your reasoning.

26. 62% of the students in Mrs. Chen's class are boys, and 48% are girls.

27. 48% of the students in Mr. Davis' class are wearing blue jeans, and 27% are wearing T-shirts.

28. Students in Mr. O'Malley's class showed an improvement in their test scores of 110%.

Mixed Review and Test Prep

On a coordinate grid, plot and label each point.

29. $Y(-5, 2)$ **30.** $K(3, 9)$ **31.** $A(6, -2)$ **32.** $M(-4, -5)$ **33.** $P(-3, 4)$

Find the prime factorization.

34. 58 **35.** 25 **36.** 26 **37.** 95 **38.** 405 **39.** 125

40. 56 **41.** 6 **42.** 288 **43.** 88 **44.** 87 **45.** 72

46. What decimal describes the portion of the figure that is shaded?

Ⓐ 0.15 Ⓑ 0.17 Ⓒ 0.85 Ⓓ 1.70

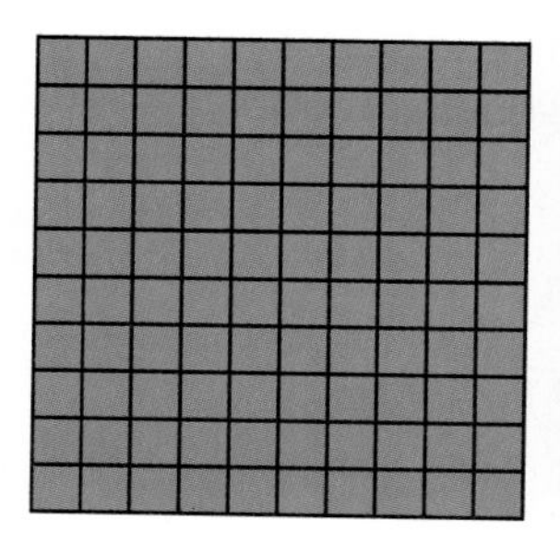

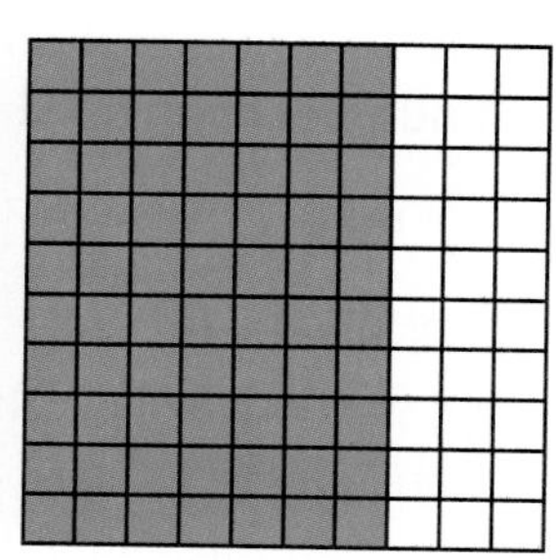

Chapter 10
Lesson
9

Estimating Percents

You Will Learn

- to estimate percents

Did You Know?

Nearly all of the earth's rain forests are located between the Tropic of Cancer (latitude 23° 26′ north) and the Tropic of Capricorn (latitude 23° 26′ south). Every continent except for Europe and Antarctica has a significant amount of land covered by rain forests.

Learn

The map shows the rain forest in Indonesia. Nika is writing a report on the rain forest. She needs to know what percent of Indonesia is made up of rain forest.

Recall that $\frac{1}{2}$ of something is 50%, $\frac{1}{4}$ is 25%, and $\frac{1}{10}$ is 10%. When estimating a percent, think of a fraction close to the given value that uses halves, fourths, or tenths. These fractions can easily be expressed as percents.

The shaded part of the map is more than $\frac{3}{4}$, but less than $\frac{4}{4}$. It is about $\frac{8}{10}$.

Your estimate should be more than 75% but less than 100%. You might estimate 80%.

About 80% of Indonesia's land is made up of rain forest.

Example 1

Estimate the percent of the figure that is shaded.

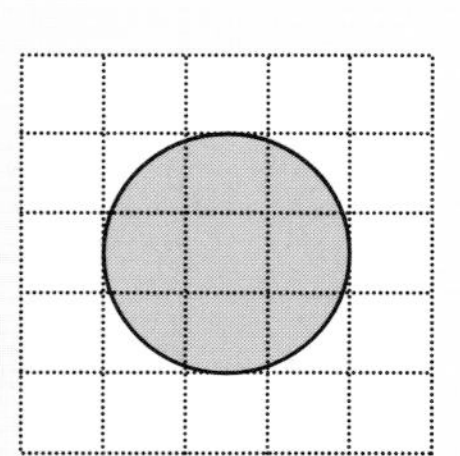

The circle covers 5 squares completely or almost completely. It covers about $\frac{1}{2}$ of 4 more squares. The combined number of covered squares is about

$5 + \frac{1}{2} + \frac{1}{2} + \frac{1}{2} + \frac{1}{2}$, or 7.

The total number of squares is 5×5, or 25.

The part shaded is about $\frac{7}{25}$, which is about $\frac{7}{28}$.

$\frac{7}{28} = \frac{1}{4}$, or 25%.

About 25% of the figure is shaded.

Example 2

Of Mr. Niemeyer's 80 students, 71 wore costumes in a play. Estimate the percent of Mr. Niemeyer's students who did *not* wear costumes.

$80 - 71 = 9$, so 9 students did *not* wear costumes.

9 is about $\frac{1}{10}$ of 80, or about 10% of 80.

About 10% did *not* wear costumes.

Example 3

Lynette counted the number of clothing stores in a local mall. She found that 66 of the 128 stores were clothing stores. Estimate the percent of clothing stores in the mall.

66 is about $\frac{1}{2}$ of 128, or 50% of 128.

About 50% of the stores in the mall sell clothes.

Talk About It

1. If you know 10% of a number, how can you use estimation to find 5% of the number? 20% of the number? 80% of the number?
2. Describe a situation where you could use mental math to find a percent exactly, instead of having to estimate.

Check

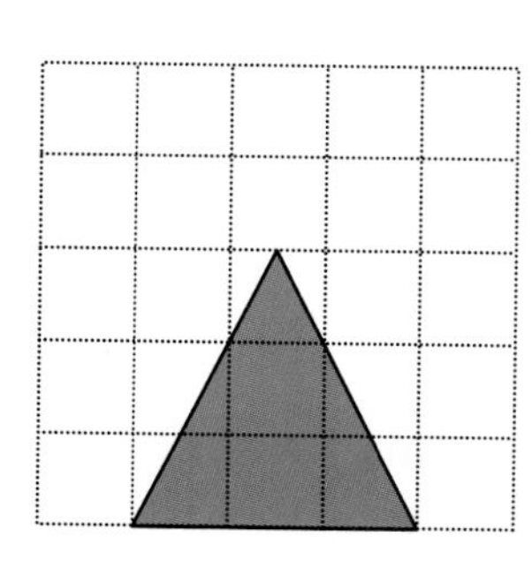

1. Estimate the percent of the figure that is shaded.
2. Estimate the percent of 15 out of 89.
3. Estimate the percent of 24 out of 49.
4. Estimate the percent of $\frac{3}{33}$.
5. **Reasoning** If you are describing a pizza that's been partially eaten, is it easier to estimate the fraction not eaten, or the percent not eaten? Explain.

Practice

Skills and Reasoning

Estimate the percent of each grid that is shaded.

6. 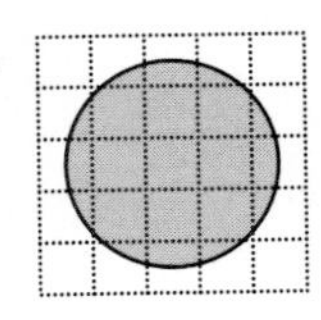

7. 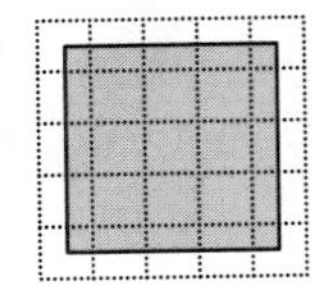

8. 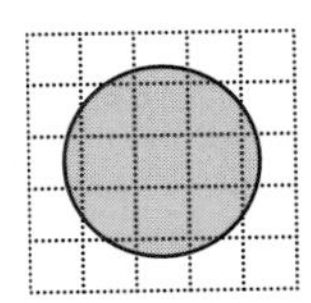

9. 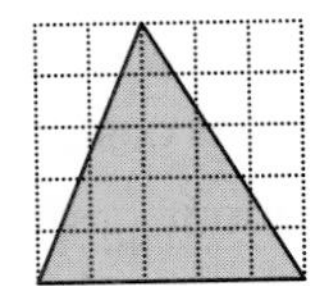

Estimate what percent of each figure is shaded.

10. 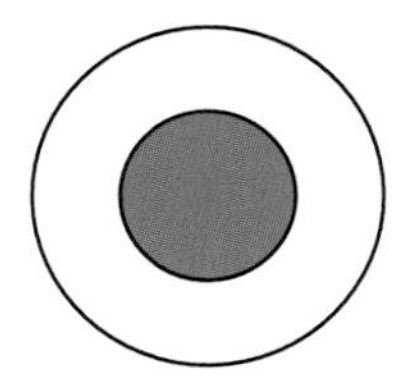

11. 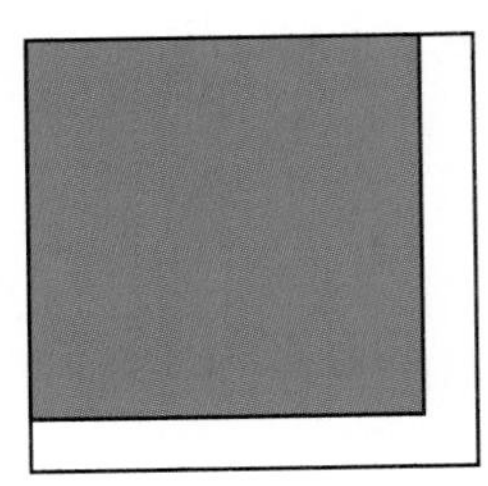

12. 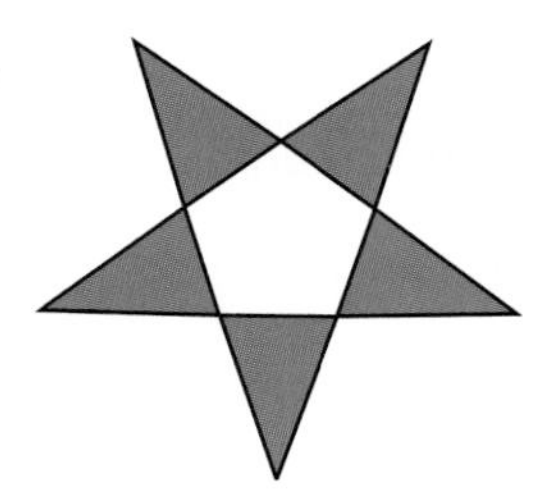

13. 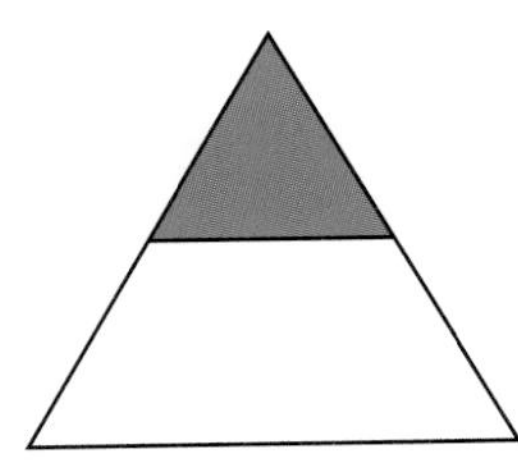

14. 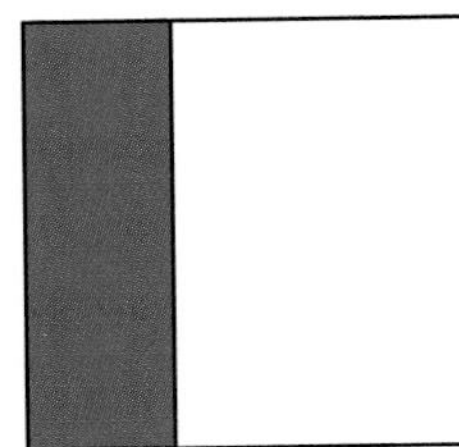

15. 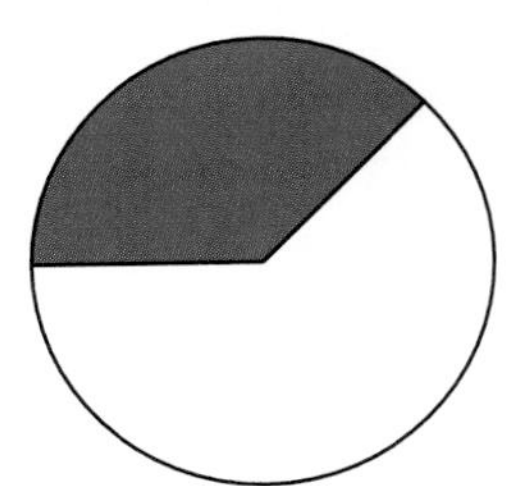

16. 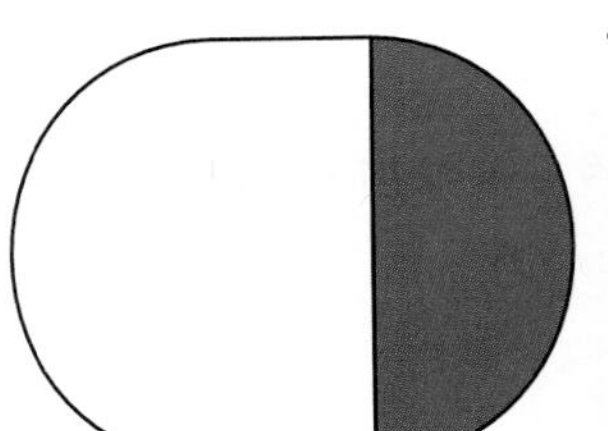

17. 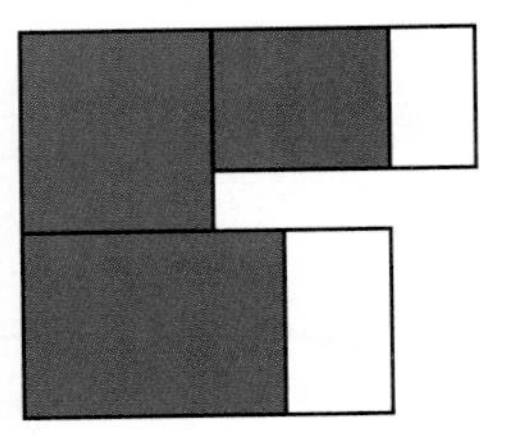

Estimate each percent.

18 8 out of 72 **19.** 12 out of 77 **20.** 93 out of 187 **21.** 318 out of 965 **22.** 12 out of 16

23. $\frac{39}{150}$ **24.** $\frac{57}{90}$ **25.** $\frac{14}{109}$ **26.** $\frac{6}{657}$ **27.** $\frac{474}{489}$

28. $\frac{16}{25}$ **29.** $\frac{21}{99}$ **30.** $\frac{56}{57}$ **31.** $\frac{1}{15}$ **32.** $\frac{47}{465}$

33. Reasoning Is it easier to estimate the percent for $\frac{7}{200}$ or $\frac{7}{310}$? Explain.

Problem Solving and Applications

34. 32 out of 45 dentists surveyed recommend GlowBrite Toothpaste. Approximately what percent recommend GlowBrite?

35. Critical Thinking If a shirt was originally $20, went on sale for 15% off, and then was put on clearance with an additional 45% off, estimate the clearance price of the shirt. Explain your reasoning.

36. Critical Thinking In a right triangle, estimate the percent of the number of angles that are not right angles. Explain your reasoning.

37. **Estimation** One researcher estimates that rain forests cover about 3,536,342 square miles of the earth's 50,500,000 square miles of land. About what percent of the earth's land is covered by rain forests?

38. **Estimation** Of the 7,800 known species of birds, about 2,600 live in rain forests. What percent of bird species live in rain forests?

Geography A rain forest is an example of a *biome,* or a particular type of environment. Use the map showing the major biomes of South America for **39–41.**

39. About what percent of South America is desert?

40. About what percent of South America is rain forest?

41. About what percent of the South American rain forest is above the equator?

Equator

Desert
Grassland
Rainforest
Chaparral
Temperate Forest

Using Data Use the Data File on page 507 for **42** and **43.**

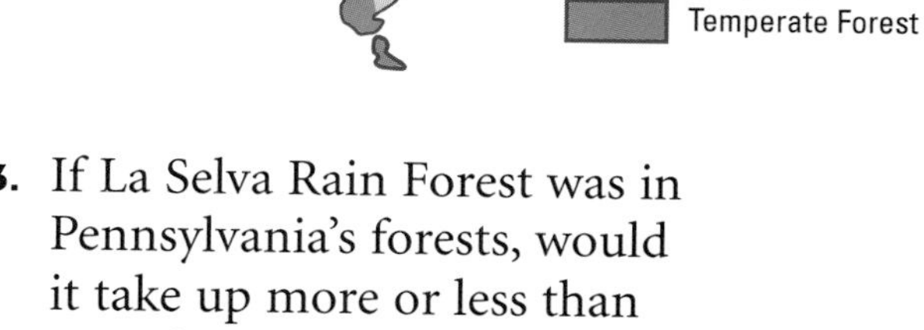

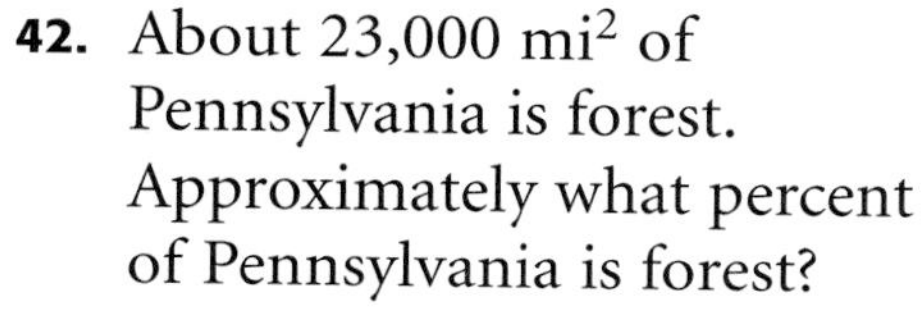

42. About 23,000 mi^2 of Pennsylvania is forest. Approximately what percent of Pennsylvania is forest?

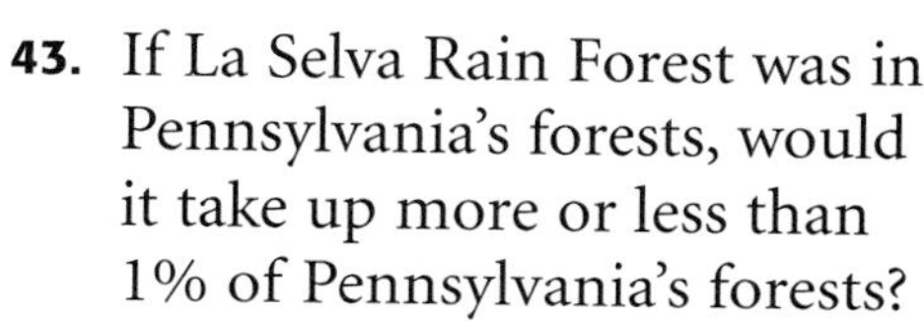

43. If La Selva Rain Forest was in Pennsylvania's forests, would it take up more or less than 1% of Pennsylvania's forests?

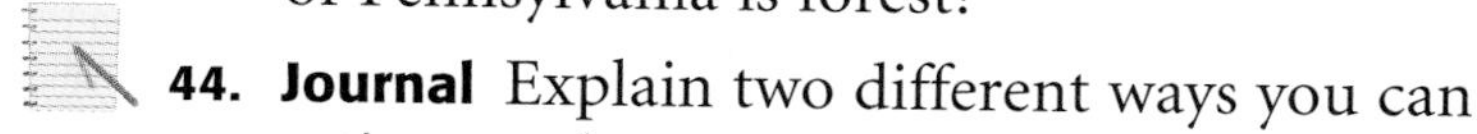

44. **Journal** Explain two different ways you can estimate what percent 75 is of 200.

Mixed Review and Test Prep

STAY SHARP!

For **45–48,** plot the image of trapezoid *JKML.*

45. Translate *JKML* 2 units down, 6 units right

46. Slide *JKML* 5 units right, 1 unit down

47. Slide *JKML* 3 units up, 4 units left

48. Translate *JKML* 2 units down

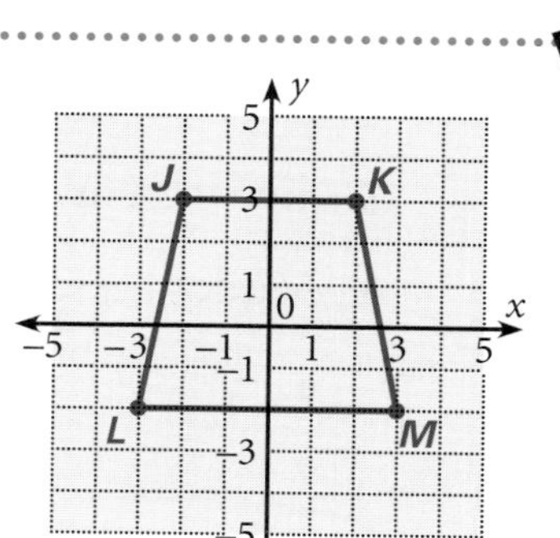

Find the LCM of each pair.

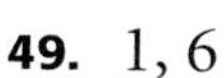

49. 1, 6	50. 10, 12	51. 6, 4	52. 8, 8	53. 5, 10
54. 25, 75	55. 5, 6	56. 12, 8	57. 14, 3	58. 12, 14
59. 3, 2	60. 13, 1	61. 12, 32	62. 4, 9	63. 40, 25

64. What is $\frac{11}{12} \times \frac{2}{5}$?

Ⓐ $\frac{79}{60}$ Ⓑ $\frac{31}{60}$ Ⓒ $\frac{11}{30}$ Ⓓ $2\frac{7}{24}$

Skills Practice Bank, page 669, Set 5

Chapter 10
Lesson
10

Connecting Percents to Fractions and Decimals

Problem Solving Connection
- Look for a Pattern

Materials
- 10 × 10 grids
- colored pencils or markers

Explore

Fractions, decimals, and percents all describe portions of a whole. So every percent can be written as both a fraction and a decimal.

Work Together

Modeling a Percent

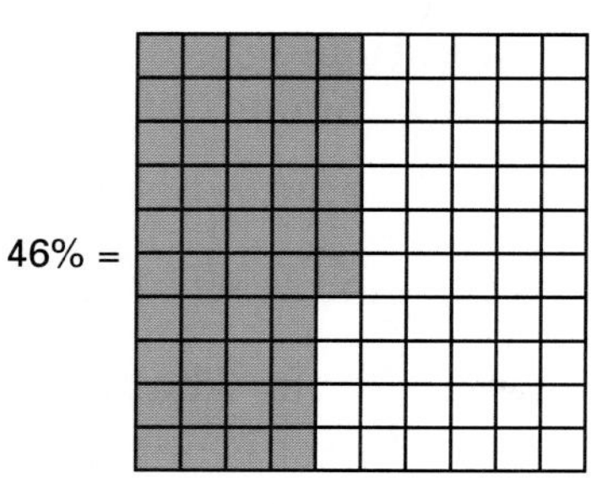

1. Color in a number of squares equal to the percent.
2. Model these percents:
   a. 21% b. 55% c. 4% d. 75%

Modeling a Decimal

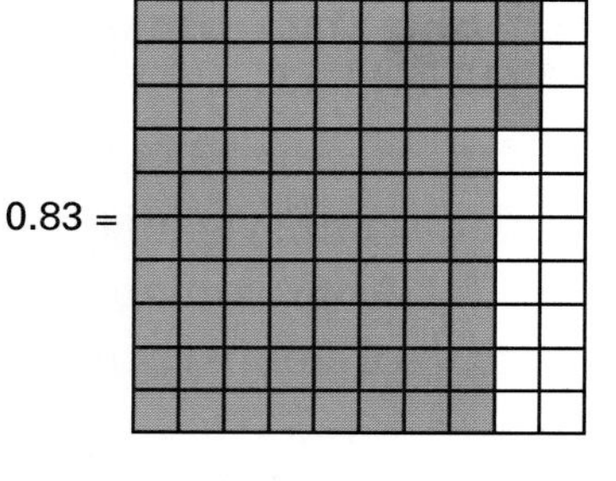

3. Color in one column for each tenth.
4. Color in one square for each hundredth.
5. Model these decimals:
   a. 0.66 b. 0.75 c. 0.02 d. 0.49

Modeling a Fraction

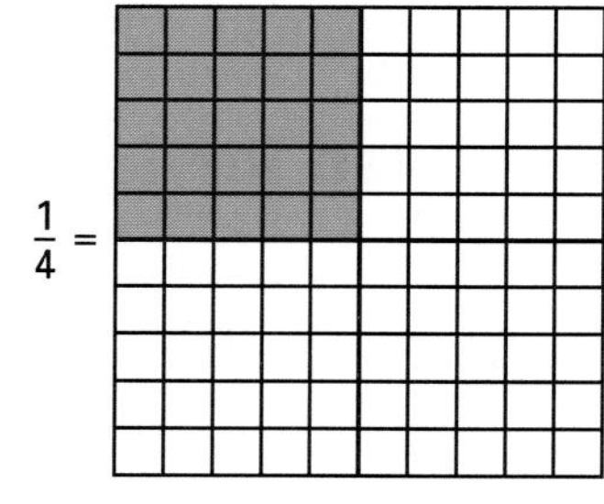

6. Divide the grid into groups of equal size. The number of groups should equal the denominator.
7. Color in as many groups as the numerator.
8. Model these fractions:
   a. $\frac{3}{4}$ b. $\frac{3}{5}$ c. $\frac{7}{10}$ d. $\frac{1}{2}$

Talk About It

9. For a given grid, can you describe the number of squares colored using either a percent or a decimal? Explain.
10. For a given grid, can you describe the number of squares colored using either a percent or a fraction? Explain.

Connect and Learn

Fractions, percents, and decimals all describe parts of a whole. To convert a percent into a fraction or a decimal, rewrite the percent as a fraction over 100.

Example 1

a. Write 53% as a fraction.

$53\% = \frac{53}{100}$

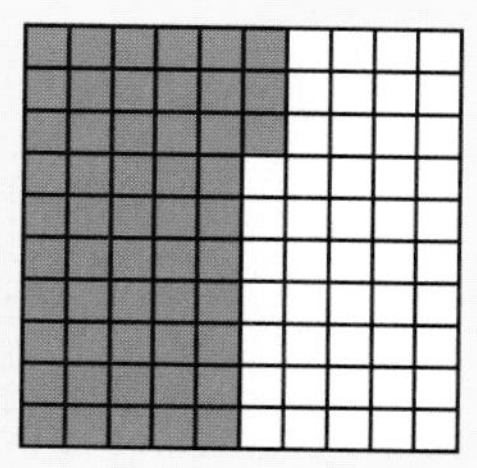

b. Write 91% as a decimal.

$91\% = \frac{91}{100} = 0.91$

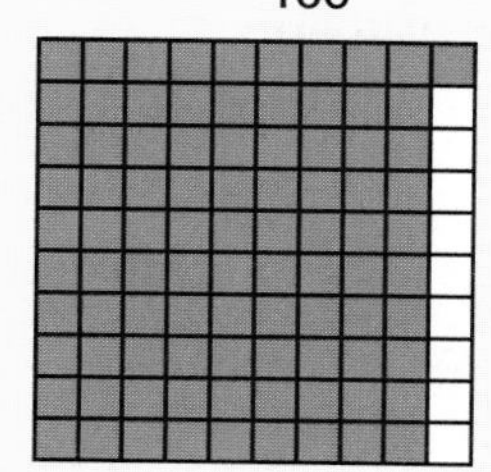

Remember

If a fraction does not have a power of 10 as a denominator, you can still convert it to a decimal by dividing the numerator by the denominator.

If you want to convert a fraction to a percent, you can do so with a proportion.

$$\frac{\text{part}}{\text{whole}} = \frac{\text{percent value}}{100}$$

Example 2

The White's tree frog is $\frac{5}{8}$ the length of the flying gecko. Rewrite this fraction as a percent.

$\frac{5}{8} = \frac{x}{100}$

$8x = 500$

$x = 62.5$

The White's tree frog is 62.5% of the length of the flying gecko.

Check

Convert each percent to a fraction in lowest terms.

1. 56% **2.** 15% **3.** 75% **4.** 66% **5.** 150% **6.** 125%

Convert each fraction to a percent.

7. $\frac{5}{8}$ **8.** $\frac{7}{10}$ **9.** $\frac{5}{16}$ **10.** $\frac{4}{8}$ **11.** $\frac{3}{4}$ **12.** $\frac{9}{16}$

13. Reasoning How can you determine without converting to a percent if a decimal is less than 10%? Greater than 100%?

14. Reasoning Which is easier, converting a fraction to a percent or converting a percent to a fraction? Explain.

Practice

Skills and Reasoning

Convert each percent to a fraction in lowest terms.

15. 89% **16.** 136% **17.** 90% **18.** 43% **19.** 234% **20.** 78%

21. 22% **22.** 37% **23.** 45% **24.** 126% **25.** 81% **26.** 68%

27. 300% **28.** 70% **29.** 9% **30.** 52% **31.** 92% **32.** 175%

Convert each decimal or fraction to a percent.

33. 0.84 **34.** 0.95 **35.** 0.04 **36.** 0.9 **37.** $\frac{55}{50}$ **38.** $\frac{14}{200}$

39. $\frac{17}{20}$ **40.** $\frac{39}{100}$ **41.** 0.53 **42.** $\frac{4}{5}$ **43.** $\frac{3}{10}$ **44.** 0.453

45. 0.56 **46.** 0.32 **47.** $\frac{12}{25}$ **48.** $\frac{98}{100}$ **49.** 0.75 **50.** 0.23

51. 0.675 **52.** $\frac{5}{100}$ **53.** 0.333 **54.** $\frac{3}{5}$ **55.** $\frac{76}{200}$ **56.** 0.01

Give the shaded part of each figure as a percent, fraction, and decimal. Write all fractions in lowest terms.

57.
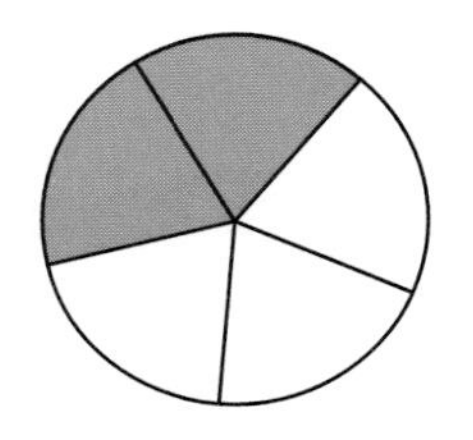

58.
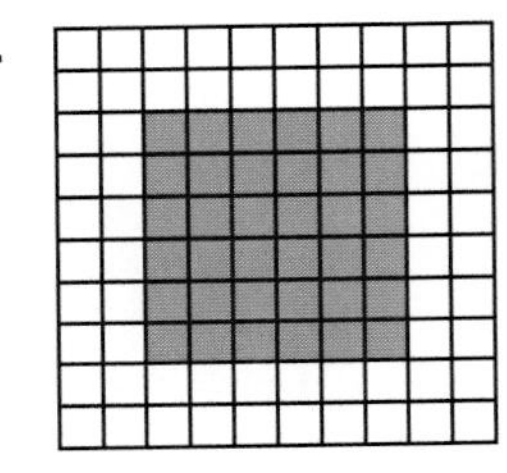

59.
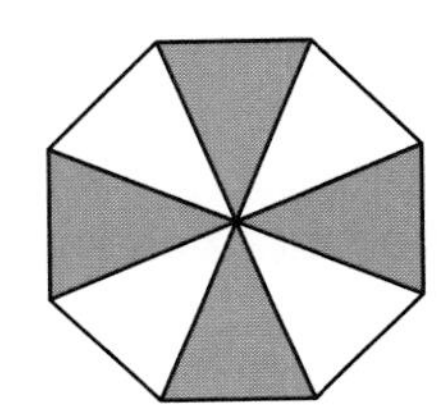

60.
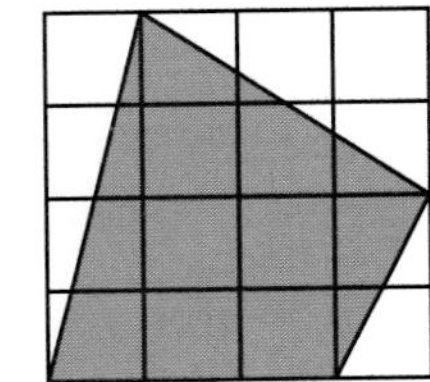

61.

62.
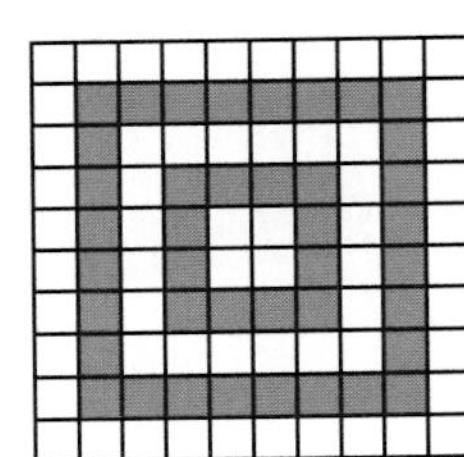

63.
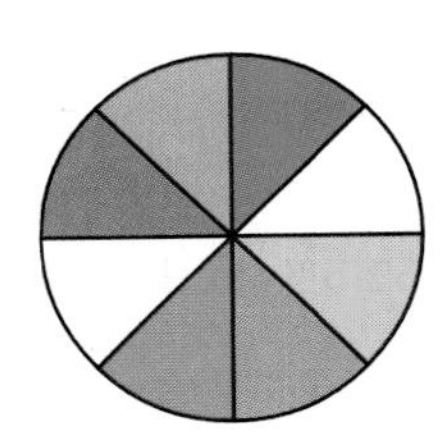

64.
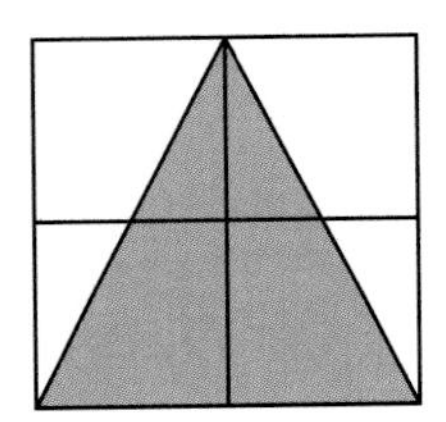

Copy and complete the table of common percents and their equivalencies. Write fractions in lowest terms.

65.	**Percent**	10%		25%			40%				70%	75%			100%
66.	**Decimal**		0.2			$0.\overline{3}$			0.6	$0.\overline{6}$				0.9	
67.	**Fraction**				$\frac{3}{10}$			$\frac{1}{2}$			$\frac{7}{10}$		$\frac{4}{5}$		

68. Reasoning Newspaper articles sometimes express relationships as percents and sometimes as fractions. Why?

Problem Solving and Applications

69. Two-thirds of the students at the Liberty Academy use the bus on the weekends. Convert this value to a percent.

70. Health 25% of all medicines in use today come from plant sources, many of which are found in rain forests. Convert this value to a decimal.

71. Number Sense Chandra has $\frac{1}{3}$ of the marbles, and Liu has 30%. Who has more? Can you tell how many each person has?

72. Critical Thinking 45% of the students at Suburban High School are boys. 30% of the boys at Suburban High School have curly hair. What fraction of the students at Suburban High School are boys with curly hair?

73. Critical Thinking Fanny's Fashion Center is advertising a sale. Everything is $\frac{1}{5}$ off. What percent of full price should you expect to pay?

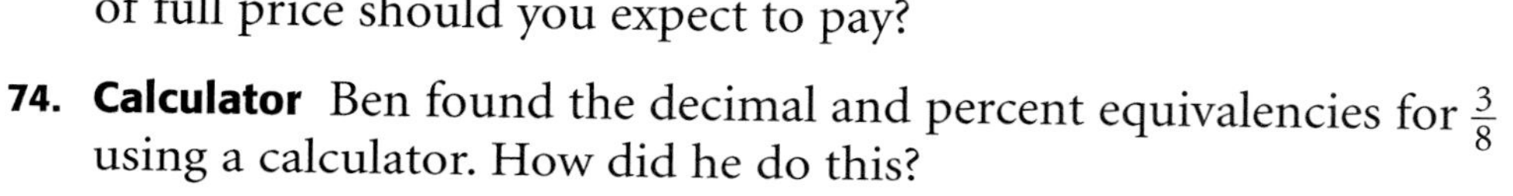

74. Calculator Ben found the decimal and percent equivalencies for $\frac{3}{8}$ using a calculator. How did he do this?

75. Estimation Marybeth estimated the percent equivalence for $\frac{19}{97}$ to be 20%. How do you think she made her estimate?

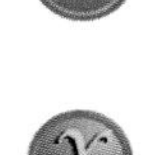

76. Algebra Readiness Write an equation you could use to convert $\frac{7}{9}$ to a percent.

77. Algebra Readiness Write a formula for converting decimals to percents.

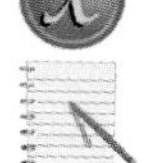

78. Journal In what situations would it be easier to work with fractions? With decimals? With percents? Explain.

Mixed Review and Test Prep

Graph each equation.

79. $y = x - 6$ **80.** $y = 6 + x$ **81.** $y = 8x$ **82.** $y = -2x$ **83.** $y = -5 + x$

Name an equivalent fraction for each.

84. $\frac{5}{6}$ **85.** $\frac{14}{20}$ **86.** $\frac{10}{32}$ **87.** $\frac{19}{50}$ **88.** $\frac{2}{7}$ **89.** $\frac{6}{10}$

90. $\frac{7}{29}$ **91.** $\frac{6}{24}$ **92.** $\frac{12}{96}$ **93.** $\frac{50}{75}$ **94.** $\frac{150}{200}$ **95.** $\frac{10}{80}$

96. Which of the following is equivalent to $\frac{23}{50}$?

Ⓐ $\frac{2}{5}$ Ⓑ $\frac{1}{2}$ Ⓒ $\frac{69}{150}$ Ⓓ $\frac{42}{100}$

Chapter 10
Lesson
11

Finding a Percent of a Number

You Will Learn

- to find a percent of a number and how to find a whole when given a percent and a part

Did You Know?
Ynez Mexia, a self-taught plant collector, documented several thousand plant species from North and South America. In one two-year trip, she collected over 65,000 plant specimens from the Amazon rain forest.

Learn

Pharmacologists have identified about 3,000 types of plants that have cancer-fighting properties. 70% of them grow in the rain forest.

To find the number of plants with cancer-fighting properties growing in the rain forest, find 70% of 3,000. (HINT: The word *of* indicates multiplication.)

70% of $3{,}000 = ?$

To work with percents, convert them to decimals or fractions.

70% of $3{,}000 = \frac{7}{10}$ of $3{,}000 = 0.7$ of $3{,}000$

$0.7 \times 3{,}000 = 2{,}100$

2,100 types of cancer-fighting plants grow in the rain forest.

Recall that you can use proportions to convert fractions into percents. You can also use proportions when looking for a percent of a whole number.

$$\frac{\text{part}}{\text{whole}} = \frac{\text{percent value}}{100}$$

Example 1

Find 53% of 62.	53% is slightly more than
Estimate: $\frac{1}{2} \times 60 = 30$	$\frac{1}{2}$, and 62 is close to 60.
part → $\frac{x}{62} = \frac{53}{100}$ ← **percent value**; **whole** → 62, 100 ← **100**	Write a proportion.
$100x = 3{,}286$	Find the cross products.
$x = 3{,}286 \div 100$	Use division to undo multiplication.
$x = 32.86$	Divide.

32.86 is close to the estimate of 30, so the answer is reasonable.

In some situations, you know the percent and the value of the percent, but you need to determine how big the "whole" is. You can also solve these problems using a proportion.

Example 2

78% of x is 39. Find the total amount.

part → **whole** → $\frac{39}{x} = \frac{78}{100}$ ← **percent value** ← **100** Write a proportion.

$78x = 3{,}900$ Find cross products.

$x = 3{,}900 \div 78$ Use division to undo multiplication.

$x = 50$ Divide.

The total amount is 50.

Example 3

The sales tax in Pennsylvania is 6%. Reuben had to pay $9 in sales tax on his purchase of a glockenspiel at Pennsylvania Percussion. Find the cost of the glockenspiel.

Let x represent the cost of the glockenspiel.

part → **whole** → $\frac{9}{x} = \frac{6}{100}$ ← **percent value** ← **100** Write a proportion.

$6x = 900$ Find the cross products.

$x = 900 \div 6$ Use division to undo multiplication.

$x = 150$ Divide.

The glockenspiel cost $150.

Talk About It

1. What happens to a percent of a whole when the whole increases?
2. Give an example of a percent you might want to find outside of the classroom. Use the word *of* to indicate multiplication.

Check

Simplify.

1. 50% of 100
2. 40% of 28
3. 65% of 940
4. 62% of 1,000

Find the total amount.

5. 25% of ▒ is 25.
6. 20% of ▒ is 2.
7. 35% of ▒ is 42.
8. 73% of ▒ is 146.
9. 65% of the 740 students at Tyler Academy have attended at least one other school. How many students have attended more than one school?
10. **Reasoning** What happens to the percent of a whole number when the percent decreases?

Practice

Skills and Reasoning

Simplify. Round each answer to the nearest hundredth.

11. 50% of 200 **12.** 25% of 80 **13.** 20% of 35 **14.** 48% of 2000

15. 34% of 65 **16.** 68% of 63.2 **17.** 22% of 84 **18.** 25% of 64

19. 99% of 106 **20.** 140% of 50 **21.** 100% of 54.3 **22.** 9% of 525

23. 33% of 68 **24.** 19% of 2.34 **25.** 2% of 18.8 **26.** 83% of 34

27. 76% of 20 **28.** 50% of 66 **29.** 25% of $10.99 **30.** 15% of $20.13

31. 13.6% of 45 **32.** 4.5% of $12.02 **33.** 37% of 23 **34.** 6% of 294

Find the total amount.

35. 30% of ■ is 75 **36.** 45% of ■ is 90 **37.** 4.3% of ■ is 8.6 **38.** 90% of ■ is 63

39. 7% of ■ is 6.16 **40.** 22% of ■ is 0.22 **41.** 7.5% of ■ is 13.2 **42.** 115% of ■ is $69

43. Winston scored about 83% on a 160-point test. About how many points did he receive credit for?

44. Reasoning If you know the percent and the part, and you want to know the whole, explain how you can use division instead of proportions.

Problem Solving and Applications

45. A test has 24 multiple choice questions. How many do you need to answer correctly to score at least 80%?

46. Of the estimated 300 species of hummingbirds, 83% can be found in rain forests. How many species can be found in rain forests?

47. Industry Argentina produced 11,100 passenger cars in 1991 and 21,000 in 1992. What percent of the number of 1992 cars was the number of 1991 cars?

48. Consumer The sales tax on the items shown is 5.25%. For each item, find the sales tax amount and the total price.

49. **Geography** At the beginning of 1994, Ethiopia had a population of 55,200,000. If the population was growing at a rate of 3% per year, how much did the population increase that year?

50. **Probability** Gloria plays a game 100 times, and her chances of winning are 60%. Esmeralda plays the same game 50 times and her chances of winning are 49%. Who will win more games?

51. Shalini earned $34,000 in 1997. If her 1998 income was 108% of her 1997 income, how much did she earn in 1998?

52. **Critical Thinking** Penelope explained how she calculated a 5% discount for a $22 meal. "First, I moved the decimal point over one place, and got $2.20. Then, I took half of that, which was $1.10. The meal is $22 minus $1.10, or $20.90." Do you agree with her answer? Will her method always work? Explain.

53. A new student's score on a spelling test was about 72% of Catherine's score. Catherine's score was about 98% of Tom's score. Tom's score was about 94% of Luanna's score. Luanna got 93 out of 100 points. How many points did the new student get?

54. **Critical Thinking** Hank bought some stock at $15 per share and later sold it at $30 per share. He told Robin his stock had gone up by 100%. Robin said he sold it for 200% of the original price. Who was right?

Mixed Review and Test Prep

Write each fraction in lowest terms.

55. $\frac{7}{14}$ **56.** $\frac{5}{25}$ **57.** $\frac{20}{30}$ **58.** $\frac{6}{18}$ **59.** $\frac{12}{36}$ **60.** $\frac{8}{10}$

61. $\frac{6}{8}$ **62.** $\frac{9}{15}$ **63.** $\frac{3}{21}$ **64.** $\frac{4}{24}$ **65.** $\frac{21}{35}$ **66.** $\frac{6}{9}$

Write each improper fraction as a mixed number and each mixed number as an improper fraction.

67. $6\frac{4}{5}$ **68.** $\frac{6}{5}$ **69.** $2\frac{8}{9}$ **70.** $\frac{10}{3}$ **71.** $5\frac{1}{7}$ **72.** $\frac{16}{7}$

73. $\frac{21}{2}$ **74.** $11\frac{3}{4}$ **75.** $3\frac{1}{2}$ **76.** $\frac{65}{8}$ **77.** $\frac{14}{5}$ **78.** $9\frac{11}{12}$

79. Find $\frac{1}{6}$ of 780.

Ⓐ 390 Ⓑ 130 Ⓒ 405.6 Ⓓ 520

Skills Practice Bank, page 669, Set 6

Technology

Using a Spreadsheet to Create a Circle Graph

There are many ways to visually display data in order to make it easier to analyze. One useful way is a circle graph, which shows how portions of a set of data compare with the whole set. Each portion of a circle graph represents a percentage of the whole set. You can use your spreadsheet software to organize data and create a circle graph.

Materials
Interactive CD-ROM Spreadsheet/Grapher Tool or other spreadsheet software

The data below represents the grades a math class received on a test. What would the data look like in a circle graph?

Test Scores												
C	A	C	B	C	B	A	B	A	D	C	B	A
B	D	C	A	B	A	C	C	B	A	C	B	C
F	A	B	C	C	A	B	C	B	C	A	C	F

Work Together

Use your spreadsheet software to create a circle graph.

1. Create a new spreadsheet like the one shown in your software program.
2. Enter the test score data into the spreadsheet as shown.
3. Select cells A2 to B6. These cells contain the grades and the number of students earning each grade.

	A	B
1	Grade	Number
2	A	10
3	B	11
4	C	14
5	D	2
6	F	2
7		
8		
9		
10		

4. Using the graph option in your spreadsheet software, choose a circle graph that shows labels and percents. The spreadsheet software will use the data from cells A2 to B6 to create a circle graph.

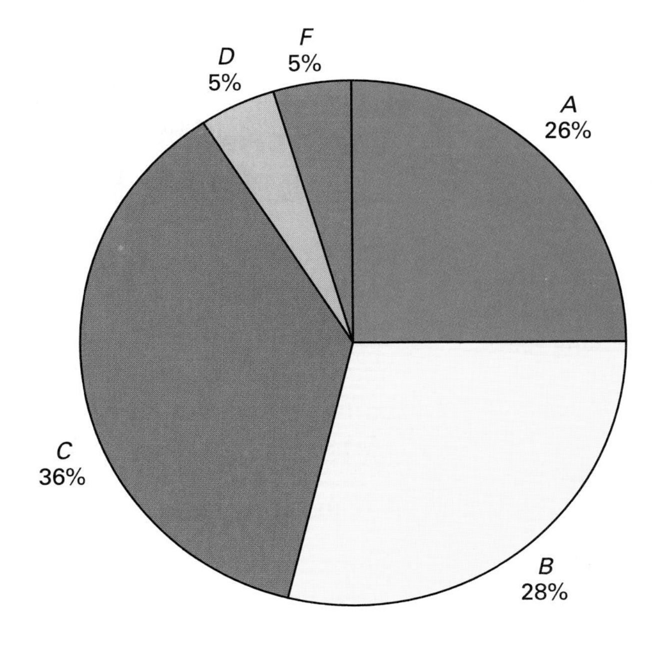

Exercises

1. Collect data from students about their favorite class. Use a spreadsheet to make a circle graph of the data.
2. Collect data from students about the kinds of pets they have. Use a spreadsheet to make a circle graph of the data.

Extensions

3. What would a circle graph look like if all the categories in column A had the same number in column B?
4. Is it easier to create a circle graph by hand or with a spreadsheet? Explain.
5. Why is a circle graph a good way to visually display data?

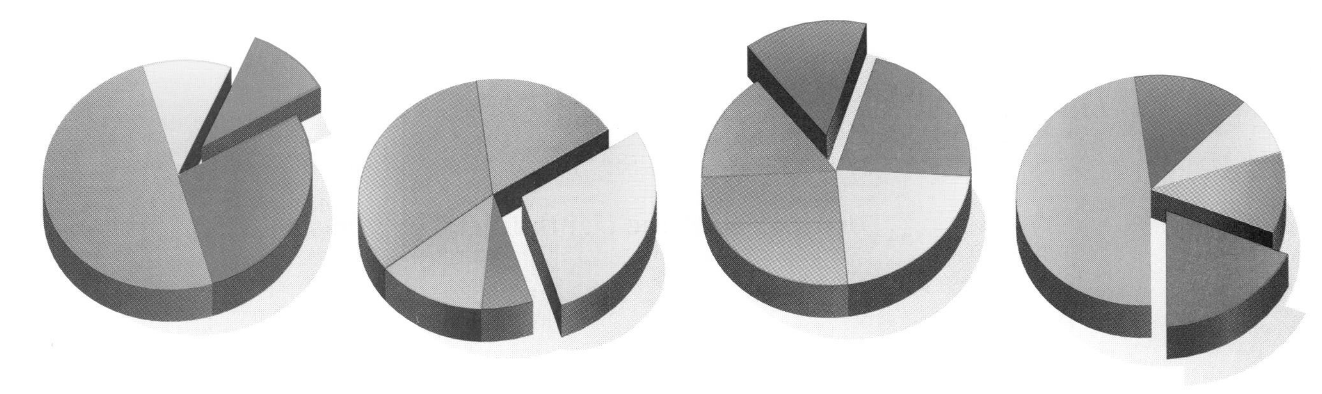

Chapter 10

Problem Solving

Comparing Strategies: Look for a Pattern/Make a Table

You Will Learn

- to solve problems by looking for patterns and making a table

Vocabulary

fractals

infinite

Vivian and Hassan are investigating fractals. A **fractal** is a design that begins with a point, a line segment, or a geometric shape. The form is constantly changed in the same way to make **infinite** patterns. An infinite pattern is a pattern that continues endlessly.

Vivian and Hassan drew these fractals.

1. 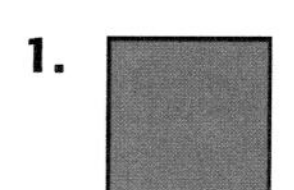
2. 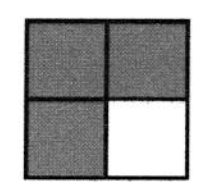
3. 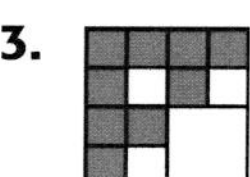

4. 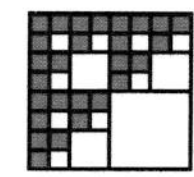

They want to find the portion of the eighth fractal that will be shaded without having to continue their drawings.

Math Tip

The strategy you use depends on the information you are given and what you are asked to find.

Vivian's Method

	Data		Pattern
1.		All shaded	
2.		$\frac{3}{4}$ shaded	$\frac{3}{2 \times 2}$
3.		$\frac{9}{16}$ shaded	$\frac{3 \times 3}{4 \times 4}$
4.		$\frac{27}{64}$ shaded	$\frac{3 \times 3 \times 3}{8 \times 8}$

Hassan's Method

Figure	Shaded		Total Squares	
1	1		1	
		× 3		× 4
2	3		4	
		× 3		× 4
3	9		16	
		× 3		× 4
4	27		64	
		× 3		× 4
5	81		256	
		× 3		× 4
6	243		1,024	
		× 3		× 4
7	729		4,096	
		× 3		× 4
8	2,187		16,384	

Pattern: Each numerator is multiplied by one more 3 than in the previous pattern. Each number in the denominator is multiplied by 2, so the denominator is multiplied by 4.

$$\frac{3 \times 3 \times 3 \times 3 \times 3 \times 3 \times 3}{128 \times 128} = \frac{2{,}187}{16{,}384}$$

So $\frac{2{,}187}{16{,}384}$, or 13.35%, of the eighth fractal will be shaded.

1. Which strategy do you think has more chances for making a mistake? Why?
2. **Calculator** What portion of the tenth fractal will be shaded?

Check

Look for a pattern or make a table to solve.

1. Vivian designed another fractal pattern shown below. She wants to know what portion of the tenth fractal will *not* be shaded.

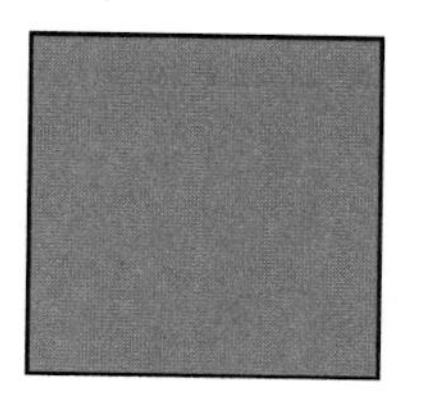
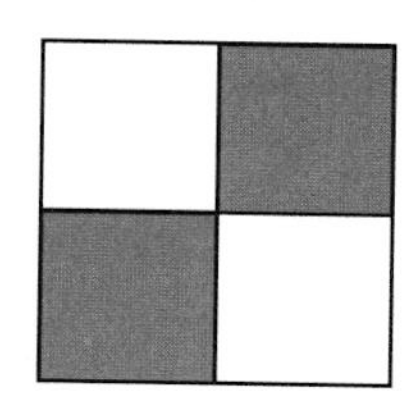
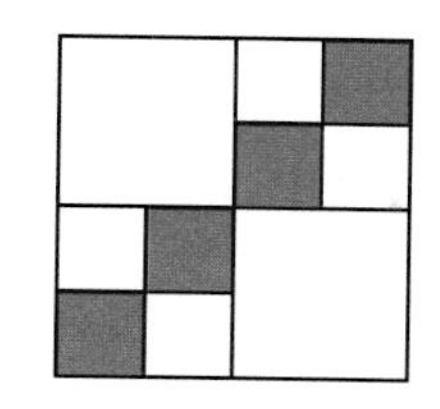
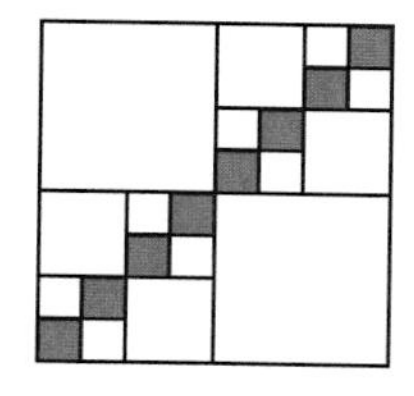

   a. Vivian estimated that the unshaded portion of the tenth fractal will be about 50%. Is her estimate reasonable?

   b. Write the fraction, in lowest terms, and percent of the unshaded portions of the first four fractals.

   c. **Calculator** What portion of the tenth fractal is unshaded?

Problem Solving Practice

Use any strategy to solve each problem.

2. According to the Yukon Tourism Board in Canada, there are about 30,000 people in Yukon Territory. That's 60% of the number of moose in the territory. Suppose the moose population grows at a rate of 5% per year and the resident population grows at a rate of 10% per year. How many people and moose will inhabit the Yukon Territory in 4 years?

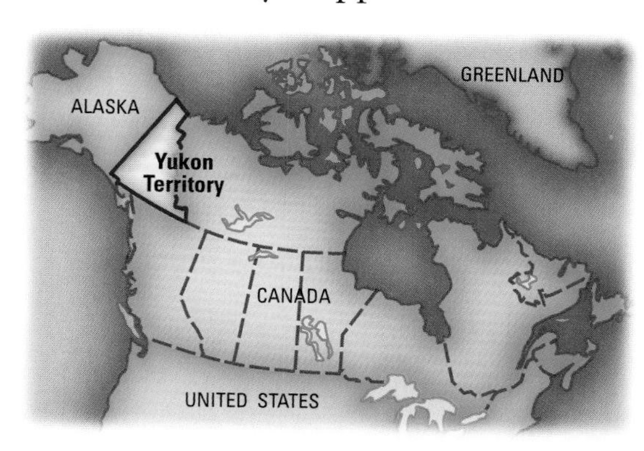

3. **Write Your Own Problem** Draw a set of fractal patterns. Write a problem about these patterns. Exchange your problems with a partner and solve.

4. Martin is using small black and white tiles to create a table top. He wants to use the fifth fractal pattern in the following series. How many black and white tiles will he need if each of the black spaces is 1 tile?

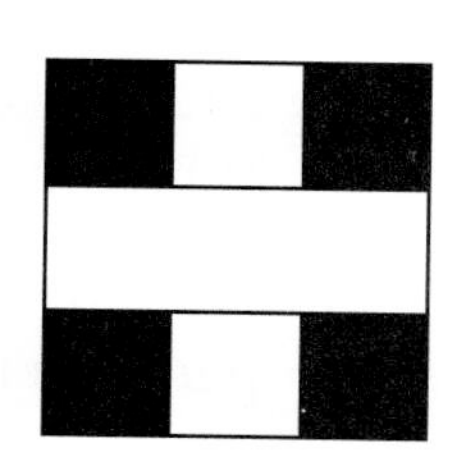

Problem Solving Strategies

- Draw a Picture
- Look for a Pattern
- Guess and Check
- Use Logical Reasoning
- Make an Organized List
- Make a Table
- Solve a Simpler Problem
- Work Backward

Choose a Tool

SECTION C

Review and Practice

(Lesson 8) Solve.

1. For every 4 carrots that Rennie grows, she grows 3 lettuce plants.
   a. What is the ratio of lettuce to carrots?
   b. What percent of Rennie's vegetables are carrots?
   c. What percent of Rennie's vegetables is lettuce?
2. The Rain Forest Explorer's Club is planning a trip to Ocalla National Forest. 45 of the 100 members plan to travel to the forest. What percent will visit the forest? What percent will not? Which is greater, the group traveling to the forest or the group that's not?

(Lesson 9) Estimate the percent of each figure that is shaded.

3. 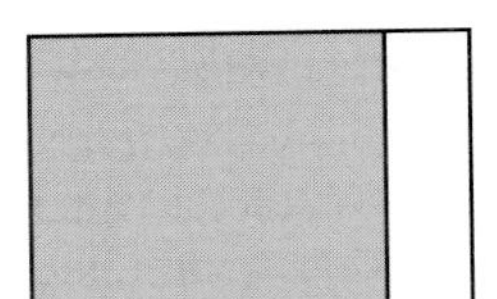

4. 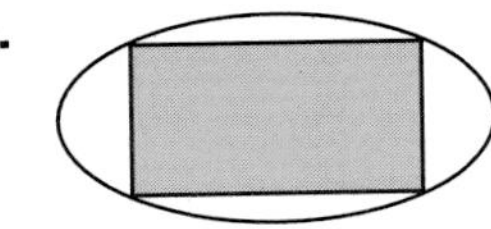

5. 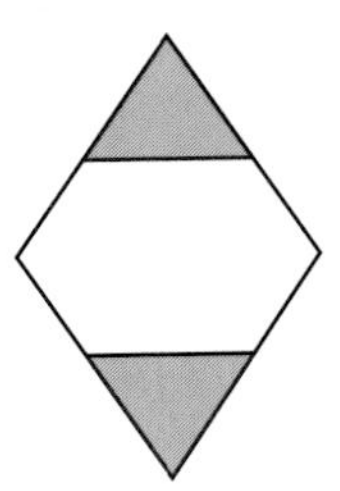

Estimate each percent.

6. 6 out of 89
7. 420 out of 772
8. 27 out of 98
9. 3 out of 45
10. $\frac{45}{75}$
11. $\frac{12}{199}$
12. $\frac{9}{700}$
13. $\frac{399}{450}$

(Lesson 10) Convert each fraction to a decimal and a percent.

14. $\frac{64}{100}$
15. $\frac{3}{5}$
16. $\frac{13}{20}$
17. $\frac{75}{200}$
18. $\frac{88}{500}$

(Lesson 11) Simplify.

19. 78% of 37
20. 8% of 46.3
21. 12% of 146
22. 230% of 57
23. The cost of a new stereo system is $328. Nisha waited until the electronics store was having a sale before buying one. She paid $223.04. What percent of the regular price did she pay?

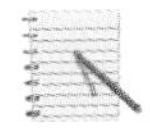

24. **Journal** When might it be easier to convert percents to decimals in order to work with them?

Skills Checklist

In this section, you have:

- **Learned About Percents**
- **Estimated Percents**
- **Connected Percents to Fractions and Decimals**
- **Found a Percent of Number**

REVIEW AND PRACTICE

Choose at least one of the following. Use what you have learned in this chapter.

1 Changing Times

Work in teams of two. Consider a year as 52 weeks of 7 days each. Find the following ratios:

- months in the year to weeks in the year
- months in the year to years in the year

- days in the week to weeks in the month
- days in the week to days in the month

2 Percent Pursuit

$100\% = 1.0 = 1$

$10\% = 0.1 = \frac{1}{10}$

$\frac{1}{5} = 0.2 = 20\%$

$33\frac{1}{3}\% = \frac{1}{3} = 0.\overline{3}$

Pick a topic of your choice to access on **www.mathsurf.com/6** that will give you data expressed as percents. Write and solve a problem with an answer as a decimal or percent.

3 Zoomin' Zoos!

For each of the animals, determine how long it would take to run the following distances. Set up and solve a proportion to find each answer. Give your answers in minutes.

a. 5 mi

b. 10 mi

c. 20 mi

	MILES PER HOUR
Lion	50
Zebra	40
Grizzly bear	30
Elephant	25

4 Spectators' Special Sports

At Home Ask at least 20 friends, family members, or members of your community to name the sport that they enjoy watching the most. Give the ratio of each sport to the total responses. Then write each ratio as a decimal and as a percent. Which was the most popular? The least popular?

REVIEW AND PRACTICE

CHAPTER 10

Review/Test

(Lesson 1) Write the ratio as a fraction in lowest terms.

1. 4 out of 32 dentists
2. One chaperone for every 6 students
3. Ninety of the 100 students passed the test.
4. 30 out of 45 cats live more than 10 years.

(Lesson 2) Supply the ratios for **5** and **6.**

5. Write four equal ratios for the ratio 5:7.
6. Write the ratio of 7 triangles to 8 squares in three ways.

(Lessons 3–5, 7) Solve each problem.

7. Why is 8 mi/5 hr = 20 hr/32 mi not a correct proportion? Rewrite it correctly.
8. Fuji apples cost $2.10 for 3 lb. Use a proportion to find out how much it would cost to buy 7 lb.
9. Are the two figures similar, congruent, or neither? Explain.

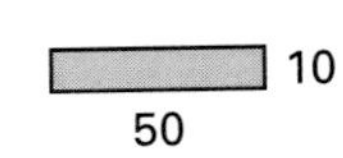

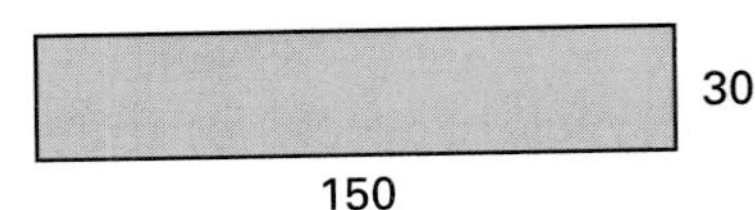

(Lessons 5–7 and 10) For **10** and **11,** determine whether the statement is true or false. If it is false, rewrite it as a true statement.

10. Cross products and unit rates are used to solve proportions.
11. A percent can be written as a fraction and compares a quantity to the number 1.

(Lessons 8 and 9) Use the circle graph for **12–14.**

12. About what percent of Akiko's weekly fruit intake is made up of bananas?
13. About what percent of Akiko's fruit diet is made up of oranges?
14. Which does Akiko eat more of, bananas or apples?

Pears
Bananas
Oranges
Apples
Akiko's Weekly Fruits

(Lesson 10) Write each percent as a ratio of a number to 100, as a fraction in lowest terms, and as a decimal.

15. 70%
16. 27%
17. 40%
18. 5%

(Lesson 11) Solve.

19. Jonah had 84 baseball cards. He threw 25% of them away. How many did he throw away?
20. Jessica had 6 Florida Marlin cards, which was 3 percent of her total collection. How many cards did she have in her collection?

CHAPTER 10

Performance Assessment

You are an architect who has designed some community buildings. You need to make scale models of them using measurements that are in proportion to the full-sized buildings. Also, all the models must be made in the same proportion to each other.

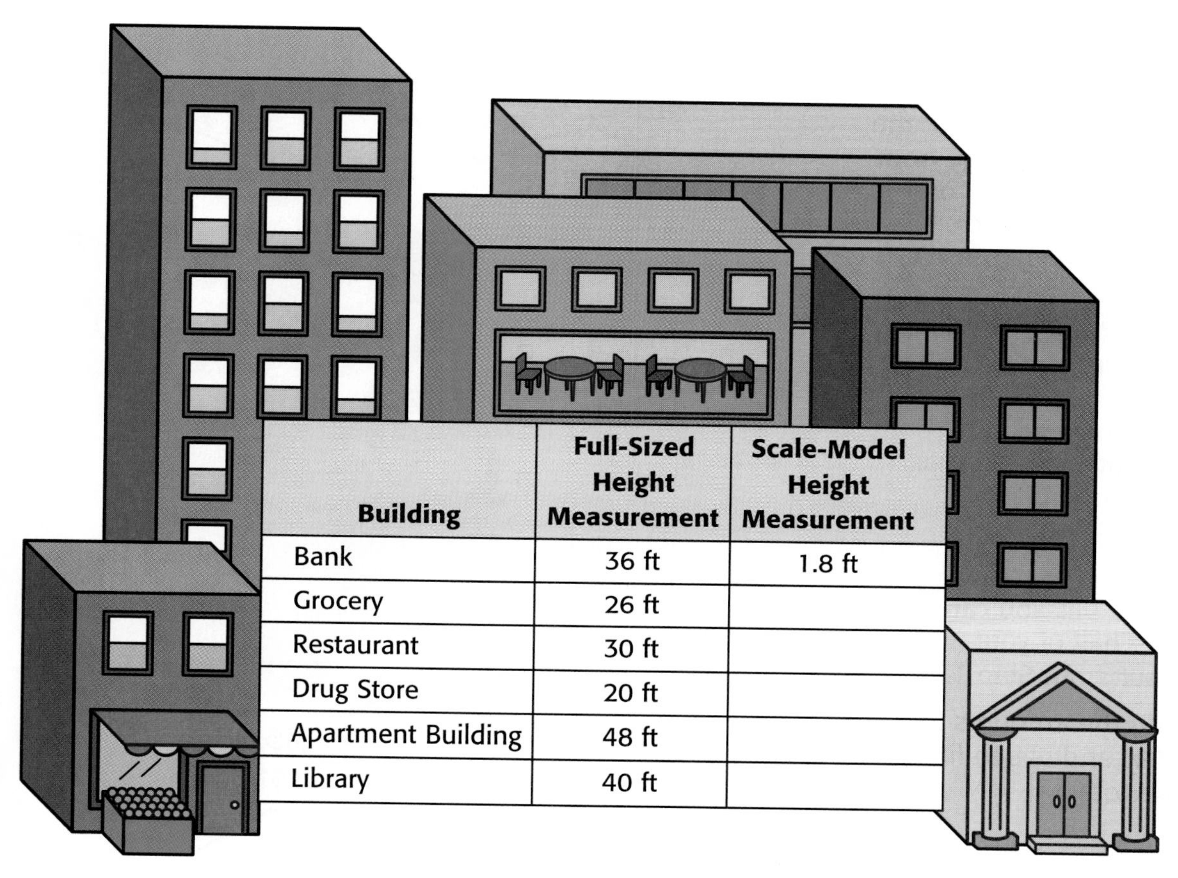

Building	Full-Sized Height Measurement	Scale-Model Height Measurement
Bank	36 ft	1.8 ft
Grocery	26 ft	
Restaurant	30 ft	
Drug Store	20 ft	
Apartment Building	48 ft	
Library	40 ft	

1. **Recording** Copy and complete the table. Find all of the scale model measurements using a ratio that matches the ratio of the bank building's full-sized height and its scale-model height.

2. **Decision Making** Suppose you want to make larger scale models than the ones that would be made using the ratio in the above table. Choose a new ratio to use. Find the new measurements of the model buildings. List the full-sized and scale measurements in a table.

3. **Critical Thinking** Suppose each building has the same border decoration that runs along the entire height of the building. The border decoration is sold by the foot. For the bank, the cost of the border decoration is $99 for one corner. What is the cost per foot of the border decoration? What would be the cost of the border decoration for one corner of the grocery building?

Math Magazine

South of the Border Cafe

Here's a Hot Tip . . .

In the United States, when you are served in a restaurant by a waiter or waitress, it is customary to leave a tip. The tip is equal to a percent of the bill for the food. Most tips range from 10% to 20%, based on the quality of the service. Leaving a 15% tip is common. You can use mental math to find the percent of the bill.

1. First, calculate 10% of the bill. You can divide the bill by 10, or move the decimal point one place to the left.
2. Next, calculate 5% of the bill. You can take half of your result from Step 1.
3. Add the amounts for 10% and 5% to find the total tip.

CHECK 00131

taco platter	4.50
tostada salad	4.00
veggie burrito	3.15
2 med. root beers	1.50
1 large iced tea	1.00
	14.15
tax	0.93
	15.08

Thank You for Visiting Us

10% of $15.08 is about $1.50

Half of $1.50 is $0.75

15% = $1.50 + $0.75, or $2.25

Try These!

Find 15% of each amount.

1. $10.62 **2.** $4.67 **3.** $13.59

4. $20.31 **5.** $47.53 **6.** $28.47

If the service is excellent, many people will leave a 20% tip. Use the ideas above to help you find 20% of each amount.

7. $9.81 **8.** $14.63 **9.** $16.67

10. $23.31 **11.** $27.20 **12.** $37.14

Cumulative Review

Test Prep Strategy: Make Smart Choices

Estimate the area of a circle with a radius of 4.1 in.

Ⓐ 7 in² Ⓑ 12 in² Ⓒ 48 in² Ⓓ 72 in²

The formula for finding the area of a circle is $A = \pi r^2$. Round the radius to 4 and square: $4 \times 4 = 16$. Choices Ⓐ and Ⓑ are already eliminated as being too small. Round π to 3 and multiply the rounded value of r^2. $3 \times 16 = 48$, or choice Ⓒ.

Write the letter of the correct answer. Choose any strategy.

1. Find the next three numbers in this pattern: 15, 25, 23, 33, 31, . . .

   Ⓐ 29, 39, 37 Ⓑ 41, 39, 49 Ⓒ 41, 51, 49 Ⓓ not here

2. Find the quotient of 88.88 ÷ 44.

   Ⓐ 2.02 Ⓑ 2.2 Ⓒ 20.2 Ⓓ 22

3. How many millimeters are in 3 meters?

   Ⓐ 30 Ⓑ 300 Ⓒ 3,000 Ⓓ 30,000

4. What is the approximate area of a circle with a diameter of 10 ft?

   Ⓐ 15.7 ft² Ⓑ 31.4 ft² Ⓒ 78.5 ft² Ⓓ 314 ft²

5. Tell whether 495 is divisible by 2, 3, 5, 9, or 10.

   Ⓐ 5 Ⓑ 3, 5, 9 Ⓒ 3, 5 Ⓓ 2, 3, 5, 9

6. Solve the equation $x - \frac{3}{5} = \frac{2}{3}$.

   Ⓐ $x = 1\frac{4}{15}$ Ⓑ $x = \frac{5}{8}$ Ⓒ $x = \frac{2}{5}$ Ⓓ $x = \frac{1}{15}$

7. How many $\frac{2}{3}$-cup servings are contained in 12 cups of juice?

   Ⓐ 6 Ⓑ 8 Ⓒ 18 Ⓓ not here

8. What is the least rotation clockwise that will land the figure on top of itself?

   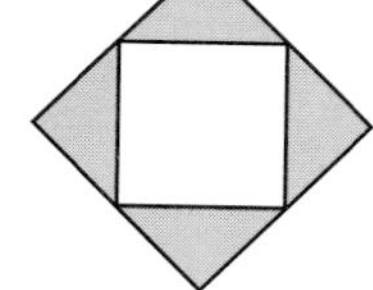

   Ⓐ 360° Ⓑ 270° Ⓒ 180° Ⓓ 90°

9. Simplify: $-3 - (-5)$.

   Ⓐ −8 Ⓑ −2 Ⓒ 2 Ⓓ 8

10. What are the cross products for $\frac{m}{7} = \frac{12}{21}$?

    Ⓐ $21m = 84$ Ⓑ $7m = 252$ Ⓒ $12m = 147$ Ⓓ not here

Test Prep Strategies

- Read Carefully
- Follow Directions
- Make Smart Choices
- Eliminate Choices
- Work Backward from an Answer

DATA FILE

Chapter 11

Solids and Measurement

The Grapes of Wrap

Solids and Surface Area

577

Imagine trying to eat the world's largest box of popcorn! The box measured 39 ft $11\frac{1}{2}$ in. long, 20 ft $8\frac{1}{2}$ in. wide, and 8 ft high and was covered with paper decorated with drawings of popcorn. It took the students at Beauclerc Elementary School in Jacksonville, Florida, more than 6 days to fill the box.

How could you figure out how much paper would be needed to cover the surface of the box?

The Grapes of Wrap
Page 577

LINKS

People of the World

Many African tribes build cylindrical houses with cone-shaped roofs, such as the traditional houses built by the Kikuyu of Kenya.
www.mathsurf.com/6/ch11/social

Arts & Literature

Cubism is a style of art that often shows objects and scenes as basic geometric shapes.
www.mathsurf.com/6/ch11/science

Entertainment

A standard basketball and a 16-lb bowling ball have approximately the same surface area (283 in^2 and 227 in^2). A basketball weighs about 22 oz, about $8\frac{1}{2}$% of the weight of a bowling ball.

SECTION B

A Pet From a Different World

Volume

597

The Living Seas Aquarium at the Epcot Center near Orlando, Florida holds the greatest volume of water in the world. More than 3,000 fish, representing 65 species, can be found swimming in 6.25 million gallons of water.

The Monterey Bay Aquarium in California contains the most marine life. 6,500 specimens from 525 species of fauna and flora are held in 1 million gallons of water.

About how many gallons of water are there for each fish in the Living Seas Aquarium?

A Pet From a Different World
Page 597

Science

In zero gravity, water "drops" are shaped like spheres, forming the most compact shape possible for their volume.

Social Studies

The Great Pyramid in Giza, Egypt, is made from more than 2,000,000 blocks of stones. Each block weighs 2,500 lb.

Materials
posterboard, rulers, graph paper or graphing software

In this project, you will plan an aquarium for your classroom.

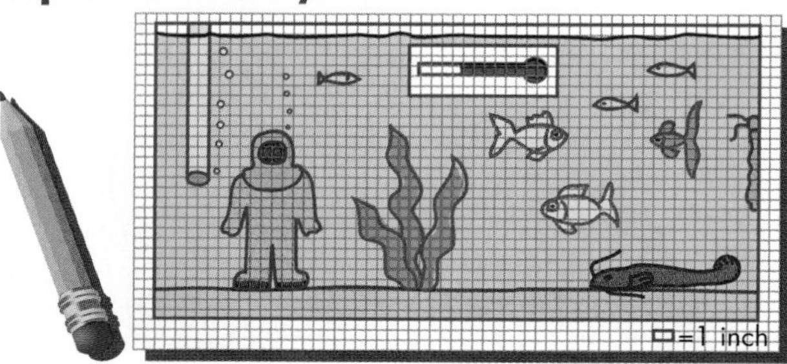

Make a Plan

- What are some fish that you like? Are the fish you selected compatible? Remember that while most aquarium fish are fresh-water fish, some fish only like warm and salty water. Other fish are bitter enemies and will fight if put together in the same aquarium.

Carry It Out

1. Decide how large an aquarium your classroom can accommodate.
2. Determine how many fish do you think an aquarium of this size can hold.
3. Find out the average adult size of the fish you have selected and record the length in inches.
4. Sketch your design on a sheet of graph paper. Be sure to have a key that tells how many squares equal one inch.
5. Color in your design and display it for the class.

Talk About It

- How did the size of your classroom influence the design of your aquarium?
- How did measuring all aspects of the aquarium in inches help in designing your project? Would it have been better to have measured everything in a different unit? Explain.

Present the Project

Share your design with the class.

Solids and Surface Area

Package designers create containers in a variety of shapes, sizes, designs, and colors. But designing a package isn't as easy as it sounds. Consumers notice large, fancy, or unusual containers, but these are expensive to manufacture.

What do you notice about the shapes of these containers?

Finding Surface Area of Solids

Review area of polygons and circles. Find the area of each shape.

1. 3.5 cm

2. 12.3 ft; 27.4 ft

3. 4 in.; 12 in.

4. 8 in.; 16 in.

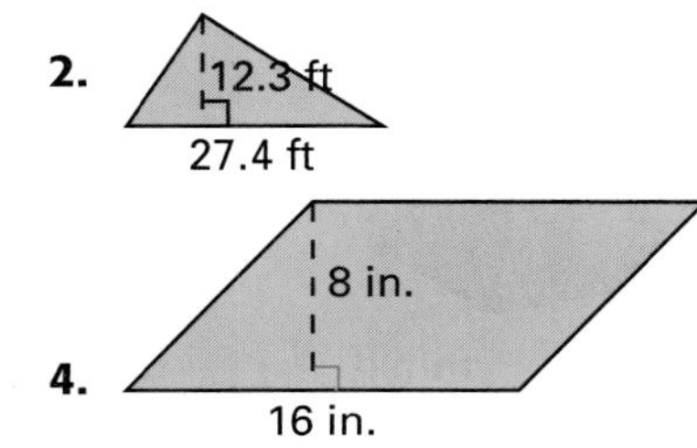

Skills Checklist

In this section, you will:

- ❒ Classify Solids
- ❒ Explore Surface Area
- ❒ Learn About Surface Area Formulas
- ❒ Find the Surface Area of Cylinders

Chapter 11
Lesson
1

Classifying Solids

You Will Learn
how to classify different solids

Vocabulary
solid
face
edge
polyhedron
prism
base
pyramid
cylinder
cone
sphere
net
cube

Learn

Three-dimensional objects are all around us. They come in all shapes and sizes. What if familiar objects took on different shapes? Maybe some already have!

We call these three-dimensional figures that take up space **solids**.

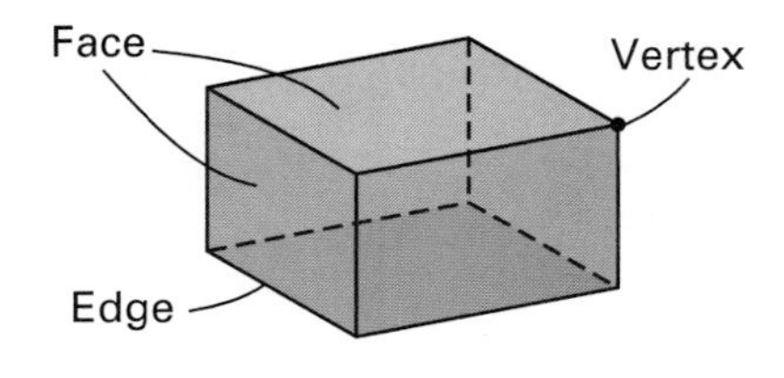

A **polyhedron** is a solid with flat surfaces called **faces**. The outline of each face is a polygon. The line where two faces come together is an **edge**. The point where several edges come together is a *vertex*.

A **prism** is a polyhedron that has two parallel congruent faces called **bases**. All other faces are rectangles. A prism is named by the shape of its bases.

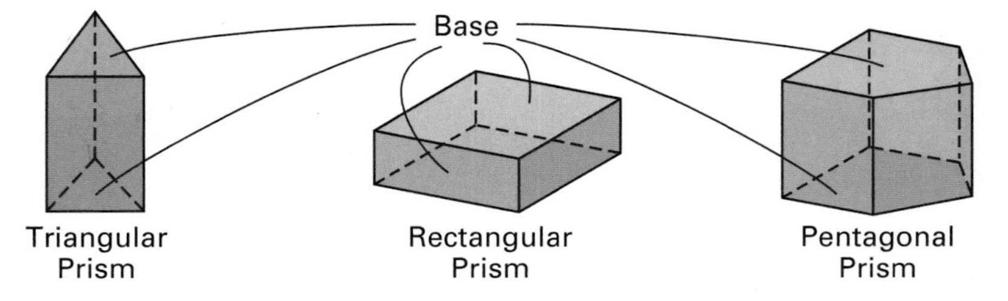

A **pyramid** is a polyhedron with one base. All the other faces are triangles. A pyramid is named for the shape of its base.

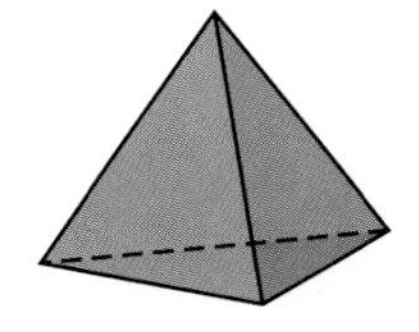
Triangular Pyramid

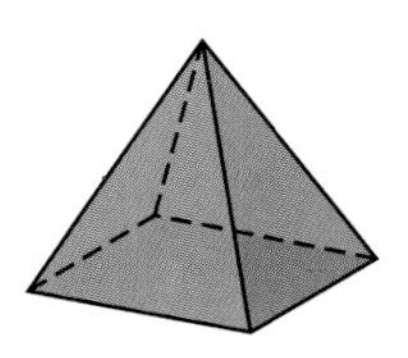
Rectangular Pyramid

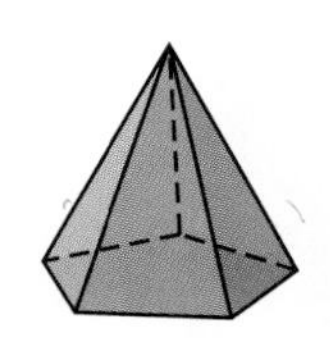
Pentagonal Pyramid

Solids with curved surfaces are not polyhedrons.

A **cylinder** has two parallel, congruent circular bases. A **cone** has one circular base.

A **sphere** has no base.

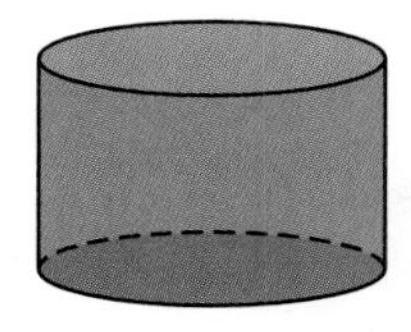

Cylinder

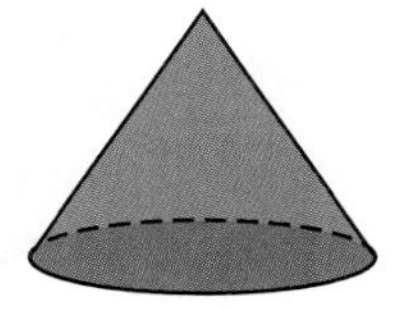

Cone

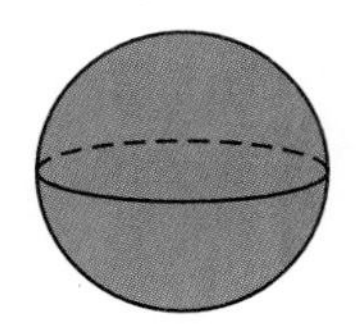

Sphere

Example

Classify each solid. If the solid is a polyhedron, tell how many faces, edges, and vertices it has.

a. The solid is a triangular prism with 5 faces, 9 edges, and 6 vertices.

b. The solid is a square (or rectangular) pyramid with 5 faces, 8 edges, and 5 vertices.

c. The solid is a cylinder. It is not a polyhedron.

A flat pattern that can be folded into a solid is called a **net**. A solid may have several different nets. This net forms a solid with six square sides, called a **cube**.

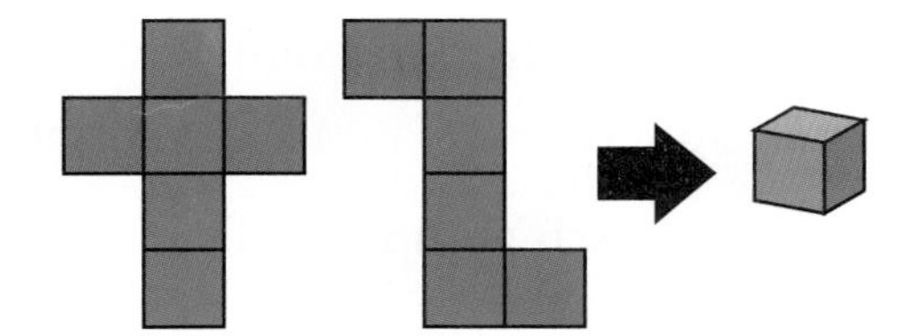

Talk About It

1. Is a pyramid a prism? Is a sphere a polyhedron? Explain.
2. In a prism, what shapes appear as the bases and the other faces?

Check

Classify each solid. Tell how many edges, vertices, and faces it has.

1.

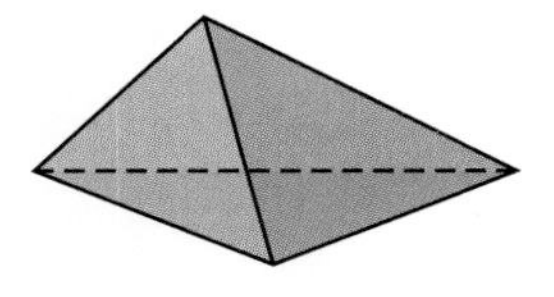

2.

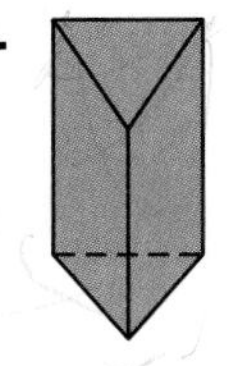

What solid does each net make?

3.

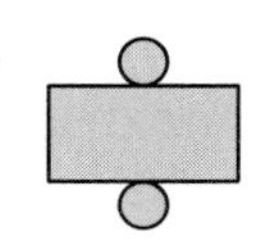

4.

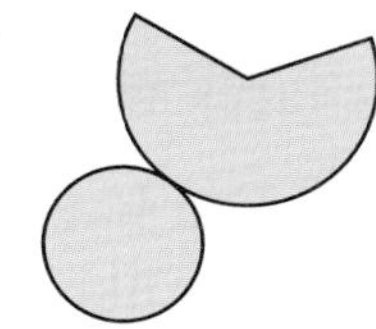

5. **Reasoning** Etta says that each face of a pyramid is a triangle. Is she right? Explain.

Practice

Skills and Reasoning

State the shape of each face of each figure.

6. 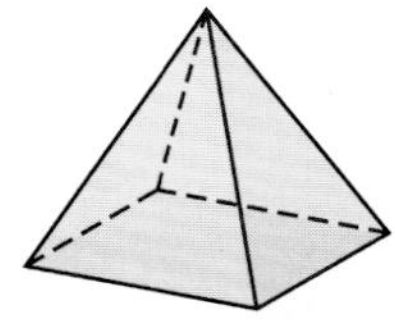

7. 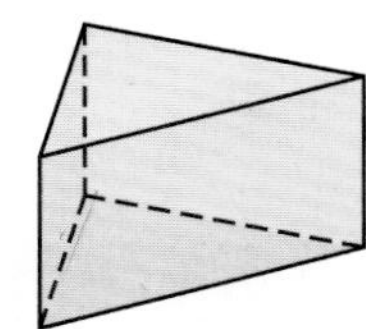

8. 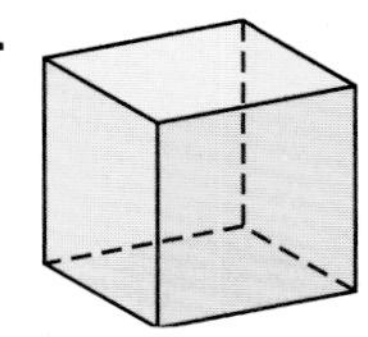

9. 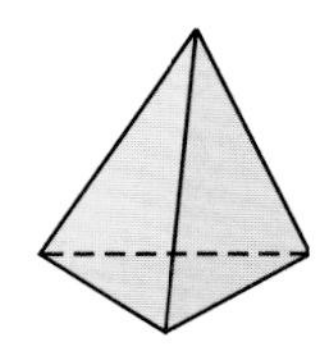

Geometry Classify each solid. If it is a polyhedron, tell how many vertices, edges, and faces it has.

10. 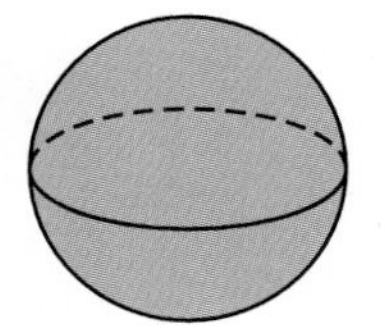

11. 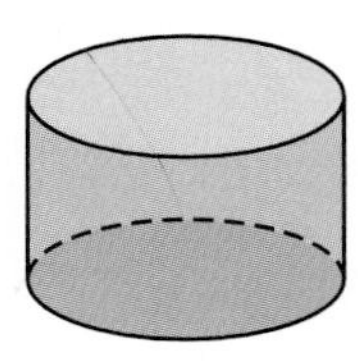

12. 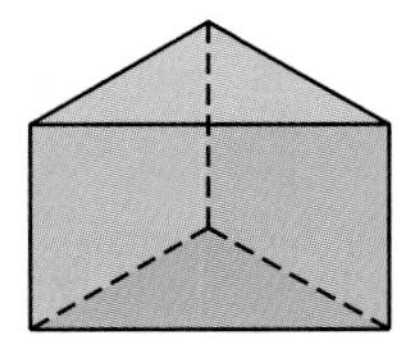

13. 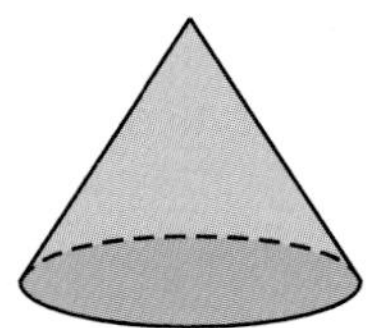

14. 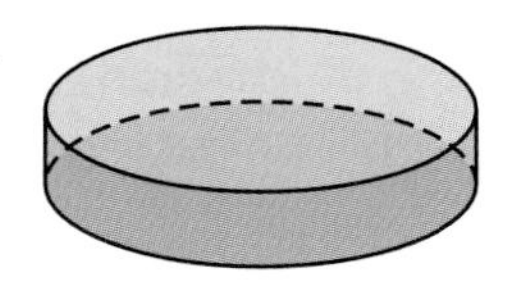

15. 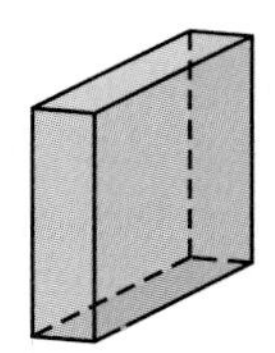

16. 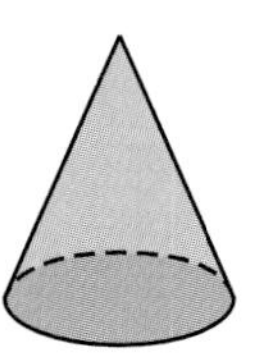

17. 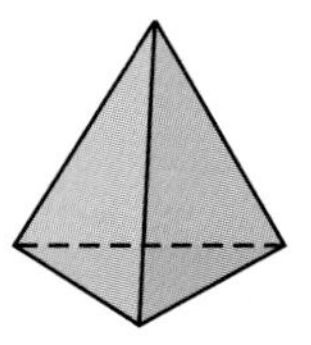

Geometry Draw an example of each.

18. Sphere **19.** Triangular prism **20.** Cylinder **21.** Cone

Classify each group of solids.

22. 

23. 

24. 

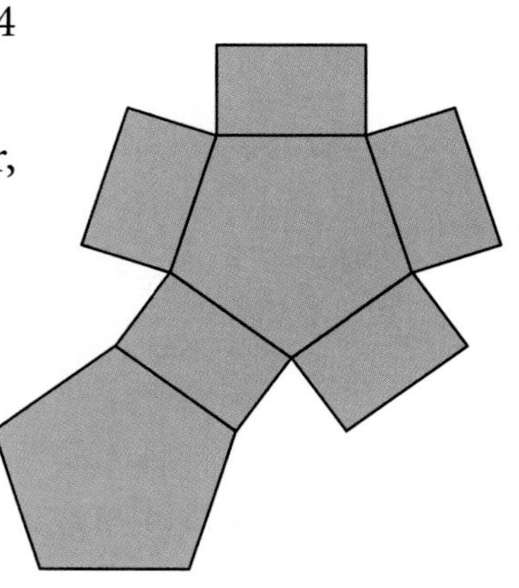

25. Reasoning Can you classify a polyhedron if you know that it has 4 edges? 5 vertices? 12 faces? Explain.

26. Critical Thinking Use what you know about triangular, rectangular, and pentagonal prisms to draw a hexagonal prism. Classify each of the faces and explain your drawing.

27. What If You have to inform someone what a triangular prism looks like. What would you write?

28. Name the solid that is formed from this net.

Problem Solving and Applications

29. **History** Pyramids in the Americas are four-sided flat-topped polyhedrons that were used as platforms for temples. Egyptian pyramids are square pyramids with four triangular sides that were used as royal tombs. Design a net for an Egyptian pyramid.

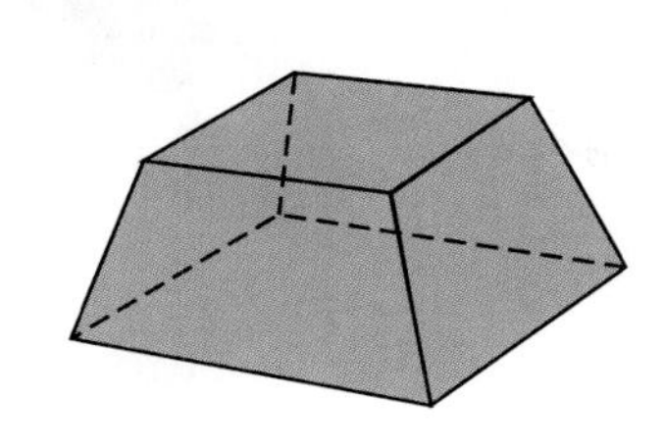

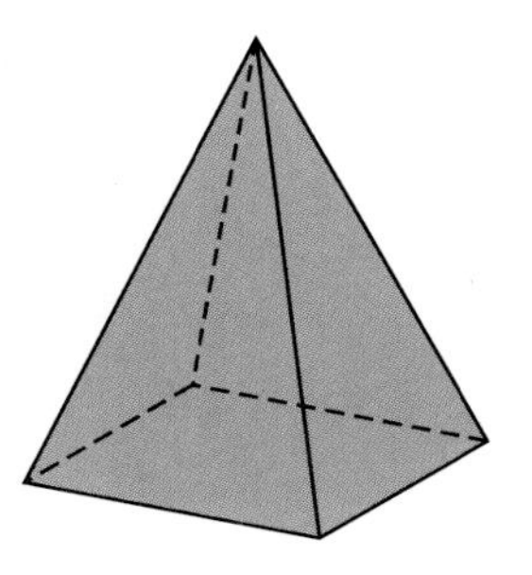

30. **Collecting Data** Make a list of six different polyhedrons you see in objects around you. Name the object. Classify each. Tell how many vertices, edges, and faces each has.

31. **Critical Thinking** Heidi is mailing a set of building blocks to her cousin. She needs to decide which box to use. Most of the blocks are rectangular or triangular prisms, and the types of boxes she can use are shown. Explain to Heidi what shape box she should use and why.

Name the solids in each figure.

32. 

33. 

Rickey, George. "Cluster of Four Cubes," 1992, stainless steel. National Gallery of Art, Washington D.C. Gift of George Rickey and Patrons Permanent Fund.

34. **Journal** Choose a polyhedron and explain how you would determine the number of faces, edges, vertices, and its name.

Mixed Review and Test Prep

STAY SHARP!

35. What is the ratio of vowels to letters in the alphabet?

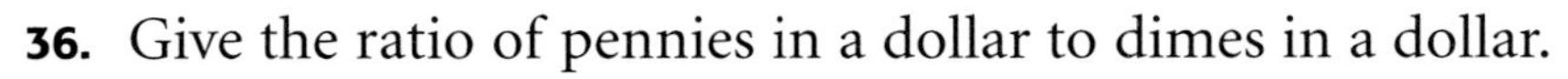

36. Give the ratio of pennies in a dollar to dimes in a dollar.

Write each as a decimal.

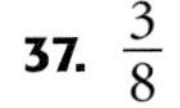

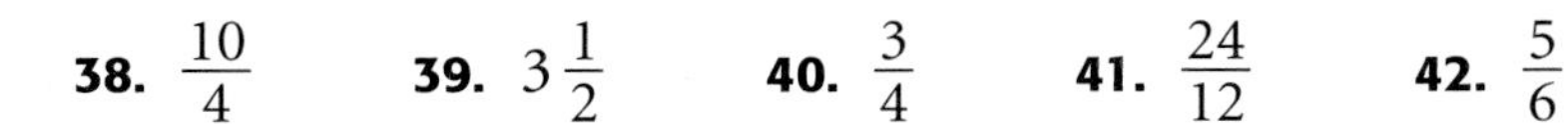

37. $\frac{3}{8}$ 38. $\frac{10}{4}$ 39. $3\frac{1}{2}$ 40. $\frac{3}{4}$ 41. $\frac{24}{12}$ 42. $\frac{5}{6}$

43. The cross product for $\frac{m}{6} = \frac{3}{2}$ is:

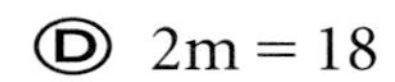

Ⓐ $3m = 12$ Ⓑ $2m = 9$ Ⓒ $6m = 6$ Ⓓ $2m = 18$

Chapter 11
Lesson
2

Exploring Surface Area

Problem Solving Connection
- Draw a Picture/ Use Objects

Materials
- Cuisenaire rods
- centimeter graph paper

Vocabulary
surface area (SA)

Explore

What does a box of dog biscuits have in common with its net? They have the same surface area!

The **surface area (SA)** of a polyhedron is the sum of the areas of all of its faces.

To find the surface area of a polyhedron, unfold it into a net of polygons. Then add their areas.

Work Together

Use four Cuisenaire rods of the same color.

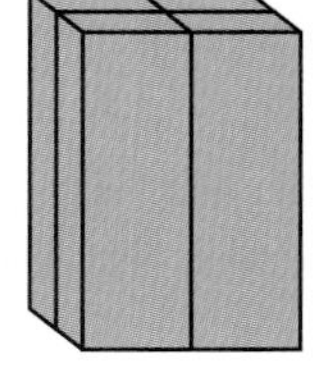

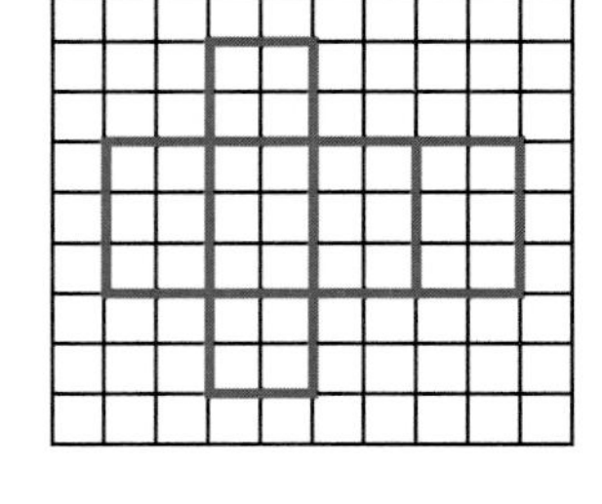

1. Create a rectangular prism by putting the rods together as shown.
   a. On centimeter graph paper, draw a net for this prism.
   b. Tell how many squares it will take to cover this prism.

2. Reassemble the same four rods as shown.
   a. On centimeter graph paper, draw a net for this prism.
   b. Tell how many squares it will take to cover this prism.

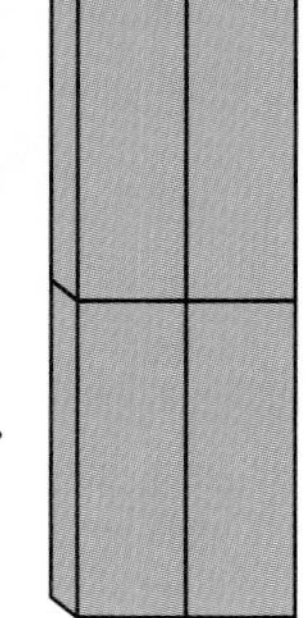

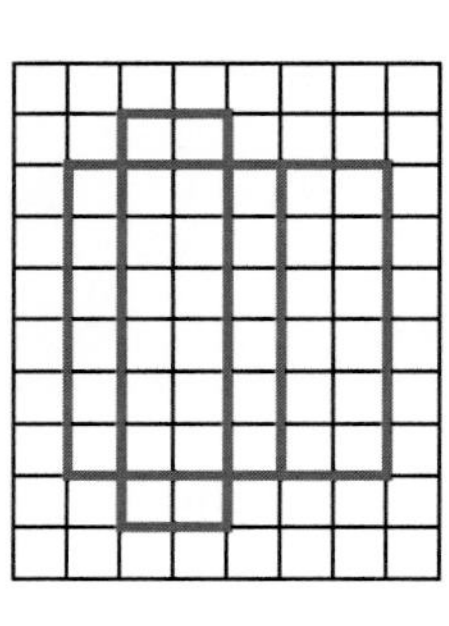

Talk About It

3. Why must you be able to find the areas of polygons in order to find the surface areas of polyhedrons?

4. Which of the two prisms has the greater surface area? Tell how you know.

5. Why is surface area measured in square units?

6. Could you make more than one net for each prism? Would a different net give a different surface area? Explain.

Connect and Learn

The surface area of a polyhedron is the sum of the areas of each face. You must first recognize the number of faces and their shapes.

Example 1

Count the number of faces of the solid, and state the shape of each face.

The solid has five faces.
The top and bottom are triangles.
The other three faces are rectangles.

Remember

base × height = Area of a rectangle

base × height = Area of a parallelogram

$\frac{1}{2}$(base × height) = Area of a triangle

You can use the formulas for area of polygons to find the area of each face of a figure.

Example 2

Find the surface area of the pyramid.

The net consists of a 5 cm by 5 cm square and 4 triangles with bases of 5 cm and heights of 6 cm.

SA = area of square + area of 4 triangles

$SA = (5 \times 5) + 4 \times \frac{1}{2}(5 \times 6)$

$= 25 + 4 \times 15$

$= 25 + 60$

$= 85$

The surface area is 85 cm^2.

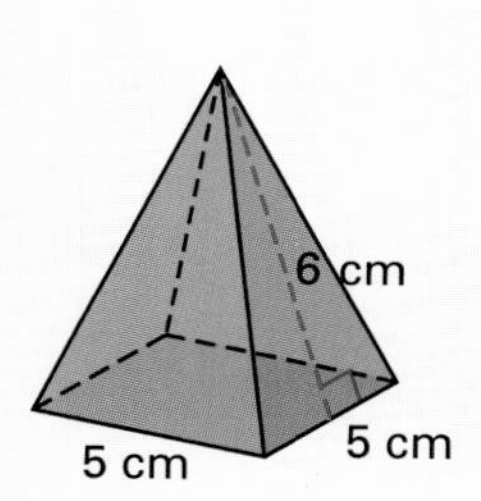

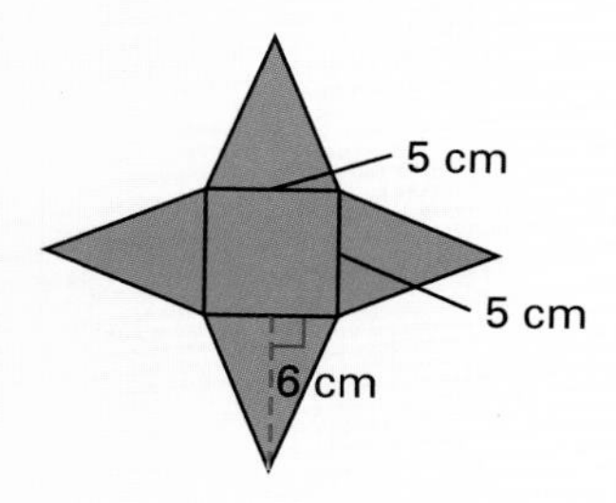

Check

Use the figure on the right for **1-3.**

1. Count the number of faces, and state the shape of each face.
2. Find the surface area of each face.
3. Find the surface area of the entire figure.

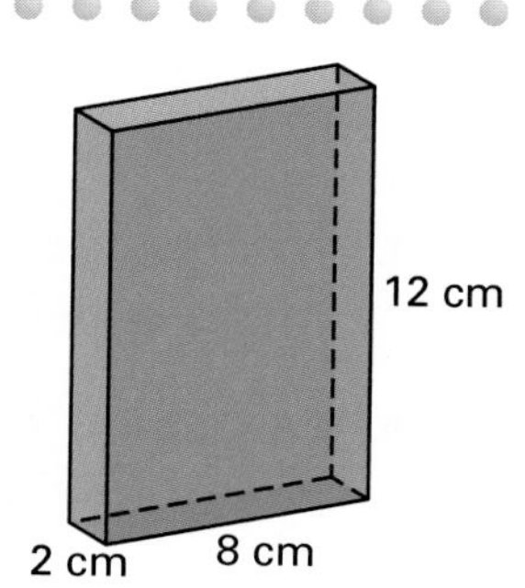

4. **Reasoning** Will the surface area of this polyhedron change if the net is changed? Explain.

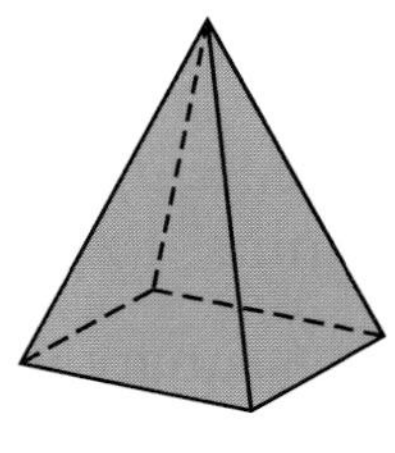

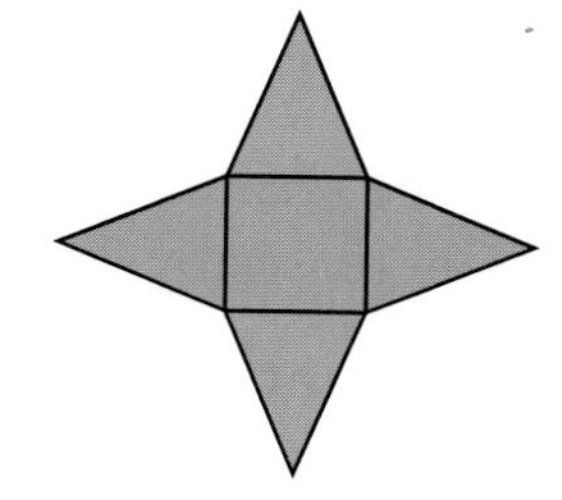

Practice

Skills and Reasoning

Find each area.

5. 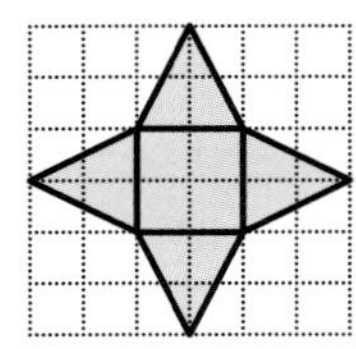

6. 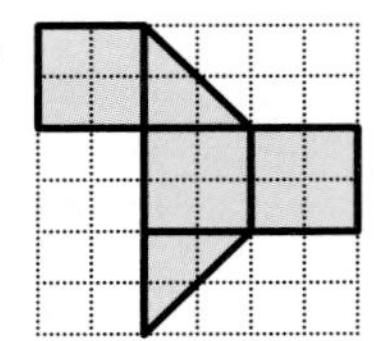

7. 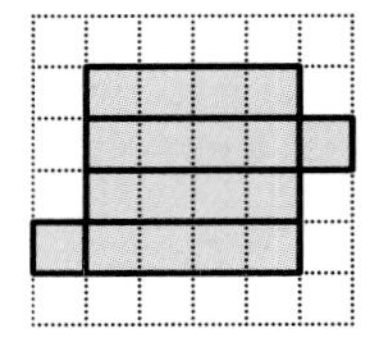

8. 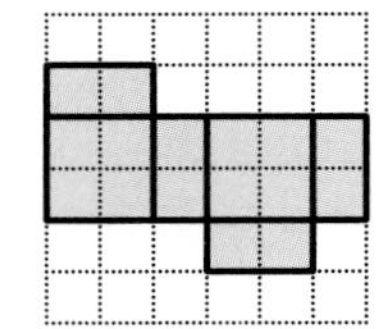

Geometry Find the area of each net. Classify the solid each net will form.

9. 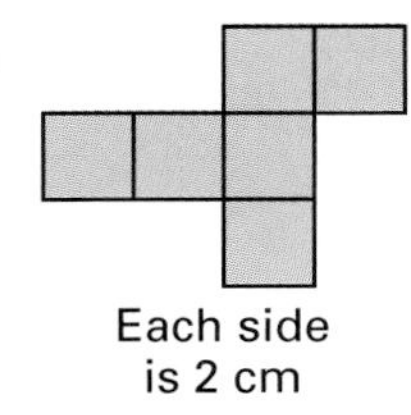

10. 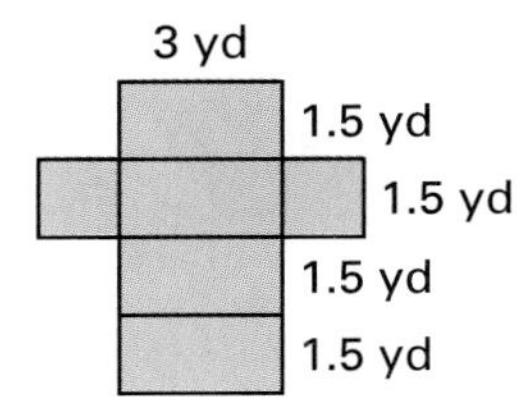

11. 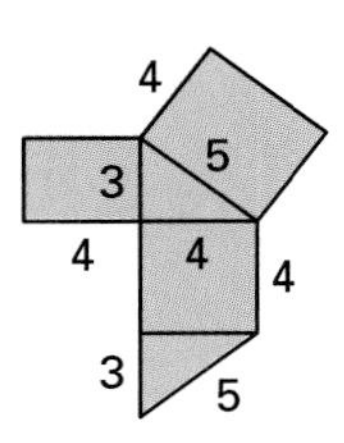

12. 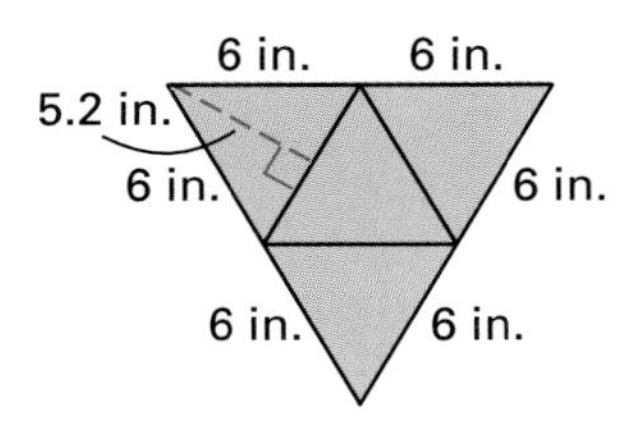

Geometry State the number of faces in each solid. Then classify each face and find the total surface area.

13. 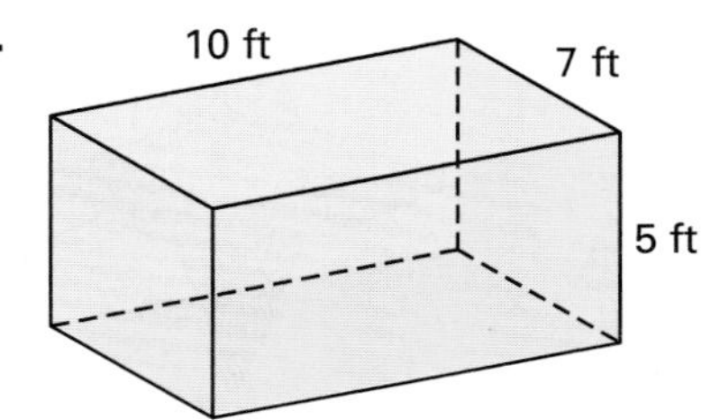

14. 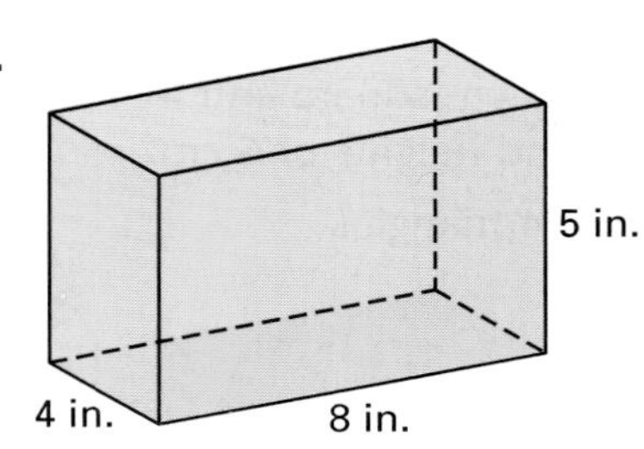

15. 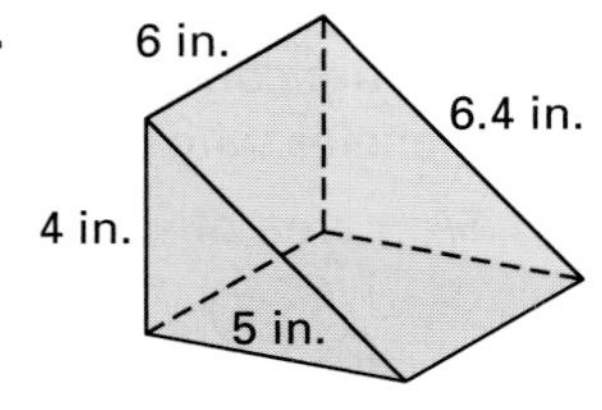

16. Which net can form a cube?

Ⓐ 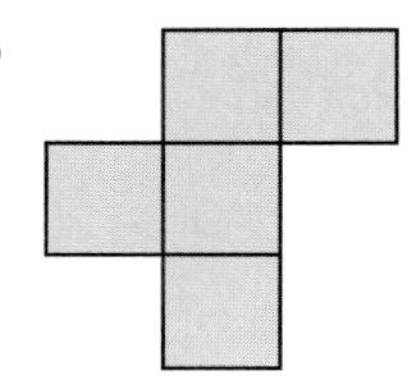

Ⓑ 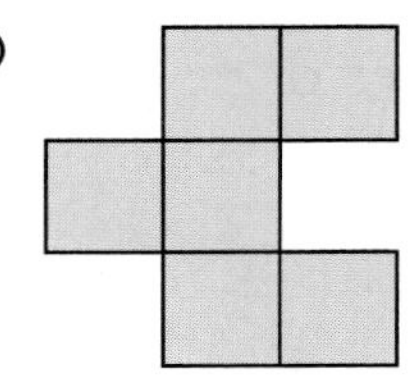

Ⓒ 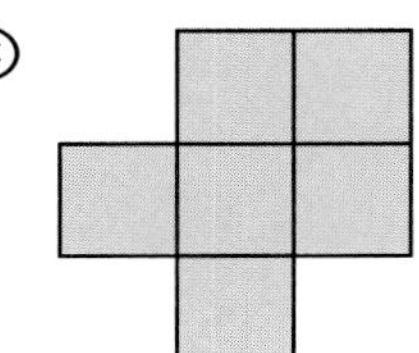

Ⓓ 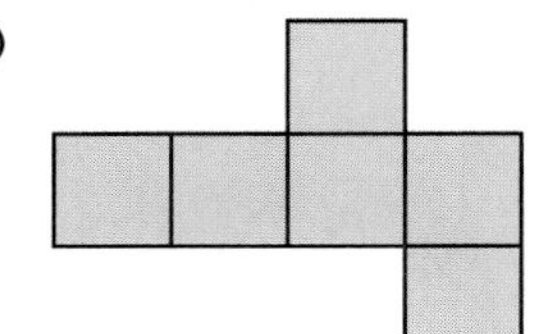

17. If each side in a net for a cube is 3 in., what is the total surface area of the cube?

18. Calculator Use a calculator to find the surface area of a square pyramid whose net consists of a 5 cm by 5 cm square and 4 triangles with bases of 4.6 cm and heights of 7.8 cm.

19. Reasoning Will the surface area of a cube increase by 2 square units if the area of each face increases by 2 square units? Explain.

20. What If Suppose the surface area of a cube is 6 square units. If you put two of these cubes end to end, would the surface area of the new polyhedron be 12 square units? Explain.

Math Tip

The M+ button adds numbers to the calculator's memory. Press 5 × 5 = M+ to store the area of the square. When you know the area of the four triangles, press + MR = to add this to the number in the memory.

Problem Solving and Applications

21. **Measurement** The United States Post Office only delivers mail that is at least 0.007 in. thick. If a piece is between 0.007 and 0.25 in. thick, it must also be at least 3.5 in. long and 5 in. wide. What is the surface area of the thinnest piece of mail that the U.S. Post Office will deliver?

22. Marie is making spaghetti for dinner. The box of spaghetti measures $1\frac{1}{2}$ in. wide, 4 in. long and 12 in. high. What is the total surface area of the package?

23. If wrapping paper costs \$0.29 a square foot, how much would it cost to cover the box shown?

24. **Critical Thinking** Regan has enough foil to cover half of the larger box shown. Since the dimensions of the smaller box are half those of the larger box, she thinks she can completely cover the smaller box instead. Do you agree with Regan? Explain.

50 cm
80 cm
20 cm
25 cm
40 cm
10 cm

25. **Patterns** A manufacturing company wants you to design a box with a surface area 4 times that of its standard 2 in. by 2 in. by 2 in. box. Find as many whole-number solutions as you can.

26. **Journal** List some differences between the perimeter of a rectangle, the area of a rectangle, and the surface area of a rectangular prism. Can any of the quantities be negative? Explain.

Mixed Review and Test Prep

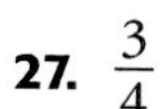

For each ratio, give two equivalent ratios.

27. $\frac{3}{4}$ 28. 6:24 29. $\frac{4}{10}$ 30. 7 to 9 31. $\frac{11}{12}$ 32. 3:8

33. $\frac{1}{9}$ 34. 2:3 35. $\frac{6}{10}$ 36. 16:3 37. $\frac{10}{15}$ 38. 4 to 7

Order from least to greatest.

39. $\frac{1}{2}$, 0.23, 1.23 40. 6.7, $\frac{1}{6}$, $\frac{5}{6}$, 41. 8.2, $8\frac{1}{4}$, 8.75 42. $\frac{1}{3}$, $\frac{3}{3}$, 3.3

43. Which shape cannot be used to make a tessellation?

Ⓐ Equilateral triangle Ⓑ Parallelogram

Ⓒ L-shaped figure Ⓓ D-shaped figure

Chapter 11
Lesson
3

Surface Area Formulas

You Will Learn
- to use surface area formulas

Remember
In the formula $6s^2$, the ^{2} is an exponent. It means that you should multiply the value of s by itself.

Learn

When it comes to finding ways to keep the cost of food down, packaging is the first place to look.
Each block of cheese weighs about two pounds. Which would need more shrink wrap?

6 cm
16 cm
8 cm
8 cm
8 cm
8 cm

You can use a formula to find the surface area of a rectangular prism.

Opposite each face of a rectangular prism is another face with the same area.

The total surface area is the sum of the areas of the three sets of faces.

$SA = (2 \times l \times w) + (2 \times l \times h) + (2 \times w \times h)$

$SA = (2 \times 50) + (2 \times 70) + (2 \times 35) = 310$

SA (rectangular prism) $= 2lw + 2lh + 2wh$

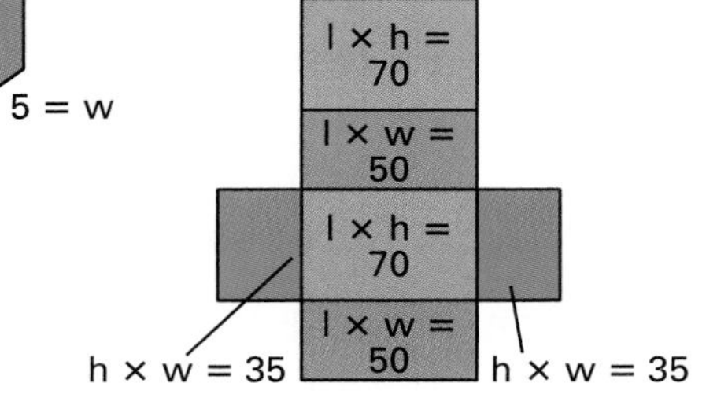

Example 1

Find the surface area of the rectangular block of cheese.

$l = 16$, $w = 8$, $h = 6$

$$\begin{aligned} SA &= 2lw + 2lh + 2wh \\ &= (2 \times 16 \times 8) + (2 \times 16 \times 6) + (2 \times 8 \times 6) \\ &= 256 + 192 + 96 \\ &= 544 \end{aligned}$$

The surface area is 544 cm^2.

If a rectangular prism is a cube, the length, width, and height are all equal.

You can use a simplified surface area formula. Let s be the length of each side.

SA (cube) $= 6s^2$

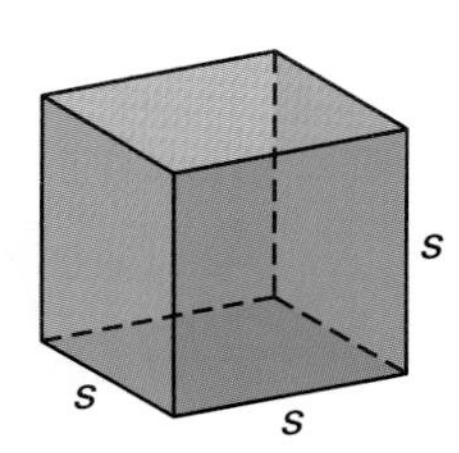

Example 2

Find the surface area of the cube of cheese.

The cheese is a cube with 8 cm on each side. $s = 8$ cm

$$\begin{aligned} SA &= 6s^2 \\ &= 6 \times 8^2 \\ &= 6 \times 64 \\ &= 384 \end{aligned}$$

The surface area is 384 cm^2.

If the triangular faces of a pyramid are congruent, you can use this formula to find the surface area of the pyramid.

SA = area of base + (number of triangular faces) × (area of each face)

Example 3

Find the surface area of the pyramid.

The base is a square 8 units on a side. Each face is a triangle with base 8 and height 6.

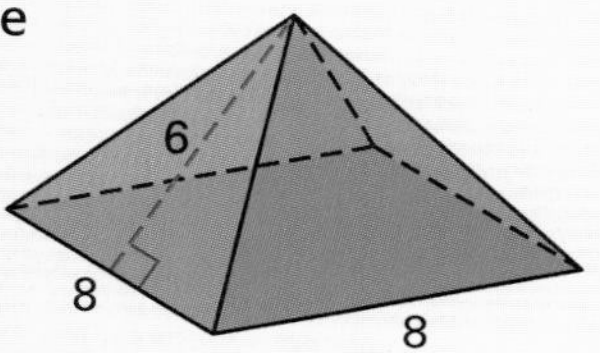

$$\begin{aligned} SA &= (8 \times 8) + 4 \times (8 \times 6 \div 2) \\ &= 64 \quad + 4 \times (24) \\ &= 160 \end{aligned}$$

The surface area is 160 units^2.

Talk About It

1. Which block of cheese on page 586 would need more shrink wrap? Explain.
2. If two prisms have the same surface area, are they the same prism? Explain.

Check

Find the surface area of each solid.

1.

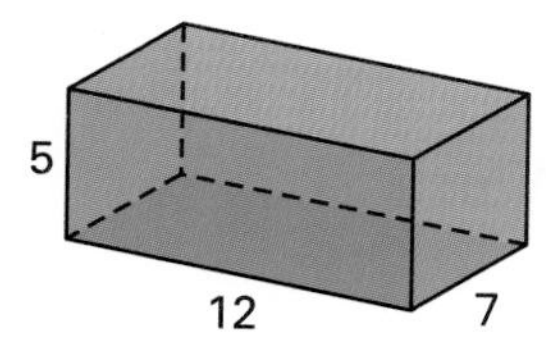

2.

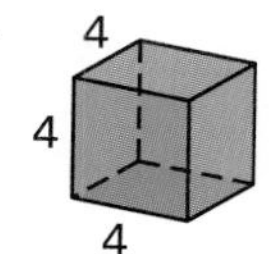

3.

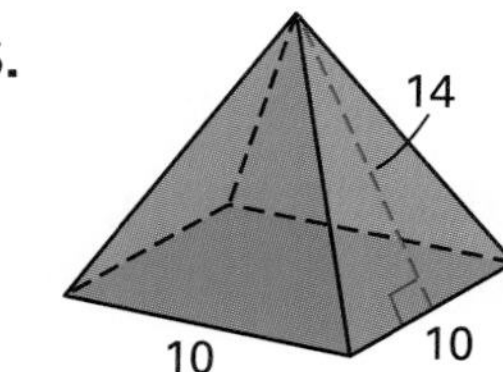

4. **Reasoning** David could not remember the formula for finding the surface area of a cube, so he used the formula for surface area of a rectangular prism. Would he get the right answer? Explain.

Practice

Skills and Reasoning

Find the surface area of each cube.

5.

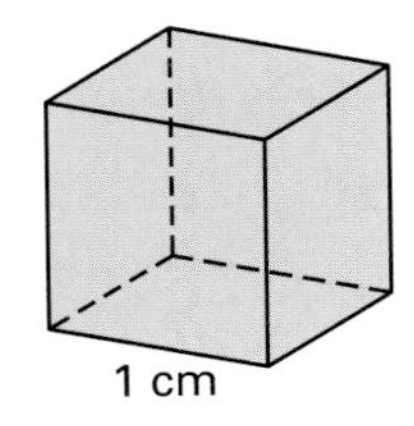

6.

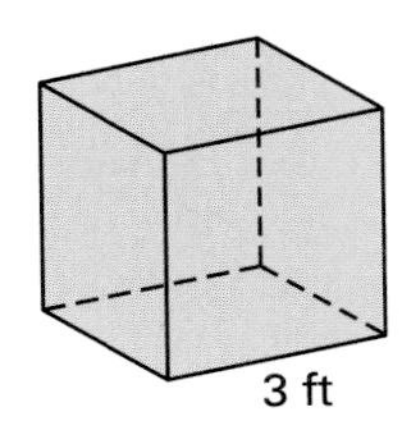

7.

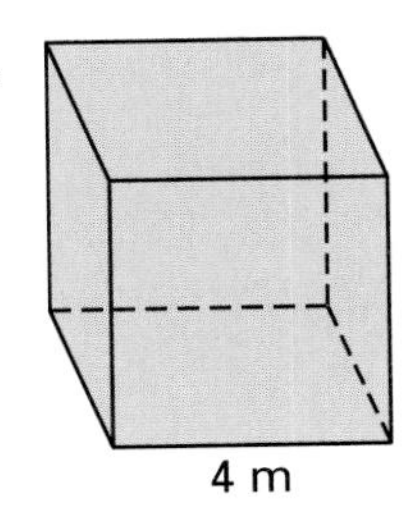

8.

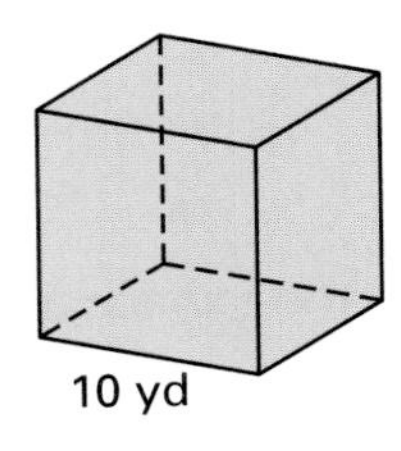

Find the surface area of each solid.

9.

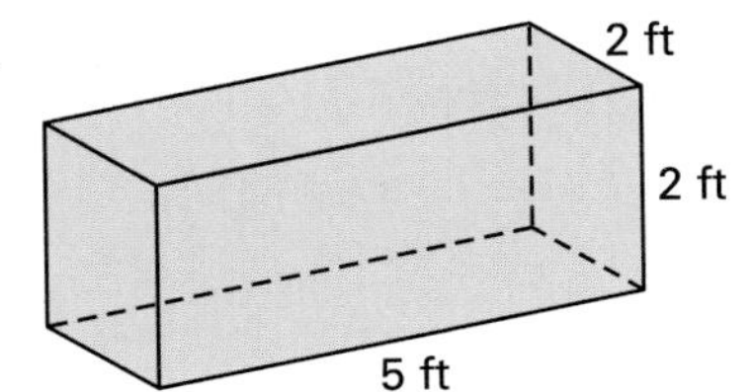

10.

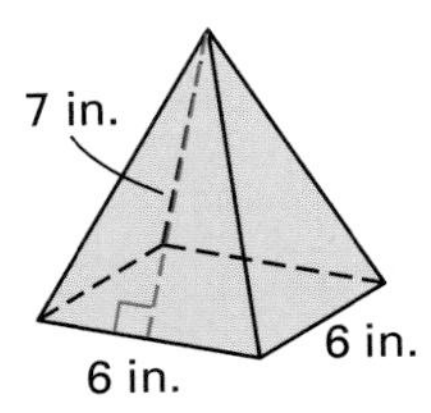

11.

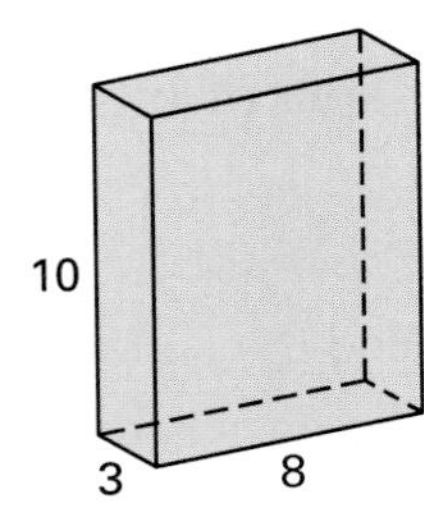

12.

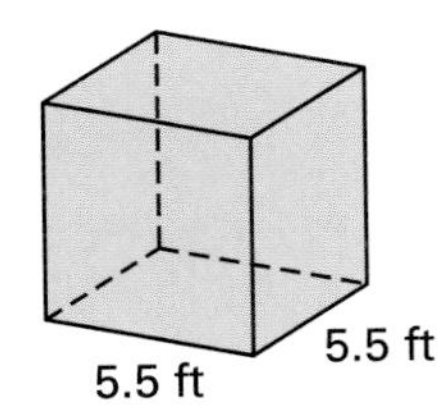

13.

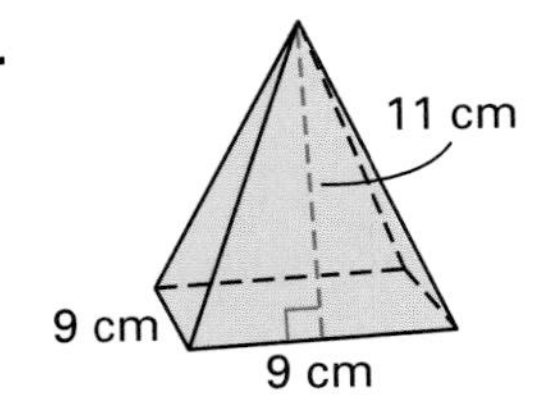

14.

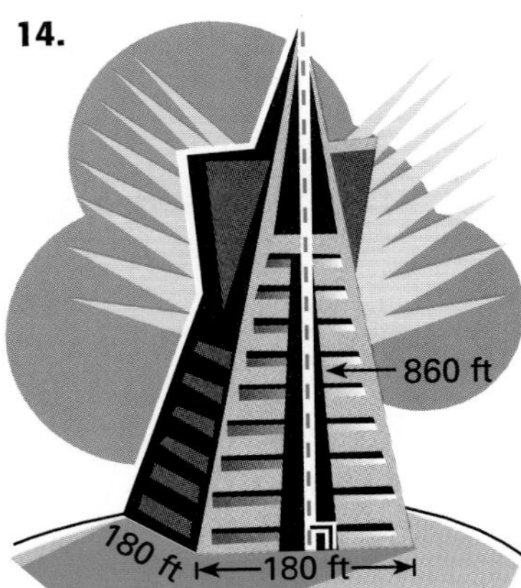

15.

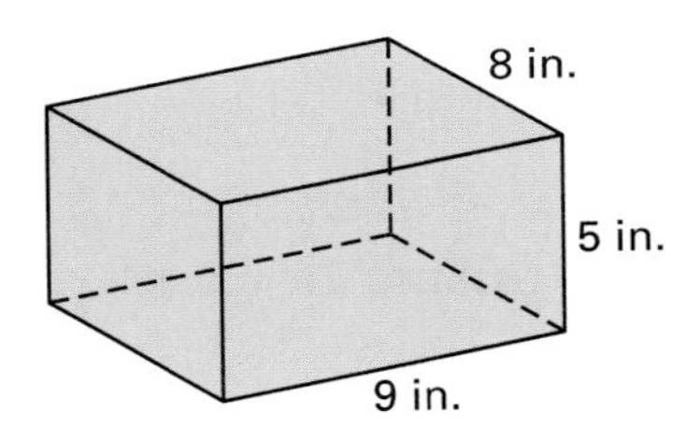

16.

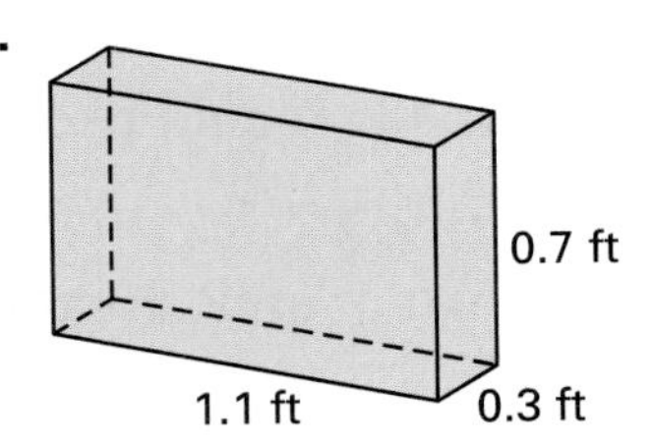

Geometry Find the surface area of each rectangular prism.

17. $l = 4.1$ cm, $w = 3$ cm, $h = 6$ cm

18. $l = 10$ in., $w = 15$ in., $h = 12$ in.

19. The side of a number cube measures 1.5 cm. What is its surface area?

20. Critical Thinking Look at the figures in Exercises 15 and 16. Which solid has the greater surface area? Explain.

21. Reasoning Hanna could not remember the formula for finding the surface area of a rectangular solid, so she used the formula for the surface area of a cube instead. She got the right answer. Is this possible? Explain.

Problem Solving and Applications

22. Critical Thinking The Wrap'n'Pack gift wrapping company has three different-sized medium boxes. What is the average surface area for a medium box?

Medium Boxes (in.)	A	B	C
Length	12	20	8
Width	12	16	6
Height	12	24	2

23. Mariana wants to cover the pyramid shown with gold foil.

a. How many square feet of foil does she need?

b. Money If the foil cost \$0.02 per square foot, how much should Mariana plan to spend?

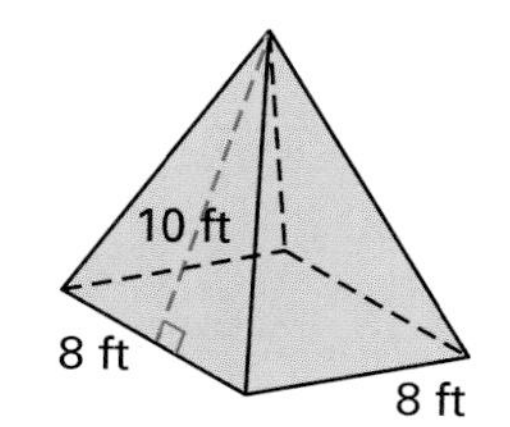

24. A trailer is 23 ft by 9 ft by 8 ft. How much aluminum siding is used for the trailer, including the top and the bottom?

Find the surface area of each box.

25.

26.

27. Using Data Use the Data File on page 574. How much paper would be needed to cover the world's largest box of popcorn? (Hint: Change all measurements to inches.)

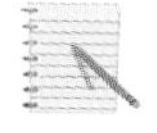

28. Journal Explain how you would find the surface area of a cube with 4-in. sides.

Mixed Review and Test Prep

STAY SHARP!

State if each ratio is a rate.

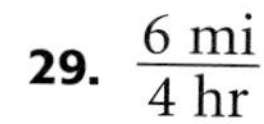

29. $\frac{6 \text{ mi}}{4 \text{ hr}}$ **30.** $\frac{1 \text{ kitten}}{7 \text{ oz}}$ **31.** $\frac{6 \text{ in.}}{11 \text{ in.}}$ **32.** $7:9$ **33.** $\frac{35 \text{ miles}}{1 \text{ hour}}$

Simplify.

34. $\frac{5}{6} - \frac{2}{3}$ **35.** $\frac{1}{4} + \frac{7}{11}$ **36.** $\frac{3}{4} - \frac{2}{7}$ **37.** $\frac{10}{12} + \frac{1}{6}$ **38.** $\frac{4}{9} - \frac{2}{7}$

39. What is the decimal form for six and thirty-four thousandths?

Ⓐ 6034.0 Ⓑ 6.340 Ⓒ 6.034 Ⓓ 60.34

PRACTICE AND APPLY

Chapter 11
Lesson
4

Surface Area of a Cylinder

You Will Learn

- to find the surface area of a cylinder

Remember

The area for a circle is $\pi \times radius^2$. You can use 3.14 as an approximation for π.

Learn

A cylinder has two bases. Each base is a circle. The side can be unrolled to form a rectangle. The length of the rectangle equals the circumference of the circle.

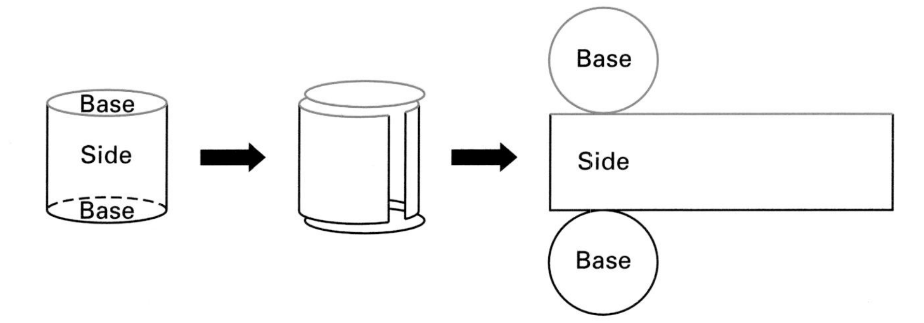

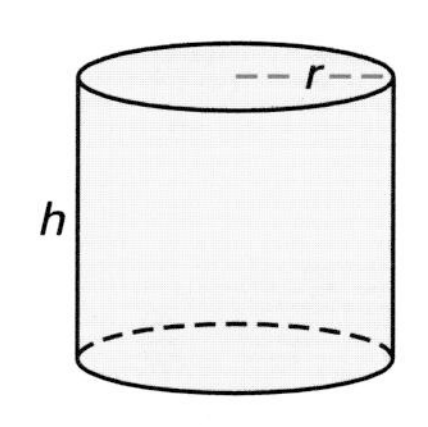

You can use this relationship to find the surface area of a cylinder whose height is h and whose bases have a radius of r.

$$SA = (2 \times \text{area of base}) + (\text{ the area of rectangular side})$$
$$= (2 \times \text{area of base}) + (\text{length of side} \times \text{height of side})$$
$$= (2 \times \text{area of base}) + (\text{circumference of base} \times \text{height of cylinder})$$
$$= (2 \times \pi r^2) \qquad + (2\pi r \times h)$$
$$SA = 2\pi r^2 + 2\pi rh$$

Example 1

Find the surface area of the ice cream container.
Use 3.14 for π.

$r = 2.5$ in. $\quad h = 6.5$ in.

$SA = 2\pi r^2 + 2\pi rh$

$SA \approx (2 \times 3.14 \times 2.5 \times 2.5) + (2 \times 3.14 \times 2.5 \times 6.5)$

$\approx 39.25 + 102.05$

≈ 141.3

The surface area is about 141.3 in^2.

If you know the diameter of the base of a cylinder, you can find the radius by dividing the diameter by 2.

Example 2

Find the surface area. Use 3.14 for π.

If the diameter is 75.5, the radius is half of that, or 37.75.

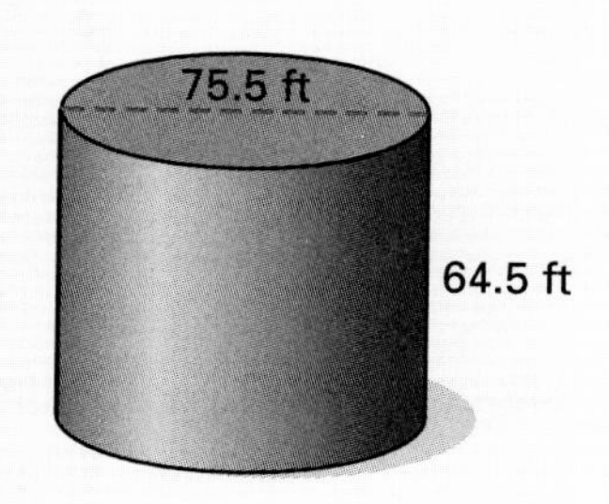

$$\begin{aligned} SA &= 2\pi r^2 + 2\pi rh \\ &\approx (2 \times 3.14 \times 37.75 \times 37.75) + (2 \times 3.14 \times 37.75 \times 64.5) \\ &\approx 8{,}949.4 + 15{,}291 \\ &\approx 24{,}240.4 \end{aligned}$$

The surface area is about 24,240.4 ft^2.

You can find the surface area of a half-cylinder. Use the formula $SA = 2\pi r^2 + 2\pi rh$ to find the area of a complete cylinder, then divide by 2. Then add the area of the rectangular top.

Example 3

Find the surface area of the half-cylinder.

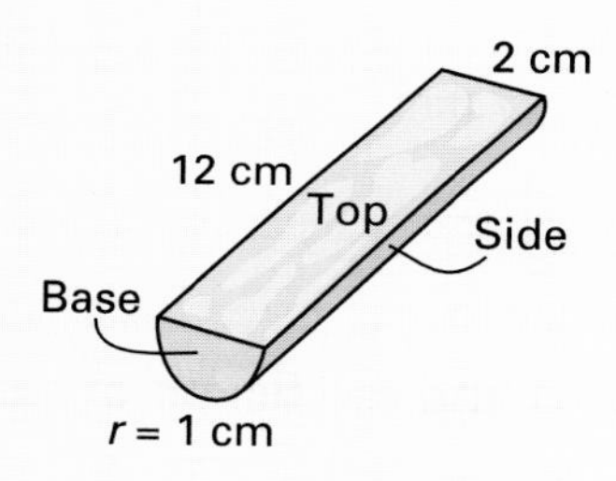

$$\begin{aligned} SA &= 2\pi r^2 + 2\pi rh \div 2 \\ &= 81.64 \div 2 \\ &= 40.82 \text{ cm}^2 \end{aligned}$$

The area of the rectangular top is $12 \text{ cm} \times 2 \text{ cm} = 24 \text{ cm}^2$.

$40.82 \text{ cm}^2 + 24 \text{ cm}^2 = 64.82 \text{ cm}^2$

The surface area is about 64.82 cm^2.

Talk About It

1. How would the surface area change if the half-cylinder did not have a top?
2. Why are the surface areas of the cylinders not exact?

Check

1. Find the surface area of the cylinder shown.

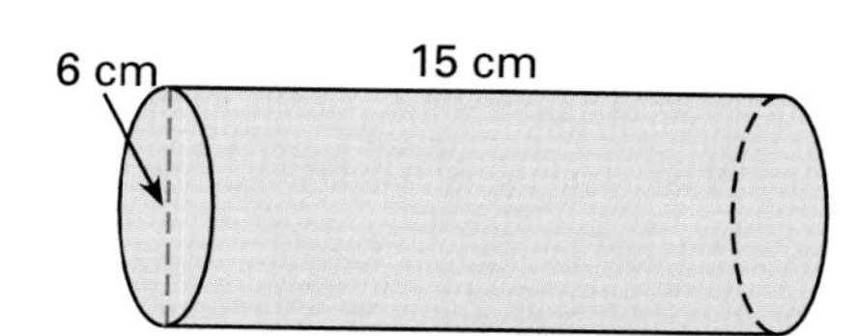

2. **Reasoning** Tom has forgotten the formula for the surface area of a cylinder. He thinks he can find the surface area of a cylinder by adding up all the areas one at a time. Is he right? Explain.

Practice

Skills and Reasoning

Find the circumference of each cylinder. Use 3.14 for π.

3.

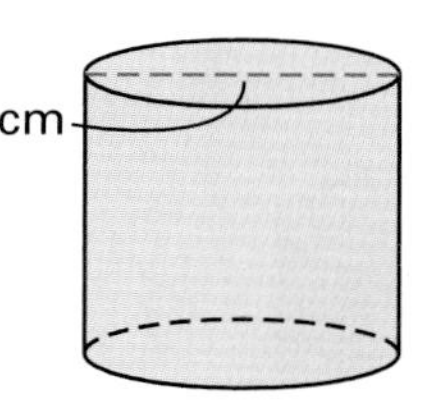

4.

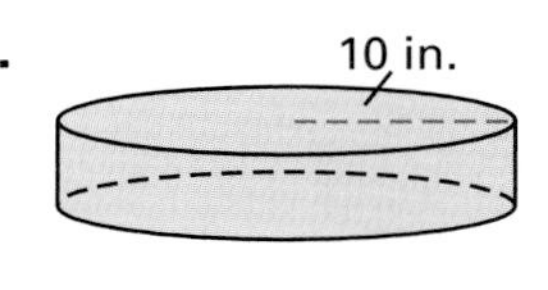

5.

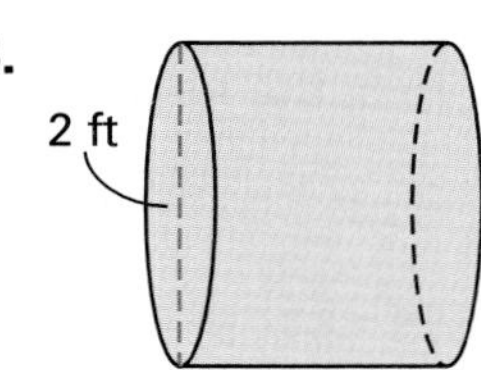

6.

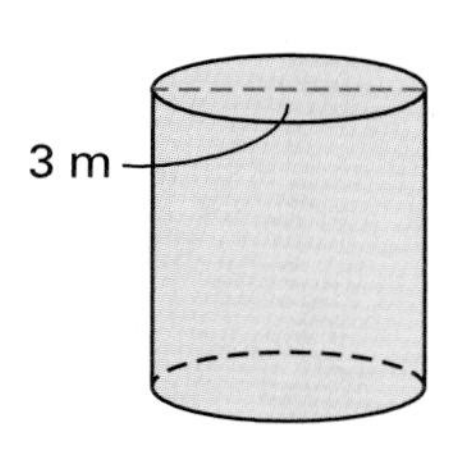

Find the surface area of each cylinder. Use 3.14 for π.

7.

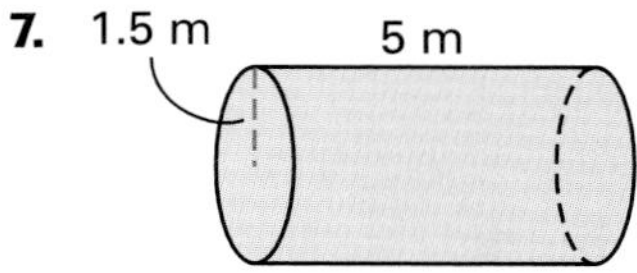

8.

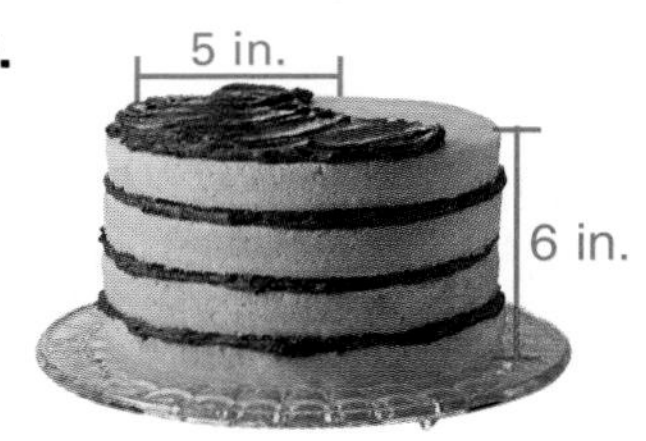

9.

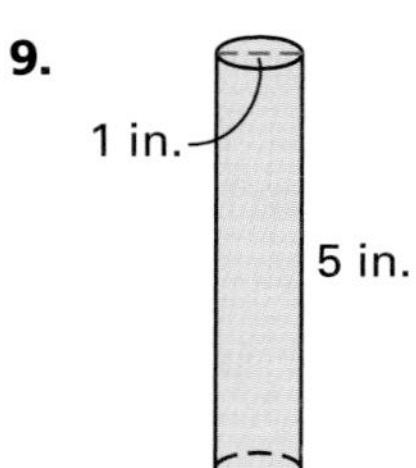

10.

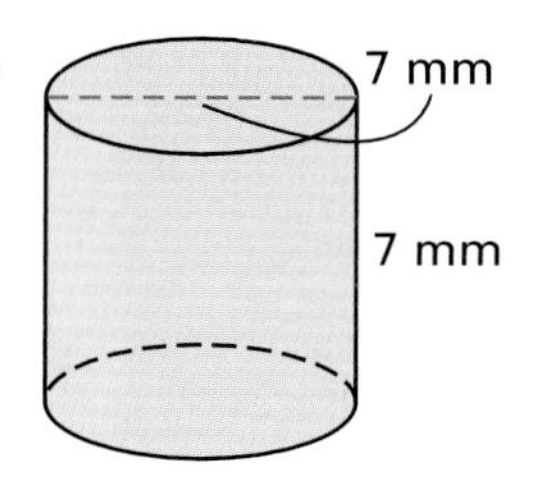

11.

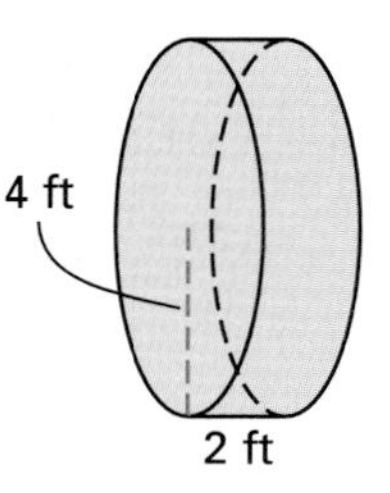

Given the radius and the height of each cylinder, find the surface area. Use 3.14 for π.

12. $r = 7, h = 10$ **13.** $r = 1, h = 21$ **14.** $r = 5, h = 3.5$ **15.** $r = 12, h = 16$

16. Reasoning Ruan found the surface area of a certain cylinder whose height is 6 cm and diameter is 4 cm to be about 251.2 cm^2. Harold told him the correct answer was 100.48 cm^2. What did Ruan do wrong? Explain.

Problem Solving and Applications

Choose any strategy to solve each problem.

17. Tito has found the surface area of four cylinders and recorded the data in the bar graph. The surface area of a fifth cylinder is greater than the second but less than the third. Find a possible height and diameter for the fifth cylinder.

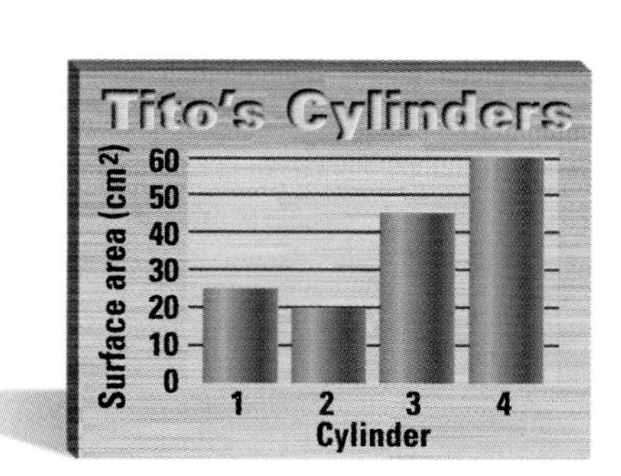

18. Industry A can of cake frosting is 4.5 inches tall and has a 3-inch diameter.

a. If there is no overlap, what is the area of the can's label?

b. What is the surface area of the entire can?

Problem Solving and HISTORY

The process of preserving food in cans was introduced into the United States in the early 1800s. Even though tin cans were much cheaper, they did not replace glass containers until the middle of the 19th century. Today we have aluminum and plastic containers as well.

19. Salt comes in a cardboard container shaped like a cylinder. The diameter of the container is 3 in. and the height is 5.25 in. What is the surface area of the salt container?

20. Some advertising companies use unusual packaging to attract customers to their products. A T-shirt in a can compelled Patricia to purchase this T-shirt. The can's radius is 2 in. and height is 4.3 in. What is the surface area of that can?

21. Critical Thinking How much advertising space is there on the label of a can with a diameter of 3 in. and a height of 4 in.? Explain.

22. Critical Thinking Some doll collectors display their dolls in cases like the one shown. The back of the case is a 12 in. by 5 in. rectangle. The bottom and top pieces are both half-circles. The front is clear plastic. What is the surface area of the entire case? Describe how you found it and explain your reasoning.

23. Write Your Own Problem Make up a problem that can be solved using the formula for finding the surface area of a cylinder. Then solve it.

Mixed Review and Test Prep

State if the pair of ratios form a proportion.

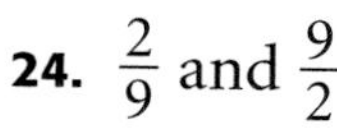

24. $\frac{2}{9}$ and $\frac{9}{2}$ **25.** $\frac{5}{10}$ and $\frac{1}{2}$ **26.** $\frac{4}{7}$ and $\frac{2}{3}$ **27.** $\frac{7}{27}$ and $\frac{21}{54}$ **28.** $\frac{4}{10}$ and $\frac{110}{27}$

29. $\frac{1}{2}$ and $\frac{32}{16}$ **30.** $\frac{1}{8}$ and $\frac{3}{24}$ **31.** $\frac{10}{16}$ and $\frac{2}{4}$ **32.** $\frac{9}{4}$ and $\frac{36}{36}$ **33.** $\frac{12}{5}$ and $\frac{60}{144}$

Simplify.

34. 62% of 200 **35.** 30% of 58 **36.** 78% of 24 **37.** 12% of 2

38. Andrea has read $\frac{2}{3}$ of her 504-page book. How many pages has she read?

Ⓐ 168 Ⓑ 336 Ⓒ 1,008 Ⓓ Not here

Technology

Using a Spreadsheet to Find the Surface Area of a Cylinder

How would you go about comparing the surface areas of two cylinders if you only had their dimensions? You'd probably use the formula for the surface area of a cylinder and do the calculations yourself. But you can use a spreadsheet to find the surface areas of these cylinders. The spreadsheet software will quickly complete the calculations for you.

Materials

Interactive CD-ROM Spreadsheet/Grapher Tool or other spreadsheet software

Which has more surface area, a cylinder with a height of 5 cm and a radius of 2 cm, or a cylinder with a height of 2 cm and a radius of 5 cm?

Work Together

Use your spreadsheet software to calculate the surface areas.

1. Create a new spreadsheet in your software program. Enter the information into the spreadsheet as shown.

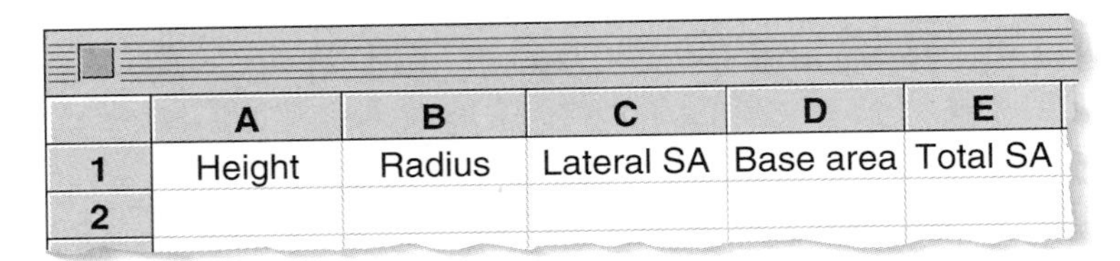

	A	B	C	D	E
1	Height	Radius	Lateral SA	Base area	Total SA
2					

2. Enter the dimensions of the first cylinder. In cell A2, enter 5. In cell B2, enter 2. In cell C2, enter the formula =2*3.14*A2*B2. In cell D2, enter the formula =3.14*(B2)^2. In cell E2, enter the formula =C2+2*D2.

3 Copy the contents of row 2 down to row 3. Then, enter the dimensions of the second cylinder. Change the height value to 2 and the radius value to 5.

	A	B	C	D	E
1	Height	Radius	Lateral SA	Base area	Total SA
2	5	2	62.8	12.56	87.92
3	2	5	62.8	78.50	219.80

4 Which cylinder has more surface area?

Exercises

1. Which has more surface area, a cylinder with a height of 3 cm and a radius of 4 cm, or a cylinder with a height of 4 cm and a radius of 3 cm?
2. Which has more surface area, a cylinder with a height of 5 cm and a radius of 3 cm, or a cylinder with a height of 6 cm and a radius of 2 cm?
3. The height and radius of a cylinder are whole numbers whose sum is 10. How much should the height and radius be so that the cylinder has the greatest surface area possible?

Extensions

4. Why do you think it's necessary to type an = at the beginning of each formula?
5. Why might someone want to set up a spreadsheet to calculate the surface area of a cylinder instead of using a calculator or pencil and paper?

SECTION A

Review and Practice

Vocabulary Copy and complete each sentence with the best term.

1. The flat surfaces of a solid are called the ________.
2. A ________ is a solid whose faces are polygons.
3. A flat pattern that can be folded to make a solid is called a ________.

(Lesson 1) Classify each solid. If it is a polyhedron, tell how many vertices, edges, and faces it has.

4. 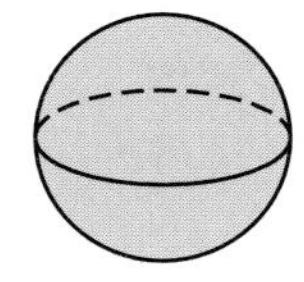

5. 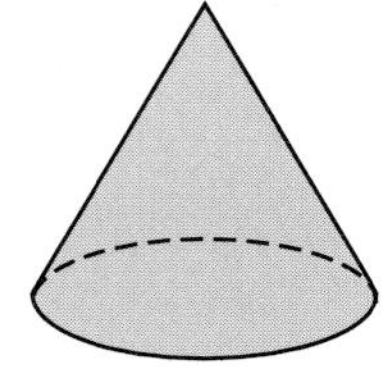

6. 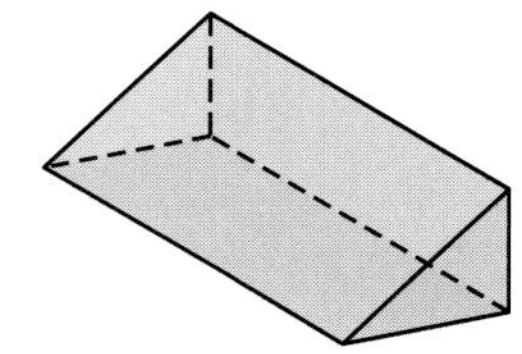

7. 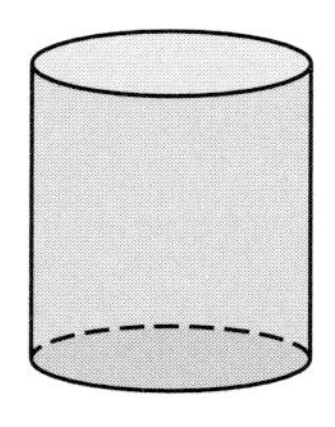

8. 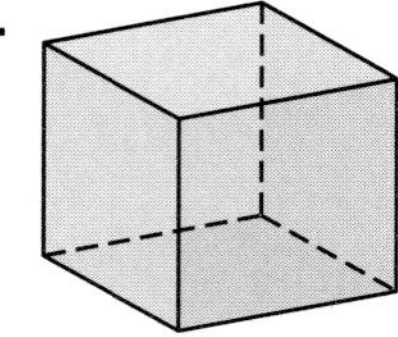

9. 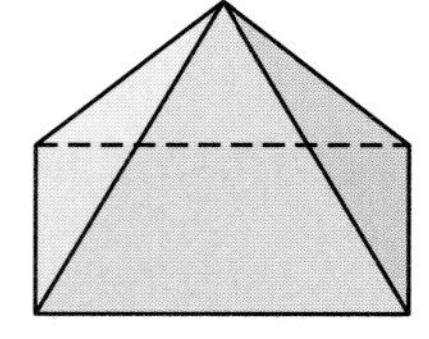

(Lessons 2 and 3) Find the surface area of each figure.

10. 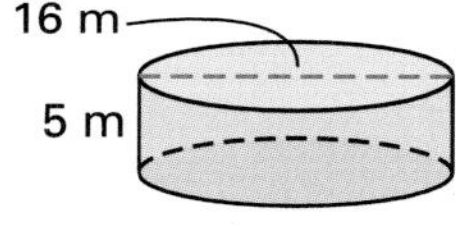

11. 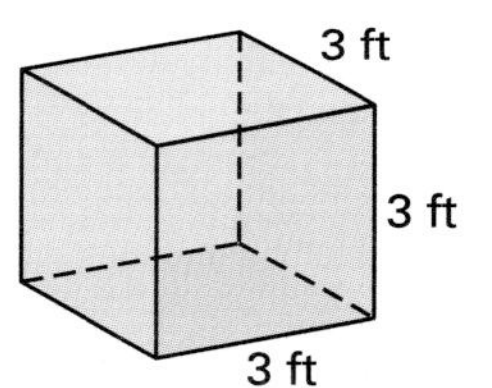

12. 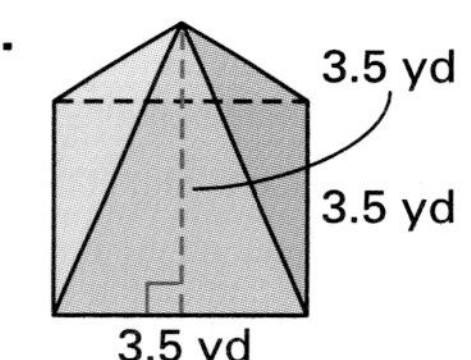

13. A box of cereal measures $1\frac{3}{4}$ in. wide, $6\frac{1}{2}$ in. long, and $8\frac{1}{2}$ in. high. What is the total surface area of the package?

(Lesson 4) Find the surface area of each cylinder. Use 3.14 for π. Round your answers to the nearest hundredth.

14. 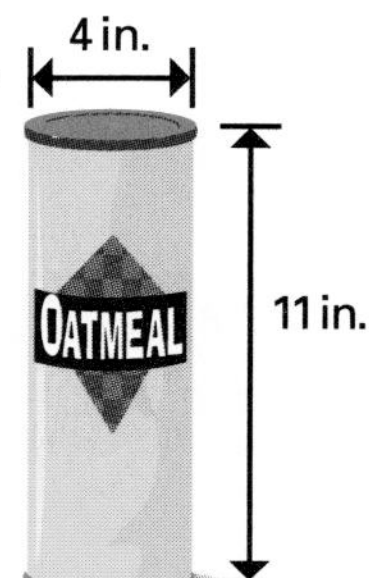

15. 

16. 

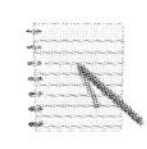

17. **Journal** Describe the difference between a rectangular pyramid and a rectangular prism.

Skills Checklist

In this section, you have:

- ☑ Classified Solids
- ☑ Explored Surface Area
- ☑ Learned About Surface Area Formulas
- ☑ Found the Surface Area of Cylinders

CHAPTER 11

SECTION

B Volume

What would it be like having a pet from another planet? Would it breathe a different kind of air? Live at a different temperature? Need a self-contained environment that you would have to control? In many ways, keeping fish is like having an alien pet. An aquarium is a self-contained environment where you control the air, temperature, and light.

How could a person who is putting together an aquarium use mathematics?

GET READY!

Finding Volume

Review multiplying with decimals. Find each product.

1. 12.6×3.4

2. 98.3×17.9

3. 12.75×20

4. $8.6 \times 1.2 \times 7$

5. $5.5 \times 10 \times 4.1$

6. $2.7 \times 1.4 \times 0.9$

7. $2(6.4 + 7.1)$

8. $10(8.3 + 1.7)$

Skills Checklist

In this section, you will:

- ❒ Explore Three-Dimensional Figures
- ❒ Explore Volume
- ❒ Calculate Volume

Chapter 11
Lesson
5

Three-Dimensional Figures

Problem Solving Connection
- Draw a Picture

Materials
- centimeter cubes
- centimeter grid paper

Explore

A drawing on a piece of paper has two dimensions: width and length. Artists try to make their paintings look life-like by adding a third dimension: depth. They do this with a technique called *perspective,* which came into use in Italy in the late 1400s.

You can look at a model of a three-dimensional shape and then draw its three dimensions: top, front, and side.

Did You Know?
Flat drawings that show the front, side, and top views of a solid are also known as *orthographic projections*. A three-dimensional picture is an *isometric projection*.

Work Together

1. Use centimeter cubes to build the stack shown.

   a. On graph paper, draw what you see when you look down on your stack. Write in each square the number of cubes each square represents.
   b. Draw what you see when you look at the front of your stack. Write the number of cubes in each square.
   c. Draw what you see when you look at each side of your stack. Write the number of cubes in each square. Do both side views give the same drawing?

2. Repeat Exercise 1 for the stack shown. There are no hidden cubes.

Talk About It

3. Can you determine the number of cubes needed to make a stack from drawings of the front, side, and top views? Explain.

4. Describe a solid with the same front, side, and top views.

Connect and Learn

A solid is a three-dimensional figure. Flat drawings show the solid from one view only. In order to record what the solid looks like in all three dimensions, you need to show three views: front, side, and top.

Example

Draw front, side, and top views of the solid. There are no hidden cubes.

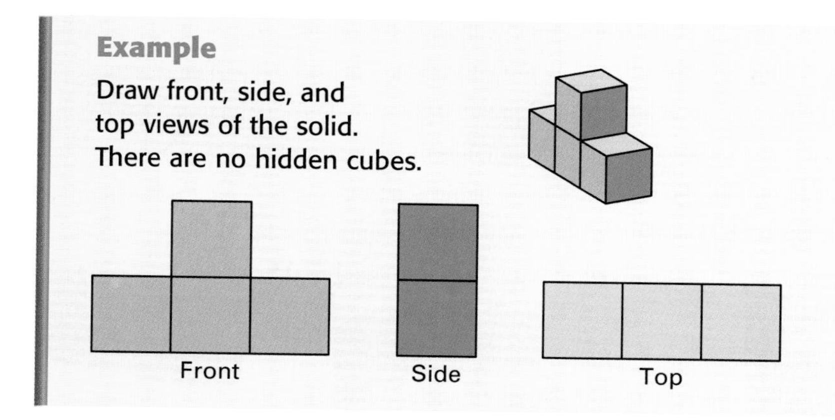

A solid has other views, such as the back view and the bottom view. Because these views are mirror images of the front, side, and top views, they are not necessary when drawing a solid.

Check

State how many cubes are in each solid.

1.

2.

3.

Draw the front, side and top view of each solid.

4.

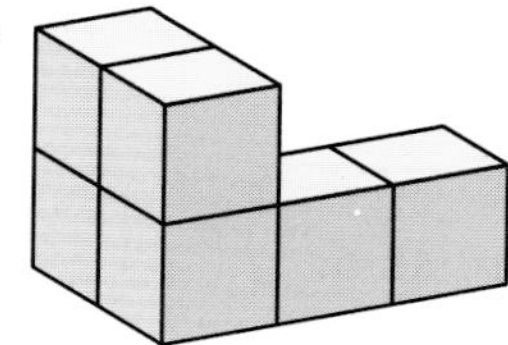

5.

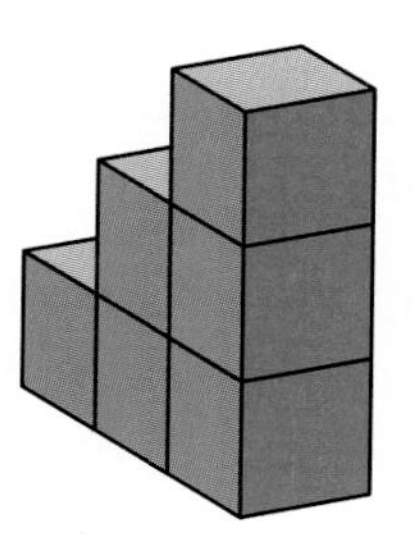

6.

7. Reasoning David looked at the front view of the figure in Exercise 4. He says that he could make a different stack of 6 cubes with the same front view. Is he right? Explain.

Practice

Skills and Reasoning

State how many cubes are in each solid.

8. 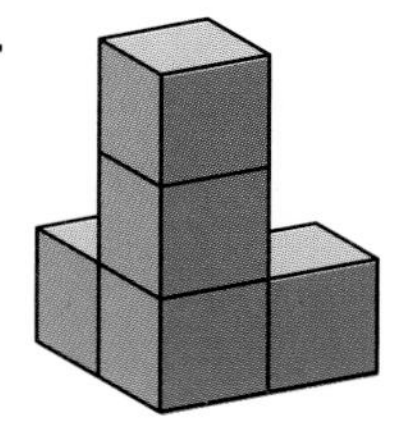

9. 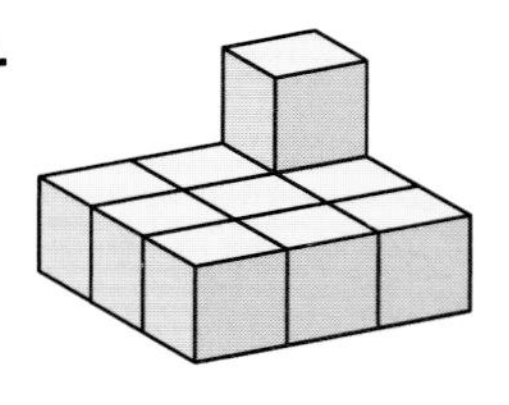

10. 

11. 

Draw the front, side, and top views of each solid.

12. 

13. 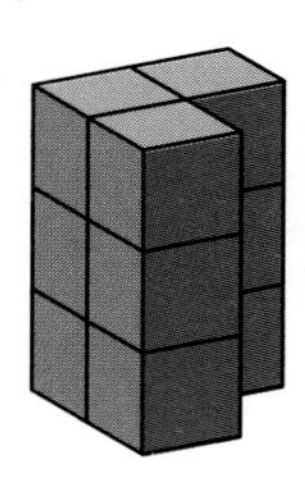

14. 

15. 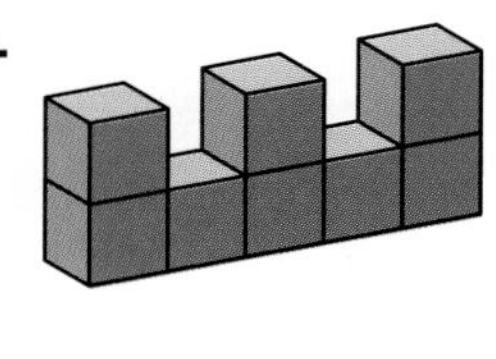

16. 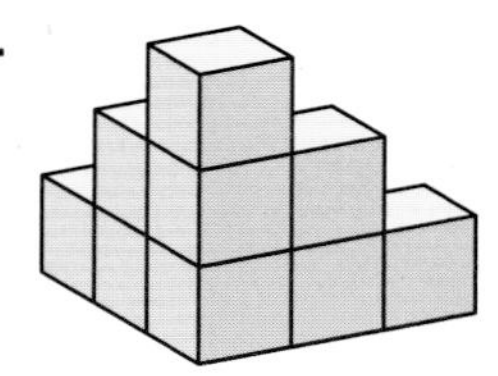

17. 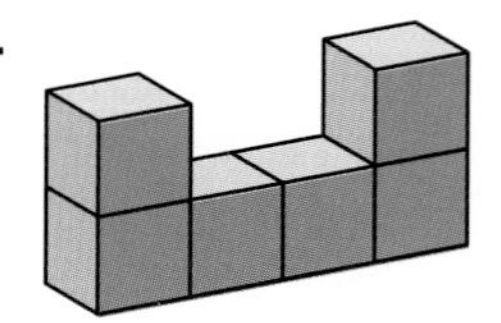

18. 

19. 

Patterns Describe each pattern. How many cubes are in the eighth solid of each pattern?

20.

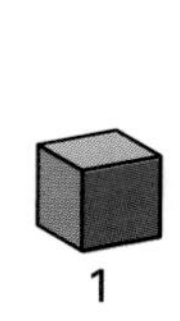
1

2

3

21.

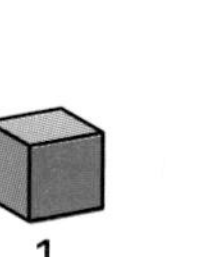
1

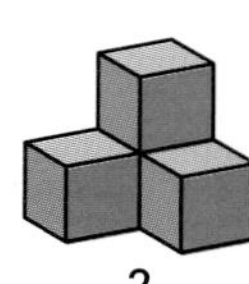
2

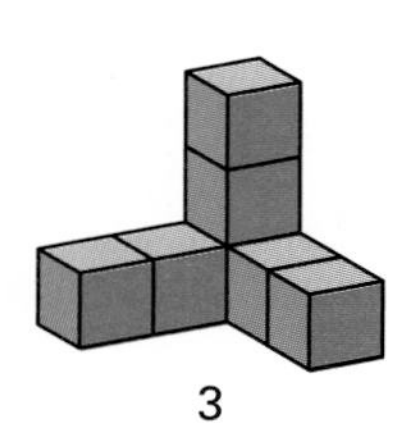
3

22. **What If** You have 24 cubes. Describe or draw the dimensions of three rectangular prisms you can make with the cubes. Explain how you decided on the dimensions of the prisms.

23. **Reasoning** Theresa looked at the top view of the figure in Exercise 8. She says that she could make a different stack of 5 cubes with the same top view. Is she right? Explain. You can use a drawing in your explanation.

24. **Reasoning** Nathaniel looked at all three views of the figure in Exercise 10. He says that he could make a different stack with the same three views. Is he right? Explain. You can use a drawing in your explanation.

Problem Solving and Applications

Tell if each set of views makes a prism. Explain.

25.

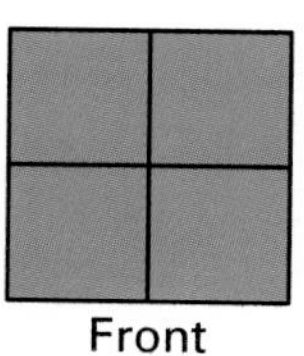

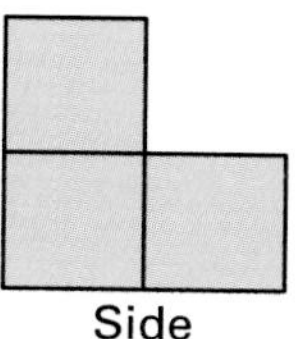

Top

26.

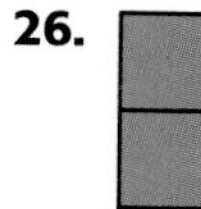

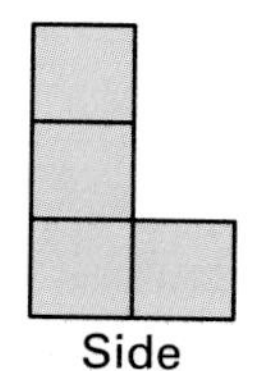

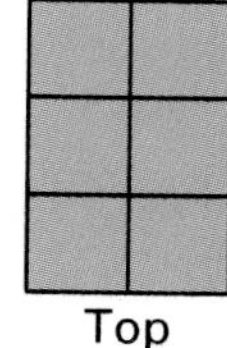

Each solid is made up of 1-centimeter cubes. Find the surface area of each. Explain your reasoning.

27.

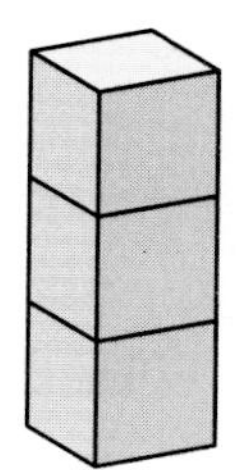

28.

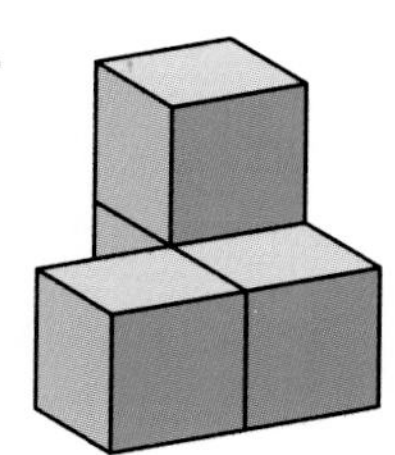

29.

30.

31. Patterns Laura and Jonathan built a replica of the Great Pyramid in Giza, Egypt for a social studies project. They used 84 sugar cubes. The top view of their pyramid was a 7×7 square. Describe the pyramid they made.

32. Geometry Each cube in the solid shown is 1.7 cm by 1.7 cm by 1.7 cm.

a. How many cubes are in the solid?

b. How tall is the solid at its highest point?

c. How wide is the solid at its widest point?

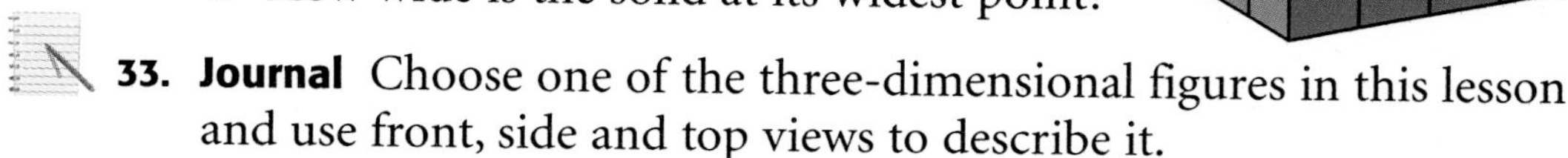

33. Journal Choose one of the three-dimensional figures in this lesson and use front, side and top views to describe it.

Mixed Review and Test Prep

STAY SHARP!

Solve each proportion.

34. $\frac{4}{6} = \frac{8}{x}$ **35.** $\frac{86}{f} = \frac{43}{24}$ **36.** $\frac{5}{y} = \frac{42}{35}$ **37.** $\frac{9}{21} = \frac{r}{7}$ **38.** $\frac{p}{11} = \frac{33}{27}$

Convert each to a percent.

39. 1.56 **40.** 0.723 **41.** $\frac{11}{20}$ **42.** 0.34 **43.** $\frac{7}{25}$ **44.** $1\frac{3}{10}$

Convert each percent to a fraction or mixed number in lowest terms.

45. 67% **46.** 83.4% **47.** 250% **48.** 99% **49.** 1% **50.** 0.6%

51. Which shape cannot be used to make a tessellation?

Ⓐ Square Ⓑ Circle Ⓒ Rectangle Ⓓ Regular hexagon

Exploring Volume

Problem Solving Connection
- Draw a Picture

Materials
- graph paper
- dried beans
- centimeter cubes
- scissors
- tape

Vocabulary
volume
cubic units

Explore

Three-dimensional figures can be described by their **volume**. You can find a figure's volume by counting the number of **cubic units** (units^3) it contains.

Work Together

1. Use centimeter graph paper and tape to build two open boxes.
   a. Draw the net of a box with a 5 cm × 5 cm base with a height of 5 cm.
   b. Cut out the net, cutting only on the outside lines.
   c. Fold up on the lines around the base and tape the four sides.
   d. Repeat for a 5 cm × 4 cm base box with a height of 3 cm.

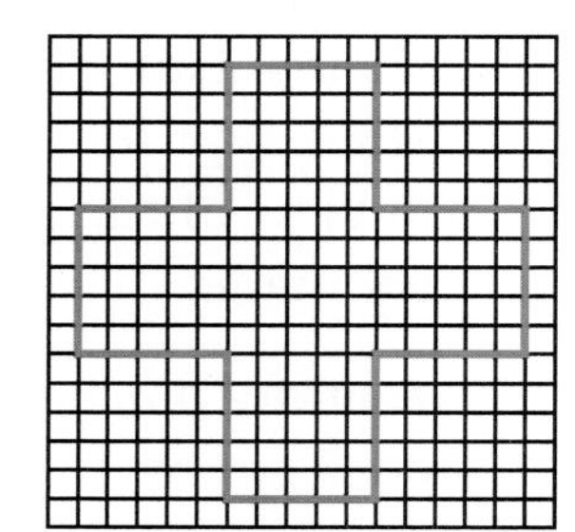

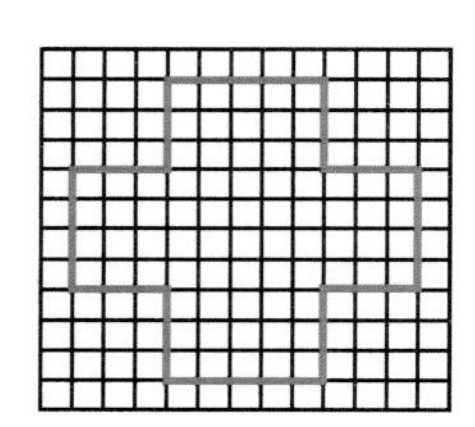

2. Make a table like the one below.
3. Fill each box first with beans, then with centimeter cubes, and record the results in the table.
4. Which box holds fewer beans? fewer cubes?

Box	Number of beans	Number of cubes
5 cm x 5 cm x 5 cm		
5 cm x 4 cm x 3 cm		

Talk About It

5. Do the beans or cubes more accurately measure the space inside each box? Explain.
6. Examine your table. Is there another way, besides counting the cubes, to determine how many cubes fill each box? Explain.

Connect and Learn

You can find the volume of a rectangular prism by counting cubes.

Example 1

Find the volume of the rectangular prism.

Each layer of the prism is 6 cubes by 2 cubes. This equals 6×2, or 12 cubes.

There are 4 layers in the prism. At 12 cubes per layer, this equals 4×12, or 48 cubes.

The volume is 48 cubic units.

You can use the exponent 3 to write the number of cubic units in a solid.

Example 2

Each cube in the prism measures 1 m by 1 m by 1 m. Find the volume of the prism. One layer of cubes is 5 m by 3 m. That's 5×3, or 15 m^2. There are 4 layers. At 15 m^2 per layer, this equals 15×4, or 60 m^3.

The volume is 60 m^3.

Check

Find the volume of each prism.

1. 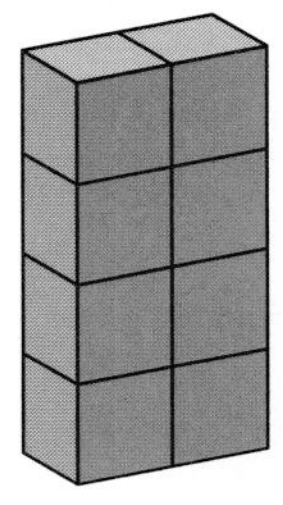

2. 

3. 

4. 

5. 

6. 

7. **Reasoning** Michael says that the volume of a 2 cm by 2 cm by 2 cm box is the same as its surface area. Is he right? Explain.

Practice

Skills and Reasoning

Find the volume of each solid.

8. 

9. 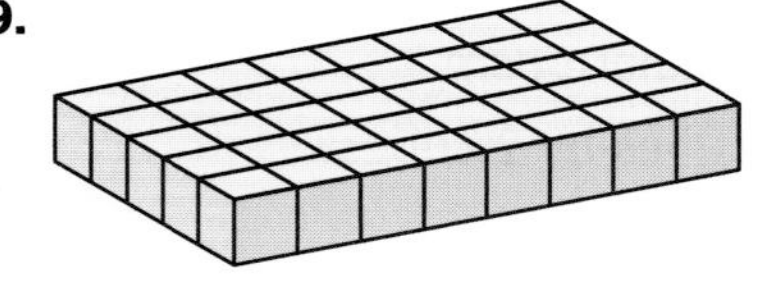

10. 

11. 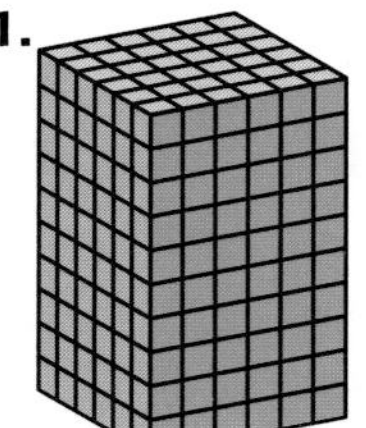

12. 

13. 

14. 

15. 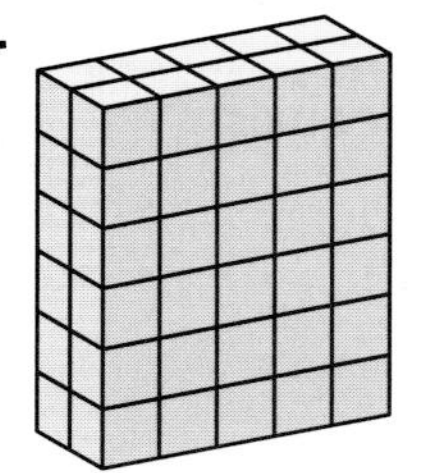

16. 

17. **Geometry** What is the volume of a rectangular prism that measures 8 cubes by 5 cubes by 4 cubes?

18. **Critical Thinking** Each cube in each solid shown measures 1 cm by 1 cm by 1 cm. Order the solids from least to greatest according to their volumes. Would your list be different if you ordered the solids by surface areas? Explain.

a. 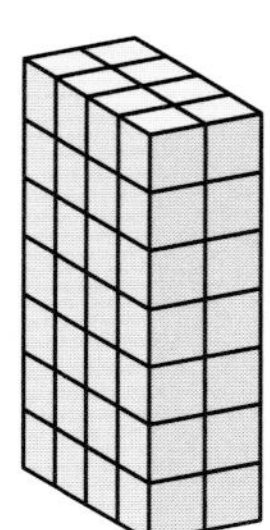

b. 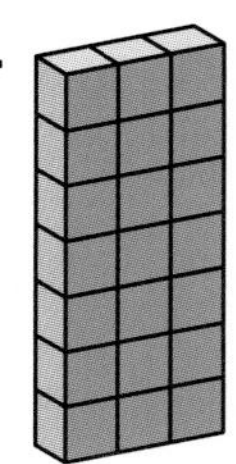

c. 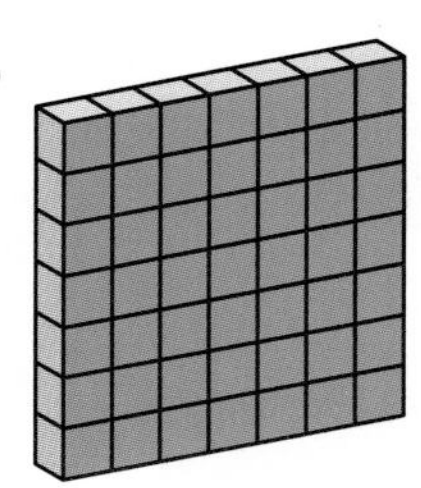

19. **Critical Thinking** Use the views shown to find the volume of each solid.

a. 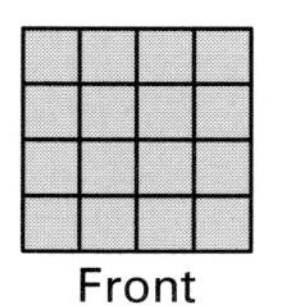 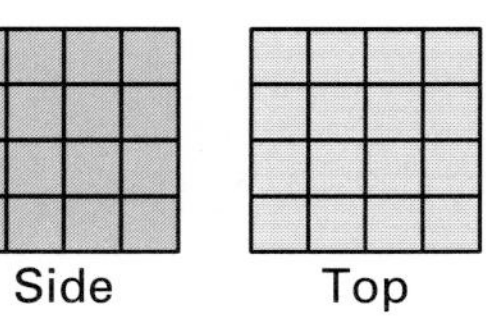

Front Side Top

b. 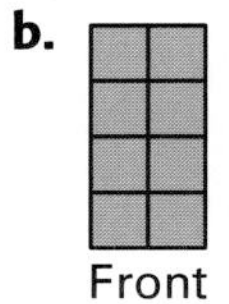 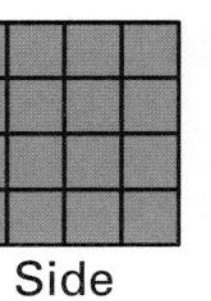

Front Side Top

c. 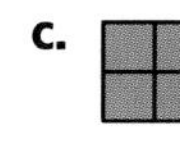 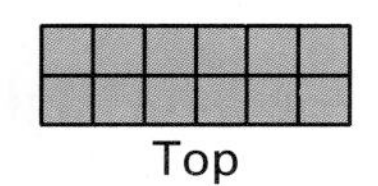

Front Side Top

Problem Solving and Applications

20. **Consumer** When sugar cubes are produced, they are put into tightly packed boxes for purchasing. If the box of sugar cubes shown is 3 cubes high, how many sugar cubes are in the box?

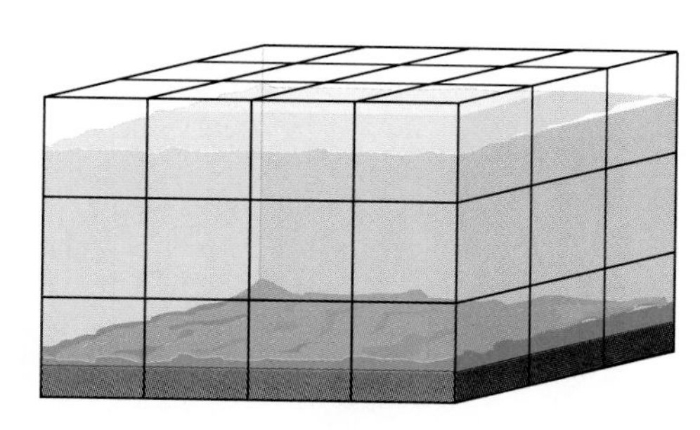

21. Each cube in the aquarium shown measures 1 ft by 1 ft by 1 ft. What is the aquarium's volume?

22. **Probability** Raquel is selling cookies for a school fund-raiser. The Raisin Delight variety comes in cube-shaped packages. Each shipment of Raisin Delights is made up of 12 packages. How many different ways can the 12 packages be arranged to form a shipment shaped like a rectangular prism? List the different ways.

23. Sonjay has 32 1-inch cubes and a box that is 5 in. by 4 in. by 2 in. Will all of Sonjay's blocks fit into the box?

24. **Logic** Marianne packed 8 layers of toy blocks in a box that held 480 blocks. She packed 10 layers of the same blocks in another box that also held 480 blocks. What can you conclude about shape of the boxes? Explain.

25. **Journal** Describe a situation that involves a box and 32 1-inch cubes.

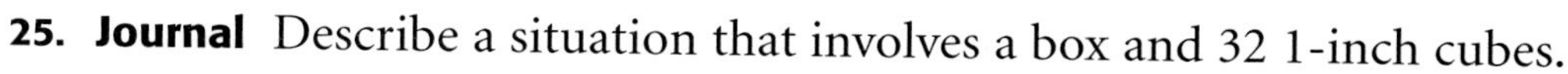

Mixed Review and Test Prep

STAY SHARP!

Find the unit rate for each.

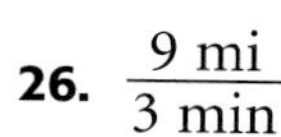

26. $\frac{9 \text{ mi}}{3 \text{ min}}$
27. $\frac{15 \text{ yd}^2}{5 \text{ rooms}}$
28. $\frac{45 \text{ bananas}}{\$9}$
29. $\frac{14 \text{ lb}}{4 \text{ sacks}}$
30. $\frac{19 \text{ m}}{60 \text{ sec}}$
31. $\frac{28 \text{ elephants}}{27 \text{ mi}^2}$
32. $\frac{9 \text{ worms}}{2 \text{ in}^2}$
33. $\frac{4 \text{ dots}}{34 \text{ sec}}$

Estimate what percent of each figure is shaded.

34. 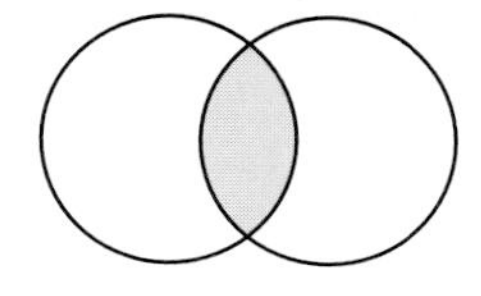

35. 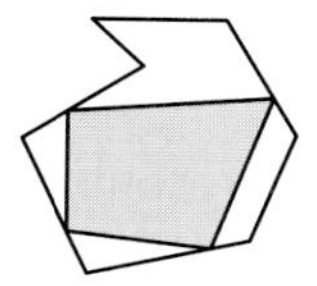

36. 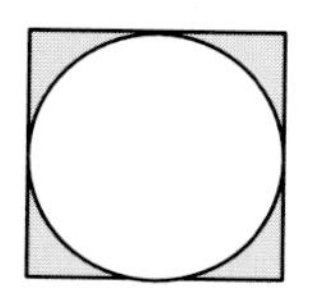

37. 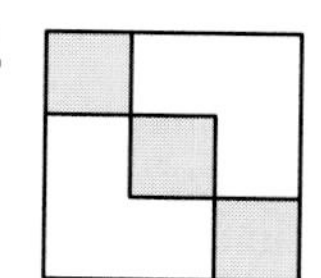

38. Which of the following is proportional to $\frac{2}{9}$?

Ⓐ $\frac{1}{4}$ Ⓑ $\frac{1}{7}$ Ⓒ $\frac{3}{10}$ Ⓓ $\frac{4}{18}$

Calculating Volume

You Will Learn

- to use the volume formula for rectangular prisms

Learn

Chris and his father enjoy visiting the Shedd Aquarium in Chicago, IL. Divers each day feed fish in a 90,000-gallon tank. This indoor aquarium also contains whales, dolphins, sea otters, harbor seals, and a colony of penguins.

Chris lives in Chicago, IL.

You can use a formula to find the volume of a rectangular prism. The volume of a rectangular prism is the product of the prism's length, width, and height.

Volume = length × width × height

Example 1

Find the volume of the rectangular prism.

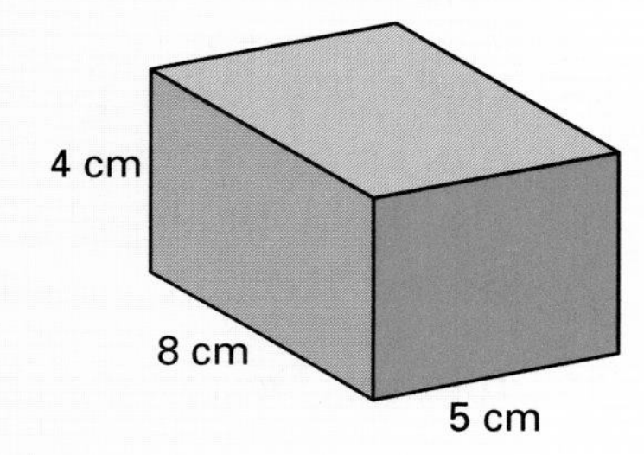

$V = l \times w \times h$	Write the formula.
$= 8 \times 5 \times 4$	Substitute known values.
$= 160$	Multiply.

The volume of the prism is 160 cm^3.

Every 231 in^3 of water represents 1 gallon of water. To find the volume of a solid, set up a proportion.

Did You Know?

There are two types of aquarium tanks: glass and acrylic. Glass tanks are cheaper and harder to scratch. Acrylic tanks are lighter and harder to break.

Example 2

Find the volume of the tank in cubic inches and in gallons.

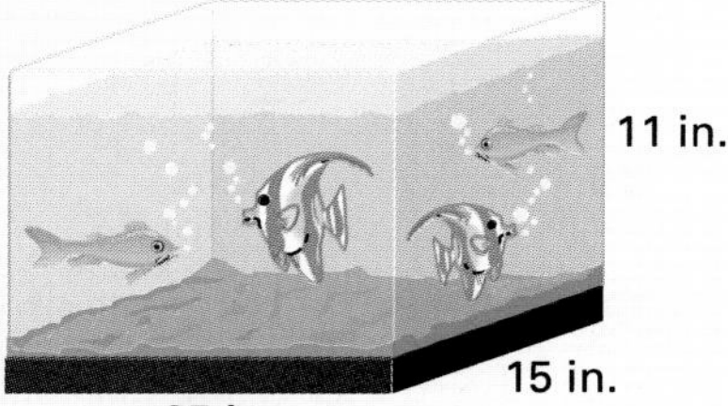

$V = l \times w \times h$	Write the formula.
$= 35 \times 15 \times 11$	Substitute known values.
$= 5{,}775$	Multiply.

The volume is 5,775 in^3.

Every 231 in^3 of water in the tank represents 1 gallon.

$\frac{\text{in.}^3}{\text{gal}}: \frac{5{,}775}{x} = \frac{231}{1} \quad 231x = 5{,}775$

Therefore, the total number of gallons in the tank is $5{,}775 \div 231 = 25$.

The tank has a volume of 25 gallons.

If you know the volume of a rectangular prism and two of its dimensions, you can find the third dimension.

Example 3

Becky built an 8 ft by 6 ft sandbox for her best friend. She bought 48 ft^3 of sand for the box. How deep was the sand?

$V = l \times w \times h$	Write the formula.
$48 = 8 \times 6 \times h$	Substitute known values.
$48 = 48h$	Simplify. Think: What number times 48 equals 48?
$h = 1$	Use mental math.

The sand was 1 ft deep.

Talk About It

1. Can you use the formula $V = 1 \times w \times h$ to find the volume of any solid? Explain.
2. Describe an easy way to find the volume of a cube. Explain.
3. How can knowing the area of the bottom face of a rectangular prism help you to find the volume of the prism? Explain.
4. How can you find the volume in cubic inches if the dimensions are given in feet?

Check

Find the volume of each rectangular prism.

1.

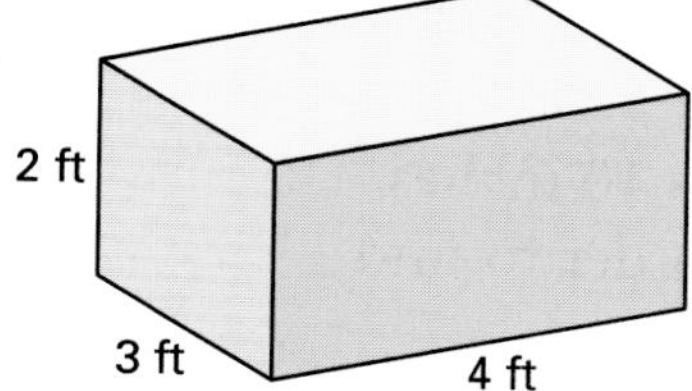

2.

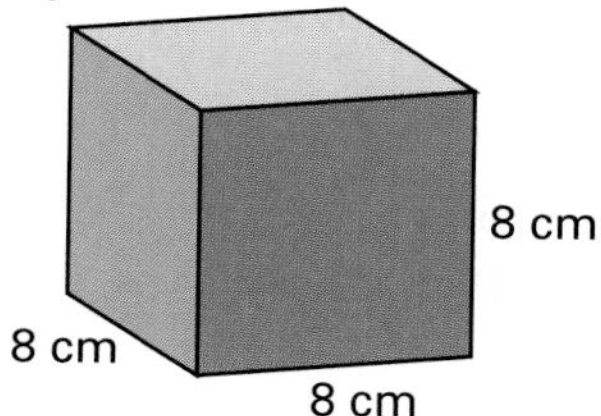

3.

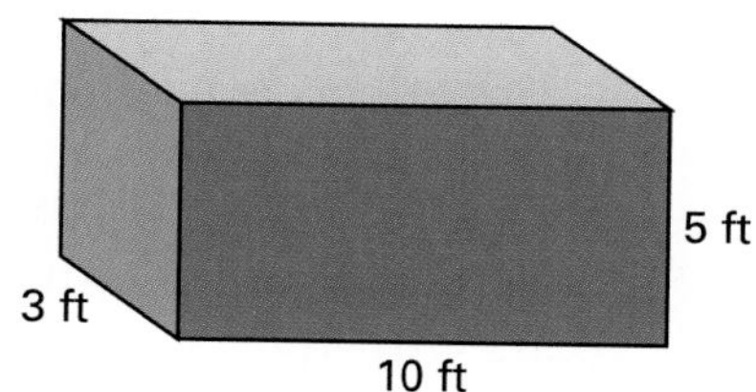

4. Find the length of a rectangular prism with a width of 15 in., a height of 8 in., and a volume of 2,160 in^3.
5. **Reasoning** Christopher told Andrew that the volume of his fish aquarium is 1,800 cubic inches. He also told him that the lid of the tank has a surface area of 150 square inches. Andrew says the height of the tank is one foot. Is he right? Explain.

Practice

Skills and Reasoning

Find the volume of each solid.

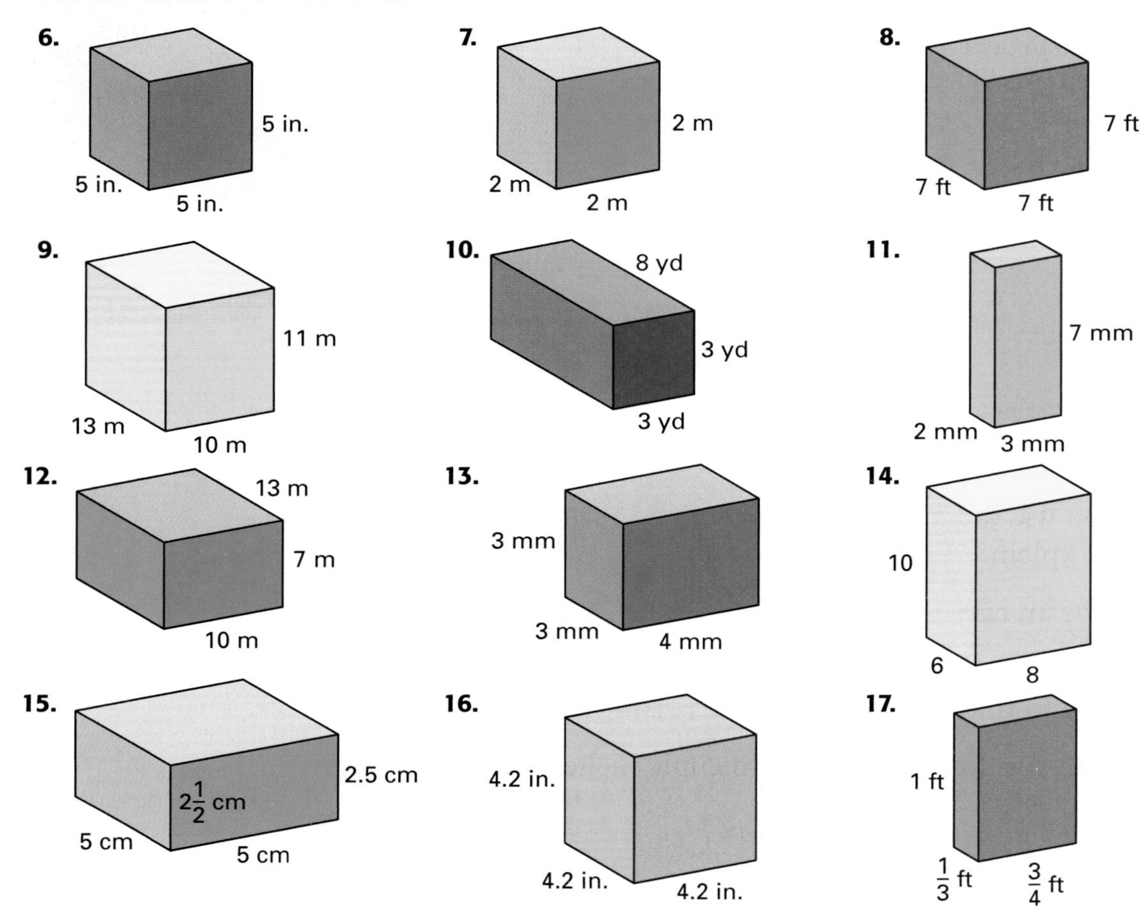

18. **Critical Thinking** The volume of a gallon of water is about 231 cubic inches. If a 25-gallon aquarium is 32 inches long and 15 inches wide, how deep is it? Explain.

19. **Reasoning** The length of a box is 28 inches. The width is 10 inches. What other information about the box do you need in order to find its volume?

Problem Solving and Applications

20. The size of a goldfish depends on the size of the pond or tank it is in. A small pond for a dozen 4-inch goldfish should be about 6 feet long, 4 feet wide, and 1.5 feet deep. What is the volume of this pond?

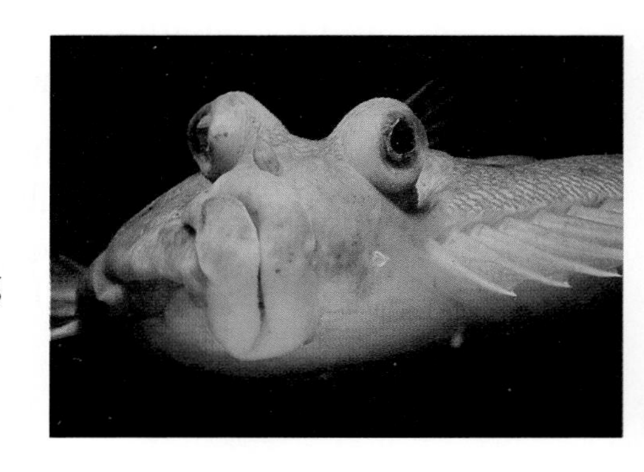

21. **Time** A toy manufacturer makes 1-inch cubical building blocks. The blocks are packed in boxes measuring 12 in. by 6 in. by 4 in. If it takes 1.5 seconds for each block to be packed, how long will it take to fill one box?

Problem Solving and GEOGRAPHY

The Great Barrier Reef along the east coast of Australia is the world's largest coral reef. It is a series of coral reefs and islands that extend for 1,250 miles. The reef is up to 150 miles wide. The tide is the lowest during the full or new moon. Low tide on the reefs usually means about 12 inches of water.

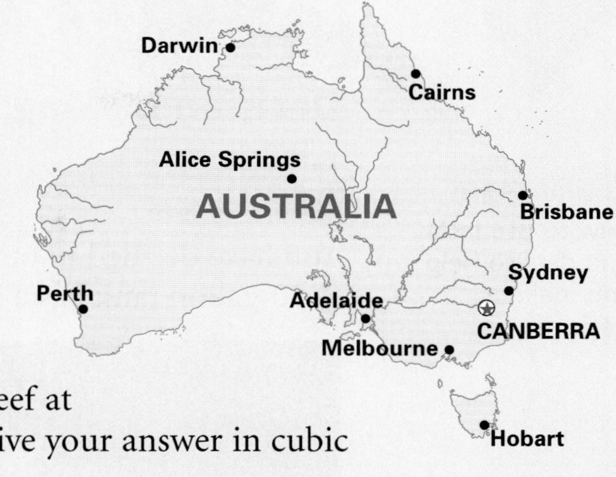

22. **Estimation** To the nearest cubic mile, what would be the volume of water in the coral reef at low tide if the level of the water is 1 foot? Give your answer in cubic miles. (HINT: 1 foot = $\frac{1}{5{,}280 \text{ mi}}$)

23. The coral reef tank at the Great Barrier Reef Aquarium in Townsville, Australia, is 38 meters long, 17 meters wide, and 4.5 meters deep. What is the volume of the tank?

24. **Using Data** Use the Data File on page 575 to determine how many cubic inches of water are held in the Monterey Bay Aquarium.

25. **Algebra Readiness** The volume of an aquarium is 5,000 cubic inches. If the width is 20 inches and the height is 10 inches, what is the length?

26. **Critical Thinking** One area in Water-Play Park has a 15-ft by 20-ft pool that is 12 feet deep. The pool is filled at the start of summer at the rate of 1,200 cubic feet of water per hour. How many hours does it take to fill the pool? Explain.

27. **Journal** Explain how you would find the volume of a rectangular prism whose width is 7 in., length is 5 in., and height is 3 in.

Mixed Review and Test Prep

Find the missing side lengths for each pair of similar figures.

28.

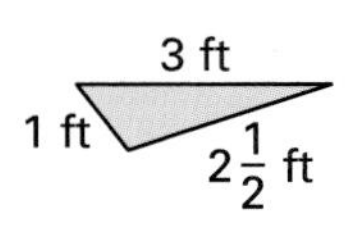

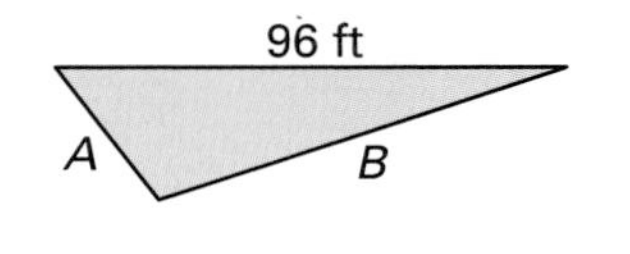

29.

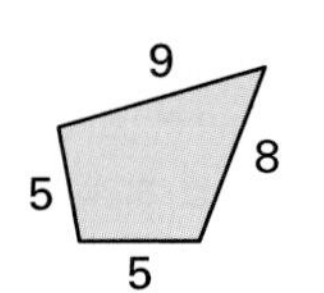

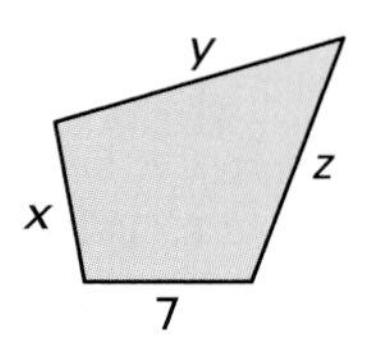

30. In a pictograph, each baseball represents 50 home runs. How many home runs do 7 baseballs represent?

Ⓐ 300 Ⓑ 350 Ⓒ 530 Ⓓ 500

Chapter 11

Problem Solving

Decision Making: Building an Aquarium

You Will Learn

- how to use facts and data to help you make a decision

Explore

You have decided to build a 50-gallon tank for tropical fish. A 50-gallon tank has a volume of 11,550 in^3.

You've decided to stock your aquarium with the following species:

Facts and Data	
Species	**Length (in.)**
White Cloud Mountainfish	1
Zebra Danios	2
Red-Striped Rasboras	3
Cherry Barbs	$1\frac{1}{2}$

- You want your tank to have a height of 22 in.
- You need to know how much glass to buy.
- You may have no more than 1 inch of fish per gallon of water.
- You have to have at least six of each species.

Work Together

Understand

1. What are you asked to do?
2. What information do you have about the fish?
3. What information do you have to help you decide the size your aquarium will be?

Plan and Solve

4. What do you need to determine before making your aquarium?
5. How will you determine the dimensions of the tank?
6. How might estimation help you make your choices?
7. How might a net of your tank help you?
8. How many gallons will one of each species of fish require?
9. How will you determine the amount of water six of each species will require?
10. How will you decide how much glass to buy?

Make a Decision

11. List the dimensions and surface area of your aquarium. Draw a net of your tank.
12. Find another set of dimensions for your tank and tell whether they would make a reasonable choice for a fish tank.
13. List the largest possible collection of fish for your aquarium. Explain how you determined how many of each species of fish should be in your collection.

Present Your Decision

14. Present your decision to your class.
15. Share your strategies for making your decisions with your class.

SECTION B

Review and Practice

(Lesson 5) Draw the front, side, and top views of each solid. There are no hidden cubes.

1. 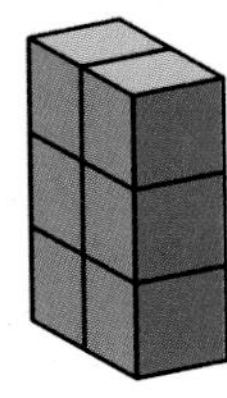

2. 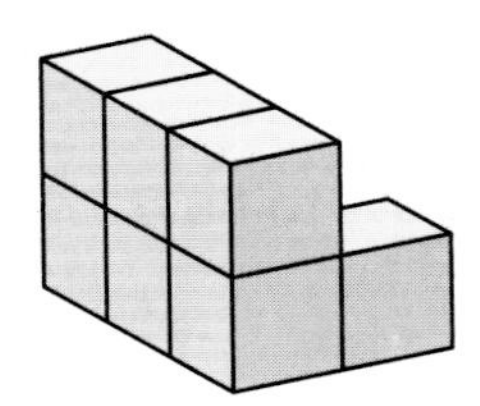

3. 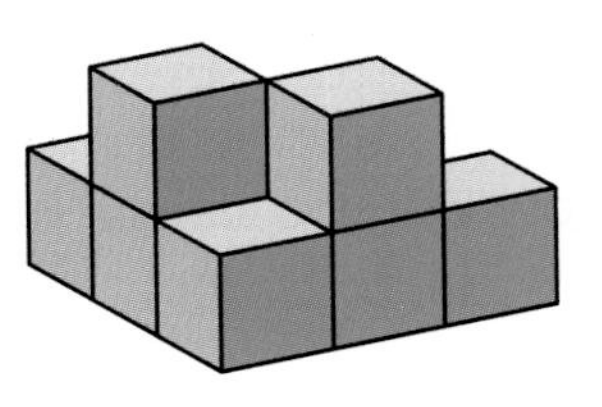

4. 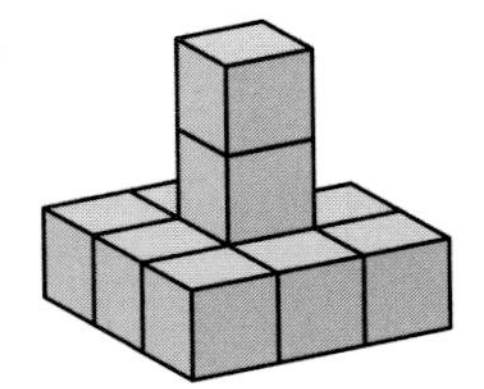

(Lesson 6) Choose the best answer.

5. Which of the following shows the volume of the figure on the right?

Ⓐ 6 units^2 Ⓑ 6 units Ⓒ 18 units Ⓓ 6 units^3

Find the volume of each solid.

6. 

7. 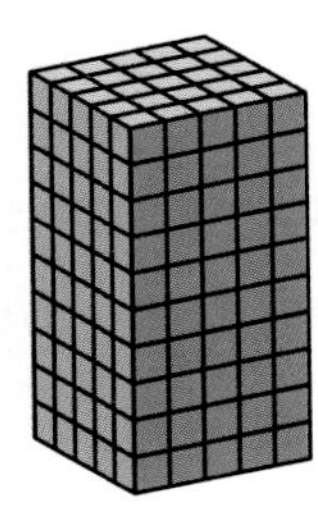

8. 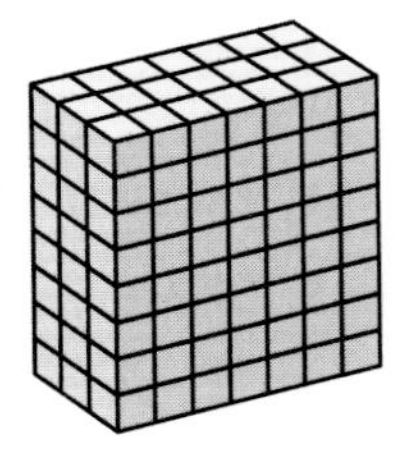

9. Each cube in the figure shown measures 1 in. by 1 in. What is the figure's volume?

(Lesson 7) Find the volume of each aquarium.

10.

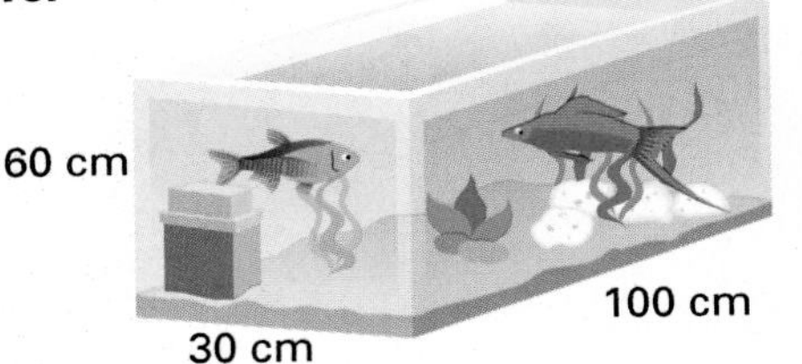

11.

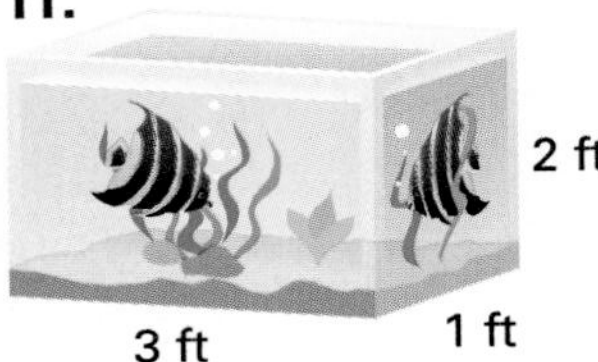

12. The volume of an aquarium is 7,500 cubic inches. If the width is 25 inches and the height is 15 inches, what is the length?

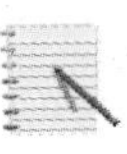

13. **Journal** Can you use the formula $V = 1 \times w \times h$ to find the volume of a sphere or cylinder? Explain.

Skills Checklist

In this section, you have:

- ☑ Explored Three-Dimensional Figures
- ☑ Explored Volume
- ☑ Calculated Volume

REVIEW AND PRACTICE

YOUR CHOICE

Choose at least one of the following. Use what you have learned in this chapter.

1 The Mystery Quadrilateral

On a coordinate plane, connect these four points in order: (5, −3); (2, 7); (−4, 7); (−7, −3). Classify the shape. Find the shape's area, and explain how you found the area.

2 A Change of Data

At Home Using a centimeter ruler, ask a parent or family member to help you measure the diameter of four different coins (for example, a penny, a nickel, a dime, a half-dollar). Find the circumference for each coin. Display the data in a bar graph, and share it with the person who helped you.

3 Round Pegs and Square Holes

Draw a circle and a square. The length of the square should be the same as the diameter of the circle. Find the area of the circle and the square. What percent of the square's area is the circle's area? Repeat this for two more pairs of circles and squares. What patterns do you notice?

4 The One That Boasts the Most

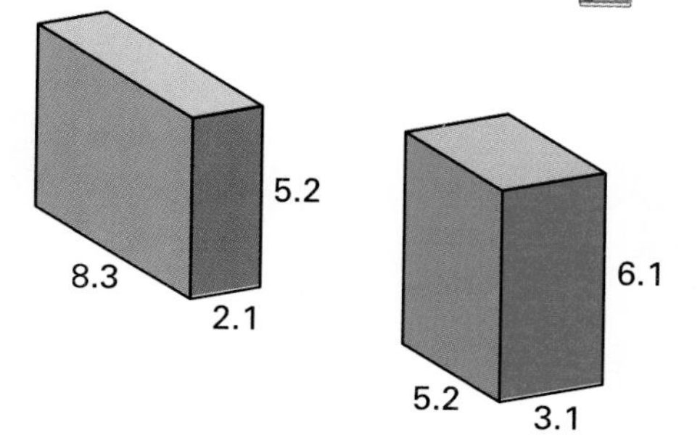

Calculate the surface area and volume for each of the two boxes. Which has more surface area? Which has the greater volume? Does the box with more surface area automatically have the greater volume? Explain.

CHAPTER 11

Review/Test

Vocabulary Complete each sentence for **1–7.**

Word List
edge
net
polyhedron
prism
pyramid
surface area
volume

1. A(n) ________ is a solid whose faces are polygons.
2. The number of cubic units needed to fill a solid is the ________.
3. A(n) ________ is a line formed where the two faces of a solid come together.
4. A solid with one base where all the other faces are triangles is a(n) ________.
5. The ________ of a solid is the sum of the areas of the faces.
6. Like a pyramid, a(n) ________ can be named by the shape of the base.
7. A ________ is a flat pattern that can be folded into a solid.
8. Is a cone a polyhedron? Is a cube a polyhedron? Explain.

(Lessons 2–4) Find the surface area of each solid.

9.

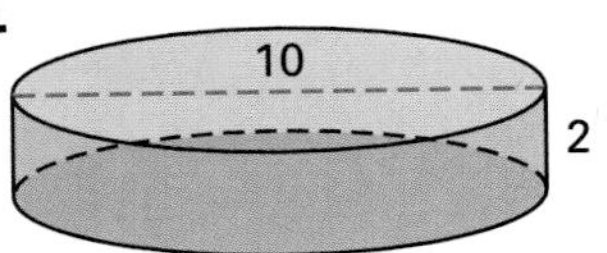

10.

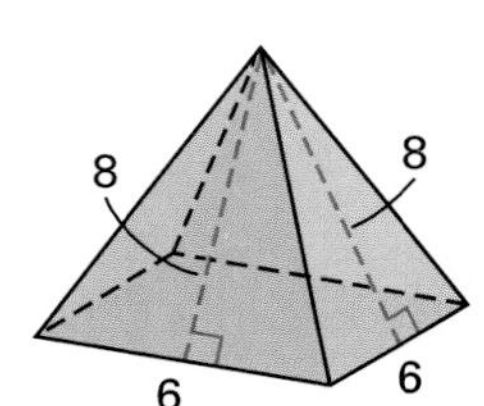

11.

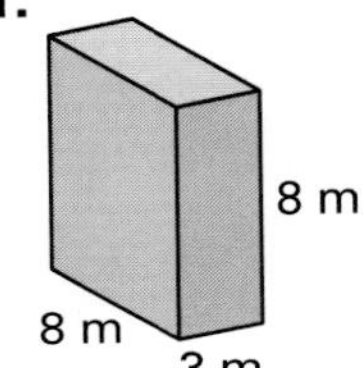

(Lesson 5) State how many cubes are in each solid.

12.

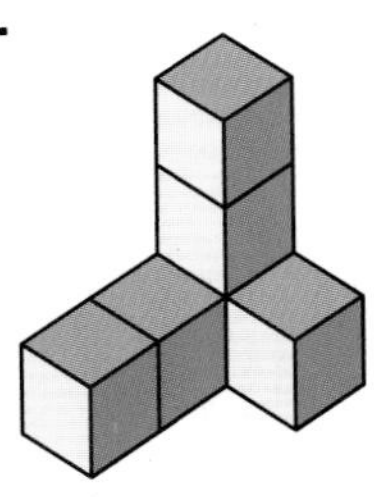

13.

14.

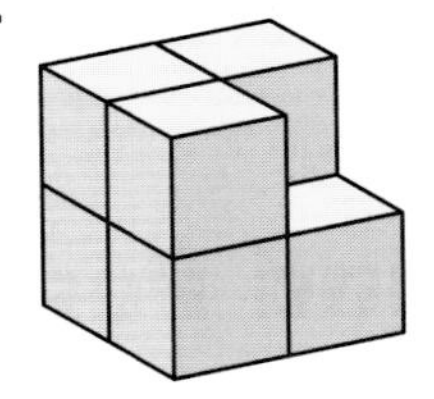

15. Draw the front, side, and top views of the solid. There are no hidden cubes.

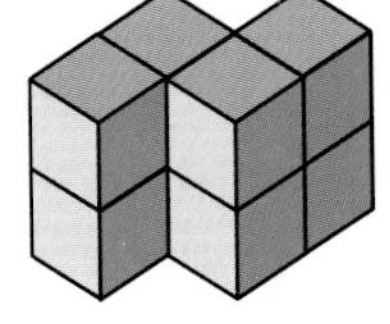

(Lessons 6 and 7) Find the volume of each solid.

16.

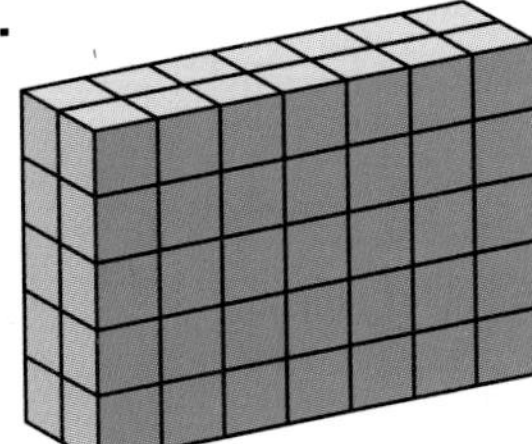

17.

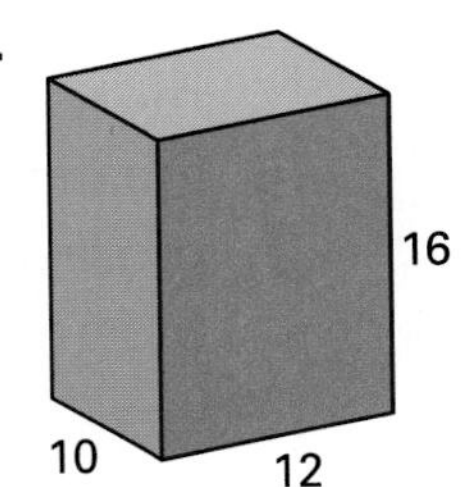

18.

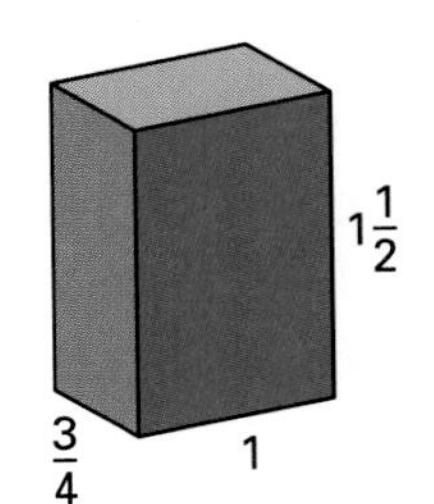

CHAPTER 11

Performance Assessment

You are designing a set of blocks for a toy company. You need to decide on the size of the blocks and the container. You also need to find the surface area of the blocks and the container so that they can be wrapped.

Your block set must include:

- three rectangular prisms
- three cubes
- three square pyramids
- one cylinder-shaped container that will hold all 9 blocks in the set

1. **Decision Making** Decide on the block shapes and the measurements needed to find the surface areas and size of the container. What measurement units will you use? What block sizes and container size would be best for a toy?

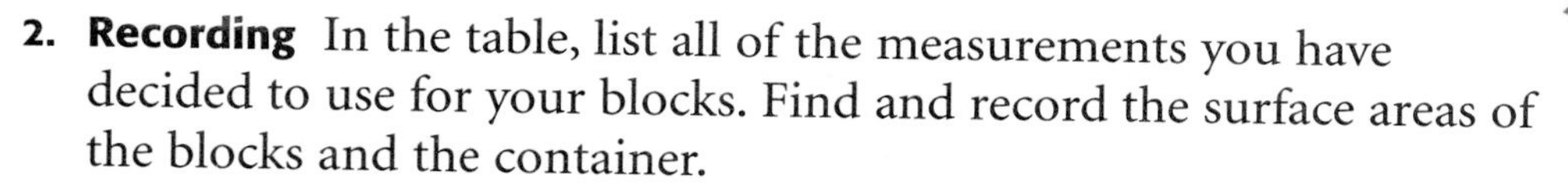

2. **Recording** In the table, list all of the measurements you have decided to use for your blocks. Find and record the surface areas of the blocks and the container.

Item	Measurement (including unit)	Surface Area (including unit)
Rectangular Prism	Length:	
	Width:	
	Height:	
Cube	Side:	
Square Pyramid	Side of Square:	
	Base of Triangle:	
	Height of Triangle:	
Cylinder Container	Radius of Base:	
	Height:	

3. **Explain Your Thinking** How did you decide on the shapes and sizes of your blocks and the size of your cylinder container?

4. **Critical Thinking** What is the volume of your rectangular prism block?

REVIEW/TEST

Math Magazine

Euler Who-ler?

Leonhard Euler, a Swiss mathematician, discovered a relationship between the faces (F), the vertices (V), and the edges (E) of polyhedrons.

Euler (1707–1783) revised almost every branch of mathematics known in his lifetime.

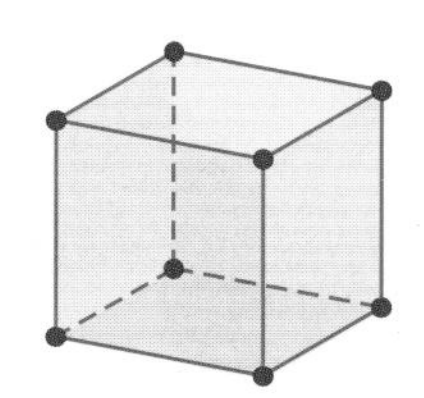

6 faces + 8 vertices – 12 edges = 2

$$F + V - E = 2$$

If you know the numbers for two of the values, you can use the formula to find the third.

Try These!

For each polyhedron, count the number of faces, the number of vertices, and the number of edges. Verify that Euler's formula works for these polyhedrons.

1.

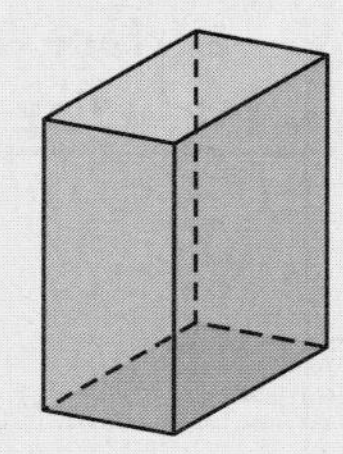

2.

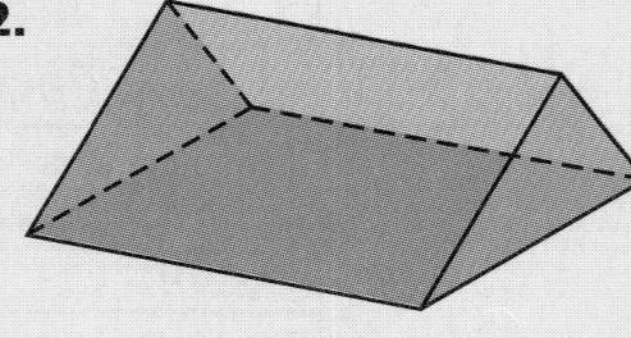

3.

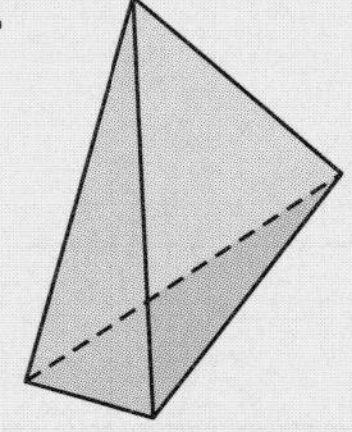

4.

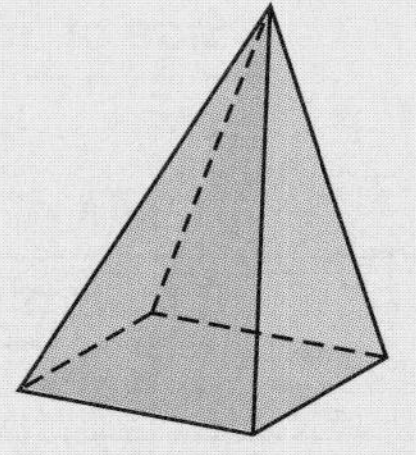

Use Euler's formula to complete the chart below.

	Number of Faces	Number of Vertices	Number of Edges
5.	7	10	
6.	8		18
7.		16	24

CHAPTERS 1–11

Cumulative Review

Test Prep Strategy: Read Carefully

Watch for extra information.

Blythe's aquarium holds 9 fish, 3 sea plants, and 1 plastic scuba diver. It measures 12 in. wide, 15 in. tall, and 18 in. long. What is its volume?

Ⓐ 180 in^3 Ⓑ 3,240 in^2 Ⓒ 3,240 in^3 Ⓓ 270 in^2

Read the entire problem first. Ask yourself, "What information do I need to answer the question?" The number of fish, plants, and divers is unnecessary information.

$12 \times 15 \times 18$ is 3,240 in^3, or choice Ⓒ.

Write the letter of the correct answer. Choose any strategy.

1. Round 7,215,628 to the ten-thousands place.
   Ⓐ 7,000,000 Ⓑ 7,200,000 Ⓒ 7,220,000 Ⓓ 7,215,000

2. Solve: $\frac{b}{2.04} = 7$.
   Ⓐ $b = 14.28$ Ⓑ $b = 1.42$ Ⓒ $b = 142.8$ Ⓓ $b = 1428$

3. Find the area of the parallelogram.
   Ⓐ 13.63 in. Ⓑ 7.6 in^2
   Ⓒ 13.63 in^2 Ⓓ 12.63 in^2

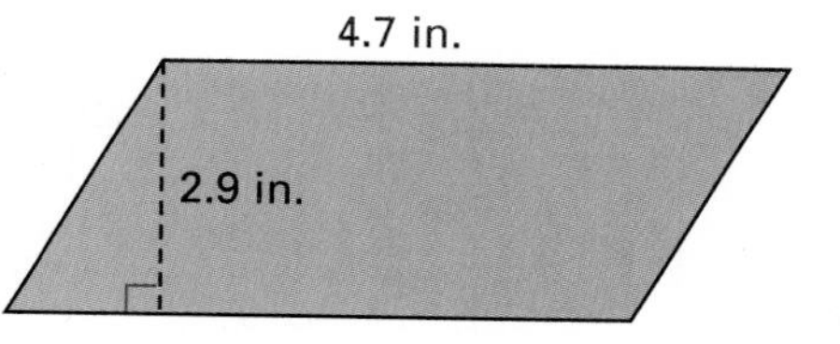

4. Which inequality is **not** true?
   Ⓐ $\frac{3}{5} > \frac{3}{4}$ Ⓑ $\frac{5}{8} < \frac{6}{7}$ Ⓒ $\frac{4}{9} > \frac{3}{10}$ Ⓓ $\frac{7}{12} < \frac{7}{8}$

5. Simplify: $\frac{2}{3} + \frac{2}{12}$. Choose the answer in lowest terms.
   Ⓐ $\frac{1}{3}$ Ⓑ $\frac{5}{6}$ Ⓒ $\frac{10}{12}$ Ⓓ $\frac{4}{12}$

6. Which pair of figures does **not** show a translation?
   Ⓐ Ⓑ Ⓒ Ⓓ

7. Order from least to greatest: 4, 3, 0, –5.
   Ⓐ –5, 0, 3, 4 Ⓑ 0, 3, 4, –5 Ⓒ 4, 3, 0, –5 Ⓓ –5, 4, 3, 0

8. Convert 45% to a fraction and a decimal.
   Ⓐ 4.5, $\frac{45}{100}$ Ⓑ 0.45, $\frac{45}{10}$ Ⓒ 0.045, $\frac{9}{20}$ Ⓓ 0.45, $\frac{9}{20}$

9. What is the surface area of a box 4 in. by 8 in. by 6 in.?
   Ⓐ 48 in^2 Ⓑ 208 in^2 Ⓒ 32 in^2 Ⓓ 192 in.

10. State how many cubes are in the solid. There are no hidden cubes.
    Ⓐ 11 Ⓑ 12 Ⓒ 13 Ⓓ 14

Test Prep Strategies

- Read Carefully
- Follow Directions
- Make Smart Choices
- Eliminate Choices
- Work Backward from an Answer

DATA FILE

Chapter 12
Probability

SECTION A Force of Nature!

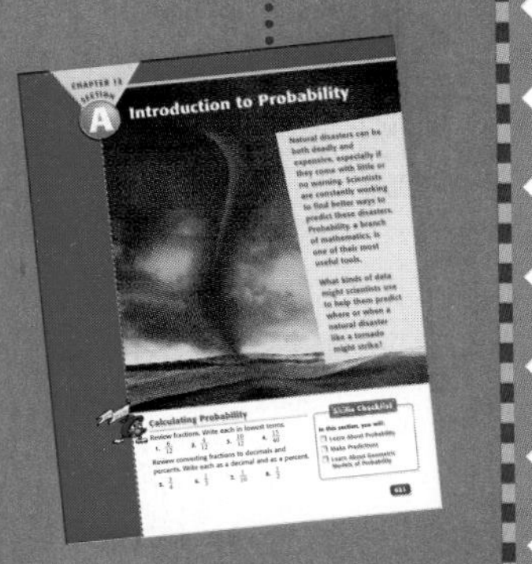

Force of Nature!
Page 621

Introduction to Probability 621

Tornadoes occur most often in the midwestern and southern states of the U.S. during spring and early summer. They are most likely to occur between 3 P.M. and 7 P.M. About 1,000 tornadoes have been recorded each year since 1990. If you lived in Portland, Oregon, how likely is it that you might experience a tornado: *very likely, likely, not likely?* Explain.

Fujita Scale (F Scale) for Rating Tornado Intensity

F Scale	Wind Velocity (mi/hr)	Damage
F0	40–72	Light—tree branches, chimneys
F1	73–112	Moderate—mobile homes, autos pushed aside
F2	113–157	Considerable—roofs torn off houses, large trees uprooted
F3	158–206	Severe—houses torn apart, trees uprooted, cars lifted off ground
F4	207–260	Devastating—houses leveled, cars thrown
F5	261–318	Incredible—structures lifted off foundations, cars become missiles
F6	318	Maximum tornado wind speed

LINKS

Arts & Literature

In Frank Stockton's short story *The Lady or the Tiger*, a young man must choose between two doors. Behind one is the woman he would marry. Behind the other is a ferocious tiger. The young man has a 50/50 chance of choosing the door with the tiger.

People of the World

"Rock-paper-scissors," a game of chance, is played throughout the world. In Japan, it's known as "jan-ken-po."

www.mathsurf.com/6/ch12/people

Free Parking

Fairness

639

Professional athletes are often expected to succeed at hard-to-do tasks. The table lists the probabilities of professional athletes succeeding at certain sports events. According to the table, who is more likely to succeed: a professional golfer trying to hit a hole in one or a professional bowler trying to score a perfect game?

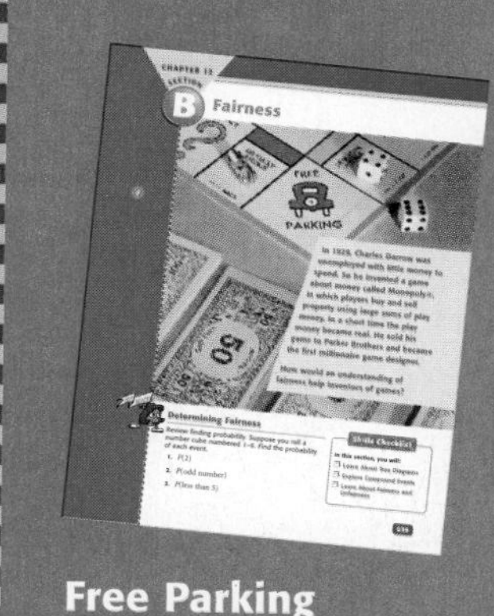

Free Parking
Page 639

What are the chances?	
Sport Event	**Probability It Will Happen**
Golf Hole in one (one round of a PGA event)	3,708 to 1
Major League Baseball Home team winning Going into extra innings	7 to 3 10 to 1
Basketball (NBA) Home team winning Going into overtime	7 to 3 23 to 1
Bowling Bowling a perfect 300 game in 1 year	4,000 to 1
Football (NFL) Returning the kickoff for a touchdown	45 to 1

Student Council Elections	Votes
Susana Alcocer	32%
Van Nguyen	28%
Maritess Estrera	20%
Peter Michaels	20%
± 5% margin of error	

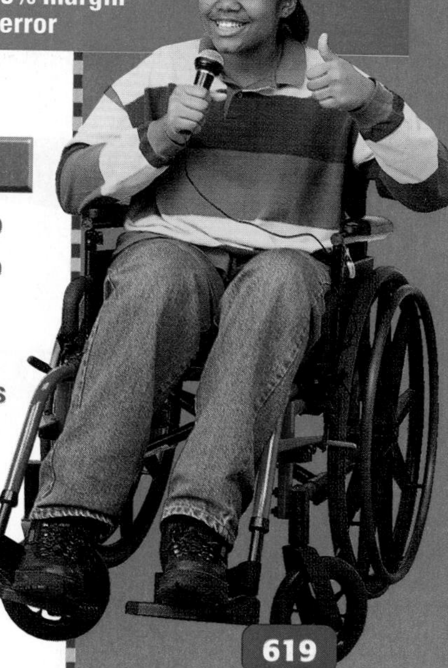

Entertainment

In the game Yahtzee®, the chances of getting a yahtzee, or five of a kind, on the first roll of the dice are 1 out of 1,296, or approximately 0.08%.

Science

The chances of a person you meet being left-handed are about 13%.

Social Studies

When polls are used to predict who is likely to win an election, they include a "margin of error," which measures how inaccurate the prediction may be.

Materials
markers, posterboard

Round and round the spinner goes, and where it stops nobody knows! In this project, you will design your own game of chance.

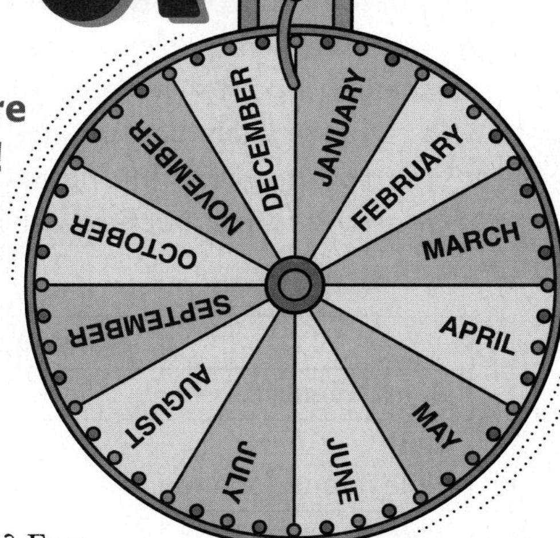

Make a Plan

- What are some games of chance you have played?
- How do you want to set up your game? For example, do you want to build a spinner, roll a ball, or toss a counter?
- How many winners do you want to have each time? Will only one person win, or will you have multiple winners?

Carry It Out

1. Make a list of all the games of chance your team might want to create. Are there any games that will give the players a better chance of winning?
2. Decide on the game of chance your team likes best. Will the game be more fun with one winner or with multiple winners each time?
3. Draw a sketch of the game. How long will it take people to play one round?
4. Calculate the probability of winning your game. How will the number of people playing and the number of winners affect the outcome?

Talk About It

- Why did your team select the game of chance that it did? How can you make sure that your game of chance is played fairly?

Present the Project

Compare your team's designs to that of another team. Are both of the games fair to the people who are playing them? If your team could play one of the two games, which game would give you the better chance of winning?

CHAPTER 12 SECTION

A Introduction to Probability

Natural disasters can be both deadly and expensive, especially if they come with little or no warning. Scientists are constantly working to find better ways to predict these disasters. Probability, a branch of mathematics, is one of their most useful tools.

What kinds of data might scientists use to help them predict where or when a natural disaster like a tornado might strike?

GET READY!

Calculating Probability

Review fractions. Write each in lowest terms.

1. $\frac{6}{12}$ **2.** $\frac{4}{12}$ **3.** $\frac{10}{12}$ **4.** $\frac{15}{40}$

Review converting fractions to decimals and percents. Write each as a decimal and as a percent.

5. $\frac{3}{4}$ **6.** $\frac{1}{5}$ **7.** $\frac{1}{10}$ **8.** $\frac{1}{2}$

Skills Checklist

In this section, you will:

- ❒ Learn About Probability
- ❒ Make Predictions
- ❒ Learn About Geometric Models of Probability

Chapter 12
Lesson
1

Probability

You Will Learn

- to find the probability of an event

Vocabulary

experiment
outcome
event
probability

Learn

Suppose you are playing a game with a spinner like the one shown.

You could use one of these words to describe the chances of landing on blue.

Impossible
EVEN CHANCE
Possible
FOR CERTAIN
PROBABLY NOT
Probable
Rare

Did You Know?
The heaviest coin was made of copper in Sweden in 1644. It weighed 43 lb and $7\frac{1}{4}$oz.

Words such as *impossible* and *even chance* are very specific. Anyone would know what you mean by them. Words such as *rare* and *possible* may mean different things to different people. To make sure everyone understands what you mean, you can use mathematics to describe the chances of something happening.

A probability **experiment** is a situation that can happen in more than one way. The **outcomes** of an experiment are the ways it can happen.

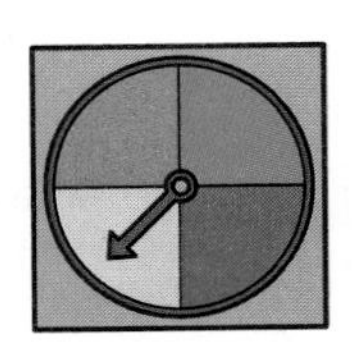

Outcomes: red, green, blue, yellow

Outcomes: 1, 2, 3, 4, 5, 6

Outcomes: heads, tails

An **event** is the particular outcome that you're looking for. You can describe the **probability** that a particular event will happen by using a ratio.

$$P(\text{event}) = \frac{\text{number of ways the event can happen}}{\text{number of possible outcomes}}$$

Example 1

What is the probability of landing on blue? Express your answer as a fraction, a decimal, and a percent.

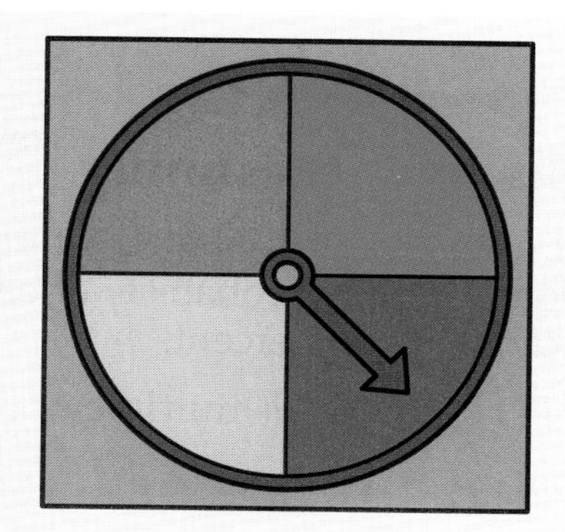

Event: Landing on blue

Number of possible outcomes: 4 (red, green, blue, yellow)

Number of ways the event can occur: 1 (blue)

$P(\text{blue}) = \frac{1}{4}$

As a decimal, this is 0.25. As a percent, this is 25%.

Sometimes an event can happen in more than one way.

Example 2

An ocean liner has 8 lifeboats, numbered 1 through 8. In the event of an emergency, every passenger is randomly assigned to one of the 8 boats. What is the probability of being assigned to a boat whose number is less than 6?

Event: A boat numbered less than 6

Number of possible outcomes: 1, 2, 3, 4, 5, 6, 7, 8

Number of ways the event can occur: 5 (boat 1, 2, 3, 4, or 5)

$P(\text{less than } 6) = \frac{5}{8}$

Talk About It

1. Give an example of a situation with 3 outcomes.
2. For Example 1, what is the probability of not landing on blue? Explain.
3. If $P(\text{event}) = 0$, what can you conclude about the event? If $P(\text{event}) = 1$?

Check

For each spinner, what is the probability of each event? Express your answer as a fraction, a decimal, and a percent.

1. $P(\text{red})$
2. $P(\text{blue or green})$
3. $P(\text{not yellow})$
4. $P(\text{yellow, blue, or green})$

A

B

5. **Reasoning** Draw a spinner with more than two sections where the probability of landing on red is 50%. Explain your reasoning.

Practice

Skills and Reasoning

A set of ten cards is labeled 1 through 10. Suppose you choose one card at random. Find the probability of each event. Express your answer as a fraction, a decimal, and a percent.

6. $P(1)$ **7.** $P(\text{multiple of } 3)$ **8.** $P(\text{2-digit number})$ **9.** $P(6 \text{ or } 2)$

10. $P(12)$ **11.** $P(\text{less than } 11)$ **12.** $P(\text{odd number})$ **13.** $P(5)$

Suppose you roll a number cube with sides labeled with the numbers 1–6. Find the probability of each event.

14. $P(6)$ **15.** $P(\text{even number})$ **16.** $P(\text{vowel})$ **17.** $P(\text{a number less than } 6)$

There are 6 cards that spell out C H A N C E. Suppose you choose one card at random. Find the probability of each event.

18. $P(A)$ **19.** $P(C)$ **20.** $P(\text{vowel})$ **21.** $P(\text{consonant})$

22. Janice's board game uses 8 playing tokens, each a different color. If she places the 8 tokens in a bag so that she can't see them, what is the probability that she picks the blue token? The red token? Explain.

23. At the Hamburger House, each kid's meal comes with a dinosaur toy. The dinosaurs are Triceratops, Stegosaurus, Tyrannosaurus rex, Brontosaurus, and Parasaurolophus. What is the probability of getting the Tyrannosaurus rex toy?

24. The probability of getting red on a spinner is 80%. What is the probability of not getting red? How are these two probabilities related?

25. Suppose the probability of an event is $\frac{7}{13}$. Which is greater, the probability that the event will occur or the probability that it will not occur? Explain.

Problem Solving and Applications

26. History The first seismograph was built in the year 132 by the Chinese philosopher Zhan Heng. Eight bronze dragons were set around a large vessel above eight bronze toads. When an earthquake occurred, a ball fell out of a dragon's mouth and was caught by a toad. If the dragons were numbered 1 to 8, what was the probability that the ball would fall out of the mouth of a dragon with a prime number?

27. **Science** A group of scientists studying earthquakes plans to observe nine different devices that monitor seismic activity. If each scientist is assigned to a monitoring device at random, what is the probability that the first scientist will monitor either the laser reflector or creepmeter?

Using Data The bar graph shows the eye color of the 32 students in Patty's class. If a student is chosen at random, find the probability of each event.

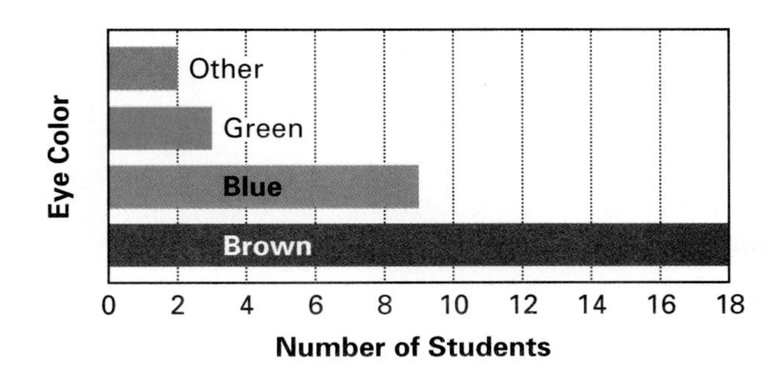

28. P(blue)

29. P(brown or green)

30. **Critical Thinking** Is it more likely that you could roll a number cube twice and get a 3 and then a 5, or a 3 and then a 3? Explain.

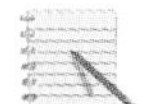

31. **Journal** Can the probability of an event be greater than 1? Less than 0? Explain.

Mixed Review and Test Prep

STAY SHARP!

Classify each solid.

32. 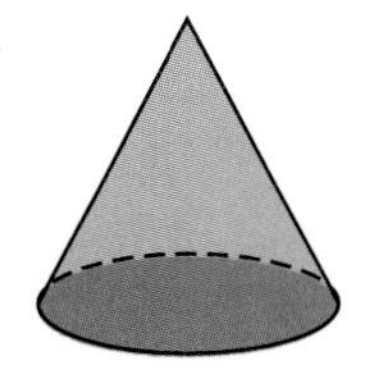

33. 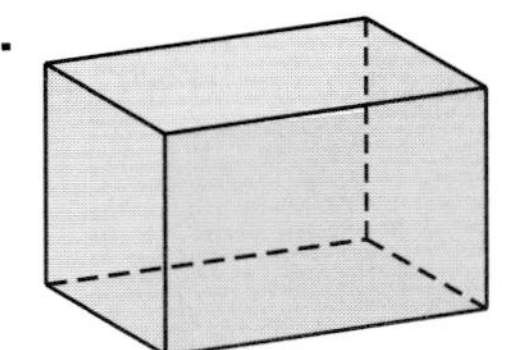

34. 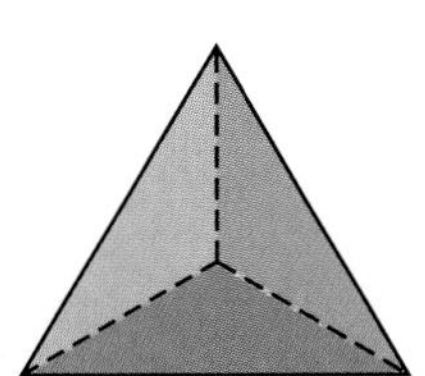

35. 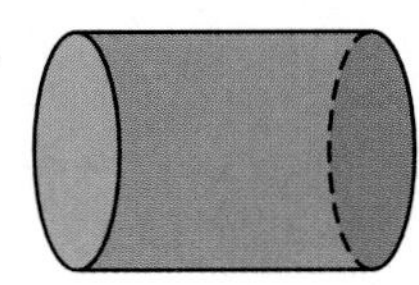

Find the surface area for each solid.

36. 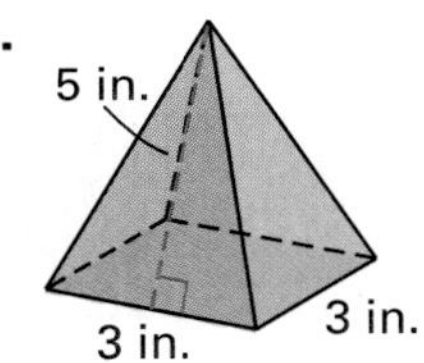

37. 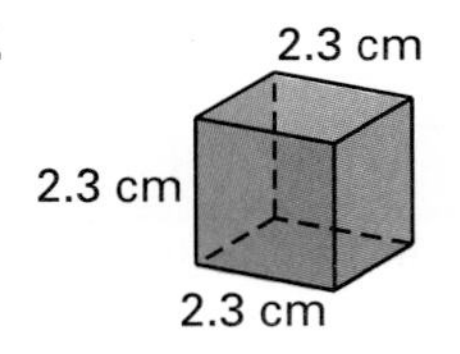

38. 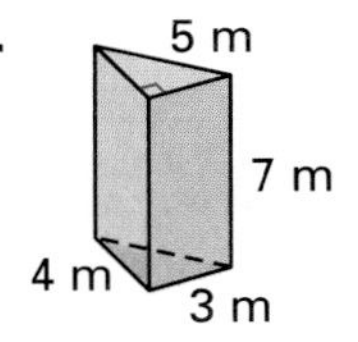

39. 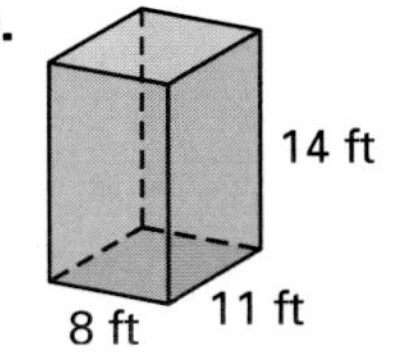

40. Choose the correct solution to $36.702 \div 3$.

Ⓐ 12.234 Ⓑ 1.2234 Ⓒ 33.702 Ⓓ 12.243

Chapter 12
Lesson
2

Making Predictions

You Will Learn
- to calculate probability from sample data

Vocabulary
sample

Learn

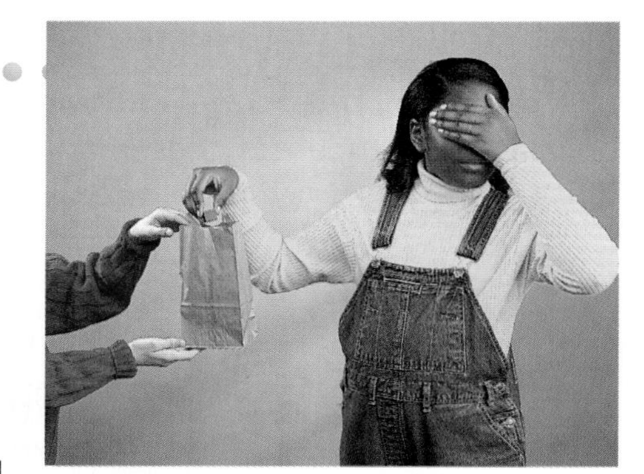

Mark put 10 cubes into a paper bag. The cubes were red, green, and blue. Mark asked Toya to guess the probability of drawing each different color cube out of the bag at random.

Sometimes it is difficult to calculate the probability of an event because you don't know all the possible outcomes or you don't know how likely each outcome is. In these situations, you can sometimes collect data and predict the probability based on the data.

Remember
When a probability is written as a fraction, the fraction should be written in lowest terms.

Example 1

Toya collected data by removing a cube from the bag without looking, recording its color, and returning it to the bag. She repeated this for 20 draws. Predict the probability of selecting each color cube.

$P(\text{red}) = \frac{8}{20} = \frac{2}{5}$

$P(\text{green}) = \frac{10}{20} = \frac{1}{2}$

$P(\text{blue}) = \frac{2}{20} = \frac{1}{10}$

Color	Tally	Frequency
red	𝍸 III	8
green	𝍸 𝍸	10
blue	II	2

A **sample** is a set of data that can be used to predict how a particular situation might happen.

Example 2

Michaleena recorded the results of 30 draws of letters from a bag. Predict the next letter Michaleena will draw. What is the probability that Michaleena will draw that letter?

a	s	d	t	n	x	i	y
II	I	III	II	III	𝍸 I	III	𝍸 𝍸

In 30 draws, the letter Michaleena drew the most was *y*. So it is more likely that Michaleena will draw a *y* on her next draw.

$P(y) = \frac{10}{30} = \frac{1}{3}$

The probability that Michaleena's next draw is a *y* is $\frac{1}{3}$.

Example 3

At a pizzeria, the manager wanted to know what kind of pizza slices customers order during lunch. He collected this data during one shift. Suppose 300 customers are expected in one week. Use the data to estimate how many cheese slices will be ordered in a week.

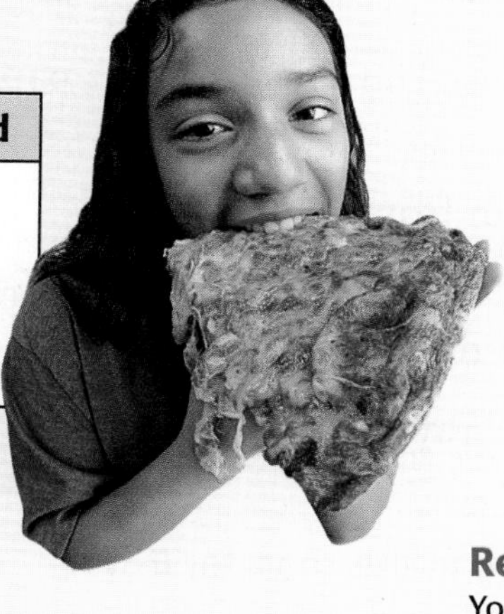

Pizza	Slices Ordered
Pepperoni	30
Veggie	12
Combination	10
Cheese	8

There were 60 slices ordered. Of the 60 slices, 8 were cheese. The probability of a customer ordering a cheese slice is $\frac{8}{60}$, or $\frac{2}{15}$.

Write and solve a proportion.

$$\frac{\text{number of ways event can happen}}{\text{number of possible outcomes}} \quad \begin{matrix}\rightarrow \\ \rightarrow\end{matrix} \frac{2}{15} = \frac{x}{300}$$

$$15x = 600$$

$$x = 40$$

About 40 customers a week could be expected to order a cheese slice.

Remember

You can use cross products to solve proportions.

Talk About It

1. Do you think Mark put exactly 4 red cubes, 5 green cubes, and 1 blue cube in the bag in Example 1? Explain.
2. Why would it be a good idea to collect as large a set of sample data as possible before making a prediction?

Check

Use the data from Example 3 to answer **1–2.**

1. What is the probability of a customer ordering a veggie slice?
2. What is the probability that a customer orders a slice that is not a combination slice?
3. **Reasoning** Which spinner most likely produced the sample data? Explain. Data: red, blue, blue, red, red, red, red, red, blue, red

A

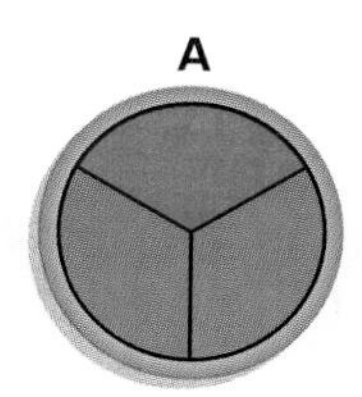

B

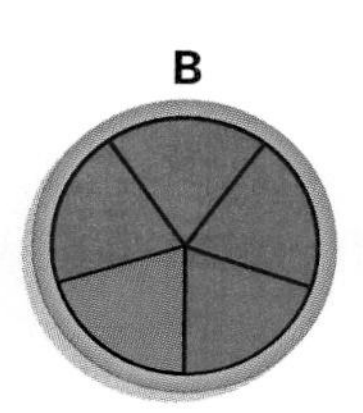

C

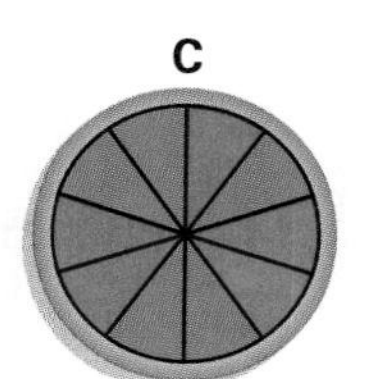

Practice

Skills and Reasoning

Tell if you need sample data to determine the probability of each situation happening.

4. A tsunami striking Hawaii next year
5. Meeting a person from Peru tomorrow
6. Rolling a 2 on a number cube
7. Choosing a red crayon out of a box

Use the data recorded in the chart for **8–11.**

Trial	1	2	3	4	5	6	7	8	9	10
Outcome	Blue	Pink	White	White	White	Pink	Blue	White	Pink	Pink
Trial	11	12	13	14	15	16	17	18	19	20
Outcome	Blue	White	White	Pink	White	Pink	White	White	Pink	White

8. How many different outcomes were there?
9. How many outcomes were blue?
10. What is the probability of the outcome not being pink or blue?
11. Predict the outcome of trial 21. Give the probability of that outcome.

Estimation Ms. Shaw's 6th-grade class conducted an in-class survey. Use the results to answer **12–15.**

Question	Result
Are you male or female?	15 female, 17 male
Do you have an emergency kit at home?	21 yes, 11 no
Is the date of your birth an odd or an even number?	20 even, 12 odd
Have you experienced a flood?	27 no, 5 yes

If there are 102 6th graders in the school, use the survey results to estimate the number of 6th graders in the school who:

12. are girls
13. have an emergency kit at home
14. have an even birth date
15. have experienced a flood

Problem Solving and SCIENCE

Using Data The table below shows the average number of tornadoes in the United States per month over 10 years.

Month	Tornadoes	Month	Tornadoes	Month	Tornadoes	Month	Tornadoes
January	15	April	112	July	90	October	25
February	29	May	181	August	62	November	26
March	55	June	169	September	42	December	20

16. In what month is the probability of a tornado the greatest? If a tornado occurs, what is the probability that it occurs during that month?

17. Tornado season is from March through August. If a tornado occurs, what is the probability that it occurs during tornado season?

18. Hurricane season in the United States is from June 1 to November 30. In an average season, there are ten tropical storms. Six are expected to reach hurricane strength and two of these are likely to strike the U.S. coast. Is the probability that a tropical storm will turn into a hurricane more than 50%?

19. Journal In 1995, there were 19 tropical storms, of which 11 reached hurricane strength. Why was 1995 considered an unusual year?

Mixed Review and Test Prep

STAY SHARP!

Tell which solid of each pair has the greater surface area.

20.

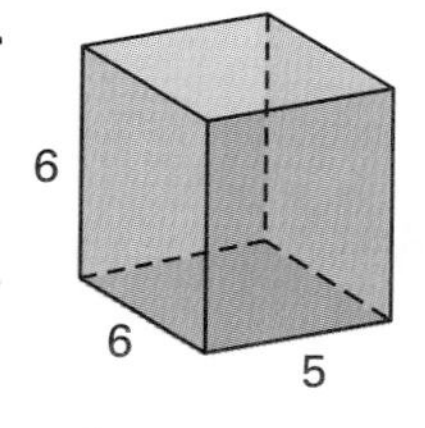

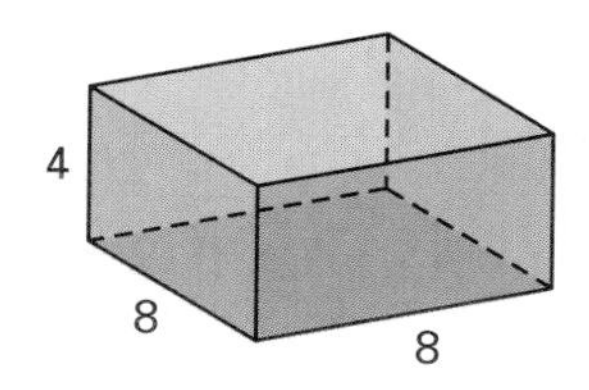

21.

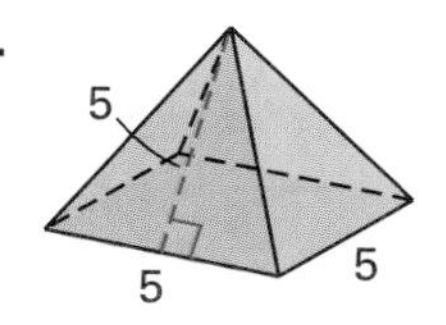

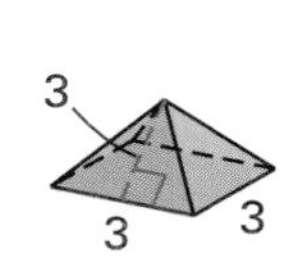

22. Choose the set of integers that is ordered from least to greatest.

Ⓐ –3, –4, –5 Ⓑ 0, –1, 2, –3 Ⓒ –7, –6, 0 Ⓓ 8, –7, 6

Chapter 12

Problem Solving

Analyze Word Problems: Checking for a Reasonable Answer

You Will Learn
- to use estimation to determine if your answer is reasonable

Learn

The Chelsea Flea Market raised money to help remodel the Chelsea Public Library. The market manager rented 31 booths at \$150 a booth. She put aside 10% of the rental fee for clean-up expenses. She estimated the clean-up expenses to be about \$500. Is this estimate too high, too low, or close enough?

Work Together

▶ Understand

What do you know?

What do you need to find out?

▶ Plan

What will you do to find out? — Find the amount to be spent on clean-up for a booth; Find the total to be spent on clean-up.

▶ Solve

Find the amount to be spent on clean-up for each booth.	10% of \$150 $0.1 \times \$150 = \$15$
Multiply to find the total amount for all the booths.	$31 \times \$15 = \$465$
Write your answer.	\$465

The manager's estimate of \$500 is close enough, so it is reasonable.

▶ Look Back

Does the answer make sense?

1. How can you use estimation to find out if your answer is reasonable?
2. What should you do if your estimate makes you think your answer is not reasonable?
3. Suppose a student calculated that the manager should plan to spend \$15 on clean-up. What would you tell that student about that answer and where a mistake might have been made?

Check

State if the estimate given is too low, too high, or close enough and explain why.

1. The flea market raised a total of $10,345. Of that money, $2,586.24 went to cover the operating expenses of the flea market. The rest went to the library. How much went to the library? *$7,800*

2. Martha's school is in the Chelsea neighborhood. The school rented a booth and sold $2,469 worth of items. The school gave $\frac{1}{4}$ of the money to the library fund. How much did the school donate? *$1,850.00*

Problem Solving Practice

Problem Solving Strategies

- Draw a Picture
- Look for a Pattern
- Guess and Check
- Use Logical Reasoning
- Make an Organized List
- Make a Table
- Solve a Simpler Problem
- Work Backward

Choose a Tool

Use any strategy to solve each problem.

3. **Logic** Greg, Bonita, Sean, and Jenny each like a different kind of book: biography, mystery, science fiction, and fiction. Bonita likes books that are true stories. Jenny likes mystery or fiction. Neither of the boys likes fiction. Greg bought his friend a science fiction book because he knew his friend liked that kind of book. What kind of book does each person like?

4. **Estimation** Emilio's Pizzeria sold pizza for $1.10 a slice. Each pizza had 8 slices and 59 pizzas were sold. Emilio planned to donate $\frac{1}{3}$ of the money collected to the library. He said this amount was $21.63. Is he correct?

5. Visitors can attend two of these events at the Chelsea Public Library: library tour, storytelling, puppet show, and computer demonstration. Make an organized list to show the combinations of events visitors could attend.

6. **Money** George owed $6 in library fines. Half of this was for an overdue video. The rest was for three books that were each 20 days overdue. What fine does the library charge per day for an overdue book?

7. **Using Data** An F4 tornado occurred in one midwestern town during May. In June, the same town experienced a tornado with $\frac{1}{3}$ the wind velocity. Use the Data File on page 618 to determine what type of tornado most likely occurred in June.

8. **Estimation** During a tornado, 13 homes received moderate damage. Estimated repairs were $12,000 per house. A local newspaper estimated the total cost for repairs to be $1,500,000. Is this estimate correct?

Technology

Using a Spreadsheet to Generate Random Numbers

You can test the expected probability of a possible outcome by performing an experiment. For instance, you may want to find out your chances of rolling a number cube and getting a 4. But rather than rolling the number cube over and over and recording the result each time, you can use a spreadsheet to simulate the experiment.

Materials

Interactive CD-ROM Spreadsheet/Grapher Tool or other spreadsheet software

How does the expected probability compare to the experimental probability of rolling two number cubes and getting a sum of 10?

Work Together

Use your spreadsheet software to simulate rolling number cubes.

1. First, determine the probability of rolling two number cubes and getting a sum of 10. There are 36 different possible outcomes when rolling two cubes. How many ways can 10 be rolled? What is the expected probability of rolling a 10?

2. Next, test the expected probability by generating random numbers to simulate rolling two number cubes. Create a new spreadsheet in your software program and enter the information as shown.

	A	B	C
1	Roll 1	Roll 2	Sum
2			

3. In cell A2, enter $=TRUNC(6*(RAND())+1)$. Copy this formula into cell B2. Then copy the formula down to row 101. This will generate 100 random numbers from 1 to 6. (Your data will look different from the data shown here.)

	A	B	C
1	Roll 1	Roll 2	Sum
2	3	5	
3	4	6	
4	6	3	
5	1	2	
6	2	1	
7	2	4	
8	3	5	
9	5	2	

4. In cell C2, enter the formula $=(A2+B2)$. Copy the formula down to row 101.

5. Count the number of times 10 appears as the sum. This can be expressed as a ratio to 100, and as a percent. How do your results compare to the probability you calculated in Step 1?

Exercises

1. Repeat the experiment by recopying the formulas in row 2 down to row 101. How do your results the second time compare to the first time?

2. Use the steps above to find the chances of getting a sum of 12.

Extensions

3. Can you roll two number cubes 100 times and record the results more quickly by hand or with a spreadsheet? Explain.

4. Change the number in front of the "*RAND" to a different number, and copy the formula to row 101. How does this change the data?

Chapter 12
Lesson
3

Geometric Models of Probability

You Will Learn

- to calculate probability from geometric models

Did You Know?

The Coast Guard uses probability when describing the chances of locating a particular ship lost at sea.

Learn

Suppose you are going to play a game. You must decide which spinner has the better chance of landing on "Move ahead 2 spaces."

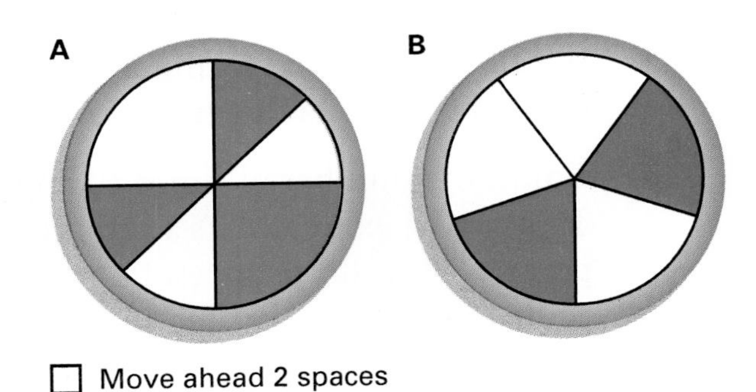

Even though the sections are not the same size, you can still determine the probability of landing on "Move ahead 2 spaces" for each spinner.

One Way

Spin each spinner 20 times and record the results in a table.

The probability of landing on "Move ahead 2 spaces" is $\frac{9}{20}$ for Spinner A and $\frac{13}{20}$ for Spinner B.

Spinner	Move Ahead	Go Back
A	𝍸 IIII	𝍸 𝍸 I
B	𝍸 𝍸 III	𝍸 II

Spinner B is the better spinner to use.

Remember, though, probability calculated from sample data is only an estimate.

Another Way

Find out the total area of each spinner covered by sections marked "Move ahead 2 spaces."

Spinner A:

$\frac{1}{8} + \frac{1}{8} + \frac{1}{4} = \frac{1}{8} + \frac{1}{8} + \frac{2}{8} = \frac{4}{8} = \frac{1}{2}$

Spinner B:

$\frac{1}{5} + \frac{1}{5} + \frac{1}{5} = \frac{3}{5}$

There is a better chance on landing on "Move ahead 2 spaces" on Spinner B.

If you can determine each area within the figure, you can determine the probability of the situation.

Example 1

A tornado has a very irregular path. When the funnel touches the ground, it might go straight, double back, or hop over places. If a tornado touches down in the area pictured, what is the probability that it will touch down in a shaded area?

The total area is 25 square units. The shaded area is 9 square units.

The probability that the tornado will hit the shaded region is $\frac{9}{25}$.

Sometimes you will need to recall the formulas for areas of figures.

Example 2

If a coin is tossed onto the carnival game board at random, what is the probability that it will land in the circle?

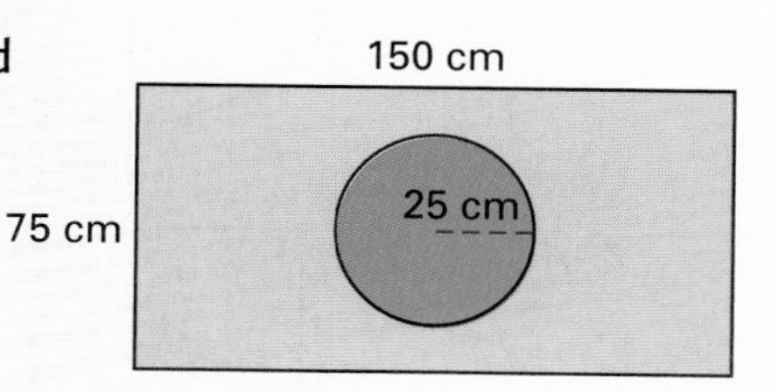

$$P(\text{land in circle}) = \frac{\text{area of circle}}{\text{area of rectangle}}$$

$$= \frac{3.14 \times 25 \times 25}{75 \times 150}$$

$$= \frac{1{,}962.5}{11{,}250} \approx 0.17, \text{ or } 17\%$$

The probability that the coin will land in the circle is approximately 17%.

Remember

The area of a circle is $\pi \times \text{radius}^2$

Talk About It

1. Why are the results from both ways on page 634 different?
2. For Example 2, why couldn't you write a ratio of the number of ways the event could occur to the number of possible outcomes?

Check

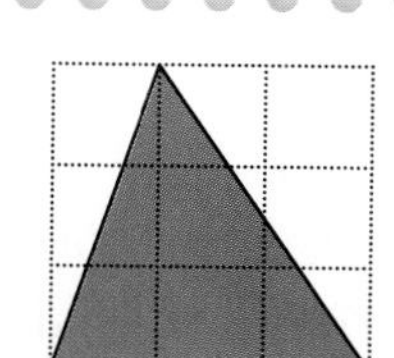

1. Find the probability of tossing a coin onto the carnival gameboard and hitting the shaded region.
2. **Reasoning** One dart board has a bull's eye of 20 square cm. Another of the same size has two bull's eyes, each 10 square cm. Which dart board would you choose to play? Why?

Practice

Skills and Reasoning

Use the figure shown to answer **3–5.**

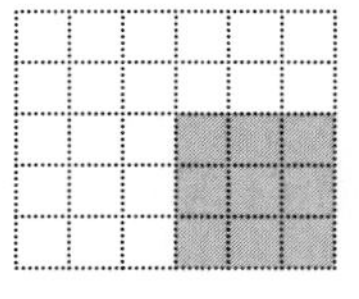

3. Find the area of the shaded square.
4. Find the area of the rectangle.
5. Find the probability that a token thrown at random will land on the shaded square.

Calculator Suppose you drop a token on each shape in **6–13.** Find the probability of the token landing on the shaded area. Write your answer as a percent.

6. 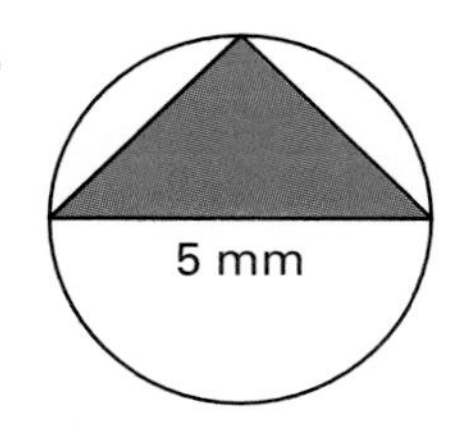

7. 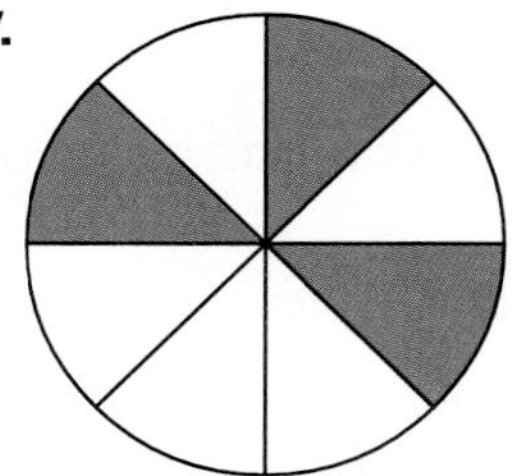

8. 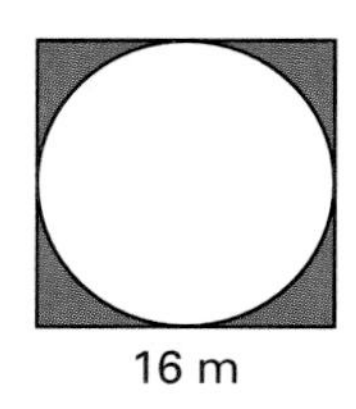

9. 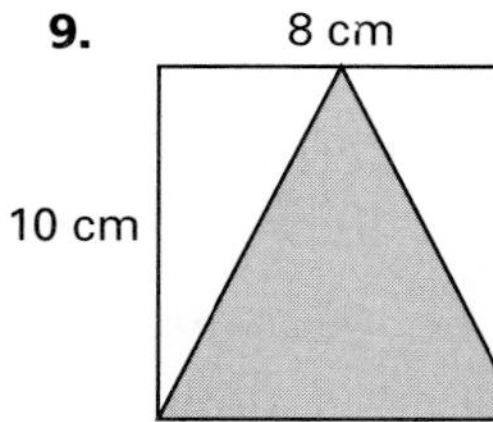

10. 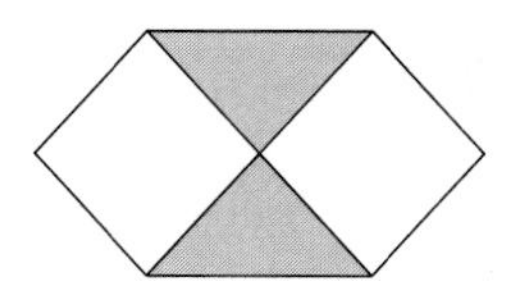

11. 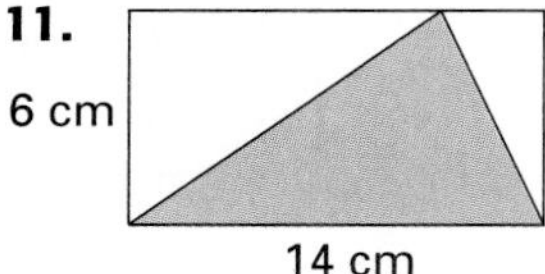

12. 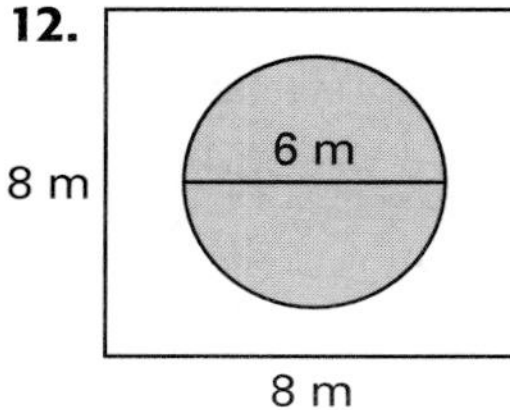

13. 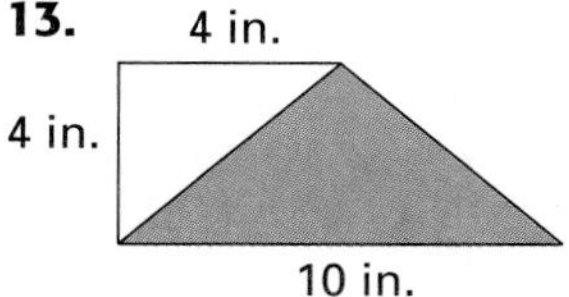

14. If you throw 200 darts at the dart board shown, how many do you expect will land in the shaded area?

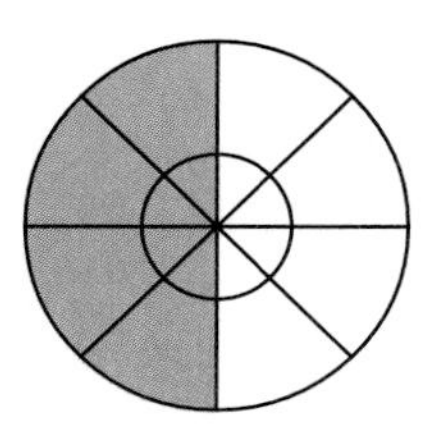

Problem Solving and Applications

Using Data Use the floor plan of the Northrop City Branch Public Library to find the following probabilities.

15. Probability of a person being in the main reading room
16. Probability of a person being in the children's room
17. Probability of a person leaving by Exit 3

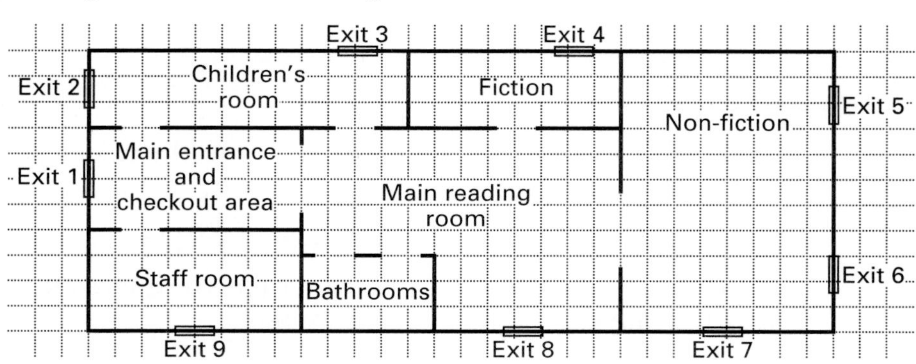

18. **Science** Hurricanes blow in a spiral around a circular center known as the "eye." If a storm covers a circular area 400 miles wide and its eye is 20 miles wide, what is the probability of an object in a hurricane being in the eye of the hurricane?

19. **Choose a Strategy** On Jerome's gameboard, the probability of a coin randomly landing on a blue square is $\frac{1}{4}$, on a green square $\frac{1}{3}$, and on a red square $\frac{3}{14}$. What is the smallest number of squares that could be on Jerome's board.

20. **Critical Thinking** In a geometric model of probability, if the entire model is reduced in size, what happens to the probability of randomly landing on the shaded area? Explain.

21. **Write Your Own Problem** Draw a gameboard or spinner. Then write a geometric probability problem that involves your drawing. Remember to label measurements if needed.

22. **Journal** Draw a dart board so that the probability of hitting the bull's eye is $\frac{2}{3}$. Explain your drawing.

Mixed Review and Test Prep

Draw front, side, and top views for each figure. There are no hidden cubes.

23. 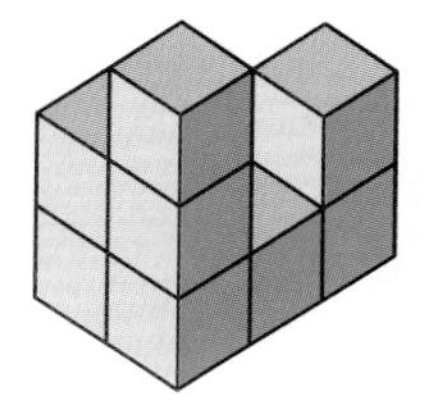

24. 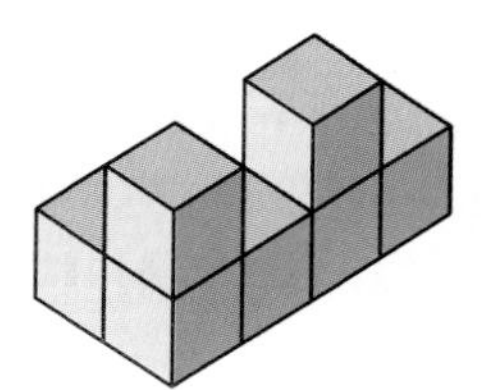

25. 

26. 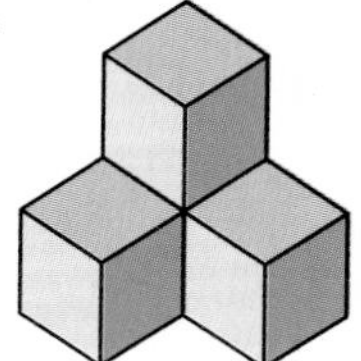

Find the volume.

27. 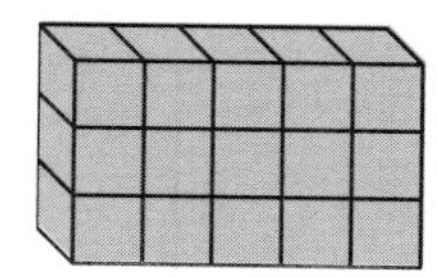

28. 

29. 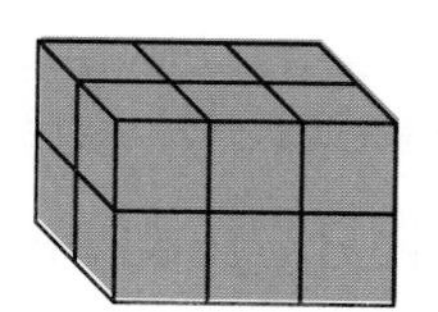

30. 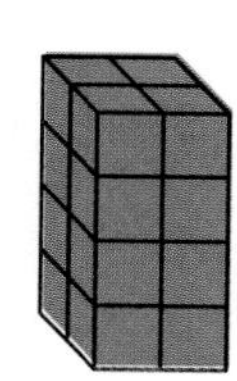

31. A parachutist is scheduled to land somewhere in the open field shown. Which is the best estimate of the ratio of grassy area to total area?

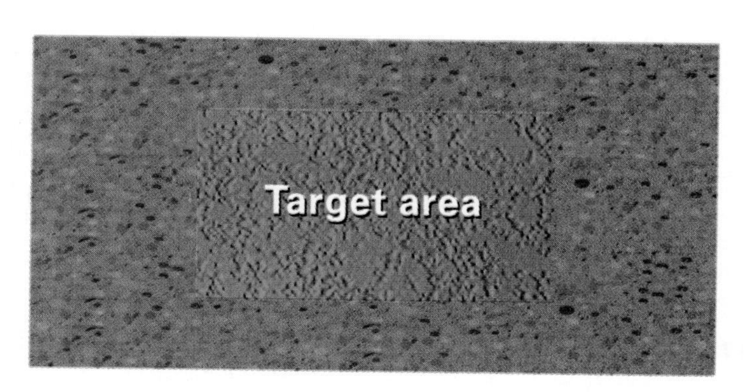

Ⓐ $\frac{1}{4}$ Ⓑ $\frac{1}{2}$

Ⓒ $\frac{3}{4}$ Ⓓ 1

Skills Practice Bank, page 672, Set 3

SECTION A

Review and Practice

(Lesson 1) Choose the best answer.

1. How many outcomes are possible when you flip a coin?

   Ⓐ 1   Ⓑ 4   Ⓒ 2   Ⓓ 0

2. Which of the following best describes the probability of landing on red on this spinner?

   Ⓐ $\frac{1}{4}$ Ⓑ $\frac{1}{3}$ Ⓒ $\frac{2}{3}$ Ⓓ $\frac{3}{3}$

A number cube labeled 1-6 is rolled. Find the probability of each event.

3. $P(1)$ 4. $P(3 \text{ or } 4)$ 5. $P(7)$ 6. $P(<7)$ 7. $P(\text{not } 3)$

Use the spinner to find each probability.

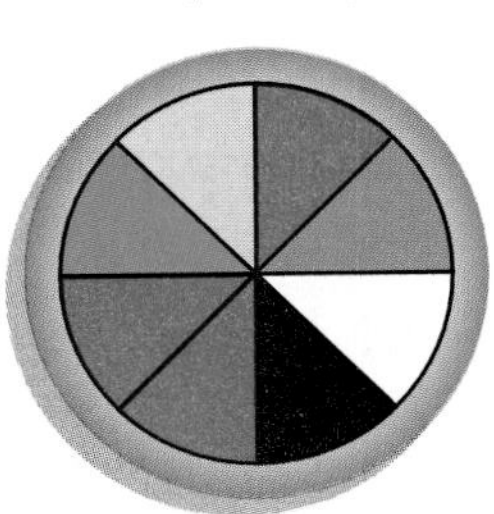

8. $P(\text{red})$ 9. $P(\text{not red})$

10. $P(\text{green})$ 11. $P(\text{not yellow})$

12. Which probability is greater, 1 out of 10 or 15 out of 15,000? Explain.

(Lessons 2 and 3) Solve.

13. The probability of drawing a red marble out of a bag is $\frac{1}{5}$. For a green marble it is $\frac{1}{10}$, for a blue marble it is $\frac{3}{10}$, and for a yellow marble it is $\frac{2}{5}$. What are the chances of randomly drawing a marble that's either red or blue?

14. On average, there are 100,000 thunderstorms in the United States every year. The probability that a thunderstorm will develop into a tornado is approximately $\frac{1}{100}$. About how many tornadoes are there every year?

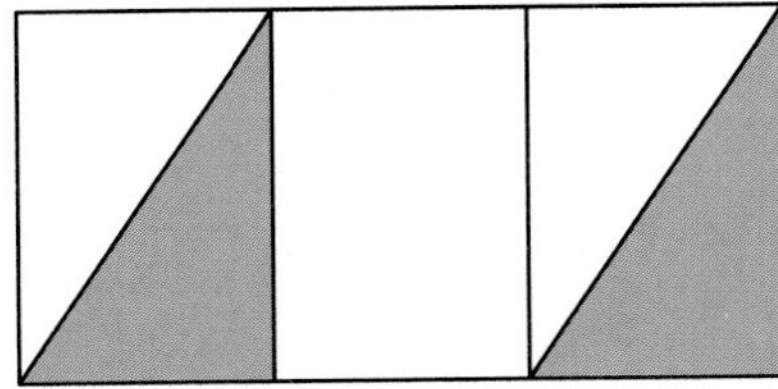

15. If 100 tokens were dropped on the figure shown, how many would you expect to hit the shaded region?

16. Marie is designing a contest. She wants to fill a bag with table-tennis balls, some of which she has painted different colors. Prizes will be awarded to people who pull colored table-tennis balls out of the bag. If she wants the probability of getting a red ball to be $\frac{1}{7}$, of a yellow ball to be $\frac{1}{5}$, and of a green ball to be $\frac{1}{10}$, what is the minimum number of balls she must have in the bag?

17. **Journal** Draw a dart board so that the probability of hitting the bull's-eye is $\frac{1}{4}$. Explain your drawing.

Skills Checklist

In this section, you have:

- ☑ Learned About Probability
- ☑ Made Predictions
- ☑ Learned About Geometric Models of Probability

CHAPTER 12

SECTION

B Fairness

In 1929, Charles Darrow was unemployed with little money to spend. So he invented a game about money called Monopoly®, in which players buy and sell property using large sums of play money. In a short time the play money became real. He sold his game to Parker Brothers and became the first millionaire game designer.

How would an understanding of fairness help inventors of games?

GET READY!

Determining Fairness

Review finding probability. Suppose you roll a number cube numbered 1–6. Find the probability of each event.

1. $P(2)$
2. $P(\text{odd number})$
3. $P(\text{less than } 5)$

Skills Checklist

In this section, you will:

- ❒ **Learn About Tree Diagrams**
- ❒ **Explore Compound Events**
- ❒ **Learn About Fairness and Unfairness**

Chapter 12
Lesson
4

Tree Diagrams

You Will Learn

- to make tree diagrams

Vocabulary

tree diagram

Learn

John plays many computer games. Before he can start playing one game, he must decide what level he wants to play (easy, intermediate, hard), how many players there will be (1 or 2), and whether there will or will not be sound. John wondered how many different ways he could play the game.

John lives in San Antonio, Texas.

It is often easy to list the outcomes for a single experiment. It can be more complicated to list the outcomes for a series of experiments. To list the outcomes for a series, you can use a **tree diagram**. This type of diagram shows one branch for each possible outcome.

1. List the level choices.

Level
E
I
H

2. List the choices for the number of players.

Level — **Number of Players**

E — 1, 2
I — 1, 2
H — 1, 2

3. List the choices for sound. Then list all the outcomes. H,2,NS means hard, 2 players, no sound.

Level — **Number of Players** — **Sound**

E
- 1
  - S = E,1,S
  - NS = E,1,NS
- 2
  - S = E,2,S
  - NS = E,2,NS

I
- 1
  - S = I,1,S
  - NS = I,1,NS
- 2
  - S = I,2,S
  - NS = I,2,NS

H
- 1
  - S = H,1,S
  - NS = H,1,NS
- 2
  - S = H,2,S
  - NS = H,2,NS

Example 1

If you flip a penny, a nickel, and a dime, how many different ways can the three coins land?

There are two ways the penny can land: heads or tails. There are also two outcomes for the nickel, heads or tails, as well as for the dime.

Make a tree diagram. There are eight different possible outcomes.

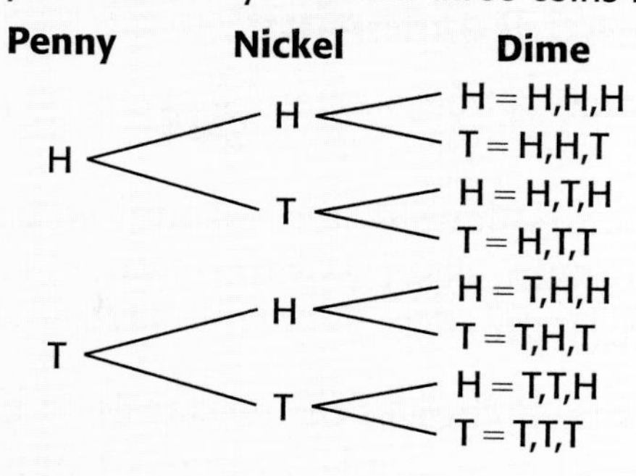

You can also use multiplication to find the number of possible outcomes.

Example 2

Multiply to find the number of possible outcomes in Example 1.

(number of ways penny can land)	×	(number of ways nickel can land)	×	(number of ways dime can land)	=	(number of possible outcomes)
2	×	2	×	2	=	8

Talk About It

1. In Example 1, what is the difference between the outcome H,H,T and the outcome H,T,H?
2. Suppose that in Example 1 you first flip the dime, then the penny, then the nickel. How would this change the tree diagram? The number of possible outcomes?
3. How could multiplication be used to find the number of different ways John could play the game?

Check

1. Conway's Restaurant has three flavors of ice cream (chocolate, vanilla, and mint) and two toppings (hot fudge and butterscotch). Draw a tree diagram showing all the possible ice cream servings with one flavor of ice cream and one topping.
2. **Reasoning** Jessie is drawing a tree diagram to show possible combinations. She has red, orange, yellow, and green blocks. They come in three shapes: triangles, squares, and circles. How many branches will her tree diagram have if Jessie first lists the choices for color? If she first lists the choices for shape? Explain.

Practice

Skills and Reasoning

For **3–5,** draw a tree diagram showing all possible outcomes for each situation.

3. In the first level of a computer game, a player chooses a path (mountain, desert, swamp, water) and an item of assistance (net, board, helmet).

4. The lunch choices of the day are a bologna or peanut butter sandwich with either an apple, orange, or banana, and either juice or milk.

5. A baseball team has five pitchers and three catchers. Only one pitcher and one catcher are on the field at the same time.

6. Prizes for first, second, and third place were wrapped in separate boxes. The labels identifying the prizes fell off.

a. How many ways can the labels be put on the boxes?

b. If one of the three labels is put on a box, what is the probability that it is the correct label?

7. The Wild Outback Resort has ten different board games, five different card games, and six different water games for their guests to play. Sam wants to borrow one of each type of game for the weekend. How many combinations of board, card, and water games are there?

8. **Calculator** A Texas license plate consists of "letter, letter, letter, number, number, letter." If all 26 letters of the alphabet and all 10 digits, 0–9, can be used, how many different license plates are possible?

9. The Wheel Shop sells five different brands of bikes. Each brand comes in three different models: 1-speed, 3-speed, or 10-speed. Each bike can also be red or blue. How many different kinds are there?

Problem Solving and CAREERS

A retail sales manager makes sure that a store has a variety of merchandise for its customers to choose from. One clothing store stocks a sweater in two styles (turtleneck and crew neck), four sizes (small, medium, large, and extra large), and eight colors (white, red, green, black, blue, yellow, brown, purple).

10. To have at least one of each style, size, and color, how many sweaters must the store have in stock?

11. Suppose the store manager placed one of each style, size, and color sweater on a table. A customer picks up a sweater at random. Find each probability.

a. The customer picks up a blue sweater.

b. The customer picks up a medium or large sweater.

c. The customer picks up a medium-sized yellow crew-neck sweater.

12. **Critical Thinking** Would you recommend that the manager have the same number of each different sweater in stock? Explain.

13 **Money** Sweaters are regularly priced at $34.00. Some colors are not selling as fast as others, so the manager puts them on sale for 25% off. What is the sale price of the sweaters?

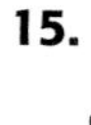

14. **Journal** To find the number of different possible combinations, do you prefer making a tree diagram or using multiplication? Explain.

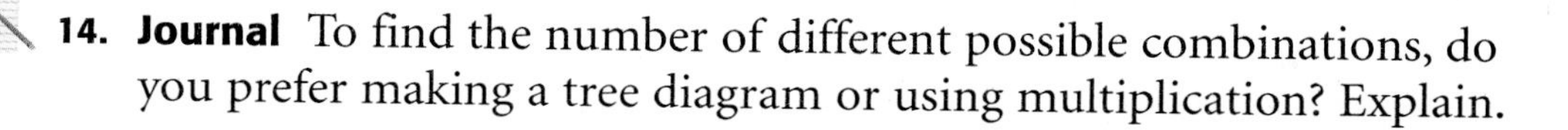

Mixed Review and Test Prep

Find the volume of each solid.

15.

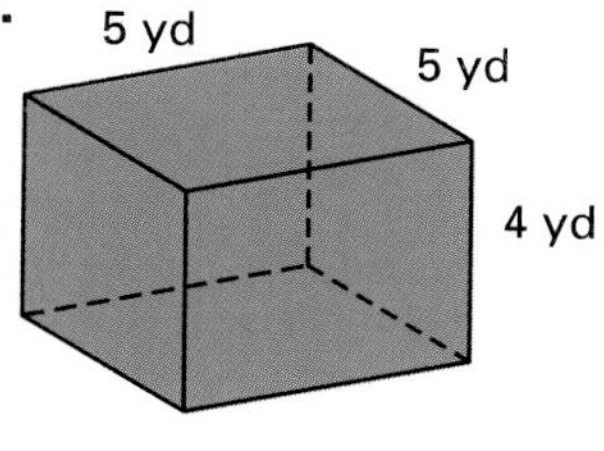

16.

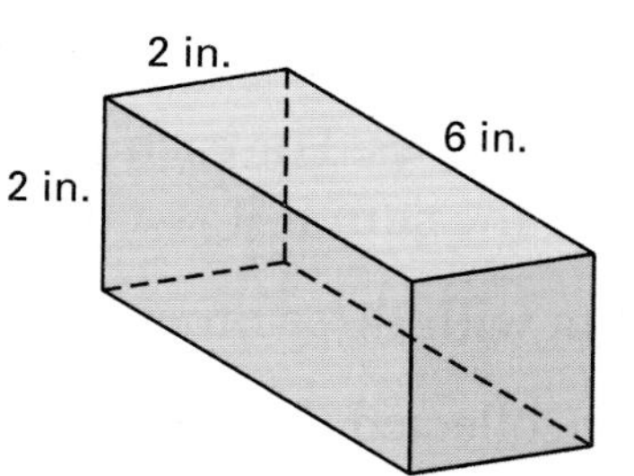

17.

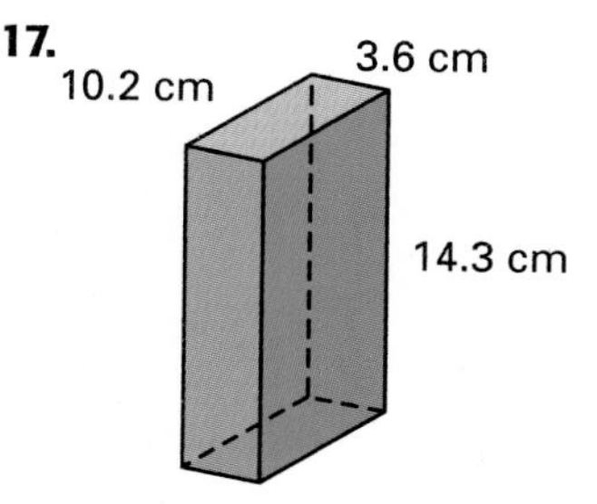

Suppose you roll a decahedron with faces numbered 1–10. Find the probability of each event.

18. $P(1,6, \text{or } 9)$ **19.** $P(10)$ **20.** $P(5 \text{ or } 3)$ **21.** $P(12)$ **22.** $P(\text{factor of } 10)$

23. Jenny has 3 red sweaters, 2 blue sweaters, and 4 yellow sweaters. What is the probability that she will not wear a yellow sweater?

Ⓐ $\frac{2}{9}$ Ⓑ $\frac{3}{9}$ Ⓒ $\frac{4}{9}$ Ⓓ $\frac{5}{9}$

Skills Practice Bank, page 671, Set 4

Compound Events

Problem Solving Connection
- Guess and Check

Materials
Number cubes

Vocabulary
compound event

Explore

You have learned how to find all of the possible outcomes for a series of experiments. But how do you find the probability of one of those outcomes?

Work Together

In the game Monopoly®, you can get out of jail if you roll a 7, an 11, or doubles (the same number on both number cubes).

1. Predict the number of times out of 100 rolls of two cubes that you can roll a 7. Then predict the number of 11s and the number of doubles.
2. Roll the cubes 25 times. For each roll, write down the sum of the numbers. Circle the sum if it is a double.
3. Share your data with three other groups.
4. Based on your collected data, determine the probability of getting just a 7, just an 11, or just doubles. Also, determine the probability for getting either a 7, an 11, or doubles.

Talk About It

5. Did your data match your prediction? Explain.
6. Why might it be a good idea to add the data from three other groups to your own data?

Connect and Learn

A single event is the outcome of a single experiment, such as tossing a coin and getting heads, or rolling a 6 on a number cube. A **compound event** is a combination of two or more single events, such as tossing a coin and getting heads *and then* rolling 6 on a number cube.

To find the probability for a compound event, first calculate the number of possible outcomes. Then calculate the number of ways the compound event can happen. The probability is the ratio of these values.

> **Example**
>
> Find P(H and 6) for tossing a coin and rolling a number cube.
>
> | | |
> |---|---|
> | Number of possible outcomes: | 2 outcomes for the coin; 6 outcomes for the cube; 2×6 or 12 possible outcomes |
> | Number of ways event can happen: | 1 way to get heads on the coin |
> | | 1 way to get 6 on the cube |
> | | 1×1 or 1 way to get heads and 6 |
>
> $P(\text{H and } 6) = \frac{1}{12}$

Check

Use the spinners to answer **1–3.**

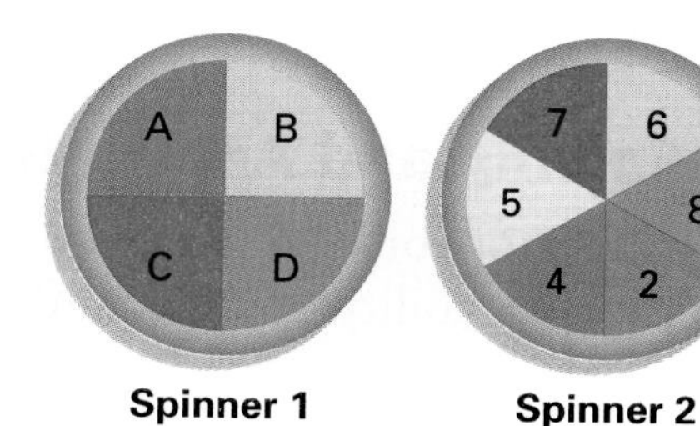

Spinner 1 **Spinner 2**

1. Find the probability of Spinning A on Spinner 1 and an odd number on Spinner 2.
2. Find the probability of spinning a consonant (B, C, or D) on Spinner 1 and a prime number on Spinner 2.
3. Find the probability of spinning a letter in the word "DAD" on Spinner 1 and an even number on Spinner 2.
4. What are the chances of flipping three coins and getting all heads?

Practice

Three cards numbered 1, 4, and 7 are in a paper bag. Each time a card is drawn it is replaced. Find the probability of each event.

5. P(odd, then even)
6. P(even, then even)
7. P(odd, then odd)
8. P(odd, even, odd)
9. P(even, then odd)
10. P(even, even, even)
11. Use the menu shown to find the probability of a customer ordering an egg roll, sweet and sour pork, and juice.

For **12–14,** the spinner is spun twice.

12. Find the probability of spinning white both times.
13. Find the probability of spinning white and then red.
14. Find the probability of not spinning red either time.
15. Two 1–6 number cubes are tossed. What is the probability that the number on each cube is the same? Different?
16. Three number cubes are tossed. What is the probability that the number on each cube is 4? Is an even number?

Problem Solving and Applications

17. **Science** The probability of a newborn child being a girl is about $\frac{1}{2}$. What is the probability of all 5 children in a family being girls?
18. **Recreation** The probability of Josh winning the 50-yard dash at the school track meet is 0.6, and his probability of winning the hurdles is 0.7. Which pair of outcomes listed in the chart does Josh have the greatest chance of accomplishing?

Dash	Hurdles
Win	Lose
Win	Win
Lose	Win
Lose	Lose

19. **Using Data** Some athletes are professional in more than one sport. Use the Data File on page 619 to find the probability that a professional golfer and bowler would make a hole in one and bowl a perfect game during one year.

20. Suppose you have 26 cards, each with a different letter of the alphabet. Find the probability of the following if you draw cards, putting each one back before drawing another. The vowels are A, E, I, O, and U.

a. *P*(vowel and then consonant)

b. *P*(vowel and then vowel)

c. *P*(consonant and then consonant)

d. *P*(X and then Y)

e. *P*(vowel, vowel, and then vowel)

f. *P*(A, B, and then C)

21. Paul has 6 argyle socks, 8 blue socks, and 4 white socks in his drawer. While getting dressed, he picks out 1 sock at random, puts it on and then picks out another. What is the probability that he picks an argyle sock on both tries?

22. If you flip a coin 4 times, which is greater, *P*(3 heads and then 1 tail) or *P*(2 heads and then 2 tails)? Explain.

23. **Critical Thinking** Zack has two spinners with numbers on them. The probability of spinning a 7 on both spinners is $\frac{3}{20}$. If the probability of getting a 7 on the first spinner alone is $\frac{1}{4}$, what is the probability of getting a 7 on the second spinner alone?

24. **Journal** How can you use a tree diagram to find the probability of a two-step event? Explain.

Mixed Review and Test Prep

STAY SHARP!

25. Which of the three spinners is most likely to have produced the sample data?

green, green, yellow, yellow, yellow, yellow, green, green, yellow, green, yellow

#1

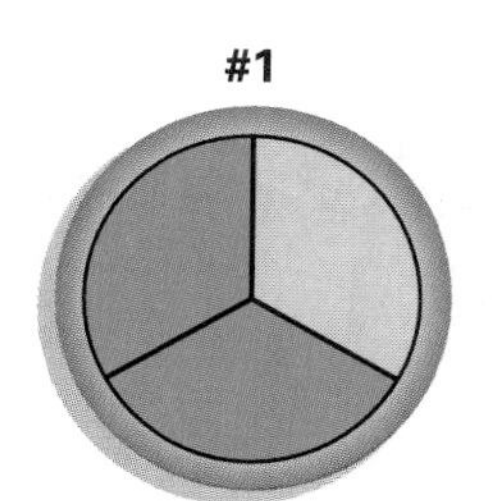

#2

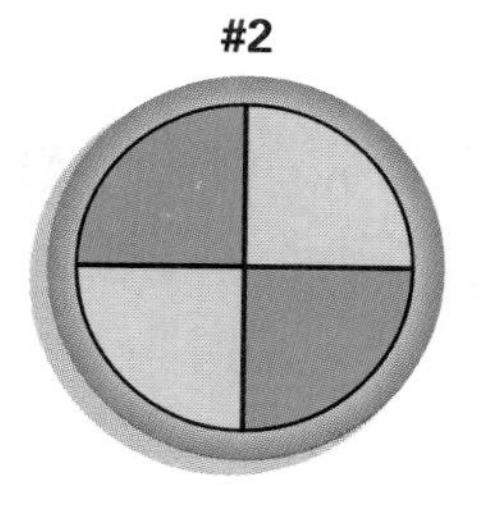

#3

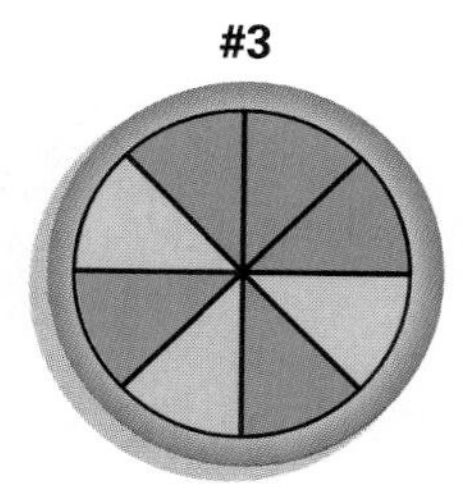

26. Suppose you drop a token on the rectangle shown. Find the probability of the token landing on the red area.

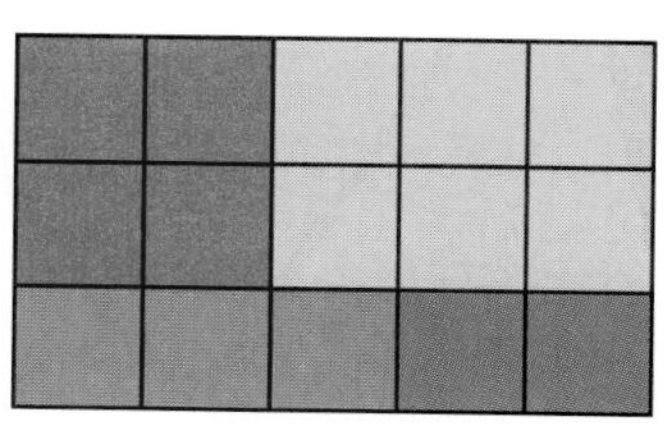

27. The temperature outside is −10°C. It drops 2° at night. What is the new temperature?

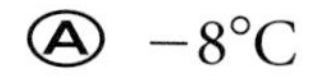

Ⓐ −8°C Ⓑ 12°C Ⓒ 8°C Ⓓ −12°C

Probability Game

Players
2 players

Materials
gameboard
drawing paper
crayons, markers, or colored pencils
posterboard
paper clips
pencils
counter for each player

Object
The object of the game is to design a spinner that will help in advancing a counter on the game board as quickly as possible.

How to Play

1. Players make one gameboard as shown.
2. Players examine the gameboard as they study the game rules:

   Game Rules
   Players place counters on the START space.

   Players take turns spinning their own designed spinners. If the spinner dial lands on a color that matches the color of the next adjacent space, the player can move his or her counter to that space.

   The first player who reaches the END space wins.
3. Each player designs a spinner that he or she will use during the game.
4. Players play the game. Each player uses his or her own designed spinner.

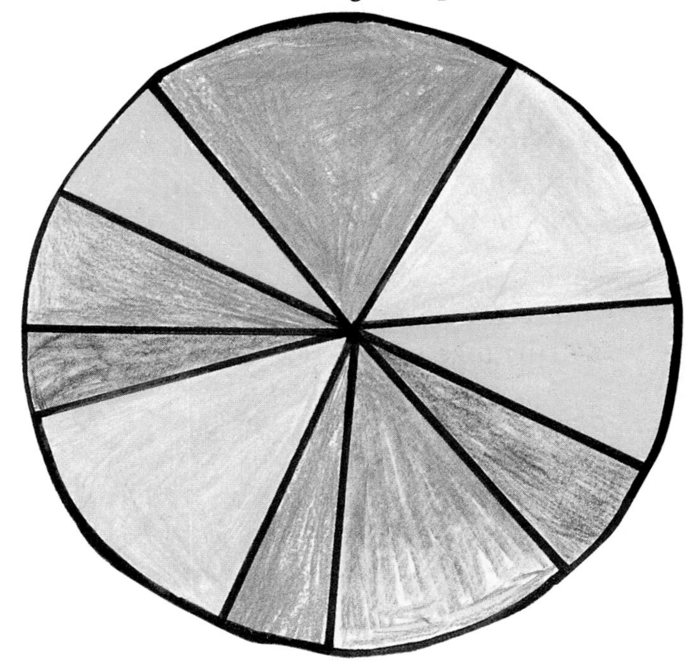

Talk About It

1. How did you decide on the design of your spinner?
2. How did the rules of the game affect your spinner design?

More Ways to Play

- Players change the design of their spinners, if they wish, and play again.
- Players work together to design a spinner that will make it hard to advance on the gameboard. Both players use this spinner to play.

Reasoning

1. Suppose you designed a spinner with color areas that match the proportions of color spaces on the gameboard. Then suppose you have difficulty getting to the first space when playing. Would you change your spinner design? Explain.
2. How would you change the game-board and your spinner design to make the game easier?

Fairness and Unfairness

You Will Learn
- to tell if a game is fair

Vocabulary
fair
unfair

Did You Know?
Bowlers use fairness when determining game handicaps that will make games more even for less experienced players.

Learn

Catherine and Van are getting ready to play a number game. In this game, two 1–6 number cubes are rolled. If the product of the resulting numbers is less than 18, Player A wins. Otherwise Player B wins. Catherine and Van want to know if this is a fair game.

A game is **fair** if each player has the same probability of winning. The game is **unfair** if one player has a greater probability of winning. You can determine if a game is fair or unfair by comparing the probabilities for winning.

First, Catherine and Van complete a table to list the products of the numbers.

×	**1**	**2**	**3**	**4**	**5**	**6**
1	1	2	3	4	5	6
2	2	4	6	8	10	12
3	3	6	9	12	15	18
4	4	8	12	16	20	24
5	5	10	15	20	25	30
6	6	12	18	24	30	36

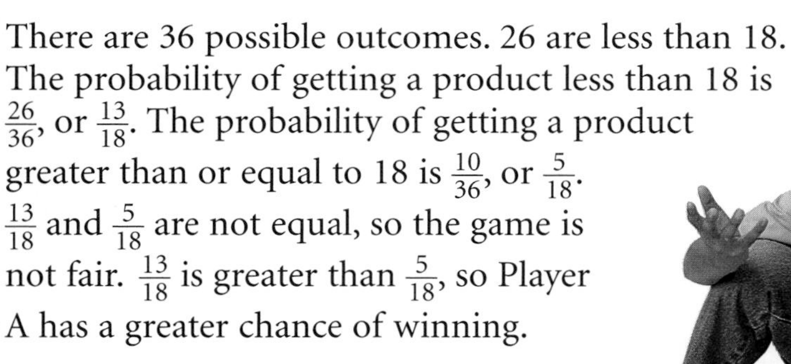

There are 36 possible outcomes. 26 are less than 18. The probability of getting a product less than 18 is $\frac{26}{36}$, or $\frac{13}{18}$. The probability of getting a product greater than or equal to 18 is $\frac{10}{36}$, or $\frac{5}{18}$. $\frac{13}{18}$ and $\frac{5}{18}$ are not equal, so the game is not fair. $\frac{13}{18}$ is greater than $\frac{5}{18}$, so Player A has a greater chance of winning.

Example 1

In a game, each letter of the alphabet is written on a separate card. A card is drawn at random. If the letter is before the letter *M*, Player A wins. Otherwise, Player B wins. Is the game fair?

There are 26 possible outcomes. There are 12 ways for Player A to win (drawing an A, B, C, D, E, F, G, H, I, J, K, or L). The probability of Player A winning is $\frac{12}{26}$, or $\frac{6}{13}$. There are 14 ways for Player B to win. The probability of Player B winning is $\frac{14}{26}$, or $\frac{7}{13}$. The game is not fair.

When a game involves compound events, you can use a tree diagram or multiplication to determine the possible outcomes.

Example 2

In a game, two coins are flipped. If the coins match, Player A wins. If the coins don't match, Player B wins. Is the game fair?

There are 2 outcomes for each coin. There are 2×2 or 4 possible outcomes.

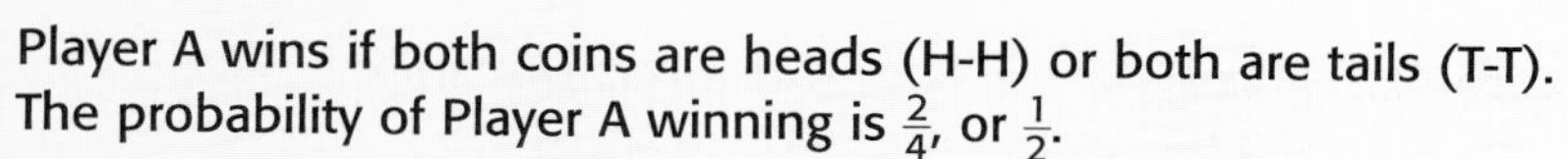

Player A wins if both coins are heads (H-H) or both are tails (T-T). The probability of Player A winning is $\frac{2}{4}$, or $\frac{1}{2}$.

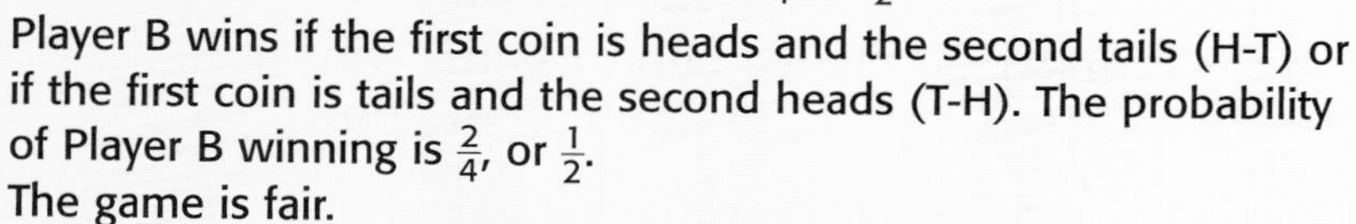

Player B wins if the first coin is heads and the second tails (H-T) or if the first coin is tails and the second heads (T-H). The probability of Player B winning is $\frac{2}{4}$, or $\frac{1}{2}$.
The game is fair.

Talk About It

1. Why is it important to consider whether or not a game is fair?
2. In Examples 1 and 2, which player has the greater probability of winning?
3. How could the game in Example 1 be changed to make it a fair game? Explain.

Check

1. Players A and B each write down a whole number less than 10. If one number is a factor of the other, Player A wins. If not, Player B wins. Is the game fair?
2. Players A and B each write down a whole number. If the difference between the numbers is even, Player A wins. If not, Player B wins. Is the game fair?
3. **Reasoning** In a game, there are 3 ways for Player A to win. The probability of Player A winning is $\frac{1}{3}$. How many different outcomes must this game have?

Practice

Skills and Reasoning

For **4–7,** use the spinner and determine if the game is fair. If it is not, tell which player has the higher probability of winning.

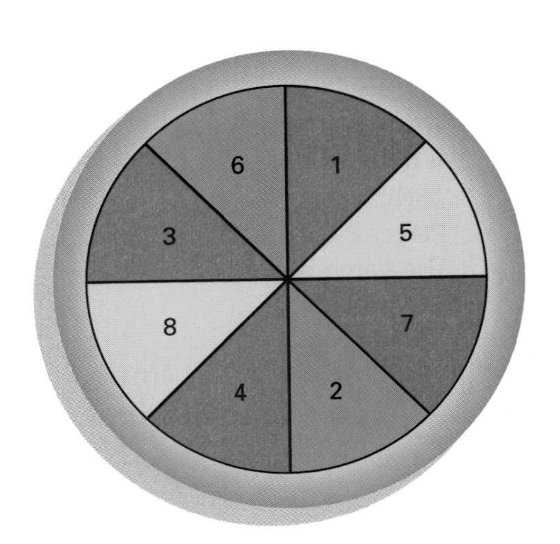

4. If the spinner lands on blue or yellow, Player A wins. Otherwise Player B wins.

5. If the spinner lands on an even prime number, Player A wins. Otherwise, Player B wins.

6. If the spinner lands on red or an odd number, Player A wins. Otherwise, Player B wins.

7. If the spinner lands on a factor of 4, Player A wins. Otherwise Player B wins.

For **8–13,** determine if the game is fair. If it is not, tell which player has the higher probability of winning.

8. A blue number cube is labeled $-3, 3, 3, -5, 6, 6$ and a red number cube is labeled $-1, 2, 2, 4, 4, 6$. Sheila wins if the number on the blue cube is greater than the number on the red cube. Manda wins if the number on the red cube is greater, or if both numbers are the same.

9. A nickel and a dime are tossed. The winner is determined as shown.

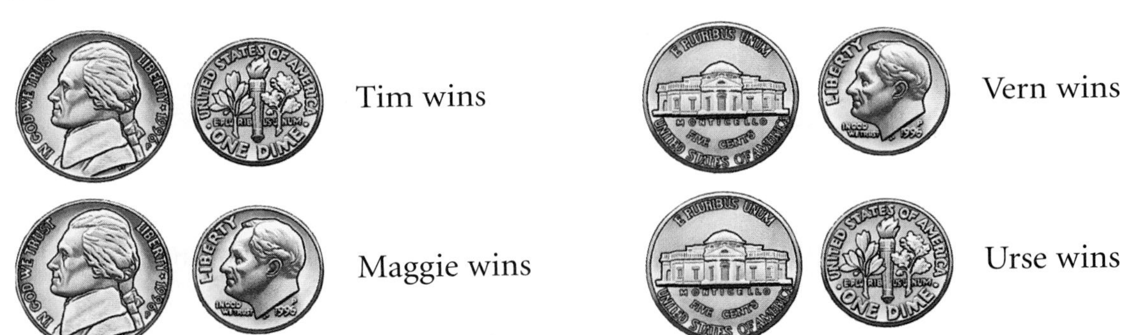

10. A number cube is tossed. Player 1 wins if the number is less than 3. Otherwise, Player 2 wins.

11. Two number cubes are tossed. If a proper fraction in lowest terms can be written using the numbers rolled, Player 1 wins. Otherwise Player 2 wins.

12. Bill and Ben tossed 2 coins 30 times. Bill won $\frac{11}{15}$ of the time. Ben won the rest of the time.

13. Edna and Charity played a number game 20 times. Charity won 35% of the time. Edna won 65% of the time.

14. Algebra Readiness Suppose you played a game in which you won w times. You said that this must be a fair game. Write an expression to represent how many times you played the game.

Problem Solving and Applications

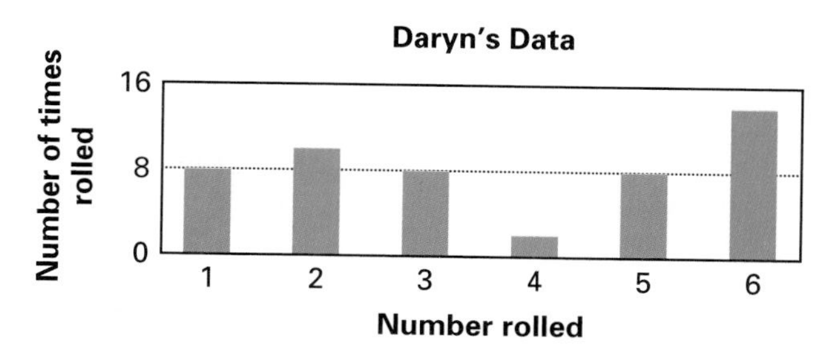

15. **Using Data** Daryn rolled a number cube 50 times and recorded how many times he got each number. His bar graph is shown. Is it possible that Daryn is using a fair cube?

16. In many games, the team or person that goes first is determined by flipping a coin. Heads goes first, tails goes second. Why do you think this is such a common method?

17. **Critical Thinking** You and a friend toss a coin to decide who will go first for a game. Your friend says, "Heads I win. Tails you lose." Is this method fair or unfair? Explain.

18. In a game, the probability that Player A wins is 40%. The probability that Player B wins is 40%. The probability that neither player wins is 20%. Is this game fair? Explain your reasoning.

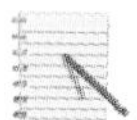

19. **Journal** How would you try to determine whether a spinner game is fair or unfair?

Mixed Review and Test Prep

20. Draw a tree diagram showing the following.
    - **a.** The possible outcomes for tossing 3 coins.
    - **b.** The possible pizza combinations using 5 different toppings, 2 different cheeses, and 3 different crusts. Assume each pizza has one topping, one cheese, and one crust.

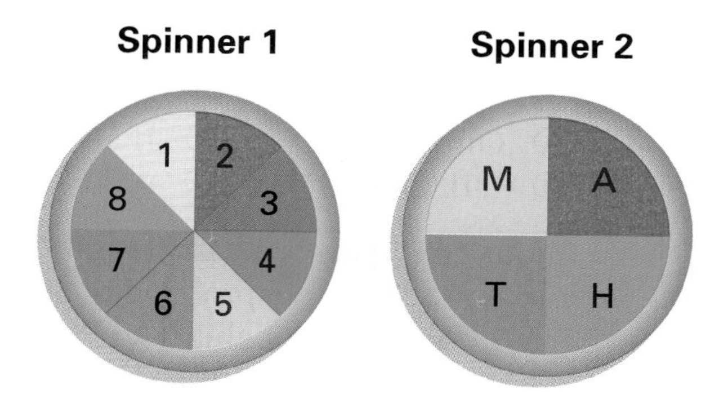

21. What is the probability of spinning a number less than 5 on Spinner 1 and an A on Spinner 2?

22. Simplify: $2\frac{7}{8} + 5\frac{3}{4}$.

    Ⓐ $5\frac{3}{4}$ Ⓑ $8\frac{5}{8}$ Ⓒ $8\frac{3}{4}$ Ⓓ $8\frac{1}{8}$

Skills Practice Bank, page 671, Set 6

SECTION B

Review and Practice

(Lessons 4–6) Solve each problem.

1. Suppose you toss three coins.
   - a. How many possible outcomes are there?
   - b. What is the probability for each outcome happening?

2. Laurel baked 12 oatmeal cookies, 10 sugar cookies, and 15 chocolate chip cookies. Her brother took a cookie at random. What is the probability that Laurel's brother *didn't* take a chocolate chip cookie?

3. There is one of four different prizes inside each box of Toastie Oaties. If you buy three boxes, what is the probability of getting the same prize in each box?

4. Suppose you toss a quarter onto a 2-foot square that has a 1-foot diameter circular region shaded. Does the probability of the quarter landing outside the circular region depend on the location of the circle? Explain.

5. A locker combination has three numbers. Each number is a whole number from 1 to 35.
   - a. How many locker combinations are possible if the numbers can be repeated?
   - b. What is the probability that someone could choose the correct combination in one try?

6. Two coins are tossed. Player A wins if they both land with the same side up. Player B wins if they land differently. Is the game fair? Explain.

7. The following percentages list the chances of each player winning different 3-player games. Which game is fair?

   I. 20%, 30%, 40% II. 40%, 40%, 20% III. 50%, 50%, 0%

   Ⓐ Only I Ⓑ II and III
   Ⓒ I, II, and III Ⓓ not here

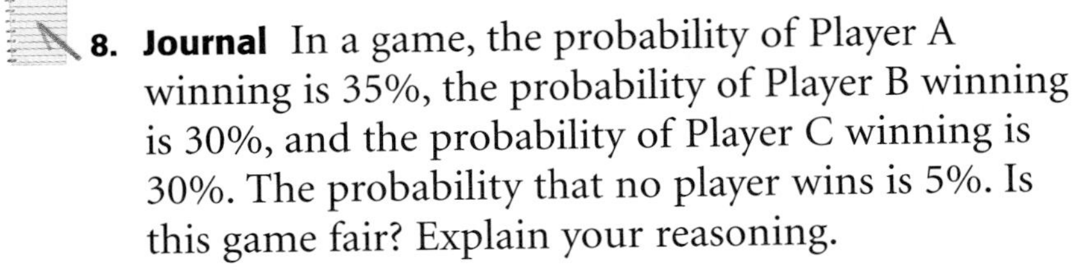

8. **Journal** In a game, the probability of Player A winning is 35%, the probability of Player B winning is 30%, and the probability of Player C winning is 30%. The probability that no player wins is 5%. Is this game fair? Explain your reasoning.

Skills Checklist

In this section, you have:

- ☑ **Learned About Tree Diagrams**
- ☑ **Explored Compound Events**
- ☑ **Learned About Fairness and Unfairness**

Choose at least one of the following. Use what you have learned in this chapter.

1 The Name Game

Create a spinner that is divided into equal portions, one for each letter in your name. Find the probability of the spinner landing on a vowel. Write the probability as a percent. Now spin the spinner 100 times and record your results. Compare the probability and the event. Explain possible reasons for any difference.

2 Luck of the Draw

At Home Place 8 blue and 2 red marbles or plastic chips in a bag. Ask five family members or friends to draw from the bag five times, returning their selection to the bag after each pick. Record the results. Repeat the experiment, without returning the selections. How do the results of the first and second selections differ?

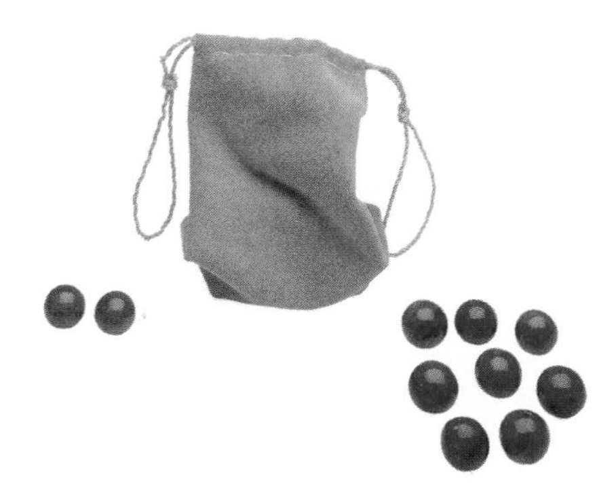

3 Whither the Weather?

Surf the World Wide Web to find data on when a weather event is likely to occur. When is the probability of the weather event greatest? What is the likelihood of the event occuring during vacation?

4 Clothes Combo

Draw a small icon to represent your three favorite pairs of pants, three favorite sweaters or jackets, and three favorite pairs of footwear. Then create a tree diagram showing all the possible combinations you can make.

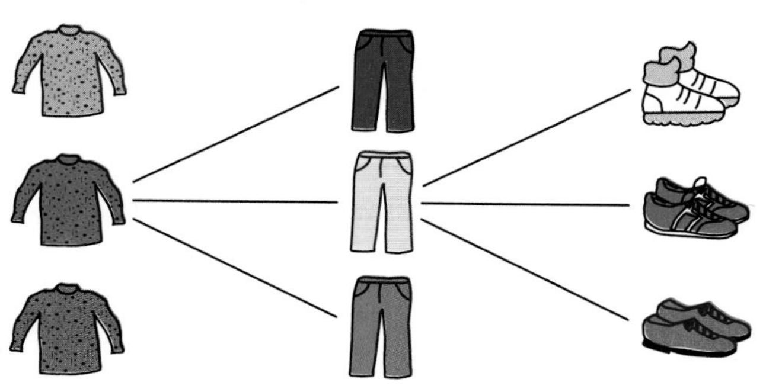

CHAPTER 12

Review/Test

(Lessons 1 and 5) For **1–3,** write *true* or *false.* Rewrite each false statement to make it true.

1. The probability of an event compares the number of possible outcomes to the number of ways an event can happen.
2. The outcomes of a situation are all the ways something can happen.
3. A compound event lists the outcomes of a series of experiments.

(Lessons 2–6) Choose a strategy to solve.

4. One event has a probability of 65%, and one has a probability of $\frac{4}{5}$. Which is more likely to occur?
5. In an election poll, 320 out of 500 people said they would vote for a school bond issue. The bond issue needs 51% of the votes to pass. What are its chances of passing? Explain.

6. Two number cubes numbered 1–6 are tossed.
   a. How many outcomes are possible?
   b. What is the probability that the number on each cube is a multiple of 3?

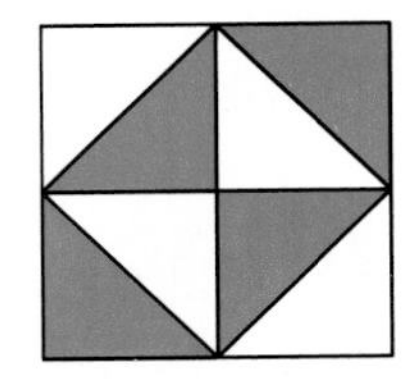

7. If a button lands on the game board shown, what is the chance it will land on a shaded triangle?
8. a. Name two methods of finding the number of possible kinds of sundaes that can be made with vanilla, chocolate, and strawberry ice creams; fudge, pineapple, raspberry, and cherry syrups; and toppings of peanuts, coconut, raisins or candies.

   b. How many different sundaes can be made if each contains one flavor of ice cream, one flavor of syrup, and one topping?

9. If you spin both spinners, what is the probability that the pointers will land on a circle and a triangle?

Spinner 1

Spinner 2

10. In a game, each letter of the alphabet is written on a card. Julia draws a card at random. If the letter is a vowel, Julia wins. Otherwise Annie wins. Is the game fair?

CHAPTER 12

Performance Assessment

You work for a company that designs spinners and number cubes for probability games. You are given two games and asked to design spinners and number cubes for them.

For Game 1:

- Design a spinner with a probability of $\frac{1}{4}$ of landing in a section that is yellow.
- The spinner must include at least three colors.
- Use the spinner to get a sample of 20 spins.
- Use the sample to determine which color section has the greatest probability of being spun on the next spin. If more than one color has the same probability, list each of the colors.

For Game 2:

- Design a six-faced number cube with a probability of $\frac{1}{3}$ of landing on the number 2.
- Design another six-faced number cube that when combined with your first number cube gives a probability of $\frac{1}{4}$ of landing on the number 2.
- Use a tree diagram to list all of the possible outcomes of rolling your two number cubes together. Find the number of possible outcomes.
- Use your two number cubes to make up rules for a game for two players. Make up one game that is fair. Make up one game that is unfair. If you need to change the numbers on the cubes, you may do so.

1. **Decision Making** For Game 1, decide on the colors and sizes of the sections of your spinner. Do your spinner sections need to be the same size? For Game 2, decide on the numerals and the number of times each numeral will appear on your number cubes. Does it matter which numerals you choose?

2. **Recording** For the spinner in Game 1, record your chosen colors and section sizes by drawing and making a spinner. For the number cubes in Game 2, draw the net of a number cube and write the numerals in the sections of the net.

3. **Explain Your Thinking** How did you decide on the colors and sections of your spinner and the numerals in your number cubes?

Math Magazine

What are the Chances? Not Likely!

Probability does not only express the chances of something happening. It can also express the chances of something *not* happening.

One way to find the probability that an event does not happen is to first count the number of ways the event cannot occur. On this spinner, there are three outcomes that are not red. There are four possible outcomes. The probability of not getting red is $\frac{3}{4}$.

The probability of an event happening and the probability of an event not happening always equals 1, or 100%. You can use this idea as another way to find the probability of an event not happening. First find the probability of the event happening, and then subtract that number from 1, or 100%. The probability of getting red is $\frac{1}{4}$, or 25%. The probability of not getting red is $1 - \frac{1}{4} = \frac{3}{4}$, or $100\% - 25\% = 75\%$.

Try These!

Using the spinner, find the probability for each event.

1. Not landing on red
2. Not landing on a letter
3. Not landing on an odd number
4. Not landing on a two-digit number

Using the spinner, determine which event is more likely. Explain.

5. Landing on blue or not landing on blue
6. Landing on a number or not landing on a number
7. Not landing on the "?" or not landing on a letter
8. Not landing on a letter or not landing on a number

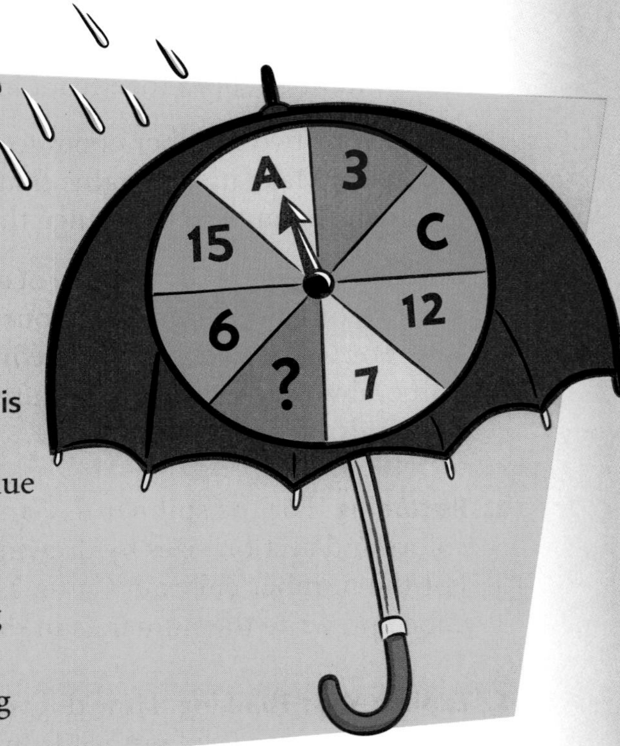

CHAPTERS 1–12

Cumulative Review

Test Prep Strategy: Read Carefully

Watch for tricky problems.

Noah has a spinner numbered from 1 to 8. If he spins once, what is the probability the spinner will **not** land on a number divisible by 3?

Ⓐ $\frac{2}{8}$ Ⓑ $\frac{6}{8}$ Ⓒ $\frac{1}{8}$ Ⓓ not here

Take the time to read the problem carefully. Did you notice the word "not?" You are looking for all the numbers from 1 to 8 that are not divisible by 3. Six of the eight numbers are not divisible by 3. Choice Ⓑ is the only possible answer.

Write the letter of the correct answer. Choose any strategy.

1. Divide 8.442 by 0.42.

   Ⓐ 0.021 Ⓑ 0.201 Ⓒ 20.1 Ⓓ 21

2. What conversion factor do you use to convert from quarts to pints?

   Ⓐ 4 Ⓑ 2 Ⓒ $\frac{1}{2}$ Ⓓ $\frac{1}{4}$

3. Find the least common multiple of 36 and 54.

   Ⓐ 2 Ⓑ 9 Ⓒ 18 Ⓓ 108

4. If a figure with point $A(-3, -4)$ is reflected over the x-axis, what is its image point?

   Ⓐ $(3, 4)$ Ⓑ $(3, -4)$ Ⓒ $(-3, 4)$ Ⓓ not here

5. Which point does **not** lie on the graph of $y = -3x$?

   Ⓐ $(10, -30)$ Ⓑ $(-30, 10)$ Ⓒ $(-2, 6)$ Ⓓ $(6, -18)$

6. The sides of one triangle measure 3 ft, 5 ft, and 6 ft. The shortest side of a similar triangle measures 18 ft. What are the lengths of its other two sides?

   Ⓐ 30 ft, 48 ft Ⓑ 30 ft, 36 ft Ⓒ 11 ft, 15 ft Ⓓ 6 ft, 10 ft

7. If Sean saves 35% on the purchase of a $22 shirt, how much does he save?

   Ⓐ $77.70 Ⓑ $14.30 Ⓒ $7.70 Ⓓ not here

8. Find the volume of a box 7 inches long, 4 inches wide, and 3 inches high.

   Ⓐ 84 in^3 Ⓑ 66 in^3 Ⓒ 33 in^3 Ⓓ 84 in^2

9. Eleven cards spell MATHEMATICS. What is the probability of picking an A card?

   Ⓐ $\frac{2}{11}$ Ⓑ $\frac{11}{2}$ Ⓒ $\frac{1}{5}$ Ⓓ not here

Test Prep Strategies

- Read Carefully
- Follow Directions
- Make Smart Choices
- Eliminate Choices
- Work Backward from an Answer

Set 1 For use after page 9.

Use the line graph to answer **1** and **2.**

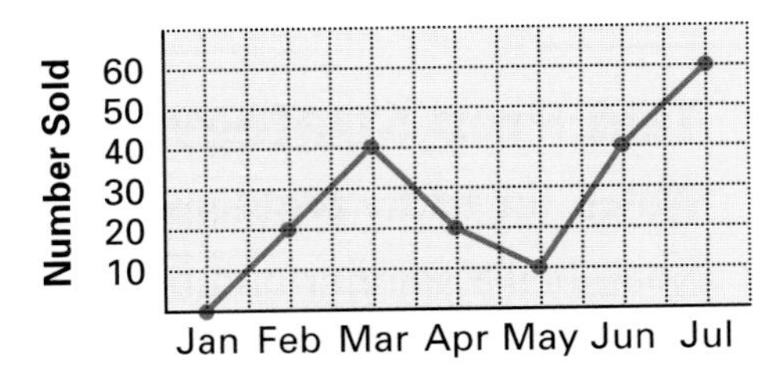

1. In which month did the sales of hot dogs increase the most when compared to the month before?
2. In how many months were the sales greater than 30?
3. A pictograph's key shows that a symbol equals 10 bicycles. How many symbols would be needed to represent 115 bicycles?

Set 2 For use after page 17.

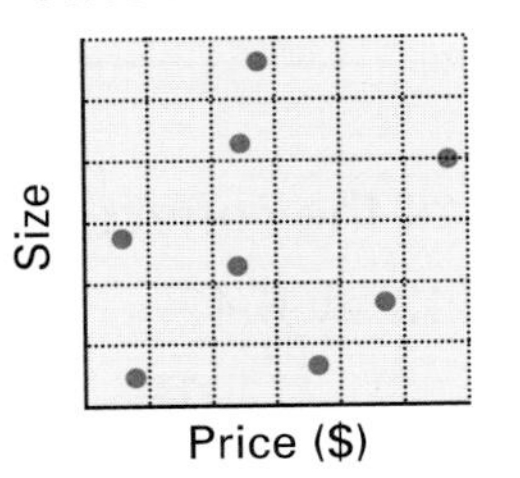

1. Does the scatterplot show a trend? Explain.
2. Describe a scatterplot that shows a trend.

Set 3 For use after page 25.

Use the Science Test Scores data for **1** and **2.**

Science Test Scores						
86	72	98	79	84	63	72
98	92	75	81	76	93	94
86	89	72	88	64	77	

1. Use tallies to make a frequency chart of test scores in these groups: under 70; 70–79; 80–89; 90–99.
2. Use the test score data to make a line plot.

Set 4 For use after page 29.

1. Make a bar graph using the number of Supreme Court justices appointed by these presidents: Clinton, 2; Bush, 2; Reagan, 3; Carter, 0; Ford, 1; and Nixon, 4.

Set 5 For use after page 33.

1. Make a stem-and-leaf diagram for the following data: 43, 41, 56, 37, 42, 48, 45, 43, 51, 54, 39, 44, 42, 47, 42, 40.

Set 6 For use after page 43.

1. Find the median, mode, and mean for these stolen-base records: Henderson, 1,117; Brock, 938; Cobb, 892; Raines: 777; Collins, 742; Carey, 738; Wagner, 703; Morgan, 689; Wilson, 661; and Campaneris, 649.
2. For any data set, which of the three measures (mean, median, or mode) is most likely to be affected by an outlier? Explain.

Set 1 For use after page 65.

1. Give the place value of 4 in 2,549,013.
2. Write 81,294,537 in word form.

Set 2 For use after page 73.

1. Round 81,294,537 to the given place:
   a. Thousands b. Millions
2. Use $>$ or $<$ and compare 593,293 and 593,392.
3. Order from least to greatest: 3,192,536; 31,925,006; 3,492,426.

Set 3 For use after page 77.

1. Give the base and exponent of 13^6. 2. Write 6^5 in expanded form.
3. Write 3 squared in exponential notation.
4. Write each in standard form:
   a. 7^2 b. 8 cubed c. 12^1 d. 5 to the fourth power

Set 4 For use after page 95.

Use mental math to solve each problem.

1. $170 + 30 + 64 + 36$ 2. 8×303 3. 40×700 4. $54{,}000 \div 60$

Use estimation to solve each problem.

5. $592 - 128$ 6. $4{,}518 + 3{,}179$ 7. 47×712 8. $152 \times 9 \times 12$

Use the order of operations to solve each problem.

9. $7 \times 8 \div 2 + 3$ 10. $(11 - 5)^2 \div 3 \times 7$

Set 5 For use after page 113.

Write the problem as an expression.

1. Jared went on a weekend hiking trip. He hiked 5 miles on Friday and 12 miles on Saturday. He hiked x miles on Sunday to return to the base camp. How many miles did Jared hike over the weekend?

Set 6 For use after page 121.

1. State whether each phrase describes a constant or a variable.
   a. The number of quarters in a dollar
   b. The number of quarters in your pocket

Evaluate each expression for $x = 3$, 5, and 7.

2. $3x$ 3. $x + 9$
4. Is the equation $24 - x = 15$ true for $x = 9$? For $x = 11$?
5. Solve for x: a. $x + 6 = 27$ b. $\frac{x}{3} = 6$

Set 1 For use after page 145.

1. Show each in decimal form.
   a. 41 thousandths
   b. 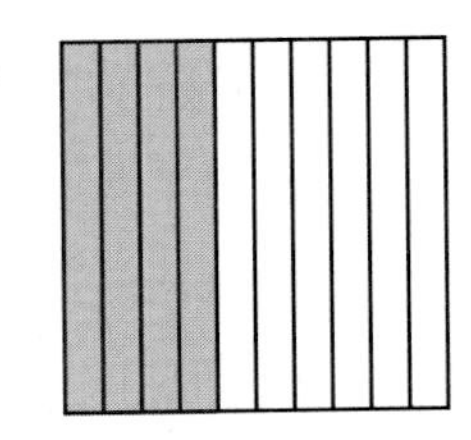
2. Round 0.6927 to the thousandths place.
3. Round 14.3015 to the hundredths place.
4. Round 6.3197 to the thousandths place.

Set 2 For use after page 155.

Compare. Write $<$, $>$, or $=$.

1. $1.057 \bigcirc 1.507$
2. $61.250 \bigcirc 61.25$
3. $52.175 \bigcirc 52.21$
4. Use the $<$ symbol to order the decimals from greatest to least: 4.018; 4.197; and 4.0182.
5. The state of New York has a population of about 17,990,000. Write this number in scientific notation.

Set 3 For use after page 171.

For **1** and **2**, write and solve an equation.

1. Kara bought this shirt with a \$20 bill. How much change did she receive?
2. Seth is 61.2 in. tall. His sister is 7.9 in. shorter. How tall is Seth's sister?

Set 4 For use after page 193.

Estimate.

1. $29.21 + 72.4$
2. $451.8 - 93.507$
3. 15.9×6
4. $46.4 \div 15$

Simplify.

5. $8.4 + 421.93$
6. $11.03 - 2.287$
7. 7.3×4.1
8. $10.8 \div 2.7$
9. 3.68×0.01
10. $4.91 \times 10{,}000$
11. $83 \div 100$
12. $638 \div 0.001$
13. The star Arcturus is about 10.3 light-years from Earth. The star Vega is about 7.5 light-years from Earth. How many more light-years away from Earth is Arcturus?

Set 5 For use after page 197.

Solve.

1. $h - 7.2 = 12.3$
2. $x + 6 = 19.3$
3. $0.5k = 0.35$
4. $\frac{n}{0.9} = 5$
5. $r + 2.6 = 15.1$
6. $m - 0.7 = 3.6$
7. $8t = 2.4$
8. $\frac{h}{4} = 3.2$

Skills Practice Bank Chapter 4

Set 1 For use after page 213.

Find the perimeter of each figure.

1. 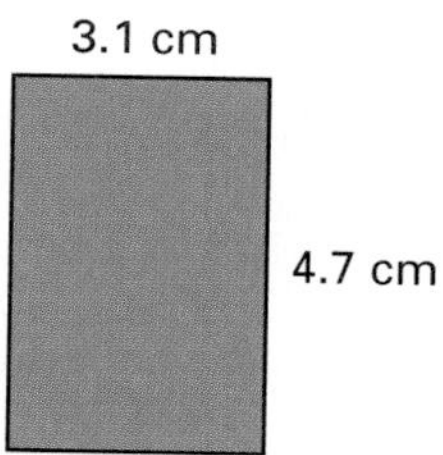

2. 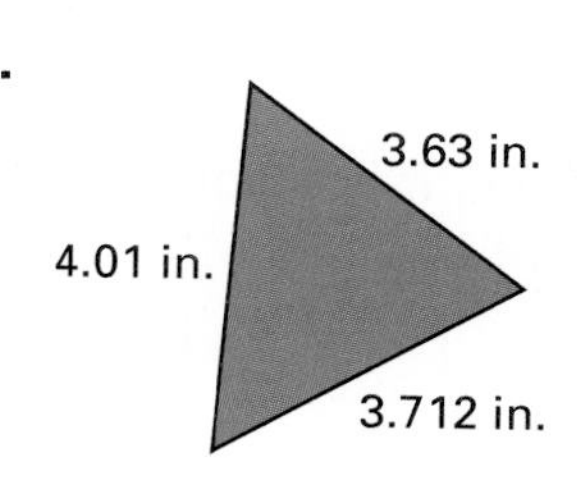

3. 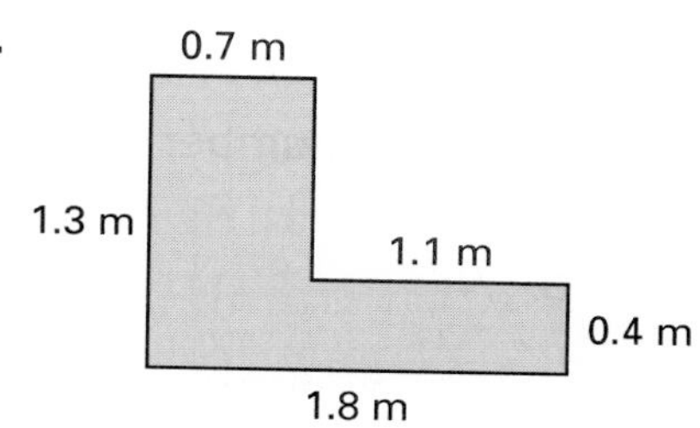

Set 2 For use after page 221.

Use powers of 10 or conversion factors to find each measure.

1. 174 g = ■ kg
2. 60 in. = ■ ft
3. 6.5 lb = ■ oz
4. 5 gal = ■ qt
5. 24.913 km = ■ m
6. 2.8 kg = ■ g

Set 3 For use after page 233.

Find the area of each figure.

1. 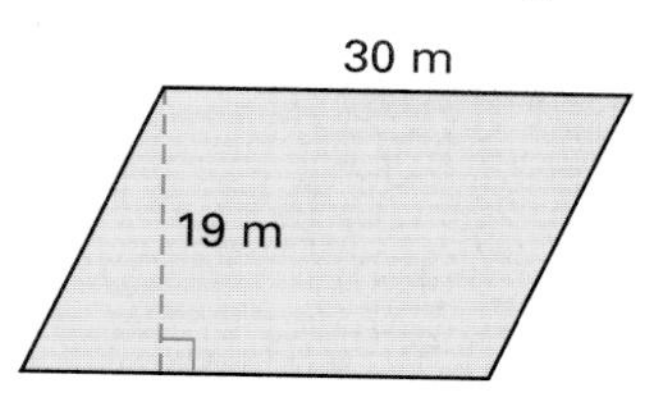

2. 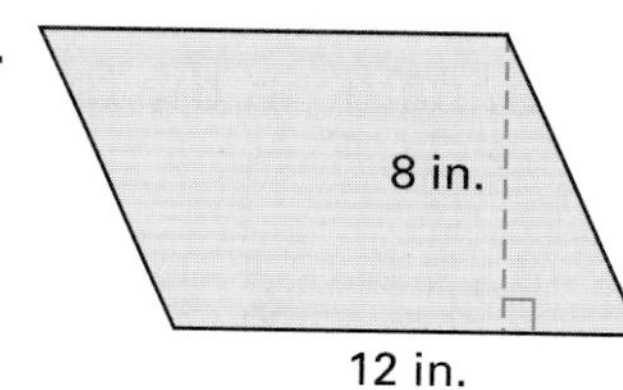

3. 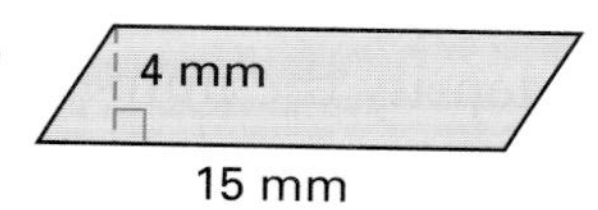

Set 4 For use after page 237.

Find the area of each triangle.

1. 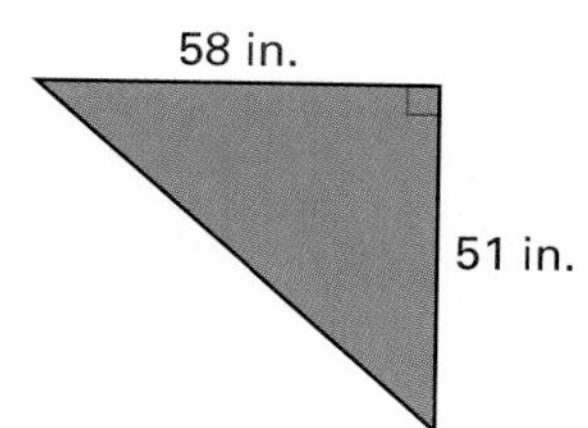

2. 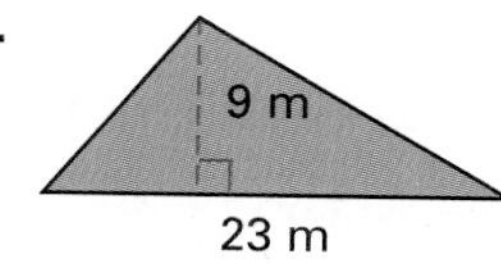

3. 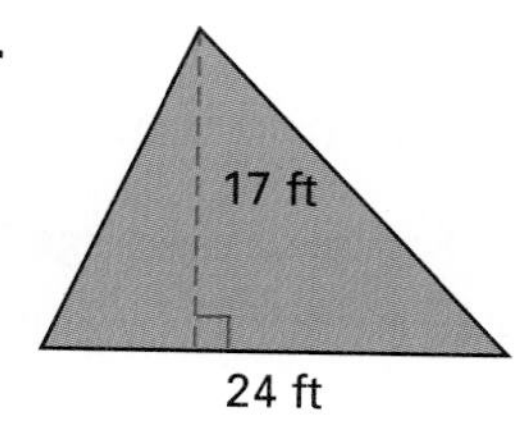

Set 5 For use after page 251.

1. The diameter of a circle is 12 mm.
   a. Find the circumference. Use 3.14 for π.
   b. Find its area.

Set 6 For use after page 255.

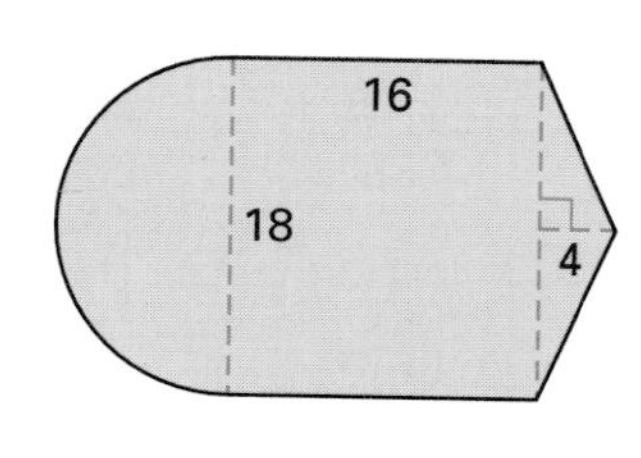

1. Find the area of the irregular shape.
2. Describe how you found the area of the shape.

SKILLS PRACTICE BANK

Set 1 For use after page 273.

Test each number for divisibility by 2, 3, 5, 6, 9, and 10.

1. 104
2. 660
3. 450
4. 1,200

Label each number as prime or composite. If it is composite, find its prime factorization.

5. 76
6. 101
7. 243
8. 85

Set 2 For use after page 277.

Find the least common multiple for each number pair.

1. 14, 24
2. 21, 35
3. 15, 25
4. 36, 18

Set 3 For use after page 289.

What fraction does the shaded part of each model represent?

1. 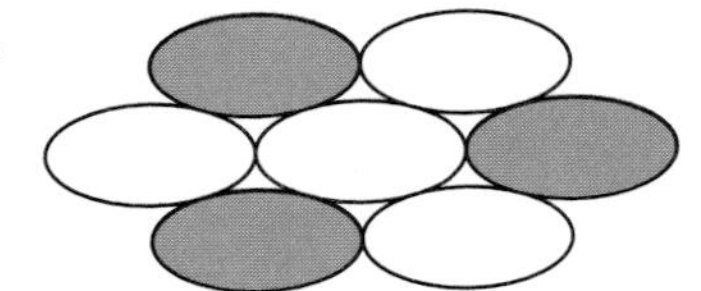

2. 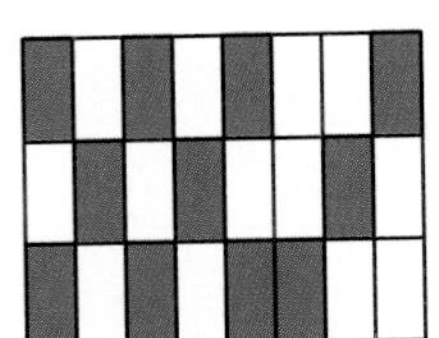

3. Identify the numerator and denominator in the fraction $\frac{7}{12}$.

Write each fraction in the lowest terms.

4. $\frac{45}{60}$
5. $\frac{48}{128}$
6. $\frac{18}{63}$
7. $\frac{420}{480}$

Set 4 For use after page 293.

Rewrite each as a mixed number or as an improper fraction.

1. $\frac{43}{5}$
2. $3\frac{5}{6}$
3. $\frac{25}{4}$
4. $7\frac{2}{7}$
5. Draw a model of the fraction $\frac{3}{5}$ and name an equivalent fraction.

Set 5 For use after page 299.

Rewrite each fraction as a decimal.

1. $\frac{7}{8}$
2. $\frac{1}{6}$
3. $\frac{13}{4}$
4. $\frac{14}{5}$

Set 6 For use after page 305.

1. Four drawings have heights of $6\frac{1}{3}$ in., $\frac{15}{2}$ in., $7\frac{3}{4}$ in., and $\frac{15}{4}$ in. List their heights in order from the shortest to the tallest.

Set 1 For use after page 323.

1. Write the equation this model represents.

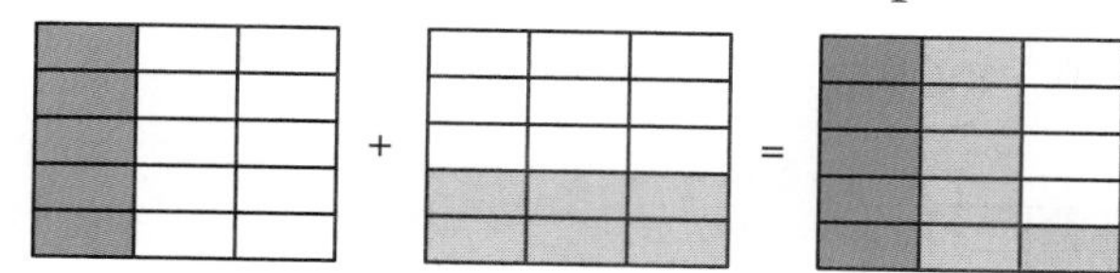

Add or subtract. Write each answer in lowest terms.

2. $\frac{8}{9} - \frac{5}{9}$
3. $\frac{3}{8} + \frac{9}{8}$
4. $\frac{2}{11} + \frac{7}{11}$
5. $\frac{7}{16} - \frac{1}{4}$
6. $\frac{7}{8} + \frac{1}{3}$
7. $\frac{7}{9} + \frac{3}{4}$
8. $\frac{6}{7} - \frac{4}{5}$
9. $\frac{3}{4} - \frac{3}{5}$

Set 2 For use after page 331.

Solve each equation.

1. $\frac{4}{15} + y = \frac{13}{15}$
2. $x - \frac{3}{10} = \frac{1}{5}$
3. $t + \frac{1}{4} = \frac{7}{8}$

Set 3 For use after page 339.

Round each mixed number to the nearest whole number.

1. $7\frac{4}{5}$
2. $12\frac{1}{2}$
3. $23\frac{9}{19}$
4. $\frac{6}{11}$

Estimate each sum or difference.

5. $6\frac{3}{4} + 3\frac{1}{8}$
6. $11\frac{1}{5} - 5\frac{2}{7}$
7. $4\frac{7}{15} + 1\frac{2}{5}$
8. $8\frac{4}{5} - 2\frac{5}{11}$

Set 4 For use after page 343.

Simplify.

1. $2\frac{3}{4} + 5\frac{1}{4}$
2. $7\frac{1}{8} + 4\frac{1}{3}$
3. $8\frac{2}{5} + 7$
4. $2\frac{7}{8} + 5\frac{1}{9}$
5. $3\frac{3}{8} + 2\frac{1}{4}$
6. $4\frac{8}{9} + 5\frac{2}{5}$
7. $3 + 3\frac{4}{5}$
8. $2\frac{7}{9} + 3\frac{1}{9}$

Set 5 For use after page 347.

Simplify.

1. $7\frac{3}{5} - 2\frac{1}{5}$
2. $6\frac{5}{7} - 4\frac{1}{4}$
3. $10\frac{7}{9} - 3\frac{2}{9}$
4. $5\frac{11}{16} - 4\frac{3}{16}$
5. $7\frac{4}{15} - 5\frac{1}{9}$
6. $3\frac{2}{3} - 1\frac{1}{4}$
7. $6\frac{4}{5} - 2\frac{1}{3}$
8. $19 - 4\frac{7}{12}$

Set 1 For use after page 363.

Estimate.

1. $3\frac{1}{2} \times 7\frac{1}{8}$
2. $15\frac{5}{7} \div 3\frac{3}{4}$
3. $28\frac{1}{8} \times 6\frac{1}{3}$
4. $2\frac{3}{8} \div 1\frac{1}{4}$

Set 2 For use after page 371.

1. Write the multiplication problem the model represents.

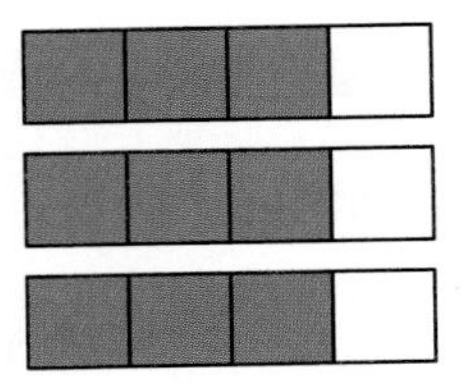

Simplify.

2. $\frac{2}{5} \times 6$
3. $\frac{3}{7} \times \frac{3}{8}$
4. $\frac{1}{6} \times \frac{5}{6}$
5. $4\frac{3}{5} \times \frac{8}{13}$
6. Is the product of two mixed numbers always greater than either number? Explain.

Set 3 For use after page 379.

Simplify.

1. $4 \div \frac{5}{8}$
2. $2 \div \frac{1}{2}$
3. $5 \div \frac{2}{5}$
4. $1 \div \frac{1}{8}$
5. $8 \div 2\frac{1}{4}$
6. $3 \div 1\frac{1}{3}$
7. $6 \div \frac{7}{9}$
8. $7 \div \frac{5}{8}$

Set 4 For use after page 383.

1. Write the equation that the model represents.

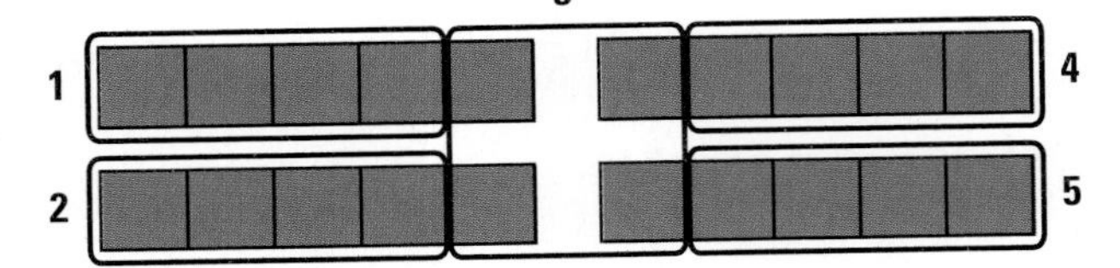

Simplify.

2. $4\frac{1}{2} \div \frac{3}{4}$
3. $\frac{1}{3} \div \frac{6}{5}$
4. $\frac{1}{4} \div \frac{3}{8}$
5. $\frac{3}{12} \div 2\frac{1}{2}$

Set 5 For use after page 391.

Solve.

1. $\frac{2}{3}x = \frac{5}{6}$
2. $\frac{3}{4}t = \frac{15}{20}$
3. $\frac{4}{5}j = \frac{8}{35}$
4. $\frac{3}{10}h = \frac{21}{80}$
5. $\frac{1}{7}t = \frac{3}{35}$
6. $\frac{1}{8}n = \frac{3}{4}$
7. $\frac{2}{5}y = \frac{3}{10}$
8. $\frac{7}{8}a = \frac{1}{2}$

Set 1 For use after page 409.

1. Draw and label a segment with end points C and D.

2. Draw and label an acute angle through points A, B, and C with B as the vertex.

Set 2 For use after page 423.

1. Classify the triangle whose angles measure 73°, 24°, and 83°.

2. What kind of triangle has two sides with length 4 cm and one side with length 5 cm?

Set 3 For use after page 431.

1. Which quadrilaterals have two pairs of parallel sides?

2. Explain why all squares are rectangles, but not all rectangles are squares.

Set 4 For use after page 441.

1. Tell if the picture has line symmetry. If it does, tell how many lines of symmetry.

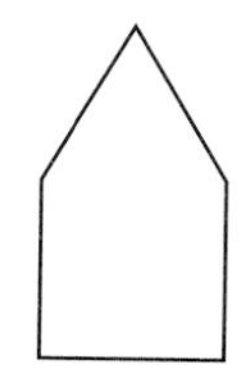

2. Tell if the line is a line of symmetry.

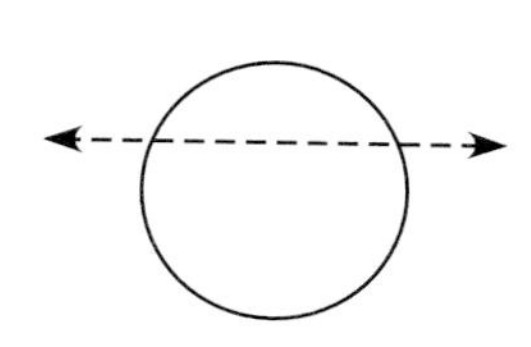

Set 5 For use after page 449.

Tell whether each transformation is a reflection, translation or rotation.

1.

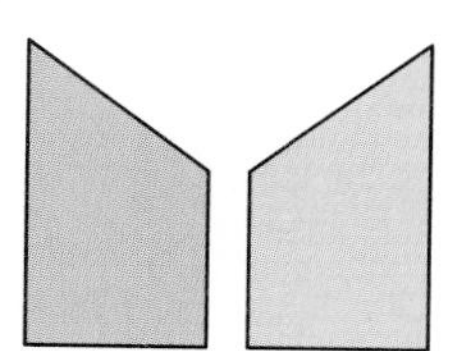

2.

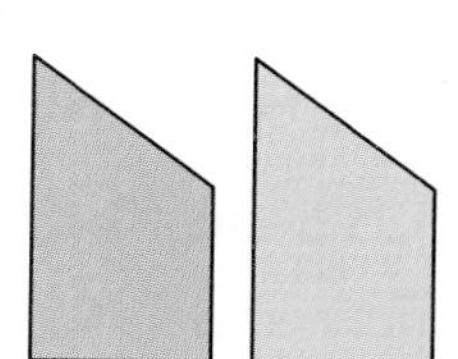

3.

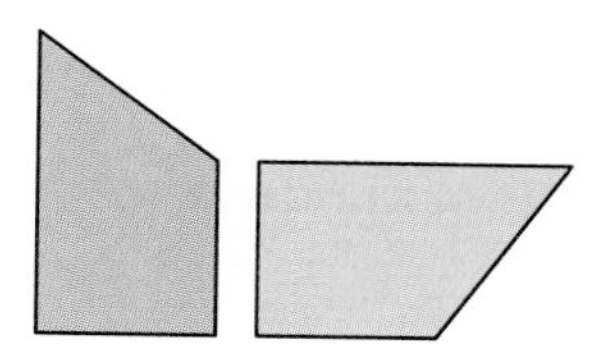

4. Trace the figure and draw its reflection over the line.

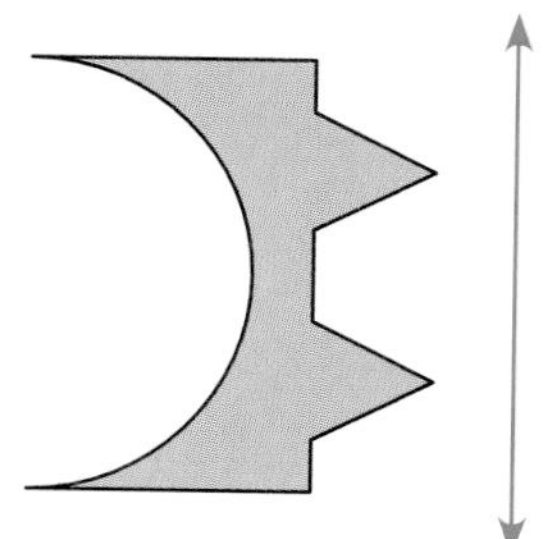

5. Give the number of degrees and the direction the figure has been rotated.

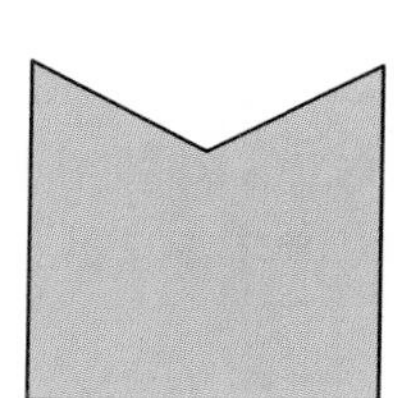

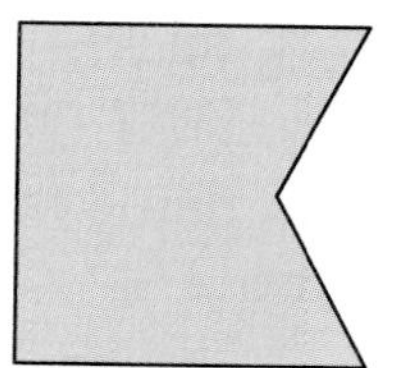

Skills Practice Bank Chapter 9

Set 1 For use after page 465.

1. Locate the integers $-3, 2, -5, 6, 1$, and -1 on a number line.

2. What is the closest integer to the right of $-5\frac{2}{3}$ on a number line?

Set 2 For use after page 473.

Write the equation that is shown by each model.

1.

2.

Move left 7

$-5 \quad -4 \quad -3 \quad -2 \quad -1 \quad 0 \quad 1 \quad 2$

Simplify.

3. $-3 + (-9)$

4. $2 + (-6)$

5. $-4 + 11$

6. $-6 - (-1)$

Set 3 For use after page 477.

Simplify.

1. $-7 \times (-7)$

2. $8 \times (-5)$

3. $-4 \times (-9)$

4. -7×3

5. $-24 \div 4$

6. $-45 \div (-9)$

Set 4 For use after page 487.

1. Name the ordered pair for the point 2 units to the right of the origin and 7 units down.

2. Name the quadrant where the point $(-1, -4)$ is located.

3. Name a point the same distance from the origin as $(0, 3)$ and located:

   a. On the x-axis

   b. On the y-axis

Set 5 For use after page 493.

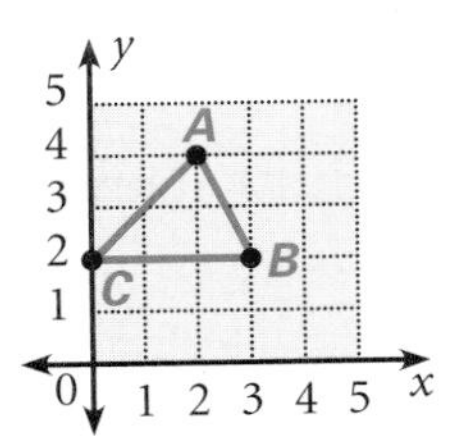

1. Create $A'B'C'$ by translating the triangle ABC 3 units to the left and 2 units down. Give the coordinates of A', B', and C'.

2. Rectangle $QRST$ has coordinates $Q(-5, 1)$, $R(-5, 3)$, $S(-1, 3)$, and $T(-1, 1)$. If $QRST$ is reflected on the y-axis, name the coordinates of Q', R', S', and T'.

Set 6 For use after page 497.

1. Graph the equations $y = x - 2$ and $y = x + 3$ on the same coordinate grid.

2. Explain why one of the graphs is a translation of the other.

Set 1 For use after page 517.

1. Show three ways to write the ratio of four lemons to seven limes.
2. Write the ratio $\frac{35}{60}$ in lowest terms.
3. Each bag contains 8 red marbles and 11 blue marbles. If there are 4 bags, what is the ratio in the lowest terms:

   a. Of red marbles to blue marbles? b. Of blue marbles to red marbles?
4. Which of the following ratios is **not** equal to the ratio 8 to 24?

   Ⓐ $\frac{5}{15}$ Ⓑ $\frac{30}{10}$ Ⓒ 7:21 Ⓓ $\frac{1}{3}$

Set 2 For use after page 521.

1. Which of the following is not a rate?

   Ⓐ $\frac{5 \text{ ft}}{4 \text{ sec}}$ Ⓑ $\frac{4 \text{ ft}}{1 \text{ sec}}$ Ⓒ $\frac{4 \text{ sec}}{5 \text{ ft}}$ Ⓓ $\frac{4 \text{ sec}}{5 \text{ sec}}$
2. Use a table to find four equal rates that describe boiling 2 gallons of water in 4 minutes.
3. What is the unit rate of a car's travel time if the car travels 240 miles in 5 hours?

Set 3 For use after page 537.

1. Can the ratio 5 mi/8 s and 35 s/56 mi form a proportion? Explain.
2. Apples cost $1.20 per pound. How much do 40 oz of apples cost?

Set 4 For use after page 543.

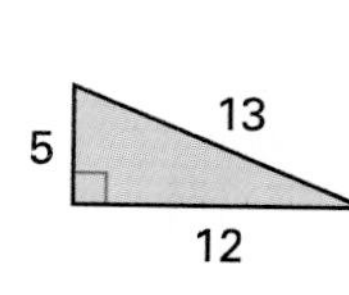

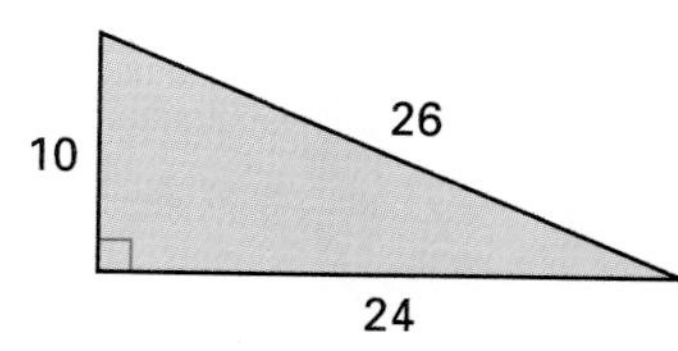

1. Explain why the two triangles are similar.

Set 5 For use after page 555.

Estimate the percent.

1. 6 out of 61
2. 203 out of 611
3. $\frac{51}{254}$
4. $\frac{4}{411}$
5. In 1980, the population of the metropolitan area of Naples, Florida was 85,971. By 1990, it had increased by 66,128. About what percent was the increase?

Set 6 For use after page 563.

Write each percent as a ratio of a number to 100, as a fraction in lowest terms, and as a decimal.

1. 60%
2. 12%
3. 45%
4. 52%

Set 1 For use after page 581.

Classify each solid. If it is a polyhedron, state the number of faces, edges and vertices.

1. 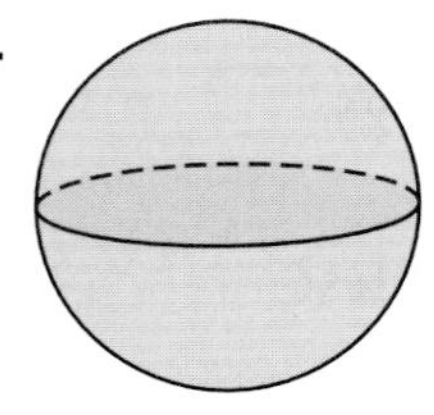

2. 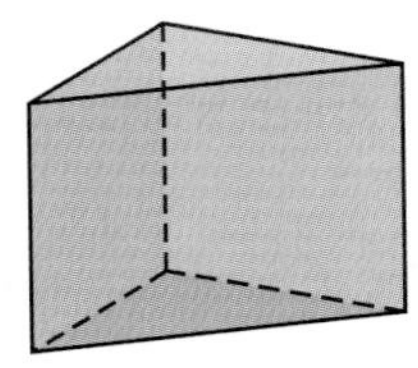

3. 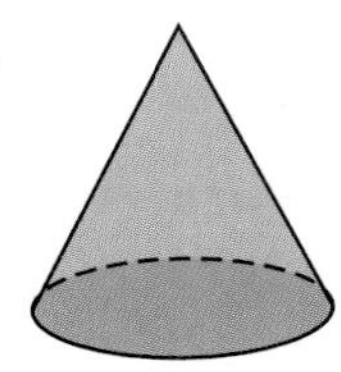

Set 2 For use after page 593.

Find the surface area of each figure. Use 3.14 for π.

1. 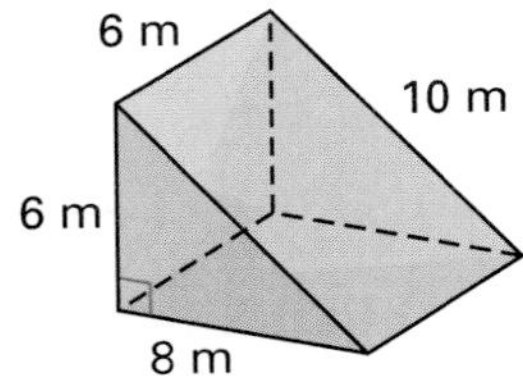

2. 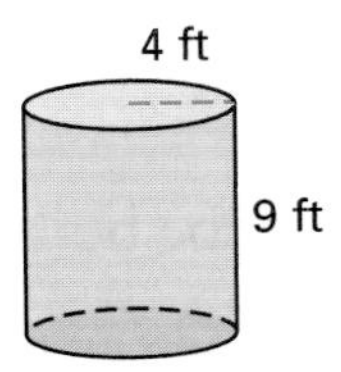

3. 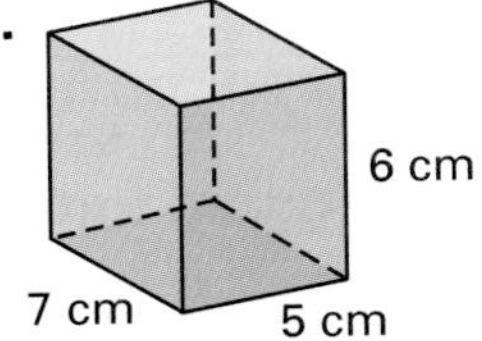

Set 3 For use after page 601.

For each solid, draw the front view, the side view, and the top view.

1. 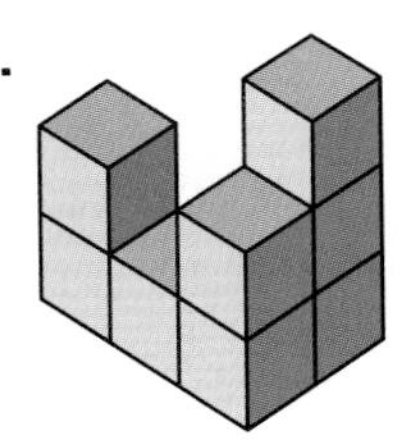

2. 

3. 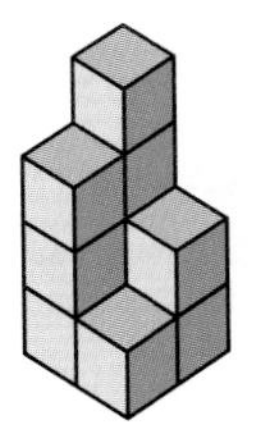

Set 4 For use after page 609.

Find each volume.

1. 

2. 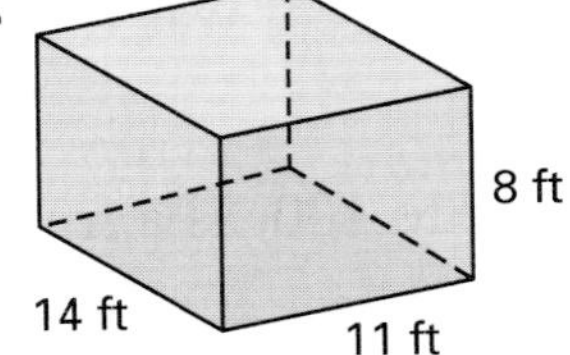

3. 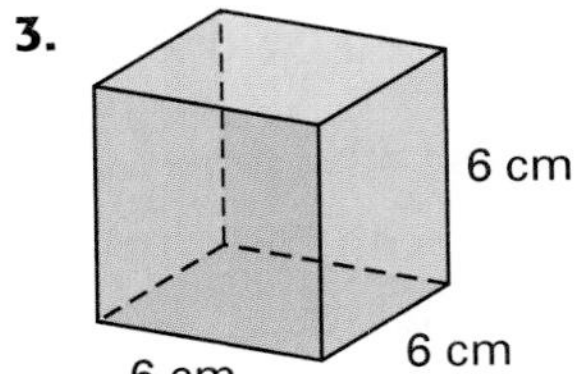

Set 1 For use after page 625.

1. In a classroom, students' desks are arranged in rows and columns that form a rectangle. There are 7 desks in each row and 7 desks in each column. The last column of desks is next to a wall of windows. What is the probability of sitting at a desk next to the windows?

Set 2 For use after page 629.

1. Estimate the probability of choosing a person at random whose birthday falls on a Monday next year.

2. If P (event) $= \frac{2}{3}$, what is the probability that the event will **not** occur?

Set 3 For use after page 637.

1. A spinner has 6 equal sections labeled A, B, C, D, E, and F.
   a. What is the probability of landing in the B section?
   b. What is the probability of **not** landing in the B section?

Set 4 For use after page 643.

1. Complete a tree diagram that shows how many different lunches can be made if there are 4 kinds of sandwiches (tuna, peanut butter, turkey and cheese); 2 kinds of snacks (chips and fruit); and 3 kinds of drinks (milk, juice, and soda).

Set 5 For use after page 647.

1. Use multiplication to find the possible number of stereo systems that could be assembled using one each of 3 tuners, 5 compact disc players, 4 cassette players, and 3 amplifiers.

2. If you spin both of the spinners, how many possible outcomes are there?

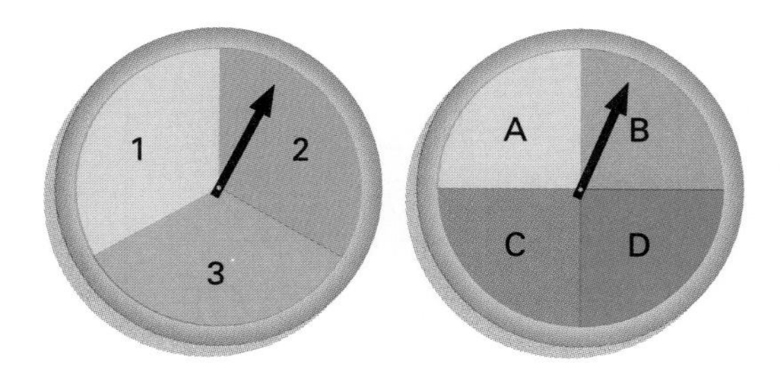

3. What is the probability of spinning A or B on Spinner 1 and an odd number on Spinner 2?

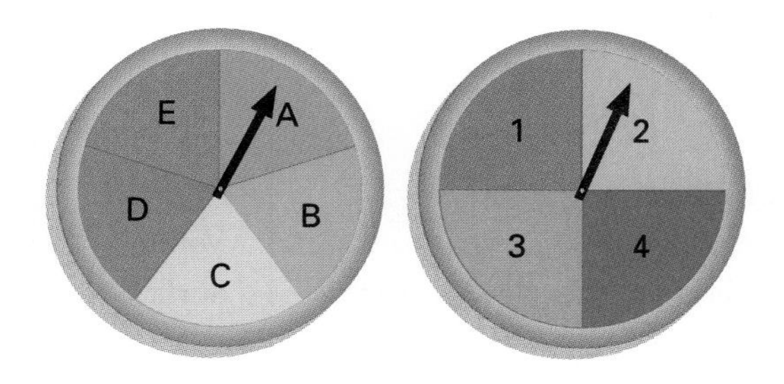

Set 6 For use after page 653.

1. Player A and Player B each roll a number cube numbered 1–6. If the sum of the two numbers is greater than 5, Player A wins. Otherwise, Player B wins. Is the game fair? Explain.

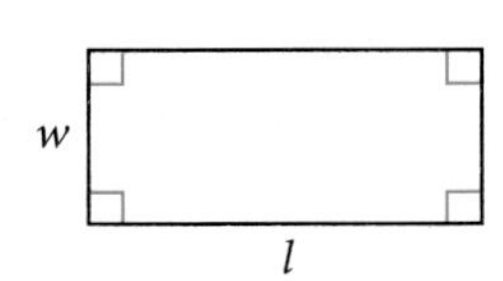

Rectangle
Area: $A = lw$
Perimeter: $p = 2l + 2w$

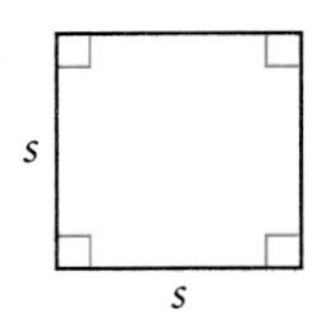

Square
Area: $A = s^2$
Perimeter: $p = 4s$

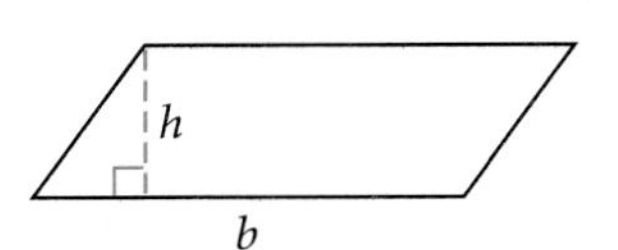

Parallelogram
Area: $A = bh$

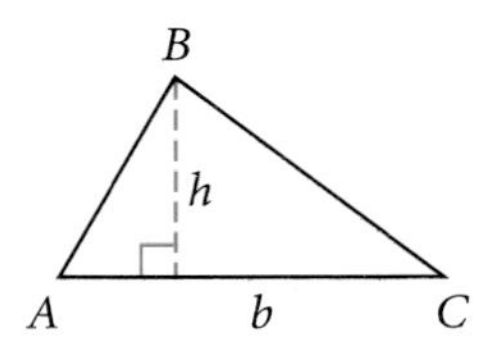

Triangle
Area: $A = \frac{1}{2}bh$
$m\angle A + m\angle B + m\angle C = 180°$

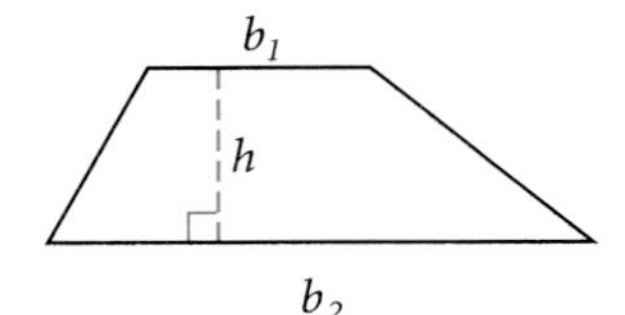

Trapezoid
Area: $A = \frac{1}{2}h(b_1 + b_2)$

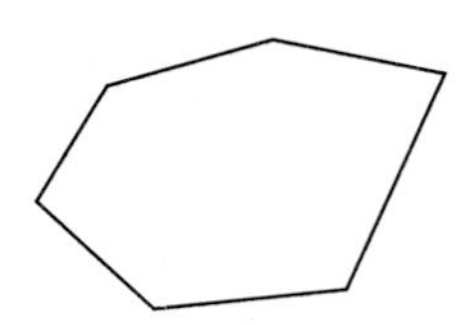

Polygon
Sum of angle measures for n-sided polygon: $S = (n - 2)180°$
Perimeter: sum of measures of all sides

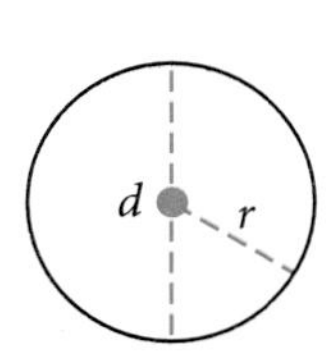

Circle
Area: $A = \pi r^2$
Circumference: $C = \pi d = 2\pi r$

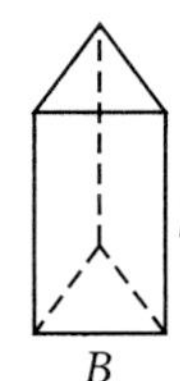

Prism
Volume: $V = Bh$
Surface Area: $SA = ph + 2B$

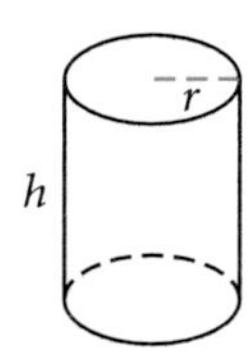

Cylinder
Volume: $V = \pi r^2 h$
Surface Area: $SA = 2\pi rh + 2\pi r^2$

Measurement Conversion Factors

Metric Units of Measure

Length

1,000 meters (m) = 1 kilometer (km)
100 centimeters (cm) = 1 m
10 decimeters (dm) = 1 m
1,000 millimeters (mm) = 1 m
10 cm = 1 decimeter (dm)
10 mm = 1 cm

Area

100 square millimeters (mm^2) = 1 square centimeter (cm^2)
10,000 cm^2 = 1 square meter (m^2)
10,000 m^2 = 1 hectare (ha)

Volume

1,000 cubic millimeters (mm^3) = 1 cubic centimeter (cm^3)
1,000 cm^3 = 1 cubic decimeter (dm^3)
1,000,000 cm^3 = 1 cubic meter (m^3)

Capacity

1,000 milliliters (mL) = 1 liter (L)
1,000 L = 1 kiloliter (kL)

Mass

1,000 kilograms (kg) = 1 metric ton (t)
1,000 grams (g) = 1 kg
1,000 milligrams (mg) = 1 g

Temperature in Degrees Celsius (°C)

0°C = freezing point of water
37°C = normal body temperature
100°C = boiling point of water

Customary Units of Measure

Length

12 inches (in.) = 1 foot (ft)
3 ft = 1 yard (yd)
36 in. = 1 yd
5,280 ft = 1 mile (mi)
1,760 yd = 1 mi
6,076 ft = 1 nautical mile

Area

144 square inches (in^2) = 1 square foot (ft^2)
9 ft^2 = 1 square yard (yd^2)
43,560 sq ft^2 = 1 acre (A)

Volume

1,728 cubic inches (cu in.) = 1 cubic foot (cu ft)
27 cu ft = 1 cubic yard (cu yard)

Capacity

8 fluid ounces (fl oz) = 1 cup (c)
2 c = 1 pint (pt)
2 pt = 1 quart (qt)
4 qt = 1 gallon (gal)

Weight

16 ounces (oz) = 1 pound (lb)
2,000 lb = 1 ton (T)

Temperature in Degrees Fahrenheit (°F)

32°F = freezing point of water
98.6°F = normal body temperature
212°F = boiling point of water

Time

60 seconds (sec) = 1 minute (min)
60 min = 1 hour (hr)
24 hr = 1 day

Symbols

$+$	plus or positive
$-$	minus or negative
$\cdot$	times
$\times$	times
$\div$	divided by
$\pm$	positive or negative
$=$	is equal to
$\neq$	is not equal to
$<$	is less than
$>$	is greater than
$\leq$	is less than or equal to
$\geq$	is greater than or equal to
$\approx$	is approximately equal to
%	percent
$a{:}b$	the ratio of a to b, or $\frac{a}{b}$
$\cong$	is congruent to
$\sim$	is similar to
$^\circ$	degree(s)
$\overleftrightarrow{AB}$	line containing points A and B
$\overline{AB}$	line segment with endpoints A and B
$\overrightarrow{AB}$	ray with endpoint A and containing B
∟	right angle
$\perp$	is perpendicular to
$\parallel$	is parallel to
AB	length of $\overline{AB}$; distance between A and B
$\triangle ABC$	triangle with vertices A, B, and C
$\angle ABC$	angle with sides $\overrightarrow{BA}$ and $\overrightarrow{BC}$
$\angle B$	angle with vertex B
$m\angle ABC$	measure of angle ABC
$'$	prime
a^n	the nth power of a
$\lvert x \rvert$	absolute value of x
$\sqrt{x}$	principal square root of x
π	pi (approximately 3.1416)
(a, b)	ordered pair with x-coordinate a and y-coordinate b
$P(\text{A})$	the probability of event A
$n!$	n factorial

TABLES

Glossary

acute angle An angle smaller than a right angle. (p. 406)

acute triangle A triangle with three acute angles. (p. 417)

addend A number added to one or more others.

addition An operation that gives the total number when two or more numbers are put together.

algebra A branch of mathematics in which arithmetic relations are explored using letter symbols to represent numbers.

algebraic expression An expression that contains at least one variable. *Example:* $n - 7$.

angle Two rays with the same endpoint. (p. 406)

area The amount of surface a figure covers. (p. 227)

Associative Property The fact that changing the grouping of addends or factors does not change the sum or product. *Example:* $(5 + 3) + 7 = 15$ and $5 + (3 + 7) = 15$. (p. 81)

average See *mean.*

axes See *x-axis* and *y-axis.*

bar graph A graph using vertical or horizontal bars to display numerical information. (p. 7)

base [of an exponent] A number multiplied by itself the number of times shown by an exponent. *Example:* $6^2 = 6 \times 6$, where 6 is the base. (p. 74); **[of a figure]** On a two-dimensional figure, the distance across the bottom. (p. 227) On a prism, one of the two parallel and congruent faces. (p. 578)

binary number system A base-2 place-value system.

bisect Dividing a geometric figure into two equal parts. (p. 456)

box-and-whisker plot A graph showing the shape of a data set. (p. 56)

capacity The volume of a figure, given in terms of liquid measure.

center The point at the exact middle of a circle.

centi- A prefix meaning $\frac{1}{100}$. (p. 214)

circle See examples below. (p. 244)

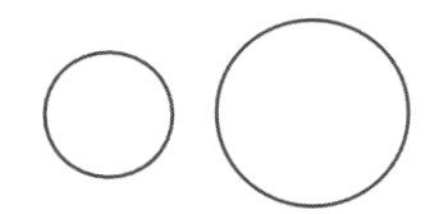

circle graph A round graph that uses different-sized wedges to show how portions of a set of data compare with the whole set. (p. 8)

circumference The perimeter of a circle. (p. 245)

clockwise The direction of rotation when the top of a figure turns to the right. (p. 443)

clustering An estimation method where numbers that are approximately equal are treated as if they were equal. *Example:* $26 + 24 + 23$ is about $25 + 25 + 25$, or 3×25. (p. 84)

common denominator A denominator that is the same in two fractions. (p. 302)

common factor A number that is a factor of two different numbers. *Example:* 4 is a common factor of 8 and 12. (p. 286)

common multiple A number that is a multiple of each of two given numbers. *Example:* 44 is a common multiple of 2 and 11. (p. 274)

Commutative Property The fact that changing the order of addends or factors does not change the sum or product. *Example:* $4 \times 7 = 28$ and $7 \times 4 = 28$. (p. 80)

compatible numbers Pairs of numbers that can be computed easily. *Example:* $30 + 70$. (p. 80)

compensation Choosing numbers close to the numbers in a problem, and then adjusting the answer to compensate for the numbers chosen. (p. 81)

complementary angles Two angles whose measures add up to 90°. (p. 411)

composite number A whole number greater than 1 that is not prime. (p. 271)

compound event A combination of two or more single events. *Example:* getting heads on a coin toss and then rolling 4 with a number cube. (p. 645)

cone See example below. (p. 579)

congruent Having the same size and shape. (p. 439)

constant A quantity that does not change. (p. 106)

conversion factor The number of measurement units that another unit is equal to. *Example:* To convert inches to feet, divide by the conversion factor 12 (12 inches = 1 foot). (p. 219)

coordinate One of the numbers in an ordered pair. (p. 484)

coordinate plane A set of lines used to locate points in a plane. (p. 484)

counterclockwise The direction of rotation when the top of a figure turns to the left. (p. 443)

cross product For two ratios, the product of the top value from one and the bottom value from the other. (p. 527)

cube A prism whose faces are all squares of the same size. (p. 578)

cubed Raised to the power of 3. *Example:* 2 cubed $= 2^3 = 8$. (p. 75)

cubic unit A unit measuring volume, consisting of a cube with edges one unit long. (p. 602)

customary system (of measurement) The measurement system often used in the United States, using inches, feet, miles, ounces, pounds, quarts, gallons, etc. (p. 218)

cylinder See example below. (p. 579)

deci- A prefix meaning $\frac{1}{10}$. *Example:* 1 decimeter = 0.1 meter. (p. 215)

decimal system A base-10 place-value system.

degree A unit of angle measure, $\frac{1}{360}$ of a complete circle. (p. 410)

deka- A prefix meaning 10. *Example:* 1 dekameter = 10 meters. (p. 215)

denominator The bottom number in a fraction, telling how many parts the whole is divided into. (p. 282)

diameter A line connecting two points on a circle and passing through the circle's center. (p. 245)

difference The result of subtracting one number from another. (p. 110)

digit The symbols used to write the numerals 0, 1, 2, 3, 4, 5, 6, 7, 8, and 9.

Distributive Property The fact that numbers can be broken into lesser numbers for calculating. *Example:* $(32 \times 5) = (30 + 2) \times 5 = (30 \times 5) + (2 \times 5) = 160$. (p. 81)

dividend A number being divided by another number. *Example:* In $5 \div 3$, 5 is the dividend. (p. 186)

divisible Can be divided by another number without leaving a remainder. *Example:* 18 is divisible by 6. (p. 266)

division An operation that tells how many equal sets or how many in each equal set.

divisor A number that another number is being divided by. *Example:* In $4 \div 9$, 9 is the divisor. (p. 186)

edge The line where two faces of a solid come together. (p. 578)

endpoint A point at the end of a segment or ray. (p. 402)

equality A mathematical relation of being exactly the same.

equation A mathematical sentence stating that two expressions are equal. *Example:* $14 = 2x$. (p. 114)

equilateral triangle A triangle with three sides of the same length. (p. 421)

equivalent fractions Two fractions naming the same amount. (p. 283)

estimate An approximation for the result of a calculation.

Euler's formula A formula about edges, faces, and vertices of polyhedrons stating: $F + V - E = 2$. (p. 616)

evaluate To find the number that an algebraic expression names.

even number A whole number that has 0, 2, 4, 6, or 8 in the ones place.

event The particular outcome one is looking at in a probability experiment. (p. 622)

expanded form A way of writing an exponential number showing all of the factors individually. *Example:* $9 \times 9 \times 9$. (p. 75)

experiment A situation that can turn out in more than one way. (p. 622)

exponent A raised number telling how many times another number, the base, is being multiplied by itself. *Example:* $9^3 = 9 \times 9 \times 9$, where 3 is the exponent and 9 is the base. (p. 74)

exponential notation A way of writing repeated multiplication of a number using exponents. *Example:* 9^3. (p. 74)

expression A mathematical phrase containing variables, constants, and operation symbols. *Example:* $12 - x$. (p. 106)

face A flat surface on a solid. (p. 578)

factor A number that divides another number without a remainder. *Example:* 6 is a factor of 42. (p. 75)

factor tree A diagram showing how a composite number breaks down into its prime factors. (p. 271)

fair game A game in which each player has the same probability of winning. (p. 650)

flip See *reflection.*

foot A unit in the customary system of measurement equal to 12 inches. (p. 218)

formula A rule showing relationships among quantities. *Example:* $A = bh$.

fraction A number describing part of a whole when the whole is cut into equal pieces. (p. 282)

frequency chart A table listing each value that appears in a data set followed by the number of times it appears. (p. 22)

front-end estimation An estimation method where only the first digit of each number is used for computation, and the result is adjusted based on the remaining digits. (p. 84)

gallon A unit in the customary system of measurement equal to 4 quarts. (p. 218)

geometry A branch of mathematics in which the relations between points, lines, figures, and solids are explored.

gram The basic unit of mass in the metric system. (p. 214)

graph A diagram that shows information in an organized way.

greatest common factor (GCF) The greatest whole number that divides two whole numbers. *Example:* 16 is the GCF of 32 and 48. (p. 287)

hecto- A prefix meaning 100. *Example:* 1 hectometer = 100 meters. (p. 215)

height The distance along a figure that is perpendicular to the base. (p. 227)

hexagon A polygon with 6 sides. (p. 424)

horizontal axis The horizontal line of the two lines on which a graph is built. (p. 26)

improper fraction A fraction whose numerator is greater than or equal to its denominator. *Example:* $\frac{22}{7}$. (p. 290)

inch A unit of length in the customary measurement system. (p. 218)

inequality A statement that two expressions are not equal. *Example:* $7 > 5$.

integers The set of positive whole numbers, their opposites, and 0: $\ldots -3, -2, -1, 0, 1, 2, 3, \ldots$. (p. 463)

intersect To cross through the same point. (p. 402)

interval The amount of space between the values on a bar graph scale. (p. 26)

irregular polygon A polygon whose sides and angles do not all have the same measure.

isosceles triangle A triangle with at least two sides of the same length. (p. 421)

kilo- A prefix meaning 1,000. (p. 214)

least common denominator (LCD) The least common multiple (LCM) of two denominators. *Example:* 30 is the LCD of $\frac{1}{6}$ and $\frac{1}{15}$. (p. 321)

least common multiple (LCM) The least number other than zero that is a multiple of two numbers. *Example:* 60 is the LCM of 10 and 12. (p. 274)

like denominators Denominators that are the same in two fractions. (p. 317)

line A one-dimensional figure that extends forever in both directions. (p. 402)

line graph A graph in which a line shows changes in data, often over time. (p. 8)

line of symmetry The imaginary "mirror" in line symmetry. (p. 439)

line plot A plot that shows the shape of a data set by stacking $\times$'s above each value on a number line. (p. 23)

line symmetry The ability of a figure to be folded into congruent halves. (p. 439)

liter The basic unit of volume in the metric system. (p. 214)

lowest terms The name for a fractional amount where the numerator and denominator have a greatest common factor of 1. (p. 286)

mass The amount of matter that something contains.

mean The sum of the values in a data set divided by the number of values. (p. 41)

median The middle value in a data set when the values are listed from lowest to highest. (p. 36)

mental math Performing calculations in your mind, without using pencil and paper or a calculator.

meter The basic unit of length in the metric system. (p. 214)

metric system (of measurement) A system of measurements used to describe how long, heavy, or big something is. (p. 214)

mile A unit in the customary system of measurement equal to 5,280 feet. (p. 218)

milli- A prefix meaning $\frac{1}{1000}$. (p. 214)

mixed number A number combining a whole number with a fraction. *Example:* $2\frac{7}{8}$. (p. 290)

mode One of the values appearing most often in a data set. (p. 36)

multiple The product of a given number and any whole number. (p. 274)

multiplication An operation that combines two numbers, called factors, to give one number, called the product.

negative numbers Numbers less than 0. (p. 462)

net A flat pattern that can be folded into a solid. (p. 579)

number line A line that shows numbers in order.

number-word form A way of writing a number using digits and words. *Example:* 45 trillion. (p. 62)

numeral A symbol for a number.

numerator The top number in a fraction, telling how many parts of the whole are being named. (p. 282)

obtuse angle An angle greater than a right angle but smaller than a straight angle. (p. 406)

obtuse triangle A triangle with an obtuse angle. (p. 417)

octagon A polygon with 8 sides. (p. 424)

odd number A whole number that has 1, 3, 5, 7, or 9 in the ones place.

operation A mathematical procedure. *Examples:* addition, subtraction, multiplication, division.

opposite The integer on the opposite side of zero from a given number, but at the same distance from zero. *Example:* 7 and -7 are opposites of each other. (p. 466)

order of operations The rules telling what order to do operations in: (1) simplify inside parentheses, (2) simplify exponents, (3) multiply and divide from left to right, and (4) add and subtract from left to right. (p. 92)

ordered pair A pair of numbers, such as $(3, -7)$, used to locate a point on a coordinate plane. (p. 484)

origin The point (0, 0), where the x- and y-axes of a coordinate plane intersect. (p. 484)

ounce A unit of weight in the customary measurement system. (p. 218)

outcome One of the ways an experiment can turn out. (p. 622)

outlier A number very different from the other numbers in a data set. (p. 46)

parallel Two lines, segments, or rays that do not cross, no matter how far they extend. (p. 402)

parallelogram A four-sided figure whose opposite sides are parallel and of the same length. (p. 230)

pentagon A polygon with 5 sides. (p. 424)

percent A ratio comparing a part to a whole using the number 100. The percent is the number of hundredths that the part is equal to. (p. 548)

perimeter The distance around the outside of a figure. (p. 210)

perpendicular Two lines are perpendicular if they cross at right angles. (p. 402)

pi (π) For any circle, the ratio of the circumference to the diameter. π equals 3.14159265. . . . (p. 245)

pictograph A graph using symbols to represent data. (p. 7)

place value The multiple of ten telling how much a digit represents. *Example:* In 374, the 7 is in the tens place. (p. 62)

polygon A closed figure made of line segments. (p. 424)

polyhedron A solid consisting entirely of flat faces. (p. 578)

positive numbers Numbers greater than 0. (p. 462)

pound A unit in the customary system of measurement equal to 16 ounces. (p. 218)

power An exponent. (p. 74)

prime factorization The set of primes whose product is a given composite. *Example:* $70 = 2 \times 5 \times 7$. (p. 271)

prime number A whole number greater than 1 with exactly two whole positive factors: 1 and itself. *Examples:* 2, 3, 5, 7, 11, ... (p. 271)

prism A polyhedron that has two congruent and parallel faces. See examples below. (p. 578)

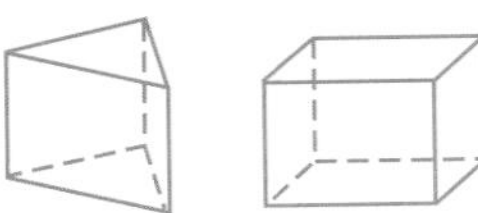

probability A ratio of the number of ways an event can happen to the total number of possible outcomes. (p. 622)

product The result of multiplying numbers. (p. 110)

proportion A pair of equal ratios. (p. 526)

protractor A tool that measures angles. (p. 410)

pyramid A solid with one base and whose other sides are all triangles. See examples below. (p. 578)

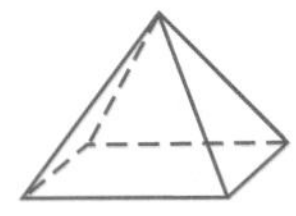

quadrants The four regions into which the two axes of a coordinate grid divide the plane. (p. 484)

quadrilateral A polygon with 4 sides. (p. 424)

quart A unit of volume in the customary measurement system. (p. 218)

quotient The result of dividing one number by another. (p. 110)

radius A line from the center of a circle to any point on the circle. (p. 245)

range The difference between the highest and lowest values in a data set. (p. 27)

rate A ratio in which two quantities with different units of measure are compared. *Example:* 18 dollars per 2 hours. (p. 518)

ratio A comparison of two quantities, often written as a fraction. (p. 510)

ray A part of a line that has one endpoint and extends forever in the other direction. (p. 402)

reciprocal A fraction whose numerator and denominator have been switched. (p. 376)

rectangle A parallelogram with opposite sides the same length and all angles measuring 90°. (p. 428)

reflection The mirror image of a figure that has been "flipped" over a line. (p. 439)

regular polygon A polygon whose sides and angles all have the same measure. (p. 424)

remainder The number less than the divisor that remains after the division process is completed.

repeating decimal A decimal number that repeats a pattern of digits continuously on the right. *Example:* 6.141414. . . . (p. 297)

rhombus A parallelogram with all sides the same length. (p. 428)

right angle An angle like the corner of an index card. It measures 90°. (pp. 227, 406)

right triangle A triangle with a right angle. (p. 417)

rotation The image of a figure that has been "turned," as if on a wheel. (p. 443)

rotational symmetry The ability of a figure to be rotated less than a full circle and exactly match its original image. (p. 443)

rounding Adjusting a number to make it more convenient to use, according to a given place value. *Example:* 2,571 rounded to the nearest hundred is 2,600. (p. 66)

sample A set of data used to predict how a particular situation might happen. (p. 626)

scale The "ruler" that measures the heights of the bars in a bar graph. (p. 26)

scalene triangle A triangle with no sides of equal length. (p. 421)

scatterplot A graph showing paired data values. (p. 14)

scientific notation Writing a number as the product of a number greater than or equal to 1 but less than 10 and a power of 10. *Example:* $350 = 3.50 \times 10^2$. (p. 152)

segment Part of a line, with two endpoints. (p. 402)

side Each of the rays forming an angle. (p. 406)

similar Figures having the same shape but possibly different sizes. (p. 540)

slide See *translation.*

solid A three-dimensional figure. (p. 578)

sphere See example below. (p. 579)

square A quadrilateral with all sides the same length and all angles measuring 90°. (p. 428)

square centimeter The area of a square with 1-centimeter sides. (p. 227)

square inch The area of a square with 1-inch sides. (p. 227)

square root The length of one side of a square with an area equal to a given number. (p. 260)

squared Raised to the power of 2. *Example:* 3 squared $= 3^2 = 9$. (p. 79)

standard form A way of writing a number using digits. *Example:* 45,000,000,000,000. (p. 75)

stem-and-leaf diagram A graph showing the shape of a data set by breaking each value into a "stem" part and a "leaf" part. (p. 30)

straight angle An angle formed by two rays pointing in opposite directions. (p. 406)

subtraction An operation that tells the difference between two numbers, or how many are left when some are taken away.

sum The result of adding numbers. (p. 110)

supplementary angles Two angles whose measures add up to 180°. (p. 411)

surface area (SA) The sum of the areas of each face of a polyhedron. (p. 582)

symmetry See *line symmetry* and *rotational symmetry.*

T-table A table showing corresponding *x*- and *y*-values for an equation. (p. 495)

tally marks Marks used to organize a large set of data. Each mark indicates one time a value appears in the data set. (p. 22)

terminating decimal A decimal number that ends on the right. (p. 297)

tessellation A pattern of congruent shapes covering a surface without gaps or overlaps. (p. 447)

translation The image of a figure that has been slid to a new position without flipping or turning. (p. 447)

trapezoid A quadrilateral with exactly two parallel sides. (p. 428)

tree diagram A branching, tree-like diagram showing all possible outcomes of a situation. (p. 640)

trend A relationship between two sets of data that shows up as a pattern in a scatterplot. (p. 14)

triangle A closed figure made from three line segments. (p. 416)

turn See *rotation.*

unfair game A game in which all players do not have the same probability of winning. (p. 650)

unit One of something; an amount or quantity used as a standard of measurement.

unit fraction A fraction with a numerator of 1.

unit rate A rate in which the second number in the comparison is one unit. *Example:* 25 gallons per minute. (p. 518)

unlike denominators Denominators that are different in two fractions. (p. 320)

variable A quantity that can change or vary, often represented with a letter. (p. 106)

Venn diagram A diagram that uses regions to show relationships between sets of things. (p. 310)

vertex The common endpoint of two rays forming an angle. Plural: vertices. (p. 406)

vertical axis The vertical line of the two lines on which a graph is built. (p. 26)

volume The number of cubic units an object contains. (p. 602)

weight A measure of the force that gravity exerts on a body.

whole number Any number in the set {0, 1, 2, 3, 4, . . . }.

word form A way of writing a number using only words. *Example:* forty-five trillion. (p. 62)

***x*-axis** The horizontal axis on a coordinate plane. (p. 484)

***x*-coordinate** The first number in an ordered pair, locating a point on the *x*-axis of a coordinate plane. (p. 484)

***y*-axis** The vertical axis on a coordinate plane. (p. 484)

***y*-coordinate** The second number in an ordered pair, locating a point on the *y*-axis of a coordinate plane. (p. 484)

yard A unit in the customary system of measurement equal to 3 feet. (p. 218)

zero pair A number and its opposite. *Example:* 7 and (-7).

GLOSSARY

Credits

Photographs

Front Matter **viTC** David Sams/Stock, Boston **xviii** Chuck Mason/International Stock **xx** Mark C. Burnett/Stock, Boston **xxi** Jean-Marc Giboux/Liaison International **xxii** Fridman Damm/Leo de Wys, Inc. **xxiv** Pictor/Uniphoto Picture Agency **xxvii** John Lund/Tony Stone Images

Chapter 1 **2(inset)** Christopher Liu/China Stock **2BL** John Michael/International Stock **3T** Dennis O'Clair/Tony Stone Images **3B** ZEFA/The Stock Market **7** Blake/Reuters/Corbis-Bettmann **12** W. Gregory Brown/Animals, Animals **13** Bob Daemmrich/Stock, Boston **15TR** David Madison/Bruce Coleman Inc. **15MR** Dr. Nigel Smith/Earth Scenes **16TL** Marc Chamberlain/Tony Stone Images **16TR** Paul Humann/Jeff Rotman Photography **17** Lee F. Snyder/Photo Researchers **19TC (inset)** Jeff Rotman Photography **19BR (inset)** Marc Chamberlain/Tony Stone Images **19(background)** Warren Bolster/Tony Stone Images **21** Jon Feingersh/The Stock Market Formata Medium UPI/Corbis-Bettmann **27BL** FPG International **27MR** Mark Reinstein/FPG International **27ML** Popperfoto/Archive Photos **27BR** Ron Thomas/Reuters/Corbis Bettmann **28** from HERBLOCK: A CARTOONIST'S LIFE(Macmillan Publishing, 1993) **30** AFP/Archive Photos **35(inset)** Mississippi Valley State University **36BR** Mitchell Layton/Duomo **36TR** Taro Yamasaki **37** Bill Reitzel **39** Kevin Lamarque/Reuters/Corbis-Bettmann **41** Paul Souders/Allsport **42BR** Al Bello/Allsport **43** Gail Shumway/FPG International **47BL** Culver Pictures **49** Brad Mangin/Duomo **50MR** National Baseball Hall of Fame © Topps/Hank Aaron Foundation. Courtesy of Hank Aaron and the Hank Aaron Chasing the Dream Foundation **50ML** TM©Family Babe Ruth and the Babe Ruth Baseball League, Inc. under license authorized by CMG Worldwide Inc., Indianapolis, Indiana, 46202 USA http://ww.cmgww.com. Photo by Geoffrey Nilsen Photography **51TL** Archive Photos **51BR** Archive Photos **53TR** Stewart L. Craig Jr./Bruce Coleman Inc.

Chapter 2 **58C** Jack Zehrt/FPG International **61** NASA **62** Peter Tenzer/International Stock **63** Alan Carey/The Image Works **64** Frank Rossotto/The Stock Market **65** NASA/Lunar & Planetary Institute **65**ML NASA/Science Source/Photo Researvhers **67**TR SuperStock 69TL Lunar & Planetary Institute **69**TR NASA **71** Lunar & Planetary Institute **72ML** Sovfoto/Eastfoto **76** lower NASA **76** upper NASA/JPL/TSADO/Tom Stack & Associates **77TR** CNRI/SPL/Photo Researchers **77ML** NASA/JPL/TSADO/Tom Stack & Associates **77TR (inset)** NIBSC/SPL/Photo Researchers **80** Randy Anderson **81(insets)** Underwood Collection/Corbis Bettmann **83** Carl Yarbrough/Uniphoto Picture Agency **88BR** Bob Daemmrich/The Image Works **92** Hewlett Packard **93** Texas Instruments **97** Jack Zehrt/FPG International **98(background)** Alaska Stock **99BR** John Terence Turner/FPG International **99TR** Mark Gamba/The Stock Market **100** Gregory Sams/SPL/Photo Researchers 103MR IFA-Bildesteam/Uniphoto Picture Agency **105** Barry E. Parker/Bruce Coleman Inc. **106** Steve Starr/Stock, Boston **107** Carleton Ray/Photo Researchers **110** Barbara Filet/Tony Stone Images **111BR** Comstock **111TC** Topham/The Image Works **112MR** Eric A. Wessman/Stock, Boston **115** Gregory Ochocki/Photo Researchers **117TR** Navaswan/FPG International **119** Brian Parker/Tom Stack & Associates **121MR** Mark Gamba/The Stock Market **121TR** Monteath C./Hedgehog House N. Zeal./Explorer/Photo Researchers **122** Greg Johnson/International Stock **123BR** Myron J. Dorf/The Stock Market **126BR** Darryl Torckler/Tony Stone Images **126BR (inset)** Peter David/Photo Researchers **126C** Richard Pasley/Stock, Boston **128TR** Thomas Kitchin/Tom Stack & Associates

Chapter 3 **134C** Buddy Mays/FPG International **134ML** J.P. Courau/DDB Stock Photo **134T** Rod Planck/Tony Stone Images **134BR** Steven E.Sutton/Duomo **137(insets)** Stephen Cooper/Tony Stone Images **138** G.C. Kelley/Photo Researchers **141TR** Andrew Syred/SPL/Photo Researchers **141MR** Popperfoto/Archive Photos **142TR** Ray Coleman/Photo Researchers **143BR** Rod Planck/Tony Stone Images **146C** Richard Gaul/FPG International **148** Jan C. Taylor/Bruce Coleman Inc. **150BL** James H. Carmichael, Jr./Photo Researchers **150MR** L.West/National Audubon Society/Photo Researchers **151** Bob Llewellyn/Uniphoto Picture Agency **152** James Carmichael/Bruce Coleman Inc. **154** Astrid & Hanns-Frieder Michler/SPL/Photo Researchers **155TR** Kim Taylor/Bruce Coleman Inc. **156TL** Buddy Mays/FPG International **156TR** Buddy Mays/FPG International **161** Martin Rogers/Tony Stone Images **165** Jeff Greenberg/The Image Works **168** Craig Weiman **175** Western History Department/Denver Public Library **176** Antman Archive/The Image Works **178** Nathan Bilow/Tony Stone Images **179** Norman Currie/Corbis-Bettmann **182B** Archive Photos **182T** Culver Pictures **187** Pictos/Uniphoto Picture Agency **189MR** Doug Pensinger/Allsport **189TR** McLaughlin Historical File 1/FPG International **195** Western History Department/Denver Public Library **197** Western History Department/Denver Public Library **201BL** Bob Daemmrich/Stock, Boston **201BR** Lawrence Migdale/Stock, Boston **201TR** Roy Morsch/The Stock Market **203C** Art Wolfe/Tony Stone Images **203TR** Jack S. Grove/Tom Stack & Associates

Chapter 4 **206ML** Prim & Ray Manley/SuperStock **206C** Ted Russell/The Image Bank **207TL** Kunio Owaki/The Stock Market **207BR (lower)** Michael Macor/San Francisco Chronicle **207BR** (upper) Richard Martin/Agency Vandystadt/ Allsport **209** John Elk/Stock,Boston **212BR** Margaret Hensel/Positive Images **213** Jenny Wachter/Photo Resaerchers **216BL** Telegraph Colour Library/FPG International **217MR** Norman O. Tomalin/Bruce Coleman Inc. **217TR** Steve Dunwell/The Image Bank **218** Chris Doyal **220BL** Susan Kuklin/Photo Researchers **222TR** Jack Zehrt/FPG International **222(inset, l)** NASA **222BC (spread)** NASA/SPL/Photo Researchers **222(inset, r)** NASA/The Image Works **223inset** Owen Franken/Stock, Boston **225** Kunio Owaki/The Stock Market **228** NMAA, Smithsonian Institution/Art Resource, NY **229** John Riley/Tony Stone Images **234TR** Alan Choisnet/The Image Bank **240** Kunio Owaki/ The Stock Market **243inset** Dewitt Jones/Tony Stone Images **246MR (upper)** Arthur Tilley/FPG International **246MR (lower)** David Sams/Stock, Boston **246BC** FPG International **250** James Carmichael/ The Image Bank **251** Georg Gerster/Comstock

Chapter 5 **263BR** Ellen Beach/Bruce Coleman Inc. **263ML** Kevin Schafer/Tony Stone Images **265** NASA **266** Tom Tracy/The Stock Market **268** FPG International **269TR** ET Archive/SuperStock **269MR** George Hunter/Tony Stone Images **272** Jay Thomas International Stock **273TL** M. Fischer/Art Resource, NY **275** The Cartoon Bank **277TR** Pat Lanza Field/Bruce Coleman Inc. **277MR** SuperStock **278** David Stoecklein/The Stock Market **279MR** (left) Diana Miller/Tony Stone Images **279MR (right)** SuperStock **280** Photri/The Stock Market **282TR** James Granger **288** AKG/SuperStock **299TR** M. Greenlan/The Image Works **299TC** SuperStock **304BR** Rindy Nyberg/Southern Card & Novelty Inc. **304MR** V. Rousel/Southern Card & Novelty Inc. **307ML** Larry Gatz/The Image Bank

Chapter 6 **312R** Custom Medical Stock Photo **312L** Tom Till/Tony Stone Images **313CR** Jane Gifford/Tony Stone Images **313CL** Jane Grushow/Grant Heilman Photographer **316** Rick Dole **317** AP Wide World Photos **319** Pictos/Uniphoto Picture Agency **322** David Scharf **325BR** Texas Instruments **328** SIU/Peter Arnold, Inc. **331** Jay Freis/The Image Bank **333** Comstock **334** Michael Tamborrino/FPG International **335** Tom Dietrich/Tony Stone Images **336** Doug Mc Kay/Tony Stone Images **337** Owen Franken/Stock, Boston **338** Tom Till/DRK Photo **342** Thomas Dimock/ The Stock Market **348** Tom Dietrich/Tony Stone Images **349** Bob Firth/International Stock **350** UPI Corbis-Bettmann

Chapter 7 **356CR** David Barnes/Tony Stone Images **356BR** Dimitri Messinis/Agence France/Corbis-Bettman **357BR** Draeger/Culver Pictures **357CL** Michelle Burgess/The Stock Market **359** Lawrence Migdale/Stock, Boston **360BR** R. Dahlquist/SuperStock **362BL** Archive Photos **362BR** Kunio Owaki/The Stock Market **363** George F. Godfrey/Earth Scenes **364** Robert A. Tyrell **367** Karl & Kay Ammann/Bruce Coleman Inc. **368** James Carmichael/Bruce Coleman Inc. **369** SuperStock **370** James H. Robinson/Photo Researchers **372** Bruce M. Herman/Photo Researchers **374ML** Akos Szilvasi/Stock, Boston **375(inset)** Stanley Tretick/People Weekly **375** Steve Liss / People Weekly **376** James Keyser **377** SuperStock **379ML** Kwok Leung Paul/Liaison International **381** Simon Bruty/Allsport **391** Bob Daemmrich/Stock, Boston **392** Jack Daniels/Tony Stone Images **393TR** Bruce Wilson/Tony Stone Images **393BR** David Madison **393BL** Henry Ausloos/Animals, Animals

Chapter 8 **398BR (lower)** Kim Taylor/Bruce Coleman **398BR (upper)** William Johnson/Stock, Boston **399BL** John David Fleck/Liaison International **399C** Symmetry Drawing E67 by M. C. Escher. © 1997 Cordon Art-Baarn, Holland. All rights reserved. **402** SuperStock **404** Bob Llewellyn/Uniphoto Picture Agency **407** Peter Gridley/FPG International **410** Chris Doyal **422BR** Jenny Thomas **424** Comstock **423BR** Corbis- Bettmann **426MR**

Dave B. Fleetham/Tom Stack & Associates **427CR** Archive Photos **427ML** Eduardo Garcia/FPG International **427MR** Michele & Tom Grimm/International Stock **427CL** Peter Menzel/Stock, Boston **427TR** SuperStock **431TR** SuperStock **437** Adam Woolfitt/Woodfin Camp & Associates **439** ©1994, Asian Art Museum of San Francisco **440ML (right)** Barry L. Runk/Grant Heilman Photography **440MR (left)** Carl Zeiss/Bruce Coleman Inc. **440ML (left)** Chris Arend/Tony Stone Images **440MR (right)** Noble Stock/International Stock **440BR** Robert Fried/Stock, Boston **441** Wolfgang Kaehler/Liaison International **444** ©1994, Asian Art Museum of San Francisco **447** Barry Brukoff/Woodfin Camp & Associates **448ML** A.K.G. Berlin/SuperStock **448BL** Bruce Hands/Comstock **448TR** Sylvain Grandadam/Tony Stone Images **448MR** Wolfgang Kaehler/Liaison International **452TR** Paula Massood **452BC** Paula Massood **455** Jerry Jacka Photography/Courtesy, Hubbell Trading Post, Ganado, AZ

Chapter 9 **462TR** Charles Thatcher/Tony Stone Images, Chris & Donna McLaughlin/The Stock Market **465** Telegraph Colour Library/FPG International **467** Michael Collier/Stock,Boston **468BR** Ken Chernus/FPG International **468BL** Lambert/Archive Photos **471** Lawrence Migdale/Tony Stone Images **472** Comstock **477ML** Don Smetzer/Tony Stone Images **480** Jenny Thomas **481(background)** Chuck Davies/Tony Stone Images **482** Michael Kevin Daly/The Stock Market **484** Bruce Silverstein **488B** Fritz Prenzel/Animals,Animals **497** Jeffrey Myers/Stock, Boston **501BL** Andrew Unangst/The Image Bank **501BR** Gary S. Chapman/The Image Bank

Chapter 10 **506TR** Gary Irving/Tony Stone Images **507TC** Ron Chapelle/FPG International **507MR** Stuart Westmoreland/Tony Stone Images **507BR** SuperStock **508TR** Chris Cole/Duomo 508MR David Madison/Tony Stone Images **509** SuperStock **513** Gary Irving /Tony Stone Images **517TR** John Running/Tony Stone Images **517ML** Stan Osolinski/Tony Stone Images **518TR** Jack Daniels/Tony Stone Images **518MR** Jurgen Vogt/The Image Bank **519TR** GK & Vikki Hart/The Image Bank **522BL** Ken Frick/International Stock **522TR** Steve Payne **525** SuperStock **527** Christian Michaels/FPG International **528** Jonathan Wright/Bruce Coleman Inc. **530TR** Rafael Macia/Photo Researchers **531** Russell D. Curtis/Photo Researchers **532C** Mike Nazzaschi/Stock, Boston **532ML** S.L. Craig, Jr./Bruce Coleman Inc. **534** Paul Harris/Tony Stone Images **535BR** S. Purdy Matthews/Tony Stone Images **536** E. Nagele/FPG International **537TR** Robert Frerck/Tony Stone Images **542CR** FPG International **542ML** SuperStock **544TR** Kunio Owaki/The Stock Market **545BR** Margaret Hensell/ Positive Images **545ML** Patricia J. Bruno/Positive Images **546** Jeff Gnass/The Stock Market **547(background)** Art Wolfe/Tony Stone Images **547(inset, br)** David M. Dennis/Tom Stack & Associates **547(inset,bc)** Gregory G. Dimijian/Photo Researchers **547(inset, tr)** Nancy Adams/Tom Stack & Associates **547(inset, bl)** Roy Toff/Tom Stack & Associates **549** SuperStock **552MR** Robert Frerck/Tony Stone Images **555TR (left)** Fritz Prenzel/Animals, Animals **555TR (right)** John Cancalosi/Stock, Boston **557** Jeff Lepore/Photo Researchers **559** David Austen/Stock, Boston **560** Phillipe Plailly/Eurelios/SPL/Photo Researchers **562MR** Robert A. Tyrell

Chapter 11 **575C** Michael Salas/The Image Bank **575BR** Sylvain Grandadam/Tony Stone Images **579MR** C. G. Maxwell/National Audubon Society/Photo Researchers **579ML** Corbis-Bettmann **581BL** Joseph Nettis/Stock, Boston **581BR** National Gallery of Art, photo by Phillip A. Charles **589MR** Alan Carey/The Image Works **597** Mike Stevens/ Tony Stone Images **598** SCALA/Art Resource **606TR** Chris Doyal **608** Jeff Rotman/Tony Stone Images **609MR** Jeff Hunter/The Image Bank **610** Jeffrey Sylvester/FPG International **616** Culver Pictures

Chapter 12 **618ML** Howard Bluestein/Photo Researchers **618CL** Howard Bluestein/Photo Researchers **619TC** Chris Trotman/Duomo **621** Paul & Lindamarie Ambrose/FPG International **623MR** Harvey Lloyd/The Stock Market **624BR** China Stock **628** Warren Bolster/Tony Stone Images **629MR** NASA/GSFC/Science Source/Photo Researchers **631** Rafael Macia/Photo Researchers **635** Howard Bluestein/Photo Researchers **640** Randy Anderson **642BR** Bob Daemmrich/Stock, Boston **642TC** Dennis O'Clair/Tony Stone Images **386–387C (spread)** Texas Instruments

Anne Dowie* 103TL, 104, 163, 164, 203BR (middle), 220MR, 293TR, 321, 346 **Cheryl Fenton*** xTC, xiiiBC, 58B, 59B, 123BL, 135BR, 225(inset), 246C, 249, 254, 262ML, 282ML, 283MR, 285TR, 289, 298ML, 305, 388, 393TL, 401, 405, 412, 415, 417, 418, 422ML, 425, 426BL, 426BR, 426BC, 448C, 461, 483, 506BL, 524, 562BR, 579C, 605TR, 613BL, 624MR, 630, 639, 642MR, 646 **George B. Fry III*** 627, 647 **Dennis Geaney*** ivTR, vTC, viiiTL, xivTR, xviiBR (center and left), 42TR, 252BL, 650BL **Richard Hutchings*** iiiTC, ivMR, ixBL (inset), vMR, viiTR, viiBL, 56TR, 127, 132ML, 204MR (lower), 260TR, 287, 292, 302, 310ML, 343MR, 354(insets), 396BR, 504, 529, 548MR, 572MR, 658TL (inset) **Ken Karp*** viTR, viiMR, xiMR, xiBC, xiiBC, xiiiMR, xivC, xivBR, xviiBR (left), xxv, 31, 56TL, 74, 85, 86BR, 89TR (lower), 98(inset), 147R, 172, 173, 181, 234BL, 234BR, 241, 244, 276, 281, 286, 295, 303, 351BR, 371, 420, 442, 446, 456, 469, 481(inset), 492, 499, 511, 519BR, 521, 523, 530TC, 535TR, 539MR, 544BR, 548C, 561, 574MR (upper), 602, 611, 618BR, 619BR, 626, 643, 644, 648BC, 649, 650BR, 653, 655TR, 656, 300–301B (spread) **Ana Nance*** 428, 429 **Geoffrey Nilsen Photography*** 16BR, 35, 82, 86TR, 87TR, 88TR, ML, 95, 143TR, 144ML, 155ML, 160, 171TC, 185TR, 201TL, 203BR (upper/lower), 219, 233ML, 262MR, 284, 298BR, 323, 366, 382, 574MR (lower), 577, 583, 585TR, 592C **Parker/Boon Productions and Dorey Sparre Photography*** ivBL, viBC, viiiMR, xMR, xBL, xiiTC, xiiTR, xviiTR, 144MR, 252, 515 **Robie Price*** iiiBL, viiiBL, ixMR, xxiii, 5, 40, 48, 53BL (lower), 90, 137(background), 157, 170, 171BL, 185BR, 212MR, 216TR, 237MR, 245, 291, 313BR (bottom), 378, 383TL, 459BR, 493, 537ML, 553, 607, 613TR, 654

*Photographs provided expressly for Scott Foresman-Addison Wesley

Illustrations

Jenny Ahrens 409 **Karin Batten** 508TC **Christine Benjamin** 142BR, 220C **Eliot Bergman** 359 **Ken Bowser** 56BR, 260T, 582 **Irene Chernisov** 498ML, 503, 576 **Dave Coulson** 658TR, 658TL, 658BR **Mike Dean** 129BR, 180, 310TR, 400TR, 569BR, 578, 655TL, 655BL, 655BR **Lisa Donovan** 136TC, 264TC, 358TC **Cameron Eagle** 66, 67C, 257, 351TR, 351BL, 385, 450, 569TL **Frank Frisari** 109, 193, 196, 274 **Cynthia Gamo** 114 **Ginger Graziano** 60TC, 620TC **Colin Hayes** 53BR, 108, 145TR, 207C, 263C, 290, 533, 543, 565, 569MR, 574C, 612, 650MR, 657, 124–125C (spread), 238–239(spread), 44–45C (spread), 632–633C (spread) **David Healy** 208TC (inset), 208MR, 234TL, 352 **Marlene Howerton** 339 **Dave Jonason** 128MR, 153, 353, 514, 551 **Matt Kania** 60MR **Rita Lascaro** ixBL, 3C, 47TR, 129BL, 131, 132TL, 136MR, 204ML, 204MR (upper), 221, 247, 334MR, 354, 357C, 373, 396inset , 408, 458C, 510BR, 571, 572TC, 593TR, 593TL, 620TR, 622, 623TR, 662, 326–327B (spread) **Ginidir Marshall** 4, 445, 460TC, 498TC **Jane Mc Creary** 512 **Shelly Meredith** 113, 330, 539TR **Patrick Merewether** 520BR **Karen Minot** 262TR, 307BL **Andrew Muonio** 53BL (upper), 68 **Ortelius Design** 24, 135C, 314, 413, 459C, 460MR, 609TR **Bill Pasini** 185TL, 186, 233TR, 542BR, 552TR, 563, 567 **Matt Perry** 542CL, 542MR **Precision Graphics** 605TL, 606BR **Bill Rieser** 285MR, 293ML, 307MR, 588 **Saul Rosenbaum** 432, 433, 435, 462B Rob Schuster 8, 20, 72TR, 112MR (inset), 117TR, 194, 235, 237BR, 242, 273TR, 285ML, 313BR (top), 343BC, 344B, 347, 360TR, 374MR, 379TR, 375TC, 421, 473, 477MR, 501TR, 510TC, 580, 589ML, 589MR, 593ML, 613TL, 629TR, 651 **Fran Strauss** 648TC **Blake Thornton** 167, 259, 325, 395, 479, 506C, 586, 596 **Bob Ting** xiTC, 572C **Twelve Dozen Graphics** 208TC, 314TC, 400TC **Joe Van Der Bos** 69C, 237TR **Tom Ward** 2C, 6, 18, 32, 33, 55, 59T, 59C, 73, 86ML, 198, 199, 214, 264TR, 383TR, 414, 453, 488B, 489, 569TR, 594, 595, 615 **Sarah Woodward** 315 **Rose Zgodzinski** 520MR, 589TR

All tech art by Precision Graphics and York Graphic Services.

Index

A

Aaron, Hank, 3, 50–51
Acute angle, 406–408, 410–412, 453
Acute triangle, 416–418
Addition, 157, 162–164, 168–170, 201, 316–318, 320–322, 326–327, 328–330, 340–342, 351, 466–468
  of angles in quadrilateral, 238–239
  estimation, 84–86, 158–160
  of mixed numbers, 336–338, 340–342
Algebra
  expression. *See* Expression, algebraic
  glossary entry, 675
  introduction to, 59, 105
  variable, 106–108
Algebra Readiness, 192, 289, 292, 363, 366, 378, 419, 464, 559, 609, 652
Angle
  acute, 406–408
  bisecting, 456
  classifying, 406–408
  constructing, 410–412, 456
  defined, 406
  glossary entry, 675
  measuring, 410–412
  obtuse, 406–408
  right, 406–408
  sides of, 406–408
  straight, 406–408
  sum of, in quadrilateral, 428–430
Applications Real–world applications of mathematics are found throughout this book. A few instances are shown below. *See also* specific subject areas.
  architectural design, 440
  art, 444
  Aztec calendar, 269
  automobiles, 33
  basketball, 49
  biking, 178, 247
  blood system, 331
  calories, 17, 112, 185
  calendar, 269, 273
  carpentry, 289, 293
  CD-ROM, 9
  Crystal Palace, 431
  distance, 189
  Dome of the Rock, 448
  Egypt, 537
  elevation, 472
  fairness, 650–653
  forest fires, 517
  garden design, 213
  geology, 299
  geography, 29, 117, 255
  geometry, 82, 228, 233, 284
  heart rate, 496
  health, 160, 185, 193, 371, 496
  history, 25, 109, 141, 179, 185, 269, 277, 289, 363
  industry, 91, 383, 585
  interior design, 449
  Islamic Art, 444
  law enforcement, 427
  life span, 366
  literature, 86, 112
  New York Stock Exchange, 346
  oceanography, 9
  origami, 408
  optometry, 217
  paleontology, 299
  probability, 33, 273
  population, 13, 185, 362, 379
  rain forests, 555
  recipe, 323, 395
  rock crystal, 422
  spiders, 144, 155
  social studies, 13, 103, 185, 362
  sports, 141, 151
  sunscreen, 371
  temperature, 465
  tennis, 39, 43
  time, 269, 273, 277
  urban planning, 413
  U. S. flag, 109
  U. S. Capitol, 413
Area, 225, 307, 613. *See also* Surface area (SA)
  of circle, 248–250
  glossary entry, 675
  of irregular figure, 252–254
  of parallelogram, 230–232
  of rectangle, 226–228
  of square, 226–228
  of triangle, 234–236
Arts and Literature, 3, 58, 135, 206, 262, 312, 356, 398, 458, 506, 574, 618
Athletes, 3, 35–49
Average, 40–42, 46–48, 52
Avoirdupois system of weight measurement, 391
Axis, 26–28, 484–486

B

Bar graph, 6, 26–29, 53
Base, 226–228, 234–236, 578–580, 613
Bermuda Triangle, 237
Braille, 351
Brantland, Gro, 27
Browser software, 488–489
Butcher, Susan, 41

C

Calculator, 86, 92–94, 121, 276, 307, 326–327, 449, 559, 566, 584, 642
Careers, 161, 217, 229, 293, 299, 342, 427, 465, 643
CD-ROM, 43, 124, 146, 238–239, 300–301, 432–433. *See also* Computers; Geometry Software; Spreadsheet
***Centi–* prefix,** 214–216
Choose a strategy, 91, 117, 193, 323, 343, 370, 473
Circle, 207, 243, 613
  area of, 248–250, 613
  circumference of, 245, 613
  diameter of, 245, 257, 613
  glossary entry, 675
  pi and, 244–246
  radius of, 245
Circle graph, 7, 351, 352, 564–565
Circumference, 245, 249, 613
Clocks, 277, 408
Clockwise rotation, 442–444
Collecting data, 28, 121, 151, 289, 319, 371, 378, 383, 533
Common denominator, 302–304
Common factor, 286–288
Common multiple, 274–276
Comparing
  decimals, 148–150, 556–558
  fractions, 302–304
  numbers, 70–72
Compound event, 644–646
Computer, 9, 43, 53, 58, 59, 124, 129, 146, 201, 206, 207, 238–239, 257, 262, 263, 300–301, 312, 313, 351, 356, 357, 398, 399, 432–433, 453, 458, 459, 488–489, 506, 507, 569. *See also* CD-ROM; World Wide Web
Cone, 578–580
Congress, 25
Congruent, 540
Congruent figure, 540–542
Constructions, 456
Consumer, 42, 496, 529, 562, 605
Conversion factor, 218–220
Coordinate, 484–486
Coordinate grid, 484–486, 501
Coordinate plane
  defined, 484
  glossary entry, 676
  graphing, 483, 484–486
Counterclockwise rotation, 442–444
Critical Thinking, 12, 16, 25, 29, 33,

39, 43, 48, 49, 65, 68, 69, 77, 83, 85, 90, 91, 95, 102, 103, 109, 121, 141, 144, 151, 160, 161, 164, 170, 171, 179, 184, 185, 189, 193, 213, 217, 221, 229, 237, 247, 269, 288, 293, 304, 309, 318, 323, 330, 339, 346, 347, 363, 379, 382, 405, 409, 419, 431, 441, 464, 469, 472, 477, 486, 493, 497, 513, 520, 521, 537, 554, 559, 563, 571, 580, 581, 585, 588, 589, 593, 604, 608, 609, 615, 625, 637, 642, 647, 653, 657

Cross product, 526–528, 530–532
Cube, 578–580, 613
Cubic units, 597, 602–604
Cuisenaire rods, 420–422
Customary system of measurement, 218–220
Cylinder, 578–580, 590–592, 594–595

D

Data, *See* Using Data
Decagon, 424–426
***Deci-* prefix,** 214–26
Decimals
adding, 162–164, 168–170
comparing, 148–150
connecting fractions to, 282–284
connecting percents to, 556–558
converting, 296–298
dividing, 190–192, 194–196
equations, solving, 194–196
estimating with, 158–160
multiplying, 176–178, 180–181, 182–184, 194–196
notation, 138–140
ordering, 148–150
repeating, 297
rounding, 142–144
scientific notation, 152–154
subtracting, 162–164, 168–170
terminating, 297
Decision making, 50–51, 126–127, 198–199, 240–241, 348–349, 480–481, 522–523, 610–611. *See also* Explore; Problem Solving
Degree, 410–412
***Deka-* prefix,** 214–216
Denominator, 316–318, 320–322
Diameter, 245, 613
Difference. *See also* Subtraction
glossary entry, 676
Divers, 6
Divisibility, 266–268, 278–279
Division. *See also* Quotient
with decimals, 190–192, 194–196
estimation, 88–90, 158–160
with fractions, 376–378, 380–382, 386–387
glossary entry, 676
of integers, 474–476
solving fraction equations by, 388–390
with whole numbers, 176–178, 186–188, 376–378
Dodecagon, 424–426

E

Entertainment, 2, 58, 134, 207, 263, 312, 356, 399, 458, 507, 574, 618
Equal ratio, 514–516
Equations
decimal, 168–170, 194–196
fraction, 388–390
graphing, 494–496
solving, 118–120, 194–196
using, 114
Equilateral triangle, 420–422
Estimation, 8, 12, 16, 32, 48, 69, 120, 144, 158–160, 160, 217, 221, 233, 331, 339, 360–362, 382, 472, 552–554, 609, 628, 631
of area, 233
with decimals, 144, 158–160
of differences, 84–86, 158–160, 336–338
of fractions, 292
of large numbers, 69
of mixed numbers, 336–338, 339
of percents, 552–554, 559
of products, 88–90, 158–160, 360–362
of probability, 628, 630–631
of quotients, 88–90, 158–160, 360–362
of rate, 517
of sums, 84–86, 158–160, 336–338
of variables, 120
Event, 622–624
compound, 644–646
Experiment, 622
Experimental probability, 622–624
Explore, 40–42, 74–76, 118–120, 152–154, 162–164, 190–192, 226–228, 244–246, 248–250, 270–272, 296–298, 340–342, 344–346, 380–382, 416–418, 420–422, 438–440, 442–444, 446–448, 462–464, 466–468, 470–472, 474–476, 494–496, 514–516, 526–528, 540–542, 556–558, 582–584, 598–600, 602–604, 644–646
Exponent, 74–76, 129, 501
Exponential notation, 501
Expression, algebraic
glossary entry, 677
variable and, 106–108
writing, 110–112

F

Fairness, 619, 639, 650–652, 653
Fine Arts, 112, 228, 233, 405, 409, 440, 444, 445, 448, 529. *See also* Applications
Flips, 490–492
Foot, 218–220
Formula, 226–228, 234–236, 248–250, 586–588, 606–608
Fractal, 566–568
Fraction calculator, 326–327, 386–387
Fractions
adding, 316–318, 320–322, 328–330
comparing, 302–304
connecting decimals to, 282–284
connecting percents to, 556–558
converting, 296–298
denominator of, 316–318, 320–322
dividing, 380–382, 388–390
equations, 388–390
improper, 290–292
in lowest terms, 286–288
multiplying, 360–362, 364–366, 368–370, 388–390
numerator of, 316–318, 320–322
ordering, 302–304
proper, 290–292
quotient of, 360–362
subtracting, 316–318, 320–322, 328–330
understanding, 282–284
Frequency chart, 22–24

G

Gallon, 218–220
Gandhi, Indira, 27
Gems, 399
Geography, 24, 38, 72, 86, 112, 117, 121, 237, 255, 319, 542, 550, 555, 563, 609. *See also* Applications
Geometric models of probability, 634–636
Geometry *See also* Angle; Applications; Lines; Triangle
angles, 406–408, 410–412, 416–418
flips, 434–435, 490–492
of gems, 398
glossary entry, 677
irregular figures, 252–254
lengths, missing, 543

INDEX

lines, 402–404
line symmetry, 434–435
polygon, 424–426, 428–430
polyhedron, 578–580
quadrilateral, 424–426, 428–430, 486
rotational symmetry, 442–444
sides, 446–448, 490–492
tessellation, 446–448
three-dimensional figures, 601
transformational, 399, 437
translation, 447, 490–492
turns, 442–444
Geometry readiness, 363
Geometry software, 238–239, 432–433
Gram, 214–216
Graph
axis, 26–28
bar, 27–29
circle, 7, 351, 352
of coordinate plane, 459, 483, 490–492, 501
of equations, 494–496
of flips, 490–492
glossary entry, 677
line, 7
misleading, 10
scatterplot, 14–16
of slides, 490–492
Great Lakes, 27

H

Health, 42, 109, 160, 185, 189, 193, 216, 366, 371, 496, 520, 559. *See also* Applications
***Hecto-* prefix,** 214–216
Height, 226–228, 234–236, 393
Henderson, Rickey, 7
Hexagon, 424–426
History, 24, 109, 141, 179, 185, 269, 277, 289, 367, 390, 422, 431, 532, 581, 593, 625. *See also* Applications
Horizontal axis, 26–28

I

Improper fractions, 290–292
Inches, 218–220
Industry, 91, 383, 513, 520, 562, 592
Integers, 458, 461
adding, 466–468
dividing, 474–476
glossary entry, 677
multiplying, 474–476
negative number, 462–464
opposite of, 466–468
positive number, 462–464, 501
subtracting, 470–472
zero, 462–464
Interval, 26–28
Irregular figure, 252–254
Irregular polygon, 424–426
Islamic art, 437, 444
Isometric projection, 598
Isosceles triangle, 420–422

J

Jordan, Michael, 49
Journal, 17, 25, 33, 39, 52, 76, 83, 86, 91, 103, 109, 113, 117, 128, 141, 145, 151, 155, 161, 165, 171, 173, 174, 179, 185, 189, 193, 197, 213, 217, 221, 229, 242, 247, 251, 255, 256, 269, 273, 277, 279, 280, 285, 289, 293, 299, 305, 306, 331, 343, 347, 363, 367, 371, 374, 383, 391, 405, 409, 413, 414, 419, 423, 427, 431, 441, 445, 449, 465, 469, 477, 482, 487, 497, 500, 513, 521, 524, 533, 537, 546, 555, 559, 568, 581, 585, 589, 601, 609, 612, 625, 637, 638, 643, 647, 653, 654

K

Kennedy, President John F., 23, 30
***Kilo-* prefix,** 214–216
Kondakova, Elena, 72

L

Least common denominator (LCD), 320–322
Least common multiple (LCM), 274–276, 307
Length. *See* Measurement
Lincoln, President Abraham, 31
Line graph. *See* Graph
Line of symmetry, 434–435
Line plot, 22–24
Lines, 398, 401
bisecting, 456
construction, 456
classifying, 402–404
defined, 402
endpoints of, 402–404
glossary entry, 677
intersection of, 402–404
parallel, 402–404, 453
perpendicular, 402–404
ray, 402–404
segment, 402–404
Line symmetry, 438–440
Liter, 214–216
Literature, 86, 112, 537
Logic, 39, 72, 86, 193, 319, 343, 366, 422, 605, 631
Lowest terms, 286–288

M

Math History, 273
Math Magazine, 56, 132, 204, 260, 310, 354, 396, 456, 504, 572, 616, 658
Mean, 40–42, 46–48
Measurement, 49, 71, 91, 173, 184, 189, 206, 209, 217, 221, 273, 292, 298, 305, 330, 367, 378, 382, 383, 445, 468, 585. *See also* Area; Surface area (SA); Volume
of angle, 410–412
Avoirdupois system of weight, 391
circumference, 245, 613
conversion factor, 218–220
customary system of, 218–220
diameter, 245, 613
irregular figure, 252–254
metric system conversion, 214–216
and proportion, 532
perimeter, 210–212
pi and, 244–246
radius, 245
of temperature, 378, 465
of time, 33, 65, 155, 173, 185, 251, 323, 378, 408, 543, 569, 608
Troy system of weight, 391
units of, 206, 209
weight, 379, 391
Median, 36–38, 44, 46–48, 52
Meir, Golda, 27
Mental Math, 8, 17, 25, 39, 80–81, 85, 188, 212, 289, 319, 322, 338, 367, 382, 418
problem solving, 39
techniques, 80–81, 367
Meter, 214–216
Metric system conversion, 214–216
Metric system. *See* Measurement
Mile, 218–220
***Milli-* prefix,** 214–216
Mixed numbers
adding, 313, 335, 336–338, 340–342
and decimals, 393
difference of, estimating, 336–338
improper fractions and, 290–292
subtracting, 313, 335, 336–338, 344–346
sum of, estimating, 336–338
Mixed Review and Test Prep
Mixed Review and Test Prep problems are found on the last page of each lesson throughout this book.
Mode, 36–38, 46–48, 52
Money, 33, 103, 173, 193, 273, 322, 351, 367, 373, 413, 427, 449, 536, 589, 613, 631, 642

Multiplication. *See also* Product
with decimals, 135, 175, 176–178, 182–184, 194–196
estimating, 88–90, 158–160
with fractions, 356, 359, 364–366, 386–387
glossary entry, 678
of integers, 474–476
solving fraction equation by, 388–390
of whole number, 364–366
Music, 155

N

Native Americans, 47
Net, 578–585
Net patterns, 578–585
Number
common multiple of, 274–277
comparing and ordering, 70–72, 148–150, 302–304
decimal. *See* Decimals
dividing, whole, 35, 186–188, 376–378
divisibility of, 266–268
estimation. *See* Estimation
exponent, 74–76
fractional. *See* Fractions
integer. *See* Integers
large, 58, 61–64, 66–68, 129
least common multiple of, 274–276, 307
mixed. *See* Mixed number
multiplying, whole, 176–178, 364–366
negative, 462–464, 501
ordering, 70–72, 148–150, 302–304
order of operations, 92–94
patterns, 100–102, 129
percent of, 560–562
positive, 462–464, 501
prime factorization and, 270–272
rounding large, 66–68
sense, 59, 79, 539, 551, 559
theory, 262, 265
whole, 35, 176–178, 186–188, 364–366, 376–378
Number sense, 59, 79, 468, 539, 551, 559
Number theory
decimal conversion, *See* Decimals
divisibility, 266–268
least common multiple, 274–276, 307
prime factorization, 270–272
Numerator, 320–322, 368–370
Numerical pattern, 100–102, 192, 201, 262, 279, 319, 339

O

Obtuse angle, 406–408, 410–412, 453
Obtuse triangle, 416–418
Oceanography, 9
Octagon, 424–426
Olympics, 16
Operations, *See* Addition; Division; Multiplication; Order of operations; Subtraction
Operation sense, 59, 79
Opposite, 466–468
Ordered pair, 484–486
Ordering, 70–72, 148–150, 302–304
Order of operations, 92–94
Orthographic projection, 598
Ounce, 218–220
Outcome, 622
Outcome of experiment, 622–624
Outliers, 46–48

P

Parallel, 402–404
Parallel lines, 402–404
Parallelogram, 230–232, 428–430
Patterns, 17, 49, 82, 100–102, 140, 171, 192, 201, 262, 279, 319, 339, 373, 513, 556–558, 566–568, 585, 600, 601
data sets, 49
numerical, 82, 100–102, 192, 201, 262, 279, 319, 339
triangular and square numbers, 132
Pentagon, 424–426
People of the World, 2, 59, 135, 207, 262, 312, 356, 399, 459, 506, 574, 618
Percent, 506, 507, 547
connecting to fractions and decimals, 556–558
defined, 548
estimating, 552–554
glossary entry, 678
of a number, 560–562
understanding, 547, 548–550
Performance Assessment, 55, 131, 203, 259, 309, 353, 395, 455, 503, 571, 615, 657
Perimeter, 210–212, 351
Perpendicular lines, 402–404, 453
Perspective, 598–600
Pi, 244–246
Polygon, 415, 424–426, 428–430, 453
Polyhedron, 578–580, 598–601
Positive number, 462–464, 501
Pound, 218–220
Power, 74–76
Prediction, 626–628
Presidents, 3, 21, 23–26, 28, 30–31
Prime factorization, 270–272, 307
Prime number, 270–272
Prism, 578–580, 586–588
Probability, 618–620. *See also* Applications
compound event, 644–646
defined, 622
event, 348–349, 622–624
experiment, 622–624
fairness and unfairness, 620, 639, 650–653
game, 648–649
geometric models of, 634–636
glossary entry, 678
of experimental outcome, 622–624, 655
percents and, 563
prediction and, 626–628
problem solving, 348–349, 655
tree diagram and, 640–642
understanding, 618–620
Problem Solving
and careers, 161, 229, 299, 427, 642
and geography, 533, 609
and health, 371
and history, 25, 277, 593
and recreation, 87, 347, 487, 521
and science, 69, 73, 113, 145, 331, 629
and social studies, 165, 251, 413
Problem Solving, analyze word problems
checking for a reasonable answer, 544–545, 630–631
finding unnecessary information, 98–99, 222–223
identifying missing information, 332–333, 372–373
interpreting math phrases, 122–123
Problem Solving and Applications, 9, 12, 17, 29, 33, 39, 43, 49, 68, 72, 77, 82, 86, 90, 95, 103, 109, 112, 116, 141, 144, 150, 155, 160, 164, 171, 178, 185, 189, 193, 196, 213, 217, 221, 233, 237, 246, 255, 268, 272, 284, 288, 292, 298, 304, 319, 323, 339, 343, 346, 362, 367, 370, 378, 382, 405, 408, 419, 422, 431, 440, 444, 449, 464, 468, 472, 477, 486, 493, 496, 512, 516, 520, 528, 532, 537, 554, 559, 562, 581, 585, 589, 592, 601, 605, 608, 624, 636, 646, 653
Problem Solving, compare strategies
look for a pattern/make a table, 566–567
solve a simpler problem/make an organized list, 278–279
use logical reasoning/draw a picture,

434–435, 688, 690
work backward/guess and check, 172–173
Problem Solving Connection
draw a picture, 162, 190, 270, 296, 380, 582, 598, 602
guess and check, 118, 420, 438, 442, 644
look for a pattern, 74, 152, 226, 244, 248, 416, 420, 438, 446, 466, 470, 474, 494, 526, 540, 556
make a table, 226, 244, 248, 416, 514
make an organized list, 40, 74, 474
use logical reasoning, 340, 344, 470
work backward, 118
Problem Solving, decision making
18–19, 50–51, 126–127, 198–199, 240–241, 348–349, 480–481, 522–523, 610–611
Problem Solving Strategies
draw a picture, xx
guess and check, xxii
look for a pattern, xxi
make a table, xxv
make an organized list, xxiv
solve a simpler problem, xxvi
use logical reasoning, xxiii
work backward, xxvii
Product. *See also* Decimals; Fractions; Multiplication
glossary entry, 678
Proper fractions, 290–292
Proportion, 506
cross product and, 526–528, 530–532
defined, 526
glossary entry, 678
solving, 530–532, 534–536
understanding, 525
Protractor, 410–412
Pyramid, 578–580

Q

***Quad-* prefix,** 424–426
Quadrant, 484–486
Quadrilateral, 424–426, 428–430, 486, 613
Quart, 218–220
Quotient. *See also* Division
glossary entry, 679

R

Radius, 245, 248–250
Random number, 632–633
Range, 27–28, 32
Rate, 506, 509, 518–520, 569
Ratio, 506, 509. *See also* Percent; Proportion
defined, 510
equal, 514–516
glossary entry, 679
and probability, 622–624
rate, 506, 509
understanding, 510–512
Ray, 402–404
Rectangle, 226–228, 428–430
Recreation, 347, 487, 521, 646
Regular polygon, 424–426
Repeating decimal, 297
Rhombus, 428–430
Right angle, 406–408, 410–412, 453
Right triangle, 416–418
Rotation, 442–444
Rotational symmetry, 442–444
Rounding
decimals, 142–144
glossary entry, 679
large numbers, 66–68
Ruth, Babe, 50–51

S

SA. *See* Surface area
Sample, 626–628
Scale, 26–28
Scalene triangle, 420–422
Scatterplot, 14–16
Science, 2, 12, 32, 58, 64, 72, 77, 83, 103, 112, 135, 141, 144, 145, 154, 155, 197, 206, 263, 313, 318, 322, 331, 357, 367, 370, 373, 379, 391, 399, 418, 426, 448, 459, 473, 507, 517, 536, 575, 619, 625, 637. *See also* Applications
Scientific notation, 152–154
Segment, 402–404
Sharks, 2, 8, 10, 12, 14, 16, 18–20
Sides, 406–408, 420–422, 424–426, 446–448, 490–492
of angle, 406–408
glossary entry, 679
of triangle, 420–422, 424–426
Skills Practice Bank, 660–671
Slides 446–448, 490–492
Similar, 540–542
Social Studies, 3, 27, 59, 77, 91, 137, 155, 206, 251, 262, 280, 313, 357, 362, 379, 398, 413, 458, 506, 575, 619. *See also* Applications
Software, 44–45, 124–125, 146–147, 238–239, 300–301, 432–433, 488–489, 564–565, 594–595, 632–633. *See also* CD-ROM; Computers; Spreadsheet; Technology
Solid, 574, 577
base of, 578–580
classifying, 578–580
cylinder, 590–592, 594–595
defined, 578
edge of, 578–580
faces of, 578–580
glossary entry, 679
three-dimensional figure, 598–600
Soyer, Alexis, 286
Sphere, 578–580
Sports, 50–51, 141, 569, 619
Spreadsheet, 44–45, 124–125, 146–147, 300–301, 564–565, 594–595, 632–633
Square, 226–228, 428–430, 613
Stem-and-leaf diagram, 30–32
Straight angle, 406–408
Subtraction. *See also* Difference
of decimals, 135, 162–164, 168–170
estimation, 84–86, 157–160
of fractions, 312, 315–318, 320–322, 328–330, 351
glossary entry, 679
of integers, 470–472
of mixed numbers, 313, 335–338, 344–346
Sum. *See also* Addition
glossary entry, 679
Surface area (SA), 574, 577
of cylinder, 590–592, 594–595
defined, 582
formulas, 586–588
glossary entry, 680
of solid, 598–600
understanding, 577

T

Tally mark, 22–24
Team Project, 4, 60, 136, 208, 264, 314, 358, 400, 460, 508, 576, 620
Technology, *See also* Calculator; CD-ROM; Computer; Fraction calculator; Geometry software; Spreadsheet; World Wide Web
Terminating decimal, 297
Tessellation, 399, 446–448
Thatcher, Margaret, 27
Three-dimensional figure, 598–600. *See also* specific types of figure
Time, 33, 65, 155, 173, 185, 251, 323, 378, 408, 543, 569, 608
Titanic, 111
Translation, 446–448
Transportation. *See* Applications
Trapezoid, 428–430, 613
Tree diagram, 640–642, 655
Trends, 14–16
Triangle

acute, 416–418, 453
angles in, 416–418, 420–422, 424–426
area of, 234–236
defined, 234–236, 416, 424–426
equilateral, 420–422
glossary entry, 680
isosceles, 420–422
obtuse, 416–418, 453
relationships in, 432–433
right, 416–418, 453
scalene, 420–422
sides of, 420–422, 424–426

Troy system of weight measurement, 391
Turns, 442–444
Two-dimensional figure, *See* specific types

U

Unfair game, 619, 639, 650–653
Unit rates, 518–520, 534–536
Using Data, 12, 25, 43, 72, 83, 86, 116, 141, 161, 213, 217, 221, 228, 237, 246, 255, 269, 273, 285, 292, 319, 339, 363, 373, 378, 408, 419, 423, 445, 449, 469, 472, 473, 512, 532, 555, 589, 609, 625, 631, 646, 653

V

Van Gogh, Vincent, 58
Vertical axis, 26–28
Volume, 575, 597, 602–604
defined, 602–604
glossary entry, 680
measuring, 597, 602–604, 613
of solid, 602–604
understanding, 602–604

W

Weight, *See* Measurement
Wentworth, C. K., 113
Whole number, 176–178, 186–188, 364–366, 376–378
World Wide Web, 2–3, 53, 58–59, 129, 134–135, 201, 206–207, 257, 262–263, 312–313, 351, 356–357, 398–399, 453, 458–459, 488–489, 501, 506–507, 569, 574–575, 618–619, 655
Williams, Ted, 3

X

***x*-axis,** 484–486
***x*-coordinate,** 484–486

Y

Yard, 218–220
***y*-axis,** 484–486
***y*-coordinate,** 484–486
Your Choice, 53, 129, 201, 257, 307, 351, 393, 453, 501, 569, 613, 655

Z

Zero. *See* Integer